W9-BJH-747

New Perspectives on

Microsoft® Office 2003

Premium Edition

First Course

THOMSON

COURSE TECHNOLOGY

Australia • Canada • Mexico • Singapore • Spain • United Kingdom • United States

What does this logo mean?

It means this courseware has been approved by the Microsoft® Office Specialist Program to be among the finest available for learning Microsoft Office Word 2003, Microsoft Office Excel 2003, Microsoft Office Access 2003, and Microsoft Office PowerPoint® 2003. It also means that upon completion of this courseware, you may be prepared to take an exam for Microsoft Office Specialist qualification.

This text, when used in conjunction with the *New Perspectives on Microsoft Office 2003 Second Course* text, will prepare students for Microsoft Office Specialist certification for Microsoft Word 2003, Microsoft Excel 2003, and Microsoft Access 2003.

What is a Microsoft Office Specialist?

A Microsoft Office Specialist is an individual who has passed exams for certifying his or her skills in one or more of the Microsoft Office desktop applications such as Microsoft Word, Microsoft Excel, Microsoft PowerPoint, Microsoft Outlook®, Microsoft Access, or Microsoft Project. The Microsoft Office Specialist Program is the only program in the world approved by Microsoft for testing proficiency in Microsoft Office desktop applications and Microsoft Project.* This testing program can be a valuable asset in any job search or career advancement.

More Information:

To learn more about becoming a Microsoft Office Specialist, visit www.microsoft.com/officespecialist

To learn about other Microsoft Office Specialist approved courseware from Course Technology, visit **www.course.com/newperspectives/teacherslounge**

www.course.com/NewPerspectives

New Perspectives on

Microsoft® Office 2003

Premium Edition

First Course

Ann Shaffer
Patrick Carey
June Jamrich Parsons
Dan Oja
Kathleen T. Finnegan

Roy Ageloff
University of Rhode Island

Joseph J. Adamski
Grand Valley State University

Lisa Ruffolo
Robin M. Romer
Katherine T. Pinard
Jane E. Pedicini

S. Scott Zimmerman
Brigham Young University

Beverly B. Zimmerman
Brigham Young University

THOMSON

COURSE TECHNOLOGY

Australia • Canada • Mexico • Singapore • Spain • United Kingdom • United States

THOMSON
COURSE TECHNOLOGY

New Perspectives on Microsoft® Office 2003, First Course—Premium Edition
is published by Thomson Course Technology.

Executive Editor:
Rachel Goldberg

Senior Editor:
Amanda Shelton

Senior Product Manager:
Kathy Finnegan

Product Manager:
Brianna Hawes

Associate Product Manager:
Shana Rosenthal

Editorial Assistant:
Janine Tangney

Marketing Manager:
Joy Stark

Marketing Coordinator:
Melissa Marcoux

Developmental Editors:
Pam Conrad, Kim Crowley, Jane Pedicini, Katherine T. Pinard, Robin Romer, Lisa Ruffolo

Production Editors:
Kelly Robinson, Jennifer Goguen McGrail, Pamela Elizian, Summer Hughes, Philippa Lehar, Elena Montillo

Composition:
GEX Publishing Services

Text Designers:
Steve Deschene, Abby Scholz

Cover Designers:
Nancy Goulet, Abby Scholz

Cover Artist:
Ed Carpenter
www.edcarpenter.net

Preface

Real, Thought-Provoking, Engaging, Dynamic, Interactive—these are just a few of the words that are used to describe the New Perspectives Series' approach to learning and building computer skills.

Without our critical-thinking and problem-solving methodology, computer skills could be learned but not retained. By teaching with a case-based approach, the New Perspectives Series challenges students to apply what they've learned to real-life situations.

Our ever-growing community of users understands why they're learning what they're learning. Now you can too!

See what instructors and students are saying about the best-selling New Perspectives Series:

"The New Perspectives format is a pleasure to use. The Quick Checks and the tutorial Review Assignments help students view topics from a real world perspective."
— Craig Shaw, Central Community College – Hastings

...and about New Perspectives on Microsoft Office 2003 First Course:

"Our school has used the New Perspectives on Microsoft Office First Course book for several years, and we have found no reason to consider changing to another text-book, despite considerable efforts from other publishers. We recently completed another textbook evaluation project, and we determined there simply is not a better solution for our student population. The book is extremely student friendly, the screen shots are very meaningful and visually appealing, and the actual student instructions are easily identifiable, easy to follow and accurate."
— Glen Johansson, Spokane Community College

"The layout in this textbook is thoughtfully designed and organized. It is very easy to locate concepts and step-by-step instructions. The Case Problems provide different scenarios that cover material in the tutorial with plenty of exercises."
— Shui-lien Huang, Mt. San Antonio College

"The 'Managing Your Files' tutorial covers all the basic skills students need to have a good working knowledge of files and file management. It is clear, concise, and easy to understand."
— Mary Logan, Delgado Community College

www.course.com/NewPerspectives

Why *New Perspectives* will work for you

Review

Apply

Reference Window

Task Reference

Reinforce

Context
Each tutorial begins with a problem presented in a "real-world" case that is meaningful to students. The case sets the scene to help students understand what they will do in the tutorial.

Hands-on Approach
Each tutorial is divided into manageable sessions that combine reading and hands-on, step-by-step work. Colorful screenshots help guide students through the steps. **Trouble?** tips anticipate common mistakes or problems to help students stay on track and continue with the tutorial.

Review
In New Perspectives, retention is a key component to learning. At the end of each session, a series of Quick Check questions helps students test their understanding of the concepts before moving on. Each tutorial also contains an end-of-tutorial summary and a list of key terms for further reinforcement.

Assessment
Engaging and challenging Review Assignments and Case Problems have always been a hallmark feature of the New Perspectives Series. Colorful icons and brief descriptions accompany the exercises, making it easy to understand, at a glance, both the goal and level of challenge a particular assignment holds.

Reference
While contextual learning is excellent for retention, there are times when students will want a high-level understanding of how to accomplish a task. Within each tutorial, Reference Windows appear before a set of steps to provide a succinct summary and preview of how to perform a task. In addition, a complete Task Reference at the back of the book provides quick access to information on how to carry out common tasks. Finally, each book includes a combination Glossary/Index to promote easy reference of material.

Lab Assignments
Certain tutorials in this book contain Lab Assignments, which provide additional reinforcement of important skills in a simulated environment. These labs have been hailed by students and teachers alike for years as the most comprehensive and accurate on the market. Great for pre-work or remediation, the labs help students learn concepts and skills in a structured environment.

Student Online Companion
This book has an accompanying online companion Web site designed to enhance learning. This Web site includes:
- Internet Assignments and Lab Assignments for selected tutorials
- Student Data Files and PowerPoint presentations
- Microsoft Office Specialist Certification Grids

Certification
This logo on the front of this book means that this book has been independently reviewed and approved by ProCert Labs. If you are interested in acquiring Microsoft Office Specialist certification, you may use this book as courseware in your preparation. For more information on this certification, go to www.microsoft.com/officespecialist.

www.course.com/NewPerspectives

New Perspectives offers an entire system of instruction

The New Perspectives Series is more than just a handful of books. It's a complete system of offerings:

New Perspectives catalog
Our online catalog is never out of date! Go to the catalog link on our Web site to check out our available titles, request a desk copy, download a book preview, or locate online files.

Coverage to meet your needs!
Whether you're looking for just a small amount of coverage or enough to fill a semester-long class, we can provide you with a textbook that meets your needs.

- Brief books typically cover the essential skills in just 2 to 4 tutorials.
- Introductory books build and expand on those skills and contain an average of 5 to 8 tutorials.
- Comprehensive books are great for a full-semester class, and contain 9 to 12+ tutorials.
- Power Users or Advanced books are perfect for a highly accelerated introductory class or a second course in a given topic.

So if the book you're holding does not provide the right amount of coverage for you, there's probably another offering available. Go to our Web site or contact your Course Technology sales representative to find out what else we offer.

Instructor Resources

We offer more than just a book. We have all the tools you need to enhance your lectures, check students' work, and generate exams in a new, easier-to-use and completely revised package. This book's Instructor's Manual, ExamView testbank, PowerPoint presentations, data files, solution files, figure files, and a sample syllabus are all available on a single CD-ROM or for downloading at www.course.com.

How will your students master Microsoft Office?

SAM (Skills Assessment Manager) 2003 helps you energize your class exams and training assignments by allowing students to learn and test important computer skills in an active, hands-on environment. With SAM 2003, you create powerful interactive exams on critical Microsoft Office 2003 applications, including Word, Excel, Access, and PowerPoint. The exams simulate the application environment, allowing your students to demonstrate their knowledge and to think through the skills by performing real-world tasks. Designed to be used with the New Perspectives Series, SAM 2003 includes built-in page references so students can create study guides that match the New Perspectives textbooks you use in class. Powerful administrative options allow you to schedule exams and assignments, secure your tests, and run reports with almost limitless flexibility. Find out more about SAM 2003 by going to www.course.com or speaking with your Course Technology sales representative.

Distance Learning

Enhance your course with any of our online learning platforms. Go to www.course.com or speak with your Course Technology sales representative to find the platform or the content that's right for you.

www.course.com/NewPerspectives

About the Premium Edition

The *New Perspectives on Microsoft Office 2003, First Course—Premium Edition* transforms the way students learn Microsoft Office skills with the following features, **new to this edition**:

- **SAM 2003 Training Companion CD!** This fully customized training companion is integrated with each tutorial in this book, providing students with hands-on practice and reinforcement of important skills. The SAM CD icon (shown on the left) appears at key points throughout each tutorial, prompting students to go to the CD for "just-in-time" training on the tasks they are learning in that tutorial.
- **New listing of tutorial objectives and SAM training tasks!** The first page of each tutorial now includes a listing of the learning objectives for each tutorial session and the corresponding tasks on the SAM 2003 Training Companion CD. This map shows, at a glance, exactly which training tasks are available to students in each session to enhance their learning experience.
- **Enhanced Data File listings!** The "Read This Before You Begin" page, which appears at the beginning of each application section, now includes a complete listing of all the starting Data Files needed for that section, as well as the ending files, which students create and save. This new format makes it easy for students and instructors to ensure they have all the necessary files, both before working on a tutorial and upon completion of a tutorial. These redesigned pages also provide important information about storing Data Files, using the new SAM 2003 Training Companion CD, and completing any Course Labs available for the application.
- **SAM 2003 Training Companion Task Reference!** This task reference appears at the back of the book and provides a complete list of all the tasks available on the SAM 2003 Training Companion CD, which tutorial and session they map to, and which pages in the book students can go to for coverage of each task.
- **Increased emphasis on file management!** The "Managing Your Files" tutorial has been updated with coverage of USB drives and explains how students can use these popular storage devices. Also, the new tear-off File Management FastCARD on the back of the book offers students a handy way to have file management tips and techniques at their fingertips.

System Requirements

For students who will work through this text using their own computers, please note the following system requirements:

- **Operating System** This text assumes a typical installation of Microsoft Windows XP Professional (although the Microsoft Windows XP Home version is acceptable as well).
- **Internet** This text assumes a typical installation of Microsoft Internet Explorer 6.0 or higher and Microsoft Outlook Express 6 or higher.
- **Microsoft Office 2003** This text assumes a typical installation of Microsoft Word 2003, Microsoft Excel 2003, and Microsoft Access 2003. For Microsoft PowerPoint 2003, a complete installation is required.

NOTE: For system requirements information related to the SAM 2003 Training Companion CD that accompanies this text, please refer to the insert provided with the CD on the inside front cover.

www.course.com/NewPerspectives

Brief Contents

Table of Contents

File Management   FM 1

Read This Before You Begin................... FM 2

Managing Your Files   FM 3

Creating and Working with Files and Folders in Windows XP ....FM 3

Internet   BEB 1

Read This Before You Begin................... BEB 2

Browser and E-mail Basics   BEB 3

Introduction to Microsoft Internet Explorer and Microsoft Outlook Express ....BEB 3

Word

Tutorial 4   AC 129

Integration   INT 2-1

Tutorial 2   INT 2-3

PowerPoint

Tutorial 1   PPT 3

Tutorial 2   PPT 41

New Perspectives on

Essential Computer Concepts

Essential Computer Concepts

Photo Credits

Figure 1:   © PhotoDisc/Getty Images

Figure 3:   Courtesy of Acer America Inc.; Courtesy of Gateway Inc.; Courtesy of ViewSonic Corporation

Figure 4:   Courtesy of palmOne, Inc. palmOne, Zire, and Tungsten are among the trademarks owned by or exclusively licensed to palmOne, Inc.

Figure 5:   Courtesy of IBM Corporation

Figure 6:   Courtesy of NASA

Figure 7:   Courtesy of Microsoft Corporation

Figure 8:   Courtesy of Microsoft Corporation

Figure 10:   Courtesy of ViewSonic Corporation

Figure 11:   Courtesy of Lexmark International Inc.

Figure 20:   Courtesy of Seagate Technology

Figure 22:   Courtesy of Acer America Inc.

Essential Computer Concepts

Case | Paik's Oriental Rug Gallery

Paik's Oriental Rug Gallery, located in the university town of Lake Thompson, specializes in the sale of new and used Oriental carpets. Paik's also performs beautiful renovations of damaged or old Oriental rugs. Thanks to his excellent customer service and professional reputation, owner Sang Kee Paik has broadened his customer base over the course of the last two years and is finding it hard to keep up with the paperwork. He recently hired you, a college graduate of the school of business, to assist him.

After several days on the job, you suggest to Mr. Paik that he would find it much easier to manage his inventory and payroll if he purchased several computers. He tells you he's considered that before, but hasn't had time to shop around. He asks you to research the features and prices of today's computers and recommend what he should purchase.

You go to the library to review computer trade magazines and examine the features of current models. Computers and their prices are constantly changing, but most of today's computers are well-suited to running a small business. You are sure you will be able to find computers that will meet Mr. Paik's needs. Figure 1 (on the next page) shows an advertisement for a computer you think might be appropriate for Mr. Paik's business.

| Objectives

- Describe the components of a computer system
- Compare the types of computers
- Define a personal computer's hardware in terms of its functions: input, output, processing, and storage
- Examine data representation and the ASCII code
- Describe how peripheral devices are connected to a personal computer
- Identify the hardware and software that are used to establish a network connection
- Explain how Internet access, e-mail, and the World Wide Web affect the use of computers
- Discuss the types of system software and their functions
- Identify popular application software
- Describe how data is shared among different types of application software

| Labs

Using a Mouse

Using a Keyboard

Peripheral Devices

Using Files

The Internet: World Wide Web

User Interfaces

Multimedia

Student Data Files There are no student Data Files needed for this tutorial.

Figure 1 ▶ **Computer ad**

Our award-winning computers offer strong performance at a reasonable price. MicroPlus computers feature superior engineering, starting with a genuine Intel processor and a motherboard designed specifically to take advantage of the latest chnological advancements. Of course, you are covered by our one-year on-site parts and labor warranty.*

All Credit Cards Welcome Call Toll Free 1-800-555-0000 and order today!

*ON-SITE SERVICE AVAILABLE FOR HARDWARE ONLY AND MAY NOT BE AVAILABLE IN CERTAIN REMOTE AREAS. SHIPPING AND HANDLING EXTRA. ALL RETURNS WILL BE EXCHANGED FOR LINE PRODUCT ONLY. ALL RETURNS MUST BE IN ORIGINAL BOX WITH ALL MATERIALS CALL FOR AN RMA NUMBER. DEFECTIVE PRODUCTS WILL BE REPAIRED AT MICROPLUS DISCRETION. THE COST FOR RETURNED MERCHANDISE IS NOT INCLUDED WITH ANY MONEY-BACK GUARANTEE. PRICES AND AVAILABILITY SUBJECT TO CHANGE WITHOUT NOTICE.

This high-end desktop PC is powerful enough to meet the most demanding computing needs today and beyond.

Specifications:

- Processor: Intel® Pentium® 4 Processor 2.66GHz with 512K L2 Advanced Transfer Cache Compare
- Memory: 512MB SDRAM expandable to 2GB (2048MB)
- Hard Drive: 80GB 6 ms UATA100 7200RPM Hard Drive
- Floppy Drive: 3.5" 1.44MB diskette drive
- DVD±RW/±R/CD-RW: 4x Recordable DVD drive
- Operating System: Microsoft® Windows® XP Professional Edition
- Application Software: Microsoft® Office 2003
- Monitor: 15" LCD Flat Panel Display (15" viewable), 1,024 X 768
- Video: 64MB NVIDIA™ GeForce2 MX400 AGP Graphics with DVI and TV Out
- Keyboard: Multi-function Keyboard
- Mouse: Logitech USB Optical Wheel Mouse
- Sound System: SoundBlaster Audigy Audio w/ IEEE 1394
- Speakers: built into the monitor
- Case: Mid-Tower Case
- Expansion Slots: 5 PCI and 1 AGP
- External ports: (6) USB (2 in front and 4 more in back), Parallel, Serial, and (2) PS/2
- Controller: Integrated Ultra ATA Controller
- Modem: 56K PCI Voice Modem 2
- Network card: intergrated 10/100 Ethernet

Limited Warranty Program: 1 Year Limited Parts / Labor / Onsite / 1 Year Limited Support3

AntiVirus Software: Norton AntiVirus 90 day Introductory Offer at no additional charge

What Is a Computer?

Computers have become essential tools in almost every type of activity in virtually every type of business. A **computer** is defined as an electronic device that accepts input, processes data, stores data, and produces output. It is a versatile tool with the potential to perform many different tasks.

A **computer system** includes a computer, peripheral devices, and software. The physical components of a computer are referred to as **hardware**. The design and construction of a particular computer is referred to as its **architecture**, or **configuration**. The technical details about each component are called **specifications**. For example, a computer system might be *configured* to include a printer; a *specification* for that printer might be a print speed of eight pages per minute or the capacity to print in color. The computer itself takes care of the processing function, but it needs additional components, called **peripheral devices**, to accomplish its input, output, and storage functions. In this tutorial, you will learn more about the hardware that performs these basic computer functions.

Software refers to the intangible components of a computer system, particularly the **programs**, or lists of instructions, that the computer needs to perform a specific task. Software is the key to a computer's versatility. When your computer is using word processing software—for example, the Microsoft Word program—you can type memos, letters, and reports. When your computer is using accounting software, you can maintain information about what your customers owe you or display a graph showing the timing of customer payments.

The hardware and the software of a computer system work together to process data—the words, figures, sounds, and graphics that describe people, events, things, and ideas. Figure 2 illustrates how you and the computer system interact to complete a task. Suppose you want to use the computer to write a report. First you instruct the computer to use the word processing program. After activating the word processing program, you begin typing the text of your report. The data you type into the computer is called **input**. You use an **input device**, such as a keyboard or a mouse, to input data and issue commands. **Commands** are another type of input that instruct the computer on how to process the data. For example, in your report, you might want to center the title and double-space the text of the report. You issue the appropriate commands in the word processing program that will instruct the computer to modify the data you have input so the text is double-spaced and the title of the report is centered. Modifying data in this way is referred to as **processing**. In a computer, processing tasks occur on the **motherboard**, which is the main circuit board of the computer. The motherboard contains the **processing hardware**, the computer's major electronic components.

How a computer works ◄ **Figure 2**

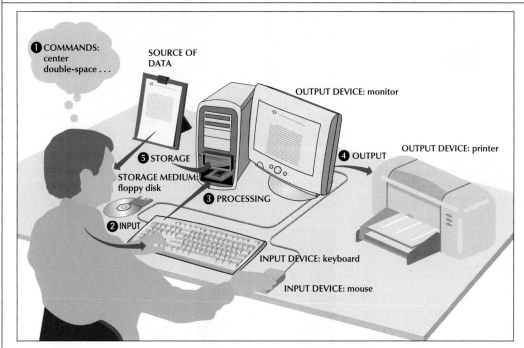

The result of the computer processing your input is referred to as **output**. Output can be in many different forms, for example reports, documents, graphs, sounds, and pictures. Computers produce output using **output devices**, such as a computer monitor or a printer. The output you create using a computer can be stored either inside the computer itself, or on an external storage device, such as a floppy disk. You will learn more about storage devices later in this tutorial.

Using a computer has several advantages. The first is the speed at which you can perform tasks. Second, the capability of storing the output and using it over and over again, in so many different ways, makes using a computer the most effective way to perform many personal and business tasks. Finally, an important advantage is sharing data and output with others. You make a note to find out whether Paik employees will need to share their data.

Types of Computers

There are many types of computers, which are classified by their size, speed, capabilities, and cost. Computers are categorized as personal computers, hand-held computers, mainframes, and supercomputers.

Personal computers, originally called **microcomputers**, are the computers typically used by a single user, for use in the home or office. Examples of personal computers are shown in Figure 3.

Figure 3	Examples of personal computers

A desktop computer fits on a desk and runs on power from an electrical wall outlet. The monitor can be a flat panel monitor (like the one shown) or a CRT monitor, which takes up more space on the desk, but is less expensive.

A notebook computer is small and lightweight, giving it the advantage of portability. It can run on power supplied by an electrical outlet, or it can run on battery power.

A Tablet PC is a portable computer that has a screen on which the user can execute commands and write with a stylus. The computer recognizes the handwriting and integrates it into the program being used. On some models, the screen can be moved out of the way so that the user can access an attached keyboard; on other models, you can attach a keyboard if you wish.

A personal computer is used for general computing tasks such as word processing, working with photographs or graphics, e-mail, and Internet access. A personal computer is available as a **desktop computer**, which is designed to sit compactly on a desk; as a **notebook computer** (also referred to as a **laptop computer**), which is designed for portability; or as a **Tablet PC**, which is also designed for portability, but includes the capability of recognizing ordinary handwriting on the screen. Tablet PCs also include speech recognition software. Personal computers cost between $500 and $3000, but the average computer user spends $800 to $1300 when purchasing a personal computer. A notebook computer with similar capability is usually more expensive than a desktop computer, and Tablet PCs are more expensive than notebook computers.

Hand-held computers, also known as **PDAs** (Personal Digital Assistants), are small computers designed to fit in the palm of your hand, as shown in Figure 4. Hand-held computers are compact enough to fit in your pocket, and they run on batteries. Hand-held computers have more limited capabilities than personal computers, and are generally used to maintain an electronic appointment book, address book, calculator, and notepad, although high-end PDAs are all-in-one devices that can be used to send and receive e-mails and make phone calls. Hand-held computers cost between $100 and $700.

Example of a hand-held computer ◄ Figure 4

You assume that your recommendation to Mr. Paik will include personal computers because most daily tasks can be performed very efficiently using them. However, you wonder whether some employees might need the portability of notebook computers or Tablet PCs, and whether others might need a PDA. You add these notes to your list of questions to ask Mr. Paik.

Many small and large businesses use personal computers extensively. But some businesses, government agencies, and other institutions also use larger and faster types of computers such as mainframes and supercomputers. Usually, a company decides to purchase a mainframe computer when it must carry out the processing tasks for many users, especially when the users share large amounts of data. Each user inputs processing requests and views output through a terminal. A **terminal** has a keyboard for input and a monitor for output, but is not capable of processing data on its own.

Mainframe computers, like the one shown in Figure 5, are typically used to provide centralized storage, processing, and management for large amounts of data. The price of a mainframe computer varies widely, from several hundred thousand dollars to several million dollars.

Figure 5 ▶ **The system unit for the IBM S/390 G5 mainframe computer**

The largest and fastest computers, called **supercomputers**, were first developed for high-volume computing tasks such as weather prediction. Supercomputers, like the one shown in Figure 6, are also being used by large corporations and government agencies when the tremendous volume of data would seriously delay processing on a mainframe computer. Although its cost can be tens of millions of dollars, a supercomputer's processing speed is so much faster than that of personal computers and mainframes that the investment can be worthwhile.

Figure 6 ▶ **A supercomputer**

How would you classify the computer in the advertisement shown in Figure 1 at the beginning of the tutorial? If your answer is a desktop personal computer, you are correct. The computer in that ad fits on a desk and is not portable.

Based on what you have learned about the computing process and types of computers, you decide to recommend that Mr. Paik purchase some personal computers. When you look at the ad, however, you realize that there are several specifications that Mr. Paik may not understand. Your recommendation will have to explain what each listed component does, and why it is important. The remainder of this tutorial will focus on personal computer hardware and software in more detail, so you can learn what you need to know to make a better recommendation.

Computer Hardware

As you've already learned, computer hardware can be defined as the physical components of a computer. Now look at the hardware you might use in a typical personal computer system.

Input Devices

You input data and commands by using an input device such as a keyboard or a mouse. The computer can also receive input from a storage device. This section takes a closer look at the input devices you might use. Output and storage devices are covered in later sections.

The most frequently used input device is a **keyboard**. The top keyboard in Figure 7 is a standard 101-key keyboard. Newer keyboards, such as the bottom keyboard in Figure 7, are **ergonomic**, which means that they have been designed to fit the natural placement of your hands and should reduce the risk of repetitive-motion injuries. All keyboards consist of three major parts: the main keyboard, the keypads, and the function keys.

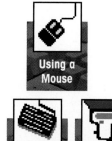

Using a
Mouse

Using a
Keyboard

Peripheral
Devices

Keyboards ◄ **Figure 7**

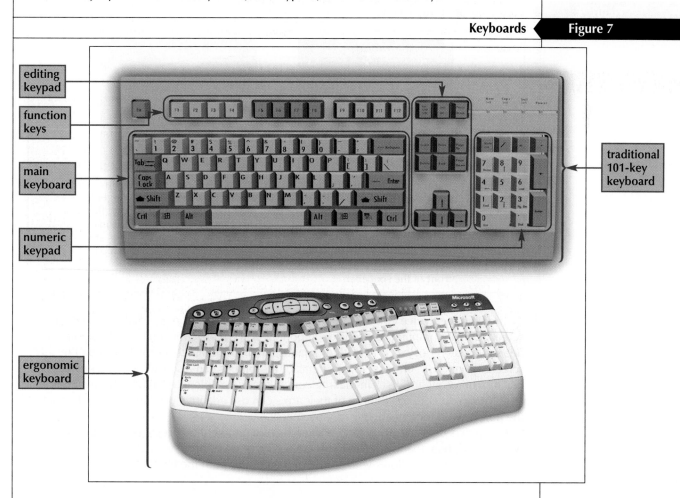

All personal computers are equipped with a pointing device. The most popular is a **mouse**, such as the ones shown in Figure 8; notebook computers are usually equipped with one of the other options pictured in Figure 9.

Figure 8 ▶ **Personal computer pointing devices**

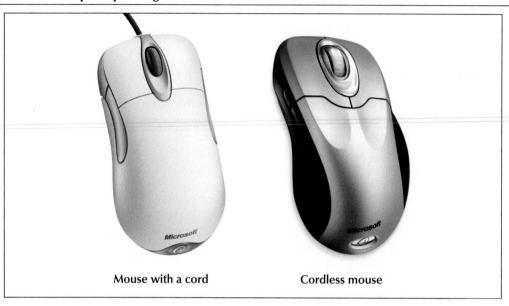

Mouse with a cord   Cordless mouse

Figure 9 ▶ **Notebook pointing devices**

Track point

Touch pad

A **track point** is a small eraser-like device embedded among the typing keys. To control the on-screen pointer, you push the track point up, left, right, or down. Buttons for clicking and double-clicking are located in front of the spacebar.

A **touch pad** is a touch-sensitive device. By dragging your finger over the surface, you control the on-screen pointer. Two buttons equivalent to mouse buttons are located in front of the touch pad.

The **pointing device** controls a **pointer**, a small arrow or other symbol, on the display screen. Using a pointing device is an important skill because most personal computers depend on such devices to select commands and manipulate text or graphics on the screen. People with physical impairments or disabilities can also use pointing devices because of recent advances in making computers accessible to everyone. For example, people who do not have the use of their arms can use adaptive pointing devices to control the pointer with foot, head, or eye movements.

Computers used for presentations often feature remote input devices, sometimes called **wireless pointers**, that work like the remote control used for a TV, VCR, or DVD. The remote input device allows you to control the pointer from the back of the auditorium.

Now that you have read about input devices, refer back to the computer advertisement shown in Figure 1 at the beginning of the tutorial. Can you list the input devices included with the advertised system? A mouse and a keyboard are considered essential peripheral devices, so advertisements do not always list them. Unless the ad specifies some other input device, such as a track ball, you can safely assume the computer comes equipped with a traditional keyboard and mouse.

Output Devices

As stated earlier, output is the result of processing data; output devices show you those results. The most commonly used output devices are monitors and printers. A **monitor** is the device that displays the output from a computer, as shown in Figure 10. The monitor on the left is a **CRT (cathode ray tube) monitor**, which uses gun-like devices that direct beams of electrons toward the screen to activate dots of color to form the image you see on the screen. The monitor on the right is a **flat panel monitor**. Most flat panel monitors use **LCD (liquid crystal display)** technology, which creates the image you see on the screen by manipulating light within a layer of liquid crystal. This is the same technology used in digital watches or the time display on a microwave oven. Flat panel display monitors take up very little room on the desktop, are lightweight, and are very easy to read, but are much more expensive than CRT monitors. However, many graphic artists prefer CRT technology because it displays uniform color from any viewing angle.

Monitor types   Figure 10

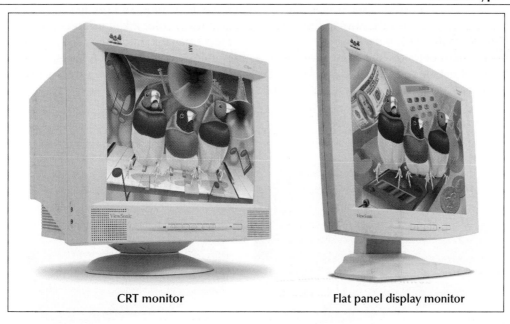

CRT monitor   Flat panel display monitor

Factors that influence the quality of a monitor are screen size, resolution, and dot pitch. **Screen size** is the diagonal measurement in inches from one corner of the screen to the other. Measurements for today's desktop monitors range from 15" to 23". The monitors on notebook computers range from 12" to 17". The first personal computer monitors and many terminals still in use today are character-based. A **character-based display** divides the screen into a grid of rectangles, one for each typed character. A monitor that is capable of displaying graphics, called a **graphics display**, divides the screen into a matrix of small dots called **pixels**. **Resolution** is the maximum number of pixels the monitor can display. Standard resolutions are 640 × 480, 800 × 600, 1,024 × 768, 1,280 × 1,024, and 1,600 × 1,200. The resolution you use depends on your monitor size. If your screen is small, 1,600 × 1,200 resolution will make the objects on the screen too small to see clearly. Resolution is easy to adjust on most monitors. **Dot pitch** measures the distance between pixels, so a smaller dot pitch means a sharper image. A .28 or .26 dot pitch (dp) is typical for today's monitors.

A computer display system consists of a monitor and a **graphics card**, also called a **video display adapter** or **video card**. A **card** is a rigid piece of insulating material with circuits on it. The circuits control the functions of the card. The graphics card is installed inside the computer on the motherboard, and controls the signals the computer sends to the monitor. If you plan to display a lot of images on the monitor, you may also need a **graphics accelerator card** to speed up the computer's ability to display them. When purchasing a monitor, you must be sure that it comes with a video card that is compatible with your computer.

Refer back to the computer ad in Figure 1. Does this personal computer include a monitor and video card? The correct answer is yes, both are included. What is the type, size, and resolution of the monitor? The monitor is a 15" 1,024 × 768 flat panel monitor.

A **printer** produces a paper copy of the text or graphics processed by the computer. A printed copy of computer output is called **hard copy**, because it is more tangible than the electronic or magnetic copies found on a disk, in the computer memory, or on the monitor. There are three popular categories of printers, and each has special capabilities.

The most popular printers for business use are **laser printers**, like the one shown on the left in Figure 11, because they use the same technology as a photocopier. A temporary laser image is transferred onto paper with a powdery substance called **toner**. This produces high-quality output quickly and efficiently. The speed of laser printers is measured in **pages per minute (ppm)**. Color laser printers use several toner cartridges to apply color to the page. Non-color laser printers are less expensive than color laser printers.

A less expensive alternative to the laser printer is to use a color **inkjet printer** such as the one shown on the right in Figure 11. These printers spray ink onto paper. The quality of the inkjet output is almost comparable to a laser printer's output. Inkjet printers, with and without color capabilities, are very popular printers for home use. The speed of inkjet printers is also measured in pages per minute.

| Figure 11 | Types of printers |

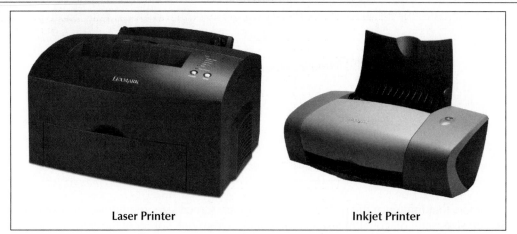

Laser Printer   **Inkjet Printer**

Another type of printer is the dot matrix printer, the oldest printing technology currently found on the computer market. Dot matrix printers transfer ink to the paper by striking a ribbon with pins. Using more pins controls the quality of the print, so a 24-pin dot matrix printer produces better quality print than a 9-pin. Dot matrix printers are most often used when a large number of pages need to be printed fairly quickly or when a business needs to print on multi-page continuous forms. The speed of dot matrix printers is measured in characters per second (cps). Some examples of their usefulness are the printing of grade reports, bank statements, or payroll checks.

You notice that the computer ad in Figure 1 does not include a printer, so you make a note to ask Mr. Paik if your recommendation should include one. If so, you decide to recommend a color laser printer to print correspondence, advertisements, and brochures.

Multimedia devices are another category of peripheral devices. **Multimedia** refers to an integrated collection of computer-based media including text, graphics, sound, animation, and video. Most personal computers come equipped with a sound card and speakers that can play digital sounds. The sound card converts sounds so that they can be broadcast through speakers.

The computer advertised in Figure 1 includes a sound card and speakers that are built into the monitor. These are also output devices that you need to mention in your recommendation. Mr. Paik will need these output devices for a variety of activities, such as participating in teleconferences on product availability attended by suppliers in widespread locations, or recording announcements that employees can play back at their convenience. Later in this tutorial, you will learn how business users are sharing a variety of data resources, including digital sound.

Processing Hardware

The most important computer function is processing data. Before you can understand this function and the hardware that executes it, you first need to learn how the computer represents and stores data.

Using Files

Data Representation

The characters used in human language are meaningless to a computer because it is an electronic device. Like a light bulb, the computer must interpret every signal as either "on" or "off." To do so, a computer represents data as distinct or separate numbers. Specifically, it represents "on" with a 1 and "off" with a 0. These numbers are referred to as **binary digits**, or **bits**.

A series of eight bits is called a **byte**. As Figure 12 shows, the byte that represents the integer value 0 is 00000000, with all eight bits "off" or set to 0. The byte that represents the integer value 1 is 00000001, and the byte that represents 255 is 11111111.

Binary representation of numbers ◄ **Figure 12**

Number	Binary Representation
0	00000000
1	00000001
2	00000010
3	00000011
4	00000100
5	00000101
6	00000110
7	00000111
8	00001000
⋮	⋮
253	11111101
254	11111110
255	11111111

Personal computers commonly use the **ASCII** code to represent character data. ASCII (pronounced "ASK-ee") stands for **American Standard Code for Information Interchange**. The ASCII system translates the decimal numbers 0 through 255 into binary data. Each ASCII code represents a letter or character on the keyboard; for example, the ASCII code 65 represents the character *A*, and the ASCII code 97 represents *a*. Computers translate ASCII code into binary data so that they can process it. Figure 13 shows sample ASCII code.

Figure 13 | **Sample ASCII code representing letters and symbols**

Character	ASCII code	Binary Number
(space)	32	00100000
$	36	00100100
A	65	01000001
B	66	01000010
a	97	01100001
b	98	01100010

As a computer user, you don't have to know the binary representations of numbers, characters, and instructions, because the computer handles all the necessary conversions internally. However, because the amount of memory in a computer and its storage capacity are expressed in bytes, you should be aware of how data is represented. **Storage**, or **memory capacity**, is the amount of data, or number of characters, that the device can handle at any given time. A **kilobyte** (KB or simply K) is 1,024 bytes, or approximately one thousand bytes. A **megabyte** (MB) is 1,048,576 bytes, or about one million bytes. A **gigabyte** (GB) is 1,073,741,824 bytes, or about one billion bytes. You will see the symbols KB, MB, and GB refer to both processing and storage capacity.

The Microprocessor

The two most important components of personal computer hardware are the **microprocessor**, a silicon chip designed to manipulate data, and the **memory**, which stores instructions and data. The type of microprocessor and the memory capacity are two factors that directly affect the price and performance of a computer.

The microprocessor, such as the one shown in Figure 14, is an integrated circuit (an electronic component called a **chip**) which is located on the motherboard inside the computer. The terms **processor** and **central processing unit** (CPU) also refer to this device, which is responsible for executing instructions to process data.

Figure 14 | **An Intel Pentium 4 microprocessor**

The speed of a microprocessor is determined by its clock speed, word size, and cache size. Think of the **clock speed** as the pulse of the processor. It is measured in millions of cycles per second, or **megahertz** (MHz), or **gigahertz** (GHz), a billion cycles per second. **Word size** refers to the number of bits that are processed at one time. A computer with a large word size can process faster than a computer with a small word size. The earliest personal computers had an 8-bit word size, but now a 64-bit word size is common. **Cache**, sometimes called **RAM cache** or **cache memory**, is special high-speed memory reserved for the microprocessor's use. It speeds up the processing function by accessing data the computer anticipates you will request soon, while you are still working on something else.

Take another look at the computer advertised in Figure 1. What is the type and speed of its microprocessor? Your answer should be that it has a Pentium 4 microprocessor that can operate at 2.66 GHz and has 512 K cache.

Memory

Computer **memory** is a set of storage locations on the motherboard. Your computer has four types of memory: random access memory, virtual memory, read-only memory, and complementary metal oxide semiconductor (CMOS) memory.

Random access memory (RAM) is active during the processing function. It consists of electronic circuits on the motherboard that temporarily hold programs and data while the computer is on. RAM is **volatile**, which means that it is constantly changing as long as the computer is on and is cleared when the computer is turned off. The microprocessor uses RAM to store and retrieve instructions and data as they are needed. For example, if you are writing a paper, the word processing program that you are using is temporarily copied into RAM so the microprocessor can quickly access the instructions that you will need as you type and format your paper. As you type, the characters are also stored in RAM, along with the many fonts, special characters, graphics, and other objects that you might use to enhance the paper. How much you can include in your paper depends on the RAM capacity of the computer you are using. Most personal computers on the market today use **SDRAM** (synchronous dynamic RAM) or **RDRAM** (Rambus dynamic RAM). SDRAM is plenty fast for the average computer user and inexpensive. RDRAM was originally designed for use in computer game systems and is more expensive than SDRAM. When paired with a microprocessor of 1 GHz or faster, RDRAM can improve a computer system's overall performance.

Look at the computer ad in Figure 1. Notice that this computer has 512 MB of SDRAM. In other words, it has the capacity to temporarily store over 512 million characters at any one time. Although your paper might not be that long, the computer uses a lot of that available memory for programs and other data it needs to process your paper. The notation "expandable to 2 GB (2048 MB)" tells you that you can add more RAM to this computer. Expandability is an important feature of any computer; you need to be able to change your computer's capability as your needs change.

When the programs running on a computer use all the available RAM, the software uses space on the computer's storage devices to simulate RAM. This extra memory is called **virtual memory**. Figure 15 explains how it works. The disadvantage of using virtual memory is that it is much slower than RAM, so expanding the RAM capacity of a computer will improve its performance.

Figure 15 ▶ **How virtual memory works**

1. Your computer is running a word processing program that takes up most of the program area in RAM, but you want to run a spreadsheet program at the same time.

2. The operating system moves the least-used segment of the word processing program into virtual memory on disk.

3. The spreadsheet program can now be loaded into the RAM vacated by the least-used segment of the word processing program.

4. If the least-used segment of the word processing program is later needed, it is copied from virtual memory back into RAM. To make room, some other infrequently used segment of a program will need to be transferred into virtual memory.

Read-only memory (ROM) is another set of electronic circuits on the motherboard inside the computer. Although you can expand your RAM capacity, you cannot add to ROM capacity. In fact, the manufacturer of the computer permanently installs ROM. It is the permanent storage location for a set of instructions that the computer uses when you turn it on. Because ROM never changes and it remains intact when the computer is turned off, it is called **nonvolatile**.

The events that occur between the moment you turn on the computer and the moment you can actually begin to use the computer are called the **boot process**, as shown in Figure 16, and the act of turning on the computer is sometimes called **booting up**. When the computer is off, RAM is empty. When the computer is turned on, the set of instructions in ROM checks all the computer system's components to make sure they are working, and activates the essential software that controls the processing function.

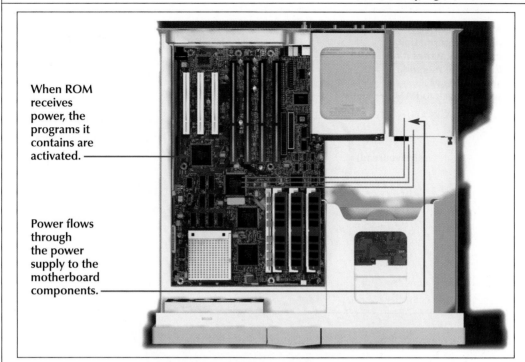

When ROM receives power, the programs it contains are activated. ——

Power flows through the power supply to the motherboard components.——

Complementary metal oxide semiconductor (CMOS) memory (pronounced "SEE-Moss") is another chip that is installed on the motherboard. It is also activated during the boot process and contains information about where the essential software is stored. A small rechargeable battery powers CMOS so its contents will be saved between computer uses. Unlike ROM, which cannot be changed, CMOS must be changed every time you add or remove hardware to your computer system. Thus, CMOS is often referred to as semipermanent memory, ROM as permanent memory, and RAM as temporary memory.

Storage Devices and Media

Because RAM retains data only while the power is on, your computer must have a more permanent storage option. As Figure 17 shows, a storage device receives data from RAM and writes it on a storage medium, such as a disk. Later the data can be read and sent back to RAM to use again.

Figure 17	Storage devices and RAM

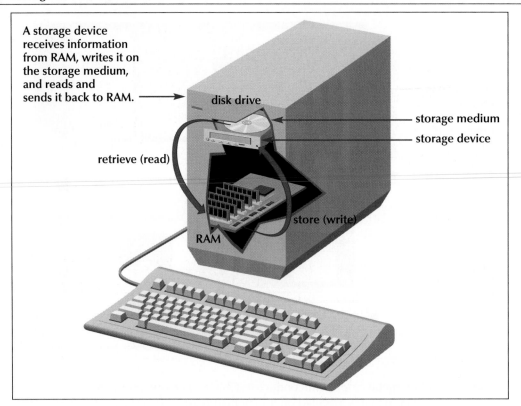

A storage device receives information from RAM, writes it on the storage medium, and reads and sends it back to RAM.

disk drive

storage medium

storage device

retrieve (read)

store (write)

RAM

Before you can understand the hardware that stores data, you need to know how data is stored. All data and programs are stored as files. A computer **file** is a named collection of related bits that exists on a storage medium. There are two categories of files: executable files and data files. An **executable file** contains the instructions that tell a computer how to perform a specific task. The files that are used during the boot process, for instance, are executable. Users create **data files**, usually with software. For instance, a paper that you write with a word processing program is data, and must be saved as a data file if you want to use it again.

The storage devices where computer files are kept can be categorized by the method they use to store files. **Magnetic storage devices** use oxide-coated plastic storage media called **mylar**. Figure 18 illustrates the process of storing data on magnetic media.

Storing data on magnetic media ◄ Figure 18

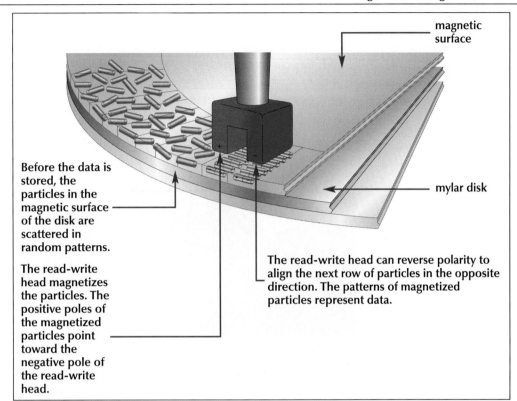

magnetic surface

mylar disk

Before the data is stored, the particles in the magnetic surface of the disk are scattered in random patterns.

The read-write head magnetizes the particles. The positive poles of the magnetized particles point toward the negative pole of the read-write head.

The read-write head can reverse polarity to align the next row of particles in the opposite direction. The patterns of magnetized particles represent data.

The most common magnetic storage devices are floppy disk drives, hard disk drives, and tape drives. **Floppy disks**, sometimes called **diskettes**, are flat circles of iron oxide-coated plastic enclosed in a hard plastic case (see Figure 19). Floppy disks are sometimes called 3½" disks because of the size of the hard plastic case. Floppy disks have the capacity to store 1.44 MB, or 1,440,000 bytes, of data. Although some computers are now manufactured without a floppy disk drive, floppy disks are still very common. The computer shown in the advertisement in Figure 1 has a floppy disk drive that accepts 3½" floppy disks with 1.44 MB capacity.

3½" disk ◄ Figure 19

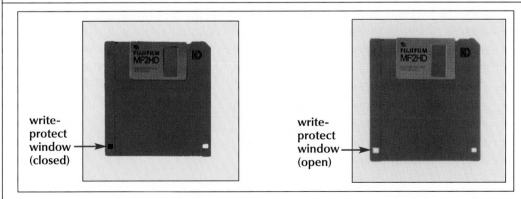

write-protect window (closed)

write-protect window (open)

Write protection prevents additional files from being stored on the disk and any file from being erased from the disk. To write protect a 3½" floppy disk, you open the write-protect window, as shown in Figure 19.

The other most common magnetic storage device is a **hard disk drive**, such as the one shown in Figure 20. This drive contains several iron oxide-covered metal platters that are usually sealed in a case inside the computer. Hard disk storage has two advantages over floppy disk storage: speed and capacity.

Figure 20 ⟩ **Internal components of a hard disk drive**

The speed of a disk drive is measured by its **access time**, the time required to read or write one record of data. Access time is measured in **milliseconds** (ms), one-thousandths of a second. The hard disk drive included in Figure 1, for instance, has 6 ms access time. Its capacity is 80 GB. Although this seems like a very high number, a Windows-based computer fully loaded with typical software can use up to 1 GB, and the addition of data and multimedia files can add up quickly.

Another magnetic storage device is a **tape drive**, which provides inexpensive archival storage for large quantities of data. Tape storage is much too slow to be used for day-to-day computer tasks; therefore, tapes are used to make backup copies of data stored on hard disks. If a hard disk fails, data from the backup tape can be reloaded on a new hard disk with minimal interruption of operations. Large corporations use tape drives for backup, but smaller companies and home computer systems rely on other storage methods.

Optical storage devices use laser technology to read and write data on silver platters. The first standard optical storage device on personal computers was the **CD-ROM** drive, which stands for **Compact Disk Read Only Memory**. One CD-ROM can store up to 700 MB, equivalent to more than 450 floppy disks. Today's personal computers are also equipped with **DVD**, or **Digital Video Disk**, drives. DVDs, though the same size as CD-ROMs, can store up to 4.7 GB of data, depending on whether data is stored on one or two sides of the disk, and how many layers of data each side contains. This is a little less than seven times the capacity of a CD. A DVD has more than enough storage capacity for an entire feature-length film—up to 9 hours of video or 30 hours of CD-ROM-quality audio.

Optical storage technology records data as a trail of tiny pits in the disk surface. The data that these pits represent can then be "read" with a beam of laser light. Figure 21 shows how data is stored on optical media.

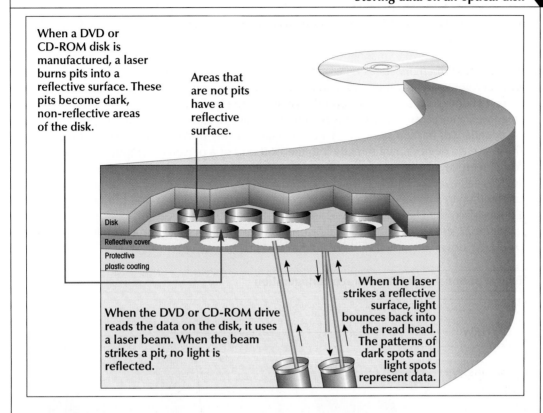

When a DVD or CD-ROM disk is manufactured, a laser burns pits into a reflective surface. These pits become dark, non-reflective areas of the disk.

Areas that are not pits have a reflective surface.

Disk

Reflective cover

Protective plastic coating

When the DVD or CD-ROM drive reads the data on the disk, it uses a laser beam. When the beam strikes a pit, no light is reflected.

When the laser strikes a reflective surface, light bounces back into the read head. The patterns of dark spots and light spots represent data.

The most common uses of CD-ROMs or DVDs are for software distribution and storing large files that typically include graphics, animation, and video. Optical storage media are very durable. Unlike magnetic media, such as floppy and hard disks, CD and DVD platters are not susceptible to humidity, dust, fingerprints, or magnets. They are not indestructable, however. Take care not to scratch the disk surface or expose the disk to high temperatures.

CD-ROMs are for "read-only" access, meaning you can read data stored on them, but you cannot use them to record or store your own data. In order to record data on a CD, you need a **CD-R** (compact disc recordable) drive and a CD-R disk. Instead of storing data in pits made on the surface of the disk, as with a CD-ROM drive, the drive is designed so that a laser changes the reflectivity of a dye layer on a blank CD-R disk, creating dark spots on the disk's surface that represent the data. Once the data is recorded, you cannot erase or modify it, but you can append new data to the data currently stored on the CD-R disk. A **CD-RW** (compact disk rewritable) drive is designed so that you can write data on a special CD-RW disk and continually access and modify that data. CD-R disks can be read by a standard CD-ROM drive or a DVD drive; CD-RW disks can be read only by CD-RW drives or CD-ROM drives labeled "multi-read."

Both CD-Rs and CD-RWs are useful for storing large amounts of data, or for transferring large files from one computer to another. The original CD-ROM drive had a relatively slow access time: 600 ms. As the technology has improved, that access time has decreased to less than 200 ms. A lower number means faster access. Also consider the drive's data transfer rate, measured in kilobits per second (**Kbps**), to classify it as 1X (the original), 2X (twice the original), 3X, and so on.

Recordable DVD drives are becoming more common. As with CDs, you can buy a DVD to which you can record only once, or a rewritable DVD to which you can record and then re-record data. Recordable and rewriteable DVDs come in several formats; for example, recordable DVDs are available as DVD-R and DVD+R. Make sure you know which type of DVD your DVD drive uses. The computer shown in Figure 1 includes a 4x recordable/rewritable DVD drive. It supports both the -RW and +RW formats, and it can read and record CDs as well.

Another alternative to magnetic storage are **flash memory storage devices**. Small and portable, flash memory stores data on a silicon chip (normally encased in hard plastic) and does not need power to maintain the information. Commonly used for storing data for cell phones, digital cameras, and PDAs, (under the brand names CompactFlash, SmartMedia and Memory Stick) flash memory storage devices are growing in popularity as secondary or backup storage devices for data typically stored on a hard disk drive. These storage devices plug directly into the USB port of a personal computer, where your computer recognizes it as another disk drive. With no moving parts, flash memory storage devices can even be attached to a keychain! Flash storage devices for personal computers can hold up to 512 MB of data, well exceeding the amount of data that can be stored on a floppy disk. The computer shown in Figure 1 has six USB ports.

Figure 22 shows the typical storage configuration of a personal computer. It includes a DVD±RW drive, a floppy disk drive, and a hard drive.

Figure 22 ▶ **Typical personal computer storage configuration**

You decide that your recommendation to Mr. Paik should include computers with at least CD-RW drives, and some computers with DVD±RW drives. As computers are used, the storage devices fill up quickly with software and data, so it's a good idea to purchase as much storage capacity as your budget allows. Even though floppy disks are becoming less popular as recordable CD and DVD drives drop in price and flash memory storage devices become more readily available, Mr. Paik still has plenty of data stored on floppy disks, so you will recommend floppy disk drives as well. You also decide to recommend at least 80 GB hard drives and perhaps 120 GB hard drives for some of the machines. You will also recommend at least 512 MB of RAM for each machine.

Data Communications

The transmission of text, numeric, voice, or video data from one computer to another is called **data communications**. This broad-based definition encompasses many critical business activities, from sending a letter to the printer upstairs to sending an **e-mail** (**electronic mail**) message to the company offices around the globe.

The four essential components of data communications are a sender, a receiver, a channel, and a protocol. The computer that originates the message is the **sender**. The message is sent over some type of **channel**, such as telephone or coaxial cable, a microwave signal, or optical fibers. The computer at the message's destination is called the **receiver**. The rules that establish an orderly transfer of data between the sender and the receiver are called **protocols**. Communication software and hardware establish these protocols at the beginning of the transmission, and both computers follow them strictly to guarantee an accurate transfer of data.

Data Bus

As noted earlier, peripherals are devices that can be added to a computer system to enhance its usefulness. Starting at the microprocessor, and passing through a continuous channel, the data travels out to the appropriate device. From an input device back to the microprocessor, the path is reversed. This communication between the microprocessor, RAM, and the peripherals is called the **data bus**.

An external peripheral device must have a corresponding **port** and **cable** that connect it to the back of the computer. Inside the computer, each port connects to a **controller card**, sometimes called an **expansion** or **interface card**. These cards, which provide an electrical connection to a variety of peripheral devices, plug into electrical connectors on the motherboard called **slots** or **expansion slots**. Figure 23 shows the data path that connects a printer to a computer. An internal peripheral device such as a hard disk drive may plug directly into the motherboard, or it may have an attached controller card. The transmission protocol is handled by a **device driver**, or simply **driver**, which is a computer program that can establish communication because it contains information about the characteristics of your computer and of the device.

Components for connecting a printer to a computer ◀ **Figure 23**

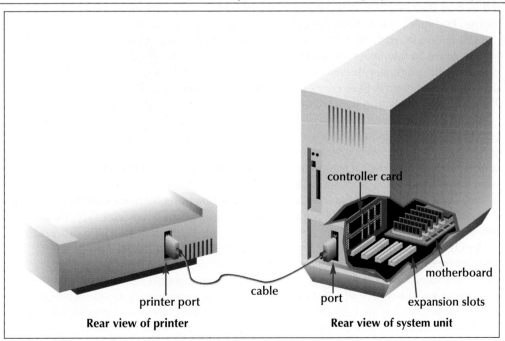

controller card

motherboard

printer port | cable | port | expansion slots

Rear view of printer | **Rear view of system unit**

Personal computers can have several types of ports, including USB, parallel, serial, SCSI, and MIDI. Figure 24 diagrams how the ports on a desktop personal computer might appear.

Figure 24 ▶ **Computer expansion ports**

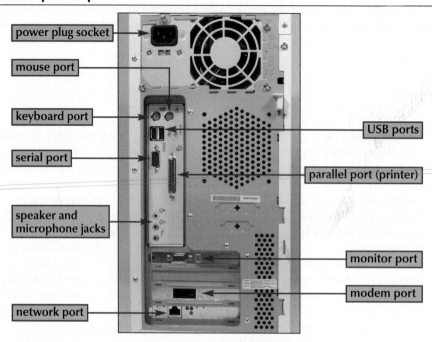

power plug socket

mouse port

keyboard port

USB ports

serial port

parallel port (printer)

speaker and microphone jacks

monitor port

modem port

network port

A **parallel port** transmits data eight bits at a time. Parallel transmissions are relatively fast, but increase the risk for interference, so they are typically used to connect a printer that is near the computer. A **serial port** transmits data one bit at a time. Typically, a mouse, keyboard, and modem are connected with serial interfaces.

SCSI (pronounced "scuzzy") stands for **small computer system interface**. One SCSI port provides an interface for one or more peripheral devices. The first is connected directly to the computer through the port, and the second device is plugged into a similar port on the first device. SCSI connections can allow many devices to use the same port. They are particularly popular on Macintosh computers and notebook computers.

Figure 24 shows some other ports for telephone cables to connect a modem, a video port to connect a monitor, and a network port. The interface to a sound card usually includes jacks for speakers and a microphone, which are designed to work with a **MIDI (musical instrument digital interface) card**, which is pronounced "middy." MIDI cards are used to record and play back musical data.

Notebook computers may also include a **Personal Computer Memory Card International Association (PCMCIA) device**. PCMCIA devices are credit-card-sized cards that plug directly into the PCMCIA slot and can contain additional memory, a modem, or a hard disk drive.

Another type of port found in computers is a **USB (Universal Serial Bus) port**. USB is a high-speed technology that facilitates the connection of external devices, such as joysticks, scanners, keyboards, video conferencing cameras, speakers, modems, and printers, to a computer. The device you install must have a **USB connector**, a small rectangular plug. You simply plug the USB connector into the USB port, and the computer recognizes the device and allows you to use it immediately. USB-compatible computers work more like stereo systems, in that you don't have to completely disassemble the unit to add a component. Any USB device can use any USB port, interchangeably and in any order. You can "daisy chain" up to 127 devices, plugging one device into another, or you can connect multiple devices to a single inexpensive hub. Data is transferred through a USB port 10 times faster than through a serial port, for example. For many USB devices, power is supplied via the port, so there is no need for extra power cables. Older computers can have numerous connectors—a keyboard connector, a mouse port, a parallel port, a joystick port, two audio ports, and two serial ports. USB computers replace this proliferation of ports with one standardized plug and port combination.

Look at the computer advertised in Figure 1. Does this computer include any of the ports illustrated in Figure 24? It mentions PS/2, USB, and parallel ports. Ports for a monitor, mouse, and keyboard are also included, because the advertisement lists those devices.

Networks

One of the most important types of data communications in the business world is a network connection. A **network** connects one computer to other computers and peripheral devices, enabling you to share data and resources with your coworkers. There are a variety of network configurations, too many to discuss thoroughly here. However, any type of network has some basic characteristics and requirements that you should know.

In a **local area network** (LAN), computers and peripheral devices are located relatively close to each other, generally in the same building. If you are using such a network, it is useful to know three things: the location of the data, the type of network card in your computer, and the communications software that manages protocols and network functions.

Some networks have one or more computers, called **servers**, that act as the central storage location for programs and provide mass storage for most of the data used on the network. A network with a server and computers dependent on the server is called a **client/server network**. The dependent computers are the **clients**. These networks are dependent on the server because it contains most of the data and software. When a network does not have a server, all the computers essentially are equal, and programs and data are distributed among them. This is called a **peer-to-peer network**.

Each computer that is part of the network must have a **network interface card (NIC)** installed. This card creates a communications channel between the computer and the network. A cable is used to connect the NIC port to the network. **Wi-Fi** (short for wireless fidelity) refers to a high-frequency **wireless local area network (WLAN)**. Wi-Fi is used to connect computers in a network by transmitting data through the air from an alternative to a wired LAN. Wi-Fi can be especially useful in buildings with older wiring. **Network software** is also essential, establishing the communications protocols that will be observed on the network and controlling the "traffic flow" as data travels throughout the network.

A personal computer that is not connected to a network is called a **standalone computer**. When it is connected to the network, it becomes a **workstation**. You have already learned that a terminal has a keyboard and monitor used for input and output, but it is not capable of processing on its own. A terminal is connected to a network that uses mainframes as servers. Any device connected to the network is called a **node**. Figure 25 illustrates a typical network configuration.

Network nodes include workstations, printers, and servers ◄ **Figure 25**

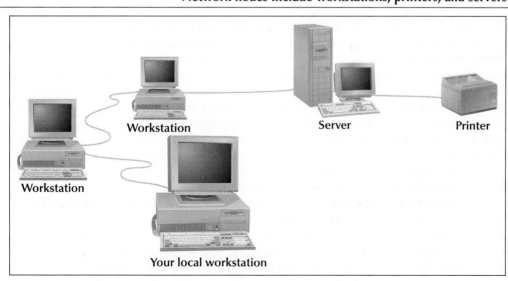

Workstation

Workstation

Server

Printer

Your local workstation

Look at the computer ad in Figure 1. Is this computer networked? Can it be networked? Why or why not? Your answer should be that the computer is not currently part of a network but does include an integrated network adapter card. With the appropriate network software, this computer can be connected to a network.

Telecommunications

Telecommunications means communicating over a comparatively long distance using a phone line. When it is not possible to connect users on one network, then telecommunications allows you to send and receive data over the telephone lines. To make this connection, you must use a communications device called a **modem**. A modem, which stands for *modulator-demodulator*, is a device that connects your computer to a standard telephone jack. The modem converts the **digital**, or stop-start, **signals** your computer outputs into **analog**, or continuous wave, **signals** (sound waves) that can traverse ordinary phone lines. Figure 26 shows the telecommunications process, in which a modem converts digital signals to analog signals at the sending site (modulates) and a second modem converts the analog signals back into digital signals at the receiving site (demodulates).

| Figure 26 | Using modems to send and receive a memo |

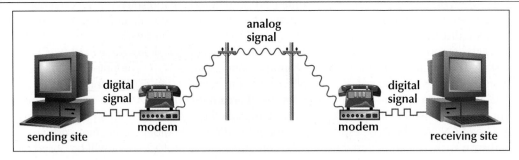

Most computers today come with a built-in 56K modem. The number 56 represents the modem's capability to send and receive about 56,000 **bits per second (bps)**. Actual speed may be reduced by factors such as distance, technical interference, and other issues. This speed is adequate for Paik employees to connect to suppliers at other locations around the world.

The Internet

The Internet was originally developed for the government to connect researchers around the world who needed to share data. Today, the **Internet** is the largest network in the world, connecting millions of people. It has become an invaluable communications channel for individuals, businesses, and governments around the world.

The first Internet experience most people have is to use **electronic mail**, more commonly called **e-mail**. This is the capability to send a message from one user's computer to another user's computer where it is stored until the receiver opens it. The vast network of networks that make up the Internet pass the message along through electronic links called **gateways**. E-mail has become such an integral part of business that you know you must recommend it to Mr. Paik. Your recommendation will list its advantages: speed and ease of communication with vendors and customers, lower postage costs, lower long-distance charges, and increased worker productivity.

Another benefit of using the Internet is the emergence of the **World Wide Web**, sometimes referred to simply as the **Web**. The Web is a huge database of information that is stored on network servers in places that allow public access. The information is stored as text files called **Web pages**, which can include text, graphics, sound, animation, and video. A collection of Web pages is called a **Web site**. Figure 27 shows a sample Web page.

A Web page on the World Wide Web ◄ Figure 27

The evolution of multimedia and Internet technologies has made the World Wide Web the perfect communications tool for marketing business services and products. Hyperlinks are the primary resource for making the Web possible. A **hyperlink**, or **link**, is a place on a Web page that is programmed to connect to a particular file on the same network server, or even on a network server on the other side of the globe. The communications software that helps you navigate the World Wide Web is called **Web browsing software**, or a **Web browser**. You decide to include the benefits of Internet and World Wide Web access in your recommendation to Mr. Paik. Specifically, you plan to convince him that he could sell carpets and advertise his carpet renovation services through the Web.

Computer Software

Just as a tape player or DVD player is worthless without tapes or DVDs, computer hardware is useless without software. **Software** is defined as the instructions and associated data that direct the computer to accomplish a task. Sometimes the term *software* refers to a single program, but often the term refers to a collection of programs and data that are packaged together. A **software package** contains disks or a CD-ROM and reference manual. The CD-ROM contains one or more programs and possibly some data. For example, the Microsoft Office 2003 software includes programs that help you draw graphics, create documents, and make calculations. The software includes some data, such as a thesaurus of words and their synonyms.

Software can be divided into two major categories: system software and application software. **System software** helps the computer carry out its basic operating tasks. **Application software** helps the user carry out a variety of tasks.

User Interfaces

System Software

System software manages the fundamental operations of your computer, such as loading programs and data into memory, executing programs, saving data to disks, displaying information on the monitor, and transmitting data through a port to a peripheral device. There are four types of system software: operating systems, utilities, device drivers, and programming languages.

An **operating system** controls basic input and output, allocates system resources, manages storage space, maintains security, and detects equipment failure. You have already learned the importance of data communications, both from a standalone computer and from a workstation to other users on a network. The flow of data from the microprocessor to memory to peripherals and back again is called basic **I/O**, or **i**nput/**o**utput. The operating system controls this flow of data just as an air-traffic controller manages airport traffic.

A system resource is any part of the computer system, including memory, storage devices, and the microprocessor, that can be used by a computer program. The operating system allocates system resources so programs run properly. Most of today's computers are capable of **multitasking**—opening and running more than one program at a time—because the operating system is allocating memory and processing time to make multitasking possible. An example of multitasking is producing a document in your word processing program while you check a resource on the Internet. Both the word processing program and the Web browsing program are allowed to use parts of the computer's resources, so you can look at the resource periodically while you are writing about it in your paper. The operating system is also responsible for managing the files on your storage devices. Not only does it open and save files, but it also keeps track of every part of every file for you and lets you know if any part is missing. This activity is like a filing clerk who puts files away when they are not being used, and gets them for you when you need them again.

While you are working on the computer, the operating system is constantly guarding against equipment failure. Each electronic circuit is checked periodically, and the moment a problem is detected, the user is notified with a warning message on the screen.

The operating system's responsibility to maintain security may include requiring a username and password or checking the computer for virus infection. Unscrupulous programmers deliberately construct harmful programs, called **viruses**, which instruct your computer to perform destructive activities, such as erasing a disk drive. Some viruses are more annoying than destructive, but some can be harmful, erasing data or causing your hard disk to require reformatting. Computer users should protect themselves from viruses by using virus protection software. **Virus protection software** searches executable files for the sequences of characters that may cause harm and disinfects the files by erasing or disabling those commands. The computer advertised in Figure 1 comes with virus protection software pre-installed, and with the operating system Windows XP Professional.

Microsoft Windows, used on many personal computers, and the MAC OS, used exclusively on Macintosh computers, are referred to as **operating environments** because they provide a **graphical user interface (GUI**, pronounced "goo-ey") that acts as a liaison between the user and all of the computer's hardware and software. In addition to the operating system, Windows and the Mac OS also include utilities, device drivers, and some application programs that perform common tasks.

Utilities are another category of system software that augment the operating system by taking over some of its responsibility for allocating hardware resources. There are many utilities that come with the operating system, but some independent software developers offer utilities for sale separately. For example, Norton Utilities is a very popular collection of utility software.

Each peripheral device requires a **device driver**, or simply **driver**, which is system software that helps the computer communicate with that particular device. When you add a device to an existing computer, part of its installation includes adding its device driver to the computer's configuration.

The last type of system software is computer **programming languages**, which a programmer uses to write computer instructions. The instructions are translated into electrical signals that the computer can manipulate and process. Some examples of popular programming languages are BASIC, Visual Basic, C, C++, Ada, Java, JavaScript, CGI, and Perl.

As you get ready to make your recommendations to Mr. Paik, you realize that the primary factor in deciding the computer specifications you choose to purchase is the software his employees will be using.

Application Software

Multimedia

Application software enables you to perform specific computer tasks. In the business world, some examples of tasks that are accomplished with application software are document production, spreadsheet calculations, and database management. In addition, businesses sometimes use graphics and presentation software, including multimedia applications.

Document production software includes word processing software, desktop publishing software, e-mail editors, and Web authoring software. All of these production tools have a variety of features that assist you in writing and formatting documents. Most offer **spell checking** to help you avoid typographical and spelling errors, as shown in Figure 28.

Spell checking a document ◄ Figure 28

a wiggly red line indicates a possible spelling error

Natural Pest Control

Your garden produces bushels of tender green beans, tons of succulent tomatoes, scads of juicy strawberries, and plenty of six-foot pests. What to do when the cutworms bigin munching on those beans?

Many also assist you with grammar checking and thesaurus tools to improve your writing by offering suggestions and alternatives. Most document production software allows you to perform **copy-and-paste** and **cut-and-paste operations**; these operations allow you to copy or move words around. Document production software may also include **search** or **replace** features that allow you to look for a sequence of characters and substitute new text.

A **document template** is a preformatted document into which you type your text. A template might include format settings such as margins, line spacing, **font** (the style of type), and font size. Templates make it easier to produce consistent documents, such as letterhead or business cards. Figure 29 shows some of the document templates available with Microsoft Word, a popular word processing software package.

Figure 29 ▸ **Document templates**

Template categories include letters, memos, reports, and publications.

Within each category you can choose from several different templates.

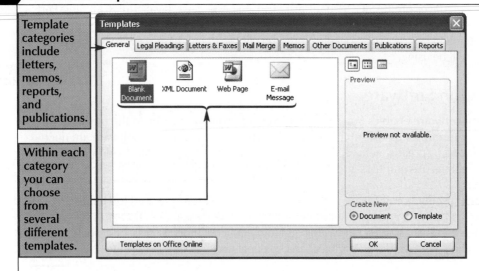

Desktop publishing software is a variation of word processing software that focuses on the format or printed appearance of documents. It is particularly useful for the design of brochures, posters, newsletters, and other documents that are printed in special sizes and formats. Desktop publishing features, such as automatic page numbering and the use of styles, facilitate the development of multiple-page documents. A **style** is a collection of formatting options that are given a name and used repeatedly throughout a document to maintain consistency. Most word processing software includes desktop publishing features such as the automatic generation of a table of contents or index and the ability to insert graphics.

Data communications makes possible the production of documents referred to as **electronic publishing**. Instead of printing and distributing documents on paper, many businesses and individuals are transmitting them electronically by including them in e-mail messages, posting them to the World Wide Web, or participating in electronic conferences where participants can view documents simultaneously. **Web authoring software** allows you to easily create Web pages. With Web authoring software, you can add text, images, links, animation, and sound to a Web page for a Web site. You can also transform word processing documents into Web pages.

Spreadsheet software is a numerical analysis tool that both businesses and individuals use extensively. You can use spreadsheet software, for example, to maintain your checkbook register. Most people use a calculator to keep track of their bank accounts, but using a spreadsheet has several advantages. Spreadsheet software creates a **worksheet**, composed of a grid of columns and rows. Each column is lettered, and each row is numbered. The intersection of a column and row is a **cell**, and each cell has a unique address, called its **cell reference**. Figure 30 shows a typical worksheet that includes a simple calculation.

A typical worksheet | Figure 30

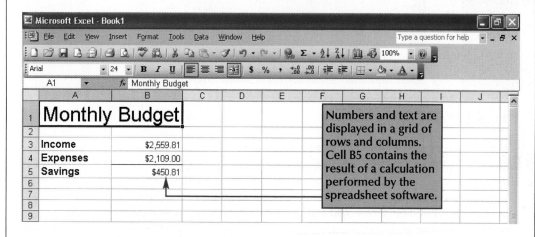

You type numbers into the grid, then create formulas that perform calculations using these numbers. In many ways, a spreadsheet is the ultimate calculator. Once your numbers are on the screen, you don't have to reenter them when you want to redo a calculation with revised or corrected numbers.

With the appropriate data and formulas, you can use an electronic spreadsheet to prepare financial reports, analyze investment portfolios, calculate amortization tables, examine alternative bid proposals, and project income, as well as perform many other tasks involved in making informed business decisions. As an additional benefit, spreadsheet software allows you to produce graphs and reports based upon the data. Figure 31 shows the data in the spreadsheet in Figure 30 represented as a simple graph.

Figure 31 ▶ **Worksheet data displayed as a graph**

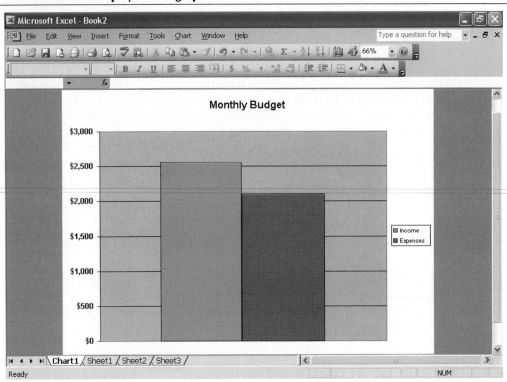

One of the most common types of application software is database management software, which lets you collect and manage data. A database is a collection of information stored on one or more computers. The explosion of information in our society is primarily organized and managed in databases. A structured database is organized in a uniform format of records and fields. A record is a collection of data items in a database. A **field** is one piece of information in the record. Data is the actual information in a field. A familiar example of a structured database is the online catalog of books at a library. This database contains one record for each book in the library, and within each record, several fields that identify the title, the author, and the subjects that the book can be classified under. The information in each field is the data for that record.

Structured databases typically store data that describes a collection of similar entities. Some other examples are student academic records, medical records, a warehouse inventory, or an address book.

A **free-form database** is a loosely structured collection of information, usually stored as documents rather than as records. The collection of word processing documents you have created and stored on your computer is an example of a free-form database. Another example is an encyclopedia stored on a CD-ROM containing documents, photographs, and even video clips. The most familiar example of a free-form database in our society is the World Wide Web with its millions of documents stored worldwide.

Graphics and **presentation software** allow you to create illustrations, diagrams, graphs, and charts that can be projected before a group, printed out for quick reference, or transmitted to remote computers. Most application software allows you to include graphics that you can create yourself using graphics software, such as Microsoft Paint or Adobe PhotoShop. You can also use **clip art**, simple drawings that are included as collections with many software packages. Figure 32 shows a slide from a presentation created in Microsoft PowerPoint—a popular presentation software program that allows you to create colorful presentations and transparencies.

Presentation software | Figure 32

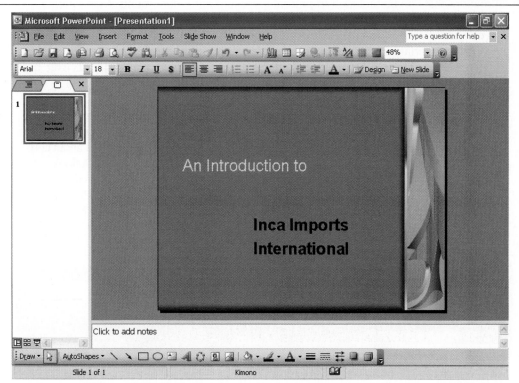

Many programs allow users to use data created in one application in a document created by another application. In fact, it is so easy to add a graphic to your word processing document that you may forget the graphic was created and saved using graphics software. **Object linking and embedding** (**OLE**) refers to the ability to use data from another file, called the **source**. **Embedding** occurs when you copy and paste the source data in the new file. Think of embedding as taking a snapshot of the original. No matter what happens to the original, you still have the copy, as it appeared when you first copied it. **Linking** allows you to create a connection between the source data and the copy in the new file. The link updates the copy every time a change is made to the source data. The seamless nature of OLE among some applications is referred to as **integration**, and the ability to integrate data from all of your applications has become an important skill in business.

Photo editing software allows you to manipulate digital photos. You can make the images brighter, add special effects to the photo, add additional images to a photo, or crop the photo to include only relevant parts of the image. Examples of photo editing software are Adobe Photoshop and Microsoft Picture It!

Multimedia authoring software allows you to record digital sound files, video files, and animations that can be included in presentations and other documents. Macromedia Director and MicroMedium Digital Trainer Professional are two examples of software that you can use to create files that include multimedia. You can sequence and format the screens into tutorials or presentations. Like Web authoring software, multimedia authoring software also uses hypertext to link documents so that the reader can easily navigate from one document to another. Most application software allows users to integrate these multimedia elements into other types of files.

Finally, you must also consider **information management** software. Business people benefit greatly from using this type of software, which keeps track of their schedules, appointments, contacts, and "to-do" lists. Most e-mail software allows users to add all the information about contacts to the list of e-mail addresses. In addition, some software, such as Microsoft Outlook, combines a contact list with information management components, such as a calendar and to-do list. Some information software allows you to synchronize information between a PDA and a desktop or notebook computer. The main screen of Microsoft Outlook is shown in Figure 33.

| Figure 33 | **Information management software** |

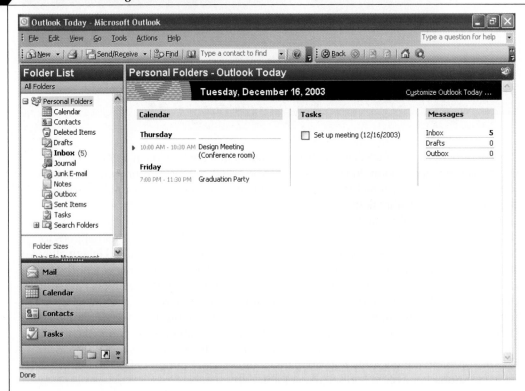

You are now ready to approach Mr. Paik with your recommendations for personal computer hardware, network access, and software. Look back at Figure 1 to be sure that you understand each specification listed. Also consider the software options you should recommend. What will you include? The computer ad already lists Microsoft Windows, so your recommendation should include document production, spreadsheet, and database management software that is compatible with Microsoft Windows. Current versions of Windows include e-mail and network communication software, including Web browsing and Web authoring software. Here's hoping that Mr. Paik approves your recommendations. Good luck!

Tutorial Summary

In this tutorial, you learned about computers and their components. You learned about the different types of computers and their uses. You also learned about peripheral devices and how they are connected to the computer. You learned to distinguish between input and output, and you learned how a computer processes data. You then learned about the motherboard and its components, how a computer stores information, and how information is transmitted. You learned that computers can be connected to form networks and that networks can communicate with each other. Finally, you learned about software and how to distinguish between system and application software.

Key Terms

access time

analog signals

application software

architecture

ASCII (American Standard Code for Information Interchange)

binary digits (bits).

boot process

booting up

bps

byte

cable

cache

cache memory

card

CD-R

CD-ROM (Compact Disk Read Only Memory)

CD-RW

cell

cell reference

central processing unit (CPU)

channel

character-based display

cps

chip

client

client/server network

clip art

clock speed

commands

complementary metal oxide semiconductor (CMOS)

computer

computer system

configuration

controller card

copy-and-paste operation

CRT (cathode ray tube) monitor

cut-and-paste operation

data

data bus

data communications

data files

database

database management software

desktop computer

desktop publishing software

device driver

digital signals

diskette

document production software

document template

dot matrix printer

dot pitch

driver

DVD (Digital Video Disk)

e-mail (electronic mail)

electronic publishing

embed

ergonomic

executable file

expansion card

expansion slot

field

file

flash memory storage device

flat panel monitor

floppy disk

font

free-form database

gateway

gigabyte (GB)

gigahertz (GHz)

graphics software

graphical user interface (GUI)

graphics accelerator card

graphics card

graphics display

hand-held computer

hard copy

hard disk drive

hardware

hyperlink (link)

I/O

information management software

ink-jet printer

input

input device

integration

interface card

Internet

Kbps

keyboard

Review Questions

1. What is the key to a computer's versatility?
   a. software
   b. hardware
   c. price
   d. peripherals

2. Which one of the following would not be considered a personal computer?
   a. desktop
   b. notebook
   c. mainframe
   d. personal digital assistant

3. Keyboards, monitors, hard disk drives, printers, and motherboards are all examples of which of the following?
   a. input devices
   b. output devices
   c. peripherals
   d. hardware

4. The selection of components that make up a particular computer system is referred to as the _____.
   a. configuration
   b. specification
   c. protocol
   d. device driver

5. Moving text, sorting lists, and performing calculations are examples of which of the following?
   a. input
   b. output
   c. processing
   d. storage

6. What do you call each 1 or 0 used in the representation of computer data?
   a. a bit
   b. a byte
   c. an ASCII
   d. a pixel

7. What usually represents one character of data?
   a. a bit
   b. a byte
   c. an integer
   d. a pixel

8. What is a megabyte?
   a. 10 kilobytes
   b. about a million bytes
   c. one-half a gigabyte
   d. about a million bits

9. Which one of the following microprocessors is fastest?
   a. 200 MHz
   b. 2.66 GHz
   c. 2.4 GHz
   d. 233 MHz

10. Which of the following temporarily stores data and programs while you are using them?
    a. ROM
    b. a floppy disk
    c. RAM
    d. a hard disk

11. What do you call a collection of data stored on a disk under a name that you assign it?
    a. a file
    b. the operating system
    c. a protocol
    d. a pixel

12. Which of the following storage media does not allow you to recycle by writing over old data?
    a. hard disk
    b. floppy disk
    c. CD-ROM
    d. tape
13. A computer display system consists of a monitor and a _____.
    a. parallel port
    b. network card
    c. graphics card
    d. sound card
14. A personal computer that is connected to a network is called a _____.
    a. desktop
    b. workstation
    c. terminal
    d. PDA
15. What telecommunications hardware is needed to convert digital signals to analog signals?
    a. mouse
    b. device driver
    c. modem
    d. slot
16. Which one of the following is system software?
    a. Microsoft Excel
    b. Microsoft Windows
    c. Microsoft Paint
    d. Microsoft Word
17. Which of the following is not a function of an operating system?
    a. controls basic input and output
    b. allocates system resources
    c. manages storage space
    d. carries out a specific task for the user
18. Random access memory (RAM) is measured in _____.
19. Disk access time is measured in _____.
20. The clock speed of a microprocessor is measured in _____.
21. _____ is the maximum number of pixels a monitor can display.
22. The transmission of text, numeric, voice, or video data from one computer to another is called _____.
23. A(n) _____ includes a computer, peripheral devices, and software.
24. The capability to send a text message from one user to another user's account where it is stored until the receiver opens it is called _____.
25. The _____ is a huge database of information that is stored on network servers around the world, and which users access by using browser software.
26. For each of the following data items, indicate how many bytes of storage would be required:

Data Item	Number of Bytes
North	
U.S.A.	
General Ledger	

27. Read the following requirements for using Microsoft Office 2003 Professional (taken from the documentation that accompanies the software). Then turn back to the computer advertisement shown in Figure 1 at the beginning of the tutorial and determine if the computer specifications listed in the ad are sufficient to run Office 2003.
    To use Microsoft Office 2003 Professional, you need:
    - PC with a Pentium III or equivalent, 233 MHz or higher processor; Pentium 4 or equivalent recommended
    - 128 MB of RAM plus an additional 8 MB of RAM for each Office application running simultaneously; 256 MB recommended
    - 400 MB of available hard disk space minimum; 880 MB recommended

28. Using the system requirements listed in Question 27, look through a recent computer magazine and find the least expensive computer that will run the Microsoft Office 2003 Professional software. Make a photocopy of the ad showing the specifications, price, and vendor. Write the name of the magazine and the issue date at the top of the photocopied ad. Write a short paper that supports your selection.

29. You have learned that the use of multimedia requires special hardware and software. Look for current prices and specifications of multimedia hardware in advertisements in magazines or in your local newspaper. What are the highest priced devices, and why are they so expensive? In the following chart, add the specifications and price for the most expensive examples of these devices that you can find. Look at the computer advertisement shown in Figure 1 and determine if the computer specifications listed in the ad are sufficient to run multimedia. If not, write a statement that justifies adding the cost of the higher-quality device you listed here.

Multimedia Device	Specifications	Price
DVD-ROM drive		
Speakers		
Headphones		
Large, high-resolution monitor		

Lab Assignments

The New Perspectives Labs are designed to help you master some of the key concepts and skills presented in this text. The steps for completing the Labs are located on the Course Technology Web site. Log on to the Internet and use your Web browser to go to the Student Online Companion for New Perspectives Office 2003 at **www.course.com/np/office2003**. Click the Lab Assignments link, and then navigate to the assignments for this tutorial.

Reinforce

Using a Mouse

Using a Keyboard

Peripheral Devices

Using Files

The Internet: World Wide Web

User Interfaces

Multimedia

New Perspectives on

Exploring the Basics of Microsoft® Windows XP

Investigating the Windows XP   WIN 3
Operating System

Read This Before You Begin

Data Files

The "Exploring the Basics of Microsoft Windows XP" tutorial does not require any starting student Data Files. Also, you do not have to save any files for this tutorial or any end-of-tutorial exercises, so you will not need a USB drive or other storage medium in order to complete this tutorial.

SAM 2003 Training Companion CD

The SAM 2003 Training Companion CD that comes with this text gives you "just-in-time" training and reinforcement of important Microsoft Office skills. Look for the SAM CD logo throughout each tutorial for opportunities to complete the hands-on tasks included on this CD.

Course Labs

The "Exploring the Basics of Microsoft Windows XP" tutorial features two interactive Course Labs to help you understand mouse and keyboard concepts. There are Lab Assignments at the end of the tutorial that relate to these labs. Contact your instructor or technical support person for assistance in accessing the labs.

Exploring the Basics of Microsoft Windows XP

Investigating the Windows XP Operating System

Case | Your Computer Training

Your Computer Training is a small business in Tampa, Florida, that provides lessons and instruction on how to use a computer, offering courses for beginning, intermediate, and advanced computer users. The instruction includes detailed explanations, definitions, and descriptions as well as hands-on practice of computer skills. First-time and novice users learn a full range of basic tasks—from starting the computer and opening and closing programs to shutting down the computer. Steve Laslow teaches an introductory course on the fundamentals of using the Microsoft Windows XP operating system.

In this tutorial you will start Windows XP and practice some basic computer skills. Then you'll learn how to navigate with My Computer and Windows Explorer. Finally, you'll use the Windows XP Help system.

Session	Objectives		SAM Training Tasks	
Session 1	• Start Windows XP and tour the desktop • Explore the Start menu • Run software programs, switch between them, and close them	• Manipulate windows • Identify and use the controls in menus, toolbars, and dialog boxes	• Close a program • Close a window • Close open windows and save changes from the taskbar • Log on to the computer • Maximize a window • Minimize a window • Move a window • Open an inactive window • Redisplay a minimized window • Scroll by dragging the scroll box	• Scroll using scroll arrows • Select a menu option • Select a toolbar button • Select an option in a list box • Size a window • Switch between programs • Use a scroll bar • Use ScreenTips to identify desktop icons and toolbar buttons • View the contents of the Recycle Bin
Session 2	• Navigate your computer with Windows Explorer and My Computer • Change the view of the items in your computer	• Get help when you need it • Shut down Windows	• Bookmark a Help Topic • Change the appearance of the My Documents window • Change the format of the icons in a window • Change the view in the My Documents folder • Control the toolbar display • Log off from the computer • Navigate through the Windows hierarchy • Return to a previous Help Topic	• Search for a topic in Help and Support • Sort files in Details view • Start Windows XP Help • Turn off the computer • Turn off Windows XP • Use Details view to examine file characteristics • Use the Index tab in Help and Support • Use the topic menus in Help and Support • View files and folders with My Computer

Student Data Files   There are no student Data Files needed for this tutorial.

Session 1

For hands-on practice of key tasks in this session, go to the SAM 2003 Training Companion CD included with this text.

Starting Windows XP

Steve Laslow begins the course by discussing the operating system. The **operating system** is software that helps the computer perform essential tasks such as displaying information on the computer screen and saving data on disks. (Software refers to the **programs**, or **applications**, that a computer uses to complete tasks.) Your computer uses the **Microsoft Windows XP** operating system—**Windows XP** for short. Windows is the name of the operating system, and XP indicates the version you are using. Microsoft has released many versions of Windows since 1985, and is currently developing new versions.

Much of the software created for Windows XP shares the same look and works the same way. This similarity in design means that once you learn how to use one Windows XP program, such as Microsoft Word (a word-processing program), you are well on your way to understanding how to use other Windows XP programs. Windows XP allows you to use more than one program at a time, so you can easily switch between your word-processing program and your appointment book program, for example. Windows XP also makes it easy to access the **Internet**, a worldwide collection of computers connected to one another to enable communication. All in all, Windows XP makes your computer an effective and easy-to-use productivity tool.

Windows XP starts automatically when you turn on your computer. After completing some necessary startup tasks, Windows XP displays a Welcome screen. Depending on the way your computer is set up, the Welcome screen might simply welcome you to Windows XP or it might list all the users for the computer. If a list of users appears, you must click your user name and perhaps type a password to start using Windows XP. A **user name** is a unique name that identifies you to Windows XP, and a **password** is text—often a confidential combination of letters and numbers—that you must enter before you can work with Windows XP. The Welcome screen might reappear if there's been no activity on the computer for a while.

To start Windows XP:

1. Turn on your computer. After a moment, Windows XP starts and the Welcome screen appears.

   Trouble? If you are asked to select an operating system, do not take action. Windows XP should start automatically after a designated number of seconds. If it does not, ask your instructor or technical support person for help.

   Trouble? If this is the first time you have started your computer with Windows XP, messages might appear on your screen informing you that Windows is setting up components of your computer.

2. On the Welcome screen, click your user name, if necessary. The Windows XP screen appears, as shown in Figure 1.

   Trouble? If your user name does not appear in the list of users on the Welcome screen, ask your instructor or technical support person which name you should click.

   Trouble? If you need to enter a user name and a password, type your assigned user name, press the Tab key, type your password, and then click the Continue button or press the Enter key to continue.

Windows XP desktop **Figure 1**

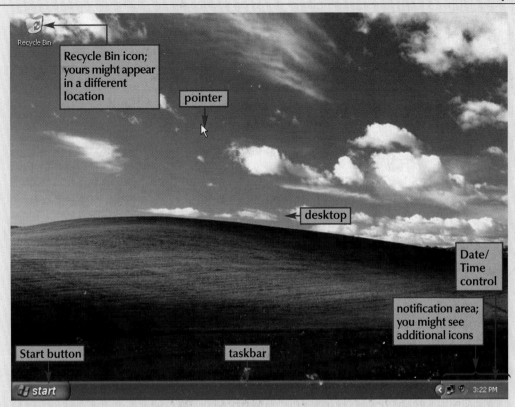

Recycle Bin icon; yours might appear in a different location

pointer

desktop

Date/Time control

notification area; you might see additional icons

Start button

taskbar

start 3:22 PM

3. Look at your screen and locate the objects labeled in Figure 1. The objects on your screen might appear larger or smaller than those in Figure 1, depending on your monitor's settings. Figure 2 describes the function of each of these objects.

Elements of the Windows XP desktop **Figure 2**

Element	Description
Icon	A small picture that represents an object available to your computer
Pointer	A small object, such as an arrow, that moves on the screen when you move the mouse
Desktop	Your workplace on the screen
Date/Time control	Shows the current date and time and lets you set the clock
Taskbar	Contains buttons that give you quick access to common tools and the programs currently running
Start button	Provides access to Windows XP programs, documents, and information on the Internet
Notification area	Displays icons corresponding to services running in the background, such as an Internet connection

Trouble? If a blank screen or animated design replaces the Windows XP desktop, your computer might be set to use a screen saver, a program that causes a monitor to go blank or to display an animated design after a specified amount of idle time. Press any key to restore the Windows XP desktop.

The Windows XP screen uses a **graphical user interface** (**GUI**, pronounced "gooey"), which displays icons that represent items stored on your computer, such as programs and files. **Icons** are pictures of familiar objects, such as file folders and documents. Windows XP gets its name from the rectangular work areas, called "windows," that appear on your screen as you work (although no other windows should be open right now). You will learn more about windows later in this tutorial.

Touring the Windows XP Desktop

In Windows terminology, the area displayed on your screen when Windows XP starts represents a **desktop**—a workspace for projects and the tools that you need to manipulate your projects. When you first start a computer, it uses **default** settings, those preset by the operating system. The default desktop you see after you first install Windows XP, for example, displays an image of green hills and clouds in a blue sky. However, Microsoft designed Windows XP so that you can easily change the appearance of the desktop. You can, for example, change images or add patterns and text to the desktop background.

Using a
Mouse

Interacting with the Desktop

To interact with the objects on your desktop, you use a **pointing device**. Pointing devices come in many shapes and sizes. The most common one is called a **mouse**, so this book uses that term. If you are using a different pointing device, such as a trackball, substitute that device whenever you see the term "mouse." Some pointing devices are designed to ensure that your hand won't suffer fatigue while using them. Some are attached directly to your computer via a cable, whereas others work like a TV remote control and allow you to access your computer without being right next to it.

You use a pointing device to move the mouse pointer over objects on the desktop, or to **point** to them. The pointer is usually shaped like an arrow ⌕, although it changes shape depending on the pointer's location on the screen and what tasks you are performing. As you move the mouse on a surface, such as a mouse pad, the pointer on the screen moves in a corresponding direction.

When you point to certain objects, such as the objects on the taskbar, a "tip" appears in a yellow box. These tips are called **ScreenTips**, and they tell you the purpose or function of the object to which you are pointing.

To view ScreenTips:

▶ 1. Use the mouse to point to the **Start** button on the taskbar. After a few seconds, you see the ScreenTip "Click here to begin," as shown in Figure 3.

Figure 3 ▶ **Viewing ScreenTips**

▶ 2. Point to the time displayed at the right end of the taskbar. A ScreenTip for today's date (or the date to which your computer's time clock is set) appears.

Clicking refers to pressing a mouse button and immediately releasing it. Clicking sends a signal to your computer that you want to perform an action on the object you click. In Windows XP you perform most actions with the left mouse button. If you are told to click an object, position the mouse pointer on that object and click the left mouse button, unless instructed otherwise.

When you click the Start button, the Start menu opens. A **menu** is a group or list of commands, and a **menu command** is a word that you can click to complete tasks. If a right-pointing arrow follows a menu command, then you can point to the command to open a **submenu**, which is a list of additional choices related to the command. The **Start menu** provides you with access to programs, documents, and much more. You can click the Start button to open the Start menu.

To open the Start menu:

1. Point to the **Start** button on the taskbar.

2. Click the left mouse button. The Start menu opens. An arrow ▷ follows the All Programs command on the Start menu, indicating that you can view additional choices by navigating to a submenu. See Figure 4; your Start menu might show different commands.

Start menu ◀ Figure 4

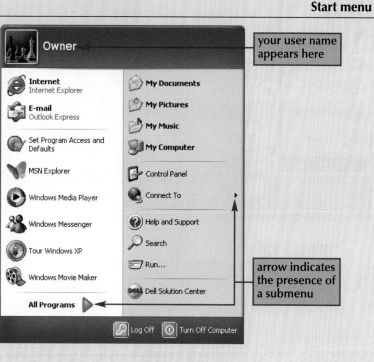

3. Click the **Start** button on the taskbar to close the Start menu.

You need to select an object to work with it. To **select** an object in Windows XP, you point to and then click that object. Windows XP shows you which object is selected by highlighting it, usually by changing the object's color, putting a box around it, or making the object appear to be pushed in.

In Windows XP, depending on your computer's settings, you can select certain objects by pointing to them and others by clicking them. You'll point to the All Programs command on the Start menu to open the All Programs submenu.

To select a menu command:

▶ **1.** Click the **Start** button on the taskbar. The button appears to be pushed in, indicating that it is selected.

▶ **2.** Point to (but don't click) **All Programs** on the Start menu. When you first point to the All Programs command, it is highlighted to indicate it is selected. After a short pause, the All Programs submenu opens. See Figure 5.

Figure 5 ▶ | **All Programs submenu**

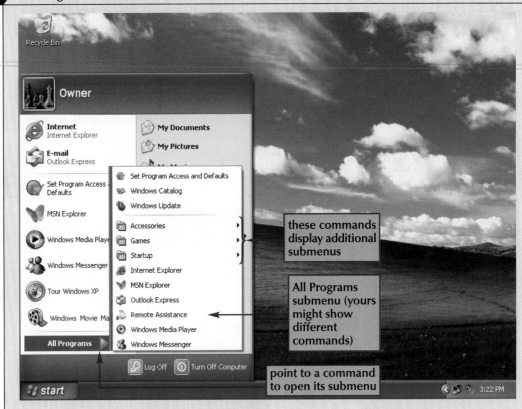

Trouble? If a submenu other than the All Programs menu opens, you pointed to the wrong command. Move the mouse so that the pointer points to All Programs.

▶ **3.** Click the **Start** button on the taskbar to close the Start menu. You return to the desktop.

In addition to clicking an object to select it, you can double-click an object to open or start the item associated with it. For example, you can double-click a folder icon to open the folder and see its contents. Or you can double-click a program icon to start the program. **Double-clicking** means to click the left mouse button twice in quick succession.

You can practice double-clicking now by opening the Recycle Bin. The Recycle Bin holds deleted items such as folders until you remove them permanently.

To view the contents of the Recycle Bin:

▶ **1.** Click the desktop, and then point to the **Recycle Bin** icon on the desktop. After a few moments, a ScreenTip appears that describes the Recycle Bin.

▶ **2.** Click the left mouse button twice quickly to double-click the **Recycle Bin** icon. The Recycle Bin window opens, as shown in Figure 6.

Contents of the Recycle Bin | **Figure 6**

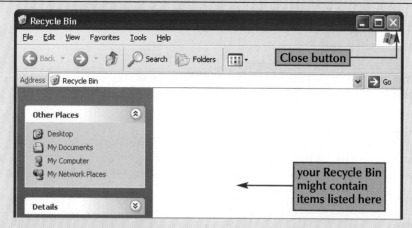

Trouble? If the Recycle Bin window does not open, and you see only the Recycle Bin name highlighted below the icon, you double-clicked too slowly. Double-click the icon again more quickly.

Now you can close the Recycle Bin window.

3. Click the **Close** button ☒ in the upper-right corner of the Recycle Bin window.

You'll learn more about opening and closing windows later in this session.

Your mouse has more than one button—in addition to the left button, the mouse has a right button that you can use for performing certain actions in Windows XP. However, the term "clicking" continues to refer to the left button; clicking an object with the *right* button is called **right-clicking**.

In Windows XP, right-clicking selects an object and opens its **shortcut menu**, which is a list of commands directly related to the object that you right-clicked. You can right-click practically any object—the Start button, a desktop icon, the taskbar, and even the desktop itself—to view commands associated with that object. Recall that you clicked the Start button with the left mouse button to open the Start menu. Now you can right-click the Start button to open the shortcut menu for the Start button.

To right-click an object:

1. Position the pointer over the **Start** button on the taskbar.

2. Right-click the **Start** button on the taskbar to open its shortcut menu. This menu offers a list of commands related to the Start button. See Figure 7.

Start button shortcut menu | **Figure 7**

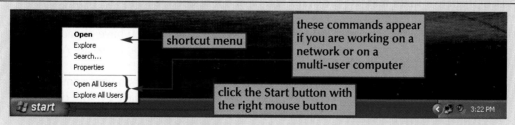

Trouble? If the shortcut menu does not open and you are using a trackball or a mouse with three buttons or a wheel, make sure you click the button on the far right, not the one in the middle.

> **Trouble?** If your menu looks slightly different from the one in Figure 7, don't worry; different computers often have different commands.
>
> **3.** Press the **Esc** key to close the shortcut menu. You return to the desktop.

Now that you've opened the Start menu and its shortcut menu, you're ready to explore the contents of the Start menu.

Exploring the Start Menu

Recall that the Start menu is the central point for accessing programs, documents, and other resources on your computer. The Start menu is organized into two panels, as shown in Figure 8, and each panel lists items you can point to or click.

| Figure 8 | Start menu |

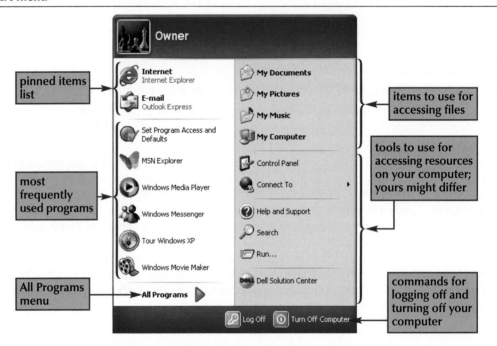

The left panel organizes programs for easy access. The area at the top of the left panel is called the **pinned items list**. Pinned items stay on the Start menu unless you remove them. By default, Windows XP lists the Web browser and e-mail program on your computer in the pinned items list. You can pin other items to this list if you like. When you use a program, Windows XP adds it to the **most frequently used programs list**, which appears below the pinned items list. Windows XP can list only a certain number of frequently used programs—after that, the programs you have not opened recently are replaced by the programs you used last.

The last item in the left panel is the All Programs menu, which you have already used to display a list of programs currently installed on your computer. You'll use the All Programs menu shortly to start a program.

From the right panel, you can access common locations and tools on your computer. For example, **My Documents** is your personal folder, a convenient place to store documents, graphics, and other work. **My Computer** is a tool that you use to view, organize, and access the programs, files, and drives on your computer.

From the lower section of the right panel, you can open windows that help you work effectively with Windows XP, including the **Control Panel**, which contains specialized tools that you can use to change the way Windows XP looks and behaves, and the **Help and Support Center**, which provides tutorials, demonstrations, and steps for performing tasks in Windows XP. (You'll explore the Help and Support Center later in this tutorial.) Finally, you also log off and turn off your computer from the Start menu. When you **log off**, you end your session with Windows XP but leave the computer turned on.

Now that you've explored the Start menu, you're ready to use it to start a program.

Starting a Program

Reference Window

- Click the Start button on the taskbar, and then point to All Programs.
- If necessary, point to the submenu that contains the program you want to start.
- Click the name of the program you want to start.
or
- Click the name or icon of the program you want to start in the pinned items list or the most frequently used programs list on the Start menu.

Windows XP includes an easy-to-use word-processing program called WordPad. Suppose you want to start the WordPad program and use it to write a letter or report. You open Windows XP programs from the Start menu. Programs are usually located on the All Programs submenu or on one of its submenus. To start WordPad, for example, you navigate to the All Programs and Accessories submenus.

To start the WordPad program from the Start menu:

1. Click the **Start** button on the taskbar to open the Start menu.

2. Point to **All Programs** to open the All Programs submenu.

3. Point to **Accessories**. The Accessories submenu opens. Figure 9 shows the open menus.

Start menu and related submenus   Figure 9

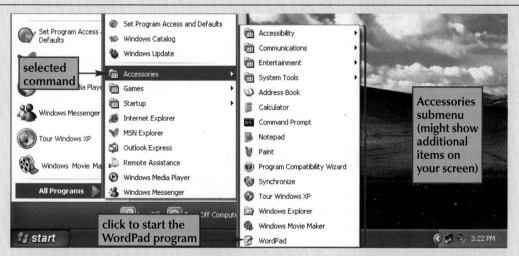

Trouble? If a different menu opens, you might have paused the pointer over a different menu command, which opened its submenu. Move the pointer back to All Programs, and then move the pointer up or down to point to Accessories.

4. Click **WordPad** on the Accessories submenu. The WordPad program window opens, as shown in Figure 10.

Figure 10 **WordPad program window**

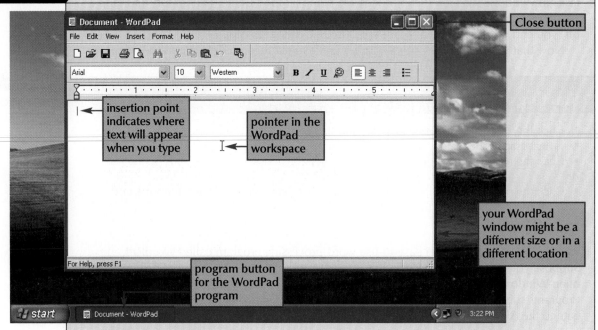

Trouble? If the WordPad program window fills the entire screen, don't worry. You will learn how to manipulate windows shortly.

When a program is started, it is said to be open or running. A **program button** appears on the taskbar for each open program. You click a program button to switch between open programs. When you are finished using a program, you can click the Close button located in the upper-right corner of the program window to **exit**, or close, that program.

To exit the WordPad program:

1. Click the **Close** button ⊠ on the WordPad title bar. The WordPad program closes and you return to the Windows XP desktop.

Running Multiple Programs

One of the most useful features of Windows XP is its ability to run multiple programs at the same time. This feature, known as **multitasking**, allows you to work on more than one task at a time and to switch quickly between projects. For example, you can start WordPad and leave it running while you start the Paint program.

To run WordPad and Paint at the same time:

▶ **1.** Start WordPad again.

▶ **2.** Click the **Start** button on the taskbar.

▶ **3.** Point to **All Programs**, and then point to **Accessories**.

▶ **4.** Click **Paint**. The Paint program window opens, as shown in Figure 11. Now two programs are running at the same time.

Two programs open ◀ **Figure 11**

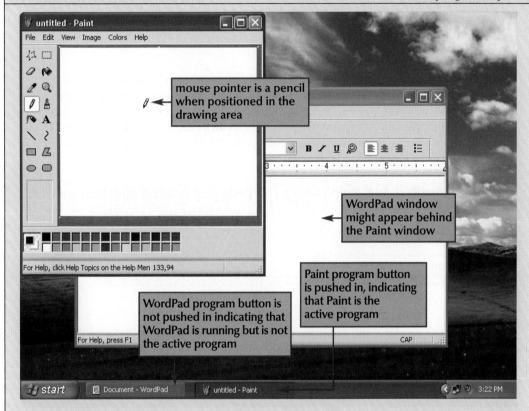

Trouble? If the Paint program fills the entire screen, continue with the next set of steps. You will learn how to manipulate windows shortly.

The **active program** is the one you are currently using—Windows XP applies your next keystroke or command to the active program. Paint is the active program because it is the one in which you are currently working. The WordPad program button is still on the taskbar, indicating that WordPad is still running even if you can't see its program window. Imagine that the WordPad program window is stacked behind the Paint program window.

Switching Between Programs

Because only one program is active at a time, you'll need to switch between programs if you want to work in one or the other. The easiest way to switch between programs is to use the program buttons on the taskbar.

To switch between WordPad and Paint:

▶ 1. Click the program button labeled **Document - WordPad** on the taskbar. The WordPad program window moves to the front, and now the Document - WordPad button looks pushed in, indicating that WordPad is the active program.

▶ 2. Click the program button labeled **untitled - Paint** on the taskbar to switch to the Paint program. The Paint program is again the active program.

In addition to using the taskbar to switch between open programs, you can also close programs from the taskbar.

Closing Programs from the Taskbar

You should always close a program when you are finished using it. Each program uses computer resources, such as memory, so Windows XP works more efficiently when only the programs you need are open. You've already seen how to close an open program using the Close button on the title bar of the program window. You can also close a program, whether active or inactive, by using the shortcut menu associated with the program button on the taskbar.

To close WordPad and Paint using the program button shortcut menus:

▶ 1. Right-click the **untitled - Paint** button on the taskbar. The shortcut menu for the Paint program button opens. See Figure 12.

| Figure 12 | Program button shortcut menu |

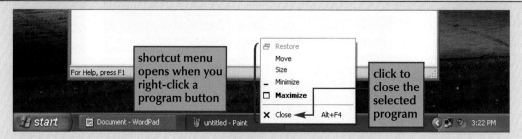

▶ 2. Click **Close** on the shortcut menu. The Paint program closes and the program button labeled "untitled - Paint" disappears from the taskbar.

▶ 3. Right-click the **Document - WordPad** button on the taskbar, and then click **Close** on the shortcut menu. The WordPad program closes and its program button no longer appears on the taskbar.

Now that you've learned the basics of using the Windows XP desktop, you're ready to explore other Windows XP features, including windows and dialog boxes.

Using Windows and Dialog Boxes

Recall that when you run a program in Windows XP, the program appears in a window. A **window** is a rectangular area of the screen that contains a program, text, graphics, or data. Windows, spelled with an uppercase "W," is the name of the Microsoft operating system. The word "window" with a lowercase "w" refers to one of the rectangular areas on the screen. A window also contains **controls**, which are graphical or textual objects used for manipulating the window and for using the program. Figure 13 describes the controls you are likely to see in most windows.

Window controls ◄ **Figure 13**

Control	Description
Menu bar	Contains the titles of menus, such as File, Edit, and Help
Sizing buttons	Let you enlarge, shrink, or close a window
Status bar	Provides you with messages relevant to the task you are performing
Title bar	Contains the window title and basic window control buttons
Toolbar	Contains buttons that provide you with shortcuts to common menu commands
Window title	Identifies the program and document contained in the window
Workspace	Part of the window you use to enter your work—to enter text, draw pictures, set up calculations, and so on

The WordPad program is a good example of a typical window. You'll start WordPad and identify its window controls.

To look at the window controls in WordPad:

▶ **1.** Make sure that Windows XP is running and the Windows XP desktop is displayed.

▶ **2.** Start WordPad.

▶ **3.** On your screen, identify the controls that are labeled in Figure 14.

WordPad window controls ◄ **Figure 14**

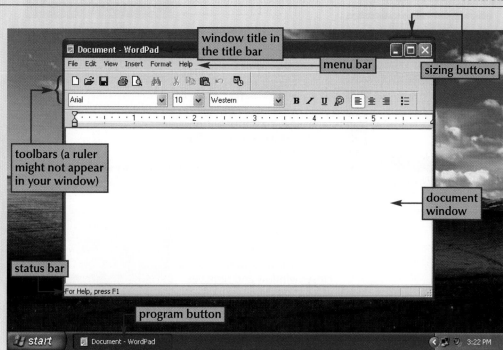

Trouble? If your WordPad program window fills the entire screen or differs in size, you can still identify all the controls.

After you open a window, you can manipulate it by changing its size and position.

Manipulating Windows

On the right side of the title bar are three buttons. The Minimize button, which is the first of the three buttons, hides a window so that only its program button is visible on the taskbar. The other button changes name and function depending on the status of the window (it either maximizes the window or restores it to a predefined size). You are already familiar with the last button—the Close button. Figure 15 shows how these buttons work.

Figure 15 ▶ **Window buttons**

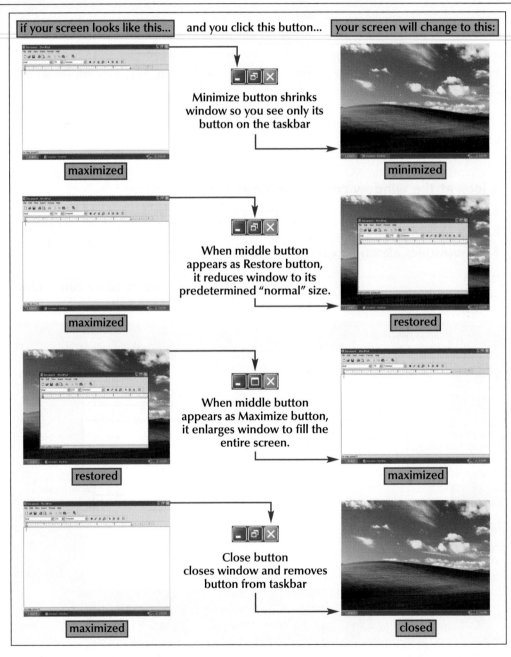

You can use the Minimize button when you want to temporarily hide a window but keep the program running.

To minimize the WordPad window:

1. Click the **Minimize** button ▬ on the WordPad title bar. The WordPad window shrinks so that only the Document - WordPad button on the taskbar is visible.

   Trouble? If the WordPad program window closed, you accidentally clicked the Close button. Use the Start button to start WordPad again, and then repeat Step 1. If you accidentally clicked the Maximize or Restore button, repeat Step 1.

You can redisplay a minimized window by clicking the program's button on the taskbar. When you redisplay a window, it becomes the active window.

To redisplay the WordPad window:

1. Click the **Document - WordPad** button on the taskbar. The WordPad window is restored to its previous size.

   The taskbar button provides another way to switch a window between its minimized and active states.

2. Click the **Document - WordPad** button on the taskbar again to minimize the window.

3. Click the **Document - WordPad** button once more to redisplay the window.

The Maximize button enlarges a window so that it fills the entire screen. You will probably do most of your work using maximized windows because they allow you to see more of the program and your data.

To maximize the WordPad window:

1. Click the **Maximize** button ▢ on the WordPad title bar.

   Trouble? If the window is already maximized, it will fill the entire screen, and the Maximize button won't appear. Instead, you'll see the Restore button. Skip Step 1.

The Restore button reduces the window so that it is smaller than the entire screen. This feature is useful if you want to see more than one window at a time. Also, because the window is smaller, you can move the window to another location on the screen or change the dimensions of the window.

To restore a window:

1. Click the **Restore** button ▣ on the WordPad title bar. Once a window is restored, the Restore button ▣ changes to the Maximize button ▢.

You can use the mouse to move a window to a new position on the screen. When you click an object and then press and hold down the mouse button while moving the mouse, you are said to be **dragging** the object. You can move objects on the screen by dragging them to a new location. If you want to move a window, you drag the window by its title bar. You cannot move a maximized window.

To drag the restored WordPad window to a new location:

1. Position the mouse pointer on the WordPad title bar.
2. Press and hold down the left mouse button, and then move the mouse up or down a little to drag the window. The window moves as you move the mouse.
3. Position the window anywhere on the desktop, and then release the left mouse button. The WordPad window appears in the new location.
4. Drag the WordPad window to the upper-left corner of the desktop.

You can also use the mouse to change the size of a window. Notice the sizing handle at the lower-right corner of the window. The **sizing handle** provides a visible control for changing the size of a window.

To change the size of the WordPad window:

1. Position the pointer over the sizing handle in the lower-right corner of the WordPad window. The pointer changes to. See Figure 16.

Figure 16	Preparing to resize a window

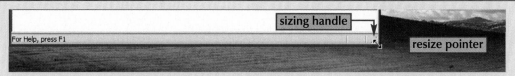

For Help, press F1

sizing handle

resize pointer

2. Press and hold down the mouse button, and then drag the sizing handle down and to the right.
3. Release the mouse button. Now the window is larger.
4. Practice using the sizing handle to make the WordPad window larger or smaller, and then maximize the WordPad window.

You can also use the resize pointer to drag the left, right, top, or bottom window borders left, right, up, or down to change a window's size in any one direction.

Selecting Options from a Menu

Most Windows XP programs use menus to organize the program's features and available functions. The menu bar is typically located at the top of the program window and shows the names of the menus, such as File, Edit, and Help. Windows XP menus are relatively standardized—most programs designed for Windows XP include similar menus. This makes it easier to learn new programs because you can make a pretty good guess about which menu contains the task you want to perform.

When you click any menu name, the choices for that menu appear below the menu bar. Like choices on the Start menu, these choices are referred to as menu commands. To select a menu command, you click it. For example, the File menu is a standard feature in most Windows XP programs and contains the commands typically related to working with a file: creating, opening, saving, and printing. Menu commands that are followed by an ellipsis open a dialog box. A **dialog box** is a special kind of window where you enter or choose settings for how you want to perform a task. For example, you use the Page Setup dialog box to set margins and some printing options. If you open a menu, and then decide not to select a command, you can close the menu by clicking its name again or pressing the Esc key.

To select the Page Setup menu command from the File menu:

▶ **1.** Click **File** on the WordPad menu bar to open the File menu. See Figure 17.

File menu ◀ **Figure 17**

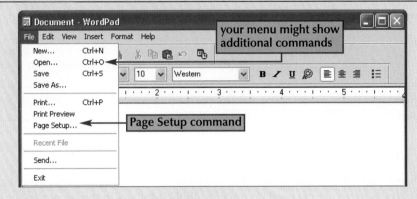

▶ **2.** Click **Page Setup** to open the Page Setup dialog box.

▶ **3.** After examining the dialog box, click the **Cancel** button to close the Page Setup dialog box.

If you had selected options in the Page Setup dialog box that you wanted to retain, you would click the OK button instead of the Cancel button.

Not all menu items and commands immediately carry out an action—some show submenus or ask you for more information about what you want to do. The menu gives you visual hints about what to expect when you select an item. These hints are sometimes referred to as **menu conventions**. Figure 18 shows examples of these menu conventions.

Examples of menu conventions ◀ **Figure 18**

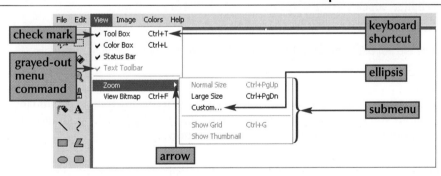

Figure 19 describes the Windows XP menu conventions.

| Figure 19 | ▶ | **Menu conventions** |

Convention	Description
Check mark	Indicates a toggle, or "on-off" switch (like a light switch) that is either checked (turned on) or not checked (turned off).
Ellipsis	Three dots that indicate you must make additional selections after you select that command. Commands without dots do not require additional choices—they take effect as soon as you click them. If a command is followed by an ellipsis, a dialog box opens that allows you to enter specifications for how you want a task carried out.
Triangular arrow	Indicates the presence of a submenu. When you point to a menu option that has a triangular arrow, a submenu automatically appears.
Grayed-out command	Command that is not currently available. For example, a graphics program might display the Text Toolbar command in gray if there is no text in the graphic to work with.
Keyboard shortcut	A key or combination of keys that you can press to select the menu command without actually opening the menu.

Using Toolbars

Although you can usually perform all program commands by using menus, you also have one-click access to frequently used commands on the toolbars in the program window. Using the buttons on the toolbars, you can quickly access common commands. Just as menu commands are grouped on menus according to task, the buttons on a toolbar are also grouped and organized by task.

Recall that Windows XP programs often display ScreenTips, which indicate the purpose and function of a window component such as a button. You'll explore the WordPad toolbar buttons by looking at their ScreenTips.

To determine the names and descriptions of the buttons on the WordPad toolbar:

▶ **1.** Position the pointer over the **Print Preview** button 🔍 on the WordPad toolbar. After a short pause, the ScreenTip for the button appears below the button, and a description of the button appears in the status bar just above the Start button.

   Trouble? If you closed WordPad after the previous set of steps, restart the program.

▶ **2.** Move the pointer to each button on the toolbar to display its name and purpose.

You select a toolbar button by clicking it, which performs the button's command. One of the buttons you pointed to on the WordPad toolbar is called the Undo button. Clicking the Undo button reverses the effects of your last action.

To use the Undo button on the WordPad toolbar:

▶ **1.** Type your name in the WordPad window.

▶ **2.** Click the **Undo** button 🔄 on the WordPad toolbar. WordPad reverses your last action by removing your name from the WordPad window.

Besides menus and toolbars, windows can contain list boxes and scroll bars, which you'll learn about next.

Using List Boxes and Scroll Bars

As you might guess from the name, a **list box** displays a list of available choices from which you can select one item. In WordPad, you can choose a date and time format from the Available formats list box in the Date/Time dialog box. List box controls usually include arrow buttons, a scroll bar, and a scroll box. A scroll bar appears when the list of available options is too long or wide to fit in the list box. The arrows and scroll box enable you to move through the complete list.

To use the Date/Time list box:

▶ **1.** Click the **Date/Time** button 🖳 on the WordPad toolbar to open the Date and Time dialog box, which lists the current date in many formats. See Figure 20.

List box ◀ **Figure 20**

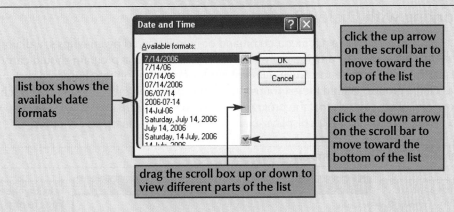

list box shows the available date formats

click the up arrow on the scroll bar to move toward the top of the list

click the down arrow on the scroll bar to move toward the bottom of the list

drag the scroll box up or down to view different parts of the list

▶ **2.** To scroll down the list, click the **down arrow** button on the scroll bar three times.

▶ **3.** Drag the **scroll box** to the top of the scroll bar by pointing to the scroll box, pressing and holding down the left mouse button, dragging the scroll box up, and then releasing the left mouse button. The list scrolls back to the beginning.

▶ **4.** Find a date format similar to "July 14, 2006" in the Available formats list box, and then click that date format to select it.

▶ **5.** Click the **OK** button to close the Date and Time dialog box. The current date is inserted into your document.

A list box is helpful because it only includes options that are appropriate for your current task. For example, you can select only dates and times in the available formats from the list box in the Date and Time dialog box—no matter which format you choose, WordPad will recognize it. Sometimes a list might not include every possible option, so you can type the option you want to select. In this case, the list box includes a **list arrow** on its right side. You can click the list arrow to view options and then select one, or you can type appropriate text.

Buttons can also have list arrows. The list arrow indicates that there is more than one option for that button. Rather than crowding the window with a lot of buttons, one for each possible option, including a list arrow on a button organizes its options logically and compactly into a list. Toolbars often include list boxes and buttons with list arrows. For example, the Font Size button list box on the WordPad toolbar includes a list arrow. To select an option other than the one shown in the list box or on the button, you click the list arrow, and then click the option that you want to use.

To select a new font size from the Font Size button list box:

▶ **1.** Click the **Font Size** button list arrow 10 ▾ on the WordPad toolbar.

▶ **2.** Click **18**. The Font Size list closes, and the font size you selected appears in the list box.

▶ **3.** Type a few characters to test the new font size.

▶ **4.** Click the **Font Size** button list arrow 10 ▾ on the WordPad toolbar again.

▶ **5.** Click **12**.

▶ **6.** Type a few characters to test this type size. The text appears in the smaller font size.

Dialog boxes also contain scroll bars and list boxes. You'll examine a typical dialog box next.

Working with Dialog Boxes

Recall that when you select a menu command or item followed by an ellipsis, a dialog box opens that allows you to provide more information about how a program should carry out a task. Some dialog boxes organize different kinds of information into bordered rectangular areas called groups. Within these groups, you will usually find tabs, option buttons, check boxes, and other controls that the program uses to collect information about how you want it to perform a task. Figure 21 displays examples of common dialog box controls.

| Figure 21 | Examples of dialog box controls |

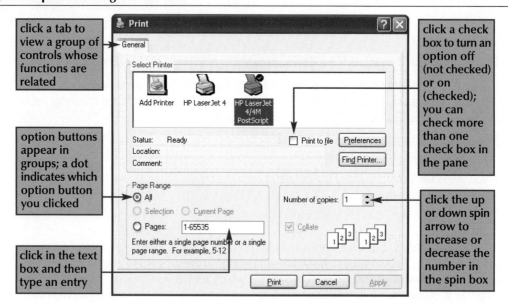

Now you can open a typical Windows XP dialog box in WordPad. To learn how dialog box controls work, you'll open the Options dialog box, which you use to determine how text fits in the WordPad window and which toolbars appear. You'll remove the check mark from a check box and select an option button, and then see how these settings affect the WordPad window. Note that by default the status bar appears at the bottom of the WordPad window and that the ruler uses inches.

To work with a typical Windows XP dialog box:

1. Click **View** on the WordPad menu bar, and then click **Options**. The Options dialog box opens, by default, to the Rich Text tab.

   Trouble? If the Options dialog box does not display the Rich Text options, click the Rich Text tab.

2. Click the **Status bar** check box to remove the check mark.
3. Click the **Options** tab to select the measurement units that the WordPad ruler uses.
4. Click the **Centimeters** option button.
5. Click the **OK** button. WordPad accepts your changes and closes the Options dialog box.

Examine the WordPad window and note that the ruler now uses centimeters instead of inches and the status bar no longer appears at the bottom of the window. You can use the Options dialog box again to restore the WordPad window to its original condition.

To restore the WordPad window:

1. Click **View** on the WordPad menu bar, and then click **Options**. The Options dialog box opens.
2. On the Rich Text tab, click the **Status bar** check box to insert a check mark.
3. Click the **Options** tab, and then click the **Inches** option button.
4. Click the **OK** button. The WordPad window now includes a status bar and a ruler that uses inches as its measurement unit.
5. Click the **Close** button ⊠ on the WordPad title bar to close WordPad.
6. When you see the message "Save changes to Document?" click the **No** button.

In this session, you started Windows XP and toured the desktop, learning how to interact with the items on the desktop and on the Start menu. You also started two Windows programs, manipulated windows, and learned how to select options from a menu, toolbar, and dialog box.

Session 1 Quick Check

1. What is the purpose of the taskbar?
2. What is a ScreenTip?
3. The _____ is a list of options that provides you with access to programs, documents, submenus, and more.
4. Which feature of Windows XP allows you to run more than one program at a time?
5. Even if you can't see an open program on your desktop, the program might be running. How can you tell if a program is running?
6. Why should you close each program when you are finished using it?
7. A(n) _____ consists of a group of buttons, each of which provides one-click access to important program functions.
8. A(n) _____ is helpful because it only includes options that are appropriate for your current task.

Review

To reinforce the tasks you learned in this session, go to the SAM 2003 Training Companion CD included with this text.

Session 2

For hands-on practice of key tasks in this session, go to the SAM 2003 Training Companion CD included with this text.

Exploring Your Computer

To discover the contents and resources on your computer, you explore, or navigate, it. **Navigating**, in this context, means to move from one location to another on your computer, such as from one window to another. Windows XP provides two different ways to navigate, view, and work with the contents and resources on your computer—My Computer and Windows Explorer.

Navigating with My Computer

The My Computer icon on the Start menu represents your computer, its storage devices, printers, and other objects. The My Computer icon opens the My Computer window, which contains an icon for each of the storage devices on your computer, as shown in Figure 22. These icons appear in the right pane of the My Computer window. By default, the My Computer window also has a left pane, which shows icons and links to other resources. You'll learn more about the left pane shortly.

Figure 22	Relationship between computer and My Computer window

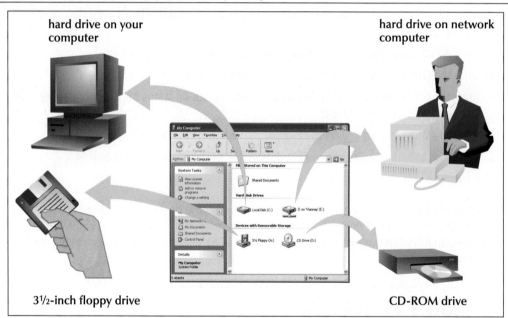

Each storage device you have access to on your computer has a letter associated with it. The first floppy drive on a computer is usually designated as drive A (if you add a second drive, it is usually designated as drive B), and the first hard drive is usually designated as drive C (if you add additional hard drives, they are usually designated D, E, and so on). If you have a CD or DVD drive, it usually has the next letter in the alphabetic sequence. If you have access to hard drives located on other computers in a network, those drives will sometimes (although not always) have letters associated with them as well. Naming conventions for network drives vary. In the example shown in Figure 22, the network drive has the drive letter E.

You can use the My Computer window to keep track of where your files are stored and to organize your files. In this session, you will explore the contents of your hard disk, which is assumed to be located in drive C. If you use a different drive on your computer, such as drive E, substitute its letter for "C" throughout this session.

Now you'll open the My Computer window and explore the contents of your computer.

To explore the contents of your computer using the My Computer window:

▶ 1. If you took a break after the previous session, make sure that your computer is on and Windows XP is running.

▶ 2. Click the **Start** button on the taskbar, and then click **My Computer**. The My Computer window opens. See Figure 23. Your window might look different. For example, in addition to the Shared Documents folder, your window probably lists folders with names for each user on your computer, such as "Andrea's Documents."

My Computer window | Figure 23

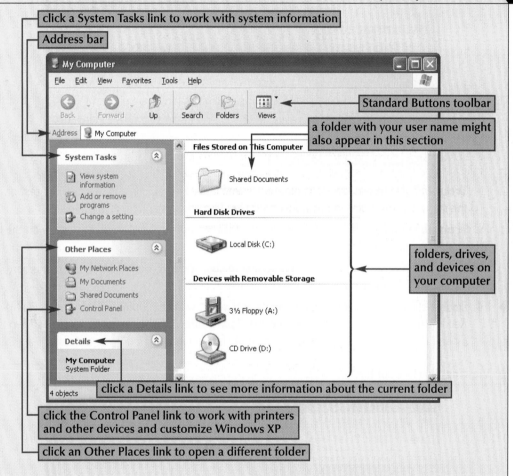

3. In the Files Stored on This Computer section, double-click the folder with your user name. A window opens showing the contents of that folder. See Figure 24.

Figure 24 | Contents of the folder with your user name

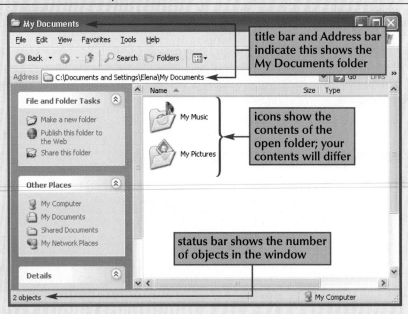

Trouble? If your window looks different from Figure 24, you can still perform the rest of the steps. For example, your window might contain additional folders and files.

Trouble? If you see a list of folder names or filenames instead of icons, click View on the menu bar, and then click Tiles.

Trouble? If the status bar does not appear in your window, click View on the menu bar, and then click Status Bar.

4. Double-click each folder in the My Documents window until you find one that contains files. Record the name of the folder you opened. Your window will be similar to the one shown in Figure 25, which shows the contents of the My Music folder.

Figure 25 | Viewing files in a folder

The tasks in the left pane change so that they are appropriate for the new location—in Figure 25, the left pane lists music tasks and other folders you might want to open. The right pane shows the contents of the folder you double-clicked. The file icon indicates its type. In Figure 25, the icon indicates that these are music files.

You can change the appearance of most windows to suit your preferences. You'll change the view of the My Computer window next.

Changing the View

Windows XP offers several options that control how toolbars, icons, and buttons appear in the My Computer window. The My Computer window, in addition to featuring a Standard Buttons toolbar, allows you to display the same toolbars that can appear on the Windows XP taskbar, such as the Address bar or the Links toolbar. You can use these toolbars to access the Web from the My Computer window. In this tutorial, however, you need to see only the Address bar and Standard Buttons toolbar.

To display only the Address bar and Standard Buttons toolbar:

▶ 1. Click **View** on the menu bar, and then point to **Toolbars**. The Standard Buttons and Address Bar commands on the Toolbars submenu should be checked, indicating that they are displayed in the My Computer window. The Links option should not be checked.

▶ 2. If the Standard Buttons or Address Bar commands *are not checked*, click the command to select it. Or if the Links command *is checked*, click it to deselect it. You must display the Toolbars submenu to select or deselect each command.

▶ 3. If necessary, click **View** on the menu bar, and then point to **Toolbars**. Make sure that only Standard Buttons, Address Bar, and Lock the Toolbars are checked.

▶ 4. Press the **Esc** key twice to close the menus.

Windows XP also provides five ways to view the contents of a disk—Thumbnails, Tiles, Icons, List, and Details. The default view, Tiles view, displays a large icon, title, file type, and file size for each file. The icon provides a visual cue to the type of file. You can also find this same information with the smaller icons displayed in the Icons and List views, but in less screen space. In Icons and List views, you can see more files and folders at one time, which is helpful when you have many files in one location.

All of the three icon views (Tiles, Icons, and List) help you quickly identify a file and its type, but what if you want more information about a set of files? Details view shows more information than the other three views. Details view shows the file icon, filename, file size, program used to create the file, and the date and time the file was created or last modified.

If you have graphic files, you can use Thumbnails view, which displays a small preview image of the graphic. In Thumbnails view, you can quickly see not only the filename, but also which picture or drawing the file contains. Thumbnails view is great for browsing a large collection of graphic files, but switching to this view can be time-consuming because Windows XP must first create all the preview images.

To practice switching from one view to another, you'll start by displaying the contents of the folder you opened earlier in Details view. So far, you've used the View menu to change the window view. Now you can use the Views button, which displays the same commands for changing views as the View menu.

To view a detailed list of files:

▶ **1.** Click the **Views** button ⊞ on the Standard Buttons toolbar, and then click **Details** to display details for the files on your disk. See Figure 26. Your files might differ or be listed in a different order.

Figure 26 ▶ **Details view**

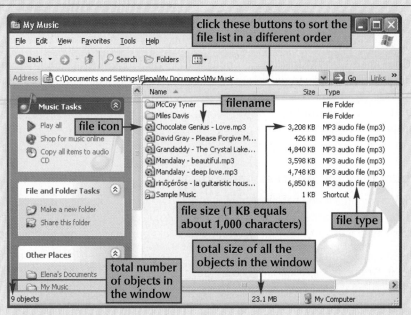

▶ **2.** Look at the file sizes. Which files are the largest?

▶ **3.** Look at the Type column. Which file is a shortcut?

Note that in Figure 26, the Sample Music item is a **shortcut**, a special type of file that serves as a direct link to another location that your computer can access, such as a folder, a document in a file, a program, a Windows tool, or a Web site.

One of the advantages of Details view is that you can sort the file list by filename, size, type, or date. This helps if you're looking for a particular file in a long file listing. For example, suppose you know that you created a file recently, but can't remember its name. You could sort the file list by date so that the most recent files appear at the top of the list.

To sort the file list by date:

▶ **1.** Click **View** on the menu bar, click **Choose Details**, click the **Date Modified** check box if it is not checked, and then click the **OK** button.

▶ **2.** Click the **Date Modified** button at the top of the list of files. The files are now sorted in descending order by date, starting with the most recent files.

▶ **3.** Click the **Date Modified** button again. The sort order is reversed, with the oldest files now at the top of the list.

▶ **4.** Click the **Name** button at the top of the file list. The files are now sorted in alphabetical order by filename.

Now that you have looked at the file details, you can switch back to Tiles view.

To switch to Tiles view:

▶ **1.** Click the **Views** button 🎛 on the Standard Buttons toolbar, and then click **Tiles** to return to Tiles view.

▶ **2.** Click the **Close** button 🗙 to close the window.

Now you can compare My Computer to Windows Explorer, another navigation tool.

Navigating with Windows Explorer

Like My Computer, Windows Explorer also lets you easily navigate the resources on your computer. Many of the techniques you use with the My Computer window apply to Windows Explorer—and vice versa. Both let you display and work with files and folders. By default, however, Windows Explorer also lets you see the hierarchy of all the folders on your computer. Viewing this hierarchy makes it easier to navigate your computer, especially if it contains many files and folders.

You will use Windows Explorer to open the same folders you opened in My Computer. As with other Windows XP programs, you start Windows Explorer using the Start menu.

To start Windows Explorer:

▶ **1.** Click the **Start** button on the taskbar, point to **All Programs**, point to **Accessories**, and then click **Windows Explorer**. The Windows Explorer window opens, as shown in Figure 27. By default, this window shows the contents of your My Documents folder when you first open it.

Windows Explorer window　　　　**Figure 27**

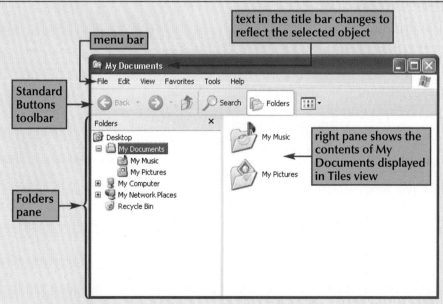

Trouble? If your Windows Explorer window looks slightly different from the one displayed in Figure 27, the configuration of your computer probably differs from the computer used to take this figure. Continue with Step 2.

▶ **2.** If the Windows Explorer window is not maximized, click the **Maximize** button 🗖 on the Windows Explorer title bar.

Windows Explorer is divided into two sections called **panes**. The left pane, also called the **Explorer bar**, shows different ways of locating specific files or folders on your computer. The right pane lists the contents of these files and folders, similar to the view of files and folders in My Computer.

The Explorer bar can be displayed in one of five ways: as a Search, Favorites, Media, History, or Folders pane. The Search pane includes tools to help you search for a particular file or folder on your computer. The Favorites pane lists your favorite files and folders on your computer and sites on the World Wide Web. The Media pane lists multimedia files, such as videos and music. The History pane organizes the files and folders on your computer by the date you last worked with them. The Folders pane organizes your files and folders based on their location in the hierarchy of objects on your computer. To move between these different panes, you click the appropriate command on the View menu. You can also quickly open the Search and Folders panes by clicking either the Search button 🔎 or the Folders button 📂 on the Standard Buttons toolbar. Note that the Explorer bar is available in any Windows XP window that displays files and folders. You can, for example, use the Explorer bar in the My Computer window.

You'll start working with Windows Explorer using the Folders pane.

To view the Folders pane:

1. Click **View** on the menu bar, and then point to **Explorer Bar**.

2. If necessary, click **Folders** to check that option; otherwise, click a blank area of the screen to close the View menu. Your Windows Explorer window should now resemble Figure 28.

| Figure 28 | Folders pane in the Windows Explorer window |

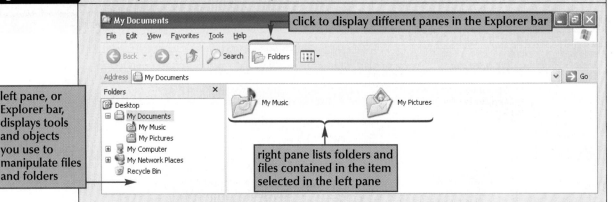

Trouble? If your Windows Explorer window looks slightly different from the one displayed in Figure 28, the configuration of your computer probably differs from the computer used to take this figure. For example, you might have different folders listed in the left and right panes of the window.

The Folders pane initially displays a list of the objects on your desktop: the My Documents folder, the My Computer window, the My Network Places window, and the Recycle Bin. If your desktop contains other folders or objects, those are displayed as well. The right pane of the Windows Explorer window displays the contents of the object selected in the Folders pane. In this case, the My Documents folder is the selected object, and it contains two items—the My Music and My Pictures folders. Icons for these objects are therefore displayed in the right pane.

Now you can open the same folder you opened before in the My Computer window.

To open a folder:

▶ 1. Double-click the folder you double-clicked earlier in the My Computer window, such as the My Music folder. The contents of that folder appear in the right pane of the Windows Explorer window, and the folder you opened is selected in the left pane.

▶ 2. Click the **Close** button ☒ on the title bar to close the window.

Getting Help

Windows XP **Help** provides on-screen information about the program you are using. Help for the Windows XP operating system is available by clicking the Start button on the taskbar and then clicking Help and Support on the Start menu. If you want Help for a particular program, such as WordPad, you must first start the program, and then click Help on the program's menu bar.

When you start Help for Windows XP, a Windows Help and Support Center window opens, which gives you access to Help files stored on your computer as well as Help information stored on Microsoft's Web site. If you are not connected to the Web, you only have access to the Help files stored on your computer.

To start Windows XP Help:

▶ 1. Click the **Start** button on the taskbar.

▶ 2. Click **Help and Support**. The Help and Support Center window opens. See Figure 29.

Windows XP Help and Support Center window | **Figure 29**

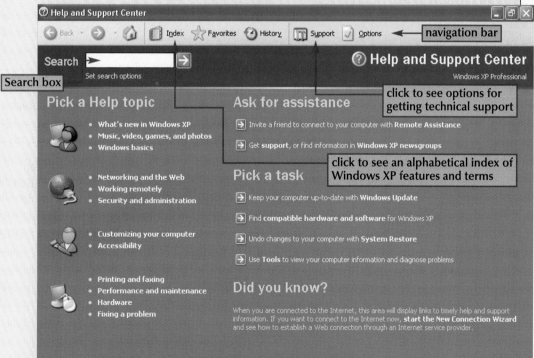

Trouble? If the Help and Support window does not display the information you see in Figure 29, click the Home icon on the navigation bar at the top of the window to view Help contents.

The Windows XP Help and Support Center window organizes the vast amount of help and support information into pages. These six pages—the Home, Index, Favorites, History, Support, and Options page—are designed to aid users in locating information on a particular topic quickly. To open one of these pages, click its button on the navigation bar. The Home page lists common tasks under the heading "Pick a Help topic" in the left pane on the page. Click a task to see detailed information or instructions about that task in the right pane of the page. The right pane of the Home page lists common tasks, tips, and ways you can ask for assistance. For example, you can contact a support professional or download the latest version of Windows XP.

The Index page displays an alphabetical list of all the Help topics from which you can choose. The Favorites page shows Help topics you've added to your Favorites list. To add a topic to the Favorites list, open the topic, and then click the Favorites button on the Help window. The History page lists links you've recently selected in Help. The Support page includes links that you can click to connect to the Microsoft Web site, if possible, for additional assistance. The Options page provides ways you can customize Help. For example, you can change the appearance of the navigation bar.

If you can't find the topic you want listed on any of the six Help and Support Center pages, the word that you are using for a feature or topic might be different from the word that Windows XP uses. You can use the Search box to search for all keywords contained in the Help pages, not just the topic titles. In the Search box, you can type any word or phrase, click the Search button, and Windows XP lists all the Help topics that contain that word or phrase.

Viewing Topics on the Windows XP Help and Support Center Home Page

Windows XP Help includes instructions on using Help itself. You can learn how to find a Help topic by using the Help and Support Center Home page.

To use the Help and Support Center Home page:

1. Click **Windows basics**. A list of topics related to using Windows XP appears in the left pane of the Help and Support Center window.

2. Click **Tips for using Help**. A list of Help topics appears in the right pane of the Help window.

3. Click **Change fonts in Help and Support Center**. The instructions appear in the right pane of the Help and Support Center window.

   Besides listing the pages in the Help and Support Center window, the navigation bar contains two buttons—the Back button and the Forward button . You use these buttons to navigate the pages you've already opened. You'll use the Back button next to return to the previous page you viewed. Once you do, you activate the Forward button, which you can click to go to the next page of those you've opened.

4. Click the **Back** button on the navigation bar. You return to the Tips for using Help page. The Forward button is now active.

Selecting a Topic from the Index

The Index page allows you to jump to a Help topic by selecting a topic from an alphabetical list. For example, you can use the Index page to learn how to arrange open windows on your desktop.

To find a Help topic using the Index page:

1. Click **Index** ⬜ on the navigation bar. A long list of indexed Help topics appears in the left pane.

2. Drag the **scroll box** down to view additional topics in the list box.

   You can quickly jump to any part of the list by typing the first few characters of a word or phrase in the box that appears above the Index list.

3. If necessary, click in the Type in the keyword to find text box above the Index list, and then type **windows**. As you type each character in the word, the list of Index topics scrolls and eventually displays topics that relate to windows.

4. Under the "windows and panes on your computer screen" topic, click the topic **reducing windows to taskbar buttons**, and then click the **Display** button. When there is just one topic, it appears immediately in the right pane; otherwise, the Topics Found window opens, listing all topics indexed under the selected entry.

   The information you requested appears in the right pane. This topic has two underlined phrases, "taskbar" and "Related Topics," which you can click to view definitions or additional information.

5. Click the underlined phrase **taskbar**. A ScreenTip shows the definition of "taskbar."

6. Click a blank area of the Help and Support Center window to close the ScreenTip.

If you have an Internet connection, you can use another Help page, Support, to contact Microsoft support or get in touch with other users of Windows XP. The Support page works like the Home page. To get support on a particular feature, you click a support option and then click the topic for which you need help. Continue clicking topics, if necessary, until you get help from a Microsoft support person or an experienced Windows XP user.

Searching the Help Pages

If you can't find the topic you need by using the Home or Index pages, or if you want to quickly find Help pages related to a particular topic, you can use the Search box. Suppose you want to know how to exit Windows XP, but you don't know if Windows refers to this as exiting, quitting, closing, or shutting down. You can search the Help pages to find just the right topic.

To search the Help pages for information on exiting Windows XP:

1. Click in the Search box. A blinking insertion point appears.

2. Type **shutdown** and then click the **Start Searching** button ➡. A list of Help pages containing the word "shutdown" appears in the left pane of the Help and Support Center window. The ones listed under Suggested Topics are topics where "shutdown" has been assigned as a keyword—meaning the topics have to do with shutting something down.

3. Click the **Full-text Search Matches** button. In these topics, "shutdown" is included in the text of the Help topic.

4. Click the **Suggested Topics** button, and then click **Turn off the computer**. A Help topic appears in the right pane of the Help and Support Center window, as shown in Figure 30.

Figure 30 **Using search to find a Help page**

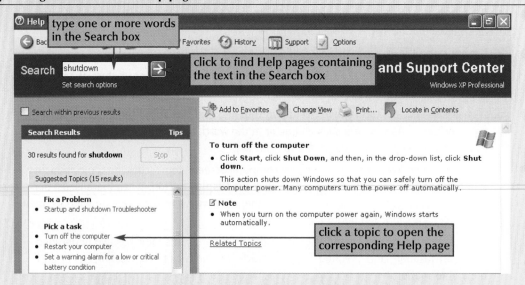

If this topic were longer than the Help and Support Center window, you could use the scroll bar to read the entire topic.

5. Click the **Close** button ☒ on the title bar to close the Help and Support Center window.

Now that you know how Windows XP Help works, don't forget to use it. Use Help when you need to perform a new task or when you forget how to complete a procedure.

Shutting Down Windows XP

You should always shut down Windows XP before you turn off your computer. If you turn off your computer without shutting it down correctly, you might lose data and damage your files.

Typically you will use the Turn Off Computer command on the Start menu when you want to turn off your computer. However, your school might prefer that you select the Log Off command on the Start menu. This command logs you out of Windows XP but leaves the computer turned on, allowing another user to log on without restarting the computer. Check with your instructor or technical support person for the preferred method at your lab.

When you select the Turn Off Computer command on the Start menu, the Turn Off Computer dialog box opens with four buttons: Standby, Turn Off, Restart, and Cancel. You choose Standby when you want to put your computer into an idle state in which it consumes less power, but is still available for immediate use. Choose Turn Off to shut down Windows and turn off the power, and choose Restart to shut down Windows and then immediately start it again. Choose Cancel if you do not want to end your Windows session, but want to return to your previous task.

To shut down Windows XP:

1. Click the **Start** button on the taskbar.

2. Click the **Turn Off Computer** command at the bottom of the Start menu. The Turn Off Computer dialog box opens. See Figure 31.

Shutting down the computer ◄ Figure 31

click to put
Windows XP
into an idle state

Turn off computer

click to
shut down
Windows XP

click to shut down
and then restart
Windows XP

Stand By   Turn Off   Restart

Cancel

Trouble? If you are supposed to log off rather than shut down, click Log Off instead and follow your school's logoff procedure.

3. Click the **Turn Off** button.

4. Wait until you see a message indicating that it is safe to turn off your computer. If your lab procedure includes switching off your computer after shutting it down, do so now; other-wise, leave the computer running. Some computers turn themselves off automatically.

In this session you learned how to start and close programs and how to use multiple programs at the same time. You learned how to work with windows and the controls they employ. Finally, you learned how to get help when you need it and shut down Windows XP. After completing Steve's introductory course, you are well on your way to mastering the fundamentals of using the Windows XP operating system.

Session 2 Quick Check

Review

1. The _____ icon on the Start menu represents your computer, its storage devices, printers, and other objects.
2. Explain the difference between the left pane in My Computer (the Tasks pane) and the Folders pane in Windows Explorer.
3. What information does Details view supply about a list of folders and files?
4. True or false: A shortcut is a special type of file that serves as a direct link to another location that your computer can access, such as a folder or a document in a file.
5. Name the five ways that you can display the Explorer bar in Windows Explorer.
6. In the Help and Support Center window, the _____ page displays an alphabetical list of all the Help topics from which you can choose.
7. To learn how to perform new tasks, you can use _____.
8. You should always _____ Windows XP before you turn off your computer.

To reinforce the tasks you learned in this session, go to the SAM 2003 Training Companion CD included with this text.

Tutorial Summary

Review

In this tutorial, you learned the basics of Windows XP. You toured the desktop and learned how to open objects on the desktop. You explored the Start menu and opened its sub-menus. You started programs from the Start menu, and then switched between multiple programs. You worked with windows by manipulating them. You selected options from a menu and buttons on a toolbar. You also examined typical dialog boxes and their controls. Then you explored your computer with My Computer and Windows Explorer, learned how to get help when you need it, and finally shut down Windows XP.

Key Terms

active program	list arrow	pinned items list
application	list box	point
click	log off	pointing device
control	menu	program
Control Panel	menu command	program button
default	menu convention	right-click
desktop	Microsoft Windows XP	ScreenTip
dialog box	most frequently used	select
double-click	programs list	shortcut
drag	mouse	shortcut menu
exit	multitask	sizing handle
Explorer bar	My Computer	Start menu
graphical user interface (GUI)	My Documents	submenu
Help	navigate	user name
Help and Support Center	operating system	window
icon	pane	Windows XP
Internet	password	

Review Assignments

There are no Data Files needed for the Review Assignments.

Steve Laslow offers a practice session as a follow-up to his basic Windows XP course. You'll start working on the Windows XP desktop, with no windows opened or minimized. Complete the following steps, recording your answers to any questions according to your instructor's preferences:

1. Start Windows XP and log on, if necessary.
2. Use the mouse to point to each object on your desktop. Record the names of each object as they appear in the ScreenTips.
3. Click the Start button. How many menu items or commands are on the Start menu?
4. Run the WordPad program located on the Accessories menu. How many program buttons are now on the taskbar (don't count toolbar buttons or items in the notification area)?
5. Run the Paint program and maximize the Paint window. How many programs are running now?
6. Switch to WordPad. What are two visual clues that tell you that WordPad is the active program?
7. Close WordPad, and then restore the Paint window.
8. Open the Recycle Bin window. Record the number of items it contains.
9. Drag the Recycle Bin window so that you can see it and the Paint window.
10. Close the Paint window from the taskbar.
11. Open the File menu in the Recycle Bin window. Write down the commands on the menu. Press the Esc key to close the menu.
12. Use any menu in the Recycle Bin window to open a dialog box. What steps did you perform? What dialog box did you open? For what do you think you use this dialog box? Click Cancel to close the dialog box.
13. Close the Recycle Bin window.

14. Open the My Computer window, and then open the My Documents folder that is designed to contain your documents.
15. Open a folder in the My Documents window that you did not open in the tutorial. List the name and contents of that folder.
16. Close the My Documents window.
17. Start Windows Explorer. Use the Folders pane to navigate to the same folder you opened in Step 14. What steps did you perform?
18. Change the view of the icons in the right pane of the Windows Explorer window. What view did you select? Describe the icons in the Windows Explorer window.
19. Close the Windows Explorer window.
20. Open the Help and Support Center window.
21. Use the Help and Support Center window to learn something new about Windows Explorer. What did you learn? How did you find this topic?
22. Use the Index page to find information about the topic of speech recognition, a feature new to Windows XP. How many topics are listed? What is their primary subject matter?
23. Use the Search box to find information about the topic of speech recognition. How many topics are listed?
24. Open the Home page in the Help and Support Center window, click What's new in Windows XP, and then click Windows XP Articles: Walkthrough ways to use your PC.
25. Click Walkthrough: Making Music.
26. Read the Get Started page. (*Hint:* The contents of the article are listed in a box in the upper-left corner of the window. Each topic is a link you can click to go to another page in the article.)
27. Click the links in the contents box, and then answer the following questions using the information you find:
    a. How can you listen to music using Windows XP?
    b. What is a playlist? What is the first step you take to create one?
    c. What is the advantage of listening to Internet radio?
28. Close Help, and then close WordPad.
29. Shut down or log off Windows.

Case Problem 1

There are no Data Files needed for this Case Problem.

JL Productions JL Productions is a company in Fort Wayne, Indiana, that produces videos and hosts advertising events for businesses in the Midwest. You have recently been hired by Julian Letice, the owner of JL Productions, to help him with office management. Your first task is to explore Julian's new Windows XP computer. Because he is visually oriented, he is particularly interested in features that improve the appearance of his desktop or that would enhance the materials he sends to his clients. Complete the following steps:

1. Start Windows XP and log on, if necessary.
2. From the desktop or the Start menu, open My Computer, and then maximize the window.
3. If necessary, change the My Computer window to Tiles view, arrange icons by type, and organize icons by group. (*Hint:* Click View on the menu bar, point to Arrange Icons by, and then click Show in Groups.) List the names of the drives on your computer.
4. Click the Shared Documents link in the Other Places area of the Tasks pane. What are the names of the Shared folders within this folder?
5. Display the Folders pane in the My Computer window. (*Hint:* Click the Folders button on the Standard Buttons toolbar.) Where is the Shared Documents folder located in the folder structure of your computer? Describe its relation to the My Documents folder.

Apply

Use the skills you learned in the tutorial to explore the contents of other folders on your computer for JL Productions.

Explore

6. Close the Folders pane, open the My Pictures folder, click the View as a slide show link in the Picture Tasks dynamic menu, and enjoy the slide show. When you are ready to exit the slide show, press the Esc key.

7. Navigate to a folder that contains graphics, music, or other media files, such as My Pictures or My Music. Switch to Details view. What types of files are contained in this folder?

8. Double-click the icon for one of the files in this folder. What happens? Close any windows that open.

9. Close the My Computer window, if necessary, and then start Windows Explorer. Open the Search pane in the Windows Explorer window. (*Hint:* Click the Search button on the Standard Buttons toolbar.)

10. Open the Help and Support Center window and then find and read topics that explain how to use the Search pane to find types of files.

Explore ▶ 11. Use the Search pane to find .bmp files, a common type of graphics file, on your computer. (*Hint:* Use *.bmp as the search text.) Name at least two locations where your computer stores .bmp files.

12. Close all open windows.

Apply

Apply what you learned in the tutorial to work with Windows XP installed on a computer for a landscaping business.

Case Problem 2

There are no Data Files needed for this Case Problem.

Rolling Hills Landscaping After working for a number of gardening and landscaping firms in Towson, Maryland, Elaine Rodriguez founded her own company, named Rolling Hills Landscaping. She works with property owners and businesses to create garden and landscaping designs, and contracts with local professional gardeners to plant and maintain the landscapes. She hired you to help her perform office tasks, and asks you to start by teaching her the basics of using her computer, which runs Windows XP. She especially wants to know which programs are installed on her computer and what they do. Complete the following:

1. Open the Start menu and write down the programs on the pinned items list.

2. Start one of the programs on the pinned items list and then describe what it does. Close the program.

3. Open the Start menu and write down the programs on the most frequently used programs list.

4. Start one of the programs on the most frequently used programs list and then describe what it does. Close the program.

5. Open the All Programs menu, point to the Accessories folder, and then open a program in the Accessories folder. What program did you start?

6. Use the Help and Support Center to research the program you started in Step 5. Find out how to perform a task using that program.

7. Perform the steps you researched in Step 6. What task did you complete? Write down the steps you performed and the results.

8. Close all open windows.

9. Start another program using the Start menu. Make sure the program includes a Help menu on its menu bar. Describe the steps you performed.

10. Click Help on the menu bar and then click each command on the menu until you open a window listing Help topics for this program. Describe the typical tasks users perform when they use this program.

Explore ▶ 11. If possible, perform one set of steps you researched in Step 10. Describe the task you performed and the results. Then close the program.

Challenge

Extend what you've learned to customize the My Computer window for a consumer research organization.

Explore

Explore

Explore

Explore

Case Problem 3

There are no Data Files needed for this Case Problem.

Yamamoto Research Ken Yamamoto runs a small business called Yamamoto Research, which researches and tests consumer products, focusing on those used in the home health care industry. Ken has created many files and folders on his new Windows XP computer, and asks you to catalog his options for working in the My Computer window. Complete the following steps:

1. Open the My Computer window. Open each menu in the My Computer window, and write down any items that seem related to changing the appearance of the window.
2. Display the My Computer window so that no toolbars appear. Then restore the window to its original condition.
3. Navigate to a folder containing graphic files. Display the icons using Thumbnail view.
4. Change the view to Icons view. Describe the differences among Icons, Thumbnail, and Tiles view.
5. In Icons view, arrange the icons by type. Then arrange them by name.
6. Switch to Details view. On the View menu, open a dialog box that lets you choose the details displayed in Details view. Note which items are currently checked.
7. Use the Choose Details dialog box to show only the name, type, and size of the items in Details view. Close the Choose Details dialog box and then sort the contents of the My Computer window by size.
8. Use the Choose Details dialog box to restore your original settings. Then sort the contents of the My Computer window by name.
9. On the Tools menu, click Folder Options to open the Folder Options dialog box. Select the option that uses Windows Classic folders, and then click the OK button. Describe the changes in the My Computer window.
10. Open the Folder Options dialog box again and click the Restore Defaults button.
11. Open the Help and Support Center window from the My Computer window and search for information about folder options. Find a definition of hidden files, and how to hide and show hidden files in the My Computer window. Record your findings.
12. Close all open windows.

Research

Work with the skills you've learned, and use the Internet, to provide information to a translation company.

Explore

Case Problem 4

There are no Data Files needed for this Case Problem.

Janus Translation Several years ago, Doug Janus and Mohammed Amos started a company that translates software programs so that they can be used in Europe, Asia, and South America. Doug often works from home, and recently set up a computer running Windows XP. He asks you to help him get connected to the Internet. You suggest using the Help and Support Center to find information. Doug also needs to know more about the Help and Support Center itself. Complete the following steps:

1. In the Help and Support Center, find information about the hardware and software Doug needs to connect to the Internet.
2. Use the Help and Support Center to find two ways that Doug can connect to the Internet. Describe these two methods.
3. Choose a topic you'd like to research using the Windows XP online Help system. Look for information on your topic using the Help and Support Center Home page, Index page, Search box, and Support page. (*Hint*: Click the Support button on the navigation bar to open the Support page.) From the Support page, go to a Windows Web site forum to research your topic. (You must be connected to the Internet to complete this step.)

4. Once you've found all the information you can, compare the four methods (Home page, Index page, Search box, and Support page) of looking for information. Write a paragraph that discusses which method proved the most useful. Did you reach the same information topics using all four methods? In a second paragraph, summarize what you learned about your topic. Finally, in a third paragraph, indicate under what circumstances you'd use which method.

Assess

SAM Assessment and Training

If your instructor has chosen to use the full online version of SAM 2003 Assessment and Training, you can go beyond the "just-in-time" training provided on the CD that accompanies this text. Simply log in to your SAM account (http://sam2003.course.com) to launch any assigned training activities or exams that relate to the skills covered in this tutorial.

Reinforce

Lab Assignments

Using a Mouse · Using a Keyboard

The New Perspectives Labs are designed to help you master some of the key concepts and skills presented in this text. The steps for completing this Lab are located on the Course Technology Web site. Log on to the Internet and use your Web browser to go to the Student Online Companion for New Perspectives Office 2003 at **www.course.com/np/office2003**. Click the Lab Assignments link, and then navigate to the assignments for this tutorial.

Review

Quick Check Answers

Session 1

1. to provide access to common tools and programs currently running
2. text that displays the purpose and function of a window component, such as a button
3. Start menu
4. multitasking
5. its button appears on the taskbar
6. to conserve computer resources such as memory
7. toolbar
8. list box

Session 2

1. My Computer
2. The Tasks pane (the left pane) of My Computer lists tasks that change so that they are appropriate for the new location. When the left pane in Windows Explorer shows the Folders pane, it shows different ways of locating specific files or folders on your computer.
3. filename, file size, file type, and date modified
4. true
5. Search, Favorites, Media, History, and Folders panes
6. Index
7. online Help or Help and Support Center
8. shut down

New Perspectives on
Managing Your Files

Creating and Working with Files   **FM 3**
and Folders in Windows XP

Read This Before You Begin

Data Files

To complete the "Managing Your Files" tutorial, you need the starting Data Files. See the inside back or front cover for information on downloading these files from course.com, or ask your instructor for assistance. The following table identifies each starting Data File and the folder it is stored in, as well as the ending files, which you create and save in each tutorial.

Folders		Starting Files	Ending Files
FM	Tutorial	Agenda.doc, Holiday.bmp, New Logo.bmp, Proposal.doc, Resume.doc, Salinas members.eml, Stationery.bmp, Vinca.jpg	Final Tutorial files.zip, Holiday.bmp, New Logo.bmp, Playground Project Logo.bmp, Proposal.doc, Resume.doc, Salinas Meeting Agenda.doc, Salinas members.eml, Stationery.bmp, Vinca.jpg
	Review	Billing Worksheet.wk4, Car Savings Plan.xls, Commissions.xls, Contracts.xls, Customer Accounts.xls, Filenames.pps, Personal Loan.doc, Speech.wav, Water lilies.jpg	Ask Not.wav, Billing Worksheet.wk4, Car Savings Plan.xls, Commissions.xls, Contracts.xls, Customer Accounts.xls, Filenames.pps, Final Review files.zip, Personal Loan.doc, Sample Loan.doc, Water lilies.jpg
	Cases	Invoice Feb.xls, Invoice Jan.xls, Invoice March.xls, Painting Class – Agenda.doc, Painting Class – Questionnaire.doc, Painting Class – Teaching Manual.doc, Paris.jpg, Vegetables.jpg	Agenda.doc, Feb.xls, Jan.xls, March.xls, Questionnaire.doc, Teaching Manual.doc

Storing Your Files

It is recommended that you store all your Data Files on a USB drive. Refer to the tutorial "Managing Your Files" for information on using USB drives. If you need to store your Data Files on floppy disks, you will need two high-density disks to store all the files for the "Managing Your Files" tutorial.

SAM 2003 Training Companion CD

The SAM 2003 Training Companion CD that comes with this text gives you "just-in-time" training and reinforcement of important Microsoft Office skills. Look for the SAM CD logo throughout each tutorial for opportunities to complete the hands-on tasks included on this CD.

Course Labs

The "Managing Your Files" tutorial features an interactive Course Lab to help you understand file management concepts. There are Lab Assignments at the end of the tutorial that relate to this lab. Contact your instructor or technical support person for assistance in accessing this lab.

Managing Your Files

Creating and Working with Files and Folders in Windows XP

Case | Distance Learning Company

The Distance Learning Company specializes in distance learning courses for individuals who want to participate in college-level classes to work toward a degree or for personal enrichment. Distance learning is formalized education that typically takes place using a computer and the Internet, replacing normal classroom interaction with modern communications technology. The company's goal is to help students gain new skills and stay competitive in the job market. The head of the Customer Service Department, Shannon Connell, interacts with the Distance Learning Company's clients on the phone and from her computer. Shannon, like all other employees, is required to learn the basics of managing files on her computer.

In this tutorial, you'll help Shannon devise a strategy for managing files. You'll learn how Windows XP organizes files and folders, and you'll examine Windows XP file management tools. You'll create folders and organize files within them. You'll also explore options for working with compressed files.

| Objectives

- Develop file management strategies
- Explore files and folders
- Create, name, copy, move, and delete folders
- Name, copy, move, and delete files
- Work with compressed files

| SAM Training Tasks

- Change the appearance of the My Documents window
- Collapse an area
- Compress files
- Copy a file in Explorer by right-dragging
- Copy a file to a different folder
- Copy a folder
- Copy files to a folder on a floppy disk
- Create a folder
- Create a folder in the My Documents folder
- Delete a file
- Delete multiple files from a folder
- Expand a folder using Windows Explorer
- Extract compressed files
- Move a file
- Move a folder
- Navigate through the Windows hierarchy
- Rename a file
- Restore files
- Select a menu option
- Select a toolbar button
- Select more than one file at a time
- View contents of a folder using Windows Explorer

Student Data Files For a complete list of the Data Files needed for this tutorial, see page FM 2.

Organizing Files and Folders

Knowing how to save, locate, and organize computer files makes you more productive when you are working with a computer. A **file**, often referred to as a **document**, is a collection of data that has a name and is stored in a computer. Once you create a file, you can open it, edit its contents, print it, and save it again—usually using the same program you used to create it. You organize files by storing them in **folders**, which are containers for your files. You need to organize files so you can find them easily and work efficiently.

A file cabinet is a common metaphor for computer file organization. A computer is like a file cabinet that has two or more drawers—each drawer is a storage device, or **disk**. Each disk contains folders that hold documents, or files. To make it easy to retrieve files, you arrange them logically into folders. For example, one folder might contain financial data, another might contain your creative work, and another could contain information you're collecting for an upcoming vacation.

A computer can store folders and files on different types of disks, ranging from removable media—such as **USB drives** (also called USB flash drives), **compact discs (CDs)**, and **floppy disks**—to **hard disks**, or fixed disks, which are permanently stored in a computer. Hard disks are the most popular type of computer storage because they can contain many gigabytes of data, millions of times more data than a floppy disk, and are economical.

To have your computer access a removable disk, you must insert the disk into a **drive**, which is a computer device that can retrieve and sometimes record data on a disk. See Figure 1. A hard disk is already contained in a drive, so you don't need to insert it each time you use the computer.

| Figure 1 | Computer drives and disks |

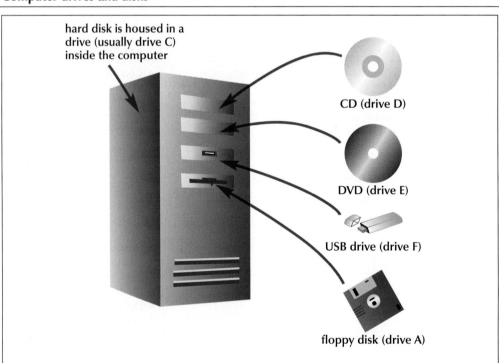

A computer distinguishes one drive from another by assigning each a drive letter. The floppy disk drive is drive A. (Most computers have only one floppy disk drive—if your computer has two, the second one is called drive B.) The hard disk is usually assigned to drive C. The remaining drives can have any other letters, but are usually assigned in the order that the drives were installed on the computer—so your USB drive might be drive D or drive F.

Understanding the Need for Organizing Files and Folders

Windows XP stores thousands of files in many folders on the hard disk of your computer. These are system files that Windows XP needs to display the desktop, use drives, and perform other operating system tasks. To ensure system stability and find files quickly, Windows organizes the folders and files in a hierarchy, or **file system**. At the top of the hierarchy, Windows stores folders and important files that it needs when you turn on the computer. This location is called the **root directory**, and is usually drive C (the hard disk). The term "root" refers to another popular metaphor for visualizing a file system—an upside-down tree, which reflects the file hierarchy that Windows uses. In Figure 2, the tree trunk corresponds to the root directory, the branches to the folders, and the leaves to files.

Windows file hierarchy ◄ Figure 2

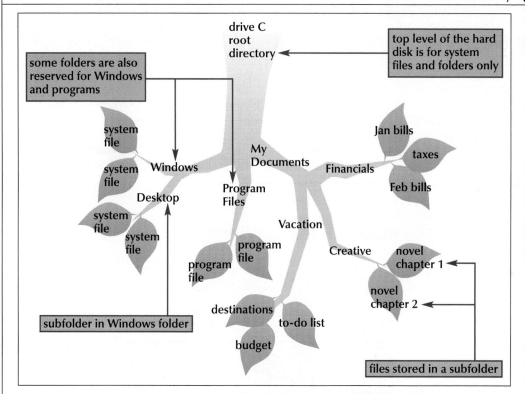

Note that some folders contain other folders. An effectively organized computer contains a few folders in the root directory, and those folders contain other folders, also called **subfolders**.

The root directory, or top level, of the hard disk is for system files and folders only—you should not store your own work here because it could interfere with Windows or a program. (If you are working in a computer lab, you might not be allowed to access the root directory.)

Do not delete or move any files or folders from the root directory of the hard disk—doing so could mean that you cannot run or start the computer. In fact, you should not reorganize or change any folder that contains installed software, because Windows XP expects to find the files for specific programs within certain folders. If you reorganize or change these folders, Windows XP cannot locate and start the programs stored in that folder. Likewise, you should not make changes to the folder that contains the Windows XP operating system (usually named Windows or Winnt).

Because the top level of the hard disk is off limits for your files—the ones that you create, open, and save on the hard disk—you must store your files in subfolders. If you are working on your own computer, you should store your files within the My Documents folder. If you are working in a computer lab, you will probably use a different location that your instructor specifies. If you simply store all your files in one folder, however, you will soon have trouble finding the ones you want. Instead, you should create folders within a main folder to separate files in a way that makes sense for you.

Likewise, if you store most of your files on removable media, such as USB drives, you need to organize those files into folders and subfolders. Before you start creating folders, whether on a hard disk or removable disk, you should plan the organization you will use.

Developing Strategies for Organizing Files and Folders

The type of disk you use to store files determines how you organize those files. Figure 3 shows how you could organize your files on a hard disk if you were taking a full semester of distance learning classes. To duplicate this organization, you would open the main folder for your documents, create four folders—one each for the Basic Accounting, Computer Concepts, Management Skills II, and Professional Writing courses—and then store the writing assignments you complete in the Professional Writing folder.

| Figure 3 | Organizing folders and files on a hard disk |

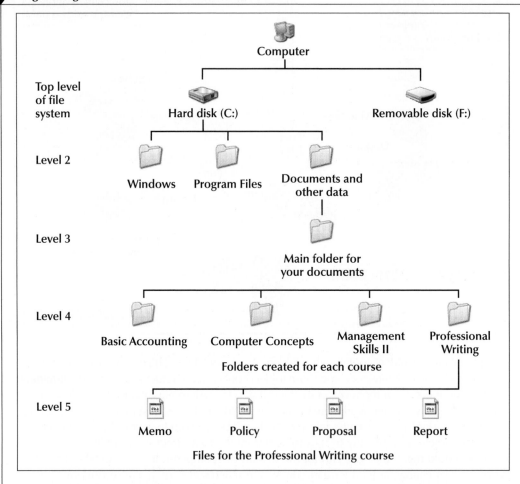

If you store your files on removable media, such as a USB drive or rewritable CD, you can use a simpler organization because you do not have to account for system files. In general, the larger the medium, the more levels of folders you should use because large media can store more files, and therefore need better organization. For example, you could organize your files on a 128 MB USB drive. In the top level of the USB drive, you could create folders for each general category of documents you store—one each for Courses, Creative, Financials, and Vacation. The Courses folder could then include one folder for each course, and each of those folders could contain the appropriate files.

You could organize these files on 1.44 MB floppy disks. Because the storage capacity of a floppy disk is much less than that of a USB drive, you would probably use one floppy disk for your courses, another for creative work, and so on. If you had to create large documents for your courses, you could use one floppy disk for each course.

If you work on two computers, such as one computer at an office or school and another computer at home, you can duplicate the folders you use on both computers to simplify transferring files from one computer to another. For example, if you have four folders in your My Documents folder on your work computer, you would create these same four folders on your removable media as well as in the My Documents folder of your home computer. If you change a file on the hard disk of your home computer, you can copy the most recent version of the file to the corresponding folder on your removable media so that it is available when you are at work. You also then have a **backup**, or duplicate copy, of important files that you need.

Planning Your Organization

Now that you've explored the basics of organizing files on a computer, you can plan the organization of your files for this book by writing in your answers to the following questions:

1. How do you obtain the files for this book (on a USB drive from your instructor, for example)? _____
   _____

2. On what drive do you store your files for this book (drive A, C, D, for example)? _____
   _____

3. Do you use a particular folder on this drive? If so, which folder do you use? _____
   _____

4. Is this folder contained within another folder? If so, what is the name of that main folder?
   _____

5. On what type of disk do you save your files for this book (hard disk, USB drive, CD, or network drive, for example)? _____

   If you cannot answer any of these questions, ask your instructor for help.

Exploring Files and Folders

Windows XP provides two tools for exploring the files and folders on your computer—Windows Explorer and My Computer. Both display the contents of your computer, using icons to represent drives, folders, and files. However, by default, each presents a different view of your computer. **Windows Explorer** shows the files, folders, and drives on your computer, making it easy to navigate, or move from one location to another within the file hierarchy. **My Computer** shows the drives on your computer and makes it easy to perform system tasks, such as viewing system information.

The Windows Explorer window is divided into two sections, called **panes**. The left pane, also called the **Explorer bar** or **Folders pane**, shows the hierarchy of the folders and other locations on your computer. The right pane lists the contents of these folders and other locations. If you select a folder in the left pane, for example, the files stored in that folder appear in the right pane. The My Computer window is also divided into panes—the left pane, called the task pane, lists tasks related to the items displayed in the right pane.

If the Folders pane in Windows Explorer showed all the folders on your computer at once, it could be a very long list. Instead, Windows Explorer allows you to open drives and folders only when you want to see what they contain. If a folder contains subfolders, an expand icon ⊞ appears to the left of the folder icon. (The same is true for drives.) To view the folders contained in an object, you click the expand icon. A collapse icon ⊟ then appears next to the folder icon; click the collapse icon to close the folder. To view the files contained in a folder, you click the folder icon, and the files appear in the right pane. See Figure 4.

Figure 4 ▶ **Viewing folder contents in Windows Explorer**

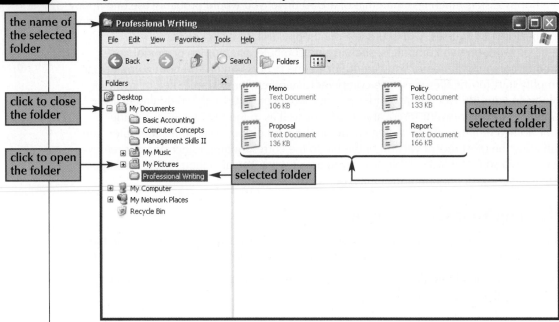

Using the Folders pane helps you navigate your computer and orients you to your current location. As you move, copy, delete, and perform other tasks with the files in the right pane of Windows Explorer, you can refer to the Folders pane to see how your changes affect the overall organization.

Like Windows Explorer, My Computer also lets you view, organize, and access the drives, folders, and files on your computer. Instead of using the Folders pane, however, you can navigate your computer in four other ways:

- **Opening drives and folders in the right pane:** To view the contents of a drive or folder, double-click the drive or folder icon in the right pane of the My Computer window. For example, to view the contents of the Professional Writing folder shown in Figure 5, you open the My Documents folder and then the Professional Writing folder.
- **Using the Standard Buttons toolbar:** Click the buttons on the Standard Buttons toolbar to navigate the hierarchy of drives, folders, subfolders, and other objects in your computer.
- **Using the Address bar:** By clicking the Address bar list arrow, you can view a list of drives, folders, and other locations on your computer. This gives you a quick way of moving to an upper level of the Windows XP file system without navigating the intermediate levels.
- **Using the task pane:** The Other Places area of the My Computer task pane lists links you can click to quickly open folders or navigate to other useful places.

By default, when you first open My Computer, it shows all the drives available on your computer, whereas Windows Explorer shows the files, folders, and drives on your computer. However, by changing window settings, you can make the two tools interchangeable. You can change settings in the My Computer window to show the Folders pane instead of the task pane. If you do, you have the same setup as Windows Explorer. Likewise, if you close the Folders pane in the Windows Explorer window, the task pane opens, giving you the same setup as in the My Computer window.

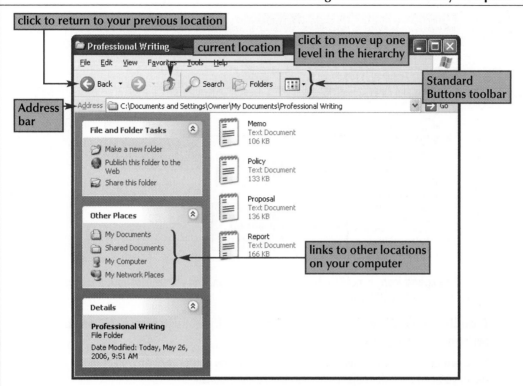

Viewing folder contents in My Computer — Figure 5

Shannon prefers to use Windows Explorer to manage her files. You'll use Windows Explorer to manage files in the rest of this tutorial.

Using Windows Explorer

Windows XP also provides a folder for your documents—the **My Documents folder**, which is designed to store the files and folders you work with regularly. On your own computer, this is where you can keep your data files—the memos, videos, graphics, music, and other files that you create, edit, and manipulate in a program. If you are working in a computer lab, you might not be able to access the My Documents folder, or you might be able to store files there only temporarily because that folder is emptied every night. Instead, you might permanently store your Data Files on removable media or in a different folder on your computer or network.

When you start Windows Explorer, it opens to the My Documents folder by default. If you cannot access the My Documents folder, the screens you see as you perform the following steps will differ. However, you can still perform the steps accurately.

To examine the organization of your computer using Windows Explorer:

1. Click the **Start** button on the taskbar, point to **All Programs**, point to **Accessories**, and then click **Windows Explorer**. The Windows Explorer window opens.

2. Click the **expand** icon + next to the My Computer icon. The drives and other useful locations on your computer appear under the My Computer icon, as shown in Figure 6. The contents of your computer will differ.

Figure 6   ▶ **Viewing the contents of your computer**

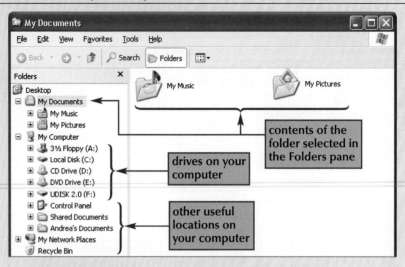

3. Click the **expand** icon ➕ next to the Local Disk (C:) icon. The contents of your hard disk appear under the Local Disk (C:) icon.

   Trouble? If you do not have permission to access drive C, skip Step 3 and read but do not perform the remaining steps.

   My Documents is still the selected folder. To view the contents of an object in the right pane, you can click the object's icon in the Folders pane.

4. Click **Documents and Settings** in the Folders pane. Its contents appear in the right pane. Documents and Settings is a built-in Windows XP folder that contains a folder for each user installed on the system.

You've already mastered the basics of navigating your computer with Windows Explorer. You click expand icons in the left pane until you find the folder that you want. Then you click the folder icon in the left pane to view the files it contains in the right pane.

Navigating to Your Data Files

The **file path** is a notation that indicates a file's location on your computer. The file path leads you through the Windows file system to your file. For example, the Holiday file is stored in the Tutorial subfolder of the FM folder. If you are working on a USB drive, for example, the path to this file might be as follows:

F:\FM\Tutorial\Holiday.bmp

This path has four parts, and each part is separated by a backslash (\ ):

- **F**: The drive name; for example, drive F might be the name for the USB drive. If this file were stored on the hard disk, the drive name would be C.
- **FM**: The top-level folder on drive F.
- **Tutorial**: A subfolder in the FM folder.
- **Holiday.bmp**: The full filename with the file extension.

If someone tells you to find the file F:\FM\Tutorial\Holiday.bmp, you know you must navigate to your USB drive, open the FM folder, and then open the Tutorial folder to find the Holiday file. My Computer and Windows Explorer can display the full file path in their Address bars so you can keep track of your current location as you navigate.

You can use Windows Explorer to navigate to the Data Files you need for the rest of this tutorial. Refer back to the information you provided in the "Planning Your Organization" section and note the drive on your system that contains your Data Files. In the following steps, this is drive F, a USB drive. If necessary, substitute the appropriate drive on your system when you perform the steps.

To navigate to your Data Files:

1. Make sure your computer can access your Data Files for this tutorial. For example, if you are using a USB drive, insert the drive into the USB port.

   Trouble? If you don't have the Data Files, you need to get them before you can proceed. Your instructor will either give you the Data Files or ask you to obtain them from a specified location (such as a network drive). In either case, be sure that you make a backup copy of your Data Files before you start using them, so that the original files will be available on your copied disk in case you need to start over because of an error or problem. If you have any questions about the Data Files, see your instructor or technical support person for assistance.

2. In the Windows Explorer window, click the **expand** icon ➕ next to the drive containing your Data Files, such as UDISK 2.0 (F:). A list of the folders on that drive appears.

3. If the list of folders does not include the FM folder, continue clicking the **expand** icon ➕ to navigate to the folder that contains the FM folder.

4. Click the **FM** folder. Its contents appear in the Folders pane and in the right pane of the Windows Explorer window. The FM folder contains the Cases, Review, and Tutorial folders, as shown in Figure 7. The other folders on your system might vary.

Navigating to the FM folder   Figure 7

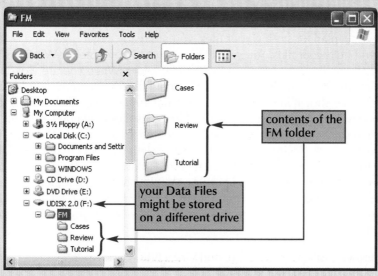

5. In the left pane, click the **Tutorial** folder. The files it contains appear in the right pane. You want to view them as a list.

6. Click the **Views** button ⊞ on the Standard Buttons toolbar, and then click **List**. The files appear in List view in the Windows Explorer window. See Figure 8.

Figure 8 **Files in the Tutorial folder in List view**

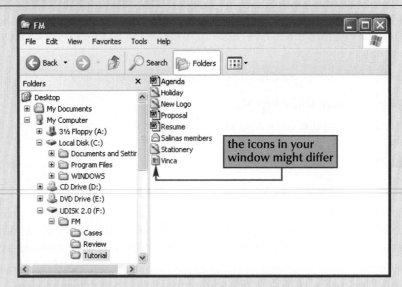

The file icons in your window depend on the programs installed on your computer, so they might be different from the ones shown in Figure 8.

Leave the Windows Explorer window open so you can work with the files in the Tutorial folder.

Working with Folders and Files

After you devise a plan for storing your files, you are ready to get organized by creating folders that will hold your files. You can do so using My Computer or Windows Explorer. For this tutorial, you'll create folders in the Tutorial folder. When you are working on your own computer, you will usually create folders within the My Documents folder.

Examine the files shown in Figure 8 again and determine which files seem to belong together. Holiday, New Logo, and Vinca are all graphics files containing pictures or photographs. The Resume and Stationery files were created for a summer job hunt. The other files were created for the Salinas neighborhood association project to update a playground.

One way to organize these files is to create three folders—one for graphics, one for the job hunt files, and another for the Salinas files. When you create a folder, you give it a name, preferably one that describes its contents. A folder name can have up to 255 characters, except / \ : * ? " < > or |. With these guidelines in mind, you could create three folders as follows:

- **Graphics folder**: Holiday, New Logo, and Vinca files
- **Job Hunt folder**: Resume and Stationery files
- **Playground folder**: Agenda, Proposal, and Salinas members files

Shannon asks you to create three new folders. Then you'll move the files to the appropriate subfolder.

Creating Folders

You've already seen folder icons in the windows you've examined. Now, you'll create folders in the Tutorial folder using the Windows Explorer menu bar.

Creating a Folder Using Windows Explorer

- In the left pane, click the drive or folder where you want to create a folder.
- Click File on the menu bar, point to New, and then click Folder (*or* right-click a blank area in the folder window, point to New, and then click Folder).
- Type a name for the folder, and then press the Enter key.

Now you can create three folders in your Tutorial folder as you planned—the Graphics, Job Hunt, and Playground folders. The Windows Explorer window should show the contents of the Tutorial folder in List view.

To create folders using Windows Explorer:

1. Click **File** on the menu bar, point to **New** to display the submenu, and then click **Folder**. A folder icon with the label "New Folder" appears in the right pane, and the expand icon appears next to the Tutorial folder because it now contains a subfolder. See Figure 9.

Creating a folder in the Tutorial folder ◄ **Figure 9**

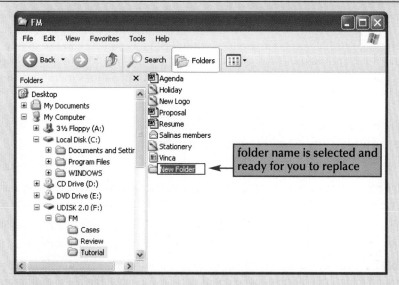

folder name is selected and ready for you to replace

Trouble? If the "New Folder" name is not selected, right-click the new folder, click Rename, and then continue with Step 2.

Windows uses "New Folder" as a placeholder, and selects the text so that you can replace it with the name you want.

2. Type **Graphics** as the folder name, and then press the **Enter** key. The new folder is named "Graphics" and is the selected item in the right pane.

You are ready to create a second folder. This time you'll use a shortcut menu to create a folder.

3. Right-click a blank area next to the Graphics folder, point to **New** on the shortcut menu, and then click **Folder**. A folder icon with the label "New Folder" appears in the right pane with the "New Folder" text selected.

4. Type **Job Hunt** as the name of the new folder, and then press the **Enter** key.

5. Using the menu bar or the shortcut menu, create a folder named **Playground**. The Tutorial folder contains three new subfolders.

Now that you've created three folders, you're ready to organize your files by moving them into the appropriate folders.

Moving and Copying Files and Folders

If you want to place a file into a folder from another location, you can either move the file or copy it. **Moving** a file removes it from its current location and places it in a new location you specify. **Copying** places the file in both locations. Windows XP provides several techniques for moving and copying files. The same principles apply to folders—you can move and copy folders using a variety of methods.

Reference Window	**Moving a File or Folder in Windows Explorer or My Computer**

- Right-click and drag the file you want to move to the destination folder.
- Click Move Here on the shortcut menu.
or
- Click the file you want to move, and then click Move this file in the File and Folder Tasks area.
- In the Move Items dialog box, navigate to the destination folder, and then click the Move button.

Shannon suggests that you continue to work in List view so you can see all the files in the Tutorial folder, and then move some files from the Tutorial folder to the appropriate subfolders. You'll start by moving the Agenda, Proposal, and Salinas members files to the Playground folder.

To move a file using the right mouse button:

1. Point to the **Agenda** file in the right pane, and then press and hold the *right* mouse button.

2. With the right mouse button still pressed down, drag the **Agenda** file to the **Playground** folder. When the Playground folder icon is highlighted, release the button. A shortcut menu opens.

3. With the left mouse button, click **Move Here** on the shortcut menu. The Agenda file is removed from the main Tutorial folder and stored in the Playground subfolder.

   Trouble? If you release the mouse button before dragging the Agenda file to the Playground folder, the shortcut menu opens, letting you move the file to a different folder. Press the Esc key to close the shortcut menu without moving the file, and then repeat Steps 1 through 3.

4. In the right pane, double-click the **Playground** folder. The Agenda file is in the Playground folder.

5. In the left pane, click the **Tutorial** folder to see its contents. The Tutorial folder no longer contains the Agenda file.

The advantage of moving a file or folder by dragging with the right mouse button is that you can efficiently complete your work with one action. However, this technique requires polished mouse skills so that you can drag the file comfortably. Another way to move files and folders is to use the File and Folder Tasks links in the task pane of the Windows Explorer or My Computer window. Although using the File and Folder Tasks links takes more steps, some users find it easier than dragging with the right mouse button.

You'll move the Resume file to the Job Hunt folder next. First, you'll close the Folders pane so that the task pane replaces it.

To move files using the File and Folder Tasks area:

1. Click the **Folders** button on the Standard Buttons toolbar. The task pane replaces the Folders pane, so that this window now resembles the My Computer window. Switch to List view, if necessary.

2. Click the **Resume** file to select it. The task pane links change so that they are appropriate for working with files.

3. In the File and Folder Tasks area, click **Move this file**. The Move Items dialog box opens. See Figure 10.

Move Items dialog box | **Figure 10**

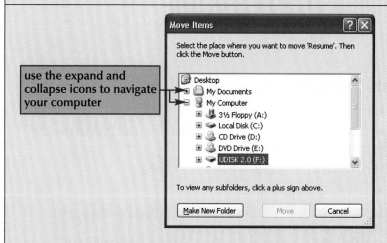

use the expand and collapse icons to navigate your computer

4. Click the **expand** icon ⊞ next to the drive containing your Data Files. Continue clicking **expand** icons ⊞ to navigate to the Tutorial folder provided with your Data Files.

5. Click the **Job Hunt** folder.

6. Click the **Move** button. The Move Items dialog box closes; Windows moves the Resume file to the Job Hunt folder, and then displays the contents of the Tutorial folder, which no longer contains the Resume file.

   You'll move the Stationery file from the Tutorial folder to the Job Hunt folder.

7. Click the **Stationery** file in the Tutorial window, and then click **Move this file** in the File and Folder Tasks area. The Move Items dialog box opens again, with the Job Hunt folder already selected for you.

8. Click the **Move** button.

You can also copy a file using the same techniques as when you move a file—by dragging with the right mouse button or by using the File and Folder Tasks links. Another easy way to copy a file is to use the file's shortcut menu. You can copy more than one file at the same time by selecting all the files you want to copy, and then clicking them as a group. To select files that are listed together in a window, click the first file in the list, hold down the Shift key, click the last file in the list, and then release the Shift key. To select files that are not listed together, click one file, hold down the Ctrl key, click the other files, and then release the Ctrl key.

Reference Window

Copying a File or Folder in Windows Explorer or My Computer

- Click the file or folder you want to copy, and then click Copy this file or Copy this folder in the File and Folder Tasks area.
- In the Copy Items dialog box, navigate to the destination folder, and then click the Copy button.

or

- Right-click the file or folder you want to copy, and then click Copy on the shortcut menu.
- Navigate to the destination folder.
- Right-click a blank area of the destination folder window, and then click Paste on the shortcut menu.

You'll copy the three graphics files from the Tutorial folder to the Graphics folder now. It's easiest to select multiple files in List view or Details view.

To copy files using the shortcut menu:

1. In the Tutorial window, switch to List view, if necessary, and then click the **Holiday** file.

2. Hold down the **Ctrl** key, click the **New Logo** file, click the **Vinca** file, and then release the **Ctrl** key. Three files are selected in the Tutorial window.

3. Right-click a selected file, and then click **Copy** on the shortcut menu.

4. In the right pane, double-click the **Graphics** folder to open it.

5. Right-click the background of the Graphics folder, and then click **Paste** on the shortcut menu. Windows copies the three files to the Graphics folder.

6. Switch to List view, if necessary.

Now that you are familiar with two ways to copy files, you can use the technique you prefer to copy the Proposal and Salinas members files to the Playground folder.

To copy the two files:

1. In the Graphics folder window, click the **Back** button on the Standard Buttons toolbar to return to the Tutorial folder.

2. Use any technique you've learned to copy the **Proposal** and **Salinas members** files from the Tutorial folder to the Playground folder.

You can move and copy folders in the same way that you move and copy files. When you do, you move or copy all the files contained in the folder. You'll practice moving and copying folders in the Case Problems at the end of this tutorial.

Naming and Renaming Files

As you work with files, pay attention to **filenames**—they provide important information about the file, including its contents and purpose. A filename such as Car Sales.doc has three parts:

- **Main part of the filename:** The name you provide when you create a file, and the name you associate with a file
- **Dot:** The period (.) that separates the main part of the filename from the file extension
- **File extension:** Usually three characters that follow the dot in the filename

The main part of a filename can have up to 255 characters—this gives you plenty of room to name your file accurately enough so that you'll know the contents of the file just by looking at the filename. You can use spaces and certain punctuation symbols in your filenames. Like folder names, however, filenames cannot contain the symbols \ / ? : * " < > | because these characters have special meaning in Windows XP.

A filename might display an **extension**—three or more characters following a dot—that identifies the file's type and indicates the program in which the file was created. For example, in the filename Car Sales.doc, the extension "doc" identifies the file as one created by Microsoft Word, a word-processing program. You might also have a file called Car Sales.xls—the "xls" extension identifies the file as one created in Microsoft Excel, a spreadsheet program. Though the main parts of these filenames are identical, their extensions distinguish them as different files. You usually do not need to add extensions to your filenames because the program that you use to create the file adds the file extension automatically. Also, although Windows XP keeps track of extensions, not all computers are set to display them.

Be sure to give your files and folders meaningful names that will help you remember their purpose and contents. You can easily rename a file or folder by using the Rename command on the file's shortcut menu.

Shannon recommends that you rename the Agenda file in the Playground folder to give it a more descriptive filename—that file could contain the agenda for any meeting. The Agenda file was originally created to store a list of topics to discuss at a meeting of the Salinas neighborhood association. You'll rename the file "Salinas Meeting Agenda."

To rename the Agenda file:

1. Click **Tutorial** in the Other Places menu, and then double-click the **Playground** folder.

2. In the Playground window, right-click the **Agenda** file, and then click **Rename** on the short-cut menu. The filename is highlighted and a box appears around it.

3. Type **Salinas Meeting Agenda**, and then press the **Enter** key. The file now appears with the new name.

   Trouble? If you make a mistake while typing and you haven't pressed the Enter key yet, press the Backspace key until you delete the mistake, and then complete Step 3. If you've already pressed the Enter key, repeat Steps 1 through 3 to rename the file again.

   Trouble? If your computer is set to display file extensions, a message might appear asking if you are sure you want to change the file extension. Click the No button, right-click the Agenda file, click Rename on the shortcut menu, type "Salinas Meeting Agenda.doc", and then press the Enter key.

All the files that originally appeared in the Tutorial folder are now stored in appropriate subfolders. Shannon mentions that you can streamline the organization of the Tutorial folder by deleting the files you no longer need.

Deleting Files and Folders

You should periodically delete files and folders you no longer need so that your main folders and disks don't get cluttered. In My Computer or Windows Explorer, you delete a file or folder by deleting its icon. Be careful when you delete a folder, because you also delete all the files it contains. When you delete a file from a hard disk, Windows XP removes the filename from the folder, but stores the file contents in the Recycle Bin. The **Recycle Bin** is an area on your hard disk that holds deleted files until you remove them permanently; an icon on the desktop allows you easy access to the Recycle Bin. If you change your mind and want to retrieve a file deleted from your hard disk, you can use the Recycle Bin to recover it or return it to its original location. However, after you empty the Recycle Bin, you can no longer recover the files that were in it.

When you delete a file from removable media, it does not go into the Recycle Bin. Instead, it is deleted as soon as its icon disappears—and you cannot recover it.

Shannon reminds you that because you copied the Holiday, New Logo, Proposal, Salinas members, and Vinca files to the Graphics and Playground folders, you can safely delete the original files in the Tutorial folder. As with moving, copying, and renaming files and folders, you can delete a file or folder in many ways, including using a shortcut menu or the File and Folder Tasks menu.

To delete files in the Tutorial folder:

1. Use any technique you've learned to navigate to and open the **Tutorial** folder.

2. Switch to List view (if necessary), click **Holiday** (the first file in the file list), hold down the **Shift** key, click **Vinca** (the last file in the file list), and then release the **Shift** key. All the files in the Tutorial folder are now selected. None of the subfolders should be selected.

3. Right-click the selected files, and then click **Delete** on the shortcut menu. Windows XP asks if you're sure you want to delete these files.

4. Click the **Yes** button.

So far, you've worked with files using Windows Explorer and My Computer, but you haven't viewed any of their contents. To view file contents, you open the file. When you double-click a file in Windows Explorer or My Computer, Windows XP starts the appropriate program and opens the file.

Working with Compressed Files

If you transfer files from one location to another, such as from your hard disk to a removable disk or vice versa, or from one computer to another via e-mail, you can store the files in a **compressed (zipped) folder** so that they take up less disk space. You can then transfer the files more quickly. When you create a compressed folder, Windows XP displays a zipper on the folder icon.

You compress a folder so that the files it contains use less space on the disk. Compare two folders—a folder named My Pictures that contains about 8.6 MB of files and a compressed folder containing the same files, but requiring only 6.5 MB of disk space. In this case, the compressed files use about 25 percent less disk space than the uncompressed files.

You can create a compressed folder using the Compressed (zipped) Folder command on the New submenu of the File menu or shortcut menu in Windows Explorer or My Computer. Then you can compress files or other folders by dragging them into the compressed folder. You can open files directly from a compressed folder, or you can extract the files first. When you **extract** a file, you create an uncompressed copy of the file and folder in a folder you specify. The original file remains in the compressed folder.

If a different compression program has been installed on your computer, such as WinZip or PKZip, the Compressed (zipped) Folder command does not appear on the New submenu. Instead, it is replaced by the name of your compression program. In this case, refer to your compression program's Help system for instructions on working with compressed files.

Shannon suggests you compress the files and folders in the Tutorial folder so you can more quickly transfer them to another location.

To compress the folders and files in the Tutorial folder:

▶ **1.** In Windows Explorer, navigate to the Tutorial folder.

▶ **2.** Right-click a blank area of the right pane, point to **New** on the shortcut menu, and then click **Compressed (zipped) Folder**. A new compressed folder with a zipper icon appears in the Tutorial window. See Figure 11. Your window might appear in a different view.

Creating a compressed folder ◀ **Figure 11**

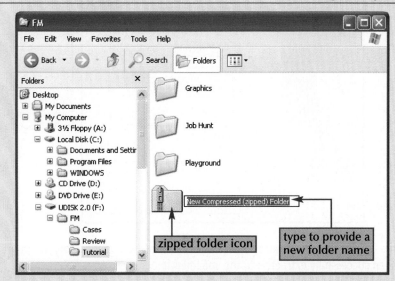

zipped folder icon

type to provide a new folder name

Trouble? If the Compressed (zipped) Folder command does not appear on the New submenu, a different compression program is probably installed on your computer. Click a blank area of the Tutorial window to close the shortcut menu, and then read but do not perform the remaining steps.

▶ **3.** Type **Final Tutorial files**, and then press the **Enter** key. Windows XP creates the compressed folder in the Tutorial folder.

▶ **4.** Click the **Graphics** folder in the right pane, hold down the **Shift** key, click the **Playground** folder in the right pane, and then release the **Shift** key. Three folders are selected in the Tutorial window.

▶ **5.** Drag the three folders to the **Final Tutorial files** compressed folder. Windows XP copies the files to the folder, compressing them to save space.

You open a compressed folder by double-clicking it. You can then move and copy files and folders in a compressed folder, though you cannot rename them. If you want to open, edit, and save files in a compressed folder, you should first extract them. When you do, Windows XP uncompresses the files and copies them to a location that you specify, preserving them in their folders as appropriate.

To extract the compressed files:

▶ **1.** Right-click the **Final Tutorial files** compressed folder, and then click **Extract All** on the shortcut menu. The Extraction Wizard starts and opens the Welcome to the Compressed (zipped) Folders Extraction Wizard dialog box.

▶ **2.** Click the **Next** button. The Select a Destination dialog box opens.

3. Press the **End** key to deselect the path in the text box, press the **Backspace** key as many times as necessary to delete "Final Tutorial files," and then type **Extracted**. The last three parts of the path in the text box should be "\FM\Tutorial\Extracted." See Figure 12.

| Figure 12 | Select a Destination dialog box |

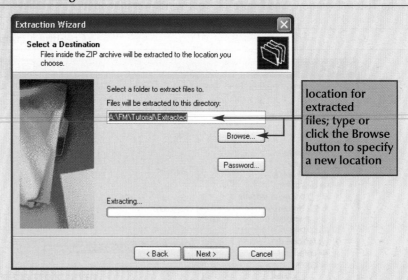

location for extracted files; type or click the Browse button to specify a new location

4. Click the **Next** button. The Extraction Complete dialog box opens, indicating that your files have been successfully extracted to the specified folder.

5. Make sure the **Show extracted files** check box is checked, and then click the **Finish** button. The Extracted folder opens, showing the Graphics, Job Hunt, and Playground folders.

6. Open each folder to make sure it contains the files you worked with in this tutorial.

7. Close all open windows.

Shannon says you have successfully completed basic Windows XP file management tasks, and are ready to use Windows XP to organize your files.

| Review |

To reinforce the tasks you learned in this tutorial, go to the SAM 2003 Training Companion CD included with this text.

Quick Check

1. What is the term for a collection of data that has a name and is stored on a disk or other storage medium?
2. Name two types of removable media for storing files.
3. The letter C is typically used for the _____ drive of a computer.
4. What are the two tools that Windows XP provides for exploring the files and folders on your computer?
5. What is the notation you can use to indicate a file's location on your computer?
6. True or False: The advantage of moving a file or folder by dragging with the right mouse button is that you can efficiently complete your work with one action.
7. In a filename, the _____ identifies the file's type and indicates the program in which the file was created.
8. True or False: When you extract a file, the original file is deleted from the compressed folder.

Review

Tutorial Summary

In this tutorial, you examined Windows XP file organization, noting that you need to organize files and folders to work efficiently. You learned about typical file management strategies, whether you are working on a hard disk or a removable disk. Then you applied these strategies to organizing files and folders by creating folders, moving and copying files, and renaming and deleting files. You also learned how to copy files to a compressed (zipped) folder, and then extract files from a compressed folder.

Key Terms

backup	extract	move
compact disc (CD)	file	My Computer
compressed (zipped) folder	file path	My Documents folder
copy	file system	pane
disk	filename	Recycle Bin
document	floppy disk	root directory
drive	folder	subfolder
Explorer bar	Folders pane	USB drive
extension	hard disk	Windows Explorer

Practice

Practice the skills you learned in the tutorial.

Review Assignments

Data Files needed for the Review Assignments: Commissions.xls, Contracts.xls, Customer Accounts.xls, Billing Worksheet.wk4, Car Savings Plan.xls, Personal Loan.doc, Speech.wav, Filenames.pps, Water lilies.jpg

Complete the following steps, recording your answers to any questions in the spaces provided:

1. Use My Computer or Windows Explorer as necessary to record the following information:
   - Where are you supposed to store the files you use in the Review Assignments for this tutorial? _____
   - Describe the method you will use to navigate to the location where you save your files for this book. _____
     _____
   - Do you need to follow any special guidelines or conventions when naming the files your save for this book? For example, should all the filenames start with your course number or tutorial number? If so, describe the conventions. _____
     _____
   - When you are instructed to open a file for this book, what location are you supposed to use? _____
   - Describe the method you will use to navigate to this location. _____
     _____

2. Use My Computer or Windows Explorer to navigate to and open the FM\Review folder provided with your Data Files.
3. Examine the nine files in the Review folder included with your Data Files, and then answer the following questions:
   - How will you organize these files? _____
     _____
   - What folders will you create? _____
     _____

- Which files will you store in these folders? _____
  _____
- Will you use any built-in Windows folders? If so, which ones? For which files?
  _____

4. In the Review folder, create three folders: Business, Personal Finances, and Project Media.
5. Move the **Commissions**, **Contracts**, **Customer Accounts**, and **Billing Worksheet** files from the Review folder to the Business folder.
6. Move the **Car Savings Plan** and **Personal Loan** files to the Personal Finances folder.
7. Copy the remaining files to the Project Media folder.
8. Delete the files in the Review folder (do *not* delete any folders).
9. Rename the **Speech** file in the Project Media folder to **Ask Not**.
10. Create a compressed (zipped) folder in the Review folder named **Final Review files** that contains all the files and folders in the Review folder.
11. Extract the contents of the Final Review files folder to a new folder named **Extracted**. (*Hint:* The file path will end with "\FM\Review\Extracted.")
12. Use Windows Explorer or My Computer to locate all copies of the **Personal Loan** file in the subfolders of the Review folder. In which locations did you find this file?
    _____
13. Close all open windows.

Case Problem 1

Apply

Use the skills you learned in the tutorial to manage files and folders for an arts organization.

Data Files needed for this Case Problem: Invoice Jan.xls, Invoice Feb.xls, Invoice March.xls, Painting Class – Agenda.doc, Painting Class – Questionnaire.doc, Painting Class – Teaching Manual.doc, Paris.jpg, Vegetables.jpg

Jefferson Street Fine Arts Center Rae Wysnewski owns the Jefferson Street Fine Arts Center (JSFAC) in Pittsburgh, and offers classes and gallery, studio, and practice space for aspiring and fledgling artists, musicians, and dancers. Rae opened JSFAC two years ago, and this year the center has a record enrollment in its classes. Knowing you are multitalented, she hires you to teach a painting class for three months and to show her how to manage her files on her new Windows XP computer. Complete the following steps:

1. In the FM\Cases folder provided with your Data Files, create two folders: Invoices and Painting Class.
2. Move the **Invoice Jan**, **Invoice Feb**, and **Invoice March** files from the Cases folder to the Invoices folder.
3. Rename the three files in the Invoices folder to remove "Invoice" from each name.
4. Move the three text documents from the Cases folder to the Painting Class folder. Rename the three documents, using shorter but still descriptive names.
5. Copy the remaining files to the Painting Class folder.

Explore

6. Using My Computer or Windows Explorer, switch to Details view and then answer the following questions:
   a. What is the largest file in the Painting Class folder? _____
   b. How many files (don't include folders) are in the Cases folder? _____
   c. How many word-processed documents are in the Cases folder and its subfolders? ____
   d. How many files in the Painting Class folder are JPEG images? (*Hint:* Look in the Type column to identify JPEG images.) _____
7. Delete the **Paris** and **Vegetables** files from the Painting Class folder.

8. Open the Recycle Bin folder by double-clicking the Recycle Bin icon on the desktop. Do the Paris and Vegetables files appear in the Recycle Bin folder? Explain why or why not. _____

_____

9. Copy the Painting Class folder to the Cases folder. The name of the duplicate folder appears as "Copy of Painting Class." Rename the "Copy of Painting Class" folder as "Graphics."

10. Create a new folder in the Cases folder named "JSFAC." Move the Invoices, Painting Class, and Graphics folders to the JSFAC folder.

Challenge

Extend what you've learned to discover other methods of managing files for a social service organization.

Case Problem 2

There are no Data Files needed for this Case Problem.

First Call Outreach   Victor Crillo is the director of a social service organization named First Call Outreach in Toledo, Ohio. Its mission is to connect people who need help from local and state agencies to the appropriate service. Victor has a dedicated staff, but they are all relatively new to Windows XP. In particular, they have trouble finding files that they have saved on their hard disks. He asks you to demonstrate how to find files in Windows XP. Complete the following:

Explore

1. Windows XP Help and Support includes topics that explain how to search for files on a disk without looking through all the folders. Click the Start button and then click Help and Support to start Windows Help and Support. Use one of the following methods to locate topics on searching for files.
   - On the Home page, click the Windows Basics link. On the Windows Basics page, click the Finding and organizing files link, and then click the Searching for files or folders topic. In the article, click the Related Topics link, and then click Search for a file or folder.
   - On the Index page, type "files" (no quotation marks) in the Type in the keyword to find text box. In the list of entries for "files," double-click "searching for." In the Topics found dialog box, double-click "Searching for files or folders."
   - In the Search box, type "searching for files," and then click Search. Click the Searching for files or folders link.

Explore

2. Read the topic and click the Related Topics link at the end of the topic, if necessary, to provide the following information:
   a. To display the Search dialog box, you must click the _____ button, point to _____ from the menu, and finally click _____ from the submenu.
   b. Do you need to type in the entire filename to find the file? _____
   c. Name three file characteristics you can use as search options. _____

   _____

Explore

3. Use the Index page in Windows XP Help and Support to locate topics related to managing files and folders. Write out two procedures for managing files and folders that were not covered in the tutorial. _____

_____

_____

_____

SAM Assessment and Training

If your instructor has chosen to use the full online version of SAM 2003 Assessment and Training, you can go beyond the "just-in-time" training provided on the CD that accompanies this text. Simply log in to your SAM account (http://sam2003.course.com) to launch any assigned training activities or exams that relate to the skills covered in this tutorial.

Lab Assignments

Using Files

The New Perspectives Labs are designed to help you master some of the key concepts and skills presented in this text. The steps for completing this Lab are located on the Course Technology Web site. Log on to the Internet and use your Web browser to go to the Student Online Companion for New Perspectives Office 2003 site at **www.course.com/np/office2003**. Click the Lab Assignments link, and then navigate to the assignments for this tutorial.

Quick Check Answers

1. file
2. USB drives, CDs, DVDs, and floppy disks
3. hard disk
4. Windows Explorer and My Computer
5. file path
6. true
7. extension
8. false

New Perspectives on

Browser and E-mail Basics

Introduction to Microsoft Internet Explorer and Microsoft Outlook Express

BEB 3

Read This Before You Begin

Data Files

To complete the "Browser and E-mail Basics" tutorial, you need the starting Data Files. See the inside back or front cover for information on downloading these files from course.com, or ask your instructor for assistance. The following table identifies each starting Data File and the folder it is stored in, as well as the ending files, which you create and save in each tutorial.

Folders	Starting Files	Ending Files
BEB / Tutorial	B&B Ideas.doc	B&B Ideas.doc, B&B Page.htm, Web Page Graphic.jpg
Review	(no starting Data Files)	(files vary per student)
Cases	(no starting Data Files)	(files vary per student)

Storing Your Files

It is recommended that you store all your Data Files on a USB drive. Refer to the tutorial "Managing Your Files" for information on using USB drives. If you need to store your Data Files on floppy disks, you will need one high-density disk to store all the files for the "Browser and E-mail Basics" tutorial.

SAM 2003 Training Companion CD

The SAM 2003 Training Companion CD that comes with this text gives you "just-in-time" training and reinforcement of important Microsoft Office skills. Look for the SAM CD logo throughout each tutorial for opportunities to complete the hands-on tasks included on this CD.

Course Labs

The "Browser and E-mail Basics" tutorial features an interactive Course Lab to help you understand Internet and browser concepts. There are Lab Assignments at the end of the tutorial that relate to this lab. Contact your instructor or technical support person for assistance in accessing this lab.

Browser and E-mail Basics

Introduction to Microsoft Internet Explorer and Microsoft Outlook Express

Case | McKiernan's Irish B&B

Susan McKiernan and her husband, Preston, moved to Lewistown, Pennsylvania, from Ballyconnell, Ireland, several years ago because Preston's company relocated its manufacturing division. In Ireland Susan's family ran a bed-and-breakfast (B&B) for many years, and eager to begin her own business, Susan decided to open a B&B in Lewistown.

The house that she and Preston bought was perfect for a B&B, having once provided lodging during the late 1800s and early 1900s for travelers. The house has three floors, a large kitchen, a large living room, and a dining room in the front of the house, separated by a large foyer. There are three bedrooms on the second floor, each with its own bathroom, and two bedrooms that share a bath on the third floor. There is also an attached barn, which has been converted into a master suite.

The business has grown steadily to the point that Preston now manages the front desk while Susan attends to the daily running of the inn. Most of their business comes by word of mouth, and they have decided to expand using more formal marketing channels. Susan and Preston have recently hired an advertising firm, Capital Ads Online, to develop a marketing campaign that will utilize the Internet as an advertising medium. Next week, Susan, who will be responsible for implementing and managing the inn's Web site, will meet with Martha Kent, the account executive at Capital Ads assigned to the McKiernans' account. In preparation for the meeting, Martha suggested that Susan view the design and layout of Web sites for other B&Bs to give her some ideas for her own advertisements on the Internet. Martha also gave Susan her e-mail address so they can communicate electronically.

You work for Susan and Preston as an intern, getting hands-on experience in the hotel management industry. They want you to help Susan prepare for her meeting with Martha by researching other B&Bs that advertise using the Internet. You explain to them that, although you are familiar with computers, you haven't spent much time

Session	Objectives		SAM Training Tasks	
Session 1	• Learn the relationship between the Internet and the World Wide Web • Learn about Web pages and Web browsers • Learn about Web addresses • Navigate links on Web pages	• Return to Web sites using the History list • Create and organize favorites • Print a Web page • Save a Web page and a graphic from a Web page	• Add a Web site to your list of Favorites/ Bookmarks • Enter a URL in the Address bar • Find a previously displayed Web page • Go to a Web page by using links • Home button • Hyperlink navigation with the mouse • Open and save URLs • Organize Favorites	• Print a Web page • Refresh a Web page • Remove Favorites • Return to a Web page • Save a Web page • Save a Web page graphic to a disk • Search the Web using another search engine • Stop a Web page transfer • Use the Favorites feature • Use the history list
Session 2	• Learn about e-mail and e-mail software • Send, receive, reply to, and print an e-mail message • Gain an understanding of e-mail etiquette	• Add and delete contacts in the Address Book • Add an attachment to a message	• Send a Web page	

Student Data Files   For a complete list of the Data Files needed for this tutorial, see page BEB 2.

"surfing" the Internet. Susan is familiar with computers and the Internet. She will help you get up to speed and familiarize you with the kind of information she wants you to research. Your goal is to learn as much as you can about using the Internet and the World Wide Web for finding information and about communicating using electronic mail.

Session 1

For hands-on practice of key tasks in this session, go to the SAM 2003 Training Companion CD included with this text.

The Internet and the World Wide Web

The **Internet**, in the simplest of terms, is a worldwide collection of networks. A **network** is composed of two or more computers that are linked together and that share and exchange information. The Internet is the world's largest network, made up of computers located all over the world. The computers and networks that make up the Internet are connected by fiber-optic cables, satellites, phone lines, and other forms of electronic communication media, as shown in Figure 1.

| Figure 1 | How computers are connected to the Internet and World Wide Web |

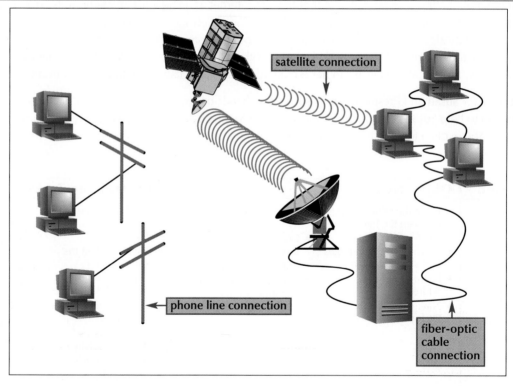

The Internet and the services it provides allow people all over the world to communicate and share information quickly and easily. The **World Wide Web (WWW)**, or simply the **Web**, is a service the Internet offers that enables individuals and businesses to test and market products and services to a global audience. The Web is a system of electronic documents, called **Web pages**, that are linked together by **hyperlinks** (or just **links**), which are words, phrases, or graphics in a Web page that target another place in the document or another document altogether. When a user clicks a hyperlink, the information at the target location is displayed, as shown in Figure 2.

Using hyperlinks to go to related information ◄ **Figure 2**

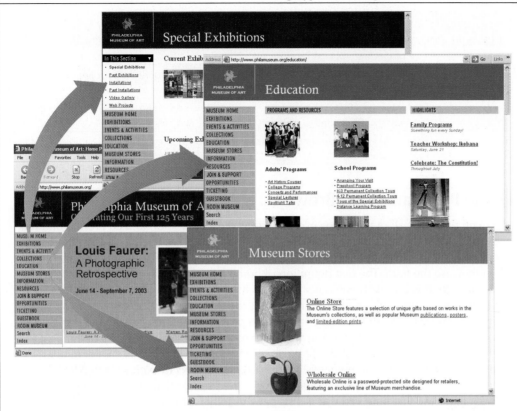

   Web pages are ordinary text files, much like the files created by word-processing software. However, the text must be formatted according to a generally accepted standard,
and the standard format used on the Web is the **Hypertext Markup Language (HTML)**.
HTML provides a variety of text-formatting tags that you can use to indicate headings,
paragraphs, bulleted lists, numbered lists, and other useful text formats in an HTML document. The real power of HTML, however, lies in its ability to enable you to access multiple HTML documents through hyperlinks.

   The computers on the Internet that store Web pages are called **Web servers**. A **Web site**
is a collection of hyperlinked Web pages that have a common theme or focus and are
stored on a Web server belonging to an organization or individual. Web sites can be used
to provide information about an organization or an individual. They can also be used by
businesses to sell or advertise their products and to communicate information to their customers or employees. The McKiernans want to create a Web site to advertise their inn.

   To help locate and navigate the large number of Web sites and Web pages, you can
use a Web directory or a search engine. A **Web directory** is a special type of Web page
that contains a list of Web sites organized by topical categories, such as education or
recreation. The hyperlinks on a Web directory page lead either to other pages containing lists of subcategories or to Web pages that relate to the category topics. **Web
search engines** are Web pages that conduct searches of the Web to find the words or
expressions that you enter as search criteria. The result of such a search is a Web page
that contains hyperlinks to Web pages that contain matching text or expressions. There
are general search engines, such as Google, that you can use to find a wide variety of
information. There are also business search engines, such as Business.com, that you
can use to find news, finance, technology, and industry-specific information. Figure 3
provides a list of common search engines.

Figure 3	Examples of search engines

Search Engine	Description
AltaVista	One of the first full-text Internet search engines
AskJeeves	A real-language search engine that lets users ask questions without knowledge of specialized search techniques
Business.com	Features a database of companies, with profiles, news, and stock quotes; also includes industry-specific updates, research-based data, and resources
Google	Returns keyword search results based on relevance of content and the number of links to other sites

Home Pages and Web Browsers

The main page that all of the pages in a particular Web site are organized around and link back to is called the site's **home page**. The term "home page" is used in at least three different ways on the Web, and it is sometimes difficult to tell which meaning people intend when they use the term. The first definition of home page indicates the main page for a particular site; this use of "home page" refers to the first page that opens when you visit a Web site. The second definition of home page is the first page that opens when you start your Web browser. A **Web browser** is a software program used to retrieve and display Web pages and to navigate them. You will learn more about Web browsers in the next section. This type of home page might be an HTML document on your own computer. Some people create such home pages and include hyperlinks to Web sites that they frequently visit. The third definition of home page is the Web page that a particular Web browser loads the first time you use it. This page usually is stored at the Web site of the firm or organization that created the Web browser software. Home pages that fall within the second or third definitions are sometimes called **start pages**.

To use your computer to gather information from the Internet and have access to the HTML documents stored on the Web, your computer needs to have a Web browser installed on it. As stated earlier, Web browser software is designed to access, retrieve, and display Web pages on your computer. Although the Internet connects many different types of computers running different operating system software, Web browser software lets your computer communicate with all of these different types of computers easily and effectively. Two popular browsers are Microsoft Internet Explorer, or simply Internet Explorer, and Netscape Navigator, or simply Navigator.

In addition to Web browser software, you also need a means of connecting to the Internet. If you are a student at a university, you might be connected to the Internet through the university's computer network. If you use a computer from your home, you might have a connection to the Internet through your phone line and a modem. This is called a **dial-up connection**. Another connection option for home-based Internet users is a **DSL (Digital Subscriber Line) connection**, which uses your phone line to establish a high-speed connection. Home connections require an account with an **Internet service provider (ISP)**, a company that sells Internet access. This company guides you in configuring your computer to connect to one of its servers via a telephone or cable modem. When you are logged on to your ISP account, meaning you are connected to your ISP's server, you can use the browser software on your computer to access files and other resources located anywhere on the Internet.

Starting Microsoft Internet Explorer

Microsoft Internet Explorer is the Web browser that installs with Windows 9x, Windows 2000, and Windows XP. It provides all the tools you need to communicate, access, and share information on the Web. Your first step in helping Susan find information about other B&Bs is to start Internet Explorer.

To start Internet Explorer:

1. Click the **Start** button on the taskbar, point to **All Programs**, and then click **Internet Explorer**. The Internet Explorer program window opens.

   Trouble? This tutorial assumes that you have Internet Explorer 6 or later installed on your computer. If you are using another Web browser, ask your instructor or technical support person for assistance or program-specific instructions.

   Trouble? If you cannot find Internet Explorer on the All Programs menu, check to see if an Internet Explorer shortcut icon appears on the desktop, and then double-click it. If you do not see the shortcut icon, ask your instructor or technical support person for help. The program might be installed in a different folder on your computer.

   Trouble? If a Dial-up Connection dialog box opens, enter your user name and password into the appropriate text boxes, and then click the Connect button. If you do not know your user name or password, ask your instructor or technical support person for assistance; you must have an Internet connection to complete the steps in this tutorial. After a connection is made, continue with Step 2.

2. If the program window does not fill the screen entirely, click the **Maximize** button ▣ on the Internet Explorer title bar. Your screen should look similar to the one shown in Figure 4.

MSN home page displayed in Internet Explorer ◄ **Figure 4**

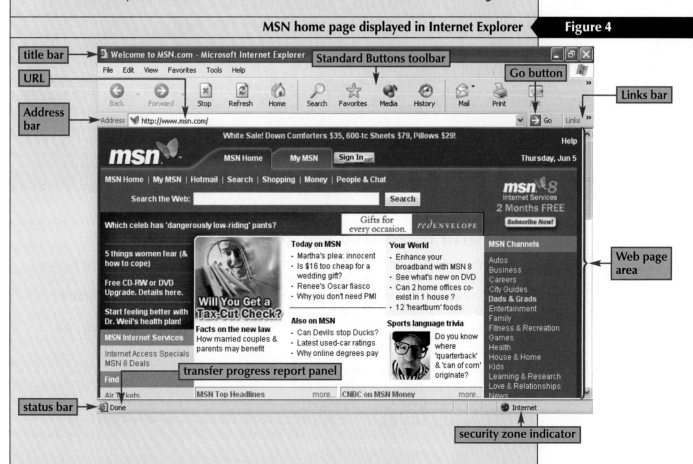

> **Trouble?** Your computer might be configured to open to a different Web page or to no page at all. Figure 4 shows the MSN home page, which is the home page that Internet Explorer opens the first time it starts.
>
> **Trouble?** If the Standard Buttons toolbar does not look like the one shown in Figure 4, you need to change its appearance. Click View on the menu bar, point to Toolbars, and then click Customize. In the Customize dialog box, click the Text options list arrow, and then click Show text labels; click the Icon options list arrow, and then click Large icons. Click the Close button. The Standard Buttons toolbar should now look like the one in the figure.

The design of Internet Explorer is similar to other Office 2003 programs. Most Windows programs use a standard graphical user interface (GUI) design that includes a number of common Windows components. These common elements include a title bar at the top of the window, a scroll bar on the right side of the window, and a status bar at the bottom of the window. Some of the other components in Internet Explorer, such as the Address bar and Links bar, are program-specific. Figure 5 describes the elements of the Internet Explorer window.

Figure 5 ▶ **Elements of the Internet Explorer window**

Element	Description
Title bar	Shows the name of the open Web page and includes the sizing buttons
Standard Buttons toolbar	Contains buttons you can click to perform commonly used tasks, such as moving to the next or previous page and printing a Web page
Address bar	Shows the address of the current Web page or the address you have entered for the Web page you want to go to
Web page area	Shows the contents of the current Web page
Status bar	Shows information about the browser's actions, for example, indicates a page is loading or is done loading
Scroll bars	Enable you to display the contents of a Web page that is wider or longer than the browser window by scrolling up and down or left and right
Home button	Returns you to the Web page that you have set as the home or start page
Go button	Displays the Web page for the address you have entered in the Address bar
Links bar	Contains links to Web pages you visit often
URL	Uniform Resource Locator, which is the address of the Web page you want to visit

Uniform Resource Locators

When you use a Web browser to access a Web page stored on a Web server, the browser software locates and retrieves the Web page content and downloads it to your computer. For this to occur, you need to provide the browser with a **Uniform Resource Locator (URL)**. A URL is a Web page's address and identifies where the Web page is stored on the Internet. The URL is a four-part addressing scheme that provides the Web browser the following information:

- Protocol to use when transporting the Web page
- Server address of the computer on which the Web page resides
- Pathname of the folder or directory on the computer on which the Web page resides
- Filename of the Web page

Figure 6 identifies the parts of a URL.

Structure of a URL ◄ **Figure 6**

$$\text{http://}\underbrace{\underbrace{\text{www.centralpenn.edu}}_{\text{server address}}}_{}\underbrace{\text{/library/}}_{}\underbrace{\text{index.html}}_{\text{filename}}$$

protocol   pathname

server address   filename

Web pages transmitted over the Internet use a communication protocol for transferring information. A **protocol** is a standardized procedure that computers use to exchange data. The most common protocol used on the Internet is the **Hypertext Transfer Protocol (HTTP)**. A Web page whose URL begins with "http://" indicates that the Web browser should use HTTP when retrieving the page.

The server address portion of a URL may consist of numbers or letters. Every computer on the Internet has an **IP (Internet Protocol) address**. An IP address is a unique number that consists of four sets of numbers from 0 to 255, separated by periods (such as 216.35.148.4), and identifies the specific server or computer connected to the Internet. Because IP addresses can be difficult for people to remember, domain names were created as another means of identifying computers and servers connected to the Internet. A **domain name** is a name that identifies one or more IP addresses, such as course.com. Domain names are used in the server address portion of a URL to identify a particular Web site. The URL shown in Figure 6 has a domain name of centralpenn.edu. In the server address for this URL, *www* indicates that the server is a Web server; *centralpenn* is the identifying name chosen by the organization to which the Web site belongs, in this case Central Pennsylvania College; and *.edu* indicates that the server is operated by an educational entity. Other common types of Web servers in the United States are .com (commercial business), .org (not-for-profit organization), and .gov (government). A more complete list is given in Figure 7.

Types of Web servers ◄ **Figure 7**

Web Server Types	Description
.com	Businesses and other commercial enterprises
.edu	Educational institutions
.gov	U.S. government agencies, bureaus, or departments
.int	International organizations
.mil	U.S. military units or agencies
.net	Network service providers or resources
.org	Other organizations, usually charitable or not-for-profit

In addition, all Web pages stored on Web servers have unique pathnames, just like files stored on a disk. The pathname in a URL includes the folder name(s) where the Web page is stored and its filename and file extension. The file extension for most Web pages is either .htm or .html. In the sample URL shown in Figure 6, the pathname that follows the server address www.centralpenn.edu specifies a file named *index.html*, which is stored in a folder named *library*.

Not all URLs include a filename. If a URL does not include a filename, most Web browsers will load the file named index.htm. The **index.htm** filename is the default name for a Web site's home page.

As stated earlier, you need to know a Web page's URL in order to open it in Internet Explorer. You can find URLs in many places; for example, newspapers and magazines often publish URLs of Web sites that might interest their readers. Friends who know about the subject area in which you are interested are also good sources. Once you have the URL of the Web page you want to view, you can enter it in the Address bar.

Entering a URL in the Address Bar

As discussed, you navigate from one Web page to another by clicking hyperlinks. Another way to display a specific Web page in Internet Explorer is to enter its URL in the Address bar. In most cases, URLs are not case-sensitive; however, in situations where the computer storing the Web page uses the UNIX operating system, URLs *are* case-sensitive. Therefore, if you are entering a URL that includes mixed cases and you do not know the type of computer on which the file resides, it is safer to retain the mixed-case format of the URL.

Reference Window

Entering a URL in the Address Bar

- Select the current URL in the Address bar.
- Type the URL of the Web page you want to retrieve.
- Press the Enter key to display the Web page in the browser window.

For this exercise, you will enter the URL for the New Perspectives Student Union Web page. In this tutorial, you will go to this Course Technology page and then click hyperlinks to go to other Web pages.

To enter the URL for the New Perspectives Student Union Web page:

1. Click the **Address bar** to select the current URL.

   Trouble? If you double-click in the Address bar, you switch to edit mode. If this occurs, click a blank space in the browser window to deactivate edit mode, and then repeat Step 1.

2. Type **www.course.com/NewPerspectives/studentunion/** in the Address bar. This is the URL for the New Perspectives Student Union Web page on the Course Technology Web site.

   Trouble? If a list box appears on the Address bar while you are typing the URL, just finish typing the URL. When the AutoComplete feature is enabled on your computer, Internet Explorer opens the Address bar list box as you begin typing a URL so that if you have gone to this location previously you can select the URL from a list, instead of typing it again.

3. Press the **Enter** key. As soon as you press the Enter key, Internet Explorer adds the http:// protocol to the URL for you, and then it transfers and displays the New Perspectives Student Union Web page in the browser window. Sometimes when a Web page contains a large amount of text and graphics, it takes a short amount of time to transfer to your computer and display fully in the browser window. The transfer time depends on the speed of your Internet connection, the amount of traffic on the Internet, and the complexity of the Web page being transferred. When the entire page has been transferred, the graphical transfer progress indicator in the status bar will stop moving, and the transfer progress report panel will display the text "Done."

   Trouble? If a Dial-up Connection dialog box opens after you press the Enter key, click the Connect button. You must have an Internet connection to complete the steps in this tutorial.

4. Scroll down the list of Student Online Companion links, and then click the **Microsoft Office 2003** link to open the Microsoft Office 2003 Student Online Companion page.

5. Scroll down and click the link for **Microsoft Office 2003 First Course**, and then click the **Browser and E-mail Basics** link to open the page that contains the links for this tutorial.

Martha Kent has suggested that Susan locate some Web sites advertising B&Bs to give her an idea of designs and layouts that appeal to her. This will help her in planning and designing the Web site for McKiernan's Irish B&B. Susan asks you to work with her to find some appropriate sites.

To go to the Web site for a B&B:

1. Scroll down to the Browser and E-mail Basics page to the Session 1 heading for this text.

2. Click one of the links listed under this heading to open the home page for a bed-and-breakfast. The home page for the B&B opens and may look similar to the sample shown in Figure 8.

Centre Mills Bed and Breakfast home page ◀ **Figure 8**

3. Read the Web page using the scroll bar on the right, if necessary, but do not click any area on the page.

4. Scroll back to the top of the page.

Once you arrive at the Web site in which you are interested, you can begin moving around the site by clicking the different links that are available. To help you navigate a Web site, you can also use the Back and Forward buttons on the Standard Buttons toolbar.

Navigating Links on a Web Page

The easiest way to move from one Web page to another is to use the hyperlinks that the authors of Web pages embed in their HTML documents. Web page authors use a word, phrase, or graphic image as a hyperlink. Sometimes, it is difficult to identify which objects and text are hyperlinks just by looking at a Web page. Fortunately, when you move the mouse pointer over a hyperlink in a Web browser, the pointer changes to 🖑 and the URL of the Web page is displayed in the status bar. Sometimes, depending on the design of the page, a ScreenTip will also appear, indicating the purpose of the link or its target destination.

Susan likes the layout of the Web site shown in Figure 8, so you will check out some of the links provided on the left side of the page.

To navigate Web pages on the bed-and-breakfast Web site:

1. Move your pointer over the link for **Rooms** until the pointer changes to 🖑, and then click that link. The address for this Web page appears in the Address bar, and the Back button is active. Figure 9 shows the Rooms page for the Centre Mills Bed and Breakfast.

Figure 9	Rooms Web page

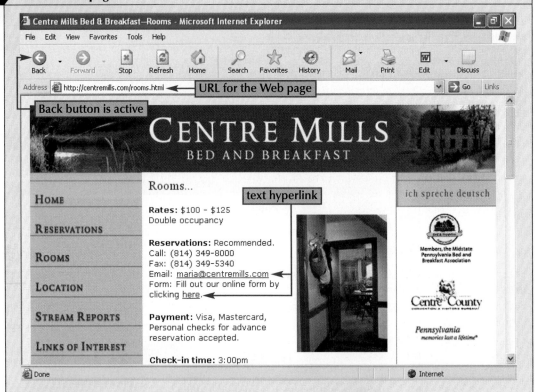

Trouble? If the Web site you chose in the previous set of steps does not have a Rooms link, then select another link of interest on the page, such as Rates or Reservations.

2. Click the **Back** button on the Standard Buttons toolbar to return to the home page for the bed-and-breakfast. The Back and Forward buttons are now active.

3. Position the pointer on the **Forward** button on the Standard Buttons toolbar to display information about the Rooms page. Clicking the Forward button now would return you to that page.

4. Locate another link on the page, and then click it. The target Web page for the link appears in the browser window.

Trouble? If the Web page appears in its own window, the Back button will not be available. Click the Close button to close the window and then skip Step 5. The home page for the bed-and-breakfast will be redisplayed.

▶ **5.** Click the **Back** button on the Standard Buttons toolbar to return to the home page for the bed-and-breakfast.

The Back and Forward buttons also have list arrows that, when clicked, display a list of the Web pages you have recently visited. You can also click the Address bar list arrow to display a list of Web sites that you have visited.

To return to the Browser and E-mail Basics page using the Back button list arrow:

▶ **1.** Click the **Back** button list arrow to view the list of Web pages you have just navigated.

▶ **2.** Click **New Perspectives on Microsoft Office 2003** in the list to return to the Browser and E-mail Basics page.

Trouble? If the New Perspectives Student Union or Student Online Companion page appears, you clicked its URL in the list. Navigate to the Browser and E-mail Basics link by clicking the Forward button.

▶ **3.** If necessary, scroll down the Browser and E-mail Basics page to display the Session 1 heading for this text.

Returning to the Home Page

As you browse different Web sites, you can always return to your home or start page for your browser by clicking the **Home button** on the Standard Buttons toolbar. Once you return to the home page, you can begin browsing again by clicking a link on the home page or by using any of the other available tools provided there.

Reloading a Web Page

When you visit a Web site, your browser loads the Web page from a remote Web server and stores a copy of the Web page in a folder on the hard drive of your computer. Storing copies of the Web pages you have visited increases the speed at which the browser can redisplay these pages as you navigate back and forward between them. When you click the **Refresh button** on the Standard Buttons toolbar, the browser contacts the remote Web server to see if the Web page has changed since it was stored on your computer. If the Web page has changed, the browser gets the new page from the Web server; otherwise, it loads the copy that is already stored on your computer.

Stopping a Web Page Transfer

If a Web page seems to be taking a long time to load, you can stop the page from loading altogether. If you accidentally click a hyperlink that you do not want to follow, you can stop the transfer of the Web page. To stop the transfer of a Web page from its server, click the **Stop button** on the Standard Buttons toolbar. In the case of the Web page taking too long to transfer, you might want to try reloading the page again by clicking the Refresh button.

Unavailable Sites

The Internet and WWW are dynamic—they are always changing, and inherent in that change is the fact that some Web sites may no longer exist or their addresses might change. Web sites are consistently being updated as well. If you click a link, you might encounter an error message. Two common messages that appear in dialog boxes are "server busy" and "DNS entry not found." Either of these messages means that your browser was unable to communicate successfully with the Web server that stores the page you requested. The cause of this inability might be temporary—in which case, you will be able to use the hyperlink later—or the cause might be permanent, and the Web site or Web page no longer exists. The browser has no way of determining the cause of the connection failure, so it provides the same error messages in both cases. Another error message that you might receive is displayed as a Web page and includes the text "File not Found." This error message usually means that the Web page's location has changed permanently or that the Web page no longer exists.

As you continue to research information for Susan, you may not be able to remember all the URLs of the sites you visit. The Back and Forward buttons only store URLs for a current session, but what if you want to return to sites you visited two days ago? Internet Explorer has a feature, the History list, that tracks sites visited for a specified period of time, and you can access this information using the History Explorer bar.

Using the History List

You have used the Back and Forward buttons as a means for navigating through Web pages viewed in your current browser session. Once you close the browser, the trail of visited sites is lost. However, Internet Explorer provides another feature, the History list, which tracks the Web sites that you have visited over a time period, not just during a browsing session. The **History list** contains the URLs for the Web sites and pages that you have visited. You click the History button on the Standard Buttons toolbar to open the History Explorer bar, which displays the History list. To return to a particular page, click that page's entry in the list. You can see the full URL of any item in the History Explorer bar by moving the mouse pointer over the History list item. The entries in the History Explorer bar are listed in alphabetical order and not in the order in which you visited the sites. You change the way in which the sites are listed by clicking View in the History Explorer bar, and choosing to view By Date, By Site, By Most Visited, and By Order Visited Today. You can also search the History list by clicking Search in the History Explorer bar.

The History list displays not only sites visited today, but also sites visited yesterday, the day before that, even last week, depending on the number of days specified in the Internet Options dialog box. You open the Internet Options dialog box from the Tools menu. (Changing Internet Explorer settings goes beyond the scope of this tutorial.)

To view the History list for this session:

▶ **1.** Click the **History** button on the Standard Buttons toolbar to open the History Explorer bar in the left pane of the Internet Explorer window. The History list stores each URL you have visited today and for other specified time periods (for example, 2 Weeks Ago, 3 Weeks Ago, and Last Week) in folders. It also maintains the hierarchy of each Web site; that is, pages you visit at a particular Web site are stored in a separate folder for that site. You can right-click any entry in the History list and copy the URL or delete it from the list. Internet Explorer stores each entry in the History list as a shortcut in the History folder, which is in the Windows folder.

As you become more and more familiar with Web sites on the Internet, you will probably want to return to certain sites because they provide information that you need on a regular basis. When you find a site that you know you will return to more than once, you can save it as a "favorite."

Using the Favorites Feature

Web addresses can be very long and, as a result, difficult to remember. Using the History list to locate important pages will be a terrific asset as you collect the information you need. In Internet Explorer, you can also save the URL of a Web site as a favorite in the Favorites list. The **Favorites list** is a feature that you can use to store and organize a list of Web pages you want to revisit. You click the Favorites button on the Standard Buttons toolbar to open the Favorites Explorer bar, which displays your list of favorites.

Susan wants you to save as a favorite any Web site that you think is well designed and easy to navigate. Then, when she has time, she will choose a few to show Martha Kent at their planning meeting next week.

To open the Favorites Explorer bar and then save a Web page as a favorite:

▶ **1.** Display the Web page you want to save as a favorite.

▶ **2.** Click the **Favorites** button on the Standard Buttons toolbar. The Favorites Explorer bar opens in the left pane of the Internet Explorer window.

▶ **3.** Click the **Add** button in the Favorites Explorer bar. The Add Favorite dialog box opens. See Figure 10. The text in the Name text box is the name of the currently displayed Web page as it appears in the Internet Explorer title bar. You can change the name of the favorite, but make sure you give it a meaningful name.

Add Favorite dialog box ◀ **Figure 10**

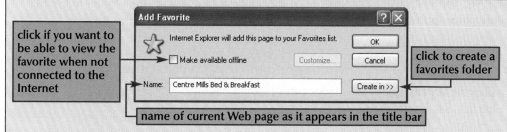

Trouble? If your Add Favorite dialog box is expanded and displays the Create in list box, click the Create in << button to reduce the size of the dialog box so it matches the one shown in the figure.

▶ **4.** Select the text in the Name text box, and then type an appropriate name. For example, if you were to create a favorite for the Centre Mills Bed and Breakfast site, you might enter "Centre Mills" in the Name text box.

▶ **5.** Click the **OK** button to close the Add Favorite dialog box. The favorite you just created appears in the Favorites list in the Favorites Explorer bar.

If you select the Make available offline option in the Add Favorite dialog box, Internet Explorer saves a copy of the Web page in a special folder on your hard drive. This means that you can display the Web page without connecting to the Internet. For example, if you are using a laptop in a place where there is no Internet access available, you can still display the Web page.

Saving Web sites as favorites is easy and will come in handy as you gather more information. However, having a long list of favorites may not be as helpful as you want. If the list is too long, you will waste time scrolling through the list, which defeats the purpose of the Favorites list—having ready access to a frequently visited Web page. To address this potential pitfall, you can create folders to organize and store multiple favorites.

Organizing Favorites

Internet Explorer offers an easy way to organize your favorite sites. You can use the Organize Favorites dialog box to create folders for storing your favorites. This dialog box provides options for creating folders, moving favorites into different folders, renaming favorites and folders, and deleting favorites and folders.

Reference Window	**Organizing the Favorites List**

- Click the Favorites button on the Standard Buttons toolbar, and then click the Organize button in the Favorites Explorer bar to open the Organize Favorites dialog box.
- To create a new folder, click the Create Folder button, and then type the name for the new folder.
- To move a favorite into a folder, select the item, click the Move to Folder button, select the folder for the item in the Browse for Folder dialog box, and then click the OK button.
- To remove an item from the Favorites list, select the item from the list in the Organize Favorites dialog box, and then click the Delete button.

Because Susan likes the Centre Mills Bed and Breakfast Web site and Preston hasn't seen it yet, you will save it as a favorite. Susan suggests that you create a folder to be used to store other appropriate Web sites that you find.

To create a new Favorites folder and move a favorite into it:

1. Click the **Organize** button in the Favorites Explorer bar to open the Organize Favorites dialog box. See Figure 11.

Organize Favorites dialog box   Figure 11

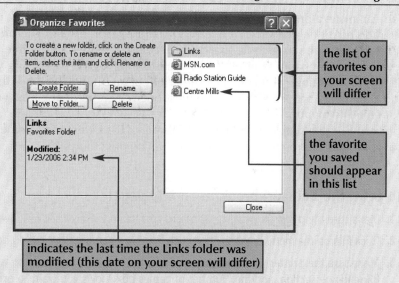

indicates the last time the Links folder was
modified (this date on your screen will differ)

2. Click the **Create Folder** button, type **B&B Sites** for the new folder name, and then press
the **Enter** key. Now you can move the favorite you created in the previous steps into this
new folder.

3. Click the name of the favorite you created earlier, and then click the **Move to Folder** button. The Browse for Folder dialog box opens. You can use this dialog box to locate the
folder in which you want to store the selected favorite.

4. Click the **B&B Sites** folder, and then click the **OK** button.

5. Click the **Close** button to close the Organize Favorites dialog box. Now the favorite you created is saved as a favorite in the B&B Sites folder, which appears in the Favorites list in the
Favorites Explorer bar.

6. Click the **B&B Sites** folder in the Favorites Explorer bar. The contents of the folder appear,
displaying the name of the favorite you created.

As you use the Web to find information about bed-and-breakfasts and other items, you
might find yourself creating many favorites so you can return to sites of interest. Sometimes
you will find you no longer need a favorite or a folder of favorites. You can remove the
folder and any favorites contained within it using the Delete button in the Organize
Favorites dialog box. You also can delete an item from the Favorites list by right-clicking the
item in the Favorites Explorer bar, and clicking Delete on the shortcut menu. Because you
may be working in a computer lab and sharing this computer with other users, you need to
delete the folder you just created.

To delete the item from the Favorites list:

1. Right-click the **B&B Sites** folder in the Favorites list in the Favorites Explorer bar. A shortcut menu displays commands for working with favorites.

2. Click **Delete** on the shortcut menu, and then click the **Yes** button in the Confirm Folder
Delete dialog box. The B&B Sites folder and the favorite you created are removed from the
Favorites list.

3. Click the **Close** button ☒ in the Favorites Explorer bar to close it.

Printing a Web Page

You can make a printed copy of most Web pages. Web pages can be any size and often do not fit on one sheet of 8 ½ × 11 (letter) paper. Instead, the browser automatically reformats the page to fit on standard letter-size paper, so one Web page may take several sheets of paper to print. If you want to print a Web page using your computer's default print settings, you can click the Print button on the Standard Buttons toolbar. If you want to change the settings, you must open the Print dialog box, which you access from the File menu.

Susan likes the simple, straightforward layout of the Centre Mills home page, and she wants to show Preston the design. She asks you to print this page.

To print the bed-and-breakfast home page:

1. Make sure the page you want to print is displayed in the browser window.

2. Click **File** on the menu bar, and then click **Print** to open the Print dialog box.

3. Make sure the printer you need to use is selected, the **All** option button is selected in the Page Range section, and the Number of copies box shows you want to print one copy.

4. Click the **Print** button to print the Web page and close the Print dialog box.

Saving a Web Page

You have learned how to use most of the Internet Explorer tools for loading Web pages and saving favorites. Now, you'll learn how to save a Web page.

You need to display the Web page that you want to save and then open the Save Web Page dialog box from the File menu. There are several options for saving a Web page, depending on what portion of the Web page you want. The "Web Page, complete" option (the default) saves the entire Web page, including its graphics and other elements that make up the page. When you save the complete Web page, Internet Explorer saves an HTML file and a folder with all of the site's related files, including page elements such as images and sounds. If you select the "Web Archive, single file" option, you will save a "picture" of the current Web page. You might use this option if you want to send a copy of the Web page to someone in an e-mail message.

The two other options—"Web Page, HTML only" and "Text File"—let you save just the HTML code or the text from the Web page, respectively, without saving the graphics, frames, or styles on the Web page.

Susan and Preston like the design layout of the Centre Mills Bed and Breakfast home page, and they want you to save the home page so they can show it to Martha at Capital Ads.

To save the bed-and-breakfast home page:

1. Make sure the B&B home page you want to save is displayed in the browser window. (Note that this can be a B&B Web page of your choice; it doesn't have to be the home page for Centre Mills.)

   Trouble? If you cannot display a B&B home page, display the Browser and E-mail Basics page.

2. Click **File** on the menu bar, and then click **Save As** to open the Save Web Page dialog box.

3. Navigate to the BEB\Tutorial folder included with your Data Files.

4. Change the default filename to **B&B Page**.
5. Click the **Save as type** list arrow, and then click **Web Page, HTML only (*.htm or *.html)**, if necessary, as shown in Figure 12.

Save Web Page dialog box ◀ **Figure 12**

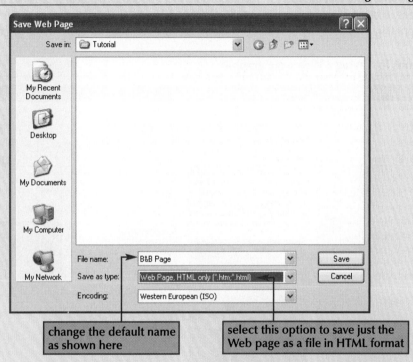

change the default name as shown here

select this option to save just the Web page as a file in HTML format

6. Click the **Save** button. The Save Web Page dialog box closes. Internet Explorer saves the Web page as an HTML file and automatically adds the .html file extension.

Saving a Web Page Graphic

You can also save images that you find. In this case, Susan wants you to save an image of one of the rooms on the Centre Mills Bed and Breakfast site.

Saving an Image from a Web Page to a Disk

Reference Window

- Open the Web page in Internet Explorer.
- Position the pointer over the graphic and then click the Save as Picture button on the shortcut toolbar (or right-click the image you want to save, and then click Save Picture As on the shortcut menu).
- Navigate to where you want to save the image, and then change the default filename if you want.
- Click the Save button.

To save the image from the Web page:

1. Go to the Web page that displays images of the B&B or rooms offered.

2. Right-click an image on the page to display the shortcut menu. See Figure 13. A toolbar of graphic commands may also display; you can use either one of these elements to save the graphic. Note that the shortcut menu provides more options. The toolbar provides quick and easy access to the four most frequently performed graphics-related tasks: saving an image, printing an image, sending an image in an e-mail message, and opening the My Pictures folder.

| Figure 13 | Options for saving a Web page graphic |

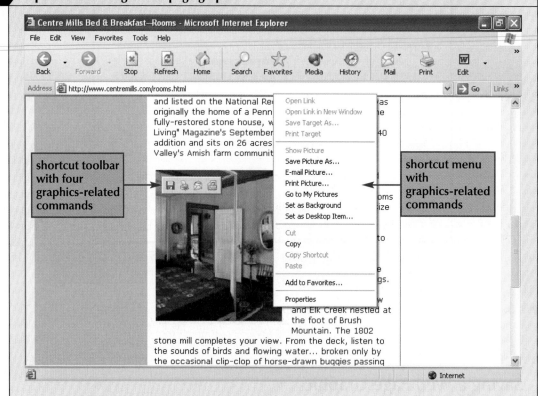

3. Click **Save Picture As** on the shortcut menu to open the Save Picture dialog box, and then navigate to the BEB\Tutorial folder.

4. Change the default filename to **Web Page Graphic**, and make sure **JPEG (*.jpeg)** appears in the Save as type list box. A JPEG file is a common file type for an image or picture.

5. Click the **Save** button.

6. Close your Web browser.

There are many graphics used on Web pages that you can save for use in your own materials. Some graphics, however, are copyrighted, and you need permission to copy and use them.

Copyright Law for the Internet

The term **copyright** applies to the exclusive legal right to reproduce, publish, or sell a product (in its literary, musical, or artistic form) by its originator. Copyright laws have served to protect the use of original and creative products of individuals and groups for many years. You have probably seen the copyright symbol © on the inside cover of almost every book you have ever read and have been made aware of the repercussions of copying someone else's work without giving that person credit—in other words, **plagiarism**.

Now, with the availability of and accessibility to a seemingly infinite amount of products and information, the scope of copyright law has taken a new direction and given rise to the term **cyberlaw**. Whether you refer to copyright law or cyberlaw, you need to be aware of the legal issues that revolve around the use and reproduction of the information that is readily available on the World Wide Web.

Before you download or copy the graphics, maps, images, sounds, or information on Web sites that you visit, you need to find out if and how you can use the materials. If you want to use materials that you have found on a Web site, you need to get permission from the owner of the site. Often, Web sites include their copyright and permission-request information on their home pages. Some Web sites indicate that the material is "free," but almost everything on the Internet is copyrighted. Even if you think that information or material you have found on a Web site does not fall within the scope of copyright protection, you should always request permission to use it. For example, you might be able to copy a picture to your computer, but you do not have a right to reproduce it in your own work.

You may also encounter the term **fair use**. This term applies to material that can be used for educational or nonprofit purposes, as opposed to commercial profit. Information that is considered factual or materials that are so old that copyright protection no longer exists fall under the category of fair use. You should still give credit to any Web site that you used in your research.

You have learned about the Internet and the World Wide Web, and how to use Internet Explorer to browse Web pages. You have saved a Web page and a graphic that Susan wants to send to the ad agency. In the next session, you will learn about e-mail.

Session 1 Quick Check

Review

1. Describe the relationship between the Internet and the World Wide Web.
2. What is the purpose of a Web browser?
3. Identify and define each part of the following URL:
   http://www.savethetrees.org/main.html.
4. Not all URLs include a filename, so most Web browsers load the file
   _____ as the default name for a Web site's home page.
5. Briefly define the term "home page."
6. What are some of the ways you can return to a Web site you have previously visited?
7. What are search engines and why are they important to people using the Internet?
8. To save an entire Web page, including graphics, frames, and styles, you select the
   _____ option in the Save Web Page dialog box.

To reinforce the tasks you learned in this session, go to the SAM 2003 Training Companion CD included with this text.

Session 2

Exploring E-mail

Electronic mail, or better known simply as **e-mail**, enables you to communicate with other users on a network such as the Internet. Sending and receiving e-mail messages is more efficient than using ground or air mail services. Instead of composing a message on a piece of paper, inserting it into an envelope, attaching the correct postage and address to the envelope, and then depositing it in a mailbox, you compose, address, and send a message directly from your computer to someone's electronic mailbox. You can avoid making many phone calls or printing memos by sending one message to many people. You can also attach files, such as word-processing documents, graphics, or spreadsheets, to an e-mail message.

Examining How E-mail Works

When you exchange e-mail, you send and receive messages with another person on your network, such as a LAN (local area network) or the Internet. An **e-mail message** is a simple text document that you can compose and send using an **e-mail program**, also called **e-mail client software,** such as Microsoft Outlook Express. When you send a message, it travels from your computer, through the network, and arrives at a computer that has been designated and set up as an **e-mail server**. Typically, the system administrator of your network or ISP manages the e-mail server.

The e-mail server stores the e-mail messages until the recipients request them. Then the server forwards the messages to the appropriate computers. Because e-mail uses this **store-and-forward technology**, you can send messages to anyone on the network, even if they do not have their computers turned on. When it's convenient, your recipients log on to the network and use their e-mail programs to receive and read their messages. The process of sending and receiving e-mail messages is illustrated in Figure 14.

Figure 14 ▶	**Sending and receiving e-mail**

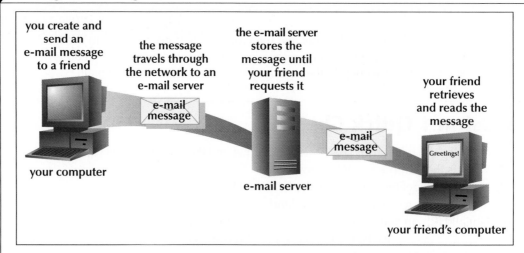

As shown in the figure, to send and receive e-mail, you must be able to access an e-mail server on a network. If your computer is part of a network at a college or university, for example, you log on to the network to access its services. An e-mail server provides mail services to faculty, staff, and students who have access to the network. When someone sends you a message, it is stored on your e-mail server until you log on to the network and use an e-mail program to check your mail. The e-mail server then transfers new messages to your electronic mailbox. You use an e-mail program to open, read, print, delete, reply to, forward, and save the mail.

If your computer is not part of a network, you can access an e-mail server on the Internet. To do so, you open an **e-mail account** with a service that provides Internet access. For example, e-mail accounts are included as part of the subscription fee for America Online (AOL) and most ISPs. E-mail accounts are also provided free of charge by advertiser-supported Web sites, such as Yahoo! and Hotmail. After you establish an e-mail account, you can connect to the Internet, most likely by using a phone line and your computer's modem, to send and receive your e-mail messages.

Reference Window

Signing Up for a Hotmail Account

- Start Internet Explorer (or any Web browser).
- Type *www.hotmail.com* in the Address Bar to go to the Hotmail Web site, and then click the New Account Sign Up tab to open the Registration page.
- Complete the Profile Information and the Account Information sections.
- Complete the .NET Passport Profile, and indicate how much information you want shared with other .NET Passport sites.
- Read the Hotmail Terms of Use and the .NET Passport Terms of Use, and then click the button to accept the terms to the agreement.

Addressing E-mail

You address an e-mail message just as you would an ordinary piece of mail. The e-mail address you enter directs the message to its destination. Your e-mail address is included in the message as a return address, so your recipients can easily respond to your message. Anyone who has an e-mail address can send and receive electronic mail. If you work for a company or attend a school that provides e-mail, there is probably a system administrator of your e-mail server who will assign you an e-mail address. Other times, such as when you sign up for a Hotmail account, you create your own e-mail address, though it must follow a particular format. Figure 15 illustrates a typical format of an e-mail address.

Typical format of an e-mail address | **Figure 15**

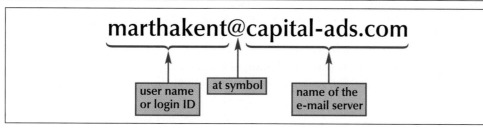

The **user name**, or login ID, is the name that you enter or are assigned when your e-mail account is being set up. The @ symbol signifies that the e-mail server name will be provided next. In the figure, *marthakent* is the user name and *capital-ads.com* is the e-mail server.

The easiest way to find an e-mail address is to ask someone. You can also look up an e-mail address in a LAN or Internet directory. Most businesses and schools publish a directory listing e-mail addresses of those who have e-mail accounts on their network. Many Web sites also provide e-mail directories for people with e-mail accounts on the Internet, such as *www.worldemail.com* and *www.people.yahoo.com*.

When you sign up for an e-mail account, you can send your new e-mail address to friends, colleagues, and clients. If your e-mail address changes—for example, if you use a different network or e-mail service—you can subscribe to an e-mail forwarding service so you don't miss any mail sent to your old address.

Before you begin sending e-mail, Susan wants you to understand some of the basic rules for appropriate e-mail communication.

Observing E-mail Etiquette

With the emergence of e-mail as a widespread form of communication, there are guidelines that will serve you well to follow. Many of these guidelines are common-sense practices, such as using appropriate language. One guiding principal that you may not realize, but should be aware of, is that e-mail is not private. When you correspond with others using e-mail, the information you send can be read by other users, especially if you work for a corporation or private institution. Your correspondents can easily forward your message to others, deliberately or inadvertently revealing information you consider confidential. Therefore, it's a good idea to be professional and careful about what you say to and about others.

Another guideline is providing meaningful information in the subject line. Most e-mail programs show the subject line, date, and sender address for incoming mail. Let your correspondents know what your message concerns by including information in the subject line that concisely and accurately describes the message contents. For example, a subject such as "Staff meeting rescheduled" is more informative than "Meeting." Even after people read your message, the subject helps them quickly locate information they might need later.

If you attach a large file to an e-mail message, it can take a long time for your recipient to download your message. Most e-mail servers have a limit to the size of the files you can attach; some allow files no larger than 1 MB. Check with your correspondents before sending large file attachments to find out about size restrictions and set up a convenient time to send the attachment.

Sending and Receiving E-mail Using Outlook Express

The Outlook Express e-mail program installs as part of Internet Explorer. You can use this program to send, receive, and manage e-mail.

Susan knows that e-mail will be the primary source of communication with Martha and the staff at Capital Ads as they develop the Web site for the McKiernans. She suggests that you practice creating and sending a few messages. First, you will start Outlook Express and review its components and layout.

Note: This tutorial assumes your installation of Outlook Express is already configured to send and receive e-mail. See your instructor or technical support person if this is not the case.

To start Outlook Express:

1. Click the **Start** button on the taskbar, point to **All Programs**, and then click **Outlook Express**. After a moment, Outlook Express opens, as shown in Figure 16. The default name that appears in this window is "Main Identity." Outlook Express can be configured to manage mail for more than one user on a computer, and for each account, there is an "identity." One of the accounts is considered the default account, or main identity. The other accounts are identified by the user name. The account shown in the figures in this tutorial belongs to the fictitious character Susan McKiernan. The account you are using will be the main identity or another identity that has been added to the account you are using.

Outlook Express window ◄ **Figure 16**

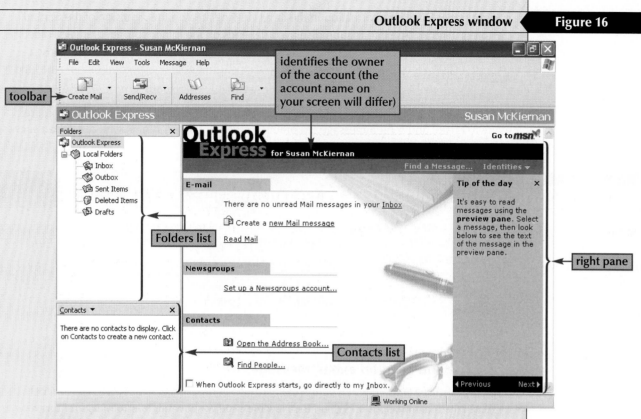

Trouble? If you cannot find Outlook Express on the All Programs menu, check to see if an Outlook Express shortcut icon appears on the desktop or on the taskbar, and then double-click it. If you do not see the shortcut icon, ask your instructor or technical support person for help. The program might be installed in a different folder on your computer.

Trouble? If you see a dialog box with the message "Outlook Express is not currently your default mail client. Would you like to make it your default mail client?" click the No button and then continue with the tutorial.

Trouble? If the title bar on the open window says "Microsoft Outlook" instead of "Microsoft Outlook Express," click the Close button to exit the program, and then repeat Step 1.

Trouble? If a Dial-up Connection dialog box opens, enter your user name and password into the appropriate text boxes, and then click the Connect button. If you do not know your user name or password, ask your instructor or technical support person for assistance. After you make a connection, continue with the tutorial.

In addition to the standard Windows components, such as the title bar, menu bar, scroll bars, Close button, and status bar, the Outlook Express window includes the following elements:

- **Toolbar**: Provides the buttons for frequently performed commands, such as composing a new message, sending or receiving mail, or replying to a message you receive.
- **Folders list**: Displays the default Outlook Express folders, which include the Inbox, Outbox, Sent Items, Deleted Items, and Draft folders. Your mail is organized in these folders automatically. You can create additional folders for the messages you create and receive.
- **Contacts list**: Displays the list of the people, companies, and organizations to which you send mail. The Contacts list appears below the Folders list.

- **Right pane**: Displays information in the large viewing area on the right side of the Outlook Express window. The information displayed depends on the folder you select in the Folders list. For example, when you click the Inbox folder, the right pane displays two sections: a message list of all the messages in your Inbox appears in the upper portion of the pane, and a preview pane displays the contents of the selected message in the lower portion.

Now that you have identified the components of the Outlook Express window, you are ready to create and send a message. To practice creating and sending messages, Susan suggests that you send yourself a test e-mail message.

Reference Window

Creating and Sending an E-mail Message

- Click the Create Mail button on the toolbar to open the New Message window.
- In the To and/or Cc text boxes, type the e-mail address of each recipient, separating names with a comma or semicolon.
- In the Subject text box, type a subject or title for the message.
- Click in the message area, and then type your message.
- Click the Send button on the Standard Buttons toolbar.

To create and send an e-mail message:

▶ 1. Click the **Create Mail** button on the toolbar to open the New Message window, and then click the **Maximize** button [□] on the New Message window title bar to maximize this window, as shown in Figure 17.

Figure 17 ▶ **New Message window**

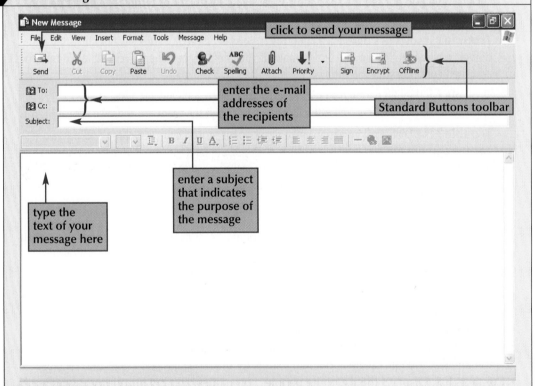

Trouble? If you do not see the toolbar, click View on the menu bar, point to Toolbars, and then click Standard Buttons.

2. Type your e-mail address in the To text box. For example, type *yourname@hotmail.com*.

   Trouble? Check with your instructor or technical support person if you are not sure what e-mail address you should enter.

3. Click the **Subject** text box, and then type **Test**.

4. Click in the message area, type **This is just a practice test message**, press the **Enter** key twice, and then type *your name*.

5. Click the **Send** button on the Standard Buttons toolbar. Outlook Express sends the message to the Outbox, and then to your e-mail address. You may see a number enclosed in parentheses appear briefly to the right of the Outbox folder in the Folders list. The number indicates that Outlook Express has moved the message to the Outbox, which in turn will send the message to the e-mail server for delivery.

If you wanted to send this message to many people, you could have typed more than one e-mail address in the To or Cc text box. You must separate each address with a comma or semicolon. You can also add the e-mail addresses of people (your contacts) to your Address Book, which you will do shortly.

Viewing Sent Messages

When you click the Send button, Outlook Express moves your message to the Outbox folder, and from there the mail server sends the message out. Usually the message remains in the Outbox folder for a brief moment. Sometimes the transmission happens so quickly, you might not notice the number that appears beside the Outbox folder because it just flashes. To make sure your message has been sent, you can open the Sent Items folder to see all the messages you have sent or replied to.

To view the message you sent:

1. Click the **Sent Items** folder in the Folders list. Your message appears in the pane on the right, as shown in Figure 18.

Sent Items folder | **Figure 18**

indicates the number of messages in the Sent Items folder

Trouble? If you do not see the Folders list in the Outlook Express window, click View on the menu bar, click Layout, click the Folder List check box in the Window Layout Properties dialog box to select this option, and then click the OK button. Repeat Step 1.

Working with E-mail Messages

Outlook Express transfers, or downloads, messages addressed to you from your e-mail server to your Inbox. Once your messages have been downloaded, they appear in a list with the name of the sender and the subject displayed. To preview a message, you click the message in the list to display its contents in the preview pane, or you can double-click the message to open it in a separate window. You can also print the messages that you receive.

To receive, read, and print the Test e-mail message:

1. Click the **Send/Recv** button on the toolbar. Outlook Express contacts your e-mail server and downloads your e-mail messages. When messages are retrieved from the e-mail server, the number of messages retrieved appears to the right of the Inbox folder. This list of messages appears in the upper portion of the right pane.

   Trouble? If a dialog box opens, asking for your user name and password, enter the information and continue with Step 2. See your instructor or technical support person if you need help entering the correct user name or password.

2. Click the **Inbox** folder in the Folders list. The number of new, unread messages in the Inbox appears to the right of the Inbox folder in the Folders list. A list of e-mail messages you have received appears in the message list, and the content of the selected message in the list appears in the preview pane. The status bar indicates how many messages there are and if any have been read. See Figure 19.

Figure 19	Inbox folder

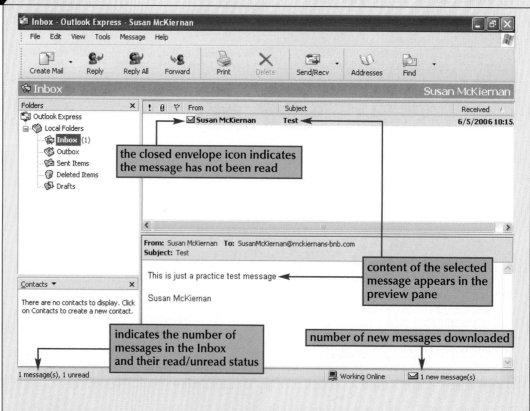

Trouble? Your message list might differ. Just make sure that the Test message you sent to yourself is listed.

3. Click **Test** in the message list. The message is displayed in the preview pane.

4. Double-click **Test** in the message list to open the test message in its own window, and then click the **Maximize** button 🔲 in the Test message window to maximize it. (Note: You do not need to open a message in its own window to work with the message.)

5. Click the **Print** button on the toolbar. The Print dialog box opens.

6. Click the **Print** button to print the message, and then click the **Close** button ⊠ on the title bar of the Test message window.

Next you'll perform another common e-mail task: replying to the messages you receive.

Replying to E-mail Messages

Some of the e-mail you receive asks you to provide information, answer questions, or confirm decisions. Instead of creating a new e-mail message, you can reply directly to the message. As part of the reply, Outlook Express fills in the To and Subject text boxes and includes the text of the original message.

Susan suggests that you practice replying to your own e-mail message.

To reply to the Test e-mail message:

1. Make sure the Test message is selected in the message list, and then click the **Reply** button on the toolbar. The Re: Test window, shown in Figure 20, opens. Click the **Maximize** button 🔲 in the Re: Test window to maximize it. The sender's e-mail address is automatically entered in the To text box, and the subject appears as "Re: Test." If copies of the message have been sent to more than one person, you can send a reply to everyone by clicking the Reply All button.

Replying to a message ◀ **Figure 20**

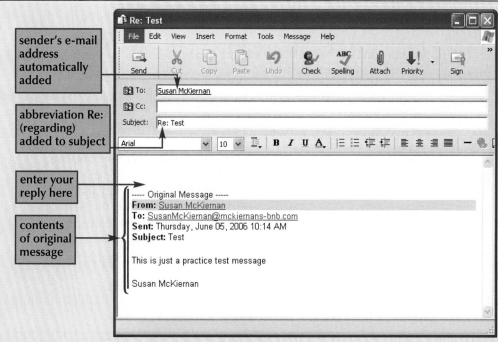

2. In the message area, type **This test was successful!**

3. Click the **Send** button on the toolbar. Note that Susan's name (or your name) now appears in the Contacts list. The name was automatically added to the Address Book. You will learn more about the Address Book later in this session.

   Trouble? If the Contacts list is not displayed in your Outlook Express window, click Tools on the menu bar, click Layout to open the Window Layout Properties dialog box, click the Contacts check box to select it, and then click the OK button. The Contacts list should appear in the lower-left corner of the window under the Folders list.

Deleting E-mail Messages

After you read and respond to your messages, you should delete any message that you no longer need. To delete a message, simply click the message in the message list, and then click the Delete button on the toolbar. When you delete a message, it moves to the Deleted Items folder. This folder might be set up to "empty" its contents automatically when you exit the program; if not, you should empty it periodically. Emptying the contents of the Deleted Items folder permanently removes those items from your computer. To empty the Deleted Items folder, right-click the Deleted Items folder in the Folders list, click Empty 'Deleted Items' Folder on the shortcut menu, and then click the Yes button to confirm the deletion. You can move a deleted message from the Deleted Items folder to another folder if you don't want the message permanently deleted; however, once the Deleted Items folder is emptied, the message no longer exists.

You are done practicing sending and replying to messages, so you can delete the test message you sent to yourself.

To delete the Test e-mail message:

1. Click **Test** in the message list, and then click the **Delete** button on the toolbar.

   The message list no longer displays the Test message.

Adding Contacts to the Address Book

You can use the **Address Book** to keep track of all the people and organizations with which you correspond electronically. In addition to storing e-mail addresses, you can keep all related information about your **contacts** in the Address Book. You can enter home addresses, home phone numbers, business addresses, business phone numbers, and personal information, such as anniversaries and birthdays.

To retrieve a contact's information quickly and easily, you can give the contact a **nickname**, a shortened version of the individual's name. You enter the nickname as the recipient and the correct e-mail address is automatically entered. You can also select the "Automatically put people I reply to in my Address Book" option on the Send tab in the Options dialog box so contacts are automatically added when you reply to a message.

Adding a Contact to the Address Book

- Click the Addresses button on the toolbar (or click Tools on the menu bar, and then click Address Book) to open the Address Book window, click the New button, and then click New Contact.
- In the Properties dialog box, enter the first and last names (the middle name, title, and nickname are optional). Modify the display name if necessary.
- Enter the e-mail address and then click the Add button.
- Enter additional information on the remaining tabs (optional).
- Click the OK button, and then close the Address Book.

or

- Display a message from the sender you want to add as a contact.
- Right-click the sender's name in the From text box, and then click Add to Address Book on the shortcut menu.

Martha at Capital Ads wants to set up an initial meeting with Susan at her earliest convenience. Susan asks you to send Martha an e-mail message with the times she could meet with Martha. Susan also wants you to attach a list of the ideas and questions she has regarding the design of the Web site. But first she wants you to add Martha Kent to the Address Book.

To add a contact to the Address Book:

1. Click the **Addresses** button on the toolbar to open the Address Book window, and then, if necessary, click the **Maximize** button ▣ on the Address Book window title bar to maximize the window.

2. Click the **New** button on the toolbar, and then click **New Contact**. The Properties dialog box opens with the Name tab displayed. You enter the basic e-mail address information here.

3. Type **Martha** in the First text box, press the **Tab** key twice, and then type **Kent** in the Last text box. As you enter the information in this top row of text boxes, the information appears in the Display list box. The display name is the name that appears when the message is displayed in the message list. The first and last names also appear in the title bar, changing the "Properties" dialog box to "Martha Kent Properties."

4. Click the **Nickname** text box, and then type **Martha**. When creating a message, you can easily and quickly retrieve an e-mail address saved in the Address Book by typing the nickname of the contact.

5. Click the **E-Mail Addresses** text box, type **marthakent@capital-ads.com**, and then click the **Add** button. See Figure 21.

Figure 21   Properties dialog box for contact Martha Kent

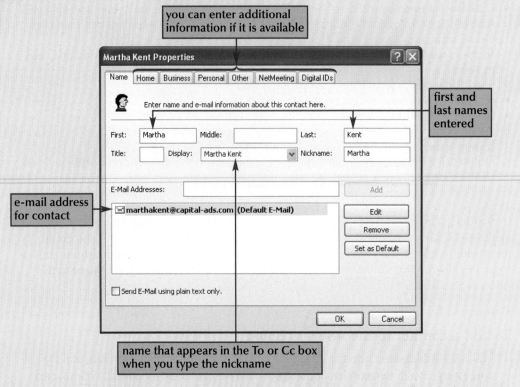

6. Click the **Business** tab in the Martha Kent Properties dialog box, and then enter **Capital Ads Online** in the Company text box. You can enter as much or as little additional informa-tion as you have available and deem important. For now, this is all you have on Martha, so you can close the Address Book.

7. Click the **OK** button to save the contact information to the Address Book, and then click the **Close** button ☒ to close the Address Book. Martha's name now appears in the Contacts list.

You can make changes to the contact entries in the Address Book or delete a contact when you no longer need to communicate with that individual. To edit contact informa-tion or to delete a contact, open the Address Book, select the contact, and then click the Properties button to make changes, or click the Delete button on the toolbar and then click the Yes button to confirm the deletion. The Properties and Delete commands are available on the shortcut menu that appears when you right-click a contact in the Contacts list.

Although you can easily open the Address Book from the toolbar, you also may want to have the Contacts list displayed on a regular basis. You can double-click a name in the Contacts list to create a new message addressed to the contact.

Attaching a File to a Message

Recall that Susan wants to send Martha a list of ideas as an attachment to an e-mail mes-sage. Before you send the message with the attachment, Susan suggests you try sending it to yourself first.

To create a message with an attachment:

1. Click the **Create Mail** button on the toolbar to open the New Message window, and then click the **Maximize** button 🔲 on the New Message window title bar to maximize this window.

2. Type your e-mail address in the To text box. Your display name automatically appears.

3. Type **First Meeting** in the Subject text box.

4. Click in the message area, and then, using Figure 22 as a guide, enter the message text, pressing the **Enter** key between paragraphs and substituting your name for Susan McKiernan's.

First Meeting message to Martha Kent 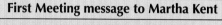 Figure 22

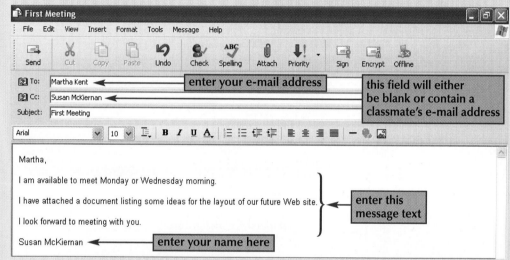

5. Click the **Attach** button on the toolbar to open the Insert Attachment dialog box, navigate to the BEB\Tutorial folder included with your Data Files, click **B&B Ideas** in the file list, and then click the **Attach** button. The file attachment information appears in the Attach text box, as shown in Figure 23.

First Meeting message with file attached ◀ Figure 23

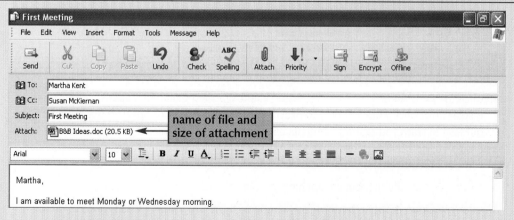

6. Click the **Send** button on the toolbar. Outlook Express moves your message to the Outbox folder before sending it to the e-mail server. You might see a "1" appear briefly next to the Outbox folder.

If you receive a message that contains an attachment, you can choose to save or open the attachment. To open the attachment, you need to make sure the program used to create the attachment is installed on your computer. If the program is not installed, sometimes you can use a text editor, such as WordPad or Notepad, to open and read the attached file. The file attached to the First Meeting message will open in Microsoft Word.

To open the message containing the attachment:

▶ **1.** Click the **Send/Recv** button on the toolbar.

▶ **2.** Click the **First Meeting** message in the message list so the contents appear in the preview pane. See Figure 24. The paperclip icon in the upper-right corner of the preview pane indicates that the message contains an attachment.

| **Figure 24** | **Message with attachment** |

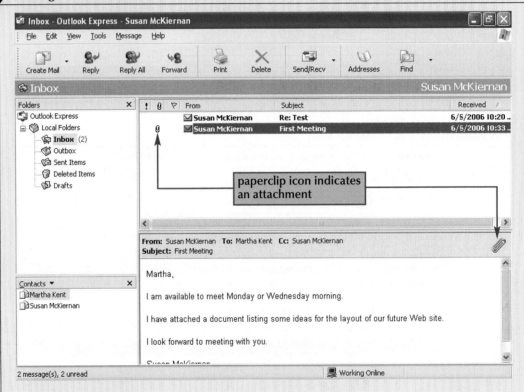

▶ **3.** Click the **paperclip** icon to display a list of attachments and the Save Attachments option.

▶ **4.** Click the **B&B Ideas** file. The Open Attachment Warning dialog box opens. Outlook Express displays this dialog box not only to provide options for saving or opening the attachments, but also to warn you that attachments can contain **viruses**, which are programs that can harm your computer. Only open or save a file from known sources to ensure that the files you download to your computer are safe and virus-free.

You could save the file, but try opening the file instead.

▶ **5.** Click the **Open it** option button. The file opens in the program in which it was created (in this case, Word). Opening the file before saving it can save time in the end. You can read the file and then decide if you want to save it. You can save it from within the program with the same name or a new name.

6. Click the **Close** button ⊠ on the Word title bar to close the document and exit the program.
7. Close Outlook Express.

Susan congratulates you for completing the basic tasks in Outlook Express and for sending Martha the message with the attached file. She is sure that you will be able to research the information that she wants and to send and receive messages easily.

Session 2 Quick Check

Review

1. What is the role of an e-mail server?
2. What are the default folders in Outlook Express?
3. Which toolbar button do you click to compose a message?
4. List three guidelines that you should follow when composing e-mail messages.
5. What are two ways that you can enter an e-mail address in the To text box?
6. Multiple e-mail addresses in the To text box must be separated by a(n) _____ or _____.
7. Describe two ways to enter contacts in the Address Book.
8. When attaching a file to an e-mail message, why must you consider the size of the file before sending the message with the attachment?

To reinforce the tasks you learned in this session, go to the SAM 2003 Training Companion CD included with this text.

Tutorial Summary

Review

In this tutorial you were introduced to the basics of Web browsers, specifically Internet Explorer. You learned about the major components of the Internet Explorer window. You also learned how to navigate to Web sites and between Web pages on a Web site. You learned how to return to visited sites and pages using the Back and Forward buttons and the History Explorer bar. You also learned how to save a Web site as a favorite so you can return to the site with one click.

The tutorial presented some basic information on e-mail using Outlook Express. You learned the components and features of Outlook Express. You learned how to create and send an e-mail message, receive and reply to a message, and attach a file to a message. You also learned about the Address Book and how to add contacts to it.

Key Terms

Address Book	e-mail account	Hypertext Markup
contact	e-mail client software	Language (HTML)
copyright	e-mail message	Hypertext Transfer
cyberlaw	e-mail program	Protocol (HTTP)
dial-up connection	e-mail server	index.htm
domain name	fair use	Internet
DSL (Digital Subscriber	Favorites list	Internet Protocol (IP) address
Line) connection	History list	Internet service provider (ISP)
electronic mail	home page	link
e-mail	hyperlink	network

nickname	store-and-forward technology	Web directory
plagiarism	Uniform Resource	Web page
protocol	Locator (URL)	Web search engine
Refresh button	user name	Web server
start page	virus	Web site
Stop button	Web browser	World Wide Web (WWW)

Practice

Practice the skills you learned in the tutorial using the same case scenario.

Review Assignments

There are no Data Files needed for the Review Assignments.

In preparation for her meeting with Martha Kent, Susan wants you to compile some additional information about the Web sites that specialize in Irish food, which she and Preston want to feature at their B&B.

Complete the following:

1. Start your Web browser, go to the New Perspectives Student Union Web page (*http://www.course.com/NewPerspectives/studentunion.htm*), click the **Microsoft Office 2003** link, click the **Microsoft Office 2003 First Course** link, click the **Browser and E-mail Basics** link, and then click the **Review Assignments** link.
2. Click the hyperlinks listed under the category heading Irish Foods to explore the Web pages for each entry.
3. Using the History Explorer bar, return to three sites that have the most interesting home pages, and then print the home page of each.
4. Create a favorites folder named "Irish Foods," and save as favorites the three sites whose home pages you printed in the preceding step.
5. Using the Favorites Explorer bar, return to each site and answer the following questions:
   a. Which sites include graphic links?
   b. Which sites include links to other Web sites? (*Hint*: If the Back button is not available when the Web page is displayed, the link has taken you to a new Web site. Click the Close button to return to the previous site.)
   c. Which sites include download links?
6. Choose your favorite image from any one of the sites, and save it in the BEB\Review folder provided with your Data Files.
7. Start your e-mail program and create a message addressed to your instructor and copied to yourself. Write the answers to Assignment 5 as the message text, attach the image you saved in Assignment 6, send the message, and then close Outlook Express.
8. In Internet Explorer, delete the Irish Foods favorites folder (and all its contents) that you created in Assignment 4, and then close Internet Explorer.

Apply

Use the skills that you learned about Internet Explorer to research several business Web sites.

Case Problem 1

There are no Data Files needed for this Case Problem.

Businesses on the Web   Business Web sites range from very simple informational sites to comprehensive sites that offer information about a firm's products or services, history, current employment openings, and finances. An increasing number of businesses offer products or services for sale on their Web sites. You just started a position on the public relations staff of Value City Central, a large retail chain of television and appliance stores. Your first assignment is to research and report on the types of information that other large firms offer on their Web sites.

Complete the following:

1. Start your Web browser, go to the New Perspectives Student Union Web page (*http://www.course.com/NewPerspectives/studentunion/*), click the **Microsoft Office 2003** link, click the **Microsoft Office 2003 First Course** link, click the **Browser and E-mail Basics** link, and then click the **Case Problems** link.
2. Use the Case Problem 1 hyperlinks to open the business sites on that page.
3. Choose three business sites that you believe would be most relevant to your assignment.
4. Print the home page for each Web site that you have chosen.
5. Select one site that you feel does the best job in each of the following five categories: overall presentation of the corporate image, description of featured products or services, presentation of the history or background of the firm, description of employment opportunities, and presentation of financial statements or other financial information about the company.
6. Prepare a report that includes one paragraph describing why you believe each of the sites you identified in the preceding step did the best job. Save your report in the BEB\Cases folder provided with your Data Files.
7. Close your Web browser and your Internet connection, if necessary.

Apply

Use the skills you learned about Internet Explorer to investigate how charitable or not-for-profit organizations use the Internet to present themselves.

Case Problem 2

There are no Data Files needed for this Case Problem.

Columbus Suburban Area Council   The Columbus Suburban Area Council is a charitable organization devoted to maintaining and improving the general welfare of people living in the suburbs of Columbus, Ohio. As the director of the council, you are interested in encouraging donations and other support from local citizens and would like to stay informed of grant opportunities that might benefit the council. You are especially interested in developing an informative and attractive presence on the Web.

Complete the following:

1. Start your Web browser, go to the New Perspectives Student Union Web page (*http://www.course.com/NewPerspectives/studentunion/*), click the **Microsoft Office 2003** link, click the **Microsoft Office 2003 First Course** link, click the **Browser and E-mail Basics** link, and then click the **Case Problems** link.
2. Follow the Case Problem 2 hyperlinks to charitable organizations to find out more about what other organizations are doing with their Web sites.

3. Select three of the Web sites you visited and, for each, prepare a list of the site's contents. Note whether each site includes financial information and whether the site discloses how much the organization spends on administrative, or nonprogram, activities. Also note whether the site lets visitors communicate with the organization via e-mail.

4. Identify which site you believe would be a good model for the Columbus Suburban Area Council's new Web site. Explain why you think your chosen site would be the best example to follow. Save any documents you create for this exercise in the BEB\Cases folder provided with your Data Files.

5. Close your Web browser and your Internet connection, if necessary.

Case Problem 3

Research

Use the skills you learned about Internet Explorer to research two of today's most popular advertising vehicles on the Internet.

There are no Data Files needed for this Case Problem.

Pretzel Piazza   You are working for the Pretzel Piazza during your summer break. This shop offers a large variety of coffees and teas, but its specialty is gourmet pretzels. The pretzels come in a wide variety of flavors, from the standard salted pretzel to the most decadent Belgium chocolate-covered pretzels. There are pretzels covered with a variety of chocolate, caramel, nuts, and candies. The owners of Pretzel Piazza have a Web site, but they are wondering if using a pop-up ad and junk mail campaign for a short period of time might be a better way to advertise their products to a wider customer base. One of your assignments is to research information and articles dealing with pop-up ads, which are independent windows that appear when you are online, and junk mail, also known as spam. After researching these topics, you will report back to the owners with your recommendation.

Complete the following:

1. Start your Web browser, go to the New Perspectives Student Union Web page (*http://www.course.com/NewPerspectives/studentunion/*), click the **Microsoft Office 2003** link, and then click the **Microsoft Office 2003 First Course** link.

2. Click the **Browser and E-mail Basics** link, and then click the **Case Problems** link.

3. Use the hyperlinks under the Case Problem 3 heading to learn more about pop-up advertising.

4. Send an e-mail message to your instructor listing the pros and cons of pop-up ads on the Internet. Give your opinion on whether pop-ups are effective advertising tools.

5. Return to the Case Problem 3 links, and use the hyperlinks to learn more about spam.

6. Send an e-mail message to your instructor listing the pros and cons of spam on the Internet. Provide the names of the Web sites that you feel were the most helpful, and explain what kind of information they provided. Indicate whether you feel spam is an effective advertising tool.

Challenge

Learn more about the features and tools of Outlook Express.

Case Problem 4

There are no Data Files needed for this Case Problem.

Learning More About Outlook Express Outlook Express is a convenient way to handle e-mail. Although not considered a full-featured or robust e-mail program, Outlook Express does offer many useful tools and features. To learn more about this application, you will use Microsoft Outlook Express Help.

Complete the following:

1. Start Outlook Express.

Explore

2. Use Outlook Express Help to learn about stationery. (*Hint*: Click Help on the menu bar, click Contents and Index, click the Index tab, type "stationery" in the text box, click the Search button to display a list of related topics, and then click the "Use stationery with outgoing messages" topic.)

Explore

3. Compose a message to your instructor using stationery. The content of the message should include the steps you used to add the stationery to the message. Also include how to set stationery as the default background for all new messages that you create. Send a copy of the message to yourself.

Explore

4. Use Outlook Express Help to learn how to set up Outlook Express to receive e-mail from a Hotmail account. (*Hint*: Click Help on the menu bar, point to Microsoft on the Web, click Search the Web to open the Search Companion pane, type "How do I set up Outlook Express to receive Hotmail" in the text box, and then click the Search button to go to the Microsoft Support Web page for information on Outlook Express and Hotmail.)

5. Compose a message to your instructor, with a copy to yourself, explaining the steps for the setup procedure. If you have a Hotmail account, *do not* set up Outlook Express to receive your e-mail unless your instructor or technical support person instructs you to do so.

Assess

SAM Assessment and Training

If your instructor has chosen to use the full online version of SAM 2003 Assessment and Training, you can go beyond the "just-in-time" training provided on the CD that accompanies this text. Simply log in to your SAM account (http://sam2003.course.com) to launch any assigned training activities or exams that relate to the skills covered in this tutorial.

Research

The Internet: World Wide Web

Lab Assignments

The New Perspectives Labs are designed to help you master some of the key concepts and skills presented in this text. The steps for completing this Lab are located on the Course Technology Web site. Log on to the Internet and use your Web browser to go to the Student Online Companion for New Perspectives Office 2003 at **www.course.com/np/office2003**. Click the Lab Assignments link, and then navigate to the assignments for this tutorial.

Quick Check Answers

Session 1

1. The Internet is a collection of networked computers, and located on these computers is a system of electronic documents that are linked together and referred to as the World Wide Web. You need to be connected to the Internet to have access to the World Wide Web.
2. A Web browser is the software that runs on your computer so it can communicate with all different types of computers connected to the Internet and access the HTML documents that reside on those computers.
3. The *http* stands for Hypertext Transfer Protocol (HTTP), used to transport the file; the *www.savethetrees* indicates the domain name of the computer on which the file resides; the *.org* identifies the Web server type; and *main.html* is the name of the file.
4. index.htm
5. A home page is the main page that all of the pages on a particular Web site are organized around and link back to.
6. You can click the Back or Forward button, use the History list, or save a site as a favorite.
7. Search engines are Web pages that conduct searches of the Web to find the words or expressions that you enter. The result of a search is a Web page that contains hyperlinks to Web pages with matching text or expressions. These pages can give users an easy way to find information on the Web.
8. Web Page, complete

Session 2

1. An e-mail server uses store-and-forward technology to store e-mail messages until recipients request them and to forward the messages to the requesting computers.
2. Inbox, Outbox, Sent Items, Drafts, and Deleted Items
3. Create Mail
4. Remember e-mail is not private; provide meaningful information in the subject line; check with recipients before sending large file attachments to find out about size restrictions and set up a convenient time to send the attachment.
5. Type the e-mail address in the To text box; select a contact from the Address Book; double-click the contact in the Contacts list.
6. comma or semicolon
7. Enter the information manually in the Address Book; or reply to an e-mail address or right-click the name of the sender in the From column, then click Add Sender to Address Book on the shortcut menu.
8. Messages with large attachments can take a long time for the recipient to download. Most e-mail servers have a limit to the size of the files you can attach; some allow files no larger than 1 MB. You need to check with your recipients before sending large file attachments to find out about size restrictions.

New Perspectives on

Using Common Features of Microsoft® Office 2003

Preparing Promotional Materials   OFF 3

Read This Before You Begin

Data Files

To complete the "Using Common Features of Microsoft Office 2003" tutorial, you need the starting Data Files. See the inside back or front cover for information on downloading these files from course.com, or ask your instructor for assistance. The following table identifies each starting Data File and the folder it is stored in, as well as the ending files, which you create and save in each tutorial.

Folders	Starting Files	Ending Files
OFF / Tutorial	(no starting Data Files)	French Sales Report.xls, Stockholder Meeting Agenda.doc
Review	Finances.xls, Letter.doc	Delmar Finances.xls, Delmar Letter.doc

Storing Your Files

It is recommended that you store all your Data Files on a USB drive. Refer to the tutorial "Managing Your Files" for information on using USB drives. If you need to store your Data Files on floppy disks, you will need one high-density disk to store all the files for the "Using Common Features of Microsoft Office 2003" tutorial.

SAM 2003 Training Companion CD

The SAM 2003 Training Companion CD that comes with this text gives you "just-in-time" training and reinforcement of important Microsoft Office skills. Look for the SAM CD logo throughout each tutorial for opportunities to complete the hands-on tasks included on this CD.

Using Common Features of Microsoft Office 2003

Preparing Promotional Materials

Case | Delmar Office Supplies

Delmar Office Supplies, a company in Wisconsin founded by Jake Alexander in 1996, sells recycled office supplies to businesses and home-based offices around the world. The demand for quality recycled papers, reconditioned toner cartridges, and renovated office furniture has been growing each year. Jake and all his employees use Microsoft Office 2003, which provides everyone in the company the power and flexibility to store a variety of information, create consistent files, and share data. In this tutorial, you'll review how the company's employees use Microsoft Office 2003.

Objectives		SAM Training Tasks	
• Explore the programs that comprise Microsoft Office	• Use personalized menus and toolbars	• Close a program	• Save a file
	• Work with task panes	• Create a new document	• Select a menu option
• Start programs and switch between them	• Create, save, close, and open a file	• Maximize a window	• Select a Start menu option
• Explore common window elements	• Use the Help system	• Minimize a window	• Select a toolbar button
	• Print a file	• Open a file from within a program	• Select text
• Minimize, maximize, and restore windows	• Exit programs	• Print a file	• Switch between programs
		• Redisplay a minimized window	

Student Data Files   For a complete list of the Data Files needed for this tutorial, see page OFF 2.

For hands-on practice of key tasks in this tutorial, go to the SAM 2003 Training Companion CD included with this text.

Exploring Microsoft Office 2003

Microsoft Office 2003, or simply **Office**, is a collection of the most popular Microsoft programs: Word, Excel, PowerPoint, Access, and Outlook. Each Office program contains valuable tools to help you accomplish many tasks, such as composing reports, analyzing data, preparing presentations, compiling information, sending e-mail, and planning schedules.

Microsoft Word 2003, or simply **Word**, is a word-processing program you use to create text documents. The files you create in Word are called **documents**. Word offers many special features that help you compose and update all types of documents, ranging from letters and newsletters to reports, brochures, faxes, and even books—all in attractive and readable formats. You can also use Word to create, insert, and position figures, tables, and other graphics to enhance the look of your documents. The Delmar Office Supplies sales representatives create their business letters using Word.

Microsoft Excel 2003, or simply **Excel**, is a spreadsheet program you use to display, organize, and analyze numerical data. You can do some of this in Word with tables, but Excel provides many more tools for recording and formatting numbers as well as performing calculations. The graphics capabilities in Excel also enable you to display data visually. You might, for example, generate a pie chart or a bar chart to help readers quickly see the significance of and the connections between information. The files you create in Excel are called **workbooks**. The Delmar Office Supplies operations department uses a line chart in an Excel workbook to visually track the company's financial performance.

Microsoft Access 2003, or simply **Access**, is a database program you use to enter, organize, display, and retrieve related information. The files you create in Access are called **databases**. With Access you can create data entry forms to make data entry easier, and you can create professional reports to improve the readability of your data. The Delmar Office Supplies operations department tracks the company's inventory in a table in an Access database.

Microsoft PowerPoint 2003, or simply **PowerPoint**, is a presentation graphics program you use to create a collection of slides that can contain text, charts, pictures, and so on. The files you create in PowerPoint are called **presentations**. You can show these presentations on your computer monitor, project them onto a screen as a slide show, print them, share them over the Internet, or display them on the World Wide Web. You can also use PowerPoint to generate presentation-related documents such as audience handouts, outlines, and speakers' notes. The Delmar Office Supplies sales department has created an effective slide presentation with PowerPoint to promote the company's latest product line.

Microsoft Outlook 2003, or simply **Outlook**, is an information management program you use to send, receive, and organize e-mail; plan your schedule; arrange meetings; organize contacts; create a to-do list; and jot down notes. You can also use Outlook to print schedules, task lists, phone directories, and other documents. Jake Alexander uses Outlook to send and receive e-mail, plan his schedule, and create a to-do list.

Although each Office program individually is a strong tool, their potential is even greater when used together.

Integrating Office Programs

One of the main advantages of Office is **integration**, the ability to share information between programs. Integration ensures consistency and accuracy, and it saves time because you don't have to re-enter the same information in several Office programs. The staff at Delmar Office Supplies uses the integration features of Office daily, including the following examples:

- The accounting department created an Excel bar chart on the previous two years' fourth-quarter results, which they inserted into the quarterly financial report created in Word. They included a hyperlink in the Word report that employees can click to open the Excel workbook and view the original data.
- The operations department included an Excel pie chart of sales percentages by divisions of Delmar Office Supplies on a PowerPoint slide, which is part of a presentation to stockholders.
- The marketing department produced a mailing to promote the company's newest products by combining a form letter created in Word with an Access database that stores the names and addresses of customers.
- A sales representative wrote a letter in Word about a sales incentive program and merged the letter with an Outlook contact list containing the names and addresses of his customers.

These are just a few examples of how you can take information from one Office program and integrate it into another.

Starting Office Programs

You can start any Office program by clicking the Start button on the Windows taskbar, and then selecting the program you want from the All Programs menu. Once the program starts, you can immediately begin to create new files or work with existing ones. If you or another user has recently used one of the Office programs, then that program might appear on the most frequently used programs list on the left side of the Start menu. You can click the program name to start the program.

Starting Office Programs	Reference Window

- Click the Start button on the taskbar.
- Point to All Programs.
- Point to Microsoft Office.
- Click the name of the program you want to start.

or

- Click the name of the program you want to start on the most frequently used programs list on the left side of the Start menu.

You'll start Excel using the Start button.

To start Excel and open a new, blank workbook:

1. Make sure your computer is on and the Windows desktop appears on your screen.

   Trouble? If your screen varies slightly from those shown in the figures, then your computer might be set up differently. The figures in this book were created while running Windows XP in its default settings, but how your screen looks depends on a variety of things, including the version of Windows, background settings, and so forth.

2. Click the **Start** button on the taskbar, and then point to **All Programs** to display the All Programs menu.

3. Point to **Microsoft Office** on the All Programs menu, and then point to **Microsoft Office Excel 2003**. See Figure 1. Depending on how your computer is set up, your desktop and menu might contain different icons and commands.

Figure 1	Start menu with All Programs submenu displayed

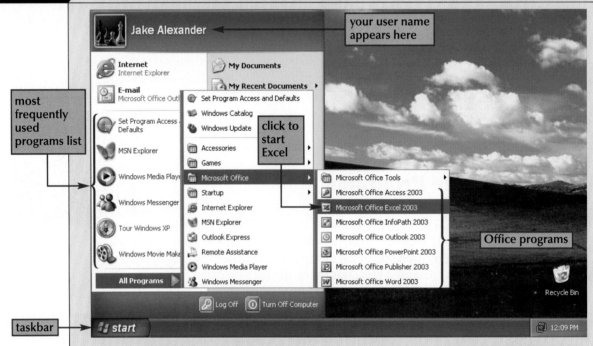

Trouble? If you don't see Microsoft Office on the All Programs menu, point to Microsoft Office Excel 2003. If you still don't see Microsoft Office Excel 2003, ask your instructor or technical support person for help.

4. Click **Microsoft Office Excel 2003** to start Excel and open a new, blank workbook. See Figure 2.

New, blank Excel workbook Figure 2

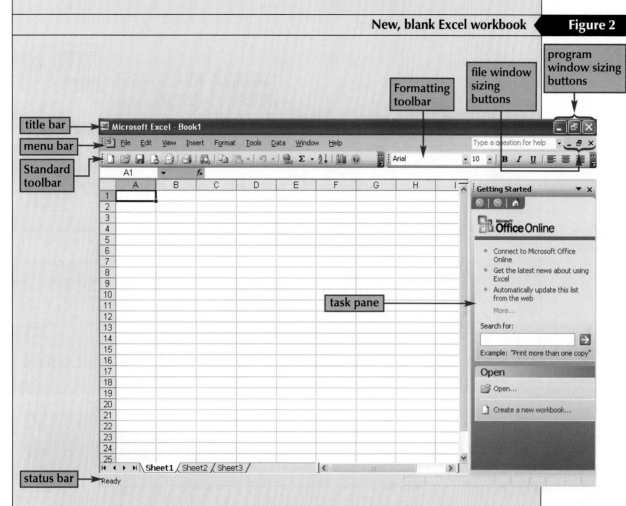

program window sizing buttons

file window sizing buttons

Formatting toolbar

title bar

menu bar

Standard toolbar

task pane

status bar

Trouble? If the Excel window doesn't fill your entire screen, the window is not maximized, or expanded to its full size. You'll maximize the window shortly.

You can have more than one Office program open at once. You'll use this same method to start Word and open a new, blank document.

To start Word and open a new, blank document:

▶ 1. Click the **Start** button on the taskbar.

▶ 2. Point to **All Programs** to display the All Programs menu.

▶ 3. Point to **Microsoft Office** on the All Programs menu.

   Trouble? If you don't see Microsoft Office on the All Programs menu, point to Microsoft Office Word 2003. If you still don't see Microsoft Office Word 2003, ask your instructor or technical support person for help.

▶ 4. Click **Microsoft Office Word 2003**. Word opens with a new, blank document. See Figure 3.

Figure 3 ▶ | **New, blank document in Word**

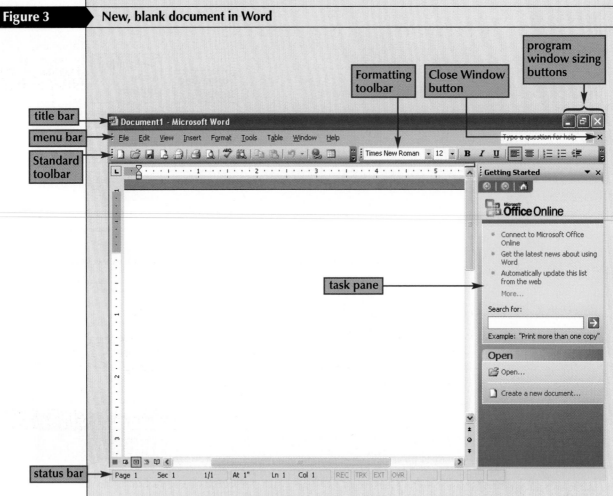

Trouble? If the Word window doesn't fill your entire screen, the window is not maximized. You'll maximize the window shortly.

When you have more than one program or file open at a time, you can switch between them.

Switching Between Open Programs and Files

Two programs are running at the same time—Excel and Word. The taskbar contains buttons for both programs. When you have two or more programs running, or two files within the same program open, you can use the taskbar buttons to switch from one program or file to another. The employees at Delmar Office Supplies often work in several programs at once.

To switch between Word and Excel:

1. Click the **Microsoft Excel – Book1** button on the taskbar to switch from Word to Excel. See Figure 4.

Excel and Word programs opened simultaneously | **Figure 4**

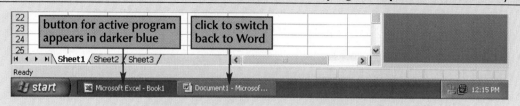

2. Click the **Document1 – Microsoft Word** button on the taskbar to return to Word.

As you can see, you can start multiple programs and switch between them in seconds.

Exploring Common Window Elements

The Office programs consist of windows that have many similar features. As you can see in Figures 2 and 3, many of the elements you see in both the Excel program window and the Word program window are the same. In fact, all the Office programs have these same elements. Figure 5 describes some of the most common window elements.

Common window elements | **Figure 5**

Element	Description
Title bar	A bar at the top of the window that contains the filename of the open file, the program name, and the program window sizing buttons
Menu bar	A collection of menus for commonly used commands
Toolbars	Collections of buttons that are shortcuts to commonly used menu commands
Sizing buttons	Buttons that resize and close the program window or the file window
Task pane	A window that provides access to commands for common tasks you'll perform in Office programs
Status bar	An area at the bottom of the program window that contains information about the open file or the current task on which you are working

Because these elements are the same in each program, once you've learned one program, it's easy to learn the others. The next sections explore the primary common features—the window sizing buttons, the menus and toolbars, and the task panes.

Using the Window Sizing Buttons

There are two sets of sizing buttons. The top set controls the program window and the bottom set controls the file window. There are three different sizing buttons. The Minimize button ▬, which is the left button, hides a window so that only its program button is visible on the taskbar. The middle button changes name and function depending on the status of the window—the Maximize button ▢ expands the window to the full screen size or to the program window size, and the Restore button ⧉ returns the window to a predefined size. The right button, the Close button ☒, exits the program or closes the file.

Most often you'll want to maximize the program and file windows as you work to take advantage of the full screen size you have available. If you have several files open, you might want to restore the files so that you can see more than one window at a time or you might want to minimize the programs with which you are not working at the moment. You'll try minimizing, maximizing, and restoring windows now.

To resize windows:

1. Click the **Minimize** button 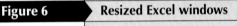 on the Word title bar to reduce the Word program window to a taskbar button. The Excel window is visible again.

2. If necessary, click the **Maximize** button on the Excel title bar. The Excel program window expands to fill the screen.

3. Click the **Restore Window** button on the Excel menu bar. The file window, referred to as the workbook window in Excel, resizes smaller than the full program window. See Figure 6.

Figure 6 ▶ **Resized Excel windows**

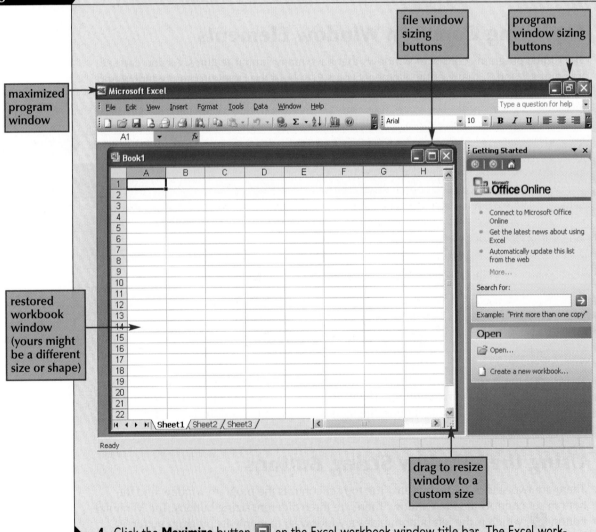

4. Click the **Maximize** button on the Excel workbook window title bar. The Excel workbook window expands to fill the program window.

5. Click the **Document1 - Microsoft Word** button on the taskbar. The Word program window returns to its previous size.

6. If necessary, click the **Maximize** button 🔲 on the Word title bar. The Word program window expands to fill the screen.

The sizing buttons give you the flexibility to arrange the program and file windows on your screen to best fit your needs.

Using Menus and Toolbars

In each Office program, you can perform tasks using a menu command, a toolbar button, or a keyboard shortcut. A **menu command** is a word on a menu that you click to execute a task; a **menu** is a group of related commands. For example, the File menu contains commands for managing files, such as the Open command and the Save command. The File, Edit, View, Insert, Format, Tools, Window, and Help menus appear on the menu bar in all the Office programs, although some of the commands they include differ from program to program. Other menus are program specific, such as the Table menu in Word and the Data menu in Excel.

A **toolbar** is a collection of buttons that correspond to commonly used menu commands. For example, the Standard toolbar contains an Open button and a Save button. The Standard and Formatting toolbars (as well as other toolbars) appear in all the Office programs, although some of the buttons they include differ from program to program. The Standard toolbar has buttons related to working with files. The Formatting toolbar has buttons related to changing the appearance of content. Each program also has program-specific toolbars, such as the Tables and Borders toolbar in Word for working with tables and the Chart toolbar in Excel for working with graphs and charts.

A **keyboard shortcut** is a combination of keys you press to perform a command. For example, Ctrl+S is the keyboard shortcut for the Save command (you hold down the Ctrl key while you press the S key). Keyboard shortcuts appear to the right of many menu commands.

Viewing Personalized Menus and Toolbars

When you first use a newly installed Office program, the menus and toolbars display only the basic and most commonly used commands and buttons, streamlining the program window. The other commands and buttons are available, but you have to click an extra button to see them (the Expand button on a menu and the Toolbar Options button on a toolbar). As you select commands and click buttons, the ones you use often are put on the short, personalized menu and on the visible part of the toolbars. The ones you don't use remain available on the full menus and toolbars. This means that the Office menus and toolbars might display different commands and buttons on each person's computer.

To view a personalized and full menu:

1. Click **Insert** on the Word menu bar to display the short, personalized menu. See Figure 7. The Bookmark command, for example, does not appear on the short menu.

Figure 7 Short, personalized menu

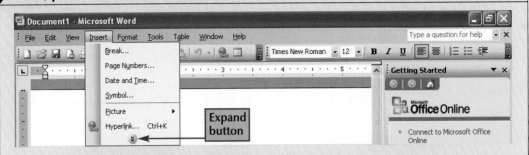

Trouble? If the Insert menu displays different commands than those shown in Figure 7, you need to reset the menus. Click Tools on the menu bar, click Customize (you might need to pause until the full menu appears to see the command), and then click the Options tab in the Customize dialog box. Click the Always show full menus check box to remove the check mark, if necessary, and then click the Show full menus after a short delay check box to insert a check mark, if necessary. Click the Reset menu and toolbar usage data button, and then click the Yes button to confirm that you want to reset the commands. Click the Close button. Repeat Step 1.

You can display the full menu in one of three ways: (1) pause until the full menu appears, which might happen as you read this; (2) click the Expand button at the bottom of the menu; or (3) double-click the menu name on the menu bar.

2. Pause until the full Insert menu appears, as shown in Figure 8. The Bookmark command and other commands are now visible.

Figure 8 Full, expanded menu

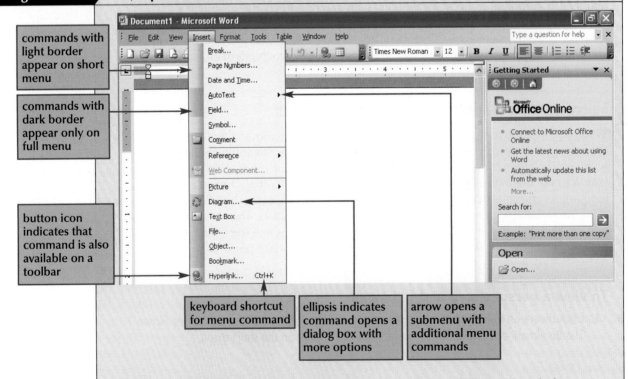

3. Click the **Bookmark** command. A dialog box opens when you click a command whose name is followed by an ellipsis (...). In this case, the Bookmark dialog box opens.

4. Click the **Cancel** button to close the Bookmark dialog box.

5. Click **Insert** on the menu bar again to display the short, personalized menu. The Bookmark command appears on the short, personalized menu because you have recently used it.

6. Press the **Esc** key on the keyboard twice to close the menu.

As you can see, the menu changed based on your actions. Over time, only the commands you use frequently will appear on the personalized menu. The toolbars work similarly.

To use the personalized toolbars:

1. Observe that the Standard and Formatting toolbars appear side by side below the menu bar.

   Trouble? If the toolbars appear on two rows, you need to reset them to their default state. Click Tools on the menu bar, click Customize, and then click the Options tab in the Customize dialog box. Click the Show Standard and Formatting toolbars on two rows check box to remove the check mark. Click the Reset menu and toolbar usage data button, and then click the Yes button to confirm you want to reset the commands. Click the Close button. Repeat Step 1.

2. Click the **Toolbar Options** button ⬚ on the Standard toolbar. See Figure 9.

Toolbar Options palette ◀ **Figure 9**

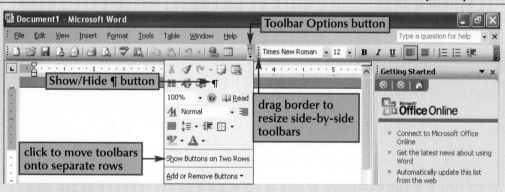

Trouble? If you see different buttons on the Toolbar Options palette, your side-by-side toolbars might be sized differently than the ones shown in Figure 9. Continue with Step 3.

3. Click the **Show/Hide ¶** button ¶ on the Toolbar Options palette to display the nonprinting screen characters. The Show/Hide ¶ button moves to the visible part of the Standard toolbar, and another button may be moved onto the Toolbar Options palette to make room for the new button.

   Trouble? If the Show/Hide ¶ button already appears on the Standard toolbar, click another button on the Toolbar Options palette. Then click that same button again in Step 4 to turn off that formatting, if necessary.

   Some buttons, like the Show/Hide ¶ button, act as a toggle switch—one click turns on the feature and a second click turns it off.

4. Click the **Show/Hide ¶** button ¶ on the Standard toolbar again to hide the nonprinting screen characters.

Some people like that the menus and toolbars change to meet their work habits. Others prefer to see all the menu commands or to display the default toolbars on two rows so that all the buttons are always visible. You'll change the toolbar setting now.

To turn off the personalized toolbars:

1. Click the **Toolbar Options** button ⬚ on the right side of the Standard toolbar.

2. Click the **Show Buttons on Two Rows** command. The toolbars move to separate rows (the Standard toolbar on top) and you can see all the buttons on each toolbar.

You can easily access any button on the Standard and Formatting toolbars with one mouse click. The drawback is that when the toolbars are displayed on two rows, they take up more space in the program window, limiting the space you have to work.

Using Task Panes

A **task pane** is a window that provides access to commands for common tasks you'll perform in Office programs. For example, the Getting Started task pane, which opens when you first start any Office program, enables you to create new files and open existing ones. Task panes also help you navigate through more complex, multi-step procedures. All the Office programs include the task panes described in Figure 10. The other available task panes vary by program.

Figure 10 ▶ **Common task panes**

Task pane	Description
Getting Started	The home task pane; allows you to create new files, open existing files, search the online and offline Help system by keyword, and access Office online
Help	Allows you to search the online and offline Help system by keyword or table of contents, and access Microsoft Office Online
Search Results	Displays available Help topics related to entered keyword and enables you to initiate a new search
New	Allows you to create new files; name changes to New Document in Word, New Workbook in Excel, New File in Access, and New Presentation in PowerPoint
Clip Art	Allows you to search for all types of media clips (pictures, sound, video) and insert clips from the results
Clipboard	Allows you to paste some or all of the items that have been cut or copied from any Office program during the current work session
Research	Allows you to search a variety of reference material and other resources from within a file

No matter what their purpose, you use the same processes to open, close, and navigate between the task panes.

Opening and Closing Task Panes

When you first start any Office program, the Getting Started task pane opens by default along the right edge of the program window. You can resize or move the task pane to suit your work habits. You can also close the task pane to display the open file in the full available program window. For example, you might want to close the task pane when you are typing the body of a letter in Word or entering a lot of data in Excel.

You will open and close the task pane.

To open and close the task pane:

▶ 1. If necessary, click **View** on the menu bar, and then click **Task Pane**. The most recently viewed task pane opens on the right side of the screen. See Figure 11.

Getting Started task pane ◀ Figure 11

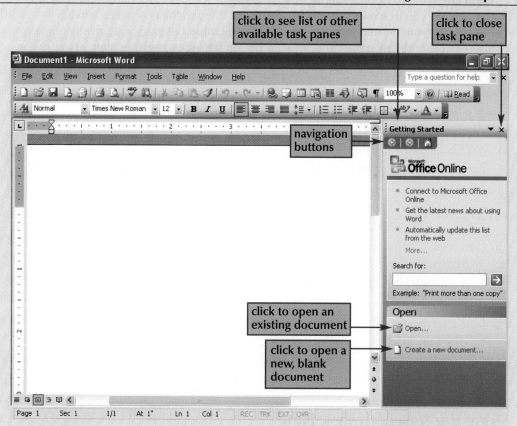

Trouble? If you do not see the task pane, you probably closed the open task pane in Step 1. Repeat Step 1 to reopen the task pane.

Trouble? If a different task pane than the Getting Started task pane opens, then another task pane was the most recently viewed task pane. You'll learn how to open different task panes in the next section; continue with Step 2.

▶ 2. Click the **Close** button ⊠ on the task pane title bar. The task pane closes, leaving more room on the screen for the open file.

▶ 3. Click **View** on the menu bar, and then click **Task Pane**. The task pane reopens.

There are several ways to display different task panes.

Navigating Among Task Panes

Once the task pane is open, you can display different task panes to suit the task you are trying to complete. For example, you can display the New task pane when you want to create a new file from a template. The name of the New task pane varies, depending on the program you are using: Word has the New Document task pane, Excel has the New Workbook task pane, PowerPoint has the New Presentation task pane, and Access has the New File task pane.

One of the quickest ways to display a task pane is to use the Other Task Panes button. When you point to the name of the open task pane in the task pane title bar, it becomes the Other Task Panes button. When you click the Other Task Panes button, all the available task panes for that Office program are listed. Just click the name of the task pane you want to display to switch to that task pane.

There are three navigation buttons at the top of the task pane. The Back and Forward buttons enable you to scroll backward and forward through the task panes you have opened during your current work session. The Back button becomes available when you display two or more task panes. The Forward button becomes available after you click the Back button to return to a previously viewed task pane. The Home button returns you to the Getting Started task pane no matter which task pane is currently displayed.

You'll use each of these methods to navigate among the task panes.

To navigate among task panes:

▶ 1. Point to **Getting Started** in the task pane title bar. The title bar becomes the Other Task Panes button.

▶ 2. Click the **Other Task Panes** button. A list of the available task panes for Word is displayed. The check mark before Getting Started indicates that this is the currently displayed task pane.

▶ 3. Click **New Document**. The New Document task pane appears and the Back button is available.

▶ 4. Click the **Back** button 🔄 in the task pane. The Getting Started task pane reappears and the Forward button is available.

▶ 5. Click the **Forward** button 🔄 in the task pane. The New Document task pane reappears and the Back button is available.

▶ 6. Click the **Home** button 🏠 in the task pane. The Getting Started task pane reappears.

Using the Research Task Pane

The Research task pane allows you to search a variety of reference materials and other resources to find specific information while you are working on a file. You can insert the information you find directly into your open file. The thesaurus and language translation tools are installed with Office and therefore are stored locally on your computer. If you are connected to the Internet, you can also use the Research task pane to access a dictionary, an encyclopedia, research sites, as well as business and financial sources. Some of the sites that appear in the search results are fee-based, meaning that you'll need to pay to access information on that site.

To use the Research task pane, you type a keyword or phrase into the Search for text box and then select whether you want to search all the books, sites, and sources; one category; or a specific source. The search results appear in the Research task pane. Some of the results appear as links, which you can click to open your browser window and display that information. If you are using Internet Explorer 5.01 or later as your Web browser, the Research task pane is tiled (appears side by side) with your document. If you are using another Web browser, you'll need to return to the task pane in your open file to click another link.

The Research task pane functions independently in each file. So you can open multiple files and perform a different search in each. In addition, each Research task pane stores the results of up to 10 searches, so you can quickly return to the results from any of your most recent searches. To move among the saved searches, click the Back and Forward buttons in the task pane.

Using the Research Task Pane

- Type a keyword or phrase into the Search for text box.
- Select a search category, individual source, or all references.
- If necessary, click a link in the search results to display more information.
- Copy and paste selected content from the task pane into your file.

Jake plans to send a copy of the next quarter's sales report to the office in France. You'll use the bilingual dictionaries in the Research task pane to begin entering labels in French into an Excel workbook for the sales report.

To use the bilingual dictionaries in the Research task pane:

1. Click the **Microsoft Excel – Book1** button on the taskbar to switch to the Excel window.

2. Click the **Other Task Panes** button on the Getting Started task pane, and then click **Research**. The Research task pane opens.

3. Click in the **Search for** text box, and then type **paper**.

4. Click the **Search for** list arrow and then click **Translation**. The bilingual dictionary opens in the Research task pane. You can choose from among 12 languages to translate to and from, including Japanese, Russian, Spanish, Dutch, German, and French.

   Trouble? If a dialog box opens stating the translation feature is not installed, click the Yes button to install it.

5. If necessary, click the **To** list arrow, and then click **French (France)**. See Figure 12.

Research task pane | **Figure 12**

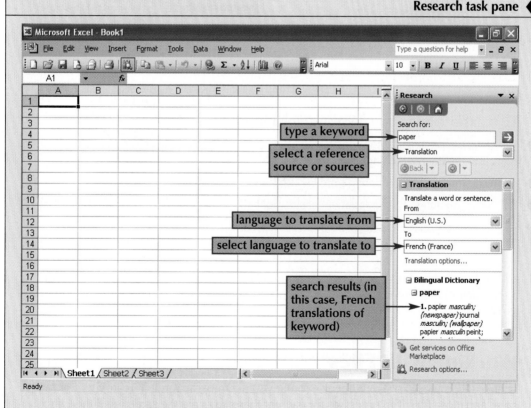

6. Scroll to read the different translations of "paper" in French.

After you locate specific information, you can quickly insert it into your open file. The information can be inserted by copying the selected content you want to insert, and then pasting it in the appropriate location in your file. In some instances, such as MSN Money Stock Quotes, a button appears enabling you to quickly insert the indicated information in your file at the location of the insertion point. Otherwise, you can use the standard Copy and Paste commands.

You'll copy the translation for "paper" into the Excel workbook.

To copy information from the Research task pane into a file:

▶ 1. Select **papier** in the Research task pane. This is the word you want to copy to the workbook.

▶ 2. Right-click the selected text, and then click **Copy** on the shortcut menu. The text is duplicated on the Office Clipboard.

▶ 3. Right-click cell **A1**, and then click **Paste**. The word "papier" is entered into the cell. See Figure 13.

Figure 13 ▶ Translation copied into Excel

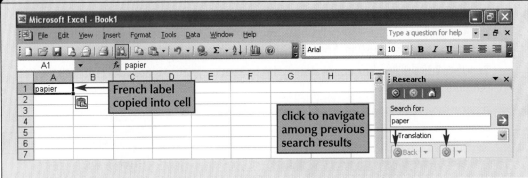

You'll repeat this process to look up the translation for "furniture" and copy it into cell A2.

To translate and copy another word into Excel:

▶ 1. Double-click **paper** in the Search for text box to select the text, type **furniture**, and then click the **Start searching** button ➡ in the Research task pane.

▶ 2. Verify that you're translating from English (U.S) to French (France).

▶ 3. Select **meubles** in the translation results, right-click the selected text, and then click **Copy**.

▶ 4. Right-click cell **A2**, and then click **Paste**. The second label appears in the cell.

The Research task pane works similarly in all the Office programs. You'll use other task panes later in this tutorial to perform specific tasks, including opening a file and getting assistance.

Working with Files

The most common tasks you'll perform in any Office program are to create, open, save, and close files. The processes for each of these tasks are the same in all the Office programs. In addition, there are several methods for performing most tasks in Office. This flexibility enables you to use Office in a way that fits how you like to work.

Creating a File

To begin working in a program, you need to create a new file or open an existing file. When you start Word, Excel, or PowerPoint, the program opens along with a blank file—ready for you to begin working on a new document, workbook, or presentation. When you start Access, the Getting Started task pane opens, displaying options for opening a new database or an existing one.

Jake has asked you to start working on the agenda for the stockholder meeting, which he suggests you create using Word. You enter text in a Word document by typing.

To enter text in a document:

1. Click the **Document1 – Microsoft Word** button on the taskbar to activate the Word program window.

2. Type **Delmar Office Supplies**, and then press the **Enter** key. The text you typed appears on one line in the Word document.

   Trouble? If you make a typing error, press the Backspace key to delete the incorrect letters, and then retype the text.

3. Type **Stockholder Meeting Agenda**, and then press the **Enter** key. The text you typed appears on the second line.

Next, you'll save the file.

Saving a File

As you create and modify Office files, your work is stored only in the computer's temporary memory, not on a hard disk. If you were to exit the programs, turn off your computer, or experience a power failure, your work would be lost. To prevent losing work, save your file to a disk frequently—at least every 10 minutes. You can save files to the hard disk located inside your computer or to portable storage disks, such as floppy disks, Zip disks, or read-write CD-ROMs.

The first time you save a file, you need to name it. This name is called a **filename**. When you choose a filename, select a descriptive one that accurately reflects the content of the document, workbook, presentation, or database, such as "Shipping Options Letter" or "Fourth Quarter Financial Analysis." Filenames can include a maximum of 255 letters, numbers, hyphens, and spaces in any combination. Office appends a **file extension** to the filename, which identifies the program in which that file was created. The file extensions are .doc for Word, .xls for Excel, .ppt for PowerPoint, and .mdb for Access. Whether you see file extensions depends on how Windows is set up on your computer.

You also need to decide where to save the file—on which disk and in what folder. A **folder** is a container for your files. Just as you organize paper documents within folders stored in a filing cabinet, you can organize your files within folders stored on your computer's hard disk or a removable disk. Store each file in a logical location that you will remember whenever you want to use the file again.

Reference Window	Saving a File

- Click the Save button on the Standard toolbar (*or* click File on the menu bar, and then click Save or Save As).
- In the Save As dialog box, click the Save in list arrow, and then navigate to the location where you want to save the file.
- Type a filename in the File name text box.
- Click the Save button.
- To resave the named file to the same location, click the Save button on the Standard toolbar (*or* click File on the menu bar, and then click Save).

The two lines of text you typed are not yet saved on disk. You'll do that now.

To save a file for the first time:

1. Click the **Save** button 🖫 on the Standard toolbar. The Save As dialog box opens. The first few words of the first line appear in the File name text box, as a suggested filename. You'll replace this with a more descriptive filename.

2. Click the **Save in** list arrow, and then click the location that contains your Data Files.

   Trouble? If you don't have the Common Office Features Data Files, you need to get them before you can proceed. Your instructor will either give you the Data Files or ask you to obtain them from a specified location (such as a network drive). In either case, be sure that you make a backup copy of your Data Files before you start using them, so that the original files will be available on your copied disk in case you need to start over because of an error or problem. If you have any questions about the Data Files, see your instructor or technical support person for assistance.

3. Double-click the **OFF** folder in the list box, and then double-click the **Tutorial** folder. This is the location where you want to save the document. See Figure 14.

4. Type **Stockholder Meeting Agenda** in the File name text box.

Figure 14	Completed Save As dialog box

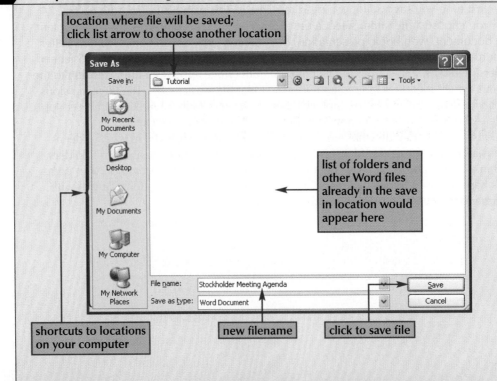

location where file will be saved;
click list arrow to choose another location

list of folders and other Word files already in the save in location would appear here

shortcuts to locations on your computer

new filename

click to save file

Trouble? If the .doc file extension appears after the filename, then your computer is configured to show file extensions. Continue with Step 5.

5. Click the **Save** button. The Save As dialog box closes, and the name of your file appears in the program window title bar.

The saved file includes everything in the document at the time you last saved it. Any edits or additions you then make to the document exist only in the computer's memory and are not saved in the file on the disk. As you work, remember to save frequently so that the file is updated to reflect the latest content of the document.

Because you already named the document and selected a storage location, the second and subsequent times you save, the Save As dialog box doesn't open. If you wanted to save a copy of the file with a different filename or to a different location, you would reopen the Save As dialog box by clicking File on the menu bar, and then clicking Save As. The previous version of the file remains on your disk as well.

You need to add your name to the agenda. Then you'll save your changes.

To modify and save a file:

1. Type your name, and then press the **Enter** key. The text you typed appears on the next line.
2. Click the **Save** button 🔲 on the Standard toolbar to save your changes.

When you're done with a file, you can close it.

Closing a File

Although you can keep multiple files open at one time, you should close any file you are no longer working on to conserve system resources as well as to ensure that you don't inadvertently make changes to the file. You can close a file by clicking the Close command on the File menu or by clicking the Close Window button in the upper-right corner of the menu bar.

As a standard practice, you should save your file before closing it. If you're unsure whether the file is saved, it cannot hurt to save it again. However, Office has an added safeguard: If you attempt to close a file or exit a program without saving your changes, a dialog box opens asking whether you want to save the file. Click the Yes button to save the changes to the file before closing the file and program. Click the No button to close the file and program without saving changes. Click the Cancel button to return to the program window without saving changes or closing the file and program. This feature helps to ensure that you always save the most current version of any file.

You'll add the date to the agenda. Then, you'll attempt to close the document without saving.

To modify and close a file:

1. Type the date, and then press the **Enter** key. The text you typed appears under your name in the document.
2. Click the **Close Window** button ☒ on the Word menu bar to close the document. A dialog box opens, asking whether you want to save the changes you made to the document.

3. Click the **Yes** button. The current version of the document is saved to the file, and then the document closes, and Word is still running.

   Trouble? If Word is not running, then you closed the program in Step 2. Start Word, click the Close Window button on the menu bar to close the blank document.

Once you have a program open, you can create additional new files for the open program or you can open previously created and saved files.

Opening a File

When you want to open a blank document, workbook, presentation, or database, you create a new file. When you want to work on a previously created file, you must first open it. Opening a file transfers a copy of the file from the storage disk (either a hard disk or a portable disk) to the computer's memory and displays it on your screen. The file is then in your computer's memory and on the disk.

| Reference Window | **Opening an Existing or a New File** |

- Click the Open button on the Standard toolbar (*or* click File on the menu bar, and then click Open *or* click the More link in the Open section of the Getting Started task pane).
- In the Open dialog box, click the Look in list arrow, and then navigate to the storage location of the file you want to open.
- Click the filename of the file you want to open.
- Click the Open button.

or

- Click the New button on the Standard toolbar (*or* click File on the menu bar, click New, and then (depending on the program) click the Blank document, Blank workbook, Blank presentation, or Blank database link in the New task pane).

Jake asks you to print the agenda. To do that, you'll reopen the file. You'll use the Open button on the Standard toolbar.

To open an existing file:

1. Click the **Open** button 📄 on the Standard toolbar. The Open dialog box, which works similarly to the Save As dialog box, opens.

2. Click the **Look in** list arrow, and then navigate to the **OFF\Tutorial** folder included with your Data Files. This is the location where you saved the agenda document.

3. Click **Stockholder Meeting Agenda** in the file list. See Figure 15.

Open dialog box ◄ **Figure 15**

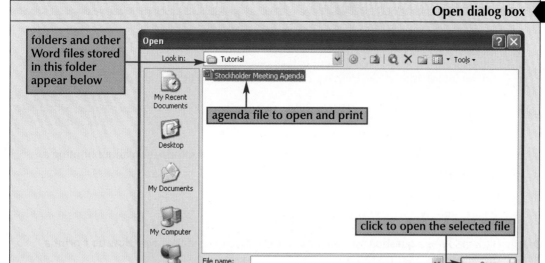

folders and other Word files stored in this folder appear below

agenda file to open and print

click to open the selected file

4. Click the **Open** button. The file containing the agenda opens in the Word program window.

Next, you'll get information about printing files in Word.

Getting Help

If you don't know how to perform a task or want more information about a feature, you can turn to Office itself for information on how to use it. This information, referred to simply as **Help**, is like a huge encyclopedia available from your desktop. You can access Help in a variety of ways, including ScreenTips, the Type a question for help box, the Help task pane, and Microsoft Office Online.

Using ScreenTips

ScreenTips are a fast and simple method you can use to get help about objects you see on the screen. A **ScreenTip** is a yellow box with the button's name. Just position the mouse pointer over a toolbar button to view its ScreenTip.

Using the Type a Question for Help Box

For answers to specific questions, you can use the **Type a question for help box**, located on the menu bar of every Office program, to find information in the Help system. You simply type a question using everyday language about a task you want to perform or a topic you need help with, and then press the Enter key to search the Help system. The Search Results task pane opens with a list of Help topics related to your query. You click a topic to open a Help window with step-by-step instructions that guide you through a specific procedure and explanations of difficult concepts in clear, easy-to-understand language. For example, you might ask how to format a cell in an Excel worksheet; a list of Help topics related to the words you typed will appear.

Getting Help from the Type a Question for Help Box

- Click the Type a question for help box on the menu bar.
- Type your question, and then press the Enter key.
- Click a Help topic in the Search Results task pane.
- Read the information in the Help window. For more information, click other topics or links.
- Click the Close button on the Help window title bar.

You'll use the Type a question for help box to obtain more information about printing a document in Word.

To use the Type a question for help box:

1. Click the **Type a question for help box** on the menu bar, and then type **How do I print a document?**

2. Press the **Enter** key to retrieve a list of topics. The Search Results task pane opens with a list of topics related to your query. See Figure 16.

Figure 16 Search Results task pane displaying Help topics

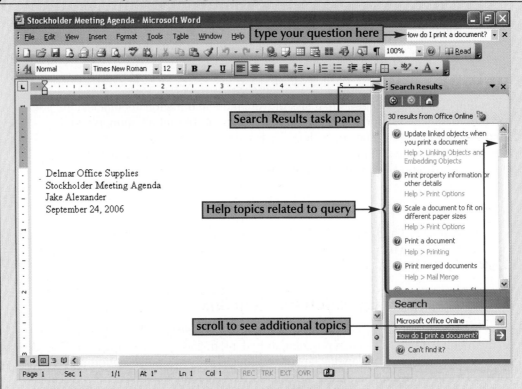

Trouble? If your search results list differs from the one shown in Figure 16, your computer is not connected to the Internet or Microsoft has updated the list of available Help topics since this book was published. Continue with Step 3.

3. Scroll through the list to review the Help topics.

4. Click **Print a document** to open the Help window and learn more about the various ways to print a document. See Figure 17.

Print a document Help window ◀ **Figure 17**

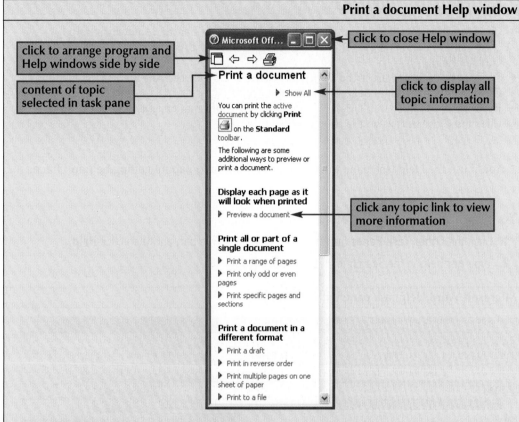

click to arrange program and Help windows side by side

content of topic selected in task pane

click to close Help window

click to display all topic information

click any topic link to view more information

Trouble? If the Word program window and the Help window do not appear side by side, then you need to tile the windows. Click the Auto Tile button on the toolbar in the Help window.

▶ **5.** Read the information, and then when you're done, click the **Close** button ⊠ on the Help window title bar to close the Help window.

The Help task pane works similarly.

Using the Help Task Pane

For more in-depth help, you can use the **Help task pane**, a task pane that enables you to search the Help system using keywords or phrases. You type a specific word or phrase in the Search for text box, and then click the Start searching button. The Search Results task pane opens with a list of topics related to the keyword or phrase you entered. If your computer is connected to the Internet, you might see more search results because some Help topics are stored only online and not locally on your computer. The task pane also has a Table of Contents link that organizes the Help system by subjects and topics, like in a book. You click main subject links to display related topic links.

Reference Window	**Getting Help from the Help Task Pane**

- Click the Other Task Panes button on the task pane title bar, and then click Help (*or* click Help on the menu bar, and then click Microsoft Word/Excel/PowerPoint/Access/Outlook Help).
- Type a keyword or phrase in the Search for text box, and then click the Start searching button.
- Click a Help topic in the Search Results task pane.
- Read the information in the Help window. For more information, click other topics or links.
- Click the Close button on the Help window title bar.

You'll use the Help task pane to obtain more information about getting help in Office.

To use the Help task pane:

1. Click the **Other Task Panes** button on the task pane title bar, and then click **Help**.
2. Type **get help** in the Search for text box. See Figure 18.

Figure 18	**Microsoft Word Help task pane with keyword**

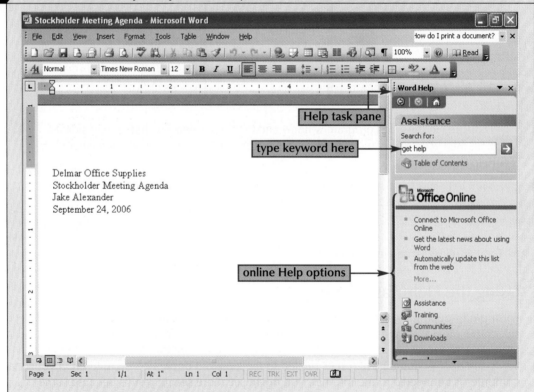

3. Click the **Start searching** button →. The Search Results task pane opens with a list of topics related to your keywords.
4. Scroll through the list to review the Help topics.
5. Click **About getting help while you work** to open the Microsoft Word Help window and learn more about the various ways to obtain help in Word. See Figure 19.

About getting help while you work Help window ◄ **Figure 19**

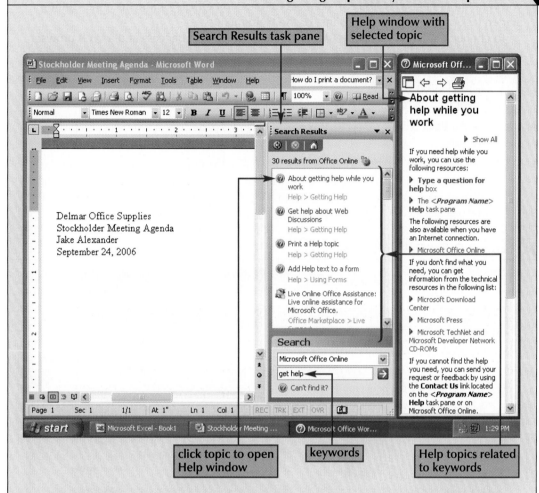

Trouble? If your search results list differs from the one shown in Figure 19, your computer is not connected to the Internet or Microsoft has updated the list of available Help topics since this book was published. Continue with Step 6.

Trouble? If the Word program window and the Help window do not appear side by side, then you need to tile the windows. Click the Auto Tile button on the toolbar in the Help window.

► **6.** Click **Microsoft Office Online** in the right pane to display information about that topic. Read the information.

► **7.** Click the other links about this feature and read the information.

► **8.** When you're done, click the **Close** button ⊠ on the Help window title bar to close the Help window. The task pane remains open.

If your computer has a connection to the Internet, you can get more help information from Microsoft Office Online.

Using Microsoft Office Online

Microsoft Office Online is a Web site maintained by Microsoft that provides access to additional Help resources. For example, you can access current Help topics, read how-to articles, and find tips for using Office. You can search all or part of a site to find information about tasks you want to perform, features you want to use, or anything else you want more help with. You can connect to Microsoft Office Online from the Getting Started task pane, the Help task pane, or the Help menu.

To connect to Microsoft Office Online, you'll need Internet access and a Web browser such as Internet Explorer.

To connect to Microsoft Office Online:

1. Click the **Back** button ⬅ in the Search Results task pane. The Word Help task pane reappears.

2. Click the **Connect to Microsoft Office Online** link in the task pane. Internet Explorer starts and the Microsoft Office Online home page opens. See Figure 20. This Web page offers links to Web pages focusing on getting help and for accessing additional Office resources, such as additional galleries of clip art, software downloads, and training opportunities.

| Figure 20 | Microsoft Office Online home page |

Trouble? If the content you see on the Microsoft Office Online home page differs from the figure, the site has been updated since this book was published. Continue with Step 3.

3. Click the **Assistance** link. The Assistance page opens. From this page, you browse for help in each of the different Office programs. You can also enter a keyword or phrase pertaining to a particular topic you wish to search for information on using the Search box in the upper-right corner of the window.

4. Click the **Close** button ☒ on the Internet Explorer title bar to close the browser.

The Help features enable the staff at Delmar Office Supplies to get answers to questions they have about any task or procedure when they need it. The more you practice getting information from the Help system, the more effective you will be at using Office to its full potential.

Printing a File

At times, you'll want a paper copy of your Office file. The first time you print during each session at the computer, you should use the Print menu command to open the Print dialog box so you can verify or adjust the printing settings. You can select a printer, the number of copies to print, the portion of the file to print, and so forth; the printing settings vary slightly from program to program. For subsequent print jobs, you can use the Print button to print without opening the dialog box, if you want to use the same default settings.

Printing a File	Reference Window

- Click File on the menu bar, and then click Print.
- Verify the print settings in the Print dialog box.
- Click the OK button.

or

- Click the Print button on the Standard toolbar.

Now that you know how to print, you'll print the agenda for Jake.

To print a file:

▶ **1.** Make sure your printer is turned on and contains paper.

▶ **2.** Click **File** on the menu bar, and then click **Print**. The Print dialog box opens. See Figure 21.

Print dialog box | **Figure 21**

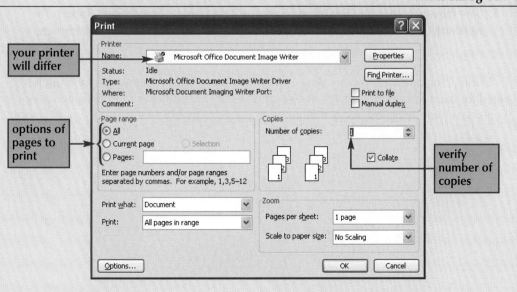

3. Verify that the correct printer appears in the Name list box in the Printer area. If the wrong printer appears, click the **Name** list arrow, and then click the correct printer from the list of available printers.

4. Verify that **1** appears in the Number of copies text box.

5. Click the **OK** button to print the document.

Trouble? If the document does not print, see your instructor or technical support person for help.

Now that you have printed the agenda, you can close Word and Excel.

Exiting Programs

Whenever you finish working with a program, you should exit it. As with many other aspects of Office, you can exit programs with a button or from a menu. You'll use both methods to close Word and Excel. You can use the Exit command to exit a program and close an open file in one step. If you haven't saved the final version of the open file, a dialog box opens, asking whether you want to save your changes. Clicking the Yes button saves the open file, closes the file, and then exits the program.

To exit a program:

1. Click the **Close** button ⊠ on the Word title bar to exit Word. The Word document closes and the Word program exits. The Excel window is visible again on your screen.

   Trouble? If a dialog box opens, asking whether you want to save the document, you may have inadvertently made a change to the document. Click the No button.

2. Click **File** on the Excel menu bar, and then click **Exit**. A dialog box opens asking whether you want to save the changes you made to the workbook.

3. Click the **Yes** button. The Save As dialog box opens.

4. Save the workbook in the **OFF\Tutorial** folder with the filename **French Sales Report**. The workbook closes, saving a copy to the location you specified, and the Excel program exits.

Exiting programs after you are done using them keeps your Windows desktop unclut-tered for the next person using the computer, frees up your system's resources, and prevents data from being lost accidentally.

Review

Quick Check

1. List the five programs included in Office.
2. How do you start an Office program?
3. Explain the difference between Save As and Save.
4. What is one method for opening an existing Office file?
5. What happens if you attempt to close a file or exit a program without saving the current version of the open file?
6. What are four ways to get help?

To reinforce the tasks you learned in this tutorial, go to the SAM 2003 Training Companion CD included with this text.

Review

Tutorial Summary

You have learned how to use features common to all the programs included in Microsoft Office 2003, including starting and exiting programs; resizing windows; using menus and toolbars; working with task panes; saving, opening, closing, and printing files; and getting help.

Key Terms

Access	menu	Outlook
database	menu bar	PowerPoint
document	menu command	presentation
Excel	Microsoft Access 2003	ScreenTip
file extension	Microsoft Excel 2003	task pane
filename	Microsoft Office 2003	toolbar
folder	Microsoft Office Online	Type a question for help box
Help	Microsoft Outlook 2003	Word
Help task pane	Microsoft PowerPoint 2003	workbook
integration	Microsoft Word 2003	
keyboard shortcut	Office	

Practice

Review Assignments

Practice the skills you learned in the tutorial using the same case scenario.

Data Files needed for the Review Assignments: Finances.xls, Letter.doc

Before the stockholders meeting at Delmar Office Supplies, you'll open and print documents for the upcoming presentation. Complete the following steps:

1. Start PowerPoint.
2. Use the Help task pane to learn how to change the toolbar buttons from small to large, and then do it. Use the same procedure to change the buttons back to regular size. Close the Help window when you're done.
3. Start Excel.
4. Switch to the PowerPoint window using the taskbar, and then close the presentation but leave open the PowerPoint program. (*Hint:* Click the Close Window button on the menu bar.)
5. Open a new, blank PowerPoint presentation from the Getting Started task pane. (*Hint:* Click Create a new presentation in the Open section of the Getting Started task pane.)

6. Close the PowerPoint presentation and program using the Close button on the PowerPoint title bar; do not save changes if asked.
7. Open the **Finances** workbook located in the **OFF\Review** folder included with your Data Files using the Open button on the Standard toolbar in Excel.
8. Use the Save As command to save the workbook as **Delmar Finances** in the **OFF\Review** folder.
9. Type your name, press the Enter key to insert your name at the top of the worksheet, and then save the workbook.
10. Print one copy of the worksheet using the Print command on the File menu.
11. Exit Excel using the File menu.
12. Start Word, and then use the Getting Started task pane to open the **Letter** document located in the **OFF\Review** folder included with your Data Files. (*Hint:* Click the More link in the Getting Started task pane to open the Open dialog box.)
13. Use the Save As command to save the document with the filename **Delmar Letter** in the **OFF\Review** folder.
14. Press and hold the Ctrl key, press the End key, and then release both keys to move the insertion point to the end of the letter, and then type your name.
15. Use the Save button on the Standard toolbar to save the change to the Delmar Letter document.
16. Print one copy of the document, and then close the document.
17. Exit the Word program using the Close button on the title bar.

SAM Assessment and Training

If your instructor has chosen to use the full online version of SAM 2003 Assessment and Training, you can go beyond the "just-in-time" training provided on the CD that accompanies this text. Simply log in to your SAM account (http://sam2003.course.com) to launch any assigned training activities or exams that relate to the skills covered in this tutorial.

Quick Check Answers

1. Word, Excel, PowerPoint, Access, Outlook
2. Click the Start button on the taskbar, point to All Programs, point to Microsoft Office, and then click the name of the program you want to open.
3. Save As enables you to change the filename and storage location of a file. Save updates a file to reflect its latest contents using its current filename and location.
4. Either click the Open button on the Standard toolbar or click the More link in the Getting Started task pane to open the Open dialog box.
5. A dialog box opens asking whether you want to save the changes to the file.
6. ScreenTips, Type a question for help box, Help task pane, Microsoft Office Online

New Perspectives on
Microsoft® Office Word 2003

Data Files

To complete Word Tutorials 1-4, you need the starting Data Files. See the inside back or front cover for information on downloading these files from course.com, or ask your instructor for assistance. The following table identifies each starting Data File and the folder it is stored in, as well as the ending files, which you create and save in each tutorial.

Folders		Starting Files	Ending Files
Tutorial .01	Tutorial	(no starting Data Files)	Web Time Contract Letter.doc
	Review	(no starting Data Files)	Call Memo.doc
	Cases	(no starting Data Files)	Congratulations Letter.doc, HigherEdVest Letter.doc, Key Card Meeting Memo.doc, Lecture Series Letter.doc
Tutorial .02	Tutorial	FAQ.doc	Flowering Shrub FAQ.doc, Tree FAQ.doc
	Review	Statmnt.doc	Customer Service Contact.doc, Monthly Statement.doc
	Cases	Form.doc, Moths.doc, Resume.doc, Tribune.doc	Encarta Definition.doc, Formatted Resume.doc, Gypsy Moth Management.doc, Invoice Authorization Form.doc, Tribune Brochure.doc, Tribune Brochure Landscape.doc
Tutorial .03	Tutorial	WAN.doc	New Hope WAN Report.doc
	Review	Trouble.doc	Equipment List.doc, Troubleshooting Report.doc
	Cases	Budget.doc, Contacts.doc, Textiles.doc, Tour.doc	Advertising Budget.doc, Dark Sky Protocol.doc, Masterpiece Tour Report.doc, Noblewood Textiles Report.doc, Sales Contacts.doc
Tutorial .04	Tutorial	Addresses.doc, Clothes.doc, Letter.doc	Addresses.doc, Cover Letter.doc, Merged Cover Letters.doc, Travel Clothes.doc
	Review	Addresses.doc, Highlights.doc, Travel.doc	Addresses.doc, Highlights Cover Letter.doc, Merged Highlights Cover Letters.doc, Travel Highlights.doc
	Cases	Convert.doc, Hill.doc, Island.jpg, News.doc	Conversion Newsletter.doc, Flannery Newsletter.doc, Hill Star Brochure.doc, Job Search Cover Letter.doc, Job Search Cover Letter Merged.doc, Job Search Data Source.doc, Job Search Envelopes.doc, Job Search Envelopes Merged.doc

Storing Your Files

It is recommended that you store all your Data Files on a USB drive. Refer to the tutorial "Managing Your Files" for information on using USB drives. If you need to store your Data Files on floppy disks, you will need one high-density disk to store all the files for Word Tutorials 1-4.

SAM 2003 Training Companion CD

The SAM 2003 Training Companion CD that comes with this text gives you "just-in-time" training and reinforcement of important Microsoft Office skills. Look for the SAM CD logo throughout each tutorial for opportunities to complete the hands-on tasks included on this CD.

Course Labs

Word Tutorial 1 features an interactive Course Lab to help you understand word processing concepts. There are Lab Assignments at the end of Tutorial 1 that relate to this lab. Contact your instructor or technical support person for assistance in accessing this lab.

Creating a Document

Writing a Business Letter

Case | Art4U, Inc.

Megan Grahs is the owner and manager of Art4U, Inc., a graphics design firm in Tucson, Arizona. When Megan founded Art4U in the early 1980s, the company drew most of its revenue from design projects for local magazines, newspapers, advertising circulars, and other print publications. The artists at Art4U laboriously created logos, diagrams, and other illustrations by hand, using watercolors, ink, pastels, and a variety of other media. Since the advent of the Internet, however, Art4U has become one of the Southwest's leading creators of electronic artwork. The firm's artists now work exclusively on computers, saving each piece of art as an electronic file that they can e-mail to a client in a matter of minutes.

Thanks to e-mail, Art4U is no longer limited to the local Tucson market. As a result, Art4U has nearly doubled in size over the past ten years. Most of the increase in business has come from Web page designers, who continually need fresh and innovative graphics to use in their Web pages. In fact, Megan has just signed a contract with Web Time Productions agreeing to create a series of logos for a high-profile Web site. She needs to return the signed contract to Web Time Productions' office in Chicago.

In this tutorial, you will create the cover letter that will accompany the contract. You will create the letter using **Microsoft Office Word 2003** (or simply **Word**), a popular word-processing program. Before you begin typing the letter, you will learn how to start the Word program, identify and use the elements of the Word screen, and adjust some Word settings. Next, you will create a new Word document, type the text of the cover letter, save the letter, and then print the letter for Megan. In the process of entering the text, you'll learn several ways to correct typing errors.

Session	Objectives		SAM Training Tasks	
Session 1.1	• Plan a document • Identify the components of the Word window	• Choose commands using toolbars and menus • Create a new document	• Display formatting marks • Insert text • Modify default font • Open a new document window	• Save a document • Start Word • Zoom page width • Zoom text width
Session 1.2	• Scroll a document and move the insertion point • Correct errors and undo and redo changes • Save, preview, and print a document	• Enter the date with AutoComplete • Remove Smart Tags • Create an envelope	• Check spelling and grammar as you type • Close a document and exit Word • Insert a date • Insert a date with AutoComplete • Move to a specific location in a document	• Print documents • Use AutoCorrect • Use print preview • Use the Smart Tag action button • Use Undo and Redo buttons • Use Word Wrap

Student Data Files   There are no student Data Files needed for this tutorial.

For hands-on practice of key tasks in this session, go to the SAM 2003 Training Companion CD included with this text.

Four Steps to a Professional Document

Word helps you produce quality work in minimal time. Not only can you type a document in Word, but you can also quickly make revisions and corrections, adjust margins and spacing, create columns and tables, and add graphics to your documents. The most efficient way to produce a document is to follow these four steps: (1) planning, (2) creating and editing, (3) formatting, and (4) printing.

In the long run, planning saves time and effort. First, you should determine what you want to say. State your purpose clearly and include enough information to achieve that purpose without overwhelming or boring your reader. Be sure to organize your ideas logically. Decide how you want your document to look as well. In this case, your letter to Web Time Productions will take the form of a standard business letter. It should be addressed to Web Time's president, Nicholas Brower. Megan has given you a handwritten note indicating what she would like you to say in the letter. This note is shown in Figure 1-1.

Figure 1-1	Megan's notes for the contract letter

Notes for Contract Letter

Please include the following questions in the Web Time Productions cover letter:

• When will we receive a complete schedule for the project?

• How many preliminary designs do you require?

• Will you be available to discuss the project with our artists via a conference call next week?

Send the letter to Web Time Productions' president, Nicholas Brower. The address is: 2015 Dubuque Avenue, Chicago, IL 60025.

After you plan your document, you can go ahead and create and edit it using Word. Creating the document generally means typing the text of your document. Editing consists of reading the document you've created, correcting your errors, and, finally, adding or deleting text to make the document easy to read.

Once your document is error-free, you can format it to make it visually appealing. Formatting features, such as adjusting margins to create white space (blank areas of a page), setting line spacing, and using bold and italic, can help make your document easier to read.

Printing is the final phase in creating an effective document. In this tutorial, you will preview your document before you spend time and resources to print it.

Exploring the Word Window

Before you can apply these four steps to produce a letter in Word, you need to start Word and learn about the general organization of the Word window. You'll do that now.

To start Microsoft Word:

1. Click the **Start** button on the taskbar, point to **All Programs**, point to **Microsoft Office**, and then click **Microsoft Office Word 2003**. The Word window opens. See Figure 1-2.

   Trouble? If you don't see the Microsoft Office Word 2003 option on the Microsoft Office submenu, look for it in a different submenu or as an option on the All Programs menu. If you still can't find the Microsoft Office Word 2003 option, ask your instructor or technical support person for help.

Maximized Word window | Figure 1-2

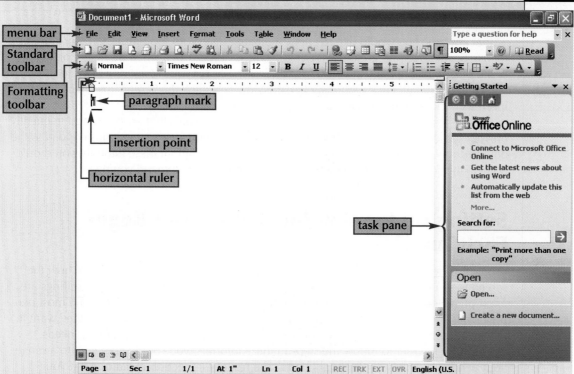

2. If the Word window does not fill the entire screen, click the **Maximize** button ▣ in the upper-right corner of the Word window. Your screen should now resemble Figure 1-2.

   Trouble? If your screen looks slightly different from Figure 1-2, just continue with the steps. You will learn how to change the appearance of the Word window shortly.

   Word is now running and ready to use. Don't be concerned if you don't see everything shown in Figure 1-2. You'll learn how to adjust the appearance of the Word window soon.

   The Word window is made up of a number of elements, which are described in Figure 1-3. You are already familiar with some of these elements, such as the menu bar and toolbars, because they are common to all Windows programs.

Figure 1-3 ▶ **Parts of the Word window**

Screen Element	Description
Formatting toolbar	Contains buttons that affect how the document looks.
horizontal ruler	Shows page margins, tabs, and column widths.
insertion point	Shows where characters will appear when you start typing.
menu bar	Contains lists, or menus, of all the Word commands. When you first display a menu, you see a short list of the most frequently used commands. To see the full list of commands in the menu, you can click the menu and then wait a few seconds for the remaining commands to appear, double-click the menu, or click the menu and then click or point to the downward-facing double-arrow at the bottom of the menu.
paragraph mark	Marks the end of a paragraph.
Standard toolbar	Contains buttons for activating frequently used commands.
task pane	Provides links and buttons that you can use to perform common tasks.

If at any time you would like to check the name of a Word toolbar button, position the mouse pointer over the button without clicking. A ScreenTip, a small box with the name of the button, will appear. (If you don't see ScreenTips on your computer, click Tools on the Word menu bar, click Options, click the View tab, click the ScreenTips check box to insert a check, and then click OK.)

Keep in mind that the menus initially display the commands that are used most frequently on your particular computer. When you leave a menu open for a few seconds or point to the double-arrow, a complete list of commands appears. Throughout these tutorials, you should point to the double-arrow on a menu if you do not see the command you need.

Setting Up the Window Before You Begin Each Tutorial

Word provides a set of standard settings, called **default settings**, which control how the screen is set up and how a document looks when you first start typing. These settings are appropriate for most situations. However, these settings are easily changed, and most people begin a work session by adjusting Word to make sure it is set up the way they want it.

As you gain experience, you will learn how to customize Word to suit your needs. But to make it easier to follow the steps in these tutorials, you should take care to arrange your window to match the tutorial figures. The rest of this section explains what your window should look like and how to make it match those in the tutorials. Depending on how many people use your computer (and how much they adjust Word's appearance), you might have to set up the window to match the figures each time you start Word.

Setting the Document View to Normal

The View buttons in the lower-left corner of the Word window change the way your document is displayed. You will learn how to select the appropriate view for a document in a later tutorial. For now, you want the document displayed in Normal view.

To make sure the document is displayed in Normal view:

▶ **1.** Click the **Normal View** button ▤ to the left of the horizontal scroll bar. See Figure 1-4. If your Document window was not in Normal view, it changes to Normal view now. The Normal View button is now highlighted, indicating that it is selected.

Changing to Normal view ◀ **Figure 1-4**

Displaying the Toolbars, Task Pane, and Ruler

The Word toolbars allow you to perform common tasks quickly by clicking a button. To eliminate on-screen clutter while you work through these tutorials, you should check to make sure that only the Formatting and Standard toolbars appear on your screen. The Standard toolbar should be positioned on top of the Formatting toolbar, as shown previously in Figure 1-2.

Depending on the choices made by the last person to use your computer, you may not see both toolbars or you may see both toolbars on one row. You also may see additional toolbars. In the following steps, you will make sure that your Word window shows only the Standard and Formatting toolbars. At the same time, you will verify that the task pane is displayed as it is in Figure 1-2.

To verify that your Word window shows the correct toolbars and the task pane:

▶ **1.** Position the pointer over any toolbar and click the right mouse button. A shortcut menu appears. The menu lists all available toolbars with a check mark next to those currently displayed. If the Standard and Formatting toolbars are currently displayed on your computer, you should see check marks next to their names. You should also see a check mark next to "Task Pane," indicating that the task pane is displayed on the right side of the screen. (You saw the task pane earlier in Figure 1-2.)

▶ **2.** Verify that you see a check mark next to the word "Standard" in the shortcut menu. If you do not see a check mark, click **Standard** now. (Clicking any item on the shortcut menu closes the menu, so you will need to re-open it in the next step.)

▶ **3.** Redisplay the shortcut menu, and click **Formatting** if you don't see a check mark next to it.

▶ **4.** If you don't see the task pane, click View on the menu bar and then click **Task Pane**.

▶ **5.** Redisplay the shortcut menu. If any toolbar besides the Formatting and Standard toolbars is open, click the toolbar name to remove the check mark and hide the toolbar.

Trouble? If you see a task pane other than the Getting Started task pane, click the down pointing arrow at the top of the task pane, and then click Getting Started.

If the toolbars appear on one row, perform the next steps to arrange them in two rows.

To arrange the Standard and Formatting toolbars on two rows:

1. Click **Tools** on the menu bar, and then click **Customize**. The Customize dialog box opens.
2. Click the **Options** tab if it is not already selected, and then click the **Show Standard and Formatting toolbars on two rows** check box to select it (that is, to insert a check).
3. Click **Close**. The Customize dialog box closes. The toolbars and task pane on your screen should now match those shown earlier in Figure 1-2.

Setting Up Other Screen Elements

Next, you'll take care of a few other parts of the screen, including:

- The horizontal ruler, which appears below the Formatting toolbar and is used to adjust margins and align parts of a document
- The Zoom setting, which controls the document's on-screen magnification; a setting of 100% displays the text in the same size as it will appear when printed
- The default font setting, which controls the size and shape of the characters that appear when you start typing

You'll learn more about these topics later. For now, you simply need to make your screen match the figures in this book by displaying the horizontal ruler, setting the Zoom setting to 100%, and verifying that 12-point Times New Roman is the default font.

To display the ruler, check your Zoom setting, and select the correct default font:

1. Click **View** on the menu bar, and then point to the double-arrow at the bottom of the menu to display the hidden menu commands.
2. If "Ruler" does not have a check mark next to it, click **Ruler**. The horizontal ruler should now be displayed, as shown earlier in Figure 1-2.
3. Click the **Zoom** list arrow `100%` on the Standard toolbar. A list of screen magnification settings appears. In Figure 1-5, the currently selected setting is 100%.

Figure 1-5 ▶ **Zoom settings**

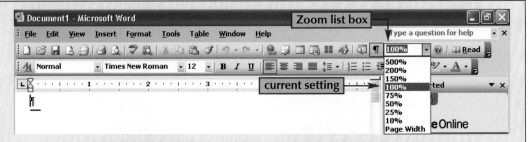

4. If 100% is not selected on your computer, click **100%** to select it. If you don't need to change your Zoom setting, press the **Esc** key to close the Zoom list. Next, you will check the default font setting.
5. Click **Format** on the menu bar, and then click **Font**. The Font dialog box opens. Click the **Font** tab if it is not already selected. See Figure 1-6.

Font dialog box | **Figure 1-6**

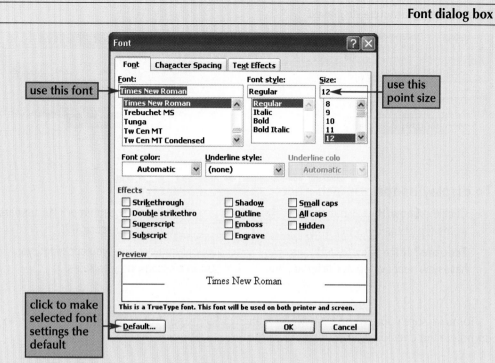

use this font

use this point size

click to make selected font settings the default

6. In the Font list box, click **Times New Roman**.

7. In the Size list box, click **12** if it is not already selected.

8. Click the **Default** button to make Times New Roman and 12 point the default settings. Word displays a message asking you to verify that you want to make 12-point Times New Roman the default font.

9. Click the **Yes** button.

Displaying Nonprinting Characters

Nonprinting characters are symbols that can appear on the screen but are not visible on the printed page. For example, one nonprinting character marks the end of a paragraph (¶) and another marks the space between words (•). It's helpful to display nonprinting characters so you can see whether you've typed an extra space, ended a paragraph, and so on.

Depending on how your computer is set up, nonprinting characters might have appeared automatically when you started Word. In Figure 1-7, you can see the paragraph symbol (¶) in the blank Document window. Also, the Show/Hide ¶ button is highlighted in the Standard toolbar. Both of these indicate that nonprinting characters are displayed. If they are not displayed on your screen, you need to perform the following step.

Figure 1-7 ▶ **Nonprinting characters displayed**

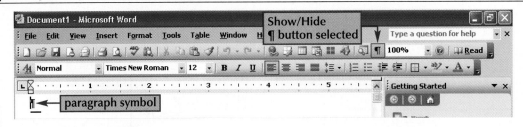

To display nonprinting characters:

▶ 1. Click the **Show/Hide** ¶ button [¶] on the Standard toolbar. A paragraph mark (¶) appears at the top of the Document window. Your screen should now match Figure 1-7.

Trouble? If the Show/Hide ¶ button was already highlighted before you clicked it, you have now deactivated it. Click the Show/Hide ¶ button a second time to select it.

To make sure your window always matches the figures in these tutorials, remember to complete the checklist in Figure 1-8 each time you sit down at the computer.

Figure 1-8 ▶ **Word window checklist**

Screen Element	Setting
Default font	Times New Roman
Default font size	12 point
Document view	Normal view
Formatting toolbar	Displayed below Standard toolbar
Horizontal ruler	Displayed
Nonprinting characters	Displayed
Other toolbars	Hidden
Standard toolbar	Displayed below menu bar
Task pane	Displayed
Word window	Maximized
Zoom box	Setting identical to setting shown in figures

Now that you have planned your letter, opened Word, identified screen elements, and adjusted settings, you are ready to begin typing a letter.

Beginning a Letter

You're ready to begin typing Megan's letter to Nicholas Brower at Web Time Productions. Figure 1-9 shows the completed letter printed on company letterhead. You will create this letter by completing the steps in this tutorial.

Completed letter **Figure 1-9**

Art4U, Inc.
5725 Mesa Avenue
Tucson, AZ 85703
Art4U@Earth-World-Art.com

February 15, 2006

Nicholas Brower
Web Time Productions
2015 Dubuque Avenue
Chicago, IL 60025

Dear Nicholas:

Enclosed you will find the signed contract. As you can see, I am returning all three pages, with my signature on each.

Now that we have finalized the contract, I have a few questions: When will we receive a complete schedule for the project? Also, how many preliminary designs do you require? Finally, will you be available to discuss the project with our artists via a conference call some afternoon next week? Thursday or Friday afternoon would be ideal, if either of those options work for you.

Thanks again for choosing Art4U. We look forward to working with you.

Sincerely yours,

Megan L. Grahs

You'll begin by opening a new blank document (in case you accidentally typed something in the current page). Whenever you need to perform a common task such as opening a document, you can usually start with the task pane. In this case, you can use a special task pane that is devoted to creating new documents.

To open a new document:

► **1.** Click the **Create a new document** button ▢ in the Open section at the bottom of the Getting Started task pane. Instead of the Getting Started task pane, you now see the New Document task pane. See Figure 1-10.

Figure 1-10	New Document task pane

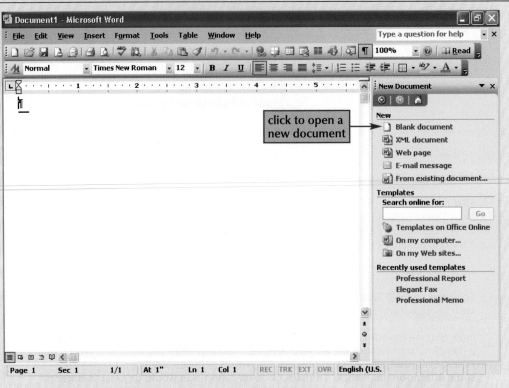

2. Click the **Blank document** button in the New Document task pane. A new document named Document2 opens and the task pane closes.

Now that you have opened a new document, you need to insert some blank lines in the document to ensure that you leave enough room for the company letterhead.

To insert blank lines in the document:

1. Press the **Enter** key eight times. Each time you press the Enter key, a nonprinting paragraph mark appears. In the status bar (at the bottom of the Document window), you should see the setting "At 2.5"," indicating that the insertion point is approximately 2.5 inches from the top of the page. Another setting in the status bar should read "Ln 9," indicating that the insertion point is in line 9 of the document. See Figure 1-11. (Your settings may be slightly different.)

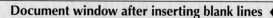
Document window after inserting blank lines

Figure 1-11

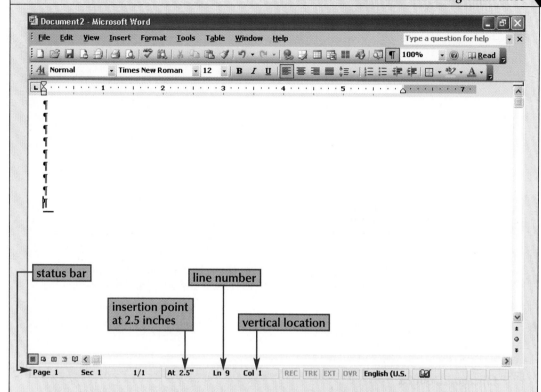

Trouble? If the paragraph mark doesn't appear each time you press the Enter key, the non-printing characters might be hidden. Click the Show/Hide ¶ button on the Standard toolbar.

Trouble? If you pressed the Enter key too many times, press the Backspace key to delete each extra line and paragraph mark. If you're on line 9 but the "At" number is not 2.5", don't worry. Different monitors produce slightly different measurements when you press the Enter key.

Pressing Enter is a simple, fast way to insert space in a document. When you are a more experienced Word user, you'll learn how to insert space without using the Enter key.

Entering Text

Normally, you begin typing a letter by entering the date. However, Megan tells you that she's not sure whether the contract will be ready to send today or tomorrow. So she asks you to skip the date for now and begin with the inside address. Making changes to documents is easy in Word, so you can easily add the date later.

In the following steps, you'll type the inside address (shown on Megan's note, in Figure 1-1). If you type a wrong character, press the Backspace key to delete the mistake and then retype the correct character.

To type the inside address:

1. Type **Nicholas Brower**, and then press the **Enter** key. As you type, a nonprinting character (•) appears between words to indicate a space. See Figure 1-12.

Figure 1-12 **First line of inside address**

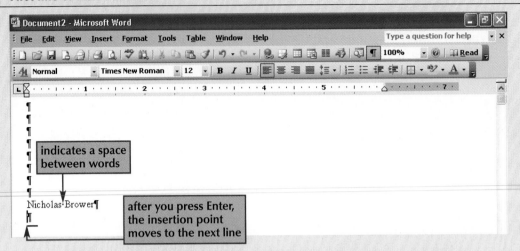

Trouble? If a wavy line appears beneath a word, check to make sure you typed the text correctly. If you did not, use the Backspace key to remove the error, and then retype the text correctly.

2. Type the following text, pressing the **Enter** key after each line to complete the inside address:

   Web Time Productions
   2015 Dubuque Avenue
   Chicago, IL 60025

   Be sure to press the Enter key after you type the ZIP code. Ignore the dotted underline below the street address. You'll learn the meaning of this underline later in this tutorial.

3. Press the **Enter** key again to add a blank line after the inside address. (You should see a total of two paragraph marks below the inside address.) Now you can type the salutation.

4. Type **Dear Nicholas:** and then press the **Enter** key twice to double space between the salutation and the body of the letter. See Figure 1-13.

Figure 1-13 **Letter with inside address and salutation**

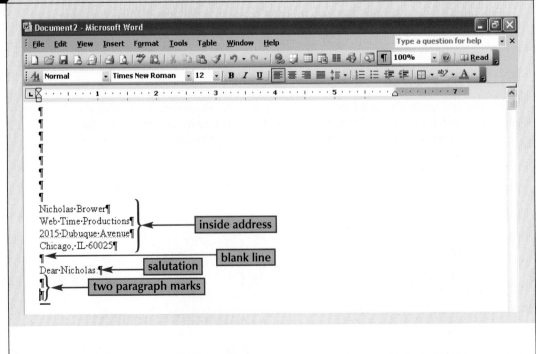

Before you continue with the rest of the letter, you should save what you have typed so far.

To save the document:

▶ 1. Click the **Save** button 🖫 on the Standard toolbar. The Save As dialog box opens. Note that Word suggests using the first few words of the letter ("Nicholas Brower") as the filename. You will replace the suggested filename with something more descriptive.

▶ 2. Type **Web Time Contract Letter** in the File name text box. Next, you need to tell Word where you want to save the document. In this case, you want to use the Tutorial subfolder in the Tutorial.01 folder.

▶ 3. Click the **Save in** list arrow, click the drive containing your Data Files, double-click the **Tutorial.01** folder, and then double-click the **Tutorial** folder. The word "Tutorial" is now displayed in the Save in box, indicating that the Tutorial folder is open and ready for you to save the document. See Figure 1-14.

Trouble? The Tutorial.01 folder is included with the Data Files for this text. If you don't have the Word Data Files, you need to get them before you can proceed. Your instructor will either give you the Data Files or ask you to obtain them from a specified location (such as a network drive). In either case, be sure that you make a backup copy of your Data Files before you start using them, so that the original files will be available on your copied disk in case you need to start over because of an error or problem. If you have any questions about the Data Files, see your instructor or technical support person for assistance.

Save As dialog box ◀ **Figure 1-14**

Trouble? If Windows XP is configured for Web style, you can single-click, rather than double-click, folders to open them in the Save As dialog box.

Trouble? If Word automatically adds the .doc extension to your filename, your computer is configured to show file extensions. Just continue with the tutorial.

▶ 4. Click the **Save** button in the Save As dialog box. The dialog box closes, and you return to the Document window. The new document name (Web Time Contract Letter) appears in the title bar.

Note that Word automatically appends the .doc extension to document filenames to identify them as Microsoft Word documents. However, unless your computer is set up to display file extensions, you won't see the .doc extension in any of the Word dialog boxes or in the title bar. These tutorials assume that file extensions are hidden.

You've made a good start on the letter, and you've saved your work so far. In the next session, you'll finish typing the letter and then you'll print it.

Review

To reinforce the tasks you learned in this session, go to the SAM 2003 Training Companion CD included with this text.

Session 1.1 Quick Check

1. In your own words, list the steps in creating a document.
2. Define each of the following in your own words:
   a. nonprinting characters
   b. Zoom setting
   c. font settings
   d. default settings
3. Explain how to change the document view to Normal view.
4. Explain how to display or hide the Standard toolbar.
5. True or False: To display the Formatting toolbar, you need to use a button on the Standard toolbar.
6. True or False: Each time you press the Enter key, a nonprinting paragraph character (¶) appears in the status bar.
7. Word automatically appends the _____ extension to all document file names, even if you can't see the file extensions on the screen.

Session 2.1

For hands-on practice of key tasks in this session, go to the SAM 2003 Training Companion CD included with this text.

Continuing Work on the Letter

Now that you have saved your document, you're ready to continue working on Megan's letter. As you type the body of the letter, you do not have to press the Enter key at the end of each line. Instead, when you type a word that extends into the right margin, both the insertion point and the word move automatically to the next line. This automatic line breaking is called **word wrap**. You'll see how word wrap works as you type the body of the letter.

To continue typing the letter:

1. If you took a break after the previous session, make sure that Word is running. Also, review the check list in Figure 1-8 and verify that your screen is set up to match the figures in this tutorial.
2. Make sure the insertion point is at Ln 16 (according to the setting in the status bar). If it's not, move it to line 16 by pressing the arrow keys.
3. Type the following sentence: **Enclosed you will find the signed contract.**
4. Press the **spacebar**.
5. Type the following sentence: **As you can see, I am returning all three pages, with my signature on each.** Notice how Word moves the last few words to a new line when the preceding line is full.
6. Press the **Enter** key to end the first paragraph, and then press the **Enter** key again to create a double space between the two paragraphs.

7. Type the following text:

Now that we have finalized the contract, I have a few questions: When will we receive a complete schedule for the project? Also, how many preliminary designs do you require?

When you are finished, your screen should look similar to Figure 1-15, although the line breaks on your screen might be slightly different.

Beginning of second main paragraph ◄ | **Figure 1-15**

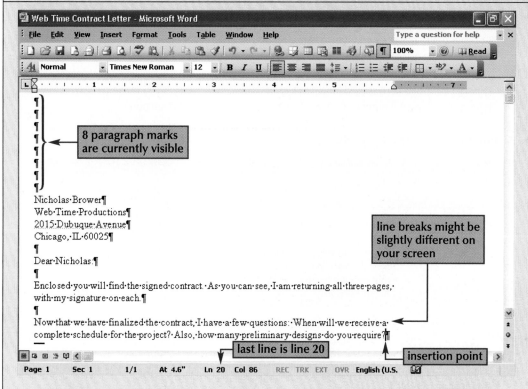

Trouble? If your screen does not match Figure 1-15 exactly, don't be concerned. The letter widths of the Times New Roman font can vary, which produces slightly different measurements on different monitors. As a result, the word or letter where the line wraps in your document might be different from the one shown in Figure 1-15.

Scrolling a Document

After you finish the last set of steps, the insertion point should be near the bottom of the Document window. Unless you are working on a large monitor, your screen probably looks like there's not enough room to type the rest of Megan's letter. However, as you continue to add text at the end of your document, the text that you typed earlier will **scroll** (or shift up) and disappear from the top of the Document window. You'll see how scrolling works as you enter the rest of the second paragraph.

To observe scrolling while you're entering text:

1. Make sure the insertion point is positioned to the right of the question mark after the word "require." The insertion point should be positioned at the end of line 20. See Figure 1-15.

2. Press the **spacebar**, and then type the following text:

   Finally, will you be available to discuss the project with our artists via a conference call some afternoon next week? Thursday or Friday afternoon would be ideal, if either of those options works for you.

3. Press the **Enter** key twice. The document scrolls up.

   At some point (either as you type the text in Step 2 or when you press the Enter key in Step 3), one or more paragraph marks at the top of the letter scroll off the top of the Document window. (Exactly when this happens depends on the size of your monitor.) When you are finished typing, your document should look like Figure 1-16. (Don't worry if you make a mistake in your typing. You'll learn a number of ways to correct errors in the next section.)

Figure 1-16 ▶ Part of document scrolled off the screen

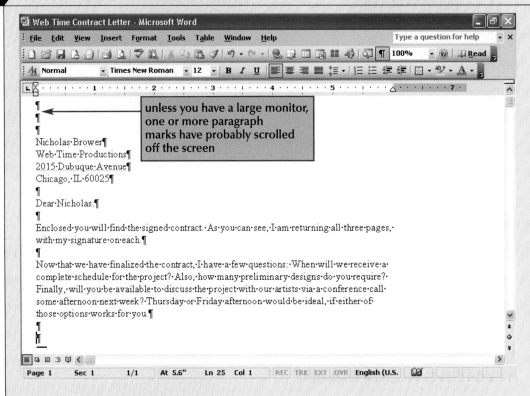

4. Type the following text:

   Thanks again for choosing Art4U. We look forward to working with you.

5. Press the **Enter** key twice.

6. Type **Sincerely yours,** (including the comma) to enter the complimentary closing.

7. Press the **Enter** key five times to allow space for a signature. Unless you have a very large monitor, part or even all of the inside address scrolls off the top of the Document window.

8. Type **Megan Grahs**, and then press the **Enter** key. A wavy red line appears below "Grahs." In Word, such lines indicate possible spelling errors. Because Megan's last name is not in the Word dictionary, Word suggests that it might be spelled incorrectly. You'll learn more about Word's error checking features in the next section. For now, you can ignore the wavy red line.

   You've completed the letter, so you should save your work.

9. Click the **Save** button 🔲 on the Standard toolbar. Word saves your letter with the same name and in the same location you specified earlier. Don't be concerned about any typing errors. You'll learn how to correct them in the next section.

In the last set of steps, you watched the text at the top of your document move off your screen. You can scroll this hidden text back into view so you can read the beginning of the letter. When you do, the text at the bottom of the screen will scroll out of view. To scroll the Document window, you can click the up or down arrows in the vertical scroll bar, click anywhere in the vertical scroll bar, or drag the scroll box. See Figure 1-17.

Note: If you are using a very large monitor, your insertion point may still be some distance from the bottom of the screen. In that case, you may not be able to perform the scrolling steps that follow. Read the steps to familiarize yourself with the process of scrolling. You'll have a chance to scroll longer documents later.

Parts of the scroll bar ◄ **Figure 1-17**

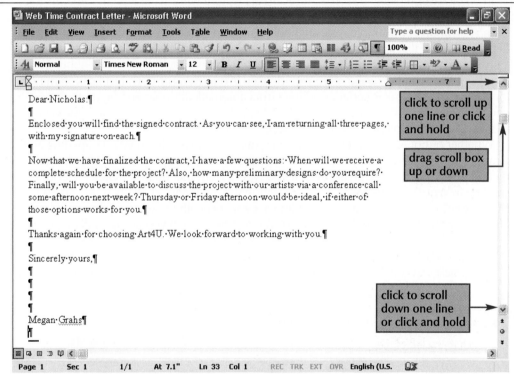

In the next set of steps, you will practice using the vertical scroll bar.

To scroll the document using the vertical scroll bar:

1. Position the mouse pointer on the up arrow at the top of the vertical scroll bar. Press and hold the mouse button to scroll the text. When the text stops scrolling, you have reached the top of the document and can see the beginning of the letter. Note that scrolling does not change the location of the insertion point in the document.

2. Click the down arrow on the vertical scroll bar several times. The document scrolls down one line at a time.

▶ **3.** Click anywhere in the vertical scroll bar, below the scroll box. The document scrolls down one full screen.

▶ **4.** Drag the scroll box up until the first line of the inside address ("Nicholas Brower") is positioned at the top of the Document window.

▶ **5.** Scroll down to show the last line of the letter.

Correcting Errors

If you notice a typing error as soon as you make it, you can press the Backspace key, which deletes the characters and spaces to the left of the insertion point one at a time. Backspacing erases both printing and nonprinting characters. After you erase the error, you can type the correct character(s). You can also press the Delete key, which deletes characters to the right of the insertion point one at a time.

In many cases, however, Word's **AutoCorrect** feature will do the work for you. Among other things, AutoCorrect automatically corrects common typing errors, such as typing "adn" for "and." For example, you might have noticed AutoCorrect at work if you forgot to capitalize the first letter in a sentence as you typed the letter. AutoCorrect can automatically correct this error as you type the rest of the sentence. You'll learn more about using AutoCorrect as you become a more experienced Word user. For now, just keep in mind that AutoCorrect corrects certain spelling errors automatically. Depending on how your computer is set up, some or all AutoCorrect features might be turned off. You'll learn how to turn AutoCorrect on in the following steps.

Whether or not AutoCorrect is turned on, you can always rely on Word's **Spelling and Grammar checker**. This feature continually checks your document against Word's built-in dictionary and a set of grammar rules. If you type a word that doesn't match the correct spelling in Word's dictionary or if a word isn't in the dictionary at all (as is the case with Megan's last name, Grahs), a wavy red line appears beneath the word. A wavy red line also appears if you type duplicate words (such as "the the"). If you accidentally type an extra space between words or make a grammatical error (such as typing "He walk to the store." instead of "He walks to the store."), a wavy green line appears beneath the error.

The easiest way to see how these features work is to make some intentional typing errors.

To correct intentional typing errors:

▶ **1.** Click to the left of the last paragraph mark to position the insertion point there (if it is not already there), and then press the **Enter** key to create a double space after Megan's last name, which is in the signature line. Before you start typing, you'll check to make sure AutoCorrect is turned on.

▶ **2.** Click **Tools** on the menu bar, and then click **AutoCorrect Options**. The AutoCorrect: English (U.S.) dialog box opens.

▶ **3.** Click the **Capitalize first letter of sentences** check box and the **Replace text as you type** check box to insert checks if these options are not already checked, and then click **OK**. (It is okay if other check boxes have checks.)

▶ **4.** Carefully and slowly type the following sentence exactly as it is shown, including the spelling errors and the extra space between the last two words: **microsoft Word corects teh commen typing misTakes you make**. Press the **Enter** key when you are finished typing.

Notice that as you press the spacebar after the word "commen," a wavy red line appears beneath it, indicating that the word might be misspelled. Notice also that Word automatically capitalized the word "Microsoft" because it's the first word in the sentence. And, when you pressed the spacebar after the words "corects," "teh," and "misTakes," Word automatically corrected the spelling. After you pressed the Enter key, a wavy green line appeared under the last two words, alerting you to the extra space. See Figure 1-18.

Document with intentional typing errors | **Figure 1-18**

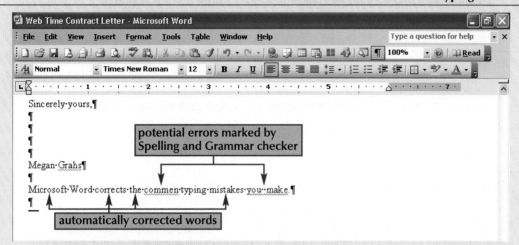

Trouble? If red and green wavy lines do not appear beneath mistakes, Word is probably not set to check spelling and grammar automatically as you type. Click Tools on the menu bar, and then click Options to open the Options dialog box. Click the Spelling & Grammar tab. If necessary, insert check marks in the "Check spelling as you type" and the "Check grammar as you type" check boxes, and then click OK.

Working with AutoCorrect

Whenever AutoCorrect makes a change, Word inserts an **AutoCorrect Options button** in the document. You can use this button to undo a change, or to prevent AutoCorrect from making the same change in the future. To see an AutoCorrect Options button, you position the mouse pointer over a word that has been changed by AutoCorrect.

To display an AutoCorrect Options button:

1. Position the mouse pointer over the word "corrects." A small blue rectangle appears below the first few letters of the word, as shown in Figure 1-19.

Word changed by AutoCorrect | **Figure 1-19**

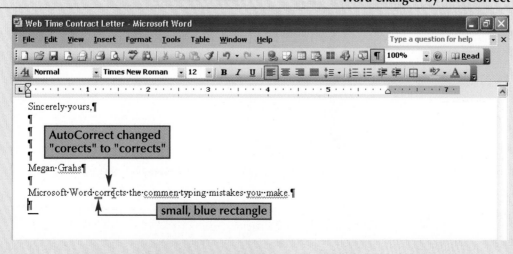

Trouble? If you see a blue button with a lightning bolt, move the pointer slightly to the right so that only the rectangle is visible, and then continue with the next step.

2. Point to the blue rectangle below "corrects." The blue rectangle is replaced by the AutoCorrect Options button and the entire word "corrects" is highlighted.

3. Click the **AutoCorrect Options** button ![AutoCorrect Options button]. A menu with commands related to AutoCorrect appears. You could choose to change "corrects" back to "corects." You could also tell AutoCorrect to stop automatically correcting "corects." This second option might be useful if you found that AutoCorrect continually edited a word, such as a brand name or technical term, which was in fact spelled correctly. In the "corects" example, the change made by AutoCorrect is acceptable, so you can simply close the AutoCorrect menu.

4. Click anywhere in the document. The AutoCorrect menu closes.

Correcting Spelling and Grammar Errors

After you verify that AutoCorrect made changes you want, you should review your document for wavy underlines. Again, the red underlines indicate potential spelling errors, while the green underlines indicate potential grammar or punctuation problems. In the following steps, you will learn a quick way to correct such errors.

To correct spelling and grammar errors:

1. Position the I-Beam pointer over the word "commen," and then click the right mouse button. A shortcut menu appears with suggested spellings. See Figure 1-20.

Figure 1-20 | **Shortcut menu with suggested spellings**

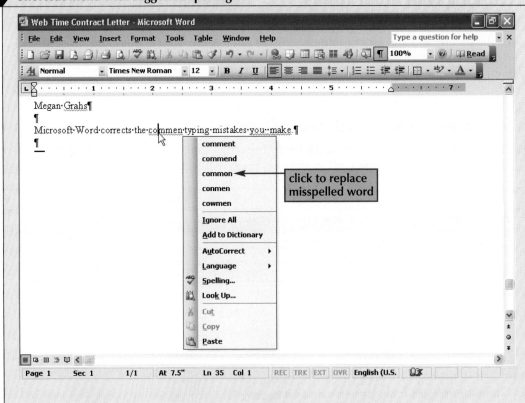

Trouble? If the shortcut menu doesn't appear, repeat Step 1, making sure you click the right mouse button, not the left one. If you see a different menu from the one shown in Figure 1-20, you didn't right-click exactly on the word "commen." Press the Esc key to close the menu, and then repeat Step 1.

2. Click **common** in the shortcut menu. The menu disappears, and the correct spelling appears in your document. Notice that the wavy red line disappears after you correct the error.

3. Click to the right of the letter "u" in the word "you." Press the **Delete** key to delete the extra space.

You can see how quick and easy it is to correct common typing errors with AutoCorrect and the Spelling and Grammar checker. Remember, however, to proofread each document you create thoroughly. AutoCorrect will not catch words that are spelled correctly, but used improperly (such as "your" for "you're").

Proofreading the Letter

Before you can proofread your letter, you need to delete the practice sentence.

To delete the practice sentence:

1. Confirm that the insertion point is to the right of "you" in the sentence you just typed, and then press the **Delete** key repeatedly to delete any spaces and characters to the right of the insertion point, including one paragraph mark.

2. Press the **Backspace** key repeatedly until the insertion point is to the left of the paragraph mark below Megan's name. There should only be one paragraph mark below her name. If you accidentally delete part of the letter, retype it, using Figure 1-17 as a guide.

Now you can proofread the letter for any typos. You can also get rid of the wavy red underline below Megan's last name.

To respond to possible spelling errors:

1. Be sure the signature line is visible. Because Word doesn't recognize "Grahs" as a word, it is marked as a potential error. You need to tell Word to ignore this name wherever it occurs in the letter.

2. Right-click **Grahs**. A shortcut menu opens.

3. Click **Ignore All**. The wavy red underline disappears from below "Grahs."

4. Scroll up to the beginning of the letter, and proofread it for typos. If a word has a wavy red or green underline, right-click it and choose an option in the shortcut menu. To correct other errors, click to the right or left of the error, use the Backspace or Delete key to remove it, and then type a correction.

5. Click the **Save** button on the Standard toolbar. Word saves your letter with the same name and to the same location you specified earlier.

Inserting a Date with AutoComplete

The beauty of using a word-processing program such as Microsoft Word is that you can easily make changes to text you have already typed. In this case, you need to insert the current date at the beginning of the letter. Megan tells you that she wants to send the contract to Web Time Productions on February 15, so you need to insert that date into the letter now.

Before you can enter the date, you need to move the insertion point to the right location. In a standard business letter, the date belongs approximately 2.5 inches from the top. (As you recall, this is where you started the inside address earlier.) You also need to insert some blank lines to allow enough space between the date and the inside address.

To move the insertion point and add some blank lines:

▶ 1. Scroll up to display the top of the document.

▶ 2. Click to the left of the "N" in "Nicholas Brower" in the inside address. The status bar indicates that the insertion point is on line 9, 2.5 inches from the top. (Your status bar might show slightly different measurements.)

▶ 3. Press the **Enter** key four times, and then press the ↑ key four times. Now the insertion point is positioned at line 9, with three blank lines between the inside address and the line where you will insert the date. See Figure 1-21.

Figure 1-21 ▶ **Position of insertion point**

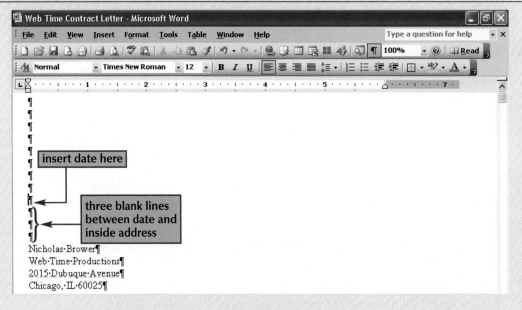

You're ready to insert the date. To do this you can take advantage of Word's **AutoComplete** feature, which automatically inserts dates and other regularly used items for you. In this case, you can type the first few characters of the month, and let Word insert the rest. (This only works for long month names like February.)

To insert the date:

1. Type **Febr** (the first four letters of February). A rectangular box appears above the line, as shown in Figure 1-22. If you wanted to type something other than February, you could continue typing to complete the word. In this case, though, you want to accept the AutoComplete suggestion, which you will do in the next step.

AutoComplete suggestion | Figure 1-22

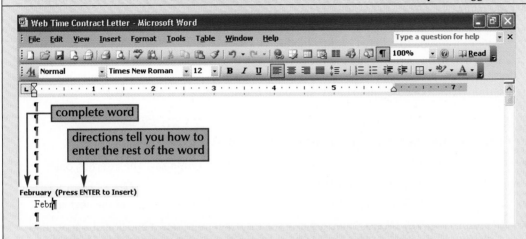

Trouble? If the AutoComplete suggestion doesn't appear, this feature may not be active. Click Tools on the menu bar, click AutoCorrect Options, click the AutoText tab, click the Show AutoComplete suggestions check box to insert a check, and then click OK. Delete the characters "Febr" and begin again with Step 1.

2. Press the **Enter** key. The rest of the word "February" is inserted in the document.

3. Press the **spacebar**, and then type **15, 2006**.

Trouble? If February happens to be the current month, you will see a second AutoComplete suggestion displaying the current date after you press the spacebar. To ignore that AutoComplete suggestion, continue typing the rest of the date as instructed in Step 3.

4. Click one of the blank lines below the date. Depending on how your computer is set up, you may see a dotted underline below the date. (You will learn the meaning of this underline later in this tutorial.) You have finished entering the date. See Figure 1-23.

Date entered in the document | Figure 1-23

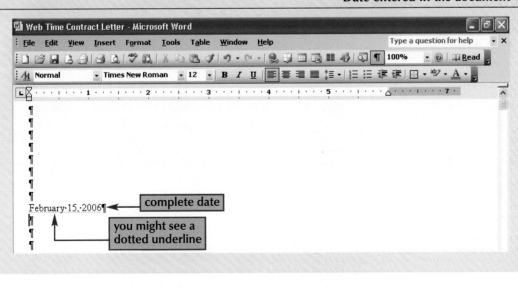

Moving the Insertion Point Around a Document

When you scroll a document, you change the part of the document that is displayed on the screen. But to change the location in the document where new text will appear when you type, you need to move the insertion point. In the last section, you moved the insertion point by scrolling up and then clicking where you wanted to insert new lines and text. You can also use the arrow keys on your keyboard, ←, →, ↑, and ↓, to move the insertion point one character at a time to the left or right, or one line at a time up or down. In addition, you can press a combination of keys to move the insertion point. As you become more experienced with Word, you'll decide which method you prefer.

Megan asks you to add her middle initial to the signature line. Before you can do that, you need to make sure you're comfortable moving the insertion point around the document. To see how quickly you can move through the document, you'll use keystrokes to move the insertion point to the beginning and end of the document.

To move the insertion point with keystrokes:

1. Press the **Ctrl** key and hold it down while you press the **Home** key. The insertion point moves to the beginning of the document.

2. Press the **Page Down** key to move the insertion point down to the top of the next screen.

3. Press the ↓ key several times to move the insertion point down one line at a time, and then press the → key several times to move the insertion point to the right one character at a time.

4. Press the **Ctrl+End** keys. The insertion point moves to the end of the document.

5. Use the arrow keys to position the insertion point to the right of the "n" in "Megan."

6. Press the **spacebar**, and then type the letter **L** followed by a period.

Figure 1-24 summarizes the keystrokes you can use to move the insertion point around the document. When you simply need to display a part of a document, you'll probably want to use the vertical scroll bar. But when you actually need to move the insertion point to a specific spot, it's helpful to use these special keystrokes.

Figure 1-24 **Keystrokes for moving the insertion point**

Press	To move the insertion point
← or →	Left or right one character at a time
↑ or ↓	Up or down one line at a time
Ctrl+← or Ctrl+→	Left or right one word at a time
Ctrl+↑ or Ctrl+↓	Up or down one paragraph at a time
Home or End	To the beginning or to the end of the current line
Ctrl+Home or Ctrl+End	To the beginning or to the end of the document
Page Up or Page Down	To the previous screen or to the next screen
Alt+Ctrl+Page Up or Alt+Ctrl+Page Down	To the top or to the bottom of the document window

Using the Undo and Redo Commands

To undo (or reverse) the very last thing you did, click the **Undo button** on the Standard toolbar. If you want to restore your original change, the **Redo button** reverses the action of the Undo button (or redoes the undo). To undo more than your last action, you can click the Undo list arrow on the Standard toolbar. This list shows your most recent actions. Undo reverses the action only at its original location. You can't delete a word or phrase, move the surrounding text, and then undo the deletion at a different location.

Megan asks you to undo the addition of her middle initial, to see how the signature line looks without it.

To undo the addition of the letter "L":

1. Place the mouse pointer over the **Undo** button ↺ on the Standard toolbar. The label "Undo Typing" appears in a ScreenTip, indicating that your most recent action involved typing. See Figure 1-25.

Using the Undo button ◀ | Figure 1-25

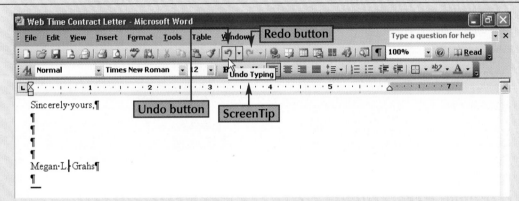

2. Click the **Undo** button ↺. The letter "L," the period, and the space you typed earlier are deleted.

   Trouble? If something else changes, you probably made another edit or change to the document between the addition of Megan's middle initial and the undo. Click the Undo button on the Standard toolbar until the letter "L," the period, and the space following it are deleted. If a list of possible changes appears under the Undo button, you clicked the list arrow next to the Undo button rather than the Undo button itself. Press the Esc key to close the list.

   As she reviews the signature line, Megan decides that she does want to include her middle initial after all. Instead of retyping it, you'll redo the undo.

3. Place the mouse pointer over the **Redo** button ↻ on the Standard toolbar and observe the "Redo Typing" ScreenTip.

4. Click the **Redo** button ↻. Megan's middle initial (along with the period and an additional space) are reinserted into the signature line.

5. Click the **Save** button 🖫 on the Standard toolbar to save your changes to the document.

Your letter is nearly finished. All that remains is to remove the straight dotted underlines and then print the letter.

Removing Smart Tags

A straight dotted underline below a date or address indicates that Word has inserted a Smart Tag in the document. A **Smart Tag** is a feature that allows you to perform actions (such as sending e-mail or scheduling a meeting) that would normally require a completely different program. When you point to Smart Tag text, a Smart Tag Actions button appears, which you can click to open a menu with commands related to that item. (For example, you might click a Smart Tag on an address to add that address to your e-mail address book.) You don't really need Smart Tags in this document, though, so you will delete them. (Your computer may not be set up to show Smart Tags at all, or it might show them on dates but not addresses. If you do not see any Smart Tags in your document, simply read the following steps.)

To remove the Smart Tags from the document:

▶ 1. Scroll up so you can see the inside address. If you see a straight dotted underline below the street address (2015 Dubuque Avenue), position the mouse pointer over that line. A Smart Tag icon ⓘ appears over the street address.

▶ 2. Move the mouse pointer over the **Smart Tag** icon ⓘ. The icon is transformed into the Smart Tag Actions button ⓘ ▾, as shown in Figure 1-26.

Figure 1-26 ▶ Displaying the Smart Tag Actions button

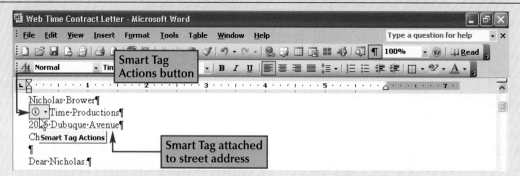

▶ 3. Click the **Smart Tag Actions** button ⓘ ▾. A menu of commands related to addresses appears.

▶ 4. Click **Remove this Smart Tag**. The Smart Tag menu closes. The address is no longer underlined, indicating that the Smart Tag has been removed. Depending on how your computer is set up, the Smart Tag on the street address may have been the only one in your document. But it's possible you see others.

▶ 5. Remove any other Smart Tags in the document, including any on the date or elsewhere in the inside address.

▶ 6. Click the **Save** button 🖫 on the Standard toolbar.

Previewing and Printing a Document

Do you think the letter is ready to print? You could find out by clicking the Print button on the Standard toolbar and then reviewing the printed page. With that approach, however, you risk wasting paper and printer time. For example, if you failed to insert enough space for the company letterhead, you would have to add more space, and then print the letter all over again. To avoid wasting paper and time, you should first display the document in the **Print Preview window**. By default, the Print Preview window shows you the full page; there's no need to scroll through the document.

To preview the document:

▸ 1. Proof the document one last time and correct any new errors. Always remember to proof your document immediately before printing it.

▸ 2. Replace "Megan L. Grahs" with your first and last name, at the end of the letter. This will ensure that you will be able to identify your copy of the letter.

▸ 3. Click the **Print Preview** button 🔍 on the Standard toolbar. The Print Preview window opens and displays a full-page version of your letter, as shown in Figure 1-27. This shows how the letter will fit on the printed page. The Print Preview toolbar includes a number of buttons that are useful for making changes that affect the way the printed page will look.

Full page displayed in Print Preview window ◀ Figure 1-27

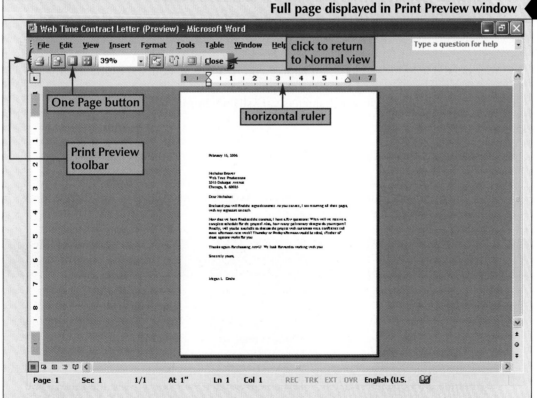

Trouble? If your letter in the Print Preview window is smaller and off to the left rather than centered in the window, click the One Page button on the Print Preview toolbar.

Trouble? If you don't see a ruler above the document, your ruler is not displayed. To show the ruler in the Print Preview window, click View on the menu bar and then click Ruler.

▸ 4. Click the **Close** button on the Print Preview toolbar to return to Normal view.

▸ 5. Click the **Save** button 🖫 on the Standard toolbar.

Note that it is especially important to preview documents if your computer is connected to a network so that you don't keep a shared printer tied up with unnecessary printing. In this case, the text looks well spaced and the letterhead will fit at the top of the page. You're ready to print the letter.

When printing a document, you have two choices. You can use the Print command on the File menu, which opens the Print dialog box in which you can adjust some printer settings. Or, if you prefer, you can use the Print button on the Standard toolbar, which prints the document using default settings, without opening a dialog box. In these tutorials, the first time you print from a shared computer, you should check the settings in the Print dialog box and make sure the number of copies is set to 1. After that, you can use the Print button.

To print the letter document:

▶ 1. Make sure your printer is turned on and contains paper.

▶ 2. Click **File** on the menu bar, and then click **Print**. The Print dialog box opens.

▶ 3. Make sure the Printer section of the dialog box shows the correct printer. If you're not sure what the correct printer is, check with your instructor or technical support person. Also, make sure the number of copies is set to 1.

   Trouble? If the Print dialog box shows the wrong printer, click the Name list arrow, and then select the correct printer from the list of available printers.

▶ 4. Click the **OK** button. Assuming your computer is attached to a printer, the letter prints.

Your printed letter should look similar to Figure 1-9, but without the Art4U letterhead. The word wraps, or line breaks, might not appear in the same places on your letter because the size and spacing of characters vary slightly from one printer to the next.

Creating an Envelope

After you print the letter, Megan asks you to print an envelope in which to mail the contracts. Creating an envelope is a simple process because Word automatically uses the inside address from the letter as the address on the envelope.

Reference Window | **Printing an Envelope**

- Click Tools on the menu bar, point to Letters and Mailings, and then click Envelopes and Labels.
- In the Envelopes and Labels dialog box, verify that the Delivery address box contains the correct address. If necessary, you can type a new address or edit the existing one.
- If necessary, type a return address. If you are using preprinted stationery that already includes a return address, click the Omit check box to insert a check.
- To print the envelope immediately, insert an envelope in your printer, and then click Print.
- To store the envelope along with the rest of the document, click Add to Document.
- To print the envelope after you have added it to the document, open the Print dialog box and print the page containing the envelope.

Megan tells you that your printer is not currently stocked with envelopes. She asks you to create the envelope and add it to the document. Then she will print the envelope later, when she is ready to mail the contracts to Web Time Productions.

To create an envelope:

▶ 1. Click **Tools** on the menu bar, point to **Letters and Mailings**, and then click **Envelopes and Labels**. The Envelopes and Labels dialog box opens, as shown in Figure 1-28. By default, Word uses the inside address from the letter as the delivery address. Depending on how your computer is set up, you might see an address in the Return address box. Because Megan will be using Art4U's printed envelopes, you don't need to include a return address on this envelope.

Envelopes and Labels dialog box ◀ **Figure 1-28**

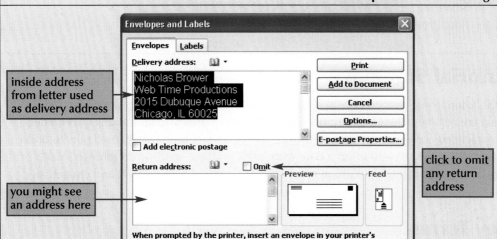

▶ 2. Click the **Omit** check box to insert a check, if necessary.

▶ 3. Click the **Add to Document** button. The dialog box closes, and you return to the Document window. The envelope is inserted at the top of the document, above a double line with the words "Section Break (Next Page)." The double line indicates that the envelope and the letter are two separate parts of the document. The envelope will print in the standard business envelope format. The letter will still print on standard 8.5 x 11-inch paper. (You'll have a chance to print an envelope in the exercises at the end of this tutorial.)

▶ 4. Click the **Save** button 🖫 on the Standard toolbar.

You are finished with the letter and the envelope, so you can close the document.

To close the document:

▶ 1. Click the **Close Window** button ☒ on the menu bar. The Web Time Contract Letter document closes.

   Trouble? If you see a dialog box with the message "Do you want to save the changes to 'Web Time Contract Letter?'," click the Yes button.

▶ 2. Close any other open documents without saving them.

Congratulations on creating your first letter in Microsoft Word. You'll be able to use the skills you learned in this tutorial to create a variety of professional documents.

Review

To reinforce the tasks you learned in this session, go to the SAM 2003 Training Companion CD included with this text.

Session 1.2 Quick Check

1. True or False: The term "word wrap" refers to automatic line breaking.
2. Explain how to enter the name of a month using AutoComplete.
3. What button can you use to reverse your most recent edit immediately?
4. List the steps required to print an envelope.
5. In your own words, define each of the following:
   a. scrolling
   b. AutoComplete
   c. Redo button
   d. Smart Tag
   e. Print Preview

Review

Tutorial Summary

In this tutorial you learned how to set up your Word window to match the figures in this book, create a new document from scratch, and type a professional-looking cover letter. You practiced correcting errors, and moving the insertion point. You learned how to undo and redo changes, how to insert a date with AutoComplete and how to remove Smart Tags from a document. Finally, you previewed and printed a document, and created an envelope.

Key Terms

AutoComplete

AutoCorrect

AutoCorrect Options button

default settings

nonprinting characters

Print Preview window

Redo button

scroll

Smart Tag

Spelling and Grammar
  checker

Undo button

word wrap

Pr ...

Pra
lea
usi
sce

Review Assignments

... **eeded for the Review Assignments.**

... l from Nicholas Brower at Web Time Productions, confirming
... ce call. Megan has e-mailed the graphic artists at Art4U, inform-
... o make sure everyone remembers, she would like you to post a
... ard in the break room. She also asks you to create an envelope so
... to freelance artists who work outside the Art4U offices. Create
... e 1-29 by completing the following steps. The steps show quota-
... u type; do not include the quotation marks in your letter.

Art4U, Inc.
5725 Mesa Avenue
Tucson, AZ 85703
Art4U@Earth-World-Art.com

...

...ns

...06

...Call

Please plan to join us for a conference call at 3 p.m. on Friday, March 1. Nicholas Brower,
president of Web Time Productions, will be taking part, as will five of his company's most
experienced Web page designers. This will be your chance to ask the designers some
important questions.

You will be able to join the call from your desk by dialing an 800 number and a special
access code. You'll receive both of these numbers via e-mail the day of the call.

1. Make sure a new blank document is open.
2. Compare your screen to the checklist in Figure 1-8 and change any settings if necessary. In particular, make sure that nonprinting characters are displayed and the Getting
   Started task pane is open.
3. Press the Enter key eight times to insert enough space for the company letterhead.
4. Type "TO:" in capital letters, and then press the spacebar.
5. Turn off capitalization if you turned it on in Step 4, and then type "Art4U Staff
   Artists". Throughout the rest of this exercise, turn capitalization on and off as needed.
6. Press the Enter key twice, type "FROM:", press the spacebar, turn off capitalization,
   and then type your name.

7. Press the Enter key twice, type "DATE:", and then press the spacebar.

8. Enter the date February 20, 2006 using AutoComplete when possible to reduce the amount of typing required.

9. Press the Enter key twice, type "SUBJECT:", press the spacebar, type "Conference Call", and then press the Enter key three times.

10. Continue typing the rest of the memo as shown in Figure 1-29. (You will have a chance to correct any typing errors later.) Ignore any AutoCorrect suggestions that are not relevant to the text you are typing.

11. Save your work as **Call Memo** in the Tutorial.01\Review folder provided with your Data Files.

12. Practice using the keyboard to move the insertion point around the document. Use the arrow keys so the insertion point is positioned immediately to the left of the "A" in "Art4U" in the "TO" line.

13. Type "All" and a space, so the TO line reads "TO: All Art4U Staff Artists".

14. Undo the change and then redo it.

15. Scroll to the beginning of the document and proofread your work.

16. Correct any misspelled words marked by wavy red lines. If the correct spelling of a word does not appear in the shortcut menu, close the list, and then make the correction yourself. Remove any red wavy lines below words that are actually spelled correctly. Then correct any grammatical or other errors indicated by wavy green lines. Delete any extra words or spaces.

17. Remove any Smart Tags.

18. Save your most recent changes.

19. Preview and print the memo.

20. Add an envelope to the document. Use your own address as the delivery address. Do not include a return address.

21. Save your changes and close the Call Memo document. If any other documents are open, close them without saving any changes.

Case Problem 1

Apply

Apply the skills you learned to create a letter about a health care lecture.

There are no Data Files needed for this Case Problem.

Wingra Family Practice Clinic You are a nurse at Wingra Family Practice Clinic. You have organized a lunchtime lecture series for the clinic staff in which regional medical professionals will discuss topics related to pediatric healthcare. You have hired your first speaker and need to write a letter confirming your agreement and asking a few questions. Create the letter by completing the following steps. The steps show quotation marks around text you type; do not include the quotation marks.

1. Open a new blank document if one is not already open, and then check your screen to make sure your settings match those shown earlier in Figure 1-8.

2. Locate the Undo and Redo buttons on the Standard toolbar and be prepared to use them as necessary as you work on the letter.

3. Type your name, press Enter, and then type the following address:
   Wingra Family Practice Clinic
   2278 Norwood Place
   Middleton, WI 52247

4. Press the Enter key four times, and then type "May 8, 2007" as the date.

5. Press the Enter key four times, and using the proper business letter format, type this inside address:
   Dr. Susanna Trevay
   James Madison Medical Center
   56 Ingersoll Drive
   Madison, WI 53788

6. Double space after the inside address (that is, press the Enter key twice), type the salutation "Dear Dr. Trevay:", and then insert a blank line.

7. Type the paragraph as follows: "Thank you so much for agreeing to lecture about early childhood vaccinations on Friday, May 25. Before I can publicize your talk, I need some information. Please call by Tuesday with your answers to the following questions:"

8. Save your work as **Lecture Series Letter** in the Tutorial.01\Cases folder provided with your Data Files.

9. Insert one blank line, and then type these questions on separate lines with one blank line between each:
   Which vaccines will you cover in detail?
   Will you discuss common immune responses to vaccine antigens?
   Will you provide hand-outs with suggested vaccination schedules?

10. Move the insertion point to the beginning of the third question (which begins "Will you provide…"). Insert a new line, and add the following as the new third question in the list: "Would you be willing to take questions from the audience?"

11. Correct any spelling or grammar errors indicated by red or green wavy lines. Because "Wingra" is spelled correctly, use the shortcut menu to remove the wavy red line under the word "Wingra" and prevent Word from marking the word as a misspelling. Repeat to ignore "Trevay," "Ingersoll," and any other words that are spelled correctly but that are marked as misspellings.

12. Insert a blank line after the last question, and type the complimentary closing "Sincerely," (including the comma).

13. Press the Enter key four times to leave room for the signature, and type your full name. Then press the Enter key and type "Wingra Family Practice Clinic". Notice that "Wingra" is not marked as a spelling error this time.

14. Scroll up to the beginning of the document, and then remove any Smart Tags in the letter.

15. Save your changes to the letter, and then preview it using the Print Preview button.

16. Print the letter, and then close the document.

Case Problem 2

Apply

Apply the skills you learned to create a letter informing a client about a new investment program.

There are no Data Files needed for this Case Problem.

Pear Tree Investment Services As a financial planner at Pear Tree Investment Services, you are responsible for keeping your clients informed about new investment options. You have just learned about a program called HigherEdVest, which encourages parents to save for their children's college education. Write a letter to a client introducing the program and asking him to call for more information. Create the letter by completing the following steps. The steps show quotation marks around text you type; do not include the quotation marks in your letter.

1. Open a new, blank document if one is not already open, and then check your screen to make sure your settings match those shown earlier in Figure 1-8.

2. Locate the Undo and Redo buttons on the Standard toolbar and be prepared to use them as necessary as you work on the letter.

3. Press the Enter key until the insertion point is positioned about two inches from the top of the page. (Remember that you can see the exact position of the insertion point, in inches, in the status bar.)

4. Type the name of the current month. (If an AutoComplete suggestion appears, accept it to complete the name of the month.) Press the spacebar. After you press the spacebar, an AutoComplete suggestion appears with the current date. Accept the suggestion.

5. Press the Enter key four times after the date, and, using the proper business letter format, type the inside address: "Joseph Robbins, 5788 Rugby Road, Hillsborough, CO 77332".

6. Double space after the inside address (that is, press the Enter key twice), type the salutation "Dear Joseph:", and then double space again.

7. Write one paragraph introducing the HigherEdVest program, explaining that you think the client might be interested, and asking him to call your office at 555-5555 for more details.

8. Insert a blank line and type the complimentary closing "Sincerely,".

9. Press the Enter key four times to leave room for the signature, and then type your name and title.

10. Save the letter as **HigherEdVest Letter** in the Tutorial.01\Cases folder provided with your Data Files.

11. Remove any Smart Tags. Reread your letter carefully, and correct any errors. Use the arrow keys to move the insertion point, as necessary.

12. Save any new changes, and then preview and print the letter.

13. Create an envelope for the letter. Click the Omit check box if necessary to deselect it, and then, for the return address, type your own address. Add the envelope to the document. If you are asked if you want to save the return address as the new default return address, click No. If your computer is connected to a printer that is stocked with envelopes, click File on the menu bar, click Print, click the Pages option button, type 1 in the Pages text box, and then click OK.

14. Save your work, and then close the document.

Case Problem 3

There are no Data Files needed for this Case Problem.

Boundary Waters Technical College Liza Morgan, professor of e-commerce at Boundary Waters Technical College in northern Minnesota, was recently honored by the Northern Business Council for her series of free public seminars on developing Web sites for nonprofit agencies. She also was recently named Teacher of the Year by a national organization called Women in Technology. As one of her former students, you decide to write a letter congratulating her on these honors. To create the letter, complete the following steps:

1. Open a new blank document if one is not already open, and then check your screen to make sure your settings match those in Figure 1-8.

2. Create the letter shown in Figure 1-30. Replace "Your Name" with your first and last name.

Figure 1-30

August 13, 2006

Professor Liza Morgan
Department of Business Administration
Boundary Waters Technical College
1010 Sturgeon Drive
Blue Pines, Minnesota 50601

Dear Professor Morgan:

I was happy to hear about your recent honors. You certainly deserve to be recognized for your Web site development seminars. As a grateful former student, I heartily endorse your Teacher of the Year award. Congratulations!

Sincerely,

Your Name

3. Save the document as **Congratulations Letter** in the Tutorial.01\Cases folder provided with your Data Files.
4. Correct any typing errors, remove any Smart Tags, and then preview and print the letter.
5. Create an envelope, using your address as the return address, and then add the envelope to the document. (*Hint*: Click the Omit check box to deselect it if it is selected before attempting to type the return address.) Do not save the return address as the default.
6. Save the document and close it.

Challenge

Go beyond what you've learned to write a memo for a small e-business company.

Case Problem 4

There are no Data Files needed for this Case Problem.

Head for the Hills You are the office manager for Head for the Hills, a small company that sells hiking equipment over the Internet. The company has just moved to a new building, which requires a special security key card after hours. Some employees have had trouble getting the key cards to work properly. You decide to hold a meeting to explain the security policies for the new building and to demonstrate the key cards. But first you need to post a memo announcing the meeting. The recently ordered letterhead (with the company's new address) has not yet arrived, so you will use a Word template to create the memo. Word provides templates—that is, models with predefined formatting—to help you create complete documents (including a professional-looking letterhead) quickly. To create the memo, do the following steps. The steps show quotation marks around text you type; do not include the quotation marks in your letter.

1. Open a new blank document if one is not already open, and then check your screen to make sure your settings match those in Figure 1-8.
2. Open the New Document task pane. You see a number of options related to creating new documents.

Explore 3. In the "Templates" section, click On my computer. The Templates dialog box opens.

Explore 4. Click the Memos tab, click Professional Memo, and then click the OK button. A memo template opens containing generic, placeholder text that you can replace with your own information.

5. Display the template in Normal view, if it is not already. Click immediately to the right of the last "e" in the text "Company Name Here" (at the top of the document), press the Backspace key repeatedly to delete the text, and type "Head for the Hills".
6. Click the text "Click here and type name" in the To: line, and type "All Employees". Click the text after "From:", and replace it with your name.
7. Click the text after "CC:", press Delete to delete the placeholder text, and then delete the entire "CC:" line. Note that Word inserts the current date automatically after the heading "Date."
8. Click the text after "Re:", and then type "Using key cards".
9. Delete the placeholder text that begins "How to Use..." but do not delete the paragraph mark (¶) at the end of the line, and then type "Meeting Tomorrow".

Explore 10. Delete the text in the body of the letter but do not delete the paragraph mark (¶) at the end of the paragraph, and then type a paragraph announcing the meeting, which is scheduled for tomorrow at 2 p.m. in the Central Conference Room.

11. Save the letter as **Key Card Meeting Memo** in the Tutorial.01\Cases folder provided with your Data Files.

Explore 12. To make it easier to review your work, you can change the Zoom setting in Normal view. Click the Zoom box in the Standard toolbar, type 110%, and then press the Enter key. Continue to type values in the Zoom text box until the document fills the window.

13. Review the memo. Correct any typos and delete any Smart Tags. Save the memo again, preview it, and then print it.
14. Close the document.

Research

Go to the Web to find information you can use to create documents.

Internet Assignments

The purpose of the Internet Assignments is to challenge you to find information on the Internet that you can use to work effectively with this software. The actual assignments are updated and maintained on the Course Technology Web site. Log on to the Internet and use your Web browser to go to the Student Online Companion for New Perspectives Office 2003 at **www.course.com/np/office2003**. Click the Internet Assignments link, and then navigate to the assignments for this tutorial.

Assess

SAM Assessment and Training

If your instructor has chosen to use the full online version of SAM 2003 Assessment and Training, you can go beyond the "just-in-time" training provided on the CD that accompanies this text. Simply log in to your SAM account (http://sam2003.course.com) to launch any assigned training activities or exams that relate to the skills covered in this tutorial.

Reinforce

Word Processing

Lab Assignments

The New Perspectives Labs are designed to help you master some of the key concepts and skills presented in this text. The steps for completing this Lab are located on the Course Technology Web site. Log on to the Internet and use your Web browser to go to the Student Online Companion for New Perspectives Office 2003 at **www.course.com/np/office2003**. Click the Lab Assignments link, and then navigate to the assignments for this tutorial.

Review

Quick Check Answers

Session 1.1

1. (1) Plan the content, purpose, organization, and look of your document. (2) Create and then edit the document. (3) Format the document to make it visually appealing. (4) Preview and then print the document.
2. a. symbols you can display on-screen but that don't print
   b. controls the document's on-screen magnification
   c. settings that control the size and shape of the characters that appear when you start typing
   d. standard settings
3. Click the Normal View button.
4. Right-click a toolbar or the menu bar, and then click Standard.
5. False
6. False
7. .doc

Session 1.2

1. True
2. Type the first few characters of the month. When an AutoComplete suggestion appears, press the Enter key.
3. Undo
4. Click Tools on the menu bar, point to Letters and Mailings, and then click Envelopes and Labels. In the Envelopes and Labels dialog box, verify that the Delivery address contains the correct address. If necessary, you can type a new address or edit the existing one. If necessary, type a return address. If you are using preprinted stationery that already includes a return address, click the Omit check box to insert a check. To print the envelope immediately, insert an envelope in your printer, and then click Print. To store the envelope along with the rest of the document, click Add to Document. To print the envelope after you have added it to the document, open the Print dialog box, and then print the page containing the envelope.
5. a. the means by which text at the bottom of the document shifts out of view when you display the top of the document, and text at the top shifts out of view when you display the bottom of a document
   b. a feature that automatically enters dates and other regularly used items
   c. a button that redoes changes
   d. a window in which you can see how the document will look when printed
   e. a feature that that allows you to perform actions (such as sending e-mail or scheduling a meeting) that would normally require a completely different program.

Editing and Formatting a Document

Preparing an FAQ Document

Case | Long Meadow Gardens

Marilee Brigham is the owner of Long Meadow Gardens, a landscape and gardening supply company. The firm's large nursery provides shrubs and trees to professional landscape contractors throughout the Minneapolis/St. Paul area. At the same time, Long Meadow Gardens' retail store caters to home gardeners, who often call the store with questions about planting and caring for their purchases.

Marilee has noticed that retail customers tend to ask the same set of questions. To save time, she would like to create a series of handouts designed to answer these common questions. (Such a document is sometimes known as an FAQ—which is short for "frequently asked questions.") The company's chief horticulturist, Peter Chi, has just finished creating an FAQ containing information on planting trees. Now that Marilee has commented on and corrected the draft, Peter asks you to make the necessary changes and print the document.

In this tutorial, you will edit the FAQ document according to Marilee's comments. You'll also change the overall look of the document by changing margins and line spacing, indenting and justifying paragraphs, and copying formatting from one paragraph to another. You'll use various formatting techniques to enhance and draw attention to specific parts of the document. Finally, before you print the FAQ document, you will add a comment, and look up information using the Research task pane.

Session	Objectives		SAM Training Tasks	
Session 2.1	• Check spelling and grammar • Select and delete text	• Move text within the document • Find and replace text	• Check grammar • Check spelling • Check spelling and grammar as you type • Collect and paste using the clipboard task pane • Copy and paste text • Cut and paste text • Cut text • Delete selected text from a document	• Find and replace text • Move text • Open a document • Select a line • Select nonadjacent text • Select text • Set default dictionary • Use Save As • Use the Paste Options button
Session 2.2	• Change margins, line spacing, alignment, and paragraph indents • Copy formatting with the Format Painter • Change fonts and adjust font sizes	• Emphasize points with bullets, numbering, bold, underlining, and italics • Preview formatted text • Add a comment to a document • Use the Research task pane	• Add bullets • Add numbering • Add picture bullets to a list • Adjust line spacing • Bold text • Center a paragraph • Change font • Change font size • Change the page orientation • Create a hanging indent • Delete comments	• Edit a comment • First-line indent paragraph • Indent paragraphs • Insert comments • Italicize text • Justify a paragraph • Modify page margins • Print documents • Right-align a paragraph • Underline a word • Use Format Painter • Use print preview • Use the Research task pane

Student Data Files For a complete list of the Data Files needed for this tutorial, see page WD 2.

Session 2.1

For hands-on practice of key tasks in this session, go to the SAM 2003 Training Companion CD included with this text.

Reviewing the Document

Marilee's editing marks and notes on the first draft are shown in Figure 2-1. Notice that the edits specify changes both to the text of the document and to how the document is formatted. For example, Marilee would like to add bullets to emphasize the species of water-tolerant trees, and she would like to format the steps involved in removing the burlap from around the base of a tree as a numbered list. You'll begin by opening the first draft of the document, which has the filename FAQ.

Figure 2-1 ▶ **Draft of FAQ with Marilee's edits (page 1)**

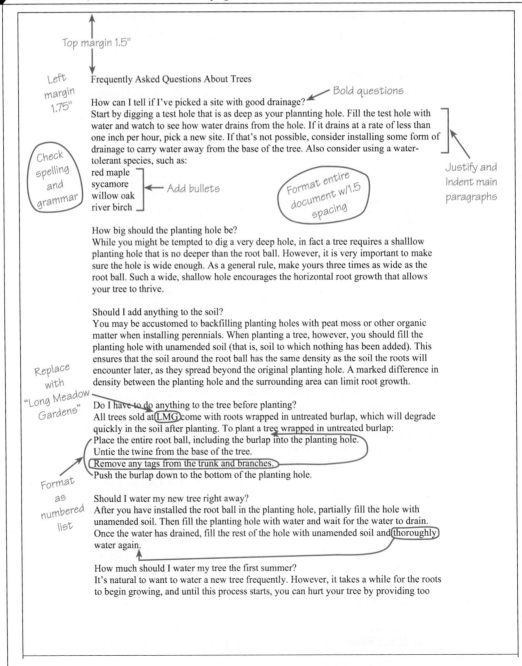

Draft of FAQ with Marilee's edits (page 2) ◀ **Figure 2-1 (cont.)**

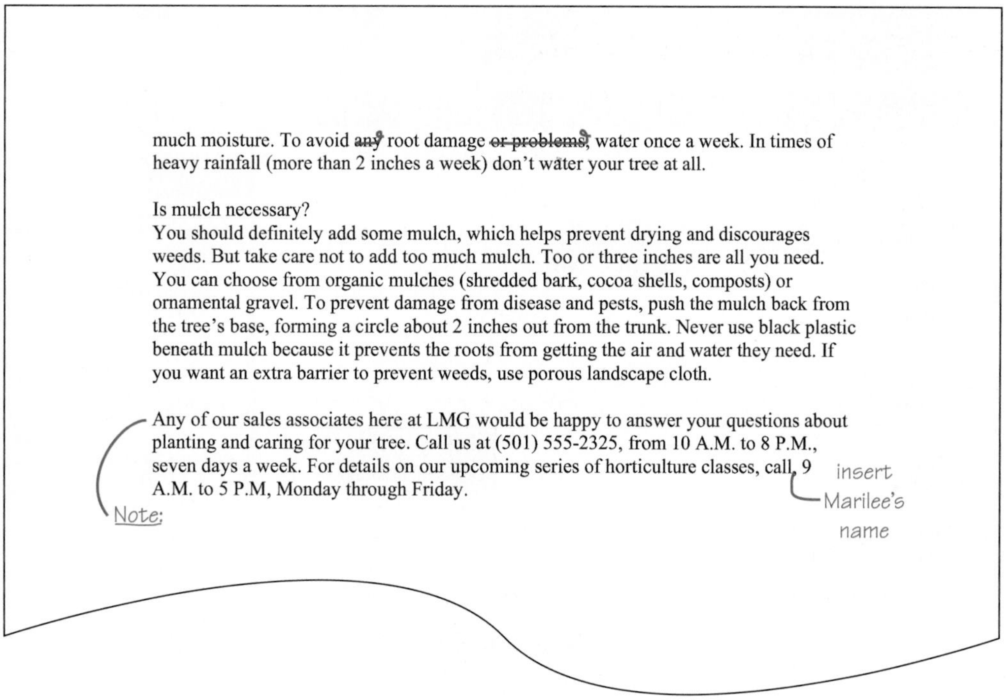

much moisture. To avoid ~~any~~ root damage ~~or problems~~, water once a week. In times of heavy rainfall (more than 2 inches a week) don't water your tree at all.

Is mulch necessary?
You should definitely add some mulch, which helps prevent drying and discourages weeds. But take care not to add too much mulch. Too or three inches are all you need. You can choose from organic mulches (shredded bark, cocoa shells, composts) or ornamental gravel. To prevent damage from disease and pests, push the mulch back from the tree's base, forming a circle about 2 inches out from the trunk. Never use black plastic beneath mulch because it prevents the roots from getting the air and water they need. If you want an extra barrier to prevent weeds, use porous landscape cloth.

Any of our sales associates here at LMG would be happy to answer your questions about planting and caring for your tree. Call us at (501) 555-2325, from 10 A.M. to 8 P.M., seven days a week. For details on our upcoming series of horticulture classes, call 9 A.M. to 5 P.M, Monday through Friday.

insert
Marilee's
name

Note;

To open the document:

▶ **1.** Start Word, and then verify that the Getting Started task pane is displayed.

▶ **2.** In the Open section of the Getting Started task pane, click the **Open** button 📂. You may have to point to the down arrow at the bottom of the task pane to scroll down in order to display the Open button. (Depending on how your computer is set up, the label next to this button might read "More" or "Open.") The Open dialog box opens, as shown in Figure 2-2. (Note that you could also use the Open button on the Standard toolbar to open this dialog box.)

Figure 2-2	Open dialog box

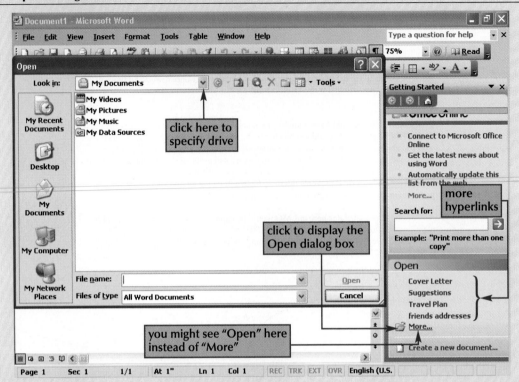

3. Click the **Look in** list arrow, and then navigate to the Tutorial.02 folder included with your Data Files.

4. Double-click the **Tutorial.02** folder, and then double-click the **Tutorial** folder.

5. Click **FAQ** to select the file, if necessary.

   Trouble? If you see "FAQ.doc" in the folder, Windows is configured to display file extensions. Click FAQ.doc and continue with Step 6. If you can't find the file with or without the file extension, make sure you're looking in the Tutorial subfolder within the Tutorial.02 folder included with your Data Files, and check to make sure the Files of type text box displays All Word Documents or All Files. If you still can't locate the file, ask your instructor or technical support person for help.

6. Click the **Open** button. The document opens with the insertion point at the beginning of the document. Notice that the document consists of a series of questions and answers.

7. Verify that the document is displayed in Normal view, and then scroll down until you can see the question "Is mulch necessary?" Notice the dotted line in the middle of the preceding paragraph. This line shows where Word has inserted a page break, dividing the document into two pages. See Figure 2-3. Word automatically inserts a page break (called an **automatic page break**) whenever your text fills up all the available lines on a page. In Normal view, a page break is represented by the dotted line shown in Figure 2-3. In some views, page breaks are not visible at all.

Document with automatic page break ◀ Figure 2-3

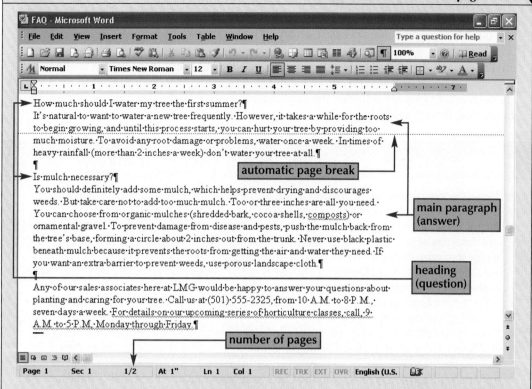

8. Check that your screen matches Figure 2-3. If necessary, click the **Show/Hide ¶** button ¶ to display nonprinting characters. This will make formatting elements (paragraph marks, spaces, and so forth) visible and easier to change.

Now that you've opened the document, you can save it with a new name. To avoid altering the original file, FAQ, you will save the document using the filename Tree FAQ. Saving the document with another filename creates a copy of the file and leaves the original file unchanged in case you want to work through the tutorial again.

To save the document with a new name:

1. Click **File** on the menu bar, and then click **Save As**. The Save As dialog box opens with the current filename highlighted in the File name text box. You could type an entirely new filename, or you could edit the current one.

2. Click to the left of "FAQ" in the File name text box, type **Tree**, and then press the **spacebar**.

3. Verify that the Tutorial.02\Tutorial folder is selected in the Save in box.

4. Click the **Save** button. The document is saved with the new filename "Tree FAQ".

Now you're ready to begin working with the document. First, you will check it for spelling and grammatical errors.

Using the Spelling and Grammar Checker

When typing a document, Word highlights possible spelling and grammatical errors. You can quickly recognize these possible errors by looking for words underlined in red (for possible spelling errors) or green (for possible grammatical errors). When you're working on a document that someone else typed, it's a good idea to start by using the Spelling and Grammar checker. This feature automatically checks a document word by word for a variety of errors. Among other things, the Spelling and Grammar checker can sometimes find words that, though spelled correctly, are not used properly.

Reference Window	Checking a Document for Spelling and Grammatical Errors

- Move the insertion point to the beginning of the document, and then click the Spelling and Grammar button on the Standard toolbar.
- In the Spelling and Grammar dialog box, review any errors highlighted in color. Possible grammatical errors appear in green; possible spelling errors appear in red. Review the suggested corrections in the Suggestions list box.
- To accept a suggested correction, click on it in the Suggestions list box, click Change to make the correction, and then continue searching the document for errors.
- Click Ignore Once to skip the current instance of the highlighted text and continue searching the document for errors.
- Click Ignore All to skip all instances of the highlighted text and continue searching the document for spelling errors. Click Ignore Rule to skip all instances of a highlighted grammatical error.
- To type your correction directly in the document, click outside the Spelling and Grammar dialog box, make the correction, and then click Resume in the Spelling and Grammar dialog box.
- To add an unrecognized word to the dictionary, click Add to dictionary.

The Spelling and Grammar Checker compares the words in your document to the default dictionary that is installed automatically with Word. If you regularly use terms that are not included in the main dictionary, you can create a custom dictionary and then select it as the new default dictionary. A custom dictionary includes all the terms in the main dictionary, plus any new terms that you add. To create a custom dictionary and select it as the new default dictionary, you would follow these steps:

1. Click **Tools** on the menu bar, click **Options**, click the **Spelling & Grammar** tab, and then click **Custom Dictionaries**. The Custom Dictionaries dialog box opens.
2. Click **New**. The Create Custom Dictionary dialog box opens.
3. Type a name for the custom dictionary in the File name text box, and click **Save**. You return to the Custom Dictionaries dialog box.
4. In the **Dictionary list** box, click the new custom dictionary to select it, click **Change Default**, and then click **OK**.

You'll see how the Spelling and Grammar checker works as you check the Tree FAQ document for mistakes.

To check the Tree FAQ document for spelling and grammatical errors:

1. Press **Ctrl+Home** to verify that the insertion point is located at the beginning of the document, to the left of the "F" in "Frequently Asked Questions."

2. Click the **Spelling and Grammar** button 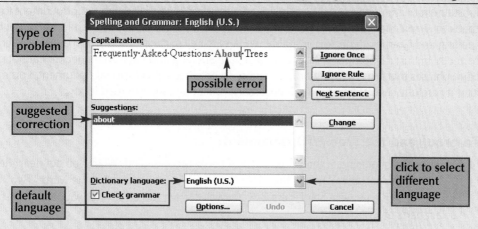 on the Standard toolbar. The Spelling and Grammar dialog box opens with the word "About" highlighted in green, indicating a possible grammatical error. The word "about" (with a lowercase "a") is suggested as a possible replacement. The line immediately under the dialog box title bar indicates the possible type of problem, in this case, Capitalization. See Figure 2-4. Prepositions of five or more letters are capitalized in titles so no change is required here.

   Trouble? If you see the word "plannting" selected instead of "About," your computer is not set up to check grammar. Click the Check grammar check box to insert a check, and then click Cancel to close the Spelling and Grammar dialog box. Repeat Steps 1 and 2.

Spelling and Grammar dialog box ◄ **Figure 2-4**

Figure 2-4 shows the Spelling and Grammar: English (U.S.) dialog box with labels:
- **type of problem** → Capitalization:
- Frequently·Asked·Questions·About·Trees (with **possible error** pointing to "About")
- Buttons: Ignore Once, Ignore Rule, Next Sentence
- **suggested correction** → Suggestions: about
- Button: Change
- Dictionary language: English (U.S.) with **click to select different language** pointing to the dropdown
- **default language** → ✓ Check grammar
- Buttons: Options..., Undo, Cancel

3. Click the **Ignore Rule** button. The word "plannting" is highlighted in red, with "planting," "planning," and "plantings" listed as possible corrections.

4. Verify that "planting" is highlighted in the Suggestions list box, and then click the **Change** button. "Planting" is inserted into the document, and the misspelled word "shalllow" is highlighted in the document.

5. Verify that "shallow" is selected in the Suggestions list box, and then click the **Change** button. The word "composts" is highlighted in green, with "and composts" listed as a possible correction. The type of problem "Comma Use" has to do with using a comma without "and" before the last item in a list. Marilee likes the list as it stands, so you'll ignore this suggestion.

6. Click the **Ignore Rule** button. You click Ignore Rule to ignore the rule throughout the entire document. (You can click Ignore Once to ignore a grammatical rule in the currently selected text.)

The last sentence of the document is selected. According to the type of problem listed at the top of the dialog box, the highlighted text is a sentence fragment. In this case, Word is correct. The word "call" lacks a direct object—that is, you need to indicate whom the reader should call. You can fix this problem by clicking outside the Spelling and Grammar dialog box and typing the change directly in the document.

▶ 7. Click outside the Spelling and Grammar dialog box just to the right of "call," press the **spacebar**, type **Marilee Brigham**, and then click the **Resume** button in the Spelling and Grammar dialog box. A message box opens indicating that the spelling and grammar check is complete. Notice that the last sentence is no longer a sentence fragment; that is because "Marilee Brigham" completes the sentence.

Trouble? If you don't see the word "call," the Spelling and Grammar checker dialog box is covering it. Click the title bar of the Spelling and Grammar dialog box, and drag the dialog box out of the way.

▶ 8. Click the **OK** button. The Spelling and Grammar dialog box closes. You return to the Tree FAQ document.

Although the Spelling and Grammar checker is a useful tool, remember that there is no substitute for careful proofreading. Always take the time to read through your document to check for errors the Spelling and Grammar checker might have missed. Keep in mind that the Spelling and Grammar checker probably won't catch *all* instances of words that are spelled correctly but used improperly. And, of course, the Spelling and Grammar checker cannot pinpoint phrases that are confusing or inaccurate. To produce a professional document, you must read it carefully several times, and, if necessary, ask a co-worker to read it, too.

To proofread the Tree FAQ document:

▶ 1. Scroll to the beginning of the document and begin proofreading. When you get near the bottom of the document, notice that the word "Too" is used instead of the word "Two" in the paragraph on mulch. See Figure 2-5. You will correct this error after you learn how to select parts of a document.

Figure 2-5 | **Word "Too" used incorrectly**

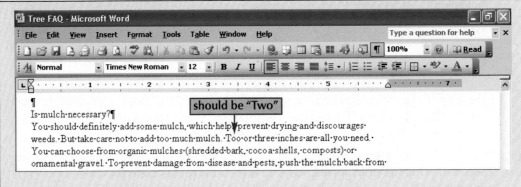

▶ 2. Finish proofreading the Tree FAQ document.

To make all of Marilee's changes, you need to learn how to select parts of a document.

Selecting Parts of a Document

Before you can do anything to text (such as deleting, moving, or formatting it), you often need to highlight, or **select** it. You can select text by using the mouse or the keyboard, although the mouse is usually easier and more efficient. With the mouse you can quickly select a line or paragraph by clicking the **selection bar** (the blank space in the left margin area of the Document window). You can also select text using various combinations of keys. Figure 2-6 summarizes methods for selecting text with the mouse and the keyboard. The notation "Ctrl+Shift" means you press and hold the two keys at the same time. Note that you will use the methods described in Figure 2-6 as you work on the Tree FAQ document.

Methods for selecting text ◀ Figure 2-6

To Select	Mouse	Keyboard	Mouse and Keyboard
A word	Double-click the word.	Move the insertion point to the beginning of the word, hold down Ctrl+Shift, and then press →.	
A line	Click in the selection bar next to the line.	Move the insertion point to the beginning of the line, hold down Shift, and then press →.	
A sentence	Click at the beginning of the sentence, then drag the pointer until the sentence is selected.		Press and hold down the Ctrl key, and click within the sentence.
Multiple lines	Click and drag in the selection bar next to the lines.	Move the insertion point to the beginning of the first line, hold down Shift, and then press → until all the lines are selected.	
A paragraph	Double-click in the selection bar next to the paragraph, or triple-click within the paragraph.	Move the insertion point to the beginning of the paragraph, hold down Ctrl+Shift, and then press ↓.	
Multiple paragraphs	Click in the selection bar next to the first paragraph in the group, and then drag in the selection bar to select the paragraphs.	Move the insertion point to the beginning of the first paragraph, hold down Ctrl+Shift, and then press ↓ until all the paragraphs are selected.	
An entire document	Triple-click in the selection bar.	Press Ctrl+A.	Press and hold down the Ctrl key and click in the selection bar.
A block of text	Click at the beginning of the block, then drag the pointer until the entire block is selected.		Click at the beginning of the block, press and hold down the Shift key, and then click at the end of the block.
Nonadjacent blocks of text	Press and hold the Ctrl key, then drag the mouse pointer to select multiple blocks of nonadjacent text.		

Deleting Text

When editing a document, you frequently need to delete text. You already have experience using the Backspace and Delete keys to delete a few characters. To delete an entire word or multiple words, you select the text. After you select the text, you can either replace it with something else by typing over it, or delete it by pressing the Delete key. You need to delete the word "Too" and replace it with "Two," so you'll use the first method now.

To replace "Too" with "Two":

1. Press **Ctrl+End**. The insertion point moves to the end of the document.

2. Press and hold the **Ctrl** key while you press the ↑ key three times. The insertion point is now positioned at the beginning of the paragraph that begins "You should definitely add some mulch." (The status bar indicates that this is line 5 of page 2.)

3. In the second line of the paragraph, double-click the word **Too** (in the phrase "Too or three inches"). The entire word is highlighted.

4. Type **Two**. The selected word is replaced with the correction. The sentence now correctly reads: "Two or three inches are all you need."

Next, Marilee wants you to delete the phrase "or problems" and the word "any" in the paragraph before the one you've just corrected. Peter explains that you can do this quickly by selecting multiple items and then pressing Delete. As you'll see in the following steps, selecting parts of a document by clicking and dragging takes a little practice, so don't be concerned if you don't get it right the first time. You can always try again.

To select and delete multiple items:

1. Press the ↑ key five times. As shown in Figure 2-7, the insertion point is now located in the sentence that begins "To avoid any root damage or problems." The status bar indicates that this is line 1 of page 2.

Figure 2-7 ▶ **Text to be deleted**

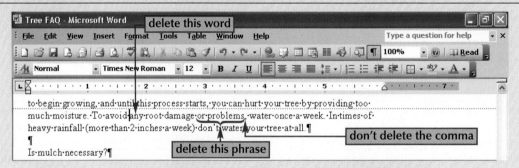

2. Double-click the word **any**. The word and the space following it are selected.

3. Press and hold the **Ctrl** key, click to the left of "or" and drag to select the phrase "or problems," and then release the **Ctrl** key. Do not select the comma after the word "problems." At this point the word "any" and the phrase "or problems" should be selected.

Trouble? If you don't get Step 3 right the first time (for instance, if you accidentally selected the word "damage"), click anywhere in the document and then repeat Steps 2 and 3.

4. Press the **Delete** key. The selected items are deleted and the words around them move in to fill the space. As you can see in Figure 2-8, you still need to delete the extra space before the comma.

Paragraph after deleting phrase | **Figure 2-8**

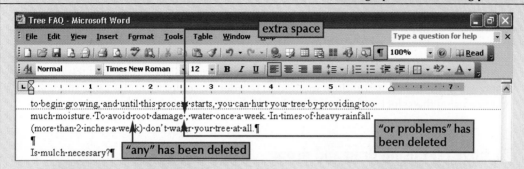

Trouble? If you deleted the wrong text, click the Undo button 🔟 (not the Redo button) on the Standard toolbar to reverse your mistake, and then begin again with Step 2.

Trouble? If your screen looks slightly different from Figure 2-8, don't be concerned. The text may wrap differently on your monitor. Just make sure you deleted the correct text.

5. Click to the right of the word "damage," and then press the **Delete** key. The extra space is deleted.

6. Scroll down to display the last line of the document (if necessary), drag the mouse pointer to select "Marilee Brigham," press the **Delete** key, press the **spacebar**, and then type your first and last name. This change will make it easier for you to retrieve your document if you print it on a network printer used by other students.

You have edited the document by replacing "Too" with "Two" and by removing the text that Marilee marked for deletion. Now you are ready to make the rest of the edits she suggested.

Moving Text within a Document

One of the most useful features of a word-processing program is the ability to move text. For example, Marilee wants to reorder the four points Peter made in the section "Do I have to do anything to the tree before planting?" on page 1 of his draft. You could reorder the list by deleting an item and then retyping it at a new location, but it's easier to select and then move the text. Word provides several ways to move text: drag and drop, cut and paste, and copy and paste.

Dragging and Dropping Text

One way to move text within a document is called drag and drop. With **drag and drop**, you select the text you want to move, press and hold down the mouse button while you drag the selected text to a new location, and then release the mouse button.

Dragging and Dropping Text

- Select the text you want to move.
- Press and hold down the mouse button until the drag-and-drop pointer appears, and then drag the selected text to its new location.
- Use the dotted insertion point as a guide to determine exactly where the text will be inserted.
- Release the mouse button to drop the text at the insertion point.

Marilee wants you to change the order of the items in the list on page 1 of the document. You'll use the drag-and-drop method to reorder these items. At the same time, you'll practice using the selection bar to highlight a line of text.

To move text using drag and drop:

1. Scroll up until you see "Do I have to do anything to the tree before planting?" (line 29 of page 1). In the list of steps involved in planting a tree, Marilee wants you to move the third step ("Remove any tags from the trunk and branches.") to the top of the list.

2. Move the pointer to the selection bar to the left of the line "Remove any tags from the trunk and branches." The pointer changes from an I-beam ⌶ to a right-facing arrow ⌀.

3. Click to the left of the line "Remove any tags from the trunk and branches." The line is selected. Notice that the paragraph mark at the end of the line is also selected. See Figure 2-9.

Figure 2-9   **Selected text to drag and drop**

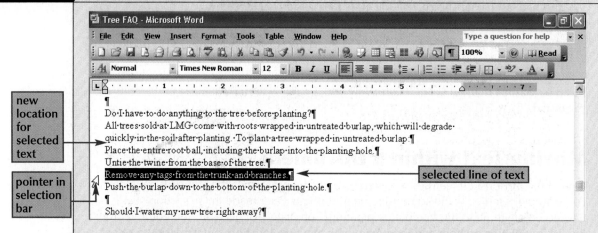

new location for selected text

pointer in selection bar

selected line of text

4. Position the pointer over the selected text. The pointer changes from a right-facing arrow ⌀ to a left-facing arrow ⌀.

5. Press and hold down the mouse button until the drag-and-drop pointer ⌀ appears. Note that a dotted insertion point appears within the selected text. (You may have to move the mouse pointer slightly left or right to see the drag-and-drop pointer or the dotted insertion point.)

6. Drag the selected text up until the dotted insertion point appears to the left of the word "Place." Make sure you use the dotted insertion point, rather than the mouse pointer, to guide the text to its new location. The dotted insertion point indicates exactly where the text will appear when you release the mouse button. See Figure 2-10.

Moving text with drag-and-drop pointer | Figure 2-10

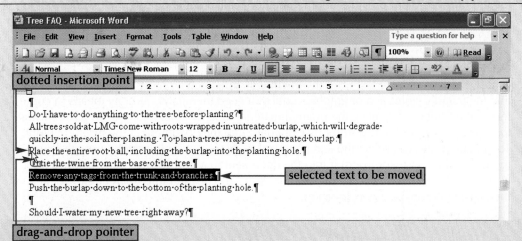

7. Release the mouse button. The selected text moves to its new location as the first step in the list. A Paste Options button appears near the newly moved text, as shown in Figure 2-11. When you move the mouse pointer over the Paste Options button, it changes to include a list arrow.

Paste Options button | Figure 2-11

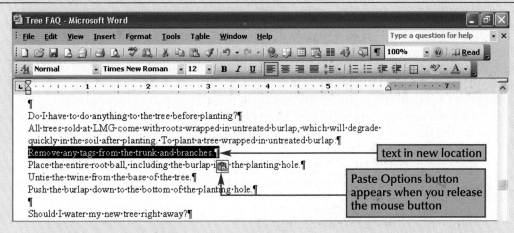

Trouble? If the selected text moves to the wrong location, click the Undo button ⟳ on the Standard toolbar, and then repeat Steps 2 through 7. Remember to hold down the mouse button until the dotted insertion point appears to the left of the word "Place."

Trouble? If you don't see the Paste Options button, your computer is not set up to display it. Read Step 8, and then continue with Step 9.

8. Click the **Paste Options** button 🖹 ▾. A menu of text-moving commands appears. These commands are useful when you are inserting text that looks different from the surrounding text. For instance, suppose you selected text formatted in the Times New Roman font and then dragged it to a paragraph formatted in the Arial font. You could then use the Match Destination Formatting command to format the moved text in Arial.

9. Deselect the highlighted text by clicking anywhere in the document. The Paste Options menu closes, but the button remains visible. It will disappear as soon as you perform another task.

Dragging and dropping works well if you're moving text a short distance in a document. However, Word provides another method, called cut and paste, that works well for moving text both long and short distances.

Cutting or Copying and Pasting Text

To **cut** means to remove text from the document and place it on the **Clipboard**, a feature that temporarily stores text or graphics until you need them later. To **copy** means to copy text to the Clipboard, leaving the original material in its original location. To **paste** means to transfer a copy of the text from the Clipboard into the document at the insertion point. To **cut and paste**, you select the text you want to move, cut (or remove) it from the document, and then paste (or insert) it into the document in a new location. If you don't want to remove the text from its original location, you can copy it (rather than cutting it), and then paste the copy in a new location.

| Reference Window | **Cutting or Copying and Pasting Text** |

- Select the text you want to cut or copy.
- To remove the text, click the Cut button on the Standard toolbar.
- To make a copy of the text, click the Copy button on the Standard toolbar.
- Move the insertion point to the target location in the document.
- Click the Paste button on the Standard toolbar.

Depending on how your computer is set up, when you cut or copy more than one item, the **Clipboard task pane** may open automatically, making it easier for you to select which items you want to paste into the document. (To have the Clipboard task pane open automatically, click Options at the bottom of the Clipboard task pane, and then select Show Clipboard Automatically.) You can also choose to open the Clipboard task pane via the Office Clipboard command on the Edit menu. The Clipboard task pane contains a list of all the items currently stored on the Clipboard. The Clipboard can store a maximum of 24 items. The last item cut or copied to the Clipboard is the first item listed in the Clipboard task pane.

As indicated in Figure 2-1, Marilee suggested moving the word "thoroughly" (in the paragraph under the heading "Should I water my new tree right away?") to a new location. You'll use cut and paste to move this word.

To move text using cut and paste:

1. If necessary, scroll down until you can see the paragraph below the heading "Should I water my new tree right away?" near the bottom of page 1.

2. Double-click the word **thoroughly**. As you can see in Figure 2-12, you need to move this word to the end of the sentence.

Text to move using cut and paste | Figure 2-12

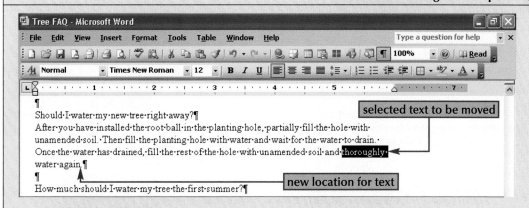

3. Click the **Cut** button on the Standard toolbar to remove the selected text from the document.

4. If the Clipboard task pane opens, click its **Close** button for now. You'll have a chance to use the Clipboard task pane shortly.

5. Click between the "n" in "again" and the period that follows it. The insertion point marks the position where you want to move the text.

6. Click the **Paste** button on the Standard toolbar. The word "thoroughly" appears in its new location, along with a Paste Options button. Note that Word also included a space before the word, so that the end of the sentence reads "and water again thoroughly." The Paste Options button that appeared in the previous set of steps (when you dragged text to a new location) disappears.

   Trouble? If the Paste Options buttons on your computer do not behave exactly as described in these steps—for instance, if they do not disappear as described—this is not a problem, just continue with the tutorial.

Peter mentions that he'll be using the paragraph on mulch and the paragraph on watering for the FAQ he plans to write on flowering shrubs. He asks you to copy that information and paste it in a new document that he can use as the basis for the new FAQ. You can do this using copy and paste. In the process you'll have a chance to use the Clipboard task pane.

To copy and paste text:

1. Click **Edit** on the menu bar, and then click **Office Clipboard**. The Clipboard task pane opens on the right side of the Document window. It contains the word "thoroughly," which you copied to the Clipboard in the last set of steps. See Figure 2-13.

Figure 2-13 | **Clipboard task pane**

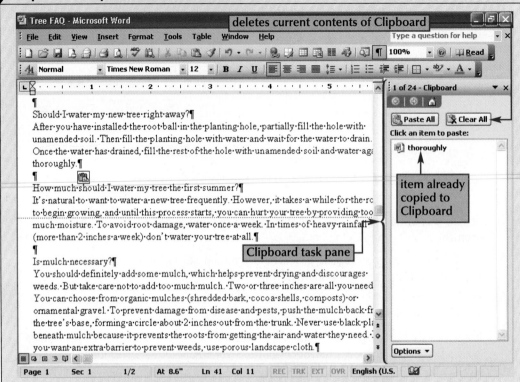

2. Click the **Clear All** button near the top of the task pane. The current contents of the Clipboard are deleted, and you see the following message on the Clipboard task pane: "Clipboard empty. Copy or cut to collect items."

3. Move the mouse pointer to the selection bar and double-click next to the paragraph that begins "After you have installed the root ball." The entire paragraph is selected.

4. Click the **Copy** button 📋 on the Standard toolbar. The first part of the paragraph appears in the Clipboard task pane.

5. If necessary, scroll down until you can see the paragraph below the heading "Is mulch necessary?"

6. Select the paragraph below the heading (the paragraph that begins "You should definitely add . . . ").

7. Click the **Copy** button 📋 on the Standard toolbar. The first part of the paragraph appears in the Clipboard task pane, as shown in Figure 2-14. Note the Clipboard icon 📋 on the Windows taskbar indicating that the Clipboard task pane is currently active.

Trouble? If you do not see the Clipboard icon in the task pane, click the Options button at the bottom of the Clipboard task pane, and then click Show Office Clipboard Icon on Taskbar. When a check mark is next to this option, the Clipboard icon appears in the far right side of the Windows taskbar to the left of the time.

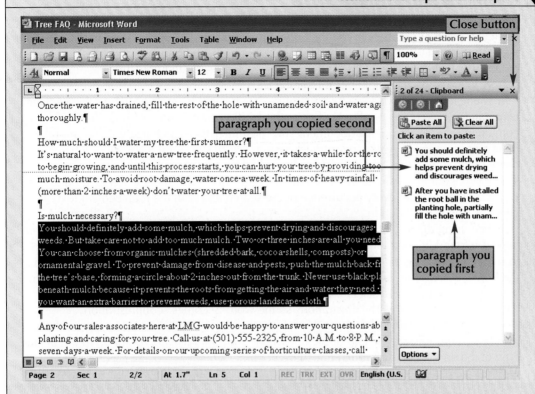

Items in the Clipboard task pane ◄ Figure 2-14

8. Click the **New Blank Document** button ▢ on the Standard toolbar. A new, blank document opens. The Clipboard icon 📋 on the Windows taskbar indicates that although the Clipboard task pane is no longer visible, it is still active.

9. Double-click the **Clipboard** icon 📋 on the right side of the Windows taskbar. The Clipboard task pane is now visible.

Now you can use the Clipboard task pane to insert the copied text into the new document.

To insert the copied text into the new document:

1. In the Clipboard task pane, click the item that begins "You should definitely add . . . " The text is inserted in the document.

2. Press the **Enter** key to insert a blank line, and then click the item that begins "After you have installed the root ball . . . " in the task pane. The text is inserted in the document.

3. Save the document as **Flowering Shrub FAQ** in the Tutorial.02\Tutorial folder, and then close the document. You return to the Tree FAQ document, where the Clipboard task pane is still open. You are finished using the Clipboard task pane, so you will delete its contents.

4. Click the **Clear All** button on the Clipboard task pane. The copied items are removed from the Clipboard task pane.

5. Click the **Close** button ✖ on the Clipboard task pane. The Clipboard task pane closes.

6. Click anywhere in the document to deselect the highlighted paragraph.

7. Save the document.

Finding and Replacing Text

When you're working with a longer document, the quickest and easiest way to locate a particular word or phrase is to use the **Find command**. To use the Find command, you type the text you want to find in the Find what text box, and then you click the Find Next button. The text in the Find what text box is the search text. After you click the Find Next button, Word finds and highlights the search text.

If you want to replace characters or a phrase with something else, you use the **Replace command**, which combines the Find command with a substitution feature. The Replace command searches through a document and substitutes the search text with the replacement text you specify. As you perform the search, Word stops and highlights each occurrence of the search text. You must determine whether or not to substitute the replacement text. If you want to substitute the highlighted occurrence, you click the Replace button. If you want to substitute every occurrence of the search text with the replacement text, you click the Replace All button.

When using the Replace All button with single words, keep in mind that the search text might be found within other words. To prevent Word from making incorrect substitutions in such cases, it's a good idea to select the Find whole words only check box along with the Replace All button. For example, suppose you want to replace the word "figure" with "illustration." Unless you select the Find whole words only check box, Word replaces "figure" in "configure" with "illustration" so the word becomes "conillustration."

As you search through a document, you can search from the current location of the insertion point down to the end of the document, from the insertion point up to the beginning of the document, or through the entire document.

Reference Window	**Finding and Replacing Text**

- Click Edit on the menu bar, and then click either Find or Replace.
- To find text, click the Find tab. To find and replace text, click the Replace tab.
- Click the More button to expand the dialog box to display additional options (including the Find whole words only option). If you see the Less button, the additional options are already displayed.
- In the Search list box, select Down if you want to search from the insertion point to the end of the document, select Up if you want to search from the insertion point to the beginning of the document, or select All to search the entire document.
- Type the characters you want to find in the Find what text box.
- If you are replacing text, type the replacement text in the Replace with text box.
- Click the Find whole words only check box to search for complete words. Click the Match case check box to insert the replacement text using the same case specified in the Replace with text box.
- Click the Find Next button.
- Click the Replace button to substitute the found text with the replacement text and find the next occurrence.
- Click the Replace All button to substitute all occurrences of the found text with the replacement text.

Marilee wants the company initials, LMG, to be spelled out as "Long Meadow Gardens" each time they appear in the text. You'll use the Replace command to make this change quickly and easily.

To replace "LMG" with "Long Meadow Gardens":

▸ 1. Press **Ctrl+Home** to move the insertion point to the beginning of the document.

▸ 2. Click **Edit** on the menu bar, and then click **Replace**. The Find and Replace dialog box opens.

▸ 3. If you see a **More** button, click it to display the additional search options. (If you see a Less button, the additional options are already displayed.) Also, click the **Search** list arrow, and then click **All** if it is not already selected in order to search the entire document.

▸ 4. Click the **Find what** text box, type **LMG**, press the **Tab** key, and then type **Long Meadow Gardens** in the Replace with text box.

   Trouble? If you already see the text "LMG" and "Long Meadow Gardens" in your Find and Replace dialog box, someone has recently performed these steps on your computer. Skip Step 4 and continue with Step 5.

▸ 5. Click the **Find whole words only** check box to insert a check.

▸ 6. Click the **Match case** check box to insert a check. This ensures that Word will insert the replacement text using initial capital letters, as you specified in the Replace with text box. Your Find and Replace dialog box should look like Figure 2-15.

Find and Replace dialog box ◂ **Figure 2-15**

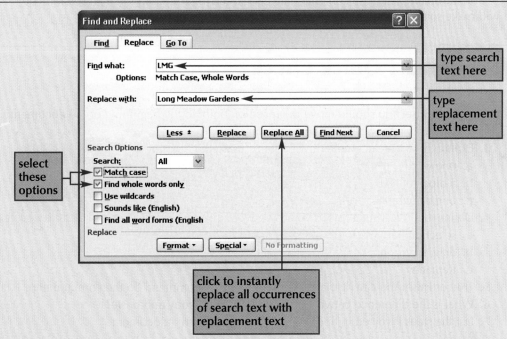

▸ 7. Click the **Replace All** button to replace all occurrences of the search text with the replacement text. When Word finishes making the replacements, you see a message box telling you that two replacements were made.

▸ 8. Click the **OK** button to close the message box, and then click the **Close** button in the Find and Replace dialog box to return to the document. The full company name has been inserted into the document, as shown in Figure 2-16. (You may have to scroll down to see this section.)

Figure 2-16 **Document with "Long Meadow Gardens" inserted**

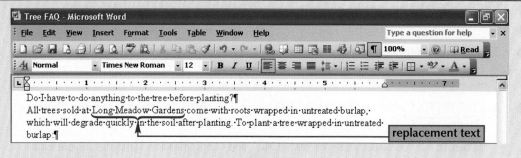

9. Save the document.

Note that you can also search for and replace formatting, such as bold and special characters, in the Find and Replace dialog box. Click in the Find what text box, enter the search text, click the Format button, click Font to open the Font dialog box, and then select the formatting for the search text. Repeat this process for the replacement text, and then complete the search or replacement operation as usual.

You have completed the content changes Marilee requested. In the next session you will make some changes that will affect the document's appearance.

Review

To reinforce the tasks you learned in this session, go to the SAM 2003 Training Companion CD included with this text.

Session 2.1 Quick Check

1. Explain how to use the Spelling and Grammar checker.
2. True or False: You should move the insertion point to the beginning of the document before starting the Spelling and Grammar checker.
3. Explain how to select the following items using the mouse:
   a. one word
   b. a block of text
   c. one paragraph
4. Define the following terms in your own words:
   a. selection bar
   b. drag and drop
   c. Replace
5. True or False: You can display the Clipboard via a command on the Format menu.
6. What is the difference between cut and paste, and copy and paste?
7. List the steps involved in finding and replacing text in a document.

Session 2.2

For hands-on practice of key tasks in this session, go to the SAM 2003 Training Companion CD included with this text.

Changing Margins and Page Orientation

By default, text in a Word document is formatted in **portrait orientation**, which means the page is longer than it is wide (like a typical business letter). In Portrait orientation, the default margins are 1.25 inches for the left and right margins and 1 inch for the top and bottom margins. In **landscape orientation**, the page is wider than it is long, with slightly different margins, so that text spans the widest part of the page.

When working with margins, note that the numbers on the ruler indicate the distance in inches from the left margin, not from the left edge of the paper. You can change both page margins and page orientation from within the Page Setup dialog box.

Changing Margins and Page Orientation for the Entire Document

- With the insertion point anywhere in your document and no text selected, click File on the menu bar, and then click Page Setup.
- If necessary, click the Margins tab to display the margin settings.
- Click the Landscape icon if you want to switch to Landscape orientation.
- Use the arrows to change the settings in the Top, Bottom, Left, or Right text boxes, or type a new margin value in each text box.
- Make sure the Apply to list box displays Whole document.
- Click the OK button.

You need to change the top margin to 1.5 inches and the left margin to 1.75 inches, per Marilee's request. The left margin needs to be wider than usual to allow space for making holes so that the document can be inserted in a three-ring binder. In the next set of steps, you'll change the margins using the Page Setup command. You can also change margins in Print Layout view by dragging an icon on the horizontal ruler. You'll have a chance to practice this technique in the Case Problems at the end of this tutorial.

To change the margins in the Tree FAQ document:

1. If you took a break after the previous session, make sure Word is running, the Tree FAQ document is open in Normal view, and nonprinting characters are displayed.

2. Press **Ctrl+Home** to move the insertion point to the top of the document.

3. Click **File** on the menu bar, and then click **Page Setup** to open the Page Setup dialog box.

4. Click the **Margins** tab, if it is not already selected, to display the margin settings. Portrait orientation is selected by default. The Top margin setting is selected. See Figure 2-17. As you complete the following steps, keep an eye on the document preview, which changes to reflect changes you make to the margins.

Page Setup dialog box ◄ **Figure 2-17**

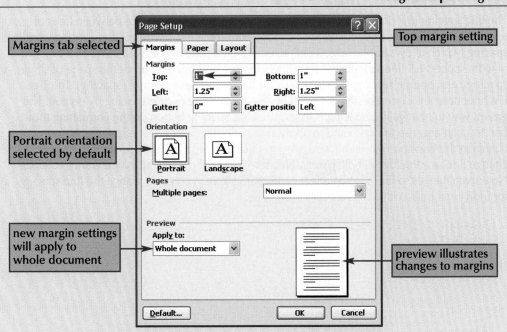

5. Type **1.5** to change the Top margin setting. (You do not have to type the inches symbol.)

6. Press the **Tab** key twice to select the Left text box and highlight the current margin setting. The text area in the Preview box moves down to reflect the larger top margin.

7. Verify that the insertion point is in the Left text box, type **1.75**, and then press the **Tab** key. The left margin in the Preview box increases.

8. Make sure the **Whole document** option is selected in the Apply to list box, and then click the **OK** button to return to your document. Notice that the right margin on the ruler has changed to reflect the larger left margin setting and the resulting reduced page area. The document text is now 5.5 inches wide. See Figure 2-18.

Figure 2-18 ▶ **Ruler after setting left margin to 1.75 inches**

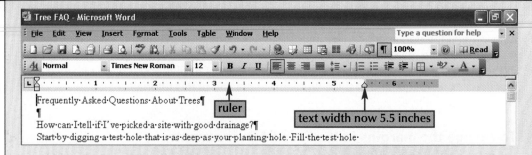

Trouble? If a double dotted line and the words "Section Break" appear in your document, Whole document wasn't specified in the Apply to list box. If this occurs, click the Undo button ⟳ on the Standard toolbar and repeat Steps 2 through 8, making sure you select the Whole document option in the Apply to list box.

Next, you will change the amount of space between lines of text.

Changing Line Spacing

The **line spacing** in a document determines the amount of vertical space between lines of text. In most situations, you will want to choose from three basic types of line spacing: **single spacing** (which allows for the largest character in a particular line as well as a small amount of extra space); **1.5 line spacing** (which allows for one and one-half times the space of single spacing); and **double spacing** (which allows for twice the space of single spacing). The Tree FAQ document is currently single-spaced because Word uses single spacing by default. The easiest way to change line spacing is to use the Line Spacing button on the Formatting toolbar. You can also use the keyboard to apply single, double, and 1.5 line spacing. Before changing the line-spacing setting, you need to click in the paragraph you want to change. To change line spacing for multiple paragraphs, select all of the paragraphs you want to change. Note that changes to line spacing affect entire paragraphs; you can't change the line spacing for individual lines within a paragraph.

Changing Line Spacing in a Document

- Click in the paragraph you want to change, or select multiple paragraphs.
- Click the list arrow next to the Line Spacing button on the Formatting toolbar, and then click the line spacing you want.

or

- Click in the paragraph you want to change, or select multiple paragraphs.
- Press Ctrl+1 for single spacing, Ctrl+5 for 1.5 line spacing, or Ctrl+2 for double spacing.

Marilee thinks the document will be easier to read with more spacing between the lines. She has asked you to change the line spacing for the entire Tree FAQ document to 1.5 line spacing. You will begin by selecting the entire document.

To change the document's line spacing:

1. Triple-click in the selection bar to select the entire document.

2. Move the mouse pointer over the **Line Spacing** button ⊞ ▾ on the Formatting toolbar to display its ScreenTip. You see the text "Line Spacing (1)," indicating that single spacing is currently selected.

3. Click the **Line Spacing** list arrow ⊞ ▾ on the Formatting toolbar. A list of line spacing options appears, as shown in Figure 2-19. To double space the document, you click 2.0, while to triple space it, you click 3.0. In this case, you need to apply 1.5 line spacing.

Line Spacing list box | **Figure 2-19**

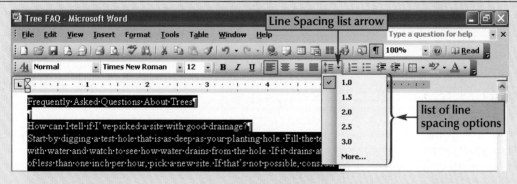

4. Click **1.5**. Notice the additional space between every line of text in the document.

5. Move the mouse pointer over the **Line Spacing** button ⊞ ▾ on the Formatting toolbar to display a ScreenTip that reads "Line Spacing (1.5)." This tells you that 1.5 spacing is currently selected.

6. Click the title to deselect the text.

Now you are ready to make formatting changes that affect individual paragraphs.

Aligning Text

As you begin formatting individual paragraphs in the Tree FAQ document, keep in mind that in Word, a **paragraph** is defined as any text that ends with a paragraph mark symbol (¶). A paragraph can be a group of words that is many lines long, a single word, or even a blank line, in which case you see a paragraph mark alone on a single line. (The Tree FAQ document includes one blank paragraph before each question heading.)

The term **alignment** refers to how the text of a paragraph lines up horizontally between the margins. By default, text is aligned along the left margin but is **ragged**, or uneven, along the right margin. This is called **left alignment**. With **right alignment**, the text is aligned along the right margin and is ragged along the left margin. With **center alignment**, text is centered between the left and right margins and is ragged along both the left and right margins. With **justified alignment**, full lines of text are spaced between both the left and the right margins and the text is not ragged. Text in newspaper columns is often justified. The easiest way to apply alignment settings is by using the alignment buttons on the Formatting toolbar.

Marilee indicates that the title of the Tree FAQ should be centered and that the main paragraphs should be justified. First, you'll center the title.

To center-align the title:

▶ **1.** Verify that the insertion point is located in the title "Frequently Asked Questions About Trees" at the beginning of the document.

▶ **2.** Click the **Center** button ▤ on the Formatting toolbar. The text centers between the left and right margins. See Figure 2-20.

Figure 2-20 | **Centered title**

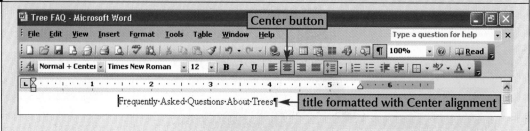

Next, you'll justify the text in the first two main paragraphs.

To justify the first two paragraphs using the Formatting toolbar:

▶ **1.** Click anywhere in the paragraph that begins "Start by digging a test hole . . . "

▶ **2.** Click the **Justify** button ▤ on the Formatting toolbar. The paragraph text spreads out so that it lines up evenly along the left and right margins.

▶ **3.** Scroll down so you can move the insertion point to anywhere in the paragraph that begins "While you might be tempted . . . "

▶ **4.** Click the **Justify** button ▤ on the Formatting toolbar again. The text is evenly spaced between the left and right margins. See Figure 2-21.

Justified paragraphs

Figure 2-21

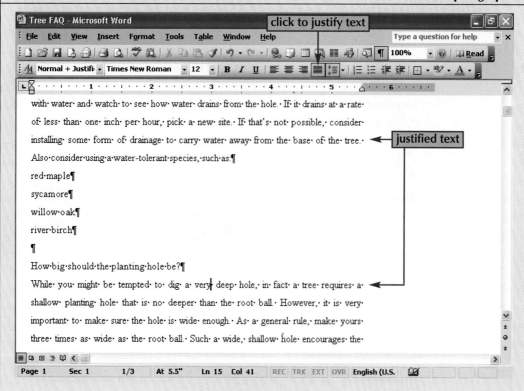

You'll justify the other paragraphs later. Now that you've learned how to change the paragraph alignment, you can turn your attention to indenting a paragraph.

Indenting a Paragraph

When you become a more experienced Word user, you might want to do some paragraph formatting, such as a **hanging indent** (where all lines except the first line of the paragraph are indented from the left margin) or a **right indent** (where all lines of the paragraph are indented from the right margin). You can select these types of indents on the Indents and Spacing tab of the Paragraph dialog box. To open this dialog box, you click Format on the menu bar and then click Paragraph.

In this document, though, you need to indent only the main paragraphs 0.5 inches from the left margin. This left indent is a simple paragraph indent. You can use the Indent buttons on the Formatting toolbar to increase or decrease paragraph indenting quickly. According to Marilee's notes, you need to indent all of the main paragraphs.

To indent a paragraph using the Increase Indent button:

1. Press **Ctrl+Home**, and then click anywhere in the paragraph that begins "Start by digging a test hole . . . "

2. Click the **Increase Indent** button 📊 on the Formatting toolbar twice. (Don't click the Decrease Indent button by mistake.) The entire paragraph moves right 0.5 inches each time you click the Increase Indent button. The paragraph is indented 1 inch, 0.5 inches more than Marilee wants.

3. Click the **Decrease Indent** button on the Formatting toolbar to move the paragraph left 0.5 inches. The paragraph is now indented 0.5 inches from the left margin. Don't be concerned about the list of tree species. You will indent the list later, when you format it as a bulleted list.

4. Move the insertion point to anywhere in the paragraph that begins "While you might be tempted . . . " You may have to scroll down to see the paragraph.

5. Click the **Increase Indent** button on the Formatting toolbar. The paragraph is indented 0.5 inches. See Figure 2-22.

Figure 2-22 ▶ **Indented paragraphs**

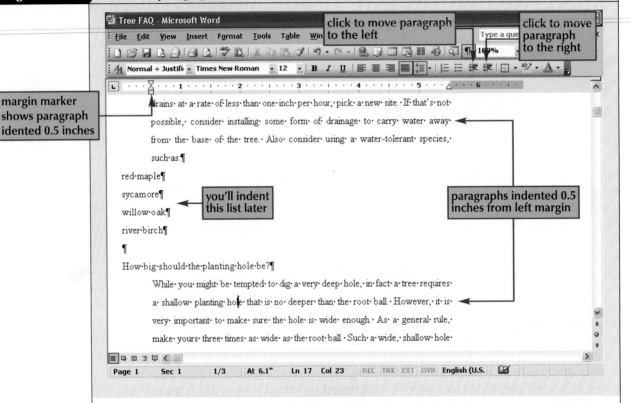

You can continue to indent and then justify each paragraph, or simply use the Format Painter command. The Format Painter allows you to copy both the indentation and alignment changes to all paragraphs in the document.

Using the Format Painter

The **Format Painter** makes it easy to copy all the formatting features of one paragraph to other paragraphs. You can use this button to copy formatting to one or multiple items.

Using the Format Painter

- Select the item whose formatting you want to copy.
- To copy formatting to one item, click the Format Painter button, and then use the mouse pointer to select the item you want to format.
- To copy formatting to multiple items, double-click the Format Painter button, and then use the mouse pointer to select each item you want to format. When you are finished, click the Format Painter button again to deselect it.

Use the Format Painter now to copy the formatting of the second paragraph to other main paragraphs. You'll begin by moving the insertion point to the paragraph whose format you want to copy.

To copy paragraph formatting with the Format Painter:

1. Verify that the insertion point is located in the paragraph that begins "While you might be tempted . . . "

2. Double-click the **Format Painter** button on the Standard toolbar. The Format Painter button will stay highlighted until you click the button again. When you move the pointer over text, the pointer changes to to indicate that the format of the selected paragraph can be painted (or copied) onto another paragraph.

3. Scroll down, and then click anywhere in the paragraph that begins "You may be accustomed . . . " The format of the third paragraph shifts to match the format of the first two main paragraphs. See Figure 2-23. All three paragraphs are now indented and justified. The Format Painter pointer is still visible.

Formats copied with Format Painter | **Figure 2-23**

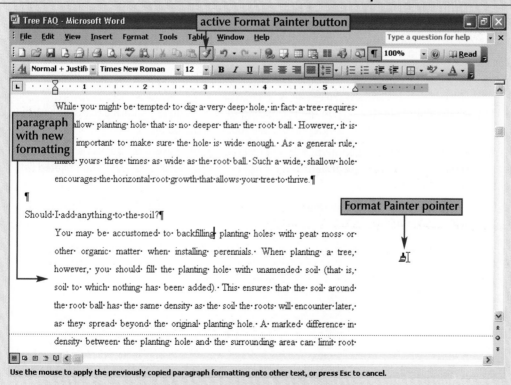

4. Scroll down to click the remaining paragraphs that are preceded by a question heading. Take care to click only the paragraphs below the question headings. Do not click the document title, the one-line questions, the lists, or the last paragraph in the document.

   Trouble? If you click a paragraph and the formatting doesn't change to match the second paragraph, you single-clicked the Format Painter button rather than double-clicked it. Move the insertion point to a paragraph that has the desired format, double-click the Format Painter button, and then repeat Step 4.

   Trouble? If you accidentally click a title or one line of a list, click the Undo button 🔄 on the Standard toolbar to return the line to its original formatting. Then select a paragraph that has the desired format, double-click the Format Painter button 🖌, and finish copying the format to the desired paragraphs.

5. After you are finished formatting paragraphs with the Format Painter pointer, click the **Format Painter** button 🖌 on the Standard toolbar to turn off the feature.

6. Save the document.

All the main paragraphs in the document are formatted with the correct indentation and alignment. Your next job is to make the lists easier to read by adding bullets and numbers.

Adding Bullets and Numbers

You can emphasize a list of items by adding a heavy dot, or **bullet**, before each item in the list. For consecutive items, you can use numbers instead of bullets. Marilee requests that you add bullets to the list of tree species on page 1 to make them stand out.

To apply bullets to the list of items:

1. Scroll to the top of the document until you see the list of tree species below the text "Also consider using a water-tolerant species such as:".

2. Select the four items in the list (from "red maple" to "river birch"). It doesn't matter whether or not you select the paragraph mark after "river birch."

3. Click the **Bullets** button 📃 on the Formatting toolbar. A bullet, a dark circle, appears in front of each item. Each line indents to make room for the bullet.

4. In order to make the bullets align with the first paragraph, make sure the list is still selected, and then click the **Increase Indent** button 📄 on the Formatting toolbar. The bulleted list moves to the right.

5. Click anywhere within the document window to deselect the text. Figure 2-24 shows the indented bulleted list.

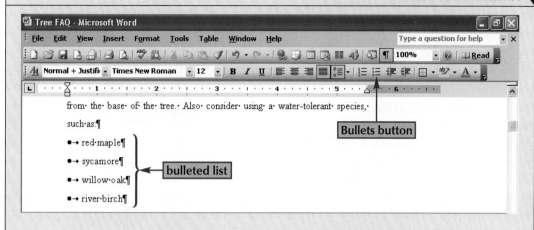

The bulleted list you just created includes the default bullet style. To select a different style of bullets (such as check marks or arrows) you can use the Bullets and Numbering command on the Format menu. You'll have a chance to try that command in the Case Problems at the end of this tutorial.

Next, you need to format the list of steps involved in planting a tree. Marilee asks you to format this information as a numbered list because this list shows sequential steps. This is an easy task thanks to the Numbering button, which automatically numbers selected paragraphs with consecutive numbers. If you insert a new paragraph, delete a paragraph, or reorder the paragraphs, Word automatically adjusts the numbers to make sure they remain consecutive.

To apply numbers to the list of steps:

1. Scroll down until you see the list that begins "Remove any tags . . . " and ends with "of the planting hole."

2. Select the entire list. It doesn't matter whether or not you select the paragraph mark at the end of the last item.

3. Click the **Numbering** button 📇 on the Formatting toolbar. Consecutive numbers appear in front of each item in the list. The list is indented, similar to the bulleted list. The list would look better if it was indented to align with the paragraph.

4. Click the **Increase Indent** button 📑 on the Formatting toolbar. The list moves to the right, so that the numbers align with the preceding paragraph.

5. Click anywhere in the document to deselect the text. Figure 2-25 shows the indented and numbered list.

| Figure 2-25 | **Indented numbered list** |

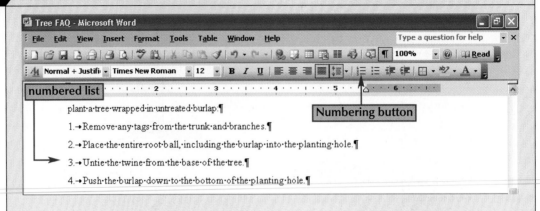

The text of the document is now properly aligned and indented. The bullets and numbers make the lists easy to read and give readers visual clues about the type of information they contain. Next, you need to adjust the formatting of individual words.

Changing the Font and Font Size

All of Marilee's remaining changes concern changing fonts, adjusting font sizes, and emphasizing text with font styles. The first step is to change the font of the title from 12-point Times New Roman to 14-point Arial. This will make the title stand out from the rest of the text.

| Reference Window | **Changing the Font and Font Size** |

- Select the text you want to change.
- Click the Font list arrow on the Formatting toolbar to display the list of fonts.
- Click the font you want to use.
- Click the Font Size list arrow, and then click the font size you want to use.

or

- Select the text that you want to change.
- Click Format on the menu bar, and then click Font.
- In the Font tab of the Font dialog box, select the font and font size you want to use.
- Click the OK button.

Marilee wants you to change the font of the title as well as its size and style. To do this, you'll use the Formatting toolbar. Marilee wants you to use a **sans serif font**, which is a font that does not have the small additional lines (called serifs) at the tops and bottoms of the letters. Sans serif fonts are often used in titles so they contrast with the body text. A **serif font** is a font that does include these small lines. Times New Roman is a serif font, and Arial is a sans serif font.

To change the font of the title:

1. Press **Ctrl+Home** to move the insertion point to the beginning of the document, and then click to the left of the title **Frequently Asked Questions About Trees** to select it.

2. Click the **Font** list arrow on the Formatting toolbar. A list of available fonts appears in alphabetical order, with the name of the current font in the Font text box. See Figure 2-26. Fonts that have been used recently might appear above a double line. Note that each name in the list is formatted with the relevant font. For example, "Arial" appears in the Arial font, and "Times New Roman" appears in the Times New Roman font.

Font list ◀ **Figure 2-26**

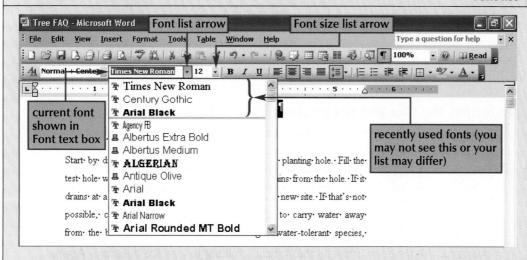

Trouble? If you don't see the fonts beginning with "A" at the top of your Font list, scroll up until you do.

3. Click **Arial** to select it as the new font. As you click, watch the font in the title change to reflect the new font.

Trouble? If Arial doesn't appear in the font list, use another sans serif font.

4. Click the **Font Size** list arrow on the Formatting toolbar, and then click **14** in the size list. As you click, watch the title's font increase from 12 to 14 points.

5. Save your work, and then click within the title to deselect it. See Figure 2-27. Note that the font settings in the Formatting toolbar reflect the font settings of the text that is currently selected, or, if no text is selected, of the text currently containing the insertion point.

Title font and font size changed ◀ **Figure 2-27**

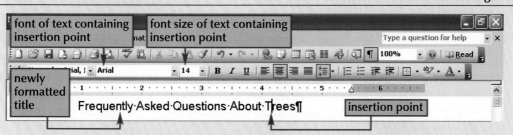

Trouble? If your font and font size settings don't match those in Figure 2-27, you might not have clicked the title. Click the title, view the font and font size settings displayed on the Formatting toolbar, and then make the necessary changes. Because of differences in fonts and monitors, the characters in your document might look different from the figure.

Emphasizing Text Using Bold, Underline, and Italic Styles

You can emphasize words in your document by formatting them with bold, underline, or italic styles. These styles help make specific thoughts, ideas, words, or phrases stand out. (You can also add special effects such as shadows to characters.) Marilee marked a few words on the document draft (shown in Figure 2-1) that need special emphasis. You add bold, underline, or italic styles by using the corresponding buttons on the Formatting toolbar. These buttons are **toggle buttons**, which means you can click them once to format the selected text, and then click again to remove the formatting from the selected text.

Bolding Text

Marilee wants to draw attention to the title and all of the question headings. You will do this by formatting them with the bold style.

To format the title and the questions in bold:

1. Select the title **Frequently Asked Questions About Trees**. It doesn't matter whether or not you select the paragraph mark following the title.

2. Press and hold the **Ctrl** key, and then select the first question in the document ("How can I tell if I've picked a site with good drainage?"). Again, whether or not you select the paragraph mark following the question is of no concern. Both the title and the first question are now selected. You can continue to select nonadjacent information by using the Ctrl key and scroll arrows.

3. Continue to hold down the **Ctrl** key, and then scroll down and select each of the remaining questions. Use the down arrow on the vertical scroll bar to view the questions. Again, whether or not you select the paragraph mark following each question is of no concern.
   Trouble? If you accidentally select something other than a question, keep the Ctrl key pressed while you click the incorrect item. This should deselect the incorrect item.

4. Release the **Ctrl** key, click the **Bold** button B on the Formatting toolbar, click anywhere in the document to deselect the text, and then scroll up to return to the beginning of the document. The title and the questions appear in bold, as shown in Figure 2-28.

Figure 2-28	Text in bold

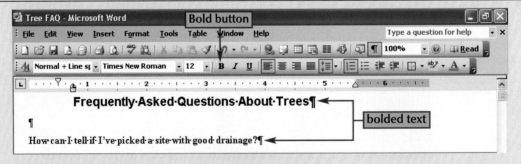

After reviewing this change, Marilee wonders if the title would look better without bold. You can easily remove bold by selecting the text and clicking the Bold button again to turn off, or toggle, bold.

5. To remove the bold, select the title, and then click the **Bold** button B on the Formatting toolbar. The title now appears without bold. Marilee decides she prefers to emphasize the title with bold after all.

6. Verify that the title is still selected, and then click the **Bold** button B on the Formatting toolbar. The title appears in bold again.

Underlining Text

The Underline button works in the same way as the Bold button. Marilee's edits indicate that the word "Note" should be inserted and underlined at the beginning of the final paragraph. Using the Underline button, you'll make both of these changes at the same time.

To underline text:

1. Press **Ctrl+End** to move the insertion point to the end of the document, then press **Ctrl+↑** to move the insertion point to the left of the word "Any" in the first line of the final paragraph.

2. Click the **Underline** button ⓤ on the Formatting toolbar to turn on underlining. The Underline button is highlighted. Whatever text you type now will be underlined on your screen and in your printed document.

3. Type **Note:** and then click the **Underline** button ⓤ on the Formatting toolbar to turn off underlining. The Underline button is no longer highlighted, and "Note:" is now underlined.

4. Press the **spacebar**. See Figure 2-29.

Word typed with underline ◄ **Figure 2-29**

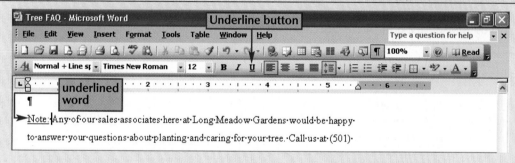

Italicizing Text

Next, you'll format each instance of "Long Meadow Gardens" in italic. This helps draw attention to the company name.

To italicize the company name:

1. Scroll up to the first question on the second page ("Do I have to do anything to the tree before planting?").

2. In the first line below the question, select **Long Meadow Gardens**.

3. Click the **Italic** button ⓘ on the Formatting toolbar. The company name changes from regular to italic text. In the next step, you'll learn a useful method for repeating the task you just performed.

4. Scroll down to the last paragraph of the document, select the company name, and then press the **F4** key. The F4 key enables you to repeat your most recent action. It is especially helpful when formatting parts of a document.

5. Save the document.

Previewing Formatted Text

You have made all the editing and formatting changes that Marilee requested for the Tree FAQ document. It's helpful to preview a document after formatting it, because the Print Preview window makes it easy to spot text that is not aligned correctly.

To preview and print the document:

1. Press **Ctrl+Home**, click the **Print Preview** button on the Standard toolbar, click the **One Page** button on the Print Preview toolbar if you see more than one page, and examine the first page of the document. Use the vertical scroll bar to display the second page. (If you notice any alignment or indentation errors, click the Close button on the Print Preview toolbar, correct the errors in Normal view, save your changes, and then return to the Print Preview window.)
2. Click the **Print** button on the Print Preview toolbar. After a pause, the document prints.
3. Click the **Close** button on the Print Preview toolbar. You return to Normal view.
4. If you made any changes to the document after previewing it, save your work.

You now have a printed copy of the final Tree FAQ document, as shown in Figure 2-30.

Figure 2-30 Final version of Tree FAQ document

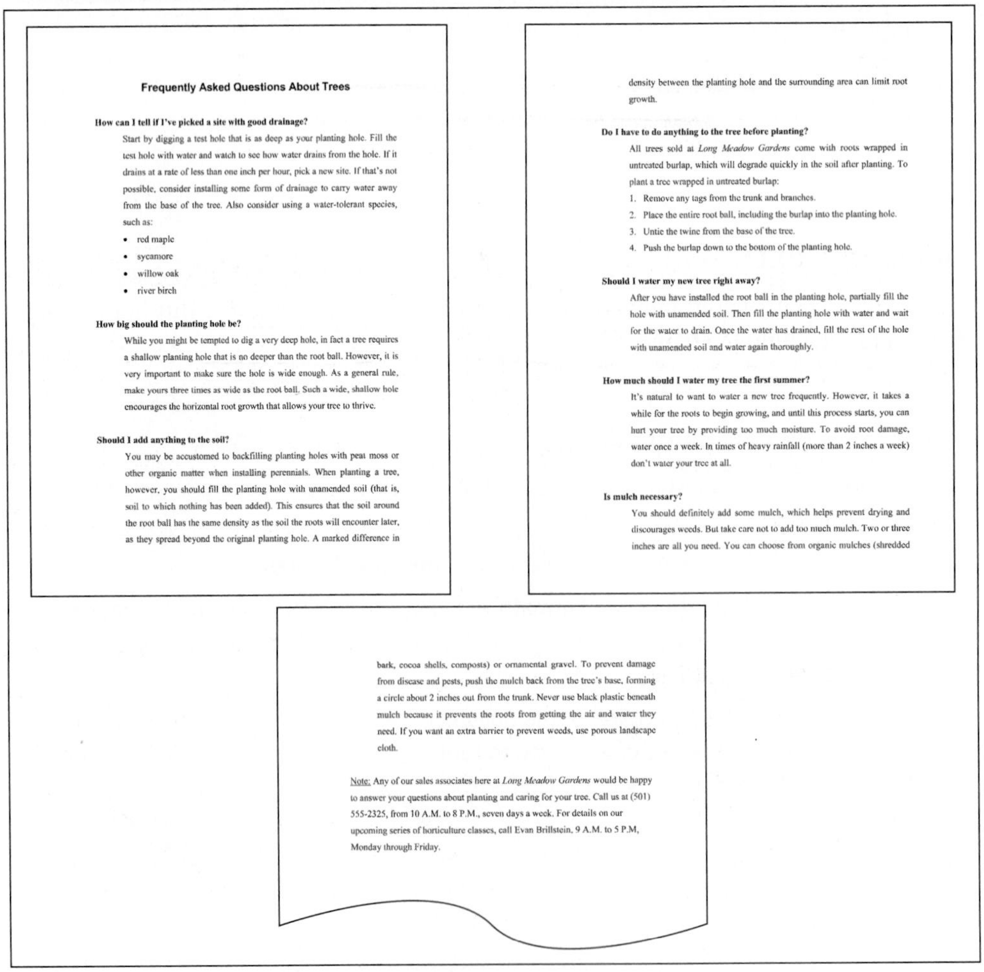

Frequently Asked Questions About Trees

How can I tell if I've picked a site with good drainage?

Start by digging a test hole that is as deep as your planting hole. Fill the test hole with water and watch to see how water drains from the hole. If it drains at a rate of less than one inch per hour, pick a new site. If that's not possible, consider installing some form of drainage to carry water away from the base of the tree. Also consider using a water-tolerant species, such as:

- red maple
- sycamore
- willow oak
- river birch

How big should the planting hole be?

While you might be tempted to dig a very deep hole, in fact a tree requires a shallow planting hole that is no deeper than the root ball. However, it is very important to make sure the hole is wide enough. As a general rule, make yours three times as wide as the root ball. Such a wide, shallow hole encourages the horizontal root growth that allows your tree to thrive.

Should I add anything to the soil?

You may be accustomed to backfilling planting holes with peat moss or other organic matter when installing perennials. When planting a tree, however, you should fill the planting hole with unamended soil (that is, soil to which nothing has been added). This ensures that the soil around the root ball has the same density as the soil the roots will encounter later, as they spread beyond the original planting hole. A marked difference in density between the planting hole and the surrounding area can limit root growth.

Do I have to do anything to the tree before planting?

All trees sold at *Long Meadow Gardens* come with roots wrapped in untreated burlap, which will degrade quickly in the soil after planting. To plant a tree wrapped in untreated burlap:

1. Remove any tags from the trunk and branches.
2. Place the entire root ball, including the burlap into the planting hole.
3. Untie the twine from the base of the tree.
4. Push the burlap down to the bottom of the planting hole.

Should I water my new tree right away?

After you have installed the root ball in the planting hole, partially fill the hole with unamended soil. Then fill the planting hole with water and wait for the water to drain. Once the water has drained, fill the rest of the hole with unamended soil and water again thoroughly.

How much should I water my tree the first summer?

It's natural to want to water a new tree frequently. However, it takes a while for the roots to begin growing, and until this process starts, you can hurt your tree by providing too much moisture. To avoid root damage, water once a week. In times of heavy rainfall (more than 2 inches a week) don't water your tree at all.

Is mulch necessary?

You should definitely add some mulch, which helps prevent drying and discourages weeds. But take care not to add too much mulch. Two or three inches are all you need. You can choose from organic mulches (shredded bark, cocoa shells, composts) or ornamental gravel. To prevent damage from disease and pests, push the mulch back from the tree's base, forming a circle about 2 inches out from the trunk. Never use black plastic beneath mulch because it prevents the roots from getting the air and water they need. If you want an extra barrier to prevent weeds, use porous landscape cloth.

Note: Any of our sales associates here at *Long Meadow Gardens* would be happy to answer your questions about planting and caring for your tree. Call us at (501) 555-2325, from 10 A.M. to 8 P.M., seven days a week. For details on our upcoming series of horticulture classes, call Evan Brillstein, 9 A.M. to 5 P.M, Monday through Friday.

Adding Comments

Peter reviews the Tree FAQ document and is happy with its appearance. He wonders if he should add some information about fertilizing new trees. He asks you to insert a note to Marilee about this using Word's Comment feature. A **comment** is an electronic version of a self-sticking note that you might attach to a piece of paper. To insert a comment in a Word document, select a block of text, click Comment on the Insert menu, and then type your comment in the comment box. To display a comment, place the mouse pointer over text where the comment has been inserted. Comments are very useful when you are exchanging Word documents with co-workers electronically, whether via e-mail, disks, or on CDs, because they allow you to make notes or queries without affecting the document itself.

You'll insert Peter's comment at the document title so that Marilee will be sure to see it as soon as she opens the document. It's easiest to work with comments in Print Layout view.

To add the comment to the document:

1. Click the **Print Layout View** button 🔲 in the lower-left corner of the Word window, then click the **Zoom** list arrow and click **100%** in the list if it is not already selected. The document view changes, allowing you to see the document margins.

2. Scroll up and down through the document and notice that, in Print Layout view, a page break is represented by something more noticeable than a dotted line. You can actually see the end of one page and the beginning of another.

3. Scroll up to the beginning of the document, and then select the title **Frequently Asked Questions About Trees**. (Do not select the paragraph mark after the title.)

4. Click **Insert** on the menu bar, and then click **Comment**. A comment balloon appears in the right margin, with the insertion point ready for you to type your comment. The Reviewing toolbar opens, displaying buttons that are useful for working with comments. See Figure 2-31.

Inserting a comment   Figure 2-31

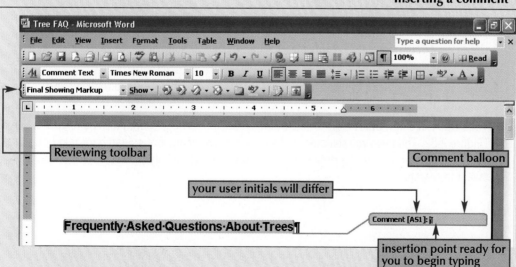

Trouble? If you can't see the entire comment balloon, scroll right to display it fully.

The comment is preceded by the user's initials and a number. Initials depend on the information entered on the Information tab in the Options dialog box. The numbers are sequential, with the first comment labeled #1, the second #2, and so on.

5. Type **Should we add a section on fertilizing new trees?** The newly typed comment is displayed in the comment balloon. Depending on the size of your monitor, you may need to scroll right to read the entire comment.

6. Click the **Normal View** button ☰ in the lower-left corner of the Word window. The title is highlighted in color with brackets around it, indicating that a comment has been inserted at this point in the document.

7. Place the mouse pointer over the title. The comment is displayed in a ScreenTip over the pointer. When you move the mouse pointer away from the title, the ScreenTip closes.

8. Save the document.

Note that to delete a comment, you can right-click the comment box in Print Layout view and click Delete Comment. To edit a comment, click in the comment box and make any deletions or additions you desire. After you insert comments in a document, you can choose to print the document with or without comments in the margin. To print the comments, select Document showing markup in the Print what list box of the Print dialog box. To print a document without comments, select Document in the Print what list box. You'll find comments useful when you need to collaborate on a document with your fellow students or co-workers.

Using the Research Task Pane

Before you finish your work for the day, Peter suggests that you use the Research task pane to look up information on plants sold at Long Meadow Gardens. The **Research task pane** provides a number of research tools, including a thesaurus, an Internet search engine, and access to the Encarta Encyclopedia and Dictionary. To take full advantage of these options, your computer must be connected to the Internet. To get started, Peter asks you to use the Research task pane to find the Latin name for "red maple."

To look up "red maple" in the Research task pane:

1. Verify that your computer is connected to the Internet. If your computer is not connected to the Internet, read, but do not attempt to perform, the following steps.

2. Use the Find command to locate and select the text "red maple". Close the Find and Replace dialog box.

3. Click the **Research** button 📖 on the Standard toolbar. The Research task pane opens. See Figure 2-32. The term you selected in the document appears in the Search for text box, ready for you to look up the definition. Next, you need to specify the reference source you want to search.

Opening the Research task pane | **Figure 2-32**

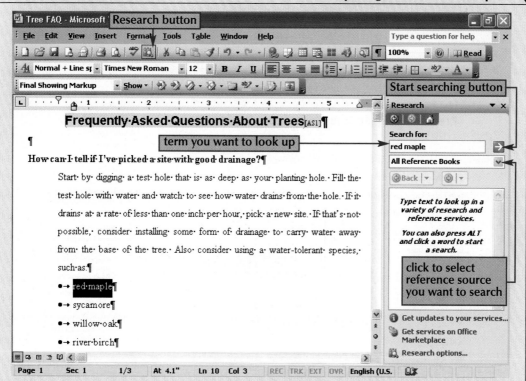

4. Verify that **All Reference Books** is selected in the list box below the Search for text box, and then click the **Start searching** button. A list of research results appears, as shown in Figure 2-33. At the top of the list is the Encarta Dictionary definition for "red maple," with the Latin name, *Acer rubrum*, at the end. If the initial search results don't provide the information you need, scroll down and click the "Can't find it?" link at the bottom of the Research task pane to display more research options. In some cases, when you click a link in the Research task pane, Internet Explorer might open a Web page with further information.

Trouble? If All Reference Books is not selected in the list box below the Search for text box, click the list arrow and select All Reference Books. At that point the search will begin; you do not have to click the Start searching button.

Figure 2-33 | **Research results**

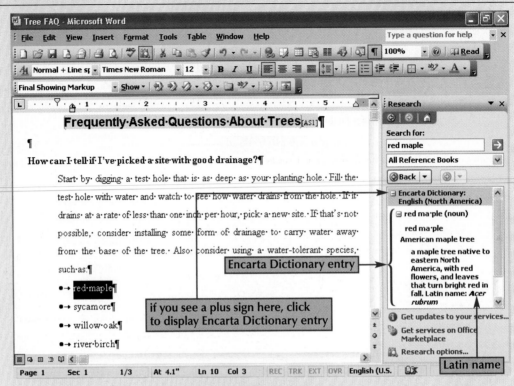

Trouble? If you see "Encarta Dictionary: English (North America)" but not the dictionary entry for "red maple," click the plus sign as indicated in Figure 2-33.

▶ **5.** Click the **Close** button [X] at the top of the Research task pane. The Research task pane closes.

▶ **6.** Close the Reviewing toolbar, save, and then close the document.

In this tutorial, you have helped Peter edit and format the Tree FAQ document that will be handed out to all customers purchasing a tree at Long Meadow Gardens. Peter will e-mail the file to Marilee later so that she can review your work and read the comment you inserted.

Review

Session 2.2 Quick Check

1. What are Word's default values for the left and right margins? For the top and bottom margins?
2. Describe the steps involved in changing the line spacing in a document.
3. Describe the four types of text alignment.
4. Explain how to indent a paragraph 1 inch or more from the left margin.
5. Describe a situation in which you would use the Format Painter.
6. Explain how to transform a series of short paragraphs into a numbered list.
7. Explain how to add underlining to a word as you type it.
8. True or False: Before you can take full advantage of the Research task pane, your computer must be connected to the Internet.

To reinforce the tasks you learned in this session, go to the SAM 2003 Training Companion CD included with this text.

Tutorial Summary

In this tutorial you learned how to use the Spelling and Grammar checker, select parts of a document, delete text, and move text within a document. You also learned how to find and replace text. Next, you focused on formatting a document, including changing margins and line spacing, aligning text, indenting paragraphs, using the Format Painter, changing the font and font size, and emphasizing text with bold, underlining, and italic styles. Finally, you learned how to add a comment to a document, preview formatted text, and look up information using the Research task pane.

Key Terms

¶	cut and paste	portrait orientation
1.5 line spacing	double spacing	ragged
alignment	drag and drop	Replace command
automatic page break	Find command	Research task pane
bullet	Format Painter	right alignment
center alignment	hanging indent	right indent
Clipboard	justified alignment	sans serif font
Clipboard task pane	landscape orientation	select
comment	left alignment	selection bar
copy	paragraph	serif font
copy and paste	paragraph symbol (¶)	single spacing
cut	paste	toggle button

Apply the skills you learned in the tutorial using the same case scenario.

Review Assignments

Data File needed for the Review Assignments: Statmnt.doc

Now that you have completed the Tree FAQ document, Marilee asks you to help her create a statement summarizing customer accounts for Long Meadow Gardens' wholesale nursery. She would also like you to create a document that contains contact information for Long Meadow Gardens. Remember to use the Undo and Redo buttons as you work to correct any errors.

1. Open the file **Statmnt** located in the Tutorial.02\Review folder included with your Data Files, and then check your screen to make sure your settings match those in the tutorial.
2. Save the document as **Monthly Statement** in the same folder.
3. Change the left and right margins to 1.5 inches using the Page Setup dialog box.
4. Make all edits and formatting changes shown in Figure 2-34, and then save your work.

Figure 2-34

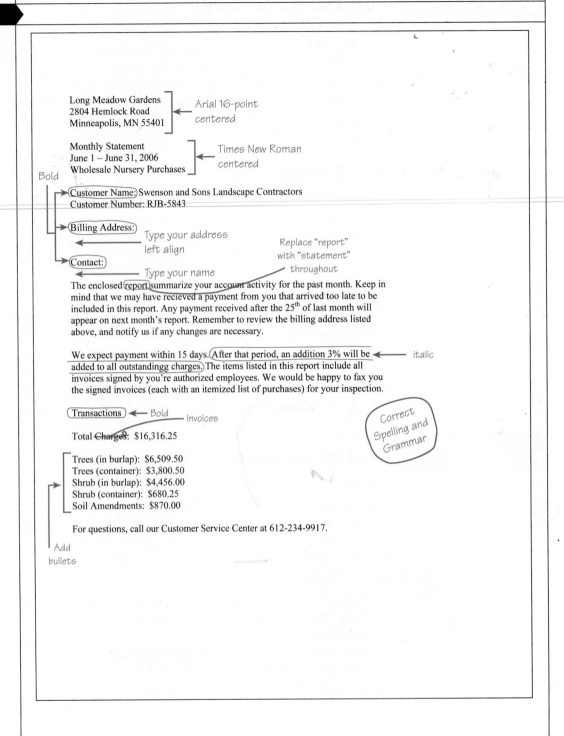

Long Meadow Gardens
2804 Hemlock Road
Minneapolis, MN 55401

Arial 16-point centered

Monthly Statement
June 1 – June 31, 2006
Wholesale Nursery Purchases

Times New Roman centered

Bold

Customer Name: Swenson and Sons Landscape Contractors
Customer Number: RJB-5843

Billing Address: *Type your address left align*

Contact: *Type your name*

Replace "report" with "statement" throughout

The enclosed report summarize your account activity for the past month. Keep in mind that we may have recieved a payment from you that arrived too late to be included in this report. Any payment received after the 25th of last month will appear on next month's report. Remember to review the billing address listed above, and notify us if any changes are necessary.

We expect payment within 15 days. After that period, an addition 3% will be added to all outstandingg charges. The items listed in this report include all invoices signed by you're authorized employees. We would be happy to fax you the signed invoices (each with an itemized list of purchases) for your inspection.

italic

Transactions *Bold* *Invoices*

Total Charges: $16,316.25

Correct Spelling and Grammar

Trees (in burlap): $6,509.50
Trees (container): $3,800.50
Shrub (in burlap): $4,456.00
Shrub (container): $680.25
Soil Amendments: $870.00

For questions, call our Customer Service Center at 612-234-9917.

Add bullets

5. Proofread the document carefully to check for any additional errors. Look for and correct two errors that were not reported when you used the Spelling and Grammar checker.

6. Remove any Smart Tags in the document.

7. Move the last sentence of the document (which begins "For questions, call . . . ") to create a new paragraph, just above the heading "Transactions."

8. Select the Transactions portion of the document, from the heading "Transactions" down to the end of the document. Increase the indentation by 0.5 inch.

9. Open the Clipboard task pane. Select the company name and address at the top of the document and copy it to the Clipboard. Then copy the Customer Service Center phone number (above Transactions) to the Clipboard.

10. Open a new, blank document. Type your name on the first line, and then "Customer Service Center" on the next line. Move the insertion point to the third line. Open the Clipboard task pane, and then click the company address to insert this information at the insertion point. Be sure the insertion point is below the address, and then click the phone number to insert it in the document. Notice that text inserted from the Clipboard retains its original formatting, though the alignment may not carry over perfectly.

11. Left-align any centered text, clear the contents of the Clipboard task pane, close the task pane, and print the document.

12. Switch to Print Layout view. Then select the company name and insert the following comment: "Marilee, please let me know how you want this document formatted."

13. Save the document as **Customer Service Contact** in the Tutorial.02\Review folder. Close the document.

14. Save the Monthly Statement document, and then preview and print it.

15. Select the term "Amendments," which appears in the bulleted list at the end of the document. Open the Research task pane and look up the definition of "amendment." *Note*: you must have an active Internet connection to complete this step.

16. Type an asterisk (*) after "Amendments," and then on a blank line at the end of the document type an asterisk (*) followed by the definition of "amendment." After the definition include a sentence indicating that the definition is taken from the Encarta Dictionary.

17. Close the Research task pane and the Reviewing toolbar, save the Monthly Statement document, and then close it.

Case Problem 1

Apply

Apply the skills you learned to create a one-page advertising brochure.

Data File needed for this Case Problem: Tribune.doc

Blue Ridge Tribune The *Blue Ridge Tribune* is a student-run newspaper published through the Blue Ridge College Student Services Association. The newspaper is distributed around campus each Friday. The online version of the newspaper is posted on the Blue Ridge College Web site. Local businesses have a long-established tradition of advertising in the print version of the newspaper, and the paper's advertising manager, Noah McCormick, would like to ensure that this same tradition carries over to the online newspaper. When he sends out the monthly statements to his print advertisers, he would like to include a one-page brochure encouraging them to purchase an online ad. He typed the text about online advertising that is currently found on the Blue Ridge Tribune Web site and saved it as unformatted text in a Word document.

1. Open the file **Tribune** located in the Tutorial.02\Cases folder included with your Data Files, and save the file as **Tribune Brochure** in the same folder.

2. Correct any spelling or grammar errors. Make sure the right correction is selected in the Suggestions list box before you click Change.

3. Proofread for other errors, such as words that are spelled correctly but used incorrectly.
4. In the second to last sentence, replace "the BRT Advertising Office" with your name.
5. Change the right margin to 1.5 inches and the left margin to 2 inches.
6. Format the entire document in 12-point Times New Roman font.
7. Format the four paragraphs below "Did you know?" as a bulleted list.
8. Drag the third bullet (which begins "You can include . . . ") up to make it the first bullet in the bulleted list.
9. Format the first line of the document using a font, font size, and alignment of your choice. Use bold or italic for emphasis.
10. Format the entire document using 1.5 line spacing.
11. Save your work, preview the document, and then switch back to Normal view to make any changes you think necessary.
12. Print the document and then return to the Print Preview window. Open the Page Setup dialog box and switch to Landscape orientation. (Don't change any margin settings.) Observe the change in the Print Preview window.
13. Save the document as **Tribune Brochure Landscape** in the Tutorial.02\Cases folder and print it.
14. Switch to Print Layout view, and add a comment to the first line (*Blue Ridge Tribune*) asking Noah if he would like you to leave a printed copy of the brochure in his mailbox.
15. As Noah reviews the brochure, he wonders if the word "Web" should actually be capitalized. Use the Research task pane to look up "Web" in the Encarta Dictionary. In the first definition, you can see that "Web" is short for "World Wide Web." You will use this information to explain to Noah that indeed Web should be capitalized. Close the Research task pane.
16. Close the Reviewing toolbar, save, and then close the document.

Case Problem 2

Apply

Use your skills to format the summary document shown in Figure 2-35.

Data File needed for this Case Problem: Moths.doc

Hamilton Polytechnic Institute Finn Hansen is an associate researcher in the Department of Entomology at Hamilton Polytechnic Institute. He is working on a nationwide program that aims to slow the spread of a devastating forest pest, the gypsy moth. He has created a one-page document that will be used as part of a campaign to inform the public about current efforts to manage gypsy moths in North America. Format the document by completing the following steps.

1. Open the file **Moths** located in the Tutorial.02\Cases folder included with your Data Files, and then check your screen to make sure your settings match those in the tutorials.
2. Save the file as **Gypsy Moth Management** in the same folder.
3. Format the document as shown in Figure 2-35.

Figure 2-35

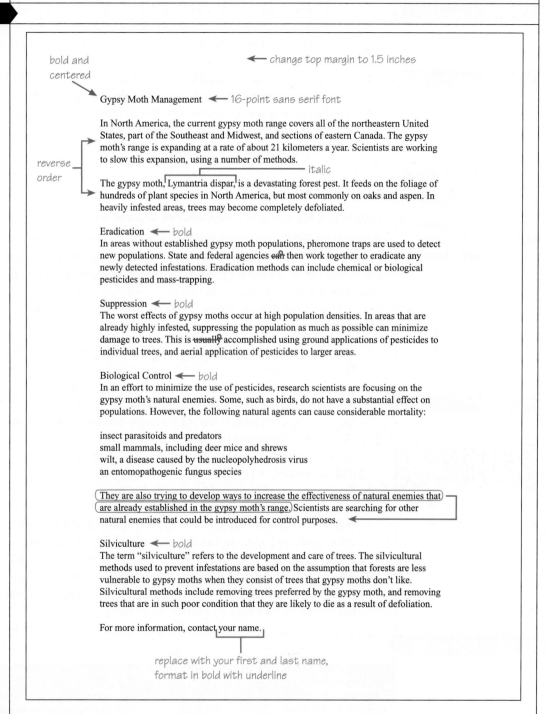

bold and
centered

← change top margin to 1.5 inches

Gypsy Moth Management ← 16-point sans serif font

In North America, the current gypsy moth range covers all of the northeastern United States, part of the Southeast and Midwest, and sections of eastern Canada. The gypsy moth's range is expanding at a rate of about 21 kilometers a year. Scientists are working to slow this expansion, using a number of methods.

reverse
order

italic

The gypsy moth, Lymantria dispar, is a devastating forest pest. It feeds on the foliage of hundreds of plant species in North America, but most commonly on oaks and aspen. In heavily infested areas, trees may become completely defoliated.

Eradication ← bold
In areas without established gypsy moth populations, pheromone traps are used to detect new populations. State and federal agencies can then work together to eradicate any newly detected infestations. Eradication methods can include chemical or biological pesticides and mass-trapping.

Suppression ← bold
The worst effects of gypsy moths occur at high population densities. In areas that are already highly infested, suppressing the population as much as possible can minimize damage to trees. This is usually accomplished using ground applications of pesticides to individual trees, and aerial application of pesticides to larger areas.

Biological Control ← bold
In an effort to minimize the use of pesticides, research scientists are focusing on the gypsy moth's natural enemies. Some, such as birds, do not have a substantial effect on populations. However, the following natural agents can cause considerable mortality:

insect parasitoids and predators
small mammals, including deer mice and shrews
wilt, a disease caused by the nucleopolyhedrosis virus
an entomopathogenic fungus species

They are also trying to develop ways to increase the effectiveness of natural enemies that are already established in the gypsy moth's range. Scientists are searching for other natural enemies that could be introduced for control purposes. ←

Silviculture ← bold
The term "silviculture" refers to the development and care of trees. The silvicultural methods used to prevent infestations are based on the assumption that forests are less vulnerable to gypsy moths when they consist of trees that gypsy moths don't like. Silvicultural methods include removing trees preferred by the gypsy moth, and removing trees that are in such poor condition that they are likely to die as a result of defoliation.

For more information, contact your name.

replace with your first and last name,
format in bold with underline

Explore

4. Indent the entire document using the ruler, as follows:
   a. Make sure the horizontal ruler is displayed and the document is shown in Normal view.
   b. Select the entire document.
   c. Position the pointer on the small gray square on the ruler at the left margin. A ScreenTip with the words "Left Indent" appears.
   d. Press and hold down the mouse button. A vertical dotted line appears in the document window, indicating the current left margin. Drag the Left Indent marker to the 0.5-inch mark on the ruler, and then release the mouse button. Click anywhere to deselect the document.

Explore

5. Select the list of the four natural agents that can cause mortality in gypsy moths (in the "Biological Control" section), click Format on the menu bar, and then use the Bullets and Numbering dialog box to create a bulleted list using a square as the bullet symbol.

Explore

6. Select the headings "Eradication", "Suppression", "Biological Control", and "Silviculture". Press Ctrl+I to format the selected text in italic.
7. Use the Spelling and Grammar checker to make corrections as needed, proofread for additional errors, save, and preview the document.
8. Print the document, and then close it.

Challenge

Case Problem 3

Expand your formatting skills to create a resume for an aspiring editor.

Data File needed for this Case Problem: Resume.doc

Educational Publishing Elena Pelliterri has over a decade of experience in education. She worked as a writing teacher, and then as a college supervisor of student teachers. Now she would like to pursue a career as sales representative for a company that publishes textbooks and other educational materials. She has asked you to edit and format her resume. Complete the resume by completing the following steps. The steps show quotation marks around text you type; do not include the quotation marks.

1. Open the file **Resume** located in the Tutorial.02\Cases folder included with your Data Files, and then check your screen to make sure your settings match those in the tutorials.
2. Save the file as **Formatted Resume** in the same folder.

Explore

3. Read the comment inserted at the first line of the document. Right-click the comment (point to the comment in the right margin and press the right mouse button), and then click Delete Comment on the shortcut menu.
4. Switch to Normal view, search for the text "your name", and replace it with your first and last name.
5. Replace all occurrences of "Aroyo" with "Arroyo".
6. Use the Spelling and Grammar checker to correct any errors in the document. Note that this document contains text that the Spelling and Grammar checker might consider sentence fragments but that are acceptable in a resume.
7. Delete the word "traveling" from the sentence below the "OBJECTIVE" heading.
8. Format the resume as described in Figure 2-36. Use one sans serif font and one serif font throughout. Be sure to pick fonts that look professional and are easy to read. Use the Format Painter to copy formatting as necessary.

Figure 2-36

Resume Element	Format
Name "Elena Pelliterri"	18-point, sans serif font, bold, with underline
Address, phone number, and e-mail address	12-point, sans serif font, bold
Uppercase headings (OBJECTIVE, EXPERIENCE, etc.)	12-point, serif font, bold, italic
Subheadings below EXPERIENCE, which begin "Rio Mesa College..." and "Middleton Public Schools..."	12-point, serif font, bold
Lists of teaching experience, educational history, and so on, below the resume headings and subheadings	12-point, serif font, bulleted list

9. Reorder the two items under the "COMPUTER SKILLS" heading so that the second item becomes the first.

Explore

10. Experiment with two special paragraph alignment options: first line and hanging. First, select the two bulleted items under the subheading "Middleton Public Schools." Click the Bullets button on the Formatting toolbar to remove the bulleted list format. Next, click Format on the menu bar, click Paragraph, and then click the Indents and Spacing tab. Click the Special list arrow in the Paragraph dialog box, and notice the special alignment options. Experiment with both the First line and the Hanging options. When you are finished, return the document to its original format by choosing the (none) option, and then reapplying the bulleted list format.
11. Save and preview the document.
12. Print the document and close it.

Explore

13. The Research task pane provides access to a variety of resources. Some (such as the Encarta Dictionary) are free, while others (such as the Encarta Encyclopedia) require you to pay a subscription fee. After you find the information you need in the Research task pane, you can copy and paste it into your document. Keep in mind that you must always cite your source when you use copyrighted material, such as the definitions from the Encarta Dictionary. To practice using the Research task pane, open a new, blank document, connect your computer to the Internet (if necessary), and open the Research task pane. Change the document's Zoom setting to 75% so you can see the entire document next to the Research task pane. Type the word "publishing" in the Search for text box, click the list arrow below the Search for text box, and select an option that interests you. Experiment by clicking topics in the Research task pane. To display a topic more fully, click the box that contains a plus sign (to the left of the topic). In some cases, when you click a topic, Internet Explorer opens (with the Research task pane on the left) to display more information.

Explore

14. When you are finished experimenting, close Internet Explorer, if necessary, and return to the Word window. Click the list arrow below the Search for text box and select Encarta Dictionary: English (North America). Scroll down and then drag the mouse pointer to select the definition that begins "the trade, profession, or activity…", press Ctrl+C to copy the information to the Clipboard, click in the document, and then use the Paste button to paste the definition into the document. Add some text explaining that you copied the definition from the Encarta Dictionary to demonstrate how to copy and paste information from the Research task pane.
15. Save the document as **Encarta Definition** in the Tutorial.02\Cases folder, print it, close the Research task pane, and close the document.

Case Problem 4

Challenge

Explore new ways to format an Invoice Authorization Form for a high-tech computer company.

Data File needed for this Case Problem: Form.doc

Gygs and Bytes Melissa Martinez is the purchasing manager for Gygs and Bytes, a wholesale distributor of computer parts based in Portland, Oregon. Most of the company's business is conducted via catalog or through the company's Web site, but local customers sometimes drop by to pick up small orders. In the past Melissa has had problems determining which of her customers' employees were authorized to sign credit invoices. To avoid confusion, she has asked all local customers to complete a form listing employees who are authorized to sign invoices. She plans to place the completed forms in a binder at the main desk, so the receptionist at Gygs and Bytes can find the information quickly.

1. Open the file **Form** located in Tutorial.02\Cases folder included with your Data Files, and save the file as **Invoice Authorization Form** in the same folder.
2. Correct any spelling or grammar errors. Ignore the name of the company "Gygs and Bytes."

Explore

3. When you type Web addresses or e-mail addresses in a document, Word automatically formats them as links. When you click a Web address formatted as a link, Windows automatically opens a Web browser (such as Microsoft Internet Explorer) and, if your computer is connected to the Internet, displays that Web page. If you click an e-mail address formatted as a link, Windows opens a program in which you can type an e-mail message. The address you clicked is automatically included as the recipient of the e-mail. You'll see how this works as you add a Web address and e-mail address to the statement. In the address at the top of the document, click at the end of the ZIP code, add a new line, and then type the address for the company's Web site: **www.G&B.com**. When you are finished, press Enter. Notice that as soon as you press Enter, Word formats the address in blue with an underline, marking it as a link. Move the mouse pointer over the link and read the ScreenTip. The company is fictitious and does not have a Web site.

Explore

4. In the line below the Web address, type G&B@worldlink.com and then press Enter. Word formats the e-mail address as a link. Press and hold the Ctrl key and then click the e-mail link. Your default e-mail program opens, displaying a window where you could type an e-mail message to Gygs and Bytes. (If your computer is not set up for e-mail, close any error messages that open.) Close the e-mail window without saving any changes. The link is now formatted in a color other than blue, indicating that the link has been clicked.

5. Change the top and left margins to 1.5 inches.

6. Center the first six lines of the document (containing the form title and the company addresses).

7. Format the first line of the document (the form title) in 16-point Arial, with italic.

8. Format lines 2 through 6 (the addresses, including the Web and e-mail addresses) in 12-point Arial.

Explore

9. Replace all instances of G&B, except the first two (in the Web and e-mail addresses), with the complete company name, Gygs and Bytes. In the Find and Replace dialog box, select the Match case check box to ensure that the replacement text is inserted exactly as you typed it in the Replace with text box. (Be sure to use the Find Next button to skip an instance of the search text.)

10. Format the blank ruled lines as a numbered list. Customers will use these blank lines to write in the names of authorized employees.

Explore

11. Format the entire document using 1.5 spacing. Then triple-space the numbered list (with the blank lines) and the Signature and Title lines as follows:
    a. Select the numbered list with the blank lines.
    b. Triple-space the selected text using the Line Spacing button on the Formatting toolbar.
    c. Select the "Signed:" and the "Title:" lines, and then press F4.

12. Save the document.

13. Drag "Customer Name:" up to position it before "Customer Number:".

Explore

14. Select "Customer Name:", "Customer Number:", and "Address:". Press Ctrl+B to format the selected text in bold. Note that it is sometimes easier to use this keyboard shortcut instead of the Bold button on the Formatting toolbar.

15. Delete the phrase "all employees" and replace it with "all authorized personnel".

Explore

16. Select the phrase "all authorized personnel will be required to show a photo I.D." Press Ctrl+I to format the selected text in italic. It is sometimes easier to use this keyboard shortcut instead of the Italic button on the Formatting toolbar.

17. Insert your name in the form to the right of "Customer Name:". Format your name without bold, if necessary.

18. Insert your address, left aligned, without bold, below the heading "Address:".

Explore ▶ 19. Click the Print Preview button on the Standard toolbar to check your work.

Explore ▶ 20. Click the Shrink to Fit button on the Print Preview toolbar to reduce the entire document to one page. Word reduces the font sizes slightly in order to fit the entire form on one page. Close the Print Preview window and save your work.

Explore ▶ 21. Use the Print command on the File menu to open the Print dialog box. Print two copies of the document by changing the Number of copies setting in the Print dialog box.

Explore ▶ 22. You can find out useful statistics about your documents by using the Word Count command on the Tools menu. Use this command to determine the number of words, characters (not including spaces), and paragraphs in the document, and then write these statistics in the upper-right corner of the printout.

23. Save and close the document.

Internet Assignments

Research

Go to the Web to find information you can use to create documents.

The purpose of the Internet Assignments is to challenge you to find information on the Internet that you can use to work effectively with this software. The actual assignments are updated and maintained on the Course Technology Web site. Log on to the Internet and use your Web browser to go to the Student Online Companion for New Perspectives Office 2003 at **www.course.com/np/office2003**. Click the Internet Assignments link, and then navigate to the assignments for this tutorial.

SAM Assessment and Training

Assess

If your instructor has chosen to use the full online version of SAM 2003 Assessment and Training, you can go beyond the "just-in-time" training provided on the CD that accompanies this text. Simply log in to your SAM account (http://sam2003.course.com) to launch any assigned training activities or exams that relate to the skills covered in this tutorial.

Quick Check Answers

Review

Session 2.1

1. Click at the beginning of the document, and then click the Spelling and Grammar button on the Standard toolbar. In the Spelling and Grammar dialog box, review each error, which is displayed in color. Grammatical errors appear in green; spelling errors appear in red. Review the possible corrections in the Suggestions list box. To accept a suggested correction, click it in the Suggestions list box, and then click Change to make the correction and continue searching the document for errors.

2. True

3. a. double-click the word
   b. click at the beginning of the block, and then drag until the entire block is selected
   c. double-click in the selection bar next to the paragraph, or triple-click in the paragraph

4. a. the blank space in the left margin area of the Document window that allows you to select entire lines or large blocks of text easily
   b. the process of moving text by first selecting the text, then pressing and holding the mouse button while moving the text to its new location in the document, and finally releasing the mouse button
   c. a command on the Edit menu that is used to search for a set of characters and replace them with a different set of characters

5. False
6. Cut and paste removes the selected material from its original location and inserts it in a new location. Copy and paste makes a copy of the selected material and inserts the copy in a new location; the original material remains in its original location.
7. Click Edit on the menu bar, click Replace, type the search text in the Find what text box, type the replacement text in the Replace with text box, click Find Next, Replace, or click Replace all.

Session 2.2

1. The default top and bottom margins are 1 inch. The default left and right margins are 1.25 inches.
2. Select the text you want to change, click the Line Spacing list arrow on the Formatting toolbar, and then click the line spacing option you want. Or select the text, and then press Ctrl+1 for single spacing, Ctrl+5 for 1.5 line spacing, or Ctrl+2 for double spacing.
3. Left alignment: each line flush left, ragged right; Right alignment: each line flush right, ragged left; Center: each line centered, ragged right and left.; Justify: each line flush left and flush right.
4. To indent a paragraph, place the insertion point in the paragraph and then click the Increase Indent button on the Formatting toolbar. Each click indents the text .5 inches, so to indent 1 inch, click the button two times. Use the horizontal ruler to confirm that the text is indented to the correct position.
5. You might use the Format Painter to copy the formatting of a heading to the other headings in a document.
6. Select the paragraphs, and then click the Numbering button on the Formatting toolbar.
7. Click the Underline button on the Formatting toolbar, type the word, and then click the Underline button again to turn off underlining.
8. True

Creating a Multiple-Page Report

Writing a Recommendation

Case | Tyger Networks

Tyger Networks is a consulting company in Madison, Wisconsin, that specializes in setting up computer networks for small businesses and organizations. Susan Launspach, the program director at New Hope Social Services, recently contacted Tyger Networks about linking the computer networks at New Hope's three main offices. The offices are scattered throughout southern Wisconsin in Madison, Janesville, and Milwaukee. Each office has its own self-contained computer network. To make it easier for a social worker in one office to access data stored on a computer in another office, Susan would like to establish some kind of connection between the three networks.

Caitlyn Waller, an account manager at Tyger Networks, is responsible for the New Hope account. In a phone call, she explained to Susan that connecting the three offices will create a new type of a network known as a wide area network (WAN). Because Susan is unfamiliar with networking terminology, Caitlyn offered to write a report that summarizes the options for creating this type of a network. Working with a task force of sales and technical personnel, Caitlyn compiled the necessary information in a multi-page document. Now Caitlyn would like you to help her finish formatting the report. She also needs some help adding a table to the end of the report. Once the report is completed, Susan will present it to the board of directors at New Hope Social Services.

In this tutorial, you will format the report's title page so that it has a different layout from the rest of the report. The title page will contain only the title and subtitle and will not have page numbers like the rest of the report. You also will add a table to the report that summarizes the costs involved in creating a WAN.

Session	Objectives		SAM Training Tasks	
Session 3.1	• Set tab stops • Divide a document into sections • Center a page between the top and bottom margins	• Create a header with page numbers • Create a table	• Change the vertical alignment of a section • Create a document header • Create a hanging indent • Create a header different from previous section header • Create tables • Delete a page break • Enter data into a Word table	• First-line indent paragraph • Format sections • Insert a next page section break • Insert page breaks • Insert page numbers • Modify tabs • Set Decimal tabs • Use Page Setup options to format sections • Use print preview
Session 3.2	• Sort the rows in a table • Modify a table's structure	• Format a table • Explore Reading Layout view	• Apply AutoFormats to tables • Delete table columns • Insert rows in a table • Modify cell formats • Modify table borders • Modify table formats by merging table cells	• Modify table formats by splitting table cells • Print documents • Rotate text in a table cell • Sort table data • Use formulas in tables • Use Reading layout and other views

Student Data Files   For a complete list of the Data Files needed for this tutorial, see page WD 2.

Planning the Document

Caitlyn divided the responsibility for the report among the members of the group. Each person gathered information about one topic and wrote the appropriate section of the report. Then Caitlyn compiled all the information into a coherent and unified report. In addition, she took care to follow the company's guidelines for content, organization, style, and format.

Because Caitlyn knows that some members of the New Hope board of directors will not have time to read the entire report, she began the report with an executive summary. The body of the report provides an in-depth explanation of the options for establishing a WAN. At the end of the report, she summarizes the costs of these options. The report's style follows established standards of business writing, and emphasizes clarity, simplicity, and directness.

In accordance with the company style guide, Caitlyn's report will begin with a title page, with the text centered between the top and bottom margins. Every page except the title page will include a line of text at the top, giving a descriptive name for the report, as well as the page number. The text and headings will be formatted to match all reports created at Tyger Networks, and will follow company guidelines for layout and text style.

Opening the Report

Caitlyn already has combined the individual sections into one document. She also has begun formatting the report by changing the font size of headings, adding formatting such as bold and italic, and by indenting paragraphs. You'll open the document and follow the steps in this section to perform the remaining formatting tasks, as indicated in Figure 3-1.

Options for Establishing a Wide Area Network

make this a vertically centered title page

Prepared for
Susan Launspach, Program Director
New Hope Social Services

set tab stop

Written by Tyger Networks:

type list of task force members and their titles

start new page

Executive Summary

This report presents options for connecting the three computer networks run by New Hope Social Services. First we describe the networks in the Madison, Janesville, and Milwaukee offices, and then we explain the options for integrating these networks into a larger structure, known as a Wide Area Network (WAN). Finally, in a table at the end of this report, we summarize the costs for implementing the various WAN connections.

New Hope's Existing LANs

The term Local Area Network (LAN) refers to a network of computers and other devices (such as printers) that are geographically close to each other (for example, on the same floor of a building). A LAN is managed via a special computer known as a server. The majority of the computers on the three New Hope LANs are used to run Microsoft Office applications. The network operating system on the Janesville and Madison servers has been upgraded to Windows 2000 Server, while the Milwaukee server continues to run Windows NT 4. Because the three LANs are separate, a social worker in one office cannot directly access data stored on a computer in one of the other two offices.

insert header in this section

WAN Technology

To allow inter-office data access, we propose connecting the three LANs, thereby creating a Wide Area Network (WAN). A WAN is a network that spans a geographical distance (between buildings, cities, or even countries). Strictly speaking, a WAN consists of one link between two points. It does not usually connect one site to several other sites in the way that a LAN connects multiple computers. Thus, to connect the three New Hope LANs, we would need to establish multiple WAN links. The following sections describe various options for creating these links. The

To open the document:

▸ 1. Start Word, and then open the file **WAN** located in the Tutorial.03\Tutorial folder included with your Data Files.

▸ 2. To avoid altering the original file, save the document as **New Hope WAN Report** in the same folder.

▸ 3. Check your settings to make sure your screen matches figures in this tutorial. In particular, be sure to display the nonprinting characters and switch to Normal view if necessary. Note that throughout this tutorial, your Zoom settings may not automatically match the Zoom settings shown in the figures. As you work through the tutorial steps, adjust your Zoom settings as necessary if you want to make your screen match the figures exactly.

Setting Tab Stops

Tabs are useful for indenting paragraphs and for vertically aligning text or numerical data in columns. A **tab** adds space between the margin and text in a column or between text in one column and text in another column. A **tab stop** is the location where text moves when you press the Tab key. When Show/Hide ¶ is selected, the nonprinting tab character → appears wherever you press the Tab key. A tab character is just like any other character you type; you can delete it by pressing the Backspace key or the Delete key.

Word provides several **tab-stop alignment styles**. The five major styles are left, center, right, decimal, and bar, as shown in Figure 3-2. The first three tab-stop styles position text in a similar way to the Align Left, Center, and Align Right buttons on the Formatting toolbar. The difference is that with a tab, you determine line by line precisely where the left, center, or right alignment should occur.

Figure 3-2 ▸ **Tab stop alignment styles**

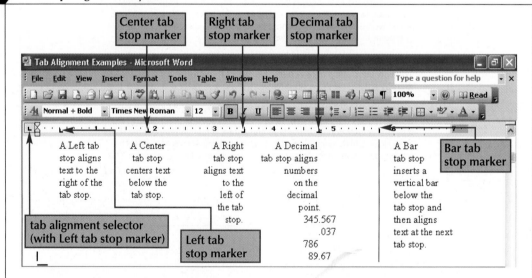

Left tabs position the left edge of text at the tab stop and extend the text to the right. **Center tabs** position text so that it's centered evenly on both sides of the tab stop. **Right tabs** position the right edge of text at the tab stop and extend the text to the left. **Decimal tabs** position numbers so that their decimal points are aligned at the tab stop.

Bar tabs insert a vertical bar at the tab stop and then align text to the right of the next tab stop. In addition, you can use a **First Line Indent tab**, which indents the first line of a paragraph, and a **Hanging Indent tab**, which indents every line of a paragraph *except* the first line.

The Word default tab-stop settings are every one-half inch, as indicated by the small gray tick marks at the bottom of the ruler shown in Figure 3-3. You set a new tab stop by selecting a tab-stop alignment style (from the tab alignment selector at the left end of the horizontal ruler) and then clicking the horizontal ruler to insert the tab stop. You can remove a tab stop from the ruler by clicking it and dragging the tab stop off the ruler.

Ruler with tab stops ◄ | Figure 3-3

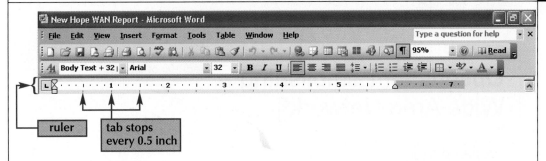

You should never try to align columns of text by adding extra spaces with the spacebar. Although the text might seem precisely aligned in the document window, it might not be aligned when you print the document. Furthermore, if you edit the text, the extra spaces might disturb the alignment. One of the main advantages of tab stops is that, if you edit text aligned with tabs, the alignment remains intact. If you want to align a lot of text in many columns, you'll find it easier to use a table, as described later in this tutorial.

To align columns using tabs, set tab stops on the horizontal ruler, type text in the first column, and then press the Tab key. The insertion point then moves to the next tab stop to the right, where you can type more text. You can continue in this way until you type the first row of each column. Then you can press the Enter key, and begin typing the next row of each column. However, sometimes you'll find that text in a column stretches beyond the next default tab stop, and as a result the columns fail to line up evenly.

Setting Tab Stops

Reference Window

- To set a tab stop, click the tab alignment selector on the far left of the horizontal ruler until the appropriate tab-stop alignment style appears, and then click the horizontal ruler where you want to position the tab stop. Press the Tab key to move the insertion point from one tab stop to another.
- To change the tab alignment or location for text that already contains tab stops, select the text and then move an existing tab stop to a new location, or click the tab alignment selector on the far left of the horizontal ruler until the appropriate tab-stop alignment style appears and then click the horizontal ruler where you want to set the tab stop.
- To remove a tab stop, click it and drag it off the horizontal ruler.

In the Tyger Networks report, you need to type the list of task force members and their titles. As you type, you'll discover whether Word's default tab stops are appropriate for this document, or whether you need to add a new tab stop.

To enter the task force list using tabs:

▶ 1. Verify that nonprinting characters are displayed, and then move the insertion point to the line below the text "Written by Tyger Networks:."

▶ 2. Type **Caitlyn Waller**, and then press the **Tab** key. A tab character appears, and the insertion point moves to the first tab stop after the "r" in "Waller." This tab stop is located at the 1.5-inch mark on the horizontal ruler. See Figure 3-4.

Figure 3-4 ▶ **Tab character**

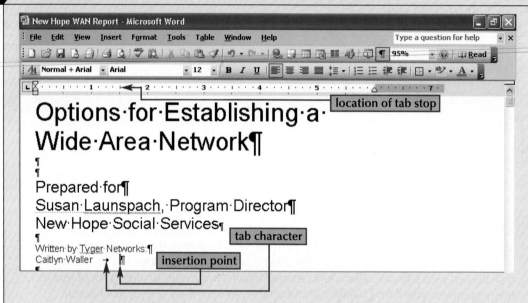

▶ 3. Type **Account Manager**, and then press the **Enter** key. The insertion point moves to a new line, ready for you to enter the next name in the list.

▶ 4. Type **Melissa J. Curlington**, and then press the **Tab** key. The insertion point moves to the first available tab stop, at the 2-inch mark on the horizontal ruler.

▶ 5. Type **Product Manager**, and then press the **Enter** key.

As you can see, Melissa J. Curlington's title does not align with Caitlyn Waller's title on the line above. You'll fix this in a moment by inserting a new tab stop that overrides the default tab stops. But first continue typing the list of names.

▶ 6. Type **Angelo Zurlo-Cuva**, press the **Tab** key, type **Sales Engineer**, press the **Enter** key, type your first and last name, press the **Tab** key, and then type **Network Engineer**. When you are finished, your document should look like Figure 3-5.

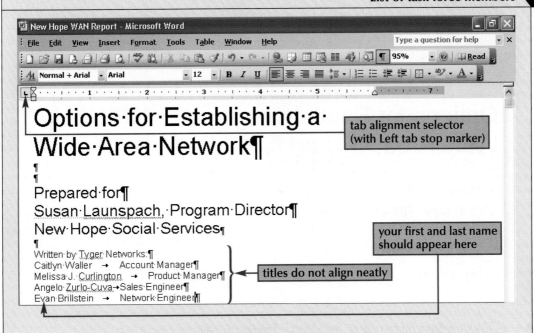

The list of names and titles is not aligned properly. You'll fix this by inserting a new tab stop.

To add a new tab stop to the horizontal ruler:

▶ **1.** Click and drag the mouse pointer to select the list of task force members and titles.

▶ **2.** Make sure the current tab-stop alignment style is Left tab ⌊L⌋, as shown in Figure 3-5. If ⌊L⌋ is not selected, click the **tab alignment selector** one or more times until ⌊L⌋ appears.

▶ **3.** Click the **tick mark** on the ruler that occurs at 2.5 inches. Word automatically inserts a Left tab stop at that location and removes the tick marks to its left. The column of titles shifts to the new tab stop.

▶ **4.** Deselect the highlighted text and then move the insertion point anywhere in the list of names and titles. See Figure 3-6.

Figure 3-6 | **Left tab stop on ruler**

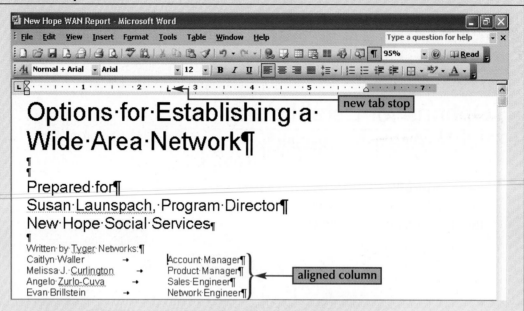

5. Click the **Save** button on the Standard toolbar to save your work.

The two columns of information are now aligned, as Caitlyn requested. Notice that Word changed the tab stops only for the selected paragraphs, not for all the paragraphs in the document. In the Case Problems at the end of this tutorial you'll have a chance to work with tab stops using the Tabs dialog box (which you can open via the Tabs command on the Format menu). Among other things, the Tabs dialog box allows you to insert a leader, which is a row of dots (or other characters) between tabbed text. A dot leader makes it easier to read a long list of tabbed material because the eye can follow the dots from one item to the next. You can also use the Tabs dialog box to clear (or remove) tab stops from a document. Next, you need to change the layout of the title page.

Formatting the Document in Sections

According to the company guidelines, the title page of the report should be centered between the top and bottom margins of the page. To format the title page differently from the rest of the report, you need to divide the document into sections. A **section** is a unit or part of a document that can have its own page orientation, margins, headers, footers, and vertical alignment. Each section, in other words, is like a mini-document within a document.

To divide a document into sections, you insert a **section break**, which appears in a document as a dotted line with the words "Section Break." A section break marks the point at which one section ends and another begins. A section can start on a new page, or a section can continue on the same page as text not included in the new section. You insert a section break with the Break command on the Insert menu. To delete a section break (or a page break), click the line representing the break and press the Delete key.

To insert a section break after the title:

▶ 1. Position the insertion point immediately to the left of the "E" in the heading "Executive Summary." You want the text above this heading to be on a separate title page and the executive summary to begin on the second page of the report.

▶ 2. Click **Insert** on the menu bar, and then click **Break** to open the Break dialog box. See Figure 3-7.

Break dialog box ◀ **Figure 3-7**

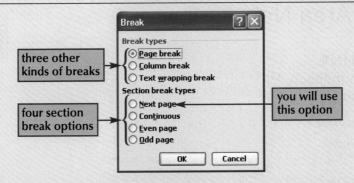

three other kinds of breaks

four section break options

you will use this option

The Break dialog box can be a bit confusing, so you should study it carefully before continuing with these steps. The option buttons under "Break types" allow you to insert three different types of breaks, including a **page break**, which moves the text after it onto a new page. (You don't need to be concerned with the other options right now.) The four option buttons under "Section break types" allow you to insert four types of section breaks. Of these, the two most important types of section breaks are a Next page section break, which starts a new section on a new page, and a Continuous section break, which inserts a section break without starting a new page. If you simply want to start a new page, you can click the Page break option button in the Break dialog box. If you want to start a new page *and* insert a section break, you should click the Next page option button in the Break dialog box. Because you want the document to have a title page, and because you want to format the title page differently than the rest of the document, you will insert a section break that starts a new page. In other words, you need to click the Next page option button.

▶ 3. Under "Section break types," click the **Next page** option button, and then click the **OK** button. A double-dotted line and the words "Section Break (Next Page)" appear before the heading "Executive Summary," indicating that you have inserted a break that starts a new section on the next page. The status bar indicates that the insertion point is on page 2, section 2. See Figure 3-8.

| Figure 3-8 | Section break |

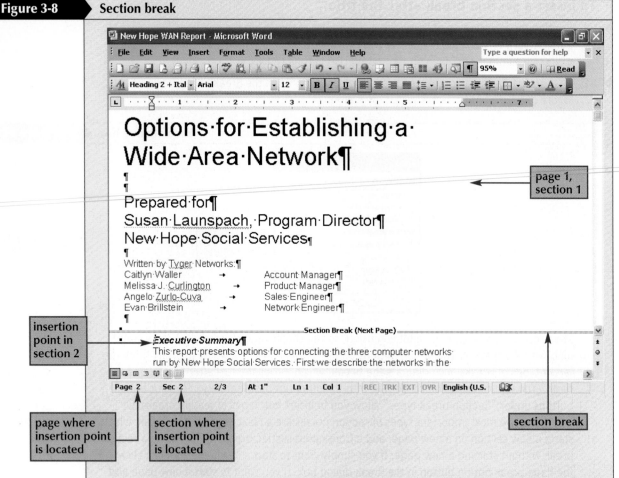

Trouble? If you see a single dotted line and the words "Page Break," you inserted a page break rather than a section break. Click the Undo button ⟲ on the Standard toolbar, and then repeat Steps 1 through 3.

▶ **4.** To practice deleting a section break, click the Section break line, and then press the **Delete** key. The section break line disappears and the status bar indicates that the insertion point is located in section 1, which is now the only section.

▶ **5.** Click the **Undo** button ⟲ on the Standard toolbar. The section break reappears.

▶ **6.** Save your work.

Now that the title page is a separate section and page from the rest of the report, you can make changes affecting only that section, leaving the rest of the document unchanged.

Changing the Vertical Alignment of a Section

You're ready to center the text of page 1 vertically on the page. But first you will switch to the Print Preview window, so you can more easily observe your changes to page 1.

To see the document in Print Preview:

▶ 1. Click the **Print Preview** button 🔍 on the Standard toolbar to open the Print Preview window.

▶ 2. If you don't see all three pages (as shown in Figure 3-9) click the **Multiple Pages** button ▦ on the Print Preview toolbar, and then click and drag across the top three pages in the list box to select "1 × 3 Pages." The three pages of the report are reduced in size and appear side by side. See Figure 3-9. Although you cannot read the text on the pages, you can see the general layout.

Report in Print Preview window ◀ **Figure 3-9**

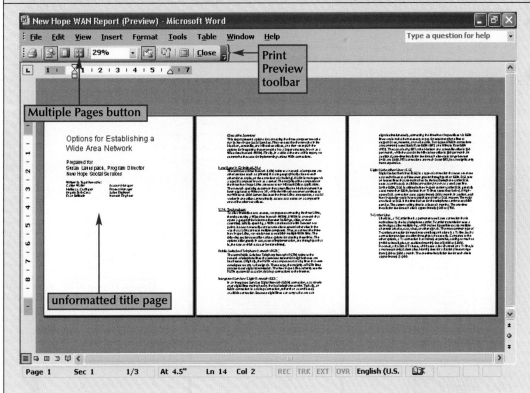

Now you can change the vertical alignment to center the lines of text between the top and bottom margins. The **vertical alignment** specifies how a page of text is positioned on the page between the top and bottom margins—flush at the top, flush at the bottom, or centered between the top and bottom margins.

You'll center the title page text from within the Print Preview window.

To change the vertical alignment of the title page:

1. Click the **Magnifier** button 🔍 on the Print Preview toolbar once to deselect it. When the magnifier button is deselected, you can edit the document.

2. Click the **leftmost page** in the Print Preview window to move the insertion point to page 1 (the title page). The status bar indicates that page 1 is the current page.

   Trouble? If the size of page 1 increases when you click it, you selected the Magnifier button 🔍 in Step 1 instead of deselecting it. Click the Multiple Pages button 🔳 on the Print Preview toolbar, drag to select "1 × 3 Pages," and then repeat Steps 1 and 2.

3. Click **File** on the menu bar, and then click **Page Setup**. The Page Setup dialog box opens.

4. Click the **Layout** tab. In the Apply to list box, select **This section** (if it is not already selected) so that the layout change affects only the section containing the insertion point (that is, the first section) and not both sections of your document.

5. Click the **Vertical alignment** list arrow, and then click **Center** to center the pages of the current section—in this case, just page 1—vertically between the top and bottom margins.

6. Click the **OK** button to return to the Print Preview window. The text of the title page is centered vertically, as shown in Figure 3-10.

Figure 3-10	Title page vertically centered

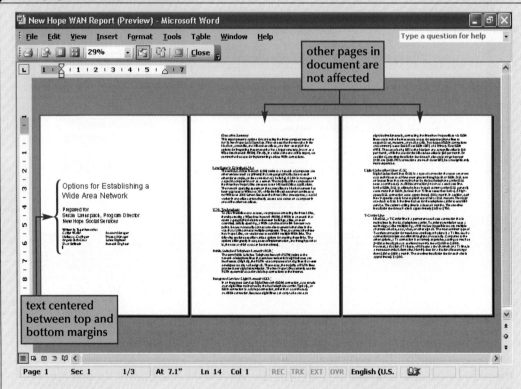

7. Click the **Close** button on the Print Preview toolbar to return to Normal view.

You have successfully centered the title page text. Next, you turn your attention to inserting a header with a descriptive name for the report and the page number at the top of every page in section 2.

Adding Headers

The report guidelines at Tyger Networks require a short report title and the page number to be printed at the top of every page except the title page. Text that is printed at the top of every page is called a **header**. For example, the information printed at the top of the page you are reading is a header. Similarly, a **footer** is text that is printed at the bottom of every page. (You'll have a chance to work with footers in the Case Problems at the end of this tutorial.)

When you insert a header or footer into a document, you switch to Header and Footer view. The Header and Footer toolbar is displayed, and the insertion point moves to the top of the document, where the header will appear. The document text is dimmed, indicating that it cannot be edited until you return to Normal or Print Layout view.

You'll create a header for the main body of the report (section 2) that prints "Options for Establishing a Wide Area Network" at the left margin and the page number at the right margin.

To insert a header for section 2:

1. Click anywhere after the section break so that the insertion point is located in section 2 and not in section 1. Refer to the status bar to verify that the insertion point is in section 2.

2. Click **View** on the menu bar, and then click **Header and Footer**. The Word window changes to Header and Footer view, and the Header and Footer toolbar appears. The header area is located in the top margin of your document, surrounded by a dashed line, and displays the words "Header -Section 2-." See Figure 3-11. (If the Header and Footer toolbar covers the header area, drag the toolbar below the header area, similar to its position in Figure 3-11.) Currently, the header is set up so that any text you type in the section 2 header will also appear in the section 1 header. In other words, the headers for sections 1 and 2 are linked. In order to create separate headers for the two sections, you need to deselect the Link to Previous button in the Header and Footer toolbar. You'll do that in the next step.

Creating a header ◄ **Figure 3-11**

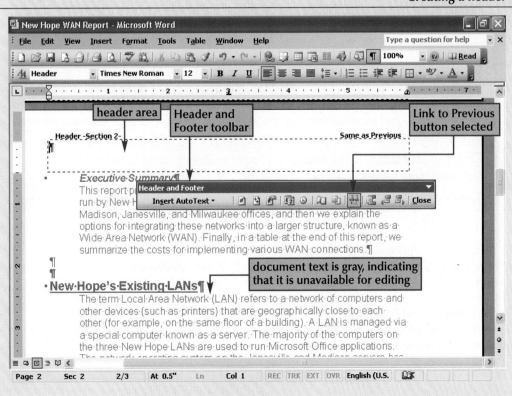

Trouble? If the header area displays "Header -Section 1-," click the Show Next button 🗐 on the Header and Footer toolbar until the header area displays "Header -Section 2-."

Trouble? If the text of the document doesn't appear on the screen, click the Show/Hide Document Text button 🗐 on the Header and Footer toolbar, and continue with Step 3.

▶ **3.** Click the **Link to Previous** button 🗒 on the Header and Footer toolbar to deselect it. When Link to Previous is selected, Word automatically inserts the header text you create in one section in the previous section. You deselected it to ensure that the header text you create in section 2 applies only to the current section (section 2), and not to the previous section (section 1).

▶ **4.** Type **Options for Establishing a Wide Area Network**. The title is automatically aligned on the left. See Figure 3-12.

Figure 3-12	Header text

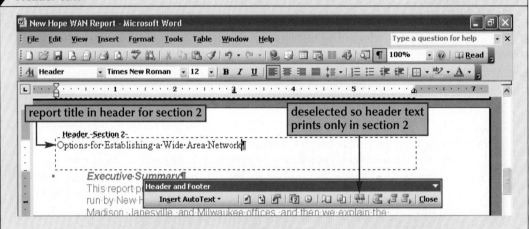

▶ **5.** Press the **Tab** key to move the insertion point to the next available tab stop, on the right margin of the header area. (Notice that by default the header contains Center and Right tab stops.)

▶ **6.** Type the word **Page**, and then press the **spacebar** once.

▶ **7.** Click the **Insert Page Number** button 🗐 on the Header and Footer toolbar. The page number "2" appears at the right-aligned tab. The page number in the header looks like you simply typed the number 2, but you actually inserted a special instruction telling Word to insert the correct page number on each page. Now consecutive page numbers will print on each page of the header within this section.

▶ **8.** Click the **Close** button on the Header and Footer toolbar to return to Normal view, and then save your changes.

Trouble? If your document is not displayed in Normal view, switch to Normal view now.

You can use the Header and Footer toolbar to insert a page number in the style of "Page 1 of 2." In a header or footer, type the word "Page" followed by a space, click the Insert Page Number button 🗐 on the Header and Footer toolbar, type a space followed by the word "of", type another space, and then click the Insert Number of Pages button 🗐 on the Header and Footer toolbar to insert the total number of pages in the document.

Notice that you can't see the header in Normal view. To see exactly how the header will appear on the printed page, you need to switch to the Print Preview window or to Print Layout view.

To view the header and margins in Print Preview:

1. Click the **Print Preview button** 🔍 on the Standard toolbar. The three pages of the document are displayed as they were earlier in the Print Preview window, although this time you can see a line of text at the top of pages 2 and 3. To read the header text, you need to increase the magnification.

2. Verify that the **Magnifier** button 🔍 on the Print Preview toolbar is selected.

3. Move the pointer ⊕ over the second page of the document, and then click the header text at the top of the page. The Print Preview window zooms in on the header text for page 2, as shown in Figure 3-13.

Header text for page 2 in Print Preview ◀ Figure 3-13

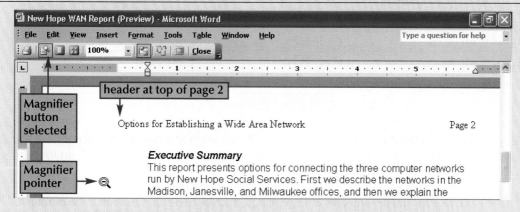

4. Use the vertical scroll bar to scroll down until you can see the header for page 3.

5. Scroll up until you can see the top of page 1. Notice that the header appears only on pages 2 and 3. The header does not appear on the title page because the title page is in a different section of the document. The correct page numbers appear on pages 2 and 3.

6. Use the **Multiple Pages** button 🔳 to display all three pages of the document again.

7. Click the **Close** button on the Print Preview toolbar to return to Normal view.

8. Save your work.

The report now has the required header. You have formatted Caitlyn's report so that the results are professional-looking, presented clearly, and easy to read. Next, you will add a table that summarizes the costs of the various WAN options.

Inserting Tables

Using Word, you can quickly organize data and arrange text in an easy-to-read table format. A **table** is information arranged in horizontal rows and vertical columns. As shown in Figure 3-14, table rows are commonly referred to by number (row 1, row 2, and so forth), while columns are commonly referred to by letter (column A on the far left, then column B, and so forth). However, you do not see row and column numbers on the screen. The area where a row and column intersect is called a **cell**. Each cell is identified by a column and row label. For example, the cell in the upper-left corner of a table is cell A1 (column A, row 1), the cell to the right of that is cell B1, the cell below cell A1 is A2, and so forth. The table's structure is shown by **gridlines**, which are light gray lines that define the rows and columns. By default, gridlines do not appear on the printed page. You can emphasize specific parts of a table on the printed page by adding a **border**, which is a line that prints along the side of a table cell.

Figure 3-14 ▶ **Elements of a Word table**

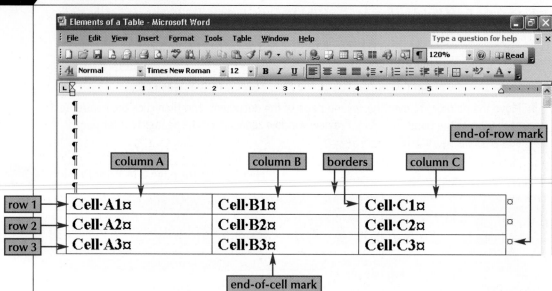

Depending on your needs, you can create a blank table and then insert information into it (as you'll do next), or you can convert existing text into a table (as you'll do in the Case Problems at the end of this tutorial).

You may be wondering why you would use a table instead of tabs to align text in columns. Tabs work well for smaller amounts of information, such as two columns with three or four rows, but tabs and columns become tedious and difficult to work with when you need to organize a larger amount of more complex information. The Word Table feature allows you to organize data quickly and to place text and graphics in a more legible format.

Creating a Table

You can create a table with equal column widths quickly by using the Insert Table button on the Standard toolbar. (You will use this technique to create the table Caitlyn requested.) You also can create a table by dragging the Draw Table pointer to draw the table structure you want. (You'll practice this method in the Case Problems.) However you create a table, you can modify it by using commands on the Table menu or the buttons on the Tables and Borders toolbar.

Caitlyn wants you to create a table that summarizes information in the Tyger Networks report. Figure 3-15 shows a sketch of what Caitlyn wants the table to look like. The table will allow the members of the New Hope board of directors to see at a glance the cost of each option. The top row of the table, called the **heading row**, identifies the type of information in each column.

Figure 3-15 ▶ **Table sketch**

Type of Connection	Monthly Charge
ISDN	$50 to $60
DSL	$80
T1	$1000 to $2000

Inserting a Page Break

Before you begin creating the table, you need to insert a page break because you want the table to appear on a separate page.

To insert a page break:

1. Verify that the document is displayed in Normal view.
2. Press **Ctrl+End** to position the insertion point at the end of the report.
3. Press **Ctrl+Enter**. A dotted line with the words "Page Break" appears in the document window. *Note*: You also can add a page break using the Break dialog box (the same dialog box you used earlier to insert a section break).

   Trouble? If you do not see the words "Page Break," check to make sure the document is displayed in Normal view.
4. Scroll down until the page break is positioned near the top of the document window.

The insertion point is now at the beginning of a new page, where you want to insert the table.

Inserting a Blank Table

You'll use the Insert Table button to insert a blank table structure into the new page. Then you can type the necessary information directly into the table.

To create a blank table using the Insert Table button:

1. Click the **Insert Table** button on the Standard toolbar. A drop-down grid resembling a miniature table appears below the Insert Table button. The grid opens with four rows and five columns for the table. You can drag the pointer to select as many rows and columns as you need. In this case, you need four rows and two columns.
2. Position the pointer in the upper-left cell of the grid, and then drag the pointer down and across the grid until you highlight four rows and two columns. As you drag the pointer across the grid, Word indicates the size of the table (rows by columns) at the bottom of the grid.
3. When the table size is 4 × 2, click the mouse button. An empty table, four rows by two columns, appears in your document with the insertion point blinking in the upper-left corner (cell A1). The two columns are of equal width. Each cell contains an end-of-cell mark, and each row contains an end-of-row mark. See Figure 3-16.

Empty table in Normal view | Figure 3-16

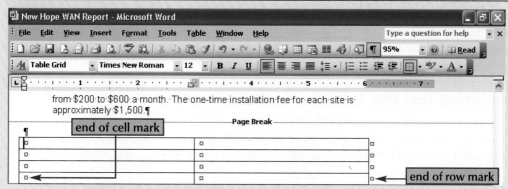

Trouble? If your table is displayed in Print Layout view, switch to Normal view and then compare your table to Figure 3-16.

Trouble? If you don't see the end-of-cell and end-of-row marks, you need to show non-printing characters. Click the Show/Hide ¶ button ¶ on the Standard toolbar to show nonprinting characters.

Trouble? If you see the Tables and Borders toolbar displayed along with the new blank table, close it. You will learn how to use the Tables and Borders toolbar later in this tutorial.

When working with tables and graphics, it's helpful to switch to Print Layout view, which allows you to get a better sense of the overall layout of the page, including the headers. Also, some special table features are only available in Print Layout view. You'll switch to Print Layout view in the following steps.

To display the table structure in Print Layout view:

1. Click the **Print Layout View** button ▣. Note that a Zoom setting of 100% or greater should make it easy for you to see the entire table on the screen. The table is displayed in Print Layout view, where you can see the column widths indicated on the horizontal ruler. Also, notice that the document header is visible in Print Layout view.

2. Move the mouse pointer over the empty table. The Table Move handle appears in the table's upper-left corner, and the Table Resize handle appears in the lower-right corner. See Figure 3-17. You don't need to use either of these handles now, but you should understand their function. To select the entire table quickly, you can click the Table Move handle. Then you can move the entire table by dragging the Table Move handle. To change the size of the entire table, you could drag the Table Resize handle.

| Figure 3-17 | Empty table in Print Layout view |

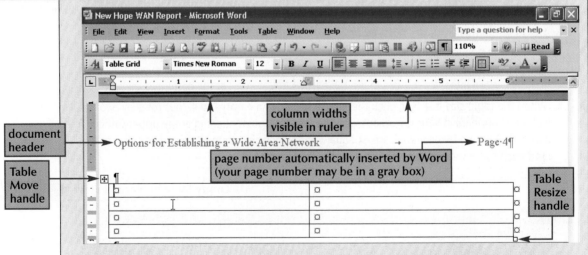

Entering Text in a Table

You can enter text in a table by moving the insertion point to a cell and typing. If the text takes up more than one line in the cell, Word automatically wraps the text to the next line and increases the height of that cell and all the cells in that row. To move the insertion point to another cell in the table, you can either click in that cell or use the Tab key. Figure 3-18 summarizes the keystrokes for moving the insertion point within a table.

Keystrokes for moving around a table

Figure 3-18

Press	To move the insertion point
Tab or →	One cell to the right, or to the first cell in the next row
Shift+Tab or ←	One cell to the left, or to the last cell in the previous row
Alt+Home	To the first cell of the current row
Alt+End	To the last cell of the current row
Alt+PageUp	To the top cell of the current column
Alt+PageDown	To the bottom cell of the current column
↑	One cell up in the current column
↓	One cell down in the current column

Now you are ready to insert information into the table.

To insert data into the table:

1. Verify that the insertion point is located in cell **A1** (in the upper-left corner).

2. Type the heading **Type of Connection**.

3. Press the **Tab** key to move to cell B1. See Figure 3-19.

Entering text in the table

Figure 3-19

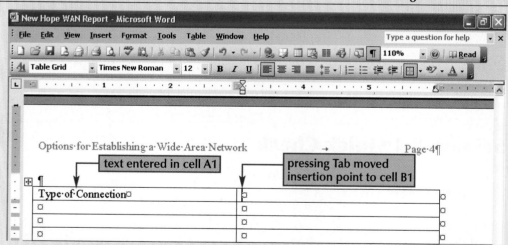

Trouble? If Word created a new paragraph in cell A1 rather than moving the insertion point to cell B1, you pressed the Enter key instead of the Tab key. Press the Backspace key to remove the paragraph mark, and then press the Tab key to move to cell B1.

4. Type **Monthly Charge**, and then press the **Tab** key to move to cell A2. Notice that when you press the Tab key in the last column of the table, the insertion point moves to the first column in the next row.

You have finished entering the heading row, the row that identifies the information in each column. Now you can enter the information about the various WAN options.

To continue entering information in the table:

➤ **1.** Type **ISDN**, and then press the **Tab** key to move to cell B2.

➤ **2.** Type **$50 to $60**, and then press the **Tab** key to move the insertion point to cell A3.

➤ **3.** Type the remaining information for the table, as shown in Figure 3-20, pressing the **Tab** key to move from cell to cell. You'll change the column widths in the next session.

Figure 3-20 | Table with completed information

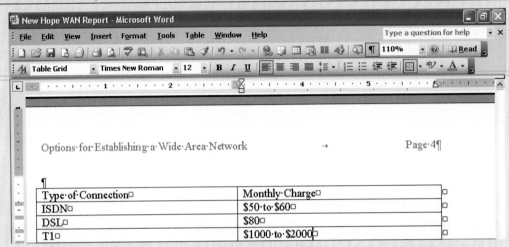

Trouble? If a new row (row 5) appeared at the bottom of your table, you pressed the Tab key when the insertion point was in cell B4, the last cell in the table. Click the Undo button ⤺ on the Standard toolbar to remove row 5 from the table.

➤ **4.** Save your work.

Keep in mind that many document-editing features, such as the Backspace key, the copy-and-paste feature, the Undo button, and the AutoCorrect feature, work the same way in a table as they do in the rest of the document. You will edit and format this table in the next session.

Review

To reinforce the tasks you learned in this session, go to the SAM 2003 Training Companion CD included with this text.

Session 3.1 Quick Check

1. Define the following in your own words:
   a. section break
   b. cell
   c. table
   d. header
   e. tab stop

2. Explain how to insert a new tab stop.

3. Describe a situation in which you would want to divide a document into sections.

4. Explain how to center the title page vertically between the top and bottom margins.

5. What is the difference between a header and a footer?

6. How do you insert the page number in a header?

7. Describe how to insert a blank table consisting of three columns and two rows.

8. How do you move the insertion point from one row to the next in a table?

9. Describe a situation in which it would be better to use a table rather than tab stops.

10. Explain how to select an entire table.

Session 3.2

Displaying the Tables and Borders Toolbar

The **Tables and Borders toolbar** contains a number of useful buttons that simplify the process of working with tables. You'll display the Tables and Borders toolbar in the following steps.

For hands-on practice of key tasks in this session, go to the SAM 2003 Training Companion CD included with this text.

To open the Tables and Borders toolbar:

1. If you took a break after the previous session, make sure Word is running and that the New Hope WAN Report document is open. Check that the nonprinting characters are displayed, that the document is displayed in Print Layout view, and that the document is scrolled so that the table is visible.

2. Click the **Tables and Borders** button ⬚ on the Standard toolbar. The Tables and Borders toolbar appears.

3. Move the mouse pointer over the table. The Draw Table pointer ⌀ appears. You can use this pointer to add new rows or columns in a table, and to add borders between cells. You'll have a chance to practice using this pointer in the Case Problems at the end of this tutorial. For now you'll turn it off.

4. Click the **Draw Table** button ⬚ on the Tables and Borders toolbar. The pointer changes to an I-beam pointer Ⅰ.

5. If necessary, drag the Tables and Borders toolbar down and to the right, so that it doesn't block your view of the table, as shown in Figure 3-21.

Positioning the Tables and Borders toolbar | **Figure 3-21**

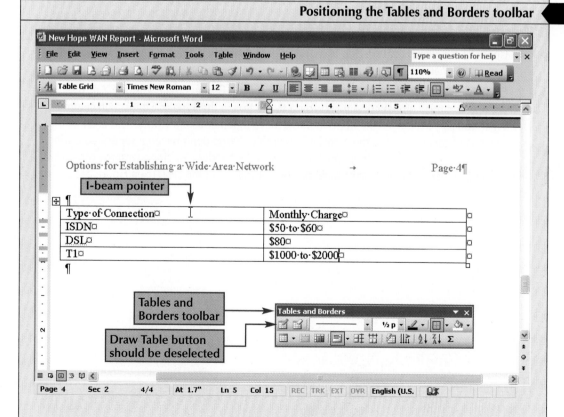

6. Move the mouse pointer over the buttons on the Tables and Borders toolbar and read the name of each button as it is displayed in a ScreenTip. In particular, notice the Merge Cells button, which you can use to combine multiple cells into one cell; the Split Cells button, which you can use to divide one cell into multiple cells; and the AutoSum button, which you can use to total a column of numbers. You'll have a chance to practice using these buttons in the Case Problems at the end of this tutorial. Notice also the two Sort buttons, which you can use to rearrange the rows in a table. You will use the Sort Ascending button in the next section.

Sorting Rows in a Table

The term **sort** refers to the process of rearranging information in alphabetical, numerical, or chronological order. When you sort a table, you arrange the rows based on the contents of one of the columns. For example, you could sort the table you just created based on the contents of the Type of Connection column—either in ascending alphabetical order (from *A* to *Z*) or in descending alphabetical order (from *Z* to *A*). Alternately, you could sort the table based on the contents of the Monthly Charge column—either in ascending numerical order (lowest to highest) or in descending numerical order (highest to lowest). When you sort table data, Word usually does not sort the heading row along with the other information; instead, the heading row remains unsorted at the top of the table.

Caitlyn would like you to sort the table in ascending alphabetical order, based on the contents of the Type of Connection column. You start by positioning the insertion point in that column.

To sort the information in the table:

1. Click cell **A2** (which contains the text "ISDN"). The insertion point is now located in the Type of Connection column.

2. Click the **Sort Ascending** button 🔼 on the Tables and Borders toolbar. Rows 2 through 4 are now arranged alphabetically according to the text in the Type of Connection column. When you sort a table, all the items in a row move together as one entity. This ensures that the type of connection and the associated monthly charge don't become separated during the sort process. Also note that Word did not sort the header row along with the other rows. The header row remains in its original position at the top of the table. See Figure 3-22.

Table after being sorted 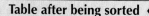 **Figure 3-22**

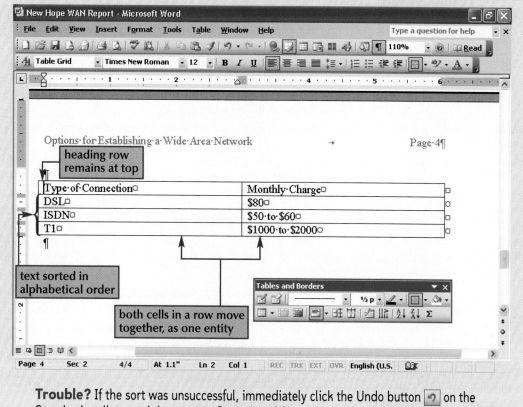

Trouble? If the sort was unsuccessful, immediately click the Undo button 🔄 on the Standard toolbar, and then repeat Steps 1 and 2.

Caitlyn stops by and asks you to add an "Installation Charge" column. She also would like you to insert a new row with information about a Fractional T1 connection.

Modifying an Existing Table Structure

You will often need to modify a table structure by adding or deleting rows and columns. When you select part of a table, new buttons sometimes appear on the Standard toolbar to help you modify the table structure. For instance, when you select a column, the Insert Columns button appears to help you insert a new column in the table. In most cases, however, you'll find it easiest to use menu commands to add and delete rows and columns, because the menu commands allow you to specify exactly how you want to modify the table. For instance, by using a menu command, you can indicate whether you want to insert a column to the right or left of the selected column. By contrast, the Insert Columns button always inserts a new column to the left of the selected column.

Figure 3-23 summarizes ways to insert or delete rows and columns in a table.

Figure 3-23	Ways to insert or delete table rows and columns

To	Do this
Insert a row within a table	Select the row above or below where you want the row added, click Table on the menu bar, point to Insert, and then click Rows Above or Rows Below.
	Select the row below where you want the row added, and then click the Insert Rows button on the Standard toolbar.
Insert a row at the end of a table	Position the insertion point in the cell at the far right of the bottom row, then press the Tab key.
Insert a column within a table	Select the column to the right or left of where you want the column added, click Table on the menu bar, point to Insert, then click Columns to the Left or Columns to the Right.
	Select the column to the right of where you want the column added, then click the Insert Columns button on the Standard toolbar.
Insert a column at the end of a table	Select the rightmost column in the table, click Table on the menu bar, point to Insert, and then click Columns to the Right.
	Select the end-of-row markers to the right of the table, and then click the Insert Columns button on the Standard toolbar.
Delete a row	Select the row or rows to be deleted including the end-of-row marker(s), click Table on the menu bar, point to Delete, and then click Rows.
Delete a column	Select the column or columns to be deleted, click Table on the menu bar, point to Delete, and then click Columns.

Inserting Columns in a Table

Your first task is to insert a new column between the Type of Connection column and the Monthly Charge column. This column will contain information on the Installation Charge for each WAN option. You need to begin by selecting the column to the left of the location where you want to insert a column.

To insert a column in the table:

1. Click in cell **A1** (which contains the heading "Type of Connection"), and then drag the mouse pointer down until the entire Type of Connection column is selected.

2. Click **Table** on the menu bar, point to **Insert**, and then click **Columns to the Right**. A new column is inserted in the table to the right of the Type of Connection column.

   Note: Word inserts the same number of new columns as are selected. For example, if you had selected two columns in Step 1, Word would have inserted two new columns in the table.

3. Click in the new cell **B1** (the blank cell at the top of the new column), and then enter the **Installation Charge** heading and data shown in Figure 3-24.

New Installation Charge column ◄ **Figure 3-24**

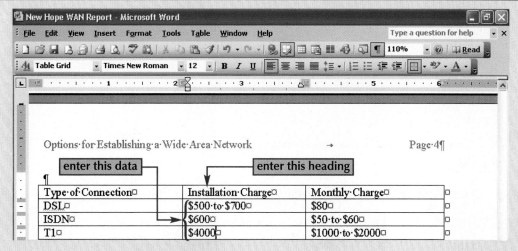

Inserting Rows in a Table

Next, you need to insert a row with information on a more economical type of T1 connection, called a fractional T1 connection. You could insert this row in its alphabetical position in the table (below the DSL row). But it's quicker to add the row to the end of the table, and then resort the table.

To insert a row at the bottom of the table:

1. Click the last cell in the Monthly Charge column (which contains "$1000 to $2000"). The insertion point is now located in the last cell in the table.

2. Press the **Tab** key. A blank row is added to the bottom of the table.

   Trouble? If a blank row is not added to the bottom of the table, click the Undo button on the Standard toolbar. Check to make sure the insertion point is in the rightmost cell of the bottom row, and then press the Tab key.

3. Enter the following information in the new row:
   Type of Connection: **Fractional T1**
   Installation Charge: **$1500**
   Monthly Charge: **$200 to $600**

4. Click anywhere in the Type of Connection column, and then click the **Sort Ascending** button on the Tables and Borders toolbar. The table rows are rearranged in alphabetical order, with the Fractional T1 row positioned below the DSL row, as shown in Figure 3-25.

Figure 3-25	Sorted table with new row

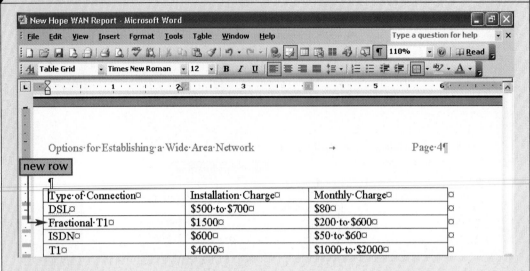

5. Save your work.

After reviewing the table, Caitlyn decides not to include the information on the full T1 connection, because it is far too expensive for New Hope's current budget. She asks you to delete the T1 row.

Deleting Rows and Columns in a Table

With Word, you can delete either the contents of table cells or the structure of the cells themselves. To delete the contents only, you select one or more cells and then press the Delete key. However, to delete both the contents and structure of a selected row or column from the table entirely, you must use one of the methods described earlier in Figure 3-23. Right now you'll use a menu command to delete the T1 row.

To delete a row using the Table menu:

1. Click the selection bar next to the T1 row, at the bottom of the table. The entire T1 row including the end-of-row marker is selected. (Take care to select the T1 row, at the bottom of the table, *not* the Fractional T1 row.)

2. Click **Table** on the menu bar, point to **Delete**, and then click **Rows**. The selected row is deleted from the table. See Figure 3-26.

Table after deleting row | Figure 3-26

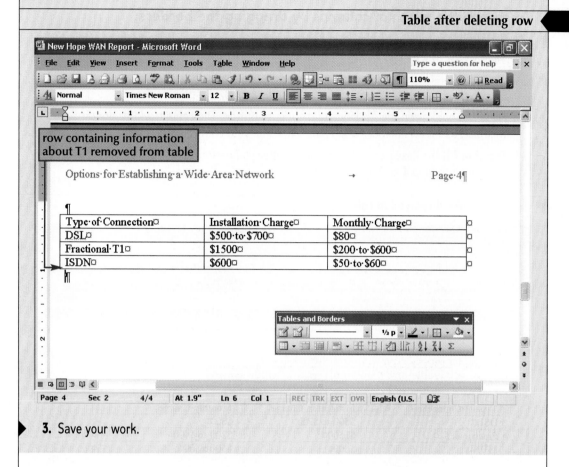

3. Save your work.

Formatting Tables

Word provides a variety of ways to enhance the appearance of the tables you create. You can alter the width of the columns and the height of the rows, or change the alignment of text within the cells or the alignment of the table between the document's left and right margins. You can change the appearance of the table borders, and add a shaded background. You can format an entire table at once using the **Table AutoFormat command** on the Table menu. (You'll have a chance to practice using this command in the Case Problems at the end of this tutorial.) In general, however, making formatting changes individually (using the mouse pointer along with various toolbar buttons and menu commands) gives you more options and more flexibility.

Changing Column Width and Row Height

Sometimes you'll want to adjust the column widths in a table to make the text easier to read. If you want to specify an exact width for a column, you should use the Table Properties command on the Table menu. However, it's usually easiest to drag the column's right border to a new position. Alternately, you can double-click a column border to make the column width adjust automatically to accommodate the widest entry in the column.

The columns in the table you have been working with are too wide for the information they contain. You'll change these widths by dragging the column borders, using the ruler as a guide. Keep in mind that to change the width of a column, you need to drag the column's right border.

To change the width of columns by dragging the borders:

▶ **1.** Verify that the table is displayed in Print Layout view, and then click anywhere within the table. Verify that no part of the table is selected.

▶ **2.** Move the pointer over the border between columns A and B (in other words, over the right border of column A, the "Type of Connection" column). The pointer changes to ◀║▶.

▶ **3.** Press and hold down the **Alt** key and the mouse button. The column widths are displayed in the ruler, as shown in Figure 3-27. (The widths on your computer might differ slightly.)

   Trouble? If the Research task pane opens after you perform Step 3, leave it open until you complete Step 4 and then close it.

| **Figure 3-27** | **Column widths displayed in ruler** |

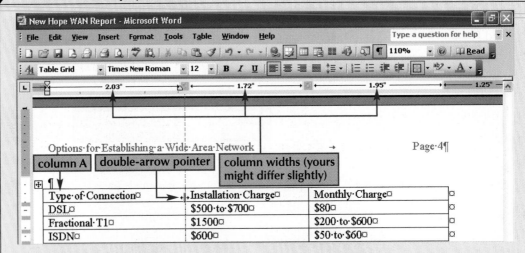

▶ **4.** While holding down the **Alt** key and the mouse button, drag the pointer to the left until column A is about **1.4** inches wide, and then release the mouse button and the Alt key. As the width of column A decreases, the width of column B (the Installation Charge column) increases. The overall width of the table does not change.

   Trouble? If you can't adjust the column width to exactly 1.4 inches, make it as close to that width as possible.

Now you need to adjust the width of both columns B and C. You could do this by dragging the column border, as you did for column A. But it's much faster to double-click the right border of each column.

To change the width of columns B and C:

▶ **1.** Position the mouse pointer over the right border of column B until the pointer changes to ◀║▶, and then double-click the right border of column B (the Installation Charge column). The column shrinks, leaving just enough room for the widest entry in the column (the column heading "Installation Charge").

▶ **2.** Repeat this procedure to adjust the width of column C (the Monthly Charge column). All three columns in the table are now just wide enough to accommodate the column headings.

You can change the height of rows by dragging a border. You'll make row 1 (the header row) taller so it is more prominent.

To change the height of row 1:

1. Position the pointer over the bottom border of the header row. The pointer changes to ⬍.

2. Press and hold down the **Alt** key and the mouse button. The row heights are displayed in the vertical ruler.

3. While holding down the **Alt** key, drag the pointer down until row 1 is about **0.45** inches high, then release the mouse button and the Alt key. Notice that the height of the other rows in the table is not affected by this change. See Figure 3-28.

   Trouble? If the Research task pane opens, close it.

Table with narrower columns and a wider heading row	**Figure 3-28**

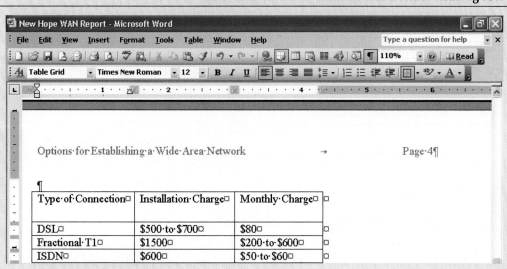

Aligning Text Within Cells

Aligning the text within the cells of a table makes the information easier to read. For example, aligning a column of numbers or percentages along the right margin helps the reader to compare the values quickly. At the same time, centering a row of headings makes a table more visually appealing. You can align text within the active cell the same way you do other text—with the alignment buttons on the Formatting toolbar. However, the Alignment buttons on the Tables and Borders toolbar provide more options.

Caitlyn would like you to align the data in the Installation Charge and Monthly Charge columns along the right side of the columns. The table also would look better with the headings centered. You'll begin by selecting and formatting all of columns B and C. For simple left and right alignment, you can use the Align buttons on the Formatting toolbar. For more sophisticated options, such as centering text horizontally and vertically in a cell, use the Align button on the Tables and Borders toolbar.

To right-align the numerical data and center the headings:

1. Move the pointer to the top of column B until the pointer changes to ⬇. Press and hold the left mouse button, and then drag right to select columns B and C.

2. Click the **Align Right** button 📄 on the Formatting toolbar. The column heads and numbers line up along the right edges of the cells.

   Notice that in the process of formatting columns B and C, you right-aligned two of the headings ("Installation Charge" and "Monthly Charge"). You will reformat those headings in the next three steps when you center the text in row 1 both horizontally and vertically in each cell.

3. Click the selection bar next to row 1. All of row 1 is selected.

4. Click the **Align** list arrow 📄▾ on the Tables and Borders toolbar to display a palette of nine alignment options.

5. Click the **Align Center** button 📄 in the middle of the palette. The text is centered both horizontally and vertically in the row.

6. Click anywhere in the table to deselect the row, and then save your work. See Figure 3-29.

| Figure 3-29 ▶ | **Table with newly aligned text** |

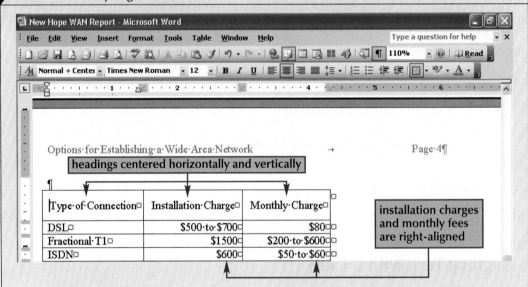

Trouble? If more than just the heading row is centered, click the Undo button 🔄 on the Standard toolbar, and then repeat Steps 3 through 6.

Changing Borders

While gridlines and borders may seem to be the same things, they are different elements of a table. Gridlines are light gray lines that indicate the structure of the table on the screen but do not show on the printed page. Borders are darker lines overlaying the gridlines, which do show on the printed page. When you create a table using the Insert Table button, Word automatically applies a thin black border, so you can't actually see the underlying gridlines.

After you have created a table, you can add new borders or erase existing borders by using the buttons on the Tables and Borders toolbar. You can modify an existing border by changing its **line weight** (its thickness). You can also choose a different **line style**—for instance, you can change a single straight-line border to a triple dotted line. If you prefer, you can create a table without any borders at all. You can also turn off the underlying gridlines by using the Hide Gridlines command on the Table menu. (Depending on how your computer is set up, gridlines might be hidden by default.)

Altering Table Borders

Reference Window

- Select the cell (or cells) whose borders you want to change.
- Click the Line Weight list arrow on the Tables and Borders toolbar, and then select a line weight.
- Click the Line Style list arrow on the Tables and Borders toolbar, and then select a line style.
- Click the Borders list arrow on the Tables and Borders toolbar, and then select a position for the new border.

or

- Use the Draw Table pointer to click the parts of the table that you want formatted with the selected line weight and line style.

To modify the table's borders:

1. Click the selection bar to the left of row 1 to select the heading row.

2. Click the **Line Weight** list arrow [½ ▾] on the Tables and Borders toolbar, and then click **2 ¼ pt**. Next, you will examine the options available in the Line Style list. Currently, a single straight-line border is selected.

3. Click the **Line Style** list arrow [——— ▾] on the Tables and Borders toolbar, and then scroll to view the various options. Note that you can remove borders (without removing the underlying gridlines) by selecting the No Border option. Caitlyn prefers a simple border, so you decide not to change the current selection.

   Trouble? If a single, straight-line border is not selected in the Line Style list, click the first line style under "No Border" now.

4. Press the **Esc** key. The Line Style list closes. You have selected a single straight-line border, with a thickness of 2 ¼ points.

5. Click the **Outside Border** list arrow [▦ ▾] on the Tables and Borders toolbar. (The exact name shown in the ScreenTip for this list arrow will vary, depending on what option is currently selected in the list. For example, it may currently be called the All Borders list arrow instead of the Outside Border list arrow.) A palette of options appears. You want to insert a thick border at the bottom of Row 1, so you need to use the Bottom Border option.

6. Click the **Bottom Border** [▦] option (in the bottom row of the Borders palette, third from the left). The new border style is applied to the bottom border of row 1.

7. Click anywhere in the table to deselect the row. See Figure 3-30.

Figure 3-30 **Row 1 with new border**

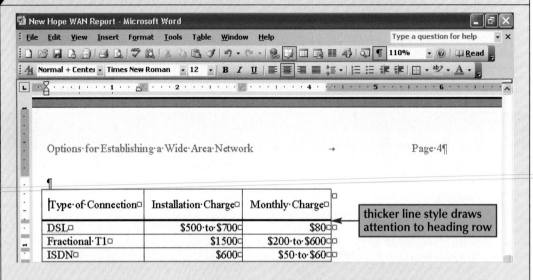

8. Save your work.

Changing the borders has made the table more attractive. You'll finish formatting the table by adding shading to the cells containing the headings.

Adding Shading

Adding **shading** (a gray or colored background) is useful in tables when you want to emphasize headings, totals, or other important items. Generally, when you add shading to a table, you also need to bold the shaded text to make it easier to read.

You will now add a light gray shading to the heading row and then format the headings in bold.

To add shading to the heading row and change the headings to bold:

1. Click the selection bar to the left of row 1 to select the heading row.

2. Click the **Shading Color** list arrow on the Tables and Borders toolbar. A palette of shading options opens.

3. Point to the fifth gray square from the left, in the top row. The ScreenTip "Gray-15%" appears.

4. Click the **Gray-15%** square. A light gray background appears in the heading row. Now you need to format the text in bold to make the headings stand out from the shading.

5. Click the **Bold** button [B] on the Formatting toolbar to make the headings bold. The wider letters take up more space, so Word breaks one or more of the headings into two lines within row 1.

Trouble? If any of the headings break incorrectly (for example, if the last "n" in "Installation" moves to the next line), you might need to widen columns to accommodate the bold letters. Drag the column borders as necessary to adjust the column widths so no word is split incorrectly.

6. Click in the table to deselect row 1. Your table should look like Figure 3-31, although the line breaks in your heading row may differ.

Row with shading and bold headings ◄ **Figure 3-31**

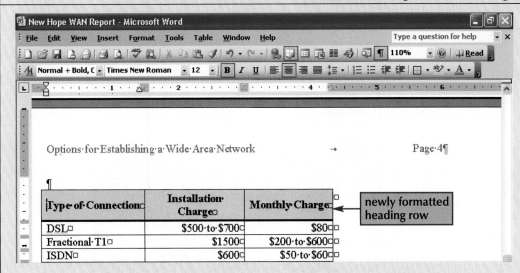

7. Save your changes.

Centering a Table

If a table doesn't fill the entire page width, you can center it between the left and right margins. The Center button on the Formatting toolbar centers only text within each selected cell. It does not center the entire table across the page. To center a table across the page (between the left and right margins), you need to use the Table Properties command.

Caitlyn thinks the table would look better if it was centered between the left and right margins.

To center the table across the page:

1. Click anywhere in the table, click **Table** on the menu bar, and then click **Table Properties**. The Table Properties dialog box opens.

2. Click the **Table** tab, if necessary.

3. In the Alignment section, click the **Center** option. See Figure 3-32.

Figure 3-32 Table Tab of the Table Properties dialog box

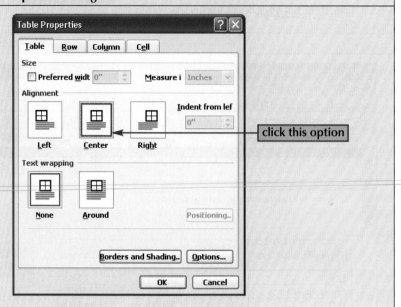

4. Click the **OK** button. The table centers between the left and right margins.

5. Save your work, and then close the Tables and Borders toolbar.

Now that you're finished with the table, you need to review the entire report quickly to make sure it requires no further work. To do that, you'll use Reading Layout view.

Reviewing a Document in Reading Layout View

As you've already seen, when you need to check the overall formatting in a document, it's useful to use the Whole Page zoom setting in Print Layout view, or the Print Preview window. But when you are only interested in the content of the document—that is, the text, tables and graphics, regardless of how they are laid out on the page—it's best to use **Reading Layout view**. This view allows you to peruse a document quickly, displaying the entire content of a page in a single screen, in a font that is large enough to read easily. Reading Layout view is designed to let you review a document online, without paying attention to margins and other page layout issues. When you're ready to concern yourself again with the document layout and formatting, you should return to Print Layout view.

Caitlyn asks you to skim the report now in Reading Layout view, to ensure that the document is completely finished.

To review the report in Reading Layout view:

1. Click the **Reading Layout** button 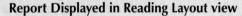 in the lower-left corner of the document window, just to the left of the horizontal scroll bar. Exactly what you see in Reading Layout view will depend on the choices made by the last person to use Reading Layout view on your computer, though you should see the Reading Layout toolbar below the menu bar. You will probably see the Reviewing toolbar too.

2. Scroll up to display the top of the document, click the **Allow Multiple Pages** button to select it (if it is not already selected), and then verify that the **Actual Page** button is *not* selected. (If it is selected, click it to deselect it now.) Finally, verify that the **Thumbnails** button is *not* selected. (If it is selected, click it to deselect it now.) Your screen should resemble Figure 3-33. Note that instead of dividing a document into pages, Reading Layout view divides a document into screens. The content of the report fills up multiple screens. Only the first two of these screens are currently displayed.

Report Displayed in Reading Layout view | Figure 3-33

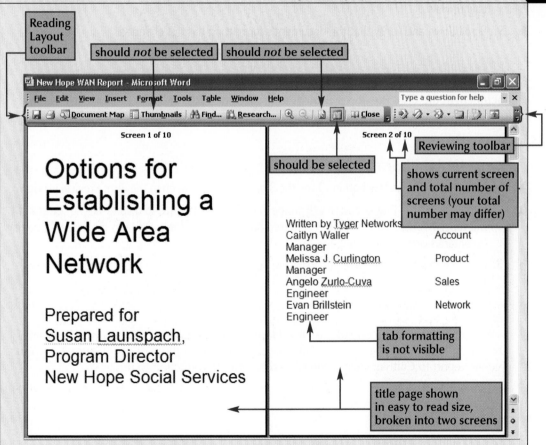

▶ **3.** Click the **down arrow** button ⏷ on the vertical scroll bar. Screen 2 is now displayed on the left, with screen 3 on the right.

▶ **4.** Continue scrolling through the document until you have reviewed all the screens, and then return to the beginning of the document.

▶ **5.** Click screen 1 to move the insertion point there.

▶ **6.** Click the **Increase Text Size** button 🔍 on the Reading Layout toolbar three times. Notice how the text increases in size, making it easier to read. The line breaks change to accommodate the larger sized text. These changes affect only how the text is displayed on the screen. When you return to Print Layout view later, you will see that the document has retained its original formatting.

▶ **7.** Click the **Decrease Text Size** button 🔍 on the Reading Layout toolbar three times to reverse the change made in Step 6. When you finish, the Decrease Text Size button should be a light shade of blue, indicating that the text cannot be made any smaller.

▶ **8.** Click the **Close** button on the Reading Layout toolbar. The document returns to Print Layout view.

▶ **9.** Scroll down and verify that the document's formatting has not changed.

To verify that the document's page layout settings haven't changed, you can review the document in the Print Preview window. You'll do that next, and then print a copy of the full report for Caitlyn.

To preview and print the report:

▶ **1.** Click the **Print Preview** button 🔍 on the Standard toolbar to open the Print Preview window.

▶ **2.** Use the **Multiple Pages** button 🔲 on the Print Preview toolbar to display all four pages of the report. Verify that the table is centered horizontally on the page, and that the title page is centered vertically on the page.

▶ **3.** Click the **Print** button 🖨 on the Print Preview toolbar to print the report, and then close the document.

You now have a hard copy of the New Hope report including the table, which summarizes the costs for creating a WAN. Your four-page report should look like Figure 3-34. You give the report to Caitlyn, so that she can add a brief introduction to the table.

New Hope WAN report | **Figure 3-34**

Options for Establishing a Wide Area Network

Prepared for
Susan Launspach, Program Director
New Hope Social Services

Written by Tyger Networks:
Caitilyn Waller	Account Manager
Melissa J. Curlington	Product Manager
Angelo Zurlo-Cuva	Sales Engineer
Evan Brillstein	Network Engineer

Options for Establishing a Wide Area Network   Page 2

Executive Summary
This report presents options for connecting the three computer networks run by New Hope Social Services. First we describe the networks in the Madison, Janesville, and Milwaukee offices, and then we explain the options for integrating these networks into a larger structure, known as a Wide Area Network (WAN). Finally, in a table at the end of this report, we summarize the costs for implementing various WAN connections.

New Hope's Existing LANs
The term Local Area Network (LAN) refers to a network of computers and other devices (such as printers) that are geographically close to each other (for example, on the same floor of a building). A LAN is managed via a special computer known as a server. The majority of the computers on the three New Hope LANs are used to run Microsoft Office applications. The network operating system on the Janesville and Madison servers has been upgraded to Windows XP, while the Milwaukee server continues to run Windows 2000 Server. Because the three LANs are separate, a social worker in one office cannot directly access data stored on a computer in one of the other two offices.

WAN Technology
To allow interoffice data access, we propose connecting the three LANs, thereby creating a Wide Area Network (WAN). A WAN is a network that spans a geographical distance (between buildings, cities, or even countries). Strictly speaking, a WAN consists of one link between two points. It does not usually connect one site to several other sites in the way that a LAN connects multiple computers. Thus, to connect the three New Hope LANs, we would need to establish multiple WAN links. The following sections describe various options for creating these links. The options differ greatly in cost, ease of implementation, and throughput (that is, the rate at which data can be transferred).

Public Switched Telephone Network (PSTN)
The term Public Switched Telephone Network (PSTN) refers to the network of telephone lines that services residential neighborhoods and businesses. Originally, the PSTN was composed of analog lines that were developed to carry voice signals. These days, the majority of PSTN lines provide faster digital transmission. The New Hope LANs currently use the PSTN system for occasional dial-up connections to the Internet.

Integrated Services Digital Network (ISDN)
In an Integrated Services Digital Network (ISDN) connection, data travels over digital lines maintained by the local telephone carrier. Typically, an ISDN connection is a dial-up connection, rather than a continuously available connection. Because digital lines can carry voice and data

---

Options for Establishing a Wide Area Network   Page 3

signals simultaneously, connecting the three New Hope offices via ISDN lines would make it unnecessary to pay for separate phone lines to support faxes, modems, and voice calls. Two types of ISDN connections are commonly used: Basic Rate ISDN (BRI) and Primary Rate ISDN (PRI). The cost of using BRI at the Madison and Janesville office is $50 per month, while the cost for the Milwaukee office is $60 per month. An additional, one-time installation fee for each site will range between $400 and $600. PRI connections are much faster BRI, but are significantly more expensive.

Digital Subscriber Lines (DSL)
Digital Subscriber Lines (DSL) is a type of connection that uses advanced data techniques to achieve even greater throughput than ISDN. DSL runs on leased lines that are maintained by the local telephone carrier. DSL uses a continuously available connection, known as a dedicated line. Unlike ISDN, DSL is offered by New Hope's current carrier. DSL generally costs more than ISDN, but less than T1 lines (described below). A high-speed DSL connection costs approximately $80 a month. In addition, each New Hope site would have to purchase or rent a DSL modem. The major drawback to DSL is the time it takes for the telephone carrier to establish service. The current waiting time is at least six months. The one-time installation fee for each site is approximately $500 to $700.

T-Carrier Line
Like DSL, a T-Carrier line is a permanent dedicated connection that is maintained by the local telephone carrier. T-carrier transmission uses a technology called multiplexing, which makes it possible to carry multiple channels of voice, data, video, or other signals. The most common type of T-carrier connection for medium to small organizations is a T1 line. Such a connection provides excellent throughput and security. Compared to the other options, a T1 connection is extremely expensive, costing as much as $4000 to install, plus an additional monthly fee of $1000 to $2000. However, a fractional T1 lease, which uses a few channels on a T1 line, is a more economical alternative. Monthly fees for a fractional lease range from $200 to $600 a month. The one-time installation fee for each site is approximately $1,500.

Options for Establishing a Wide Area Network   Page 4

Type of Connection	Installation Charge	Monthly Charge
DSL	$500 to $700	$80
Fractional T1	$1500	$200 to $600
ISDN	$600	$50 to $60

To reinforce the tasks you learned in this session, go to the SAM 2003 Training Companion CD included with this text.

Session 3.2 Quick Check

1. Define the following terms in your own words:
   a. line weight
   b. line style
   c. gridline
   d. shading
2. In what order would the following numbers appear in a table if you sorted them in ascending numerical order: 26, 12, 65, 44?
3. Explain how to add a row to the bottom of a table.
4. What's the fastest way to modify a column to accommodate the widest entry in the column?
5. Explain how to adjust the height of a row in a table.
6. Explain how to alter the border on the bottom of a heading row.
7. How do you center a table between the left and right margins?

Review

Tutorial Summary

In this tutorial you learned how to set tab stops, divide a document into sections, center text on a page between the top and bottom margins, create a header, and create a table. You also learned how to display the Tables and Borders toolbar and how to sort the rows of a table. Finally, you learned how to add and delete rows and columns, how to format a table to improve its appearance, and how to review a document in Reading Layout view.

Key Terms

Bar tab	heading row	shading
border	Left tab	sort
cell	line style	tab
Center tab	line weight	tab stop
Decimal tab	page break	table
First Line Indent tab	Reading Layout view	Table AutoFormat command
footer	Right tab	Tables and Borders toolbar
gridlines	section	tab-stop alignment style
Hanging Indent tab	section break	vertical alignment
header		

Practice

Apply the skills you learned in the tutorial using the same case scenario.

Review Assignments

Data File needed for the Review Assignments: Trouble.doc

Susan Launspach, the program director at New Hope Social Services, has contacted Caitlyn Waller about another issue related to the agency's local area networks (LANs). Since last January, employees at the Madison office have experienced a number of problems, including malfunctioning printers and difficulty retrieving e-mail. Susan would like to hire Tyger Networks to resolve the network problems, a process known as troubleshooting. To secure the necessary funding, she needs a report outlining the basic issues, which she can then distribute to New Hope's board of directors. Working with a task force at

Tyger Networks, Caitlyn has completed a draft of this report. It's your job to format the report and add a table at the end. When you're finished, she would like you to create a separate document that lists only the new equipment recommended by Tyger Networks. Complete the following:

1. Open the file **Trouble** located in the Tutorial.03\Review folder included with your Data Files, and then save it as **Troubleshooting Report** in the same folder.
2. Check your screen to make sure your settings match those in the tutorial. Display nonprinting characters as necessary and switch to Print Layout view.
3. Select the list of task force members and their titles, and then insert a left tab stop 2.5 inches from the left margin.
4. Replace "Evan Brillstein" with your name.
5. Divide the document into two sections. Insert a section break so that the executive summary begins on a new page.
6. Vertically align the first section of the document using the Center alignment option, and view the results in Print Preview.
7. Create a header for section 2 that aligns your name at the left margin and centers the page number preceded by the word "Page." Don't forget to deselect the Link to Previous button. (*Hint*: To center the page number, use the second tab stop.) Close the Header and Footer toolbar, and then save your work.
8. Insert a page break at the end of the document.
9. Create the table shown in Figure 3-35.

Figure 3-35 ▶

Troubleshooting Option	Explanation	Cost
Cable Checker	3 devices for each office, at $225 a piece	$675
Onsite Troubleshooting	40 hours of onsite troubleshooting, at $120 an hour	$4800
Cable Tester	1 device to be shared among the three offices	$1400

10. Display the Tables and Borders toolbar.
11. Sort the table by the contents of the Troubleshooting Option column in ascending order.
12. Insert a new row just below the Cable Tester row, and then enter the following information into the new row:
    Troubleshooting option: Onsite Training
    Explanation: Informational seminar for all Madison employees
    Cost: $300
13. Modify the widths of columns A and C to accommodate only the widest entry in each, and then right-align the data in the Cost column.
14. Increase the height of the heading row and format it appropriately using shading and boldface. Center the headings vertically and horizontally in their cells.
15. Select the entire table, select the 2 ¼ pt line weight, select the single line style, and then use the Outside Border option in the Borders list box. Select the heading row and add a double ½-point border at the bottom of the heading row.
16. Center the table between the page's left and right margins and then save your work.
17. Use the Table Move handle to select the entire table. Copy the table, open a new, blank document, and paste a copy of the table into the new document. Use the Delete command on the Table menu to delete the Onsite Training and Onsite Troubleshooting rows. Adjust border formatting as needed. Save the document as **Equipment List** in the Tutorial.03\Review folder. Close the document.

18. Close the Tables and Borders toolbar.
19. Save your work, review it in Reading Layout view, preview the report, and then print it.
20. Close the document.

Case Problem 1

Apply

Apply the skills you learned to create an annual report for a textile store.

Data File needed for this Case Problem: Textiles.doc

Noblewood Textiles, Inc. As an assistant manager of Noblewood Textiles in San Diego, California, you must help prepare an annual report for the board of directors. Complete the following:

1. Open the file **Textiles** located in the Tutorial.03\Cases folder included with your Data Files, and then save it as **Noblewood Textiles Report** in the same folder.
2. Check your screen to make sure your settings match those in the tutorials. Switch to Print Layout view.
3. Divide the document into two sections. Begin section 2 with the introduction on a new page.
4. Format the title ("Annual Report") and the subtitle ("Noblewood Textiles") using 16-point Arial. Center the first section vertically. Select the title and subtitle, and center them horizontally using the Center button on the Formatting toolbar. Note that you can combine horizontal and vertical alignment styles. Use the Print Preview window to check your work.
5. Create a header for section 2 that aligns your name to the left margin and "Noblewood Textiles Annual Report" to the right margin. Click the Link to Previous button on the Header and Footer toolbar to deselect it. Select the header text and format it in 8-point Times New Roman.
6. While in Header and Footer view, click the Switch between Header and Footer button on the Header and Footer toolbar to switch to the footer area for section 2. Press the Tab key to move the insertion point to the center tab stop, and then type the word "Page" followed by a space and the page number (using the Insert Page Number button on the Header and Footer toolbar). Insert a space, type the word "of", insert another space, and then click the Insert Number of Pages button on the Header and Footer toolbar to insert the total number of pages in the document. Click the Link to Previous button on the Header and Footer toolbar to deselect it, if necessary. Close Header and Footer view when you are finished.
7. Select the list of members under the heading "Board of Directors," click Format on the menu bar, and then click Tabs. To insert a tab stop with a dot leader at the 4-inch mark, type 4 in the Tab stop position text box, verify that the Left option button is selected in the Alignment section, and then click the 2..... option button in the Leader section. Click the Set button. Notice the Clear button, which you can use to clear the tab stop you just set, and the Clear All button, which you can use to clear all the custom tab stops (that is, tab stops other than the default ones) from a document. Click the OK button to close the Tabs dialog box.
8. Insert a page break at the end of the document, and then insert a table consisting of five rows and three columns.
9. Insert the headings "Name", "Title", and "Duties". Fill in the rows with the relevant information about the store personnel who are mentioned by name in the "Store Management and Personnel" section.
10. Adjust the table column widths so the information is presented attractively.
11. Bold and italicize the headings. Increase the height of the heading row, and use the Tables and Borders toolbar to center the column headings horizontally and vertically.

12. Insert a row in the middle of the table, and add your name to the list as another assistant manager. Adjust the column widths as needed.
13. Format the heading row with a light gray shading of your choice, and then change the outside border of the table to a double ¾-point weight.
14. Center the table horizontally on the page.
15. Save and preview the document. Review it in Reading Layout view, print it, and then close the document. Close the Tables and Borders toolbar.

Case Problem 2

Data File needed for this Case Problem: Tour.doc

Top Flight Travel's "Masterpiece Tour" Report Each year Top Flight Travel sponsors a "Masterpiece" tour, which shepherds travelers through a two-week, whirlwind tour of the artistic masterpieces of Europe. The tour director has just completed a report summarizing the most recent tour. It's your job to format the report, which includes one table. Complete the following:

1. Open the file named **Tour** located in the Tutorial.03\Cases folder included with your Data Files, and then save it as **Masterpiece Tour Report** in the same folder.
2. Check your screen to make sure your settings match those in the tutorials. Switch to Print Layout view.
3. Replace "Your Name" in the first page with your first and last name.
4. Divide the document into two sections. Begin the second section on a new page, with the summary that starts "This report summarizes and evaluates."
5. Vertically align the first section using the Center alignment option.
6. Create a header for section 2 only that contains the centered text "Top Flight Travel." (*Hint*: To center text in the header, use the second tab stop. If necessary, deselect the Link to Previous button before you begin.) Format the header text using italic and the font size of your choice.
7. On the Header and Footer toolbar, click the Switch Between Header and Footer button to move to the footer area of the document. Using the same techniques you used to create a header in the tutorial, create a footer for section 2 only that aligns "Evaluation Report" to the left margin and the date to the right margin. (*Hint*: Deselect the Link to Previous button if necessary, and then use the Insert Date button on the Header and Footer toolbar to insert the date.) Close Header and Footer view.
8. Display the Tables and Borders toolbar, and turn off the Draw Table pointer if it is active. In the table, select the text in column A (the left column), bold the text, and then click the Change Text Direction button (on the Tables and Borders toolbar) twice so that text is formatted vertically (that is, the text reads from bottom to top). Adjust the width of column A to accommodate the newly rotated text.
9. Adjust the other column width so it is approximately 5" wide.
10. Delete the blank row 2.
11. Format column A with a light colored shading of your choice.
12. Change the border around column A to 2¼-point line weight. Adjust the row heights, if necessary, to display each row heading in one line.
13. Save and preview the document. Close the Tables and Borders toolbar.
14. Review the document in Reading Layout view, print it, and then close the document.

Apply

Apply skills you learned to create a report summarizing information on a European tour.

Explore

Explore

Challenge

Go beyond what you've learned to convert text into a table and then use other advanced table commands to enhance the table.

Case Problem 3

Data Files needed for this Case Problem: Contacts.doc and Budget.doc

Contact List for Flower Box Bakery Ken Yamamoto recently opened Flower Box Bakery, a wholesale bakery catering to upscale cafes and tea shops in suburban St. Louis. He has just acquired a list of potential sales contacts from the local chamber of commerce via e-mail. The information consists of names, phone numbers, and managers for a number of new cafes and restaurants in the St. Louis area. The information is formatted as simple text, with the pieces of information separated by commas. Ken asks you to convert this text into a table and then format the table to make it easy to read. When you're finished, he needs you to sum a column of numbers in his Advertising Budget table. Complete the following:

1. Open the file named **Contacts** located in the Tutorial.03\Cases folder included with your Data Files, and then save it as **Sales Contacts** in the same folder. Check your screen to make sure your settings match those in the tutorials.

Explore
2. Select the entire document, click Table on the menu bar, point to Convert, and then click Text to Table. In the Convert Text to Table dialog box, make sure the settings indicate that the table should have three columns. Select the AutoFit to contents option button to ensure that columns are sized appropriately, select the Commas option button, and then click the OK button. Word converts the list into a table.

3. Replace the name "Enrique Mendoza" with your first and last name.

4. Insert a new row at the top of the table, and then insert appropriate column headings.

Explore
5. When you need to format a table quickly, you can allow Word's AutoFormat command to do the work for you. Click anywhere in the table, click Table on the menu bar, and then click Table AutoFormat to open the Table AutoFormat dialog box. Scroll down the Table styles list box to see the available options. Click options that interest you, and observe the sample tables in the Preview box. Note that you can deselect the check boxes in the "Apply special formats to" section to remove boldface or shading from columns or rows that don't require it. Select a table style that you think is appropriate for the Contacts table, deselect check boxes as you see fit, and then click the Apply button.

6. Sort the table alphabetically by column A.

Explore
7. Place the pointer over the Table Resize handle, just outside the lower-right corner of the table. Drag the double-arrow pointer to increase the height and width of each cell to a size of your choice. Notice that all the parts of the table increase proportionally.

8. Save your work, preview the table, print it, and then close the document.

9. Open the file **Budget** located in the Tutorial.03\Cases folder included with your Data Files, and then save it as **Advertising Budget** in the same folder. If necessary, open the Tables and Borders toolbar.

Explore
10. Select the cell containing the word "Total" and the blank cell to its right. Click the Merge Cells button on the Tables and Borders toolbar. The two cells are merged into one. Format the word "Total" so that it aligns on the right side of the new, larger cell.

Explore
11. Click the blank cell to the right of the Total cell, and then click the AutoSum button on the Tables and Borders toolbar. Word automatically sums the costs in the third column and displays the total ($400.00) in the selected cell.

Explore
12. Change the cost of the Missouri Monthly advertisement to $250, click the cell containing the total ($400.00), and then click the AutoSum button again. Word updates the total.

13. Save your work, preview the document, and then close it.

Challenge

Use your table skills to create the instruction sheet shown in Figure 3-36.

Case Problem 4

There are no Data Files needed for this Case Problem.

Hammond Astronomical Society Sarah Vernon coordinates star-gazing tours for the Hammond Astronomical Society. To ensure that participants can see as well as possible in the night sky, they are asked to follow a set of rules that astronomers refer to as a dark sky protocol. You can use Word table features to create an instruction sheet describing the club's dark sky protocol. Figure 3-36 shows Sarah's sketch. Complete the following steps.

Figure 3-36

Dark Sky Protocol		Hammond Astronomical Society
	Personal Items	**Vehicles**
	Turn off flashlights.	Turn off all interior lights before arrival.
	Shield computers with red foil.	Turn off headlights.
	Shield all lights for charts and confine them to the target area.	Park so backup lights are not required upon exit.
	Rationale: Most people need 30 minutes to achieve optimum night vision. Accidental exposure to light from cars, computers or flashlights means the period of dark adaptation must begin again. Some individuals can tolerate small amounts of red light without significant vision degradation, as long as the light source is dim and does not shine into the eyes. For more information, see Sarah Vernon.	

1. Open a new, blank document, and save it as **Dark Sky Protocol** in the Tutorial.03\Cases folder included with your Data Files.
2. If necessary, switch to Print Layout view, display rulers, and then open the Tables and Borders toolbar.
3. Click the Draw Table button on the Tables and Borders toolbar, if necessary, to select the button and change the pointer to the Draw Table pointer.
4. Select a single-line line style, with a line weight of 1½ points.

Explore

5. Change the Zoom setting to 60%. In the upper-left corner of the document (near the paragraph mark), click and then drag down and to the right to draw a rectangle about 6 inches wide and 5 inches high.

Explore

6. Continue to use the Draw Table pointer to draw the columns and rows shown in Figure 3-36. For example, to draw the column border for the "Dark Sky Protocol" column, click at the top of the rectangle, where you want the column to begin, and drag down to the bottom of the rectangle. Use the same technique to draw rows. If you make a mistake, use the Undo button. To delete a border, click the Eraser button on the Tables and Borders toolbar, click the border you want to erase, and then click the Eraser button again to turn it off. Don't expect to draw the table perfectly the first time. You may have to practice until you become comfortable with the Draw Table pointer, but once you can use it well, you will find it a helpful tool for creating complex tables. Click the Draw Table button on the Tables and Borders toolbar again to turn off the Draw Table pointer.

Explore

7. Change the Zoom setting to 100%. In the left column, type the text "Dark Sky Protocol". With the pointer still in that cell, click the Change Text Direction button on the Tables and Borders toolbar twice to position the text vertically. Format the text in 28-point Times New Roman, and then center it in the cell using the Align Center option on the Tables and Borders toolbar. (*Hint*: You will probably have to adjust and readjust the row and column borders throughout this project, until all the elements of the table are positioned properly.)

8. Type the remaining text, as shown in Figure 3-36. Replace the name "Sarah Vernon" with your own name. Use boldface as shown in Figure 3-36 to draw attention to key elements. Use the font styles, font sizes, and alignment options you think appropriate.

Explore

9. Click the blank cell in the top row of the table. Click the Drawing button on the Standard toolbar to display the Drawing toolbar, if necessary. Click the AutoShapes button on the Drawing toolbar, point to Stars and Banners, and then click the 5-Point Star shape. A box appears in the cell with the text "Create your drawing here." If the Drawing Canvas toolbar opens, close it. Click anywhere within the blank cell. The star shape is inserted in the cell or somewhere nearby. The star is selected, as indicated by the small circles, called selection handles, that surround it. If necessary, drag the star to position it neatly within the cell. If the star is not the right size, click the lower-right selection handle, and drag up or down to adjust the size of the star so that it fits within the cell borders more precisely. With the star still selected, click the Fill Color list arrow on the Drawing toolbar, and then click a yellow square in the color palette.

10. Adjust column widths and row heights so that the table is attractive and easy to read.

Explore

11. Now that you have organized the information using the Word table tools, you can remove the borders so that the printed information sheet doesn't look like a table. Click the Table Move handle to select the entire table, click Table on the menu bar, click Table Properties, click the Table tab if it is not already selected, click the Borders and Shading button, click the Borders tab if it is not already selected, click the None option, click the OK button, and then click the OK button again. The borders are removed from the table; gridlines will not be visible on the printed page. (Depending on how your computer is set up, they may not be visible on your screen, either. If gridlines are not displayed, click Table on the menu bar, and then click Show Gridlines.)

12. Save your work, preview the document, make any necessary adjustments, print it, and then close the document.

Research

Go to the Web to find information you can use to create documents.

Internet Assignments

The purpose of the Internet Assignments is to challenge you to find information on the Internet that you can use to work effectively with this software. The actual assignments are updated and maintained on the Course Technology Web site. Log on to the Internet and use your Web browser to go to the Student Online Companion for New Perspectives Office 2003 at **www.course.com/np/office2003.** Click the Internet Assignments link, and then navigate to the assignments for this tutorial.

Assess

SAM Assessment and Training

If your instructor has chosen to use the full online version of SAM 2003 Assessment and Training, you can go beyond the "just-in-time" training provided on the CD that accompanies this text. Simply log in to your SAM account (http://sam2003.course.com) to launch any assigned training activities or exams that relate to the skills covered in this tutorial.

Review

Quick Check Answers

Session 3.1

1. a. in Normal view, a dotted line with the words "Section Break" that marks the point at which one section ends and another begins
   b. the intersection of a row and a column in a table
   c. information arranged in horizontal rows and vertical columns
   d. text entered one time but that is printed at the top of every page
   e. the location where text moves when you press the Tab key
2. Select the text whose tab alignment you want to change, click the tab alignment selector on the far left of the horizontal ruler until the appropriate tab stop alignment style appears, and then click in the horizontal ruler where you want to set the new tab stop.
3. You could divide a document into sections if you wanted to center only part of the document between the top and bottom margins.
4. Insert a section break, move the insertion point within the section you want to align, click File, click Page Setup, click the Layout tab, select Center in the Vertical alignment list box, make sure "This section" is selected in the Apply to list box, and then click OK.
5. A header appears at the top of a page, whereas a footer appears at the bottom of a page.
6. Click View on the menu bar, click Header and Footer, verify that the insertion point is located in the Header area, press Tab to move the insertion point to where you want the page number to appear, and then click the Insert Page Number button on the Header and Footer toolbar.
7. Move the insertion point to the location where you want the table to appear. Click the Insert Table button on the Standard toolbar. In the grid, click and drag to select three columns and two rows, and then release the mouse button.

8. If the insertion point is in the cell at the far right in a row, press the Tab key. Otherwise, press the ↓ key.
9. It's better to use a table rather than tab stops when you need to organize more than a few columns of information.
10. Click the Table Move handle.

Session 3.2

1. a. the thickness of the line used to create a border
   b. the style of the line used to create a border
   c. the outline of a row, cell, column, or table, which is hidden when the document is printed
   d. a gray or colored background used to highlight parts of a table
2. 12, 26, 44, 65
3. Click the cell at the far right in the bottom row of the table, and then press the Tab key.
4. Double-click the column's right-hand border.
5. Drag the bottom border of the row to a new position.
6. Select the row. Click the Line Style list arrow on the Tables and Borders toolbar, and select a line style. Click the Line Weight list arrow on the Tables and Borders toolbar, and select a line weight. Click the Borders list arrow on the Tables and Borders toolbar, and then click the Bottom Border option.
7. Click anywhere in the table, click Table on the menu bar, click Table Properties, click the Table tab, click Center, and then click OK.

Desktop Publishing and Mail Merge

Creating a Newsletter and Cover Letter

Case | Wide World Travel, Inc.

Wide World Travel, Inc. hosts international tours for travelers of all ages. Recently, the company has expanded its business by selling clothes and shoes specifically designed for the frequent traveler. Max Stephenson, one of the Wide World tour guides, has taken on the job of managing this new retail venture. In order to generate business, he wants to create an informational newsletter. He has asked you to help him create the newsletter, as well as the form letter that will accompany each copy of the newsletter.

Max has already written the text of the newsletter, which describes some of the most popular items sold by Wide World Travel. Now Max wants you to transform this text into a publication that is neat, organized, and professional-looking. He would like the newsletter to contain headings (so the customers can scan it quickly for interesting items) as well as a headline that will give the newsletter a memorable look. He wants you to include a picture that will reinforce the newsletter content.

In this tutorial, you'll plan the layout of the newsletter and then add some information about the Wide World Travel Web site. Then you'll get acquainted with some desktop-publishing features available in Word that you'll use to create the newsletter. You'll format the title using an eye-catching design and divide the document into newspaper-style columns to make it easier to read. To add interest and focus to the text, you'll include a piece of art. You'll then fine-tune the newsletter layout, give it a more professional appearance with typographic characters, and put a border around the page to give the newsletter a finished look.

After you create the newsletter, you will use Word's mail merge feature to insert personalized information into the cover letter that will accompany the newsletter.

Session	Objectives		SAM Training Tasks	
Session 4.1	• Identify desktop-publishing features • Create a title with WordArt	• Work with hyperlinks • Create newspaper-style columns	• Apply columns • Convert a hyperlink to regular text • Create WordArt • Display the Web page associated with a hyperlink	• Hide white space • Insert hyperlinks • Modify hyperlinks • Use advanced text wrapping
Session 4.2	• Insert and edit graphics • Wrap text around a graphic • Incorporate drop caps	• Use symbols and special typographic characters • Add a page border • Perform a mail merge	• Add a page border • Apply the superscript font effect • Autoformat text as you type • Complete an entire mail merge process for form letters • Crop and rotate graphics • Flip a graphic • Format a letter as a drop cap • Insert a column break • Insert a symbol	• Insert a symbol automatically • Insert Clip Art • Insert graphics in documents • Insert symbols • Modify a document footer • Modify graphics • Position a graphic • Resize a graphic • Revise column layout • Use AutoCorrect

Student Data Files   For a complete list of the Data Files needed for this tutorial, see page WD 2.

Session 4.1

For hands-on practice of key tasks in this session, go to the SAM 2003 Training Companion CD included with this text.

Planning the Newsletter Document

The newsletter will provide a brief overview of some popular items sold by Wide World Travel. Like most newsletters, it will be written in an informal style that conveys information quickly. The newsletter title will help readers quickly identify the document. The newsletter text will be split into two columns to make it easier to read, and headings will help readers scan the information quickly. A picture will add interest and illustrate the newsletter's content. Drop caps and other desktop-publishing elements will help draw readers' attention to certain information and make the newsletter design attractive and professional.

Elements of Desktop Publishing

Desktop publishing is the production of commercial-quality printed material using a desktop computer system from which you can enter and edit text, create graphics, compose or lay out pages, and print documents. In addition to newsletters, you can desktop publish brochures, posters, and other documents that include text and graphics. In the Case Problems, you'll have the chance to create a brochure. The following elements are commonly associated with desktop publishing:

- High-quality printing. A laser printer or high-resolution inkjet printer produces final output.
- Multiple fonts. Two or three font types and sizes provide visual interest, guide the reader through the text, and convey the tone of the document.
- Graphics. Graphics, such as horizontal or vertical lines (called rules), boxes, electronic art, and digitized photographs help illustrate a concept or product, draw a reader's attention to the document, and make the text visually appealing.
- Typographic characters. For example, long dashes, called em dashes (—), are used in place of double hyphens (--) to separate dependent clauses; typographic medium-width dashes, called en dashes (–), are used in place of hyphens (-) as minus signs and in ranges of numbers; and typographic bullets (•) are used to draw attention to items in a list.
- Columns and other formatting features. Columns of text, pull quotes (small portions of text pulled out of the main text and enlarged), page borders, and other special formatting features that you don't frequently see in letters and other documents distinguish desktop-published documents.

Professional desktop publishers use software specially designed for desktop-publishing tasks. You can, however, use Word to create simple desktop-published documents. You'll incorporate many of the desktop-publishing elements listed above to produce the newsletter shown in Figure 4-1.

Travel in Style!

Wide World Travel Clothes

After countless trips abroad, our tour leaders have mastered the art of traveling light. The secret, they explain, is to pack a few well-made, light-weight items that you can wash in a sink and dry overnight on a line. Unless you lived in a large city with numerous specialty stores, finding good traveling clothes used to be nearly impossible. But now you can purchase everything you need for a fast-paced Wide World tour at the Wide World Web site. This newsletter describes a few of our most popular items. To learn more about other Wide World products, call us at 555-281-9010 or visit our Web site at www.wide-world-travel.com.

Travel Time Knitware

Unbelievably versatile, these knit garments are so adaptable that you can wear them from the train station to the outdoor market to the theater with just a change of accessories. They combine the softness of cotton with the suppleness of Flexistyle®, a wrinkle-resistant synthetic fabric.

The cardigan has side vents for a graceful drape and looks great layered over the knit shell. The pants have comfortable elasticized waistbands and side-seam pockets. Available in Midnight Black, Azure, and Coffee. Sizes: XS, S, M, L, and XL.

Pack It Straw Hat

If you're planning a trip to sunny climes, bring along this eminently packable broad-brimmed hat. Crunch it in a ball and stuff it into your suitcase. When you unpack, the hat will spring back to its original, elegant shape—guaranteed! Available in Cream and Taupe. Sizes: S, M, L, and XL.

Comfort Trekkers

These amazingly supportive walking shoes combine the comfort of hiking boots with the style of light-weight athletic shoes, giving your feet both stability and support. Wear them to explore a mysterious medieval city in the morning, and then hike a mountain trail after lunch. Available in Antique Black and Desert Brown, in whole and half sizes.

Prepared by Student Name 10/16/2006

Working with Hyperlinks

Web pages often include special text called **hyperlinks** (or simply **links**) that you can click to display other Web pages. You can also use hyperlinks in Word documents that will be read online (that is, on a computer). For example, if you type an e-mail address and then press the Enter key, Word automatically formats the e-mail address as a hyperlink. Hyperlink text is usually formatted in blue with an underline. When you press Ctrl and click an e-mail hyperlink, an e-mail program opens automatically, ready for you to type a message. If you completed the Case Problems for Tutorial 2, you already have experience using e-mail hyperlinks.

In addition to e-mail addresses, Word also automatically formats Web page addresses, or **URLs**, as hyperlinks. (One example of a Web address is *www.microsoft.com*.) When you press Ctrl and click a Web page address that has been formatted as a hyperlink, your computer's browser opens automatically and attempts to display that Web page. The browser may not actually be able to display the Web page if your computer is not currently connected to the Internet, or if the Web page is unavailable for some other reason.

Including hyperlinks in a Word document is very useful when you plan to distribute the document via e-mail so others can read it online. For instance, if you include your e-mail address in a memo to a potential customer, the customer can click the e-mail address to begin typing an e-mail message to you in reply. However, when you know that your document will only be distributed on paper, it's a good idea to remove any hyperlinks so that the e-mail address or Web address is formatted without the underline, in the same color font as the surrounding text. To remove a hyperlink, right-click the hyperlink, and then click Remove Hyperlink in the shortcut menu. Once you remove the hyperlink, the Web address or e-mail address remains in the document, but is no longer formatted in blue with an underline.

Max would like you to complete the newsletter text by adding a reference to the Wide World Travel Web site. He does not want the company's Web address formatted as a hyperlink, so you will have to remove the hyperlink after typing the Web address. He has saved the newsletter text in a document named Clothes. You'll begin by opening the document that contains the unformatted text, often called copy, that will serve as the content for your desktop-published document.

To open the newsletter document and add the Web address:

1. Start Word, and make sure your screen matches the figures in this tutorial. In particular, be sure to display nonprinting characters.

2. Open the file **Clothes** from the Tutorial.04\Tutorial folder included with your Data Files.

3. To avoid altering the original file, save the document as **Travel Clothes** in the same folder.

4. If necessary, change the Zoom setting on the Standard toolbar to **100%** and switch to Normal view.

5. Read the document to preview its content.

6. Click to the right of the phone number (at the end of the first main paragraph), press the **spacebar**, and then type the following: **or visit our Web site at www.wide-world-travel.com**

7. Type a period at the end of the Web address, and then press the **Enter** key. The Web address is formatted as a hyperlink, in a blue font with an underline.

8. Move the mouse pointer over the hyperlink. A ScreenTip appears, with the complete URL (including some extra characters that a browser needs to display the Web page). The ScreenTip also displays instructions for displaying the Wide World Travel Web site. See Figure 4-2.

Figure 4-2 | **Hyperlink with ScreenTip**

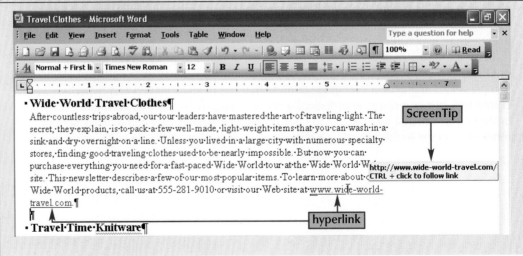

Max tells you that users will be viewing the document in printed form only. He asks you to remove the hyperlink. This will ensure that the format of the Web address matches the rest of the paragraph.

To remove the hyperlink:

► **1.** Right-click the text **www.wide-world-travel.com**. A shortcut menu opens.

► **2.** Click **Remove Hyperlink**. The shortcut menu closes, and the text is now formatted in black to match the rest of the paragraph.

You have finished adding the information about the company's Web site to the newsletter. Now that the newsletter contains all the necessary details, you can turn your attention to your first desktop-publishing task, adding a headline.

Using WordArt to Create a Headline

Max wants the title of the newsletter, "Travel in Style," to be eye-catching and dramatic. **WordArt** is a Word feature that allows you to insert specially formatted text into a document. WordArt provides great flexibility in designing text with special effects that express the image or mood you want to convey in your printed documents. With WordArt, you can apply color and shading, as well as alter the shape and size of the text.

You begin creating WordArt text by clicking a button on the Drawing toolbar. When you first display the Drawing toolbar, Word switches to Print Layout view. As a rule, Print Layout view is the most appropriate view to use when you are desktop publishing because it shows you exactly how the text and graphics fit on the page. The vertical ruler in Print Layout view helps you position graphical elements more precisely.

Creating Special Text Effects Using WordArt

Reference Window

- Click the Drawing button on the Standard toolbar to display the Drawing toolbar.
- Click the Insert WordArt button on the Drawing toolbar.
- Click the style of text you want to insert, and then click the OK button.
- Type the text you want in the Edit WordArt Text dialog box.
- Click the Font and Size list arrows to select the font and font size you want.
- If you want, click the Bold or Italic button, or both.
- Click the OK button.
- Click the WordArt to select it, and then drag any handle to resize and reshape it. To avoid altering the WordArt's proportions, press and hold down the Shift key while you drag a handle.

You're ready to use WordArt to create the newsletter title. First you will display the Drawing toolbar. Then you will choose a WordArt style and type the headline text.

To create the title of the newsletter using WordArt:

1. Press **Ctrl+Home** to move the insertion point to the beginning of the document.

2. Click the **Drawing** button on the Standard toolbar. The Drawing toolbar appears at the bottom of the screen. Word switches to Print Layout view.

   Trouble? If the Drawing toolbar is not positioned at the bottom of the Document window, drag it there by its title bar. If you do not see the Drawing toolbar anywhere, right-click the Standard toolbar, and then click Drawing on the shortcut menu.

3. If necessary, click **View** on the menu bar, click **Ruler** to display the vertical and horizontal rulers, type **90** in the Zoom text box, and then press the Enter key to change the Zoom setting to 90%. This Zoom setting should allow you to see the entire width of the newsletter. Throughout this tutorial, feel free to zoom in or zoom out if you prefer to see more or less of the newsletter.

4. Click the **Insert WordArt** button on the Drawing toolbar. The WordArt Gallery dialog box opens, displaying 30 different WordArt styles.

5. Click the WordArt style in the second row from the top, second column from the right, as shown in Figure 4-3.

Figure 4-3   **WordArt styles**

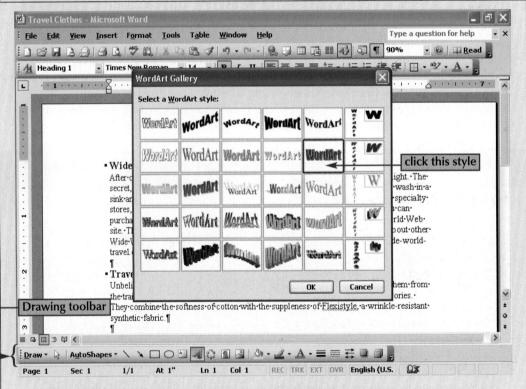

6. Click the **OK** button. The Edit WordArt Text dialog box opens, displaying the default text "Your Text Here," which you will replace with the newsletter title. Note that you can also select text in the document that you want to format as WordArt before you click the Insert WordArt button. In that case, the text you selected is displayed in the Edit WordArt Text dialog box instead of the default text "Your Text Here."

7. Type **Travel in Style** to replace the default text with the newsletter title. Notice the toolbar at the top of the Edit WordArt Text dialog box, which you can use to apply bold and italic, or to change the font or font style. You don't need to use these options now, but you might choose to when creating headlines for other documents.

8. Click the **OK** button. The Edit WordArt Text dialog box closes, and the WordArt image is inserted at the beginning of the newsletter. The "Wide World Travel Clothes" heading moves to the right to accommodate the new headline. See Figure 4-4.

| WordArt headline inserted into document | Figure 4-4 |

Trouble? If you see a border around the headline, the WordArt is currently selected. Click anywhere outside of the border to deselect the WordArt.

Eventually, you will position the headline so that it appears at the very top of the document, stretching from margin to margin. But for now, you can leave it in its current position.

Selecting a WordArt Object

The WordArt image you have created is not regular text. You cannot edit it as you would other text, that is, by moving the insertion point to it and typing new letters or by selecting part of it and using the buttons on the Formatting toolbar. Unlike regular text, a WordArt headline is considered an **object**—that is, something that you can manipulate independently of the text. You can think of the WordArt object as a thing that lies on top of, or next to, the text in a document. To edit a WordArt object in Word, you must first click it to select it. Then you can make changes using special toolbar buttons and dialog boxes, or by dragging it with the mouse.

Max would like you to make several changes to the newsletter headline. Before you can do this, you need to select it.

To select the WordArt headline:

1. Click the WordArt headline. The headline is surrounded by a black border with eight small black squares (called **sizing handles**). The WordArt toolbar also appears. The black sizing handles indicate that the WordArt is an **inline graphic**, that is, a graphic that is part of the line of text in which it was inserted. See Figure 4-5.

Figure 4-5 | Selected headline

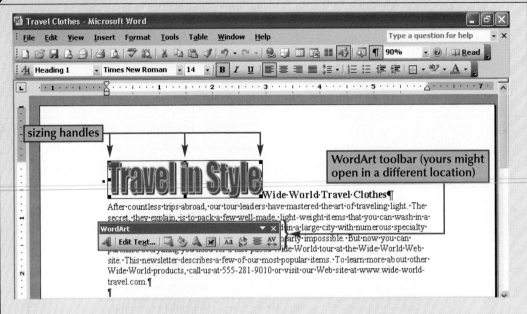

Editing a WordArt Object

Now that the WordArt object is selected, you can modify its appearance (color, shape, size, and so forth) using the buttons on the Drawing toolbar or the WordArt toolbar. First of all, Max would like you to edit the WordArt by adding an exclamation point at the end of the headline. While you're making that change, he would like you to format the headline in italic.

To change the font and formatting of the WordArt object:

1. Verify that the WordArt object is selected, as indicated by the sizing handles.

2. Click the **Edit Text** button on the WordArt toolbar. The Edit WordArt Text dialog box opens. As you recall, you used this dialog box earlier when you first created the WordArt headline.

3. Click at the end of the headline (after the "e" in Style"), and then type **!** (an exclamation point).

4. Click the **Italic** button I in the Edit WordArt Text dialog box. The headline in the Text box is now formatted in italic, with an exclamation point at the end.

5. Click the **OK** button. The Edit WordArt Text dialog box closes, allowing you to see the edited headline in the document.

Changing the Shape of a WordArt Object

You can quickly change the shape of a WordArt object using the **WordArt Shape** button on the WordArt toolbar. Right now, the WordArt headline has a straight shape, without any curve to it. Max wants to use an arched shape.

To change the shape of the WordArt object:

1. Verify that the WordArt headline is selected, and then click the **WordArt Shape** button 🄰 on the WordArt toolbar. A palette of shape options opens.

2. Move the mouse pointer over each option in the palette to display a ScreenTip with the name of each shape. As you can see, the Plain Text shape (a straight line) is currently selected.

3. Point to the **Inflate Top** shape (fourth row down, fifth column from the left), as shown in Figure 4-6.

WordArt shapes ◄ Figure 4-6

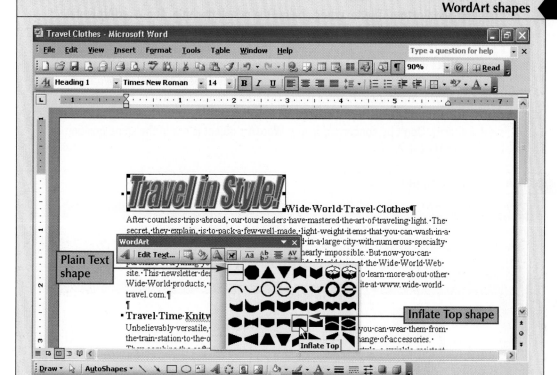

4. Click the **Inflate Top** shape. The newsletter title is formatted in the new WordArt shape.

The headline has the shape you want. Now you can take care of positioning the WordArt object above the newsletter text.

Wrapping Text Below the WordArt Object

At this point, the WordArt object is on the same line as the heading "Wide World Travel Clothes." Max would like you to set the WordArt on its own line at the top of the document. To do this, you need to change the way the text flows, or **wraps**, around the WordArt object.

You can wrap text around objects many different ways in Word. For example, you can have the text wrap above and below the object, through it, or so the text follows the shape of the object, even if it has an irregular shape. Text wrapping is often used in newsletters to prevent text and graphics from overlapping, to add interest, and to prevent excessive open areas, called **white space**, from appearing on the page. The Text Wrapping button on the WordArt or Picture toolbar provides some basic choices, whereas the Layout tab of the Format WordArt dialog box provides more advanced options. (To open the Format WordArt dialog box, click the Format WordArt button on the WordArt toolbar.) Because you want to use a relatively simple option—wrapping text so that it flows below the WordArt headline—you'll use the Text Wrapping button on the WordArt toolbar. You'll have a chance to use the Format WordArt dialog box in the Case Problems at the end of this tutorial.

To wrap the newsletter text below the WordArt headline:

1. With the WordArt object selected, click the **Text Wrapping** button 🖼 on the WordArt toolbar. A menu of text wrapping options opens.

2. Click **Top and Bottom**. The text drops below the newsletter title. The WordArt is still selected, but instead of black sizing handles, you see small white circles. Like the black squares, the white circles are sizing handles. The white sizing handles indicate that the graphic object is a **floating graphic**, which means the graphic can be moved independently of the surrounding text. A number of other items appear around the WordArt object, as shown in Figure 4-7. You can use the sizing handles shown in Figure 4-7 to change the size and position of the WordArt object. You'll learn the meaning of the anchor symbol shortly. Don't be concerned if your WordArt object is not in the same position as the one in Figure 4-7.

| Figure 4-7 | WordArt after wrapping text |

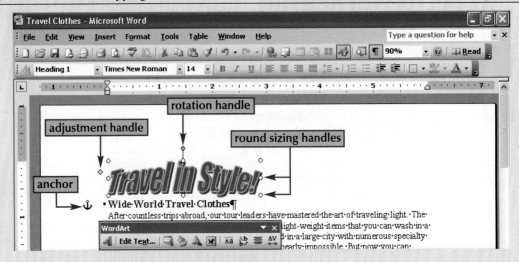

Trouble? If you can't see the anchor symbol, your Zoom setting is probably too high. Change it to 90%.

Positioning and Sizing the WordArt Object

After you choose a text wrapping style for a WordArt object, you can adjust its size and position in the document. To position a WordArt object, click it and drag it with the mouse pointer. To widen any WordArt object, drag one of its sizing handles. To keep the object the same proportion as the original, hold down the Shift key as you drag the sizing handle. This prevents "stretching" the object more in one direction than the other.

Max asks you to widen the headline so it fits neatly within the newsletter margins. As you enlarge the headline, you can practice dragging the WordArt object to a new position.

To position and enlarge the WordArt object:

1. Move the mouse pointer over the headline.

2. Use the ⬚ pointer to drag the WordArt object to the right, until it is centered below the 3-inch mark in the horizontal ruler, over the top of the newsletter.

3. Click the **Undo** button ⬚ on the Standard toolbar to undo the move. The headline returns to its original position, aligned along the left margin. Note that you can use this same technique to drag a WordArt object to any location in a document. (You'll learn more about dragging objects later in this tutorial, when you insert a picture into the newsletter.)

4. With the WordArt object still selected, position the pointer over the lower-right sizing handle. The pointer changes to ⬚.

5. Press and hold the **Shift** key while you drag the sizing handle to the right margin, using the horizontal ruler as a guide. As you drag the handle, the pointer changes to ─├─ and a dotted outline appears to show you how big the WordArt will be when you release the mouse button. See Figure 4-8.

Resizing the WordArt Object ◄ **Figure 4-8**

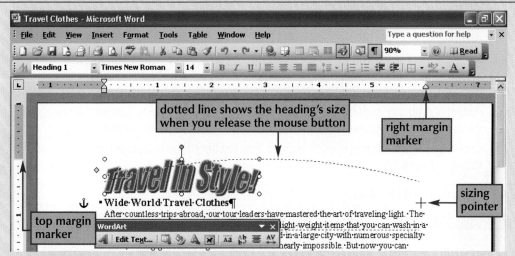

6. Release the mouse button when the dotted horizontal line stretches from the left to the right margin. The WordArt heading should be about six inches wide and a little less than 1.5 inches high at its tallest. If necessary, repeat the procedure to make the exclamation point line up with the right margin.

   Trouble? If the WordArt heading spans the margins, but is not tall enough to read easily, you probably didn't hold down the Shift key when you dragged the mouse pointer. Undo the change and begin again with Step 4.

7. If necessary, drag the headline down slightly, so that the top of the headline does not extend into the top margin, as shown in Figure 4-9. Notice that when you drag the headline down, the newsletter text also moves down to accommodate the headline.

   Trouble? If the headline jumps to the middle of the first paragraph of text, you dragged it too far. Click the Undo button ⬚, and then repeat Step 7.

In addition to moving and resizing the WordArt headline, you can drag the rotation handle to rotate the headline. You can also use the adjustment handle to increase or decrease the arch at the top of the headline. Right now you need to turn your attention to the WordArt object anchor symbol.

Anchoring the WordArt Object

After you wrap text around a WordArt object, you need to make sure the WordArt object is properly positioned within the document as a whole—a process known as anchoring. The process draws its name from the anchor symbol in the left margin, which indicates the position of the WordArt relative to the text. The anchor symbol is only visible after you wrap text around the document and when nonprinting characters are displayed. To ensure that changes to the text (such as section breaks) do not affect the WordArt, you need to anchor the WordArt to a blank paragraph before the text. At this point, the WordArt anchor symbol is probably located to the left of the first paragraph (the heading "Wide World Travel Clothes"). However, yours may be in a different position (for instance, it might be positioned above and to the left of the WordArt). In the next set of steps, you will move the anchor to a new, blank paragraph at the beginning of the document.

To anchor the WordArt object to a blank paragraph:

1. Press **Ctrl+Home**. The insertion point moves to the beginning of the newsletter text (that is, to the left of the first "W" in the heading "Wide World Travel Clothes"). The WordArt object is no longer selected; you cannot see the anchor at this point.

2. Press the **Enter** key. A new paragraph symbol is inserted either above or below the Word-Art object.

3. If the new paragraph symbol is inserted above the WordArt heading, drag the WordArt heading up slightly until the paragraph mark moves below the WordArt heading.

4. Click the WordArt object. The selection handles and the anchor symbol appear. The anchor symbol is probably positioned to the left of the "Wide World Travel Clothes" heading, though it might be located to the left of the new blank paragraph instead.

5. Click the anchor and drag it up to position it to the left of the new, blank paragraph as shown in Figure 4-9, if it is not already positioned there.

Figure 4-9 | **Properly anchored WordArt**

Trouble? If your WordArt headline is positioned below the new paragraph symbol, drag it up slightly to position it above the new paragraph symbol. If you notice any other differences between your headline and the one shown in Figure 4-9, edit the headline to make it match the figure. For example, you may need to drag the WordArt left or right slightly, or you may need to adjust its size by dragging one of its sizing handles.

6. Click anywhere in the newsletter to deselect the WordArt, and then save your work.

Your WordArt is now finished. Max congratulates you on your excellent work. The headline will definitely draw attention to the newsletter, encouraging potential customers to read the entire document.

Formatting Text in Newspaper-Style Columns

Because newsletters are meant for quick reading, they are usually laid out in newspaper-style columns. In **newspaper-style columns**, a page is divided into two or more vertical blocks, or columns. Text flows down one column, continues at the top of the next column, flows down that column, and so forth. The narrow columns and small type size allow the eye to take in a lot of text, thus allowing a reader to scan a newspaper quickly for interesting information.

When formatting a document in columns, you can click where you want the columns to begin and then click the Columns button on the Formatting toolbar. However, the Columns command on the Formatting menu offers more options. Using the Columns command, you can insert a vertical line between columns. The Columns command also gives you more control over exactly what part of the document will be formatted in columns.

Max wants you to divide the text below the title into two columns and add a vertical line between them.

To apply newspaper-style columns to the body of the newsletter:

▶ **1.** Position the insertion point at the beginning of the second paragraph (to the left of the first "W" in "Wide World Travel Clothes").

▶ **2.** Click **Format** on the menu bar, and then click **Columns**. The Columns dialog box opens.

▶ **3.** In the Presets section, click the **Two** icon.

▶ **4.** Click the **Line between** check box to select it. The text in the Preview box changes to a two-column format with a vertical rule between the columns.

You want these changes to affect only the paragraphs after the WordArt headline, so you'll need to insert a section break and apply the column formatting to the text after the insertion point.

▶ **5.** Click the **Apply to** list arrow, and then click **This point forward** to have Word automatically insert a section break at the insertion point. See Figure 4-10.

Completed Columns dialog box | **Figure 4-10**

creates two columns of the same width

adds section break at insertion point

places a line between columns

shows how columns will look with current settings

6. Click the **OK** button to return to the Document window. A continuous section break appears below the WordArt title. The word "continuous" indicates that the new section continues on the same page as the preceding text—in other words, the WordArt title and the newsletter text will print on the same page, even though they are in different sections of the newsletter. The text in Section 2 is formatted in two columns. The insertion point is in Section 2 as indicated by the information displayed in the status bar.

To get a good look at the columns, you need to change the Zoom setting so you can see the entire page at one time.

To zoom out to display the whole page:

1. Click the **Zoom** list arrow on the Standard toolbar, and then click **Whole Page**. Word displays the entire page of the newsletter so that you can see how the two-column format looks on the page. See Figure 4-11. Note that the Whole Page Zoom setting is only available in Print Layout view. You should use it whenever you want to have the entire page displayed as you edit it. Some details, such as the line between the columns, are not visible in the Whole Page Zoom setting.

| Figure 4-11 | Whole Page view showing two columns |

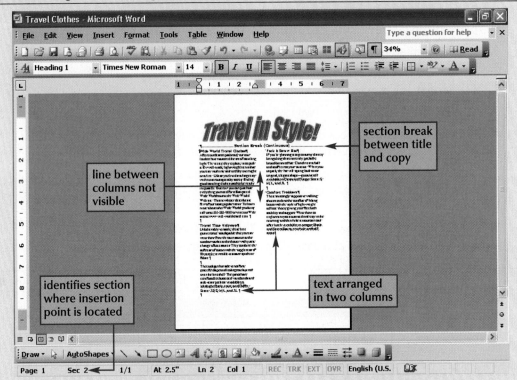

Trouble? Your columns may break at a slightly different line from those shown in the figure. This is not a problem; just continue with the tutorial.

The newsletter headline is centered on the page, and the copy is in a two-column format. The text fills the left column but not the right column. You'll fix this later, after you add a graphic and format some of the text.

2. Click the **Zoom** list arrow again, and then click **Page Width**. The Page Width option changes the Zoom setting enough to make the page span the width of the document window. Now you can read the text again.

3. Save your work.

Keep in mind that you can modify the structure of columns in a document by reformatting the document with three or more columns, or return the document to its original format by formatting it as one column. You can also insert column breaks to force text to move from one column to the next. You'll have a chance to practice modifying the columns in the Case Problems at the end of this tutorial.

Session 4.1 Quick Check

Review

1. Describe four elements commonly associated with desktop publishing.
2. True or False: When using Word's desktop-publishing features, you should display your document in Print Layout view.
3. In your own words, define the following terms:
   a. desktop publishing
   b. WordArt
   c. copy
   d. anchor
4. True or False: You can edit WordArt just as you would edit any other text in Word.
5. How do you change the text of a WordArt object after you have inserted it into a Word document?
6. What is the purpose of the WordArt Shape button on the WordArt toolbar?
7. True or False: When you first format a document into newspaper-style columns, the columns will necessarily be of equal length.

To reinforce the tasks you learned in this session, go to the SAM 2003 Training Companion CD included with this text.

Session 4.2

Inserting Graphics

Graphics, which can include drawings, paintings, photographs, charts, tables, designs, or even designed text such as WordArt, add variety to documents and are especially appropriate for newsletters. You can use the buttons on Word's Drawing toolbar to draw pictures in your document. However, it's usually easier to create a picture in a special graphics program and then save the picture as an electronic file. (You may already be familiar with one graphics program, **Paint**, which is included as part of the Windows operating system.)

For hands-on practice of key tasks in this session, go to the SAM 2003 Training Companion CD included with this text.

Instead of creating your own art in a graphics program, you can take a piece of art on a piece of paper (such as a photograph) and scan it—that is, run it through a special machine called a scanner. A **scanner** is similar to a copy machine except that it saves a copy of the image as an electronic file, instead of reproducing it on a piece of paper. (As you may know, many modern copy machines also function as scanners.) You can also use a digital camera to take a photograph that is then stored as an electronic file.

Electronic files come in several types, many of which were developed for use in Web pages. In desktop publishing, you will often work with **bitmaps**—a type of file that stores an image as a collection of tiny dots, which, when displayed on a computer monitor or printed on a page, make up a picture. There are several types of bitmap files, the most common of which are:

- BMP: Used by Microsoft Paint, and other graphics programs, to store graphics you create. These files, which have the .bmp file extension, tend to be very large.
- GIF: Suitable for most types of simple art. A GIF file is compressed, so it doesn't take up much room on your computer. A GIF file has the file extension .gif.
- JPEG: Suitable for photographs and drawings. Files stored using the JPEG format are even more compressed than GIF files. A JPEG file has the file extension .jpg.
- TIFF: Commonly used for photographs or scanned images. TIFF files have the file extension .tif and are usually much larger than GIF or JPEG files, but smaller than BMP files.

Once you have stored a piece of art as an electronic file, you can insert it into a document using the Picture command options on the Insert menu. You'll have a chance to explore some of these options in the Case Problems at the end of this tutorial.

If you don't have time to prepare your own art work, you can take advantage of **clip art**—a collection of ready-made images. A number of clip art selections are stored on your computer when you install Microsoft Word. You can also download additional clip art from the Web. (You'll have a chance to look for clip art on the Web in the Case Problems at the end of this tutorial.) You begin inserting clip art by opening the Clip Art task pane. From there you can search for images that are stored on your computer or on the Web. Then you copy an image to the Clipboard, and paste the image into the document.

To add visual appeal to the Travel in Style newsletter, you will insert a piece of clip art. Max wants you to use a clip art object that reflects the newsletter content.

To insert the clip art image of an airplane into the newsletter:

1. If you took a break after the previous session, make sure Word is still running, the file Travel Clothes is open, the document is in Print Layout view, and the nonprinting characters are displayed. Also verify that the Drawing toolbar is displayed.

2. Click the **Insert Clip Art** button 🖻 on the Drawing toolbar. The Clip Art task pane opens, as shown in Figure 4-12. You use the top part of the Clip Art task pane to search for graphics related to a specific topic. You can click the Organize clips option (near the bottom) to open the Clip Organizer window, where you can browse among the various clip art images stored on your computer. You'll use the Clip Organizer to insert an image into the newsletter. You'll have a chance to try the Search for option in the Case Problems at the end of this tutorial. If someone recently used your Clip Art task pane to search for graphics, you may see the search topic in the Search for text box.

Figure 4-12 ▸ **Clip Art task pane**

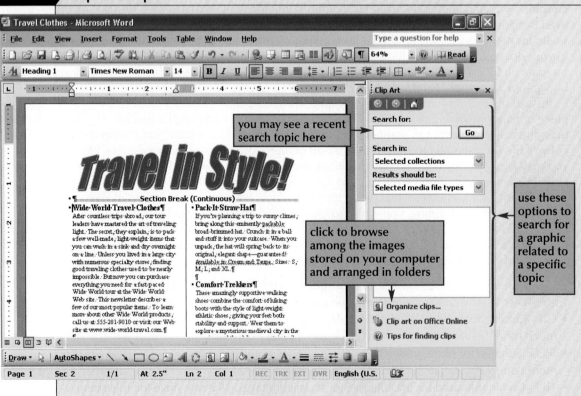

3. Click **Organize clips** near the bottom of the Clip Art task pane. The Favorites - Microsoft Clip Organizer window opens. This window is similar to Windows Explorer. For example, you click the plus sign next to a folder to display its subfolders. You select a subfolder to display its contents in the right pane. The default Microsoft Office clip art is stored in sub-folders within the Office Collections folder. See Figure 4-13. You might see different folders from those shown in Figure 4-13, but you should see the Office Collections folder.

Trouble? If you see the Add Clips to Organizer dialog box, click Now. This will organize the clip art installed on your computer into folders, so that you can then use the Clip Organizer dialog box to select a piece of clip art. The Add Clips to Organizer dialog box appears the first time you attempt to use clip art on your computer. After the clip organiz-ing process concludes, continue with Step 4.

Microsoft Clip Organizer   Figure 4-13

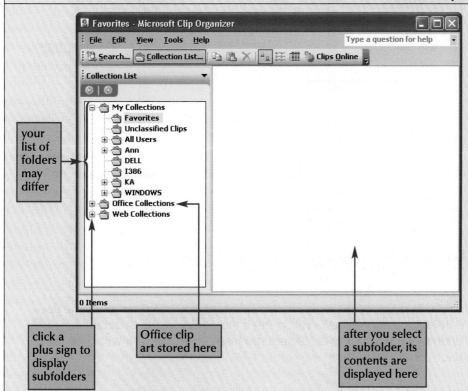

your list of folders may differ

click a plus sign to display subfolders

Office clip art stored here

after you select a subfolder, its contents are displayed here

4. Scroll as needed to view the Office Collections folder, and then click the plus sign next to the **Office Collections** folder. A list of subfolders within the Office Collections folder appears. This list of folders, which is created when you install Word, organizes clip art images into related categories. The folders with plus signs next to them contain subfolders or clip art images.

5. Scroll down and examine the list of folders. Click any plus signs to open subfolders, and then click folders to display clip art images in the right pane.

6. Click the plus sign next to the **Transportation** folder to display its subfolders, and then click the **Transportation** folder to select it. Three images stored in the Transportation folder are displayed in the right pane.

Trouble? If you don't see any images in the Transportation folder, click the Travel folder to select it and display an image of an airplane in a blue circle.

> **7.** Move the pointer over the image of the airplane in the blue circle. An arrow button appears on the right side of the image.

> **8.** Click the arrow button. A menu of options opens, as shown in Figure 4-14.

Figure 4-14 | **Image in Transportation folder selected**

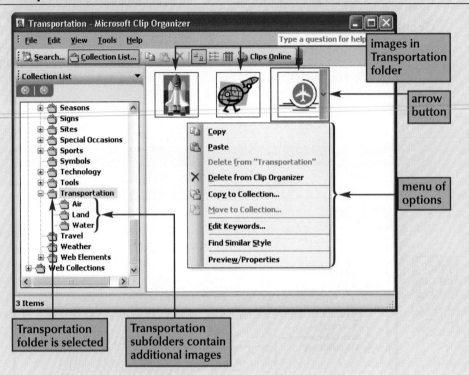

> **9.** Click **Copy** in the menu. The image is copied to the Clipboard.

Now that you have copied the image to the Clipboard, you can paste it into the document at the insertion point. Max asks you to insert the graphic in the paragraph below the heading "Wide World Travel Clothes." Before you insert the image, you will close the Clip Art task pane.

To paste the clip art into the document:

> **1.** Click the **Close** button ☒ in the Microsoft Clip Organizer title bar, and then click **Yes** when you see a dialog box asking if you want the item to remain on the Clipboard. You return to the Document window.

> **2.** Click the **Close** button ☒ on the Clip Art task pane.

> **3.** Position the insertion point to the left of the word "After" in the beginning of the first paragraph below the heading "Wide World Travel Clothes."

> **4.** Click the **Paste** button 🖺 on the Standard toolbar. The image is inserted into the document at the insertion point. The image nearly fills the left column.

> **5.** Save the document.

> **6.** Click the airplane image to select it. Like the WordArt object you worked with earlier, the clip art image is a graphic object with sizing handles that you can use to change its size. The Picture toolbar appears whenever a graphic object is selected. See Figure 4-15.

Newsletter with the Clip Art object inserted | **Figure 4-15**

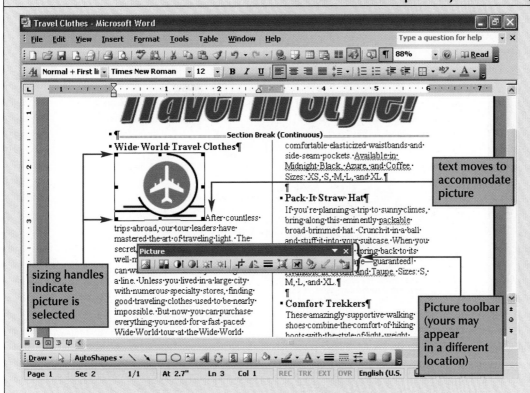

Trouble? If the Picture toolbar does not appear when you click the airplane image, right-click any toolbar, and then click Picture.

Max would like the image to be smaller so it doesn't divert attention from the text. You'll make that change in the next section.

Resizing a Graphic

It's often necessary to change the size of a graphic to make it fit into a document. This is called **scaling** the image. You can resize a graphic either by dragging its sizing handles or, for more precise control, by using the Format Picture button on the Picture toolbar.

For Max's newsletter, the dragging technique will work fine.

To resize the clip art graphic:

1. Make sure the clip art graphic is selected.

2. Drag the lower-right sizing handle up and to the left until the dotted outline forms a rectangle slightly less than 1.5 inches wide. Remember to use the horizontal ruler as a guide. See Figure 4-16. *Note*: You don't have to hold down the Shift key, as you do with WordArt, to resize the picture proportionally.

Figure 4-16 Resizing the graphic

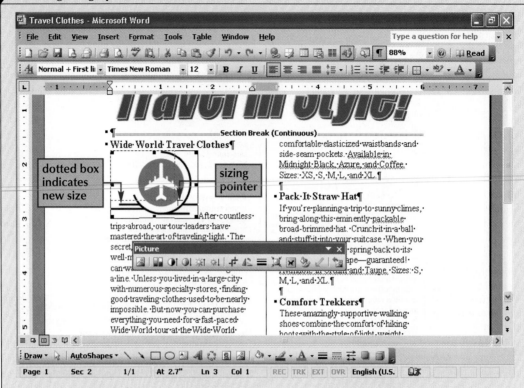

3. Release the mouse button. The airplane image is now about half as wide as the left column.

Max wonders if the graphic would look better if you deleted part of the horizontal lines on the left side of the image. You'll make that change in the next section.

Cropping a Graphic

You can **crop** the graphic—that is, cut off one or more of its edges—using either the Crop button on the Picture toolbar or the Format Picture dialog box. Once you crop a graphic, the part you cropped is hidden from view. It remains a part of the graphic image, so you can change your mind and restore a cropped graphic to its original form.

To crop the airplane graphic:

1. If necessary, click the clip art to select it. The sizing handles appear.
2. Click the **Crop** button ⌐⁺ on the Picture toolbar. The pointer changes to ⇗. To crop the graphic, you must position this pointer over a middle handle on any side of the graphic.
3. Position the ⇗ pointer directly over the middle sizing handle on the left side of the picture.
4. Press and hold down the mouse button. The pointer changes to ⊣.
5. Drag the handle to the right. As you drag, a dotted outline appears to indicate the new shape of the graphic. Position the left border of the dotted outline along the left border of the blue circle. See Figure 4-17.

Cropping the graphic | **Figure 4-17**

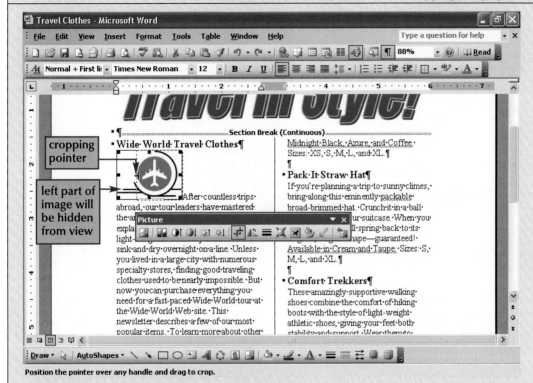

Position the pointer over any handle and drag to crop.

6. Release the mouse button.

Max decides he prefers to display the whole airplane, so he asks you to return to the original image.

7. Click the **Undo** button on the Standard toolbar. The cropping action is reversed, and the full image reappears.

Rotating a Graphic

Max still isn't happy with the appearance of the graphic because of the amount of white space on the left side. He suggests rotating the image so that the airplane is positioned horizontally on the page. You can use the Rotate Left button on the Picture toolbar to rotate the image.

To rotate the airplane graphic:

1. If necessary, click the clip art to select it. The sizing handles appear.

2. Click the **Rotate Left 90°** button on the Picture toolbar. The graphic rotates 90 degrees to the left.

3. Click the **Rotate Left 90°** button again. The graphic rotates another 90 degrees, leaving the airplane upside down.

4. Click the **Rotate Left 90°** button again. The graphic rotates another 90 degrees. Now the airplane appears to be flying across the page from left to right. The selection handles become circles. See Figure 4-18. If you needed to rotate the image with the text wrapped around it, you could drag the rotation handle, which is the round green circle.

Figure 4-18 | **Rotated graphic**

Now Max wants you to make the text wrap to the right of the graphic, making the airplane look as if it's flying into the text.

Wrapping Text Around a Graphic

For the airplane to look as though it flies into the newsletter text, you need to make the text wrap around the image. Earlier, you used Top and Bottom text wrapping to position the WordArt title above the columns of text. Now you'll apply Tight text wrapping to make the text follow the shape of the plane.

To wrap text around the airplane graphic:

1. Verify that the airplane graphic is selected.

2. Click the **Text Wrapping** button [image] on the Picture toolbar. A menu of text wrapping options appears.

3. Click **Tight**. The text wraps to the right of the airplane, following its shape. Your screen should look similar to Figure 4-19.

4. Click anywhere in the text to deselect the graphic, and then save the newsletter. Don't be concerned if the heading "Wide World Travel Clothes" wraps around the top of the graphic. You will move the graphic away from the heading in the next section. If the heading does not wrap around the graphic, that's fine too.

Text wrapped around graphic | **Figure 4-19**

The Text Wrapping button should provide all the options you need for most situations. In some cases, however, you might want to use the more advanced options available in the Format Picture or Format WordArt dialog box. You'll have a chance to explore these options in the Case Problems at the end of this tutorial.

Moving a Graphic

Finally, Max asks you to move the graphic down to the middle of the paragraph so that it is not so close to the heading. You can do this by dragging the graphic to a new position. Like WordArt, a clip art graphic is anchored to a specific paragraph in a document. When you drag a graphic (including WordArt) to a new paragraph, the anchor symbol moves to the top of that paragraph. When you drag a graphic to a new position within the same paragraph, the anchor symbol remains in its original position and only the graphic moves. You'll see how this works when you move the airplane graphic.

To move the graphic:

1. Select the graphic. You should see an anchor symbol either within the graphic or to the left of the heading "Wide World Travel Clothes."

2. Move the mouse pointer ⁺⁺↕ over the graphic.

3. Click and slowly drag the ⁺⁺↕ pointer down. As you move the pointer, a dotted outline appears indicating the new position of the graphic.

4. Position the dotted outline so it is in the middle of the paragraph and aligned along the left margin, and then release the mouse button. The graphic moves to its new position, but the anchor remains at the top of the paragraph, to the left of the first line of the paragraph. Your newsletter should look similar to Figure 4-20.

Figure 4-20 Graphic in new position

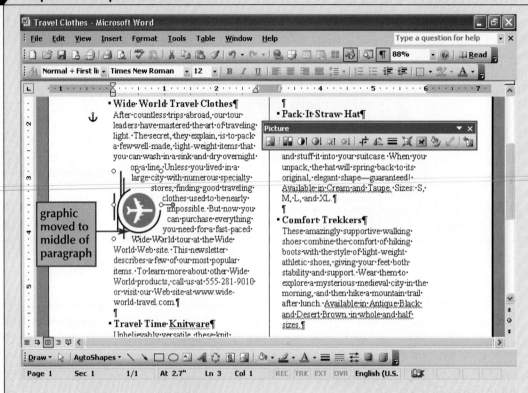

5. Click anywhere outside the graphic to deselect it.

   Trouble? If paragraph text wraps to the left of the graphic, you need to drag the graphic further to the left, so that it aligns along the left margin.

The image of the airplane draws the reader's attention to the beginning of the newsletter, but the rest of the text looks plain. Max suggests adding a drop cap at the beginning of each section.

Inserting Drop Caps

A **drop cap** is a large, capital letter that highlights the beginning of the text of a newsletter, chapter, or some other document section. The drop cap usually extends from the top of the first line of the paragraph down two or three succeeding lines of the paragraph. The text of the paragraph wraps around the drop cap. Word allows you to create a drop cap for the first letter of the first word of a paragraph.

You will create a drop cap for the first paragraph following each heading in the newsletter. The drop cap will extend two lines into the paragraph.

To insert drop caps in the newsletter:

1. If necessary, click in the paragraph below the heading "Wide World Travel Clothes" (the paragraph where you inserted the graphic).

2. Click **Format** on the menu bar, and then click **Drop Cap**. The Drop Cap dialog box opens.

3. In the Position section, click the **Dropped** icon.

4. Click the **Lines to drop** down arrow once to change the setting from 3 to 2. You don't need to change the default distance from the text. See Figure 4-21.

Drop Cap dialog box ◄ **Figure 4-21**

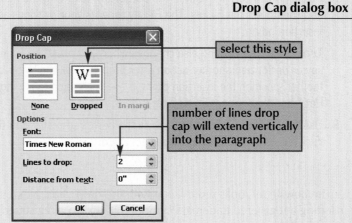

5. Click the **OK** button to close the dialog box, and then click anywhere in the newsletter to deselect the new drop cap. Word formats the first character of the paragraph as a drop cap.

Word re-wraps the text around the graphic to accommodate the drop cap above. See Figure 4-22. If the paragraph text wraps to the left of the graphic, drag the graphic closer to the left margin.

Drop Cap begins the paragraph ◄ **Figure 4-22**

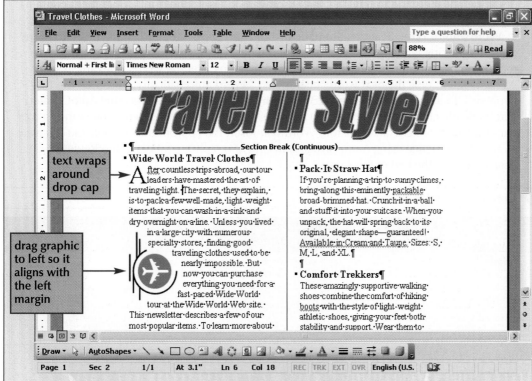

Trouble? Don't be concerned if Word now marks the "fter" of "After" as a grammatical error. Word considers drop caps to be objects, not regular text. By formatting the *A* in "After" as a drop cap, you essentially deleted the regular character *A*. Because the remaining regular characters "fter" do not appear in the Word dictionary, Word might mark it as a potential error.

6. Position the insertion point in the paragraph following the heading "Travel Time Knitware," and then repeat Steps 2-5.

7. Position the insertion point in the paragraph following the heading "Pack It Straw Hat," and then press the **F4** key. The F4 key repeats your previous action at the location of the insertion point.

   Trouble? If something else changes when you press the F4 key, you pressed another key or performed another action after Step 6. Click the Undo button ↻ on the Standard toolbar, position the insertion point in the paragraph following the heading "Pack It Straw Hat," and then repeat Steps 2 through 5.

8. Use the **F4** key to add a drop cap to the paragraph following the last heading, and then click anywhere in the text to deselect the drop cap.

The newsletter looks more lively with the drop caps. Next, you turn your attention to inserting a registered trademark symbol (®) next to a registered trademark name.

Inserting Symbols and Special Characters

In printed publications, it is customary to change some of the characters available on the standard keyboard into more polished-looking characters called **typographic symbols**. For instance, while you might type two hyphens to indicate a dash, in a professionally-produced version of that document the two hyphens would be changed to one long dash (called an em dash because it is approximately as wide as the letter "m"). In the past, desktop publishers had to rely on special software to insert and print a document containing typographic symbols, but now you can let Microsoft Word do the work for you.

Word's AutoCorrect feature automatically converts some standard characters into more polished-looking typographic symbols as you type. For instance, as Max typed the information on the Pack It Straw Hat, he typed two hyphens after the words "elegant shape." As he began to type the next word "guaranteed," Word automatically converted the two hyphens into an em dash. Figure 4-23 lists some of the other characters that AutoCorrect automatically converts to typographic symbols. In most cases you need to press the spacebar and type more characters before Word will insert the appropriate symbol. You'll have a chance to practice using AutoCorrect to insert typographic symbols in the Review Assignments at the end of this tutorial.

Figure 4-23 ▶ **Common typographic symbols**

To insert this symbol or character	Type	Word converts it to
em dash	word--word	word—word
smiley	:)	☺
copyright symbol	(c)	©
registered trademark symbol	(r)	®
trademark symbol	(tm)	™
ordinal numbers	1st, 2nd, 3rd, etc.	1st, 2nd, 3rd, etc.
fractions	1/2, 1/4	½ ¼
arrows	--> or <--	→ or ←

To insert typographic symbols into a document after you've finished typing it, you can use the Symbol command on the Insert menu.

Inserting Symbols and Special Characters

- Move the insertion point to the location where you want to insert a particular symbol or special character.
- Click Insert on the menu bar, and then click Symbol to open the Symbol dialog box.
- Click the appropriate symbol, or click the name from the list on the Special Characters tab.
- Click the Insert button.
- Click the Close button.

Max noticed that he forgot to insert a registered trademark symbol (®) after "Flexistyle." He asks you to insert this symbol now, using the Symbol command on the Insert menu.

To insert the registered trademark symbol:

1. Scroll down to display the paragraph below the heading "Travel Time Knitware," and then click to the right of the word "Flexistyle." (Take care to click between the final "e" and the comma.)

2. Click **Insert** on the menu bar, and then click **Symbol** to open the Symbol dialog box.

3. If necessary, click the **Special Characters** tab. See Figure 4-24.

Inserting a typographic symbol ◀ Figure 4-24

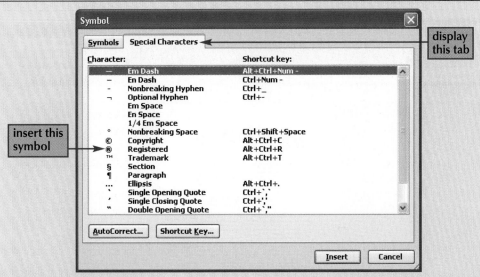

4. Click **Registered** to select it, and then click the **Insert** button.

5. Close the Symbol dialog box. Word inserts an ® immediately after the word "Flexistyle." Finally, you need to format the symbol as superscript, so that it is raised slightly above the surrounding text.

6. Select the symbol, click **Format** on the menu bar, click **Font**, verify that the Font tab is selected, click the **Superscript** check box to insert a check (in the Effects section of the Font dialog box), and then click **OK.** The registered trademark symbol is now smaller and raised slightly above the surrounding text.

Next, you need to adjust the columns of text so they are approximately the same length.

Balancing the Columns

You can shift text from one column to another by adding blank paragraphs to move the text into the next column or by deleting blank paragraphs to shorten the text so it will fit into one column. The problem with this approach is that any edits you make could throw off the balance. Instead, Word can automatically **balance** the columns, or make them of equal length. You'll balance the columns in the newsletter next.

To balance the columns:

1. Position the insertion point at the end of the text in the right column, just after the period following the word "sizes."

   Next, you need to change the zoom to Whole Page so you can see the full effect of the change.

2. Click the **Zoom** list arrow on the Standard toolbar, and then click **Whole Page**.

3. Click **Insert** on the menu bar, and then click **Break**. The Break dialog box opens.

4. Below "Section break types," click the **Continuous** option button.

5. Click the **OK** button. Word inserts a continuous section break at the end of the text. As shown in Figure 4-25, Word balances the text between the two section breaks.

Figure 4-25 ▶ **Newsletter with balanced columns**

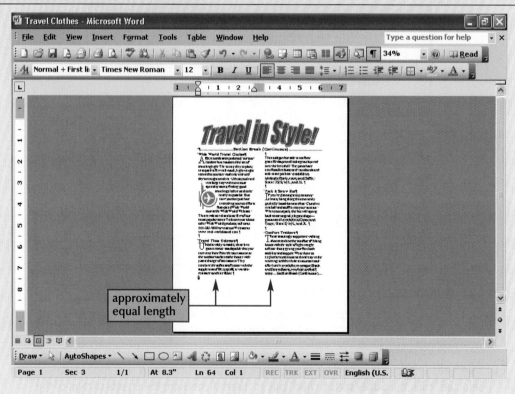

Drawing a Border Around the Page

You can add definition to a paragraph or an entire page by adding a border. You can also emphasize individual paragraphs within a document by putting a border around one or more paragraphs and by adding shading. Right now, Max wants to add a border around the entire newsletter page. (In the Case Problems at the end of this tutorial, you'll have a chance to add a border around individual paragraphs.)

To draw a border around the newsletter:

1. Make sure the document is in Print Layout view and that the Zoom setting is set to Whole Page so that you can see the entire newsletter.

2. Click **Format** on the menu bar, and then click **Borders and Shading**. The Borders and Shading dialog box opens.

3. Click the **Page Border** tab. You use the Setting options on the left side to specify the type of border you want. In this case, you want a simple box.

4. In the Setting section, click the **Box** option. Now that you have selected the type of border you want, you can choose the style of line that will be used to create the border.

5. In the Style list box, scroll down and select the ninth style down from the top (the thick line with the thin line underneath), and then verify that the Apply to option is set to **Whole document**. See Figure 4-26. (While the Borders and Shading dialog box is open, notice the Shading tab, which you can use to add a colored background to a page. You'll have a chance to use this tab in the Case Problems at the end of this tutorial.)

Adding a border to the newsletter | **Figure 4-26**

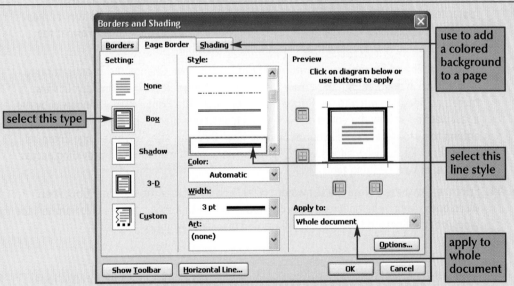

6. Click the **Options** button in the lower-right corner of the Borders and Shading dialog box. The Border and Shading Options dialog box opens. See Figure 4-27. Here you can change settings that control where the border is positioned on the page. Currently, the border is positioned 24 points from the edge of the page. To ensure that your printer will print the entire border, you need to change the Measure from setting so that it is positioned relative to the outside edge of the text rather than the edge of the page.

Figure 4-27 ▶ **Border and Shading Options dialog box**

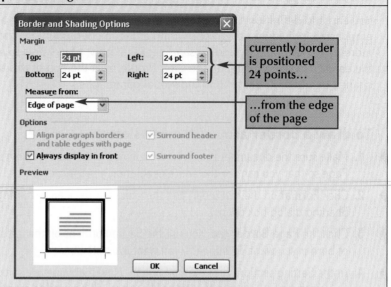

7. Click the **Measure from** list arrow, and then click **Text.** The settings in the Top and Bottom boxes change to 1 pt, and the settings in the Left and Right boxes change to 4 pts, indicating the border's position relative to the edge of the text.

8. Click the **OK** button in the Border and Shading Options dialog box, click **OK** in the Borders and Shading dialog box, and then save your work. The newsletter is now surrounded by an attractive border, as shown earlier in Figure 4-1.

9. Switch to Header and Footer view, change the Zoom setting to Page Width, create a footer that centers **Prepared by your name** and the current date at the bottom of the document. (Be sure to replace "your name" with your first and last name.) Format the footer in a small font to make it as unobtrusive as possible.

10. Close Header and Footer view to return to Print Layout view. Change the Zoom setting to Whole Page. Note that with the Whole Page Zoom setting selected in Print Layout view, there's no need to switch to the Print Preview window. (The Print Preview window provides a fast way to see how the entire document will look at one glance, but does not include the editing tools found in Print Layout or Normal view. By contrast, the Whole Page Zoom setting in Print Layout view allows you to view one page at a time while still providing access to the usual Word editing tools.)

11. Print the newsletter, close the Drawing toolbar, and then close the document but keep Word open, saving the document if prompted to do so. Unless you have a color printer, the WordArt headline and the airplane will print in black and white.

You give the printed newsletter to Max, along with a copy on disk. He thinks it looks great and thanks you for your help. He'll print it later on a high-quality color printer (to get the best resolution for printing multiple copies).

Now that the newsletter is finished, you need to create an accompanying cover letter. Max would like to use Word's mail merge feature to insert customer names and addresses into a form letter.

Understanding the Merge Process

The term **mail merge** refers to the process of combining information from two separate documents to create many final documents, each containing customized information. The two separate documents are called a main document and a data source.

A **main document** is a document (such as a letter) that contains standard text and placeholders (called **merge fields**) that tell Word where to insert variable information (such as a name or an address). You can distinguish merge fields from the other text of the main document, because each merge field name is enclosed by pairs of angled brackets—like this: << >>.

Max's main document is a letter that contains the text shown in Figure 4-28. You will replace the text in brackets with merge fields.

Max's main document ◀ **Figure 4-28**

May 25, 2006

[insert address]

Dear [insert first name]:

Enclosed you'll find a newsletter describing Wide World Travel's exciting new Web site, where you can purchase travel clothes selected by our in-house travel experts. From now on, when you are looking for practical and elegant travel attire, think of Wide World Travel. This publication describes just a few of our most popular items. For more information, visit our Web site at www.wide-world-travel.com.

Sincerely,

Max Stephenson
Senior Travel Guide

A **data source** is a document that contains information, such as clients' names and addresses, which will be inserted into the main document. Max plans to send the newsletter to a small test group of clients for starters. His data source is a table in a Word document that contains the names and addresses of five Wide World Travel clients. This table is shown in Figure 4-29. The header row in the table contains the names of the merge fields. Each row in the table contains information about an individual client and, in mail merge terminology, is called a **record**.

Max's data source ◀ **Figure 4-29**

a merge field name

header row includes all merge field names for this data source

First Name	Last Name	Street Address	City	State	ZIP
Deborah	Browne	3519 Olbrich Avenue	Hartford	CT	06115
Tom	Finnegan	634 Bay View Court	Hartford	CT	06114
Nikki	Nijhawan	2276 Fairlawn Avenue	Good Hope	CT	06117
Alessandra	Ramirez	1 West Main Street	Hartford	CT	06115
Melissa	Sobek	654 State Street	Newark	DE	19716

record for individual client

During a mail merge, the merge fields in the main document instruct Word to retrieve information from the data source. For example, one merge field in the main document might retrieve a first name from the data source; another merge field might retrieve a street address. For each record in the data source, Word will create a separate letter in the final document, which is called the **merged document**. Thus, if the data source contains five sets of client names and addresses, the merged document will contain five separate letters, each one containing a different client name and address in the appropriate places.

Using the Mail Merge Task Pane

Word's Mail Merge task pane walks you through the steps involved in merging documents. When you first open the Mail Merge task pane, the steps you see described there will vary, depending on what document you have open in the main Word window. To ensure that you see the same thing in the Mail Merge task pane each time, it's helpful to open a new, blank document before you open the Mail Merge task pane. Max asks you to start the mail merge process now.

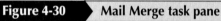

To begin the mail merge process:

▶ **1.** Click the **New Blank Document** button 🗋 on the Standard toolbar to open a blank document. Verify that Print Layout view is selected and change the Zoom setting to 100%.

▶ **2.** Click **Tools** on the menu bar, point to **Letters and Mailings**, and then click **Mail Merge**. The Mail Merge task pane opens. Depending on how your computer is set up, you might also see the Mail Merge toolbar. If you do see the Mail Merge toolbar, close it. See Figure 4-30.

Figure 4-30	**Mail Merge task pane**

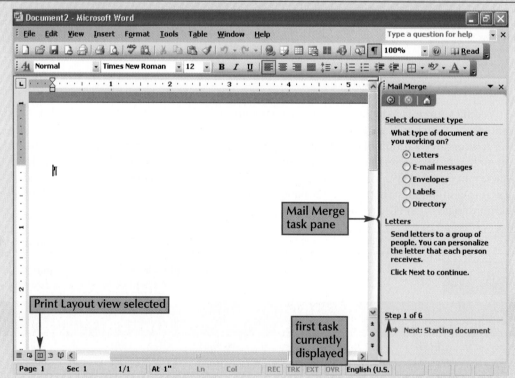

The Mail Merge task pane currently shows the first of six tasks related to completing a mail merge. Your first task is to specify the type of main document you want to use for the merge.

▶ **3.** Verify that the **Letters** option button is selected in the Mail Merge task pane.

4. At the bottom of the Mail Merge task pane, click **Next: Starting document**. The Mail Merge task pane displays information and options that you can use to select a starting document—that is, to select a main document. In this case, you want to start from an existing document. Specifically, you want to use the Letter document included with your Data Files.

5. Click the **Start from existing document** option button. The task pane displays options for opening an existing document.

6. Verify that **(More files...)** is selected, click the **Open** button on the task pane, and then use the Open dialog box to select and open the file **Letter** located in the Tutorial.04\Tutorial folder. Word inserts the text of the Letter file into the new, blank document, leaving the original Letter file untouched.

7. Check your screen to make sure your document window is in Print Layout view at 100% zoom and with nonprinting characters displayed.

8. Save the document as **Cover Letter** in the Tutorial.04\Tutorial folder, and then scroll down if necessary to display the entire letter. Close the rulers if they are open.

When he first typed the letter, Max included the text in brackets as placeholder text. You will replace the bracketed text with merge fields. First, you need to tell Word where to find the list of recipients for Max's letter.

Selecting a Data Source

You can use many kinds of files as data sources for a mail merge including Word tables, Excel worksheets, Access databases, or a special file designed to store addresses for Microsoft Office applications. You can select a pre-existing file, or you can create a new data source from scratch. In this situation, you will use a pre-existing document containing a simple Word table.

To select the data source:

1. In the bottom of the Mail Merge task pane, click **Next: Select recipients**, and then verify that the **Use an existing list** option button in the task pane is selected.

2. Click **Browse** in the Mail Merge task pane. The Select Data Source dialog box opens. This dialog box is similar to Word's Open dialog box, which you've already used many times.

3. Use the Look in list arrow to open the Tutorial.04\Tutorial folder, select the **Addresses** document, and then click the **Open** button. The table from the Addresses document is displayed in the Mail Merge Recipients dialog box.

4. Click the **OK** button. The Mail Merge Recipients dialog box closes, and you return to the Cover Letter document with the Mail Merge task pane open. Under "Use an existing list," you see the name of the file selected as the data source. (Depending on where you store your Data Files, you may see only the beginning of a directory path, which identifies the location where the data source file is stored.)

5. Click **Next: Write your letter** at the bottom of the Mail Merge task pane. The task pane displays options related to inserting merge fields in the main document.

Inserting Merge Fields

Max's letter is a standard business letter, so you'll place the client's name and address below the date. You could insert individual merge fields for the client's first name, last name, address, city, and ZIP code. But it's easier to use the Address block link in the Mail Merge task pane, which inserts a merge field for the entire address at one click.

To insert an Address Block merge field:

1. Select the text **[insert address]**, and then delete it. Remember to delete the opening and closing brackets. Do not delete the paragraph mark following the text.
2. Verify that there are four blank paragraphs between the date and the salutation, and that the insertion point is positioned in the third blank paragraph below the date.
3. Click **Address block** in the Mail Merge task pane. The Insert Address Block dialog box opens. See Figure 4-31. The options in this dialog box allow you to fine-tune the way the address will be inserted in the letter.

Figure 4-31	Insert Address Block dialog box

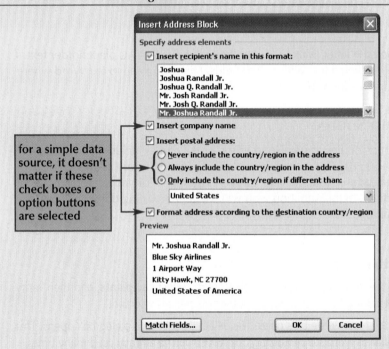

for a simple data source, it doesn't matter if these check boxes or option buttons are selected

4. Verify that the **Insert recipient's name in this format** check box is selected, and then click **Joshua Randall Jr.** in the list box to ensure that Word will insert each recipient's first and last name. (The other options in this list are only useful with more complicated data sources.)
5. Verify that the **Insert postal address** check box is selected. It doesn't matter whether any of the other check boxes and option buttons are selected. (These options are only useful with more complicated data sources.)
6. Click the **OK** button. An Address Block merge field is inserted in the letter. See Figure 4-32. Depending on how your computer is set up, you might see a gray background behind the merge field. Notice the angled brackets that surround the merge field. The angled brackets are automatically inserted when you insert a merge field. It is important to note that you cannot type the angled brackets and merge field information—you must enter it via a dialog box selection.

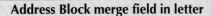

Address Block merge field in letter | Figure 4-32

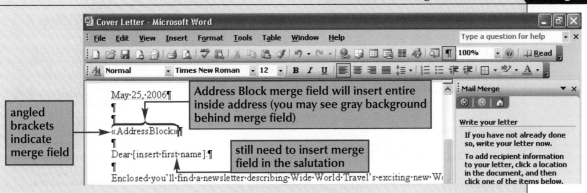

Later, when you merge the main document with the data source, Word will replace the Address Block merge field with information from the data source. Your next job is to insert a merge field that will include each client's first name in the salutation. To insert individual merge codes (rather than a code for the entire address), you need to use the More items option in the Mail Merge task pane.

To insert the merge field for the salutation:

▶ **1.** Select and delete **[insert first name]** in the salutation. Remember to delete the opening and closing brackets. Do not delete the colon.

▶ **2.** If necessary, insert a space to the left of the colon. When you finish, the insertion point should be positioned between the space and the colon.

▶ **3.** Click **More items** in the Mail Merge task pane. The Insert Merge Field dialog box opens. The Fields list shows all the merge fields in the data source. See Figure 4-33. Note that merge fields cannot contain spaces, so Word replaces any spaces in the merge field names with underlines. You want to insert the client's first name into the main document, so you need to make sure the First_Name merge field is selected.

Insert Merge Field dialog box | Figure 4-33

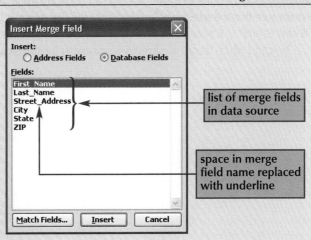

▶ **4.** Verify that **First_Name** is selected, click the **Insert** button, and then close the Insert Merge Field dialog box. The First_Name merge field is inserted in the document. See Figure 4-34.

| Figure 4-34 | First_Name merge field inserted in document |

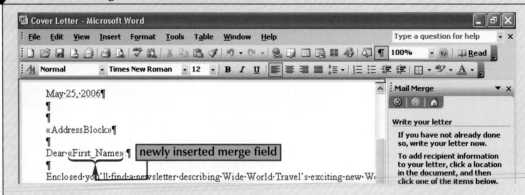

Trouble? If you make a mistake and insert the wrong merge field, click the Undo button on the Standard toolbar, and then repeat Steps 3 and 4.

5. Save your changes to the main document.

The main document now contains all the necessary merge fields, but not the data. To include data, you merge the main document and the data source. First, however, you should preview the merged document.

Previewing the Merged Document

When you preview the merged document, you can check one last time for any missing spaces between the merge codes and the surrounding text. You can also look for any other formatting problems, and, if necessary, make final changes to the main document.

To preview the merged document:

1. In the Mail Merge task pane, click **Next: Preview your letters**. The data for the first client in the data source (Deborah Browne) replaces the merge fields in the form letter. See Figure 4-35. Carefully check the letter to make sure the text and formatting are correct. In particular, check to make sure that the spacing before and after the first name in the salutation is correct because it is easy to omit spaces or add extra spaces around merge fields. Finally, notice that the task pane indicates which record is currently displayed in the document.

Previewing the merge document ◄ **Figure 4-35**

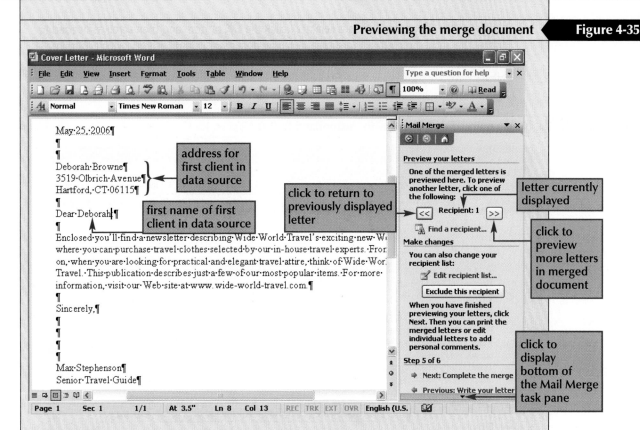

Trouble? If you need to make any changes to the form letter, click the down arrow at the bottom of the Mail Merge task pane to scroll to the bottom of the task pane, click Previous: Write your letter in the task pane, edit the document, save your changes, and then click Next: Preview your letters in the task pane. When you are finished, your screen should look like Figure 4-35.

You are ready for the final step, completing the merge.

Merging the Main Document and Data Source

Now that you've previewed the merge, you're ready to complete the merge between the main document and the data source. The result will be personalized letters to Wide World Travel clients. Because the data source consists of five records, you'll create a merged document with five pages, one letter per page.

To complete the mail merge:

▶ **1.** In the Mail Merge task pane, click **Next: Complete the merge**. The task pane displays options related to merging the main document and the data source. You can use the Print option to have Word print the customized letters immediately, without displaying them on the screen. Instead, you'll use the Edit individual letters option to merge to a new document.

▶ **2.** Click **Edit individual letters** in the Mail Merge task pane. The Merge to New Document dialog box opens. Here, you need to specify which records you want to include in the merge. You want to include all the records in the data source.

3. Verify that the **All** option button is selected, click the **OK** button, and then scroll as needed to display the entire first letter. Word creates a new document called Letters1, which contains five pages, one for each record in the data source. Each letter is separated from the one that follows it by a section break. See Figure 4-36. The main document with the merge fields (Cover Letter) remains open, as indicated by its button in the taskbar.

Figure 4-36	Newly merged document with customized letters

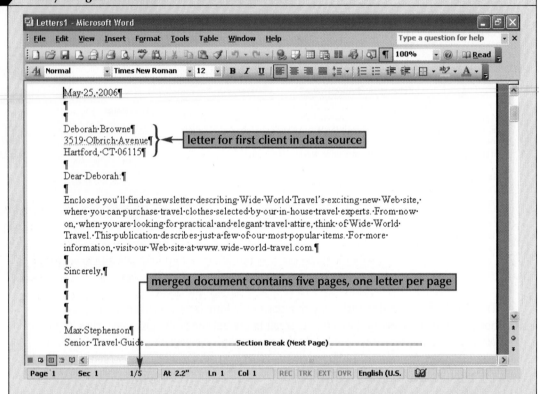

4. Save the merged document in the Tutorial.04\Tutorial folder, using the filename **Merged Cover Letters**. You saved this merged document because it is a small one. However, there's usually no need to waste disk space by saving large merged documents. Typically, you would just print the merged document and close it without saving it. If you need another copy of the merged document later, you can simply merge the data source and main document again.

5. Scroll down and review the five letters. Note the different address and salutation in each.

6. Close the Merged Cover Letters document. The document named Cover Letter reappears, along with the Mail Merge task pane.

7. Close the document and the task pane, and then click the **Yes** button if you are asked to save changes.

You have completed a mail merge and generated a merged document. Max will send the cover letters out with five sample copies of his newsletter right away.

Review

To reinforce the tasks you learned in this session, go to the SAM 2003 Training Companion CD included with this text.

Session 4.2 Quick Check

1. Define the following in your own words:
   a. drop cap
   b. scaling
   c. clip art
   d. main document
   e. data source
2. Explain how to insert a clip art graphic in Word.
3. True or False: When inserting a drop cap, you cannot specify the number of lines you want the drop cap to extend into the document vertically.
4. Describe two different methods for inserting the registered trademark symbol in a document.
5. Describe the process for drawing a border around a page.
6. Describe the steps involved in performing a mail merge.

Review

Tutorial Summary

In this tutorial you planned a newsletter and learned about the elements of desktop publishing. You worked with hyperlinks, created a WordArt headline, anchored a WordArt object, and formatted text in newspaper-style columns. You also inserted a graphic into a document, edited the graphic, inserted drop caps, and inserted symbols and special characters. Finally, you balanced the newsletter columns, drew a border around the page, and used mail merge to create customized cover letters to accompany the newsletter.

Key Terms

balance	links	scanner
bitmap	mail merge	sizing handle
clip art	main document	typographic symbols
crop	merge fields	URL
data source	merged document	Web page
drop cap	newspaper-style column	white space
floating graphic	object	WordArt
graphics	Paint	WordArt Shape button
hyperlinks	record	wrap
inline graphic	scaling	

Practice

Apply the skills you learned in the tutorial using the same case scenario.

Review Assignments

Data Files needed for the Review Assignments: Travel.doc, Highlights.doc, and Addresses.doc

Max's Wide World Travel newsletter was a success; the sales for the advertised items were brisk. Now he has been asked to create a newsletter describing the highlights of some recent Wide World Travel tours. Max has already written the text of the newsletter and asks you to transform it into a professional-looking newsletter. He asks you to create an accompanying cover letter using Word's mail merge feature. Complete the following:

1. Open the file **Travel** from the Tutorial.04\Review folder included with your Data Files, and then check your screen to make sure your Word document is displayed in Print Layout view at 100% zoom, that the nonprinting characters are displayed, and that the Drawing toolbar is open.
2. Save the document as **Travel Highlights** in the same folder.
3. In the first paragraph, replace "YOUR NAME" with your first and last name.
4. Insert "or visit our Web site at www.wide-world-travel.com" at the end of the first paragraph, immediately after the phone number (do not include the quotation marks). Add a period to complete the sentence. Then insert a blank line and remove the hyperlink from the Web address.
5. At the top of the document, create the headline "Wide World Highlights" using WordArt. In the WordArt Gallery, choose the fourth style from the left in the third row down from the top (the rainbow style with the shadow).
6. Change the shape of the WordArt object to Triangle Up, and then italicize the WordArt text.
7. Apply the Top and Bottom wrapping style to the WordArt object.
8. Insert a blank paragraph at the beginning of the document, anchor the WordArt headline to the new paragraph, and then save your work. If the WordArt moves below the new paragraph symbol, drag it up above the new paragraph. When you are finished, the anchor symbol should be positioned to the left of the new paragraph symbol, with the WordArt object positioned above the new paragraph symbol.
9. If necessary, enlarge the WordArt object to span the entire width of the page. Be sure to hold down the Shift key while you drag. When you are finished, the WordArt object should be approximately .5 inches high on the left end, and about 1 inch tall at the center.
10. Position the insertion point to the left of the first word in the paragraph (which begins "Wide World Travel, Inc."), and then format the newsletter text in two columns using the Columns dialog box. Insert a section break so that the two-column formatting is applied to the part of the newsletter after the insertion point. Do not insert a line between columns. View the new columns in Print Layout view, using the Whole Page Zoom setting.
11. Switch to Page Width zoom, and then click to the left of the paragraph that begins "We prefaced our adventure . . . "
12. Insert the clip art graphic of the Eiffel Tower from the Buildings folder in the Office Collections folder.
13. Select and resize the graphic so it is approximately 1.5 inches square.
14. Crop the image vertically about .25" on both the left and right so that, when you are finished, the image is approximately 1 inch wide.
15. Wrap text around the graphic using Tight text wrapping
16. Create a drop cap in the first paragraph under each heading, including the first paragraph below the WordArt headline, using the default settings for the Dropped position.

17. In the first paragraph below the WordArt headline, insert the trademark symbol after "Wide World Adventures." Format the symbol as superscript if it appears in the same size as the surrounding text.

18. Balance the columns. If the words in the last line of the newsletter text are spaced too far apart after you insert the section break, click at the end of the line, and then press the Enter key to move the section break to the next line.

19. Add a border around the page using a border style of your choice.

20. Preview, save, and print the newsletter. When you are finished, close the document.

21. Open the file **Highlights** located in the Tutorial.04\Review folder, and then save the document as **Highlights Cover Letter** in the same folder.

22. Merge the Highlights Cover Letter document with the Addresses file found in the Tutorial.04\Review folder. Use the Address Block merge field for the inside address. Then include a merge field that will insert the customer's first name in the salutation. Preview the merged letters and make any necessary changes before completing the merge.

23. Save the merged document as **Merged Highlights Cover Letters** and close it. Save your changes to the main document and close it. Close the task pane.

Case Problem 1

Data File needed for this Case Problem: Convert.doc

City of Santa Fe, New Mexico   Caroline Hestwood is the manager of information systems for the city of Santa Fe. She and her staff are planning to convert all city computers from the Windows 2000 operating system to Windows XP and to standardize application software on the latest version of Microsoft Office. Caroline writes a monthly newsletter on computer operations and training, so this month she has devoted the newsletter to the conversion. She asks you to finalize the newsletter. Complete the following:

1. Open the file **Convert** located in the Tutorial.04\Cases folder included with your Data Files, and then check your settings to be sure your document is displayed in Print Layout view at 100% zoom, that the nonprinting characters are displayed, and that the Drawing toolbar is open.

2. Save the document as **Conversion Newsletter** in the same folder.

3. If the text you want to format as WordArt has already been typed, you can begin creating your WordArt by selecting the text in the document. Select the text of the newsletter title, "Software Update." (Do not select the paragraph symbol at the end of the title.) Click the Insert WordArt button on the Drawing toolbar, and then create a Word Art title, using the style in the third row down, first column on the left.

4. Set the text wrapping style to Top and Bottom, and then verify that the WordArt is anchored to the blank paragraph at the top of the document.

5. Edit the WordArt object to set the font to 32-point Arial bold, and then apply the Arch Up (Curve) shape to the object. Resize the WordArt object so that it spans the width of the page from left margin to right margin and so that its maximum height is about 1 inch. (*Hint*: Use the sizing handles while watching the horizontal and vertical rulers in Print Layout view to adjust the object to the appropriate size.) Drag the WordArt down, if necessary, so that it is positioned below the top margin.

6. Center and italicize the subtitle of the newsletter, "Newsletter from the Santa Fe Information Management Office." Verify that the WordArt is anchored to the first paragraph in the document (which is a blank paragraph).

7. Replace "INSERT YOUR NAME HERE" with your name, then center and italicize the line containing your name.

8. Select the subtitle and the line after it (containing your name). Apply a Box style border, with Gray–15% shading. Be sure Paragraph is selected in the Apply to list box of the Borders and Shading dialog box.

9. Format all the text below the WordArt heading in two newspaper style columns. Notice that the text you italicized and centered now appears centered over the left column.

10. Undo the column formatting, click to the left of "The Big Switch," insert a continuous section break, and then format the text below the section break in two columns. The subtitle is now centered over the two columns.

11. Position the insertion point at the beginning of the first paragraph under the heading "Training on MS Office," and then open the Clip Art task pane. If any text appears in the Search for text box, delete it, type "computer," and then click Go. A group of clip art images appears in the Clip Art task pane. Click the image of a woman in a purple shirt typing on a keyboard. Close the Clip Art task pane.

Explore ▶ 12. Resize the picture so that it is 55% of its original size. Instead of dragging the sizing handles as you did in the tutorial, select the picture, and then click the Format Picture button on the Picture toolbar to open the Format Picture dialog box. Click the Size tab. Adjust the Height and Width settings to 55% in the Scale section, and make sure the Lock aspect ratio check box is selected. If you do not like the result, you can drag the sizing handles to fine-tune the adjustment.

13. Apply the Tight text wrapping option. Drag the picture down so it is positioned to the left of the second and third bullets.

14. Use the Clip Organizer to insert a second computer-related graphic in the right column, in the paragraph under the italicized heading "Why are we switching to Windows XP?" Open the Office Collections folder, open the Technology folder, and then open the Computing folder. Use the black and white image of a computer and a mouse on a blue background. Size the image to span half the column, apply the Square wrapping option, and drag the picture down so it is positioned halfway down the paragraph along the left column margin.

Explore ▶ 15. You can use the Replace command to replace standard word processing characters with typographic symbols. To replace every occurrence of two hyphens (--) with an em dash (—), position the insertion point at the beginning of the first paragraph of text (at the beginning of the paragraph under the heading "The Big Switch"). Click Edit on the menu bar, and then click Replace. Click the More button to display additional options. In the Find what text box, type two hyphens (--), and then press the Tab key to move the insertion point to the Replace with text box. Click the Special button at the bottom of the dialog box. Click Em Dash in the list. Word displays the special code for em dashes in the Replace with text box. Click the Replace All button. When the operation is complete, click the OK button, and then click the Close button.

16. Insert a drop cap in the first paragraph under each heading, using the default settings for the Dropped option.

17. Switch to Whole Page zoom and insert a border around the newsletter. Use a border style of your choice.

18. Save and print the newsletter, and then close it.

Apply

Apply the skills you learned to create an employee newsletter.

Case Problem 2

Data Files needed for this Case Problem: News.doc and Island.jpg

Flannery Investments   Jamie Kiesling is the director of personnel for Flannery Investments, a national investment company with headquarters in Minneapolis, Minnesota. Kiesling assigned you the task of preparing the monthly newsletter *Flannery News*, which provides news about employees of Flannery Investments. You decide to update the layout and to use the desktop-publishing capabilities of Word to design the newsletter. You will use text assembled by other employees for the body of the newsletter. Complete the following:

1. Open the file **News** located in the Tutorial.04\Cases folder included with your Data Files, and then save it as **Flannery Newsletter** in the same folder.
2. Use the Find and Replace command to replace all instances of the name "Daniela" with your first name. Then replace all instances of "Alford" with your last name.
3. Click at the end of the second section (to the right of the space after "contact her at"), and then type your e-mail address followed by a period. Press the Enter key to insert a blank line, remove the hyperlink, and then delete the new blank line.
4. Create a "Flannery News" WordArt title for the newsletter. Use the WordArt style in the second row down, third column from the left, and set the font to 24-point Arial bold. Set the wrapping style to Top and Bottom, and then anchor the WordArt to the blank paragraph at the top of the document (if it isn't already).
5. Resize the WordArt object proportionally so that the title spans the width of the page and the height of the title is about .5 inches. (*Hint*: Use the sizing handles while watching the horizontal and vertical rulers in Print Layout view to adjust the object to the appropriate size.)
6. Make sure the WordArt object is positioned above the blank paragraph, click to the left of the heading "Win a Vacation Get-Away," and then format the body of the newsletter into two newspaper-style columns. Place a vertical rule between the columns. (*Hint*: Click the Undo button and repeat the steps if the columns do not start where expected. If the vertical line crosses the WordArt, click Format on the menu bar, click Columns, click the Apply to list arrow, and then click This point forward.)
7. You can change the structure of a newsletter by reformatting it with additional columns. Change the number of columns from two to three using the Columns command on the Format menu. Make sure that the Equal column width check box is selected.

Explore

8. Position the insertion point at the beginning of the paragraph below the heading "Win a Vacation Get-Away." Click Insert on the menu bar, point to Picture, and then click From File. Look in the Tutorial.04\Cases folder, select the file named **Island**, and then click the Insert button.

Explore

9. You can make precise cropping changes using the Format Picture dialog box. Keep in mind that any cropping changes are relative to the original size of the image. For example, the photograph you inserted was created by a digital camera as a six-inch by eight-inch image, so to remove half the image's width, you would need to crop three inches. To try cropping the photograph, verify that it is selected, click the Format Picture button on the Picture toolbar, click the Picture tab, and in the Crop from text boxes, change the Left value to 2.8 and the Right value to 2. Then click the OK button.

Explore

10. You already know how to wrap text around a graphic or WordArt object using the Text Wrapping button. In some situations, however, you might need additional options to gain even more control over how text wraps in a document. To view these options now, verify that the photo is selected, click the Format Picture button on the Picture toolbar, click the Layout tab, and then click the Advanced button. Click the Tight icon, and notice the additional settings at the bottom of the Advanced Layout dialog box. Among other things, you can specify to what side the text should wrap and the distance to preserve between the text and the graphic. Click the Right only option button, click the OK button, and then click the OK button again. Keep in mind that you can also access the Advanced Layout dialog box from the Format WordArt dialog box.

11. Insert a drop cap in the first paragraph after each heading except the "Win a Vacation Get-Away" heading. Use the Dropped default settings for number of lines, but change the font of the drop cap to Arial.

12. Balance the columns and then preview the document.

13. Add a border around the entire page of the newsletter.

14. Save the newsletter, and then preview and print it. Close the document.

Challenge

Explore new techniques as you create the two-sided brochure shown in Figure 4-37.

Case Problem 3

Data File needed for this Case Problem: Hill.doc

Hill Star Dairy Cooperative   Haley Meskin is the publicity director for Hill Star Dairy Cooperative in Lawrence, Kansas. Local residents pay a membership fee to join the co-op, and then receive a 10% discount on purchases of organic dairy products. Many members don't realize that they can take advantage of other benefits, such as free cooking classes and monthly mailings with recipe cards and coupons. To spread the word, Haley would like to create a brochure describing the benefits of joining the co-op. She has already written the text of the brochure. She would like the brochure to consist of one piece of paper folded in three parts, with text on both sides of the paper, as shown in Figure 4-37.

Figure 4-37

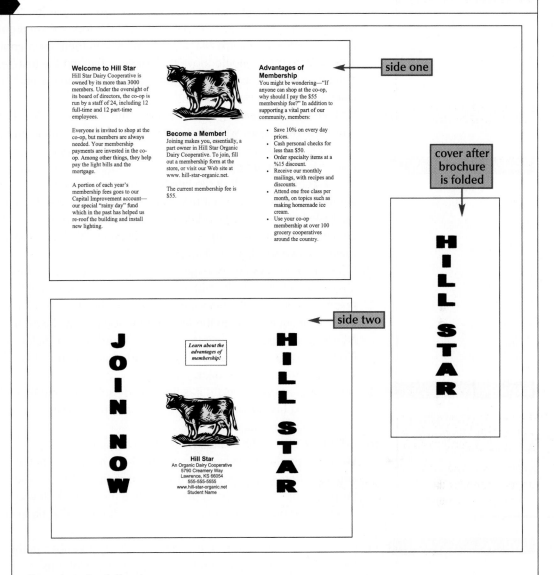

Complete the following:

1. Open the file **Hill** located in the Tutorial.04\Cases folder included with your Data Files, and then save it as **Hill Star Brochure** in the same folder. If necessary, switch to Print Layout view.

2. On the second page, below the cow graphic, click after the Web address, insert a blank line, and then type your first and last name. Remove the hyperlink from the Web address.

3. Format the entire document in three columns of equal width. Do not include a vertical line between columns. Don't be concerned that part of the text overflows onto a second page.

4. Click at the end of the list of member benefits (after "country."), and then press Ctrl+Enter to insert a page break. Remove the bullet from the new paragraph.

Explore

5. You are already familiar with adding section breaks and page breaks to a document. You can also add a column break, which forces the text after the insertion point to move to the next column. Click at the beginning of the heading "Become a Member!" (just to the left of the "B"), click Insert on the menu bar, and then click

Break. Under Break types, click the Column break option button, and then click the OK button. Insert another column break before the heading "Advantages of Membership." On the second page, click at the top of the left column, press Enter three times to insert some blank paragraphs, and then insert another column break. This column break should move the cow graphic and the text below it to the middle column. Press Ctrl+End to move the insertion point to the end of the document, and insert another column break.

6. Change the Zoom setting to Whole Page and review your work. The document should consist of two pages, with three columns each. The graphic and the co-op address should appear in the middle column on the second page.

Explore ▶ 7. Click the cow graphic in the second page, click the Copy button on the Standard toolbar, click to the left of the heading "Become a Member!", and then add two blank paragraphs. Click in the first new paragraph (at the top of the column), and then click the Paste button on the Standard toolbar. The middle column of the first page now contains another cow graphic, with the heading "Become a Member!" below, followed by two paragraphs of text.

8. Click in the left column of page 2, and then delete all but one of the paragraph marks above the column break. With the insertion point located at the only remaining paragraph mark in the left column, insert the WordArt text "JOIN NOW". In the WordArt Gallery, select the style in the left column, fourth row down. Be sure to type "JOIN NOW" in all uppercase letters in the Edit WordArt Text dialog box. Save your work. Don't be concerned if part of the WordArt object is truncated. You'll fix that in Step 9, when you rotate the WordArt.

Explore ▶ 9. Select the WordArt object if it is not already selected, and then click the WordArt Vertical Text button on the WordArt toolbar. The heading is positioned vertically in the left column of page 2.

10. Adjust the size of the WordArt object (by dragging a sizing handle) so that the WordArt spans the height of the column—do *not* press Shift as you drag the handle— and the letters spread out to fill the height of the column. When you are finished, the WordArt object should be approximately 6 inches high. If you increase the size too much, the WordArt will jump to the next column. If that happens, click the Undo button and try again.

Explore ▶ 11. Click the Format WordArt button on the WordArt toolbar. In the Format WordArt dialog box, click the Colors and Lines tab, click the Color list arrow, click the black square in the upper-left corner of the palette, and then click the OK button. The WordArt changes from a marbleized brown to all black. Save your work.

12. Use the Copy button on the Formatting toolbar to copy the "JOIN NOW" WordArt object to the Clipboard. Paste a copy of the WordArt object in the right column of page 2, double-click the WordArt object, and then change the text to "HILL STAR". When you are finished, page 2 should consist of the "JOIN NOW" WordArt in the left column, the graphic and address information in the middle column, and the "HILL STAR" WordArt in the right column. Verify that Zoom is still set to Whole Page view and examine your work.

13. Use the Center button on the Formatting toolbar to center both WordArt objects in their respective columns. Then use the Page Setup command on the File menu to center both pages vertically. (*Hint*: Use the Vertical alignment setting in the Layout tab.) Save your work.

Explore ▶ 14. If you need to add a small amount of text to a document that's formatted in a complicated way, you can use a text box, which is a kind of miniature Word document. Like a graphic, a text box is an object that you can select and resize. You can edit and format the text in a text box using the usual Word tools. In Print Layout view, change the Zoom setting to 100% and scroll to display the top of the middle column on the second page. Click at the top of the middle column, insert one blank paragraph, move the insertion point to the top of the column, and click the Text Box button on the Drawing toolbar. A gray box called a drawing canvas appears at the top of the middle column. The drawing canvas contains the text "Create your drawing here." Drag the mouse pointer inside the drawing canvas to draw a rectangle about 1.5 inches wide and one inch tall, and then release the mouse button. Type "Learn about the advantages of membership!" (without the quotation marks). Select the text in the text box and format it in 14-point Times New Roman, italic, bold. Use the Center button on the Formatting toolbar to center the text in the text box, and then click anywhere outside the drawing canvas to deselect the text box and the drawing canvas. Switch the Zoom setting to Whole Page, and adjust the text box size and the position of the graphic as needed so that the content of the center column fits nicely on the page. Save your work.

Explore

15. To print the brochure, you need to print the first page and then print the second page on the reverse side. Click File on the menu bar, click Print, click the Pages option button, type 1, and then click the OK button. Retrieve the printed page, and then insert it into your printer's paper tray so that "JOIN NOW" prints on the reverse side of the list of member benefits; likewise, "HILL STAR" should print on the reverse side of the "Welcome to Hill Star" text. Whether you should place the printed page upside down or right-side up depends on your printer. You may have to print a few test pages until you get it right. When you finish, you should be able to turn page 1 (the page with the heading "Welcome to Hill Star") face up, and then fold it inward in thirds, along the two column borders. Fold the brochure so that the "HILL STAR" column lies on top. *Note*: Ask your instructor if you should print the brochure before doing so.

16. Close the document.

Create

Create the table shown in Figure 4-38, and then use it as the data source for a mail merge resulting in cover letters and envelopes for your own job search.

Case Problem 4

There are no Data Files needed for this Case Problem.

Job Search Cover Letters You're ready to start looking for a job, and plan to use Word's mail merge feature to create customized cover letters to accompany your resume. You'll start by creating the table shown in Figure 4-38 and filling it with address information for potential employers. Then you'll create a cover letter to use as a main document, and customize it by inserting the appropriate mail merge fields.

Figure 4-38

First Name	Last Name	Company Name	Street Address	City	State	ZIP

Complete these steps:

1. Open a new, blank document, and then save it as **Job Search Data Source** in the Tutorial.04\Cases folder included with your Data Files.

2. Create the table shown in Figure 4-38, and then enter information for three potential employers. The information can be real or fictitious. For the First Name and Last Name columns, use the name of an appropriate contact at each company. Save your work and close the document.

3. Open a new, blank document and save it as **Job Search Cover Letter** in the Tutorial.04\Cases folder.

4. Create a cover letter that introduces yourself and describes your experience and education. Instead of an inside address, include the placeholder text "[Inside Address]". For the salutation, use "Dear Ms. [Last Name]". (You'll have a chance to change "Ms." to "Mr." where necessary when you edit the individual merged letters.) Refer the reader to your resume for more information. Use the correct business letter style for your cover letter. Include a sentence in the cover letter that mentions the company name. Use the placeholder "[Company Name]" to remind you to insert the appropriate merge field later. Save your work and close the document.

5. Open a new, blank document, open the Mail Merge task pane, and follow the steps outlined in the Mail Merge task pane. Use the Job Search Cover Letter document as the main document, and select the **Job Search Data Source** file as the data source. Use the Address block merge field for the inside address (and verify that the Insert company name check box is selected in the Insert Address Block dialog box). Add a merge field for the last name in the salutation of the letter, and add a merge field to replace the Company Name placeholder text in the body of the letter. Save your changes to the main document before completing the merge.

6. Preview your letters, and then complete the merge (choosing the Edit individual letters option). Review the letters, and edit them as necessary to use Ms. or Mr. appropriately in the salutation. Save the merged document as **Job Search Cover Letter Merged** in the Tutorial.04\Cases folder, close it, and close the Mail Merge task pane.

7. Print your main document, and then close it.

8. Open a new, blank document, and then save it as **Job Search Envelopes** in the Tutorial.04\Cases folder.

Explore ▶ 9. Open the Mail Merge task pane, click the Envelopes option button under Select document type, click Next: Starting document, click Envelope options, and then click OK in the Envelope Options dialog box to select the default settings. The document layout changes to resemble a business size envelope.

10. Continue with the steps in the Mail Merge task pane, selecting the **Job Search Data Source** file as the data source.

Explore ▶ 11. Click Next: Arrange your envelope, and then type your name and address as the return address. Notice that the insertion point is positioned in the return address, ready for you to begin typing. (Change the Zoom setting if necessary to make the text easier to read.) Click the paragraph mark in the center of the document and insert an Address block merge field. Save your work.

12. Preview the envelopes, and complete the merge (choosing the Edit individual envelopes option). Save the merged document as **Job Search Envelopes Merged** in the Tutorial.04\Cases folder, and then close it. If your computer is connected to a printer that is stocked with envelopes, print the main document. Close the main document and the Mail Merge task pane.

Research

Go to the Web to find information you can use to create documents.

Internet Assignments

The purpose of the Internet Assignments is to challenge you to find information on the Internet that you can use to work effectively with this software. The actual assignments are updated and maintained on the Course Technology Web site. Log on to the Internet and use your Web browser to go to the Student Online Companion for New Perspectives Office 2003 at **www.course.com/np/office2003**. Click the Internet Assignments link, and then navigate to the assignments for this tutorial.

Assess

SAM Assessment and Training

If your instructor has chosen to use the full online version of SAM 2003 Assessment and Training, you can go beyond the "just-in-time" training provided on the CD that accompanies this text. Simply log in to your SAM account (http://sam2003.course.com) to launch any assigned training activities or exams that relate to the skills covered in this tutorial.

Review

Quick Check Answers

Session 4.1

1. List any four of the following: The document uses multiple fonts; the document incorporates graphics; the document uses typographic symbols; the document uses columns and other special formatting features; the printing is of high-quality.
2. True
3. a. using a desktop computer system to produce commercial-quality printed material; with desktop publishing, you can enter and edit text, create graphics, lay out pages, and print documents
   b. a Word feature that allows you to insert specially formatted text into a document.
   c. unformatted text
   d. a symbol that appears in the left margin, which shows a WordArt object's position in relation to the text
4. False
5. To change the text of a WordArt object, click the object to select it, click the Edit Text button on the WordArt toolbar, edit the text in the Edit WordArt Text dialog box, and then click OK.
6. The WordArt Shape button allows you to change the basic shape of a WordArt object.
7. False

Session 4.2

1. a. a large, uppercase letter that highlights the beginning of the text of a newsletter, chapter, or some other document section
   b. resizing an image to fit a document better
   c. premade artwork that you can insert into your document
   d. a document (such as a letter) that contains standard text and placeholders (called merge fields) that tell Word where to insert variable information (such as a name or an address)
   e. a document that contains information, such as clients' names and addresses, which will be inserted into the main document

2. Position the insertion point at the location where you want to insert the image, click the Insert Clip Art button on the Drawing toolbar, click Organize clips in the Clip Art task pane, open the folder containing the image you want, click the arrow button on the image, click Copy, and then close the Clip Organizer. Finally, paste the graphic into the document.

3. False

4. Click where you want to insert the symbol in the document, click Insert on the menu bar, click Symbol, click the Special Characters tab in the Symbol dialog box, click Registered Trademark in the list, click the Insert button, and then click the Close button. Another option is to type "(r)" and press the spacebar.

5. Click Format on the menu bar, click Borders and Shading, click the Page Border tab in the Borders and Shading dialog box, select the border type you want in the Setting section, choose a line style from the Style list box, make sure Whole document appears in the Apply to list box, and then click OK.

6. Select or create a main document. Select or create a data source. Use the Mail Merge task pane to insert merge fields into the main document. Preview the merged document. Merge the data source and the main document.

New Perspectives on

Microsoft® Office Excel 2003

Read This Before You Begin: Tutorials 1-4

Data Files

To complete Excel Tutorials 1-4, you need the starting Data Files. See the inside back or front cover for information on downloading these files from course.com, or ask your instructor for assistance. The following table identifies each starting Data File and the folder it is stored in, as well as the ending files, which you create and save in each tutorial.

Folders		Starting Files	Ending Files
Tutorial .01	Tutorial	(no starting Data Files)	Dalton.xls
	Review	(no starting Data Files)	Dalton2.xls, Dalton3.xls
	Cases	Altac1.xls, Halley1.xls, Site1.xls	Altac2.xls, Budget.xls, Halley2.xls, Site2.xls, Site3.xls
Tutorial .02	Tutorial	Budget1.xls	Budget2.xls, Budget3.xls
	Review	Family1.xls	Family2.xls, Family3.xls
	Cases	Chem1.xls, Sales1.xls, Sonic1.xls, Soup1.xls, Works1.xls	Chem2.xls, Sales2.xls, Sonic2.xls, Soup2.xls, Works2.xls
Tutorial .03	Tutorial	Back.jpg, Sales1.xls	Sales2.xls
	Review	Region1.xls	Region2.xls
	Cases	Blades1.xls, Frosti1.xls, Packing1.xls	Blades2.xls, Frosti2.xls, Packing2.xls, Payroll1.xls, Payroll2.xls
Tutorial .04	Tutorial	Space.jpg, Vega1.xls	Vega2.xls
	Review	VegaUSA1.xls	VegaUSA2.xls
	Cases	Oil1.xls, Park1.xls, Powder1.xls	BCancer.xls, Oil2.xls, Park2.xls, Powder2.xls

Storing Your Files

It is recommended that you store all your Data Files on a USB drive. Refer to the tutorial "Managing Your Files" for information on using USB drives. If you need to store your Data Files on floppy disks, you will need two high-density disks to store all the files for Excel Tutorials 1-4.

SAM 2003 Training Companion CD

The SAM 2003 Training Companion CD that comes with this text gives you "just-in-time" training and reinforcement of important Microsoft Office skills. Look for the SAM CD logo throughout each tutorial for opportunities to complete the hands-on tasks included on this CD.

Course Labs

Excel Tutorial 1 features an interactive Course Lab to help you understand spreadsheet concepts. There are Lab Assignments at the end of Tutorial 1 that relate to this lab. Contact your instructor or technical support person for assistance in accessing this lab.

www.course.com/NewPerspectives

Using Excel to Manage Data

Creating a Sales Order Report

Case | Dalton Food Co-op

Sandra Dalton and her husband, Kevin, own a farm in northern Florida. Recently, Sandra has been selling produce to local families to earn extra income. When she started, Sandra kept a paper record of customer orders, and all of the data was entered into a paper ledger with the calculations done on a tabletop calculator. Several months ago, Sandra and Kevin purchased a computer for the co-op. Bundled with the other software installed on the computer was a copy of **Microsoft Office Excel 2003** (or simply **Excel**), a computer program used to enter, analyze, and present quantitative data.

Sandra, who handles most of the financial aspects of the business, has been using Excel for several months, but as the business continues to grow and its busy season approaches, she has asked you to help. She wants you to use an Excel workbook to keep track of orders recently made at the Dalton Food Co-op.

Session	Objectives		SAM Training Tasks	
Session 1.1	• Learn about spreadsheets and how they work • Identify major components of the Excel window • Navigate within and between worksheets	• Enter text, dates, data, and formulas into a worksheet • Change the size of a column or row	• Create formulas using the formula bar • Enter data in a selected range of cells • Enter formulas using Point mode • Enter numbers with format symbols • Go to a specific cell	• Modify column widths • Modify row height • Range finder • Select a cell • Use Save • Use the Select All button to assign formats to the entire worksheet
Session 1.2	• Select and move cell ranges • Calculate totals with AutoSum • Insert and delete a column or row • Work in edit mode • Undo an action	• Insert, move, and rename a worksheet • Check the spelling in a workbook • Preview and print a workbook • Display the formulas within a worksheet	• Check spelling in a worksheet • Clear cell content • Copy cells • Create formulas using the SUM function • Delete a worksheet from a workbook • Delete rows and columns • Delete selected cells • Display formula contents • Edit a formula • Edit numbers in cells • Edit text in cells • Fit to print • Format cells before entering data	• Insert a cell • Insert columns and rows • Insert worksheets into a workbook • Modify worksheet names • Modify worksheet orientation • Move cells • Print a worksheet • Print all worksheets in a workbook • Print-preview a worksheet • Reposition worksheets in a workbook • Select non-adjacent cells • Undo and Redo an entry

Student Data Files   For a complete list of the Data Files needed for this tutorial, see page EX 2.

Session 1.1

For hands-on practice of key tasks in this session, go to the SAM 2003 Training Companion CD included with this text.

Introducing Excel

Before you begin working with the recent orders at the co-op, you need to understand some of the key terms and concepts associated with a program such as Excel.

Understanding Spreadsheets

Excel is a computerized spreadsheet. A **spreadsheet** is an important tool used for analyzing and reporting information. Spreadsheets are often used in business for budgeting, inventory management, and decision making. For example, an accountant might use a paper-based spreadsheet like the one shown in Figure 1-1 to record a company's estimated and actual monthly cash flow.

| Figure 1-1 | A sample spreadsheet |

Cash Flow Comparison
Actual versus Budget

		Jan-06
	Estimated	**Actual**
Cash balance(start of month)	$ 1,500.00	$ 1,500.00
Receipts		
Cash sales	1700.00	1852.00
Cash expenditures		
Advertising	200.00	211.00
Wages	900.00	900.00
Supplies	100.00	81.00
Total cash expenditures	1200.00	1192.00
Net cash flow	500.00	660.00
Cash balance(end of month)	$ 2,000.00	$ 2,160.00

In this spreadsheet, the accountant has recorded the estimated and actual cash flow for the month of January. Each line, or row, in this spreadsheet displays a different cash flow value. Each column contains the predicted or actual values, or text that describes those values. The accountant has also entered the total cash expenditures, net cash flow, and closing cash balance for the month, perhaps having used a calculator to do the calculations.

Figure 1-2 shows the same spreadsheet in Excel. The spreadsheet is now laid out in a grid in which the rows and columns are easily apparent. As you will see later, calculations are also part of this electronic spreadsheet, so that total cash expenditures, net cash flow, and cash balances are calculated automatically rather than entered manually. When you change an entry in the electronic spreadsheet, the spreadsheet automatically updates any calculated values based on the entry. You can also use an electronic spreadsheet to perform a **what-if analysis** in which you change one or more of the values in the worksheet and then examine the recalculated values to determine the effect of the change. (You will have a chance to explore this feature at the end of the tutorial.) So, an electronic spreadsheet provides more flexibility in entering and analyzing your data than the paper version.

The same spreadsheet in Excel   Figure 1-2

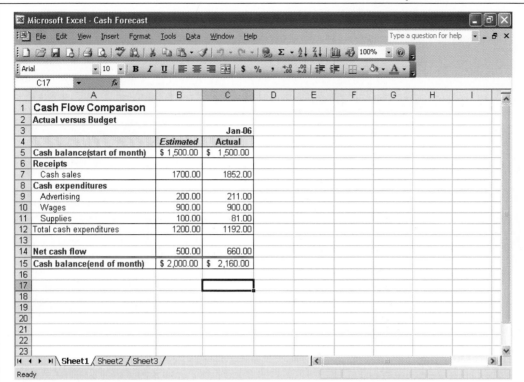

Excel stores electronic spreadsheets in files called **workbooks**. Each workbook is made up of individual **worksheets**, or **sheets**, just as a spiral-bound ledger, which an accountant would use, is made up of sheets of paper. You will learn more about multiple worksheets later in the tutorial. For now, keep in mind that the terms *worksheet* and *sheet* are often used interchangeably.

Parts of the Excel Window

Excel displays workbooks within a window that contains many tools for entering, editing, and viewing data. You will learn about some of these tools after starting Excel. By default, Excel opens with a blank workbook.

To start Excel:

1. Click the **Start** button on the taskbar, point to **All Programs**, point to **Microsoft Office**, and then click **Microsoft Office Excel 2003**. The Excel window opens. See Figure 1-3.

Figure 1-3 Parts of the Excel window

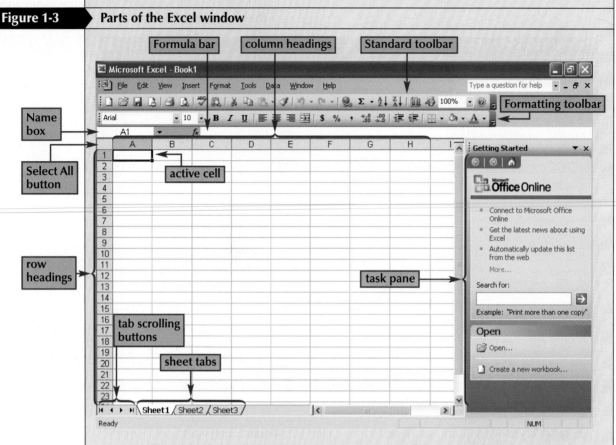

Trouble? If you don't see the Microsoft Office Excel 2003 option on the Microsoft Office submenu, look for it in a different submenu or as an option on the All Programs menu. If you still cannot find the Microsoft Office Excel 2003 option, ask your instructor or technical support person for help.

The Excel window contains many of the components that you find in other Windows programs, including a title bar, a menu bar, scroll bars, and a status bar. The Excel window also contains features that are unique to Excel. Within the Excel program window is another window, referred to as the **workbook window** or **worksheet window**. The worksheet window provides a grid of **columns** and **rows**, and the intersection of a column and row is called a **cell**. Each cell is identified by a **cell reference**, which is its column and row location. For example, the cell reference B6 indicates that the cell is located where column B and row 6 intersect. The column letter is always first in the cell reference: B6 is a correct reference; 6B is not. The cell in which you are working is called the **active cell**. Excel identifies the active cell by outlining it with a dark border. In Figure 1-3, cell A1 is the active cell. Notice that the cell reference for the active cell appears in the **Name box** next to the **Formula bar**. You can change the active cell by selecting another cell in the worksheet. As you review the layout of the Excel window shown in Figure 1-3, refer to Figure 1-4 for a description of each component.

Excel window components ◀ **Figure 1-4**

Feature	Description
Active cell	The cell in which you are currently working. A dark border outlining the cell identifies the active cell.
Column headings	The letters that appear along the top of the worksheet window. Columns are listed alphabetically from A to IV (a total of 256 possible columns).
Formula bar	The bar located immediately below the toolbars that displays the contents of the active cell. As you type or edit data, the changes appear in the Formula bar.
Name box	The box that displays the cell reference, or column and row location, of the active cell in the workbook window.
Row headings	The numbers that appear along the left side of the worksheet window. Rows are numbered consecutively from 1 to 65,536.
Select All button	Square button located at the intersection of the column and row headings that you click to select the entire contents of the worksheet.
Sheet tabs	Tabs located at the bottom of each worksheet in the workbook that display the names of the sheets. To move between worksheets, click the appropriate sheet tab.
Task pane	The pane that provides access to frequently used tasks. When you start Excel, the Getting Started task pane appears. The task pane disappears once you open a workbook. There are several task-specific panes available in Excel.
Tab scrolling buttons	Series of buttons located to the left of the sheet tabs that you can click to move between worksheets in the workbook.
Toolbars	Toolbars that provide quick access to commonly used commands. The Standard toolbar contains buttons for the most frequently used program commands, such as Save and Print. The Formatting toolbar contains buttons used to format the appearance of the workbook, such as Bold and Italics. Additional toolbars are available.

Now that you are familiar with the basic layout of an Excel window, you can try moving around within the workbook.

Navigating a Worksheet

Excel provides several ways of moving around within a worksheet. You can use your mouse to click a cell to make it the active cell, or you can use the vertical and horizontal scroll bars to display the area of the worksheet containing the cell you want to make active. You can also navigate a worksheet by using your keyboard. Figure 1-5 describes some of these keyboard shortcuts that Excel provides so you can move from cell to cell within the worksheet quickly and easily.

Shortcut keys for navigating a worksheet ◀ **Figure 1-5**

Keystroke	Action
↑, ↓, ←, →	Moves the active cell up, down, left, or right one cell
Ctrl + Home	Moves the active cell to cell A1
Ctrl + End	Moves to the last cell in the worksheet that contains data
Enter	Moves the active cell down one cell, or moves to the start of the next row in the selected range of cells
F5	Opens the Go To dialog box, in which you specify the cell you want to move to
Home	Moves the active cell to column A of the current row
Page Up, Page Down	Moves the active cell up or down one full screen
Tab, Shift + Tab	Moves the active cell to the right or left one cell

Try navigating the worksheet now.

To move around in the worksheet:

1. Click the **Close** button ☒ in the task pane to close it because you will not be using it in this session. The active cell is A1. The cell A1 is surrounded by a black border, indicating it is the active cell, and the Name box displays the cell reference A1.

2. With cell A1 the active cell, press the ↓ key on your keyboard four times to move to cell A5, and then press the → key twice to make cell C5 the active cell, as shown in Figure 1-6. Note that the column and row headings are highlighted and the cell reference appears in the Name box.

Figure 1-6	Making cell C5 the active cell

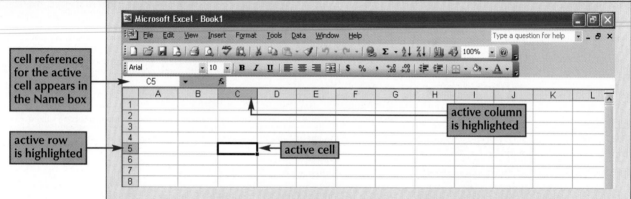

3. Press the **Enter** key to move down one cell, and the press the **Tab** key to move to the right one cell. The active cell is now D6.

4. Press the **Page Down** key to move the display down one screen. The active cell should now be cell D29. If the actual number of columns and rows displayed on your screen differs from that shown in Figure 1-2, the active cell on your screen might not be cell D29. You will learn more about working with the number of columns and rows on your screen later in this tutorial; for now the active cell on your screen should be a screen full of rows down the worksheet.

5. Press the **Page Up** key to move the display back up one screen, making cell D6 the active cell again.

6. Press the **Home** key to move to the first cell in the current row, and then press the **Ctrl + Home** keys to make cell A1 active.

You will probably use the keyboard keys to navigate a worksheet the most frequently, but there will also be situations in which you will want to go directly to a cell on your worksheet. Although you can use the Page Up and Page Down keys or use the scroll bars, you have two other options: the Name box and the Go To dialog box. You can just click in the Name box and type the cell reference you want to go to, or you can open the Go To dialog box from any location in the worksheet by pressing the F5 function key. Try using these methods to navigate the worksheet.

To use the Go To dialog box and Name box:

1. Press the **F5** key to open the Go To dialog box, type **K55** in the Reference text box, and then click the **OK** button to make cell K55 the active cell.

2. Click in the **Name** box, type **E6**, and then press the **Enter** key to make cell E6 the active cell.

Navigating Between Worksheets

By default, a new Excel workbook contains three worksheets, labeled Sheet1, Sheet2, and Sheet3. Each sheet can be used to display different information. To move from one sheet to another, click the sheet tabs at the bottom of each sheet.

To move between worksheets:

1. Click the **Sheet2** tab. Sheet2, which is blank, appears in the workbook window. Notice that the Sheet2 tab is now white with the name "Sheet2" in a bold font. This is a visual indicator that Sheet2 is the active worksheet.

2. Click the **Sheet3** tab to move to the next worksheet in the workbook.

3. Click the **Sheet1** tab to make it the active worksheet.

Now that you have some basic skills navigating through a worksheet and a workbook, you can begin work on Sandra's worksheet.

Developing a Worksheet

Before you begin to enter data in a worksheet, you should think about the purpose of the worksheet and what will be needed to meet the challenge of that purpose. Effective worksheets are well planned and carefully designed. A well-designed worksheet should clearly identify its overall goal. It should present information in a clear, well-organized format and include all the data necessary to produce results that address the goal of the application. The process of developing a good worksheet includes the following planning and execution steps:

- Determine the worksheet's purpose, what it will include, and how it will be organized.
- Enter the data and formulas into the worksheet.
- Test the worksheet, and then edit the worksheet to correct any errors or to make modifications.
- Document the worksheet and format the worksheet's appearance.
- Save and print the complete worksheet.

To develop a worksheet that records orders made at the co-op, Sandra wants to develop a planning analysis sheet that will help her answer the following questions:

1. What is the goal of the worksheet? This helps to define its purpose or, in other words, the problem to solve.
2. What are the desired results? This information describes the output—the information required to help solve the problem.
3. What data is needed to calculate the results you want to see? This information is the input—data that must be entered.
4. What calculations are needed to produce the desired output? These calculations specify the formulas used in the worksheet.

After careful consideration of these questions, Sandra has developed the planning analysis sheet shown in Figure 1-7.

| Figure 1-7 | Planning analysis sheet |

Planning Analysis Sheet
Author: Sandra Dalton, Dalton Food Co-op
Date: 4/26/2006

My goal
To develop a worksheet in which I can enter food co-op orders, calculating the total
quantity of the items ordered and the revenue generated.

What results do I need to see?
- A listing of each order made by customers
- The total amount of each order
- The total quantity of items ordered by all of the customers
- The total revenue generated by all of the orders

What data do I need?
- The customer's name and address
- The date of the order
- The item purchased by the customer
- The price of each item
- The quantity of items ordered by the customer

What calculations must be performed by the worksheet?
- The total amount of each order (= price of the item x the quantity ordered)
- The total quantity of items ordered (= sum of the order quantities)
- The total revenue generated by all of the orders (= sum of the total amount of each order)

Sandra also knows the information that needs to go into the worksheet, including titles, column headings, row labels, and data values. Figure 1-8 shows how Sandra wants the sales data laid out, based on a sampling of customer orders.

| Figure 1-8 | Sales data for co-op worksheet |

Name	Address	Date	Item	Price	Qty	Total
Alison Wilkes	45 Lincoln Street Midtown, FL 80481	4/16/2006	Red Grapefruit	$14	2	
David Wu	315 Oak Lane Midtown, FL 80422	4/16/2006	Navel Oranges	$17	1	
Carl Ramirez	900 South Street Crawford, FL 81891	4/17/2006	Navel Oranges	$17	2	
Jerry Dawson	781 Tree Lane Midtown, FL 80313	4/18/2006	Deluxe Combo	$21	4	
TOTAL						

The first two columns contain the name and address of the person ordering items from the co-op. The Date and Item columns indicate the date that the order was placed and the item ordered. The Price column displays the price of the item. The Qty column indicates the quantity of each item ordered by the customer. The Total column will display the total amount of each order. The TOTAL row will display the total quantity of items ordered and the total revenue generated by all of the sales. With this information in hand, you are now ready to create Sandra's worksheet in Excel.

Entering Data into a Worksheet

A worksheet can contain the following types of data: text, numeric values, dates, and calculated values. A text entry is simply any combination of words, letters, and numbers, typically used to label key features of the worksheet. Numeric values are numbers on which calculations can be made. Numeric values do not contain alphabetic characters, but may contain characters such as commas, dollar signs, and percent signs. Dates are special numeric values recognized by Excel and can be used to determine date-related calculations. The power of Excel lies in the formulas that you can enter into the worksheet cells, whose calculated values are based on the text, dates, and numeric values entered into other cells in the workbook (or in more complicated cases, other workbooks). If those values are changed, the calculated values will also be changed.

Worksheet cells in Excel can also be formatted to improve or enhance the appearance of the cell contents or an entire worksheet. You'll learn about formatting later in Tutorial 3.

Entering Text

To insert text into a worksheet cell, you first make the cell active by using one of the navigation techniques discussed earlier, and then you type the text you want the cell to contain. Excel automatically aligns the text with the left edge of the cell.

First, you'll enter the column headings that Sandra wants across the top row of her worksheet.

To enter the column headings in row 1:

1. Press the **Ctrl + Home** keys to make cell A1 the active cell on the Sheet1 worksheet.

2. Type **Name** and then press the **Tab** key. Pressing the Tab key enters the text in the cell and moves the insertion point to the right to cell B1, making it the active cell.

3. Type **Address** in cell B1, and then press the **Tab** key again. Cell C1 becomes the active cell.

4. Enter the remaining column headings **Date**, **Item**, **Price**, **Qty**, and **Total** in cells C1 through G1. Press the **Enter** key after you type the text for cell G1. Figure 1-9 shows the column headings for the worksheet.

Entering text into the worksheet ◄ **Figure 1-9**

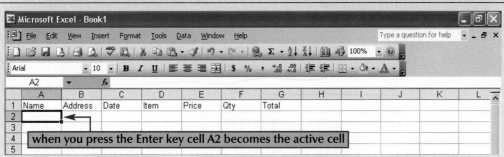

Trouble? If you make a mistake as you type, you can correct the error by clicking the cell and retyping the entry.

Note that when you press the Enter key, the active cell becomes cell A2, not cell G2. Excel recognizes that when you enter a row of data and then press the Enter key, you have completed the task of entering data in the current row, so the insertion point moves to the start of the next row. If you had started entering data in cell C1 rather than A1, pressing the Enter key would have made cell C2 the active cell.

Entering Several Lines of Text Within a Cell

In the next row, you'll enter actual sales information. One cell in this row contains the customer's address. In Sandra's records, this information is presented on two separate lines, with the street address on one line and the city, state, and ZIP code on the other. To place text on separate lines within the same cell, you press and hold the Alt key on the keyboard while pressing the Enter key.

Reference Window

Entering Multiple Lines of Text Within a Cell

- Click the cell in which you want to enter the text.
- Enter a line of text.
- Press and hold the Alt key, and then press the Enter key to move the insertion point to a new line within the cell.
- Enter the next line of text.
- Press the Alt + Enter keys for each new line of text you need to enter within the cell.

Try this technique now by entering the first customer's name and address.

To enter the address on two lines within a cell:

1. Verify that cell **A2** is the active cell, type **Alison Wilkes**, and then press the **Tab** key to move to column B, where you will enter the two-line address.

2. Type **45 Lincoln Street** in cell B2, but do *not* press the Tab or Enter key.

3. Press and hold the **Alt** key, and then press the **Enter** key to insert a line break, moving the insertion point to a new line within the cell.

4. Type **Midtown, FL 80481** on the second line of the cell, and then press the **Tab** key. Figure 1-10 shows the worksheet with the text you have entered so far.

Figure 1-10 ▶ Entering the customer name and address

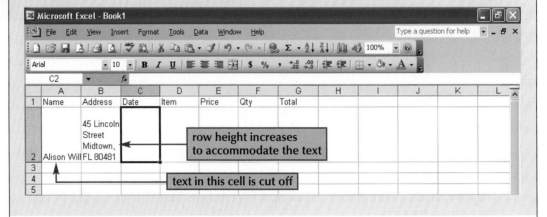

Excel has done a couple of things that you need to understand before entering more data. First, the name of the customer in cell A2 has been cut off, or truncated. When you enter more text than can be displayed within a cell, Excel will display the additional text in the cell or cells to the right as long as they are empty. If the cells to the right are not empty, Excel will truncate the display of the text when it encounters the first non-empty cell. The text itself is not affected. The complete name of the first customer is still entered in cell A2; it's just not displayed.

Second, the customer address in cell B2 does not extend into cell C2, even though that cell is empty. Instead, the height of row 2 has been increased to accommodate this text. If a cell contains multiple lines of text, Excel increases the height of the row to display all of the text entry. Note that the text in cell B2 "appears" to be on four lines, even though you entered the address on two lines. Excel wrapped the text in this way so that it would fit within the existing column width. Later in this session, you will learn how to adjust column widths and row heights to improve the worksheet's appearance.

Entering Dates

In Excel, dates are treated as numeric values, not text. This allows you to perform calculations with dates, such as determining the number of days between two dates. You'll learn how to work with date values in the next tutorial. For now, you need to know how to enter a date. You can enter a date using any of the following date formats, which are recognized by Excel:

- 4/16/2006
- 4/16/06
- 4-16-2006
- April 16, 2006
- 16-Apr-06

The appearance of a date, regardless of how you enter it in a cell, depends on the date format that has been set as the default in your version of Excel. For example, if you enter the date as the text string "April 26, 2006," Excel will automatically convert the entry to "26-Apr-2006" if the DD-MMM-YYYY format has been set as the default. You will learn about cell formats and date formats in Tutorial 3.

Sandra wants the date "4/16/2006" to appear in cell C2, so you will enter that next.

To insert the date in cell C2:

1. Verify that cell **C2** is the active cell.

2. Type **4/16/2006** and then press the **Tab** key.

   Trouble? If your computer is set up to display dates using a different date format, do not worry about their appearance at this time.

3. Type **Red Grapefruit** in cell D2, and then press the **Tab** key. Note that the text in cell D2 is completely displayed because, at this point, the cells to the right of D2 are still empty.

Entering Values

Values are numbers that represent a quantity of some type: the number of units in an inventory, stock prices, an exam score, and so on. Values can be numbers such as 378 and 25.275 or negative numbers such as –55.208. Values can also be expressed as currency such as $14.95 or as percentages such as 95%. Not all numbers are treated as values. For example, Excel treats a telephone number (1-800-555-8010) or a Social Security number (372-70-9654) as a text entry. As you type information into a cell, Excel determines whether the entry can be treated as a value, and if so, automatically right-aligns the value within the cell.

Next, you'll enter the price and quantity of the first order into cells E2 and F2.

To enter the price and quantity values:

1. Type **$14** in cell E2, and then press the **Tab** key.

2. Type **2** in cell F2, and then press the **Tab** key. Figure 1-11 shows the data for the first order. The last cell in the row is empty, but next you will enter a calculation that will give Sandra the total amount of the order.

Figure 1-11	Entering the price and quantity values

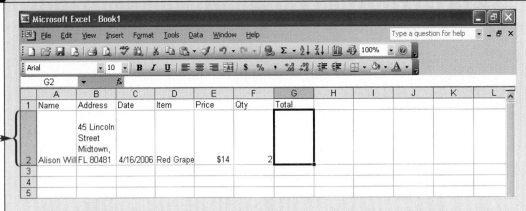

data for the first order entered

The remaining cell in this row will contain the total price of the order, which is equal to the price of the red grapefruit item multiplied by the quantity ordered. The total price of the first order is $14 multiplied by 2, or $28. Rather than entering this value into the cell, you'll let Excel calculate it for you by entering a formula.

Entering Formulas

The single most important reason for using a spreadsheet is to perform calculations on data. To accomplish that goal, you need to enter formulas. A **formula** is a mathematical expression that calculates a value. Excel formulas always begin with an equal sign (=) followed by an expression that describes the calculation to be done. A formula can contain one or more **arithmetic operators**, such as +, –, *, or /. For example, the formula $=A1+A2$ calculates the sum by adding the values of cells A1 and A2. Figure 1-12 gives examples of some other Excel formulas. Note that, by convention, cell references appear in uppercase letters, but this is not a requirement for Excel formulas. You can type the formula using either upper- or lowercase letters, and Excel will automatically convert the cell references to uppercase.

Sample Excel formulas using arithmetic operators ◀ **Figure 1-12**

Operation	Operator	Example	Description
Addition	+	=10+A5	Adds 10 to the value in cell A5
		=B1+B2+B3	Adds the values of cells B1, B2, and B3
Subtraction	–	=C9–B2	Subtracts the value in cell B2 from the value in cell C9
		=1–D2	Subtracts the value in cell D2 from 1
Multiplication	*	=C9*B9	Multiplies the value in cell C9 by the value in cell B9
		=E5*0.06	Multiplies the value in cell E5 by 0.06
Division	/	=C9/B9	Divides the value in cell C9 by the value in cell B9
		=D15/12	Divides the value in cell D15 by 12
Exponentiation	^	=B5^3	Raises the value in cell B5 to the third power
		=3^B5	Raises 3 to the power specified in cell B5

Entering a Formula

Reference Window

- Click the cell where you want the formula result to appear.
- Type = and then type the expression that calculates the value you want.
- For a formula that includes cell references, such as B2 or D78, type the cell reference, or use the mouse or arrow keys to select each cell.
- When the formula is complete, press the Enter key (or press the Tab key or click the Enter button on the Formula bar).

If an expression contains more than one arithmetic operator, Excel performs the calculation in the order of precedence. The **order of precedence** is a set of predefined rules that Excel follows to calculate a formula by determining which operator is applied first, which operator is applied second, and so forth. First, Excel performs exponentiation (^). Second, Excel performs multiplication (*) or division (/). Third, Excel performs addition (+) or subtraction (–).

For example, because multiplication has precedence over addition, the formula =3+4*5 results in the value 23. If the expression contains two or more operators with the same level of precedence, Excel applies them from left to right in the expression. In the formula =4*10/8, Excel first multiplies 4 by 10 and then divides the result by 8 to produce the value 5.

When building a formula, you must add parentheses to change the order of operations. Excel will calculate any expression contained within the parentheses before any other part of the formula. The formula =(3+4)*5 first calculates the value of 3+4 and then multiplies the total by 5, resulting in the value 35. (Note that without the parentheses, Excel would produce a value of 23, as noted in the previous paragraph.) Figure 1-13 shows other examples of Excel formulas using the order of precedence rules.

Figure 1-13 | **Examples illustrating order of precedence rules**

Formula (A1=50, B1=10, C1=5)	Order of precedence rule	Result
=A1+B1*C1	Multiplication before addition	100
=(A1+B1)*C1	Expression inside parentheses executed before expression outside	300
=A1/B1–C1	Division before subtraction	0
=A1/(B1–C1)	Expression inside parentheses executed before expression outside	10
=A1/B1*C1	Two operators at same precedence level, leftmost operator evaluated first	25
=A1/(B1*C1)	Expression inside parentheses executed before expression outside	1

Using what you know about formulas, you'll enter a formula in cell G2 to calculate the total amount of Alison Wilke's order.

To enter a formula to calculate the total amount of the first order:

1. Verify that cell **G2** is the active cell.

2. Type **=E2*F2** (the price of the item multiplied by the quantity ordered). Note that as you type the cell reference, Excel surrounds each cell with a different colored border that matches the color of the cell reference in the formula. As shown in Figure 1-14, Excel surrounds cell E2 with a blue border, matching the blue used for the cell reference. Green is used for the F2 cell border and cell reference.

Figure 1-14 | **Typing a formula into the active cell**

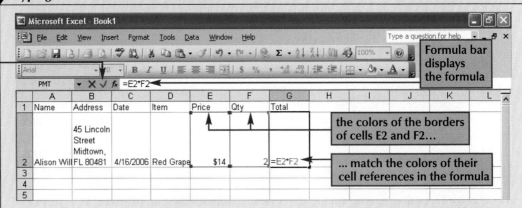

3. Press the **Enter** key. The total amount of the first order displayed in cell G2 is $28. Note that the value is displayed as currency because one of the components of the formula (cell E2) is a currency value. As you can see, the result of the formula is displayed in the worksheet. To see the formula itself, you need to select the cell and examine the formula in the Formula bar.

You can also enter formulas interactively by clicking each cell. In this technique, you type = (an equal sign) to begin the formula, and then click each cell that needs to be entered in the formula. Using this point-and-click method reduces the possibility of error caused by typing an incorrect cell reference.

Next, you'll enter the data for the second order, and then enter the formula =E3*F3 (the price of the item multiplied by the quantity ordered) using the point-and-click method.

To enter the same formula using the point-and-click method:

1. Enter **David Wu** in cell A3, **315 Oak Lane** on one line in cell B3 and **Midtown, FL 80422** on a second line in the cell, **4/16/2006** in cell C3, **Navel Oranges** in cell D3, **$17** in cell E3, and **1** in cell F3. Be sure to press the Alt + Enter keys to enter the address information on two separate lines as you did for the address in cell B2.

2. Make sure cell **G3** is the active cell, and then type **=** (but do *not* press the Enter or Tab key). When you type the equal sign, Excel knows that you are entering a formula. Any cell that you click from now on will cause Excel to insert the reference of the selected cell into the formula until you complete the formula by pressing the Enter or Tab key or by clicking the Enter button on the Formula bar (refer to Figure 1-14).

3. Click cell **E3**. Note that the cell is highlighted in the same color as the cell reference that now appears in the formula in cell G3.

4. Type ***** to enter the multiplication operator.

5. Click cell **F3** to enter this cell reference, and then press the **Enter** key. Cell G3 now contains the formula =E3*F3 and displays the value $17, which is the total amount of the second order.

Using AutoComplete

As you continue to work with Excel, you may find yourself entering the same text in different rows in the worksheet. To help make entering repetitive text easier, Excel provides the **AutoComplete** feature. Once you enter text in a worksheet, Excel tries to anticipate the text you are about to enter by displaying text that begins with the same letter as a previous entry. For example, two people—David Wu and Carl Ramirez—have ordered a box of navel oranges. You have already entered the data for David Wu's order. When you enter the data for Carl Ramirez's order, you will see how AutoComplete works.

To enter text using AutoComplete:

1. Enter **Carl Ramirez** in cell A4, **900 South Street Crawford, FL 81891** in cell B4 on two separate lines within the cell, and **4/17/2006** in cell C4. Do *not* enter the item for Carl's order yet.

2. Make sure cell **D4** is the active cell, and then type **N**. Note that Excel anticipates the entry by displaying "Navel Oranges," which is text you have already entered beginning with the letter N. See Figure 1-15. At this point, you can accept Excel's suggestion by pressing the Enter or Tab key to complete the text entry and to exit the cell. To override Excel's suggestion, you simply keep typing the text you want to enter into the cell.

| **Figure 1-15** | **Entering text with the AutoComplete feature** |

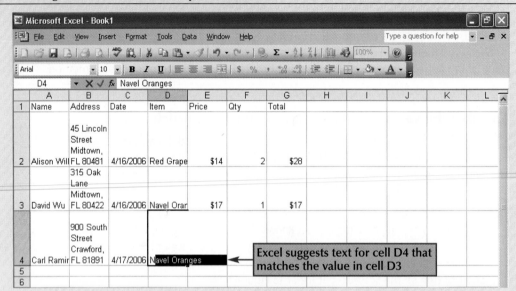

Trouble? If your version of Excel is not set up to use AutoComplete, you will not see the suggested text; therefore you must type "Navel Oranges".

3. Press the **Tab** key to accept Excel's AutoComplete suggestion and to move to cell E4.

4. Type **$17** in cell E4, press the **Tab** key, type **2** in cell F4, and then press the **Tab** key to move to cell G4.

5. Enter **=E4*F4** in cell G4 by typing the formula or by using the point-and-click method. Note that from now on in this text, when you are instructed to "enter" something versus "type" it, use the method that you most prefer; that is, press the Enter key, press the Tab key, or click the Enter button on the Formula bar. Clicking the Enter button not only enters the value in the cell, but also keeps that cell as the active cell.

Excel does not apply AutoComplete to dates or values. However, you can use another feature, AutoFill, to automatically fill in formulas. You'll learn more about AutoFill in the next tutorial.

Now you'll enter the last co-op order into the worksheet.

To enter the last order into the worksheet:

1. Enter **Jerry Dawson** in cell A5, **781 Tree Lane Midtown, FL 80313** in cell B5, **4/18/2006** in cell C5, **Deluxe Combo** in cell D5, **$21** in cell E5, and **4** in cell F5. (Remember to enter the address on two lines.)

2. In cell G5, enter the formula **=E5*F5**. Figure 1-16 shows the completed worksheet.

Four co-op orders entered — Figure 1-16

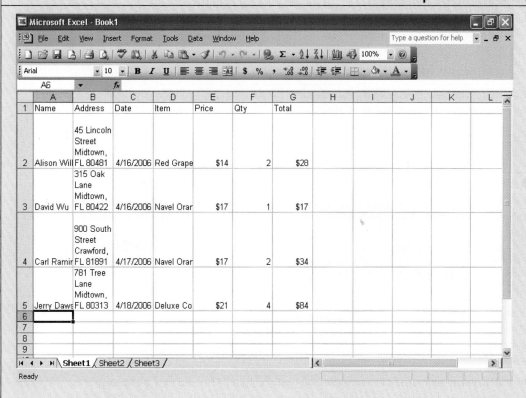

Changing the Size of a Column or Row

The default sizes of the columns and rows in an Excel worksheet may not always accommodate the information you need to enter. You can change the width of one column or multiple columns or the height of one row or multiple rows. Excel provides several methods for changing the width of a column or the height of a row. You can click the dividing line of the column or row, or you can drag the dividing line to change the width of the column or the height of the row. Heights and widths are expressed in terms of the number of characters that can be displayed in the cell, as well as the number of screen pixels, which are small units of measurement that appear as tiny dots on the screen.

Changing the Column Width or Row Height

Reference Window

- Click the column or row heading whose width or height you want to change.
- Click Format on the menu bar, point to Column or Row, and then click Width or Height (or click AutoFit or AutoFit Selection to make the column or row as large as the longest entry of the cells).
- In the Column Width or Row Height dialog box, enter the new column width or row height, and then click the OK button.

or

- Drag the column or row heading dividing line to the right or up to increase the column width or row height, or drag the dividing line to the left or down to decrease the column width or row height.

or

- Double-click the column or row heading dividing line to make the column or row as large as the longest entry of the cells in the column or row.

You'll use the drag technique to increase the width of the columns in which the data display has been truncated. As you drag the dividing line, a ScreenTip appears and displays the column width in characters and pixels.

To change the width of columns in the worksheet:

1. Move the mouse pointer to the dividing line between the column A and column B headings until the pointer changes to ⟷.

2. Click and drag the pointer to the right to a length of about **20** characters (or **145 pixels**). See Figure 1-17.

Figure 1-17	Increasing the width of column A

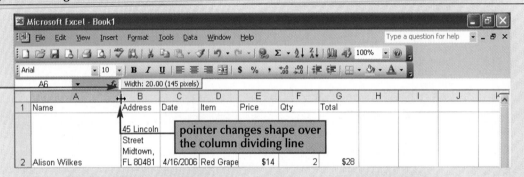

ScreenTip showing the width in characters and pixels

pointer changes shape over the column dividing line

3. Release the mouse button. All the names in column A should now be visible.

   Trouble? If the text in column A is still truncated, drag the dividing line further to the right.

4. Move the mouse pointer to the dividing line between column B and column C until the pointer changes to ⟷, and then increase the width of column B to **25** characters (or **180** pixels).

5. Use your mouse to increase the width of column D to **15** characters (or **110** pixels).

Changing the width of the columns does not affect the height of the rows. However, now that column A is wider and the rows are taller, there is a great deal of empty space. To remove the empty space, you'll resize the rows. Rather than choosing a size for the rows, you'll let Excel make the adjustment automatically. If you double-click the dividing line of a column or row heading, the column width or row height adjusts to match the length of the longest entry in that column or row. You'll use this technique now to modify the height of the second row in the worksheet.

To change the height of the second row:

1. Move the mouse pointer to the dividing line between the second and third rows until the pointer changes to ✛.

2. Double-click the dividing line between the second and third rows. See Figure 1-18.

Changing the height of the second row ◄ Figure 1-18

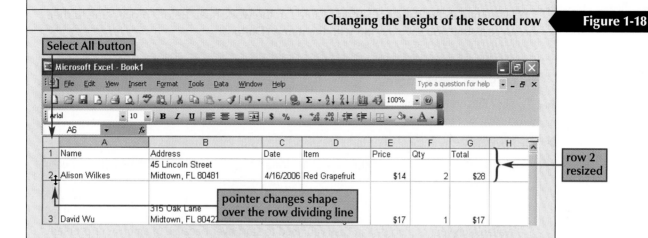

You can continue modifying the height of the remaining rows using this technique, but, for a worksheet containing a large amount of data, that would be extremely time-consuming. Another approach is to select the entire worksheet and then double-click the dividing line between any two row headings. When you do that, Excel changes the height of the rows to accommodate the data in them and reduces the amount of empty space. You can use this approach to resize columns, too.

You can select the entire worksheet by clicking the Select All button. You'll use this approach now to change the height of the remaining rows in the co-op order worksheet.

To change the height of the remaining rows:

1. Click the **Select All** button located at the junction of the row and column headings (see Figure 1-18). The row and column headings are displayed in black or dark blue, and all of the worksheet cells are displayed in light blue, indicating that the entire worksheet has been selected.

2. Move the mouse pointer to a dividing line between any two rows until the pointer changes to ✛.

3. Double-click the dividing line. Excel resizes the height of all the rows.

4. Click cell **A1** to make it the active cell and to remove the blue highlighting from the worksheet. Figure 1-19 shows the revised layout of the sheet.

Adjusting the height of the worksheet rows ◄ Figure 1-19

	A	B	C	D	E	F	G	H
1	Name	Address	Date	Item	Price	Qty	Total	
2	Alison Wilkes	45 Lincoln Street Midtown, FL 80481	4/16/2006	Red Grapefruit	$14	2	$28	
3	David Wu	315 Oak Lane Midtown, FL 80422	4/16/2006	Navel Oranges	$17	1	$17	
4	Carl Ramirez	900 South Street Crawford, FL 81891	4/17/2006	Navel Oranges	$17	2	$34	
5	Jerry Dawson	781 Tree Lane Midtown, FL 80313	4/18/2006	Deluxe Combo	$21	4	$84	
6								
7								
8								

You've entered the data that Sandra wanted in the worksheet. Before proceeding further, she suggests that you save the file with the name "Dalton".

To save the workbook:

▶ **1.** Click **File** on the menu bar, and then click **Save**. The Save As dialog box opens with the current workbook name, which is "Book1," in the File name text box.

▶ **2.** Navigate to the Tutorial.01\Tutorial folder included with your Data Files.

   Trouble? If you don't have the Excel 2003 Data Files, you need to get them before you can proceed. Your instructor will either give you the Data Files or ask you to obtain them from a specified location (such as a network drive). In either case, be sure that you make a backup copy of your Data Files before you start using them, so that the original files will be available on your copied disk in case you need to start over because of an error or problem. If you have any questions about the Data Files, see your instructor or technical support person for assistance.

▶ **3.** Replace the default filename with **Dalton**, make sure that **Microsoft Office Excel Workbook** is displayed in the Save as type list box, and then click the **Save** button. Excel saves the workbook with the name "Dalton" and closes the Save As dialog box. The new workbook name appears in the title bar of the Excel window.

   Trouble? If your computer has been set up to display file extensions, the filename "Dalton.xls" will appear in the title bar.

By default, Excel saves the workbook in Microsoft Excel Workbook format, and for most of the work you will do in this text, you will use this file format. If you are creating a workbook that will be read by applications other than Excel (or earlier versions of Excel), you can save your workbook in a different file format by following these steps:

1. Open the Save or Save As dialog box.
2. Display the location in which you want to save the file, and enter a filename, if necessary.
3. Click the Save as type list arrow, and then select the file format you want to apply.
4. Click the Save button.

Figure 1-20 describes some of the file formats in which you can save your workbooks.

Figure 1-20 ▶ **Some of the formats supported by Excel**

Format	Description
Microsoft Excel 4.0, 5.0, 97, 2000, 2002 Workbook	Saves the workbook in an earlier version of Excel
Single File Web Page	Saves the workbook as a single Web page file (MHTML file) that can be read by Internet Explorer 4.0 or later
Template	Saves the workbook as a template to be used for creating other Excel workbooks
Web Page	Saves the workbook in separate files that are used as the basis for a Web site, in a format that is readable by most browsers
XML Spreadsheet	Saves the workbook as an XML document

Sandra has some other changes to the workbook that she wants you to make. You'll continue working with the worksheet in the next session.

Session 1.1 Quick Check

Review

1. A(n) _____ is the place on the worksheet where a column and row intersect.
2. Cell _____ refers to the intersection of the fourth column and second row.
3. What combination of keys can you press to make A1 the active cell in the worksheet?
4. To make Sheet2 the active worksheet, you _____ .
5. Indicate whether Excel treats the following cell entries as text, a value, or a formula.
   a. 11/09/2006
   b. Net Income
   c. 321
   d. C11*225
   e. 201-19-1121
   f. =D1-D9
   g. 44 Evans Avenue
6. How do you enter multiple lines of text within a cell?
7. What formula would you enter to divide the value in cell E5 by the value in cell E6?

To reinforce the tasks you learned in this session, go to the SAM 2003 Training Companion CD included with this text.

Session 1.2

Working with Ranges

Sandra has had a chance to study your work from the previous session. She likes the layout of her data, but she wants to have a title at the top of the worksheet that displays information about the sheet's contents. To make room for the title, you have to move the contents of the worksheet down a few rows. Before you attempt that, you have to first understand how Excel works with groups of cells.

A group of worksheet cells is called a **cell range**, or just **range**. Ranges can be either adjacent or nonadjacent. An **adjacent range** is a single rectangular block, such as all of the data entered in cells A1 through G5 of the Dalton workbook. A **nonadjacent range** consists of two or more separate adjacent ranges. For example, a nonadjacent range might be composed of the names of the customers in the cell range A1 through A5 and the total price of their orders in the cell range G1 through G5.

Just as a cell reference indicates the location of a cell on the worksheet, a **range reference** indicates the location and size of a cell range. For adjacent ranges, the range reference identifies the cells in the upper-left and lower-right corners of the rectangle, with the individual cell references separated by a colon. For example, the range reference for the order data you entered in the last session was A1:G5 because it included the range of cells from A1 through G5. If the range is nonadjacent, a semicolon separates the rectangular blocks A1:A5 and G1:G5, as in A1:A5;G1:G5. This nonadjacent range references the customer names in the range A1:A5 and the total amounts of their orders in the range G1:G5.

For hands-on practice of key tasks in this session, go to the SAM 2003 Training Companion CD included with this text.

Selecting Ranges

Once you know how to select ranges of cells, you can move and copy the data anywhere in the worksheet or workbook.

Reference Window

Selecting Adjacent or Nonadjacent Ranges of Cells

To select an adjacent range of cells:
- Click a cell in the upper-left corner of the rectangle that comprises the adjacent range.
- Press and hold the left mouse button, and then drag the pointer through the cells you want selected.
- Release the mouse button.

To select a nonadjacent range of cells:
- Select an adjacent range of cells.
- Press and hold the Ctrl key, and then select another adjacent cell range.
- With the Ctrl key still pressed, continue to select other cell ranges until all of the ranges are selected.
- Release the mouse button and the Ctrl key.

To see how to select ranges, you'll start by selecting all of the cells containing order information.

To select the order data:

1. If you took a break at the end of the previous session, make sure that Excel is running and that the Dalton workbook is open.

2. Click cell **A1** on the Sheet1 worksheet, press and hold the left mouse button, and then drag the pointer to cell **G5**.

3. Release the mouse button. All the cells in the range A1:G5 are now highlighted, indicating that they are selected. See Figure 1-21.

Figure 1-21 Selecting the range A1:G5

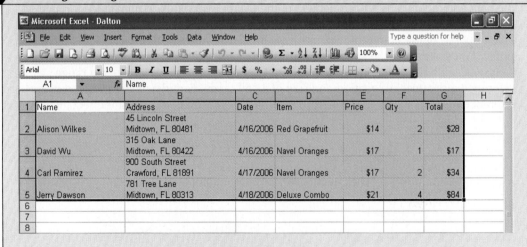

4. Click any cell in the worksheet to deselect the range.

Now try selecting the nonadjacent range A1:A5;G1:G5.

To select the nonadjacent range A1:A5;G1:G5:

▶ **1.** Select the range **A1:A5**, press and hold the **Ctrl** key, select the range **G1:G5**, and then release the mouse button and the Ctrl key. See Figure 1-22 for the selected nonadjacent range.

Selecting the nonadjacent range A1:A5;G1:G5 ◀ **Figure 1-22**

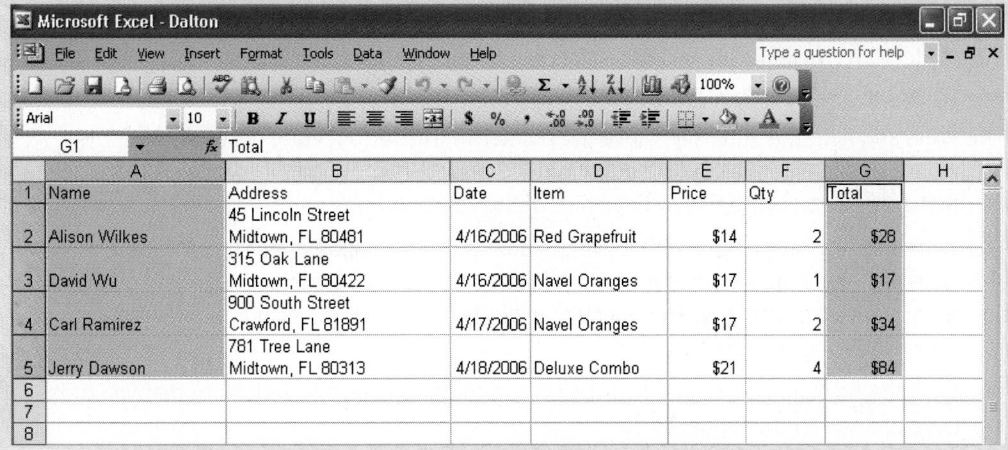

▶ **2.** Click any cell in the worksheet to deselect the range.

Other Selection Techniques

You can also select large cell ranges that extend beyond the borders of the workbook window. When this situation occurs, Excel automatically scrolls the workbook window horizontally or vertically to display additional cells in the worksheet. Selecting a large cell range using the mouse drag technique can be slow and frustrating. For this reason, Excel provides keyboard shortcuts that enable you to quickly select large blocks of data without having to drag through the worksheet to select the necessary cells. Figure 1-23 describes some of these selection techniques.

Other range selection techniques ◀ **Figure 1-23**

To Select...	Action
A large range of cells	Click the first cell in the range, press and hold down the Shift key, and then click the last cell in the range. All of the cells between the first and last cell are selected.
All cells on the worksheet	Click the Select All button, the gray rectangle in the upper-left corner of the worksheet where the row and column headings meet.
All cells in an entire row or column	Click the row or column heading.
A range of cells containing data	Click the cell where you want to begin the selection of the range, press and hold down the Shift key, and then double-click the side of the cell in the direction that you want to extend the selection. Excel selects all adjacent cells that contain data, extending the selection of the range to the first empty cell.

Try some of the techniques described to select ranges of cells in the Dalton workbook.

To select a range of cells using keyboard shortcuts:

▶ 1. Click cell **A1** to make it the active cell.

▶ 2. Press and hold the **Shift** key, click cell **A5**, and then release the Shift key. Note that all of the cells between A1 and A5 are selected.

   Trouble? If the range A1:A5 is not selected, try again, but make sure you hold the Shift key while you click cell A5.

▶ 3. Click cell **A1** to make it the active cell again. Note that you don't have to deselect one range before clicking another cell.

▶ 4. Press and hold the **Shift** key, move the pointer to the bottom edge of cell A1 until the mouse pointer changes to ⳧, and then double-click the bottom edge of cell **A1**. The selection extends to cell A5, the last cell before the empty cell A6.

▶ 5. With the Shift key still pressed, move the pointer to the right edge of the selection until, once again, the pointer changes to ⳧, double-click the right edge of the selection, and then release the Shift key. The selection extends to the last nonblank column in the worksheet, selecting the range A1:G5.

▶ 6. Click the **A** column heading. All of the cells in column A are selected. Note that you didn't have to deselect the range A1:G5.

▶ 7. Click the **1** row heading. All of the cells in the first row are selected.

Moving a Selection of Cells

Now that you know various ways to select a range of cells, you can move the co-op data down a few rows in the worksheet. To move a cell range, you first select it; then you position the pointer over the selection border, and drag the selection to a new location. Try this technique to move the order data from the cell range A1:G5 to the cell range A5:G9.

To move the order data:

▶ 1. Select the range **A1:G5**, and then move the pointer over the bottom border of the selection until the pointer changes to ⳧.

▶ 2. Press and hold the left mouse button, changing the pointer to ⬚, and then drag the selection down four rows. A ScreenTip appears indicating the new range reference of the selection. See Figure 1-24.

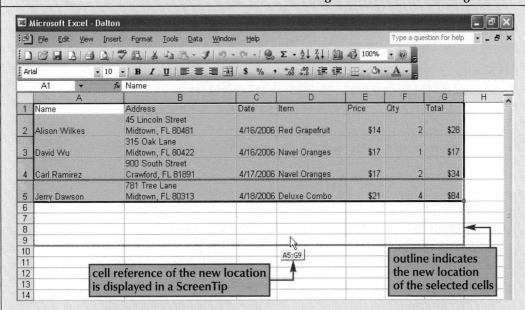

3. When the ScreenTip displays "A5:G9," release the left mouse button. The order data is now moved to range A5:G9.

   Trouble? If you selected the wrong range or moved the selection to the wrong location, click the Undo button 🔄 on the Standard toolbar, and then repeat Steps 1 through 3.

4. Click cell **A1** to remove the selection and to make cell A1 the active cell so you can enter the new titles in the worksheet.

5. Type **Dalton Food Co-op** in cell A1, **List of Orders** in cell A2, **April, 2006** in cell A3, and then press the **Enter** key. Note that moving the cell range had no impact on the values in the worksheet; the values shown by the formulas in column G are also unchanged. This is because Excel automatically updated the cell references in the formulas to reflect the new location of the data. To confirm this, you'll examine the formula in cell G6.

6. Click cell **G6** and observe what is displayed in the Formula bar. The formula in cell G6 is now *=E6*F6*. Recall that when you originally entered Alison Wilke's order, the formula for this cell was *=E2*G2* because the order was originally placed in the second row of the worksheet. When you moved the data, Excel automatically updated the formula to reflect the new location of Alison Wilke's order.

The technique you used to move the cell range is called "drag and drop." You can also use the drag-and-drop technique to copy a cell range. Copying a range of cells is similar to moving a range, except that you must press the Ctrl key while you drag the selection to its new location. A copy of the original data will then appear at the location of the pointer when you release the mouse button. You'll learn more about copying and pasting in the next two tutorials.

A cell range can also be moved from one worksheet in the workbook to another. To do this, press and hold the Alt key and then drag the selection over the sheet tab of the new worksheet. Excel will automatically make that worksheet the active sheet, so you can drag the selection into its new location on the worksheet.

Calculating Sums with AutoSum

Sandra reminds you that she wants the worksheet to also display summary information about the co-op orders, including the total number of items ordered and the amount of revenue generated from those orders. You could calculate the total quantity and total revenue using the formulas =F6+F7+F8+F9 and =G6+G7+G8+G9.

One problem with this approach is that as Sandra adds new orders to the worksheet, you will have to constantly update these formulas, adding cell references for the new orders. As you add more orders, the length of these two expressions will increase dramatically, increasing the possibility of making errors in the formulas.

One way to solve this problem is to use a **function**, which is a predefined formula that performs calculations using specific values. You will learn about and work with functions in more detail in the next tutorial. In this case, you'll insert one of Excel's most commonly used Financial functions, the SUM function, using the AutoSum button on the Standard toolbar. The **AutoSum** feature is a quick and convenient way to enter the SUM function. You use the **SUM function** to calculate the sum of values in a cell range. In this case, you want to calculate the sum of the values in the range F6:F9 and in the range G6:G9.

Now, you'll use AutoSum to calculate the total quantity and total revenue of the ordered items, putting these values in cells F10 and G10.

To calculate the total order quantity and revenue:

1. Click cell **A10**, type **TOTAL**, and then press the **Tab** key five times to move to cell F10.

2. With cell F10 as the active cell, click the **AutoSum** button Σ on the Standard toolbar. Excel automatically inserts the SUM function in the active cell and selects a cell range that it anticipates is the range of cells to be summed. See Figure 1-25. A ScreenTip also appears, showing the form of the SUM function. The mode indicator in the status bar changes to Point, indicating that you can point to the cell references. In this case, the range that Excel has selected for you is the correct range of cells, so all you need to do is indicate that you accept the range. You can complete the function and move to the next cell by pressing the Tab key.

Using the AutoSum button ◄ **Figure 1-25**

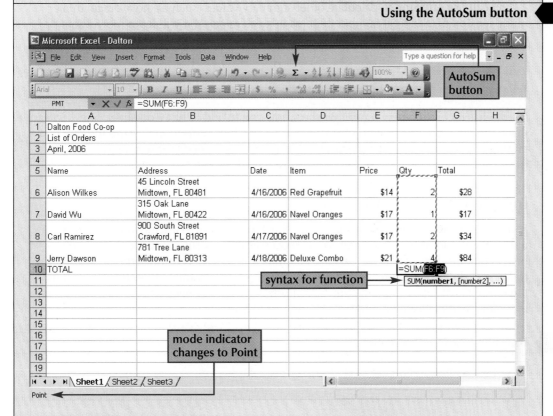

3. Press the **Tab** key to move to cell G10. The result of the formula *=SUM(F6:F9)* appears in cell F10, and you are in position to calculate the next set of values.

4. Click the **AutoSum** button ∑ on the Standard toolbar to enter the SUM function in cell G10, and then press the **Enter** key to complete the formula *=SUM(G6:G9)*, accepting the range that Excel highlighted. See Figure 1-26. Nine items were sold, for a total of $163.

Calculating the total quantity and total income for the co-op ◄ **Figure 1-26**

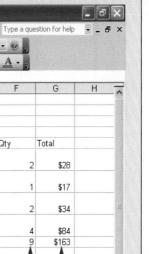

You can use AutoSum to calculate other summary values, such as the average, minimum, maximum, and total number of items in a cell range. You will learn more about using AutoSum to summarize values in Tutorial 2.

Working with Rows and Columns

Sandra has received a new order that she wants you to add to her worksheet. She wants to insert the new order right after Jerry Dawson's order, but wants to make sure the row containing the total values is still the last row. To do this, you need to insert a new row into the worksheet between row 9 and row 10.

Inserting a Row or Column

You can insert rows and columns in a worksheet, or you can insert individual cells within a row or column. When you insert rows, Excel shifts the existing rows down. When you insert columns, Excel shifts the existing columns to the right. If you insert cells within a row, Excel shifts the existing cells down; if you insert cells within a column, Excel shifts the existing cells to the right. Figure 1-27 illustrates what happens when you insert a row, a column, and cells within a row and within a column.

Figure 1-27 | **Inserting new rows and columns**

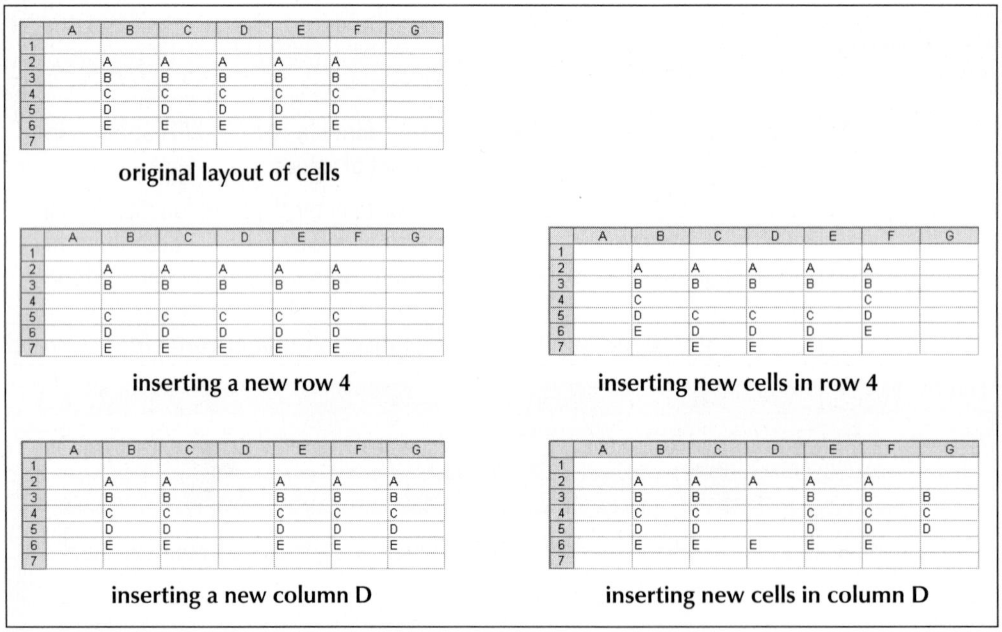

original layout of cells

inserting a new row 4

inserting new cells in row 4

inserting a new column D

inserting new cells in column D

You can use the Insert menu to insert cells, rows, and columns. You can also use the right-click method to display a shortcut menu that provides the Insert command, which opens the Insert dialog box.

Inserting a Row or Column into a Worksheet

- Select a cell where you want to insert the new row or column.
- Click Insert on the menu bar, and then click Rows or Columns.

or

- Right-click a cell where you want to insert a new row or column, and then click Insert on the shortcut menu.
- In the Insert dialog box, click the Entire row or Entire column option button, and then click the OK button.

To insert multiple rows or columns, you select a cell range that contains multiple rows or columns before applying the Insert command. For example, to insert two new blank rows, select two rows or any portion of two rows. To insert three blank columns, select three columns or any portion of three columns.

Sometimes you might need to insert individual cells, rather than an entire row or column, into a worksheet. To insert cells into a row or column, you must select the number of cells you want to insert, and then open the Insert dialog box. In this dialog box you indicate how Excel should shift the existing cells to accommodate the cells you want to insert.

Inserting Cells into a Worksheet

- Select a cell range equal to the number of cells you want to insert.
- Click Insert on the menu bar, and then click Cells; or right-click the selected range, and then click Insert on the shortcut menu.
- Click the Shift cells right option button to insert the new cells into the row, or click the Shift cells down button to insert the new cells into the column.

Sandra wants the data for the new order to be entered above the TOTAL row, row 10. You'll use the right-click method to insert a new row 10, and then you'll enter the data.

To insert a new row 10:

▸ **1.** Right-click cell **A10**, which is where you want to insert the new row.

▸ **2.** Click **Insert** on the shortcut menu. The Insert dialog box opens. See Figure 1-28.

Insert dialog box | **Figure 1-28**

▸ **3.** Click the **Entire row** option button, and then click the **OK** button. Excel inserts a new row 10 and shifts the calculations of the total values down one row.

▸ **4.** Enter the data for Karen Paulson's order into row 10, as shown in Figure 1-29. Make sure that you press the Tab key to move from cell to cell and press the Alt + Enter keys to enter the address on two lines within cell B10.

Figure 1-29 — **Data entered in the new row 10**

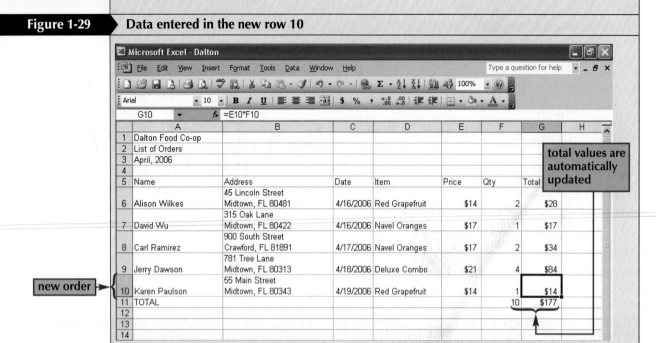

Note that Excel automatically inserts the formula *=E10*F10* into cell G10 for you. Excel recognizes that you are inserting a new set of values into a list of values and assumes that you intend to use the same formulas for the new order that you used for the previous ones. Also note that the calculations of the total quantity of items ordered and the total revenue from those orders have been updated. The functions now calculate the sums in the cell ranges F6:F10 and G6:G10. You'll learn more about how such formulas are automatically adjusted by Excel in the next tutorial.

Deleting a Row or Column

Sandra has also learned that David Wu has canceled his co-op order. You have two options for removing data from a worksheet. If you simply want to erase the contents of a cell, you can **clear** the cell, without actually removing the cell from the worksheet. If you want to remove not only the contents of the cells from the worksheet, but also the cells themselves, you can **delete** a cell range, and Excel then shifts the contents of the adjacent cells into the location of the deleted cells.

To clear the contents of a cell or range of cells, you select the range and then select the Clear command on the Edit menu or on the shortcut menu that you display by right-clicking the selection. Pressing the Delete key on the keyboard also clears the contents of the selected cells, without removing the cells themselves. To delete cells and their contents, you select the range and then choose the Delete command on the Edit menu, or right-click the selected cells, and click Delete on the shortcut menu. To adjust the adjacent cells, Excel opens the Delete Cells dialog box, which you can select to shift the remaining cells left or up, or choose to delete the entire row.

Because David Wu has canceled his order, you'll delete it from the worksheet.

To delete the row that contains David Wu's order:

1. Click the row heading for row **7**, which contains the data you want to delete.

2. Click **Edit** on the menu bar, and then click **Delete**. Excel deletes the row and shifts the next row up. See Figure 1-30. The total calculations in cells F10 and G10 are automatically updated to reflect the fact that David Wu's order has been deleted.

Deleting a row from the worksheet ◀ **Figure 1-30**

Editing Your Worksheet

When you work in Excel, you might make mistakes that you want to correct or undo. Sandra has noticed such a mistake in the Dalton workbook. The price for the Deluxe Combo box should be $23, not $21. You could simply clear the value in cell E8 and then type the correct value. However, there may be times when you will not want to change the entire contents of a cell, but merely edit a portion of the entry, especially if the cell contains a large block of text or a complicated formula. To edit the cell contents, you need to work in **edit mode**.

When you are working in edit mode, some of the keyboard shortcuts you've been using perform differently. For example, the Home, Delete, Backspace, and End keys do not move the insertion point to different cells in the worksheet; rather they move the insertion point to different locations within the cell. The Home key, for example, moves the insertion point to the beginning of whatever content has been entered into the cell. The End key moves the insertion point to the end of the cell's content. The left and right arrow keys move the insertion point backward and forward through the cell's content. The Backspace key deletes the character immediately to the left of the insertion point, and the Delete key deletes the character to the right of the insertion point.

Editing a Cell

- Switch to edit mode by double-clicking the cell, clicking the cell and pressing the F2 key, or clicking the cell and then clicking in the Formula bar.
- Use the Home, End, ←, or → keys to move the insertion point within the cell's content, or use the Delete and Backspace keys to erase characters.
- Press the Enter key when finished, or if you are working in the Formula bar, click the Enter button.

You'll switch to edit mode and then change the value in cell E8.

To edit the value in cell E8:

1. Double-click cell **E8**. Note that the mode indicator in the status bar switches from Ready to Edit. Also note that the value 21 appears in the cell, not $21. This is because the cell contains a numeric value, not a text string. The dollar sign ($) is used to format the value. You'll learn more about formats in Tutorial 3.

2. Press the **End** key to move the blinking insertion point to the end of the cell.

3. Press the **Backspace** key once to delete the 1 character, type **3** to update the value, and then press the **Enter** key to accept the change. The value $23 appears in cell E8, and the total amount of this order in cell G8 changes to $92. Note that the mode indicator on the status bar switches back to Ready.

If you make a mistake as you type in edit mode, you can press the Esc key or click the Cancel button on the Formula bar to cancel all changes you made while in edit mode.

Undoing an Action

As you revise your worksheet, you may find that you need to undo one of your changes. To undo an action, click the Undo button on the Standard toolbar. As you work, Excel maintains a list of your actions, so you can undo most of the actions you perform in your workbook during the current session. To reverse more than one action, click the list arrow next to the Undo button and click the action you want to undo from the list. To see how this works, you'll use the Undo button to remove the edit you just made to cell E8.

To undo your last action:

1. Click the **Undo** button ⟲ on the Standard toolbar. The value $21 appears again in cell E8, indicating that your last action, editing the value in this cell, has been undone.

If you find that you have gone too far in undoing your previous actions, you can go forward in the action list and redo those actions. To redo an action, you click the Redo button on the Standard toolbar. Now you'll use the Redo button to return the value in cell E8 to $23.

To redo your last action:

1. Click the **Redo** button ⟳ on the Standard toolbar. The value in cell E8 changes back to $23.

Through the use of edit mode and the Undo and Redo buttons, you should be able to correct almost any mistake you make in your Excel workbook. The Undo and Redo commands are also available on the Edit menu or by using the shortcut keys Ctrl + Z, to undo an action, and Ctrl + Y, to redo an action.

Working with Worksheets

By default, Excel workbooks contain three worksheets, labeled Sheet1, Sheet2, and Sheet3. You can add new worksheets or remove old ones. You can also give your worksheets more descriptive names. In the Dalton workbook, there is no data entered in the Sheet2 or Sheet3 worksheets. Sandra suggests that you remove these sheets from the workbook.

Adding and Removing Worksheets

To delete a worksheet, you first select its sheet tab to make the worksheet the active sheet; then right-click the sheet tab and choose Delete from the shortcut menu. Try this now by deleting the Sheet2 and Sheet3 worksheets.

To delete the Sheet2 and Sheet3 worksheets:

1. Click the **Sheet2** tab to make Sheet2 the active sheet.

2. Right-click the sheet tab, and then click **Delete** on the shortcut menu. Sheet2 is deleted and Sheet3 becomes the active sheet.

3. Right-click the **Sheet3** tab, and then click **Delete**. There is now only one worksheet in the workbook.

After you delete the two unused sheets, Sandra informs you that she wants to include a description of the workbook's content and purpose. In other words, Sandra wants to include a **documentation sheet**, a worksheet that provides information about the content and purpose of the workbook. A documentation sheet can be any information that you feel is important, for example, the name of the person who created the workbook or instructions on how to use the workbook. A documentation sheet is a valuable element if you intend to share the workbook with others. The documentation sheet is often the first worksheet in the workbook, though in this case, Sandra wants to place it at the end of the workbook.

To insert a new worksheet, you can either use the Worksheet command on the Insert menu or the right-click method. Both methods insert a new worksheet *before* the active sheet.

To insert a new worksheet in the workbook:

1. Click **Insert** on the menu bar, and then click **Worksheet**. A new worksheet with the name "Sheet4" is placed at the beginning of your workbook. Your worksheet might be named Sheet2 or another name.

Sandra wants the documentation sheet to include the following information:

- The name of the co-op
- The date that this workbook was originally created
- The person who created the workbook
- The purpose of the workbook

You'll add this information to the new sheet in the Dalton workbook.

To insert the documentation information in the new worksheet:

▶ **1.** Click cell **A1**, if necessary, type **Dalton Food Co-op**, and then press the **Enter** key twice.

▶ **2.** Type **Date:** in cell A3, and then press the **Tab** key.

▶ **3.** Enter the *current date* in cell B3, and then press the **Enter** key.

▶ **4.** Type **Created By:** in cell A4, and then press the **Tab** key.

▶ **5.** Enter *your name* in cell B4, and then press the **Enter** key.

▶ **6.** Type **Purpose:** in cell A5, and then press the **Tab** key.

▶ **7.** Type **To enter orders for the Dalton Food Co-op** in cell B5, and then press the **Enter** key.

▶ **8.** Increase the width of column A to **15** characters (**110** pixels). Figure 1-31 shows the completed documentation sheet.

Figure 1-31 ▶ **Completed documentation sheet**

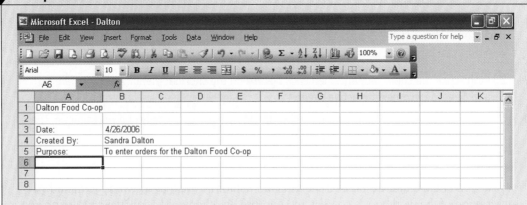

Renaming a Worksheet

The current sheet names, "Sheet4" and "Sheet1," are not very descriptive. Sandra suggests that you rename Sheet4 "Documentation" and Sheet1 "Orders." To rename a worksheet, you double-click the sheet tab to select the sheet name, and then you type a new name for the sheet. Sheet names cannot exceed 31 characters in length, including blank spaces.

To rename the worksheets:

▶ **1.** Double-click the **Sheet4** tab. Note that the name of the sheet is selected.

▶ **2.** Type **Documentation** and then press the **Enter** key. The width of the sheet tab adjusts to the length of the name you type.

▶ **3.** Double-click the **Sheet1** tab.

▶ **4.** Type **Orders** and then press the **Enter** key. Both worksheets are renamed.

Moving a Worksheet

You can change the placement of the worksheets in the workbook. To move the position of a worksheet in the workbook, click the sheet tab and then drag and drop it to a new location relative to the other worksheets. You can also make a copy of a worksheet using a similar drag-and-drop technique. To create a copy of a worksheet, press the Ctrl key as you drag and drop the sheet tab of the worksheet you want duplicated.

Moving or Copying a Worksheet

Reference Window

- Click the sheet tab of the worksheet you want to move (or copy).
- Drag the sheet tab along the row of sheet tabs until the small arrow appears in the new location. To create a copy of the worksheet, press and hold the Ctrl key as you drag the sheet tab to the new location.
- Release the mouse button. Release the Ctrl key if necessary.

Try this now by switching the location of the Documentation and Orders worksheets.

To reposition the worksheets:

1. Click the **Orders** tab, and then press and hold the left mouse button so the pointer changes to ⬚ and a small arrow appears in the upper-left corner of the tab.

2. Drag the pointer to the left of the sheet tab for the Documentation sheet, and then release the mouse button. The Documentation sheet is now the second sheet in the workbook, but Sandra would prefer that the documentation sheet be the first sheet.

3. Click the **Orders** tab, and then drag the sheet tab to the right of the Documentation sheet tab to place it back in its original location.

When you create a copy of a worksheet, you move the copy of the original worksheet to a new location, while the original sheet remains at its initial position.

Using the Spell Checker

One of Excel's editing tools is the **Spell Checker**. This feature checks the words in the workbook against the program's internal dictionary. If the Spell Checker comes across a word not in its dictionary, it displays the word in a dialog box along with a list of suggested replacements. You can replace the word with one from the list, or you can choose to ignore the word and go to the next word that might be misspelled. You can also add the word to the dictionary to prevent it from being flagged in the future. There are words that are not included in the online dictionary (for example, some uncommon personal names or last names). The Spell Checker will stop at these words. You can then choose to ignore all occurrences of the word, change the word, or add the word to the dictionary. Excel checks the spelling on the current worksheet only.

To see how the Spell Checker works, you'll make an intentional spelling error in the Orders worksheet.

To check the spelling in the Orders sheet:

▶ 1. Make sure the Orders sheet is the active sheet, and then click cell **G5**. You will enter the error in this cell.

▶ 2. Type **Totale** and then click cell **A1**. The Spell Checker always starts at the active cell in the worksheet. You can start from other cells, and the Spell Checker will cycle back to the first cell in the worksheet to continue checking each cell for spelling errors. However, you will find it helpful and more efficient to begin spell checking with the first cell in the sheet, cell A1.

▶ 3. Click the **Spelling** button 🔡 on the Standard toolbar. The Spelling dialog box opens, with the first word that the spell checker does not recognize, "Totale." See Figure 1-32.

| **Figure 1-32** | Spelling dialog box |

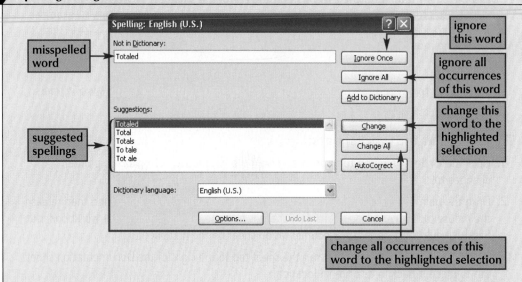

▶ 4. Click **Total** in the list of suggestions, and then click the **Change** button. The word "Totale" changes to "Total," and then Spell Checker continues to look for other potential spelling errors. There shouldn't be any other errors in this workbook.

Trouble? If there are any other errors (you may have misspelled a name, address, or item), fix them before continuing to the next step.

▶ 5. Click the **OK** button to close the Spell Checker.

Previewing and Printing a Worksheet

Sandra would like a printed hard copy of the Dalton workbook for her records. You can print the contents of your workbook either by using the Print command on the File menu or by clicking the Print button on the Standard toolbar. If you use the Print command, Excel opens the Print dialog box in which you can specify which worksheets you want to print, the number of copies, and the print quality. If you click the Print button, your worksheet will print using the options already set in the Print dialog box. If you want to change a setting, you must open the Print dialog box using the File menu.

Before sending a worksheet to the printer, you should preview how the worksheet will appear as a printed page. You can display the worksheet in the Print Preview window either by selecting the Print Preview command on the File menu or by clicking the Print Preview button on the Standard toolbar. You can also click the Preview button in the Print dialog box. Previewing the printout is a helpful way to avoid printing errors.

If you are printing to a shared printer on a network, other people might be sending print jobs at the same time you do. To avoid confusion, you will print the contents of both the Documentation sheet and the Orders sheet. You will use the Print command on the File menu because you need to print the entire workbook and not just the active worksheet (which is the default print setting).

To open the Print dialog box:

▶ **1.** Click **File** on the menu bar, and then click **Print** to open the Print dialog box.

▶ **2.** Click the **Name** list box, and then select the printer to which you want to print, if it is not already selected.

   Now you need to select what to print. To print the complete workbook, select the Entire workbook option button. To print the active worksheet, select the Active sheet(s) option button. To print the selected cells on the active sheet, click the Selection option button.

▶ **3.** Click the **Entire workbook** option button.

▶ **4.** Make sure **1** appears in the Number of copies list box, since you only need to print one copy of the workbook. Figure 1-33 shows the Print dialog box.

Print dialog box ◀ Figure 1-33

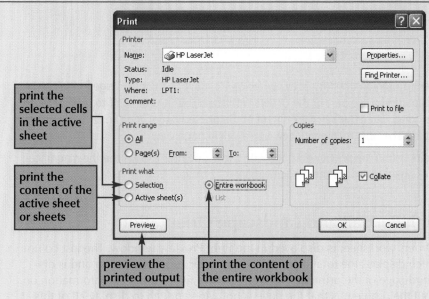

print the selected cells in the active sheet

print the content of the active sheet or sheets

preview the printed output

print the content of the entire workbook

Next you will preview the worksheet to ensure that it looks correct before printing it.

To preview the workbook before printing it:

▶ **1.** Click the **Preview** button in the Print dialog box. Excel displays a preview of the first full page of the worksheet, in this case the Documentation sheet, as it will appear printed. As you can see from the status bar in Figure 1-34, this is the first of three pages.

   Trouble? If the status bar on your screen indicates that there are just two pages, you can still complete the steps.

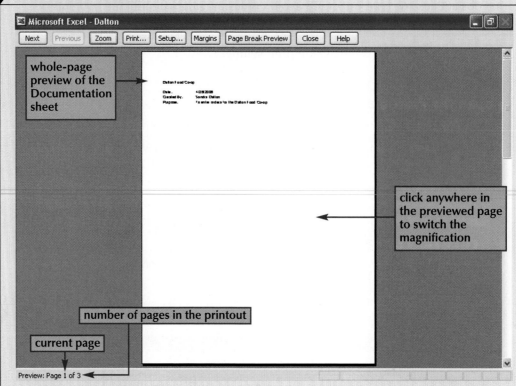

Figure 1-34 ▶ **Print Preview window**

whole-page preview of the Documentation sheet

click anywhere in the previewed page to switch the magnification

number of pages in the printout

current page

Preview: Page 1 of 3

▶ **2.** Click the **Next** button on the Print Preview toolbar to move to the next page in the preview. On this page you see part of the Orders worksheet, but it is difficult to read because the text is so small. To better see the content of the printed page, you can click the preview page to switch between a magnified view and a whole-page view.

▶ **3.** Click anywhere within the previewed page with the 🔍 pointer to increase the magnification, and click again to reduce the magnification.

Working with Portrait and Landscape Orientation

Not all of the Orders worksheet is displayed in the Print Preview window. The last column in the sheet, which displays the total amount of each order, has been cut off and is displayed on the third page of the printout. Naturally Sandra wants all of the information on a single sheet, but the problem is that the page is not wide enough to display all of this information. One way of solving this problem is to change the orientation of the page. There are two types of page orientations: portrait and landscape. In **portrait orientation** the page is taller than it is wide. In **landscape orientation** the page is wider than it is tall. In many cases, you will want to print your worksheets in landscape orientation. You'll choose this option for the Orders worksheet.

To print in landscape orientation:

▶ **1.** Click the **Setup** button on the Print Preview toolbar. The Page Setup dialog box opens.

▶ **2.** Verify that the Page tab is selected in the dialog box, and then click the **Landscape** option button. See Figure 1-35.

Print Setup dialog box ◄ **Figure 1-35**

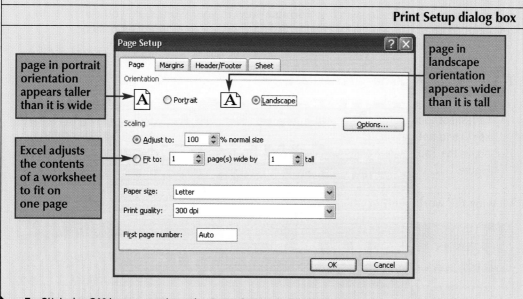

3. Click the **OK** button to close the Page Setup dialog box.

4. If necessary, click anywhere within the previewed page to switch the magnification back to a whole-page view. As shown in Figure 1-36, the entire Orders worksheet is now displayed on the second (and last) page of this printout.

Orders sheet in landscape orientation ◄ **Figure 1-36**

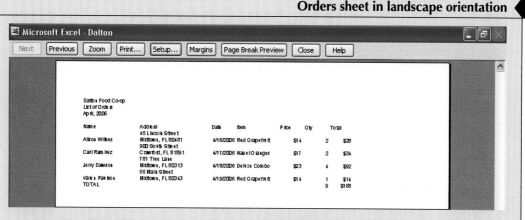

5. Click the **Print** button on the Print Preview toolbar to print the workbook and close the Print Preview window.

Note that the Documentation sheet is printed in portrait orientation, whereas the Orders worksheet is printed in landscape orientation. Changing the orientation only affects the worksheet currently displayed in the Print Preview window; it does not apply to other sheets in the workbook.

Printing the Worksheet Formulas

Sandra examines the printout and notices that none of the formulas are displayed. This is to be expected since most of the time you're only interested in the final results and not the formulas used to calculate those results. In some cases, you will want to view the formulas used in developing your workbook. This is particularly useful in situations where the results were not what you expected, and you want to examine the formulas to see if a mistake has been made. To switch to **Formula view** in your workbook, you can press the keyboard shortcut Ctrl + grave accent (`). Try this now for the Orders worksheet.

To view the worksheet formulas:

1. With the Orders worksheet active, press the **Ctrl + `** (grave accent) keys and then scroll the worksheet to the left so columns F and G are visible. (Make sure you press the grave accent key (`) and not the single quotation mark key ('). The grave accent key is usually located above the Tab key on your keyboard.) Excel displays the formulas in columns F and G. See Figure 1-37.

Figure 1-37 ▶ **Viewing the worksheet formulas**

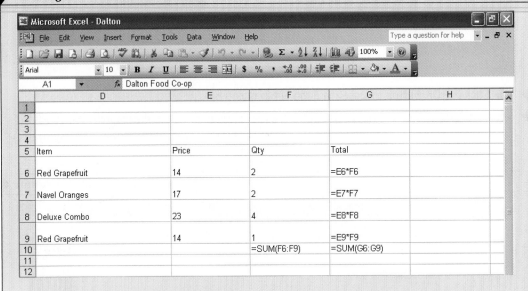

Trouble? If the Formula Auditing toolbar appears, close the toolbar.

Note that the column widths have been changed. Excel does this automatically to ensure that the entire formula can be displayed within each cell. These changed column widths will not affect the normal view of your worksheet as long as you don't change the column widths while in Formula view.

Sandra asks you to print a copy of the worksheet with the formulas displayed. First, you'll preview the worksheet.

2. Click the **Print Preview** button ⬚ on the Standard toolbar. Excel displays a preview of the Orders worksheet in Formula view. Not all of the contents of the worksheet in this view are displayed on a single page. To fit the printout to a single page, you will change the setup of the page using the Page Setup dialog box.

3. Click the **Setup** button on the Print Preview toolbar. The Page Setup dialog box opens.

4. Click the **Fit to** option button to fit the Orders worksheet on one page, and then click the **OK** button. The Formula view of the Orders worksheet should now fit on a single page.

5. Click the **Print** button on the Print Preview toolbar to print the worksheet and close the Print Preview window.

Trouble? If the Print Preview window closes and the Print dialog box opens, click the OK button to print the worksheet.

As you may have noticed while you were working in Print Preview and the Page Setup dialog box, there are a lot of options for choosing what to print and how to print. You'll examine more of these options in Tutorial 3. For now, you can switch the Orders worksheet back to Normal view and save and then close the file.

To complete your work:

1. Press the **Ctrl +`** (grave accent) keys to switch the worksheet back to Normal view. The keyboard shortcut Ctrl + ` (grave accent) works as a toggle, so you can display or hide the formulas by pressing this combination of keys.

2. Save your changes to the Dalton workbook, and then close it.

You give Sandra the hard copy of the Dalton workbook. If she needs to add new information to the workbook or if she needs you to make further changes to the structure of the workbook, she'll contact you.

Session 1.2 Quick Check

1. Describe the two types of cell ranges in Excel.
2. How do you write the cell reference for the rectangular group of cells that extends from cell A5 through cell F8?
3. The _____ button provides a quick way to enter the SUM function.
4. When you insert a new row into a worksheet, the existing rows are shifted
   _____.
5. When you insert a new column into a worksheet, the existing columns are shifted
   _____.
6. How do you change the name of a worksheet?
7. How does clearing a cell differ from deleting a cell?
8. What keyboard shortcut do you press to display the worksheet formulas?

Review

To reinforce the tasks you learned in this session, go to the SAM 2003 Training Companion CD included with this text.

Tutorial Summary

Review

In this tutorial, you learned the basics of spreadsheets and Excel. You learned about the major components of the Excel window. You also learned how to navigate within a worksheet and between worksheets in an Excel workbook. You learned how to enter text, dates, values, and formulas into a worksheet and were introduced to functions using the AutoSum button. Within the workbook, you practiced selecting and moving cell ranges. You saw how to insert new rows and columns into a workbook and how to modify the size of a column or row. You learned how to create new worksheets, rename them, and move them around the workbook. You learned how to check the spelling in a workbook, and finally, you learned how to print the contents of a workbook in different orientations and how to print the formulas in that workbook.

Key Terms

active cell	edit mode	sheet
adjacent range	formula	sheet tab
argument	Formula bar	Spell Checker
arithmetic operator	Formula view	spreadsheet
AutoComplete	function	SUM function
AutoSum	landscape orientation	tab scrolling buttons
cell	Name box	value
cell range	nonadjacent range	what-if analysis
cell reference	order of precedence	workbook
clear	portrait orientation	workbook window
column	range	worksheet
delete	range reference	worksheet window
documentation sheet	row	

Practice

Practice the skills you learned in the tutorial using the same case scenario.

Review Assignments

There are no Data Files needed for the Review Assignments.

Sandra has another set of orders she wants you to enter into a new Excel workbook. The data is shown in Figure 1-38.

Figure 1-38

Name	Address	Date	Item	Price	Qty
Wendy Battle	313 Oak Street Midtown, FL 80481 (833) 555-1284	5/1/2006	Deluxe Combo	$23	2
Eugene Burch	25 Fourth Street Cabot, FL 81121 (833) 555-3331	5/1/2006	Red Grapefruit	$14	4
Nicole Sweeny	312 Olive Street Midtown, FL 81241 (833) 555-9811	5/3/2006	Deluxe Combo	$23	1
Amy Yang	315 Maple Street Midtown, FL 80440 (833) 555-3881	5/4/2006	Navel Oranges	$17	3

Note that Sandra has added the phone numbers of the customers to her data. She wants the phone numbers entered into the customer address cell, but on a different line within that cell. To complete this task:

1. Start Excel and open a blank workbook. In the range A1:F5, enter the labels and data from Figure 1-38. Make sure that the address information is inserted with the street address on the first line; the city, state, and ZIP code on the second line; and the phone number on the third line.
2. In cell G1, enter the label "Total."
3. In the cells below G1, enter formulas to calculate the total amount of each order.
4. In cell A6, enter the label "TOTAL."

5. In cell F6, use the AutoSum button to calculate the total quantity of items ordered, and in cell G6, use the AutoSum button to calculate the total revenue generated by these orders.

6. Move sales data from the range A1:G6 to the range A5:G10.

7. In cell A1, enter the text "Dalton Food Co-op." In cell A2, enter the text "List of Orders." In cell A3, enter the text "May, 2006."

8. Change the width of columns A and B to 20 characters (or 145 pixels) each. Change the width of column D to 15 characters (or 110 pixels). Change the width of column G to 10 characters (or 75 pixels).

9. Select all of the cells in the worksheet, and then reduce the amount of empty space in the rows by reducing the row height to the height of the data contained in the rows.

10. Change the name of the worksheet to "Orders".

11. Create a worksheet named "Documentation" at the beginning of the workbook and, in the Documentation sheet, enter the following:
    - Cell A1: Dalton Food Co-op
    - Cell A3: Date:
    - Cell B3: *current date*
    - Cell A4: Created By:
    - Cell B4: *your name*
    - Cell A5: Purpose:
    - Cell B5: To enter May orders for the Dalton Food Co-op

12. Increase the width of column A in the Documentation worksheet to 20 characters.

13. Check the spelling on both worksheets, correcting any errors found.

14. Delete any empty worksheets from the workbook.

15. Print the contents of the workbook with the Documentation sheet in portrait orientation and the Orders worksheet in landscape orientation.

16. Display the formulas in the Orders worksheet. Preview the worksheet before printing it, and set up the worksheet to print as a single page.

17. Save the workbook as **Dalton2** in the Tutorial.01\Review folder included with your Data Files.

18. Insert the following new order in the Orders worksheet directly below Amy Yang's order:
    - Name: Chad Reynolds
    - Address: 100 School Lane
      Midtown, FL 80411
      (833) 555-4425
    - Date: 5/5/2006
    - Item: Navel Oranges
    - Price: $17
    - Qty: 2

19. Remove Amy Yang's order from the worksheet, and change the quantity ordered by Eugene Burch from 4 to 3.

20. Check the spelling in the Orders worksheet again, correcting any errors found.

21. Print the contents and formulas of the Orders worksheet again.

22. Save the workbook as **Dalton3** in the Tutorial.01\Review folder, and then close the workbook.

Case Problem 1

Data File needed for this Case Problem: Altac1.xls

Altac Bicycles   Deborah York is a financial consultant for Altac Bicycles, an online seller of bicycles and bicycle equipment. She has entered some financial information in an Excel workbook, which she needs for a report she is writing. She has asked that you enter the remaining data and some formulas to complete the workbook. To complete this task:

1. Open the **Altac1** workbook located in the Tutorial.01\Cases folder included with your Data Files, and then save the workbook as **Altac2** in the same folder.
2. Insert two rows at the top of the Sheet1 worksheet, and then enter the following text on two separate lines within cell A1:
   Altac Bicycles
   Financial Data*
3. Insert five rows below the Expenses label in row 9, and then enter the following labels and data in the appropriate cells in columns B, C, D, and E, beginning on row 10:

Figure 1-39

Research	1,602	1,481	1,392
Sales and Marketing	2,631	2,012	1,840
Administrative	521	410	324
Research and Development	491	404	281
Total Operating Expenses			

4. Increase the width of column A to 18 characters and the width of column B to 25 characters. Decrease the height of row 1 to 30.
5. Rename Sheet1 "Financial Data".
6. Using the AutoSum feature, calculate the total operating expenses for each year.
7. For each year, enter formulas that calculate the following values:
   - gross margin, which is the difference between the net sales and the cost of sales
   - operating income, which is the difference between the gross margin and the total operating expenses
   - pre-tax income, which is the sum of the operating income and the other income
   - net income, which is the difference between the pre-tax income and the income taxes
8. Move the contents of range G4:K9 to range A22:E27. (*Note:* The worksheet window will automatically scroll as you move the selection down and to the left.)
9. For each year, enter a formula that calculates the net income per share, which is the net income divided by the number of shares.
10. Switch to Sheet2, and then enter the following text in the cells indicated:
    - Cell A1: Altac Bicycles
    - Cell A3: Date:
    - Cell B3: *current date*
    - Cell A4: Created By:
    - Cell B4: *your name*
    - Cell A5: Purpose:
    - Cell B5: Financial data for Altac Bicycles for 2006, 2005, and 2004
11. Increase the width of column A to 18 characters and the width of column B to 15 characters. Rename the sheet as "Documentation" and then move the sheet to the first position in the workbook.
12. Delete any empty worksheets, and then check the spelling in the workbook. Correct any errors found.
13. Save the changes you have made to the workbook, print the contents of the entire workbook in portrait orientation, and then close the workbook.

Apply

Use the skills you have learned to create a balance sheet for a food retailer.

Case Problem 2

Data File needed for this Case Problem: Halley1.xls

Halley Food Co. Michael Li is working on the annual financial report for Halley Food Corporation, one of the biggest food retailers in the country. He has entered some financial data in an Excel workbook and would like you to complete the workbook by entering the remaining data and the formulas needed to calculate the total values.
To complete this task:

1. Open the **Halley1** workbook located in the Tutorial.01\Cases folder included with your Data Files, and then save the workbook as **Halley2** in the same folder.
2. Insert one row at the top of the worksheet, and then enter the following text on two separates lines within cell A1:
   Halley Food Co.
   Balance Sheet
3. Increase the width of column A to 30 characters, the width of column B to 20 characters, and the width of column C to 26 characters. Decrease the height of row 1 to 30.
4. Move range H3:I9 to B28:C34. (*Note:* The worksheet window will automatically scroll as you move the selection down and to the left.)
5. Enter the following data in columns D, E, and F for the shareholders' equity for each year:

Figure 1-40

Preferred and common stock	5,557	4,821	3,515
Retained earnings	5,666	4,007	3,401
Other comprehensive income	289	203	187

6. Using the AutoSum feature, calculate the totals for the current assets and the totals for the other assets for each year.
7. In row 17, enter formulas to calculate the total assets for each year, which is the sum of the total current assets and the total other assets.
8. Using the AutoSum feature, calculate the totals for the current liabilities and the totals for the shareholders' equity for each year.
9. In row 34, enter formulas to calculate the total liabilities and shareholders' equity for each year, which is the sum of the total current liabilities, the minority interest, and the total shareholders' equity for each year.
10. Rename Sheet1 as "Balance Sheet."
11. Switch to Sheet2, and then enter the following information in the cells indicated:
    * Cell A1: Halley Food Co.
    * Cell A3: Date:
    * Cell B3: *current date*
    * Cell A4: Created By:
    * Cell B4: *your name*
    * Cell A5: Purpose:
    * Cell B5: Balance sheet for Halley Food Co.
12. Resize column A to 20 characters and column B to 40 characters.
13. Rename Sheet2 as "Documentation" and move it to the beginning of the workbook. Delete the empty sheet.
14. Use the Spell Checker to correct any spelling errors in the workbook, and then print the entire workbook in landscape orientation.
15. Save your changes to the workbook, and then close it.

Challenge

Challenge yourself by going beyond what you've learned to create a worksheet that calculates the weighted scores of four possible locations for a new shoe factory.

Case Problem 3

Data File needed for this Case Problem: Site1.xls

Kips Shoes   Kips Shoes is planning to build a new factory. The company has narrowed the site down to four possible cities. Each city has been graded on a 1-to-10 scale for four categories: the size of the local market, the quality of the labor pool, the local tax base, and the local operating expenses. Each of these four factors is given a weight, with the most important factor given the highest weight. After the sites are analyzed, the scores for each factor will be multiplied by their weights, and then a total weighted score will be calculated.

Gwen Sanchez, the senior planning manager overseeing this project, has entered the weights and the scores for each city into an Excel workbook. She needs you to finish the workbook by inserting the formulas to calculate the weighted scores and the total overall score for each city. To complete this task:

1. Open the **Site1** workbook located in the Tutorial.01\Cases folder included with your Data Files, and then save the workbook as **Site2** in the same folder.
2. Switch to the Site Analysis sheet.
3. In cell B14, calculate the weighted Market Size score for Waukegan by inserting a formula that multiplies the value in cell B7 by the weight value in cell G7.
4. Insert formulas to calculate the weighted scores for the rest of the cells in the range B14:E17.

Explore
5. Select the range B18:E18, and then click the AutoSum button to calculate the sum of the weighted scores for all four of the cities. Note that you can apply the AutoSum button to more than one cell at a time. Which city has the highest weighted score?
6. Switch to the Documentation sheet, and enter your name and the date in the appropriate locations on the sheet.
7. Spell check the workbook, print the entire workbook in portrait orientation, and then save your changes to the workbook.

Explore
8. Gwen has another set of weighted scores she wants you to try. However, she doesn't want you to enter the new values in the Site Analysis worksheet, so you need to make a copy of the worksheet. To learn how to copy a worksheet, open the Excel Help task pane, and then enter "copy a worksheet" in the Search for text box. Scroll the list of topics in the Search Results task pane to locate the topic "Move or copy sheets." Open the topic, read the information about copying a sheet, and then close the Microsoft Excel Help window and the Search Results task pane.

Explore
9. Using what you learned in Step 8, create a copy of the Site Analysis worksheet, placing the new worksheet at the end of the workbook. Rename the new sheet "Site Analysis 2".
10. In the Site Analysis 2 worksheet, change the weighted scores of Market Size to 0.2 and Labor Pool to 0.4. Which city has the highest weighted score now?
11. Print the contents of the Site Analysis 2 worksheet.
12. Save the workbook as **Site3** in the Tutorial.01\Cases folder, and then close the workbook.

Create

Use Figure 1-41, which shows the "end results," to create a workbook containing monthly budget figures over a three-month period for a college student.

Case Problem 4

There are no Data Files needed for this Case Problem.

Monthly Budget   Alice Drake is a first-year student at MidWest University and has a part-time job in the admissions department. Her college-related expenses, such as tuition, books, and fees, are covered through grants and scholarships, so the money Alice makes goes towards her personal expenses. Being on her own for the first time, Alice is finding it difficult to keep within a budget. She has asked you to look at her finances and help her figure out how her money is being spent. Figure 1-41 shows the worksheet that you will create to help Alice analyze her budget.

Figure 1-41

enter formulas to calculate the ending cash balance and the net cash flows

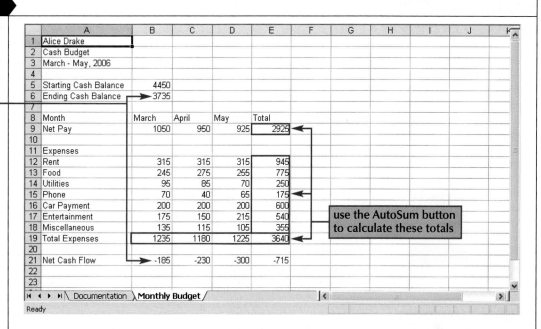

use the AutoSum button to calculate these totals

To complete this task:

1. Start Excel and save a new workbook with the name **Budget** in the Tutorial.01\Cases folder included with your Data Files.
2. On the Sheet1 worksheet, enter the labels and values as indicated in Figure 1-41. Note that the cells in which totals will be calculated have been marked. Do not enter the values shown; you will enter appropriate formulas next.
3. Using the AutoSum button, calculate the values for the total net pay, the total monthly expenses, and the total of each expense for the three months.
4. Enter formulas to calculate the net cash flow for each month and for all three months.
5. Enter a formula to calculate the ending cash balance, which is based on the value of the starting cash balance minus the total net cash flow over the three months. (*Hint:* Because two negatives make a positive, you need to *add* the total net cash flow to the starting cash balance.)
6. Rename Sheet1 as "Monthly Budget."
7. Create a worksheet named "Documentation" at the front of the workbook containing your name, the date, and the purpose of the workbook.
8. Delete any blank worksheets in the workbook.
9. Check the spelling on both worksheets, correcting any errors found.
10. Print the entire workbook in portrait orientation.
11. Save your changes to the workbook, and then close it.

Internet Assignments

Research

Use the Internet to find and work with data related to the topics presented in this tutorial.

The purpose of the Internet Assignments is to challenge you to find information on the Internet that you can use to work effectively with this software. The actual assignments are updated and maintained on the Course Technology Web site. Log on to the Internet and use your Web browser to go to the Student Online Companion for New Perspectives Office 2003 at **www.course.com/np/office2003**. Click the Internet Assignments link, and then navigate to the assignments for this tutorial.

Assess

SAM Assessment and Training

If your instructor has chosen to use the full online version of SAM 2003 Assessment and Training, you can go beyond the "just-in-time" training provided on the CD that accompanies this text. Simply log in to your SAM account (http://sam2003.course.com) to launch any assigned training activities or exams that relate to the skills covered in this tutorial.

Reinforce

Lab Assignments

Spreadsheets

The New Perspectives Labs are designed to help you master some of the key concepts and skills presented in this text. The steps for completing this Lab are located on the Course Technology Web site. Log on to the Internet and use your Web browser to go to the Student Online Companion for New Perspectives Office 2003 at **www.course.com/np/office2003**. Click the Lab Assignments link, and then navigate to the assignments for this tutorial.

Review

Quick Check Answers

Session 1.1

1. cell
2. D2
3. Ctrl + Home
4. click the Sheet2 tab
5. a. value
    b. text
    c. value
    d. text (there is no equal sign indicating a formula)
    e. text
    f. formula
    g. text
6. Press the Alt + Enter keys to enter text on a new line within a cell.
7. =E5/E6

Session 1.2

1. An adjacent cell range is a rectangular block of cells. A non-adjacent cell range consists of two or more separate adjacent ranges.
2. A5:F8
3. AutoSum
4. down
5. to the right
6. Double-click the sheet tab and then type the new name to replace the highlighted sheet tab name.
7. Clearing a cell deletes the cell's contents but does not affect the position of other cells in the workbook. Deleting a cell removes the cell from the worksheet, and other cells are shifted in the direction of the deleted cell.
8. Ctrl + ` (grave accent)

Working with Formulas and Functions

Developing a Family Budget

Case | Tyler Family Budget

As a newly married couple, Amanda and Joseph Tyler are trying to balance career, school, and family life. Amanda works full time as a legal assistant, and Joseph is in a graduate program at a nearby university. He recently was hired as a teaching assistant. In the summer, he is able to take on other jobs that bring additional income to the family. The couple also just moved into a new apartment. Although Joseph's and Amanda's salaries for the past year were greater than the years before, the couple seemed to have less cash on hand. This financial shortage has prompted them to take a closer look at their finances and figure out how to best manage them.

Because Amanda has agreed to take the lead role in the management of the family finances, she has set up an Excel workbook. Amanda has entered their salary amounts, which are their only income, and she has identified and entered several expenses that the family pays on a monthly basis, such as the rent and Joseph's tuition. She wants to calculate how much money they bring in and how much money they spend. She also wants to figure out their average monthly expenses and identify their greatest financial burden.

Amanda has asked for your help in completing the workbook. She wants you to insert formulas to perform the calculations she needs to get a better overall picture of the family's finances, which, in turn, should help the couple manage their money more effectively. Because the values entered cover a 12-month span, you will be able to copy and paste the formulas from one month to another and fill in series of data, such as the months of the year, rather than retyping formulas or entering each month individually. Finally, Amanda also wants the current date in her workbook, which you can enter using one of Excel's Date functions.

Session	Objectives		SAM Training Tasks	
Session 2.1	• Learn about the syntax of an Excel function • Use the SUM, AVERAGE, and MAX functions • Copy and paste formulas • Work with relative, absolute, and mixed references • Change the magnification of the workbook window	• Insert a function using the Insert Function dialog box • Use Auto Fill to insert formulas and complete a series • Insert the current date using a Date function	• AVERAGE function • Change zoom settings • Copy cells • Create formulas using the DATE function • Create formulas using the MAX function • Create formulas using the MIN function • Create formulas using the NOW function • Create formulas using the SUM function • Create formulas using the TODAY function	• Include a formula within a database or list • Use absolute references • Use relative references • Use the fill handle to copy a cell • Use the fill handle to copy multiple formulas to adjacent cells at one time • Use the fill handle to create a series • Use the ROUND function
Session 2.2 *(optional)*	• Work with Financial functions	• Work with Logical functions	• Create formulas using the IF function • Create formulas using the PMT function • Create formulas using the PV function	• Use logical functions (FALSE) • Use logical functions (TRUE)

Student Data Files   For a complete list of the Data Files needed for this tutorial, see page EX 2.

Once she has a better handle on the family's finances, Amanda might want to evaluate whether buying a house would be possible in the near future, especially in light of the low interest rates that are available.

Session 2.1

For hands-on practice of key tasks in this session, go to the SAM 2003 Training Companion CD included with this text.

Working with Excel Functions

In her budget worksheet, Amanda has already entered the couple's take-home salaries (that is, the amount of money in their paychecks minus taxes and other work-related deductions) and their expenses from the past year. You'll begin by opening her workbook so you can see what Amanda has done so far.

To open Amanda's workbook:

1. Start Excel and then open the **Budget1** workbook located in the Tutorial.02\Tutorial folder included with your Data Files.

2. On the Documentation sheet, enter *your name* in cell B3 and the *current date* in cell B4.

3. Save the workbook as **Budget2** in the Tutorial.02\Tutorial folder, and then click the **Budget** tab to make this sheet the active worksheet. See Figure 2-1. Amanda has recorded the couple's take-home salaries as income and has listed a variety of expenses in columns for each month. January's income and expenses are shown in column B, February's income and expenses are shown in column C, and so forth.

Figure 2-1 Budget worksheet

	A	B	C	D	E	F	G	H	I	J	K
1	Tyler Family Budget	1/1/2006 - 12/31/2006									
2											
3	MONTHLY TOTALS										
4		1/1/2006	2/1/2006	3/1/2006	4/1/2006	5/1/2006	6/1/2006	7/1/2006	8/1/2006	9/1/2006	10/1/2006
5	Income										
6	Amanda	2,400	2,400	2,400	2,400	2,400	2,400	2,400	2,400	2,400	2,400
7	Joseph	850	850	850	850	850	1,650	1,650	1,650	850	850
8	Total										
9											
10	Expenses										
11	Rent	850	850	850	850	850	850	850	850	850	850
12	Food	607	657	613	655	644	761	699	672	683	609
13	Utilities	225	210	200	175	150	130	145	165	175	175
14	Phone	58	63	63	63	59	59	64	63	64	58
15	Loan Payments	150	150	150	150	150	150	150	150	150	150
16	Car Payments	175	175	175	175	175	175	175	175	175	175
17	Insurance	50	50	50	50	50	50	50	50	50	50
18	Miscellaneous	140	191	171	135	171	272	146	182	144	140
19	Entertainment	192	160	172	166	185	310	155	164	132	150
20	Tuition	2,000	0	0	0	0	0	0	2,200	0	0
21	Books	520	0	0	0	0	0	0	572	0	0
22	Total										
23											

Cell A1: Tyler Family Budget: 1/1/2006 - 12/31/2006

Documentation / Budget

Ready

Amanda would like the worksheet to calculate the family's total income and expenses for each month. She would also like to see a year-end summary that displays the family's total income and expenses for the entire year. This summary should also display the average income and expenses so that Amanda can get a picture of what a typical month looks like for her family. Amanda realizes that some expenses increase and decrease during certain months, so she would like to calculate the minimum and maximum values for each expense category, which will give her an idea of the range of these values throughout the year. All of this information will help Amanda and Joseph budget for the upcoming year.

To perform these calculations, you'll have to add several formulas to the workbook. As discussed in the previous tutorial, formulas are one of the most useful features in Excel because they enable you to calculate values based on data entered into the workbook. For more complex calculations, you can enter formulas that contain one or more functions. Recall that a function is a predefined formula that performs calculations using specific values. Each Excel function has a name and syntax. The **syntax** is the rule specifying how the function should be written. The general syntax of all Excel functions is

FUNCTION(argument1, argument2, ...)

where *FUNCTION* is the name of the Excel function and *argument1, argument2*, and so forth are **arguments** specifying the numbers, text, or cell references used by the function to calculate a value. An argument can also be an **optional argument** that is not necessary for the function to calculate a value. If an optional argument is not included, Excel assumes a default value for it. Each argument entered in a function is separated by a comma. The convention used in this text shows optional arguments within square brackets along with the argument's default value, as follows:

FUNCTION(argument1, [argument2=value2])

where *argument2* is an optional argument and *value2* is the default value for this argument. As you learn more about individual functions, you will also learn which arguments are required and which are optional.

Another convention followed in this text is to write function names in uppercase letters, but Excel recognizes the function names entered in either uppercase or lowercase letters, converting the lowercase letters to uppercase automatically.

There are 350 different Excel functions organized into the following 10 categories:

- Database functions
- Date and Time functions
- Engineering functions
- Financial functions
- Information functions
- Logical functions
- Lookup and Reference functions
- Math and Trigonometry functions
- Statistical functions
- Text and Data functions

You can learn about each function using Excel's online Help. Figure 2-2 describes some of the more important Math and Statistical functions that you may often use in your workbooks.

Figure 2-2 **Math and Statistical functions**

Function	Description
AVERAGE(*number1*, [*number2, number3, ...*])	Calculates the average of a collection of numbers, where *number1, number2,* and so forth are numeric values or cell references
COUNT(*value1*, [*value2, value3, ...*])	Calculates the total number of values, where *value1, value2,* and so forth are numeric values, text entries, or cell references
MAX(*number*1, [*number2, number3, ...*])	Calculates the maximum of a collection of numbers, where *number1, number2,* and so forth are either numeric values or cell references
MEDIAN(*number1*, [*number2, number3, ...*])	Calculates the median, or the number in the middle, of a collection of numbers, where *number1, number2,* and so forth are either numeric values or cell references
MIN(*number1*, [*number2, number3, ...*])	Calculates the minimum of a collection of numbers, where *number1, number2,* and so forth are either numeric values or cell references
ROUND(*number, num_digits*)	Rounds a number to a specified number of digits, where *number* is the number you want to round and *num_digits* specifies the number of digits to which you want to round the number
SUM(*number1*, [*number2, number3, ...*])	Calculates the sum of a collection of numbers, where *number1, number2,* and so forth are either numeric values or cell references

For example, the **AVERAGE function** calculates the average value of a collection of numbers. The syntax of this function is AVERAGE(*number1,* [*number2, ...*]). When you enter the arguments *(number1, number2)*, you can enter these numbers directly into the function, as in AVERAGE(3, 2, 5, 8), or you can enter the references to the worksheet cells that contain those numbers, as in AVERAGE(A1:A4). You can also enter a function as part of a larger formula. For example, the formula =*MAX(A1:A100)/100* calculates the maximum value in the cell range A1:A100 and then divides that number by 100. You can include, or "nest," one function within another. For example, in the formula =*ROUND(AVERAGE(A1:A100),1)*, the first argument in the ROUND function uses the value calculated by the AVERAGE function; the second argument is a constant. The result is a formula that calculates the average value of the numbers in the range A1:A100, rounding that value to the first decimal place.

In the previous tutorial, you calculated totals using the AutoSum button on the Standard toolbar. Although using the AutoSum feature is a quick and convenient way to calculate a value, it is only one way to perform this calculation in Excel. To determine the totals Amanda wants, you can also use the **SUM function**, which calculates the sum of a collection of numbers. The syntax of the SUM function is SUM(*number1,* [*number2, ...*]), which is similar to that of the AVERAGE function.

You'll use the SUM function now to begin calculating the values Amanda needs, starting with the values for the month of January.

To calculate the total income and expenses for January using the SUM function:

1. Click cell **B8** on the Budget worksheet, type **=SUM(B6:B7)** and then press the **Enter** key. Excel displays the value 3,250 in cell B8, indicating that the total income for the month of January is $3,250.

   You can also enter the cell range for a function by selecting the cell range rather than typing it. You'll use this method to determine the total expenses for January.

2. Click cell **B22** and then type **=SUM(** to begin the function.

3. Select the range **B11:B21** using your mouse. As you drag to select the range, its cell reference is automatically entered into the SUM function, as shown in Figure 2-3.

Entering the SUM function | Figure 2-3

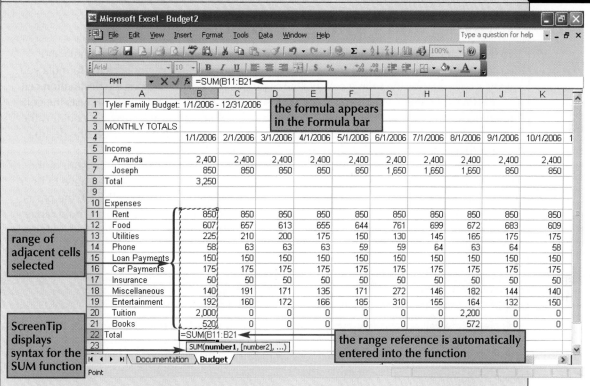

4. Press the **Enter** key to complete the formula. Note that you didn't have to type the closing parenthesis. When you press the Enter key, the closing parenthesis is inserted automatically. The value 4,967 is displayed in cell B22, indicating that the total expenses for January are $4,967.

Amanda wants to know how much money is left over at the end of each month or, in other words, the family's *net income* each month. To determine this amount, you need to enter a formula that subtracts the total monthly expenses from the total monthly income. You'll begin by calculating the net income for the month of January.

To calculate the net income for the first month:

▶ 1. Click cell **A24**, type **Net Income**, and then press the **Tab** key to move to cell B24, where you will enter the formula.

▶ 2. Type **=B8-B22** and then press the **Enter** key. Excel displays the value –1,717, which indicates that the family's net income for the month of January is a negative $1,717. Amanda and Joseph's expenses are greater than their income for that month.

Now that you've entered the formulas to calculate the total income, total expenses, and net income for January, you need to enter the same formulas for the other 11 months of the year. Entering the formulas for each of the remaining months individually would be time-consuming, but there is a quicker way.

Copying and Pasting Formulas

To use the same formula in different cells on the worksheet, you can copy the formula and paste it to a new location or locations. The cell (or range of cells) that contains the formula you copy is referred to as the **source cell** (or **source range**). The new location is the **destination cell** (or **destination range**). When you paste your selection, Excel automatically adjusts the cell references contained in the formulas. For example, if you copy cell B8, which contains the formula =SUM(B6:B7), and paste the contents of the copied cell into cell C8 (the destination cell), Excel automatically changes the formula in cell C8 to =SUM(C6:C7).

In effect, Excel recognizes that the intent of the function is to calculate the sum of the values in the two cells above the active cell. The new location does not even have to be in the same row as the copied cell. If you copy the formula in cell B8 to cell C10, the pasted formula would be =SUM(C8:C9). You can copy the formula in one cell to a whole range of cells, and Excel will correctly adjust the cell references in the formula for each cell in the range.

Reference Window	**Copying and Pasting a Cell or Range**

- Select the cell or range that you want to copy, and then click the Copy button on the Standard toolbar.
- Select the cell or range into which you want to copy the selection, and then click the Paste button on the Standard toolbar.

Next, you'll copy the formula in cell B8 to the range C8:M8 to calculate the total income for the remaining months.

To copy and paste the formula from cell B8 to the range C8:M8:

▶ 1. Click cell **B8** on the Budget worksheet, and then click the **Copy** button 📋 on the Standard toolbar. Note that the copied cell has a moving border. This border is a visual reminder that the range has been copied and is ready to be pasted.

▶ 2. Select the range **C8:M8**, and then click the **Paste** button 📋 on the Standard toolbar. Excel copies the formula in cell B8 into each of the cells in the range C8:M8, changing the cell references to match the location of each cell in the range. See Figure 2-4. Note that when you paste a selection, Excel automatically displays the Paste Options button. This button provides options that give you control over the paste process. You will learn more about this button in the next tutorial.

Copying the SUM function for the monthly income | **Figure 2-4**

Trouble? If your screen does not match the one shown in the figure, you may have scrolled the worksheet further to the right so column B is no longer visible. You can click the left scroll button on the horizontal scroll bar to reposition the worksheet in the workbook window to better match the one in the figure.

3. Press the **Ctrl + `** (grave accent) keys to display the formulas in the range B8:M8. Notice that the cell references in each formula refer to the income values for that particular month.

4. Press the **Ctrl + `** (grave accent) keys to return to Normal view.

You are not limited to copying a single formula from one cell. You can also copy a range of formulas. When you copy a range of cells, each of which contains a formula, and then paste the selection into a new location, Excel pastes the formulas in each cell to their corresponding locations in the new cell range. You don't have to select a range that is the same size as the range being copied. You just need to select the first, or upper leftmost, cell in the destination range, and Excel will paste the selection in a range that accommodates all the cells. Any existing text or values in the destination range will be overwritten. So, be sure you paste the selection in an area of the worksheet that can accommodate the selection without deleting existing data.

Next, you need to copy the formulas for January's total expenses and net income, which are in cells B22 and B24, to the ranges C22:M22 and C24:M24. Then Amanda will be able to see each month's total expenses and net income values. Although there is no formula in cell B23, you will select the range B22:B24 and paste the selection to range C22:M24, simplifying the process. No values will appear in row 23.

To copy and paste the formulas in the range B22:B24 to the range C22:M24:

1. Scroll the worksheet to the left, if necessary, so column B is visible, select the range **B22:B24**, and then click the **Copy** button 🗐 on the Standard toolbar.

Trouble? If the Clipboard task pane opens, close it. You will not need to use it in this tutorial.

> **2.** Select the range **C22:M24**, and then click the **Paste** button 🖺 on the Standard toolbar. Figure 2-5 shows the total expenses and net income values for each month in the Budget worksheet. Note that Excel has duplicated the two formulas from the first month in each succeeding month.

Figure 2-5 ▶ **Copying and pasting a cell range**

total monthly expenses

17	50	50	50	50	50	50	50	50	50	50	50	50
18	140	191	171	135	171	272	146	182	144	140	147	213
19	192	160	172	166	185	310	155	164	132	150	162	200
20	2,000	0	0	0	0	0	0	2,200	0	0	0	0
21	520	0	0	0	0	0	0	572	0	0	0	0
22	4,967	2,506	2,444	2,419	2,434	2,757	2,434	5,243	2,423	2,357	2,444	2,576
23												
24	-1,717	744	806	831	816	1,293	1,616	-1,193	827	893	806	674
25												
26												

I◄ ◄ ► ►I \ Documentation \ **Budget** /

Select destination and press ENTER or choose Paste   Sum=38,150

total monthly net income values

> **3.** Press the **Esc** key to remove the moving border from the selected range.

As you can see, Excel's ability to adjust cell references when copying and pasting formulas makes it easy to create columns or rows of formulas that share a common structure.

Using Relative and Absolute References

The type of cell reference that you just worked with is called a relative reference. A **relative reference** is a cell reference that changes when it is copied and pasted in a new location. Excel interprets the reference *relative* to the position of the active cell. For example, when you copied the formula =SUM(B6:B7) from the source cell, B8, and pasted it in the destination range, C8:M8, Excel adjusted the cell references in each pasted formula relative to the new location of the formula itself. The formula in cell C8 became =SUM(C6:C7), the formula in cell D8 became =SUM(D6:D7), and so on.

A second type of cell reference is an absolute reference. An **absolute reference** is a cell reference that doesn't change when it is copied. Excel does not adjust the cell reference because the cell reference points to a fixed, or *absolute*, location in the worksheet, and it remains fixed when the copied formula is pasted. In Excel, an absolute reference appears with a dollar sign ($) before each column and row designation. For example, $B$8 is an absolute reference, and when it is used in a formula, Excel will always point to the cell located at the intersection of column B and row 8.

Figure 2-6 provides an example in which an absolute reference is necessary to a formula. In this example, a sales worksheet records the units sold for each region as well as the overall total. If you want to calculate the percent of units sold for each region, you divide the units sold for each region by the overall total. If you use only relative references, copying the formula from the first region to the second will produce an incorrect result, because Excel shifts the location of the total sales cell down one row. To correct this problem, you use an absolute cell reference, fixing the location of the total sales cell at cell B8. In the example, this means changing the formula in cell C4 from =B4/B8 to =B4/$B$8.

Using relative and absolute references ◀ **Figure 2-6**

Formulas Using Relative References

	A	B	C	D
1	Sales			
2				
3	Regions	Units Sold	Percent	
4	Region 1	2,238	=B4/B8	
5	Region 2	1,321		
6	Region 3	3,093		
7	Region 4	1,905		
8	Total	8,557		
9				
10				

	A	B	C	D
1	Sales			
2				
3	Regions	Units Sold	Percent	
4	Region 1	2,238	0.26154026	
5	Region 2	1,321	=B5/B9	
6	Region 3	3,093		
7	Region 4	1,905		
8	Total	8,557		
9				
10				

When the formula is copied, the relative reference to the cell (B8) is shifted down and now points to an incorrect cell (B9).

Formulas Using Absolute References

	A	B	C	D
1	Sales			
2				
3	Regions	Units Sold	Percent	
4	Region 1	2,238	=B4/$B$8	
5	Region 2	1,321		
6	Region 3	3,093		
7	Region 4	1,905		
8	Total	8,557		
9				
10				

	A	B	C	D
1	Sales			
2				
3	Regions	Units Sold	Percent	
4	Region 1	2,238	0.26154026	
5	Region 2	1,321	=B5/$B$8	
6	Region 3	3,093		
7	Region 4	1,905		
8	Total	8,557		
9				
10				

When the formula is copied, the absolute reference to the cell ($B$8) continues to point to that cell.

Another type of reference supported by Excel is the mixed reference. A **mixed reference** contains both relative and absolute cell references. A mixed reference for cell B8 is either $B8 or B$8. In the case of the mixed reference $B8, the column portion of the reference remains fixed, but the row number adjusts as the formula is copied to a new location. In the B$8 reference, the row number remains fixed, whereas the column portion adjusts to each new cell location.

As you enter a formula that requires an absolute reference or a mixed reference, you can type the dollar sign for the column and row references as needed. If you have already entered a formula and need to change the type of cell reference used, you can switch to edit mode and then press the **F4** key. As you press this function key, Excel cycles through the different references for the cell in the formula at the location of the insertion point. Pressing the F4 key changes a relative reference to an absolute reference, then to a mixed reference for the row, then to a mixed reference for the column, and then back to a relative reference.

In Amanda's family budget, monthly expenses vary greatly throughout the year. For example, tuition is a major expense, and that bill must be paid once in January and once in August. Amanda knows that the family has more entertainment and miscellaneous expenses during the month of December than at other times. The family's monthly income also fluctuates as Joseph brings in more income during the summer months than at other times. Amanda would like her budget worksheet to keep a running total of the family's net income as it progresses through the year. For example, she knows that the family will start the year with less money because of the tuition bill in January. Amanda wonders how many months pass before they recover from that major expense and begin saving money again.

One way to calculate the running total is to add the net income values of consecutive months. For example, to figure out how much money the family has saved or lost after two months, you add the net income for January to the net income for February, using the formula =SUM(B24:C24). To figure out the total net income for the first three months, you use the formula =SUM(B24:D24); through the first four months the formula will be =SUM(B24:E24), and so on.

The starting point of the range in the formula needs to be fixed at the cell that contains the net income for January, cell B24. To be sure that the formula points to cell B24, you need to use the absolute reference $B$24. The ending cell of the range will shift as you copy the formula to the other months in the worksheet. You need to use a relative reference for the ending cell in the range so that Excel will adjust the reference as the formula is copied. The formula for the running total through the first two months will be =SUM($B$24:C24). When you paste this formula to the other months of the year, Excel will adjust the cell range to calculate the total for all of the months up to that point.

To calculate the running total using an absolute reference to cell B24:

1. Click cell **A25**, type **Running Total**, and then press the **Tab** key twice to move to column C.

2. Type **=SUM(B24:C24)** in cell C25, and then press the **Enter** key. Excel displays the value –973, showing that the family's expenses exceed their income by $973 through the first two months of the year.

   Now you'll change the formula to use an absolute reference for cell B24 by selecting it in the formula and pressing the F4 key.

3. Double-click cell **C25** to switch to edit mode, and then double-click **B24** within the formula to select the cell reference.

4. Press the **F4** key to change the cell reference from B24 to $B$24. See Figure 2-7.

| Figure 2-7 | Entering an absolute reference |

> **Trouble?** If you pressed the F4 key too many times and passed the absolute reference, continue pressing the F4 key to cycle through the options until $B$24 is displayed in the formula.

5. Press the **Enter** key when the correct reference is displayed. Excel displays the value –973.

   Now you can copy this formula to the remaining months of the year.

6. Click cell **C25**, and then click the **Copy** button on the Standard toolbar. The moving border indicates that cell C25 has been copied.

7. Select the range **D25:M25**, and then click the **Paste** button on the Standard toolbar. Excel copies the formula to the remaining cells, as shown in Figure 2-8. The amount shown for each month represents the cash on hand that the family accumulated during the year, up to and including that month. So, for example, at the end of the year, after paying all expenses, they have a total of $6,396.

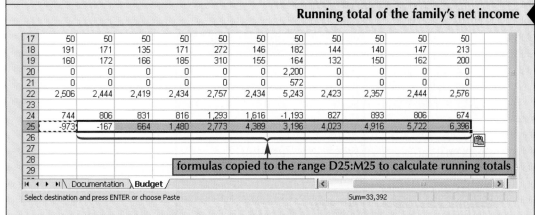

Running total of the family's net income — Figure 2-8

8. Press the **Ctrl +** ` (grave accent) keys to examine the pasted formulas in the range D25:M25. The use of absolute and relative references ensures the integrity of the formula copied in each cell used to calculate the running net income total.

9. Press the **Ctrl +** ` (grave accent) keys to return to Normal view.

Working with Other Paste Options

So far you've used the Paste button to paste formulas from a source cell or range to a destination cell or range. When Excel pastes the contents of a selected cell or range, it also pastes any formatting applied to the source cell (you'll learn about formatting in the next tutorial). If you want more control over how Excel pastes the data from the source cell, you can click the list arrow next to the Paste button and choose one of the available paste options. Figure 2-9 describes each of these options.

Paste options — Figure 2-9

Option	Description
Formulas	Pastes the formula(s), but not the formatting, of the source cell range
Values	Pastes the value(s), but not the formula(s) or formatting, of the source cell range
No Borders	Pastes the formula(s) and formatting of the source cell range, but not the format of the cell range's borders
Transpose	Pastes the formula(s) and formatting of the source cell range, except changes the orientation so that rows in the source cell range become columns, and columns become rows
Paste Link	Pastes a link to the cell(s) in the source cell range, including the formatting used
Paste Special	Opens a dialog box displaying more paste options

For example, if you want to paste the value calculated by the formula in a cell but not the formula itself, you use the Values option. This is useful in situations in which you want to "freeze" a calculated value and remove the risk of it being changed by inadvertently changing another value in the worksheet. For even more control over the paste feature, you can select the Paste Special option. When you select this option, the Paste Special dialog box opens, as shown in Figure 2-10.

Figure 2-10	Paste Special dialog box

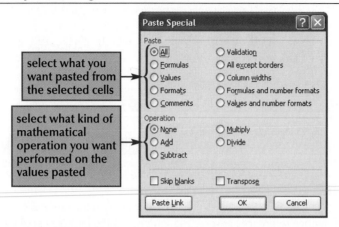

select what you want pasted from the selected cells

select what kind of mathematical operation you want performed on the values pasted

Using this dialog box, you can not only specify exactly which parts of the source cell or range—formulas, values, or formats—you want to paste, but also specify a mathematical operation you want performed as part of the paste action. For example, you can copy the value of one cell and add that value to cells in the destination range.

Another method that gives you control over the paste process is provided by the Paste Options button, which appears each time you paste a selection. By clicking this icon, you can choose from a variety of options that determine how the pasted data should be formatted. You'll explore this feature more in the next tutorial.

Changing the Magnification of a Worksheet

As you learned in Tutorial 1, an Excel worksheet can have 256 columns and more than 65,000 rows of data. You also learned that you can freeze columns and rows, so as you scroll through the data in the worksheet, the column and row headings remain visible. The number of columns and rows displayed in the workbook window depends on the zoom magnification set for the worksheet. The default zoom magnification setting is 100%. You can change this setting using the Zoom command on the View menu or the Zoom button on the Standard toolbar. Changing the zoom magnification setting allows you to see more or less of the worksheet at one time. If you decrease the magnification, you will see more of the data in the worksheet, but the data will be smaller and may be more difficult to read. If you increase the magnification, you will see less of the data in the worksheet, but the data will be larger and easier to read.

Reference Window	**Changing the Zoom Magnification of the Workbook Window**

- Click View on the menu bar, and then click Zoom.
- Click the option button for the percent magnification you want to apply, and then click the OK button.

or

- Click the Zoom list arrow on the Standard toolbar, and then click the percent option you want to apply.

You can change the magnification of the workbook window from 10% up to 400% or enter a percent not offered, for example, 65%, to further customize the display of your workbook window. You can also select a zoom magnification specific to the content of your worksheet. To do this, you select the worksheet's content and then choose the Selection option in the Zoom dialog box or on the Zoom list. Excel displays the content of the selection at a magnification that fills the entire workbook window.

Before continuing, Amanda wants to review the work done so far. Try changing the magnification so more of the worksheet is displayed at one time.

To change the zoom setting for the workbook window:

▶ **1.** Press the **Ctrl + Home** keys to make cell A1 the active cell.

▶ **2.** Click **View** on the menu bar, and then click **Zoom** to open the Zoom dialog box.

▶ **3.** Click the **75%** option button in the list of options, and then click the **OK** button. At this setting, all the data in the worksheet is displayed in the workbook window, as shown in Figure 2-11.

Budget worksheet at 75 percent magnification ◀ **Figure 2-11**

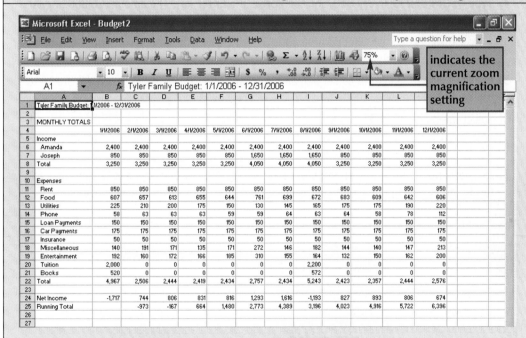

More of the worksheet is visible; however, reading the individual cell values is more difficult, so you will change the magnification back to 100%.

▶ **4.** Click the **Zoom** list arrow `100%` on the Standard toolbar, and then click **100%** to return to this higher magnification. Although the overall appearance of your screen may differ from the figures in this text, the data is not affected.

From examining the running totals, Amanda has learned several important facts. One of the family's largest expenses is Joseph's tuition, which is paid in January and August. She has also learned that the family does not recover from this January expense and show a positive overall net income until the month of April, when the total savings amount for the year up to that point is $664. Therefore, with their current income and expenses, it takes four months to "catch up" with the tuition expenditure in January, which leaves the family short on cash during February and March. The good news is that the total net income at the end of 12 months is $6,396, which represents the amount of money the family is able to save for the entire year.

Amanda now wants to know the family's total income and its total yearly expenses. You'll place these calculations in a table below the monthly figures. First, you will copy the income and expense categories to a new cell range.

To copy the income and expense categories:

1. Click cell **A27**, type **YEAR-END SUMMARY**, and then press the **Enter** key.

2. Copy the range **A5:A24** and paste it into the range **A29:A48**. If you want to remove the selection border from the copied range, you can press the Esc key. The selection border will disappear as soon as you select another range.

   Now you will enter the formula to calculate the total income for the family over the entire year.

3. Click cell **B28**, type **Total**, and then press the **Enter** key twice. You will enter the formula to calculate Amanda's salary for the year.

4. Type **=SUM(B6:M6)** in cell B30, and then press the **Enter** key. The amount 28,800 appears in the cell.

   Now you will copy this formula to calculate Joseph's yearly income, the couple's combined income, and the yearly totals for the expense categories.

5. Click cell **B30** to select this cell again, and then click the **Copy** button on the Standard toolbar.

6. Select the range **B31:B32**, press and hold the **Ctrl** key, select the range **B35:B46**, click cell **B48**, and then release the mouse button and the Ctrl key. The nonadjacent range B31:B32;B35:B46;B48 should now be selected.

7. Click the **Paste** button on the Standard toolbar. As shown in Figure 2-12, the total values for all income and expense categories should now be pasted in the worksheet.

Figure 2-12 ▶ **Year-end totals for income and expenses**

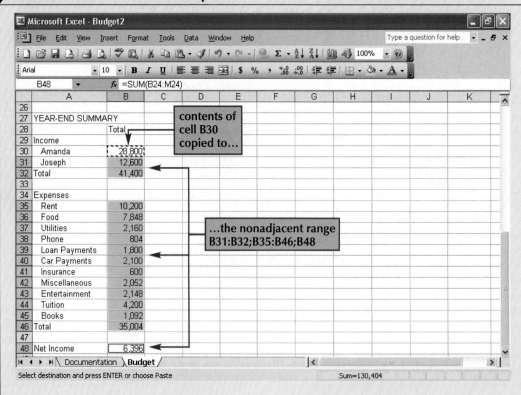

From these calculations, Amanda can quickly see that her family's yearly income is $41,400, whereas their yearly expenses total $35,004. Their largest expense is rent—a total of $10,200 per year.

Using the Insert Function Dialog Box

It's easier for Amanda to plan a budget if she knows approximately how much the family makes and spends each month. So your next task is to add a column that calculates the monthly averages for each of the income and expense categories. Rather than typing the function directly into the cell, you may find it helpful to use the Insert Function button on the Formula bar. Clicking this button displays a dialog box from which you can choose the function you want to enter. Once you choose a function, another dialog box opens, which displays the function's syntax. In this way, Excel makes it easy for you to avoid making mistakes. Try this now by entering the AVERAGE function using the Insert Function dialog box.

To insert the AVERAGE function:

▶ 1. Click cell **C28**, type **Average**, and then press the **Enter** key.

▶ 2. Click cell **C30** and then click the **Insert Function** button 𝑓𝑥 on the Formula bar. The Insert Function dialog box opens. See Figure 2-13.

Insert Function dialog box ◀ **Figure 2-13**

The Insert Function dialog box shows a list of the most recently used functions. As you can see from Figure 2-13, one of these is the AVERAGE function. However, your list may be different and might not include the AVERAGE function. You can display a different function list using the category list box. Try this now to display a list of the Statistical functions supported by Excel.

▶ 3. Click the **Or select a category** list arrow, and then click **Statistical**. Excel displays a list of Statistical functions. See Figure 2-14.

| Figure 2-14 | Excel's Statistical functions |

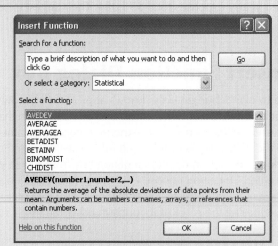

> **4.** Click **AVERAGE** in the list, and then click the **OK** button. The Function Arguments dialog box opens.

The Function Arguments dialog box provides the syntax of the selected function in an easy-to-use form. You can enter the values needed for the arguments in the reference boxes by typing them or by selecting the cell range from the worksheet. To select a cell range in the worksheet, you can click the Collapse Dialog Box button located to the right of each argument reference. Clicking this button reduces the size of the dialog box so you can see more of the worksheet. The Collapse Dialog Box button is a toggle button and, when clicked, changes to the Expand Dialog box button, which you click to restore the dialog box to its original size.

Although Amanda's salary did not change during the past year, she wants to use this workbook as a model for the next couple of years. If her salary changes in the future, the formula to calculate the average income will be in place.

You will use the Insert Function dialog box to enter the formula to calculate the average value of the cells in the range B6:M6, which contains Amanda's monthly salary amount.

To insert values into the AVERAGE function:

> **1.** Click the **Collapse Dialog Box** button located to the right of the Number1 argument reference box. The Function Arguments dialog box reduces in size to let you see more of the worksheet, and the Collapse Dialog Box button changes to the Expand Dialog Box button.
>
> **Trouble?** If the collapsed dialog box is still in the way of the range you need to select, drag the dialog box to another location on the worksheet.

> **2.** Select the range **B6:M6** on the worksheet, and then click the **Expand Dialog Box** button to restore the Function Arguments dialog box to its original size, as shown in Figure 2-15.

Function Arguments dialog box ◀ **Figure 2-15**

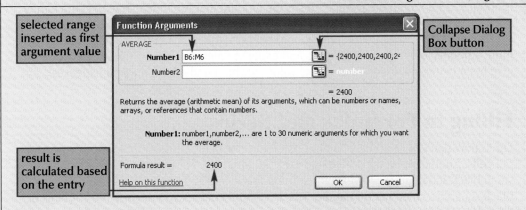

selected range inserted as first argument value

Collapse Dialog Box button

result is calculated based on the entry

3. Click the **OK** button. The value 2,400 appears in C30.

Now you will copy the formula to calculate the average of other income and expense categories.

To copy the AVERAGE function into the remaining cells:

▶ **1.** Click cell **C30**, if necessary, and then click the **Copy** button 📋 on the Standard toolbar.

▶ **2.** Select the nonadjacent range **C31:C32;C35:C46;C48**, and then click the **Paste** button 📋 on the Standard toolbar. Figure 2-16 shows the monthly averages in Amanda's budget.

Year-end average values ◀ **Figure 2-16**

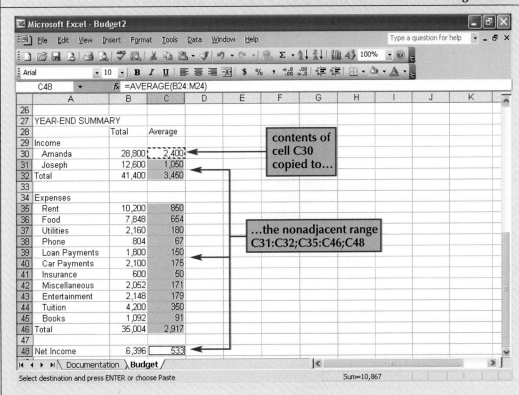

contents of cell C30 copied to...

...the nonadjacent range C31:C32;C35:C46;C48

On average, the couple makes $3,450 per month and spends $2,917. Their net income is about $533 a month on average; this is the amount that Amanda can expect the family to save. It is obvious that expenses for some months will be higher than expected. Amanda wonders how much higher? She would like to calculate the maximum and minimum amounts for each of the income and expense categories. She knows that this will give her a better picture of the range of values for her family's income and expenses.

Filling in Formulas and Series

Up to now you've used the Copy and Paste buttons to enter the same formula into multiple cells. Another approach you can use is to fill in the values. You may have noticed a small black square in the lower-right corner of a selected cell or cell range. That small black square is called the **fill handle**. This Excel tool enables you to copy the contents of the selected cells simply by dragging the fill handle over another adjacent cell or range of cells rather than going through the two-step process of clicking the Copy and Paste buttons. This technique is also referred to as **Auto Fill**.

Reference Window | **Copying Formulas Using the Fill Handle**

- Select the cell or range that contains the formula or formulas you want to copy.
- Drag the fill handle in the direction you want to copy the formula(s), and then release the mouse button.
- To select a specific fill option, click the Auto Fill Options button, and then select the option you want to apply to the selected range.

To calculate the maximum and minimum amounts for each of the income and expense categories, you will enter the **MIN** and **MAX functions**, which have a similar syntax as the AVERAGE and SUM functions. Once you enter the formulas using the MIN and MAX functions for Amanda's income, you can use Auto Fill to fill in the formulas for Joseph's income and for the expense categories.

To calculate the year-end minimum and maximum amounts:

1. Click cell **D28**, type **Minimum**, and then press the **Tab** key.

2. Type **Maximum** in cell E28, and then press the **Enter** key twice to move back to column D where you will enter the formula to calculate minimum values.

3. Type **=MIN(B6:M6)** in cell D30, and then press the **Tab** key to move to column E where you will enter the formula to calculate maximum values.

4. Type **=MAX(B6:M6)** in cell E30, and then press the **Enter** key. Excel displays the value 2,400 in both cell D30 and cell E30 because Amanda's monthly salary is $2,400 and does not vary throughout the year.

   You will use the fill handle to copy the formulas with the MIN and MAX functions into the remaining income and expense categories.

5. Select the range **D30:E30**. The fill handle appears in the lower-right corner of the selection.

6. Position the pointer over the fill handle until the pointer changes to ✛, and then drag the fill handle down the worksheet until the selection border encloses the range **D30:E48**.

7. Release the mouse button. The Auto Fill Options button appears, and by default Excel copies the formulas and formats found in the source range, D30:E30, into the destination range. Note that rows 33, 34, and 47 contain zeros. This is because those rows correspond to empty cells in the monthly table. You can delete the MIN and MAX functions in those cells.

8. Select the nonadjacent range **D33:E34;D47:E47**, and then press the **Delete** key to clear the contents of the selected cells. Figure 2-17 shows the minimum and maximum values for each income and expense category.

Year-end minimum and maximum values ◀ **Figure 2-17**

These calculations provide Amanda with an idea of the range of possible values in her budget. From these figures she can see that the maximum amount the family earned in a single month was $4,050 (cell E32), while the maximum amount the family spent in a single month was $5,243 (cell E46). How frugal can the family be? Based on her calculations, the lowest amount the family spent in a given month was $2,357 (cell D46). Amanda has also discovered that the most the family was able to save in a month was $1,616 (cell E48), while their largest deficit was $1,717—which occurred in the month of January, when a tuition payment was due. If the average values in column C give Amanda a picture of what a "typical" month looks like, the values in columns D and E give her an idea of the extremes in the family budget.

If you have a large selection to fill, you may find it difficult to use the fill handle feature of Auto Fill. If you don't want to use the fill handle, you can select the cell range that you want to fill and then use the Fill command on the Edit menu. Excel provides a list of Fill commands that you can use to fill in the selected range.

Auto Fill Options

When you use Auto Fill with formulas, Excel copies not only the formulas but also the formatting applied to the copied cell or range. However, there may be times when you only want the values in a cell copied, or maybe just the formatting. You can control what Excel does when you use the fill handle to copy formulas. When you release the mouse button, a button appears at the lower-right corner of the cell range. This is the Auto Fill Options button. Clicking this button provides a list of available options that you can choose to specify how Excel should handle the pasted selection.

The Auto Fill default option is to copy both the formulas and the formats of selected cells into the cell range. To copy only the formulas or just the formats, you can choose one of the other Auto Fill options, as shown in Figure 2-18.

| Figure 2-18 | Auto Fill options |

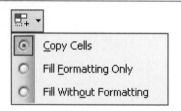

Filling a Series

The Auto Fill feature can also be used to continue a series of values, dates, or text based on an established pattern. As shown in Figure 2-19, to create a list of sequential numbers, you enter the first few numbers of the sequence and then drag the fill handle, completing the sequence. In this case, a list of numbers from 1 to 10 is quickly generated.

| Figure 2-19 | Using Auto Fill to complete a series of numbers |

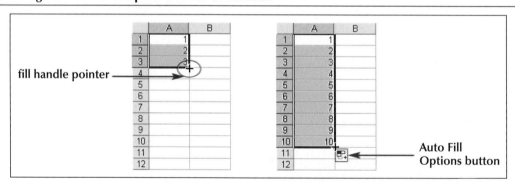

The series does not have to be numeric. It can also contain text and dates. Figure 2-20 shows a few examples of other series that can be completed using the Auto Fill feature.

Applying Auto Fill to different series | **Figure 2-20**

Type	Initial Selection	Extended Series
Values	1, 2, 3	4, 5, 6, ...
	2, 4, 6	8, 10, 12, ...
Dates and Times	Jan	Feb, Mar, Apr, ...
	January	February, March, April, ...
	Jan, Apr	Jul, Oct, Jan, ...
	15-Jan, 15-Feb	15-Mar, 15-Apr, 15-May, ...
	12/30/2005	12/31/2005, 1/1/2006, 1/2/2006, ...
	12/31/2005, 1/31/2006	2/28/2006, 3/31/2006, 4/30/2006, ...
	Mon	Tue, Wed, Thu, ...
	Monday	Tuesday, Wednesday, Thursday, ...
	11:00 AM	12:00 PM, 1:00 PM, 2:00 PM, ...
Patterned Text	1st period	2nd period, 3rd period, 4th period, ...
	Region 1	Region 2, Region 3, Region 4, ...
	Quarter 3	Quarter 4, Quarter 1, Quarter 2, ...
	Qtr3	Qtr4, Qtr1, Qtr2, ...

Amanda would like to replace dates in the Budget worksheet with the abbreviations of each month. Rather than directly typing this text, you will insert the abbreviations using the fill handle.

To fill in the abbreviations for the months of the year:

1. Press the **Ctrl + Home** keys to make the columns on the left and the top rows visible.

2. Click cell **B4**, type **Jan**, and then click the **Enter** button ☑ on the Formula bar. Because "Jan" is a commonly used abbreviation for January, Excel will recognize it as a month without your having to type in "Feb" for the next month in the series.

3. Position the pointer over the fill handle in the lower-right corner of cell B4 until the pointer changes to ✚.

4. Drag the fill handle over the range **B4:M4**, and then release the mouse button. Excel fills in the abbreviation for each month in the range of cells, as shown in Figure 2-21. As you drag the fill handle, ScreenTips for the month abbreviations appear.

Filling in the month abbreviations | **Figure 2-21**

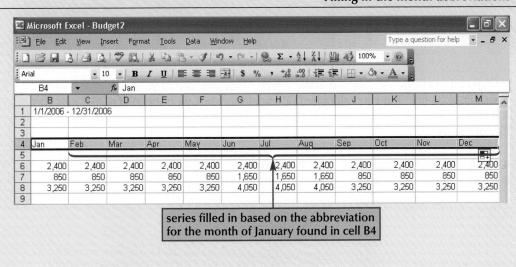

series filled in based on the abbreviation for the month of January found in cell B4

Excel provides other techniques for automatically filling in values and text. You can even create your own customized fill series. You can use Excel's online Help to explore other Auto Fill options.

Working with Date Functions

Entering the current date in a worksheet might not always address a date-related issue or need. If you want the current date to always appear in your workbook, versus the date you may have entered when you created the workbook, you can use a Date function rather than re-entering the current date each time you open the workbook. The **Date functions** provided by Excel store and calculate dates as numeric values, representing the number of days since January 1, 1900. For example, when you enter the date 1/1/2008 into a worksheet cell, you are actually entering the value 39448, because that date is 39,448 days after January 1, 1900. This method of storing dates allows you to work with dates using the same formulas you would use to work with any value. If you want to determine the number of days between two dates, you simply subtract one date from the other.

Excel automatically updates the values returned by the TODAY() and NOW() functions whenever you reopen the workbook. The **TODAY() function** displays the current date based on your computer's internal clock; the **NOW() function** displays both the date and time. If you want a permanent date (reflecting when the workbook was initially created, for example), enter the date directly into the cell without using either function.

If you have additional tasks to perform with a date or time, you can use one of the functions listed in Figure 2-22.

Figure 2-22 ▶ **Date and Time functions**

Function	Description
DATE(*year*, *month*, *day*)	Creates a date value for the date represented by the *year*, *month*, and *day* arguments
DAY(*date*)	Extracts the day of the month from the *date* value
MONTH(*date*)	Extracts the month number from the *date* value, where 1=January, 2=February, and so forth
YEAR(*date*)	Extracts the year number from the *date* value
WEEKDAY(*date*, [*return_type*])	Calculates the day of the week from the *date* value, where 1=Sunday, 2=Monday, and so forth. To choose a different numbering scheme, set the optional *return_type* value to "1" (1=Sunday, 2=Monday, ...), "2" (1=Monday, 2=Tuesday, ...), or "3" (0=Monday, 1=Tuesday, ...).
NOW()	Displays the current date and time
TODAY()	Displays the current date

You can use these functions to answer such questions as: On what day of the week does 1/1/2008 fall? You can calculate the day of the week with the **WEEKDAY function** as =*WEEKDAY(1/1/2008)*. This formula returns the value 7, which is Saturday—the seventh day of the week.

Because Amanda intends to use this worksheet as a model for future budgets, she wants the date on the Documentation sheet to always display the current date. You will replace the date you entered when you first opened the workbook with the TODAY() function.

To enter the TODAY() function on the Documentation sheet:

▶ **1.** Switch to the Documentation sheet.

▶ **2.** Click cell **B4**, type **=TODAY()**, and then click the **Enter** button  on the Formula bar. Note that there are no arguments in the TODAY() function, but you still have to include the opening and closing parentheses, and there are no spaces between the parentheses. Excel displays the current date as shown in Figure 2-23.

Inserting the current date ◄ Figure 2-23

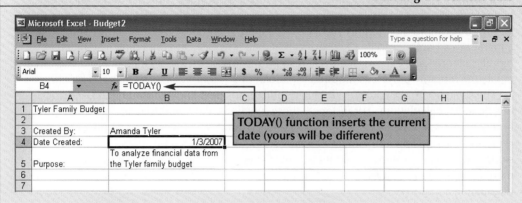

You have completed your work on the Budget2 workbook.

▶ **3.** Save your changes to the workbook, and then close it.

Using Math and Statistical functions, you have been able to calculate the monthly and end-of-year values Amanda requested. With these values in place, Amanda has a better picture of the family's finances, and she is more confident about how she will manage the family budget in the year to come.

Session 2.1 Quick Check

Review

1. What is the function you enter to calculate the minimum value in the range B1:B50?
2. Cell A10 contains the formula =*A1+B1*. When you copy the content of cell A10 and paste it into cell B11, what formula is inserted into the destination cell?
3. Cell A10 contains the formula =*$A$1+B1*. When you copy the content of cell A10 and paste it into cell B11, what formula is inserted into the destination cell?
4. Express the reference to cell A1 as (a) a relative reference, (b) an absolute reference, and (c) a mixed reference (both possibilities).
5. List the steps you use in Excel to create a series of odd numbers from 1 to 99 in column A of your worksheet.
6. To display the current date in a workbook each time you reopen it, you enter the _____ function in the cell where you want the date to appear.

To reinforce the tasks you learned in this session, go to the SAM 2003 Training Companion CD included with this text.

Session 2.2

For hands-on practice of key tasks in this session, go to the SAM 2003 Training Companion CD included with this text.

(**Note:** This session presents topics related to Financial functions and Logical functions. This session *is optional and may be skipped* without loss of continuity of the instruction.)

Working with Financial Functions

After reviewing the figures calculated in the Budget worksheet, Amanda thinks she has a better understanding of the family finances. Now she would like to determine whether the family could afford the monthly payments required to purchase a house if they were to take a loan from a bank. To do this, she wants to create a worksheet containing a "typical" month's income and expenses, and then she wants to use an Excel Financial function to calculate the monthly payments required for a loan of $175,000. Excel's **Financial functions** are the same as those widely used in the world of business and accounting to perform various financial calculations. For instance, these functions allow you to calculate the depreciation of an asset, determine the amount of interest paid on an investment, compute the present value of an investment, and so on. Although she is not a business or financial professional, Amanda's question is a financial one: Given the family budget, how great a loan payment can they afford if they want to buy a home? There are four principal factors involved in negotiating a loan:

- The size of the loan
- The length of time in which the loan must be repaid
- The interest rate charged by the lending institution
- The amount of money to be paid to the lending institution in periodic installments, called *payment periods*. (For most home loans, payments are due monthly, so the payment period is a month.)

To be sure, this is a simplified treatment of loans. Often other issues are involved, such as whether payments are due at the beginning of the payment period or at the end. For the purposes of this exercise, the above are the major factors on which Amanda will concentrate for now. Once you know any three of these factors, you can use Excel to calculate the value of the remaining fourth. Amanda is interested in a loan with the following conditions:

- The size of the loan is equal to $175,000.
- The length of time to repay the loan is equal to 30 years.
- The annual interest rate is equal to 5.5%.

She wants to calculate the fourth value—the monthly payment required by the lending institution to pay back the loan. To answer this question, you'll add a new worksheet to her workbook in which she can analyze various loan possibilities.

To create the Loan Analysis worksheet:

1. If you took a break after the last session, make sure that Excel is running and that the Budget2 workbook is open.

2. Insert a new worksheet at the end of the workbook named **Loan Analysis**, and then save the workbook as **Budget3** in the Tutorial.02\Tutorial folder included with your Data Files.

3. Click cell **A1**, type **LOAN ANALYSIS**, and then press the **Enter** key.

Now you need to copy the labels and the average values from the Budget worksheet, which you completed in the previous session.

4. Switch to the Budget worksheet, select the nonadjacent range **A29:A48;C29:C48**, and then click the **Copy** button 📋 on the Standard toolbar.

5. Switch to the Loan Analysis worksheet, and then click cell **A3** to make it the active cell.

Rather than pasting the formulas into this worksheet, you will simply paste the values.

6. Click the **Paste** list arrow 📋 ▾ on the Standard toolbar, and then click **Values** in the list of paste options. Excel pastes the labels from column A in the Budget worksheet into column A on the Loan Analysis worksheet and also pastes the average values from column C in the Budget worksheet into column B in the current worksheet. See Figure 2-24.

Pasting the income and expense categories and the average values ◀ **Figure 2-24**

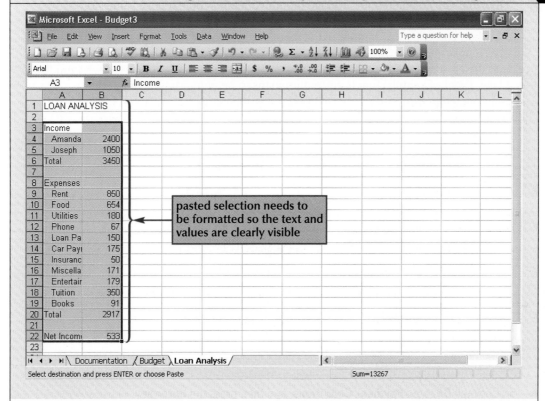

Excel pastes the cells as an adjacent range, not as a nonadjacent range. The result is that the values pasted from column C are shifted to the left into column B—right next to the labels in column A. These are the values you will need; their new location is not an issue. You will have to make some minor changes to the data, but first you need to increase the width of the columns so the values are easier to read. Then you will insert the formulas back into cells B6, B20, and B22 to calculate the total income, total expenses, and net income for a typical month.

To modify the layout of the worksheet and replace some of the values with formulas:

1. Click cell **A1** to remove the selection highlight from the pasted range.

2. Increase the width of column A to **18** characters (**131** pixels) and the width of column B to **10** characters (**75** pixels).

▶ 3. Click cell **B6**, click the **AutoSum** button Σ on the Standard toolbar, and then press the **Enter** key. Excel inserts the formula *=SUM(B4:B5)* into cell B6 to calculate the total average monthly income.

▶ 4. Click cell **B20**, click the **AutoSum** button Σ on the Standard toolbar, and then press the **Enter** key. Excel inserts the formula *=SUM(B9:B19)* into cell B20 to calculate the total average monthly expenses.

▶ 5. Click cell **B22**, type **=B6-B20** to calculate the average monthly net income, and then press the **Enter** key.

Now that you've entered the average monthly income and expense values for Amanda's budget and have widened the columns, you can enter the conditions for the loan. When you enter the amount of the loan, you will enter it as a negative value rather than as a positive value. The reason that you enter it as a negative value is because the loan is the amount owed to the lending institution; therefore, it is an expense. As you'll see later, Excel's Financial functions require loans to be entered as negative values because they represent negative cash flow. You will enter the labels and the conditions in columns D and E.

To enter the conditions of the loan in the worksheet:

▶ 1. Click cell **D3**, type **Loan Conditions**, and then press the **Enter** key to move to the next row where you will enter the Loan Amount label and the loan amount as a negative value.

▶ 2. Type **Loan Amount** in cell D4, press the **Tab** key, and then enter **-175,000** in cell E4.

Next you will enter the length of the loan in years.

▶ 3. Type **Length of Loan** in cell D5, press the **Tab** key, and then enter **30** in cell E5.

Now you will enter the annual interest rate, which is 5.5%.

▶ 4. Type **Annual Interest Rate** in cell D6, press the **Tab** key, and then enter **5.5%** in cell E6. Note that Excel may enter a zero, which doesn't change the value of the percentage.

Next, you will enter the conditions under which the loan is to be repaid. In this case, you will assume that payments are due monthly.

▶ 5. Click cell **D8**, type **Payment Conditions**, and then press the **Enter** key.

You will enter the number of payments to be made each year, which is 12.

▶ 6. Type **Payments per Year** in cell D9, press the **Tab** key, type **12** in cell E9, and then press the **Enter** key.

Next you will enter the formula to calculate the total number of payments required to pay back the loan, which is the length of the loan (found in cell E5) multiplied by the payments per year (found in cell E9).

▶ 7. Type **Total Payments** in cell D10, press the **Tab** key, type **=E5*E9** in cell E10, and then press the **Enter** key.

▶ 8. Type **Payment Amount** in cell D11, and then press the **Tab** key.

Before you continue, you will widen the columns so information is clearly visible.

▶ 9. Increase the width of column D to **18** characters (**131** pixels) and the width of column E to **10** characters (**75** pixels). Figure 2-25 shows the Loan Analysis worksheet with the values, loan conditions, and payment conditions entered.

Entering conditions for the loan and the monthly payments | Figure 2-25

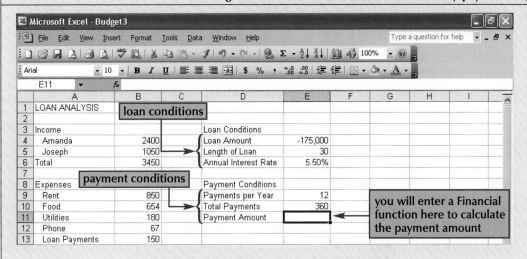

Paying off this loan will require 12 payments per year for 30 years, or 360 total payments. But how much will Amanda have to pay each month? To answer that question, you can use one of Excel's Financial functions.

Using the PMT Function

The monthly payment required to pay off a loan can be determined using the **PMT function**. The syntax of the PMT function is

=PMT(*rate, nper, pv,* [*fv*=0], [*type*=0])

where *rate* is the interest rate per payment period (determined by dividing the annual interest rate by the number of payment periods in a year), *nper* is the total number of payments, and *pv* is the present value of the future payments that will be made. In the case of a loan, the *pv* argument must be entered as a negative number. There are two optional parameters in this function: *fv* and *type*. The *fv* parameter indicates the future value of the loan and has a default value of 0. A future value of 0 means that the loan is paid off completely. The *type* parameter specifies whether payments are due at the beginning of the period (*type*=1) or at the end (*type*=0). The default value of the *type* parameter is 0.

Note that you can also use the PMT function for investments in which a specified amount of money is saved each month at a specified interest rate. In that case, the value of the *pv* argument would be positive since it represents an investment (a positive cash flow) rather than a loan (a negative cash flow).

Because the PMT function, like many Excel functions, has several required arguments, in addition to some optional arguments, you might not always remember all of the function's arguments and the order in which they should be entered. To make your task easier, you'll use the Insert Function dialog box to determine the payment amount for the loan Amanda is considering.

To select the PMT function using the Insert Function dialog box:

▶ **1.** With E11 as the active cell, click the **Insert Function** button 𝑓𝑥 on the Formula bar. The Insert Function dialog box opens.

To locate the PMT function, you'll enter a text description of this function in the Search for a function text box.

▶ **2.** Type **loan payment** in the Search for a function text box, and then click the **Go** button. Excel displays a list of functions related to loan payments. See Figure 2-26.

Figure 2-26	Searching for functions related to loan payments

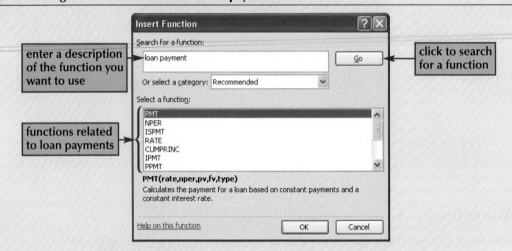

enter a description of the function you want to use

click to search for a function

functions related to loan payments

▶ **3.** Verify that **PMT** is selected in the list of functions, read the description provided in the lower portion of the dialog box, and then click the **OK** button. The Function Arguments dialog box for the PMT function opens, as shown in Figure 2-27.

Figure 2-27	Function Arguments dialog box for the PMT function

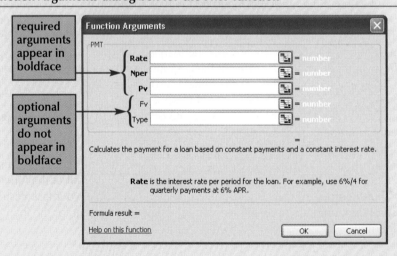

required arguments appear in boldface

optional arguments do not appear in boldface

Note that, in the Function Arguments dialog box, required arguments are displayed in a boldfaced font, whereas optional arguments are not. Neither the Fv nor Type argument is displayed in a bold font. You will use this dialog box to enter values for the PMT function's arguments. The first argument that you will enter is for the rate, which is determined by dividing the annual interest rate by the number of payment periods in a year.

To enter values for the PMT function:

▶ **1.** Click the **Collapse Dialog Box** button located to the right of the Rate box.

▶ **2.** Click cell **E6** to enter the cell reference for the annual interest rate.

To determine the rate, you will divide the value in cell E6 by the number of payment periods in a year (cell E9).

▶ **3.** Type **/** (the division sign), and then click cell **E9** to enter the cell reference.

▶ **4.** Click the **Expand Dialog Box** button to restore the Function Arguments dialog box. The expression E6/E9 should now appear in the Rate box.

Next you will enter the value for the second argument, the *nper* argument, which is the total number of payments that need to be made for the 30-year loan. This number is displayed in cell E10.

▶ **5.** Click in the **Nper** box, and then enter **E10** either by typing it directly into the reference box or by selecting the cell from the workbook.

Finally, you will enter the *pv* (present value) argument. In the case of a loan, the present value is the amount of the loan Amanda's family is seeking. This value is stored in cell E4.

▶ **6.** Click in the **Pv** box, and then enter **E4** using the method you prefer. Figure 2-28 shows the completed Function Arguments dialog box and illustrates how this dialog box relates to the function that will be inserted into cell E11.

Entering the PMT function | **Figure 2-28**

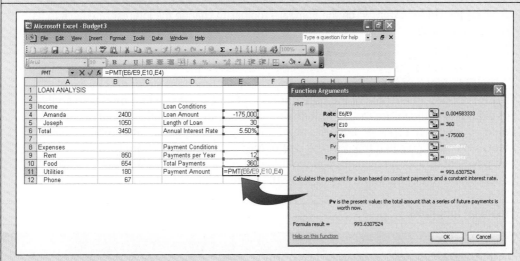

▶ **7.** Click the **OK** button. Excel displays the value $993.63 in cell E11. Therefore, the required monthly payment is $993.63 for a loan of $175,000 at a 5.5% annual interest rate for 30 years.

To see how this would affect Amanda's family budget, you will enter this information into the Expenses portion of the worksheet.

▶ **8.** Click cell **A9**, type **House Payment** to replace the word "Rent," and then press the **Tab** key.

Now you will enter a formula in cell B9 so the value House Payment is equal to the value Payment Amount.

▶ **9.** Type **=E11** in cell B9, and then press the **Enter** key. The average total monthly expenses are recalculated.

If Amanda and Joseph were to buy a home with a $175,000 mortgage under the loan conditions specified in this workbook, their average monthly expenses would increase from $2,917 to $3,060.63 (cell B20), and the amount of money they could save each month would drop from $533 to about $389 (cell B22). By replacing the rent expense with the monthly home loan payment, Amanda can quickly gauge the effects of the loan on the family budget. Because the differences don't seem too unreasonable, Amanda now wants you to increase the size of the loan to $250,000, but keep all of the other factors constant.

To explore a what-if analysis for the mortgage:

▶ 1. Click cell **E4**, type **-250,000** as the new loan amount, being sure to enter this as a negative value, and then press the **Enter** key. Under this scenario, the monthly payment increases to about $1,419 and the family's monthly expenses increase to about $3,486, which is more than they make in a typical month. Obviously a loan of this size is more than they can afford.

▶ 2. Click the **Undo** button 🔄 on the Standard toolbar to restore the worksheet to its previous condition.

   This time Amanda wants to know what would happen if the interest rate changed. To determine the difference between the low interest rate of 5.5% and a higher one, you will change the interest rate to 6.5%.

▶ 3. Click cell **E6**, type **6.5%**, and then press the **Enter** key. Excel calculates the monthly payment to be about $1,106. Amanda can see that if the interest rate increases by 1%, then the monthly payment increases by about $113. She wants you to change the interest rate back to 5.5%.

▶ 4. Click the **Undo** button 🔄 on the Standard toolbar to change the interest rate back to its previous value.

The PMT function is just one of the many Financial functions supported by Excel. Figure 2-29 describes some of the other functions that can be used for mortgage analysis. For example, you can use the PV function to calculate the size of the loan that Amanda could afford given a specific interest rate, monthly payment, and total number of payments. If Amanda wanted to know the size of the loan she could afford by using the $850 rent payment as a loan payment, you would enter the formula =PV(5.5%/12,360,850), which would return the value –$149,703.50, or a total loan of almost $150,000.

Figure 2-29 ▶ **Financial functions**

Function	Description
PMT(*rate*, *nper*, *pv*, [*fv*=0], [*type*=0])	Calculates the payments required each period on a loan or investment, where *rate* is the interest rate per period, *nper* is the total number of periods, *pv* is the present value or principal of the loan, *fv* is the future value of the loan, and *type* indicates whether payments should be made at the end of the period (0) or the beginning (1)
PV(*rate*, *nper*, *pmt*, [*fv*=0], [*type*=0])	Calculates the present value of a loan or investment based on periodic, constant payments
NPER(*rate*, *pmt*, *pv*, [*fv*=0], [*type*=0])	Calculates the number of periods required to pay off a loan or investment
RATE(*nper*, *pmt*, *pv*, [, *fv*=0], [*type*=0])	Calculates the interest rate of a loan or investment based on periodic, constant payments

You can use the other functions described in Figure 2-29 to calculate the interest rate and the total number of payment periods. Once again, if you know three of the conditions for the loan, there is an Excel function that you can use to calculate the value of the fourth.

From the calculations you have performed, Amanda now knows that a monthly mortgage payment of $993 is required to pay off a $175,000 loan in 30 years at 5.5% interest. This leaves the family with a net income of about $390 per month. The question remains whether Amanda feels that the mortgage is affordable. Amanda knows that she and Joseph will have to purchase a second car soon, that there are other expenses on the horizon, and that a new house will, no doubt, bring with it additional expenses that she may not have considered yet, such as property taxes. To prepare for those new future expenses, Amanda wants the family's net income to exceed their expenses by about $5,000 per year.

Does her current budget, with a home loan payment of $993 per month, meet that requirement? To find out, you will enter the amount of money Amanda feels that the family needs to save each year and a formula to calculate if they can achieve this goal.

To calculate the family's yearly net income:

1. Click cell **D13**, type **Is the loan affordable?** and then press the **Enter** key.

    You will enter the amount Amanda wants the family to save each year.

2. Type **Required Savings** in cell D14, press the **Tab** key, type **5,000** in cell E14, and then press the **Enter** key.

    Next, you'll enter the formula to calculate how much the family saved in one year using the average monthly net income multiplied by 12 months.

3. Type **Calculated Savings** in cell D15, press the **Tab** key, type **=B22*12** in cell E15, and then press the **Enter** key. See Figure 2-30. Note that the value in cell E15 shows five places to the right of the decimal. You'll learn how to specify the number of decimal places in Tutorial 3.

Calculating the yearly savings | **Figure 2-30**

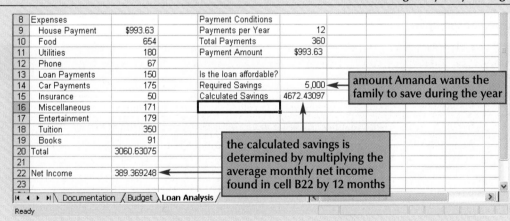

	8	Expenses			Payment Conditions			
	9	House Payment	$993.63		Payments per Year	12		
	10	Food	654		Total Payments	360		
	11	Utilities	180		Payment Amount	$993.63		
	12	Phone	67					
	13	Loan Payments	150		Is the loan affordable?			
	14	Car Payments	175		Required Savings	5,000	amount Amanda wants the	
	15	Insurance	50		Calculated Savings	4672.43097	family to save during the year	
	16	Miscellaneous	171					
	17	Entertainment	179					
	18	Tuition	350					
	19	Books	91		the calculated savings is			
	20	Total	3060.63075		determined by multiplying the			
	21				average monthly net income			
	22	Net Income	389.369248		found in cell B22 by 12 months			
	23							

Documentation / Budget \ **Loan Analysis** /

Ready

Under the proposed loan and assuming only the current expenses, the family could save about $4,672 per year, which is less than Amanda had hoped. So, Amanda would need to look at getting a smaller loan or hope that interest rates decrease in the future.

Amanda appreciates the type of information the worksheet provides, but she is concerned about getting lost in all of the numbers. She would like the worksheet to display a simple text message: "Yes" if the loan is affordable given the conditions she has set for the budget and "No" if otherwise. To add such a feature to the worksheet, you'll need to use a Logical function.

Working with Logical Functions

A **Logical function** is a function that tests, or evaluates, whether a condition in the workbook is true or false. The condition is usually entered as an expression. For example, the expression A1=10 would be true if cell A1 contains the value 10; otherwise, the expression is false.

Using the IF Function

The most commonly used Logical function is the **IF function**, which has the following syntax:

=IF(*logical_test*, *value_if_true*, [*value_if_false*])

where *logical_test* is an expression that is either true or false, *value_if_true* is the value displayed in the cell if the logical test is true, and *value_if_false* is the value displayed if the logical test is false. Note that the *value_if_false* argument is optional, though in most cases you will use it so that the function covers both possibilities.

For example, the formula *=IF(A1=10, 20, 30)* tests whether the value in cell A1 is equal to 10. If the expression A1=10 is true, the function displays the value 20 in the cell containing the function; otherwise, the cell displays the value 30. You can also construct logical tests that involve text values. The formula *=IF(A1="Retail", B1, B2)* tests whether cell A1 contains the text "Retail"; if it does, the function returns the value of cell B1; otherwise, it returns the value of cell B2.

Expressions in the logical test always include a comparison operator. A **comparison operator** indicates the relationship between two values. Figure 2-31 describes the comparison operators supported by Excel.

Figure 2-31 **Comparison operators**

Operator	Example	Description
=	A1 = B1	Tests whether the value in cell A1 *is equal to* the value in cell B1
>	A1 > B1	Tests whether the value in cell A1 *is greater than* the value in cell B1
<	A1 < B1	Tests whether the value in cell A1 *is less than* the value in cell B1
>=	A1 >= B1	Tests whether the value in cell A1 *is greater than or equal to* the value in cell B1
<=	A1 <= B1	Tests whether the value in cell A1 *is less than or equal to* the value in cell B1
<>	A1 <> B1	Tests whether the value in cell A1 *is not equal to* the value in cell B1

You'll use the IF function to display a text message in the worksheet indicating whether a $175,000 loan is affordable. In this case, the logical expression will test whether the value in cell E14 (the required savings) is less than the value in cell E15 (the calculated savings). The expression is E14 < E15. If this expression is true, then the loan is affordable for Amanda's family; otherwise, it is not. You will now enter the formula that includes the IF function *=IF(E14 < E15, "Yes", "No")*.

To insert the IF function to evaluate whether the loan is affordable:

▶ **1.** Click cell **D16**, type **Conclusion**, and then press the **Tab** key.

▶ **2.** In cell E16, type **=IF(E14<E15,"Yes","No")** and then press the **Enter** key. The text "No" appears in cell E16, indicating that the value in cell E14 is not less than the value in cell E15, and, therefore, the conditions of the mortgage are not acceptable to Amanda.

Amanda asks you to reduce the size of the loan to $165,000 to see whether this amount changes the conclusion about the mortgage's affordability.

▶ **3.** Click cell **E4**, type **-165,000** as the new loan amount, and then press the **Enter** key. As shown in Figure 2-32, the monthly payment drops to about $936 and the net yearly savings rise to about $5,354. Cell E16 displays the text string "Yes," indicating that this loan does satisfy Amanda's conditions for affordability.

Inserting a Logical function ◀ **Figure 2-32**

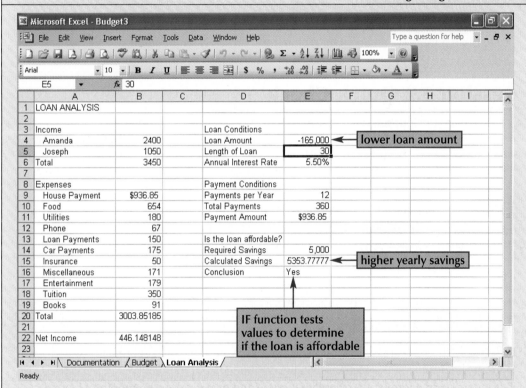

Now Amanda knows that buying a house is something that her family budget can support in the near future if she and Joseph manage their budget well. You will now save and close the Budget3 workbook.

▶ **4.** Save your changes to the workbook, and then close it.

Excel has several other Logical functions that you can use to create more complicated tests. Figure 2-33 describes the syntax of each of these functions.

Figure 2-33 ▶ **Logical functions**

Function	Description
IF(logical_test, value_if_true, [value_if_false])	Returns the value value_if_true if the logical_test expression is true and value_if_false if otherwise
AND(logical1, [logical2, logical3, ...])	Returns the value TRUE if all logical expressions in the function are true and FALSE if otherwise
OR(logical1, [logical2, logical3, ...])	Returns the value TRUE if any logical expression in the function is true and FALSE if otherwise
FALSE()	Returns the value FALSE
TRUE()	Returns the value TRUE
NOT(logical)	Returns the value FALSE if the logical expression is true and the value TRUE if the logical expression is false

Amanda's budget workbook contains much of the information that she and Joseph can use to build a more stable financial picture for themselves in the future.

Review

To reinforce the tasks you learned in this session, go to the SAM 2003 Training Companion CD included with this text.

Session 2.2 Quick Check

1. What are the four principal factors in a loan?
2. If you were to take a five-year loan for $10,000 at 7% annual interest rate, with monthly payments, what formula would you enter to calculate the monthly payment on the loan?
3. To calculate the present value of a loan based on a set, monthly payment, you could use the _____ function.
4. What formula would you use to display the text string "Yes" if the value in cell A1 is greater than the value in cell B1 and "No" if otherwise?
5. To change a logical expression from FALSE to TRUE or from TRUE to FALSE, use the _____ function.

Review

Tutorial Summary

In Session 2.1, you learned about the general syntax used by all Excel functions, and you learned about some of the Math and Statistical functions supported by Excel. You used the SUM function in a formula to calculate income and expenses for the month of January. You then learned how to copy and paste these formulas into other cells in the worksheet to calculate total figures for every month of the year. You learned the difference between the three types of cell references—relative, absolute, and mixed—and then you used an absolute reference to calculate a running total of the net income. You learned about the AVERAGE, MIN, and MAX functions, and then used them to summarize the entire year's budget figures. Once you entered the formulas that used these functions, you learned how to copy and paste the formulas using the Auto Fill feature. You also learned how to change the magnification of the workbook window so you can see more or less of the data in a worksheet. Finally, you used the TODAY() function to display the current date in the Documentation sheet.

In Session 2.2, you learned about the PMT function, which is a Financial function supported by Excel. You used the PMT function to calculate the monthly payment required to pay off a specified mortgage. You also learned about one of Excel's most commonly used Logical functions, the IF function. You used the IF function to display a text string indicating whether a loan was affordable.

Key Terms

Session 2.1	MAX function	TODAY() function
absolute reference	MIN function	WEEKDAY function
argument	mixed reference	**Session 2.2**
Auto Fill	NOW() function	comparison operator
AVERAGE function	optional argument	Financial function
Date function	relative reference	IF function
destination cell	source cell	Logical function
destination range	source range	PMT function
F4 key	SUM function	
fill handle	syntax	

Practice

Practice the skills you learned in Session 2.1 using the same case scenario.

Review Assignments

Data File needed for the Review Assignments: Family1.xls

Amanda appreciates the work you did on her family budget. Her friends Ken and Ava Giles have examined the workbook you created and have asked you to create a similar workbook for their budget.

Once you have completed a budget worksheet for the Giles family, they may want you to help them determine if they can afford to purchase their dream house in the country. The mortgage would be substantially higher than the family's current mortgage, but with Ava now working full time, the couple feels that they may be able to afford the higher mortgage. They would like you to create a workbook that will help them to determine if purchasing the house is possible.

To complete this task:

1. Open the **Family1** workbook located in the Tutorial.02\Review folder included with your Data Files, and then save the workbook as **Family2** in the same folder.
2. In the Documentation sheet, enter your name in cell B3, and then enter the current date in cell B4 using the TODAY() function.
3. Switch to the Budget worksheet, and then enter the formulas in the ranges C7:N7 and C14:N14 to calculate the total income and expenses, respectively, for each month. (*Hint*: Enter the formula in cells C7 and C14 first, and then copy and paste the formulas to the other cells in the ranges.)
4. In the range C16:N16, enter a formula to calculate the family's net income. (*Hint*: Enter the formula in cell C16 first, and then copy and paste the formula to the other cells in the range.)
5. In the range D17:N17, enter a formula using the SUM function to calculate the running total for net income from February through December. (*Hint*: Use an absolute reference for the appropriate cell reference.)
6. In the range C4:N4, use Auto Fill to fill in the month names January, February, March, and so forth.

7. In the range C21:F23, enter a formula to calculate the total, average, minimum, and maximum values of the two incomes.

8. In the range C25:F30, enter a formula to calculate the total, average, minimum, and maximum values of each expense category.

9. In the range C32:F32, enter a formula to calculate the total, average, minimum, and maximum values for net income.

10. Print the contents of the Budget worksheet, and save the changes you have made. If you are not continuing with the remaining steps, close the workbook.

Practice the skills you learned in Session 2.2 using the same case scenario.

(**Note:** The following steps are *optional*. You should attempt them only if you have completed **Session 2.2** in the tutorial.)

11. Save the workbook as **Family3** to the Tutorial.02\Review folder.

12. Add a worksheet named "Loan Analysis" to the end of the workbook, and then enter the text "Loan Analysis" in cell A1 of the worksheet.

13. Switch to the Budget worksheet, copy the nonadjacent range A21:B32;D21:D32, switch to the Loan Analysis worksheet, and then paste the values, but not the formulas, into range A3:C14, using the Paste Special option. Increase the width of columns A and C to 12 characters (89 pixels) each, and column B to 15 characters (110 pixels). Edit the entries in cells C5, C12, and C14 so they contain formulas that calculate the total income, total expense, and net income.

14. Enter the following labels in the cells as indicated:
    - Cell E3: Loan Conditions
    - Cell E4: Loan Amount
    - Cell E5: Length of Loan
    - Cell E6: Annual Interest Rate
    - Cell E8: Payment Conditions
    - Cell E9: Payments per Year
    - Cell E10: Total Payments
    - Cell E11: Payment Amount

15. Widen column E to 21 characters (152 pixels).

16. In the range F4:F9, enter values for the following loan and payment conditions:
    - Loan Amount = –300,000
    - Years = 15
    - Annual Interest Rate = 6%
    - Payments per Year = 12

17. In cell F10, enter a formula to calculate the total number of payments. In cell F11, enter a formula using the PMT function to calculate the monthly loan payment.

18. In cell C8, enter the formula to make the mortgage expense equal to the result of the calculation in cell F11.

19. Enter the following labels in the cells as indicated:
    - Cell E13: Is the loan affordable?
    - Cell E14: Minimum Loan Payment
    - Cell E15: Conclusion

20. The family does not want a monthly loan payment greater than $2,500. Enter this value into cell F14, and then in cell F15 enter a formula using the IF function to display the text string "Yes" if the monthly payment is less than or equal to the value you entered in cell F14, and "No" if otherwise. Is the loan affordable under the loan conditions you have entered?

21. Print the contents of the Loan Analysis worksheet.

22. Change the loan from a 15-year loan to a 20-year loan. What effect does this have on the monthly loan payment and the conclusion about the affordability of the loan? Print the contents of the revised Loan Analysis worksheet.

23. Save your changes to the workbook, and then close it.

Case Problem 1

Data File needed for this Case Problem: Chem1.xls

Chemistry 303 Karen Raul is a professor of chemistry at MidWest University. She has started using Excel to calculate the final grades for students in her Chemistry 303 course. The final score is a weighted total of the scores given for a student's homework, lab work, exams, and final exam. Karen needs your help in creating the formulas to calculate the final score and to calculate the class averages. One way of calculating a weighted sum is to multiply each value by the corresponding weight. For example, consider the following sample exam scores:

- Exam 1 = 84
- Exam 2 = 80
- Exam 3 = 83
- Final exam = 72

If the first three exams are each given a weight of 20% and the final exam is weighted 40%, then the weighted sum is:

$84*0.2 + 80*0.2 + 83*0.2 + 72*0.4 = 78.2$

Karen has entered the weights of the exam scores for each of her students. She needs you to calculate the weighted score as well as some statistics for each exam, including the average score, the maximum and minimum score, and the range of scores.

To complete this task:

1. Open the **Chem1** workbook located in the Tutorial.02\Cases folder included with your Data Files, and then save the workbook as **Chem2** in the same folder.

2. In the Documentation sheet, enter your name in cell B3 and then enter the current date in cell B4 using the TODAY() function. Increase the width of column B to display the date, if necessary.

3. Switch to the Grades worksheet and, in cell F7, enter a formula using cell references to calculate the weighted sum of the four exam scores using the exam values in cells B7, C7, D7, and E7 and the weights in cells B4, C4, D4, and E4.

4. In the formula in cell F7, change the cell references for cells B4, C4, D4, and E4 from relative to absolute references.

5. Use Auto Fill to copy the formula in cell F7 into the range F7:F42.

6. In cell B44, enter a formula using the COUNT function to count the Exam 1 scores in range B7:B42. In cell B45, enter a formula using the AVERAGE function to calculate the average of the Exam 1 scores in range B7:B42. In cell B46, enter a formula using the MAX function to calculate the maximum Exam 1 scores in the same range. In cell B47, enter a formula using the MIN function to calculate the minimum Exam 1 score for the same. In cell B48, enter a formula to calculate the range of the Exam 1 scores (equal to the maximum score minus the minimum score).

7. Copy and paste the formulas in range B44:B48 into the range C44:F48 to calculate the same statistics for the other three exams and the weighted total of all the exams.

8. Print the contents of the Grades sheet in landscape orientation.

9. Save your changes, and then submit the completed workbook and printout to your instructor.

Using what you have learned in Session 2.1, create a workbook that summarizes regional sales information.

Case Problem 2

Data Files needed for this Case Problem: Sales1.xls, Works1.xls

Wizard Works Andrew Howe manages orders for Wizard Works, an online seller of custom fireworks. Andrew has asked you to help him use Excel to develop some reports for an upcoming meeting. Andrew's first project is to create a sales report for three different types of Wizard Works products sold in four different regions. After you enter the sales data, Andrew wants you to calculate the total, average, minimum, and maximum sales for each product and for each region, and then for all products and all regions. You will also need to calculate the percentage of sales for each product.

To complete this task:

1. Open the **Sales1** workbook located in the Tutorial.02\Cases folder included with your Data Files, and then save the workbook as **Sales2** in the same folder.
2. Enter your name and the date in the Documentation sheet.
3. Switch to the Sales Summary sheet, and enter the sales data shown in Figure 2-34.

Figure 2-34 **Units Sold**

Region	Fountains	Firecrackers	Rockets
Region 1	1503	1380	814
Region 2	1081	1873	1103
Region 3	1773	2415	644
Region 4	2289	2103	1474

4. For each product, enter formulas to calculate the total sales for all regions, the average sales per region, and the maximum and minimum sales over all the regions.
5. For each product, enter a formula that uses absolute cell references to calculate the percentage of units sold per region.
6. Summarize the sales for all three of these Wizard Works products by calculating the total, average, maximum, and minimum units sold for all products in all regions.
7. Calculate the percent of units sold for all products in each region.
8. Print the Sales Summary worksheet in landscape orientation, and then save your changes to the workbook.

    (**Note:** The following steps are *optional*. You should attempt them only if you completed **Session 2.2** in the tutorial.)

Using what you learned in Session 2.2, create a worksheet that determines shipping costs and discounts for customer orders.

Andrew also needs your help calculating the total costs of customer orders. You need to compute the total cost of each order, which includes the shipping cost and special discount offered by the store. Customers can choose one of two shipping options: Standard shipping, which costs $8.95 or Express shipping, which costs $14.95. Wizard Works also offers a 5% discount for orders that are more than $200 (not including the shipping cost). You need to enter formulas that use the IF function to determine the shipping cost and discount, if applicable, in order to calculate the total cost of each order.

9. Open the **Works1** workbook located in the Tutorial.02\Cases folder, and then save the workbook as **Works2** in the same folder.
10. Enter your name and the date in the Documentation sheet, and then switch to the Orders sheet.
11. In cell F7, calculate the cost of each product ordered, which is equal to the price of the product multiplied by the quantity.

12. Copy the formula in cell F7 into the cells F8:F9, F15:F19, and F25:F26.
13. In cell F10, calculate the sum of the values in the range F7:F9. In cell F20, calculate the sum of the values in the range F15:F19. In cell F27, calculate the sum of the values in the range F25:F26.
14. In cell F11, enter a formula that uses the IF function to calculate the shipping cost for the order. If the text in cell G11 is equal to "Standard," then the shipping cost is equal to the value in cell D2; otherwise, the shipping cost is equal to the value in cell F2. Change the cell references in the formula for cells D2 and F2 to absolute references.
15. Copy the formula in cell F11 into cells F21 and F28.
16. In cell F12, enter a formula that uses the IF function to calculate the discount. If the value in cell F10 is greater than 200, then the discount is equal to F10 multiplied by the value in cell D4; otherwise, the discount value is 0. Change the cell reference in this formula for cell D4 to an absolute reference.
17. Copy the formula in cell F12 into cells F22 and F29.
18. In cell F13, enter a formula to calculate the total cost of the order, which is equal to the cost of the products ordered plus the shipping cost minus the discount.
19. Copy the formula in cell F13 into cells F23 and F30.
20. Print the resulting Orders worksheet in landscape orientation.
21. Save your changes, and then submit the completed workbook and printout to your instructor.

Case Problem 3

Challenge

Go beyond what you learned in Session 2.2 to use the IF function as you create a payroll worksheet.

Data File needed for this Case Problem: Sonic1.xls

Sonic Sounds   Jeff Gwydion manages the payroll at Sonic Sounds. He has asked you for help in setting up an Excel worksheet to store payroll information. The payroll contains three elements: each employee's salary, 401(k) contribution, and health insurance cost. The company's 401(k) contribution is 3% of an employee's salary for those who have worked for the company at least one year; otherwise, the company's contribution is zero. Sonic Sounds also supports two health insurance plans: Premier and Standard. The cost of the Premier plan is $6,500, and the cost of the Standard plan is $5,500. The workbook has already been set up for you. Your job is to enter the formulas to calculate the 401(k) contributions and health insurance costs for each employee. Figure 2-35 shows the worksheet as it will appear at the end of this exercise.

Figure 2-35

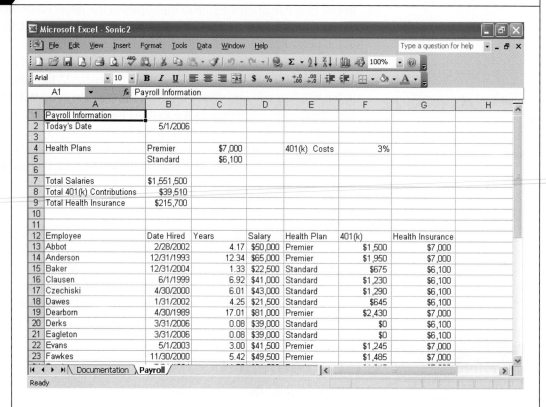

To complete this task:

1. Open the **Sonic1** workbook located in the Tutorial.02\Cases folder included with your Data Files, and then save the workbook as **Sonic2** in the same folder.
2. In the Documentation sheet, enter your name and then enter the date using the TODAY() function.
3. Switch to the Payroll worksheet. In cell C13, enter a formula to calculate the number of years the first employee has worked at Sonic Sounds. Use an absolute reference for cell B2. Divide the difference by 365. (*Hint*: You need to subtract the date the employee was hired from the current date, which is in cell B2, and then divide the difference by the number of days in a year. For the purposes of this exercise, do not try to account for leap years.)
4. Use Auto Fill to calculate the number of years the remaining employees in the table have worked for the company.

Explore 5. In the range F13:F45, insert a formula to calculate the 401(k) contributions for each employee. The formula should determine that if the number of years employed is greater than or equal to 1, then the contribution is equal to the contribution percentage in cell F4 multiplied by the employee's salary; otherwise, the contribution is zero.

Explore 6. In the range G13:G45, enter a formula to calculate the health insurance cost for each employee by testing whether the name of the employee's plan is equal to the name of the health plan in cell B4. If it is, then the cost of the health plan is equal to the value of cell C4; otherwise, the cost is equal to the value of cell C5.

7. In the range B7:B9, enter the formulas to calculate the total salaries, 401(k) contributions, and health insurance costs.
8. Print the contents of the Payroll worksheet.

9. Rework the analysis, assuming that the cost of the Premier plan has risen to $7,000 and the cost of the Standard plan has risen to $6,100.
10. Print the revised Payroll worksheet.
11. Save your changes to the workbook, and then close it.

Challenge

Go beyond what you learned in Session 2.2. Use the PMT, PPMT, and IPMT functions to create a payment schedule for a small business.

Case Problem 4

Data File needed for this Case Problem: Soup1.xls

The Soup Shop Ken Novak is the owner of a diner in Upton, Ohio, named The Soup Shop. Business has been very good lately, so Ken is considering taking out a loan to cover the cost of upgrading and expanding the diner. Ken wants your help in creating an Excel workbook that provides detailed information about the loan. He would like the workbook to calculate the monthly payment needed for a five-year, $125,000 loan at 6.5% interest. Ken believes that the expansion will increase business, so he also wants to know how much he would save on interest payments by paying off the loan after one, two, three, or four years.

To do this type of calculation, you need to know what part of each monthly payment is used to reduce the size of the loan (also referred to as payments toward the principal) and what part is used for paying interest on the loan. Excel provides two functions to calculate these values, both of which are similar to the PMT function used to calculate the total monthly payment. To calculate how much of a monthly payment is used to pay off the principal, you use the PPMT function, which has the following syntax:

=PPMT(*rate, period, nper, pv* [,*fv*=0] [,*type*=0])

where *rate* is the interest rate period, *period* is the payment period you want to examine (such as the first period, the second period, and so forth), *nper* is the total number of payment periods, *pv* is the amount of the loan, *fv* is the future value of the loan (assumed to be zero), and *type* indicates whether the payment is due at the beginning (*type*=1) or at the end (*type*=0) of the month. The function to calculate how much of the monthly payment is used for paying the interest is the IPMT function, which has a similar syntax:

=IPMT(*rate, period, nper, pv* [,*fv*=0] [,*type*=0])

As with the PMT function, the value of the *pv* argument should be negative when you are working with loans—as you are in this case.

Ken wants you to use these two functions to create a payment schedule that indicates for each of the 60 months of the loan, how much of the monthly payment is being used to pay off the loan and how much is being used to pay interest on the loan. You can then use this schedule to discover how much Ken could save in interest charges by paying off the loan early. Figure 2-36 shows the worksheet as it will appear at the end of this exercise.

Figure 2-36

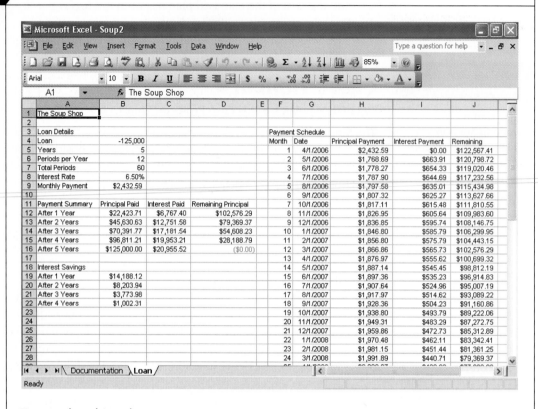

To complete this task:

1. Open the **Soup1** workbook located in the Tutorial.02\Cases folder included with your Data Files, and then save the workbook as **Soup2** in the same folder.
2. Enter your name and the current date in the Documentation sheet.
3. Switch to the Loan worksheet, and then in the range B4:B8, enter the following loan details:
   - Loan Amount = –125,000
   - Years = 5
   - Periods per Year = 12
   - Interest Rate = 6.5% (annually)

   In cell B7, enter a formula to calculate the total number of payment periods.
4. In cell B9, enter a formula using the PMT function to calculate the total monthly payment required to pay off the loan. Assume that payments are made at the beginning of each period, *not* at the end, which is the default. (*Hint:* Use the *fv* and *type* arguments.)
5. In the range F5:F64, enter the numbers 1 through 60 using Auto Fill. Each number indicates the payment period in the payment schedule.
6. Ken would like his payment schedule to include the dates on which the payments are due. In cell G5, enter the date 4/1/2006. This is the due date for the first payment. In cell G6, enter the date 5/1/2006. This is the due date for the second payment. Use the Auto Fill to enter the rest of the due dates into the range G7:G64.

Explore

7. In cell H5, enter a formula using the PPMT function to calculate the amount of the first month's payment devoted to reducing the principal of the loan. The details of the loan should reference the appropriate cells in the B4:B8 range of the worksheet using absolute references. The period number should reference the value in cell F5 using a relative reference. Be sure to indicate in the function that the payments are made at the beginning, not the end, of the month.

Explore

8. In cell I5, enter a formula using the IPMT function to calculate the amount of the first month's payment that is used for paying the interest on the loan.

Explore

9. In cell J5, enter a formula that calculates the amount of the principal remaining to be paid. Ken would like this expressed as a positive value. To calculate this value, construct a formula that is equal to the *negative* of the value in cell B4 (the amount of the loan) minus the running total of the principal payments. To calculate a running total of the principal payments, use the formula =SUM($H$5:H5). Note that this formula uses both an absolute reference and a relative reference, much like the running total example in the tutorial.

10. Using Auto Fill, copy the formulas in the range H5:J5 to the range H5:J64. (*Hint:* The value displayed in cell J64 should be $0.00, indicating that the loan is completely paid off. Also, the interest payment for the last month should be $13.11.)

11. In cell B12, enter a formula to calculate the total amount of payments made to the principal in the first 12 months of the schedule. In cell C12, enter a formula to calculate the total amount of the interest payments. In cell D12, enter a formula to calculate the amount of the remaining principal. Once again, Ken wants this expressed as a positive value, so the formula must subtract the value in cell B12 from the *negative* of the value in cell B4.

12. Repeat Step 11 for the range B13:D13, calculating the totals for the first 24 months. In the range B14:D14, calculate the totals for the first 36 months. In the range B15:D15, calculate the 48-month totals. In the range B16:D16, calculate the 60-month totals.

13. In the range B19:B22, enter a formula to calculate the amount of money Ken would save in interest payments if he paid off the loan after one year, two years, three years, and four years.

Explore

14. Preview the worksheet before printing it. Open the Page Setup dialog box, change the page orientation of the worksheet to landscape orientation, and then select the option so the worksheet will print on one page. Preview the worksheet again and then print it.

15. Save your changes to the workbook and then close it.

Internet Assignments

Research

Use the Internet to find and work with data related to the topics presented in this tutorial.

The purpose of the Internet Assignments is to challenge you to find information on the Internet that you can use to work effectively with this software. The actual assignments are updated and maintained on the Course Technology Web site. Log on to the Internet and use your Web browser to go to the Student Online Companion for New Perspectives Office 2003 at **www.course.com/np/office2003**. Click the Internet Assignments link, and then navigate to the assignments for this tutorial.

SAM Assessment and Training

Assess

If your instructor has chosen to use the full online version of SAM 2003 Assessment and Training, you can go beyond the "just-in-time" training provided on the CD that accompanies this text. Simply log in to your SAM account (http://sam2003.course.com) to launch any assigned training activities or exams that relate to the skills covered in this tutorial.

Quick Check Answers

Session 2.1

1. =MIN(B1:B50)
2. =B2+C2
3. =$A$1+C2
4. (a) A1 (b) $A$1 (c) $A1 and A$1
5. Enter the values 1 and 3 in the first two rows of column A. Select the two cells and then drag the fill handle down over the range A1:A99, completing the series.
6. TODAY()

Session 2.2

1. the loan amount, the interest rate, the number of payment periods, and the payment due each period
2. =PMT(7%/12,5*12,10000)
3. PV
4. =IF(A1>B1, "Yes", "No")
5. NOT

Developing a Professional-Looking Worksheet

Formatting a Sales Report

Case | NewGeneration Monitors

NewGeneration Monitors is a computer equipment company that specializes in computer monitors. Joan Sanchez, sales manager, has been entering sales data for three of the company's monitors into an Excel workbook. She plans on including the sales data in a report to be presented later in the week. Joan has made no attempt to change or enhance the presentation of this data. She has simply entered the numbers. She needs you to transform her raw figures into a presentable report.

To create a professional-looking document, you will learn how to work with Excel's formatting tools to modify the appearance of the data in each cell, the cell itself, and the entire worksheet. You will also learn how to format printouts, create headers and footers, and control which parts of the worksheet are printed on which pages.

Session	Objectives		SAM Training Tasks	
Session 3.1	• Format data using the Comma, Currency, and Percent styles • Copy and paste formats using the Format Painter • Modify and apply number formatting styles	• Change font type, style, size, and color • Change the alignment of cell contents • Apply borders, background colors, and patterns	• Add borders • Apply bold and italics • Apply number formats (currency and percent) • Apply number formats (dates and comma) • Center across selection • Center across selection using Alignment tab in Format Cells dialog box • Change fonts • Change the font color • Format a worksheet background	• Format cells before entering data • Format the Insert row in an empty list • Indent text • Locate and open existing workbooks • Protect worksheet cells • Right align cells • Rotate text • Set cell color • Wrap text
Session 3.2	• Merge a range of cells into a single cell • Hide rows, columns, and worksheets • Add a background image to a worksheet • Format worksheet tabs • Clear and replace formats	• Create and apply styles • Apply an AutoFormat • Set up a worksheet for printing • Add headers and footers to printouts	• Add headers to worksheets • Apply AutoFormats to worksheets • Apply styles • Center on page horizontally • Change margins in Page Setup • Clear cell formats • Control page breaks • Create a style • Format worksheet tabs	• Hide page breaks • Hide rows and columns • Hide worksheets in a workbook • Merge cells • Modify worksheet orientation • Print non-adjacent selections of worksheets in a workbook • Set print areas • Unhide columns

Student Data Files   For a complete list of the Data Files needed for this tutorial, see page EX 2.

Session 3.1

For hands-on practice of key tasks in this session, go to the SAM 2003 Training Companion CD included with this text.

Formatting Worksheet Data

The data for Joan's sales report has already been stored in an Excel workbook. Before going further, you will open the workbook and save it with a new filename.

To open the Sales report workbook:

▶ **1.** Start Excel and then open the **Sales1** workbook located in the Tutorial.03\Tutorial folder included with your Data Files.

▶ **2.** On the Documentation worksheet, enter *your name* in cell B3, and enter the *current date* in cell B4.

▶ **3.** Save the workbook as **Sales2** in the Tutorial.03\Tutorial folder.

▶ **4.** Click the **Sales** tab to display the unformatted worksheet, shown in Figure 3-1.

| Figure 3-1 | The unformatted Sales worksheet |

Microsoft Excel - Sales2

File　Edit　View　Insert　Format　Tools　Data　Window　Help　　Type a question for help

Arial　　10　　B I U 　　$ %

A1　　*fx* NewGeneration Monitors

	A	B	C	D	E	F	G	H
1	NewGeneration Monitors							
2	Sales Data							
3	1/1/2006 - 12/31/2006							
4								
5	Monthly Sales Data							
6	Month	VX100	VX300	FlatScreen	Total			
7	January	1410	1860	435	3705			
8	February	1284	1704	390	3378			
9	March	1443	1875	435	3753			
10	April	1425	1842	423	3690			
11	May	1509	1998	450	3957			
12	June	1473	1923	453	3849			
13	July	1533	1863	465	3861			
14	August	1452	1914	441	3807			
15	September	1368	1794	420	3582			
16	October	1389	1836	429	3654			
17	November	1413	1866	423	3702			
18	December	1533	2013	444	3990			
19	Total	17232	22488	5208	44928			
20								
21	Analysis of 2006 Sales							
22	Monitor	Price per Unit	Cost per Unit	Gross Profit per Unit	Units Sold	Total Revenue	Gross Profit from Sales	% of Gross Profit from Sales
23	VX100	199.99	165.2	34.79	17232	3446227.68	599501.28	0.200341795
24	VX300	299.99	234.75	65.24	22488	6746175.12	1467117.12	0.490282318
25	FlatScreen	899.99	722.23	177.76	5208	4687147.92	925774.08	0.309375888
26	Total				44928	14879550.72	2992392.48	
27								
28								

Documentation　Sales

Ready

The Sales worksheet contains two tables. The table in the upper portion of the worksheet displays the monthly sales figures for three of NewGeneration's monitors: the VX100, the VX300, and the FlatScreen. The other table presents an analysis of these sales figures. Although the data in the worksheet is accurate and complete, the numbers are not as easy to read as they could be, which also makes interpreting the data more difficult. To help improve the readability of the data presented in a worksheet, you can change its appearance by formatting it.

Formatting is the process of changing the appearance of your workbook. A properly formatted workbook can be easier to read, appear more professional, and help draw attention to the important points you want to make. Formatting only changes the appearance of the data; it does not affect the data itself. For example, if a cell contains the value 0.124168, and you format the cell to display only up to the thousandths digit (so the value appears as 0.124), the cell still contains the precise value, even though you cannot see it displayed in the worksheet.

Unless you specify different formatting, Excel automatically displays numbers in the worksheet cells using the **General number format**, which, for the most part, formats numbers just the way you enter them. There are some exceptions to this approach. For example, if the cell is not wide enough to show the entire number, the General number format rounds numbers that contain decimals and uses scientific notation for large numbers.

If you don't want to use the General number format, you can choose from a wide variety of number formats. Formats can be applied using either the Formatting toolbar or the Format menu. Formats can also be copied from one cell to another, giving you the ability to apply a common format to different cells in your worksheet.

Using the Formatting Toolbar

The Formatting toolbar is one of the fastest ways to format a worksheet. By clicking a single button on the Formatting toolbar, you can increase or decrease the number of decimal places displayed in a selected range of cells, and display a value as currency with a dollar sign or a percentage with a percent sign. You also can use the Formatting toolbar to change the font type (for example, Times New Roman or Arial), style (such as bold), color, or size.

When Joan entered the monthly sales figures for the three monitors, she was concerned with entering the figures as accurately and as efficiently as possible and wasn't concerned with the appearance of the numbers in the worksheet. She entered the sales figures without including a comma to separate the thousands from the hundreds and so forth. Now, to make the numbers easier to read, Joan wants all the values to appear with commas, and for the figures that are whole numbers, she doesn't want any zeros after the decimal point (also referred to as "trailing zeros"). She believes that these changes will make the worksheet easier to read.

To insert commas in the figures in Joan's worksheet, you will apply the Comma style using its button on the Formatting toolbar. By default, Excel automatically adds two decimal places to the numbers that you have formatted with the Comma style. You will then need to use the Decrease Decimal button on the Formatting toolbar to change the number of decimal places displayed in a number.

To apply the Comma style and remove the trailing zeros:

1. Select the range **B7:E19** in the Sales worksheet.

2. Click the **Comma Style** button ⟦ , ⟧ on the Formatting toolbar. Excel adds the comma separator to each of the values in the table and displays the values with two digits to the right of the decimal point.

   Trouble? If you do not see the Comma Style button ⟦ , ⟧ on the Formatting toolbar, click the Toolbar Options button ⟦ ⟧ on the Formatting toolbar, point to Add or Remove Buttons, point to Formatting, and then click ⟦ , ⟧ on the menu of available buttons.

   Because Joan wants whole numbers displayed without trailing zeros, you will remove any that are displayed.

3. Click the **Decrease Decimal** button ⟦ .00 → .0 ⟧ on the Formatting toolbar twice to remove the zeros. Figure 3-2 shows the worksheet with the formatting changes you have made so far.

Figure 3-2 ▶ **Applying the Comma style**

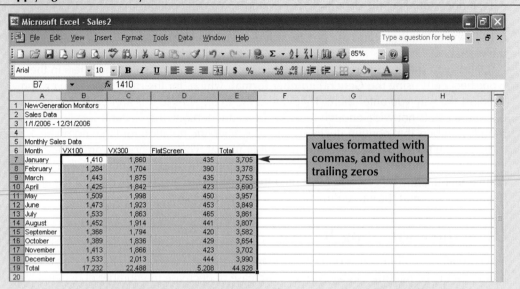

Joan wants the price and production cost of each monitor as well as last year's total sales and gross profit displayed using dollar signs, commas, and two decimal places. A quick and easy way to format the values with these attributes is to use the Currency style, which is available as a button on the Formatting toolbar. When you apply the Currency style, Excel adds a dollar sign and comma separator to the value and displays two decimal places. Try applying the Currency style to the total sales and profit values.

To apply the Currency style:

▶ 1. Select the nonadjacent range **B23:D25;F23:G26**.

   Trouble? To select a nonadjacent range, select the first range, press and hold the Ctrl key, and then select the next range.

▶ 2. Click the **Currency Style** button $ on the Formatting toolbar. As shown in Figure 3-3, Excel adds the dollar signs and commas, and keeps two decimal places to display the values as currency. Also note that the alignment of the dollar signs is along the left edge of the cell and the decimal points are aligned vertically.

Figure 3-3 ▶ **Applying the Currency style**

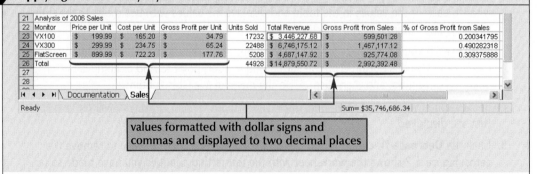

Finally, the range H23:H25 displays the percentage that each monitor contributes to the overall profit from sales. Joan wants these values displayed with a percent sign and two decimal places. To format a value as a percent, you can apply the Percent style. By default, Excel does not display any decimal places with the Percent style; therefore, you will need to increase the number of decimal places displayed.

To apply the Percent style and increase the number of decimal places:

▶ **1.** Select the range **H23:H25**.

▶ **2.** Click the **Percent Style** button % on the Formatting toolbar. The values appear with percent signs and without zeros.

▶ **3.** Click the **Increase Decimal** button on the Formatting toolbar twice to display the percentages to two decimal places. Figure 3-4 shows the values in column H formatted with percent signs and to two decimal places.

Applying the Percent style ◀ **Figure 3-4**

	21	Analysis of 2006 Sales							
	22	Monitor	Price per Unit	Cost per Unit	Gross Profit per Unit	Units Sold	Total Revenue	Gross Profit from Sales	% of Gross Profit from Sales
	23	VX100	$ 199.99	$ 165.20	$ 34.79	17232	$ 3,446,227.68	$ 599,501.28	20.03%
	24	VX300	$ 299.99	$ 234.75	$ 65.24	22488	$ 6,746,175.12	$ 1,467,117.12	49.03%
	25	FlatScreen	$ 899.99	$ 722.23	$ 177.76	5208	$ 4,687,147.92	$ 925,774.08	30.94%
	26	Total				44928	$14,879,550.72	$ 2,992,392.48	
	27								
	28								

⁞◀ ▶ ▶⁞ \ Documentation \ Sales /   ⁞<   ⁞⁞⁞   ⁞>⁞

Ready   Sum=100.00%

values formatted with percent signs and displayed to two decimal places

By displaying the percentages, you can quickly see that one monitor, the VX300, accounts for almost half of the profit from monitor sales.

Copying Formats

As you look over the sales figures, you see that one area of the worksheet still needs to be formatted. The Units Sold column in the range E23:E26 still does not display the comma separator you used with the sales figures. To fix a formatting problem like this one, you can use the Format Painter button located on the Standard toolbar. When you use the **Format Painter** option, you "paint" a format from one cell to another cell or to a range of cells. This is a fast and efficient way of copying a format from one cell to another.

Copying Formatting Using the Format Painter   Reference Window

- Select the cell or range whose formatting you want to apply to other cells.
- To apply the formatting to one cell or an adjacent range of cells, click the Format Painter button on the Standard toolbar, and then click the destination cell or drag the Format Painter pointer over the adjacent range.
- To apply the formatting to nonadjacent ranges, double-click the Format Painter button on the Standard toolbar, and then drag the Format Painter pointer over the first range and then over the other ranges you want to format.

You will use the Format Painter button to copy the format used in the sales figures and to paste that format into the range E23:E26.

To copy the formatting to the range E23:E26 using the Format Painter button:

1. Select cell **B7**, which contains the formatting that you want to copy. You do not have to copy the entire range, because the range is formatted in the same way.

2. Click the **Format Painter** button 🖌 on the Standard toolbar. As you move the pointer over the worksheet area, the pointer changes to ⊕🖌.

3. Drag the pointer over the range **E23:E26** to apply the modified Comma style format to the sales figures.

Another approach is to use the fill handle discussed in Tutorial 2 to fill in the format (not the values) from one cell to another. To use this approach, you have click the Auto Fill Options button and select the Fill Formatting option. This technique only works when the cell or cells that you want to format are adjacent to the cell containing the format you want to copy. You can also use the Paste Special command from the Copy and Paste buttons to paste only the format of a selected group of cells into a new range of cells. This technique was also discussed in Tutorial 2. One of the advantages of the Format Painter button is that it does what these two methods do, but it does so in fewer steps. However, you should use the approach with which you feel most comfortable.

The Format Painter button and the buttons on the Formatting toolbar are fast and easy ways to copy and apply cell formats, but on occasion you will need more control over your formatting choices than is provided by these toolbar buttons. In those cases, you will need to use the Format Cells dialog box.

Using the Format Cells Dialog Box

Joan agrees that formatting the values has made the worksheet easier to read, but she has a few other suggestions. She does not like the way the currency values are displayed with the dollar signs placed at the left edge of the cell, leaving a large blank space between the dollar sign and the numbers, which is characteristic of values that use an accounting format. She would rather see the dollar sign placed directly to the left of the dollar amounts, which would eliminate the blank space.

The convenience of the Formatting toolbar's one-click access to many of the formatting tasks you will want to perform does have its limits. As you can see in the worksheet, when you use the Formatting toolbar, you cannot specify how the format is applied. To make the change that Joan suggests, you will open the Format Cells dialog box, which gives you more control over the formatting by providing categories of formats from which you can choose and modify to suit your needs.

To open the Format Cells dialog box:

▶ **1.** Select the nonadjacent range **B23:D25;F23:G26**.

▶ **2.** Click **Format** on the menu bar, and then click **Cells**. The Format Cells dialog box opens, as shown in Figure 3-5. In addition to the General format category, there are 11 number format categories from which to choose.

Format Cells dialog box ◀ **Figure 3-5**

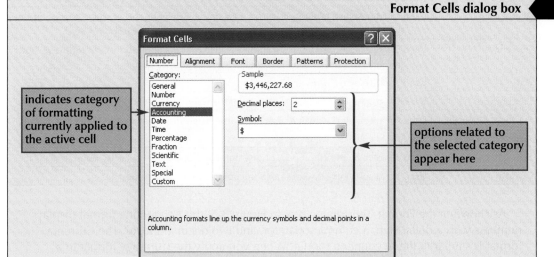

The Format Cells dialog box contains the following six tabs, each dedicated to a different set of format properties. You can apply the options available in this dialog box to any cell or range of cells that you select. The six tabs are:

- **Number:** Provides options for formatting the appearance of numbers, including dates and numbers treated as text (for example, telephone numbers)
- **Alignment:** Provides options for controlling how data is aligned within a cell
- **Font:** Provides options for selecting font types, sizes, and styles and other formatting attributes, such as underlining and colors
- **Border:** Provides options for adding borders around cells
- **Patterns:** Provides options for creating and applying background colors and patterns to cells
- **Protection:** Provides options for locking or hiding cells to prevent other users from modifying their contents

Excel supports several categories of number formats, ranging from Accounting, which you applied using the Currency Style button, to Scientific, which might be used for recording engineering data. Figure 3-6 describes the number format categories.

Figure 3-6 ▶ **Number format categories**

Category	Description
General	Default format that displays numbers as they are entered
Number	Used for a general display of numbers, with options for the formatting of negative numbers and the number of decimal places
Accounting	Used for displaying monetary values with dollar signs aligned at the left edge of the cell, the decimal points aligned vertically, and comma separators inserted
Currency	Used for displaying monetary values with dollar signs aligned next to leftmost digit and comma separators inserted (decimal points are not aligned)
Date, Time	Used for displaying date and time values
Percentage	Used for displaying decimal values as percentages
Fraction, Scientific	Used for displaying values as fractions or in scientific notation
Text	Used for displaying values as text strings
Special	Used for displaying ZIP codes, phone numbers, and social security numbers
Custom	Used for displaying numbers used in coding or specialized designs

As shown in the Format Cells dialog box in Figure 3-5, the Accounting format displays numbers with a dollar sign, a comma separator, and two decimal places. The Currency format is similar to the Accounting format. When you apply the Currency format to a number, the number appears with a dollar sign, a comma separator, and two decimal places. However, the difference between the two formats is how these attributes appear in the cell. The Accounting format lines up the decimal points and aligns the dollar signs at the left edge of the cell border (creating blank spaces between the dollar signs and the values, as you saw earlier). The Currency format aligns the dollar sign closer to the number, which removes the blank spaces. Joan prefers the Currency format, so you will apply this format to the nonadjacent range that you already selected.

To modify and apply the Currency format:

▶ 1. On the Number tab, click **Currency** in the Category list box. The Format Cells dialog box displays the options available for customizing the Currency category and provides a preview of the selected format. As shown in the Negative numbers list box, Excel displays negative currency values either with a minus sign (-) or with a combination of a red font and parentheses. Joan wants negative currency values to be displayed with a minus sign, which is one of the variations of the Currency format available to you.

▶ 2. Click the first entry in the Negative numbers list box, and then click the **OK** button. Excel changes the format of the currency values, removing the blank spaces between the dollar signs and the values and changing the alignment of the decimal points.

By using the Format Cells dialog box, you can control the formatting to ensure that text and values are displayed the way you want them to be.

Changing Font Type, Size, Style, and Color

A **font** is a set of characters that use the same typeface, style, and size. A **typeface** is the specific design of a set of printed characters, including letters, numbers, punctuation marks, and symbols. Some of the more commonly used fonts are Arial, Times Roman, and Courier. Each font can be displayed using one of the following **font styles**: regular, *italic*, **bold**, or ***bold italic***. Fonts can also be displayed with special effects, such as ~~strikeout~~, underline, and color.

Fonts can also be rendered in different sizes. **Font sizes** are measured using points. A **point** is a unit of measurement used in printing and is equal to approximately 1/72 of an inch. By default, Excel displays characters using a 10-point Arial font in a regular style. To change the font used in a selected cell, you either click the appropriate buttons on the Formatting toolbar or select options in the Format Cells dialog box.

In the logo that the company uses on all its correspondence and advertising materials, the name "NewGeneration Monitors" appears in a large Times New Roman font, which is a serif font. Characters that are designed as **serif fonts** have small lines stemming from and at an angle to the upper and lower ends of the character. **Sans serif fonts** do not include the small lines. A serif font is considered easier to read than a sans serif font. Joan wants the title in cell A1 to reflect this company-wide format, so you will format the title accordingly.

To change the font and font size of the title:

▶ **1.** Click cell **A1** to make it the active cell.

▶ **2.** Click the **Font** list arrow Arial ▾ on the Formatting toolbar, scroll down the list of available fonts, and then click **Times New Roman**.

Trouble? If you do not have the Times New Roman font installed on your computer, choose a different Times Roman font or choose MS Serif or another serif font in the list.

▶ **3.** Click the **Font Size** list arrow 10 ▾ on the Formatting toolbar, and then click **18**. Figure 3-7 shows the revised format for the title in cell A1.

Changing the font and font size ◀ **Figure 3-7**

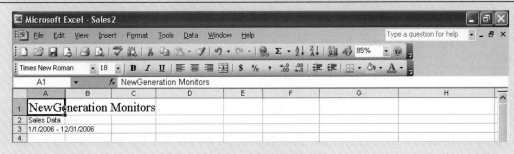

Joan wants the column titles of both tables displayed in bold font and the word "Total" in both tables displayed in italics. To make these modifications, you will again use the Formatting toolbar.

To apply the bold and italic styles:

▶ **1.** Select the nonadjacent range **A6:E6;A22:H22**.

▶ **2.** Click the **Bold** button B on the Formatting toolbar. The titles in the two tables now appear in a boldface font.

Trouble? Some of the title text may appear truncated within their cells. You'll fix this problem shortly.

> **3.** Select the nonadjacent range **A19;A26**.
>
> **4.** Click the **Italic** button I on the Formatting toolbar. The word "Total" in cells A19 and A26 is now italicized.

Joan points out that NewGeneration's logo usually appears in a red font. Color is another one of Excel's formatting tools and can dramatically enhance the presentation of your data if you have a color printer. Excel provides a palette of 40 different colors. If the color you want is not listed, you can modify Excel's color configuration to create a different color palette. Excel's default color settings will work for most situations, so in this case you will not modify Excel's color settings. You will apply a red color to the name of the company and the two subtitles, which describe the contents of this worksheet.

To change the font color of the title to red:

> **1.** Select the range **A1:A3**.
>
> **2.** Click the **Font Color** list arrow $\boxed{\mathbf{A} \cdot}$ on the Formatting toolbar to display a color palette, and then position the pointer over the Red square (third row, first column from the left) on the palette, as shown in Figure 3-8.

Figure 3-8	Choosing a font color

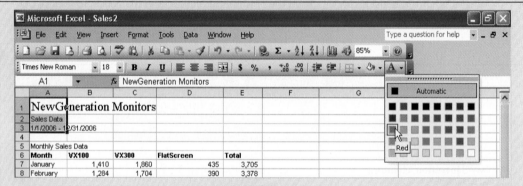

> **3.** Click the **Red** square to change the color of the font in the selected cells to red. See Figure 3-9.

Figure 3-9	Changing the font color of a cell

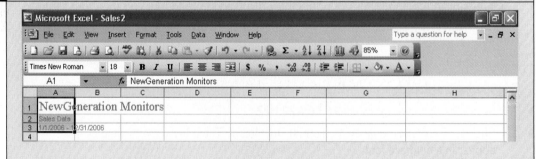

Aligning Cell Contents

When you enter numbers and formulas into a cell, Excel automatically aligns them with the cell's right edge and bottom border. Text entries are aligned with the left edge and bottom border. The default Excel alignment does not always create the most readable worksheets. As a general rule, you should center column titles, and format columns of numbers so that the decimal places are lined up within a column. You can change horizontal alignment using the alignment tools on the Formatting toolbar or the options on the Alignment tab in the Format Cells dialog box.

Next, you will center the column titles above the values in each column in the two tables.

To center the column titles:

1. Select the nonadjacent range **B6:E6;B22:H22**.

2. Click the **Center** button 🔲 on the Formatting toolbar. Excel centers the text in the selected cells in each column.

The Formatting toolbar also provides the Align Left button and the Align Right button so that you can left-align and right-align cell contents. If you want to align cell contents vertically, you have to open the Format Cells dialog box and choose the vertical alignment options on the Alignment tab.

Another alignment option available in the Format Cells dialog box is to center text across a range of cells. Joan wants the text in the cell range A1:A3 to be centered at the top of the worksheet across the first eight columns of the worksheet. This time you will open the Format Cells dialog box to make this formatting change.

To center the titles and subtitles across the first eight columns of the worksheet:

1. Select the range **A1:H3**.

2. Click **Format** on the menu bar, and then click **Cells** to open the Format Cells dialog box.

3. Click the **Alignment** tab.

4. Click the **Horizontal** list arrow in the Text alignment pane, click **Center Across Selection**, and then click the **OK** button. See Figure 3-10.

Centering text within and across columns ◄ **Figure 3-10**

The text in these cells is centered horizontally across the selection. Note that centering the text does not affect the location. The title and subtitles are still placed in cells A1 through A3. In general, you should only use this approach for text that is in the leftmost column of the selection, and there should be no text in any other column. If you had text in column B in the previous set of steps, then that text would have been centered across columns B through H, and the text in column A would have remained where it was.

Indenting and Wrapping Text

Sometimes you will want a cell's contents offset, or indented, a few spaces from the cell's edge. This is particularly true for text entries that are aligned with the left edge of the cell. Indenting is often used for cell entries that are considered "subsections" of your worksheet. Joan wants you to indent the names of the months in the range A7:A18 and the monitor titles in the range A23:A25. You will indent the text using one of the indent buttons on the Formatting toolbar.

To indent the months and monitor titles:

1. Select the nonadjacent range **A7:A18;A23:A25**.
2. Click the **Increase Indent** button on the Formatting toolbar. Excel shifts the contents of the selected cells to the right. See Figure 3-11.

Figure 3-11 **Indenting text within cells**

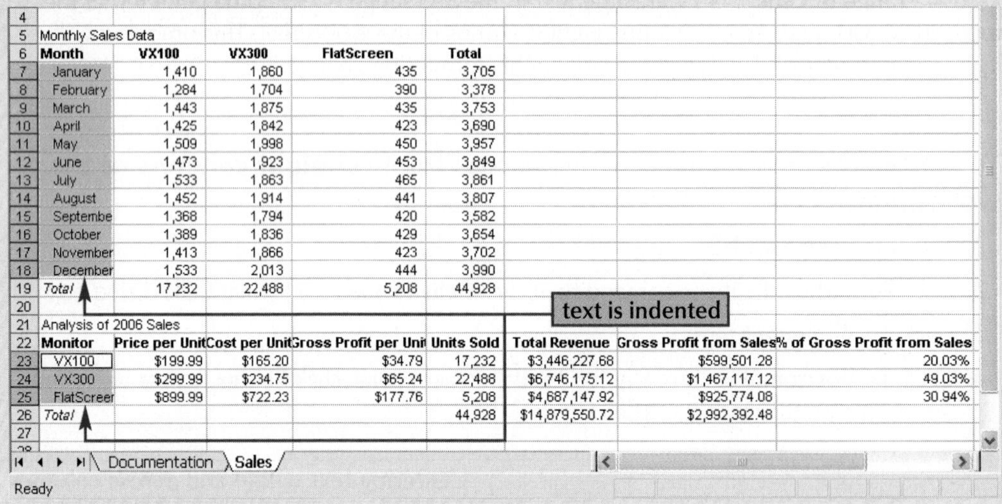

4								
5	Monthly Sales Data							
6	**Month**	**VX100**	**VX300**	**FlatScreen**	**Total**			
7	January	1,410	1,860	435	3,705			
8	February	1,284	1,704	390	3,378			
9	March	1,443	1,875	435	3,753			
10	April	1,425	1,842	423	3,690			
11	May	1,509	1,998	450	3,957			
12	June	1,473	1,923	453	3,849			
13	July	1,533	1,863	465	3,861			
14	August	1,452	1,914	441	3,807			
15	Septembe	1,368	1,794	420	3,582			
16	October	1,389	1,836	429	3,654			
17	November	1,413	1,866	423	3,702			
18	December	1,533	2,013	444	3,990			
19	*Total*	17,232	22,488	5,208	44,928			
20								
21	Analysis of 2006 Sales							
22	**Monitor**	**Price per Unit**	**Cost per Unit**	**Gross Profit per Unit**	**Units Sold**	**Total Revenue**	**Gross Profit from Sales**	**% of Gross Profit from Sales**
23	VX100	$199.99	$165.20	$34.79	17,232	$3,446,227.68	$599,501.28	20.03%
24	VX300	$299.99	$234.75	$65.24	22,488	$6,746,175.12	$1,467,117.12	49.03%
25	FlatScreer	$899.99	$722.23	$177.76	5,208	$4,687,147.92	$925,774.08	30.94%
26	*Total*				44,928	$14,879,550.72	$2,992,392.48	
27								

Clicking the Increase Indent button increases the amount of indentation by roughly one character. To decrease or remove an indentation, click the Decrease Indent button or modify the Indent value using the Format Cells dialog box.

If you enter text that is too wide for a cell, Excel either extends the text into the adjoining cells (if the cells are empty) or truncates the display of the text (if the adjoining cells contain text or values). To avoid cutting off the display of text in a cell, you can widen the columns, or place the text on several lines using the method you learned in Tutorial 1 (pressing the Alt key to move to a second line with a cell). You can also have Excel wrap the text within the cell for you. To wrap text within a cell, you click the Wrap text check box on the Alignment tab of the Format Cells dialog box.

Joan notes that some of the column titles in the second table are long. For example, the "Cost per Unit" label in cell C22 is much longer than the values below it. This formatting has caused some of the columns to be wider than they need to be. Another problem is that the text for some cells has been truncated because the columns are not wide enough. Joan suggests that you wrap the text within the column titles and then change the width of the columns where necessary. To make this change, you will use the Format Cells dialog box.

To have Excel automatically wrap text within a cell:

1. Select the range **A22:H22**.

2. Click **Format** on the menu bar, and then click **Cells** to open the Format Cells dialog box.

3. Make sure that the Alignment tab is selected, select the **Wrap text** check box in the Text control pane, and then click the **OK** button. The text in many of the selected cells now appears on two rows within the cells.

4. Change the width of columns **A** and **D** to about **12** characters (**89** pixels) each, columns **B** and **C** to about **10** characters (**75** pixels) each, columns **F** and **G** to about **13** characters (**96** pixels) each, and column **H** to about **17** characters (**124** pixels) each. See Figure 3-12.

Wrapping text and resizing the worksheet columns ◀ **Figure 3-12**

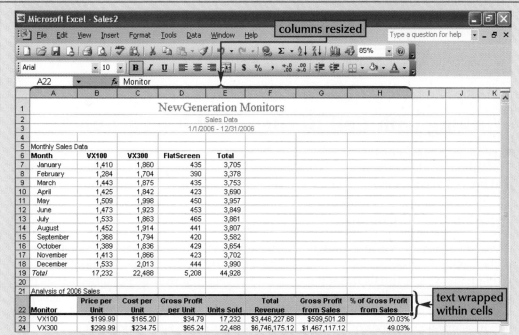

Trouble? If your screen does not match Figure 3-12, resize the columns so the values are easy to read. If some of the text is still hidden, you may need to resize the height of row 22 by dragging the bottom row border down (see Tutorial 1 for a description of resizing rows and columns).

Other Formatting Options

Excel supports even more formatting options than have been discussed so far. For example, instead of wrapping the text, you can have Excel shrink it to fit the size of the cell. If you reduce the cell later on, Excel will automatically resize the text to match. You can also rotate the contents of the cell, displaying the cell entry at almost any angle (see Figure 3-13). Joan does not need to use either of these options in her workbook, but they might be useful later for another project.

Figure 3-13 **Rotating text within a cell**

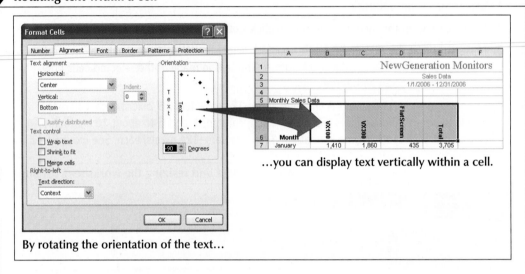

By rotating the orientation of the text…

…you can display text vertically within a cell.

Working with Cell Borders and Backgrounds

Up to now, all the formatting you have done has been applied to the contents of a cell. Excel also provides a range of tools to format the cells themselves. Specifically, you can add borders to cells and color a cell's background.

Adding a Cell Border

As you may have noticed from the printouts of other worksheets, the gridlines that appear in the worksheet window are not normally displayed on the pages that you print. **Gridlines** provide a visual cue for the layout of the cells in a worksheet. Although you can choose to print the gridlines using the Page Setup dialog box, you might want to display borders around individual cells in a worksheet. This would be particularly useful when you have different sections or tables in a worksheet, as in the Sales worksheet.

You can add a border to a cell using either the Borders button on the Formatting toolbar or the options on the Border tab in the Format Cells dialog box. The Borders button allows you to create borders quickly, whereas the Format Cells dialog box lets you further refine your choices. For example, you can specify the style, thickness, and color using the options available in the Format Cells dialog box.

Joan wants you to place a border around each cell in the two tables in the worksheet. You'll select the appropriate border style from the list of available options on the Borders palette.

To create a grid of cell borders in the two tables:

▶ **1.** Select the nonadjacent range **A6:E19;A22:H26**.

▶ **2.** Click the **Borders** list arrow ▦ ▾ on the Formatting toolbar, then move the pointer over the gallery of borders to highlight the All Borders option as shown in Figure 3-14.

Border options ◀ **Figure 3-14**

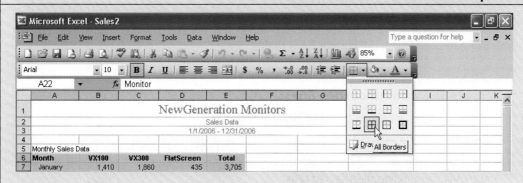

▶ **3.** Click the **All Borders** option (third row, second column from the left) in the borders gallery. A thin border appears around each cell in the selected range.

▶ **4.** Click any cell to deselect the range and to see the applied border.

You can also place a border around the entire range itself (and not the individual cells) by selecting a different border style. Try this by creating a thick border around the cell range.

To create a thick border around a selected range:

▶ **1.** Select the nonadjacent range **A6:E19;A22:H26** again.

▶ **2.** Click the **Borders** list arrow ▦ ▾ on the Formatting toolbar, and then click the **Thick Box Border** option (third row, fourth column from the left) in the borders gallery.

▶ **3.** Click any cell to deselect the range so you can see the thick border applied to the tables. The interior borders should be unchanged.

If you want a more interactive way of drawing borders on your worksheet, you can use the Draw Borders button, which is another option on the borders gallery. To see how this option works, you will add a thick black line under the column titles in both of the tables.

To draw borders using the Draw Borders button:

▶ **1.** Click the **Borders** list arrow ▦ ▾ on the Formatting toolbar, and then click the **Draw Borders** button 🖉 at the bottom of the borders gallery. The pointer changes to 🖉, and a floating Borders toolbar opens with four tools. The Draw Border button (currently selected) on the Borders toolbar draws a border line on the worksheet; the Erase Border button erases border lines; the Line Style button specifies the style of the border line; and the Line Color button specifies the line color.

▶ **2.** Click the **Line Style** list arrow ▭ ▾ to display a list of line style options, and then click the **thick line** option (the ninth from the top) in the list.

▶ 3. Click and drag the pointer over the lower border of the range **A6:E6**. The lower border thickens, matching the top border in thickness.

▶ 4. Click and drag the pointer over the lower border of the range **A22:H22**. The lower border thickens.

▶ 5. Click the **Close** button ☒ on the floating Borders toolbar to close it.

Finally, you will add a double line above the Total row in each table. You will add the line using the options in the Format Cells dialog box.

To create the double border lines:

▶ 1. Select the nonadjacent range **A18:E18;A25:H25**.

▶ 2. Click **Format** on the menu bar, and then click **Cells** to open the Format Cells dialog box.

▶ 3. Click the **Border** tab. The Border tab displays a diagram showing what borders, if any, are currently surrounding the selected cells.

  The bottom border is currently a single thin line. You want to change this to a double line.

▶ 4. Click the **double line** style in the Style list box located on the right side of the tab, and then click the **bottom border** in the border diagram to apply the double-line style. The bottom border changes to a double line. See Figure 3-15.

Figure 3-15 ▶ **Border tab in the Format Cells dialog box**

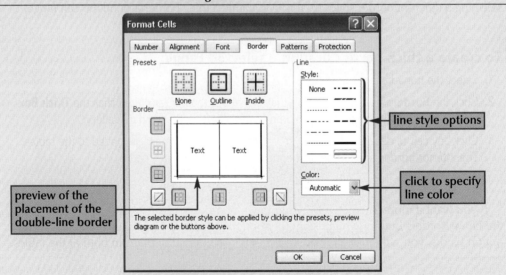

▶ 5. Click the **OK** button to close the dialog box, and then click cell **A1** to deselect the ranges. Figure 3-16 shows all of the border styles you've applied to the two tables.

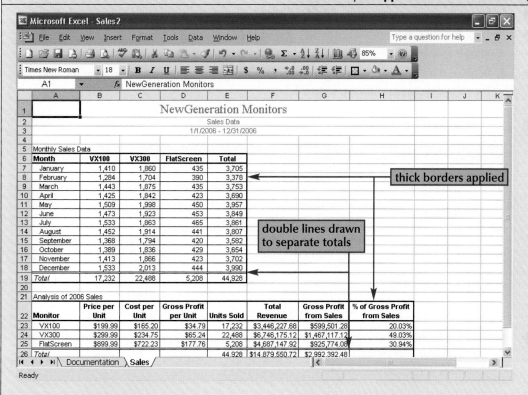

You can also specify a color for the cell borders by using the Color list box located on the Border tab (see Figure 3-15). Joan does not need to change the border colors, but she would like you to change the background color for the column title cells. When you copy the formatting of a cell, any border that you have applied is also copied.

Applying Background Colors and Patterns

Patterns and color can be used to turn a plain worksheet full of numbers and labels into a powerful presentation of information that captures your attention and adds visual emphasis to the different sections of the worksheet. If you have a color printer or a color projection device, you might want to take advantage of Excel's color tools. By default, worksheet cells are not filled with any color (the white you see in your worksheet is not a fill color for the cells). To change the background color in a worksheet, you can use the Fill Color button on the Formatting toolbar, or you can use the Format Cells dialog box, which also provides patterns that you can apply to the background. When choosing to apply color to a worksheet, you must always give consideration to the availability of a color printer. Also, if you plan to print a worksheet as an overhead, black print on a clear overhead transparency is easier to read than other colors.

Joan wants to change the background color of the worksheet. When she prints her report later in the week, she will be using the company's color laser printer. Therefore, she would like you to explore using background color in the column titles for the two sales tables. She suggests that you try formatting the column titles with a light-yellow background.

To apply a fill color to the column titles:

▶ **1.** Select the nonadjacent range **A6:E6;A22:H22**.

▶ **2.** Click the **Fill Color** button list arrow 🖉 ▾ on the Formatting toolbar. The color palette appears.

▶ **3.** Position the pointer over the **Light Yellow** square (fifth row, third column from the left) on the color palette, as shown in Figure 3-17.

Figure 3-17 Selecting a fill color

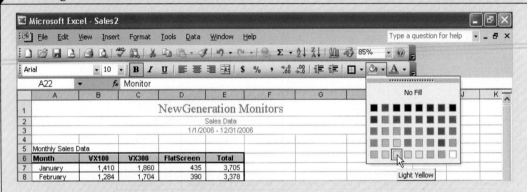

▶ **4.** Click the **Light Yellow** square to apply the color to the selected range, and then click any cell to deselect the range and to see the applied color. The column titles now have light-yellow backgrounds.

Joan would also like to investigate whether you can apply a pattern to the fill background. Excel supports 18 different fill patterns. To create and apply a fill pattern, you have to open the Format Cells dialog box.

To apply a fill pattern to the column titles:

▶ **1.** Select the nonadjacent range **A6:E6;A22:H22**.

▶ **2.** Click **Format** on the menu bar, click **Cells** to open the Format Cells dialog box, and then click the **Patterns** tab to display the options provided.

▶ **3.** Click the **Pattern** list arrow to display a gallery of patterns and a palette of colors that you can apply to the selected pattern. The default pattern color is black. First, you will choose a crosshatch pattern, which is a pattern using crossed diagonal lines.

▶ **4.** Click the **50% Gray** pattern (first row, third column) in the pattern gallery, as shown in Figure 3-18.

Selecting a fill pattern | **Figure 3-18**

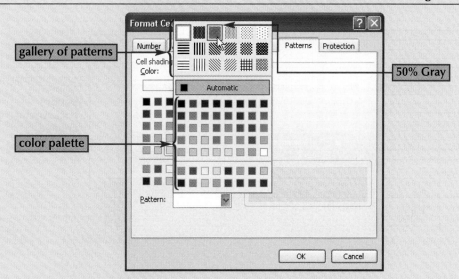

5. Click the **OK** button, and then click any cell to deselect the ranges and to see the pattern.

The background pattern you have chosen overwhelms the text in these column titles. You can improve the appearance by changing the color of the pattern itself from black to a light orange.

To change the pattern color:

1. Select the range **A6:E6;A22:H22**. The default (or automatic) color of a selected pattern is black, but you want to choose a brighter and lighter color for the pattern.

2. Click **Format** on the menu bar, and then click **Cells** to open the Format Cells dialog box again. The Patterns tab should be displayed automatically because it is the last set of options you used.

3. Click the **Pattern** list arrow to display the gallery of patterns and the color palette.

4. Click the **Light Orange** square (third row, second column) in the color palette, click the **OK** button to close the dialog box, and then click cell **A1** to deselect the range and to see the color applied to the pattern. See Figure 3-19. The column titles now appear in a light-orange patterned background. The pattern and the color do not overwhelm the column titles.

Figure 3-19 | **Cells with formatted backgrounds**

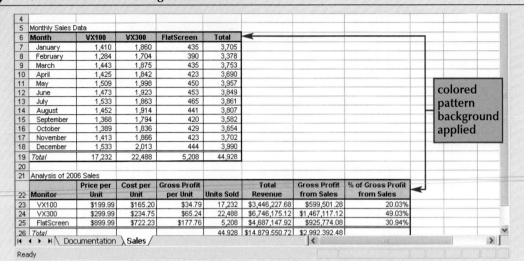

5. Save your changes to the workbook.

Joan is pleased with the progress you have made. In the next session, you will explore other formatting features.

Session 3.1 Quick Check

1. Describe two ways of applying the Currency style to cells in your worksheet.
2. If the number 0.05765 has been entered into a cell, what will Excel display if you:
   a. format the number using the Percent style with one decimal place?
   b. format the number using the Currency style with two decimal places and a dollar sign?
3. Which two buttons can you use to copy a format from one cell range to another?
4. A long text string in one of your worksheet cells has been truncated. List three ways to correct this problem.
5. How do you center the contents of a single cell across a range of cells?
6. Describe three ways of creating a cell border.
7. How would you apply a colored background pattern to a selected cell range?

Session 3.2

Formatting the Worksheet

In the previous session, you formatted individual cells within the worksheet. Excel also provides tools for formatting the columns and rows in a worksheet. You will explore some of these tools as you continue to work on Joan's sales report.

Merging Cells into One Cell

Joan has several other formatting changes that she would like you to make to the Sales worksheet. She wants you to format the titles for the two tables in her report so that they are centered in a bold font above the tables. You could do this by centering the cell title across a cell range, as you did for the title in the last session. Another way is to merge several cells into one cell and then center the contents of that single cell. Merging a range of cells into a single cell removes all of the selected cells from the worksheet, except the cell in the upper-left corner of the range. Any content in the other cells of the range is deleted. To merge a range of cells into a single cell, you can use the Merge cells check box on the Alignment tab in the Format Cells dialog box or click the Merge and Center button on the Formatting toolbar.

To merge and center the cell ranges containing the table titles:

▶ 1. If you took a break after the previous session, make sure that Excel is running and that the Sales2 workbook is open.

▶ 2. In the Sales worksheet, select the range **A5:E5**.

▶ 3. Click the **Merge and Center** button 🔳 on the Formatting toolbar. The cells in the range A5:E5 are merged into a single cell whose cell reference is A5. The text in the merged cell is centered as well.

▶ 4. Click the **Bold** button **B** on the Formatting toolbar.

▶ 5. Select the range **A21:H21**, click the **Merge and Center** button 🔳 on the Formatting toolbar, and then click the **Bold** button **B** on the Formatting toolbar.

▶ 6. Click cell **A1** to deselect the range. Figure 3-20 shows the merged and centered table titles.

Merging and centering cells ◀ **Figure 3-20**

To split a merged cell back into individual cells, regardless of the method you used to merge the cells, you select the merged cell and then click the Merge and Center button again. You can also merge and unmerge cells using the Alignment tab in the Format Cells dialog box.

Hiding Rows, Columns and Worksheets

Sometimes Joan does not need to view the monthly sales for the three monitors. She does not want to remove this information from the worksheet, but she would like the option of temporarily hiding that information. Excel provides this capability. Hiding a row or column does not affect the data stored there, nor does it affect any other cell that might have a formula referencing a cell in the hidden row or column. Hiding part of your worksheet is a good way of temporarily concealing nonessential information, allowing you to concentrate on the more important data contained in your worksheet. To hide a row or column, first you must select the row(s) or column(s) you want to hide. You can then use the Row or Column option on the Format menu or right-click the selection to open its shortcut menu.

You will hide the monthly sales figures in the first table in the worksheet.

To hide the monthly sales figures:

1. Select the headings for rows **7** through **18**.

2. Right-click the selection, and then click **Hide** on the shortcut menu. Excel hides rows 7 through 18. Note that the total sales figures in the range B19:E19 are not affected by hiding the monthly sales figures. See Figure 3-21.

Figure 3-21 ▶ **Hiding worksheet rows**

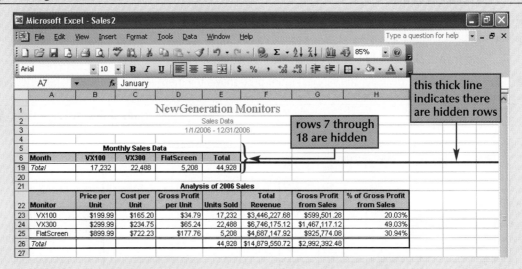

To unhide a hidden row or column, you must select the headings of the rows or columns that border the hidden area; then you can use the right-click method or the Row or Column command on the Format menu to choose the Unhide option. You will let Joan know that it is easy to hide any row or column that she does not want to view. But for now you will redisplay the hidden sales figures.

To unhide the monthly sales figures:

1. Select the row headings for rows **6** and **19**.

2. Right-click the selection, and then click **Unhide** on the shortcut menu. Excel redisplays rows 7 through 18.

3. Click cell **A1** to deselect the rows.

Hiding and unhiding a column follows the same process, except that you select the worksheet column headings rather than the row headings. For example, to hide column B, you select the column heading B. To unhide the column, you must select columns A and C.

On other occasions Joan would like to hide an entire worksheet. This could occur in situations where a worksheet contains detailed information and she only wants to display the summary figures from another sheet. To show how to hide an entire worksheet, you should suggest that she hide the documentation sheet located at the front of the workbook.

To hide the Documentation sheet:

▶ **1.** Click the **Documentation** sheet tab to make it the active sheet.

▶ **2.** Click **Format** on the menu bar, point to **Sheet**, and then click **Hide**.

The Documentation sheet disappears from the workbook. It is still present in the workbook, it is just hidden at this point. Excel maintains a list of the hidden worksheets in the current workbook, so you can always select one of those sheets to be redisplayed. Do this now to unhide the Documentation sheet.

To unhide the Documentation sheet:

▶ **1.** Click **Format** on the menu bar, point to **Sheet**, and then click **Unhide**. Excel displays the Unhide dialog box, listing all hidden worksheets in the workbook.

▶ **2.** Verify that **Documentation** is selected in the list of hidden worksheets, and click the **OK** button. The Documentation sheet should be redisplayed in the workbook and made the active sheet.

▶ **3.** Click the **Sales** sheet tab to return to the Sales worksheet.

Adding a Background Image

In the previous session you learned how to create a background color for individual cells within the worksheet. Excel also allows you to use an image file as a background for a worksheet. The image from the file is tiled repeatedly until the images fill up the entire worksheet. Images can be used to give the background a textured appearance, like that of granite, wood, or fibered paper. The background image does not affect the format or content of any cell in the worksheet, and if you have already defined a background color for a cell, Excel displays the color on top, hiding that portion of the image.

Adding a Background Image to the Worksheet

Reference Window

- Click Format on the menu bar, point to Sheet, and then click Background.
- Locate the image file that you want tiled over the worksheet background.
- Click the Insert button.

If you add a background and then decide against it, you can remove the background image by clicking Format on the menu bar, pointing to Sheet, and then clicking Delete Background. The image will automatically be removed.

Joan wants you to experiment with using a background image for the Sales worksheet. You will add the image file that she has selected.

To add a background image to the worksheet:

1. Click **Format** on the menu bar, point to **Sheet**, and then click **Background**. The Sheet Background dialog box opens.

2. Navigate to the Tutorial.03\Tutorial folder, click the **Back** image file, and then click the **Insert** button. The Back image file is applied repeatedly to, or is "tiled over," the worksheet, creating a textured background for the Sales sheet. Notice that the tiling is hidden in the cells that already contain a background color. To make the sales figures easier to read, you'll change the background color of those cells to white.

3. Select the nonadjacent range **A7:E19;A23:H26**.

4. Click the **Fill Color** list arrow ![fill color icon] on the Formatting toolbar, click the **White** square (lower-right corner) in the color palette, and then click cell **A1** to deselect the range, making the background image easier to see. Figure 3-22 shows the Sales worksheet with the formatted background.

| Figure 3-22 | Inserting a background image |

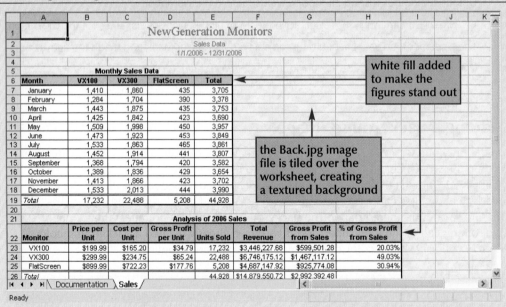

Note that you cannot apply a background image to all of the sheets in a workbook at the same time. If you want to apply the same background to several sheets, you must format each sheet separately.

Formatting Sheet Tabs

In addition to the sheet background, you can also format the background color of worksheet tabs. This color is only visible when the worksheet is not the active sheet in the workbook. By default, the tab of the active sheet in a workbook is white. If you change the color of a tab, the tab changes to white with a narrow colored stripe at the bottom of the tab when the sheet is active. You can use tab colors to better organize the various sheets in your workbook. For example, worksheets that contain sales information could be formatted with blue tabs, whereas sheets that describe the company's cash flow or budget could be formatted with green tabs. To explore how to color worksheet tabs, you will change the tab color of the Sales worksheet to light orange.

To change the tab color:

1. Right-click the **Sales** tab, and then click **Tab Color** on the shortcut menu. The Format Tab Color dialog box opens.

2. Click the **Light Orange** square (third row, second column from the left) in the color palette, and then click the **OK** button. Because the Sales sheet is the active worksheet, the tab is white with a light-orange horizontal stripe at the bottom of the tab.

3. Switch to the Documentation sheet so you can see the light-orange color of the Sales sheet tab, and then switch to the Sales sheet again.

Clearing and Replacing Formats

Sometimes you might want to change or remove some of the formatting from your workbooks. As you experiment with different formats, you can use the Undo button on the Standard toolbar to remove formatting choices that did not work out as well as you expected. Another choice is to clear the formatting from the selected cells, returning the cells to their previous format. To see how this option works, you will remove the formatting from the company name in cell A1 on the Sales worksheet.

To clear the formatting from cell A1:

1. Make sure cell **A1** is selected.

2. Click **Edit** on the menu bar, point to **Clear**, and then click **Formats**. Excel removes the formatting that was applied to the text and removes the formatting that merged the cells and then centered the text across the range.

3. Click the **Undo** button on the Standard toolbar to undo your action, restoring the formats you cleared.

Sometimes you will want to make a formatting change that applies to several different cells. If those cells are scattered throughout the workbook, you may find it time consuming to search for and replace the formats for each individual cell. If the cells share a common format that you want to change, you can use the Find and Replace command to locate the formats and modify them.

Reference Window

Finding and Replacing a Format

- Click Edit on the menu bar, and then click Replace.
- Click the Options >> button, if necessary, to display the format choices.
- Click the top Format list arrow, and then click Format.
- Specify the format you want to find in the Find Format dialog box, and then click the OK button.
- Click the bottom Format list arrow, and then click Format.
- Enter the new format, which will replace the old format, and then click the OK button.
- Click the Replace All button to replace all occurrences of the old format; click the Replace button to replace the currently selected cell containing the old format; or click the Find Next button to find the next occurrence of the old format before replacing it.
- Click the Close button.

In the Sales worksheet, the table titles and column titles are displayed in a bold font. After seeing how the use of color has made the worksheet come alive, Joan wants you to change the titles to a boldface blue. Rather than selecting the cells that contain the table and column titles and formatting them, you will replace all occurrences of the boldface text with blue boldface text.

To find and replace formats:

1. Click **Edit** on the menu bar, and then click **Replace**. The Find and Replace dialog box opens. You can use this dialog box to find and replace the contents of cells. In this case, you will use it only for finding and replacing formats, leaving the contents of the cells unchanged.

2. Click the **Options >>** button to display additional find and replace options. See Figure 3-23. The dialog box expands to display options that allow you to find and replace cell formats. It also includes options to determine whether to search within the active sheet or the entire workbook. Currently no format options have been set.

Figure 3-23 | **Find and Replace dialog box**

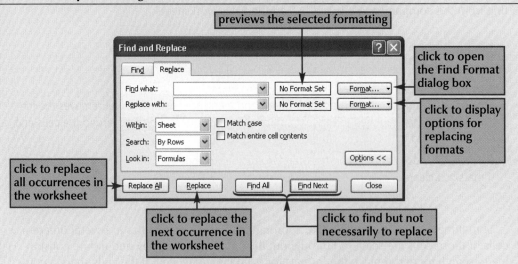

Trouble? If the button on your workbook appears as Options <<, the additional options are already displayed, and you do not need to click any buttons.

3. Click the top **Format** button to open the Find Format dialog box. Here is where you specify the format you want to search for. In this case, you are searching for cells that contain boldface text.

4. Click the **Font** tab, and then click **Bold** in the Font style list box. See Figure 3-24.

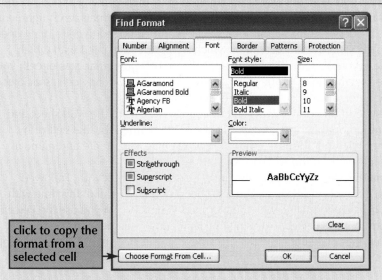

click to copy the format from a selected cell

5. Click the **OK** button.

Next, you will specify the new format that you want to use to replace the boldface text. In this case, you will specify blue boldface text.

6. Click the bottom **Format** button to open the Replace Format dialog box again, and then click **Bold** in the Font style list box.

7. Click the **Color** list box, click the **Blue** square (second row, sixth column from the left) in the color palette, and then click the **OK** button.

8. Click the **Replace All** button to replace all boldface text in the worksheet with blue bold-face text. Excel indicates that it has completed its search and made 15 replacements.

9. Click the **OK** button, and then click the **Close** button to close the Find and Replace dialog box. See Figure 3-25. The boldface text has been replaced with blue boldface text.

	Month	VX100	VX300	FlatScreen	Total
4					
5		Monthly Sales Data			
6	Month	VX100	VX300	FlatScreen	Total
7	January	1,410	1,860	435	3,705
8	February	1,284	1,704	390	3,378
9	March	1,443	1,875	435	3,753
10	April	1,425	1,842	423	3,690
11	May	1,509	1,998	450	3,957
12	June	1,473	1,923	453	3,849
13	July	1,533	1,863	465	3,861
14	August	1,452	1,914	441	3,807
15	September	1,368	1,794	420	3,582
16	October	1,389	1,836	429	3,654
17	November	1,413	1,866	423	3,702
18	December	1,533	2,013	444	3,990
19	Total	17,232	22,488	5,208	44,928

bold formatting found and replaced with bold blue formatting

	Monitor	Price per Unit	Cost per Unit	Gross Profit per Unit	Units Sold	Total Revenue	Gross Profit from Sales	% of Gross Profit from Sales
20								
21		Analysis of 2006 Sales						
22	Monitor	Price per Unit	Cost per Unit	Gross Profit per Unit	Units Sold	Total Revenue	Gross Profit from Sales	% of Gross Profit from Sales
23	VX100	$199.99	$165.20	$34.79	17,232	$3,446,227.68	$599,501.28	20.03%
24	VX300	$299.99	$234.75	$65.24	22,488	$6,746,175.12	$1,467,117.12	49.03%
25	FlatScreen	$899.99	$722.23	$177.76	5,208	$4,687,147.92	$925,774.08	30.94%
26	Total				44,928	$14,879,550.72	$2,992,392.48	

Documentation \ Sales

Ready

Using Styles

If you have several cells that employ the same format, you can create a style for those cells. This can be a faster and more efficient way of updating formats than copying and replacing formats. A **style** is a saved collection of formatting options—number formats, text alignment, font sizes and colors, borders, and background fills—that can be applied to cells in a worksheet. When you apply a style, Excel remembers which styles are associated with which cells in the workbook. If you want to change the appearance of a particular type of cell, you need only modify the specifications for the style, and the appearance of any cell associated with that style will be automatically changed to reflect the new style.

You can create a style in one of two ways: by selecting a cell from the worksheet and basing the style definition on the formatting choices already defined for that cell or by manually entering the style definitions into a dialog box. Once you create and name a style, you can apply it to cells in the workbook.

Excel has eight built-in styles: Comma, Comma [0], Currency, Currency [0], Followed Hyperlink, Hyperlink, Normal, and Percent. You have been using styles all of this time without knowing it. Most cells are formatted with the Normal style, but when you use the Percent Style button, Excel formats the selected text using the definitions contained in the Percent style. Similarly, the Currency Style button applies the format as defined in the Currency style. As you'll see, you can modify these style definitions or create some of your own.

Creating a Style

Joan wants you to further modify the appearance of the worksheet by changing the background color of the months in the first table and the monitor names in the second table to yellow. Rather than applying new formatting to the cells, you will create a new style called "Category" and then apply the new style to the category columns of the tables in the worksheet. You will create the style using the format already applied to cell A7 as a basis.

To create a style using a formatted cell:

▶ 1. Click cell **A7** to select it. The format applied to this cell becomes the basis of the new style that you want to create.

▶ 2. Click **Format** on the menu bar, and then click **Style**. The Style dialog box opens. All of the formatting options associated with the style of the active cell are listed. For example, the font is 10-point Arial. The check boxes indicate whether these various formatting categories are part of the style definition. If you deselect one of the formatting categories, such as Border, then that category will not be part of the style definition.

To create a new style for this cell, you simply type a different name into the list box.

▶ 3. Type **Category** in the Style name list box, as shown in Figure 3-26. At this point, cell A7 is no longer formatted using the Normal style; rather it is formatted using the Category style you just created.

Style dialog box ◄ **Figure 3-26**

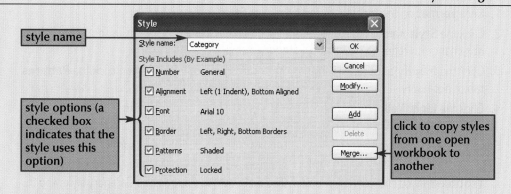

Now you will modify the properties of this style.

4. Click the **Border** check box to deselect it. Category style will not include any border format options.

Next, you will modify the pattern of the style.

5. Click the **Modify** button to open the Format Cells dialog box, and then click the **Patterns** tab.

6. Click the **Yellow** square (fourth row, third column from the left) in the color palette, and then click the **OK** button to close the Format Cells dialog box and redisplay the Style dialog box.

If you click the OK button in the Style dialog box, the style definition changes and is applied to the active cell and the Style dialog box closes. If you click the Add button in the dialog box, the style change is saved and applied, but the Style dialog box remains open for further style changes.

7. Click the **OK** button to save the new style and apply it to the background color of cell A7.

Now you need to apply this style to other cells in the workbook.

Applying a Style

To apply a style to cells in a worksheet, you first select the cells you want associated with the style and then open the Style dialog box.

To apply the Category style:

1. Select the nonadjacent range **A8:A18;A23:A25**.

2. Click **Format** on the menu bar, and then click **Style**. The Style dialog box opens.

3. Click the **Style name** list arrow, and then click **Category**. The formatting options change to reflect the associated options for the selected style.

4. Click the **OK** button to close the dialog box and apply the Category style to the selected range, and then click cell **A1** to deselect the cells. A yellow background color is applied to all of the month and monitor cells in the two tables.

The yellow background appears a bit too strong. You decide to change it to a light-yellow background. Since all the month and monitor cells are now associated with the Category style, you need only modify the definition of the Category style to make this change.

To modify the Category style:

1. Click **Format** on the menu bar, and then click **Style**.

2. Click the **Style name** list arrow, and then click **Category**. The options in the Style dialog box change to reflect the selected Category style.

3. Click the **Modify** button to open the Format Cells dialog box, and then click the **Patterns** tab, if necessary.

4. Click the **Light Yellow** square (fifth row, third column from the left) in the color palette, and then click the **OK** button.

5. Click the **Add** button in the Style dialog box. Excel changes the background color of all the cells associated with the Category style.

    Trouble? If you clicked the OK button instead of the Add button, the Category style would have been applied to the active cell as well as the ranges formatted with the Category style. Click the Undo on the Standard toolbar to undo the application of the Category style to cell A2, and then skip Step 6.

6. Click the **Close** button. See Figure 3-27. The updated Category style is applied to the ranges using that format.

| Figure 3-27 | Category style in the Sales worksheet |

The Category style becomes part of the Sales2 workbook, but it is not available to other workbooks. However, you can copy styles from one workbook to another. Copying styles allows you to create a collection of workbooks that share a common look and feel.

To copy styles from one workbook to another, open the workbook containing your customized styles, and then open the workbook into which you want to copy the styles. Open the Styles dialog box, click the Merge button, and select the first workbook. All of the styles in that workbook will be copied into the second workbook for use on that workbook's contents. Note that if you make changes to the style definitions later on, you will have to copy them again. Excel will not automatically update styles across workbooks.

Using AutoFormat

Excel's **AutoFormat** feature provides a gallery of 17 predefined formats that you can select and apply to your worksheet cells. Rather than spending time testing different combinations of fonts, colors, and borders, you can apply an existing format to your worksheet.

You have done a lot of work already formatting the data in the Sales worksheet to give it a more professional and polished look, but you decide to see how the formatting you have done compares to one of Excel's AutoFormat designs.

You'll apply an AutoFormat design to the sales figures table so that you can compare a predefined format to the format you have worked on.

To apply an AutoFormat design to the table:

▶ **1.** Select the range **A5:E19**.

▶ **2.** Click **Format** on the menu bar, and then click **AutoFormat**. The AutoFormat dialog box opens. See Figure 3-28. The dialog box displays a preview of how each format will appear when applied to cells in a worksheet.

AutoFormat gallery ◀ **Figure 3-28**

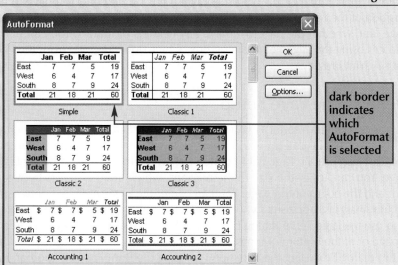

▶ **3.** Click **Classic 3** in the list of available designs, click the **OK** button, and then click cell **A1** to remove the highlighting from the table. Figure 3-29 shows the appearance of the Classic 3 design to the cells containing the monthly sales data.

Applying an AutoFormat ◀ **Figure 3-29**

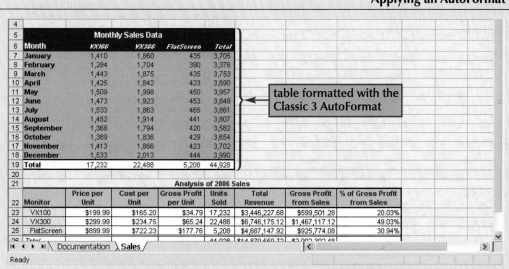

The colors and contrast of the AutoFormat design do not complement the background, so you will revert to the format you created.

4. Click the **Undo** button ⟲ on the Standard toolbar to remove the AutoFormat design.

Although you will not use AutoFormat in this case, you can see how an AutoFormat design can be a starting point. You could start with an AutoFormat design and then make modifications to the worksheet to fit your own needs.

Formatting the Printed Worksheet

You have settled on an appearance for the Sales worksheet—at least the appearance that is displayed on your screen. But that is only half of your job. Joan also wants you to format the appearance of this worksheet when it is printed out. You have to decide on the position of the report on the page, the size of the page margins, the orientation of the page, and whether the page will have any headers or footers. You can make many of these choices using the Page Setup dialog box, which you can open from the File menu or from within Print Preview.

Defining the Page Setup

As you learned in Tutorial 1, you can use the Page Setup dialog box to change the page orientation, which determines if the page is wider than it is tall or taller than it is wide. You can also use the Page Setup dialog box to control how a worksheet is placed on a page. You can adjust the size of the **margins**, which are the spaces between the page content and the edges of the page. You can center the worksheet text between the top and bottom margins (horizontally) or between the right and left margins (vertically). You can also use the Page Setup dialog box to display text that will appear in the area at the top of a page or at the bottom of a page for each page of a worksheet. You can open the Page Setup dialog box using the File menu or using the Print Preview toolbar. Working from within Print Preview can be helpful. Each time you close a dialog box in which you have made a change or selected an option, you will see how that action impacts the worksheet before printing it.

By default, Excel places a one-inch margin above and below the report and a ¾-inch margin to the left and right. Excel also aligns column A in a worksheet at the left margin and row 1 at the top margin. Depending on how many columns and rows there are in the worksheet, you might want to increase or decrease the page margins or center the worksheet between the left and right margins or between the top and bottom margins.

You will increase the margin size for the Sales worksheet to one inch all around. You will also center the worksheet between the right and left margins.

To change the margins and positioning of the worksheet:

1. Click the **Print Preview** button 🔍 on the Standard toolbar. The Print Preview window opens, displaying the worksheet as it will appear on the printed page.

2. Click the **Setup** button on the Print Preview toolbar, and then click the **Margins** tab. The Margins tab, as shown in Figure 3-30, provides a diagram that shows you the placement of the worksheet on the page. In addition to adjusting the sizes of the margins, you can also adjust the positioning of the worksheet on the printout.

Margins tab in the Page Setup dialog box ◀ Figure 3-30

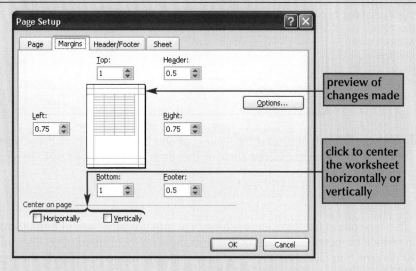

preview of changes made

click to center the worksheet horizontally or vertically

3. Click the **Left** up arrow to set the size of the left margin to **1** inch, and then click the **Right** up arrow to increase the size of the right margin to **1** inch.

4. Click the **Horizontally** check box, and then click the **OK** button to close the Page Setup dialog box and return to Print Preview.

Note that this printout does not fit on a single page. As indicated in the status line located in the lower-left corner of the Print Preview window, the worksheet covers two pages instead of one; two columns of the bottom table have been moved to the second page. You could try to reduce the left and right margins, so the worksheet fits on a single page, but as you learned in Tutorial 1, you also can change the page orientation to landscape, making the worksheet page wider than it is tall. This will accommodate all the columns of the bottom table so all the data will fit on the same page.

To change the page orientation:

1. Click the **Setup** button on the Print Preview toolbar to open the Page Setup dialog box again.

2. Click the **Page** tab and then click the **Landscape** option button, as shown in Figure 3-31.

Figure 3-31 ▸ **Changing the page orientation**

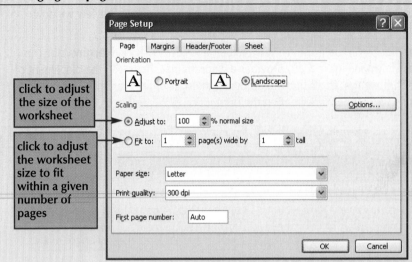

click to adjust the size of the worksheet

click to adjust the worksheet size to fit within a given number of pages

▸ **3.** Click the **OK** button to close the dialog box and return to the Print Preview window. The preview of the printed worksheet in landscape orientation shows that the report will fit on a single page.

The Page tab in the Page Setup dialog box contains other useful formatting features. You can reduce or increase the size of the worksheet on the printed page. The default size is 100 percent. You can also have Excel automatically reduce the size of the report to fit within a specified number of pages.

Working with Headers and Footers

Joan wants you to add a header and footer to the report. A **header** is text printed in the top margin of every worksheet page. A **footer** is text printed at the bottom of every page. Headers and footers can add important information to your printouts. For example, you can create a header that displays your name and the date the report was created. If the report covers multiple pages, you can use a footer to display the page number and the total number of pages. You use the Page Setup dialog box to add headers and footers to a worksheet.

Excel tries to anticipate headers and footers that you might want to include in your worksheet. Clicking the Header or Footer list arrow displays a list of possible headers or footers (the list is the same for both). For example, the "Page 1" entry inserts the page number of the worksheet prefaced by the word "Page" in the header; the "Page 1 of ?" displays the page number and the total number of pages. Other entries in the list include the name of the worksheet or workbook.

If you want to use a header or footer not available in the lists, you click the Custom Header or Custom Footer button and create your own header and footer. The Header dialog box and the Footer dialog box are similar. Each dialog box is divided into three sections: left, center, and right. If you want to enter information such as the filename or the date into the header or footer, you can either type the text or click one of the format buttons located above the three section boxes. Figure 3-32 describes the format buttons and the corresponding format codes.

Header/Footer formatting buttons ◄ Figure 3-32

Button	Name	Formatting Code	Action
A	Font	None	Sets font, text style, and font size
	Page Number	&[Page]	Inserts page number
	Total Pages	&[Pages]	Inserts total number of pages
	Date	&[Date]	Inserts current date
	Time	&[Time]	Inserts current time
	File Path	&[Path]&[File]	Inserts path and filename
	Filename	&[File]	Inserts filename
	Tab Name	&[Tab]	Inserts name of active worksheet
	Insert Picture	&[Picture]	Inserts an image file
	Format Picture	None	Opens the Format Picture dialog box

Joan wants a header that displays the filename at the left margin and today's date at the right margin. She wants a footer that displays the name of the workbook author, with the text aligned at the right margin of the footer. You'll create the header and footer now.

To add a custom header and footer to the workbook:

▶ 1. Click the **Setup** button on the Print Preview toolbar, and then click the **Header/Footer** tab. The Header/Footer dialog box opens.

▶ 2. Click the **Custom Header** button. The Header dialog box opens. See Figure 3-33.

Header dialog box ◄ Figure 3-33

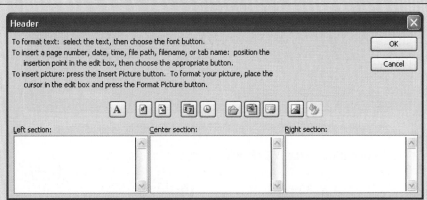

▶ 3. In the Left section box, type **Filename:** and then press the **spacebar**.

▶ 4. Click the **Filename** button 🖻 to insert the format code. The formatting code for the name of the file "&[File]" appears after the text that you entered.

▶ 5. Click the **Right section** box, and then click the **Date** button 🖫. Excel inserts the &[Date] format code into the section box.

▶ 6. Click the **OK** button to close the Header dialog box, and then click the **Custom Footer** button to open the Footer dialog box, which duplicates the layout of the Header dialog box. Now you will create a footer that centers the page number and the total number of pages at the bottom of the printout.

7. Click the **Center section** box, type **Page**, press the **spacebar**, click the **Page Number** button 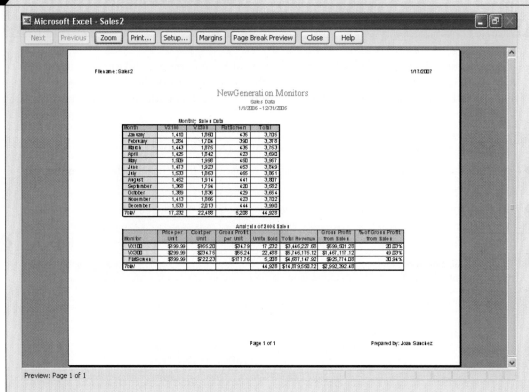, press the **spacebar**, type **of**, press the **spacebar**, and then click the **Total Pages** button. The text and codes in the Center section should appear as "Page &[Page] of &[Pages]"—which, if the worksheet was divided into five pages, would appear as "Page 1 of 5."

   Next, you will enter the workbook author in the right section of the footer.

8. Click the **Right section** box, type **Prepared by:**, press the **spacebar**, and then type your name.

9. Click the **OK** button to return to the Page Setup dialog box, which provides a preview of the custom header and footer that you created, and then click the **OK** button to return to Print Preview. As shown in Figure 3-34, the worksheet now is displayed with the new header and footer.

Figure 3-34 | Preview of the custom header and footer

10. Click the **Close** button on the Print Preview toolbar.

Note that a header or footer is added only for the printed worksheet—not the entire workbook. You can define different headers and footers for each sheet in your workbook.

Working with the Print Area and Page Breaks

When you displayed the worksheet in the Print Preview window, how did Excel know which parts of the active worksheet you were going to print? The default action is to print all parts of the active worksheet that contain text, formulas, or values, which will not always be what you want. If you want to print only a part of the worksheet, you can define a **print area** that contains the content you want to print. To define a print area, you must first select the cells you want to print, and then select the Print Area command on the File menu.

A print area can include an adjacent range or nonadjacent ranges. You can also hide rows or columns in the worksheet in order to print nonadjacent ranges. For her report, Joan might decide against printing the sales analysis information. To remove those cells from the printout, you will define a print area that excludes the cells for the second table.

To define the print area:

1. Select the range **A1:H19**.

2. Click **File** on the menu bar, point to **Print Area**, and then click **Set Print Area**. Excel places a dotted black line around the selected cells of the print area. This is a visual indicator of what parts of the worksheet will be printed.

3. Click the **Print Preview** button 🔍 on the Standard toolbar. The Print Preview window displays only the first table. The second table has been removed from the printout because it is not in the defined print area.

4. Click the **Close** button on the Print Preview toolbar.

Another way to preview the print areas in your worksheet is through **page break preview**, which displays a view of the worksheet as it is divided up into pages. Anything outside of the print area is grayed out. Try previewing the contents of the Sales worksheet using page break preview.

To switch to page break preview:

1. Click cell **A1** to remove the selection.

2. Click **View** on the menu bar, and then click **Page Break Preview**. The workbook window adjusts to display the worksheet with any page break inserted in it and the Welcome to Page Break Preview dialog box, as shown in Figure 3-35. The dialog box serves to remind you that you can adjust the page breaks. A page number appears as a watermark on each page to be printed out. Notice that the second table is grayed out because it is not part of the printed area of the worksheet.

Figure 3-35 | **Using Page Break Preview**

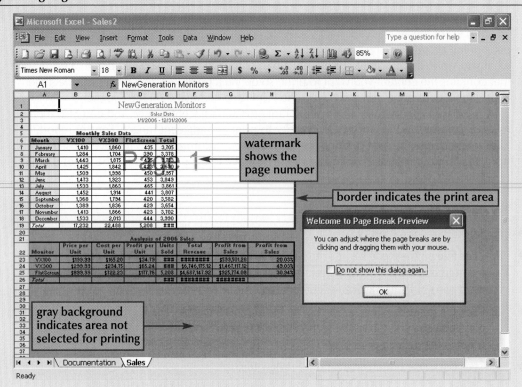

> 3. Click the **OK** button to close the dialog box before you change the dimensions of the printed area to include the other table.

> 4. Position the pointer at the bottom border of the print area (located at row 19) until the pointer changes to ↕, and then click the border and drag it down to row **26**. The print area has now been expanded to the cell range A1:H26.
>
>   **Trouble?** If you are unsure of the location of the bottom border, click row 19 to make the border easier to see, and then repeat Step 3.

> 5. Click **View** on the menu bar, and then click **Normal** to switch back to Normal view.

Another approach that Joan might take is to place the two tables on separate pages. You can do this for her by inserting a **page break**, which forces Excel to place a portion of a worksheet on a new page. Before you insert a page break, you need to indicate where in the worksheet you want the break to occur. If you select a cell in the worksheet, the page break will be placed directly above and to the left of the cell. Selecting a row or a column places the page break directly above the row or directly to the left of the column. You will place a page break directly above row 20, which will separate the first sales table from the second.

To insert a page break:

> 1. Click row **20**, click **Insert** on the menu bar, and then click **Page Break**. Another black dotted line appears—this time above row 20, indicating there is a page break at this point in the print area.

2. Click cell **A1** to remove the selection, click **View** on the menu bar, click **Page Break Preview**, and then click the **OK** button to close the Welcome to Page Break Preview dialog box. As shown in Figure 3-36, the second table will now appear on page 2 of the printout.

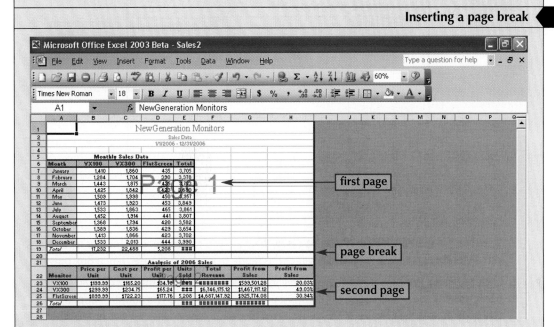

3. Click **View** on the menu bar, and then click **Normal** to return to Normal view.

As Joan reviews the preview of the worksheet, she notices that the name of the company, "NewGeneration Monitors," and the two subtitles appear on the first page, but not on the second. That is not surprising because the range that includes the titles and subtitles is limited to the first page of the printout. However, Joan would like to have this information repeated on the second page.

You can repeat information, such as the company name, by specifying which cells in the print area should be repeated on each page. This is particularly useful in long tables that extend over many pages. In such cases, you can have the column titles repeated for each page of the printout.

To set rows or columns to repeat on each page, you will open the Page Setup dialog box from the worksheet window.

To repeat the first three rows on each page:

1. Click **File** on the menu bar, click **Page Setup**, and then click the **Sheet** tab. The Sheet tab displays options you can use to control how the worksheet is printed. Note that the print area you have defined is already entered into the Print area box. Because Joan wants the first three rows of the worksheet to be repeated on each printed page, you will have to select them.

2. Click the **Rows to repeat at top** box, move your pointer over to the worksheet, and then click and drag over the range **A1:A3**. A flashing border appears around the first three rows in the worksheet. This is a visual indicator that the contents of the first three rows will be repeated on all pages of the printout. In the Rows to repeat at top box, the cell reference $1:$3 appears. See Figure 3-37.

Figure 3-37 | **Sheet tab of the Page Setup dialog box**

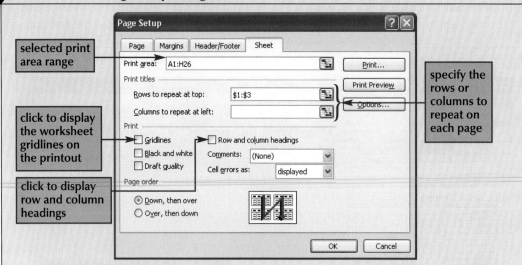

selected print area range

click to display the worksheet gridlines on the printout

click to display row and column headings

specify the rows or columns to repeat on each page

Trouble? If the Page Setup dialog box is in the way, you can move it to another location in the workbook window, or you can select the range using the Collapse Dialog Box button.

▶ **3.** Click the **Print Preview** button, and then click the **Next** button on the Print Preview toolbar to display the second page of the printout. Now the title and two subtitles appear on this page as well. See Figure 3-38.

Figure 3-38 | **Second page of the printout**

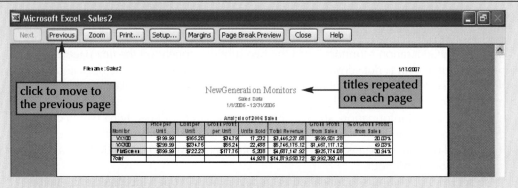

click to move to the previous page

titles repeated on each page

▶ **4.** Click the **Print** button on the Print Preview toolbar, make sure the settings in the Print dialog box are correct, and then click the **OK** button.

For now, your work is done. When you save the workbook, your printing options are saved along with the file, so you will not have to re-create the print format in the future.

▶ **5.** Save your changes to the workbook, and then close it.

Note that the Sheet tab also provides other options, such as the ability to print the worksheet's gridlines or row and column headings. You can also have Excel print the worksheet in black and white or draft quality. If there are multiple pages in the printout, you can indicate whether the pages should be ordered going down the worksheet first and then across, or across first and then down.

You show the final version of the workbook and the printout to Joan. She is very happy with the way in which you have formatted her report. She will spend some time going over the printout and will get back to you with any further changes she wants you to make.

Session 3.2 Quick Check

1. Describe two ways of merging a range of cells into one.
2. How do you clear a format from a cell without affecting the underlying data?
3. How do you add a background image to the active worksheet?
4. To control the amount of space between the content on a page and its edges, you can adjust the page's _____.
5. By default, Excel prints what part of the active worksheet?
6. How do you define a print area? How do you remove a print area?
7. How do you insert a page break into your worksheet?

Review

Tutorial Summary

In this tutorial, you learned how to use Excel's formatting tools to design your worksheet. You saw how to quickly format cells using the buttons on the Formatting toolbar, and you learned how the Format Cells dialog box can give you even more control over the appearance of your worksheet. You saw how to create and edit cell borders using the Borders button and the Draw Borders button. You also learned how to change cell backgrounds using colors and patterns and external graphic files. The tutorial also demonstrated how to apply the formats in one cell range to another through the use of the Format and Replace dialog box and through styles. Finally, you learned how to format the appearance of your printed worksheet through the use of customized headers, footers, and print areas.

Key Terms

AutoFormat	General number format	point
font	gridline	print area
font size	header	sans serif font
font style	margin	serif font
footer	page break	style
Format Painter	page break preview	typeface
formatting		

Practice

*Practice the skills you
learned in the tutorial
using the same case
scenario.*

Review Assignments

Data File needed for the Review Assignments: Region1.xls

Joan Sanchez has another report that she wants to format. The report displays regional sales for the three monitor brands you worked on earlier. As before, Joan wants to work on the overall appearance of the worksheet so the printout of the report is polished and professional looking. Figure 3-39 shows a preview of the worksheet you'll create for Joan.

Figure 3-39

	A	B	C	D	E	F	G
1		*NewGeneration Monitors*					
2		Regional Sales Report					
3		1/1/2006 - 12/31/2006					
4							
5	**Sales by Region**						
6	**Region**	**VX100**	**VX300**	**Flatscreen**	**Total**		
7	Northeast	1,723	2,248	520	4,491		
8	East	3,446	4,497	1,041	8,984		
9	Southeast	2,067	2,698	624	5,389		
10	Midwest	1,723	2,248	520	4,491		
11	Southwest	1,378	1,799	416	3,593		
12	West	4,308	5,622	1,302	11,232		
13	Canada	1,378	1,799	416	3,593		
14	Europe	861	1,124	260	2,245		
15	Asia	348	453	109	910		
16	**Total**	17,232	22,488	5,208	44,928		
17							
18	**Regional Analysis**						
19			**Region**	**Units Sold**	**Total Sales**	**Profit from Sales**	**% of Profit**
20			Domestic	14,645	$ 2,928,853	$ 509,499	17.03%
21		VX100	Foreign	2,587	$ 517,374	$ 90,001	3.01%
22			Total	17,232	$ 3,446,227	$ 599,500	20.03%
23			Domestic	19,112	$ 5,733,408	$ 1,246,866	41.67%
24		VX300	Foreign	3,376	$ 1,012,766	$ 220,250	7.36%
25			Total	22,488	$ 6,746,174	$ 1,467,116	49.03%
26			Domestic	4,423	$ 3,980,655	$ 786,232	26.27%
27		Flatscreen	Foreign	785	$ 706,492	$ 139,541	4.66%
28			Total	5,208	$ 4,687,147	$ 925,773	30.94%
29			Domestic	38,180	$12,642,918	$ 2,542,598	84.97%
30		Total	Foreign	6,748	$ 2,236,632	$ 449,793	15.03%
31			Total	44,928	$14,879,550	$ 2,992,391	100.00%
32							

To format the report:

1. Open the **Region1** workbook located in the Tutorial.03\Review folder included with your Data Files.
2. Enter your name and the current date in the Documentation sheet, and then save the workbook as **Region2** in the Tutorial.03\Review folder.
3. Switch to the Regional Sales worksheet.
4. Format the text in cell A1 with a 20-point, italicized, red, Times New Roman font. Format the text in cells A2 and A3 with a red font. Select the range A1:F3, and center the text across the selection. Do not merge the cells.
5. Select the range A5:E16, and then apply the List 2 format from the AutoFormat gallery.
6. Change the format of all values in the Sales by Region table to display a comma separator, but no decimal places. Resize column E to about 14 characters.
7. Change the format of the Units Sold values in the second table to display a comma separator, but no decimal places.
8. Indent the region names in the range A7:A15 by one character.
9. Display the text in cell A18 in bold.
10. Change the format of the values in the Total Sales and Profit from Sales columns to display a dollar sign on the left edge of the cell and no decimal places.
11. Change the format of the values in the % of Profit column to display a percent sign and two decimal places.
12. Allow the text in the range B19:F19 to wrap to a second line of text. Bold and center the text within each cell.

13. Merge and center the cells in the range A20:A22, and change the vertical text alignment to center. (*Hint*: Use the correct Text alignment option in the Format Cells dialog box to vertically align the text; see Figure 3-13.) Apply this format to the cells in the following ranges: A23:A25, A26:A28, and A29:A31.
14. Change the background color of the cells in the range A19:F19;A20:A31 to Sea Green (third row, fourth column of the color palette). Change the font color to white.
15. Change the background color of the cells in the range B20:F31 to white. Change the background color of the cells in the range B22:F22;B25:F25;B28:F28;B31:F31 to Light Green (fifth row, fourth column of the color palette).
16. Apply a thin black border to each of the cells in the range A19:F31.
17. Place a double line on the bottom border of the cells in the range B22:F22;B25:F25;B28:F28.
18. Set the print area as the range A1:F31. Insert a page break above row 18. Repeat the first three rows of the worksheet on every page of any printouts you produce from this worksheet.
19. Set up the page to print in portrait orientation with one-inch margins on all sides. Center the contents of the worksheet horizontally on the page.
20. Add a footer with the following text in the Left section box of the footer (with the date on a separate line): "Filename: *the name of the file*" and "Date: *current date*," and then the following text in the Right section box of the footer: "Prepared by: *your name*." In the Center section, place the text "Page *page_number* of *total_pages*" where *page_number* is the number of the page and *total_pages* is the total number of pages in the printout.
21. Add a header with the text "Regional Sales Report" displayed in the Center section using a 14-point Times New Roman font with a double underline. (*Hint*: Select the text in the Center section, and then click the Font button in the Footer dialog box to open the Format Cells dialog box.)
22. Preview the two-page worksheet, and then print it.
23. Save your changes to the workbook and then close it.

Apply

Use the skills you have learned to format a sales report.

Case Problem 1

Data File needed for this Case Problem: Frosti1.xls

FrostiWear Linda Young is a sales manager for FrostiWear, a new and successful online store for winter clothing. She is in charge of tracking the sales figures for FrostiWear's line of gloves. She's created a workbook containing the sales figures for three glove models organized by month and region for the past year. She would like your help in formatting the sales report and the printed output. Figure 3-40 shows a preview of the formatted worksheet you'll create for Linda.

Figure 3-40

	A	B	C	D	E	F	G	H
1				**FrostiWear**				
2				Sales Report				
3				Units Sold: 1/2007 - 12/2007				
4				Region 1	Region 2	Region 3	Region 4	Region 5	Total
5			Jan	1,150	1,690	930	2,850	1,210	7,830
6			Feb	1,100	2,200	680	2,340	1,100	7,420
7			Mar	1,070	1,290	960	2,740	1,180	7,240
8		PolyFleece Mitts	Apr	780	1,520	720	2,170	1,180	6,370
9			May	1,070	1,370	700	1,940	1,210	6,290
10			Jun	670	1,300	780	3,430	1,170	7,350
11			Jul	1,390	1,590	1,240	2,230	1,430	7,880
12			Aug	1,310	1,730	610	2,560	960	7,170
13			Sep	1,100	1,820	370	3,040	1,100	7,430
14			Oct	1,350	2,010	750	2,430	1,230	7,770
15			Nov	680	1,620	780	3,210	1,230	7,520
16			Dec	1,120	1,170	670	1,920	1,310	6,190
17			Total	12,790	19,310	9,190	30,860	14,310	86,460
18				Region 1	Region 2	Region 3	Region 4	Region 5	Total
19			Jan	790	1,160	620	2,590	760	5,920
20			Feb	1,010	1,170	610	1,950	1,010	5,750
21			Mar	710	1,270	600	2,050	930	5,560
22			Apr	890	1,190	750	2,030	980	5,840
23		ArticBlast Gloves	May	990	1,340	660	2,670	1,040	6,700
24			Jun	990	1,280	620	2,330	800	6,020
25			Jul	780	1,180	690	2,260	920	5,830
26			Aug	800	1,220	560	2,460	900	5,940
27			Sep	810	1,150	670	2,500	970	6,100
28			Oct	760	1,070	630	2,350	1,040	5,850
29			Nov	770	1,140	630	2,540	1,080	6,160
30			Dec	850	1,370	590	2,490	1,060	6,360
31			Total	10,150	14,540	7,630	28,220	11,490	72,030
32				Region 1	Region 2	Region 3	Region 4	Region 5	Total
33			Jan	340	780	280	1,670	600	3,670
34			Feb	460	810	280	1,770	480	3,800
35			Mar	410	820	310	1,490	460	3,490
36			Apr	490	890	330	1,610	650	3,970
37		Glomitts	May	470	960	290	1,580	540	3,840
38			Jun	480	740	340	1,780	640	3,980
39			Jul	470	760	320	1,500	640	3,690
40			Aug	490	690	340	1,610	600	3,730
41			Sep	420	780	340	1,660	680	3,880
42			Oct	460	820	350	1,800	660	4,090
43			Nov	550	830	440	1,250	590	3,660
44			Dec	400	790	220	1,620	540	3,570
45			Total	5,440	9,670	3,840	19,340	7,080	45,370

To complete this task:

1. Open the **Frosti1** workbook located in the Tutorial.03\Cases folder included with your Data Files, and then save the workbook as **Frosti2** in the same folder.
2. In the Documentation sheet, enter your name and the current date. Format the date so that it is displayed as *Weekday, Month Day, Year* where *Weekday* is the day of the week, *Month* is the full month name, *Day* is the day of the month, and *Year* is the four-digit year.
3. Switch to the Glove Sales worksheet. Merge the cells in the range A1:H1 into a single cell. Display the cell text in a bold white 20-point Arial font on a sky blue background. Center the text horizontally. Repeat this formatting for the cell range A2:H2 and A3:H3, except make the text size 12 points.

Explore

4. Merge range A4:A17 into a single cell. Display the text in a yellow 16-point bold Arial font on a sky blue background. Change the orientation of the text to 90 degrees, and then align the contents of the cell horizontally and vertically. (*Hint*: For more information on aligning text within a cell, read the Help topics "Indent text in a cell" and "Position data in a cell.") Apply the formatting of cell A4 to cells A18 and A32.

5. Select the noncontiguous range B4:H4;B4:B17. Display the cell text in yellow on a blue background. Right-align the contents of cells B4:B17 and indent the contents of those cells one unit. Center the contents of the cells B4:G4.

6. Select the range C5:G16. Display the contents of these cells using blue text on a light turquoise background. Apply this same formatting to cell H17.

7. Select the noncontiguous range B17:H17;H4:H17 and display the contents of those cells in bold.

8. Apply borders to the sales report as follows. First select the range C5:G16 and apply the All Borders border style to those cells. Select the range B4:G16 and apply a thick box border to the range. Also apply thick outside borders to the cell ranges B17:H17 and H4:H17 and the cell A4.

9. Copy the cell range A4:H17 and paste the format of this cell range into the range A18:H45.

10. Define the cell range A1:H45 as the print area. Repeat the first three rows on each page of the printout. Insert a page break at rows 18 and 32.

11. Create a horizontally centered header for the printout displaying the text, "FrostiWear Sales Report." Create a footer on the right corner of the page displaying your name on one line, the date on the second line, and the workbook filename on the third. Insert a centered footer displaying the text, "Page *page* of *pages*," where *page* is the page number and *pages* is the number of pages in the printout.

12. Set the orientation of the printout to landscape. Horizontally center the contents of each printed page.

13. Print the contents of the Glove Sales worksheet.

14. Save and close the workbook.

Apply

Use the skills you have learned to create a packing slip for GrillRite Grills.

Case Problem 2

Data File needed for this Case Problem: Packing1.xls

GrillRite Grills   Brian Simpko is a shipping manager at GrillRite Grills. He uses an Excel worksheet to calculate and provide shipping and order information in GrillRite's packages. He asks for your help formatting the worksheet to develop a packing slip that customers will find informative and easy to read. Figure 3-41 shows a preview of the formatted worksheet you'll create for Brian.

Figure 3-41

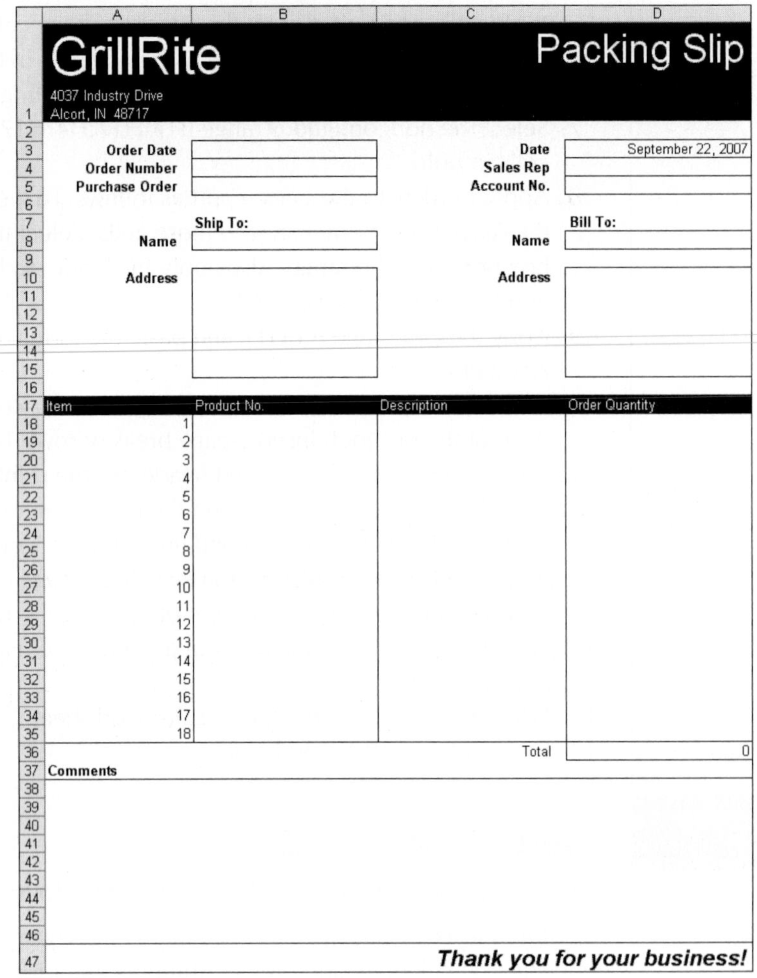

To complete this task:

1. Open the **Packing1** workbook located in the Tutorial.03\Cases folder included with your Data Files, and then save the workbook as **Packing2** in the same folder. Enter your name and the date in the Documentation sheet, and then switch to the Packing Slip sheet.
2. Select all of the cells in the worksheet and set the background color to white.
3. Select the cell range A1:D1, and change the background color to black and the font color to white. Merge cells A1 and B1. Within cell A1 select the text "GrillRite" and increase the font size to 36 points. Set the font size of the text in cell D1 to 28 points. Vertically align the contents of cells A1 and D1 with the top of the cell. Right-align the contents of cell D1.
4. Select the noncontiguous cell range A3:A5;C3:C5 and display the text in bold. Right-align the text and increase the indent by one character.

Explore
5. Change the format of the date in cell D3 to *month day*, *year* where *month* is the full name of the month, *day* is the day of the month, and *year* is the 4-digit year value.
6. Select the noncontiguous cell range B3:B5;D3:D5 and add borders around each cell in the range.
7. Display the text in cells B7, D7, A8, A10, C8, and C10 in bold. Right-align the text in cells A8, A10, C8, and C10 and indent one character. Add borders around cells B8 and D8.

8. Select the cell range B10:B15. Merge the cells and then place a border around the merged cell. Vertically align the contents of this cell with the top of the cell. Repeat these steps for the cell range D10:D15.

9. Select the cell range A17:D17 and change the background color to black and the font color to white. Place a border around the cell ranges A18:A35, B18:B35, C18:C35, and D18:D35. Place a border around cell D36. Right-align the contents of cell C36 and increase the indent by one character.

10. Display the text in cell A37 in bold. Select the cell range A38:D46 and merge the cells. Change the vertical alignment of the merged cells to top. Place a border around the merged cell. Display the text in cell D47 in a 16-point bold italic font. Right-align the contents of the cell.

11. Set the print area to the range A1:D47. Set the left and right margins to 0.5 inches. Display your name, the date, and the filename on separate lines in the lower-left footer.

12. Print the formatted Packing Slip worksheet in the portrait orientation.

13. Save and close the workbook.

Challenge

Using Figure 3-42 as your guide, challenge yourself by experimenting with more formatting techniques to enhance a worksheet presenting regional sales figures.

Case Problem 3

Data File needed for this Case Problem: Blades1.xls

Davis Blades Andrew Malki is a financial officer at Davis Blades, a leading manufacturer of roller blades. He has recently finished entering data for the yearly sales report. Andrew has asked you to help him with the design of the main table in the report. A preview of the format you will apply is shown in Figure 3-42.

Figure 3-42

Davis Blades
Sales Report
1/1/2006 - 12/31/2006

Units Sold		Northeast	East	Southeast	Midwest	Southwest	West	All Regions
Black Hawk	Qtr 1	641	748	733	676	691	783	4,272
	Qtr 2	708	826	811	748	763	866	4,722
	Qtr 3	681	795	780	719	734	833	4,542
	Qtr 4	668	779	764	705	720	816	4,452
	Total	2,698	3,148	3,088	2,848	2,908	3,298	17,988
Blademaster	Qtr 1	513	598	587	541	552	627	3,418
	Qtr 2	567	661	648	598	611	693	3,778
	Qtr 3	545	636	624	575	587	666	3,633
	Qtr 4	534	623	611	564	576	653	3,561
	Total	2,159	2,518	2,470	2,278	2,326	2,639	14,390
The Professional	Qtr 1	342	399	391	361	368	418	2,279
	Qtr 2	378	441	432	399	407	462	2,519
	Qtr 3	363	424	416	383	391	444	2,421
	Qtr 4	356	415	407	376	384	435	2,373
	Total	1,439	1,679	1,646	1,519	1,550	1,759	9,592
All Models	Qtr 1	1,496	1,745	1,711	1,578	1,611	1,828	9,969
	Qtr 2	1,653	1,928	1,891	1,745	1,781	2,021	11,019
	Qtr 3	1,589	1,855	1,820	1,677	1,712	1,943	10,596
	Qtr 4	1,558	1,817	1,782	1,645	1,680	1,904	10,386
	Total	6,296	7,345	7,204	6,645	6,784	7,696	41,970

To complete this task:

1. Open the **Blades1** workbook located in the Tutorial.03\Cases folder included with your Data Files, and then save the file as **Blades2** in the same folder.
2. Enter your name and the current date in the Documentation sheet, and then switch to the Sales worksheet.
3. Change the font of the title in cell A1 to a 16–point, dark blue, boldface, Times New Roman font. Change the subtitles in cells A2 and A3 to an 8-point, blue font. Reduce the height of row 2 and row 3 to 12 characters.
4. Add a solid black bottom border to the range A1:K1.
5. Format the text in cell A5 in a 12-point, blue, Arial font. Vertically align the text in this cell with the bottom of the cell.

Explore

6. Merge the cells in the range A6:A10, and align the contents of the cell vertically at the top of the cell. Repeat this for the following ranges: A11:A15, A16:A20, and A21:A25.
7. Change the background color of the cell range A6:I10 to light yellow. Change the background color of the range A11:I15 to light green. Change the background color of the range A16:I20 to light turquoise. Change the background color of the range A21:I25 to pale blue.
8. Reverse the color scheme for the subtotal values in the range B10:I10, so that instead of black on light yellow, the font color is light yellow on a black background. Reverse the subtotal values for the other products in the table.
9. Apply the borders, as shown in Figure 3-42, to the cells in the range A6:I25.

Explore

10. Rotate the column titles in the range C5:I5 by 45 degrees. Align the contents of each cell along the bottom-right corner of the cell. Change the background color of these cells to white, and then add a border to each cell.

Explore

11. Open the Options dialog box from the Tools menu. Deselect the Row & column headings and Gridlines options to remove the row and column headings and gridlines from the Sales worksheet window.
12. Set the print area as the range A1:K25.
13. Leave the page orientation as portrait, but center the worksheet horizontally on the page.
14. Create a custom footer with the text "Filename: *the name of the file*" left-aligned and with the text "Prepared by: *your name*" and "*the current date*" right-aligned, with your name and date on separate lines.
15. Preview the worksheet and then print it.
16. Save your changes to the workbook and then close it.

Create

Using Figure 3-43 as a guide, test your knowledge of formatting by creating your own design for a payroll worksheet.

Case Problem 4

There are no Data Files needed for this Case Problem.

Oritz Marine Services Vince DiOrio is an information systems major at a local college. He works three days a week at a nearby marina, Oritz Marine Services, to help pay for his tuition. Vince works in the business office, and his responsibilities range from making coffee to keeping the company's books.

Recently, Jim Oritz, the owner of the marina, asked Vince if he could help computerize the payroll for the employees. He explained that the employees work a different number of hours each week at different rates of pay. Jim now does the payroll manually, and finds it time consuming. Moreover, whenever he makes an error, he is annoyed at having to take the additional time to correct it. Jim is hoping that Vince can help him.

Vince immediately agrees to help. He tells Jim that he knows how to use Excel and that he can build a worksheet that will save him time and reduce errors. Jim and Vince meet to review the present payroll process and discuss the desired outcome of the payroll spreadsheet. Figure 3-43 displays the type of information that Jim records in the spreadsheet.

Figure 3-43

Employee	Hours	Pay Rate	Gross Pay	Federal Withholding	State Withholding	Total Deductions	Net Pay
Bramble	16	9.50					
Cortez	30	10.50					
DiOrio	25	12.50					
Fulton	20	9.50					
Juarez	25	12.00					
Smiken	10	9.00					
Smith	30	13.50					
Total							

To complete this task:

1. Create a new workbook named **Payroll1**, and save it in the Tutorial.03\Cases folder included with your Data Files.
2. Name two worksheets "Documentation" and "Payroll," and then delete the third sheet.
3. On the Documentation sheet, include the name of the company, your name as the author of the workbook, the date the workbook is being created, and a brief description of the purpose of the workbook.
4. On the Payroll worksheet, enter the payroll table shown in Figure 3-43.
5. Enter the formulas to calculate total hours, gross pay, federal withholding tax, state withholding tax, total deductions, and net pay, using the following information:
   a. Gross pay is equal to the number of hours multiplied by the pay rate.
   b. Federal withholding tax is equal to 15% of the gross pay.
   c. State withholding tax is equal to 4% of the gross pay.
   d. Total deductions are the sum of federal and state withholdings.
   e. Net pay is equal to the difference between the gross pay and the total amount of deductions.
6. Format the appearance of the payroll table using the techniques you learned in this tutorial. The appearance of the payroll table is up to you; however, do not use an AutoFormat design to format the table.
7. Format the printed page, setting the print area and inserting an appropriate header and footer. Only a few employees are entered into the table at present. However, after Jim Oritz approves your layout, many additional employees will be added, which will cause the report to cover multiple pages. Format your printout so that the worksheet title and column titles appear on every page.
8. Preview your worksheet, and then print it. Save your changes.
9. Add the following new employees to the worksheet. The employee list should be in alphabetical order, so these new employees should be inserted at the appropriate places in the sheet:

Name	Hours	Pay Rate
Carls	20	10.50
Lopez	35	11.50
Nelson	20	9.50

10. Preview the revised worksheet, and then print it.
11. Save this revised workbook as **Payroll2** in the Tutorial.03\Cases folder, and then close the workbook.

Research

Use the Internet to find and work with data related to the topics presented in this tutorial.

Internet Assignments

The purpose of the Internet Assignments is to challenge you to find information on the Internet that you can use to work effectively with this software. The actual assignments are updated and maintained on the Course Technology Web site. Log on to the Internet and use your Web browser to go to the Student Online Companion for New Perspectives Office 2003 at **www.course.com/np/office2003**. Click the Internet Assignments link, and then navigate to the assignments for this tutorial.

SAM Assessment and Training

Assess

If your instructor has chosen to use the full online version of SAM 2003 Assessment and Training, you can go beyond the "just-in-time" training provided on the CD that accompanies this text. Simply log in to your SAM account (http://sam2003.course.com) to launch any assigned training activities or exams that relate to the skills covered in this tutorial.

Review

Quick Check Answers

Session 3.1

1. Click the Currency Style button on the Formatting toolbar; or click Format on the menu bar, click Cells, click the Number tab, and then select Currency from the Category list box.
2. a. 5.8%
   b. $0.06
3. Format Painter button and Copy button
4. Increase the width of the column; decrease the font size of the text; or select the Shrink to fit check box or the Wrap text check box on the Alignment tab in the Format Cells dialog box.
5. Select the range, click Cells on the Format menu, click the Alignment tab, and then select Center Across Selection in the Horizontal list box.
6. Use the Borders button on the Formatting toolbar; use the Draw Borders button in the Border gallery; or click Cells on the Format menu, click the Border tab, and then choose the border options in the dialog box.
7. Click Cells on the Format menu, click the Patterns tab, click the Pattern list arrow, and then select the pattern type and color.

Session 3.2

1. Select the cells and either click the Merge and Center button on the Formatting toolbar; or click Cells on the Format menu, click the Alignment tab, and then click the Merge cells check box.
2. Select the cell, click Edit on the menu bar, point to Clear, and then click Formats.
3. Click Format on the menu bar, point to Sheet, and then click Background. Locate and select an image file to use for the background, and then click the Insert button.
4. margins
5. Excel prints all parts of the active worksheet that contain text, formulas, or values.
6. To define a print area, select a range in the worksheet, click File on the menu bar, point to Print Area, and then click Set Print Area. To remove a print area, point to Print Area on the File menu, and then click Clear Print Area.
7. Select the first cell below the row at which you want to insert the page break, and then select Page Break on the Insert menu.

Working with Charts and Graphics

Charting Sales Data

Case | Vega Telescopes

Alicia Kendall is a sales manager at Vega Telescopes, one of the leading manufacturers of telescopes and optics. She has been asked to present information on last year's sales for four of Vega's most popular telescopes: the 6- and 8-inch BrightStar and the 12- and 16-inch NightVision. Her presentation will be part of a sales conference that will be held next week in Charlotte, North Carolina.

As part of her presentation, Alicia would like to include a report that shows the sales figures for each model in the United States, Europe, and Asia. She knows that this kind of information is often best understood when presented visually, that is, in a graphical or pictorial form. She would like to use a column chart to show the sales data and a pie chart to show how each model contributes to Vega's overall sales of these four popular telescope models. Alicia is especially interested in making the charts visually appealing, and she wants to draw attention to the top-selling telescope model. She also will need printouts of the charts.

Alicia has asked you to help her create charts that will clearly and effectively present the sales data. Your task is to format the charts and individual chart components to enhance the presentation of the data, which will help Alicia explain and highlight the data at the sales conference. You will also add a drawing object that points out the top-selling telescope, and you will print the completed charts.

Session	Objectives		SAM Training Tasks	
Session 4.1	• Create column and pie charts using the Chart Wizard • Move and resize a chart • Embed a chart in a worksheet	• Place a chart on a chart sheet • Separate a slice from a pie chart	• Create charts using column chart types	• Create charts using the pie chart types
Session 4.2	• Edit the data source • Change the location of a chart • Modify chart objects • Insert and format chart text	• Create 3-D charts • Add and modify drawing objects using the Drawing toolbar • Print a chart	• Add a drop shadow to a selection • Edit a chart • Format chart data labels • Format charts	• Position a chart • Position graphics • Print a chart • Rotate and tilt a 3-D pie chart

Student Data Files   For a complete list of the Data Files needed for this tutorial, see page EX 2.

Session 4.1

For hands-on practice of key tasks in this session, go to the SAM 2003 Training Companion CD included with this text.

Excel Charts

Alicia's sales data has already been entered into a workbook for you. You will begin by opening the workbook so you can examine the sales data.

To open Alicia's workbook:

▶ **1.** Start Excel and then open the **Vega1** workbook located in the Tutorial.04\Tutorial folder included with your Data Files.

▶ **2.** Enter *your name* and the *current date* in the Documentation sheet.

▶ **3.** Save the workbook as **Vega2** to the Tutorial folder, and then switch to the Sales worksheet to view the sales data as shown in Figure 4-1.

| Figure 4-1 | Sales worksheet for Vega Telescopes |

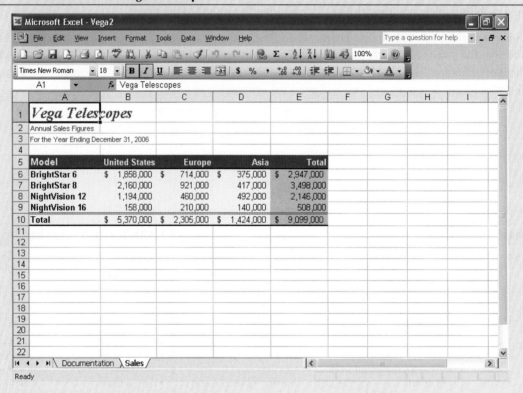

The Sales worksheet shows the annual sales, in U.S. dollars, for each of the four Vega telescope models. The sales data is broken down by world regions. As Alicia has explained, she wants two charts. The first chart should show the sales for each telescope in each region represented by columns, in which the height of the column represents the sales volume for each model. The second should be a pie chart that interprets how the total sales of each telescope model relate to overall sales. Sketches of the charts Alicia wants to create are shown in Figure 4-2.

Sketch of column and pie charts ◀ **Figure 4-2**

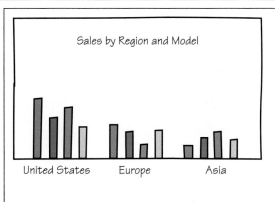
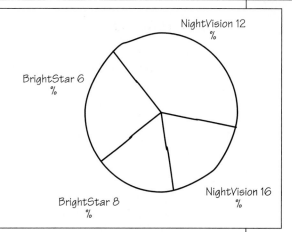

Charts, also known as graphs, provide a visual representation of the workbook data. Using charts, one can often see trends in the data that are more difficult to detect by viewing the raw numbers in a table. A chart can also be used to highlight items of interest, such as a region with low sales or an unexpectedly good sales month. Excel makes it easy to create charts through the use of the **Chart Wizard**, a series of dialog boxes that prompt you for information about the chart you want to create. This includes information such as the chart type, the cell range that the chart is based on, and features that the chart will contain. You will use the Chart Wizard to create the first chart that Alicia sketched for you—the column chart of the sales figures broken down by region and telescope model.

Creating a Chart Using the Chart Wizard

The Chart Wizard is a series of four dialog boxes, and each one is a step in the process of creating your chart. At each point in the process, you provide more detailed information about the chart you want Excel to create. Figure 4-3 describes the four steps in the Chart Wizard.

Tasks performed in each step of the Chart Wizard ◀ **Figure 4-3**

Dialog Box	Task Options
Chart Type	Select from list of available chart types and corresponding sub-types, or choose to customize a chart type
Chart Source Data	Specify the cells that contain the data on which the chart will be based and the cells that contain the labels that will appear in the chart
Chart Options	Change the appearance of the chart by selecting the options that affect titles, axes, gridlines, legends, data labels, and data tables
Chart Location	Specify where the chart will be placed: embedded as an object in the worksheet containing the data or on a separate worksheet, also called a chart sheet

You can stop the Chart Wizard at any time, and Excel will complete the remaining dialog boxes for you using the default specifications for the chart you have chosen.

Reference Window **Creating a Chart Using the Chart Wizard**

- Select the data you want to chart.
- Click the Chart Wizard button on the Standard toolbar.
- In the first step of the Chart Wizard, select the chart type and sub-type, and then click the Next button.
- In the second step, make any modifications or additions to the chart's data source, and then click the Next button.
- In the third step, make any modifications to the chart's appearance, and then click the Next button.
- In the fourth step, specify the location for the chart, and then click the Finish button.

Before starting the Chart Wizard, you can select the cell range that contains the data that will be used in the chart. If you don't select a cell range, the Chart Wizard will "guess" at the cell range. If the selected range isn't correct, you can select the correct cell range as you work with the Chart Wizard. To create the first chart that Alicia wants, you'll select the data in the cell range A5:D9. The range needs to include both the labels and the sales figures for each telescope model. You will not include the total sales within each region.

To start the Chart Wizard:

1. Select the range **A5:D9**.

2. Click the **Chart Wizard** button 🔳 on the Standard toolbar. The first step of the Chart Wizard is shown in Figure 4-4.

Figure 4-4 **Step 1 of the Chart Wizard**

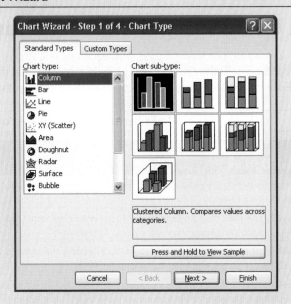

Choosing a Chart Type

The first step of the Chart Wizard provides the chart types, from which you choose the one that you feel will best display the data you want to plot. Excel supports 14 types of charts, ranging from the column chart, similar to the one shown in Alicia's first sketch, to stock market charts that can be used to record the daily behavior of stocks. Figure 4-5 provides information about some of the chart types. The charts are useful in different situations. When you want to compare the values from different categories (such as the sales of different telescope models), you will want to use a column, bar, or line chart. If you want to compare the values of individual categories to a whole collection of categories, you will want to use either a pie chart or a doughnut chart. If your data doesn't contain categories and you want to compare one set of numeric values with another, you will probably want to create an XY Scatter (scatter) chart or a bubble chart. Finally, for stock market data, you can use an Excel stock chart.

Excel chart types   Figure 4-5

Icon	Chart Type	Description
	Column	Compares values from different categories. Values are indicated by the height of the columns.
	Bar	Compares values from different categories. Values are indicated by the length of the bars.
	Line	Compares values from different categories. Values are indicated by the height of the line. Often used to show trends and changes over time.
	Pie	Compares relative values of different categories to the whole. Values are indicated by the size of the pie slices.
	XY (scatter)	Shows the patterns or relationship between two or more sets of numeric values. Often used in scientific studies and statistical analyses.
	Area	Similar to the line chart, except that areas under the lines are filled with colors indicating the different categories.
	Doughnut	Similar to the pie chart, except that it can display multiple sets of data.
	Radar	Compares a collection of values from several different data sets.
	Surface	Compares three sets of values in a three-dimensional chart.
	Bubble	Similar to the XY (scatter) chart, except the size of the data marker is determined by a third numeric value.
	Cylinder, Cone, Pyramid	Similar to the column chart, except that cylinders, cones, and pyramids are used in place of columns.

Each chart type has its own collection of sub-types that provide an alternative format for the chart's appearance. For example, the column chart type has seven different sub-types, including the clustered column and the stacked column. There are also 3-D, or three-dimensional, sub-types.

Finally, Excel also supports 20 additional "custom" chart types with additional formatting options. Some of the custom charts actually combine the properties of two or more of the main chart types. You can also create your own customized chart designs and add them to the custom chart list.

Alicia wants you to create a column chart for the sales data, in which values are arranged into separate columns. To see whether the chart you are creating is the right one, you will click the button in the first dialog box that lets you preview the chart before continuing with the Chart Wizard.

To select the chart type and preview it:

1. Verify that the **Column** chart type is selected in the Chart type list box and that the first sub-type, **Clustered Column**, is also selected.

2. Press the **Press and Hold to View Sample** button, but do not release the mouse button. A preview of the selected chart is displayed, as shown in Figure 4-6.

Figure 4-6 ▶ **Preview of the clustered column chart**

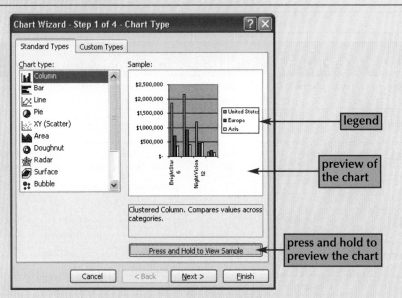

The Chart Wizard has assigned a different colored column to represent the sales values within each region. The legend on the right identifies the regions. The blue columns represent the United States, the maroon columns represent Europe, and the yellow columns represent Asia. Though the size of the Sample pane prevents you from viewing much of the chart's detail, you can see that the columns are clustered into groups; each group represents a different model. The first cluster represents sales for the BrightStar 6 telescope. The second cluster represents sales for the BrightStar 8 and so forth. Because this is the chart type that Alicia wants you to create, you can continue to the next step of the Chart Wizard.

3. Release the mouse button, and then click the **Next** button to go to step 2 of the Chart Wizard.

Choosing a Data Source

In the second step of the Chart Wizard, shown in Figure 4-7, you specify the **data source** for the chart, indicating the cell range that contains the chart's data. Excel organizes the data source into a collection of **data series**, where each data series is a range of data values that is plotted as a unit on the chart. In the case of this column chart, each data series contains the sales values of each sales region. A data series consists of **data values**, which are plotted on the chart's vertical axis, or **y-axis**. On the horizontal axis, or **x-axis**, are the data series' **category values**, or **x values**. In this chart, the data values are the sales values and the category values are the names of the different telescope models.

Specifying the data source ◄ **Figure 4-7**

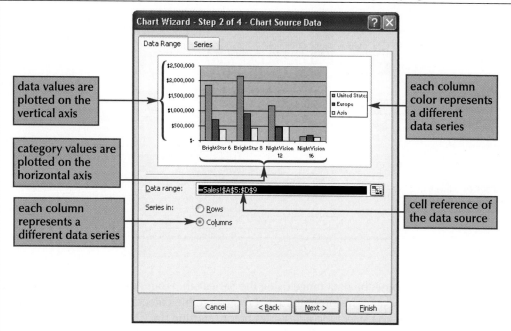

In this case, the Chart Wizard has organized the data source by columns, so that the leftmost column contains the category values and the subsequent columns each contain a different data series. The first row of the data contains the labels that identify each data series. In general, if the data spans more rows than columns, then the Chart Wizard interprets the data series by columns; otherwise, the Chart Wizard interprets the data series by rows.

In Alicia's sketch, she has indicated that she wants the name of the region to be the category value, which means that each telescope model represents a different data series. Therefore, you need to ensure that the Chart Wizard organizes the data source by rows and not columns. The first row will contain the category values, and each subsequent row will contain a data series. The first column will then contain the labels of each series.

To organize the data source by rows:

1. Click the **Rows** option button. Excel changes the orientation of the data source. The category values now represent the three regions rather than the four telescope models. See Figure 4-8.

Figure 4-8   Changing the orientation of the data source

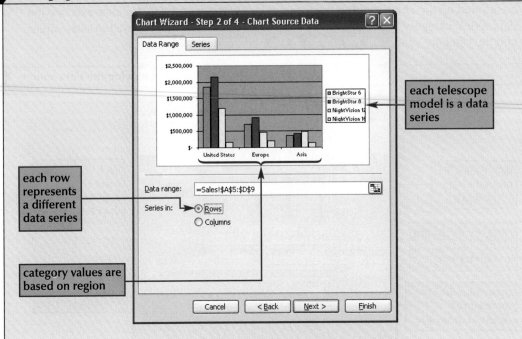

You can further define the data range using the Series tab. From this tab, you can add or remove individual data series from the chart or change the category values. Although it is recommended that you select the data series before starting the Chart Wizard, it is not necessary because you can define all of the data series and chart values using the Series tab. However, selecting the data series first does save time. You will switch to the Series tab so you can view its options.

To view the Series tab:

▶ **1.** Click the **Series** tab. The Series tab lists all of the data series used in the chart and the corresponding cell references for the cell that contains the name of the data series, the cells that contain the values for the data series, and the cells the contain the category labels. Note that the cell references include the name of the sheet from which the values are selected. See Figure 4-9.

Series tab ◀ | Figure 4-9

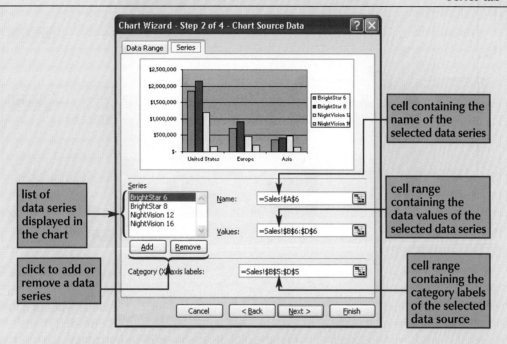

You do not have to make any changes in the data series at this point, so you will continue in the Chart Wizard.

▶ **2.** Click the **Next** button to go to step 3 of the Chart Wizard.

Choosing Chart Options

The third step of the Chart Wizard provides the options that you can use to control the appearance of the chart. To better understand the options available to you, first you'll explore the terminology that Excel uses with respect to charts. Figure 4-10 shows the elements of a typical Excel chart.

Figure 4-10 ▶ **Excel chart elements**

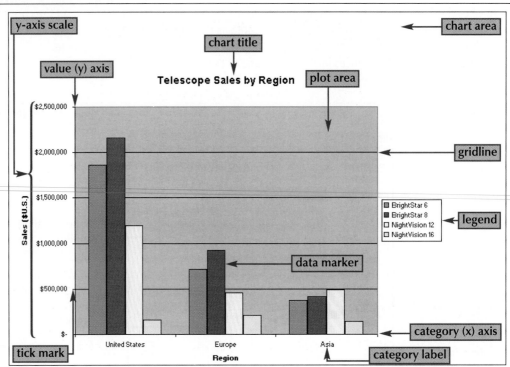

The basic element of the chart is the **plot area**, a rectangular area containing a graphical representation of the values in the data series. Each graphical representation is called a **data marker**. Each column in a column chart is an example of a data marker. Other types of data markers include the pie slices used in pie charts and the points used in XY (scatter) charts.

Most charts have two axes that border the plot area: an x-axis (or horizontal axis) and a y-axis (or vertical axis). As mentioned earlier, values from the data series are plotted along the y-axis, whereas the category labels are plotted along the x-axis. Each axis can have a title that describes the values or labels displayed on the axis. In Figure 4-10, the x-axis title is "Region" and the y-axis title is "Sales ($U.S.)."

The range of values that spans along an axis is called a **scale**. Excel automatically chooses a scale to match the range of values in the data series. In the chart shown in Figure 4-10, the scale of the y-axis ranges from $0 to $2,500,000. Next to the values on the scales are **tick marks**, which act like the division lines on a ruler, making it easier to read the scale. Your charts might also contain **gridlines**, which extend the tick marks across the plot area. Excel divides gridlines into two types. **Major gridlines** are the lines that extend the tick marks across the plot area; **minor gridlines** are the lines that divide the space between the major gridlines.

If your chart contains more than one data series, the chart will usually have a **legend** identifying the format of the data marker used for each series. Above the plot area, you can add a **chart title** to describe the contents of the plot area and the data series. The entire chart and all of the elements discussed so far are contained in the **chart area**.

You can format these various chart elements in the third step of the Chart Wizard. You can also format these features later on, after the chart has been created. As shown in Figure 4-11, step 3 of the Chart Wizard contains six tabs: Titles, Axes, Gridlines, Legend, Data Labels, and Data Table. Each tab provides tools for formatting different elements of your chart.

Step 3 of the Chart Wizard ◄ Figure 4-11

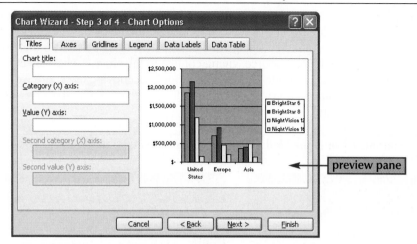

Alicia wants you to add descriptive titles to the chart and to each of the axes. She also wants you to remove the gridlines because they are not necessary in such a simple, straight-forward chart. Using the Titles and Gridlines tabs, you will make these changes now.

To insert titles into the chart:

1. Make sure that the **Titles** tab is active.

2. Click the **Chart title** text box, type **Telescope Sales by Region**, and then press the **Tab** key. The preview pane updates the chart image to reflect the addition of the chart title to the chart area.

3. Type **Region** in the Category (X) axis text box, and then press the **Tab** key.

4. Type **Sales ($U.S.)** in the Value (Y) axis text box, and then press the **Tab** key. The preview pane shows all of the new titles you entered into the chart.

5. Click the **Gridlines** tab.

6. Click the **Major gridlines** check box for the Value (Y) axis to remove the major gridlines from the chart.

7. Click the **Next** button to move to the last Chart Wizard dialog box, shown in Figure 4-12.

Step 4 of the Chart Wizard ◄ Figure 4-12

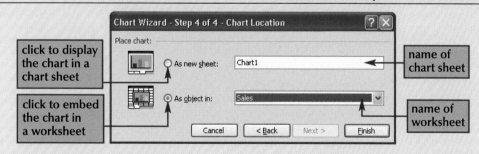

Choosing the Chart Location

In the final step of the Chart Wizard, you choose a location for the chart. You can either create an embedded chart or a chart sheet. An **embedded chart** is a chart that is displayed within a worksheet. The advantage of creating an embedded chart is that you can place the chart alongside the data source, giving context to the chart. A **chart sheet** is a new sheet that is automatically inserted into the workbook, occupying the entire workbook window and thus providing more space and details for the chart. Figure 4-13 provides examples of each type of chart.

Figure 4-13	Example of an embedded chart and a chart sheet

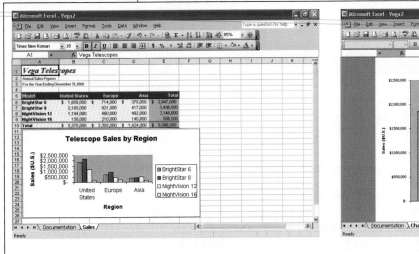

embedded chart in the Sales worksheet

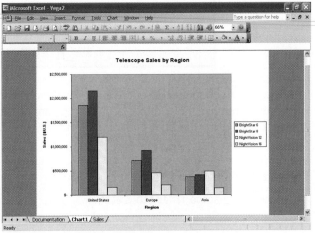

chart sheet named "Chart1"

For this first chart, you'll embed the chart in the Sales worksheet.

To embed the clustered column chart in the Sales worksheet:

1. Make sure that the **As object in** option button is selected and that **Sales** is selected in the adjacent list box.

2. Click the **Finish** button. Excel creates the column chart with the specifications you selected and embeds the chart in the Sales worksheet, as shown in Figure 4-14.

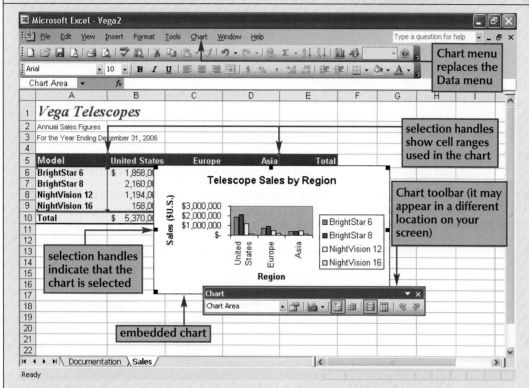

Trouble? If the Chart toolbar is not visible, it may have been closed during a previous Excel session. Click View on the menu bar, point to Toolbars, and then click Chart to redisplay the toolbar.

When the Chart Wizard creates the embedded chart, the chart appears with selection handles around it. The selection handles indicate that the chart is an **active chart** and is ready for additional formatting. The Chart toolbar also appears when the chart is selected. (Note that the Chart toolbar doesn't always appear when a chart is selected if the toolbar was closed in an earlier Excel session.) Another change that occurs is the Chart menu replaces the Data menu on Excel's menu bar. You will also find that certain Excel commands are not available to you when a chart is the active object in the workbook window. When a chart is not active, the default Excel menus return and the Chart toolbar disappears.

Try switching between the chart and the worksheet.

To switch between the embedded chart and the worksheet:

1. Click anywhere in the worksheet outside of the chart to deselect it. The Chart toolbar disappears and the Data menu replaces the Chart menu on the menu bar. There are no selection handles around the chart.

2. Move the pointer over a blank area of the chart so that the pointer changes to ⬚ and the ScreenTip "Chart Area" displays in the chart, and then click in the empty chart area. The Chart toolbar and the Chart menu reappear, and the selection handles appear around the chart.

   Trouble? If you clicked one of the chart's elements, you made that element active rather than the entire chart. Click a blank area in the chart to select the entire embedded chart.

Moving and Resizing an Embedded Chart

The Chart Wizard has a default size and location for embedded charts, which might not match what you want in your worksheet. In this case, the new chart is covering some of the data in the Sales worksheet and the chart titles seem to overwhelm the plot area. You will move the chart so you can see all of the sales data, and then you will make the chart a little larger to make it easier to read.

To move and resize the embedded chart:

1. Verify that the embedded chart is still selected, and then move the pointer over a blank area of the chart so that the pointer changes to ⬚ and the ScreenTip "Chart Area" displays.

2. Drag the embedded chart so that the upper-left corner of the chart aligns with the upper-left corner of cell A11. Note that as you drag the chart with the pointer, an outline of the chart area appears, which you can use as a guideline.

3. Release the mouse button when the chart is positioned correctly. The chart moves to a new location in the worksheet.

   To resize the chart, you drag a selection handle in the direction that you want the chart resized. To keep the proportions of the chart the same, press and hold the Shift key as you drag one of the corner selection handles.

4. Move your pointer over the lower-right selection handle until the pointer changes to ⬊.

5. Drag the lower-right corner of the embedded chart until that corner is aligned with the lower-right corner of cell F26.

6. Release the mouse button when the chart is resized, and then, if necessary, scroll the worksheet so the chart is visible. Figure 4-15 shows the chart, repositioned and resized.

Figure 4-15 **Embedded chart moved and resized**

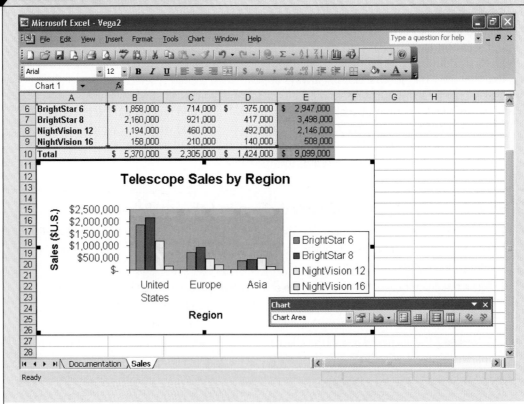

Updating a Chart

Every chart you create is connected to its data source. As a result, if you change values in the data source, Excel automatically updates the chart to reflect the change. This is true for category labels as well as for data values.

Alicia sees two changes that she would like you to make to the Sales worksheet. First, the European sales amount for the BrightStar 6 model should be $914,000, not $714,000. She also wants to change the label "United States" to "USA." You'll make these changes and observe how the embedded chart is automatically updated.

To update the column chart:

1. Scroll the worksheet so both the chart and the sales data are visible.

2. Click cell **C6**, type **914000**, and then press the **Enter** key. The data marker corresponding to European sales for the BrightStar 6 changes to reflect the new sales value.

3. Click cell **B5**, type **USA**, and then press the **Enter** key. The x-axis reflects the change to the category name.

Creating a Pie Chart

The second chart that Alicia sketched (shown in Figure 4-2) is a pie chart that shows the relative contribution of each telescope model to the total sales. In a pie chart, the size of each slice is determined by the relative value of a single data point to the sum of all values in the data series. Unlike the column chart you just created, a pie chart has only one data series, which is the total sales for each model from all regions.

To create the pie chart:

1. Select the nonadjacent range **A6:A9;E6:E9**, and then click the **Chart Wizard** button 📊 on the Standard toolbar. The first step of the Chart Wizard opens.

2. Click **Pie** in the Chart type list box, make sure that the first chart sub-type **Pie** is selected, and then click the **Next** button.

   Because you already selected the data series for the chart, which appears in columns, you do not have to make any changes, so you can bypass the second step of the Chart Wizard.

3. Click the **Next** button to move to the third step of the Chart Wizard. You will enter the chart title that Alicia wants in this dialog box.

4. Make sure that the **Titles** tab is active, click the **Chart title** text box, and then type **Total Telescope Sales**.

   Next you will add data labels to the chart that display the percentage of sales for each model.

5. Click the **Data Labels** tab, and then click the **Percentage** check box. The preview of the charts reflects the options you have chosen. See Figure 4-16.

Figure 4-16	Displaying percentage labels in a pie chart

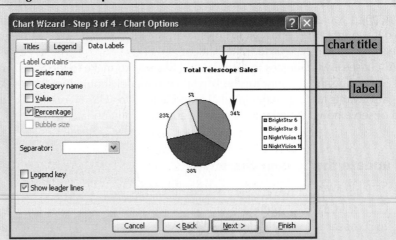

6. Click the **Next** button to display the final step of the Chart Wizard. You will place the pie chart in its own chart sheet and name the sheet "Pie Chart of Sales."

7. Click the **As new sheet** option button, and then type **Pie Chart of Sales** in the adjacent list box. The text you type in the text box will appear on the tab of the chart sheet.

8. Click the **Finish** button. Figure 4-17 shows the completed pie chart displayed on a chart sheet, which has been inserted before the Sales sheet. Note that the zoom magnification of the chart sheet on your screen might differ, depending on the settings and resolution of your monitor.

Figure 4-17	Pie chart of total telescope sales

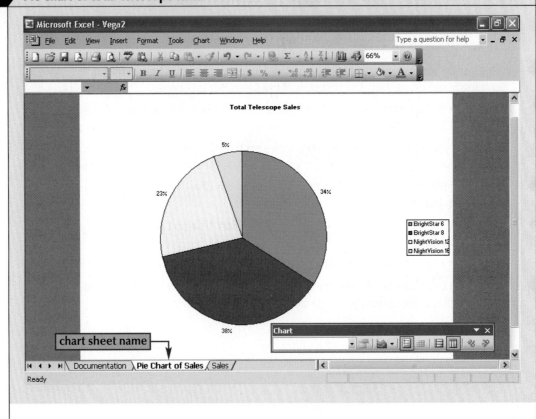

After reviewing the pie chart, Alicia has a few questions about the chart's appearance. She wonders why the slices are organized the way they are and whether the arrangement of the pie slices can be changed. The slices are arranged in a counterclockwise direction following the order that they appeared in the table. The first entry is for the BrightStar 6 telescope, the next is for the BrightStar 8, and so forth. Alicia asks whether it would be possible to move the placement of the BrightStar 6 telescope.

Rotating the Pie Chart

You cannot change the order in which the slices are arranged in the pie chart without changing their order in the data series, but you can rotate the chart. This is done by breaking the chart into 360-degree increments, starting from the top of the pie. Using this approach, the first slice starts at 0 degrees—a value that you can change. Based on Alicia's suggestion, you will change the starting point to 180 degrees, so that the first slice appears at the bottom of the pie chart.

To rotate the pie chart:

▶ **1.** Double-click the pie chart to open the Format Data Series dialog box, and then click the **Options** tab.

▶ **2.** Double-click the value in the Angle of first slice text box, and then click the **Degrees** up arrow to increase the angle of first slice value to **180**. As you click the up arrow, the pie chart in the preview pane rotates accordingly, as shown in Figure 4-18.

Rotating the pie chart 180 degrees ◀ **Figure 4-18**

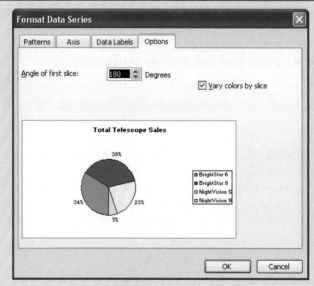

▶ **3.** Click the **OK** button to close the dialog box.

Alicia tells you that the company is particularly interested in the sales performance of the BrightStar 6 telescope, because the company is considering replacing this scope with a six-inch version of the NightVision. Alicia has seen pie charts in which a single slice is removed from the others to give it greater emphasis. She wants the slice for the BrightStar 6 removed from the other slices to draw attention to this telescope.

Exploding a Slice of a Pie Chart

This method of emphasizing a particular pie slice over others is called separating or "exploding" the slice. An exploded slice is more distinctive because it is not connected to the other slices in the pie and it appears to be bigger. Excel allows you to explode any or all of the slices in the pie. A pie chart with one or more pie slices separated from the whole is referred to as an exploded pie chart.

| Reference Window | **Creating an Exploded Pie Chart** |

To explode one pie slice from a pie chart:
- Click the pie chart to select it, and then click the pie slice you want to explode.
- Drag the selected pie slice away from the rest of the pie, and then release the mouse button.

To explode all the pie slices in a pie chart:
- Click the pie chart to select it.
- Drag any pie slice to explode all the slices an equal distance apart, and then release the mouse button.

Next, you'll separate the BrightStar 6 telescope pie slice from the rest of the pie.

To explode the slice for the BrightStar 6 telescope:

1. Make sure that the pie chart is still selected, and then click the pie slice representing the total sales for the BrightStar 6. When you position the pointer over the pie slice, a ScreenTip appears with the corresponding worksheet cell information.

2. Drag the pie slice down and to the left. As you drag the pie slice, an outline marks your progress.

3. Release the mouse button, moving the slice into its new position. See Figure 4-19 for the location of the exploded pie slice.

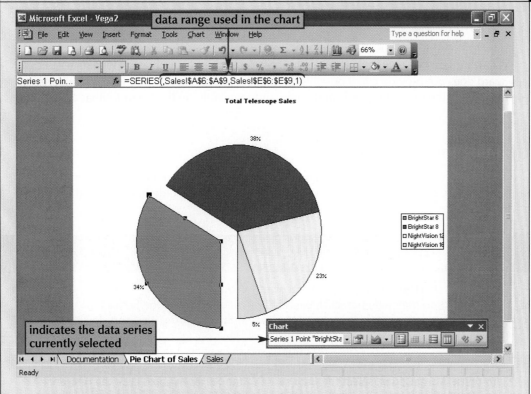

You have created the two charts that Alicia wanted, so you can save your work and then close the workbook and Excel.

4. Save your changes to the workbook, and then close it.

Rotating the pie and exploding a pie slice are both examples of formatting the appearance of an Excel chart after it has been created with the Chart Wizard. In the next session, you will learn about the other tools available that you can use to format the charts that you create.

Session 4.1 Quick Check

1. What is the difference between a chart type and a chart sub-type?
2. Which chart would you most likely use to track the daily values of a stock?
3. What is a data series?
4. What is the difference between the plot area and the chart area?
5. What are gridlines?
6. Describe the two types of chart locations.
7. A chart that shows the relative contribution of each data value to the whole is called a(n) _____ chart.
8. A pie chart in which all slices are separated from one another is called a(n) _____ chart.

Review

To reinforce the tasks you learned in this session, go to the SAM 2003 Training Companion CD included with this text.

Session 4.2

For hands-on practice of key tasks in this session, go to the SAM 2003 Training Companion CD included with this text.

Modifying a Chart

In the last session, you used the Chart Wizard to create two charts. Although the Chart Wizard presents you with a variety of choices concerning your chart's appearance, the wizard does not provide every possibility. To make further modifications to your charts, you can use the formatting tools and commands available on the Chart toolbar and the Chart menu.

Editing the Data Source

After you create a chart, you can change the data that is used in the chart. You might need to change the data if you selected the wrong data or if you decide to display a different data series.

Reference Window

Editing the Data Source of a Chart

- Select the chart whose data source you want to edit.
- Click Chart on the menu bar, click Source Data, and then click the Series tab.
- To remove a data series, select the data series in the Series list box, and click the Remove button.
- To add a data series, click the Add button, and then select the cell references for the new data series.
- To revise a data series, select the data series in the Series list box, click the reference box for the data series, and then select a new cell reference.
- Click the OK button.

Alicia can see from the charts that 16-inch telescopes comprise a small portion of Vega's sales. For this reason, she wants you to remove the NightVision 16 from the two charts you created. You will begin by removing the NightVision 16 data series from the column chart.

To remove the NightVision 16 data series from the column chart:

1. If you took a break after the previous session, make sure that Excel is running and the Vega2 workbook is open.

2. Switch to the Sales worksheet, and then click the embedded column chart to select it.

3. Click **Chart** on the menu bar, and then click **Source Data**. The Source Data dialog box opens. Note that this dialog box is identical to the second dialog box in the Chart Wizard.

4. Click the **Series** tab, click **NightVision 16** in the Series list box, and then click the **Remove** button. The preview of the chart reflects the change you have made. See Figure 4-20.

Removing the NightVision 16 from the column chart ◀ **Figure 4-20**

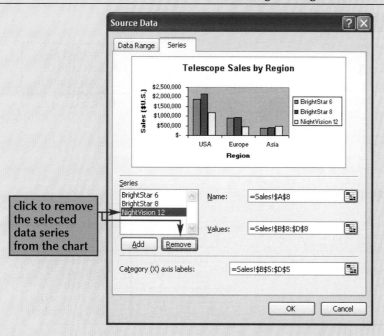

5. Click the **OK** button. The NightVision 16 sales data is no longer represented in the column chart.

Removing the NightVision 16 pie slice from the pie chart presents a slightly different challenge. Unlike the column chart (which has multiple data series), the pie chart has only one data series. To remove the NightVision 16 from the pie chart, you will have to change the cell reference of the chart's data source to exclude the NightVision 16 row.

To remove the NightVision 16 from the pie chart:

1. Switch to the Pie Chart of Sales worksheet.

2. Click **Chart** on the menu bar, click **Source Data** to open the Source Data dialog box, and then verify that the Series tab is selected. From this dialog box, you can see that the values for the data series are found in the cell range E6:E9 on the Sales worksheet and the category labels come from the range A6:A9 on the same sheet. You have to change these cell references to remove the NightVision 16 telescope from the chart.

3. Click the **Collapse Dialog Box** button 🔲 for the Values reference box, select the range **E6:E8**, and then click the **Expand Dialog Box** button 🔲 to redisplay the Source Data dialog box with the new value range.

4. Click the **Collapse Dialog Box** button 🔲 for the Category Labels reference box, select the range **A6:A8**, and then click the **Expand Dialog Box** button 🔲 to redisplay the Source Data dialog box. As shown in Figure 4-21, the preview pane displays the new pie chart with the NightVision 16 telescope excluded.

| Figure 4-21 | Removing the NightVision 16 from the pie chart |

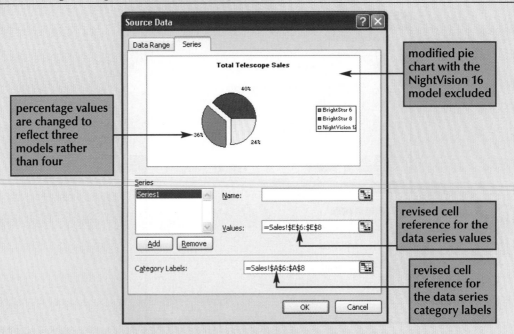

5. Click the **OK** button to save your changes to the chart.

Note that when you removed the NightVision 16 from the data series, the percentages in the pie chart changed as well to reflect a total sales figure based on only three models rather than four.

Changing the Chart Location

Alicia has decided that she prefers the chart sheet to the embedded chart. She wants you to move the embedded column chart on the Sales worksheet to a chart sheet. Rather than re-creating the chart using the Chart Wizard, you will use the Location command on the Chart menu. You will move the embedded chart to a chart sheet, which you will name "Column Chart of Sales."

To change the location of the embedded column chart:

1. Switch to the Sales worksheet, and then, if necessary, click the embedded column chart to select it.

2. Click **Chart** on the menu bar, and then click **Location**. The Chart Location dialog box opens. The dialog box is identical to the fourth dialog box in the Chart Wizard.

3. Click the **As new sheet** option button, type **Column Chart of Sales** as the name of the chart sheet, and then click the **OK** button. The column chart moves into its own chart sheet.

Changing Chart Options

As mentioned, the dialog boxes to change the chart's data source and location look identical to the dialog boxes for steps 2 and 4 of the Chart Wizard. Dialog boxes for the remaining two Chart Wizard steps are also available through commands on the Chart menu. Recall that the third step of the Chart Wizard allowed you to format the chart's appearance by adding or removing chart titles, gridlines, legends, and labels.

Alicia wants to revisit some of the chart options selected earlier. After seeing that the percent labels in the pie chart provided useful information, she wants you to add labels to the column chart displaying the actual sales values for each column. You will use the Chart Options dialog box to make this change.

To revise the chart options for the column chart:

1. Click **Chart** on the menu bar, and then click **Chart Options**. The Chart Options dialog box opens. Note that the dialog box is identical to step 3 of the Chart Wizard.

2. Click the **Data Labels** tab.

3. Click the **Value** check box, and then click the **OK** button. The sales figures for each model now appear above the corresponding column. See Figure 4-22. The values appear to be a little crowded, and you will change this next.

Adding labels to the columns | Figure 4-22

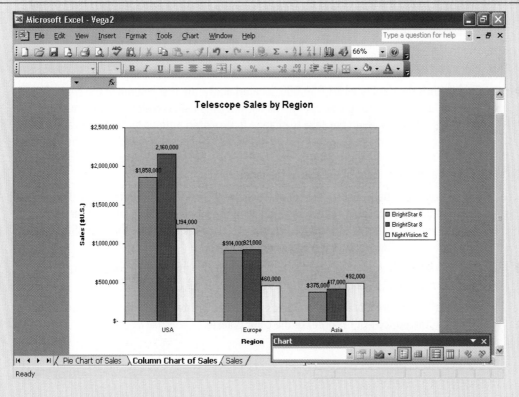

Alicia has a few changes that she wants you to make to the chart labels. You cannot make these changes by modifying the chart options. Instead, you have to format the individual elements within the chart.

Formatting Chart Elements

So far, all of the formatting that you have done has applied to the chart as a whole. You can also select and format individual chart elements, such as the chart title, legend, and axes. To select an individual chart element, you either click on the element or select the element's name from a drop-down list on the Chart toolbar. You can then use buttons on the Formatting toolbar or open a dialog box to modify the element's appearance. You can also double-click a chart element to both select it and open a dialog box or right-click the chart element and select a format from a shortcut dialog box.

In some cases, a chart element will be composed of several elements. For example, a data series will have several data markers. If you click on one data marker, you select all of the markers in the series. If you click that marker again, the selection is confined to that specific marker, removing the selection from other markers in the series. In this way, you can format all of the elements at once or confine your formatting to a specific element.

You'll have a chance to try these selection and formatting techniques in the steps that follow.

Formatting Chart Text

Alicia wants you to change the alignment of the data labels that appear above the columns. She feels that the labels would look better if you changed their alignment from horizontal to vertical. She would also like the labels to appear within and at the bottom of the columns themselves, so she suggests that you change the color of the data labels as well. You will make these changes by double-clicking the data label to open the Format Data Labels dialog box.

To format the data labels:

1. Double-click the data label **$1,858,000**, located above the first column in the chart. The Format Data Labels dialog box opens. The Format Data Labels dialog box has four tabs. You use the Font and Number tabs to change font-related options for text and values and to apply number formats to values as you did in the previous tutorial. You use the Patterns tab to change the fill color, patterns, and borders around labels. You use the Alignment tab to change the alignment of the text in the label.

   The $1,858,000 label is part of the set of labels for the BrightStar 6 data series. By double-clicking the first data label, you've selected all of the labels for this particular series. Any changes you make in this dialog box will apply to all of the labels for the BrightStar 6 sales data (but not for the labels in the other data series).

2. Click the **Font** tab, click the **Color** list box, and then click the **Yellow** square (fourth row, third column from the left) in the color palette.

   Trouble? If you are working with a black-and-white printer, select the White font color, located in the bottom-right corner of the color palette.

3. Click the **Alignment** tab.

4. In the Orientation section, change the value in the Degrees box to **90**. The text changes to a vertical orientation with an angle of 90 degrees.

5. Click the **Label Position** list arrow, and then select **Inside Base** to display the values label inside and at the base of each column in the chart. See Figure 4-23.

Changing the orientation of the data labels ◀ **Figure 4-23**

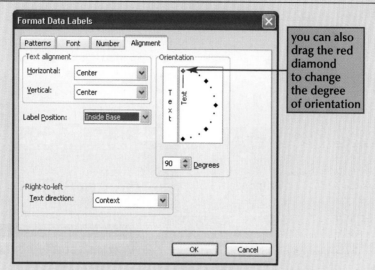

6. Click the **OK** button. The labels for the BrightStar 6 data series have been rotated 90 degrees and now appear in a yellow font at the base of the columns.

Next you'll make a similar change to the labels for the BrightStar 8 data series. Rather than double-clicking the label, you'll use the shortcut menu.

7. Right-click the **$2,160,000** label above the second column in the chart, click **Format Data Labels** from the shortcut menu, and then repeat Steps 2 through 6 to change the label to a white font rotated 90 degrees and displayed at the inside base of each column.

Finally, you'll select the data labels for the NightVision 12 data series using the Chart toolbar.

8. Click the **Chart Objects** list arrow [   ] on the Chart toolbar, scroll down the list of options, click **"NightVision 12" Data Labels** to select this chart element, and then click the **Format Data Labels** button 🖼 on the Chart toolbar.

9. Repeat Steps 3 through 6 to rotate the label to **90** degrees and display it at the inside base of each column. You don't have to change the color of the font.

10. Click the **OK** button to save your changes. Figure 4-24 shows the revised labels for all of the data series in the chart.

Figure 4-24 ▶ **Revised data labels**

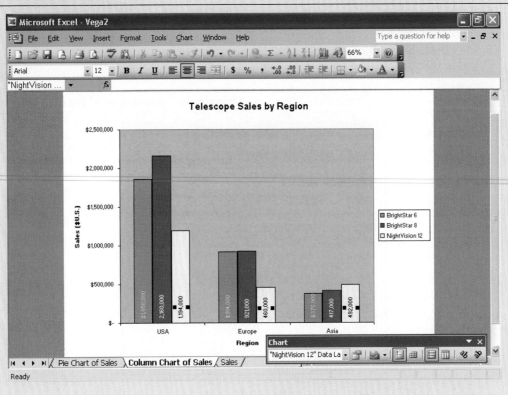

Next, Alicia wants you to add some additional text to the chart.

Inserting Unattached Text

Excel classifies chart text in three categories: label text, attached text, and unattached text. Label text includes the category names, the tick mark labels (which you've just worked with), and the legend text. Label text often is linked to cells in the worksheet. Attached text includes the chart title and the axes titles. Although the text appears in a predefined position, you can edit and move it. Unlike label text, attached text is not linked to any cells in the worksheet. Finally, unattached text is any additional text that you want to include in the chart. Unattached text can be positioned anywhere within the chart area and formatted with the same tools you use to format label and attached text.

To add unattached text to a chart, you type the text in the Formula bar. Excel automatically creates a text box for the text entry and places the text box in the chart area. You can then resize the text box and move it to another location in the chart area. You can format the text using the Format Text Box dialog box.

Inserting Unattached Text into a Chart

- Select the chart.
- In the Formula bar, type the text that you want to include in the chart.
- To resize the new unattached text box, click and drag one of the text box's selection handles.
- To move the unattached text box, click the border of the text box, and drag the text box to a new location in the chart area.
- To format the unattached text, select the text box and click the appropriate formatting buttons on the Formatting toolbar; or double-click the border of the text box to open the Format Text Box dialog box, use the options provided on the dialog box tabs, and then click the OK button.

Alicia wants you to add the text "Vega Sales from the Last Fiscal Year" to the upper-right corner of the plot area, and she wants the text to be ivory in color.

To add unattached text to the chart:

1. Click the column chart to select it, click in the Formula bar above the chart, type **Vega Sales from the Last Fiscal Year**, and then press the **Enter** key. Excel places a text box containing the new unattached text in the middle of the chart area. The text box is selected so you can modify its appearance.

2. Click the **Font Color** list arrow $\boxed{\text{A}}$ ⁃ on the Formatting toolbar, and then click the **Ivory** square (sixth row, third column from the left) in the color palette.

3. Move the pointer over the edge of the unattached text box until the pointer changes to ⁺⁺, drag the text box to the upper-right corner of the plot area, and then release the mouse button. The text should now be placed in the upper-right corner of the plot.

You can double-click an unattached text box at any time to open the Format Text Box dialog box, in which you can change the font format, alignment, and color. You can also create a border around the text. Try this now by creating a yellow border.

To create a border for the text box:

1. Verify that the text box is still selected, and then double-click the border of the selected text box to open the Format Text Box dialog box.

   Trouble? If you double-clicked the text in the text box, the Format Text Box dialog box did not open. Try double-clicking the border of the text box again.

2. Click the **Colors and Lines** tab.

3. Click the **Color** list box in the Line section, click the **Ivory** square (sixth row, third column) in the color palette, and then click the **OK** button.

4. Click outside the chart to deselect it. Figure 4-25 shows the text box with the ivory border.

Figure 4-25 **Adding unattached text to a chart**

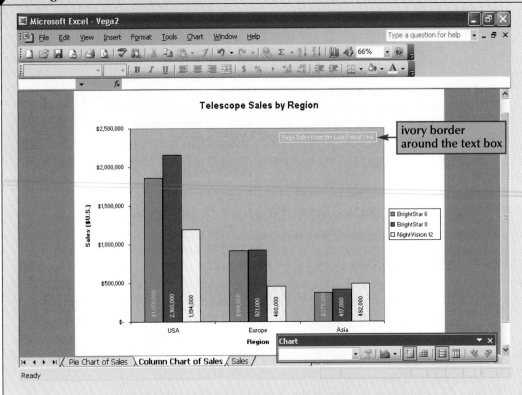

Now that you have formatted the chart labels and added unattached text, you can turn to some of the other features of Excel charts that need modifying.

Working with Colors and Fills

The formatted data labels and the unattached text help to clarify the sales data, but Alicia feels that the column chart lacks visual appeal. Alicia has seen objects filled with a variety of colors that gradually blend from one color to another. She wonders if you can do the same thing for the columns in the column chart. One idea she has is to make the columns appear more like tubes, such as telescope tubes.

When you want to fill a column (or area) in a chart with a pattern or color, you are actually modifying the appearance of the data marker in the chart. You will concentrate only on the fill color used in the data marker. Other data markers have other patterns that you can modify. For example, in an XY (scatter) chart, the data markers are points that appear in the plot. You can specify the color of those data points, their size, whether a line will connect the data points and, if so, the color, thickness, and style of that line.

You will format the data markers in the column chart beginning with the column that represents the BrightStar 6 telescope.

To format the fill color of the chart columns:

▶ **1.** Double-click the first column on the left in the chart to open the Format Data Series dialog box for that data series. You can use the options available on the different dialog box tabs to control one or more aspects of the selected data marker. For example, you use the options provided on the Patterns tab to control the border style that appears around the column as well as the interior appearance of the column. Currently, the column is formatted with a black border and filled with a pale-blue color.

2. Click the **Fill Effects** button to open the Fill Effects dialog box. The tabs in this dialog box provide a full range of options that you can use to create sophisticated and lush colors and patterns.

3. Make sure the **Gradient** tab is displayed in the dialog box.

You use the options on the Gradient tab to create fill effects that blend together different and varying amounts of color. Three color options are:

- **One color:** To create a blend that uses different shades of one color
- **Two colors:** To create a blend from one color into another
- **Preset:** To apply a predefined blend style, including Early Sunset, Nightfall, Ocean, Rainbow, and Chrome

You can also specify the direction of the blending effect, choosing from horizontal, vertical, diagonal up, diagonal down, from corner, and from center. For the selected column in the current chart, you will create a blend fill effect using a single color starting from a dark shade of the pale-blue color. You will use a vertical shading style to give the color dimension.

To create the fill effect:

1. Click the **One color** option button on the Gradient tab, and then drag the scroll box to the **Dark** end of the shading scale. Note that as you change the shading scale, the images in the Variants section reflect the degree of shading.

2. Click the **Vertical** option button in the Shading styles section. Now the images in the Variants section show the varying degrees of shading vertically.

3. Click the bottom-right Variants box, which shows the darker edges of the shading on the left and right edges of the object, as shown in Figure 4-26.

Specifying a fill effect **Figure 4-26**

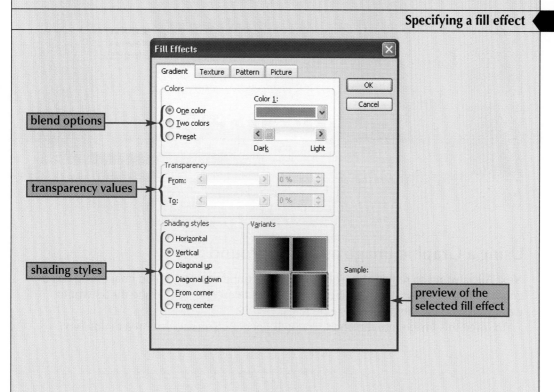

4. Click the **OK** button twice to close the dialog boxes and redisplay the chart. Excel displays the first column series with a dark-blue color on the left and right side of the column, giving it the illusion of appearing as a tube.

   Next you will create a similar blend for the other columns.

5. Double-click the second column from the left in the chart to open the Format Data Series dialog box.

6. Click the **Fill Effects** button to open the Fill Effects dialog box.

7. Click the **One color** option button, drag the scroll box to the **Dark** end of the shading scale, make sure the **Vertical** option button is selected, select the bottom-right Variants option, and then click the **OK** button twice.

8. Double-click the third column, and then repeat Steps 6 and 7 to create a one-color fill effect that goes from the dark end of the ivory scale to the light end.

9. Click outside the chart area. Figure 4-27 shows the revised column chart with blends for each of the three data series.

| Figure 4-27 | **Columns with the applied fill effects** |

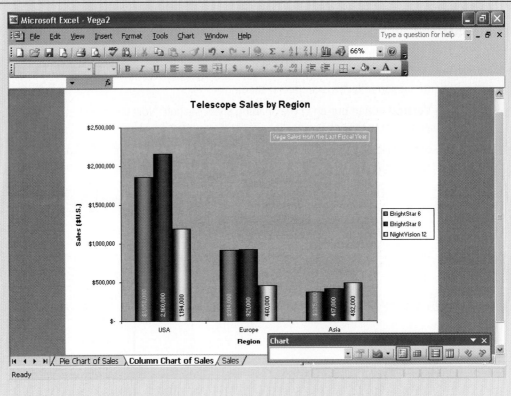

Using a Graphic Image as a Background

Next Alicia wants to replace the solid gray background with a graphic image. She has a graphic file that shows an image from the Hubble telescope, which she thinks would work well with the theme of telescope sales.

To insert this image into the chart, you will open the Format Plot Area dialog box.

To fill the plot area with an image:

1. Click the **Chart Objects** list arrow ⬚ on the Chart toolbar, click **Plot Area**, and then click the **Format Plot Area** button ⬚ on the Chart toolbar. The Format Plot Area dialog box opens.

2. Click the **Fill Effects** button on the Patterns tab to open the Fill Effects dialog box.

3. Click the **Picture** tab, and then click the **Select Picture** button. The Select Picture dialog box opens.

4. Navigate to the Tutorial.04\Tutorial folder, select the **Space** file, and then click the **Insert** button. The image appears in the Fill Effects dialog box.

5. Click the **OK** button twice to close the dialog boxes, and then click outside the chart area. Figure 4-28 shows the revised column chart with the new background image.

Chart with space background image ◀ **Figure 4-28**

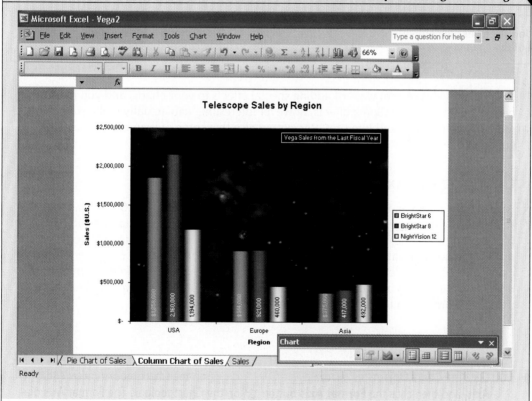

Graphic images can be applied to other elements in the chart. For example, you can replace the data markers in the chart with graphic images. To do this, select the data markers and open the Fill Effects dialog box that you used to create a background image for the chart. Select the image file that you want to use in place of the data marker. If you are working with a column chart, you can also choose to either stack or stretch the chosen image to the height of the column. Figure 4-29 shows the effect of these two options on the appearance of the column chart.

Figure 4-29 | **Replacing columns with graphics**

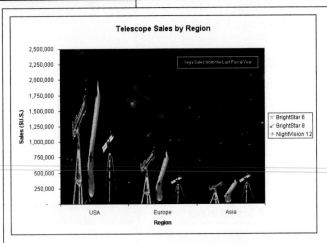
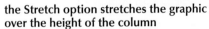
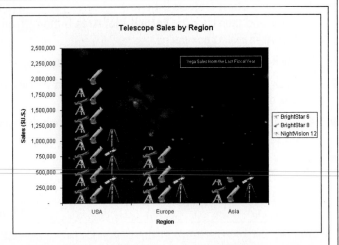

the Stretch option stretches the graphic
over the height of the column

the Stack option stacks the graphic
up to the height of the column

Excel provides several ways of adding special effects to your charts, and you must be careful not to overdo it. Some effects, however interesting, can actually make your charts more difficult to read and interpret. Remember also that some of your effects may look good in color, but will not transfer well to a black-and-white printout.

Changing the Axis Scale

Alicia might want you to make one other change to the column chart. She knows that the scale used by the chart is automatically set by Excel. Excel uses the data that you have plotted and determines an appropriate scale for the y-axis, usually designed to cover a range of reasonable values. Alicia wants you to examine the scale that Excel set for this chart to see if a change is warranted. She also thinks that expressing the sales in terms of dollars on the chart is a bit unwieldy for sales of this magnitude. She would rather have the sales expressed in terms of thousands of dollars.

To view the y-axis scale:

1. Click the **Chart Objects** list arrow [ ] on the Chart toolbar, click **Value Axis**, and then click the **Format Axis** button 🖼 on the Chart toolbar. The Format Axis dialog box opens. You can use this dialog box to format the scale's appearance and to change the range and increments used in the scale.

2. Click the **Scale** tab. See Figure 4-30.

Scale tab in the Format Axis dialog box ◀ **Figure 4-30**

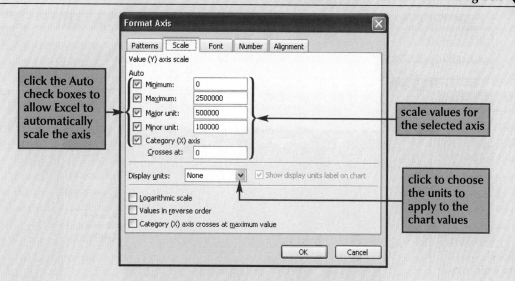

click the Auto check boxes to allow Excel to automatically scale the axis

scale values for the selected axis

click to choose the units to apply to the chart values

There are four values that comprise the scale: the minimum, maximum, major unit, and minor unit. The minimum and maximum values are the smallest and largest tick marks that appear on the axis. The major unit is the increment between the scale's **major tick marks**. The chart also has a second set of tick marks, called **minor tick marks**, that may or may not be displayed. The difference between major and minor tick marks is that axis values appear next to major tick marks, whereas no values appear next to minor tick marks.

In the current chart, the scale that Excel displayed ranges from 0 to 2,500,000 in increments of 500,000. The minor tick mark increment is 100,000, but these tick marks are not displayed on the axes. Alicia wants to reduce the increment value to 250,000 in order to show more detail on the chart. Then she wants to change the display units from none to thousands.

To revise the y-axis scale:

1. Double-click the current entry in the Major unit box, and then type **250000**. Note that when you manually change a scale value its Auto check box is automatically deselected.

2. Click the **Display units** list arrow, and then select **Thousands** in the list.

3. Make sure that the **Show display units label on chart** check box is selected, and then click the **OK** button. Figure 4-31 shows the revised y-axis scale.

Figure 4-31 — **Revised scale for the y-axis**

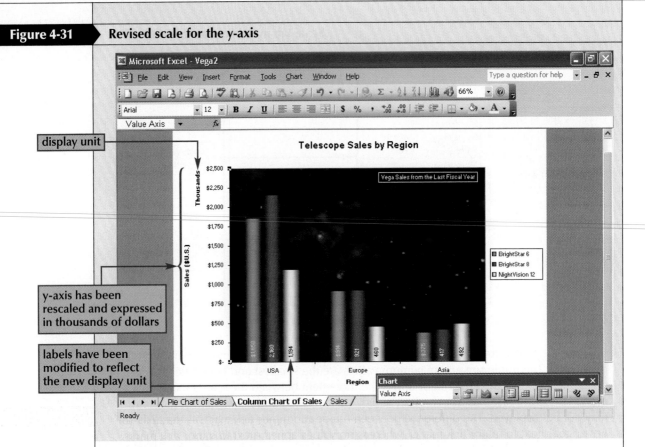

In this chart, $2,500,000 is displayed as $2,500. Because you have changed the display units in this way, you need to include information about the new value. Excel does this for you by adding the text "Thousands" to the value axis. Also note that the label values for each column now use the thousands display unit, so the Asian sales for the BrightStar 6 are displayed as $375 rather than $375,000.

Pleased with the latest version of the column chart, Alicia now wants you to go back to the pie chart and make some modifications there.

Working with Three-Dimensional Charts

Many of the Excel charts can be displayed either as two-dimensional "flat" charts or as charts that appear in three dimensions. Alicia wants you to change the pie chart to a three-dimensional pie chart. To do this, you have to change the chart type.

To change the pie chart to 3-D:

1. Switch to the Pie Chart of Sales chart sheet.
2. Click **Chart** on the menu bar, and then click **Chart Type**. The Chart Type dialog box opens.
3. Click the second chart sub-type in the top row, as shown in Figure 4-32.

Changing to a 3-D pie chart 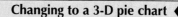 **Figure 4-32**

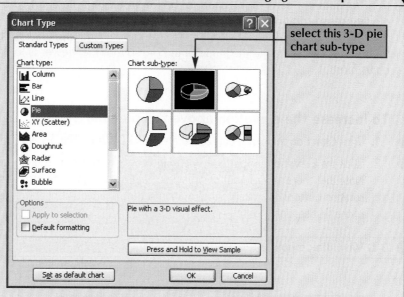

select this 3-D pie chart sub-type

4. Click the **OK** button. Excel displays the pie chart in three dimensions. Note that Excel has retained the rotation you applied to the chart in the last session, and the BrightStar 6 slice is still exploded. See Figure 4-33.

3-D pie chart **Figure 4-33**

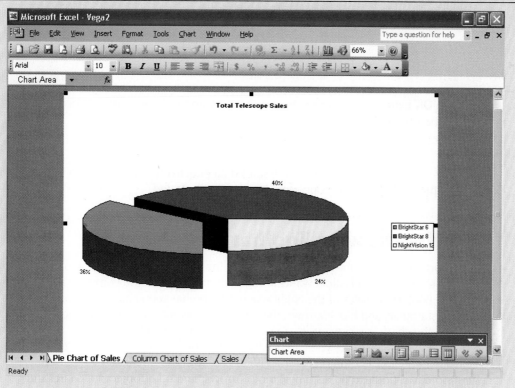

In a 3-D chart, you have several options to modify the 3-D effect. One of these is **elevation**, which is the illusion that you're looking at the 3-D chart from either above or below the chart. Another of these is **perspective**, which is the illusion that some parts of the 3-D chart are farther away from you than others. Finally, you can rotate a 3-D chart to bring different parts of the chart to the forefront. In a pie chart, you can change the elevation and rotation, but not the perspective.

Alicia likes the 3-D view of the pie chart but feels that the angle of the pie is too low. She wants you to change the angle of the pie so that the viewer is looking "down" on the chart more.

To increase the elevation above the pie chart:

1. Click **Chart** on the menu bar, and then click **3-D View**. The 3-D View dialog box opens.

2. Click the **Elevation** up button twice to increase the elevation to **25** degrees. See Figure 4-34. Note that there are also buttons that you can use to rotate the pie chart. Clicking one of the rotation buttons is similar to the rotation setting that you applied to the pie chart at the end of the first session.

Figure 4-34 ▶ 3-D View dialog box

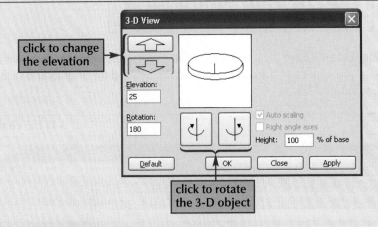

3. Click the **OK** button. Excel redraws the pie chart, giving the illusion that the observer is at an elevation above the chart.

The charts you have created present the sales data effectively, but Alicia also wants to be sure that the top-selling telescope model is clearly illustrated.

Using the Drawing Toolbar

One of the big stories from the past fiscal year was the successful introduction of the NightVision telescopes, and Alicia wants to highlight the fact that the company had in excess of $1,800,000 in sales of the NightVision 12. She has seen charts that contain shapes, like starbursts and block arrows, that give added emphasis to details and facts contained in the chart. Alicia wants to do something similar with the pie chart.

To create a graphical shape, you can use the tools provided on the Drawing toolbar. The Drawing toolbar is a common feature of all Office 2003 products. You can use the Drawing toolbar to add text boxes, lines, block arrows, and other objects to charts and worksheets. In Excel, an **object** is any entity that can be manipulated. A chart is an Excel object, as are its elements. Next, you will learn how to use the Drawing toolbar to create and format one type of object, an AutoShape.

Displaying the Drawing Toolbar

Depending on your Excel configuration, the Drawing toolbar may or may not be displayed in the Excel window when you start Excel. (The default is to not show the toolbar.) As with all toolbars, you can choose to display or hide the Drawing toolbar. Although you can display the Drawing toolbar using the View menu, you will display the toolbar by clicking the Drawing button on the Standard toolbar.

To display the Drawing toolbar:

▶ **1.** Click the **Drawing** button 🔳 on the Standard toolbar. The Drawing toolbar appears in the workbook window.

▶ **2.** If necessary, drag the Drawing toolbar to the bottom of the worksheet window, and then release the mouse button. The Drawing toolbar should now be anchored to the bottom of the window.

Now you will use the Drawing toolbar to add a drawing object to the pie chart.

Working with AutoShapes

The Drawing toolbar contains a list of predefined shapes called **AutoShapes**. These AutoShapes can be simple squares or circles or more complicated objects such as flow chart objects and block arrows. Once you insert an AutoShape into a chart or worksheet, you can resize and move it, like any other object. You can modify the fill color of an AutoShape, change the border style, and even insert text.

Inserting an AutoShape

Reference Window

- Click the AutoShapes list arrow on the Drawing toolbar.
- Point to the AutoShape category that you want to use, and then click the AutoShape that you want to create.
- Position the crosshair pointer over the location for the AutoShape in the chart or worksheet, and then drag the pointer over the area where you want the shape to appear. To draw an AutoShape in the same proportion as the shape on the palette, press and hold the Shift key as you drag the pointer to draw the shape.
- Release the mouse button.
- To resize an AutoShape, click the shape to select it, and then drag one of the nine selection handles.
- To rotate an AutoShape, click the green rotation handle that is connected to the shape, and drag the handle to rotate the shape.
- To change the shape of the AutoShape, click the yellow diamond tool, and then drag the tool to change the shape.

You will now add a multi-pointed star to the pie chart to highlight the success of the NightVision 12 telescope.

To add a multi-pointed AutoShape star to the pie chart:

1. Click the **AutoShapes** list arrow on the Drawing toolbar, point to **Stars and Banners**, and then click the **16-Point Star** AutoShape (second row, second column from the left) on the AutoShapes palette. A ScreenTip appears when you position the pointer over an AutoShape on the palette so you will know which shape you are selecting.

2. Move the pointer to the upper-right corner of the chart area, about one inch to the right of the chart title. As you move the pointer over the worksheet, the pointer shape changes to $+$.

   To draw an AutoShape in the same proportion as the shape on the palette, you must press and hold the Shift key as you drag the pointer to draw the shape.

3. Press and hold the **Shift** key, and then click and drag the pointer down and to the right about one and one-half inches. Note that pressing the Shift key allows you to create a perfect 16-point star; otherwise, the shape might be lopsided.

4. Release the mouse button. A 16-point star appears in the upper-right corner of the chart area. See Figure 4-35.

Figure 4-35 Adding an AutoShape to the pie chart

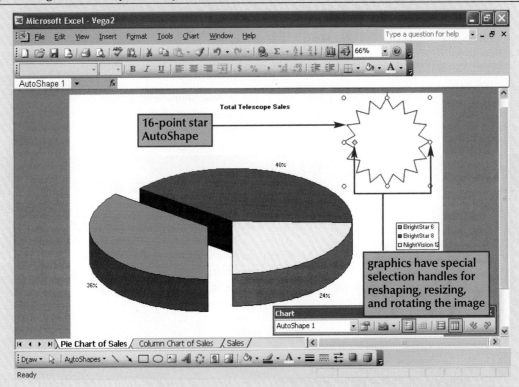

Trouble? If the AutoShape on your screen does not match the size and shape of the AutoShape shown in the figure, you can resize the object again by pressing and holding the Shift key as you drag a selection handle. Or click the Undo button 🔄 on the Standard toolbar to delete the object, and then repeat Steps 1 through 4 to redraw the AutoShape, being sure to press and hold the Shift key to draw the object proportionally.

You probably noticed that the selection handles of the AutoShape appear as open circles and that there is also a diamond tool. You can use the diamond tool to change the shape of the AutoShape. For example, you can change the size of the jagged points of the star by dragging the diamond tool either toward the center of the star (to increase the size of the points) or away from the center (to decrease the size of the points). You may have also noticed a green selection handle that is attached to the AutoShape through a vertical line. This is a rotation handle. By clicking and dragging this handle, you can rotate the AutoShape.

Formatting an AutoShape

In addition to modifying the shape, size, and rotation of an AutoShape, you can add text to it. To add text to an AutoShape, you first select it and then start typing the desired text. The text will automatically be placed within the boundaries of the shape.

Reference Window

Inserting Text into an AutoShape

- Click the border of the AutoShape to select the object.
- Type the text you want to appear in the AutoShape.
- Select the text within the AutoShape.
- Format the text using the options on the Formatting toolbar.
- Click outside of the shape to deselect it.

To highlight the success of the NightVision 12, you will add the text that Alicia wants to the AutoShape star.

To insert text into the AutoShape:

1. Make sure that the 16-point star is still selected.
2. Type **NightVision 12 Sales Exceed $1.8 Million!**
3. Click **Format** on the menu bar, click **AutoShape** to open the Format AutoShape dialog box, and then click the **Alignment** tab.

   Trouble? If there is no Alignment tab in the dialog box that opens, close the dialog box. Click the AutoShape again, making sure that the object, and not just its frame, is selected. Then repeat Step 3.

4. Click the **Horizontal** list arrow, and then click **Center**.
5. Click the **Vertical** list arrow, click **Center**, and then click the **OK** button.

   Trouble? If the text does not wrap logically within the boundaries of the AutoShape, resize the star to better accommodate the text.

The star with text adds value to the overall appearance of the chart. However, the star could use some background color to make it more visually interesting. In keeping with the other colors you have been using in the charts, you will format the AutoShape by adding a yellow background.

To change the background color of the AutoShape:

1. Make sure the 16-point star is still selected.
2. Click the **Fill Color** list arrow ![fill color icon] on the Drawing toolbar, and then click the **Ivory** square (sixth row, third column) in the color palette.

   Trouble? If the background color does not change to ivory, you may have selected the text in the star rather than the star itself. Click the Undo button ![undo icon] on the Standard toolbar, and then repeat Steps 1 and 2, being sure to select the AutoShape.

The AutoShape definitely looks better with the ivory background. You decide to try one more thing: if adding a shadow effect to the star will be too much or will add depth to the object. To add a shadow effect to an object, you can choose one of the available shadow effects provided on the Drawing toolbar.

To add a drop shadow to the AutoShape:

▶ **1.** Make sure the 16-point star is still selected.

▶ **2.** Click the **Shadow Style** button 🔲 on the Drawing toolbar to display the gallery of shadow options.

▶ **3.** Click **Shadow Style 6** (second row, second column from the left) in the shadow gallery, and then click outside the star to deselect it.

As a final step, Alicia feels that the pie chart is a little too far to the left. You will move it down and to the right to center it better.

▶ **4.** Click the **Chart Objects** list arrow [▾] on the Chart toolbar, and then click **Plot Area**.

▶ **5.** Click on the gray selection border around the plot area, drag the border down and to the right, and then click outside the chart area. Figure 4-36 shows the revised pie chart with the formatted AutoShape and the relocated pie.

| Figure 4-36 | Drop shadow added to the 16-point star AutoShape |

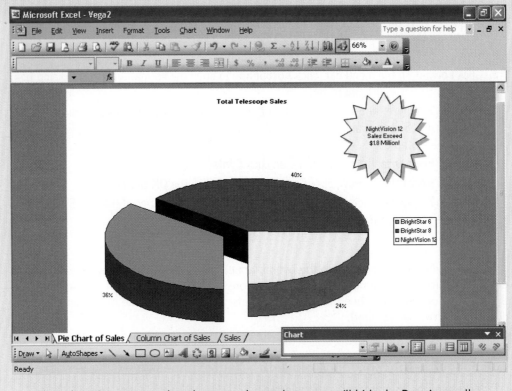

Alicia doesn't want any other changes to be made, so you will hide the Drawing toolbar, which will increase the workspace on your screen.

▶ **6.** Click the **Drawing** button 🔲 on the Formatting toolbar. The Drawing toolbar closes.

Printing Your Charts

Now that you have completed your work on the two charts for Alicia, you will make hard copies of them. Printing a chart sheet is similar to printing a worksheet. As when printing a worksheet, you should preview the printout before sending the worksheet to the printer. From the Print Preview window, you can add headers and footers and control the page layout, just as you do for printing the contents of your worksheets. You also have the added option of resizing the chart to fit within the confines of a single printed page.

To print both charts at the same time, you will select both chart sheets, open Print Preview, and then set up each chart to print on its own page.

To set up the two charts for printing:

1. Make sure the Pie Chart of Sales worksheet is the current sheet.
2. Press and hold the **Shift** key, and then click the **Column Chart of Sales** tab. Both chart sheets are selected.
3. Click the **Print Preview** button 🔍 on the Standard toolbar. The Print Preview window opens, showing the pie chart on the first of two pages.
4. Click the **Setup** button on the Print Preview toolbar to open the Page Setup dialog box. The Page Setup options are similar to the options for printing a worksheet, except that a new dialog box tab, Chart, appears.
5. Click the **Chart** tab. See Figure 4-37.

Chart tab in the Page Setup dialog box | **Figure 4-37**

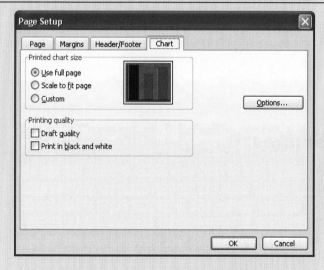

Excel provides three choices for defining the size of a chart printout. These are:

- **Use full page:** The chart is resized to fit the full page, extending to fit the full width and height of the page. The proportions of the chart may change since it is extended in all directions to fit the page. This is the default option.
- **Scale to fit page:** The chart is resized until one of the edges reaches a page margin. The chart expands in both dimensions (width and height) proportionally until one dimension fills the space between the margins.
- **Custom:** The dimensions of the printed chart are specified on the chart sheet using the Zoom tool.

You will use the Scale to fit page option because you do not want to have the charts resized disproportionately.

To set the size of the charts:

1. Click the **Scale to fit page** option button, and then click the **OK** button. The Use full page option and the Scale to fit page option will often result in charts that are close in the same size. You may not see much difference in the chart size in the Print Preview window.

2. Click the **Next** button to preview the column chart printout.

3. Click the **Setup** button, click the **Scale to fit page** option button on the Chart tab, and then click the **OK** button.

4. Click the **Print** button to open the Print dialog box, make any necessary changes, and then click the **OK** button to send both chart sheets to the printer.

   For now, there are no other changes to be made. Alicia will use the printouts of the charts at the meeting next week.

5. Save your changes to the workbook and then close it

Review

To reinforce the tasks you learned in this session, go to the SAM 2003 Training Companion CD included with this text.

Session 4.2 Quick Check

1. How would you remove a data series from a column chart?
2. How would you change the location (either embedded or as a chart sheet) of a chart?
3. What is the difference between label text, attached text, and unattached text?
4. What is the difference between major tick marks and minor tick marks?
5. How would you change a column chart into a 3-D column chart?
6. What is an AutoShape?
7. Describe the three options for sizing a chart on the printed page.

Review

Tutorial Summary

In this tutorial, you learned how to work with charts in Excel. You saw how to use Excel's Chart Wizard to create a basic chart and learned about the different types of charts that can be created by Excel. You also learned how to embed charts within a worksheet or place them on their own chart sheet in the workbook. You used Excel's editing tools to modify the chart's appearance by inserting additional text, changing font and background colors and images, rotating the chart in three dimensions, and changing the scale of the chart. This tutorial also introduced you to the Drawing toolbar, which you used to create an AutoShape, placing that shape on a chart to provide additional emphasis on key points. Finally, you learned about the different options Excel provides for printing your completed charts.

Key Terms

active chart	chart title	embedded chart
attached text	Chart Wizard	exploded pie chart
AutoShape	data marker	gridline
category values	data series	horizontal axis
chart	data source	label text
chart area	data value	legend
chart sheet	elevation	major gridline

major tick mark	plot area	vertical axis
minor gridline	scale	x-axis
minor tick mark	tick mark	x value
object	unattached text	y-axis
perspective		

Practice

Practice the skills you learned in the tutorial using the same case scenario.

Review Assignments

Data File needed for the Review Assignments: VegaUSA1.xls

Alicia has another workbook that shows the monthly United States sales for the three major telescope models. She wants you to create a column chart showing the monthly United States sales figures and a pie chart showing the total sales figures for each telescope model. To complete this task:

1. Open the **VegaUSA1** workbook located in the Tutorial.04\Review folder included with your Data Files, and then save the workbook as **VegaUSA2** to the same folder.
2. Enter your name and the current date in the Documentation sheet, and then switch to the Monthly Sales worksheet.
3. Select the range A6:D18, and then start the Chart Wizard.
4. Use the Chart Wizard to create a column chart, using the first chart sub-type. Specify "United States Telescope Sales" as the chart title, "Month" as the x-axis title, and "Sales ($U.S.)" as the y-axis title. Place the chart on a chart sheet named "Monthly Sales Chart."
5. Format the x-axis labels, changing the alignment to 90 degrees.
6. Change the scale of the y-axis using thousands as the display unit.
7. Change the background color of the plot area to white. Apply a horizontal blending effect to each column's fill color.
8. Place the chart legend at the bottom of the chart. (*Hint*: Open the Format Legend dialog box and select the Bottom option on the Placement tab.)
9. Use the Drawing toolbar to create an 8-point star located in the upper-left corner of the chart area.
10. Insert the text "NightVision 12 sales remained high in Autumn!" into the 8-point star you just created. Center the text both horizontally and vertically.
11. Change the fill color of the 8-point star to ivory, and apply Shadow Style 1 to the shape.
12. Return to the Monthly Sales worksheet, select the nonadjacent range B6:D6;B19:D19, and use the Chart Wizard to create a 3-D pie chart of the data. Assign the chart the title "Pie Chart of Total Sales" and display the sales values next to the pie slices. Place the pie chart in a chart sheet named "Pie Chart of Total Sales."
13. Apply the Late Sunset fill effect to the pie chart's chart area.
14. Select both charts, and then open the Print Preview window.
15. Use the Setup dialog box to scale both charts to fit their respective pages and to add a footer to the charts displaying your name and the date in the lower-right corner of the page. Print the charts.
16. Save your changes to the workbook and then close it.

Apply

Use the skills you have learned to create a 3-D chart of usage data for a national park.

Case Problem 1

Data File needed for this Case Problem: Park1.xls

Kenai Fjords National Park   Maria Sanford is the chief of interpretation at Kenai Fjords National Park. Part of her job is to report on park usage at the different sites and overall. She has stored last year's usage data in an Excel workbook. She would like you to represent this data in a 3-D chart, breaking down the results by sites and month. She would also like a chart that shows the monthly totals with each column organized by visitor center.

To complete this task:

1. Open the **Park1** workbook located in the Tutorial.04\Cases folder included with your Data Files, and then save the workbook as **Park2** in the same folder. Enter your name and the current date in the Documentation sheet and then switch to the Park Usage sheet.
2. Select the range A3:D15, and then start the Chart Wizard.
3. Use the Chart Wizard to create a 3-D column chart that compares values across categories and across series. The chart title should be "2006 Usage Statistics". The X axis title should be "Month". The Series axis title should be "Sites", and the Value axis title should be "Visitors". Place the chart legend at the bottom of the chart. The chart should be placed on a new chart sheet named "Usage Chart".
4. Within the Usage Chart chart sheet, change the elevation of the 3-D view to 24 degrees, the rotation to 198 degrees, and the perspective to 20 degrees. Change the color of the Exit Glacier series to blue, the Visitor Center series to red, and the Others series to green. Change the color of the walls and floor of the 3-D chart to white. Change the color of the chart area to tan. Display the chart title in a blue 18-point font.
5. Return to the Park Usage worksheet.
6. Select the range A3:D15 again (if necessary), and then start the Chart Wizard again.
7. Use the Chart Wizard to create a Stacked Column chart that compares the contribution of each value to a total across categories. The chart title should be "2006 Usage Statistics". The X axis title should be "Month" and the Value axis title should be "Visitors". The legend should be displayed at the bottom of the chart. Place the resulting chart on a chart sheet named "Usage Chart 2".
8. Change the color of the Exit Glacier series to blue, the Visitor Center series to red, and the Others series to green. Change the color of the plot area to white and the chart area to tan. Display the chart title in an 18-point blue font.
9. Move the Usage Chart and Usage Chart 2 chart sheets to the end of the workbook.
10. Format the printed output for the two chart sheets so that your name, the date, and the filename are placed on separate lines in the page's right footer.
11. Print the contents of the Usage Chart and Usage Chart 2 chart sheets.
12. Save and close the workbook.

Challenge

Broaden your knowledge and challenge your skills by exploring how to use Excel to create a Pareto quality control chart.

Case Problem 2

Data File needed for this Case Problem: Powder1.xls

Dantalia Baby Powder Kemp Wilson is a quality control engineer for Dantalia Baby Powder. Part of the company's manufacturing process involves a machine called a "filler," which pours a specified amount of powder into bottles. Sometimes the heads on the filler become partially clogged, causing the bottles to be under-filled. If that happens, the bottles must be rejected. On each assembly line, there are a certain number of bottles rejected during each shift.

Kemp's job is to monitor the number of defective bottles and locate the fillers that may have clogged filler heads. One of the tools he uses to do this is a Pareto chart. A Pareto chart is a column chart in which each column represents the total number of defects assigned to different parts of the production process. In this case, the columns would represent the 24 different fillers in the assembly line. The columns are sorted so that the part that caused the most defects is displayed first, the second-most is displayed second, and so forth. Superimposed on the columns is a line that displays the cumulative percentage of defects for all of the parts.

Thus, by viewing the cumulative percentages, you can determine, for example, what percentages of the total defects are due to the three worst parts. In this way, Kemp can isolate the problem filler heads and report how much they contribute to the total defects.

Kemp has a worksheet listing the number of defects per filler head from a recent shift. The data is already sorted going from the filler head with the most defects to the one with the fewest. The cumulative percent values have also been calculated already. Kemp wants you to create a Pareto chart based on this data. To complete this task:

1. Open the **Powder1** workbook located in the Tutorial.04\Cases folder included with your Data Files, and then save the file as **Powder2** to the same folder.
2. Enter your name and the current date in the Documentation sheet, and then switch to the Quality Control Data worksheet.
3. Select the range A5:C29, and then start the Chart Wizard.

Explore

4. Use the Chart Wizard to create a custom chart, selecting the Line – Column on 2 Axes option in the Custom Types list box. Specify "Filler Head Under Fills" as the chart title. Specify "Filler Head" as the x-axis title, "Count of Under Fills" as the y-axis title, and "Cumulative Percentage" as the second y-axis title. Do not include a legend. Place the chart on a chart sheet named "Pareto Chart."
5. Change the alignment of the x-axis labels to an angle of 90 degrees.
6. Change the alignment of the second y-axis title to –90 degrees.

Explore

Explore

7. Change the scale of the second y-axis so that the values range from 0 to 1.0.
8. Select the data series that displays the number of defects for each filler head, and add data labels that display the number of defects above each column. Do *not* display labels above the lines that represent the cumulative percentages. (*Hint*: Use the Data Labels tab in the Format Data Series dialog box.)

Explore

9. From the Format Data Series dialog box for the chart's columns, use the Options tab to reduce the gap separating the columns to 0 pixels.
10. Change the fill color of the chart columns and the plot area to white.
11. Examine the Pareto chart, and determine approximately what percentage of the total number of defects can be attributed to the three worst filler heads.
12. Add a header to the Pareto Chart sheet that displays the name of the worksheet in the center and your name and the date on the right of the page, and then print the Pareto chart.
13. Save your changes to the workbook, and then close it.

Challenge

Go beyond what you've learned in the tutorial by exploring how to use Excel to chart stock market data.

Case Problem 3

Data File needed for this Case Problem: Oil1.xls

Hardin Financial Kurt Lee is a financial analyst for Hardin Financial. As part of his job, he likes to store stock market activity in Excel workbooks. One of his workbooks contains the recent stock market activity of Mitchell Oil. He would like your help in creating a chart displaying the stock values. The chart should display the stock's opening, high, low, and closing values for each day of the past few weeks, in addition to the number of shares traded. The volume of shares traded should be expressed in terms of millions of shares.

To complete this task:

1. Open the **Oil1** workbook located in the Tutorial.04\Cases folder included with your Data Files, and then save the workbook as **Oil2** in the same folder. Enter your name and the date in the Documentation sheet and then switch to the Stock Values sheet.

2. Select the range A5:F35, and then start the Chart Wizard.

3. Use the Chart Wizard to create a stock chart using the Volume-Open-High-Low-Close subtype. Set "Mitchell Oil" as the chart title, "Date" as the Category axis title, "Shares Traded" as the Value axis title, and "Stock Value" as the Second value axis title. Hide the chart's legend. Place the chart on a chart sheet named "Stock Chart". Move the Stock Chart sheet to the end of the workbook.

4. Change the scale of the first value axis to range from 0 to 2,000,000. Set the display units to millions and display the units label on the chart. Change the scale of the second value axis to range from 10 to 30. Display values on both value axes to show two decimal places.

5. Change the alignment of the second value axis title to 90 degrees.

Explore 6. Double-click the column data series that displays the volume of shares traded and, using the Options tab, reduce the gap between adjacent columns to 0 pixels.

7. Change the fill color of the columns to blue. Change the fill color of the plot area to light turquoise.

Explore 8. In a stock chart, the daily chart values will either show an increase or a decrease from the previous day. Increases are shown with an up bar displayed in white and decreases are showed in a down bar displayed in black. Select the up bars by right-clicking one of the white bars and clicking Format Up Bars on the shortcut menu. Change the fill color of the up bar from white to green. Select the down bars by right-clicking one of the black bars and clicking Format Down Bars on the shortcut menu. Change the fill color of the down bar from black to red.

Explore 9. In the upper-left corner of the plot, use the Drawing toolbar to insert the Explosion 2 AutoShape. Insert the following text into the shape: "36% increase in 6 weeks!". Increase the Explosion 2 AutoShape sufficiently to display the entire text. Change the fill color to yellow and the font color to red.

Explore 10. Add the Shadow Style 10 drop shadow to the AutoShape.

11. Format the printed output for the chart sheet so that your name, the date, and the filename are displayed in the printout's right footer, each on a separate line.

12. Print the Stock Chart chart sheet.

13. Save and close the workbook.

Create

Test your knowledge of charts by creating a workbook with an XY (scatter) chart that presents data from a cancer research study.

Case Problem 4

There are no Data Files needed for this Case Problem.

Relating Cancer Rates to Temperature A 1965 study analyzed the relationship between the mean annual temperature in 16 regions in Great Britain and the annual mortality rates in those regions for a certain type of breast cancer. Lynn Watson is working on a symposium on the history of breast cancer research and has asked you to chart the data from this historic study. Figure 4-38 shows a preview of the workbook and chart that you'll create.

Figure 4-38

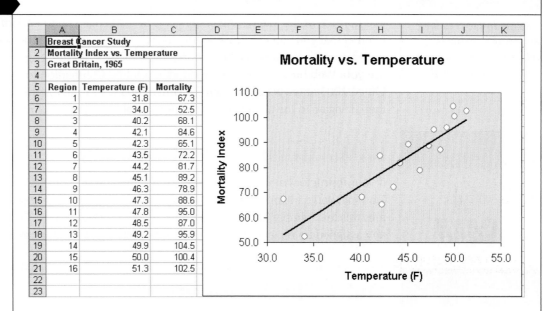

	A	B	C	D	E	F	G	H	I	J	K
1	Breast Cancer Study										
2	Mortality Index vs. Temperature										
3	Great Britain, 1965										
4											
5	Region	Temperature (F)	Mortality								
6	1	31.8	67.3								
7	2	34.0	52.5								
8	3	40.2	68.1								
9	4	42.1	84.6								
10	5	42.3	65.1								
11	6	43.5	72.2								
12	7	44.2	81.7								
13	8	45.1	89.2								
14	9	46.3	78.9								
15	10	47.3	88.6								
16	11	47.8	95.0								
17	12	48.5	87.0								
18	13	49.2	95.9								
19	14	49.9	104.5								
20	15	50.0	100.4								
21	16	51.3	102.5								
22											
23											

To complete this task:

1. Create a new workbook and save it as **BCancer** in the Tutorial.04\Cases folder included with your Data Files. The workbook should contain a Documentation sheet displaying your name, the date, and the purpose of the workbook. Name one of the other worksheets "Breast Cancer Data," and then add the titles and data shown in Figure 4-38.

Explore
2. Use the Chart Wizard to create an embedded XY (scatter) chart with no data points connected. Specify "Mortality vs. Temperature" as the chart title. Specify "Temperature (F)" as the title of the x-axis and "Mortality Index" as the title of the y-axis. Remove the gridlines. Do not include a legend. The scatter chart should be embedded on the Breast Cancer Data worksheet.

3. Change the scale of the x-axis to cover the temperature range 30 to 55 degrees Fahrenheit.

4. Change the scale of the y-axis to cover the mortality index range 50 to 110.

Explore
5. Double-click one of the data points in the chart to open the Format Data Series dialog box, and make the following changes to the appearance of the data points:
   - Change the marker style to a circle that is 7 points in size.
   - Change the background color of the circle to white.
   - Change the foreground color of the circle to red.

Explore
6. Open the Add Trendline dialog box from the Chart menu, and select the Linear trend line option on the Type tab. The purpose of the linear trend line is to display whether a linear relationship exists between the 16 regions' mean annual temperature and their annual mortality index. Does it appear that such a relationship exists? What does a high mean annual temperature imply about the annual mortality index?

7. Change the fill color of the plot area to light yellow.

8. Set up the worksheet to print in landscape orientation, centered horizontally and vertically on the page. Enter your name and the date in the right section of the page's header. Print the chart.

9. Save your changes to the workbook and close it.

Research

Use the Internet to find and work with data related to the topics presented in this tutorial.

Internet Assignments

The purpose of the Internet Assignments is to challenge you to find information on the Internet that you can use to work effectively with this software. The actual assignments are updated and maintained on the Course Technology Web site. Log on to the Internet and use your Web browser to go to the Student Online Companion for New Perspectives Office 2003 at **www.course.com/np/office2003**. Click the Internet Assignments link, and then navigate to the assignments for this tutorial.

Assess

SAM Assessment and Training

If your instructor has chosen to use the full online version of SAM 2003 Assessment and Training, you can go beyond the "just-in-time" training provided on the CD that accompanies this text. Simply log in to your SAM account (http://sam2003.course.com) to launch any assigned training activities or exams that relate to the skills covered in this tutorial.

Review

Quick Check Answers

Session 4.1

1. A chart type is one of the 14 styles of charts supported by Excel. Each chart type has various alternate formats, called chart sub-types.
2. stock chart
3. A data series is a range of data values that is plotted on a chart.
4. The plot area contains the actual data values that are plotted in the chart, as well as any background colors or images for that plot. The chart area contains the plot area and any other element (such as titles and legend boxes) that may be included in the chart.
5. Gridlines are lines that extend out from the tick marks on either axis into the plot area.
6. embedded charts, which are placed within a worksheet, and chart sheets, which contain only the chart itself
7. pie
8. exploded pie

Session 4.2

1. Click Chart on the menu bar, click Source Data, click the Series tab, select the data series in the Series list box, and then click the Remove button.
2. Click Chart on the menu bar, click Location, and then select a new location.
3. Label text is text that consists of category names, tick mark labels, and legend text. Attached text is text that is attached to other elements of the chart, such as the chart title or axes titles. Unattached text is additional text that is unassociated with any particular element of the chart.
4. Major tick marks are tick marks that appear on the axis alongside the axis values. Minor tick marks do not appear alongside any axis value, but instead are used to provide a finer gradation between major tick marks.
5. Click Chart on the menu bar, click Chart Type, and then select one of the 3-D chart sub-types for the column chart.
6. An AutoShape is a predefined shape available on the Drawing toolbar. You can add an AutoShape to any worksheet or chart. You can change the size or shape of an AutoShape, and you can change its fill color.
7. Use full page, in which the chart is resized to fit the full size of the printed page (the proportions of the chart may change in the resizing); Scale to fit page, in which the chart is resized to fit the page but retains its proportions; and Custom, in which the dimensions of the printed chart are specified in the chart sheet.

New Perspectives on

Integrating Microsoft® Office 2003

Tutorial 1   INT 1-3

Integrating Word and Excel

Creating a Letter that Includes a Chart and a Table

Read This Before You Begin

Data Files

To complete the "Integrating Word and Excel" tutorial, you need the starting Data Files. See the inside back or front cover for information on downloading these files from course.com, or ask your instructor for assistance. The following table identifies each starting Data File and the folder it is stored in, as well as the ending files, which you create and save in each tutorial.

Folders	Starting Files	Ending Files
Tutorial .01 — **Tutorial**	LHCGrowth.xls, LHCLetter.doc, LHCServiceReferrals.xls	Growth Table.xls, Hospital Letter.doc, Referrals Chart.xls
Review	LHCGrowthUpdated.xls, LHCServicesDistribution.xls, LHCMemo.doc	Distribution Chart.xls, Employee Memo.doc, Growth Table 2.xls
Cases	MusicLetter.doc, MusicRentals.xls, TutorFees.xls	Learning Expenses.xls, Parent Letter.doc, Rental Fees.xls, School Letter.doc

Storing Your Files

It is recommended that you store all your Data Files on a USB drive. Refer to the tutorial "Managing Your Files" for information on using USB drives. If you need to store your Data Files on floppy disks, you will need one high-density disk to store all the files for the "Integrating Word and Excel" tutorial.

SAM 2003 Training Companion CD

The SAM 2003 Training Companion CD that comes with this text gives you "just-in-time" training and reinforcement of important Microsoft Office skills. Look for the SAM CD logo throughout each tutorial for opportunities to complete the hands-on tasks included on this CD.

Integrating Word and Excel

Creating a Letter that Includes a Chart and a Table

Case | Lifestyles Home Care, Inc.

In 1989, Caitlin Sheehan founded Lifestyles Home Care, Inc., in Woburn, Massachusetts. Lifestyles Home Care provides in-home services for elderly and disabled people. Currently, when people are discharged from a hospital or when they become incapacitated by illness or a disability, they can obtain services that enable them to continue to live at home rather than move to a nursing home. The state of Massachusetts contracts with various agencies to coordinate and arrange for these services either free of charge or on a sliding fee scale for those people who meet established income guidelines. Lifestyles is one of the companies that various state-contracted agencies use to provide personal care and homemaking services, perform light chores, and provide transportation services for their clients. Each year, Lifestyles serves an increasing number of clients, and this year it has received more referrals from state-contracted agencies than any other home care company.

Over the past six months, Caitlin has worked on a new business plan to expand the services that Lifestyles offers and to make those services available to anyone who wants to pay for them, not just to those clients who meet the income guidelines for state-supported services. The new services are meal planning and preparation, shopping, scheduling medical appointments, driving, bill payment and mail organization, and companionship. In addition, Caitlin wants to hire care managers; care managers are coordinators who assess a client's needs and recommend and establish appropriate services. Care managers also can monitor the services once they are in place, and reassess the service plan as necessary. This service is especially helpful for those clients whose families live out of the area and, therefore, cannot check on their loved ones on a regular basis.

Objectives		**SAM Training Tasks**	
• Learn about object linking and embedding (OLE) • Embed an Excel chart in a Word document • Edit an embedded Excel chart in Word	• Link an Excel worksheet to a Word document • Update a linked Excel worksheet • Test and break a link	• Link an Excel worksheet to a Word document • Link and embed an object in a document • Use object linking to display Excel worksheet data as a Word table	• Use object linking to display Excel worksheet data as a worksheet object

Student Data Files   For a complete list of the Data Files needed for this tutorial, see page INT 1-2.

Caitlin will begin marketing the new services offered by Lifestyles to the social work departments at local hospitals. Hospital social workers help soon-to-be discharged patients by establishing a discharge plan, which frequently includes home care services. The social workers at local hospitals are already aware of Lifestyles because of the services it currently provides. Caitlin plans to send a letter to the social work departments announcing the new, expanded service offerings. She has drafted the body of the letter, which describes the new service plans and introduces the new brochure. She wants the letter to include the information from the state indicating that Lifestyles is the most referred home care company, so she used the state's information and created a pie chart. She also wants the letter to include a table she has created outlining the company's growth over the past five years.

You'll complete the letter for Caitlin using Microsoft Office 2003. She created the letter in Word, but she created the chart and table in Excel. Fortunately, Office 2003 allows you to share information between its programs.

Object Linking and Embedding

Caitlin's letter requires the chart that she created in Excel comparing the number of referrals to Lifestyles Home Care with the number of referrals to other home care companies and the table showing the company's growth. The first page of the letter, a Word document, and the chart and table, Excel files, are shown in Figure 1-1.

| Figure 1-1 | Lifestyles Home Care documents to integrate |

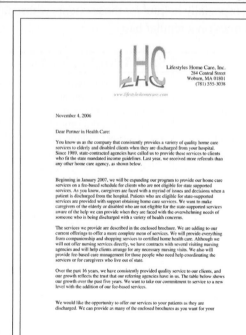

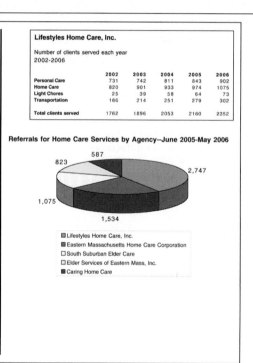

Putting all these pieces together into one Word document is possible because Office 2003 supports **object linking and embedding** (**OLE**, pronounced "oh-lay"), a way of transferring and sharing information between programs. OLE is often referred to as **integration**, which is a general term for sharing information (the terms are often used interchangeably). An **object** is anything that can be manipulated as a whole; in other words, it is the specific information that you want to share between programs and can be anything from a chart or a table (as in Caitlin's case) to a picture, video, sound clip, or almost anything else you can create on a computer. The program used to create the object is called the **source program**, and the program used to create the file where you want to insert the object is called the **destination program**. Likewise, the file that initially contains the object is called the **source file**, and the file where you want to insert the object is called the **destination file**.

Both linking and embedding involve inserting an object into a destination file; the difference lies in where their respective objects are stored. With **embedding**, a copy of the object becomes part of the destination file. You can make changes to the object in either the destination file or the source file, but the changes you make in one file do not appear in the other file. This is helpful when you do not want to change the original object. Embedding enables you to edit an object using its source program's commands, which is not possible with regular copying and pasting.

With **linking**, the object does not exist as a separate object in the destination file. Instead, OLE creates a direct connection, or **link**, between the source and destination programs, so that the object exists in only one place—the source file—but the link displays the object in the destination file as well. You edit the object in the source file, and the link ensures that the changes will appear in the destination file. Figure 1-2 summarizes embedding and linking and compares their advantages and disadvantages.

Comparing integration methods **Figure 1-2**

	Embedding	Linking
Description	Displays and stores an object in the destination file.	Displays an object in the destination file along with the source file's location; stores the object in the source file.
Use if you want to	Include the object in the destination file, and edit the object using the source program without affecting the source file.	Edit the object in the source file and have the changes appear in the destination file.
Advantages	The source file and destination file can be stored separately. You can use source program commands to make changes to the object in the destination file.	The destination file size remains fairly small. The source file and the object in the destination file remain identical.
Disadvantages	The destination file size increases to reflect the addition of the object from the source file.	The source and destination files must be stored together.

Figure 1-3 illustrates the differences between embedding and linking.

Figure 1-3 ▶ **Embedding contrasted with linking**

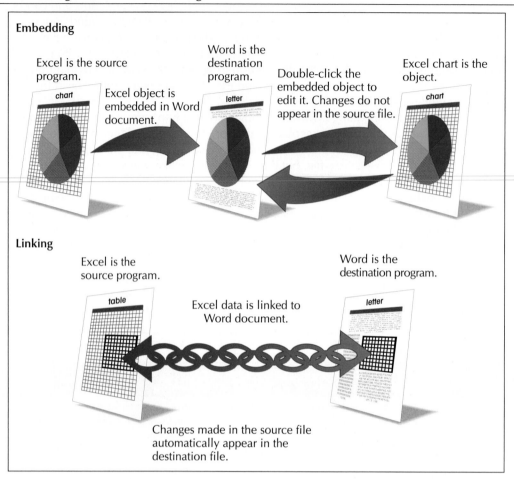

Caitlin wants to integrate the pie chart into the hospital letter. She knows that the data in the chart will not change, but she might want to modify the chart's size and appearance once it is integrated into the letter, so she asks you to embed the pie chart in the letter. Then she can use Excel commands to modify the chart from within the Word document. Caitlin wants you to link the table listing the company's growth over the past five years between the Word document and the Excel workbook, because she does not yet have the final numbers for the current year. This way, when Caitlin updates the data in the Excel table, that latest information will appear in the Word document.

Caitlin has given you the Word file containing her letter. The first thing you'll do is embed the pie chart. You need to first start Word and then open the letter.

To open the letter in Word:

▶ **1.** Start Word, and then open the document **LHCLetter**, which is located in the Tutorial.01\Tutorial folder included with your Data Files. The letter opens in Print Layout view. See Figure 1-4.

Lifestyles Home Care hospital letter | **Figure 1-4**

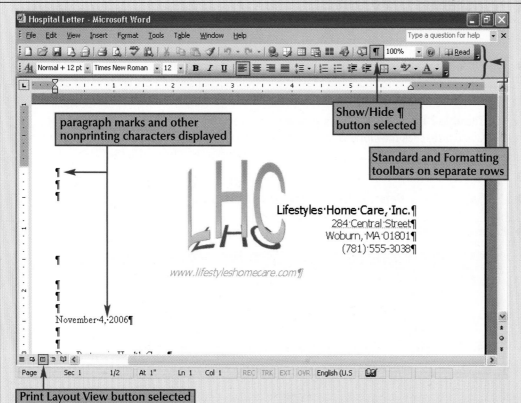

Trouble? If you don't have the Data Files for the Integration tutorials, you need to get them before you can proceed. Your instructor will either give you the Data Files or ask you to obtain them from a specific location (such as a network drive). In either case, be sure that you make a backup copy of your Data Files before you start using them, so that the original files will be available on your copied disk in case you need to start over because of an error or problem. If you have any questions about the Data Files, see your instructor or technical support person for assistance.

Trouble? If the Word toolbars appear on one row, click Tools on the menu bar, click Customize, click the Options tab in the Customize dialog box, click the Show Standard and Formatting toolbars on two rows check box to select it, and then click the Close button.

Trouble? If your document does not show the nonprinting characters, click the Show/Hide ¶ button ¶ on the Standard toolbar.

2. Click **File** on the menu bar, and then click **Save As** to display the Save As dialog box.

3. Save the file as **Hospital Letter** in the Tutorial.01\Tutorial folder.

You're ready to embed the Excel chart that shows the current distribution of services provided by Lifestyles Home Care. To do this, you need to have access to both Word and Excel. The letter is already open, so now you need to start Excel and open the file containing the pie chart.

To open the chart in Excel:

1. Start Excel as usual. You do not need to close the Word document or exit Word. Notice that a Microsoft Excel - Book 1 button appears on the taskbar next to the Hospital Letter - Microsoft Word button.

2. Open the workbook **LHCServiceReferrals**, which is located in the Tutorial.01\Tutorial folder included with your Data Files. The workbook opens with a pie chart in the active worksheet.

   Trouble? If the Excel toolbars appear on one row, click Tools on the menu bar, click Customize, click the Options tab in the Customize dialog box, click the Show Standard and Formatting toolbars on two rows check box to select it, and then click the Close button.

3. Click **File** on the menu bar, and then click **Save As** to display the Save As dialog box.

4. Save the file as **Referrals Chart** in the Tutorial.01\Tutorial folder. See Figure 1-5.

| Figure 1-5 | Referrals worksheet with pie chart |

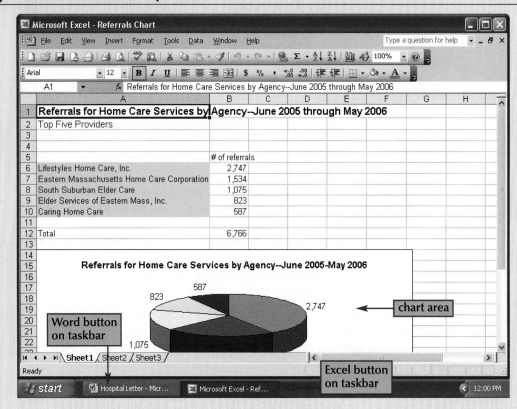

With both programs and files open, you can embed the pie chart into the letter.

Embedding an Excel Chart in a Word Document

Caitlin wants her letter to include the pie chart showing the current distribution of services provided by Lifestyles Home Care. The data for the chart will not change, so you'll embed the pie chart from the source file into the Word document. That way, if Caitlin wants to resize or modify the format of the pie chart in the letter, she can make these changes using Excel commands without affecting the source file. (Recall that when you embed an object, you automatically have access to the object's source program commands and features to manipulate the embedded object in the destination program.)

Embedding an Object

- Start the source program, open the file containing the object to be embedded, select the object or information you want to embed in the destination program, and then click the Copy button on the Standard toolbar.
- Start the destination program, open the file that will contain the embedded object, and then position the insertion point where you want to place the object.
- Click Edit on the menu bar, and then click Paste Special to open the Paste Special dialog box.
- In the Paste Special dialog box, click the Paste option button, click Microsoft Office Excel Chart Object in the As list box, and then click the OK button.

or

- In the source file, select the object or information you want to embed, and then click the Copy button on the Standard toolbar.
- Start the destination program, open the file that will contain the embedded object, and then position the insertion point where you want to place the object.
- Click the Paste button on the Standard toolbar in the destination program.
- Click the Paste Options button that appears in the document window, and then click Excel Chart (entire workbook).

Now you can embed the pie chart in the hospital letter using the Paste Special dialog box.

To embed the Excel chart in the Word document:

1. Scroll down until you can see all of the pie chart in the worksheet, and then click the chart area (the white area around the pie) to select the chart. When the chart is selected, sizing handles appear around the chart area. See Figure 1-6.

Pie chart selected in worksheet | Figure 1-6

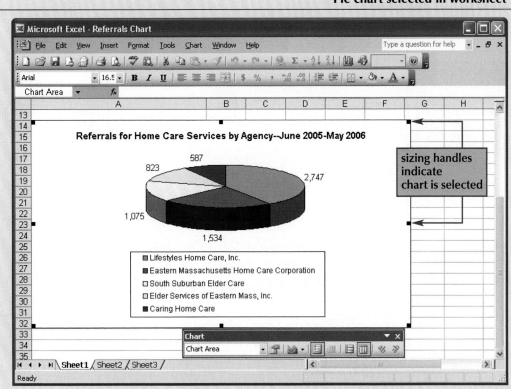

2. Click the **Copy** button on the Excel Standard toolbar to copy the chart to the Clipboard. The chart now appears with a rotating, dashed line around its frame, indicating that it has been copied.

> **Trouble?** If the Copy button is not available, you probably clicked the chart instead of the chart area. Click any cell in the worksheet to deselect the chart item, click the white area around the chart, and then repeat Step 2.

3. Click the **Hospital Letter - Microsoft Word** button on the taskbar to return to the Hospital Letter document.

4. Click to the left of the paragraph mark immediately above the second paragraph in the body of the letter, which begins "Beginning in January 2007", to position the insertion point where you need to embed the pie chart. See Figure 1-7.

Figure 1-7	Placement for the pie chart in the hospital letter

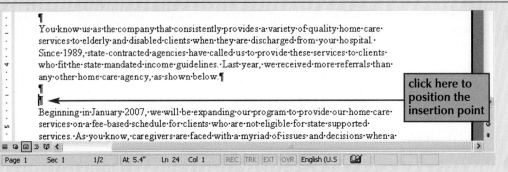

5. Click **Edit** on the menu bar, and then click **Paste Special**. The Paste Special dialog box opens. See Figure 1-8.

Figure 1-8	Paste Special dialog box

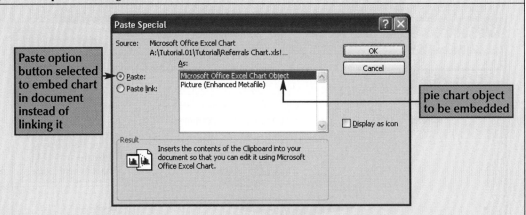

6. Make sure the **Paste** option button is selected. This option will embed the chart. If you wanted to link the chart, you would click the Paste link option button.

7. In the As list box, click **Microsoft Office Excel Chart Object**, if necessary, to select the chart as the object to embed.

> **Trouble?** If the Microsoft Office Excel Chart Object option does not appear in the As list box, you might not have selected and copied the chart correctly. Click the Cancel button in the Paste Special dialog box, click the Microsoft Excel - Referrals Chart button on the taskbar, and then repeat Steps 1 through 6, making sure that when you select the chart, sizing

handles appear around the chart area, and that when you copy the chart, a rotating dashed line appears around the chart area.

8. Click the **OK** button. The Paste Special dialog box closes, and after a few moments, the Excel pie chart appears in the letter. The Paste Options button 📋 appears in the document next to the chart. See Figure 1-9.

Pie chart embedded in the hospital letter | Figure 1-9

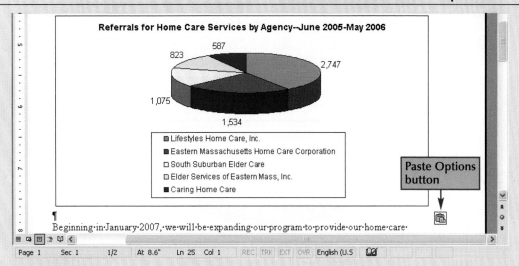

You can click the Paste Options button to select from a list of pasting options for the object (for example, you could change the object to a linked object). You'll leave the pasted object as it is.

9. Click the **Save** button 🖫 on the Word Standard toolbar to save the letter with the embedded chart.

10. Click the **Microsoft Excel - Referrals Chart** button on the taskbar, click any cell in the worksheet outside of the chart area, and then close the Referrals Chart workbook without saving any changes.

11. Click the **Hospital Letter - Microsoft Word** button on the taskbar to return to the Hospital Letter document.

After reviewing the letter with the embedded pie chart, Caitlin decides that the pie chart would be more impressive if it were rotated so that the pie slice showing the percentage of total referrals to Lifestyles appeared in front. Because you embedded the chart, you can use Excel chart commands from within the Word document to modify the chart.

Modifying an Embedded Object

When you edit an embedded object within the destination program, the changes affect only the embedded object; the original object in the source program remains unchanged. When you double-click an embedded object, the destination program's menu bar and commands change to the menu bar and commands of the embedded object's source program, which you use to modify the embedded object.

Now that you have embedded the pie chart in Word, you can rotate the chart so that the Lifestyles pie wedge appears in front.

To edit the pie chart from within Word:

1. Double-click the embedded chart in the hospital letter. After a moment, a dashed border appears around the chart, and Excel commands and buttons appear in the Word menu bar and toolbars. See Figure 1-10.

Figure 1-10   **Active Excel chart in the hospital letter**

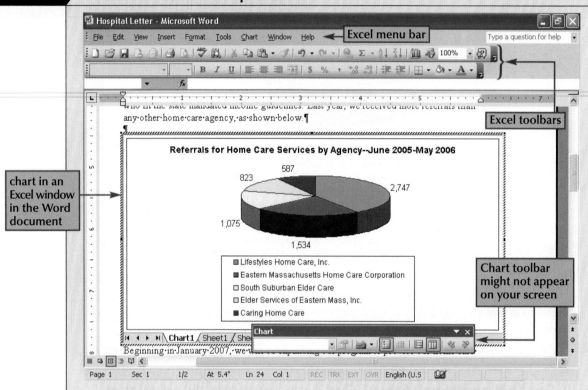

Now you can modify the chart. The chart is a 3-D pie chart, and you want to rotate it so that the Lifestyles pie wedge appears in front. You do this using the 3-D View dialog box.

2. Click **Chart** on the menu bar, and then click **3-D View**. The 3-D View dialog box opens. See Figure 1-11.

Figure 1-11   **3-D View dialog box**

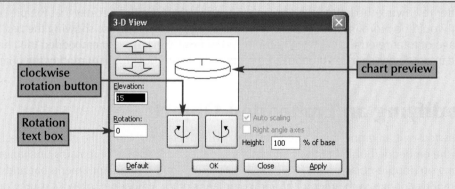

The Rotation text box shows the current value of 0, and the chart preview shows the median line pointing straight up. You want to move the Lifestyles wedge from the right side of the pie to the front of the pie, so you need to move the median line clockwise, from the right to the left.

3. Click the **clockwise rotation** button until the Rotation text box shows the value **110**. As you click the clockwise rotation button, watch the pie chart move in the preview box.

4. Click the **OK** button. The Lifestyles pie wedge appears at the front of the pie chart. See Figure 1-12.

Revised embedded pie chart ◄ **Figure 1-12**

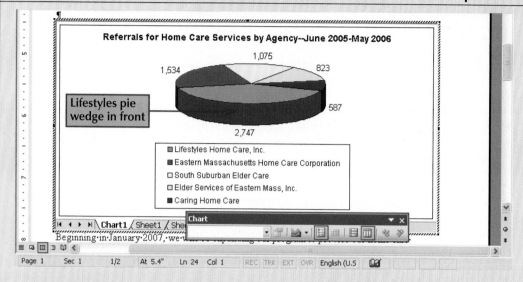

5. Click a blank area of the document outside of the selected chart to deselect the chart and return to Word's menus and toolbars.

6. Click the **Save** button 🖫 on the Standard toolbar to save the document.

If you were to open the Referrals Chart workbook, you would see that the pie chart there remained unchanged.

Your final task is to include the table outlining the growth of Lifestyles Home Care over the past five years in the letter. To do this, you will link the table from Excel to Word.

Linking an Object from Excel to Word

Caitlin created an Excel workbook named LHCGrowth showing the growth of the Lifestyles Home Care agency over the past five years. She does not yet have the final numbers for the current year, so, unlike the information in the pie chart, the table is subject to change. Because Caitlin wants you to finish setting up the letter now, you'll link the table from the LHCGrowth workbook to the Hospital Letter document instead of embedding it as you did the chart. When Caitlin receives the current year's data, she can update the table in the Excel workbook, and the changes will appear in the Word document. This will keep the information up to date in both files.

Reference Window | **Linking an Object**

- Start the source program, open the file containing the object to be linked, select the object or information you want to link to the destination program, and then click the Copy button on the Standard toolbar.
- Start the destination program, open the file that will contain the link to the copied object, position the insertion point where you want the linked object to appear, click Edit on the menu bar, and then click Paste Special.
- Click the Paste link option button in the Paste Special dialog box, select the option you want in the As list box, and then click the OK button.

or

- In the source file, select the object or information you want to link, and then click the Copy button on the Standard toolbar.
- Start the destination program, open the file that will contain the linked object, and then position the insertion point where you want to place the object.
- Click the Paste button on the Standard toolbar in the destination program.
- Click the Paste Options button that appears in the document window, and then click a linking option on the menu.

Now you will link the growth table to the letter using the Paste Options button. This button appears when you paste text or other information from one Office document to another. You first need to open the LHCGrowth workbook, and then select the table object for linking.

To link the table to the letter:

1. Click the **Microsoft Excel** button on the taskbar to switch back to Excel, click the **Open** button 📖 on the Standard toolbar to open the Open dialog box, navigate to the **Tutorial.01\Tutorial** folder included with your Data Files, and then double-click the Excel workbook **LHCGrowth**.

2. Save the workbook as **Growth Table** in the same folder.

3. Select cells **A6** through **F12**, and then click the **Copy** button 📋 on the Excel Standard toolbar to copy the data to the Clipboard.

4. Click the **Hospital Letter - Microsoft Word** button on the taskbar to return to the hospital letter.

5. Scroll the document and position the insertion point to the left of the paragraph mark above the paragraph that begins "We would like the opportunity." This is where you want the table to appear. See Figure 1-13.

Figure 1-13 | **Placement for linking the Excel worksheet to the hospital letter**

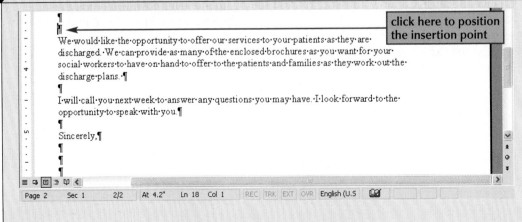

6. Click the **Paste** button ▣ on the Word Standard toolbar. The table from Excel is inserted in the letter, and the Paste Options button appears in the lower-right corner of the new table. You will use this button to link the original growth table contained in the Excel worksheet and the new growth table inserted in the letter.

7. Move the pointer over the **Paste Options** button ▣ so that it changes to ▣ ▾, and then click it to open the Paste Options shortcut menu. See Figure 1-14.

Linked growth table ◀ Figure 1-14

Figure 1-15 describes the commands on the Paste Options menu after you link an object.

Paste Options commands ◀ Figure 1-15

Choose this Paste Options command:	To do the following:
Keep Source Formatting	Paste the object without linking and match the formatting in the source file
Match Destination Table Style	Paste the object without linking and format the object in the Word default table style
Keep Text Only	Paste the object as text only, not as a table or other formatted object; Word separates table columns with tab characters and table rows with paragraph symbols
Keep Source Formatting and Link to Excel	Link the pasted object to Excel and match the formatting in the Excel source file; any formatting changes you make to the pasted object remain when you change the data in the source file
Match Destination Table Style and Link to Excel	Link the pasted object to Excel and format the linked data in the Word default table style; any formatting changes you make to the pasted object remain when you change the data in the source file
Apply Style or Formatting	Open the Style and Formatting task pane to select styles to apply to the pasted object

8. Click the **Match Destination Table Style and Link to Excel** option button. This means that the table will be linked, rather than embedded, and that its format will match the default table style in Word. The growth table in Word is now formatted in 12-point Times New Roman text, the same as the rest of the letter, the yellow fill is removed, and it is linked to the Excel worksheet.

9. Click the **Save** button ▣ on the Word Standard toolbar to save the Hospital Letter.

10. Switch to Excel, and then click the **Close Window** button ☒ on the menu bar to close the workbook.

Caitlin just received the current year's figures from her assistant. She asks you to update the growth table with the new information.

Updating Linked Objects

Now that you have linked the table from the workbook to the letter, you can edit the information in the source file (the Excel workbook), and the changes will appear in the Word document. When making changes, you can have one or both files open.

To update the table in Excel:

1. Switch back to Word, right-click the Excel table in the Word document, point to **Linked Worksheet Object** on the shortcut menu, and then click **Open Link**. The source file opens in Excel.

   Trouble? If the Linked Worksheet Object command is not on the shortcut menu, click a blank area of the document, and then try right-clicking the table again.

2. Right-click a blank area of the taskbar and then click **Tile Windows Horizontally** on the shortcut menu. The source and destination files each appear in a reduced window, stacked one on top of the other.

   Trouble? If you see more than two windows on your screen, then you had more than two documents open. Close all open documents except the Hospital Letter Word document and the Growth Table Excel workbook, and then repeat Step 2.

3. Scroll the Word window so that you can see the first item of the table in the document.

4. Click in the Excel window to make it the active window, and then scroll the Excel window so that you can see the first item of the table in the worksheet.

   The first entry you need to add is Personal Care in 2006.

5. In the Excel window, click cell **F7**, type **902**, and then press the **Enter** key.

6. Click anywhere in the Word window to make it the active window, right-click anywhere in the table, click **Update Link** on the shortcut menu, and then scroll back up the document, if necessary, to see the top of the table. The number you added in the Excel worksheet for the number of clients receiving personal care in 2006, 902, now appears in the destination document because you linked the table from Excel to Word. See Figure 1-16.

Linked documents tiled horizontally ◄ **Figure 1-16**

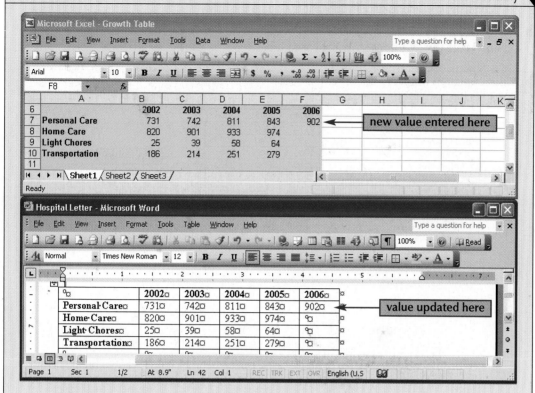

Trouble? If the Update Link command is not on the shortcut menu, click a blank area of the document, and then right-click the table again.

7. Right-click a blank area of the taskbar, and then click **Undo Tile** on the shortcut menu to view just one program window at a time.

8. Click the **Save** button on the Word Standard toolbar to save the changes to the letter.

Trouble? If Word is not the active program window, click the Hospital Letter - Microsoft Word button on the taskbar to switch to the letter.

What would happen if you were working on the new growth table in Excel without the Word document open? Would you still be able to update the information in the letter? To find out, enter the rest of the data for 2006 in the Excel workbook with the Word document closed. You can then reopen the letter to verify that the changes appear there as well.

To edit the linked object with the Word document closed:

1. Close the letter, and then click the **Microsoft Excel - Growth Table** button on the taskbar. The Growth Table worksheet becomes the active window.

2. Enter **1075** in cell F8, enter **73** in cell F9, and then enter **302** in cell F10.

3. Click the **Save** button on the Standard toolbar.

4. Click the **Microsoft Word** button on the taskbar, click **File** on the menu bar, and then look for Hospital Letter near the bottom of the File menu. The filename will be preceded by the number 1 and by the drive and folder name in which the file is stored.

5. Click **Hospital Letter** to open the letter. A dialog box opens telling you that the document contains links and asking if you want to update the links.

6. Click the **Yes** button, and then scroll the document to view the linked table. Notice that the new data for 2006 appears in the linked table in Word. See Figure 1-17.

| Figure 1-17 | Values updated in linked document |

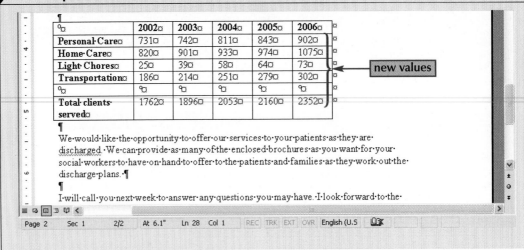

Linked documents are effective in many cases, but sometimes you'll want to break the link.

Breaking Links

Once you are finished working with linked documents, you can break the link between the two documents. You do this by using the Links command on the Edit menu in the destination file. Once you break a link, the only changes you can make to the object in the destination file are resizing, moving, and deleting. Also, any such changes you make to the object in the source file no longer appear in the destination file once the link is broken. In other words, when you break the link, the object acts as a pasted picture in the destination file.

| Reference Window | **Breaking the Link Between Linked Objects** |

- In the destination program, click Edit on the menu bar, and then click Links to open the Links dialog box.
- Select the appropriate entry in the Source file list box, click the Break Link button, and then click the Yes button.
- Save the destination file to ensure that the link will be broken.

You are finished updating the growth table with the data from the current year, and you are ready to give Caitlin the finished letter. Because the data in the table is final, Caitlin asks you to break the link between the Hospital Letter document and the Growth Table workbook, so that she can store the letter and workbook separately.

To break the link between the Hospital Letter document and the Growth Table workbook:

▶ 1. In the Word window, right-click anywhere in the linked table, point to **Linked Worksheet Object** on the shortcut menu, and then click **Links** to open the Links dialog box. There is one entry in the Source file list box. See Figure 1-18.

Links dialog box   **Figure 1-18**

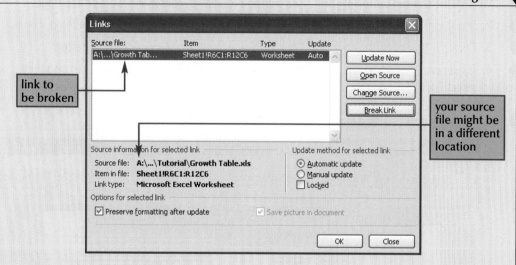

Trouble? Depending on the disk drive used for your Data Files, the filename path in the Links dialog box might be different from the one shown in Figure 1-18.

▶ 2. With the link selected in the Source file list box, click the **Break Link** button. A dialog box opens, asking you to confirm that you want to break the selected link.

▶ 3. Click the **Yes** button. The link is broken, and the dialog box closes.

You'll confirm that the link is indeed broken by editing the growth table in Excel, and then verifying that the change is not made in the letter.

▶ 4. Switch to the Excel workbook, and then enter **500** in cell F10.

▶ 5. Switch to the Word document, and then right-click the table. Note that the various Link commands no longer appear on the shortcut menu.

▶ 6. Click a blank area in the document window to close the shortcut menu, and then click **Edit** on the Word menu bar. The Links command is grayed out on the Edit menu, which means that this command is not available because there are no links in the document. This confirms that the link between the two files is broken.

▶ 7. Click a blank area in the document window to close the Edit menu.

▶ 8. Switch to the Excel workbook, click the **Close Window** button ⊠ on the Excel menu bar, and then click the **No** button when prompted to save the changes to the file. You do not want to save the change you made to the data, because this change was made simply to test the broken link. The workbook closes.

▶ 9. Switch to the Word document, and then save the **Hospital Letter** document.

If you had closed the Hospital Letter document without saving it, the link to the Excel object would still be intact. Because you saved the letter, the link remains broken.

Caitlin asks you to print a copy of the letter so that she can review it before mailing out any letters.

To finish the letter and then preview and print it:

▶ 1. Move the pointer over the table to make the Table Move Handle appear above the upper-left corner of the table, click the **Table Move** handle ⊞ to select the entire table, and then click the **Center** button ≣ on the Formatting toolbar to center the table on the page.

▶ 2. Scroll to the bottom of the letter, and then replace Caitlin Sheehan's name with your own.

▶ 3. Click the **Print Preview** button 🔍 on the Standard toolbar to preview the letter.

▶ 4. If necessary, click the **Multiple Pages** button ▦ on the Print Preview toolbar, and then select **1 x 2 Pages** to view both pages of the letter. See Figure 1-19.

Figure 1-19 ▶ **Preview of completed customer letter**

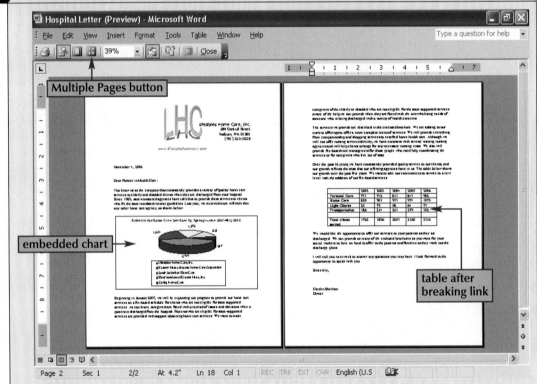

▶ 5. Print the letter, and then click the **Close** button on the Print Preview toolbar.

Trouble? If your printed letter contains a table of data instead of the pie chart, click the **Magnifier** button 🔍 on the Print Preview toolbar if it is selected, right-click the table, point to Chart Object on the shortcut menu, and then click Convert to open the Convert dialog box. Click the Activate as option button, click Microsoft Office Excel Chart, and then click the OK button. Save the document, and then print it again.

▶ 6. Save and close the letter.

▶ 7. Exit all open programs.

You have integrated the pie chart (showing the percentage of referrals to Lifestyles) and the growth table from Excel into the letter Caitlin created in Word. She is pleased with the finished letter and will send it to the local hospitals as soon as the new brochure is finished.

Review

To reinforce the tasks you
learned in this tutorial,
go to the SAM 2003
Training Companion CD
included with this text.

Quick Check

1. What is an object?
2. What is the difference between embedding an object and linking an object?
3. When an object is embedded between two programs, how many copies of the object exist?
4. If an Excel chart is linked to a Word document, which program is the source program?
5. True or False: Any changes you make to a linked object in the source file appear in both the destination and source files.
6. If you no longer want an object linked between two documents, what should you do?
7. If you break the link between the source Excel file and the destination Word file, change the number of Personal Care clients in 2006 from 902 to 1000 in the Excel file, and then close the Word file without saving changes, what will the number of Personal Care clients be when you reopen the Word file? Why?

Review

Tutorial Summary

In this tutorial, you learned how to integrate Excel data in a Word document. You learned how to copy data from an Excel workbook and how to embed the copied data in a Word document. You also accessed commands in Excel (the source program) to modify the embedded object from within the document in Word (the destination program). You also integrated data by linking copied data from Excel to a Word document. You then learned how to update the links in Word (the destination program) after the data was changed in Excel (the source program). Finally, you learned how to break the links in the destination program.

Key Terms

destination file	linking	source file
destination program	object	source program
embedding	object linking and	
integration	embedding (OLE)	
link		

Practice

Get hands-on practice of the skills you learned in the tutorial using the same case scenario.

Review Assignments

Data Files needed for the Review Assignments: LHCMemo.doc, LHCServicesDistribution.xls, and LHCGrowthUpdated.xls

Caitlin wants to send a memo to all Lifestyles employees introducing the plans for the expanded offerings and the new brochure. She already wrote the memo, and she asks you to embed an Excel chart showing the current distribution of services offered by Lifestyles. She also wants you to link an Excel worksheet listing the updated growth figures for the past five years.

To create the memo:

1. Start Word, and then open the Word document **LHCMemo** in the Tutorial.01\Review folder included with your Data Files.
2. Save the document as **Employee Memo** in the same folder.
3. Start Excel, and then open the **LHCServicesDistribution** workbook in the Tutorial.01\Review folder included with your Data Files.

4. Save the workbook as **Distribution Chart** in the same folder.

5. Embed the chart from the **Distribution Chart** workbook into the **Employee Memo** document on the blank line above the paragraph that begins "LHC has grown steadily."

6. Double-click a blank area of the chart. Describe what happens. Why does this occur?

7. Explode the Home Care wedge of the pie, and then deselect the chart. (*Hint*: Single-click the Home Care wedge twice to select only that wedge, and then drag the wedge away from the rest of the pie to explode it.)

8. Switch to Excel, and then close the **Distribution Chart** workbook without saving changes.

9. Open the **LHCGrowthUpdated** workbook in the Tutorial.01\Review folder included with your Data Files, and then save it as **Growth Table 2** in the same folder.

10. Copy the growth table.

11. Switch to the employee memo, place the insertion point in the blank paragraph mark above the heading "New Services," paste the Excel table and then use the Paste Options button to link the growth table to the Employee Memo, but keep the formatting of the *source* file when you link the table.

12. Switch to Excel, press the Esc key to deselect the table, and then change the number of home care clients in 2006 to 1354, and the number of transportation clients in 2006 to 331.

13. Switch back to the employee memo and update the link.

14. Replace Caitlin Sheehan's name at the top of the memo with your own. Center the pie chart horizontally on the page. (*Hint*: Click the chart once to select it, and then center it.) Center the table and fine-tune its format. Finally, make sure that there is one blank line between the chart and the table and any text above and below them, and that the page break is in a logical place.

15. Save the memo, and then preview and print it.

16. Break the link between the employee memo and the table.

17. Test that the link is broken by changing the number of clients in 2006 who received light chores service from 89 to 100 in the table in the Excel workbook, and then try to update the link in the Word document.

18. Exit all open programs. When prompted to save files, click the Yes button.

Case Problem 1

Data Files needed for this Case Problem: MusicLetter.doc and MusicRentals.xls

Making Music Caleb Jacobson is the owner of Making Music, a small music retail store in Danbury, Connecticut. Caleb sells instruments and accessories, sheet music, lesson books, and a few music collectibles, and he offers repair service for most common instruments. Caleb and some of his staff also teach piano and guitar lessons in a room upstairs from the store. In addition, Making Music rents and sells band instruments to middle and high school students at area schools. Currently, Making Music has arrangements with three area middle schools and two high schools to show up on the school grounds in September each year to rent or sell band instruments to interested students. Caleb wants to make arrangements with more schools to expand his business. He decides to write a letter of introduction to the music departments at several schools in nearby towns. He wants to include an updated list of instruments that he rents and sells, the current monthly rental fees, the total cost if a student rents until the instrument is paid off, and the cost if a student buys the instrument outright. He wants to be able to update this information if his prices change. He also wants to include a chart showing the instruments he sells and rents the most. You'll use Excel and Word to create the letter for Caleb.

1. Start Word, and then open the **MusicLetter** document in the Tutorial.01\Cases folder included with your Data Files.

2. Save the document as **School Letter** in the same folder.
3. At the top of the letter, replace the <Current Date> placeholder text with the current date. At the bottom of the letter, replace Caleb Jacobson's name with your own.
4. Start Excel, and then open the **MusicRentals** workbook in the Tutorial.01\Cases folder included with your Data Files.
5. Save the workbook as **Rental Fees** in the same folder.
6. Copy cells A9 through E17 in the Rental Prices worksheet to the Clipboard.
7. Switch to Word.
8. Link the Excel worksheet object into the Word document in the blank paragraph above the second paragraph in the body of the letter, matching the style of the Word document, and then save the document.
9. Switch to Excel.
10. Change the purchase price of a clarinet to $720, and then save the changes to the workbook.
11. Switch to Word and update the link. Note that the change you just made in the previous step is now reflected in the Word document.
12. Center the table, and then save the changes to the letter.
13. Switch to Excel, and then click the Rentals Chart 2005–2006 sheet tab in the Rental Fees workbook to make that worksheet active.
14. Copy the pie chart to the Clipboard. (*Hint*: There is no need to select the chart before you copy it because it is on its own chart sheet.)

Explore

15. Switch to Word, position the insertion point above the last paragraph in the body of the letter, and then click the Paste button to embed the pie chart in the school letter. When the Paste Options button appears, click it, and then click Excel Chart (entire workbook). (This is the same as using the Paste option in the Paste Special dialog box.)
16. Click the embedded chart once to select it, and then drag the lower-left sizing handle up and to the right approximately one inch to resize the chart so that it is small enough to fit on the page.
17. Edit the embedded chart so that the data labels show the percentage as well as the category name. (*Hint*: Right-click anywhere on the pie chart after you've activated Excel from within the letter, click Format Data Series on the shortcut menu, and then click the Data Labels tab in the Format Data Series dialog box.) Drag individual labels as necessary to make them readable on the chart. Click outside the chart to deselect it.
18. Switch to Excel. Note that the change you made in the previous step is not reflected in the Excel worksheet.
19. Close the **Rental Fees** workbook.
20. Save the **School Letter** document, and then preview it. Make any adjustments necessary so that the page break is in a logical spot, and then print the document.
21. Exit all open programs, saving changes if prompted.

Case Problem 2

Data File needed for this Case Problem: TutorFees.xls

Create

Expand the skills you learned in this tutorial to create a document and then link and update Excel tables to the document.

Learning Fulfillment Centers In 1997, Enrique Garcia founded Learning Fulfillment Centers in Phoenix, Arizona, to offer tutoring services for students who need extra help to keep up with their class work. He received so many requests for advanced course work that he quickly expanded his offerings to include advanced work for students who wanted to move ahead. In early 2001, Enrique opened two more offices in greater Phoenix. One of the reasons Learning Fulfillment Centers has been successful is the initial assessment that the staff conducts to evaluate each student and customize a plan for that student. Enrique plans to send out a letter to families in the area. He wants to include in the letter Excel tables that list his fees. You'll use Word and Excel to create the letter for Enrique.

1. Start Word, and create a new document. Write a letter to local families who have children. Briefly explain what Learning Fulfillment Centers offers. Include paragraphs that describe the initial assessment, the tutoring, and the advanced course work. Leave space after the tutoring and advanced course work paragraphs to link Excel tables listing the fees. Type your name and address in the inside address, and include the current date. Include a closing paragraph that mentions how successful the company is and how much it has grown. Remember to include a proper salutation and closing. Use your own name as the signatory in the letter.

2. Save the file as **Parent Letter** in the Tutorial.01\Cases folder included with your Data Files.

3. Start Excel, and open the **TutorFees** workbook in the Tutorial.01\Cases folder included with your Data Files.

4. Save the workbook as **Learning Expenses** in the same folder.

5. Link the appropriate data from the Learning Expenses workbook to appropriate paragraphs in the Parent Letter document.

6. In the Excel workbook, change the base hourly rate for writing to $55. Make this change in both worksheets.

7. Update the links in the Word document to reflect the new writing fee.

8. Save, preview, and then print the letter.

9. Close any open programs, saving files as needed.

SAM Assessment and Training

If your instructor has chosen to use the full online version of SAM 2003 Assessment and Training, you can go beyond the "just-in-time" training provided on the CD that accompanies this text. Simply log in to your SAM account (http://sam2003.course.com) to launch any assigned training activities or exams that relate to the skills covered in this tutorial.

Quick Check Answers

1. An object is anything that can be manipulated as a whole; the specific information that you want to share between programs, such as a chart, table, picture, video or sound clip, or almost anything else you can create on a computer.

2. Embedding stores a copy of the object in the destination file, and any changes made to the source file do not appear in the destination file; linking stores the object in the source file but displays it in the destination file, and any changes to the object in the source file appear in the destination file.

3. two

4. Excel

5. True

6. break the link

7. 1000. Closing the Word document without saving keeps the link intact.

New Perspectives on

Microsoft® Office Access 2003

Read This Before You Begin: Tutorials 1-4

Data Files

To complete Access Tutorials 1-4, you need the starting Data Files. See the inside back or front cover for information on downloading these files from course.com, or ask your instructor for assistance. The following table identifies each starting Data File and the folder it is stored in, as well as the ending files, which you create and save in each tutorial. Note that the Data Files you work with in each Access tutorial build on the work you did in the previous tutorial. So, when you begin Tutorial 3, for example, you will use the Data Files that resulted after you completed the steps in Tutorial 2, the Tutorial 2 Review Assignments, and the Tutorial 2 Case Problems.

Folders		Starting Files	Ending Files
Brief	Review	Globe.bmp, NEJobs.mdb, Seasonal.mdb	Globe.bmp, NEJobs.mdb, Northeast.mdb, Seasonal.mdb
	Review	Elsa.mdb, Seasons.mdb, Travel.bmp	Elsa.mdb, Recruits.mdb, Seasons.mdb, Travel.bmp
	Case1	Camcord.bmp, Events.mdb, Videos.mdb	Camcord.bmp, Events.mdb, Videos.mdb
	Case2	Fitness.mdb, Products.mdb, Weights.bmp	Fitness.mdb, Products.mdb, Weights.bmp
	Case3	Animals.bmp, Pledge.mdb, Redwood.mdb	Animals.bmp, Pledge.mdb, Redwood.mdb, Redwood97.mdb, Redwood2002.mdb
	Case4	GEM.mdb, Property.xls, Reserve.mdb, Villa.bmp	GEM.mdb, GEM97.mdb, GEM2002.mdb, Property.xls, Reserve.mdb, Villa.bmp

Storing Your Files

It is recommended that you store all your Data Files on a USB drive. Refer to the tutorial "Managing Your Files" for information on using USB drives. If you need to store your Data Files on floppy disks, you will need six high-density disks to store all the files for Access Tutorials 1-4.

SAM 2003 Training Companion CD

The SAM 2003 Training Companion CD that comes with this text gives you "just-in-time" training and reinforcement of important Microsoft Office skills. Look for the SAM CD logo throughout each tutorial for opportunities to complete the hands-on tasks included on this CD.

Course Labs

Access Tutorial 1 features an interactive Course Lab to help you understand database concepts. There are Lab Assignments at the end of Tutorial 1 that relate to this lab. Contact your instructor or technical support person for assistance in accessing this lab.

Introduction to Microsoft Access 2003

Viewing and Working with a Table Containing Employer Data

Case | Northeast Seasonal Jobs International (NSJI)

During her high school and college years, Elsa Jensen spent her summers working as a lifeguard for some of the most popular beaches on Cape Cod, Massachusetts. Throughout those years, Elsa met many foreign students who had come to the United States to work for the summer, both at the beaches and at other seasonal businesses, such as restaurants and hotels. Elsa formed friendships with several students and kept in contact with them beyond college. Through discussions with her friends, Elsa realized that foreign students often have a difficult time finding appropriate seasonal work, relying mainly on "word-of-mouth" references to locate jobs. Elsa became convinced that there must be an easier way.

Several years ago, Elsa founded Northeast Seasonal Jobs, a small firm located in Boston that served as a job broker between foreign students seeking part-time, seasonal work and resort businesses located in New England. Recently Elsa expanded her business to include resorts in the eastern provinces of Canada, and consequently she changed her company's name to Northeast Seasonal Jobs International (NSJI). At first the company focused mainly on summer employment, but as the business continued to grow, Elsa increased the scope of operations to include all types of seasonal opportunities, including foliage tour companies in the fall and ski resorts in the winter.

Elsa depends on computers to help her manage all areas of NSJI's operations, including financial management, sales, and information management. Several months ago the company upgraded to Microsoft Windows and **Microsoft Office Access 2003** (or simply **Access**), a computer program used to enter, maintain, and retrieve related data in a format known as a database. Elsa and her staff use Access to maintain data such as information about employers, positions they have available for seasonal work, and foreign students seeking employment. Elsa recently created a database named Seasonal to track the company's employer customers and data about their available positions. She asks for your help in completing and maintaining this database.

Session	Objectives		SAM Training Tasks	
Session 1.1	• Define the terms field, record, table, relational database, primary key, and foreign key • Open an existing database • Identify the components of the Access and Database windows	• Open and navigate a table • Learn how Access saves a database	• Open a form • Open Access objects in the appropriate views	• Open an existing database • Start Access
Session 1.2	• Open an existing query, and create, sort, and navigate a new query • Create and navigate a form • Create, preview, and navigate a report	• Learn how to manage a database by backing up, restoring, compacting, and converting a database	• Compact on close • Convert an Access 2000 database to 2002-2003 format • Create a report using Report Wizard • Create a summary report using Report Wizard • Create auto forms • Create queries using Wizards	• Create Select queries using the Simple Query Wizard • Open a query • Sort records in a database • Use database tools to compact a database • Use the Backup Database command

Student Data Files   For a complete list of the Data Files needed for this tutorial, see page AC 2.

Session 1.1

For hands-on practice of key tasks in this session, go to the SAM 2003 Training Companion CD included with this text.

Introduction to Database Concepts

Before you begin working on Elsa's database and using Access, you need to understand a few key terms and concepts associated with databases.

Organizing Data

Data is a valuable resource to any business. At NSJI, for example, important data includes employers' names and addresses, and available positions and wages. Organizing, storing, maintaining, retrieving, and sorting this type of data are critical activities that enable a business to find and use information effectively. Before storing data on a computer, however, you must organize the data.

Your first step in organizing data is to identify the individual fields. A **field** is a single characteristic or attribute of a person, place, object, event, or idea. For example, some of the many fields that NSJI tracks are employer ID, employer name, employer address, employer phone number, position, wage, and start date.

Next, you group related fields together into tables. A **table** is a collection of fields that describe a person, place, object, event, or idea. Figure 1-1 shows an example of an Employer table consisting of four fields: EmployerID, EmployerName, EmployerAddress, and PhoneNumber.

Figure 1-1	Data organization for a table of employers

Employer table

EmployerID	EmployerName	EmployerAddress	PhoneNumber
10122	BeanTown Tours	105 State Street, Boston, MA 02109	617-451-1970
10125	Boston Harbor Excursions	75 Atlantic Avenue, Boston, MA 02110	617-235-1800
10126	BaySide Inn & Country Club	354 Oceanside Drive, Brewster, MA 02631	508-283-5775
10190	The Briar Rose Inn	105 Queen Street, Charlottetown PE C1A 8R4	902-626-1595
10191	Windsor Alpine Tours	14 Longmeadow Road, Laconia, NH 03246	603-266-9233
10198	Trudel Spa & Resort	40 Rue Rivard, North Hatley QC J0B 2C0	819-842-7783

The specific value, or content, of a field is called the **field value**. In Figure 1-1, the first set of field values for EmployerID, EmployerName, EmployerAddress, and PhoneNumber are, respectively: 10122; BeanTown Tours; 105 State Street, Boston, MA 02109; and 617-451-1970. This set of field values is called a **record**. In the Employer table, the data for each employer is stored as a separate record. Figure 1-1 shows six records; each row of field values is a record.

Databases and Relationships

Databases

A collection of related tables is called a **database**, or a **relational database**. NSJI's Seasonal database contains two related tables: the Employer and NAICS tables, which Elsa created. (The NAICS table contains North American Industry Classification System codes, which are used to classify businesses according to their activities.) In Tutorial 2, you will create a Position table to store information about the available positions at NSJI's employer clients.

Sometimes you might want information about employers and their available positions. To obtain this information, you must have a way to connect records in the Employer table to records in the Position table. You connect the records in the separate tables through a **common field** that appears in both tables.

In the sample database shown in Figure 1-2, each record in the Employer table has a field named EmployerID, which is also a field in the Position table. For example, BaySide Inn & Country Club is the third employer in the Employer table and has an EmployerID field value of 10126. This same EmployerID field value, 10126, appears in three records in the Position table. Therefore, BaySide Inn & Country Club is the employer with these three positions available.

Database relationship between tables for employers and positions ◄ **Figure 1-2**

Employer table

EmployerID	EmployerName	EmployerAddress	PhoneNumber
10122	BeanTown Tours	105 State Street, Boston, MA 02109	617-451-1970
10125	Boston Harbor Excursions	75 Atlantic Avenue, Boston, MA 02110	617-235-1800
10126	BaySide Inn & Country Club	354 Oceanside Drive, Brewster, MA 02631	508-283-5775
10190	The Briar Rose Inn	105 Queen Street, Charlottetown PE C1A 8R4	902-626-1595
10191	Windsor Alpine Tours	14 Longmeadow Road, Laconia, NH 03246	603-266-9233
10198	Trudel Spa & Resort	40 Rue Rivard, North Hatley QC J0B 2C0	819-842-7783

primary keys

common field

foreign key

three positions for BaySide Inn & Country Club

Position table

PositionID	PositionTitle	EmployerID	Hours/Week
2040	Waiter/Waitress	10126	32
2045	Tour Guide	10122	24
2053	Host/Hostess	10190	24
2066	Lifeguard	10198	32
2073	Pro Shop Clerk	10126	24
2078	Ski Patrol	10191	30
2079	Day Care	10191	35
2082	Reservationist	10125	40
2111	Kitchen Help	10126	32

Each EmployerID value in the Employer table must be unique, so that you can distinguish one employer from another and identify the employer's specific positions available in the Position table. The EmployerID field is referred to as the primary key of the Employer table. A **primary key** is a field, or a collection of fields, whose values uniquely identify each record in a table. In the Position table, PositionID is the primary key.

When you include the primary key from one table as a field in a second table to form a relationship between the two tables, it is called a **foreign key** in the second table, as shown in Figure 1-2. For example, EmployerID is the primary key in the Employer table and a foreign key in the Position table. Although the primary key EmployerID has unique values in the Employer table, the same field as a foreign key in the Position table does not necessarily have unique values. The EmployerID value 10126, for example, appears three times in the Position table because the BaySide Inn & Country Club has three available positions. Each foreign key value, however, must match one of the field values for the primary key in the other table. In the example shown in Figure 1-2, each EmployerID value in the Position table must match an EmployerID value in the Employer table. The two tables are related, enabling users to connect the facts about employers with the facts about their employment positions.

Relational Database Management Systems

To manage its databases, a company purchases a database management system. A **database management system (DBMS)** is a software program that lets you create databases and then manipulate data in them. Most of today's database management systems, including Access, are called relational database management systems. In a **relational database management system**, data is organized as a collection of tables. As stated earlier, a relationship between two tables in a relational DBMS is formed through a common field.

A relational DBMS controls the storage of databases on disk and facilitates the creation, manipulation, and reporting of data, as illustrated in Figure 1-3. Specifically, a relational DBMS provides the following functions:

- It allows you to create database structures containing fields, tables, and table relationships.
- It lets you easily add new records, change field values in existing records, and delete records.
- It contains a built-in query language, which lets you obtain immediate answers to the questions you ask about your data.
- It contains a built-in report generator, which lets you produce professional-looking, formatted reports from your data.
- It protects databases through security, control, and recovery facilities.

Figure 1-3 ▶ **Relational database management system**

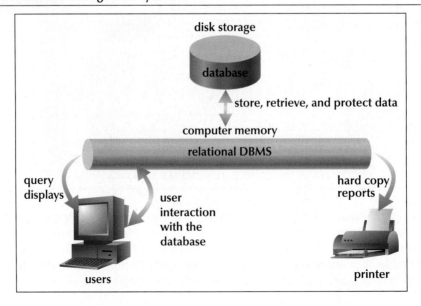

A company such as NSJI benefits from a relational DBMS because it allows users working in different departments to share the same data. More than one user can enter data into a database, and more than one user can retrieve and analyze data that was entered by others. For example, NSJI will store only one copy of the Employer table, and all employees will be able to use it to meet their specific requests for employer information.

Finally, unlike other software programs, such as spreadsheets, a DBMS can handle massive amounts of data and can easily form relationships among multiple tables. Each Access database, for example, can be up to two gigabytes in size and can contain up to 32,768 objects (tables, queries, and so on).

Opening an Existing Database

Now that you've learned some database terms and concepts, you're ready to start Access and open the Seasonal database.

To start Access:

1. Click the **Start** button on the taskbar, point to **All Programs**, point to **Microsoft Office**, and then click **Microsoft Office Access 2003**. The Access window opens. See Figure 1-4.

   Trouble? If you don't see the Microsoft Office Access 2003 option on the Microsoft Office submenu, look for it on a different submenu or as an option on the All Programs menu. If you still cannot find the Microsoft Office Access 2003 option, ask your instructor or technical support person for help.

Microsoft Access window | **Figure 1-4**

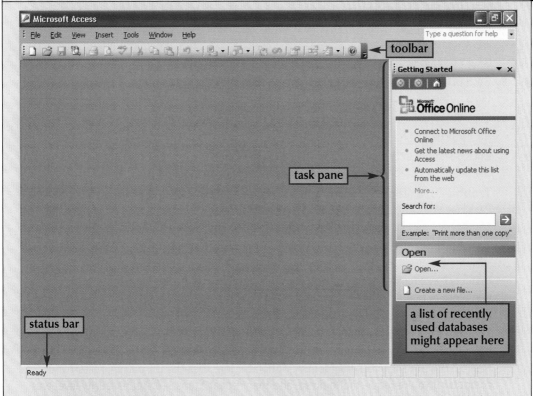

Trouble? If the Access program window on your computer is not maximized, click the Maximize button on the program window title bar.

When you start Access, the Access window contains the Getting Started task pane, which allows you to create a new database or to open an existing database. The "Create a new file" option in the task pane provides options for you to create a new database on your own, or to use one of the available online templates and let Access guide you through the steps for creating one of the standard databases provided by Microsoft.

In this case you need to open an existing database, the Seasonal database, which Elsa already created. To open an existing database, you can select the name of a database in the list of recently opened databases (if the list appears), or select a database in the Open dialog box. You need to open an existing database—the Seasonal database included with your Data Files.

To open the Seasonal database:

1. Make sure you have created your copy of the Access Data Files, and that your computer can access them. For example, if you are using a removable disk, place the disk in the appropriate disk drive.

   Trouble? If you don't have the Access Data Files, you need to get them before you can proceed. Your instructor will either give you the Data Files or ask you to obtain them from a specified location (such as a network drive). In either case, be sure that you make a backup copy of your Data Files before you start using them, so that the original files will be available on your copied disk in case you need to start over because of an error or problem. If you have any questions about the Data Files, see your instructor or technical support staff for assistance.

2. In the Open section of the task pane, click the **Open** option. The Open dialog box is displayed.

   Trouble? If your task pane doesn't provide an Open option, click the More option to display the Open dialog box.

3. Click the **Look in** list arrow, and then click the drive that contains your Data Files.

   Trouble? If you do not know where your Data Files are located, consult with your instructor about where to open and save your Data Files. Note that Access slows noticeably if you are working with a database stored on a 3 ½-inch floppy disk, and might not be able to perform some tasks, such as compacting and converting a database.

4. Click **Brief** in the list box (if necessary), and then click the **Open** button to display the contents of the Brief folder.

5. Click **Tutorial** in the list box, and then click the **Open** button to display a list of the files in the Tutorial folder.

6. Click **Seasonal** in the list box, and then click the **Open** button. The task pane closes, and the Seasonal database opens in the Access window. See Figure 1-5.

   Trouble? If a dialog box opens with a message about installing the Microsoft Jet Service Pack, see your instructor or technical support person for assistance. You must have the appropriate Service Pack installed in order to open and work with Access databases safely.

   Trouble? If a dialog box opens, warning you that the Seasonal database may not be safe, click the Open button. Your security level is set to Medium, which is the security setting that lets you choose whether or not to open a database that contains macros, VBA, or certain types of queries. The Seasonal database does not contain objects that will harm your computer, so you can safely open the database.

   Trouble? If a dialog box opens, warning you that Access can't open the Seasonal database due to security restrictions, click the OK button, click Tools on the menu bar, point to Macro, click Security, click the Medium option button, click the OK button, restart your computer if you're requested to do so, and then repeat Steps 1–6. Your security level was set to High, which is the security setting that lets you open a database that contains macros, VBA, or certain types of queries only from trusted sources. Because the Seasonal database does not contain objects that will harm your computer, you need to change the security setting to Medium and then safely open the Seasonal database.

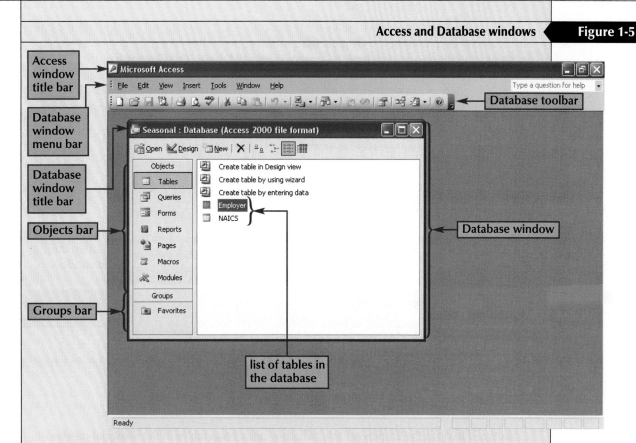

Trouble? The filename on your screen might be Seasonal.mdb instead of Seasonal, depending on your computer's default settings. The extension ".mdb" identifies the file as a Microsoft Access database.

Trouble? If Tables is not selected in the Objects bar of the Database window, click it to display the list of tables in the database.

Before you can begin working with the database, you need to become familiar with the components of the Access and Database windows.

Exploring the Access and Database Windows

The **Access window** is the program window that appears when you start the program. The **Database window** appears when you open a database; this window is the main control center for working with an open Access database. Except for the Access window title bar, all window components now on your screen are associated with the Database window (see Figure 1-5). Most of these window components—including the title bars, window sizing buttons, menu bar, toolbar, and status bar—are the same as the components in other Windows programs.

Notice that the Database window title bar includes the notation "(Access 2000 file format)." By default, databases that you create in Access 2003 use the Access 2000 database file format. This feature ensures that you can use and share databases originally created in Access 2003 without converting them to a format for an earlier version of Access, and vice versa. (You'll learn more about database file formats and converting databases later in this tutorial.)

The Database window provides a variety of options for viewing and manipulating database objects. Each item in the **Objects bar** controls one of the major object groups—such as tables, queries, forms, and reports—in an Access database. The **Groups bar** allows you to organize different types of database objects into groups, with shortcuts to those objects, so that you can work with them more easily. The Database window also provides buttons for quickly creating, opening, and managing objects, as well as shortcut options for some of these tasks.

Recall that Elsa has already created the Employer and NAICS tables in the Seasonal database. She asks you to open the Employer table and view its contents.

Opening an Access Table

As noted earlier, tables contain all the data in a database. Tables are the fundamental objects for your work in Access. To view, add, change, or delete data in a table, you first open the table. You can open any Access object by using the Open button in the Database window.

Reference Window | **Opening an Access Object**

- In the Objects bar of the Database window, click the type of object you want to open.
- If necessary, scroll the object list box until the object name appears, and then click the object name.
- Click the Open button in the Database window.

You need to open the Employer table, which is one of two tables in the Seasonal database.

To open the Employer table:

1. In the Database window, click **Employer** to select it (if necessary).
2. Click the **Open** button in the Database window. The Employer table opens in Datasheet view on top of the Database and Access windows. See Figure 1-6.

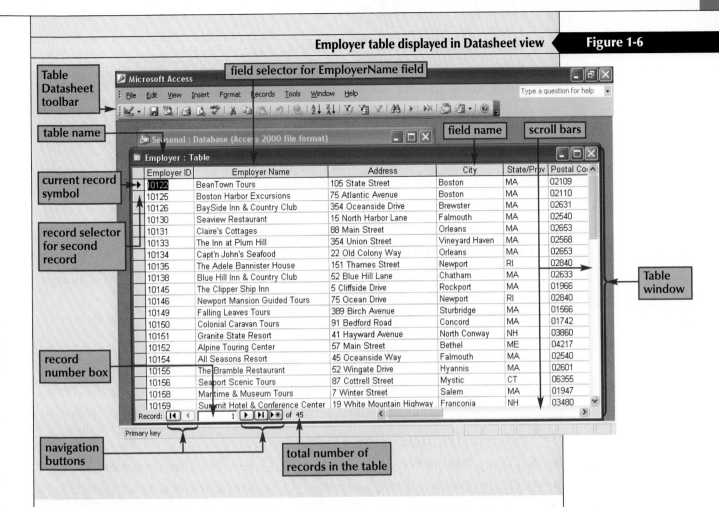

Employer table displayed in Datasheet view | Figure 1-6

Datasheet view shows a table's contents as a **datasheet** in rows and columns, similar to a table or spreadsheet. Each row is a separate record in the table, and each column contains the field values for one field in the table. Each column is headed by a field name inside a field selector, and each row has a record selector to its left. Notice that the field names are displayed with spaces between words—such as "Employer ID" instead of "EmployerID" and "Employer Name" instead of "EmployerName." (You'll learn how to change the display of field names later in this text.) Clicking a **field selector** or a **record selector** selects that entire column or row (respectively), which you then can manipulate. A field selector is also called a **column selector**, and a record selector is also called a **row selector**.

Navigating an Access Datasheet

When you first open a datasheet, Access selects the first field value in the first record. Notice that this field value is highlighted and that a darkened triangle symbol, called the current record symbol, appears in the record selector to the left of the first record. The **current record symbol** identifies the currently selected record. Clicking a record selector or field value in another row moves the current record symbol to that row. You can also move the pointer over the data on the screen and click one of the field values to position the insertion point.

The Employer table currently has 13 fields and 45 records. To view fields or records not currently visible in the datasheet, you can use the horizontal and vertical scroll bars shown in Figure 1-6 to navigate the data. The **navigation buttons**, also shown in Figure 1-6, provide another way to move vertically through the records. Figure 1-7 shows which record becomes the current record when you click each navigation button. The **record number box**, which appears between the two sets of navigation buttons, displays the current record number. The total number of records in the table appears to the right of the navigation buttons.

Figure 1-7 **Navigation buttons**

Navigation Button	Record Selected	Navigation Button	Record Selected
I◀	First record	**▶I**	Last record
◀	Previous record	**▶✳**	New record
▶	Next record		

Elsa suggests that you use the various navigation techniques to move through the Employer table and become familiar with its contents.

To navigate the Employer datasheet:

1. Click the right scroll arrow in the horizontal scroll bar a few times to scroll to the right and view the remaining fields in the Employer table.

2. Drag the scroll box in the horizontal scroll bar all the way to the left to return to the previous display of the datasheet.

3. Click the **Next Record** navigation button **▶**. The second record is now the current record, as indicated by the current record symbol in the second record selector. Also, notice that the second record's value for the EmployerID field is highlighted, and "2" (for record number 2) appears in the record number box.

4. Click the **Last Record** navigation button **▶I**. The last record in the table, record 45, is now the current record.

5. Click the **Previous Record** navigation button **◀**. Record 44 is now the current record.

6. Click the **First Record** navigation button **I◀**. The first record is now the current record.

Printing a Datasheet

At times you might want a printed copy of the records in a table. You can use the Print button 🖨 on the Table Datasheet toolbar to print the contents of a table. You can also use the Print command on the File menu to display the Print dialog box and select various options for printing.

Reference Window **Printing a Datasheet**

- Open the table datasheet you want to print.
- Click the Print button on the Table Datasheet toolbar to print the table with default settings; or click File on the menu bar, and then click Print to display the Print dialog box and select the options you want for printing the datasheet.

Elsa does not want a printed copy of the Employer table, so you do not need to print the datasheet at this time.

Saving a Database

Notice the Save button 🖫 on the Table Datasheet toolbar. Unlike the Save buttons in other Office programs, this Save button does not save the active document (database) to your disk. Instead, you use the Save button to save the design of an Access object, such as a table, or to save datasheet format changes. Access does not have a button or option you can use to save the active database. Similarly, you cannot use the Save As option on the File menu to save the active database file with a new name, as you can with other Office programs.

Access saves changes to the active database to your disk automatically, when a record is changed or added and when you close the database. If your database is stored on a removable disk, such as a floppy disk, *you should never remove the disk while the database file is open.* If you remove the disk, Access will encounter problems when it tries to save the database, which might damage the database.

You're done working with the Employer table for now, so you can close it.

To close the Employer table:

▶ **1.** Click the **Close** button ☒ on the Employer Table window to close the table. You return to the Database window.

Now that you've become familiar with database concepts and Access, opened the Seasonal database that Elsa created, and navigated an Access table, Elsa wants you to work with the data stored in the Seasonal database and to create database objects including a query, form, and report. You will complete these tasks in Session 1.2.

Session 1.1 Quick Check

1. A(n) _____ is a single characteristic of a person, place, object, event, or idea.
2. You connect the records in two separate tables through a(n) _____ that appears in both tables.
3. The _____, whose values uniquely identify each record in a table, is called a(n) _____ when it is placed in a second table to form a relationship between the two tables.
4. In a table, the rows are also called _____, and the columns are also called _____.
5. The _____ identifies the selected record in an Access table.
6. Describe two methods for navigating a table.
7. Explain how the saving process in Access is different from saving in other Office programs.

To reinforce the tasks you learned in this session, go to the SAM 2003 Training Companion CD included with this text.

Session 1.2

Working with Queries

A **query** is a question you ask about the data stored in a database. In response to a query, Access displays the specific records and fields that answer your question. When you create a query, you tell Access which fields you need and what criteria Access should use to select the records. Then Access displays only the information you want, so you don't have to navigate through the entire database for the information. In the Seasonal database, for example, Elsa might create a query to display only those records for employers located in Boston.

Before creating a new query, you will open a query that Elsa created recently so that she could view information in the Employer table in a different way.

For hands-on practice of key tasks in this session, go to the SAM 2003 Training Companion CD included with this text.

Opening an Existing Query

Queries that you create and save appear in the Queries list of the Database window. To see the results of a query, you open, or run, the query. Elsa created and saved a query named Contacts in the Seasonal database. This query shows all the fields from the Employer table, but in a different order. Elsa suggests that you open this query to see its results.

To open the Contacts query:

1. If you took a break after the previous session, make sure that Access is running and that the Seasonal database is open.

2. Click **Queries** in the Objects bar of the Database window to display the Queries list. The Queries list box contains one object—the Contacts query. See Figure 1-8.

Figure 1-8 | **List of queries in the Seasonal database**

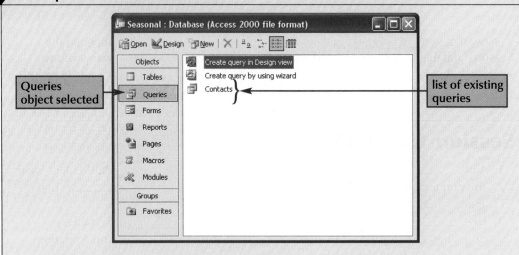

Now you will run the Contacts query by opening it.

3. Click **Contacts** to select it, and then click the **Open** button in the Database window. Access displays the results of the query in Datasheet view. See Figure 1-9.

Figure 1-9 | **Results of running the Contacts query**

Notice that the query displays the fields from the Employer table, but in a different order. For example, the first and last names of each contact, as well as the contact's phone number, appear next to the employer name. This arrangement lets Elsa view pertinent contact information without having to scroll through the table. Rearranging the display of table data is one task you can perform with queries, so that table information appears in an order more suited to how you want to work with the information.

▶ **4.** Click the **Close** button ☒ on the Query window title bar to close the Contacts query.

Even though a query can display table information in a different way, the information still exists in the table as it was originally entered. If you opened the Employer table, it would still show the fields in their original order.

Zack Ward, the director of marketing at NSJI, wants a list of all employers so that his staff can call them to check on their satisfaction with NSJI's services and recruits. He doesn't want the list to include all the fields in the Employer table (such as PostalCode and NAICSCode)—only the employer's contact information. To produce this list for Zack, you need to create a query using the Employer table.

Creating, Sorting, and Navigating a Query

You can design your own queries or use an Access **Query Wizard**, which guides you through the steps to create a query. The Simple Query Wizard allows you to select records and fields quickly, and it is an appropriate choice for producing the employer list Zack wants. You can choose this wizard either by clicking the New button to open a dialog box listing several wizards for creating a query, or by double-clicking the "Create query by using wizard" option, which automatically starts the Simple Query Wizard.

To start the Simple Query Wizard:

▶ **1.** Double-click **Create query by using wizard**. The first Simple Query Wizard dialog box opens. See Figure 1-10.

First Simple Query Wizard dialog box ◀ Figure 1-10

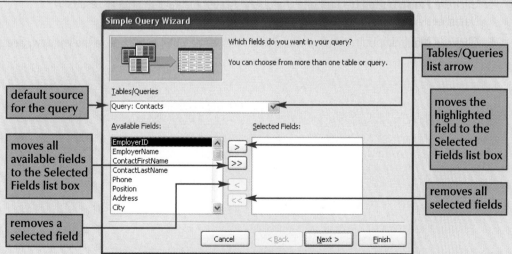

Because Contacts is the only query object in the Seasonal database, it is listed in the Tables/Queries box by default. You need to base the query you're creating on the Employer table.

2. Click the **Tables/Queries** list arrow, and then click **Table: Employer** to select the Employer table as the source for the new query. The Available Fields list box now lists the fields in the Employer table.

You need to select fields from the Available Fields list box to include them in the query. To select fields one at a time, click a field and then click the $\boxed{>}$ button. The selected field moves from the Available Fields list box on the left to the Selected Fields list box on the right. To select all the fields, click the $\boxed{>>}$ button. If you change your mind or make a mistake, you can remove a field by clicking it in the Selected Fields list box and then clicking the $\boxed{<}$ button. To remove all selected fields, click the $\boxed{<<}$ button.

Each Simple Query Wizard dialog box contains buttons on the bottom that allow you to move to the previous dialog box (Back button), move to the next dialog box (Next button), or cancel the creation process (Cancel button) and return to the Database window. You can also finish creating the object (Finish button) and accept the wizard's defaults for the remaining options.

Zack wants his list to include data from only the following fields: EmployerName, City, StateProv, ContactFirstName, ContactLastName, and Phone. You need to select these fields to include them in the query.

To create the query using the Simple Query Wizard:

1. Click **EmployerName** in the Available Fields list box, and then click the $\boxed{>}$ button. The EmployerName field moves to the Selected Fields list box.

2. Repeat Step 1 for the fields **City**, **StateProv**, **ContactFirstName**, **ContactLastName**, and **Phone**, and then click the **Next** button. The second, and final, Simple Query Wizard dialog box opens and asks you to choose a name for your query. This name will appear in the Queries list in the Database window. You'll change the suggested name (Employer Query) to "EmployerList."

3. Click at the end of the highlighted name, use the **Backspace** key to delete the word "Query" and the space after "Employer," and then type **List**. Now you can view the query results.

4. Click the **Finish** button to complete the query. Access displays the query results in Datasheet view.

5. Click the **Maximize** button 🔲 on the Query window title bar to maximize the window. See Figure 1-11.

Query results ◄ **Figure 1-11**

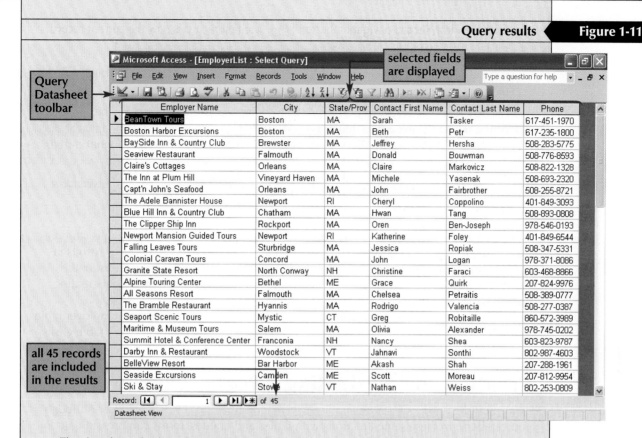

The datasheet displays the six selected fields for each record in the Employer table. The fields are shown in the order you selected them, from left to right.

The records are currently listed in order by the primary key field (EmployerID from the Employer table). This is true even though the EmployerID field is not included in the display of the query results. Zack prefers the records listed in order by state or province, so that his staff members can focus on all records for the employers in a particular state or province. To display the records in the order Zack wants, you need to sort the query results by the StateProv field.

To sort the query results:

1. Click to position the insertion point anywhere in the State/Prov column. This establishes the State/Prov column as the current field.

2. Click the **Sort Ascending** button [↓] on the Query Datasheet toolbar. Now the records are sorted in ascending alphabetical order by the values in the State/Prov column. All the records for Connecticut (CT) are listed first, followed by the records for Massachusetts (MA), Maine (ME), and so on.

   Notice that the navigation buttons are located at the bottom of the window. You navigate a query datasheet in the same way that you navigate a table datasheet.

3. Click the **Last Record** navigation button [▶|]. The last record in the query datasheet, for the Darby Inn & Restaurant, is now the current record.

4. Click the **Previous Record** navigation button [◄]. Record 44 in the query datasheet is now the current record.

▶ **5.** Click the **First Record** navigation button [I◀]. The first record is now the current record.

▶ **6.** Click the **Close Window** button [✕] on the menu bar to close the query.

A dialog box opens and asks if you want to save changes to the design of the query. This dialog box opens because you changed the sort order of the query results.

▶ **7.** Click the **Yes** button to save the query design changes and return to the Database window. Notice that the EmployerList query now appears in the Queries list box. In addition, because you maximized the Query window, now the Database window is also maximized. You need to restore the window.

▶ **8.** Click the **Restore Window** button [🗗] on the menu bar to restore the Database window.

The query results are not stored in the database; however, the query design is stored as part of the database with the name you specified. You can re-create the query results at any time by running the query again. You can also print the query datasheet using the Print button, just as you can to print a table datasheet. You'll learn more about creating and running queries in Tutorial 3.

After Zack views the query results, Elsa asks you to create a form for the Employer table so that her staff members can use the form to enter and work with data in the table easily.

Creating and Navigating a Form

A **form** is an object you use to maintain, view, and print records in a database. Although you can perform these same functions with tables and queries, forms can present data in many customized and useful ways.

In Access, you can design your own forms or use a Form Wizard to create your forms automatically. A **Form Wizard** is an Access tool that asks you a series of questions, and then creates a form based on your answers. However, an **AutoForm Wizard** does not ask you questions. Instead, it places all the fields from a selected table (or query) on a form automatically, and then displays the form on the screen, making it the quickest way to create a form.

Elsa wants a form for the Employer table that will show all the fields for one record at a time, with fields listed one below another in a column. This type of form will make it easier for her staff to focus on all the data for a particular employer. You'll use the AutoForm: Columnar Wizard to create the form.

To create the form using an AutoForm Wizard:

▶ **1.** Click **Forms** in the Objects bar of the Database window to display the Forms list. The Forms list box does not contain any forms yet.

▶ **2.** Click the **New** button in the Database window to open the New Form dialog box. See Figure 1-12.

New Form dialog box **Figure 1-12**

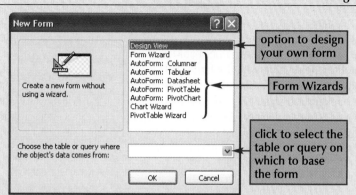

The top list box provides options for designing your own form or creating a form using one of the Form Wizards. In the bottom list box, you choose the table or query that will supply the data for the form.

▶ **3.** Click **AutoForm: Columnar** to select this AutoForm Wizard.

▶ **4.** Click the list arrow for choosing the table or query on which to base the form, and then click **Employer**.

▶ **5.** Click the **OK** button. The AutoForm Wizard creates the form and displays it in Form view. See Figure 1-13.

Form created by the AutoForm: Columnar Wizard **Figure 1-13**

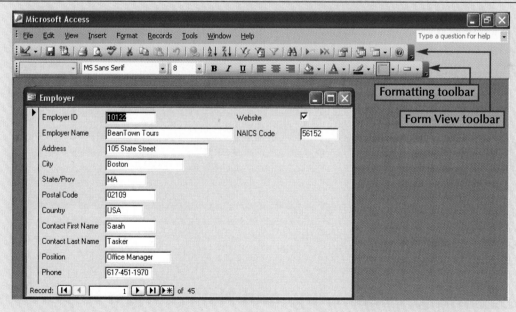

Trouble? The placement of the Form View and Formatting toolbars might be different on your screen. If you want your screen to match the figures, you can use the mouse to drag a toolbar to a new location, using the dotted line at the left edge of a toolbar. However, the position of any toolbar does not affect your ability to complete the steps.

Trouble? The background of your form might look different from the one shown in Figure 1-13, depending on your computer's settings. If so, don't worry. You will learn how to change the form's style later in this text. For now, continue with the tutorial.

The form displays one record at a time in the Employer table. Access displays the field values for the first record in the table and selects the first field value (EmployerID). Each field name appears on a separate line (spread over two columns) and on the same line as its field value, which appears in a box. The widths of the boxes are different to accommodate the different sizes of the displayed field values; for example, compare the small box for the StateProv field value with the larger box for the EmployerName field value. The AutoForm: Columnar Wizard automatically placed the field names and values on the form and supplied the background style. Note as well that field names are displayed with spaces between them, such as "Contact First Name" instead of "ContactFirstName." (You'll learn how to control the display of field names in database objects, such as tables and forms, later in this text.)

To view and maintain data using a form, you must know how to move from field to field and from record to record. Notice that the Form window contains navigation buttons, similar to those available in Datasheet view, which you can use to display different records in the form. You'll use these now to navigate the form; then you'll save and close the form.

To navigate, save, and close the form:

1. Click the **Next Record** navigation button ▶. The form now displays the values for the second record in the Employer table.

2. Click the **Last Record** navigation button ▶I to move to the last record in the table. The form displays the information for record 45, Lighthouse Tours.

3. Click the **Previous Record** navigation button ◀ to move to record 44.

4. Click the **First Record** navigation button I◀ to return to the first record in the Employer table.

   Next, you'll save the form with the name "EmployerData" in the Seasonal database. Then the form will be available for later use.

5. Click the **Save** button 🖫 on the Form View toolbar. The Save As dialog box opens.

6. In the Form Name text box, click at the end of the highlighted word "Employer," type **Data**, and then press the **Enter** key. Access saves the form as EmployerData in the Seasonal database and closes the dialog box. Note, however, that the Form window title bar still displays the name "Employer"; you'll see how to control object names in the next tutorial.

7. Click the **Close** button ☒ on the Form window title bar to close the form and return to the Database window. Note that the EmployerData form is now listed in the Forms list box.

After attending a staff meeting, Zack returns with another request. He wants the same employer list you produced earlier when you created the EmployerList query, but he'd like the information presented in a more readable format. You'll help Zack by creating a report.

Creating, Previewing, and Navigating a Report

A **report** is a formatted printout (or screen display) of the contents of one or more tables in a database. Although you can print data appearing in tables, queries, and forms, reports provide you with the greatest flexibility for formatting printed output. As with forms, you can design your own reports or use a Report Wizard to create reports automatically. Like other wizards, a **Report Wizard** guides you through the steps of creating a report.

Zack wants a report showing the same information contained in the EmployerList query that you created earlier. However, he wants the data for each employer to be grouped together, with one employer record below another, as shown in the report sketch in Figure 1-14.

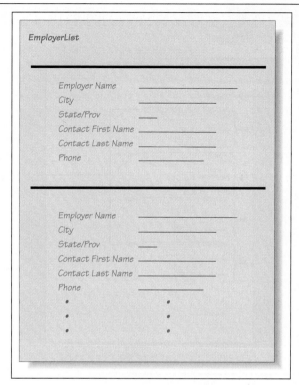

To produce the report for Zack, you'll use the AutoReport: Columnar Wizard, which is similar to the AutoForm: Columnar Wizard you used earlier when creating the EmployerData form. An **AutoReport Wizard**, like an AutoForm Wizard, places all the fields from a selected table (or query) on a report, making it the quickest way to create a report.

To create the report using the AutoReport: Columnar Wizard:

▶ 1. Click **Reports** in the Objects bar of the Database window, and then click the **New** button in the Database window to open the New Report dialog box, which is similar to the New Form dialog box you saw earlier.

▶ 2. Click **AutoReport: Columnar** to select this wizard for creating the report.

Because Zack wants the same data as in the EmployerList query, you need to choose that query as the basis for the report.

▶ 3. Click the list arrow for choosing the table or query on which to base the report, and then click **EmployerList**.

▶ 4. Click the **OK** button. The AutoReport Wizard creates the report and displays it in Print Preview, which shows exactly how the report will look when printed.

To view the report better, you'll maximize the window and change the Zoom setting so that you can see the entire page.

▶ 5. Click the **Maximize** button 🔲 on the Report window title bar, click the **Zoom** list arrow (to the right of the value 100%) on the Print Preview toolbar, and then click **Fit**. The entire first page of the report is displayed in the window. See Figure 1-15.

Figure 1-15 — **First page of the report in Print Preview**

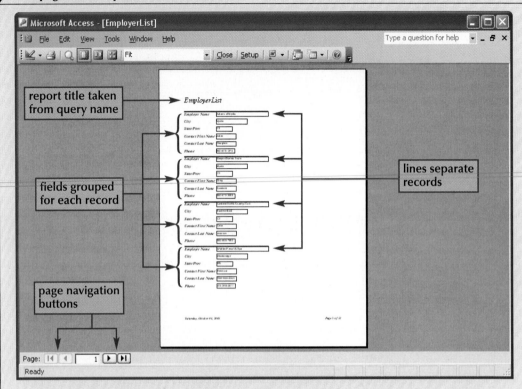

Trouble? The fonts used in your report might look different from the ones shown in Figure 1-15, depending on your computer's settings. If so, don't worry. You will learn how to change the report's style later in this text.

Each field from the EmployerList query appears on its own line, with the corresponding field value to the right and in a box. Horizontal lines separate one record from the next, visually grouping all the fields for each record. The name of the query—EmployerList—appears as the report's title.

Notice that the Print Preview window provides page navigation buttons at the bottom of the window, similar to the navigation buttons you've used to move through records in a table, query, and form. You use these buttons to move through the pages of a report.

6. Click the **Next Page** navigation button ▶. The second page of the report is displayed in Print Preview.

7. Click the **Last Page** navigation button ▶| to move to the last page of the report. Note that this page contains the fields for only one record. Also note that the box in the middle of the navigation buttons displays the number "12"; there are 12 pages in this report.

Trouble? Depending on the printer you are using, your report might have more or fewer pages, or might have more than one record on the last page. If so, don't worry. Different printers format reports in different ways, sometimes affecting the total number of pages and the number of records per page.

8. Click the **First Page** navigation button |◀ to return to the first page of the report.

Zack likes how the report looks, and he wants to show it to his staff members to see if they approve of the format. He would like a printout of the report, but he doesn't need the entire report printed—only the first page.

Printing Specific Pages of a Report

After creating a report, you typically print it to distribute it to others who need to view the report's contents. You can choose to print the entire report, using the Print toolbar button or the Print menu option, or you can select specific pages of a report to print. To specify certain pages to print, you must use the Print option on the File menu. In this case, you will print only the first page of the EmployerList report.

Note: To complete the following steps, your computer must be connected to a printer.

To print only the first page of the report:

▶ **1.** Click **File** on the menu bar, and then click **Print**. The Print dialog box opens. See Figure 1-16.

Print dialog box ◀ **Figure 1-16**

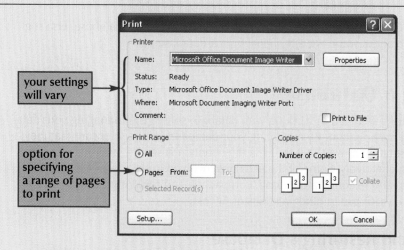

your settings will vary

option for specifying a range of pages to print

Trouble? The settings shown for the Name, Type, and Where options in your Print dialog box will vary from those shown in the figure, depending on the printer you are using.

The Print dialog box provides options for printing all the pages in the report or a specified range of pages. In this case, you will print just the first page of the report, so you need to specify a range of "From" page 1 "To" page 1.

▶ **2.** In the Print Range section, click the **Pages** option button. Notice that the insertion point now appears in the From box so that you can specify the first page to be printed.

▶ **3.** Type **1**, press the **Tab** key to move to the To box, and then type **1**. These settings will cause only the first page of the report to be printed.

▶ **4.** Click the **OK** button. The first page of the EmployerList report prints on your selected printer.

Trouble? If your report did not print, make sure that your computer is connected to a printer, and that the printer is turned on and ready to print. Then repeat Steps 1 through 4.

At this point, you could close the report without saving it because you can easily re-create it at any time. In general, it's best to save an object—report, form, or query—only if you antic-ipate using the object frequently or if it is time-consuming to create, because these objects use considerable storage space on your disk. However, Zack wants to keep the report until he receives feedback from his staff members about its layout, so he asks you to save it.

To close and save the report:

▶ 1. Click the **Close Window** button ☒ on the menu bar. *Do not* click the Close button on the Print Preview toolbar.

   Trouble? If you clicked the Close button on the Print Preview toolbar, you switched to Design view. Simply click the Close Window button ☒ on the menu bar, and then continue with the steps.

   A dialog box opens and asks if you want to save the changes to the report design.

▶ 2. Click the **Yes** button. The Save As dialog box opens.

▶ 3. Click to the right of the highlighted text in the Report Name text box, type **Report**, and then click the **OK** button. Access saves the report as "EmployerListReport" and returns to the Database window.

Now that you've become familiar with the objects in the Seasonal database, Elsa suggests that you learn about some ways to manage your database.

Managing a Database

One of the main tasks involved in working with database software is managing your databases and the data they contain. By managing your databases, you can ensure that they operate in the most efficient way, that the data they contain is secure, and that you can work with the data effectively. Some of the activities involved in database management include backing up and restoring a database, compacting and repairing a database, and converting a database for use in other versions of Access.

Backing up and Restoring a Database

Backing up a database is the process of making a copy of the database file to protect your database against loss or damage. Experienced database users make it a habit to back up a database before they work with it for the first time, keeping the original data intact, and to make frequent backups while continuing to work with a database. Because a floppy disk can hold only the smallest of databases, it is not practical to store backup copies on a floppy disk. Most users back up their databases on tapes, recordable CDs, or hard disks.

With previous versions of Access, you could only make a backup copy using one of the following methods: Windows Explorer, My Computer, Microsoft Backup, or other backup software. With Access 2003, however, a new Back Up Database option enables you to back up your database file from within the Access program, while you are working on your database. Figure 1-17 shows the Save Backup As dialog box, which opens when you choose the Back Up Database option from the File menu.

Save Backup As dialog box   **Figure 1-17**

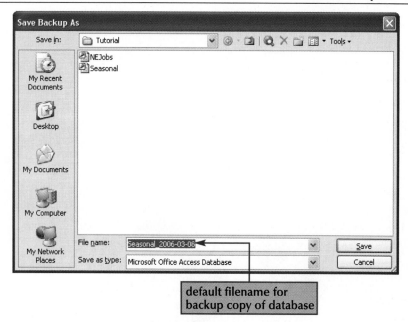

default filename for
backup copy of database

The Save Backup As dialog box is similar to the standard Save As dialog box found in Windows programs. Notice that the default filename for the backup copy consists of the same filename as the database you are backing up (in this example, "Seasonal") plus the current date. This file naming system makes it easy for you to keep track of your database backups and when they were created. (You will not actually back up the Seasonal database here; if you are working off a floppy disk, you will not have enough room on the disk to hold both the original database and its backup copy.)

To restore a backup database file, choose the same method you used to make the backup copy. For example, if you used the Microsoft Backup tool (which is one of the System Tools available from the All Programs menu and Accessories submenu in Windows), you must choose the Restore option for this tool to copy the database file to your database folder. If the existing database file and the backup copy have the same name, restoring the backup copy might replace the existing file. If you want to save the existing file, rename it before you restore the backup copy.

Compacting and Repairing a Database

Whenever you open an Access database and work in it, the size of the database increases. Further, when you delete records and when you delete or replace database objects—such as queries, forms, and reports—the space that had been occupied on the disk by the deleted or replaced records or objects does not automatically become available for other records or objects. To make the space available, you must compact the database. **Compacting** a database rearranges the data and objects in a database to decrease its file size. Unlike making a backup copy of a database file, which you do to protect your database against loss or damage, you compact a database to make it smaller, thereby making more space available on your disk and letting you open and close the database more quickly. Figure 1-18 illustrates the compacting process.

| Figure 1-18 | Compacting a database |

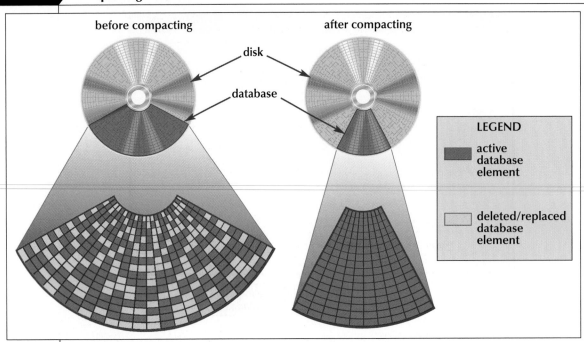

When you compact a database, Access repairs the database at the same time. In many cases, Access detects that a database is damaged when you try to open it and gives you the option to compact and repair it at that time. For example, the data in your database might become damaged, or corrupted, if you exit the Access program suddenly by turning off your computer. If you think your database might be damaged because it is behaving unpredictably, you can use the "Compact and Repair Database" option to fix it. With your database file open, point to the Database Utilities option on the Tools menu, and then choose the Compact and Repair Database option.

Compacting a Database Automatically

Access also allows you to set an option for your database file so that every time you close the database, it will be compacted automatically.

| Reference Window | **Compacting a Database Automatically** |

- Make sure the database file you want to compact automatically is open.
- Click Tools on the menu bar, and then click Options.
- Click the General tab in the Options dialog box.
- Click the Compact on Close check box to select it.
- Click the OK button.

You'll set the Compact on Close option now for the Seasonal database. Then, every time you subsequently close the Seasonal database, Access will compact the database file for you. After setting this option, you'll close the database.

Important: Because Access copies the database file and then compacts it on the same disk, you might run out of storage space if you compact a database stored on a floppy disk. Therefore, it is strongly recommended that you set the Compact on Close option *only* if your database is stored somewhere other than a floppy disk. However, if you must work with the Seasonal database on a floppy disk, per your instructor's requirements, you must also compact the database so that it will fit on the disk as you progress through the tutorials. Consult with your instructor or technical support staff to see if they recommend your using the Compact on Close option while working from a floppy disk.

To set the option for compacting the Seasonal database:

▶ **1.** Make sure the Seasonal Database window is open.

▶ **2.** Click **Tools** on the menu bar, and then click **Options**. The Options dialog box opens.

▶ **3.** Click the **General** tab in the dialog box, and then click the **Compact on Close** check box to select it. See Figure 1-19.

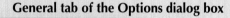

General tab of the Options dialog box | Figure 1-19

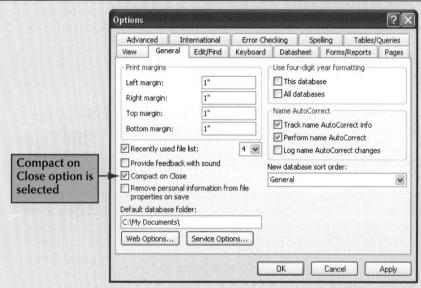

Compact on Close option is selected

▶ **4.** Click the **OK** button to set the option.

Trouble? If you are working from a floppy disk, you might receive message or warning dialog boxes when setting this option. Click OK and continue with the tutorial. See your instructor or technical support staff if you have problems with this option.

▶ **5.** Click the **Close Window** button ⊠ on the menu bar. Access closes the Seasonal database file and compacts it automatically.

Note: If the database you are compacting is located on a floppy disk, it is very important that you *wait until the compacting procedure is complete before removing the floppy disk*. Wait until the light on the floppy disk drive goes off and the whirring noise made by the floppy disk drive stops. If you remove the disk before compacting has finished, you could damage your database.

Converting an Access 2000 Database

Another important database management task is **converting** a database so that you can work with it in a different version of Access. As noted earlier in this tutorial, the default file format for databases you create in Access 2003 is Access 2000. This enables you to work with the database in either the Access 2000, 2002, or 2003 versions of the software without having to convert it. This compatibility makes it easy for multiple users working with different versions of the software to share the same database and work more efficiently.

Sometimes, however, you might need to convert an Access 2000 database to another version. For example, if you need to share an Access 2000 database with a colleague who works on a laptop computer with Access 97 installed on it, you could convert the Access 2000 database to the Access 97 format. Likewise, you might want to convert an Access 2000 database to the Access 2002 file format if the database becomes very large. The Access 2002 file format is enhanced so that large databases run faster than in earlier versions of Access, making it more efficient for you to work with the information contained in them.

To convert a database, you would follow these steps (note that you will not actually convert a database now):

1. Make sure that Access is running (the database you want to convert can be open or closed).
2. Click Tools on the menu bar, point to Database Utilities, point to Convert Database, and then choose the format you want to convert to.
3. In the Database to Convert From dialog box (which appears only if the database you want to convert is closed), select the name of the database you want to convert, and then click the Convert button.
4. In the Convert Database Into dialog box, enter a new name for the converted database in the File name text box, and then click the Save button. If a message box opens with a caution about not being able to share files with a specific version of Access, click the OK button.

After converting a database, you can use it in the version of Access to which you converted the file. Note, however, that when you convert to a previous file format, such as converting from the Access 2000 file format to the Access 97 file format, you might lose some of the advanced features of the newer version and you might need to make some adjustments to the converted database. Simple databases, such as the Seasonal database, generally retain their data and formatting when converted. However, you could lose data and other information from more complex databases when you convert them to an earlier file format.

With the Employer and NAICS tables in place, Elsa can continue to build the Seasonal database and use it to store, manipulate, and retrieve important data for NSJI. In the following tutorials, you'll help Elsa complete and maintain the database, and you'll use it to meet the specific information needs of other NSJI employees.

Review

To reinforce the tasks you learned in this session, go to the SAM 2003 Training Companion CD included with this text.

Session 1.2 Quick Check

1. A(n) _____ is a question you ask about the data stored in a database.
2. Unless you specify otherwise, the records resulting from a query are listed in order by the _____.
3. The quickest way to create a form is to use a(n) _____.
4. Describe the form created by the AutoForm: Columnar Wizard.
5. After creating a report, the AutoReport Wizard displays the report in _____.
6. _____ a database rearranges the data and objects in a database to decrease its file size.

Tutorial Summary

In this tutorial, you learned the basic concepts associated with databases, including how data is organized in a database and the functions of a relational database management system. You also learned how the Database window is the main control center for your work in Access, giving you options for viewing and manipulating all the objects in a database—tables, queries, forms, reports, and so on. By opening and navigating a table datasheet, you saw how the fields and records in a table are displayed and organized. Using various wizards, you also learned how to create queries, forms, and reports quickly in order to view and work with the data stored in a table in different ways. Finally, you were introduced to some of the important tasks involved in managing a database, including backing up, compacting, and converting a database.

Key Terms

Access	Database window	query
Access window	datasheet	Query Wizard
AutoForm Wizard	Datasheet view	record
AutoReport Wizard	field	record number box
backing up	field selector	record selector
column selector	field value	relational database
common field	foreign key	relational database
compacting	form	management system
converting	Form Wizard	(RDBMS)
current record symbol	Groups bar	report
database	navigation buttons	Report Wizard
database management	Objects bar	row selector
system (DBMS)	primary key	table

Take time to practice the skills you learned in the tutorial using the same case scenario.

Review Assignments

Data File needed for the Review Assignments: Seasons.mdb

In the Review Assignments, you'll work with the Seasons database, which is similar to Elsa's database that you worked with in the tutorial. Complete the following steps:

1. Open the **Seasons** database, which is located in the Brief\Review folder provided with your Data Files.
2. Open the **Employers** table.
3. Use the appropriate navigation buttons to move to the last record in the table, and then up three records from the last record. Write down the field values for all the fields in this record.
4. Move back to the first record in the table, print the table datasheet, and then close the table.
5. Use the Simple Query Wizard to create a query that includes the City, EmployerName, ContactFirstName, ContactLastName, and Phone fields (in that order) from the **Employers** table. Name the query **EmployerPhoneList**. Sort the query results in ascending order by City. Print the query results, and then close and save the query.
6. Use the AutoForm: Columnar Wizard to create a form for the **Employers** table. Save the form as **EmployerInfo**, and then close the form.
7. Use the AutoReport: Columnar Wizard to create a report based on the **Employers** table. Print the first page of the report, and then close the report and save it as **Employers**.

8. Set the option for compacting the **Seasons** database on close. (*Note*: If you are working from a floppy disk, check with your instructor or technical support staff to confirm that you should set this option.)
9. Close the Seasons database.

Apply

Use the skills you learned in the tutorial to work with the data contained in a video photography database.

Case Problem 1

Data File needed for this Case Problem: Videos.mdb

Lim's Video Photography   Several years ago, Youngho Lim left his position at a commercial photographer's studio and started his own business, Lim's Video Photography, located in San Francisco, California. Youngho quickly established a reputation as one of the area's best videographers, specializing in digital video photography. Youngho offers customers the option of storing edited videos on CD or DVD. His video shoots include weddings and other special events, as well as recording personal and commercial inventories for insurance purposes.

As his business continues to grow, Youngho relies on Access to keep track of information about clients, contracts, and so on. Youngho recently created an Access database named Videos to store data about his clients. You'll help Youngho complete and maintain the Videos database. Complete the following:

1. Open the **Videos** database, which is located in the Brief\Case1 folder provided with your Data Files.
2. Open the **Client** table, print the table datasheet, and then close the table.
3. Use the Simple Query Wizard to create a query that includes the ClientName, Phone, and City fields (in that order) from the **Client** table. Name the query **ClientList**. Print the query results, and then close the query.
4. Use the AutoForm: Columnar Wizard to create a form for the **Contract** table. Save the form as **ContractInfo**, and then close it.
5. Use the AutoReport: Columnar Wizard to create a report based on the **Contract** table. Print the first page of the report, and then close the report and save it as **Contracts**.
6. Set the option for compacting the **Videos** database on close. (*Note*: If you are working from a floppy disk, check with your instructor or technical support staff to confirm that you should set this option.)
7. Close the Videos database.

Apply

Apply what you learned in the tutorial to work with the data for a new business in the health and fitness industry.

Case Problem 2

Data File needed for this Case Problem: Fitness.mdb

Parkhurst Health & Fitness Center   After many years working in various corporate settings, Martha Parkhurst decided to turn her lifelong interest in health and fitness into a new business venture and opened the Parkhurst Health & Fitness Center in Richmond, Virginia. In addition to providing the usual fitness classes and weight training facilities, the center also offers specialized programs designed to meet the needs of athletes—both young and old—who participate in certain sports or physical activities. Martha's goal in establishing such programs is twofold: to help athletes gain a competitive edge through customized training, and to ensure the health and safety of all participants through proper exercises and physical preparation.

Martha created the Fitness database in Access to maintain information about the members who have joined the center and the types of programs offered. She needs your help in working with this database. Complete the following:

1. Open the **Fitness** database located in the Brief\Case2 folder provided with your Data Files.
2. Open the **Member** table, print the table datasheet, and then close the table.
3. Use the Simple Query Wizard to create a query that includes the FirstName, LastName, DateJoined, and Phone fields (in that order) from the **Member** table. Name the query **MemberList**.

Explore

4. Sort the query results in descending order by the DateJoined field. (*Hint*: Use a tool-bar button.)
5. Print the query results, and then close and save the query.
6. Use the AutoForm: Columnar Wizard to create a form for the **Member** table. Save the form as **MemberInfo**, and then close it.
7. Use the AutoReport: Columnar Wizard to create a report based on the **Member** table. Maximize the Report window and change the Zoom setting to Fit.
8. Print just the first page of the report, and then close and save the report as **Members**.
9. Set the option for compacting the **Fitness** database on close. (*Note:* If you are work-ing from a floppy disk, check with your instructor or technical support staff to confirm that you should set this option.)
10. Close the Fitness database.

Case Problem 3

Challenge

Use what you've learned, and go a bit beyond, to work with a database that contains information about a zoo.

Data File needed for this Case Problem: Redwood.mdb

Redwood Zoo The Redwood Zoo is a small zoo located in the picturesque city of Gig Harbor, Washington, on the shores of Puget Sound. The zoo is ideally situated, with the natural beauty of the site providing the perfect backdrop for the zoo's varied exhibits. Although there are larger zoos in the greater Seattle area, the Redwood Zoo is considered to have some of the best exhibits of marine animals. The newly constructed polar bear habitat is a particular favorite among patrons.

Michael Rosenfeld is the director of fundraising activities for the Redwood Zoo. The zoo relies heavily on donations to fund both ongoing exhibits and temporary displays, espe-cially those involving exotic animals. Michael created an Access database named Redwood to keep track of information about donors, their pledges, and the status of funds. You'll help Michael maintain the Redwood database. Complete the following:

1. Open the **Redwood** database, which is located in the Brief\Case3 folder provided with your Data Files.

Explore

2. Use the "Type a question for help" box to ask the following question: "How do I rename an object?" Click the topic "Rename a database object" and read the dis-played information. Close the Microsoft Office Access Help window and the task pane. Then, in the Redwood database, rename the **Table1** table as **Donor**.
3. Open the **Donor** table, print the table datasheet, and then close the table.

Explore

4. Use the Simple Query Wizard to create a query that includes all the fields in the **Donor** table *except* the MI field. (*Hint:* Use the >> and < buttons to select the necessary fields.) Name the query **Donors**.

Explore

5. Sort the query results in descending order by the Class field. (*Hint:* Use a toolbar button.) Print the query results, and then close and save the query.

Explore

6. Use the AutoForm: Columnar Wizard to create a form for the **Fund** table. Open the Microsoft Access Help task pane. (*Hint:* Click Help on the menu bar, and then click Microsoft Office Access Help.) Type the keywords "find a specific record in a form" in the Search for text box, and then click the Start searching button. Select the topic "Find a record in a datasheet or form," then choose the topic related to finding a record by record number. Read the displayed information. Close the Microsoft Office Access Help window and the task pane. Use the record number box to move to record 7 (Polar Bear Park), and then print the form for the current record only. (*Hint:* Use the Selected Record(s) option in the Print dialog box to print the current record.) Save the form as **FundInfo**, and then close it.

7. Use the AutoReport: Columnar Wizard to create a report based on the **Donor** table. Maximize the Report window and change the Zoom setting to Fit.

Explore

8. Use the View menu to view all seven pages of the report at the same time in Print Preview.

9. Print just the first page of the report, and then close and save it as **Donors**.

10. Set the option for compacting the **Redwood** database on close. (*Note:* If you are working from a floppy disk, check with your instructor or technical support staff to confirm that you should set this option.)

Explore

11. Convert the **Redwood** database to Access 2002–2003 file format, saving the converted file as **Redwood2002** in the Brief\Case3 folder. Then convert the **Redwood** database to Access 97 file format, saving the converted file as **Redwood97** in the Brief\Case3 folder. Using Windows Explorer or My Computer, view the contents of your Brief\Case3 folder, and note the file sizes of the three versions of the Redwood database. Describe the results.

12. Close the Redwood database.

Case Problem 4

Challenge

Work with the skills you've learned, and explore some new skills, to manage the data for a luxury rental company.

Data File needed for this Case Problem: GEM.mdb

GEM Ultimate Vacations As guests of a friend, Griffin and Emma MacElroy spent two weeks at a magnificent villa in the south of France. This unforgettable experience stayed with them upon returning to their home in a suburb of Chicago, Illinois. As a result, they decided to open their own agency, GEM Ultimate Vacations, which specializes in locating and booking luxury rental properties, primarily in Europe. Recently, Griffin and Emma expanded their business to include properties in Africa as well.

From the beginning, Griffin and Emma used computers to help them manage all aspects of their business. They recently installed Access and created a database named GEM to store information about guests, properties, and reservations. You'll work with the GEM database to manage this information. Complete the following:

1. Open the **GEM** database located in the Brief\Case4 folder provided with your Data Files.

2. Open the **Guest** table.

Explore

3. Open the Microsoft Access Help task pane. (*Hint*: Click Help on the menu bar, and then click Microsoft Office Access Help.) Type the keyword "print" in the Search for text box, and then click the Start searching button. Scroll down the list, click the topic "Set page setup options for printing," and then click "For a table, query, form, or report." Read the displayed information. Close the Microsoft Office Access Help window and the task pane. Set the option for printing in landscape orientation, and then print the **Guest** table datasheet. Close the table.

4. Use the Simple Query Wizard to create a query that includes the GuestName, City, StateProv, and Phone fields (in that order) from the **Guest** table. Name the query **GuestInfo**.

Explore

5. Sort the query results in descending order by StateProv. (*Hint*: Use a toolbar button.)
6. Print the query results, and then close and save the query.

Explore

7. Use the AutoForm: Columnar Wizard to create a form for the **Guest** table. Use the Microsoft Access Help task pane to search for information on how to find a specific record in a form. Select the topic "Find a record in a datasheet or form in Access," then choose the topic related to finding a record by record number. Read the displayed information. Close the Microsoft Office Access Help window and the task pane. Use the record number box to move to record 16, and then print the form for the current record only. (*Hint*: Use the Selected Record(s) option in the Print dialog box to print the current record.) Save the form as **GuestInfo**, and then close it.

Explore

8. Use the AutoReport: Tabular Wizard to create a report based on the **Guest** table. Maximize the Report window and change the Zoom setting to Fit. Use the Two Pages button on the Print Preview toolbar to view both pages of the report in Print Preview. Print the first page of the report in landscape orientation, and then close and save the report as **Guests**.
9. Set the option for compacting the **GEM** database on close. (*Note*: If you are working from a floppy disk, check with your instructor or technical support staff to confirm that you should set this option.)

Explore

10. Convert the **GEM** database to Access 2002–2003 file format, saving the converted file as **GEM2002** in the Brief\Case4 folder. Then convert the **GEM** database to Access 97 file format, saving the converted file as **GEM97** in the Brief\Case4 folder. Using Windows Explorer or My Computer, view the contents of your Brief\Case4 folder, and note the file sizes of the three versions of the GEM database. Describe the results.
11. Close the GEM database.

Research

Use the Internet to find and work with data related to the topics presented in this tutorial.

Internet Assignments

The purpose of the Internet Assignments is to challenge you to find information on the Internet that you can use to work effectively with this software. The actual assignments are updated and maintained on the Course Technology Web site. Log on to the Internet and use your Web browser to go to the Student Online Companion for New Perspectives Office 2003 at **www.course.com/np/office2003**. Click the Internet Assignments link, and then navigate to the assignments for this tutorial.

Assess

SAM Assessment and Training

If your instructor has chosen to use the full online version of SAM 2003 Assessment and Training, you can go beyond the "just-in-time" training provided on the CD that accompanies this text. Simply log in to your SAM account (http://sam2003.course.com) to launch any assigned training activities or exams that relate to the skills covered in this tutorial.

Reinforce

Databases

Lab Assignments

The New Perspectives Labs are designed to help you master some of the key concepts and skills presented in this text. The steps for completing this Lab are located on the Course Technology Web site. Log on to the Internet and use your Web browser to go to the Student Online Companion for New Perspectives Office 2003 at **www.course.com/np/office2003**. Click the Lab Assignments link, and then navigate to the assignments for this tutorial.

Review

Quick Check Answers

Session 1.1

1. field
2. common field
3. primary key; foreign key
4. records; fields
5. current record symbol
6. Use the horizontal and vertical scroll bars to view fields or records not currently visible in the datasheet; use the navigation buttons to move vertically through the records.
7. Access saves changes to the active database to disk automatically, when a record is changed or added and when you close the database. You use the Save button in Access only to save changes to the design of an object, such as a table, or to the format of a datasheet—not to save the database file.

Session 1.2

1. query
2. primary key
3. AutoForm Wizard
4. The form displays each field name to the left of its field value, which appears in a box; the widths of the boxes represent the size of the fields.
5. Print Preview
6. Compacting

Creating and Maintaining a Database

Creating the Northeast Database, and Creating, Modifying, and Updating the Position Table

Case | Northeast Seasonal Jobs International (NSJI)

The Seasonal database contains two tables—the Employer table and the NAICS table. These tables store data about NSJI's employer customers and the NAICS codes for pertinent job positions, respectively. Elsa Jensen also wants to track information about each position that is available at each employer's place of business. This information includes the position title and wage. Elsa asks you to create a third table, named Position, in which to store the position data.

Because this is your first time creating a new table, Elsa suggests that you first create a new database, named "Northeast," and then create the new Position table in this database. This will keep the Seasonal database intact. Once the Position table is completed, you then can import the Employer and NAICS tables from the Seasonal database into your new Northeast database.

Some of the position data Elsa needs is already stored in another NSJI database. After creating the Position table and adding some records to it, you'll copy the records from the other database into the Position table. Then you'll maintain the Position table by modifying it and updating it to meet Elsa's specific data requirements.

Session	Objectives		SAM Training Tasks	
Session 2.1	• Learn the guidelines for designing databases and setting field properties • Create a new database	• Create and save a table • Define fields and specify a table's primary key	• Change the format property of a field in Table Design view • Create a new database • Create a table using the Table Wizard • Create databases using the Database Wizard • Create one or more tables in Design view	• Define date/time and yes/no fields • Define number and currency fields • Define text fields • Specify a default value • Specify a multi-field primary key • Specify a required field • Specify the primary key
Session 2.2	• Add records to a table • Modify the structure of a table • Delete, move, and add fields • Change field properties • Update field property changes	• Copy records and import tables from another Access database • Delete and change records	• Add a field to a table structure • Add a field to a table between other fields • Delete a field from a table structure • Delete records from a table using a datasheet • Edit records from a table using a datasheet • Enter records into a datasheet table	• Format a table or query datasheet for display • Import a table from another Access database • Modify field properties for one or more tables in Table Design view • Move a field in a table structure • Resize to best fit • Use the New Record button to add a record

Student Data Files   For a complete list of the Data Files needed for this tutorial, see page AC 2.

Session 2.1

For hands-on practice of key tasks in this session, go to the SAM 2003 Training Companion CD included with this text.

Guidelines for Designing Databases

A database management system can be a useful tool, but only if you first carefully design the database so that it meets the needs of its users. In database design, you determine the fields, tables, and relationships needed to satisfy the data and processing requirements. When you design a database, you should follow these guidelines:

- **Identify all the fields needed to produce the required information.** For example, Elsa needs information about employers, NAICS codes, and positions. Figure 2-1 shows the fields that satisfy these information requirements.

| Figure 2-1 | Elsa's data requirements |

EmployerID	ContactFirstName
PositionID	ContactLastName
PositionTitle	Position
EmployerName	Wage
Address	HoursPerWeek
City	NAICSCode
StateProv	NAICSDesc
PostalCode	StartDate
Country	EndDate
Phone	ReferredBy
Openings	Website

- **Group related fields into tables.** For example, Elsa grouped the fields relating to employers into the Employer table and the fields related to NAICS codes into the NAICS table. The other fields are grouped logically into the Position table, which you will create, as shown in Figure 2-2.

| Figure 2-2 | Elsa's fields grouped into tables |

Employer table	NAICS table	Position table
EmployerID	NAICSCode	PositionID
EmployerName	NAICSDesc	PositionTitle
Address		Wage
City		HoursPerWeek
StateProv		Openings
PostalCode		ReferredBy
Country		StartDate
ContactFirstName		EndDate
ContactLastName		
Position		
Phone		
Website		

- **Determine each table's primary key.** Recall that a primary key uniquely identifies each record in a table. Although a primary key is not mandatory in Access, it's usually a good idea to include one in each table. Without a primary key, selecting the exact record that you want can be a problem. For some tables, one of the fields, such as a Social Security or credit card number, naturally serves the function of a primary key. For other tables, two or more fields might be needed to function as the primary key. In these cases, the primary key is referred to as a **composite key**. For example, a school grade table would use a combination of student number and course code to serve as the primary key. For a third category of tables, no single field or combination of fields can uniquely identify a record in a table. In these cases, you need to add a field whose sole purpose is to serve as the table's primary key. For Elsa's tables, EmployerID is the primary key for the Employer table, NAICSCode is the primary key for the NAICS table, and PositionID will be the primary key for the Position table.

- **Include a common field in related tables.** You use the common field to connect one table logically with another table. For example, Elsa's Employer and Position tables will include the EmployerID field as a common field. Recall that when you include the primary key from one table as a field in a second table to form a relationship, the field is called a foreign key in the second table; therefore, the EmployerID field will be a foreign key in the Position table. With this common field, Elsa can find all positions available at a particular employer; she can use the EmployerID value for an employer and search the Position table for all records with that EmployerID value. Likewise, she can determine which employer has a particular position available by searching the Employer table to find the one record with the same EmployerID value as the corresponding value in the Position table.

- **Avoid data redundancy.** When you store the same data in more than one place, **data redundancy** occurs. With the exception of common fields to connect tables, you should avoid redundancy because it wastes storage space and can cause inconsistencies, if, for instance, you type a field value one way in one table and a different way in the same table or in a second table. Figure 2-3, which contains portions of potential data to be stored in the Employer and Position tables, shows an example of incorrect database design that has data redundancy in the Position table; the EmployerName field is redundant, and one value was entered incorrectly, in three different ways.

Incorrect database design with data redundancy ◀ **Figure 2-3**

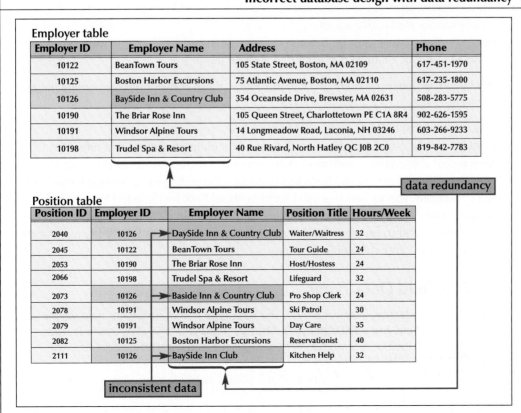

Employer table

Employer ID	Employer Name	Address	Phone
10122	BeanTown Tours	105 State Street, Boston, MA 02109	617-451-1970
10125	Boston Harbor Excursions	75 Atlantic Avenue, Boston, MA 02110	617-235-1800
10126	BaySide Inn & Country Club	354 Oceanside Drive, Brewster, MA 02631	508-283-5775
10190	The Briar Rose Inn	105 Queen Street, Charlottetown PE C1A 8R4	902-626-1595
10191	Windsor Alpine Tours	14 Longmeadow Road, Laconia, NH 03246	603-266-9233
10198	Trudel Spa & Resort	40 Rue Rivard, North Hatley QC J0B 2C0	819-842-7783

data redundancy

Position table

Position ID	Employer ID	Employer Name	Position Title	Hours/Week
2040	10126	DaySide Inn & Country Club	Waiter/Waitress	32
2045	10122	BeanTown Tours	Tour Guide	24
2053	10190	The Briar Rose Inn	Host/Hostess	24
2066	10198	Trudel Spa & Resort	Lifeguard	32
2073	10126	Baside Inn & Country Club	Pro Shop Clerk	24
2078	10191	Windsor Alpine Tours	Ski Patrol	30
2079	10191	Windsor Alpine Tours	Day Care	35
2082	10125	Boston Harbor Excursions	Reservationist	40
2111	10126	BaySide Inn Club	Kitchen Help	32

inconsistent data

- **Determine the properties of each field.** You need to identify the **properties**, or characteristics, of each field so that the DBMS knows how to store, display, and process the field values. These properties include the field's name, maximum number of characters or digits, description, valid values, and other field characteristics. You will learn more about field properties later in this tutorial.

The Position table you need to create will contain the fields shown in Figure 2-2, plus the EmployerID field as a foreign key. Before you create the new Northeast database and the Position table, you first need to learn some guidelines for setting field properties.

Guidelines for Setting Field Properties

As just noted, the last step of database design is to determine which values to assign to the properties, such as the name and data type, of each field. When you select or enter a value for a property, you **set** the property. Access has rules for naming fields, choosing data types, and setting other properties for fields.

Naming Fields and Objects

You must name each field, table, and other object in an Access database. Access then stores these items in the database, using the names you supply. It's best to choose a field or object name that describes the purpose or contents of the field or object, so that later you can easily remember what the name represents. For example, the three tables in the Northeast database will be named Employer, NAICS, and Position, because these names suggest their contents.

The following rules apply to naming fields and objects in Access:

- A name can be up to 64 characters long.
- A name can contain letters, numbers, spaces, and special characters, except for a period (.), exclamation mark (!), accent grave (`), and square brackets ([ ]).
- A name cannot start with a space.
- A table or query name must be unique within a database. A field name must be unique within a table, but it can be used again in another table.

In addition, experienced users of databases follow these conventions for naming fields and objects:

- Capitalize the first letter of each word in the name.
- Avoid extremely long names because they are difficult to remember and reference.
- Use standard abbreviations, such as Num for Number, Amt for Amount, and Qty for Quantity.
- Avoid using spaces or special characters in names. According to standard database naming conventions, spaces and special characters should not be included in names. However, you can change how a field name is displayed in database objects—tables, forms, reports, and so on—by setting the field's Caption property. (You'll learn about setting the Caption property later in this tutorial.)

Assigning Field Data Types

You must assign a data type for each field. The **data type** determines what field values you can enter for the field and what other properties the field will have. For example, the Position table will include a StartDate field, which will store date values, so you will assign the date/time data type to this field. Then Access will allow you to enter and manipulate only dates or times as values in the StartDate field.

Figure 2-4 lists the 10 data types available in Access, describes the field values allowed for each data type, explains when you should use each data type, and indicates the field size of each data type.

Data types for fields ◄ **Figure 2-4**

Data Type	Description	Field Size
Text	Allows field values containing letters, digits, spaces, and special characters. Use for names, addresses, descriptions, and fields containing digits that are not used in calculations.	0 to 255 characters; 50 characters default
Memo	Allows field values containing letters, digits, spaces, and special characters. Use for long comments and explanations.	1 to 65,535 characters; exact size is determined by entry
Number	Allows positive and negative numbers as field values. Numbers can contain digits, a decimal point, commas, a plus sign, and a minus sign. Use for fields that you will use in calculations, except calculations involving money.	1 to 15 digits
Date/Time	Allows field values containing valid dates and times from January 1, 100 to December 31, 9999. Dates can be entered in mm/dd/yy (month, day, year) format, several other date formats, or a variety of time formats, such as 10:35 PM. You can perform calculations on dates and times, and you can sort them. For example, you can determine the number of days between two dates.	8 bytes
Currency	Allows field values similar to those for the number data type. Unlike calculations with number data type decimal values, calculations performed using the currency data type are not subject to round-off error.	Accurate to 15 digits on the left side of the decimal separator and to 4 digits on the right side
AutoNumber	Consists of integers with values controlled by Access. Access automatically inserts a value in the field as each new record is created. You can specify sequential numbering or random numbering, which guarantees a unique field value, so that such a field can serve as a table's primary key.	9 digits
Yes/No	Limits field values to yes and no, on and off, or true and false. Use for fields that indicate the presence or absence of a condition, such as whether an order has been filled or whether an employee is eligible for the company dental plan.	1 character
OLE Object	Allows field values that are created in other programs as objects, such as photographs, video images, graphics, drawings, sound recordings, voice-mail messages, spreadsheets, and word-processing documents. These objects can be linked or embedded.	1 gigabyte maximum; exact size depends on object size
Hyperlink	Consists of text used as a hyperlink address. A hyperlink address can have up to three parts: the text that appears in a field or control; the path to a file or page; and a location within the file or page. Hyperlinks help you to connect your application easily to the Internet or an intranet.	Up to 64,000 characters total for the three parts of a hyperlink data type
Lookup Wizard	Creates a field that lets you look up a value in another table or in a predefined list of values.	Same size as the primary key field used to perform the lookup

Setting Field Sizes

The **Field Size property** defines a field value's maximum storage size for text, number, and AutoNumber fields only. The other data types have no Field Size property because their storage size is either a fixed, predetermined amount or is determined automatically by the field value itself, as shown in Figure 2-4. A text field has a default field size of 50 characters; you can also set its field size by entering a number from 0 to 255. For example, the PositionTitle and ReferredBy fields in the Position table will be text fields with a size of 30 characters each. This field size will accommodate the values that will be entered in each of these fields (titles and names, respectively).

When you use the number data type to define a field, you should set the field's Field Size property based on the largest value that you expect to store in that field. Access processes smaller data sizes faster, using less memory, so you can optimize your database's performance and its storage space by selecting the correct field size for each field. For example, it would be wasteful to use the Long Integer setting when defining a field that will store only whole numbers ranging from 0 to 255, because the Long Integer setting will use four bytes of storage space. A better choice would be the Byte setting, which uses one byte of storage space to store the same values. Field Size property settings for number fields are as follows:

- **Byte:** Stores whole numbers (numbers with no fractions) from 0 to 255 in one byte
- **Integer:** Stores whole numbers from −32,768 to 32,767 in two bytes
- **Long Integer** (default)**:** Stores whole numbers from −2,147,483,648 to 2,147,483,647 in four bytes
- **Single:** Stores positive and negative numbers to precisely seven decimal places and uses four bytes
- **Double:** Stores positive and negative numbers to precisely 15 decimal places and uses eight bytes
- **Replication ID:** Establishes a unique identifier for replication of tables, records, and other objects and uses 16 bytes
- **Decimal:** Stores positive and negative numbers to precisely 28 decimal places and uses 12 bytes

Setting Field Captions

The **Caption property** specifies how a field name will appear in datasheets and in other database objects, such as forms and reports. If you don't specify a caption, Access uses the field name as the default column heading in datasheets and as the default label in forms and reports. Because field names should not include spaces, some names might be difficult to read. For example, the Position table will include a field named "HoursPerWeek." This name looks awkward and might be confusing to users of the database. By setting the Caption property for this field to "Hours/Week," you can improve the readability of the field name displayed.

Elsa documented the design for the new Position table by listing each field's name, data type, size (if applicable), caption (if applicable), and description, as shown in Figure 2-5. Note that Elsa assigned the text data type to the PositionID, PositionTitle, EmployerID, and ReferredBy fields; the currency data type to the Wage field; the number data type to the HoursPerWeek and Openings fields; and the date/time data type to the StartDate and EndDate fields.

Figure 2-5	Design for the Position table

Field Name	Data Type	Field Size	Caption	Description
PositionID	Text	4	Position ID	Primary key
PositionTitle	Text	30	Position Title	
EmployerID	Text	5	Employer ID	Foreign key
Wage	Currency			Rate per hour
HoursPerWeek	Number	Integer	Hours/Week	Work hours per week
Openings	Number	Integer		Number of openings
ReferredBy	Text	30	Referred By	
StartDate	Date/Time		Start Date	Month/day/year
EndDate	Date/Time		End Date	Month/day/year

With Elsa's design in place, you're ready to create the new Northeast database and the Position table.

Creating a New Database

Access provides different ways for you to create a new database: you can use a Database Wizard, create a blank database, copy an existing database file, or use one of the database templates available on the Microsoft Web site. When you use a **Database Wizard**, the wizard guides you through the database creation process and provides the necessary tables, forms, and reports for the type of database you choose—all in one operation. Using a Database Wizard is an easy way to start creating a database, but only if your data requirements closely match one of the supplied templates. When you choose to create a blank database, you need to add all the tables, forms, reports, and other objects after you create the database file. Creating a blank database provides the most flexibility, allowing you to define objects in the way that you want, but it does require that you define each object separately. Whichever method you choose, you can always modify or add to your database after you create it.

The following steps outline the process for creating a new database using a Database Wizard:

1. If necessary, click the New button on the Database toolbar to display the New File task pane.
2. In the Templates section of the task pane, click the "On my computer" option. The Templates dialog box opens.
3. Click the Databases tab, and then choose the Database Wizard that most closely matches the type of database you want to create. Click the OK button.
4. In the File New Database dialog box, choose the location in which to save the new database, specify its name, and then click the Create button.
5. Complete each of the wizard dialog boxes, clicking the Next button to move through them after making your selections.
6. Click the Finish button when you have completed all the wizard dialog boxes.

None of the Database Wizards matches the requirements of the new Northeast database, so you'll use the Blank Database option to create it.

To create the Northeast database:

1. Start Access, and make sure your Data Files are in the proper location.
2. In the Open section of the Getting Started task pane, click **Create a new file**. The New File task pane is displayed.
3. Click **Blank database**. The File New Database dialog box opens. This dialog box is similar to the Open dialog box.
4. Click the **Save in** list arrow, and then click the drive that contains your Data Files.
5. Navigate to the **Brief\Tutorial** folder, and then click the **Open** button.
6. In the File name text box, double-click the text **db1** to select it, and then type **Northeast**.

   Trouble? If your File name text box contains an entry other than "db1," select whatever text is in this text box, and continue with the steps.
7. Click the **Create** button. Access creates the Northeast database in the Brief\Tutorial folder included with your Data Files, and then displays the Database window for the new database with the Tables object selected.

Now you can create the Position table in the Northeast database.

Creating a Table

Creating a table involves naming the fields and defining the properties for the fields, specifying a primary key for the table, and then saving the table structure. You will use Elsa's design (Figure 2-5) as a guide for creating the Position table in the Northeast database.

To begin creating the Position table:

▶ 1. Click the **New** button in the Database window. The New Table dialog box opens. See Figure 2-6.

Figure 2-6 ▶ **New Table dialog box**

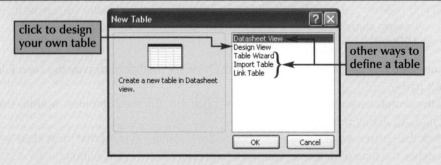

Trouble? If the New File task pane opens, you clicked the New button on the Database toolbar instead of the New button in the Database window. Click the Close button to close the task pane, and then repeat Step 1.

In Access, you can create a table from entered data (Datasheet View), define your own table (Design View), use a wizard to automate the table creation process (Table Wizard), or use a wizard to import or link data from another database or other data source (Import Table or Link Table). For the Position table, you will define your own table.

▶ 2. Click **Design View** in the list box, and then click the **OK** button. The Table window opens in Design view. (Note that you can also double-click the "Create table in Design view" option in the Database window to open the Table window in Design view.) See Figure 2-7.

Table window in Design view ◀ Figure 2-7

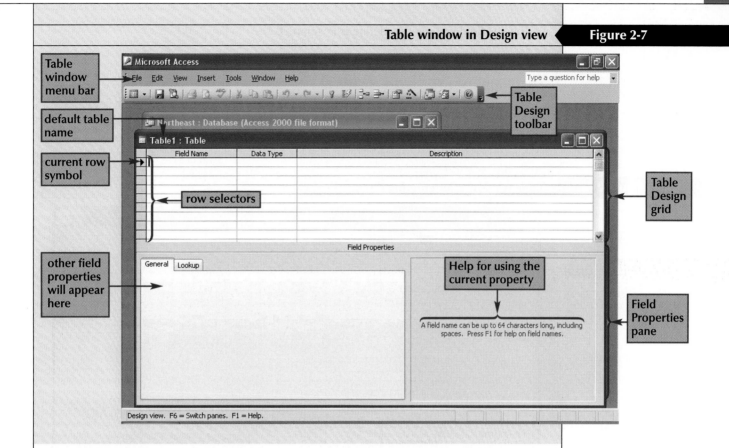

You use **Design view** to define or modify a table structure or the properties of the fields in a table. If you create a table without using a wizard, you enter the fields and their properties for your table directly in the Table window in Design view.

Defining Fields

Initially, the default table name, Table1, appears on the Table window title bar, the current row symbol is positioned in the first row selector of the Table Design grid, and the insertion point is located in the first row's Field Name text box. The purpose or characteristics of the current property (Field Name, in this case) appear in the right side of the Field Properties pane. You can display more complete Help information about the current property by pressing the **F1 key**.

You enter values for the Field Name, Data Type, and Description field properties in the Table Design grid. You select values for all other field properties, most of which are optional, in the Field Properties pane. These other properties will appear when you move to the first row's Data Type text box.

Defining a Field in a Table

Reference Window

- In the Database window, select the table, and then click the Design button to open the Table window in Design view.
- Type the field name.
- Select the data type.
- Type or select other field properties, as appropriate.

The first field you need to define is PositionID.

To define the PositionID field:

▶ 1. Type **PositionID** in the first row's Field Name text box, and then press the **Tab** key (or press the **Enter** key) to advance to the Data Type text box. The default data type, Text, appears highlighted in the Data Type text box, which now also contains a list arrow, and field properties for a text field appear in the Field Properties pane. See Figure 2-8.

Figure 2-8 | **Table window after entering the first field name**

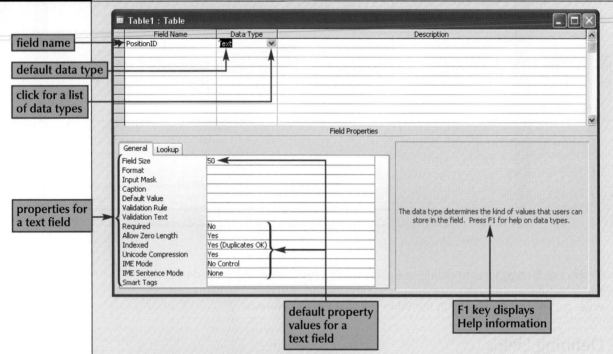

Notice that the right side of the Field Properties pane now provides an explanation for the current property, Data Type. You can display Help information about the current property by pressing the F1 key.

Trouble? If you make a typing error, you can correct it by clicking to position the insertion point, and then using either the Backspace key to delete characters to the left of the insertion point or the Delete key to delete characters to the right of the insertion point. Then type the correct text.

Because the PositionID numbers will not be used in calculations, you will assign the text data type (as opposed to the number data type) to the PositionID field.

▶ 2. Press the **Tab** key to accept Text as the data type and to advance to the Description text box.

Next you'll enter the Description property value as "Primary key." You can use the **Description property** to enter an optional description for a field to explain its purpose or usage. A field's Description property can be up to 255 characters long, and its value appears on the status bar when you view the table datasheet. Note that specifying "Primary key" for the Description property does *not* establish the current field as the primary key; you use a toolbar button to specify the primary key, which you will do later in this session.

3. Type **Primary key** in the Description text box.

Notice the Field Size property for the text field. The default setting of "50" is displayed. You need to change this number to "4" because all PositionID values at NSJI contain only 4 digits.

4. Double-click the number **50** in the Field Size property box to select it, and then type **4**.

By default, the Caption property for a field is blank. You need to set this property for the PositionID field to display "Position ID" as the column or label name in tables, forms, reports, and so on. (Refer to the Access Help system for a complete description of all the properties available for the different data types.)

5. Click to position the insertion point in the Caption property box, and then type **Position ID**. The definition of the first field is completed. See Figure 2-9.

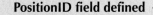

PositionID field defined Figure 2-9

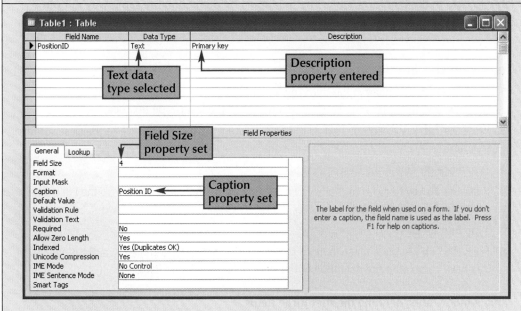

Elsa's Position table design shows PositionTitle as the second field. You will define PositionTitle as a text field with a Field Size of 30, which is a sufficient length for any title values that will be entered. You'll also set the Caption property for this field.

To define the PositionTitle field:

1. In the Table Design grid, place the insertion point in the second row's Field Name text box, type **PositionTitle** in the text box, and then press the **Tab** key to advance to the Data Type text box.

2. Press the **Tab** key to accept Text as the field's data type.

According to Elsa's design (Figure 2-5), you do not need to enter a description for this field. If you've assigned a descriptive field name and the field does not fulfill a special function (such as primary key), you usually do not enter a value for the optional Description property. PositionTitle is a field that does not require a value for its Description property.

Next, you'll change the Field Size property to 30. Note that when defining the fields in a table, you can move between the Table Design grid and the Field Properties pane of the Table window by pressing the **F6 key**.

▶ **3.** Press the **F6** key to move to the Field Properties pane. The current entry for the Field Size property, 50, is highlighted.

▶ **4.** Type **30** to set the Field Size property.

Finally, you need to set the Caption property for the field. In addition to clicking to position the insertion point in a property's box, you can press the Tab key to move from one property to the next.

▶ **5.** Press the **Tab** key three times to move to the Caption property, and then type **Position Title**. You have completed the definition of the second field.

The third field in the Position table is the EmployerID field. Recall that this field will serve as the foreign key in the Position table, allowing you to relate data from the Position table to data in the Employer table. The field must be defined in the same way in both tables—that is, a text field with a field size of 5.

To define the EmployerID field:

▶ **1.** Place the insertion point in the third row's Field Name text box, type **EmployerID** in the text box, and then press the **Tab** key to advance to the Data Type text box.

▶ **2.** Press the **Tab** key to accept Text as the field's data type and to advance to the Description text box.

▶ **3.** Type **Foreign key** in the Description text box.

▶ **4.** Press the **F6** key to move to the Field Properties pane. The current entry for the Field Size property, 50, is highlighted.

▶ **5.** Type **5** to set the Field Size property.

▶ **6.** Press the **Tab** key three times to move to the Caption property, and then type **Employer ID**. You have completed the definition of the third field. See Figure 2-10.

Figure 2-10	Table window after defining the first three fields

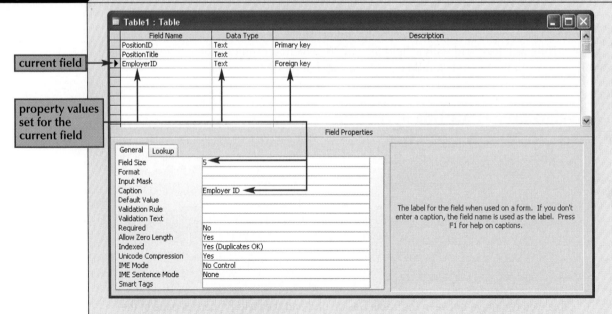

The fourth field is the Wage field, which will display values in the currency format.

To define the Wage field:

1. Place the insertion point in the fourth row's Field Name text box, type **Wage** in the text box, and then press the **Tab** key to advance to the Data Type text box.

2. Click the **Data Type** list arrow, click **Currency** in the list box, and then press the **Tab** key to advance to the Description text box.

3. Type **Rate per hour** in the Description text box.

   Elsa wants the Wage field values to be displayed with two decimal places, and she does not want any value to be displayed by default for new records. So, you need to set the Decimal Places and Default Value properties accordingly. The **Decimal Places property** specifies the number of decimal places that will be displayed to the right of the decimal point.

4. Click the **Decimal Places** text box to position the insertion point there. A list arrow appears on the right side of the Decimal Places text box.

   When you position the insertion point or select text in many Access text boxes, Access displays a list arrow, which you can click to display a list box with options. You can display the list arrow and the list box simultaneously if you click the text box near its right side.

5. Click the **Decimal Places** list arrow, and then click **2** in the list box to specify two decimal places for the Wage field values.

   Next, notice the **Default Value property**, which specifies the value that will be automatically entered into the field when you add a new record. Currently this property has a setting of 0. Elsa wants the Wage field to be empty (that is, to contain *no* default value) when a new record is added. Therefore, you need to delete the 0 so that Access, by default, will display no value in the Wage field for a new record.

6. Select **0** in the Default Value text box either by dragging the pointer or double-clicking the mouse, and then press the **Delete** key.

The next two fields in the Position table—HoursPerWeek and Openings—are number fields with a field size of Integer. Also, for each of these fields, Elsa wants the values displayed with no decimal places, and she does not want a default value displayed for the fields when new records are added. You'll define these two fields next.

To define the HoursPerWeek and Openings fields:

1. Position the insertion point in the fifth row's Field Name text box, type **HoursPerWeek** in the text box, and then press the **Tab** key to advance to the Data Type text box.

2. Click the **Data Type** list arrow, click **Number** in the list box, and then press the **Tab** key to advance to the Description text box.

3. Type **Work hours per week** in the Description text box.

4. Click the right side of the **Field Size** text box, and then click **Integer** to choose this setting. Recall that the Integer field size stores whole numbers in two bytes.

5. Click the right side of the **Decimal Places** text box, and then click **0** to specify no decimal places.

6. Move to the Caption property, and then type **Hours/Week**.

7. Select the value **0** in the Default Value text box, and then press the **Delete** key.

8. Repeat the preceding steps to define the **Openings** field as the sixth field in the Position table. For the Description, enter the text **Number of openings**. You do not have to set the Caption property for the Openings field.

According to Elsa's design (Figure 2-5), the final three fields to be defined in the Position table are ReferredBy, a text field, and StartDate and EndDate, both date/time fields. You'll define these three fields next.

To define the ReferredBy, StartDate, and EndDate fields:

1. Position the insertion point in the seventh row's Field Name text box, type **ReferredBy** in the text box, press the **Tab** key to advance to the Data Type text box, and then press the **Tab** key again to accept the default Text data type.

2. Change the default Field Size of 50 to **30** for the ReferredBy field.

3. Set the Caption property for the field to **Referred By**.

4. Position the insertion point in the eighth row's Field Name text box, type **StartDate**, and then press the **Tab** key to advance to the Data Type text box.

5. Click the **Data Type** list arrow, click **Date/Time** to select this type, press the **Tab** key, and then type **Month/day/year** in the Description text box.

Elsa wants the values in the StartDate field to be displayed in a format showing the month, the day, and a four-digit year, as in the following example: 03/11/2006. You use the Format property to control the display of a field value.

6. In the Field Properties pane, click the right side of the **Format** text box to display the list of predefined formats. As noted in the right side of the Field Properties pane, you can either choose a predefined format or enter a custom format.

Trouble? If you see a list arrow instead of a list of predefined formats, click the list arrow to display the list.

None of the predefined formats matches the exact layout Elsa wants for the StartDate values. Therefore, you need to create a custom date format. Figure 2-11 shows some of the symbols available for custom date and time formats. (A complete description of all the custom formats is available in Help.)

Figure 2-11	Symbols for some custom date formats

Symbol	Description
/	date separator
d	day of the month in one or two numeric digits, as needed (1 to 31)
dd	day of the month in two numeric digits (01 to 31)
ddd	first three letters of the weekday (Sun to Sat)
dddd	full name of the weekday (Sunday to Saturday)
w	day of the week (1 to 7)
ww	week of the year (1 to 53)
m	month of the year in one or two numeric digits, as needed (1 to 12)
mm	month of the year in two numeric digits (01 to 12)
mmm	first three letters of the month (Jan to Dec)
mmmm	full name of the month (January to December)
yy	last two digits of the year (01 to 99)
yyyy	full year (0100 to 9999)

Elsa wants the dates to be displayed with a two-digit month (mm), a two-digit day (dd), and a four-digit year (yyyy). You'll enter this custom format now.

7. Click the **Format** list arrow to close the list of predefined formats, and then type **mm/dd/yyyy**. See Figure 2-12.

Specifying the custom date format | **Figure 2-12**

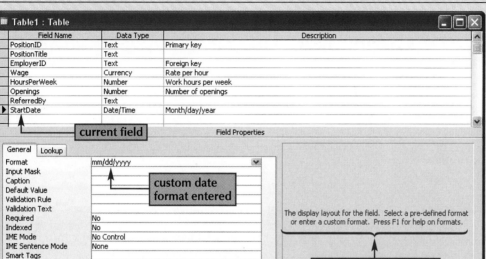

8. Set the Caption property for the field to **Start Date**.

Next, you'll define the ninth and final field, EndDate. This field will have the same definition and properties as the StartDate field.

9. Place the insertion point in the ninth row's Field Name text box, type **EndDate**, and then press the **Tab** key to advance to the Data Type text box.

You can select a value from the Data Type list box as you did for the StartDate field. Alternately, you can type the property value in the text box or type just the first character of the property value.

10. Type **d**. The value in the ninth row's Data Type text box changes to "date/Time," with the letters "ate/Time" highlighted. See Figure 2-13.

| Figure 2-13 | Selecting a value for the Data Type property |

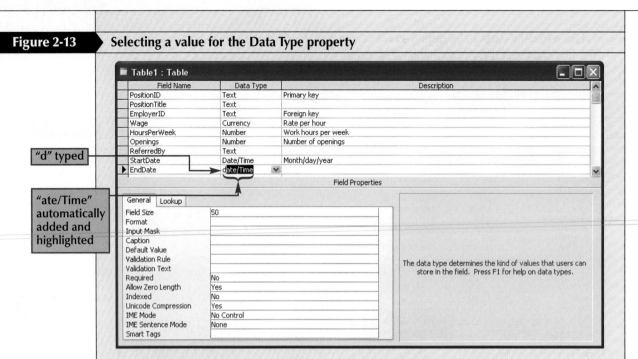

11. Press the **Tab** key to advance to the Description text box, and then type **Month/day/year**. Note that Access changes the value for the Data Type property to Date/Time.

12. In the Format text box, type **mm/dd/yyyy** to specify the custom date format for the EndDate field.

13. Set the Caption property for the field to **End Date**.

You've finished defining the fields for the Position table. Next, you need to specify the primary key for the table.

Specifying the Primary Key

Although Access does not require a table to have a primary key, including a primary key offers several advantages:

- A primary key uniquely identifies each record in a table.
- Access does not allow duplicate values in the primary key field. If a record already exists with a PositionID value of 1320, for example, Access prevents you from adding another record with this same value in the PositionID field. Preventing duplicate values ensures the uniqueness of the primary key field.
- When a primary key has been specified, Access forces you to enter a value for the primary key field in every record in the table. This is known as **entity integrity**. If you do not enter a value for a field, you have actually given the field what is known as a **null value**. You cannot give a null value to the primary key field because entity integrity prevents Access from accepting and processing that record.
- Access stores records on disk in the same order as you enter them but displays them in order by the field values of the primary key. If you enter records in no specific order, you are ensured that you will later be able to work with them in a more meaningful, primary key sequence.
- Access responds faster to your requests for specific records based on the primary key.

Specifying a Primary Key for a Table

- In the Table window in Design view, click the row selector for the field you've chosen to be the primary key.
- If the primary key will consist of two or more fields, press and hold down the Ctrl key, and then click the row selector for each additional primary key field.
- Click the Primary Key button on the Table Design toolbar.

According to Elsa's design, you need to specify PositionID as the primary key for the Position table.

To specify PositionID as the primary key:

1. Position the pointer on the row selector for the PositionID field until the pointer changes to a ➡ shape. See Figure 2-14.

Specifying PositionID as the primary key | **Figure 2-14**

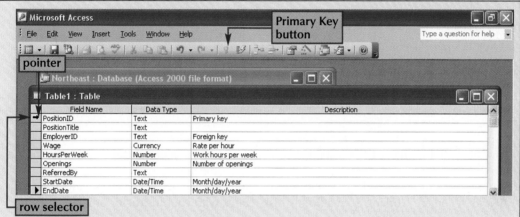

2. Click the mouse button. The entire first row of the Table Design grid is highlighted.
3. Click the **Primary Key** button 🔑 on the Table Design toolbar, and then click a row other than the first to deselect the first row. A key symbol appears in the row selector for the first row, indicating that the PositionID field is the table's primary key. See Figure 2-15.

PositionID selected as the primary key | **Figure 2-15**

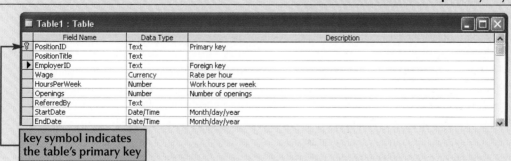

If you specify the wrong field as the primary key, or if you later change your mind and do not want the designated primary key field to be the table's primary key, you can select the field and then click the Primary Key button on the Table Design toolbar again, which will remove the key symbol and the primary key designation from the field. Then you can choose another field to be the primary key, if necessary.

You've defined the fields for the Position table and specified its primary key, so you can now save the table structure.

Saving the Table Structure

The last step in creating a table is to name the table and save the table's structure on disk. Once the table is saved, you can use it to enter data in the table.

Reference Window	**Saving a Table Structure**

- Click the Save button on the Table Design toolbar.
- Type the name of the table in the Table Name text box of the Save As dialog box.
- Click the OK button (or press the Enter key).

According to Elsa's plan, you need to save the table you've defined as "Position."

To name and save the Position table:

▶ 1. Click the **Save** button 🖫 on the Table Design toolbar. The Save As dialog box opens.

▶ 2. Type **Position** in the Table Name text box, and then press the **Enter** key. Access saves the table with the name Position in the Northeast database. Notice that Position now appears instead of Table1 in the Table window title bar.

Recall that in Tutorial 1 you set the Compact on Close option for the Seasonal database so that it would be compacted automatically each time you closed it. Now you'll set this option for your new Northeast database, so that it will be compacted automatically. (*Note*: If you are working from a floppy disk, check with your instructor or technical support staff to confirm that you should set this option.)

To set the option for compacting the Northeast database automatically:

▶ 1. Click **Tools** on the menu bar, and then click **Options**. The Options dialog box opens.

▶ 2. Click the **General** tab in the dialog box, and then click the **Compact on Close** check box to select it.

▶ 3. Click the **OK** button to set the option.

The Position table is now complete. In Session 2.2, you'll continue to work with the Position table by entering records in it, modifying its structure, and maintaining data in the table. You will also import two tables, Employer and NAICS, from the Seasonal database into the Northeast database.

Session 2.1 Quick Check

Review

1. What guidelines should you follow when designing a database?
2. What is the purpose of the Data Type property for a field?
3. For which three types of fields can you assign a field size?
4. You use the _____ property to specify how a field name appears in datasheets, forms, and reports.
5. In Design view, which key do you press to move between the Table Design grid and the Field Properties pane?
6. A(n) _____ value, which results when you do not enter a value for a field, is not permitted for a primary key.

To reinforce the tasks you learned in this session, go to the SAM 2003 Training Companion CD included with this text.

Session 2.2

Adding Records to a Table

You can add records to an Access table in several ways. A table datasheet provides a simple way for you to add records. As you learned in Tutorial 1, a datasheet shows a table's contents in rows and columns. Each row is a separate record in the table, and each column contains the field values for one field in the table. If you are currently working in Design view, you first must change from Design view to Datasheet view in order to view the table's datasheet.

Elsa asks you to add the two records shown in Figure 2-16 to the Position table. These two records contain data for positions that have recently become available at two employers.

For hands-on practice of key tasks in this session, go to the SAM 2003 Training Companion CD included with this text.

| **Records to be added to the Position table** | | **Figure 2-16** |

PositionID	PositionTitle	EmployerID	Wage	HoursPerWeek	Openings	ReferredBy	StartDate	EndDate
2021	Waiter/Waitress	10155	9.50	30	1	Sue Brown	6/30/2006	9/15/2006
2017	Tour Guide	10149	15.00	20	1	Ed Curran	9/21/2006	11/1/2006

To add the records in the Position table datasheet:

1. If you took a break after the previous session, make sure that Access is running and that the Position table of the Northeast database is open in Design view. To open the table in Design view from the Database window, right-click the **Position** table, and then click **Design View** on the shortcut menu.

   Access displays the fields you defined for the Position table in Design view. Now you need to switch to Datasheet view so that you can enter the two records for Elsa.

2. Click the **View** button for Datasheet view 🔲 on the Table Design toolbar. The Table window opens in Datasheet view. See Figure 2-17.

Figure 2-17 | **Table window in Datasheet view**

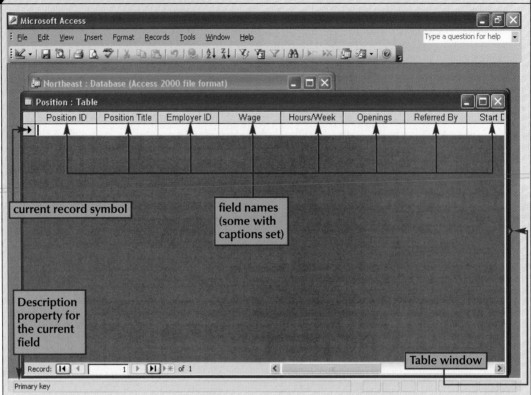

The table's nine fields appear at the top of the datasheet, with captions displayed for those fields whose Caption property you set. Some of the field names might not be visible, depending on the size of your monitor. The current record symbol in the first row's record selector identifies the currently selected record, which contains no data until you enter the first record. The insertion point is located in the first row's PositionID field, whose Description property appears on the status bar.

3. Type **2021**, which is the first record's PositionID field value, and then press the **Tab** key. Each time you press the Tab key, the insertion point moves to the right to the next field in the record. See Figure 2-18.

Datasheet for Position table after entering the first field value Figure 2-18

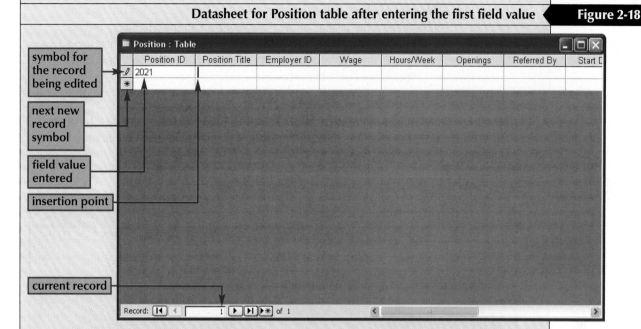

Trouble? If you make a mistake when typing a value, use the Backspace key to delete characters to the left of the insertion point or the Delete key to delete characters to the right of the insertion point. Then type the correct value. If you want to correct a value by replacing it entirely, drag to select the value, and then type the correct value.

The **pencil symbol** in the first row's record selector indicates that the record is being edited. The **star symbol** in the second row's record selector identifies the second row as the next one available for a new record. Notice that all the fields are initially empty; this occurs because you set the Default Value property for the fields (as appropriate) to remove any values and leave them blank.

4. Type **Waiter/Waitress** in the PositionTitle field, and then press the **Tab** key. The insertion point moves to the EmployerID field.

5. Type **10155** and then press the **Tab** key. The insertion point moves to the right side of the Wage field.

   Recall that the PositionID, PositionTitle, and EmployerID fields are all text fields and that the Wage field is a currency field. Field values for text fields are left-aligned in their boxes, and field values for number, date/time, and currency fields are right-aligned in their boxes.

6. Type **9.5** and then press the **Tab** key. Access displays the field value with a dollar sign and two decimal places ($9.50), as specified by the currency format. You do not need to type the dollar sign, commas, or decimal point (for whole dollar amounts) because Access adds these symbols automatically for you.

7. In the HoursPerWeek field, type **30**, press the **Tab** key, type **1** in the Openings field, and then press the **Tab** key.

8. Type **Sue Brown** in the ReferredBy field, and then press the **Tab** key. Depending on your monitor's resolution and size, the display of the datasheet might shift so that the next field, StartDate, is completely visible.

9. Type **6/30/2006** in the StartDate field, and then press the **Tab** key. Access displays the value as 06/30/2006, as specified by the custom date format (mm/dd/yyyy) you set for this field. The insertion point moves to the final field in the table, EndDate.

▶ **10.** Type **9/15/2006** in the EndDate field, and then press the **Tab** key. Access displays the value as 09/15/2006, shifts the display of the datasheet back to the left, stores the first completed record in the Position table, removes the pencil symbol from the first row's record selector, advances the insertion point to the second row's PositionID text box, and places the current record symbol in the second row's record selector.

Now you can enter the values for the second record.

▶ **11.** Refer back to Figure 2-16, and repeat Steps 3 through 10 to add the second record to the table. Access saves the record in the Position table, and moves the insertion point to the beginning of the third row. See Figure 2-19.

| Figure 2-19 | Position table datasheet after entering the second record |

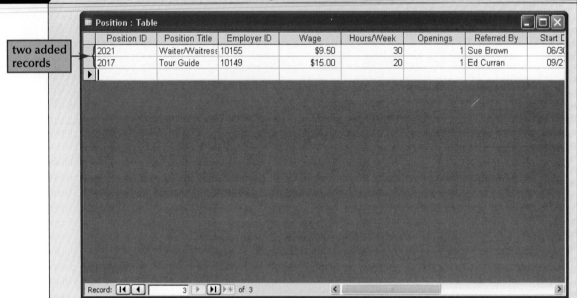

Notice that "Record 3 of 3" appears around the navigation buttons, even though the table contains only two records. Access is anticipating that you will enter a new record, which would be the third of three records in the table. If you moved the insertion point to the second record, the display would change to "Record 2 of 2."

Notice that the two records are currently listed in the order in which you entered them. However, once you close the table or change to another view, and then redisplay the table datasheet, the records will be listed in primary key order by the values in the PositionID field.

Modifying the Structure of an Access Table

Even a well-designed table might need to be modified. For example, the government at all levels and competitors place demands on a company to track more data and to modify the data it already tracks. Access allows you to modify a table's structure in Design view: you can add and delete fields, change the order of fields, and change the properties of the fields.

After holding a meeting with her staff members and reviewing the structure of the Position table and the format of the field values in the datasheet, Elsa has several changes she wants you to make to the table. First, she has decided that it's not necessary to keep track of the name of the person who originally requested a particular position, so she wants you to delete the ReferredBy field. Next, she wants the Openings field moved to the end of the table. She also wants you to add a new yes/no field, named Experience, to the table to indicate whether the available position requires that potential recruits have prior experience in that type of work. The Experience field will be inserted between the HoursPerWeek and StartDate fields. Finally, she thinks that the Wage field should remain a currency field, but she wants the dollar signs removed from the displayed field values in the datasheet so the values are easier to read. Figure 2-20 shows Elsa's modified design for the Position table.

Modified design for the Position table ◄ Figure 2-20

Field Name	Data Type	Field Size	Caption	Description
PositionID	Text	4	Position ID	Primary key
PositionTitle	Text	30	Position Title	
EmployerID	Text	5	Employer ID	Foreign key
Wage	Currency			Rate per hour
HoursPerWeek	Number	Integer	Hours/Week	Work hours per week
Experience	Yes/No			Experience required
StartDate	Date/Time		Start Date	Month/day/year
EndDate	Date/Time		End Date	Month/day/year
Openings	Number	Integer		Number of openings

You'll begin modifying the table by deleting the ReferredBy field.

Deleting a Field

After you've defined a table structure and added records to the table, you can delete a field from the table structure. When you delete a field, you also delete all the values for the field from the table. Therefore, before you delete a field you should make sure that you want to do so—and that you choose the correct field to delete.

Deleting a Field from a Table Structure

Reference Window

- In the Table window in Design view, right-click the row selector for the field you want to delete, both to select the field and to display the shortcut menu.
- Click Delete Rows on the shortcut menu.

You need to delete the ReferredBy field from the Position table structure.

To delete the ReferredBy field:

1. Click the **View** button for Design view on the Table Datasheet toolbar. The Table window for the Position table opens in Design view.

2. Position the pointer on the row selector for the ReferredBy field until the pointer changes to a ➡ shape.

3. Right-click to select the entire row for the ReferredBy field and display the shortcut menu, and then click **Delete Rows**.

A dialog box opens asking you to confirm the deletion.

> **4.** Click the **Yes** button to close the dialog box and to delete the field and its values from the table. See Figure 2-21.

Figure 2-21 **Table structure after deleting ReferredBy field**

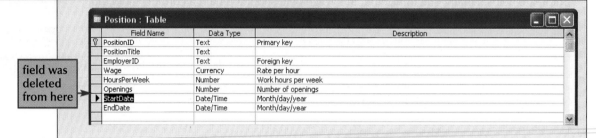

You have deleted the ReferredBy field in the Table window, but the change doesn't take place in the table on disk until you save the table structure. Because you have other modifications to make to the table, you'll wait until you finish them all before saving the modified table structure to disk.

Moving a Field

To move a field, you use the mouse to drag it to a new location in the Table window in Design view. Your next modification to the Position table structure is to move the Openings field to the end of the table, as Elsa requested.

To move the Openings field:

> **1.** Click the **row selector** for the Openings field to select the entire row.

> **2.** If necessary, scroll the Table Design grid so that you can see both the selected Openings field and the empty row below the EndDate field at the same time.

> **3.** Place the pointer in the row selector for the Openings field, click the ▷ pointer, and then drag the ▷ pointer to the row selector below the EndDate row selector. See Figure 2-22.

Figure 2-22 **Moving a field in the table structure**

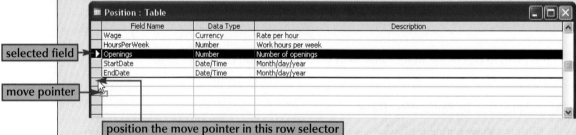

> **4.** Release the mouse button. Access moves the Openings field below the EndDate field in the table structure.
>
> **Trouble?** If the Openings field did not move, repeat Steps 1 through 3, making sure you firmly hold down the mouse button during the drag operation.

Adding a Field

Next, you need to add the Experience field to the table structure between the HoursPerWeek and StartDate fields. To add a new field between existing fields, you must insert a row. You begin by selecting the field that will be below the new field you want to insert.

Adding a Field Between Two Existing Fields

- In the Table window in Design view, right-click the row selector for the row above which you want to add a new field, to select the field and display the shortcut menu.
- Click Insert Rows on the shortcut menu.
- Define the new field by entering the field name, data type, description (optional), and any property specifications.

Reference Window

To add the Experience field to the Position table:

1. Right-click the **row selector** for the StartDate field to select this field and display the short-cut menu, and then click **Insert Rows**. Access adds a new, blank row between the HoursPerWeek and StartDate fields. See Figure 2-23.

After inserting a row in the table structure ◀ Figure 2-23

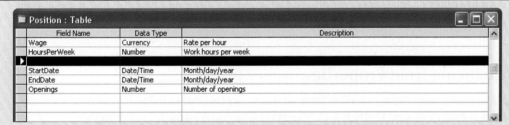

You'll define the Experience field in the new row of the Position table. Access will add this new field to the Position table structure between the HoursPerWeek and StartDate fields.

2. Click the **Field Name** text box for the new row, type **Experience**, and then press the **Tab** key.

   The Experience field will be a yes/no field that will specify whether prior work experience is required for the position.

3. Type **y**. Access completes the data type as "yes/No."

4. Press the **Tab** key to select the yes/no data type and to move to the Description text box.

   Notice that Access changes the value in the Data Type text box from "yes/No" to "Yes/No."

5. Type **Experience required** in the Description text box.

   Elsa wants the Experience field to have a Default Value property value of "No," so you need to set this property.

6. In the Field Properties pane, click the **Default Value** text box, type **no**, and then press the **Tab** key. Notice that Access changes the Default Value property value from "no" to "No." See Figure 2-24.

Figure 2-24	Experience field added to the Position table

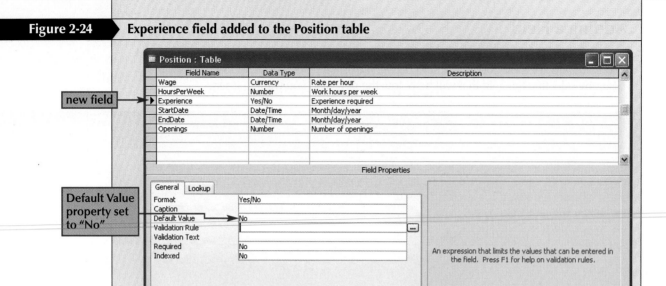

You've completed adding the Experience field to the Position table in Design view. As with the other changes you've made in Design view, however, the Experience field is not added to the Position table in the Northeast database until you save the changes to the table structure.

Changing Field Properties

Elsa's last modification to the table structure is to remove the dollar signs from the Wage field values displayed in the datasheet—repeated dollar signs are unnecessary and they clutter the datasheet. As you learned earlier when defining the StartDate and EndDate fields, you use the Format property to control the display of a field value.

To change the Format property of the Wage field:

▶ 1. Click the **Description** text box for the Wage field. The Wage field is now the current field.

▶ 2. Click the right side of the **Format** text box to display the Format list box. See Figure 2-25.

Figure 2-25

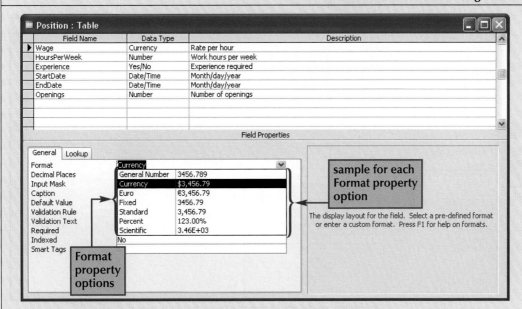

To the right of each Format property option is a field value whose appearance represents a sample of the option. The Standard option specifies the format Elsa wants for the Wage field.

3. Click **Standard** in the Format list box to accept this option for the Format property.

Notice the Property Update Options button 📝, which appears next to the Format property text box. This button allows you to have changes to properties take effect in other database objects.

Updating Field Property Changes

When you change a field's property in Design view, you can update the corresponding property on forms and reports that include the field you've modified. For example, in the preceding steps, you changed the Format property of the Wage field to Standard. If the Northeast database included forms or reports that contained the Wage field, you could choose to **propagate**, or update, the modified property in those forms and reports so that their Wage field values would be displayed in the Standard format.

To see the options for updating field property changes:

1. Position the pointer on the **Property Update Options** button 📝, and then click the list arrow that appears. A menu of related options is displayed. See Figure 2-26.

Figure 2-26 **Updating changes to field properties**

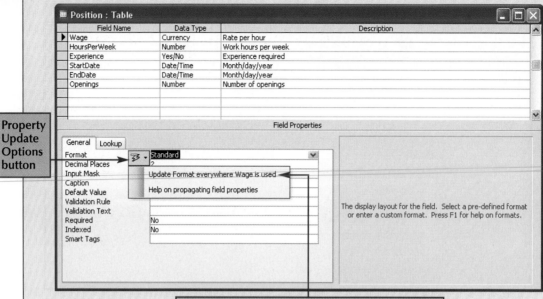

The "Help on propagating field properties" option takes you to a Help window for more information. The Update option allows you to select the objects you want to update with the property change.

▶ **2.** Click **Update Format everywhere Wage is used**. A message box opens, indicating that no objects needed to be updated. This is because the Northeast database does not currently contain any forms or reports that might include the Wage field. If the database did contain such objects, the Update Properties dialog box would open, and you could then select the forms and reports containing the field that needs to be updated.

▶ **3.** Click the **OK** button to close the message box. The Property Update Options button is no longer displayed in the Field Properties pane.

Elsa wants you to add a third record to the Position table datasheet. Before you can add the record, you must save the modified table structure, and then switch to the Position table datasheet.

To save the modified table structure, and then switch to the datasheet:

▶ **1.** Click the **Save** button 🔲 on the Table Design toolbar. The modified table structure for the Position table is stored in the Northeast database. Note that if you forget to save the modified structure and try to close the table or switch to another view, Access will prompt you to save the table before you can continue.

▶ **2.** Click the **View** button for Datasheet view 🔲 on the Table Design toolbar. The Position table datasheet opens. See Figure 2-27.

Datasheet for the modified Position table | Figure 2-27

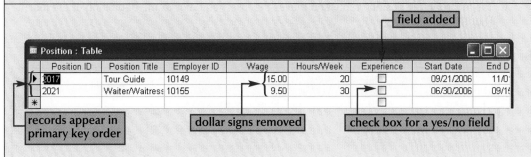

field added

Position : Table

Position ID	Position Title	Employer ID	Wage	Hours/Week	Experience	Start Date	End D
2017	Tour Guide	10149	15.00	20	☐	09/21/2006	11/0
2021	Waiter/Waitress	10155	9.50	30	☐	06/30/2006	09/1!
*					☐		

records appear in primary key order

dollar signs removed

check box for a yes/no field

Notice that the ReferredBy field no longer appears in the datasheet, the Openings field is now the rightmost column (you might need to scroll the datasheet to see it), the Wage field values do not contain dollar signs, and the Experience field appears between the HoursPerWeek and StartDate fields. The Experience column contains check boxes to represent the yes/no field values. Empty check boxes signify "No," which is the default value you assigned to the Experience field. A check mark in the check box indicates a "Yes" value. Also notice that the records appear in ascending order based on the value in the PositionID field, the Position table's primary key, even though you did not enter the records in this order.

Elsa asks you to add a third record to the table. This record is for a position that requires prior work experience.

To add the record to the modified Position table:

1. Click the **New Record** button ▶ on the Table Datasheet toolbar. The insertion point moves to the PositionID field for the third row, which is the next row available for a new record.

2. Type **2020**. The pencil symbol appears in the row selector for the third row, and the star appears in the row selector for the fourth row. Recall that these symbols represent a record being edited and the next available record, respectively.

3. Press the **Tab** key. The insertion point moves to the PositionTitle field. Recall that "PositionTitle" is the name of the field as it is stored in the database, and "Position Title" is the value specified for this field's Caption property. (This text generally refers to fields by their field names, not by their captions.)

4. Type **Host/Hostess**, press the **Tab** key to move to the EmployerID field, type **10163**, and then press the **Tab** key again. The Wage field is now the current field.

5. Type **18.5** and then press the **Tab** key. Access displays the value as "18.50" (with no dollar sign).

6. Type **32** in the HoursPerWeek field, and then press the **Tab** key. The Experience field is now the current field.

   Recall that the default value for this field is "No," which means the check box is initially empty. For yes/no fields with check boxes, you press the Tab key to leave the check box unchecked; you press the spacebar or click the check box to add or remove a check mark in the check box. Because this position requires experience, you need to insert a check mark in the check box.

7. Press the **spacebar**. A check mark appears in the check box.

8. Press the **Tab** key, type **6/15/2006** in the StartDate field, press the **Tab** key, and then type **10/1/2006** in the EndDate field.

9. Press the **Tab** key, type **1** in the Openings field, and then press the **Tab** key. Access saves the record in the Position table and moves the insertion point to the beginning of the fourth row. See Figure 2-28.

Figure 2-28 | **Position table datasheet with third record added**

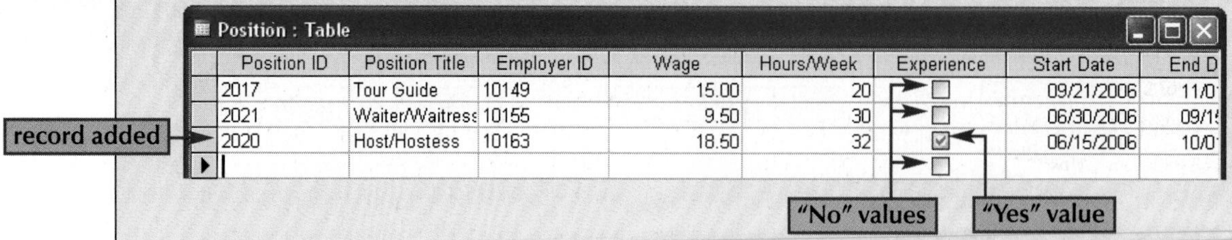

As you add records, Access places them at the end of the datasheet. If you switch to Design view and then return to the datasheet, or if you close the table and then open the datasheet, Access will display the records in primary key sequence.

For many of the fields, the columns are wider than necessary for the field values. You can resize the datasheet columns so that they are only as wide as needed to display the longest value in the column, including the field name or caption (if set). Resizing datasheet columns to their best fit improves the display of the datasheet and allows you to view more fields at the same time.

To resize the Position datasheet columns to their best fit:

1. Place the pointer on the line between the PositionID and PositionTitle field names until the pointer changes to a ↔ shape.

2. Double-click the pointer. The PositionID column is resized so that it is only as wide as the longest value in the column (the caption for the field name, in this case).

3. Double-click the ↔ pointer on the line to the right of each remaining field name to resize all the columns in the datasheet to their best fit. See Figure 2-29.

Figure 2-29 | **Datasheet after resizing all columns to their best fit**

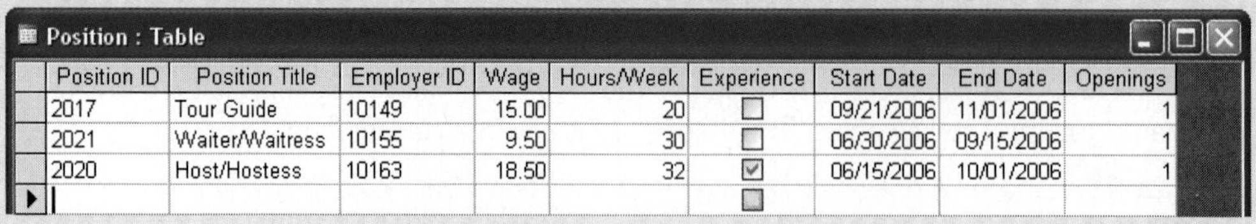

Notice that all nine fields in the Position table are now visible in the datasheet if they were not visible before.

You have modified the Position table structure and added one record. Next, you need to obtain the rest of the records for this table from another database, and then import the two tables from the Seasonal database (Employer and NAICS) into your Northeast database.

Obtaining Data from Another Access Database

Sometimes the data you need for your database might already exist in another Access database. You can save time in obtaining this data by copying and pasting records from one database table into another or by importing an entire table from one database into another.

Copying Records from Another Access Database

You can copy and paste records from a table in the same database or in a different database only if the tables have the same structure—that is, the tables contain the same fields in the same order. Elsa's NEJobs database in the Brief\Tutorial folder included with your Data Files has a table named AvailablePositions that has the same table structure as the Position table. The records in the AvailablePositions table are the records Elsa wants you to copy into the Position table.

Other programs, such as Microsoft Word and Microsoft Excel, allow you to have two or more documents open at a time. However, you can have only one database open at a time for your current Access session. Therefore, you need to close the Northeast database, open the AvailablePositions table in the NEJobs database, select and copy the table records, close the NEJobs database, reopen the Position table in the Northeast database, and then paste the copied records. (*Note*: If you have a database open and then open a second database, Access will automatically close the first database for you.)

To copy the records from the AvailablePositions table:

▶ **1.** Click the **Close** button ☒ on the Table window title bar to close the Position table. A message box opens asking if you want to save the changes to the layout of the Position table. This box appears because you resized the datasheet columns to their best fit.

▶ **2.** Click the **Yes** button in the message box.

▶ **3.** Click the **Close** button ☒ on the Database window title bar to close the Northeast database.

▶ **4.** Click the **Open** button 🖼 on the Database toolbar to display the Open dialog box.

▶ **5.** If necessary, display the list of your Data Files in the **Brief\Tutorial** folder.

▶ **6.** Open the database file named **NEJobs**. The Database window opens. Notice that the NEJobs database contains only one table, the AvailablePositions table. This table contains the records you need to copy.

▶ **7.** Click **AvailablePositions** in the Tables list box (if necessary), and then click the **Open** button in the Database window. The datasheet for the AvailablePositions table opens. See Figure 2-30. Note that this table contains a total of 62 records.

Figure 2-30   Datasheet for the NEJobs database's AvailablePositions table

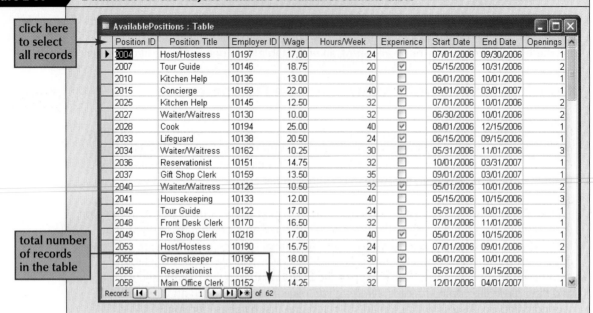

Elsa wants you to copy all the records in the AvailablePositions table. You can select all records by clicking the row selector for the field name row.

▶ 8. Click the **row selector** for the field name row (see Figure 2-30). All the records in the table are now highlighted, which means that Access has selected all of them.

▶ 9. Click the **Copy** button 🖹 on the Table Datasheet toolbar. All the records are copied to the Clipboard.

   Trouble? If a Clipboard panel opens in the task pane, click its Close button to close it, and then continue with Step 10.

▶ 10. Click the **Close** button ☒ on the Table window title bar. A message box opens asking if you want to save the data you copied to the Clipboard.

▶ 11. Click the **Yes** button in the message box. The message box closes, and then the table closes.

▶ 12. Click the **Close** button ☒ on the Database window title bar to close the NEJobs database.

To finish copying and pasting the records, you must open the Position table and paste the copied records into the table.

To paste the copied records into the Position table:

▶ 1. Click **File** on the menu bar, and then click **Northeast** in the list of recently opened databases. The Database window opens, showing the tables for the Northeast database.

▶ 2. In the Tables list box, click **Position** (if necessary), and then click the **Open** button in the Database window. The datasheet for the Position table opens.

   You must paste the records at the end of the table.

▶ 3. Click the **row selector** for row four, which is the next row available for a new record. Make sure the entire row is selected (highlighted).

▶ 4. Click the **Paste** button 🖹 on the Table Datasheet toolbar. A message box opens asking if you are sure you want to paste the records (62 in all).

Trouble? If the Paste button is not available, click the row selector for row four, make sure that the entire row is selected, and then repeat Step 4.

5. Click the **Yes** button. All the records are pasted from the Clipboard, and the pasted records remain highlighted. See Figure 2-31. Notice that the table now contains a total of 65 records—the three original records plus the 62 copied records.

Table after copying and pasting records ◄ **Figure 2-31**

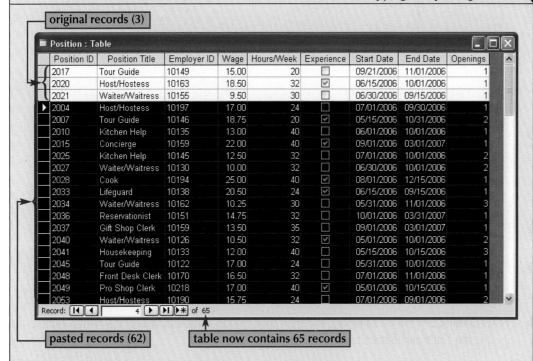

original records (3)

Position ID	Position Title	Employer ID	Wage	Hours/Week	Experience	Start Date	End Date	Openings
2017	Tour Guide	10149	15.00	20	☐	09/21/2006	11/01/2006	1
2020	Host/Hostess	10163	18.50	32	☑	06/15/2006	10/01/2006	1
2021	Waiter/Waitress	10155	9.50	30	☐	06/30/2006	09/15/2006	1
2004	Host/Hostess	10197	17.00	24	☐	07/01/2006	09/30/2006	1
2007	Tour Guide	10146	18.75	20	☑	05/15/2006	10/31/2006	2
2010	Kitchen Help	10135	13.00	40	☐	06/01/2006	10/01/2006	1
2015	Concierge	10159	22.00	40	☑	09/01/2006	03/01/2007	1
2025	Kitchen Help	10145	12.50	32	☐	07/01/2006	10/01/2006	2
2027	Waiter/Waitress	10130	10.00	32	☐	06/30/2006	10/01/2006	2
2028	Cook	10194	25.00	40	☑	08/01/2006	12/15/2006	1
2033	Lifeguard	10138	20.50	24	☑	06/15/2006	09/15/2006	1
2034	Waiter/Waitress	10162	10.25	30	☐	05/31/2006	11/01/2006	3
2036	Reservationist	10151	14.75	32	☐	10/01/2006	03/31/2007	1
2037	Gift Shop Clerk	10159	13.50	35	☐	09/01/2006	03/01/2007	1
2040	Waiter/Waitress	10126	10.50	32	☑	05/01/2006	10/01/2006	2
2041	Housekeeping	10133	12.00	40	☐	05/15/2006	10/15/2006	3
2045	Tour Guide	10122	17.00	24	☐	05/31/2006	10/01/2006	1
2048	Front Desk Clerk	10170	16.50	32	☐	07/01/2006	11/01/2006	1
2049	Pro Shop Clerk	10218	17.00	40	☑	05/01/2006	10/15/2006	1
2053	Host/Hostess	10190	15.75	24	☐	07/01/2006	09/01/2006	2

Record: ◄◄ ◄ 4 ► ►► ►* of 65

pasted records (62)   table now contains 65 records

6. Click the **Close** button on the Table window title bar to close the Position table.

Importing a Table from Another Access Database

When you **import** a table from one Access database to another, you place a copy of the table—including its structure, field definitions, and field values—in the database into which you import it. There are two ways to import a table from another Access database into your current database: using the Get External Data option on the File menu, or using the Import Table Wizard, which is available in the New Table dialog box. You'll use both methods to import the two tables from the Seasonal database into your Northeast database.

To import the Employer and NAICS tables:

1. Make sure the Northeast Database window is open on your screen.

2. Click **File** on the menu bar, point to **Get External Data**, and then click **Import**. The Import dialog box opens. This dialog box is similar to the Open dialog box.

3. Display the list of files in your Brief\Tutorial folder, click **Seasonal**, and then click the **Import** button. The Import Objects dialog box opens. See Figure 2-32.

Figure 2-32	Import Objects dialog box

The Tables tab of the dialog box lists both tables in the Seasonal database—Employer and NAICS. Note that you can import other objects as well (queries, forms, reports, and so on).

4. Click **Employer** in the list of tables, and then click the **OK** button. The Import Objects dialog box closes, and the Employer table is now listed in the Northeast Database window.

Now you'll use the Import Table Wizard to import the NAICS table. (Note that you could also use the Select All button in the Import Objects dialog box to import all the objects listed on the current tab at the same time.)

5. Click the **New** button in the Database window, click **Import Table** in the New Table dialog box, and then click the **OK** button. The Import dialog box opens.

6. If necessary, display the list of files in your Brief\Tutorial folder, click **Seasonal**, and then click the **Import** button. The Import Objects dialog box opens, again displaying the tables in the Seasonal database.

7. Click **NAICS** in the list of tables, and then click the **OK** button to import the NAICS table into the Northeast database.

Now that you have all the records in the Position table and all three tables in the Northeast database, Elsa examines the records to make sure they are correct. She finds one record in the Position table that she wants you to delete and another record that needs changes to its field values.

Updating a Database

Updating, or **maintaining**, a database is the process of adding, changing, and deleting records in database tables to keep them current and accurate. You've already added records to the Position table. Now Elsa wants you to delete and change records.

Deleting Records

To delete a record, you need to select the record in Datasheet view, and then delete it using the Delete Record button on the Table Datasheet toolbar or the Delete Record option on the shortcut menu.

Deleting a Record

- In the Table window in Datasheet view, click the row selector for the record you want to delete, and then click the Delete Record button on the Table Datasheet toolbar (or right-click the row selector for the record, and then click Delete Record on the shortcut menu).
- In the dialog box asking you to confirm the deletion, click the Yes button.

Elsa asks you to delete the record whose PositionID value is 2015 because this record was entered in error; the position for this record does not exist. The fourth record in the table has a PositionID value of 2015. This record is the one you need to delete.

To delete the record:

1. Open the Position table in Datasheet view.

2. Right-click the **row selector** for row four. Access selects the fourth record and displays the shortcut menu. See Figure 2-33.

Deleting a record ◄ **Figure 2-33**

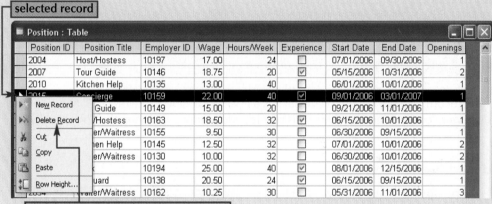

selected record

Position ID	Position Title	Employer ID	Wage	Hours/Week	Experience	Start Date	End Date	Openings
2004	Host/Hostess	10197	17.00	24	☐	07/01/2006	09/30/2006	1
2007	Tour Guide	10146	18.75	20	☑	05/15/2006	10/31/2006	2
2010	Kitchen Help	10135	13.00	40	☐	06/01/2006	10/01/2006	1
2015	Concierge	10159	22.00	40	☑	09/01/2006	03/01/2007	1
	Guide	10149	15.00	20	☐	09/21/2006	11/01/2006	1
	/Hostess	10163	18.50	32	☑	06/15/2006	10/01/2006	1
	er/Waitress	10155	9.50	30	☐	06/30/2006	09/15/2006	1
	en Help	10145	12.50	32	☐	07/01/2006	10/01/2006	2
	er/Waitress	10130	10.00	32	☐	06/30/2006	10/01/2006	2
		10194	25.00	40	☑	08/01/2006	12/15/2006	1
	uard	10138	20.50	24	☑	06/15/2006	09/15/2006	1
	er/Waitress	10162	10.25	30	☐	05/31/2006	11/01/2006	3

New Record
Delete Record
Cut
Copy
Paste
Row Height...

click here to delete the selected record

3. Click **Delete Record** on the shortcut menu. Access deletes the record and opens a dialog box asking you to confirm the deletion. Because the deletion of a record is permanent and cannot be undone, Access prompts you to make sure that you want to delete the record.

   Trouble? If you selected the wrong record for deletion, click the No button. Access ends the deletion process and continues to display the selected record. Repeat Steps 2 and 3 to delete the correct record.

4. Click the **Yes** button to confirm the deletion and close the dialog box.

Elsa's final update to the Position table involves changes to field values in one of the records.

Changing Records

To change the field values in a record, you must first make the record the current record. Then you position the insertion point in the field value to make minor changes or select the field value to replace it entirely. In Tutorial 1, you used the mouse with the scroll bars and the navigation buttons to navigate the records in a datasheet. You can also use keystroke combinations and the F2 key to navigate a datasheet and to select field values.

The **F2 key** is a toggle that you use to switch between navigation mode and editing mode:

- In **navigation mode**, Access selects an entire field value. If you type while you are in navigation mode, your typed entry replaces the highlighted field value.
- In **editing mode**, you can insert or delete characters in a field value based on the location of the insertion point.

Figure 2-34 shows some of the navigation mode and editing mode keystroke techniques.

Figure 2-34 ▶ **Navigation mode and editing mode keystroke techniques**

Press	To Move the Selection in Navigation Mode	To Move the Insertion Point in Editing Mode
←	Left one field value at a time	Left one character at a time
→	Right one field value at a time	Right one character at a time
Home	Left to the first field value in the record	To the left of the first character in the field value
End	Right to the last field value in the record	To the right of the last character in the field value
↑ or ↓	Up or down one record at a time	Up or down one record at a time and switch to navigation mode
Tab or Enter	Right one field value at a time	Right one field value at a time and switch to navigation mode
Ctrl+Home	To the first field value in the first record	To the left of the first character in the field value
Ctrl+End	To the last field value in the last record	To the right of the last character in the field value

The record Elsa wants you to change has a PositionID field value of 2125. Some of the values were entered incorrectly for this record, and you need to enter the correct values.

To modify the record:

▶ 1. Make sure the PositionID field value for the fourth record is still highlighted, indicating that the table is in navigation mode.

▶ 2. Press the **Ctrl+End** keys. Access displays records from the end of the table and selects the last field value in the last record. This field value is for the Openings field.

▶ 3. Press the **Home** key. The first field value in the last record is now selected. This field value is for the PositionID field.

▶ 4. Press the ↑ key. The PositionID field value for the previous record (PositionID 2125) is selected. This record is the one you need to change.

Elsa wants you to change these field values in the record: PositionID to 2124, EmployerID to 10163, Wage to 14.50, Experience to "Yes" (checked), and EndDate to 10/15/2006.

▶ 5. Type **2124**, press the **Tab** key twice, type **10163**, press the **Tab** key, type **14.5**, press the **Tab** key twice, press the **spacebar** to insert a check mark in the Experience check box, press the **Tab** key twice, and then type **10/15/2006**. The changes to the record are complete. See Figure 2-35.

Table after changing field values in a record | **Figure 2-35**

field values changed							
2115	Gift Shop Clerk	10154	13.00	25	☐	05/01/2006	09/30/2006	1
2117	Housekeeping	10220	13.50	30	☐	06/30/2006	09/30/2006	3
2118	Greenskeeper	10218	17.00	32	☐	05/01/2006	11/01/2006	1
2120	Lifeguard	10154	19.00	32	☑	06/15/2006	09/30/2006	2
2122	Kitchen Help	10151	13.00	35	☐	09/01/2006	03/31/2007	3
2123	Main Office Clerk	10170	14.50	32	☐	07/01/2006	11/15/2006	1
2124	Kitchen Help	10163	14.50	40	☑	06/01/2006	10/15/2006	2
2127	Waiter/Waitress	10185	10.50	40	☐	12/01/2006	05/01/2007	1
*					☐			

Record: |◄| |◄| 63 |►| |►|| |►*| of 64

You've completed all of Elsa's updates to the Position table. Now you can close the Northeast database.

6. Close the Position table, and then close the Northeast database.

Elsa and her staff members approve of the revised table structure for the Position table. They are confident that the table will allow them to easily track position data for NSJI's employer customers.

Session 2.2 Quick Check

Review

1. What does a pencil symbol in a datasheet's row selector represent? A star symbol?
2. What is the effect of deleting a field from a table structure?
3. How do you insert a field between existing fields in a table structure?
4. A field with the _____ data type can appear in the table datasheet as a check box.
5. Describe the two ways in which you can display the Import dialog box, so that you can import a table from one Access database to another.
6. In Datasheet view, what is the difference between navigation mode and editing mode?

SAM
TRAINING COMPANION

To reinforce the tasks you learned in this session, go to the SAM 2003 Training Companion CD included with this text.

Tutorial Summary

Review

In this tutorial, you learned how to create and save a new database and how to create and save a new table in that database. With this process, you also learned some important guidelines for designing databases and tables, and for setting field properties. You worked in Design view to define fields, set properties, specify a table's primary key, and modify a table's structure. Then you worked in Datasheet view to add records to the new table, both by entering them directly in the datasheet and by copying records from another Access database. To complete the database design, you imported tables from another Access database into the new database you created. Finally, you updated the database by deleting records and changing values in records.

Key Terms

Caption property	editing mode	navigation mode
composite key	entity integrity	null value
data redundancy	F1 key	pencil symbol
data type	F2 key	propagate
Database Wizard	F6 key	properties
Decimal Places property	Field Size property	set (a property)
Default Value property	import	star symbol
Description property	maintain (a database)	update (a database)
Design view		

Practice

Take time to practice the skills you learned in the tutorial using the same case scenario.

Review Assignments

Data File needed for the Review Assignments: Elsa.mdb

Elsa needs a database to track data about the students recruited by NSJI and about the recruiters who find jobs for the students. She asks you to create the database by completing the following:

1. Start Access, and make sure your Data Files are in the proper location.
2. Create a new, blank database named **Recruits** and save it in the Brief\Review folder included with your Data Files.
3. Use Design view to create a new table using the table design shown in Figure 2-36.

Figure 2-36

Field Name	Data Type	Description	Field Size	Caption	Other Properties
SSN	Text	Primary key	30		
Salary	Currency				Format: Currency Default Value: (blank)
FirstName	Text		50	First Name	
MiddleName	Text		30	Middle Name	
LastName	Text		50	Last Name	

4. Specify SSN as the primary key field, and then save the table as **Recruiter**.
5. Add the recruiter records shown in Figure 2-37 to the **Recruiter** table.

Figure 2-37

SSN	Salary	FirstName	MiddleName	LastName
892-77-1201	40,000	Kate	Teresa	Foster
901-63-1554	38,500	Paul	Michael	Kirnicki
893-91-0178	40,000	Ryan	James	DuBrava

6. Make the following changes to the structure of the **Recruiter** table:
   a. Move the Salary field so that it appears after the LastName field.
   b. Add a new field between the LastName and Salary fields, using the following properties:

Field Name:	BonusQuota
Data Type:	Number
Description:	Number of recruited students needed to receive bonus
Field Size:	Byte
Decimal Places:	0
Caption:	Bonus Quota
Default Value:	(blank)

   c. Change the format of the Salary field so that commas are displayed, dollar signs are not displayed, and no decimal places are displayed in the field values.
   d. Save the revised table structure.
7. Use the **Recruiter** datasheet to update the database as follows:
   a. Enter these BonusQuota values for the three records: 60 for Kate Foster; 60 for Ryan DuBrava; and 50 for Paul Kirnicki.
   b. Add a record to the Recruiter datasheet with the following field values:

SSN:	899-40-2937
FirstName:	Sonia
MiddleName:	Lee
LastName:	Xu
BonusQuota:	50
Salary:	39,250

8. Close the Recruiter table, and then set the option for compacting the **Recruits** database on close. (*Note*: If you are working off a floppy disk, check with your instructor or technical support staff to confirm that you should set this option.)
9. Elsa created a database with her name as the database name. In that database, the RecruiterEmployees table has the same format as the Recruiter table you created. Copy all the records from the **RecruiterEmployees** table in the **Elsa** database (located in the Brief\Review folder provided with your Data Files) to the end of the **Recruiter** table in the **Recruits** database.
10. Delete the MiddleName field from the Recruiter table structure, and then save the table structure.
11. Resize all columns in the datasheet for the Recruiter table to their best fit.
12. Print the Recruiter table datasheet, and then save and close the table.
13. Create a table named **Student** using the Import Table Wizard. The table you need to import is named **Student**, which is one of the tables in the **Elsa** database located in the Brief\Review folder provided with your Data Files.
14. Make the following modifications to the structure of the **Student** table in the **Recruits** database:
    a. Enter the following Description property values:
       StudentID: Primary key
       SSN: Foreign key value of the recruiter for this student
    b. Change the Field Size property for both the FirstName field and the LastName field to 15.
    c. Move the BirthDate field so that it appears between the Nation and Gender fields.
    d. Change the format of the BirthDate field so that it displays only two digits for the year instead of four.
    e. Save the table structure changes. (Answer "Yes" to any warning messages about property changes and lost data.)

15. Switch to Datasheet view, and then resize all columns in the datasheet to fit the data.
16. Delete the record with the StudentID value DRI9901 from the **Student** table.
17. Save, print, and then close the Student datasheet.
18. Close the Recruits database.

Apply

Using what you learned in the tutorial, create and modify two new tables containing data about video photography events.

Case Problem 1

Data Files needed for this Case Problem: Videos.mdb (*cont. from Tutorial 1*) and Events.mdb

Lim's Video Photography Youngho Lim uses the Videos database to maintain information about the clients, contracts, and events for his video photography business. Youngho asks you to help him maintain the database by completing the following:

1. Open the **Videos** database located in the Brief\Case1 folder provided with your Data Files.
2. Use Design view to create a table using the table design shown in Figure 2-38.

Figure 2-38

Field Name	Data Type	Description	Field Size	Caption	Other Properties
ShootID	Number	Primary key	Long Integer	Shoot ID	Decimal Places: 0 Default Value: (blank)
ShootType	Text		2	Shoot Type	
ShootTime	Date/Time			Shoot Time	Format: Medium Time
Duration	Number	# of hours	Single		Default Value: (blank)
Contact	Text	person who booked shoot	30		
Location	Text		30		
ShootDate	Date/Time			Shoot Date	Format: mm/dd/yyyy
ContractID	Number	Foreign key	Integer	Contract ID	Decimal Places: 0 Default Value: (blank)

3. Specify ShootID as the primary key, and then save the table as **Shoot**.
4. Add the records shown in Figure 2-39 to the Shoot table.

Figure 2-39

ShootID	ShootType	ShootTime	Duration	Contact	Location	ShootDate	ContractID
927032	AP	4:00 PM	3.5	Ellen Quirk	Elm Lodge	9/27/2006	2412
103031	HP	9:00 AM	3.5	Tom Bradbury	Client's home	10/30/2006	2611

5. Youngho created a database named Events that contains a table with shoot data named ShootEvents. The Shoot table you created has the same format as the ShootEvents table. Copy all the records from the **ShootEvents** table in the **Events** database (located in the Brief\Case1 folder provided with your Data Files) to the end of the **Shoot** table in the **Videos** database.
6. Modify the structure of the Shoot table by completing the following:
   a. Delete the Contact field.
   b. Move the ShootDate field so that it appears between the ShootType and ShootTime fields.

7. Save the revised table structure, switch to Datasheet view, and then resize all columns in the datasheet for the Shoot table to their best fit.

8. Use the **Shoot** datasheet to update the database as follows:

   a. For ShootID 421032, change the ShootTime value to 7:00 PM, and change the Location value to Le Bistro.

   b. Add a record to the Shoot datasheet with the following field values:

   ShootID: 913032
   ShootType: SE
   ShootDate: 9/13/2006
   ShootTime: 1:00 PM
   Duration: 2.5
   Location: High School football field
   ContractID: 2501

9. Switch to Design view, and then switch back to Datasheet view so that the records appear in primary key sequence by ShootID. Resize any datasheet columns to their best fit, as necessary.

10. Print the Shoot table datasheet, and then save and close the table.

11. Create a table named **ShootDesc** using the Import Table Wizard. The table you need to import is named **ShootDesc**, which is one of the tables in the **Events** database located in the Brief\Case1 folder provided with your Data Files.

12. Make the following modifications to the structure of the **ShootDesc** table in the **Videos** database:

   a. Enter the following Description property values:

   ShootType: Primary key
   ShootDesc: Description of shoot

   b. Change the Field Size property for ShootType to 2.

   c. Change the Field Size property for ShootDesc to 30.

   d. Enter the following Caption property values:

   ShootType: Shoot Type
   ShootDesc: Shoot Desc

13. Save the revised table structure (answer "Yes" to any warning messages about property changes and lost data), switch to Datasheet view, and then resize both datasheet columns to their best fit.

14. Print the ShootDesc table datasheet, and then save and close the table.

15. Close the Videos database.

Case Problem 2

Challenge

Challenge yourself by using the Table Wizard to create a new table to store data about fitness center programs.

Data Files needed for this Case Problem: Fitness.mdb (*cont. from Tutorial 1*) and Products.mdb

Parkhurst Health & Fitness Center   Martha Parkhurst uses the Fitness database to track information about members who join the center and the program in which each member is enrolled. You'll help her maintain this database by completing the following:

1. Open the **Fitness** database located in the Brief\Case2 folder provided with your Data Files.

Explore

2. Use the Table Wizard to create a new table named **Program** in the **Fitness** database, as follows:

   a. Base the new table on the Products sample table, which is one of the sample tables in the Business category.

   b. Add the following fields to your table (in the order shown): ProductID, ProductDescription, and UnitPrice.

c. Click ProductID in the "Fields in my new table" list, and then use the Rename Field button to change the name of this field to ProgramID. Follow this same procedure to rename the ProductDescription field to "Description" and to rename the "UnitPrice" field to "MonthlyFee." Click the Next button.

d. Specify the name **Program** for the new table, and choose the option for setting the primary key yourself. Click the Next button.

e. Specify ProgramID as the primary key field, and select the option "Numbers and/or letters I enter when I add new records." Click the Next button.

f. In the next dialog box, click the Relationships button, select the option "The tables aren't related" (if necessary), click the OK button, and then click the Next button.

g. In the final Table Wizard dialog box, choose the option for modifying the table design. Click the Finish button.

Explore

3. Modify the structure of the Program table as follows:

a. For the ProgramID field, make the following changes:

Data Type:	Number
Description:	Primary key
Decimal Places:	0
Caption:	Program ID
Default Value:	blank (no value specified)

b. For the Description field, make the following changes:

Description:	Full programs provide access to all facilities; limited programs restrict access to certain facilities and activities
Field Size:	35

c. For the MonthlyFee field, make the following changes:

Format:	Fixed
Decimal Places:	2
Caption:	Monthly Fee

4. Add a new field as the fourth field in the table, below MonthlyFee, with the following properties:

Field Name:	PhysicalRequired
Data Type:	Yes/No
Description:	Member must have a complete physical before joining program
Caption:	Physical Required

5. Save the modified table structure.

6. Add the records shown in Figure 2-40 to the Program table.

Figure 2-40

ProgramID	Description	MonthlyFee	PhysicalRequired
201	Junior Full (ages 13–17)	$30.00	Yes
202	Junior Limited (ages 13–17)	$20.00	Yes
203	Young Adult Full (ages 18–25)	$40.00	No
204	Young Adult Limited (ages 18–25)	$25.00	No

7. Martha created a database named Products that contains a table with program data named ProgramRecords. The Program table you created has the same format as the ProgramRecords table. Copy all the records from the **ProgramRecords** table in the **Products** database (located in the Brief\Case2 folder provided with your Data Files) to the end of the **Program** table in the **Fitness** database.

8. Resize all columns in the datasheet for the Program table to their best fit.

9. For ProgramID 209, change the PhysicalRequired field value to Yes.
10. Print the Program table datasheet, and then save and close the table.
11. Close the Fitness database.

Case Problem 3

Apply

Apply the skills you learned in the tutorial to create and work with a new table containing data about donations.

Data Files needed for this Case Problem: Redwood.mdb (*cont. from Tutorial 1*) and Pledge.mdb

Redwood Zoo   Michael Rosenfeld continues to track information about donors, their pledges, and the status of funds to benefit the Redwood Zoo. Help him maintain the Redwood database by completing the following:

1. Open the **Redwood** database located in the Brief\Case3 folder provided with your Data Files.
2. Create a table named **Pledge** using the Import Table Wizard. The table you need to import is named **PledgeRecords**, which is located in the **Pledge** database in the Brief\Case3 folder provided with your Data Files.

Explore

3. After importing the PledgeRecords table, use the shortcut menu to rename the table to **Pledge** in the Database window.
4. Modify the structure of the **Pledge** table by completing the following:
   a. Enter the following Description property values:
      PledgeID: Primary key
      DonorID: Foreign key
      FundCode: Foreign key
   b. Change the format of the PledgeDate field to mm/dd/yyyy.
   c. Change the Data Type of the TotalPledged field to Currency with the Standard format.
   d. Specify a Default Value of B for the PaymentMethod field.
   e. Specify a Default Value of F for the PaymentSchedule field.
   f. Save the modified table structure.
5. Switch to Datasheet view, and then resize all columns in the datasheet to their best fit.
6. Use the **Pledge** datasheet to update the database as follows:
   a. Add a new record to the Pledge table with the following field values:
      PledgeID: 2695
      DonorID: 59045
      FundCode: P15
      PledgeDate: 7/11/2006
      TotalPledged: 1000
      PaymentMethod: B
      PaymentSchedule: M
   b. Change the TotalPledged value for PledgeID 2499 to 150.
   c. Change the FundCode value for PledgeID 2332 to B03.
7. Print the Pledge table datasheet, and then save and close the table.
8. Close the Redwood database.

Challenge

Explore two new ways to create tables containing property rental information—by importing an Excel worksheet and by entering records first in Datasheet view.

Explore

Case Problem 4

Data Files needed for this Case Problem: GEM.mdb (*cont. from Tutorial 1*), Property.xls, and Reserve.mdb

GEM Ultimate Vacations   Griffin and Emma MacElroy use the GEM database to track the data about the services they provide to the clients who book luxury vacations through their agency. You'll help them maintain this database by completing the following:

1. Open the **GEM** database located in the Brief\Case4 folder provided with your Data Files.
2. Use the Import Spreadsheet Wizard to create a new table named **Property**. The data you need to import is contained in the **Property** workbook, which is a Microsoft Excel file located in the Brief\Case4 folder provided with your Data Files.
   a. Select the Import Table option in the New Table dialog box.
   b. Change the entry in the Files of type list box to display the list of Excel workbook files in the Brief\Case4 folder.
   c. Select the **Property** file and then click the Import button.
   d. In the Import Spreadsheet Wizard dialog boxes, choose the Sheet1 worksheet; choose the option for using column headings as field names; select the option for choosing your own primary key; specify PropertyID as the primary key; and enter the table name (**Property**). Otherwise, accept the wizard's choices for all other options for the imported data.
3. Open the **Property** table and resize all datasheet columns to their best fit.
4. Modify the structure of the Property table by completing the following:
   a. For the PropertyID field, enter a Description property of "Primary key", change the Field Size property to Long Integer, set the Decimal Places property to 0, and set the Caption property to Property ID.
   b. For the PropertyName field, change the Field Size property to 45, and set the Caption property to Property Name.
   c. For the Location field, enter a Description property of "Province, city, county", and change the Field Size property to 35.
   d. For the Country field, change the Field Size property to 15.
   e. For the NightlyRate field, change the Data Type to Currency, set the Format property to Currency, set the Decimal Places property to 0, and set the Caption property to Nightly Rate.
   f. For the Bedrooms field, enter a Description property of "Number of bedrooms", change the Field Size property to Integer, and set the Decimal Places property to 0.
   g. For the Sleeps field, enter a Description property of "Number of people who can be accommodated", change the Field Size property to Integer, and set the Decimal Places property to 0.
   h. For the PropertyType field, change the Field Size property to 20, and set the Caption property to Property Type.
   i. For the Description field, change the Data Type to Memo.
   j. Save the table structure. If you receive any warning messages about lost data or integrity rules, click the Yes button.
5. Switch to Datasheet view, and then resize all datasheet columns to their best fit (if necessary).
6. Use the **Property** datasheet to update the database as follows:
   a. For PropertyID 3395, change the NightlyRate value to $750.
   b. Add a new record to the Property table with the following field values:
      PropertyID: 3675
      PropertyName: Casa de Las Palmas

Location:	Mallorca
Country:	Spain
NightlyRate:	2500
Bedrooms:	4
Sleeps:	8
PropertyType:	Villa
Description:	Private estate; multiple terraces; beautiful sea views; pool

  c. Delete the record for PropertyID 3503.

7. Print the Property table datasheet, and then save and close the table.

Explore

8. Create a new table named **Reservation**, based on the data shown in Figure 2-41 and according to the following steps:

Figure 2-41

ReservationID	GuestID	PropertyID	StartDate	EndDate	People	RentalRate
510	220	3107	5/1/07	5/15/07	6	$1000
503	209	3488	6/12/07	6/19/07	12	$2000
511	201	3142	8/20/07	8/27/07	7	$700

  a. Select the Datasheet View option in the New Table dialog box.
  b. Enter the three records shown in Figure 2-41. (Do *not* enter the field names at this point.)
  c. Switch to Design view, supply the table name, and then answer "No" if asked if you want to create a primary key.
  d. Enter the field names and properties for the seven fields, as shown in Figure 2-42.

Figure 2-42

Field Name	Data Type	Description	Field Size	Caption	Other Properties
ReservationID	Number	Primary key	Long Integer	Reservation ID	Format: (blank) Decimal Places: 0
GuestID	Number	Foreign key	Integer	Guest ID	Format: (blank) Decimal Places: 0
PropertyID	Number	Foreign key	Long Integer	Property ID	Format: (blank) Decimal Places: 0
StartDate	Date/Time			Start Date	Format: Short Date
EndDate	Date/Time			End Date	Format: Short Date
People	Number	Number of people in the party	Byte		Format: (blank) Decimal Places: 0
RentalRate	Currency	Rate per day; includes any discounts or promotions		Rental Rate	Format: Currency Decimal Places: 0

9. Specify ReservationID as the primary key, and then save the changes to the table structure.
10. Switch to Datasheet view, and then resize all datasheet columns to their best fit.
11. Emma created a database named Reserve that contains a table with reservation data named ReserveInfo. The Reservation table you created has the same format as the ReserveInfo table. Copy all the records from the **ReserveInfo** table in the **Reserve** database (located in the Brief\Case4 folder provided with your Data Files) to the end of the **Reservation** table in the **GEM** database.

12. Resize all columns in the Reservation datasheet to their best fit (if necessary).
13. Print the Reservation datasheet, and then save and close the table.
14. Close the GEM database.

Research

Use the Internet to find and work with data related to the topics presented in this tutorial.

Internet Assignments

The purpose of the Internet Assignments is to challenge you to find information on the Internet that you can use to work effectively with this software. The actual assignments are updated and maintained on the Course Technology Web site. Log on to the Internet and use your Web browser to go to the Student Online Companion for New Perspectives Office 2003 at **www.course.com/np/office2003**. Click the Internet Assignments link, and then navigate to the assignments for this tutorial.

Assess

SAM Assessment and Training

If your instructor has chosen to use the full online version of SAM 2003 Assessment and Training, you can go beyond the "just-in-time" training provided on the CD that accompanies this text. Simply log in to your SAM account (http://sam2003.course.com) to launch any assigned training activities or exams that relate to the skills covered in this tutorial.

Review

Quick Check Answers

Session 2.1

1. Identify all the fields needed to produce the required information, group related fields into tables, determine each table's primary key, include a common field in related tables, avoid data redundancy, and determine the properties of each field.
2. The Data Type property determines what field values you can enter for the field and what other properties the field will have.
3. text, number, and AutoNumber fields
4. Caption
5. F6
6. null

Session 2.2

1. the record being edited; the next row available for a new record
2. The field and all its values are removed from the table.
3. In Design view, right-click the row selector for the row above which you want to insert the field, click Insert Rows on the shortcut menu, and then define the new field.
4. yes/no
5. Make sure the database into which you want to import a table is open, click the File menu, point to Get External Data, and then click Import; or, click the New button in the Database window, click Import Table in the New Table dialog box, and then click the OK button.
6. In navigation mode, the entire field value is selected, and anything you type replaces the field value; in editing mode, you can insert or delete characters in a field value based on the location of the insertion point.

Querying a Database

Retrieving Information About Employers and Their Positions

Case | Northeast Seasonal Jobs International (NSJI)

At a recent company meeting, Elsa Jensen and other NSJI employees discussed the importance of regularly monitoring the business activity of the company's employer clients. For example, Zack Ward and his marketing staff track employer activity to develop new strategies for promoting NSJI's services. Matt Griffin, the manager of recruitment, needs to track information about available positions, so that he can find student recruits to fill those positions. In addition, Elsa is interested in analyzing other aspects of the business, such as the wage amounts paid for different positions at different employers. You can satisfy all these informational needs for NSJI by creating and using queries that retrieve information from the Northeast database.

Session	Objectives		SAM Training Tasks	
Session 3.1	• Learn how to use the Query window in Design view • Create, run, and save queries • Update data using a query	• Define a relationship between two tables • Sort data in a query • Filter data in a query	• Add a table to the Design View query grid • Create a multi-table query • Create a one-to-many relationship using the Relationships window • Create a query in design view • Enforce referential integrity in a one-to-many relationship • Filter datasheet by form • Filter datasheet by selection • Include all fields in a query	• Include criteria in a query for a field not in the results • Order records in datasheet view • Resize panes and field lists in Query Design view • Restrict records in a join • Sort a query on multiple fields in Design View • Sort records in a database • Specify referential integrity options • Use filter by form
Session 3.2	• Specify an exact match condition in a query • Change a datasheet's appearance • Use a comparison operator to match a range of values • Use the And and Or logical operators	• Use multiple undo and redo • Perform calculations in a query using calculated fields, aggregate functions, and record group calculations	• Add a calculated field to a Select query • Build summary queries • Create calculated fields • Create queries using Wizards • Create queries with AND conditions • Create Select queries using the Simple Query Wizard • Format a table or query datasheet for display	• Format results displayed in a calculated field • Use aggregate functions in queries to perform calculations • Use date and memo fields in a query • Use text data in criteria for a query • Use the AVG function in a query • Use Undo and Redo

Student Data Files   For a complete list of the Data Files needed for this tutorial, see page AC 2.

Session 3.1

For hands-on practice of key tasks in this session, go to the SAM 2003 Training Companion CD included with this text.

Introduction to Queries

As you learned in Tutorial 1, a query is a question you ask about data stored in a database. For example, Zack might create a query to find records in the Employer table for only those employers located in a specific state or province. When you create a query, you tell Access which fields you need and what criteria Access should use to select the records.

Access provides powerful query capabilities that allow you to:

- display selected fields and records from a table
- sort records
- perform calculations
- generate data for forms, reports, and other queries
- update data in the tables in a database
- find and display data from two or more tables

Most questions about data are generalized queries in which you specify the fields and records you want Access to select. These common requests for information, such as "Which employers are located in Quebec?" or "How many waiter/waitress positions are available?" are called **select queries**. The answer to a select query is returned in the form of a datasheet. The result of a query is also referred to as a **recordset**, because the query produces a set of records that answers your question.

More specialized, technical queries, such as finding duplicate records in a table, are best formulated using a Query Wizard. A Query Wizard prompts you for information by asking a series of questions and then creates the appropriate query based on your answers. In Tutorial 1, you used the Simple Query Wizard to display only some of the fields in the Employer table; Access provides other Query Wizards for more complex queries. For common, informational queries, it is easier for you to design your own query than to use a Query Wizard.

Zack wants you to create a query to display the employer ID, employer name, city, contact first name, contact last name, and Web site information for each record in the Employer table. He needs this information for a market analysis his staff is completing on NSJI's employer clients. You'll open the Query window to create the query for Zack.

Query Window

You use the Query window in Design view to create a query. In Design view, you specify the data you want to view by constructing a query by example. When you use **query by example** (**QBE**), you give Access an example of the information you are requesting. Access then retrieves the information that precisely matches your example.

For Zack's query, you need to display data from the Employer table. You'll begin by starting Access, opening the Northeast database (which you created in Tutorial 2), and displaying the Query window in Design view.

To start Access, open the Northeast database, and open the Query window in Design view:

1. Start Access and open the **Northeast** database which you created in Tutorial 2 and saved in the Brief\Tutorial folder provided with your Data Files.

2. Click **Queries** in the Objects bar of the Database window, and then click the **New** button. The New Query dialog box opens. See Figure 3-1.

New Query dialog box ◀ **Figure 3-1**

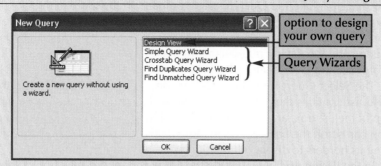

You'll design your own query instead of using a Query Wizard.

▶ **3.** If necessary, click **Design View** in the list box.

▶ **4.** Click the **OK** button. Access opens the Show Table dialog box on top of the Query window. (Note that you could also have double-clicked the "Create query in Design view" option in the Database window.) Notice that the title bar of the Query window shows that you are creating a select query.

The query you are creating will retrieve data from the Employer table, so you need to add this table to the Select Query window.

▶ **5.** Click **Employer** in the Tables list box (if necessary), click the **Add** button, and then click the **Close** button. Access places the Employer table's field list in the Select Query window and closes the Show Table dialog box.

To display more of the fields you'll be using for creating queries, you'll maximize the Select Query window.

▶ **6.** Click the **Maximize** button 🔲 on the Select Query window title bar. See Figure 3-2.

Select query in Design view ◀ **Figure 3-2**

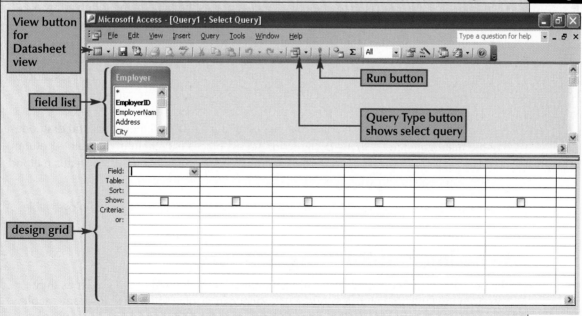

In Design view, the Select Query window contains the standard title bar, the menu bar, the status bar, and the Query Design toolbar. On the toolbar, the Query Type button shows a select query; the icon on this button changes according to the type of query you are creating. The title bar on the Select Query window displays the query type (Select Query) and the default query name (Query1). You'll change the default query name to a more meaningful one later when you save the query.

The Select Query window in Design view contains a field list and the design grid. The **field list** contains the fields for the table you are querying. The table name appears at the top of the list box, and the fields are listed in the order in which they appear in the table. You can scroll the field list to see more fields, or you can expand the field list box by dragging its borders to display all the fields and the complete field names.

In the **design grid**, you include the fields and record selection criteria for the information you want to see. Each column in the design grid contains specifications about a field you will use in the query. You can choose a single field for your query by dragging its name from the field list to the design grid. Alternatively, you can double-click a field name to place it in the next available design grid column.

When you are constructing a query, you can see the query results at any time by clicking the View button or the Run button on the Query Design toolbar. In response, Access displays the query datasheet (or recordset), which contains the set of fields and records that results from answering, or **running**, the query. The order of the fields in the query datasheet is the same as the order of the fields in the design grid. Although the query datasheet looks just like a table datasheet and appears in Datasheet view, a query datasheet is temporary, and its contents are based on the criteria you establish in the design grid. In contrast, a table datasheet shows the permanent data in a table. However, you can update data while viewing a query datasheet, just as you can when working in a table datasheet or form.

If the query you are creating includes every field from the specified table, you can use one of the following three methods to transfer all the fields from the field list to the design grid:

- Click and drag each field individually from the field list to the design grid. Use this method if you want the fields in your query to appear in an order that is different from the order in the field list.
- Double-click the asterisk in the field list. Access places the table name followed by a period and an asterisk (as in "Employer.*") in the design grid, which signifies that the order of the fields is the same in the query as it is in the field list. Use this method if you don't need to sort the query or specify conditions for the records you want to select. The advantage of using this method is that you do not need to change the query if you add or delete fields from the underlying table structure. Such changes are reflected automatically in the query.
- Double-click the field list title bar to highlight all the fields, and then click and drag one of the highlighted fields to the design grid. Access places each field in a separate column and arranges the fields in the order in which they appear in the field list. Use this method when you need to sort your query or include record selection criteria.

Now you'll create and run Zack's query to display selected fields from the Employer table.

Creating and Running a Query

The default table datasheet displays all the fields in the table, in the same order as they appear in the table. In contrast, a query datasheet can display selected fields from a table, and the order of the fields can be different from that of the table, enabling those viewing the query results to see only the information they need and in the order they want.

Zack wants the Employer table's EmployerID, EmployerName, City, ContactFirstName, ContactLastName, and Website fields to appear in the query results. You'll add each of these fields to the design grid.

To select the fields for the query, and then run the query:

▶ 1. Drag **EmployerID** from the Employer field list to the design grid's first column Field text box, and then release the mouse button. See Figure 3-3.

Field added to the design grid ◀ Figure 3-3

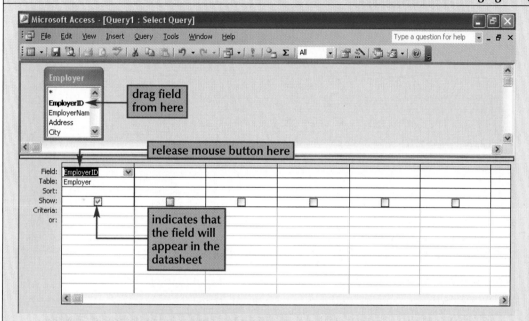

In the design grid's first column, the field name EmployerID appears in the Field text box, the table name Employer appears in the Table text box, and the check mark in the Show check box indicates that the field will be displayed in the datasheet when you run the query. Sometimes you might not want to display a field and its values in the query results. For example, if you are creating a query to show all employers located in Massachusetts, and you assign the name "EmployersInMassachusetts" to the query, you do not need to include the StateProv field value for each record in the query results—every StateProv field value would be "MA" for Massachusetts. Even if you choose not to include a field in the display of the query results, you can still use the field as part of the query to select specific records or to specify a particular sequence for the records in the datasheet.

▶ 2. Double-click **EmployerName** in the Employer field list. Access adds this field to the second column of the design grid.

▶ 3. Scrolling the Employer field list as necessary, repeat Step 2 for the **City**, **ContactFirstName**, **ContactLastName**, and **Website** fields to add these fields to the design grid in that order.

Trouble? If you double-click the wrong field and accidentally add it to the design grid, you can remove the field from the grid. Select the field's column by clicking the pointer ⬇ on the bar above the Field text box for the field you want to delete, and then press the Delete key (or click Edit on the menu bar, and then click Delete Columns).

Having selected the fields for Zack's query, you can now run the query.

4. Click the **Run** button on the Query Design toolbar. Access runs the query and displays the results in Datasheet view. See Figure 3-4.

Figure 3-4
Datasheet displayed after running the query

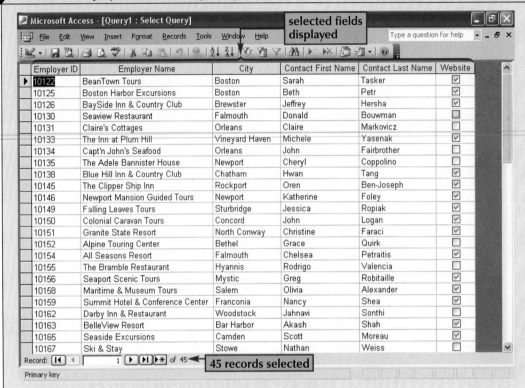

The six fields you added to the design grid—EmployerID, EmployerName, City, ContactFirstName, ContactLastName, and Website—appear in the datasheet, and the records are displayed in primary key sequence by EmployerID. Access selected a total of 45 records for display in the datasheet.

Zack asks you to save the query as "EmployerAnalysis" so that he can easily retrieve the same data again.

5. Click the **Save** button on the Query Datasheet toolbar. The Save As dialog box opens.

6. Type **EmployerAnalysis** in the Query Name text box, and then press the **Enter** key. Access saves the query with the specified name in the Northeast database and displays the name in the title bar.

When viewing the results of the query, Zack noticed a couple of changes that need to be made to the data in the Employer table. The Adele Bannister House recently developed a Web site, so the Website field for this record needs to be updated. In addition, the contact information has changed for the Alpine Touring Center.

Updating Data Using a Query

Although a query datasheet is temporary and its contents are based on the criteria in the query design grid, you can update the data in a table using a query datasheet. In this case, Zack has changes he wants you to make to records in the Employer table. Instead of making the changes in the table datasheet, you can make them in the EmployerAnalysis query datasheet. The underlying Employer table will be updated with the changes you make.

To update data using the EmployerAnalysis query datasheet:

1. For the record with EmployerID 10135 (The Adele Bannister House), click the check box in the Website field to place a check mark in it.

2. For the record with EmployerID 10152 (Alpine Touring Center), change the ContactFirstName field value to **Mary** and change the ContactLastName field value to **Grant**.

3. Click the **Close Window** button ☒ on the menu bar to close the query. Note that the EmployerAnalysis query appears in the list of queries.

4. Click the **Restore Window** button 🗗 on the menu bar to return the Database window to its original size.

   Now you will check the Employer table to verify that the changes you made in the query datasheet were also made to the Employer table records.

5. Click **Tables** in the Objects bar of the Database window, click **Employer** in the list of tables, and then click the **Open** button. The Employer table datasheet opens.

6. For the record with EmployerID 10135, scroll the datasheet to the right to verify that the Website field contains a check mark. For the record with EmployerID 10152, scroll to the right to see the new contact information (Mary Grant).

7. Click the **Close** button ☒ on the Employer table window to close it.

Matt also wants to view specific information in the Northeast database. However, he needs to see data from both the Employer table and the Position table at the same time. To view data from two tables at the same time, you need to define a relationship between the tables.

Defining Table Relationships

One of the most powerful features of a relational database management system is its ability to define relationships between tables. You use a common field to relate one table to another. The process of relating tables is often called performing a **join**. When you join tables that have a common field, you can extract data from them as if they were one larger table. For example, you can join the Employer and Position tables by using the EmployerID field in both tables as the common field. Then you can use a query, a form, or a report to extract selected data from each table, even though the data is contained in two separate tables, as shown in Figure 3-5. In the Positions query shown in Figure 3-5, the PositionID, PositionTitle, and Wage columns are fields from the Position table, and the EmployerName and StateProv columns are fields from the Employer table. The joining of records is based on the common field of EmployerID. The Employer and Position tables have a type of relationship called a one-to-many relationship.

Figure 3-5 **One-to-many relationship and sample query**

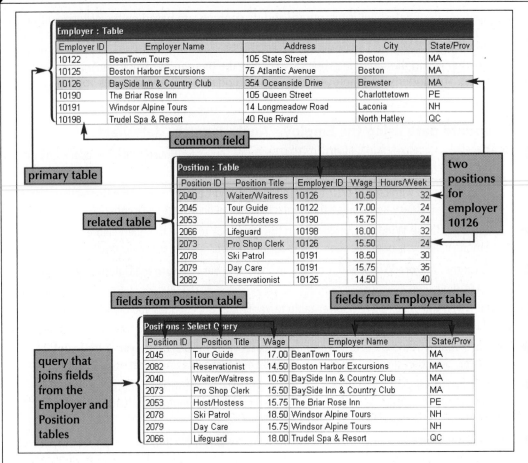

One-to-Many Relationships

A **one-to-many relationship** exists between two tables when one record in the first table matches zero, one, or many records in the second table, and when one record in the second table matches exactly one record in the first table. For example, as shown in Figure 3-5, employers 10126 and 10191 each have two available positions, and employers 10122, 10125, 10190, and 10198 each have one available position. Every position has a single matching employer.

Access refers to the two tables that form a relationship as the primary table and the related table. The **primary table** is the "one" table in a one-to-many relationship; in Figure 3-5, the Employer table is the primary table because there is only one employer for each available position. The **related table** is the "many" table; in Figure 3-5, the Position table is the related table because there can be many positions offered by each employer.

Because related data is stored in two tables, inconsistencies between the tables can occur. Consider the following scenarios:

- Matt adds a position record to the Position table for a new employer, Glen Cove Inn, using EmployerID 10132. Matt did not first add the new employer's information to the Employer table, so this position does not have a matching record in the Employer table. The data is inconsistent, and the position record is considered to be an **orphaned record**.
- Matt changes the EmployerID in the Employer table for BaySide Inn & Country Club from 10126 to 10128. Two orphaned records for employer 10126 now exist in the Position table, and the database is inconsistent.

- Matt deletes the record for Boston Harbor Excursions, employer 10125, in the Employer table because this employer is no longer an NSJI client. The database is again inconsistent; one record for employer 10125 in the Position table has no matching record in the Employer table.

You can avoid these problems by specifying referential integrity between tables when you define their relationships.

Referential Integrity

Referential integrity is a set of rules that Access enforces to maintain consistency between related tables when you update data in a database. Specifically, the referential integrity rules are as follows:

- When you add a record to a related table, a matching record must already exist in the primary table, thereby preventing the possibility of orphaned records.
- If you attempt to change the value of the primary key in the primary table, Access prevents this change if matching records exist in a related table. However, if you choose the **cascade updates option**, Access permits the change in value to the primary key and changes the appropriate foreign key values in the related table, thereby eliminating the possibility of inconsistent data.
- When you attempt to delete a record in the primary table, Access prevents the deletion if matching records exist in a related table. However, if you choose the **cascade deletes option**, Access deletes the record in the primary table and also deletes all records in related tables that have matching foreign key values. Note, however, that you should *rarely* select the cascade deletes option, because setting this option might cause you to inadvertently delete records you did not intend to delete.

Now you'll define a one-to-many relationship between the Employer and Position tables so that you can use fields from both tables to create a query that will retrieve the information Matt needs. You will also define a one-to-many relationship between the NAICS (primary) table and the Employer (related) table.

Defining a Relationship Between Two Tables

When two tables have a common field, you can define a relationship between them in the Relationships window. The **Relationships window** illustrates the relationships among a database's tables. In this window, you can view or change existing relationships, define new relationships between tables, and rearrange the layout of the tables in the window.

You need to open the Relationships window and define the relationship between the Employer and Position tables. You'll define a one-to-many relationship between the two tables, with Employer as the primary table and Position as the related table, and with EmployerID as the common field (the primary key in the Employer table and a foreign key in the Position table). You'll also define a one-to-many relationship between the NAICS and Employer tables, with NAICS as the primary table and Employer as the related table, and with NAICSCode as the common field (the primary key in the NAICS table and a foreign key in the Employer table).

To define the one-to-many relationship between the Employer and Position tables:

1. Click the **Relationships** button [icon] on the Database toolbar. The Show Table dialog box opens on top of the Relationships window. See Figure 3-6.

Figure 3-6 **Show Table dialog box**

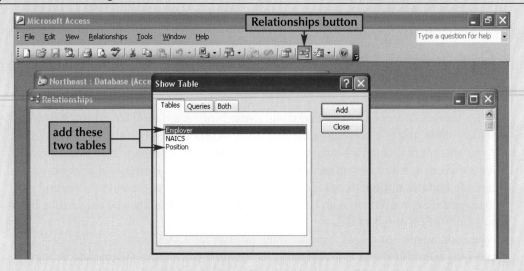

You must add each table participating in a relationship to the Relationships window.

2. Click **Employer** (if necessary), and then click the **Add** button. The Employer field list is added to the Relationships window.

3. Click **Position**, and then click the **Add** button. The Position field list is added to the Relationships window.

4. Click the **Close** button in the Show Table dialog box to close it and reveal the entire Relationships window.

So that you can view all the fields and complete field names, you'll first move the Position field list box further to the right, and then resize both field list boxes.

5. Click the Position field list title bar and drag the list to the right (see Figure 3-7), and then release the mouse button.

6. Use the ↔ pointer to drag the right side of each list box to widen it until the complete field names are displayed, and then use the ↕ pointer to drag the bottom of each list box to lengthen it until all the fields are visible. Make sure that both field list boxes no longer contain scroll bars, and that they are sized and positioned similar to those shown in Figure 3-7.

Resized field list boxes | Figure 3-7

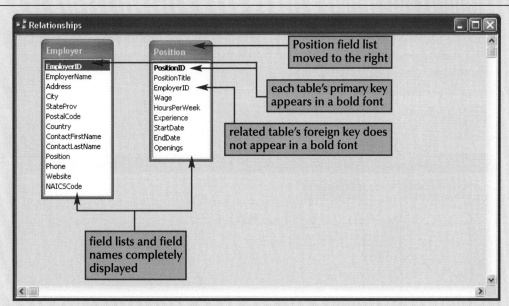

Notice that EmployerID in the Employer table appears in a bold font; this indicates that the field is the table's primary key (the same is true of PositionID in the Position table). On the other hand, the EmployerID field in the Position table is not bold, which is a reminder that this field is the foreign key in this table.

To form the relationship between the two tables, you drag the common field of EmployerID from the primary table to the related table. Then Access opens the Edit Relationships dialog box, in which you select the relationship options for the two tables.

7. Click **EmployerID** in the Employer field list, and then drag it to **EmployerID** in the Position field list. When you release the mouse button, the Edit Relationships dialog box opens. See Figure 3-8.

Edit Relationships dialog box | Figure 3-8

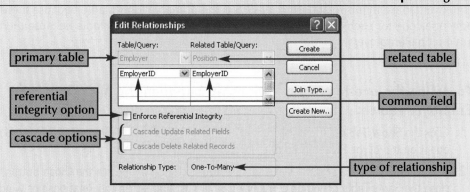

The primary table, related table, and common field appear at the top of the dialog box. The type of relationship, One-To-Many, appears at the bottom of the dialog box. When you click the Enforce Referential Integrity check box, the two cascade options become available. If you select the Cascade Update Related Fields option, Access changes the appropriate foreign key values in the related table when you change a primary key value in the primary table. You will not select the Cascade Delete Related Records option, because doing so could cause you to delete records that you did not want to delete; this option is rarely selected.

8. Click the **Enforce Referential Integrity** check box, and then click the **Cascade Update Related Fields** check box.

9. Click the **Create** button to define the one-to-many relationship between the two tables and to close the dialog box. The completed relationship appears in the Relationships window. See Figure 3-9.

Figure 3-9	Defined relationship in the Relationships window

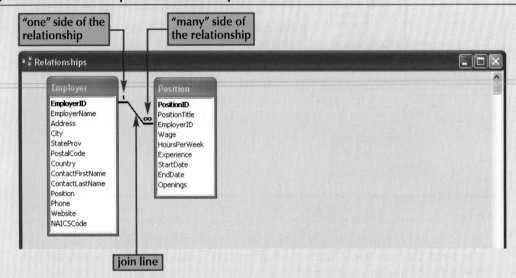

The **join line** connects the EmployerID fields, which are common to the two tables. The common field joins the two tables, which have a one-to-many relationship. The "one" side of the relationship has the digit 1 at its end, and the "many" side of the relationship has the infinity symbol ∞ at its end. The two tables are still separate tables, but you can use the data in them as if they were one table.

Now you need to define the one-to-many relationship between the NAICS and Employer tables. In this relationship, NAICS is the primary ("one") table because there is only one code for each employer. Employer is the related ("many") table because there are multiple employers with the same NAICS code.

To define the one-to-many relationship between the NAICS and Employer tables:

1. Click the **Show Table** button 🖳 on the Relationship toolbar. The Show Table dialog box opens on top of the Relationships window.

2. Click **NAICS** in the list of tables, click the **Add** button, and then click the **Close** button to close the Show Table dialog box. The NAICS field list appears in the Relationships window to the right of the Position field list. To make it easier to define the relationship, you'll move the NAICS field list below the Employer and Position field lists.

3. Click the NAICS field list title bar and drag the list until it is below the Position table (see Figure 3-10), and then release the mouse button.

Because the NAICS table is the primary table in this relationship, you need to drag the NAICSCode field from the NAICS field list to the Employer field list.

4. Click and drag the **NAICSCode** field in the NAICS field list to the **NAICSCode** field in the Employer field list. When you release the mouse button, the Edit Relationships dialog box opens.

5. Click the **Enforce Referential Integrity** check box, and then click the **Cascade Update Related Fields** check box.

6. Click the **Create** button to define the one-to-many relationship between the two tables and close the dialog box. The completed relationship appears in the Relationships window. See Figure 3-10.

Both relationships defined ◀ **Figure 3-10**

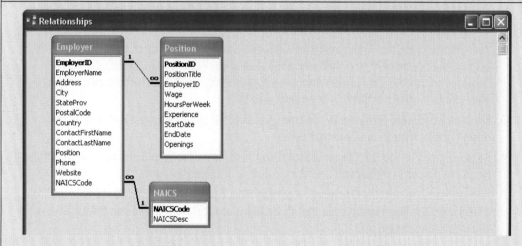

With both relationships defined, you have connected the data among the three tables in the Northeast database.

7. Click the **Save** button 🖫 on the Relationship toolbar to save the layout in the Relationships window.

8. Click the **Close** button ⊠ on the Relationships window title bar. The Relationships window closes, and you return to the Database window.

You've established relationships among the three tables in the Northeast database, so you can now create queries that let Matt view data from the Employer table and the Position table at the same time.

Creating a Multi-table Query

Now that you have joined the Employer and Position tables, you can create a query to produce the information Matt wants. To help him determine his recruiting needs, Matt wants a query that displays the EmployerName, City, and StateProv fields from the Employer table and the Openings, PositionTitle, StartDate, and EndDate fields from the Position table.

To create, run, and save the query using the Employer and Position tables:

1. Click **Queries** in the Objects bar of the Database window, and then double-click **Create query in Design view**. The Show Table dialog box opens on top of the Query window in Design view.

   You need to add the Employer and Position tables to the Query window.

2. Click **Employer** in the Tables list box (if necessary), click the **Add** button, click **Position**, click the **Add** button, and then click the **Close** button. The Employer and Position field lists appear in the Query window, and the Show Table dialog box closes. Note that the one-to-many relationship between the two tables is shown in the Query window. Also, notice that the join line is thick at both ends; this signifies that you selected the option to enforce referential integrity. If you had not selected this option, the join line would be thin at both ends and neither the "1" nor the infinity symbol would appear, even though there is a one-to-many relationship between the two tables.

   You need to place the EmployerName, City, and StateProv fields from the Employer field list into the design grid, and then place the Openings, PositionTitle, StartDate, and EndDate fields from the Position field list into the design grid. This is the order in which Matt wants to view the fields in the query results.

3. Double-click **EmployerName** in the Employer field list to place EmployerName in the design grid's first column Field text box.

4. Repeat Step 3 to add the **City** and **StateProv** fields from the Employer table, so that these fields are placed in the second and third columns of the design grid.

5. Repeat Step 3 to add the **Openings**, **PositionTitle**, **StartDate**, and **EndDate** fields (in that order) from the Position table, so that these fields are placed in the fourth through seventh columns of the design grid.

   The query specifications are completed, so you can now run the query.

6. Click the **Run** button 〔 on the Query Design toolbar. Access runs the query and displays the results in the datasheet.

7. Click the **Maximize** button 〔 on the Query window title bar. See Figure 3-11.

Figure 3-11   **Datasheet for the query based on the Employer and Position tables**

Only the seven selected fields from the Employer and Position tables appear in the datasheet. The records are displayed in order according to the values in the primary key field, EmployerID, even though this field is not included in the query datasheet.

Matt plans on frequently tracking the data retrieved by the query, so he asks you to save the query as "EmployerPositions."

> **8.** Click the **Save** button 🖫 on the Query Datasheet toolbar. The Save As dialog box opens.
>
> **9.** Type **EmployerPositions** in the Query Name text box, and then press the **Enter** key. Access saves the query with the specified name and displays the name in the title bar.

Matt decides he wants the records displayed in alphabetical order by employer name. Because the query displays data in order by the field value of EmployerID, which is the primary key for the Employer table, you need to sort the records by EmployerName to display the data in the order Matt wants.

Sorting Data in a Query

Sorting is the process of rearranging records in a specified order or sequence. Sometimes you might need to sort data before displaying or printing it to meet a specific request. For example, Matt might want to review position information arranged by the StartDate field because he needs to know which positions are available earliest in the year. On the other hand, Elsa might want to view position information arranged by the Openings field for each employer, because she monitors employer activity for NSJI.

When you sort data in a query, you do not change the sequence of the records in the underlying tables. Only the records in the query datasheet are rearranged according to your specifications.

To sort records, you must select the **sort field**, which is the field used to determine the order of records in the datasheet. In this case, Matt wants the data sorted by the employer name, so you need to specify EmployerName as the sort field. Sort fields can be text, number, date/time, currency, AutoNumber, yes/no, or Lookup Wizard fields, but not memo, OLE object, or hyperlink fields. You sort records in either ascending (increasing) or descending (decreasing) order. Figure 3-12 shows the results of each type of sort for different data types.

Sorting results for different data types ◄ **Figure 3-12**

Data Type	Ascending Sort Results	Descending Sort Results
Text	A to Z	Z to A
Number	lowest to highest numeric value	highest to lowest numeric value
Date/Time	oldest to most recent date	most recent to oldest date
Currency	lowest to highest numeric value	highest to lowest numeric value
AutoNumber	lowest to highest numeric value	highest to lowest numeric value
Yes/No	yes (check mark in check box) then no values	no then yes values

Access provides several methods for sorting data in a table or query datasheet and in a form. One method, clicking a toolbar sort button, lets you sort the displayed records quickly.

Using a Toolbar Button to Sort Data

The **Sort Ascending** and **Sort Descending buttons** on the toolbar allow you to sort records immediately, based on the values in the selected field. First you select the column on which you want to base the sort, and then you click the appropriate sort button on the toolbar to rearrange the records in either ascending or descending order. Unless you save the datasheet or form after you've sorted the records, the rearrangement of records is temporary.

Recall that in Tutorial 1 you used the Sort Ascending button to sort query results by the StateProv field. You'll use this same button to sort the EmployerPositions query results by the EmployerName field.

To sort the records using a toolbar sort button:

1. Click any visible EmployerName field value to establish the field as the current field (if necessary).

2. Click the **Sort Ascending** button ![Sort Ascending] on the Query Datasheet toolbar. The records are rearranged in ascending order by employer name. See Figure 3-13.

| Figure 3-13 | Sorting records on a single field in a datasheet |

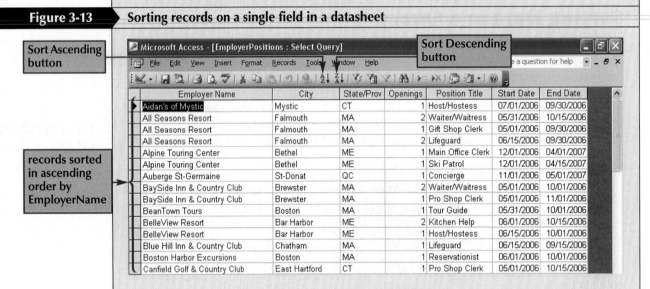

After viewing the query results, Matt decides that he'd prefer to see the records arranged by the value in the PositionTitle field, so that he can identify the types of positions he needs to fill. He also wants to display the records in descending order according to the value of the Openings field, so that he can easily see how many openings there are for each position. In addition, he wants the Openings field values to be displayed in the rightmost column of the query results so that they stand out in the query datasheet. To produce the results Matt wants, you need to sort using two fields.

Sorting Multiple Fields in Design View

Sort fields can be unique or nonunique. A sort field is **unique** if the value of the sort field for each record is different. The EmployerID field in the Employer table is an example of a unique sort field because each employer record has a different value in this field. A sort field is **nonunique** if more than one record can have the same value for the sort field. For example, the PositionTitle field in the Position table is a nonunique sort field because more than one record can have the same PositionTitle value.

When the sort field is nonunique, records with the same sort field value are grouped together, but they are not in a specific order within the group. To arrange these grouped records in a specific order, you can specify a **secondary sort field**, which is a second field that determines the order of records that are already sorted by the **primary sort field** (the first sort field specified). Note that the primary sort field is *not* the same as a table's primary key field. A table has at most one primary key, which must be unique, whereas any field in a table can serve as a primary sort field.

Access lets you select up to 10 different sort fields. When you use the toolbar sort buttons, the sort fields must be in adjacent columns in the datasheet. You highlight the adjacent columns, and Access sorts first by the first column and then by each remaining highlighted column in order from left to right.

Matt wants the records sorted first by the PositionTitle field and then by the Openings field. The two fields are adjacent, but not in the correct left-to-right order, so you cannot use the toolbar buttons to sort them. You could move the Openings field to the right of the PositionTitle field in the query datasheet. However, you can specify only one type of sort—either ascending or descending—for selected columns in the query datasheet. This is not what Matt wants; he wants the PositionTitle field values to be sorted in ascending alphabetical order and the Openings field values to be sorted in descending order. To accomplish the differing sort orders for the PositionTitle and Openings fields, you must specify the sort fields in Design view.

In the Query window in Design view, Access first uses the sort field that is leftmost in the design grid. Therefore, you must arrange the fields you want to sort from left to right in the design grid, with the primary sort field being the leftmost. In Design view, multiple sort fields do not have to be adjacent to each other, as they do in Datasheet view; however, they must be in the correct left-to-right order.

Sorting a Query Datasheet

Reference Window

- In the query datasheet, select the column or adjacent columns on which you want to sort.
- Click the Sort Ascending button or the Sort Descending button on the Query Datasheet toolbar.

or

- In Design view, position the fields serving as sort fields from left (primary sort field) to right, and then select the sort order for each sort field.

To achieve the results Matt wants, you need to switch to Design view, move the Openings field to the right of the EndDate field, and then specify the sort order for the two fields.

To select the two sort fields in Design view:

▶ 1. Click the **View** button for Design view ☒ on the Query Datasheet toolbar to open the query in Design view.

First, you'll move the Openings field to the right of the EndDate field, because Matt wants the Openings field to be the rightmost column in the query results. Remember, in Design view, the sort fields do not have to be adjacent, and non-sort fields can appear between sort fields. So, you will move the Openings field to the end of the query design, following the EndDate field.

▶ 2. If necessary, click the right arrow in the design grid's horizontal scroll bar a few times to scroll to the right so that both the Openings and EndDate fields are completely visible.

▶ 3. Position the pointer in the Openings field selector until the pointer changes to a ↓ shape, and then click to select the field. See Figure 3-14.

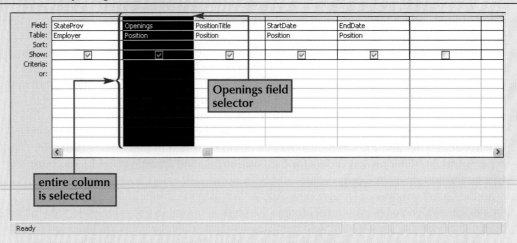

Figure 3-14 Selected Openings field

4. Position the pointer in the Openings field selector, and then click and drag the pointer to the right until the vertical line on the right of the EndDate field is highlighted. See Figure 3-15.

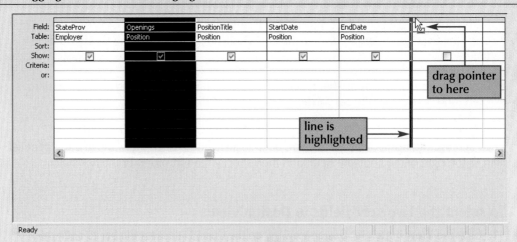

Figure 3-15 Dragging the field in the design grid

5. Release the mouse button. The Openings field moves to the right of the EndDate field.

The fields are now in the correct order for the sort. Next, you need to specify an ascending sort order for the PositionTitle field and a descending sort order for the Openings field.

6. Click the right side of the **PositionTitle Sort** text box to display the list arrow and the sort options, and then click **Ascending**. You've selected an ascending sort order for the PositionTitle field, which will be the primary sort field. The PositionTitle field is a text field, and an ascending sort order will display the field values in alphabetical order.

7. Click the right side of the **Openings Sort** text box, click **Descending**, and then click in one of the empty text boxes to the right of the Openings field to deselect the setting. You've selected a descending sort order for the Openings field, which will be the secondary sort field, because it appears to the right of the primary sort field (PositionTitle) in the design grid. See Figure 3-16.

Selecting two sort fields in Design view | Figure 3-16

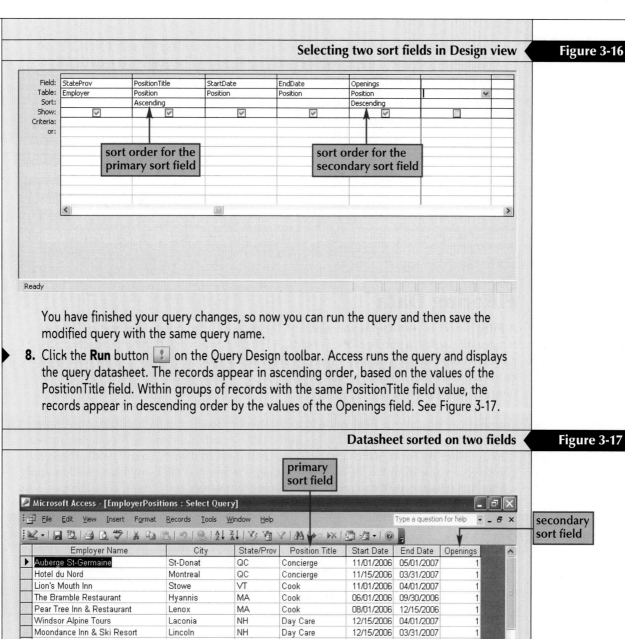

You have finished your query changes, so now you can run the query and then save the modified query with the same query name.

8. Click the **Run** button 🗓️ on the Query Design toolbar. Access runs the query and displays the query datasheet. The records appear in ascending order, based on the values of the PositionTitle field. Within groups of records with the same PositionTitle field value, the records appear in descending order by the values of the Openings field. See Figure 3-17.

Datasheet sorted on two fields | Figure 3-17

When you save the query, all of your design changes—including the selection of the sort fields—are saved with the query. The next time Matt runs the query, the records will appear sorted by the primary and secondary sort fields.

▶ 9. Click the **Save** button 🔲 on the Query Datasheet toolbar to save the revised EmployerPositions query.

Matt recently spoke with a recruit who is interested in clerk positions that are available in New Hampshire. So, Matt wants to concentrate on records that match those criteria. Selecting only the records with a PositionTitle field value that contains the word "Clerk" and a StateProv field value of "NH" is a temporary change that Matt wants in the datasheet, so you do not need to switch to Design view and change the query. Instead, you can apply a filter.

Filtering Data

A **filter** is a set of restrictions you place on the records in an open datasheet or form to *temporarily* isolate a subset of the records. A filter lets you view different subsets of displayed records so that you can focus on only the data you need. Unless you save a query or form with a filter applied, an applied filter is not available the next time you run the query or open the form.

The simplest technique for filtering records is Filter By Selection. **Filter By Selection** lets you select all or part of a field value in a datasheet or form, and then display only those records that contain the selected value in the field. Another technique for filtering records is to use **Filter By Form**, which changes your datasheet to display empty fields. Then you can select a value from the list arrow that appears when you click any blank field to apply a filter that selects only those records containing that value.

Reference Window	**Using Filter By Selection**

- In the datasheet or form, select all or part of the field value that will be the basis for the filter.
- Click the Filter By Selection button on the toolbar.

For Matt's request, you first need to select just the word "Clerk" in the PositionTitle field, and then use Filter By Selection to display only those query records with this same partial value. Then you will filter the records further by selecting only those records with a value of "NH" in the StateProv field.

To display the records using Filter By Selection:

▶ 1. In the query datasheet, locate the first occurrence of a PositionTitle field containing the word "Clerk," and then select **Clerk** in that field value.

▶ 2. Click the **Filter By Selection** button 🔲 on the Query Datasheet toolbar. Access displays the filtered results. Only the 10 query records that have a PositionTitle field value containing the word "Clerk" appear in the datasheet. The status bar's display (FLTR), the area next to the navigation buttons, and the selected Remove Filter button on the toolbar all indicate that the records have been filtered. See Figure 3-18.

Using Filter By Selection ◄ Figure 3-18

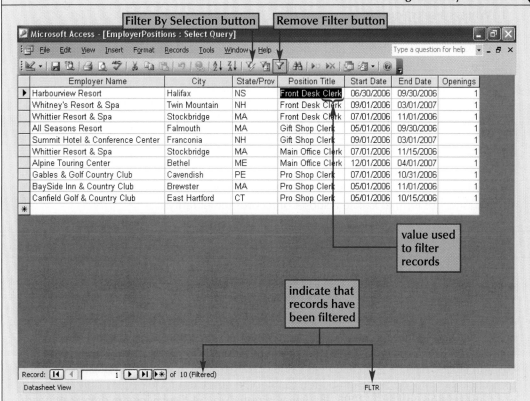

Next, Matt wants to view only those records with a StateProv value of NH, because the recruit is interested in positions in NH only.

► **3.** Click in any StateProv field value of **NH**, and then click the **Filter By Selection** button [image] on the Query Datasheet toolbar. The filtered display now shows only the 2 records for clerk positions available in New Hampshire.

Now you can redisplay all the query records by clicking the Remove Filter button; this button works as a toggle to switch between the filtered and nonfiltered displays.

► **4.** Click the **Remove Filter** button [image] on the Query Datasheet toolbar. Access redisplays all the records in the query datasheet.

► **5.** Click the **Save** button [image] on the Query Datasheet toolbar, and then click the **Close Window** button [image] on the menu bar to save and close the query and return to the Database window.

► **6.** Click the **Restore Window** button [image] on the menu bar to return the Database window to its original size.

The queries you've created will help NSJI employees retrieve just the information they want to view. In the next session, you'll continue to create queries to meet their information needs.

Session 3.1 Quick Check

1. What is a select query?
2. Describe the field list and the design grid in the Query window in Design view.
3. How are a table datasheet and a query datasheet similar? How are they different?
4. The _____ is the "one" table in a one-to-many relationship, and the _____ is the "many" table in the relationship.
5. _____ is a set of rules that Access enforces to maintain consistency between related tables when you update data in a database.
6. For a date/time field, how do the records appear when sorted in ascending order?
7. True or False: When you define multiple sort fields in Design view, the sort fields must be adjacent to each other.
8. A(n) _____ is a set of restrictions you place on the records in an open datasheet or form to isolate a subset of records temporarily.

Session 3.2

Defining Record Selection Criteria for Queries

Matt wants to display employer and position information for all positions with a start date of 07/01/2006, so that he can plan his recruitment efforts accordingly. For this request, you could create a query to select the correct fields and all records in the Employer and Position tables, select a StartDate field value of 07/01/2006 in the query datasheet, and then click the Filter By Selection button to filter the query results to display only those positions starting on July 1, 2006. However, a faster way of displaying the data Matt needs is to create a query that displays the selected fields and only those records in the Employer and Position tables that satisfy a condition.

Just as you can display selected fields from a database in a query datasheet, you can display selected records. To tell Access which records you want to select, you must specify a condition as part of the query. A **condition** is a criterion, or rule, that determines which records are selected. To define a condition for a field, you place the condition in the field's Criteria text box in the design grid.

A condition usually consists of an operator, often a comparison operator, and a value. A **comparison operator** asks Access to compare the value in a database field to the condition value and to select all the records for which the relationship is true. For example, the condition >15.00 for the Wage field selects all records in the Position table having Wage field values greater than 15.00. Figure 3-19 shows the Access comparison operators.

Figure 3-19 ▶ **Access comparison operators**

Operator	Meaning	Example
=	equal to (optional; default operator)	="Hall"
<	less than	<#1/1/99#
<=	less than or equal to	<=100
>	greater than	>"C400"
>=	greater than or equal to	>=18.75
<>	not equal to	<>"Hall"
Between ... And...	between two values (inclusive)	Between 50 And 325
In ()	in a list of values	In ("Hall", "Seeger")
Like	matches a pattern that includes wildcards	Like "706*"

Specifying an Exact Match

For Matt's request, you need to create a query that will display only those records in the Position table with the value 07/01/2006 in the StartDate field. This type of condition is called an **exact match** because the value in the specified field must match the condition exactly in order for the record to be included in the query results. You'll use the Simple Query Wizard to create the query, and then you'll specify the exact match condition.

To create the query using the Simple Query Wizard:

▶ 1. If you took a break after the previous session, make sure that Access is running, the Northeast database is open, and the Queries object is selected in the Database window.

▶ 2. Double-click **Create query by using wizard**. Access opens the first Simple Query Wizard dialog box, in which you select the tables (or queries) and fields for the query.

▶ 3. Click the **Tables/Queries** list arrow, and then click **Table: Position**. The fields in the Position table appear in the Available Fields list box. Except for the PositionID and EmployerID fields, you will include all fields from the Position table in the query.

▶ 4. Click the >> button. All the fields from the Available Fields list box move to the Selected Fields list box.

▶ 5. Scroll up and click **PositionID** in the Selected Fields list box, click the < button to move the PositionID field back to the Available Fields list box, click **EmployerID** in the Selected Fields list box, and then click the < button to move the EmployerID field back to the Available Fields list box.

   Matt also wants certain information from the Employer table included in the query results. Because he wants the fields from the Employer table to appear in the query datasheet to the right of the fields from the Position table fields, you need to click the last field in the Selected Fields list box so that the new Employer fields will be inserted below it in the list.

▶ 6. Click **Openings** in the Selected Fields list box.

▶ 7. Click the **Tables/Queries** list arrow, and then click **Table: Employer**. The fields in the Employer table now appear in the Available Fields list box. Notice that the fields you selected from the Position table remain in the Selected Fields list box.

▶ 8. Click **EmployerName** in the Available Fields list box, and then click the > button to move EmployerName to the Selected Fields list box, below the Openings field.

▶ 9. Repeat Step 8 to move the **StateProv**, **ContactFirstName**, **ContactLastName**, and **Phone** fields into the Selected Fields list box. (Note that you can also double-click a field to move it from the Available Fields list box to the Selected Fields list box.)

▶ 10. Click the **Next** button to open the second Simple Query Wizard dialog box, in which you choose whether the query will display records from the selected tables or a summary of those records. Summary options show calculations such as average, minimum, maximum, and so on. Matt wants to view the details for the records, not a summary.

▶ 11. Make sure the **Detail (shows every field of every record)** option button is selected, and then click the **Next** button to open the last Simple Query Wizard dialog box, in which you choose a name for the query and complete the wizard. You need to enter a condition for the query, so you'll want to modify the query's design.

▶ 12. Type **July1Positions**, click the **Modify the query design** option button, and then click the **Finish** button. Access saves the query as July1Positions and opens the query in Design view. See Figure 3-20.

Figure 3-20	Query in Design view

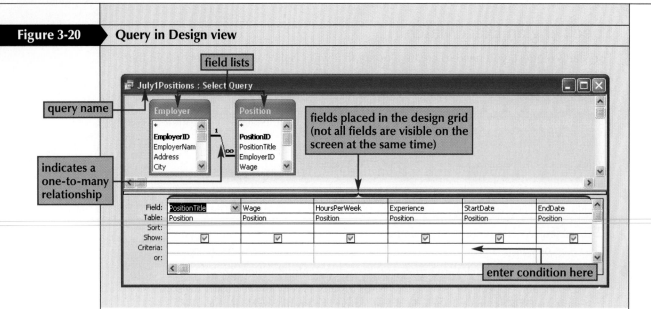

The field lists for the Employer and Position tables appear in the top portion of the window, and the join line indicating a one-to-many relationship connects the two tables. The selected fields appear in the design grid. Not all of the fields are visible in the grid; to see the other selected fields, you need to scroll to the right using the horizontal scroll bar.

To display the information Matt wants, you need to enter the condition for the StartDate field in its Criteria text box. Matt wants to display only those records with a start date of 07/01/2006.

To enter the exact match condition, and then run the query:

1. Click the **StartDate Criteria** text box, type **07/01/2006**, and then press the **Enter** key. The condition changes to #7/1/2006#.

   Access automatically placed number signs (#) before and after the condition. You must place date and time values inside number signs when using these values as selection criteria. If you omit the number signs, however, Access will include them automatically.

2. Click the **Run** button on the Query Design toolbar. Access runs the query and displays the selected field values for only those records with a StartDate field value of 07/01/2006. A total of 9 records are selected and displayed in the datasheet. See Figure 3-21.

Figure 3-21	Datasheet displaying selected fields and records

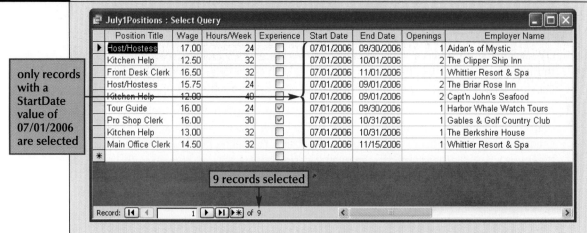

3. Click the **Save** button on the Query Datasheet toolbar to save the query.

Matt would like to see more fields and records on the screen at one time. He asks you to maximize the datasheet, change the datasheet's font size, and resize all the columns to their best fit.

Changing a Datasheet's Appearance

You can change the characteristics of a datasheet, including the font type and size of text in the datasheet, to improve its appearance or readability. As you learned in Tutorial 2, you can also resize the datasheet columns to view more columns on the screen at the same time.

You'll maximize the datasheet, change the font size from the default 10 points to 8, and then resize the datasheet columns.

To change the font size and resize columns in the datasheet:

1. Click the **Maximize** button ▣ on the Query window title bar.

2. Click **Format** on the menu bar, and then click **Font** to open the Font dialog box.

3. Scroll the Size list box, click **8**, and then click the **OK** button. The font size for the entire datasheet changes to 8.

   Next, you need to resize the columns to their best fit, so that each column is just wide enough to fit the longest value in the column. Instead of resizing each column individually, as you did in Tutorial 2, you'll select all the columns and resize them at the same time.

4. Position the pointer in the PositionTitle field selector. When the pointer changes to a ↓ shape, click to select the entire column.

5. Click the right arrow on the horizontal scroll bar until the Phone field is fully visible, and then position the pointer in the Phone field selector until the pointer changes to a ↓ shape.

6. Press and hold the **Shift** key, and then click the mouse button. All the columns are selected. Now you can resize all of them at once.

7. Position the pointer at the right edge of the Phone field selector until the pointer changes to a ↔ shape. See Figure 3-22.

Preparing to resize all columns to their best fit | Figure 3-22

8. Double-click the mouse button. All columns are resized to their best fit, which makes each column just large enough to fit the longest *visible* value in the column, including the field name at the top of the column.

9. Scroll to the left, if necessary, so that the PositionTitle field is visible, and then click any field value box (except an Experience field value) to deselect all columns. See Figure 3-23.

| Figure 3-23 | **Datasheet after changing font size and column widths** |

Trouble? Your screen might show more or fewer columns, depending on the monitor you are using.

10. Save and close the query. You return to the Database window.

After viewing the query results, Matt decides that he would like to see the same fields, but only for those records whose Wage field value is equal to or greater than 17.00. He needs this information when he recruits students who require a higher wage per hour for the available positions. To create the query needed to produce these results, you need to use a comparison operator to match a range of values—in this case, any Wage value greater than or equal to 17.00.

Using a Comparison Operator to Match a Range of Values

Once you create and save a query, you can click the Open button to run it again, or you can click the Design button to change its design. Because the design of the query you need to create next is similar to the July1Positions query, you will change its design, run the query to test it, and then save the query with a new name, which keeps the July1Positions query intact.

To change the July1Positions query design to create a new query:

1. Click the **July1Positions** query in the Database window (if necessary), and then click the **Design** button to open the July1Positions query in Design view.

2. Click the **Wage Criteria** text box, type **>=17**, and then press the **Tab** key three times. See Figure 3-24.

| Figure 3-24 | **Changing a query's design to create a new query** |

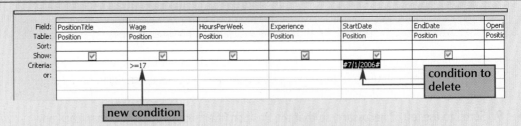

Matt's new condition specifies that a record will be selected only if its Wage field value is 17.00 or higher. Before you run the query, you need to delete the condition for the StartDate field.

3. With the StartDate field condition highlighted, press the **Delete** key. Now there is no condition for the StartDate field.

4. Click the **Run** button 🔹 on the Query Design toolbar. Access runs the query and displays the selected fields for only those records with a Wage field value greater than or equal to 17.00. A total of 19 records are selected. See Figure 3-25.

Running the modified query ◀ **Figure 3-25**

only records with a Wage value greater than or
equal to 17.00 are selected

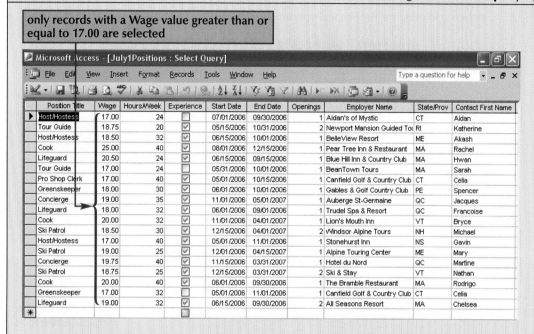

So that Matt can display this information again, as necessary, you'll save the query as HighWageAmounts.

5. Click **File** on the menu bar, and then click **Save As** to open the Save As dialog box.

6. In the text box for the new query name, type **HighWageAmounts**. Notice that the As text box specifies that you are saving the data as a query.

7. Click the **OK** button to save the query using the new name. The new query name appears in the title bar.

8. Close the Query window and return to the Database window.

Elsa asks Matt for a list of the positions with a start date of 07/01/2006 for only the employers in Prince Edward Island. She wants to increase NSJI's business activity throughout eastern Canada (Prince Edward Island in particular), especially in the latter half of the year. To produce this data, you need to create a query containing two conditions—one for the position's start date and another to specify only the employers in Prince Edward Island (PE).

Defining Multiple Selection Criteria for Queries

Multiple conditions require you to use **logical operators** to combine two or more conditions. When you want a record selected only if two or more conditions are met, you need to use the **And logical operator**. In this case, Elsa wants to see only those records with a StartDate field value of 07/01/2006 *and* a StateProv field value of PE. If you place conditions in separate fields in the *same* Criteria row of the design grid, all conditions in that row must be met in order for a record to be included in the query results. However, if you place conditions in *different* Criteria rows, a record will be selected if at least one of the conditions is met. If none of the conditions is met, Access does not select the record. When you place conditions in different Criteria rows, you are using the **Or logical operator**. Figure 3-26 illustrates the difference between the And and Or logical operators.

Figure 3-26	Logical operators And and Or for multiple selection criteria

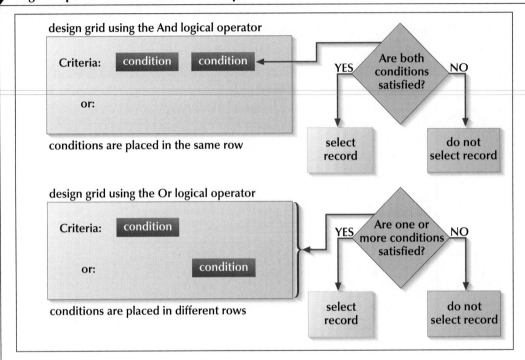

The And Logical Operator

To create Elsa's query, you need to modify the existing July1Positions query to show only the records for employers located in Prince Edward Island and offering positions starting on 07/01/2006. For the modified query, you must add a second condition in the same Criteria row. The existing condition for the StartDate field finds records for positions that start on July 1, 2006; the new condition "PE" in the StateProv field will find records for employers in Prince Edward Island. Because the conditions appear in the same Criteria row, the query will select records only if both conditions are met.

After modifying the query, you'll save it and then rename it as "PEJuly1Positions," overwriting the July1Positions query, which Matt no longer needs.

To modify the July1Positions query and use the And logical operator:

▶ 1. With the Queries object selected in the Database window, click **July1Positions** (if necessary), and then click the **Design** button to open the query in Design view.

▶ 2. Scroll the design grid to the right, click the **StateProv Criteria** text box, type **PE**, and then press the ↓ key. See Figure 3-27.

Query to find positions in PE that start on 07/01/2006 ◀ **Figure 3-27**

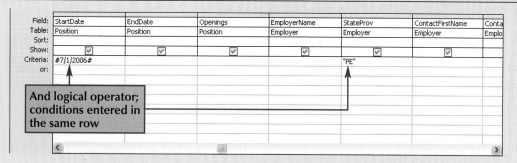

Notice that Access added quotation marks around the entry "PE"; you can type the quotation marks when you enter the condition, but if you forget to do so, Access will add them for you automatically.

The condition for the StartDate field is already entered, so you can run the query.

3. Run the query. Access displays in the datasheet only those records that meet both conditions: a StartDate field value of 07/01/2006 and a StateProv field value of PE. Two records are selected. See Figure 3-28.

Results of query using the And logical operator ◀ **Figure 3-28**

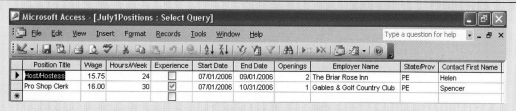

Now you can save the changes to the query and rename it.

4. Save and close the query. You return to the Database window.

5. Right-click **July1Positions** in the Queries list box, and then click **Rename** on the shortcut menu.

6. Press the **Home** key to position the insertion point to the left of the text "July," type **PE**, and then press the **Enter** key. The query name is now PEJuly1Positions.

Now Elsa can run the PEJuly1Positions query whenever she needs to know which employers in Prince Edward Island are offering positions starting on 07/01/2006.

Using Multiple Undo and Redo

Access allows you to undo and redo multiple actions when you are working in Design view for tables, queries, forms, reports, and so on. For example, when working in the Query window in Design view, if you specify multiple selection criteria for a query, you can use the multiple undo feature to remove the criteria—even after you run and save the query.

To see how this feature works, you will reopen the PEJuly1Positions query in Design view, delete the two criteria, and then reinsert them using multiple undo.

To modify the PEJuly1Positions query and use the multiple undo feature:

1. Open the **PEJuly1Positions** query in Design view.

2. Select the StartDate Criteria value, **#7/1/2006#**, and then press the **Delete** key. The StartDate Criteria text box is now empty.

3. Press the **Tab** key four times to move to and select **"PE"**, the StateProv Criteria value, and then press the **Delete** key.

4. Run the query. Notice that the results display all records for the fields specified in the query design grid.

5. Click the **View** button for Design view ⌾ on the Query Datasheet toolbar to switch back to Design view.

   Now you will use multiple undo to reverse the edits you made and reinsert the two conditions.

6. Click the **list arrow** for the Undo button ⤺ ▾ on the Query Design toolbar. A menu appears listing the actions you can undo. See Figure 3-29.

Figure 3-29	**Using multiple undo**

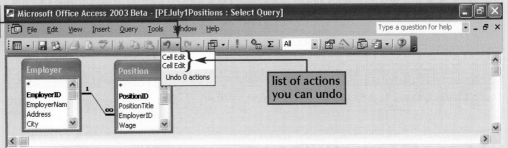

Two items, both named "Cell Edit," are listed in the Undo list box. These items represent the two changes you made to the query design—first deleting the StartDate condition and then deleting the StateProv condition. If you select an action that is below other items in the list, you will undo all the actions above the one you select, in addition to the one you select. Currently no actions are selected, so the list box indicates "Undo 0 actions."

7. Position the pointer over the second occurrence of **Cell Edit** in the list. Notice that both undo actions are highlighted, and the list box indicates that you can undo two actions.

8. Click the second occurrence of **Cell Edit**. Both actions are "undone," and the two conditions are redisplayed in the query design grid. The multiple undo feature makes it easy for you to test different criteria for a query and, when necessary, to undo your actions based on the query results.

   Notice that the Redo button and list arrow are now available. You can redo the actions you've just undone.

9. Click the **list arrow** for the Redo button ⤻ ▾ on the Query Design toolbar. The Redo list box indicates that you can redo the two cell edits.

10. Click the **list arrow** for the Redo button ⤻ ▾ again to close the Redo list box without selecting any option.

11. Close the query. Click the **No** button in the message box that opens, asking if you want to save your changes. You return to the Database window.

Matt has another request for information. He knows that it can be difficult to find student recruits for positions that offer fewer than 30 hours of work per week or that require prior work experience. So that his staff can focus on such positions, Matt wants to see a list of those positions that provide less than 30 hours of work or that require experience. To create this query, you need to use the Or logical operator.

The Or Logical Operator

For Matt's request, you need a query that selects a record when either one of two conditions is satisfied or when both conditions are satisfied. That is, a record is selected if the HoursPerWeek field value is less than 30 *or* if the Experience field value is "Yes" (checked). You will enter the condition for the HoursPerWeek field in the Criteria row and the condition for the Experience field in the "or" criteria row, thereby using the Or logical operator.

To display the information Matt wants to view, you'll create a new query containing the EmployerName and City fields from the Employer table and the PositionTitle, HoursPerWeek, and Experience fields from the Position table. Then you'll specify the conditions using the Or logical operator.

To create the query and use the Or logical operator:

1. In the Database window, double-click **Create query in Design view**. The Show Table dialog box opens on top of the Query window in Design view.

2. Click **Employer** in the Tables list box (if necessary), click the **Add** button, click **Position**, click the **Add** button, and then click the **Close** button. The Employer and Position field lists appear in the Query window, and the Show Table dialog box closes.

3. Double-click **EmployerName** in the Employer field list to add the EmployerName field to the design grid's first column Field text box.

4. Repeat Step 3 to add the **City** field from the Employer table, and then add the **PositionTitle**, **HoursPerWeek**, and **Experience** fields from the Position table.

   Now you need to specify the first condition, <30, in the HoursPerWeek field.

5. Click the **HoursPerWeek Criteria** text box, type **<30** and then press the **Tab** key.

   Because you want records selected if either of the conditions for the HoursPerWeek or Experience fields is satisfied, you must enter the condition for the Experience field in the "or" row of the design grid.

6. Press the ↓ key, and then type **Yes** in the "or" text box for Experience. See Figure 3-30.

Query window with the Or logical operator | Figure 3-30

Field:	EmployerName	City	PositionTitle	HoursPerWeek	Experience		
Table:	Employer	Employer	Position	Position	Position		
Sort:							
Show:	☑	☑	☑	☑	☑	☐	
Criteria:				<30			
or:					Yes		

Or logical operator; conditions entered in different rows

7. Run the query. Access displays only those records that meet either condition: an HoursPerWeek field value less than 30 or an Experience field value of "Yes" (checked). A total of 35 records are selected.

   Matt wants the list displayed in alphabetical order by EmployerName. The first record's EmployerName field is highlighted, indicating the current field.

8. Click the **Sort Ascending** button [↓] on the Query Datasheet toolbar.

9. Resize all datasheet columns to their best fit. Scroll through the entire datasheet to make sure that all values are completely displayed. Deselect all columns when you are finished resizing them, and then return to the top of the datasheet. See Figure 3-31.

| Figure 3-31 | Results of query using the Or logical operator |

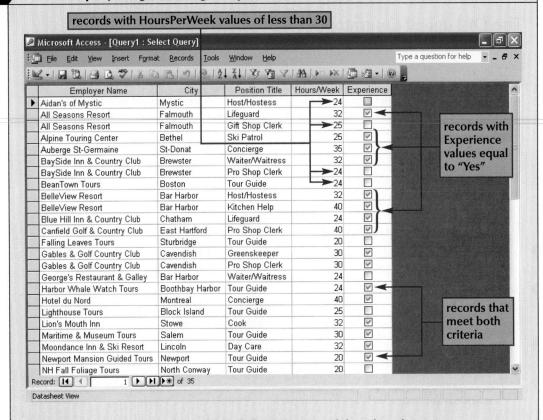

10. Save the query with the name **HoursOrExperience**, and then close the query.

Next, Elsa wants to use the Northeast database to perform calculations. She is considering offering a 2% bonus per week to the student recruits in higher paid positions, based on employer recommendation, and she wants to know exactly what these bonuses would be.

Performing Calculations

In addition to using queries to retrieve, sort, and filter data in a database, you can use a query to perform calculations. To perform a calculation, you define an **expression** containing a combination of database fields, constants, and operators. For numeric expressions, the data types of the database fields must be number, currency, or date/time; the constants are numbers such as .02 (for the 2% bonus); and the operators can be arithmetic operators (+ – * /) or other specialized operators. In complex expressions, you can enclose calculations in parentheses to indicate which one should be performed first. In expressions without parentheses, Access calculates in the following order of precedence: multiplication and division before addition and subtraction. When operators have equal precedence, Access calculates them in order from left to right.

To perform a calculation in a query, you add a calculated field to the query. A **calculated field** is a field that displays the results of an expression. A calculated field appears in a query datasheet or in a form or report; however, it does not exist in a database. When you run a query that contains a calculated field, Access evaluates the expression defined by the calculated field and displays the resulting value in the query datasheet, form, or report.

Creating a Calculated Field

To produce the information Elsa wants, you need to open the HighWageAmounts query and create a calculated field that will multiply each Wage field value by each HoursPerWeek value, and then multiply that amount by .02 to determine the 2% weekly bonus Elsa is considering.

   To enter an expression for a calculated field, you can type it directly in a Field text box in the design grid. Alternately, you can open the Zoom box or Expression Builder and use either one to enter the expression. The **Zoom box** is a large text box for entering text, expressions, or other values. To use the Zoom box, however, you must know all the parts of the expression you want to create. **Expression Builder** is an Access tool that makes it easy for you to create an expression; it contains a box for entering the expression, buttons for common operators, and one or more lists of expression elements, such as table and field names. Unlike a Field text box, which is too small to show an entire expression at one time, the Zoom box and Expression Builder are large enough to display lengthy expressions. In most cases, Expression Builder provides the easiest way to enter expressions, because you don't have to know all the parts of the expression; you can choose the necessary elements from the Expression Builder dialog box.

Using Expression Builder

Reference Window

- Open the query in Design view.
- In the design grid, position the insertion point in the Field text box of the field for which you want to create an expression.
- Click the Build button on the Query Design toolbar.
- Use the expression elements and common operators to build the expression, or type the expression directly.
- Click the OK button.

   You'll begin by copying, pasting, and renaming the HighWageAmounts query, keeping the original query intact. You'll name the new query "HighWagesWithBonus." Then you'll modify this query in Design view to show only the information Elsa wants to view.

To copy the HighWageAmounts query and paste the copy with a new name:

► **1.** Right-click the **HighWageAmounts** query in the list of queries, and then click **Copy** on the shortcut menu.

► **2.** Right-click an empty area of the Database window, and then click **Paste** on the shortcut menu. The Paste As dialog box opens.

► **3.** Type **HighWagesWithBonus** in the Query Name text box, and then press the **Enter** key. The new query appears in the query list, along with the original HighWageAmounts query.

   Now you're ready to modify the HighWagesWithBonus query to create the calculated field for Elsa.

To modify the HighWagesWithBonus query:

1. Open the **HighWagesWithBonus** query in Design view.

   Elsa wants to see only the EmployerName, PositionTitle, and Wage fields in the query results. First, you'll delete the unnecessary fields, and then you'll move the EmployerName field so that it appears first in the query results.

2. Scroll the design grid to the right until the HoursPerWeek and EmployerName fields are visible at the same time.

3. Position the pointer on the HoursPerWeek field selector until the pointer changes to a ↓ shape, click and hold down the mouse button, drag the mouse to the right to highlight the HoursPerWeek, Experience, StartDate, EndDate, and Openings fields, and then release the mouse button.

4. Press the **Delete** key to delete the five selected fields.

5. Use this same method to delete the StateProv, ContactFirstName, ContactLastName, and Phone fields from the query design grid.

   Next, you'll move the EmployerName field to the left of the PositionTitle field so that the Wage values will appear next to the calculated field values in the query results.

6. Scroll the design grid back to the left (if necessary), select the **EmployerName** field, and then use the pointer 🔓 to drag the field to the left of the PositionTitle field. See Figure 3-32.

| Figure 3-32 | Modified query before adding the calculated field |

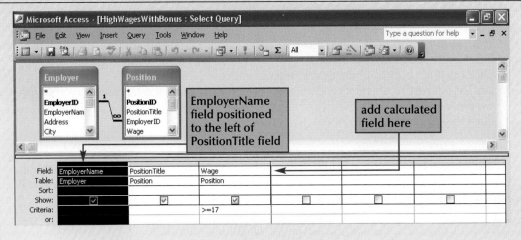

Now you're ready to use Expression Builder to enter the calculated field in the HighWagesWithBonus query.

To add the calculated field to the HighWagesWithBonus query:

1. Position the insertion point in the blank Field text box to the right of the Wage field, and then click the **Build** button 🔨 on the Query Design toolbar. The Expression Builder dialog box opens. See Figure 3-33.

Initial Expression Builder dialog box | **Figure 3-33**

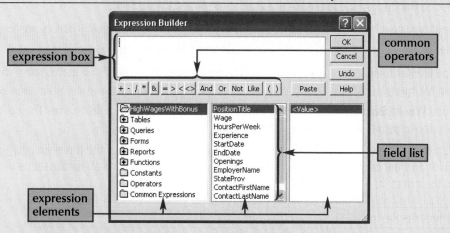

You use the common operators and expression elements to help you build an expression. Note that the HighWagesWithBonus query is already selected in the list box on the lower left; the fields included in the original version of the query are listed in the center box.

The expression for the calculated field will multiply the Wage field values by the HoursPerWeek field values, and then multiply that amount by the numeric constant .02 (which represents a 2% bonus). To include a field in the expression, you select the field and then click the Paste button. To include a numeric constant, you simply type the constant in the expression.

▶ **2.** Click **Wage** in the field list, and then click the **Paste** button. [Wage] appears in the expression box.

To include the multiplication operator in the expression, you click the asterisk (*****) button. Note that you do not include spaces between the elements in an expression.

▶ **3.** Click the ***** button in the row of common operators, click **HoursPerWeek** in the field list, and then click the **Paste** button. The expression multiplies the Wage values by the HoursPerWeek values.

▶ **4.** Click the ***** button in the row of common operators, and then type **.02**. You have finished entering the expression. See Figure 3-34.

Completed expression for the calculated field | **Figure 3-34**

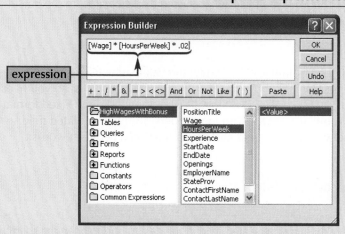

Note that you also could have typed the expression directly into the expression box, instead of clicking the field names and the operator.

> **5.** Click the **OK** button. Access closes the Expression Builder dialog box and adds the expression to the design grid in the Field text box for the calculated field.
>
> Next, you need to specify a name for the calculated field as it will appear in the query results.

> **6.** Press the **Home** key to position the insertion point to the left of the expression.
>
> You'll enter the name WeeklyBonus, which is descriptive of the field's contents; then you'll run the query.

> **7.** Type **WeeklyBonus:**. *Make sure you include the colon following the field name.* The colon is needed to separate the field name from its expression.

> **8.** Run the query. Access displays the query datasheet, which contains the three specified fields and the calculated field with the name "WeeklyBonus." Resize all datasheet columns to their best fit. See Figure 3-35.

Figure 3-35	Datasheet displaying the calculated field

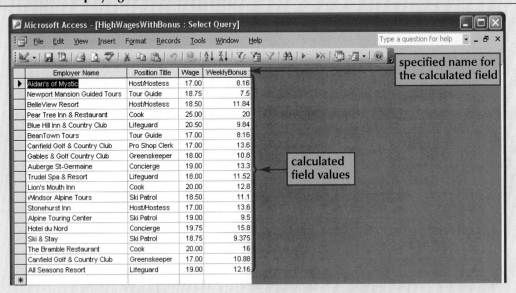

Trouble? If the calculated field name does not appear correctly, as shown in Figure 3-35, you might not have included the required colon. Switch to Design view, then repeat Steps 7 and 8, making sure that you type the colon following the field name, to separate it from the calculated field's expression.

Notice the WeeklyBonus value for Ski & Stay; the value appears with three decimal places (9.375). Currency values should have only two decimal places, so you need to format the WeeklyBonus calculated field so that all values appear in the Fixed format with two decimal places. You'll also set the Caption property for the calculated field so that it is displayed in the same way as other field names, with a space between words.

To format the calculated field:

> **1.** Switch to Design view.

> **2.** Right-click the **WeeklyBonus** calculated field in the design grid to open the shortcut menu, and then click **Properties**. The property sheet for the selected field opens. The property sheet for a field provides options for changing the display of field values in the datasheet.

3. Click the right side of the **Format** text box to display the list of formats, and then click **Fixed**. This format specifies no commas or dollar signs, which are unnecessary for the calculated field and would only clutter the worksheet.

4. Click the right side of the **Decimal Places** text box, and then click **2**.

5. Press the **Tab** key twice to move to the Caption property, and then type **Weekly Bonus**. See Figure 3-36.

Property sheet settings to format the calculated field ◀ **Figure 3-36**

Now that you have formatted the calculated field, you can run the query.

6. Close the Field Properties window, and then save and run the query. The calculated field now displays the name "Weekly Bonus," and the value for Ski & Stay now correctly appears as 9.38.

7. Close the query.

Elsa prepares a report on a regular basis that includes a summary of information about the wages paid to student recruits. She lists the minimum hourly wage paid, the average wage amount, and the maximum hourly wage paid. She asks you to create a query to determine these statistics from data in the Position table.

Using Aggregate Functions

You can calculate statistical information, such as totals and averages, on the records selected by a query. To do this, you use the Access aggregate functions. **Aggregate functions** perform arithmetic operations on selected records in a database. Figure 3-37 lists the most frequently used aggregate functions. Aggregate functions operate on the records that meet a query's selection criteria. You specify an aggregate function for a specific field, and the appropriate operation applies to that field's values for the selected records.

Figure 3-37   **Frequently used aggregate functions**

Aggregate Function	Determines	Data Types Supported
Avg	Average of the field values for the selected records	AutoNumber, Currency, Date/Time, Number
Count	Number of records selected	AutoNumber, Currency, Date/Time, Memo, Number, OLE Object, Text, Yes/No
Max	Highest field value for the selected records	AutoNumber, Currency, Date/Time, Number, Text
Min	Lowest field value for the selected records	AutoNumber, Currency, Date/Time, Number, Text
Sum	Total of the field values for the selected records	AutoNumber, Currency, Date/TIme, Number

To display the minimum, average, and maximum of all the wage amounts in the Position table, you will use the Min, Avg, and Max aggregate functions for the Wage field.

To calculate the minimum, average, and maximum of all wage amounts:

1. Double-click **Create query in Design view**, click **Position**, click the **Add** button, and then click the **Close** button. The Position field list is added to the Query window, and the Show Table dialog box closes.

   To perform the three calculations on the Wage field, you need to add the field to the design grid three times.

2. Double-click **Wage** in the Position field list three times to add three copies of the field to the design grid.

   You need to select an aggregate function for each Wage field. When you click the Totals button on the Query Design toolbar, a row labeled "Total" is added to the design grid. The Total row provides a list of the aggregate functions that you can select.

3. Click the **Totals** button Σ on the Query Design toolbar. A new row labeled "Total" appears between the Table and Sort rows in the design grid. See Figure 3-38.

Figure 3-38   **Total row inserted in the design grid**

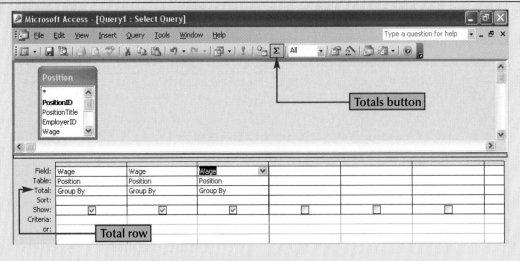

In the Total row, you specify the aggregate function you want to use for a field.

4. Click the right side of the first column's **Total** text box, and then click **Min**. This field will calculate the minimum amount of all the Wage field values.

   When you run the query, Access automatically will assign a datasheet column name of "MinOfWage" for this field. You can change the datasheet column name to a more descriptive or readable name by entering the name you want in the Field text box. However, you must also keep the field name Wage in the Field text box, because it identifies the field whose values will be calculated. The Field text box will contain the datasheet column name you specify followed by the field name (Wage) with a colon separating the two names.

5. Position the insertion point to the left of Wage in the first column's Field text box, and then type **Minimum Wage:**. *Be sure that you type the colon following the name.*

6. Click the right side of the second column's **Total** text box, and then click **Avg**. This field will calculate the average of all the Wage field values.

7. Position the insertion point to the left of Wage in the second column's Field text box, and then type **Average Wage:**.

8. Click the right side of the third column's **Total** text box, and then click **Max**. This field will calculate the maximum amount of all the Wage field values.

9. Position the insertion point to the left of Wage in the third column's Field text box, and then type **Maximum Wage:**.

   The query design is completed, so you can run the query.

10. Run the query. Access displays one record containing the three aggregate function values. The single row of summary statistics represents calculations based on the 64 records selected by the query.

    You need to resize the three columns to their best fit to see the column names.

11. Resize all columns to their best fit, and then position the insertion point in the field value in the first column. See Figure 3-39.

Results of the query using aggregate functions ◀ **Figure 3-39**

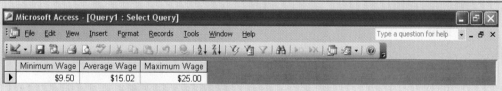

12. Save the query as **WageStatistics**, and then close the query.

Elsa also wants her report to include the same wage statistics (minimum, average, and maximum) for each type of position. She asks you to display the wage statistics for each different PositionTitle value in the Position table.

Using Record Group Calculations

In addition to calculating statistical information on all or selected records in selected tables, you can calculate statistics for groups of records. For example, you can determine the number of employers in each state or province, or the average wage amount by position.

To create a query for Elsa's latest request, you can modify the current query by adding the PositionTitle field and assigning the Group By operator to it. The **Group By operator** divides the selected records into groups based on the values in the specified field. Those records with the same value for the field are grouped together, and the datasheet displays one record for each group. Aggregate functions, which appear in the other columns of the design grid, provide statistical information for each group.

You need to modify the current query to add the Group By operator for the PositionTitle field. This will display the statistical information grouped by position for the 64 selected records in the query. As you did earlier, you will copy the WageStatistics query and paste it with a new name, keeping the original query intact, to create the new query.

To copy and paste the query, and then add the PositionTitle field with the Group By operator:

1. Right-click the **WageStatistics** query in the list of queries, and then click **Copy** on the shortcut menu.

2. Right-click an empty area of the Database window, and then click **Paste** on the shortcut menu.

3. Type **WageStatisticsByPosition** in the Query Name text box, and then press the **Enter** key.

    Now you're ready to modify the query design.

4. Open the **WageStatisticsByPosition** query in Design view.

5. Double-click **PositionTitle** in the Position field list to add the field to the design grid. Group By, which is the default option in the Total row, appears for the PositionTitle field.

    You've completed the query changes, so you can run the query.

6. Run the query. Access displays 16 records—one for each PositionTitle group. Each record contains the three aggregate function values and the PositionTitle field value for the group. Again, the summary statistics represent calculations based on the 64 records selected by the query. See Figure 3-40.

| Figure 3-40 | Aggregate functions grouped by PositionTitle |

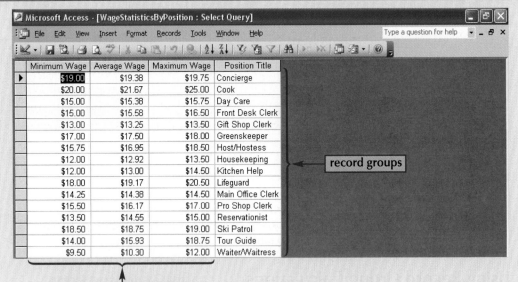

7. Save and close the query, and then close the Northeast database.

    Trouble? If a dialog box opens and asks if you want to empty the Clipboard, click the Yes button.

The queries you've created and saved will help Elsa, Zack, Matt, and other employees to monitor and analyze the business activity of NSJI's employer customers. Now any NSJI staff member can run the queries at any time, modify them as needed, or use them as the basis for designing new queries to meet additional information requirements.

Session 3.2 Quick Check

1. A(n) _____ is a criterion, or rule, that determines which records are selected for a query datasheet.
2. In the design grid, where do you place the conditions for two different fields when you use the And logical operator? The Or logical operator?
3. To perform a calculation in a query, you define a(n) _____ containing a combination of database fields, constants, and operators.
4. How does a calculated field differ from a table field?
5. What is an aggregate function?
6. The _____ operator divides selected records into groups based on the values in a field.

To reinforce the tasks you learned in this session, go to the SAM 2003 Training Companion CD included with this text.

Tutorial Summary

In this tutorial, you learned how to create queries in Design view, and how to run and save queries. You also learned how you can use the query datasheet to update the data contained in the underlying database table. This tutorial presented one of the most important database concepts—defining table relationships. You learned how to define a one-to-many relationship between two tables in a database, and how to enforce referential integrity as part of the relationship. After defining this relationship, you created a query based on data in the two tables. You learned how to sort and filter query results to view records in a particular order and to view different subsets of the displayed records. Using record selection criteria, you specified an exact match in a query, used a comparison operator to match a range of values, and used the And and Or logical operators to meet various requests for data retrieval. Finally, you created a calculated field in the Expression Builder dialog box to display the results of an expression in a query, and you used aggregate functions and the Group By operator to calculate and display statistical information in a query.

Key Terms

aggregate function	Filter By Form	recordset
And logical operator	Filter By Selection	referential integrity
calculated field	Group By operator	related table
cascade deletes option	join	Relationships window
cascade updates option	join line	run (query)
comparison operator	logical operator	secondary sort field
condition	nonunique sort field	select query
design grid	one-to-many relationship	sort
exact match	Or logical operator	Sort Ascending button
expression	orphaned record	Sort Descending button
Expression Builder	primary sort field	sort field
field list	primary table	unique sort field
filter	query by example (QBE)	Zoom box

Practice

Build on what you learned in the tutorial by practicing those skills using the same case scenario.

Review Assignments

Data File needed for the Review Assignments: Recruits.mdb (*cont. from Tutorial 2*)

Elsa needs information from the Recruits database, and she asks you to query the database by completing the following:

1. Open the **Recruits** database located in the Brief\Review folder provided with your Data Files.
2. Create a select query based on the **Student** table. Display the StudentID, FirstName, and LastName fields in the query results; sort in ascending order based on the LastName field values; and select only those records whose Nation value equals Ireland. (*Hint*: Do not display the Nation field values in the query results.) Save the query as **StudentsFromIreland**, run the query, and then print the query datasheet.
3. Use the **StudentsFromIreland** datasheet to update the **Student** table by changing the FirstName field value for StudentID OMA9956 to Richard. Print the query datasheet, and then close the query.
4. Define a one-to-many relationship between the primary **Recruiter** table and the related **Student** table. Resize the field lists, as necessary, to display all the field names. Select the referential integrity option and the cascade updates option for the relationship.
5. Use Design view to create a select query based on the **Recruiter** and **Student** tables. Select the fields FirstName, LastName, City, and Nation from the **Student** table, and the fields BonusQuota, Salary, and SSN from the **Recruiter** table, in that order. Sort in ascending order based on the Nation field values. Select only those records whose SSN equals "977-07-1798." (*Hint*: Do not display the SSN field values in the query results.) Save the query as **WolfeRecruits**, and then run the query. Resize all columns in the datasheet to fit the data. Print the datasheet, and then save and close the query.
6. Use Design view to create a query based on the **Recruiter** table that shows all recruiters with a BonusQuota field value between 40 and 50, and whose Salary field value is greater than 35000. (*Hint*: Refer to Figure 3-19 to determine the correct comparison operator to use.) Display all fields except SSN from the **Recruiter** table. Save the query as **BonusInfo**, and then run the query.
7. Switch to Design view for the **BonusInfo** query. Create a calculated field named RaiseAmt that displays the net amount of a 3% raise to the Salary values. The expression for the calculated field will begin with the Salary field, and add to it the result of multiplying the Salary field by .03. Display the results in descending order by RaiseAmt. Save the query as a new query named **SalariesWithRaises**, and then run the query.
8. Switch to Design view for the **SalariesWithRaises** query, and then change the format of the calculated field to the Standard format, with no decimal places. Also change the caption property of the calculated field to "Raise Amt." Run the query. Resize all columns in the datasheet to fit the data, print the query datasheet, and then save and close the query.
9. In the Database window, copy the **StudentsFromIreland** query, and then paste it with the new name **StudentsFromHollandPlusYoungerStudents**. Open the new query in Design view. Modify the query to display only those records with a Nation field value of Holland or with a BirthDate field value greater than 1/1/85. Also, modify the query to include the Nation field values in the query results. Save and run the query. Resize all columns in the datasheet to fit the data, print the query datasheet, and then save and close the query.

10. Create a new query based on the **Recruiter** table. Use the Min, Max, and Avg aggregate functions to find the lowest, highest, and average values in the Salary field. Name the three aggregate fields Lowest Salary, Highest Salary, and Average Salary, respectively. Save the query as **SalaryStatistics**, and then run the query. Resize all columns in the datasheet to fit the data, print the query datasheet, and then save and close the query.

11. Open the **SalaryStatistics** query in Design view. Modify the query so that the records are grouped by the BonusQuota field. Save the query as **SalaryStatisticsByBonusQuota**, run the query, print the query datasheet, and then close the query.

12. Close the Recruits database.

Case Problem 1

Data File needed for this Case Problem: Videos.mdb (*cont. from Tutorial 2*)

Lim's Video Photography Youngho Lim wants to view specific information about his clients and video shoot events. He asks you to query the Videos database by completing the following:

1. Open the **Videos** database located in the Brief\Case1 folder provided with your Data Files.

2. Define the necessary one-to-many relationships between the database tables, as follows: between the primary **Client** table and the related **Contract** table, between the primary **Contract** table and the related **Shoot** table, and between the primary **ShootDesc** table and the related **Shoot** table. (*Hint*: Add all four tables to the Relationships window, and then define the three relationships.) Resize the field lists, as necessary, to display all the field names. Select the referential integrity option and the cascade updates option for each relationship.

3. Create a select query based on the **Client** and **Contract** tables. Display the ClientName, City, ContractDate, and ContractAmt fields, in that order. Sort in ascending order based on the ClientName field values. Run the query, save the query as **ClientContracts**, and then print the datasheet.

4. Use Filter By Selection to display only those records with a City field value of Oakland in the **ClientContracts** datasheet. Print the datasheet and then remove the filter. Save and close the query.

5. Open the **ClientContracts** query in Design view. Modify the query to display only those records with a ContractAmt value greater than or equal to 600. Run the query, save the query as **ContractAmounts**, and then print the datasheet.

6. Switch to Design view for the **ContractAmounts** query. Modify the query to display only those records with a ContractAmt value greater than or equal to 600 and with a City value of San Francisco. Also modify the query so that the City field values are not displayed in the query results. Run the query, save it as **SFContractAmounts**, print the datasheet, and then close the query.

7. Close the Videos database.

Apply

Using what you learned in the tutorial, create queries to retrieve data about video photography events.

Explore

Create

Follow the steps provided and use the figures as guides to create queries for a health and fitness center.

Case Problem 2

Data File needed for this Case Problem: Fitness.mdb (*cont. from Tutorial 2*)

Parkhurst Health & Fitness Center   Martha Parkhurst is completing an analysis of the members enrolled in different programs in the fitness center. To help her find the information she needs, you'll query the Fitness database by completing the following:

1. Open the **Fitness** database located in the Brief\Case2 folder provided with your Data Files.
2. Define a one-to-many relationship between the primary **Program** table and the related **Member** table. Resize the field lists, as necessary, to display all the field names. Select the referential integrity option and the cascade updates option for the relationship.
3. Use Design view to create a select query based on the **Member** and **Program** tables. Display the fields FirstName, LastName, DateJoined, MonthlyFee, and PhysicalRequired, in that order. Sort in descending order based on the DateJoined field values. Select only those records with a PhysicalRequired field value of Yes. Save the query as **PhysicalsNeeded**, and then run the query. Switch to Design view and modify the query so that the PhysicalRequired values do not appear in the query results. Save the modified query, and then run the query.
4. Use the **PhysicalsNeeded** datasheet to update the **Member** table by changing the DateJoined value for the first record in the datasheet to 10/18/2007. Print the datasheet, and then close the query.

Explore

5. Use Design view to create a select query based on the **Member** and **Program** tables. For all members who joined the center between 06/01/2007 and 06/30/2007, display the MemberID, FirstName, LastName, DateJoined, Description, and MonthlyFee fields. Save the query as **JuneMembers**, run the query, print the query results, and then close the query.
6. Create and save the query whose results are shown in Figure 3-41. Print the query datasheet, and then close the query.

Figure 3-41

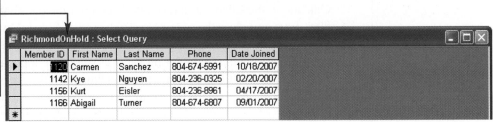

show only records for customers from Richmond whose memberships are on hold

Member ID	First Name	Last Name	Phone	Date Joined
1120	Carmen	Sanchez	804-674-5991	10/18/2007
1142	Kye	Nguyen	804-236-0325	02/20/2007
1156	Kurt	Eisler	804-236-8961	04/17/2007
1166	Abigail	Turner	804-674-6807	09/01/2007

7. Create and save the query whose results are shown in Figure 3-42. Print the query datasheet, and then close the query.

Figure 3-42

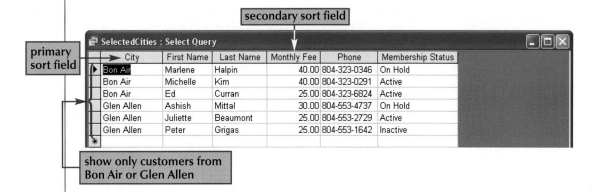

secondary sort field

primary sort field

show only customers from Bon Air or Glen Allen

8. Create and save the query whose results are shown in Figure 3-43 to display statistics for the MonthlyFee field. Print the query datasheet.

Figure 3-43

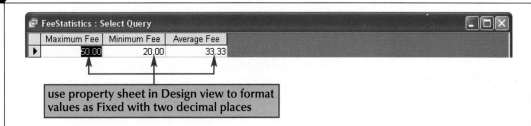

use property sheet in Design view to format values as Fixed with two decimal places

9. Change the query to display the same statistics grouped by City. (*Hint*: Use the Show Table button on the Query Design toolbar to add the **Member** table to the query.) Save the query as **FeeStatisticsByCity**. Run the query, print the query results, and then close the query.
10. Close the Fitness database.

Case Problem 3

Challenge

Use the skills you learned in the tutorial, plus some new ones, to create queries that display information about a zoo and its patrons.

Explore

Data File needed for this Case Problem: Redwood.mdb (*cont. from Tutorial 2*)

Redwood Zoo Michael Rosenfeld wants to find specific information about the donors and their pledge amounts for the Redwood Zoo. You'll help him find the information in the Redwood database by completing the following:

1. Open the **Redwood** database located in the Brief\Case3 folder provided with your Data Files.
2. Define the necessary one-to-many relationships between the database tables, as follows: between the primary **Donor** table and the related **Pledge** table, and between the primary **Fund** table and the related **Pledge** table. (*Hint*: Add all three tables to the Relationships window, and then define the two relationships.) Resize the field lists, as necessary, to display all the field names. Select the referential integrity option and the cascade updates option for each relationship.

3. Use Design view to create a select query that, for all pledges with a TotalPledged field value of greater than 200, displays the DonorID (from the **Donor** table), FirstName, LastName, PledgeID, TotalPledged, and FundName fields. Sort the query in ascending order by TotalPledged. Save the query as **LargePledges**, and then run the query.

4. Use the **LargePledges** datasheet to update the **Pledge** table by changing the TotalPledged field value for PledgeID 2976 to 750. Print the query datasheet, and then close the query.

5. Use Design view to create a select query that, for all donors who pledged less than $150 or who donated to the Whale Watchers fund, displays the PledgeID, PledgeDate, TotalPledged, FirstName, and LastName fields. Save the query as **PledgedOrWhaleWatchers**, run the query, and then print the query datasheet. Change the query to select all donors who pledged less than $150 and who donated to the Whale Watchers fund. Save the revised query as **PledgedAndWhaleWatchers**, and then run the query. Close the query.

Explore ▶

6. Use Design view to create a select query that displays the DonorID (from the **Donor** table), TotalPledged, PaymentMethod, PledgeDate, and FundName fields. Save the query as **PledgesAfterCosts**. Create a calculated field named Overhead that displays the results of multiplying the TotalPledged field values by 15% (to account for overhead costs). Save the query, and then create a second calculated field named NetPledge that displays the results of subtracting the Overhead field values from the TotalPledged field values. Format the calculated fields as Fixed and set an appropriate caption for the NetPledge field. Display the results in ascending order by TotalPledged. Save the modified query, and then run the query. Resize all datasheet columns to their best fit, print the query results, and then save and close the query.

Explore ▶

7. Use the **Pledge** table to display the sum, average, and count of the TotalPledged field for all pledges. Then do the following:
   a. Specify column names of Total Pledge, Average Pledge, and Number of Pledges.
   b. Change properties so that the values in the Total Pledge and Average Pledge columns display two decimal places and the Fixed format.
   c. Save the query as **PledgeStatistics**, run the query, resize all datasheet columns to their best fit, and then print the query datasheet. Save the query.
   d. Change the query to display the sum, average, and count of the TotalPledged field for all pledges by FundName. (*Hint*: Use the Show Table button on the Query Design toolbar to add the **Fund** table to the query.) Save the query as **PledgeStatisticsByFund**, run the query, print the query datasheet, and then close the query.

8. Close the Redwood database.

Challenge

Case Problem 4

Challenge yourself by creating queries, including a new type of query, for a luxury property rental agency.

Data File needed for this Case Problem: GEM.mdb (*cont. from Tutorial 2*)

GEM Ultimate Vacations Griffin and Emma MacElroy want to analyze data about their clients and the luxury properties they rent. Help them query the GEM database by completing the following:

1. Open the **GEM** database located in the Brief\Case4 folder provided with your Data Files.

Explore ▶

2. Define the necessary one-to-many relationships between the database tables, as follows: between the primary **Guest** table and the related **Reservation** table, and between the primary **Property** table and the related **Reservation** table. (*Hint*: Add all three tables to the Relationships window, and then define the two relationships.) Select the referential integrity option and the cascade updates option for each relationship.

3. For all guests, display the GuestName, City, StateProv, ReservationID, StartDate, and EndDate fields. Save the query as **GuestTripDates**, and then run the query. Resize all datasheet columns to their best fit. In Datasheet view, sort the query results in ascending order by the StartDate field. Print the query datasheet, and then save and close the query.

4. For all guests from Illinois (IL), display the GuestName, City, StateProv, ReservationID, People, StartDate, and EndDate fields. Sort the query in ascending order by City. Save the query as **IllinoisGuests**, and then run the query. Modify the query to remove the display of the StateProv field values from the query results. Save the modified query, run the query, print the query datasheet, and then close the query.

Explore

5. For all guests who are not from Illinois or who are renting a property beginning in the month of June 2007, display the GuestName, City, StateProv, ReservationID, StartDate, and PropertyID fields. (*Hint*: Refer to Figure 3-19 to determine the correct comparison operators to use.) Sort the query in descending order by StartDate. Save the query as **OutOfStateOrJune**, run the query, and then print the query datasheet. Change the query to select all clients who are not from Illinois and who are renting a property beginning in the month of June 2007. Sort the query in ascending order by StartDate. Save the query as **OutOfStateAndJune**, run the query, print the query datasheet, and then close the query.

6. For all reservations, display the ReservationID, StartDate, EndDate, PropertyID, PropertyName, People, and RentalRate fields. Save the query as **RentalCost**. Then create a calculated field named CostPerPerson that displays the results of dividing the RentalRate field values by the People field values. Display the results in descending order by CostPerPerson. Run the query. Modify the query design to set the following properties for the CostPerPerson field: Format set to Standard; Decimal Places set to 2; and Caption set to "Cost Per Person". Run the modified query, resize all datasheet columns to their best fit, print the query datasheet, and then save and close the query.

7. Use the **Reservation** table to determine the minimum, average, and maximum RentalRate values for all reservations. Then do the following:
   a. Specify column names of Lowest Rate, Average Rate, and Highest Rate.
   b. Use the property sheet for each column to format the results as Fixed with two decimal places.
   c. Save the query as **RateStatistics**, run the query, resize all datasheet columns to their best fit, print the query datasheet, and then save the query again.

Explore

   d. Revise the query to show the rate statistics grouped by Country. (*Hint:* Use the Show Table button on the Query Design toolbar to add the **Property** table to the query.) Save the revised query as **RateStatisticsByCountry**, run the query, print the query datasheet, and then close the query.

Explore

8. Use the "Type a question for help" box to ask the following question: "How do I create a Top Values query?" Click the topic "Show only the high or low values in a query (MDB)." Read the displayed information, and then close the Microsoft Office Access Help window and the task pane. Open the **RentalCost** query in Design view, and then modify the query to display only the top five values for the CostPerPerson field. Save the query as **TopRentalCost**, run the query, print the query datasheet, and then close the query.

9. Close the GEM database.

Research

Use the Internet to find and work with data related to the topics presented in this tutorial.

Internet Assignments

The purpose of the Internet Assignments is to challenge you to find information on the Internet that you can use to work effectively with this software. The actual assignments are updated and maintained on the Course Technology Web site. Log on to the Internet and use your Web browser to go to the Student Online Companion for New Perspectives Office 2003 at **www.course.com/np/office2003**. Click the Internet Assignments link, and then navigate to the assignments for this tutorial.

Assess

SAM Assessment and Training

If your instructor has chosen to use the full online version of SAM 2003 Assessment and Training, you can go beyond the "just-in-time" training provided on the CD that accompanies this text. Simply log in to your SAM account (http://sam2003.course.com) to launch any assigned training activities or exams that relate to the skills covered in this tutorial.

Review

Quick Check Answers

Session 3.1

1. a general query in which you specify the fields and records you want Access to select
2. The field list contains the table name at the top of the list box and the table's fields listed in the order in which they appear in the table; the design grid displays columns that contain specifications about a field you will use in the query.
3. A table datasheet and a query datasheet look the same, appearing in Datasheet view, and can be used to update data in a database. A table datasheet shows the permanent data in a table, whereas a query datasheet is temporary and its contents are based on the criteria you establish in the design grid.
4. primary table; related table
5. Referential integrity
6. oldest to most recent date
7. False
8. filter

Session 3.2

1. condition
2. in the same Criteria row; in different Criteria rows
3. expression
4. A calculated field appears in a query datasheet, form, or report but does not exist in a database, as does a table field.
5. a function that performs an arithmetic operation on selected records in a database
6. Group By

Creating Forms and Reports

Creating a Position Data Form, an Employer Positions Form, and an Employers and Positions Report

Case | Northeast Seasonal Jobs International (NSJI)

Elsa Jensen wants to continue enhancing the Northeast database to make it easier for NSJI employees to find and maintain data. In particular, she wants the database to include a form based on the Position table to make it easier for employees to enter and change data about available positions. She also wants the database to include a form that shows data from both the Employer and Position tables at the same time. This form will show the position information for each employer along with the corresponding employer data, providing a complete picture of NSJI's employer clients and their available positions.

In addition, Zack Ward would like the database to include a formatted report of employer and position data so that his marketing staff members will have printed output when completing market analyses and planning strategies for selling NSJI's services to employer clients. He wants the information to be formatted attractively, perhaps by including a picture or graphic image on the report for visual interest.

Session	Objectives		SAM Training Tasks	
Session 4.1	• Create a form using the Form Wizard • Change a form's AutoFormat • Find data using a form	• Preview and print selected form records • Maintain table data using a form	• Create forms using the Form Wizard • Delete records from a table using a form • Edit records from a table using a form	• Enter records using a form • Use AutoFormats • Use navigation controls to move among records in a form
Session 4.2	• Create a form with a main form and a subform • Create a report using the Report Wizard	• Check errors in a report • Insert a picture in a report • Preview and print a report	• Align controls • Check errors in a report • Create a report using Report Wizard • Create a summary report using Report Wizard • Enter data in OLE fields • Insert a picture in a report • Modify a subform	• Modify the properties of a form • Move controls • Preview a report • Print a report • Print specific pages of a report • Resize controls • Switch to landscape orientation

Student Data Files   For a complete list of the Data Files needed for this tutorial, see page AC 2.

Session 4.1

Creating a Form Using the Form Wizard

As you learned in Tutorial 1, a form is an object you use to maintain, view, and print records in a database. In Access, you can design your own forms or use a Form Wizard to create them for you automatically.

Elsa asks you to create a new form that her staff can use to view and maintain data in the Position table. In Tutorial 1, you used the AutoForm Wizard to create the EmployerData form in the Seasonal database. The **AutoForm Wizard** creates a form automatically, using all the fields in the selected table or query. To create the form for the Position table, you'll use the Form Wizard. The **Form Wizard** allows you to choose some or all of the fields in the selected table or query, choose fields from other tables and queries, and display the selected fields in any order on the form. You can also apply an existing style to the form to format its appearance quickly.

To open the Northeast database and activate the Form Wizard:

▶ 1. If you are working with a floppy disk, you need to delete a file from the disk to make sure you have enough space to complete this tutorial. Using My Computer or Windows Explorer, delete **NEJobs** from the Brief\Tutorial folder. (You only need to delete this file if you are working with a floppy disk.)

▶ 2. Start Access and open the **Northeast** database located in the Brief\Tutorial folder provided with your Data Files.

▶ 3. Click **Forms** in the Objects bar of the Database window.

▶ 4. Click the **New** button in the Database window. The New Form dialog box opens.

▶ 5. Click **Form Wizard**, click the list arrow for choosing a table or query, click **Position** to select this table as the source for the form, and then click the **OK** button. The first Form Wizard dialog box opens. See Figure 4-1.

| Figure 4-1 | First Form Wizard dialog box |

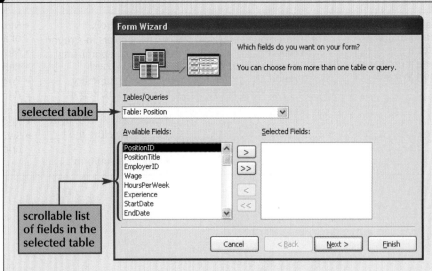

Elsa wants the form to display all the fields in the Position table, but in a different order. She would like the Experience field to appear at the bottom of the form so that it stands out, making it easier to determine if a position requires prior work experience.

To finish creating the form using the Form Wizard:

1. Click **PositionID** in the Available Fields list box (if necessary), and then click the ⎡ > ⎤ button to move the field to the Selected Fields list box.

2. Repeat Step 1 to select the **PositionTitle**, **EmployerID**, **Wage**, **HoursPerWeek**, **StartDate**, **EndDate**, **Openings**, and **Experience** fields, in that order. Remember, you can also double-click a field to move it from the Available Fields list box to the Selected Fields list box.

3. Click the **Next** button to display the second Form Wizard dialog box, in which you select a layout for the form. See Figure 4-2.

Choosing a layout for the form ◀ **Figure 4-2**

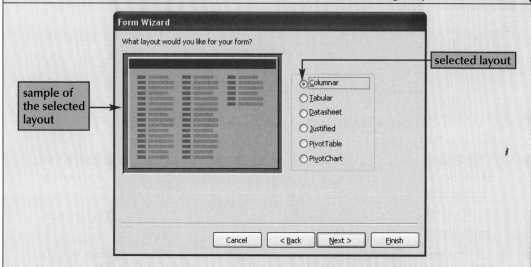

The layout choices are Columnar, Tabular, Datasheet, Justified, PivotTable, and PivotChart. A sample of the selected layout appears on the left side of the dialog box.

4. Click each of the option buttons and review the corresponding sample layout.

The Tabular and Datasheet layouts display the fields from multiple records at one time, whereas the Columnar and Justified layouts display the fields from one record at a time. The PivotTable and PivotChart layouts display summary and analytical information. Elsa thinks the Columnar layout is the appropriate arrangement for displaying and updating data in the table, so you'll choose this layout.

5. Click the **Columnar** option button (if necessary), and then click the **Next** button. Access displays the third Form Wizard dialog box, in which you choose a style for the form. A sample of the selected style appears in the box on the left. If you choose a style, which is called an **AutoFormat**, and decide you'd prefer a different one after the form is created, you can change it. See Figure 4-3.

Trouble? Don't be concerned if a different form style is selected in your dialog box instead of the one shown in Figure 4-3. The dialog box displays the most recently used style, which might be different on your computer.

Figure 4-3 | Choosing a style for the form

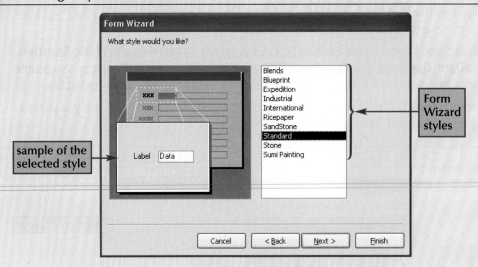

▶ **6.** Click each style and review the corresponding sample.

Elsa likes the Expedition style and asks you to use it for the form.

▶ **7.** Click **Expedition**, and then click the **Next** button. Access displays the final Form Wizard dialog box and shows the Position table's name as the default form name. "Position" is also the default title that will appear in the form's title bar.

You'll use "Position Data" as the form name and, because you don't need to change the form's design at this point, you'll display the form.

▶ **8.** Click the insertion point to the right of Position in the text box, press the **spacebar**, type **Data**, and then click the **Finish** button. The completed form opens in Form view. See Figure 4-4.

Figure 4-4 | Completed form for the Position table

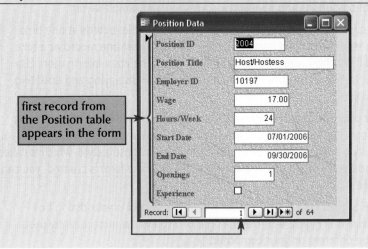

After viewing the form, Elsa decides that she doesn't like the form's style; the background makes the field names a bit difficult to read. She asks you to change the form's style.

Changing a Form's AutoFormat

You can change a form's appearance by choosing a different AutoFormat for the form. As you learned when you created the Position Data form, an AutoFormat is a predefined style for a form (or report). The AutoFormats available for a form are the ones you saw when you selected the form's style using the Form Wizard. To change an AutoFormat, you must switch to Design view.

Changing a Form's AutoFormat

- Display the form in Design view.
- Click the AutoFormat button on the Form Design toolbar to open the AutoFormat dialog box.
- In the Form AutoFormats list box, click the AutoFormat you want to apply to the form, and then click the OK button.

To change the AutoFormat for the Position Data form:

▶ **1.** Click the **View** button for Design view ☑ on the Form View toolbar. The form is displayed in Design view. See Figure 4-5.

Form displayed in Design view ◄ **Figure 4-5**

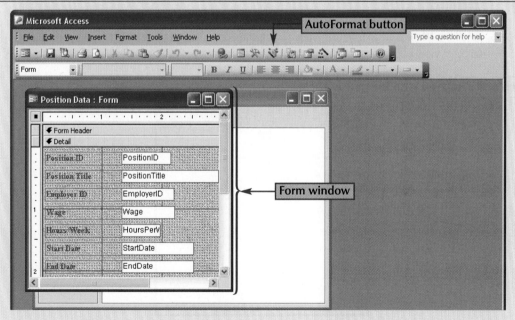

Trouble? If your screen displays any window other than those shown in Figure 4-5, click the Close button ☒ on the window's title bar to close it.

You use Design view to modify an existing form or to create a form from scratch. In this case, you need to change the AutoFormat for the Position Data form.

▶ **2.** Click the **AutoFormat** button ☒ on the Form Design toolbar. The AutoFormat dialog box opens.

▶ **3.** Click the **Options** button to display the AutoFormat options. See Figure 4-6.

Figure 4-6 | **AutoFormat dialog box**

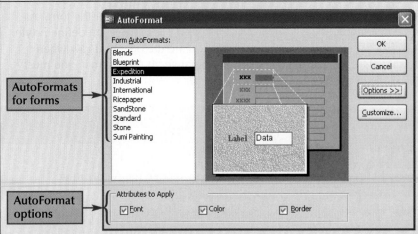

A sample of the selected AutoFormat appears to the right of the Form AutoFormats list box. The options at the bottom of the dialog box let you apply the selected AutoFormat or just its font, color, or border.

Elsa decides that she prefers the Standard AutoFormat, because its field names and field values are easy to read.

▶ **4.** Click **Standard** in the Form AutoFormats list box, and then click the **OK** button. The AutoFormat dialog box closes, the Standard AutoFormat is applied to the form, and the Form window in Design view becomes the active window.

▶ **5.** Click the **View** button for Form view 🔲 on the Form Design toolbar. The form is displayed in Form view with the new AutoFormat. See Figure 4-7.

Figure 4-7 | **Form displayed with the new AutoFormat**

Position Data	_ □ ✕
Position ID	2004
Position Title	Host/Hostess
Employer ID	10197
Wage	17.00
Hours/Week	24
Start Date	07/01/2006
End Date	09/30/2006
Openings	1
Experience	☐

Record: ◄◄ ◄ [1] ► ►► ►✳ of 64

You have finished modifying the format of the form and can now save it.

▶ **6.** Click the **Save** button 🔲 on the Form View toolbar to save the modified form.

Elsa wants to use the Position Data form to view some data in the Position table. To view data, you need to navigate the form. As you learned in Tutorial 1, you navigate a form in the same way that you navigate a table datasheet. Also, the navigation mode and editing mode keystroke techniques you used with datasheets in Tutorial 2 are the same when navigating a form.

To navigate the Position Data form:

1. Press the **Tab** key to move to the PositionTitle field value, and then press the **End** key to move to the Experience field. Because the Experience field is a yes/no field, its value is not highlighted; instead, a dotted outline appears around the field name to indicate that it is the current field.

2. Press the **Home** key to move back to the PositionID field value. The first record in the Position table still appears in the form.

3. Press the **Ctrl+End** keys to move to the Experience field for record 64, which is the last record in the table. The record number for the current record appears in the record number box between the navigation buttons at the bottom of the form.

4. Click the **Previous Record** navigation button ◀ to move to the Experience field in record 63.

5. Press the ↑ key twice to move to the EndDate field in record 63.

6. Click the insertion point between the numbers "0" and "6" in the EndDate field value to switch to editing mode, press the **Home** key to move the insertion point to the beginning of the field value, and then press the **End** key to move the insertion point to the end of the field value.

7. Click the **First Record** navigation button ◀◀ to move to the EndDate field value in the first record. The entire field value is highlighted because you have switched from editing mode to navigation mode.

8. Click the **Next Record** navigation button ▶ to move to the EndDate field value in record 2, the next record.

Elsa asks you to display the records for The Clipper Ship Inn, whose EmployerID value is 10145, because she wants to review the available positions for this employer.

Finding Data Using a Form

The **Find command** lets you search for data in a form or datasheet so you can display only those records you want to view. You choose a field to serve as the basis for the search by making that field the current field; then you enter the value you want Access to match in the Find and Replace dialog box. You can use the Find command by clicking the toolbar Find button or by using the Edit menu.

Finding Data in a Form or Datasheet

Reference Window

- Make the field you want to search the current field.
- Click the Find button on the toolbar to open the Find and Replace dialog box.
- In the Find What text box, type the field value you want to find.
- Complete the remaining options, as necessary, to specify the type of search to conduct.
- Click the Find Next button to begin the search.
- Click the Find Next button to continue searching for the next match.
- Click the Cancel button to stop the search operation.

You need to find all records in the Position table for The Clipper Ship Inn, whose EmployerID is 10145.

To find the records using the Position Data form:

▶ **1.** Click in the **EmployerID** field value box. This is the field that you will search for matching values.

▶ **2.** Click the **Find** button 🔍 on the Form View toolbar. The Find and Replace dialog box opens. Note that the Look In list box shows the name of the field that Access will search (in this case, the current EmployerID field), and the Match list box indicates that Access will find values that match the entire entry in the field. You could choose to match only part of a field value or only the beginning of each field value.

▶ **3.** If the Find and Replace dialog box covers the form, move the dialog box by dragging its title bar. If necessary, move the Position Data form window so that you can see both the dialog box and the form at the same time. See Figure 4-8.

Figure 4-8	Find and Replace dialog box

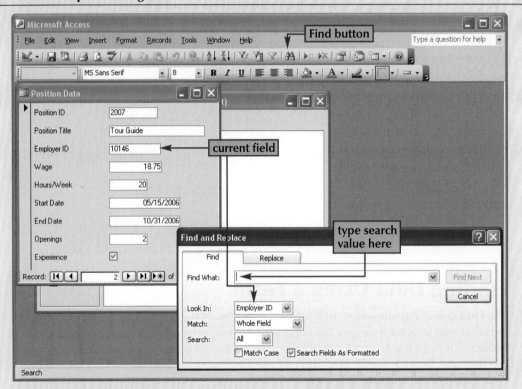

▶ **4.** In the Find What text box, type **10145** and then click the **Find Next** button. The Position Data form now displays record 7, which is the first record for EmployerID 10145.

▶ **5.** Click the **Find Next** button. Access displays record 47, which is the second record for EmployerID 10145.

▶ **6.** Click the **Find Next** button. Access displays record 48, which is the third record for EmployerID 10145.

▶ **7.** Click the **Find Next** button. Access displays a dialog box informing you that the search is finished.

▶ **8.** Click the **OK** button to close the dialog box.

The search value you enter can be an exact value, such as the EmployerID 10145 you just entered, or it can include wildcard characters. A **wildcard character** is a placeholder you use when you know only part of a value or when you want to start or end with a specific character or match a certain pattern. Figure 4-9 shows the wildcard characters you can use when finding data.

Wildcard characters ◀ Figure 4-9

Wildcard Character	Purpose	Example
*	Match any number of characters. It can be used as the first and/or last character in the character string.	th* finds the, that, this, therefore, and so on
?	Match any single alphabetic character.	a?t finds act, aft, ant, apt, and art
[]	Match any single character within the brackets.	a[fr]t finds aft and art but not act, ant, and apt
!	Match any character not within brackets.	a[!fr]t finds act, ant, and apt but not aft and art
-	Match any one of a range of characters. The range must be in ascending order (a to z, not z to a).	a[d-p]t finds aft, ant, and apt but not act and art
#	Match any single numeric character.	#72 finds 072, 172, 272, 372, and so on

Elsa wants to view the position records for two employers: George's Restaurant & Galley (EmployerID 10180) and Moondance Inn & Ski Resort (EmployerID 10185). Matt Griffin, the manager of recruitment, knows of some student recruits with prior work experience who are interested in working for these employers. Elsa wants to see which positions, if any, require experience. You'll use the * wildcard character to search for these employers' positions.

To find the records using the * wildcard character:

1. Click **10145** in the Find What text box to select the entire value, and then type **1018***. Access will match any field value in the EmployerID field that starts with the digits 1018.

2. Click the **Find Next** button. Access displays record 64, which is the first record found for EmployerID 10185. Note that the Experience field value is unchecked, indicating that this position does not require experience.

3. Click the **Find Next** button. Access displays record 25, which is the first record found for EmployerID 10180. Again, the Experience field value is unchecked.

4. Click the **Find Next** button. Access displays record 42, which is the second record found for EmployerID 10185. In this case, the Experience field value is checked, indicating that this position requires prior work experience.

5. Click the **Find Next** button. Access displays a dialog box informing you that the search is finished.

6. Click the **OK** button to close the dialog box.

7. Click the **Cancel** button to close the Find and Replace dialog box.

Of the three positions, only one requires experience—PositionID 2089. Elsa asks you to use the form to print the data for record 42, which is for PositionID 2089, so that she can give the printout to Matt.

Previewing and Printing Selected Form Records

Access prints as many form records as can fit on a printed page. If only part of a form record fits on the bottom of a page, the remainder of the record prints on the next page. Access allows you to print all pages or a range of pages. In addition, you can print the currently selected form record.

Before printing record 42, you'll preview the form record to see how it will look when printed. Notice that the current record number (in this case, 42) appears in the record number box at the bottom of the form.

To preview the form and print the data for record 42:

▶ **1.** Click the **Print Preview** button 🔍 on the Form View toolbar. The Print Preview window opens, showing the form records for the Position table in miniature. If you clicked the Print button now, all the records for the table would be printed, beginning with the first record.

▶ **2.** Click the **Maximize** button 🔲 on the form's title bar.

▶ **3.** Click the **Zoom** button 🔍 on the Print Preview toolbar, and then use the vertical scroll bar to view the entire page. Each record from the Position table appears in a separate form. See Figure 4-10.

| Figure 4-10 | **Print Preview window displaying form records** |

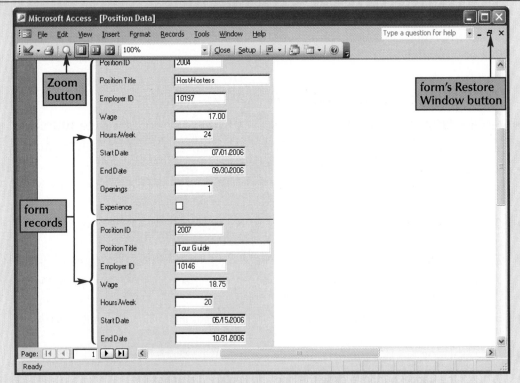

▶ **4.** Click the **Restore Window** button 🗗 on the Print Preview menu bar, and then click the **Close** button on the Print Preview toolbar to return to the table in Form view.

The record that you need to print, PositionID 2089, appears in the form. To print selected records you need to use the Print dialog box.

▸ **5.** Click **File** on the menu bar, and then click **Print**. The Print dialog box opens.

▸ **6.** Click the **Selected Record(s)** option button to print the current form record (record 42).

▸ **7.** Click the **OK** button to close the dialog box and to print the selected record.

Elsa has identified several updates, as shown in Figure 4-11, that she wants you to make to the Position table. You'll use the Position Data form to update the data in the Position table.

Updates to the Position table ◀ **Figure 4-11**

PositionID	Update Action
2033	Change HoursPerWeek to 35 Change StartDate to 6/30/2006
2072	Delete record
2130	Add new record for PositionID 2130: PositionTitle = Housekeeping EmployerID = 10151 Wage = 12.50 HoursPerWeek = 30 StartDate = 6/1/2006 EndDate = 10/15/2006 Openings = 2 Experience = No

Maintaining Table Data Using a Form

Maintaining data using a form is often easier than using a datasheet, because you can concentrate on all the changes required to a single record at one time. You already know how to navigate a form and find specific records. Now you'll make the changes Elsa requested to the Position table, using the Position Data form.

First, you'll update the record for PositionID 2033.

To change the record using the Position Data form:

▸ **1.** Make sure the Position Data form is displayed in Form view.

When she reviewed the position data to identify possible corrections, Elsa noted that 10 is the record number for PositionID 2033. If you know the number of the record you want to display, you can type the number in the record number box and press the Enter key to go directly to that record.

▸ **2.** Select **42** in the record number box, type **10**, and then press the **Enter** key. Record 10 (PositionID 2033) is now the current record.

You need to change the HoursPerWeek field value to 35 and the StartDate field value to 06/30/2006 for this record.

3. Click the insertion point to the left of the number 2 in the HoursPerWeek field value, press the **Delete** key twice, and then type **35**. Note that the pencil symbol appears in the upper-left corner of the form, indicating that the form is in editing mode.

4. Press the **Tab** key to move to and select the StartDate field value, type **6/30/2006**, and then press the **Enter** key. See Figure 4-12.

Figure 4-12	Position record after changing field values

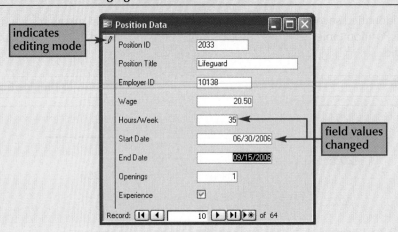

You have completed the changes for PositionID 2033. Elsa's next update is to delete the record for PositionID 2072. The employer client recently informed Elsa that a full-time, permanent employee has been hired for this position, so it is no longer available for student recruits.

To delete the record using the Position Data form:

1. Click anywhere in the PositionID field value to make it the current field.

2. Click the **Find** button 🔍 on the Form View toolbar. The Find and Replace dialog box opens.

3. Type **2072** in the Find What text box, click the **Find Next** button, and then click the **Cancel** button. The record for PositionID 2072 is now the current record.

4. Click the **Delete Record** button ▶✕ on the Form View toolbar. A dialog box opens, asking you to confirm the record deletion.

5. Click the **Yes** button. The dialog box closes, and the record for PositionID 2072 is deleted from the table.

Elsa's final maintenance change is to add a record for a new position available at the Granite State Resort.

To add the new record using the Position Data form:

1. Click the **New Record** button ▶ on the Form View toolbar. Record 64, the next record available for a new record, becomes the current record. All field value boxes are empty, and the insertion point is positioned at the beginning of the field value box for PositionID.

2. Refer to Figure 4-13 and enter the value shown for each field. Press the **Tab** key to move from field to field.

Completed form for the new record ◀ **Figure 4-13**

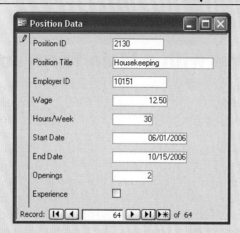

Trouble? Compare your screen with Figure 4-13. If any field value is wrong, correct it now, using the methods described earlier for editing field values.

3. After entering the value for Openings, press the **Tab** key twice (if necessary). Record 65, the next record available for a new record, becomes the current record, and the record for PositionID 2130 is saved in the Position table.

You've completed Elsa's changes to the Position table, so you can close the Position Data form.

4. Click the **Close** button ☒ on the form's title bar. The form closes, and you return to the Database window. Notice that the Position Data form is listed in the Forms list box.

So that all your database objects will be named consistently, you'll rename the form object to "PositionData" (one word). This will not affect how the form title (caption) is displayed when you work with the form in Form view; it will still appear as "Position Data" (two words).

5. Right-click **Position Data** in the Forms list box, and then click **Rename** on the shortcut menu.

6. Delete the space between the words "Position" and "Data," and then press the **Enter** key. The form object name is now "PositionData."

In the next session, you'll create another form for working with data in both the Position and Employer tables at the same time. You'll also create a report showing data from both tables.

Session 4.1 Quick Check

Review

1. Describe the difference between creating a form using the AutoForm Wizard and creating a form using the Form Wizard.
2. What is an AutoFormat, and how do you change one for an existing form?
3. Which table record is displayed in a form when you press the Ctrl+End keys while you are in navigation mode?
4. You can use the Find command to search for data in a form or _____.
5. Which wildcard character matches any single alphabetic character?
6. How many form records does Access print by default on a page?

To reinforce the tasks you learned in this session, go to the SAM 2003 Training Companion CD included with this text.

Session 4.2

For hands-on practice of key tasks in this session, go to the SAM 2003 Training Companion CD included with this text.

Elsa would like you to create a form so that she can view the data for each employer and its available positions at the same time. The type of form you need to create will include a main form and a subform.

Creating a Form with a Main Form and a Subform

To create a form based on two tables, you must first define a relationship between the two tables. In Tutorial 3, you defined a one-to-many relationship between the Employer (primary) and Position (related) tables, so you are ready to create the form based on both tables.

When you create a form containing data from two tables that have a one-to-many relationship, you actually create a **main form** for data from the primary table and a **subform** for data from the related table. Access uses the defined relationship between the tables to join them automatically through the common field that exists in both tables.

Elsa and her staff will use the form when contacting employers about their available positions. The main form will contain the employer ID and name, contact first and last names, and phone number for each employer. The subform will contain the position ID and title, wage, hours per week, experience, start and end dates, and number of openings for each position.

You'll use the Form Wizard to create the form.

To create the form using the Form Wizard:

1. If you took a break after the previous session, make sure that Access is running and the **Northeast** database is open.

2. Make sure the Forms object is selected in the Database window, and then click the **New** button. The New Form dialog box opens.

   When creating a form based on two tables, you first choose the primary table and select the fields you want to include in the main form; then you choose the related table and select fields from it for the subform.

3. Click **Form Wizard**, click the list arrow for choosing a table or query, click **Employer** to select this table as the source for the main form, and then click the **OK** button. The first Form Wizard dialog box opens, in which you select fields in the order you want them to appear on the main form.

   Elsa wants the form to include only the EmployerID, EmployerName, ContactFirstName, ContactLastName, and Phone fields from the Employer table.

4. Click **EmployerID** in the Available Fields list box (if necessary), and then click the ⟩ button to move the field to the Selected Fields list box.

5. Repeat Step 4 for the **EmployerName**, **ContactFirstName**, **ContactLastName**, and **Phone** fields.

   The EmployerID field will appear in the main form, so you do not have to include it in the subform. Otherwise, Elsa wants the subform to include all the fields from the Position table.

6. Click the **Tables/Queries** list arrow, and then click **Table: Position**. The fields from the Position table appear in the Available Fields list box. The quickest way to add the fields you want to include is to move all the fields to the Selected Fields list box, and then to remove the only field you don't want to include (EmployerID).

7. Click the >> button to move all the fields from the Position table to the Selected Fields list box.

8. Click **Position.EmployerID** in the Selected Fields list box, and then click the < button to move the field back to the Available Fields list box. Note that the table name (Position) is included in the field name to distinguish it from the same field (EmployerID) in the Employer table.

9. Click the **Next** button. The next Form Wizard dialog box opens. See Figure 4-14.

Choosing a main/subform format **Figure 4-14**

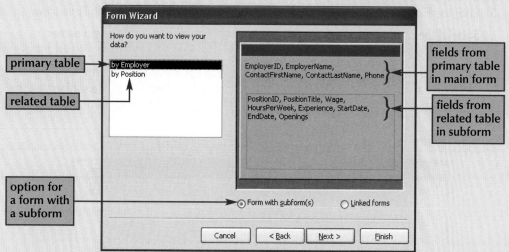

In this dialog box, the list box on the left shows the order in which you will view the selected data: first by data from the primary Employer table, and then by data from the related Position table. The form will be displayed as shown in the right side of the dialog box, with the fields from the Employer table at the top in the main form, and the fields from the Position table at the bottom in the subform. The selected option button specifies a main form with a subform. The Linked forms option creates a form structure in which only the main form fields are displayed. A button with the subform's name on it appears on the main form; you can click this button to display the associated subform records.

The default options shown in Figure 4-14 are correct for creating a form with Employer data in the main form and Position data in the subform.

To finish creating the form:

1. Click the **Next** button. The next Form Wizard dialog box opens, in which you choose the subform layout.

The Tabular layout displays subform fields as a table, whereas the Datasheet layout displays subform fields as a table datasheet. The PivotTable and PivotChart layouts display summary and analytical information. The layout choice is a matter of personal preference. You'll use the Datasheet layout.

2. Click the **Datasheet** option button (if necessary), and then click the **Next** button. The next Form Wizard dialog box opens, in which you choose the form's style.

Elsa wants all forms in the Northeast database to have the same style, so you will choose Standard, which is the same style you applied to the PositionData form.

3. Click **Standard** (if necessary), and then click the **Next** button. The next Form Wizard dialog box opens, in which you choose names for the main form and the subform.

   You will use the name "Employer Positions" for the main form and the name "Position Subform" for the subform. (Later, you'll rename the form objects so that their names do not include spaces.)

4. Click the insertion point to the right of the last letter in the Form text box, press the **spacebar**, and then type **Positions**. The main form name is now Employer Positions. The Position Subform name is already set.

   You have answered all the Form Wizard's questions.

5. Click the **Finish** button. After a few moments, the completed form opens in Form view.

   Some of the columns in the subform are not wide enough to display the field names entirely. You need to resize the columns to their best fit.

6. Double-click the pointer ↔ at the right edge of each column in the subform, scrolling the subform to the right, as necessary, to display additional columns. Scroll the subform all the way back to the left. The columns are resized to their best fit. See Figure 4-15.

| Figure 4-15 | **Main form with subform in Form view** |

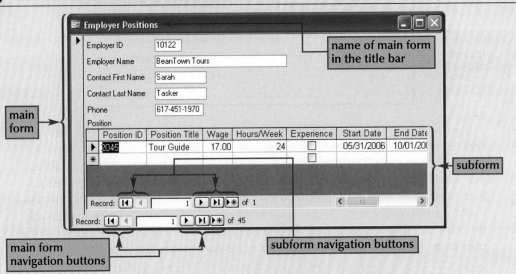

In the main form, Access displays the fields from the first record in the Employer table in columnar format. The records in the main form appear in primary key sequence by EmployerID. EmployerID 10122 has one related record in the Position table; this record is shown in the subform datasheet. The form shows that BeanTown Tours has one available position for a Tour Guide.

Notice that the subform is not wide enough to display all the fields from the Position table. Although the subform includes a horizontal scroll bar, which allows you to view the other fields, Elsa wants all the fields from the Position table to be visible in the subform at the same time. Even if you maximized the Form window, the subform would still not display all of the fields. You need to widen the main form and the subform in Design view.

Modifying a Form in Design View

Just as you use Design view to modify the format and content of tables and queries, you also use Design view to modify a form. You can change the fields that are displayed on a form, and modify their size, location, format, and so on. You need to open the Employer Positions form in Design view and resize the Position subform to display all the fields at the same time.

To widen the Position subform:

▶ 1. Click the **View** button for Design view 🖾 on the Form View toolbar to display the form in Design view.

▶ 2. Click the **Maximize** button 🔲 to enlarge the window. See Figure 4-16.

Form with subform displayed in Design view   **Figure 4-16**

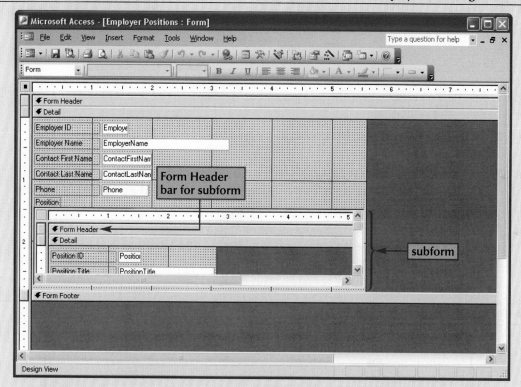

Trouble? If the subform appears as a white box instead of a datasheet as in Figure 4-16, click the View button for Form view 🔳 on the Form Design toolbar, and then click the View button for Design view 🖾 on the Form View toolbar.

▶ 3. Click the **Form Header** bar for the subform (refer to Figure 4-16) to select the subform. Notice that small boxes appear around the subform's border. These boxes, which are called **handles**, indicate that the subform is selected and can be manipulated.

▶ 4. Position the pointer on the right-center sizing handle so it changes to a ↔ shape, and then click and drag the handle to the right, to the mark just before the 6.5-inch mark on the horizontal ruler. See Figure 4-17.

Figure 4-17 Resizing the Position subform

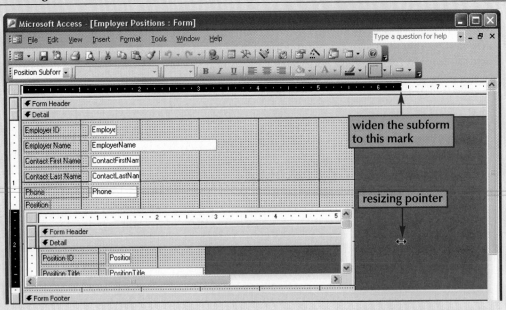

5. Release the mouse button. The subform section is resized. Notice that the main form section is also resized.

6. Switch back to Form view. Notice that all the field names in the Position subform are now visible.

7. Click the **Restore Window** button 🗗 on the menu bar to restore the form to its original size. Now you need to resize the Form window in Form view so that all the fields will be displayed when the Form window is not maximized.

8. Position the pointer on the right edge of the form so it changes to a ↔ shape, and then click and drag the right edge of the form to resize it so that it matches the form shown in Figure 4-18. Make sure the bottom of the form does not include a horizontal scroll bar; the absence of a scroll bar indicates that all fields are fully visible.

Figure 4-18 Form with all subform fields visible

Employer Positions

Employer ID	10122
Employer Name	BeanTown Tours
Contact First Name	Sarah
Contact Last Name	Tasker
Phone	617-451-1970

Position

	Position ID	Position Title	Wage	Hours/Week	Experience	Start Date	End Date	Openings
▶	2045	Tour Guide	17.00	24	☐	05/31/2006	10/01/2006	1
*					☐			

Record: ◀◀ ◀ 1 ▶ ▶▶ ▶* of 1

Record: ◀◀ ◀ 1 ▶ ▶▶ ▶* of 45

9. Save the modified form.

Two sets of navigation buttons appear at the bottom of the Form view window. You use the top set of navigation buttons to select records from the related table in the subform, and the bottom set to select records from the primary table in the main form.

You'll use the navigation buttons to view different records.

To navigate to different main form and subform records:

1. Click the **Last Record** navigation button [▶|] in the main form. Record 45 in the Employer table for Lighthouse Tours becomes the current record in the main form. The subform shows that this employer has one available Tour Guide position.

2. Click the **Previous Record** navigation button [◀] in the main form. Record 44 in the Employer table for Harbor Whale Watch Tours becomes the current record in the main form.

3. Select **44** in the record number box for the main form, type **32**, and then press the **Enter** key. Record 32 in the Employer table for Windsor Alpine Tours becomes the current record in the main form. This employer has two available positions.

4. Click the **Last Record** navigation button [▶|] in the subform. Record 2 in the Position table becomes the current record in the subform.

   You have finished your work with the form, so you can close it.

5. Close the form. Both the main form, Employer Positions, and the subform, Position Subform, appear in the Forms list box. Note that you can open each form separately in Design view and make changes to it. For example, if you open and modify the Position Subform, the changes you make will appear the next time you use the Employer Positions form, since it also contains the subform.

   Now you'll rename the two form objects so that their names do not include spaces, and all the database objects are named consistently.

6. Right-click **Employer Positions**, click **Rename**, delete the space between the words "Employer" and "Positions," and then press the **Enter** key. Repeat this procedure for the Position Subform object so that the names of both objects do not contain spaces.

You've finished your work for Elsa on the forms in the Northeast database.

Creating a Report Using the Report Wizard

As you learned in Tutorial 1, a report is a formatted printout of the contents of one or more tables in a database. In Access, you can create your own reports or use the Report Wizard to create them for you. Like the Form Wizard, the **Report Wizard** asks you a series of questions and then creates a report based on your answers. Whether you use the Report Wizard or design your own report, you can change the report's design after you create it.

Zack wants you to create a report that includes selected employer data from the Employer table and all the available positions from the Position table for each employer. Zack has sketched a design of the report he wants (Figure 4-19). Like the EmployerPositions form you just created, which includes a main form and a subform, the report will be based on both tables, which are joined in a one-to-many relationship through the common EmployerID field. As shown in the sketch in Figure 4-19, the selected employer data from the primary Employer table includes the employer ID and name, city, state or province, contact first and last names, and phone number. Below the data for each employer, the report will include the position ID and title, wage, hours per week, experience, start and end dates, and openings data from the related Position table. The set of field values for each position is called a **detail record**.

Figure 4-19 **Report sketch for the Employers and Positions report**

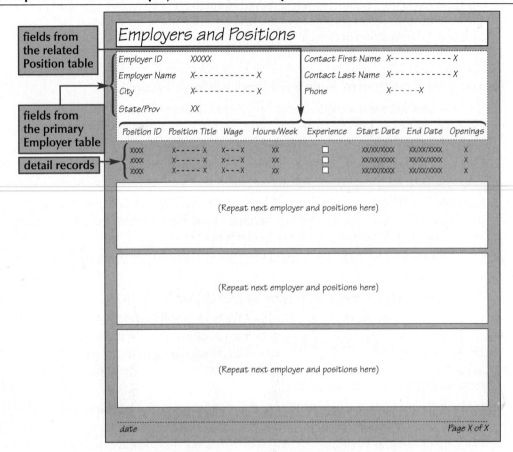

You'll use the Report Wizard to create the report according to the design in Zack's sketch.

To start the Report Wizard and select the fields to include in the report:

1. Click **Reports** in the Objects bar of the Database window to display the Reports list box. You have not yet created any reports.

2. Click the **New** button in the Database window. The New Report dialog box opens.

   As was the case when you created the form with a subform, initially you can choose only one table or query to be the data source for the report. Then you can include data from other tables. You will select the primary Employer table in the New Report dialog box.

3. Click **Report Wizard**, click the list arrow for choosing a table or query, and then click **Employer**.

4. Click the **OK** button. The first Report Wizard dialog box opens.

   In the first Report Wizard dialog box, you select fields in the order you want them to appear on the report. Zack wants the EmployerID, EmployerName, City, StateProv, ContactFirstName, ContactLastName, and Phone fields from the Employer table to appear on the report.

5. Click **EmployerID** in the Available Fields list box (if necessary), and then click the ⟩ button. The field moves to the Selected Fields list box.

6. Repeat Step 5 to add the **EmployerName**, **City**, **StateProv**, **ContactFirstName**, **ContactLastName**, and **Phone** fields to the report.

7. Click the **Tables/Queries** list arrow, and then click **Table: Position**. The fields from the Position table appear in the Available Fields list box.

The EmployerID field will appear on the report with the employer data, so you do not have to include it in the detail records for each position. Otherwise, Zack wants all the fields from the Position table to be included in the report.

8. Click the ⟩⟩ button to move all the fields from the Available Fields list box to the Selected Fields list box.

9. Click **Position.EmployerID** in the Selected Fields list box, click the ⟨ button to move the selected field back to the Available Fields list box, and then click the **Next** button. The second Report Wizard dialog box opens. See Figure 4-20.

Choosing a grouped or ungrouped report ◂ **Figure 4-20**

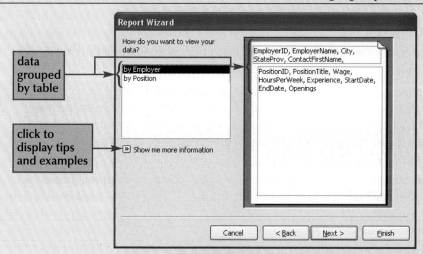

You can choose to arrange the selected data grouped by table, which is the default, or ungrouped. For a **grouped report**, the data from a record in the primary table appears as a group, followed on subsequent lines of the report by the joined records from the related table. For the report you are creating, data from a record in the Employer table appears in a group, followed by the related records for each employer from the Position table. An example of an ungrouped report would be a report of records from the Employer and Position tables in order by PositionID. Each position and its associated employer data would appear together on one or more lines of the report; the data would not be grouped by table.

You can display tips and examples for the choices in the Report Wizard dialog box by clicking the "Show me more information" button.

To display tips about the options in the Report Wizard dialog box:

1. Click the ⊠ button. The Report Wizard Tips dialog box opens. Read the information shown in the dialog box.

   You can display examples of different grouping methods by clicking the ⊠ button ("Show me examples").

2. Click the ⊠ button. The Report Wizard Examples dialog box opens.

   You can display examples of different grouping methods by clicking the ⊠ buttons.

3. Click each ⊠ button in turn, review the displayed example, and then click the **Close** button to return to the Report Wizard Examples dialog box.

4. Click the **Close** button to return to the Report Wizard Tips dialog box, and then click the **Close** button to return to the second Report Wizard dialog box.

The default options shown on your screen are correct for the report Zack wants, so you can continue responding to the Report Wizard questions.

To finish creating the report using the Report Wizard:

1. Click the **Next** button. The next Report Wizard dialog box opens, in which you choose additional grouping levels.

   Two grouping levels are shown: one for an employer's data, and the other for an employer's positions. Grouping levels are useful for reports with multiple levels, such as those containing monthly, quarterly, and annual totals, or for those containing city and country groups. Zack's report contains no further grouping levels, so you can accept the default options.

2. Click the **Next** button. The next Report Wizard dialog box opens, in which you choose the sort order for the detail records. See Figure 4-21.

Figure 4-21	Choosing the sort order for detail records

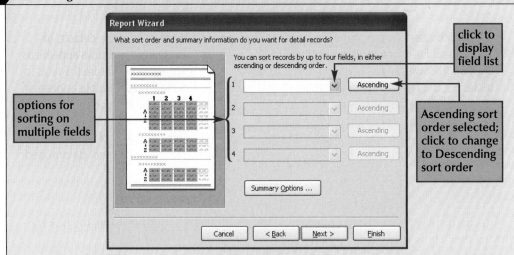

The records from the Position table for an employer represent the detail records for Zack's report. He wants these records to appear in increasing, or ascending, order by the value in the PositionID field. The Ascending option is already selected by default. To change to descending order, you simply click this button, which acts as a toggle between the two sort orders. Also, notice that you can sort on multiple fields, as you can with queries.

3. Click the **1** list arrow, click **PositionID**, and then click the **Next** button. The next Report Wizard dialog box opens, in which you choose a layout and page orientation for the report. See Figure 4-22.

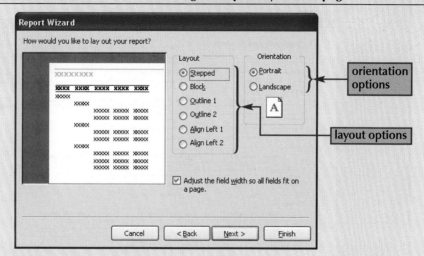

A sample of each layout appears in the box on the left.

4. Click each layout option and examine each sample that appears.

You'll use the Outline 2 layout option because it resembles the layout shown in Zack's sketch of the report. Also, because of the number of fields in the Position table, the information would fit better in a wide format; therefore, you'll choose the landscape orientation.

5. Click the **Outline 2** option button, click the **Landscape** option button, and then click the **Next** button. The next Report Wizard dialog box opens, in which you choose a style for the report.

A sample of the selected style, or AutoFormat, appears in the box on the left. You can always choose a different AutoFormat after you create the report, just as you can when creating a form. Zack likes the appearance of the Corporate AutoFormat, so you'll choose this one for your report.

6. Click **Corporate** (if necessary), and then click the **Next** button. The last Report Wizard dialog box opens, in which you choose a report name, which also serves as the printed title on the report.

According to Zack's sketch, the report title you need to specify is "Employers and Positions." (You'll rename the report object later so that its name does not contain spaces and conforms with other object names in the database.)

7. Type **Employers and Positions** and then click the **Finish** button. The Report Wizard creates the report based on your answers and saves it as an object in the Northeast database. Then Access opens the Employers and Positions report in Print Preview.

To view the report better, you need to maximize the Report window.

8. Click the **Maximize** button on the Employers and Positions title bar.

To view the entire page, you need to change the Zoom setting.

9. Click the **Zoom** list arrow on the Print Preview toolbar, and then click **Fit**. The first page of the report is displayed in Print Preview. See Figure 4-23.

Figure 4-23 | **Report displayed in Print Preview**

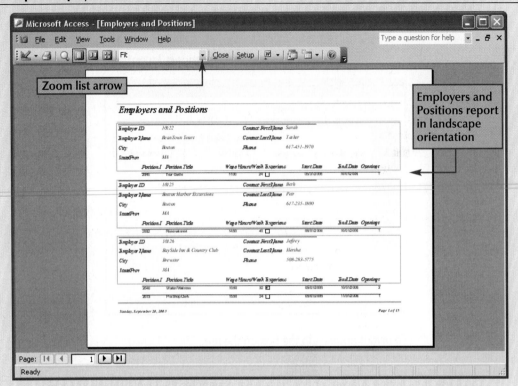

When a report is displayed in Print Preview, you can use the pointer to toggle between a full-page display and a close-up display of the report. Zack asks you to check the report to see if any adjustments need to be made. For example, some of the field titles or values might not be displayed completely, or you might need to move fields to enhance the report's appearance. To do so, you need to view a close-up display of the report.

To view a close-up display of the report:

1. Click the pointer ⊕ at the top center of the report. The display changes to show a close-up view of the report. See Figure 4-24.

Close-up view of the report 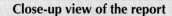 **Figure 4-24**

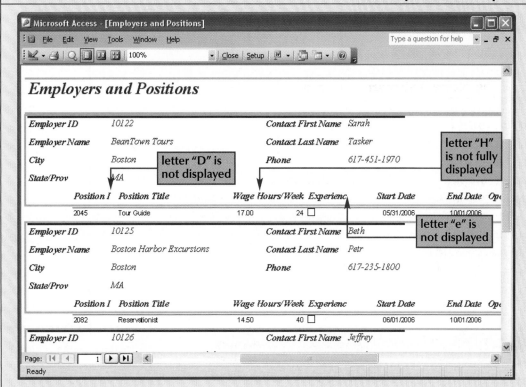

Trouble? Scroll your screen as necessary so that it matches the screen in Figure 4-24.

The letter "D" is missing from the end of the PositionID field name, the letter "H" is not fully displayed at the beginning of the HoursPerWeek field name, and the letter "e" is not visible at the end of the Experience field name. To fix these problems, you need to switch to Design view.

2. Click the **View** button for Design view ![icon] on the Print Preview toolbar. Access displays the report in Design view. See Figure 4-25.

Figure 4-25 Report displayed in Design view

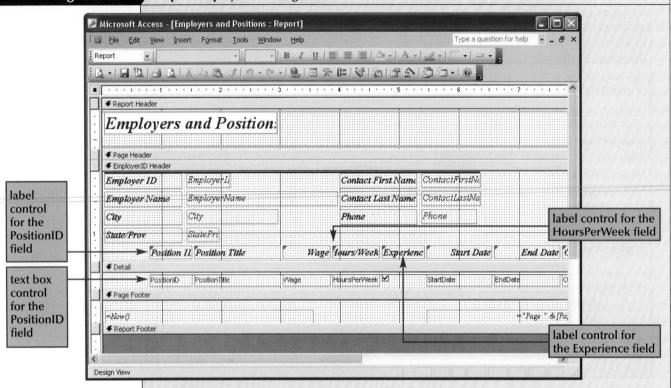

Figure 4-26 Selecting the PositionID label control

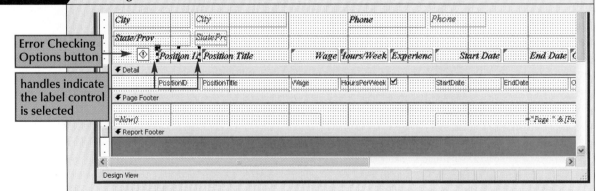

Trouble? If your screen displays any window other than the one shown in Figure 4-25, click the Close button [X] on the window's title bar to close it.

You use the Report window in Design view to modify existing reports and to create custom reports. Each item on a report in Design view is called a **control**. For example, the PositionID field consists of two controls: the **label** "Position ID," which appears on the report to identify the field value, and the PositionID **text box**, in which the actual field value appears.

3. Click the label control for the PositionID field to select it. Handles appear on the border around the control, indicating that the control is selected and can be manipulated. See Figure 4-26.

Notice also that a button appears to the left of the selected control. This button allows you to check for possible errors in your report.

Checking Errors in a Report

When you work with a report (or a form) in Design view, Access provides automatic error checking to help you make sure that your report is designed correctly. The **Error Checking Options** button (see Figure 4-26) appears any time Access identifies a possible error. You can choose one of the options provided by this button to determine if there is, indeed, an error in your report.

To check for errors in the report:

▶ **1.** Position the pointer on the **Error Checking Options** button ⬦ and then click the list arrow that appears. A menu opens listing options associated with the possible error. See Figure 4-27.

Menu displayed for possible error ◀ **Figure 4-27**

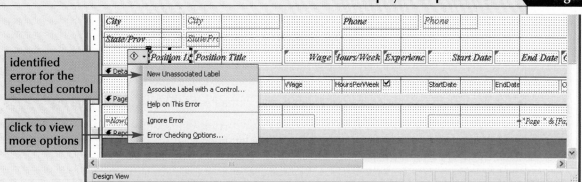

identified error for the selected control

click to view more options

In this case, the PositionID label is identified as a "new unassociated label," meaning that it does not have an associated text box in which to display the field values. Access identifies this as a potential error because the PositionID label appears in one section of the report, the EmployerID Header section, and its text box appears in another section of the report, the Detail section. Typically a label and its associated text box appear in the same section of the report. Because the selected report design places these controls in different sections, Access flags the error as an unassociated label.

▶ **2.** Click **Error Checking Options** in the menu. The Options dialog box opens. See Figure 4-28.

Options dialog box ◀ **Figure 4-28**

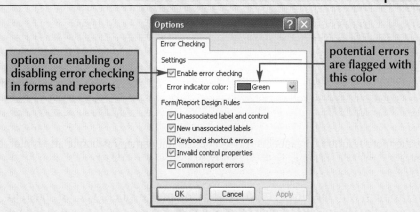

option for enabling or disabling error checking in forms and reports

potential errors are flagged with this color

The Enable error checking option allows you to turn this feature on or off (it is on by default). Note that the selected error indicator color is green. Each label in the EmployerID Header section whose associated text box is in the Detail section has a small green triangle in the upper-left corner of the label box, indicating a potential error for that label.

Because each of these labels does have an associated text box in the Detail section, there are no errors in the report design and you can safely ignore the error checking.

3. Click the **Cancel** button to close the Options dialog box.

4. Click the list arrow for the **Error Checking Options** button ⬦, and then click **Ignore Error**.

5. Click in the empty space next to the PositionID label to deselect it. Notice that the green triangle is no longer displayed in the upper-left corner of the label, because you chose to ignore the error. You could follow this same procedure for the other labels in this section, but there is no need to do so; each of the labels flagged with a green triangle does have an associated text box in the Detail section, so the report design is correct.

Now that you've determined there are no errors in the report design, you can proceed with fixing the labels that are not completely displayed.

To fix the display of the PositionID label in the report:

1. Click the **PositionID** label to select it. You need to widen the label control for the PositionID field so that the entire field name is visible in the report.

2. Position the pointer on the center-left handle of the PositionID label control until the pointer changes to a ↔ shape.

3. Click and drag the pointer to the left until the left edge of the control is aligned with the mark just after the half-inch mark on the horizontal ruler. See Figure 4-29.

| Figure 4-29 | Resizing the PositionID label control |

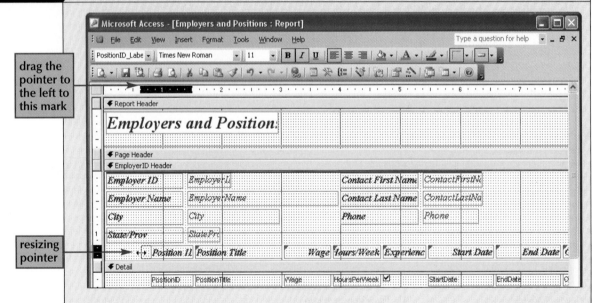

4. Release the mouse button. The label is wider, and the full name, Position ID, is visible.

To fix the problem with the HoursPerWeek and Experience labels, you first need to reduce the size of the Wage label, which currently takes up too much space in the report and crowds the other labels. However, you should also resize the Wage label's associated text box so that the displayed Wage values are aligned appropriately below the Wage label in the report. You can select multiple controls and resize them at the same time.

To fix the display of the other labels in the report:

1. Click the **Wage** label, press and hold the **Shift** key, and then click the **Wage** text box in the Detail section. Both controls have handles around them, indicating that they are selected.

2. Position the pointer on the center-right handle of the Wage label control until the pointer changes to a ↔ shape. Click and drag the pointer to the left until the right edges of both selected controls are aligned with the **3.5**-inch mark on the horizontal ruler, and then release the mouse button. Both controls are reduced in size, and you can now widen the HoursPerWeek label. Note that you do not have to widen the HoursPerWeek text box, only the label.

3. Click the **HoursPerWeek** label (which contains the text Hours/Week), position the pointer on the center-left handle, click and drag the pointer to the left to the next mark on the horizontal ruler, and then release the mouse button. The complete label is now visible.

4. Click in an empty space of the EmployerID Header section to deselect the label. See Figure 4-30.

Controls after resizing ◄ **Figure 4-30**

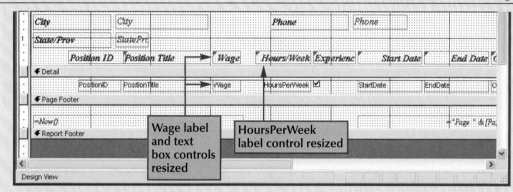

Finally, you need to correct the problem with the Experience field name. To do so, you first need to reduce the width of the StartDate label and its associated text box; then you can widen just the Experience label control.

5. Click the **StartDate** label, press and hold the **Shift** key, and then click the **StartDate** text box in the Detail section. Both controls have handles around them, indicating that they are selected.

6. Position the pointer on the center-left handle of the StartDate label control, click and drag the pointer to the right to the **5.75**-inch mark on the horizontal ruler, and then release the mouse button. Both controls are reduced in size, and you can now widen the Experience label.

7. Click the **Experience** label, position the pointer on the center-right handle, click and drag the pointer to the right to the **5.5**-inch mark on the horizontal ruler, and then release the mouse button.

   Now you need to switch back to Print Preview and make sure that the complete names for the PositionID, HoursPerWeek, and Experience fields are visible.

8. Click the **View** button for Print Preview 🔍 on the Report Design toolbar. The report appears in Print Preview. Notice that the PositionID, HoursPerWeek, and Experience labels are now completely displayed.

   Trouble? If any of the labels in your report are not completely displayed, return to Design view and use the same resizing technique to correct the size of labels and/or associated text boxes, as necessary.

9. Click **File** on the menu bar, and then click **Save** to save the modified report.

Zack decides that he wants the report to include a graphic image to the right of the report title, for visual interest. You can add the graphic to the report by inserting a picture.

Inserting a Picture in a Report

In Access, you can insert a picture or other graphic image to enhance the appearance of a report or form. Sources of graphic images include files created in Microsoft Paint and other drawing programs, and scanned files. The file containing the picture you need to insert is named Globe, and it is located in the Brief\Tutorial folder provided with your Data Files.

To insert the picture in the report:

▶ **1.** Click the **Close** button on the Print Preview toolbar to display the report in Design view. See Figure 4-31.

Figure 4-31 — Inserting a picture in Design view

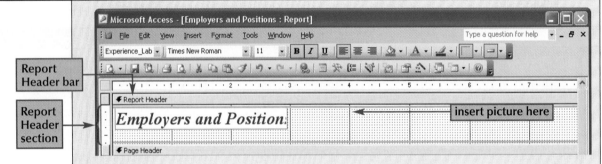

Zack wants the picture to appear on the first page of the report only; therefore, you need to insert the picture in the **Report Header** section (see Figure 4-31). Any text or picture placed in this section appears once at the beginning of the report.

▶ **2.** Click the **Report Header** bar to select this section of the report. The bar is highlighted to indicate that the section is selected.

▶ **3.** Click **Insert** on the menu bar, and then click **Picture**. The Insert Picture dialog box opens. If necessary, open the **Brief\Tutorial** folder provided with your Data Files.

▶ **4.** Click **Globe** to select the picture for the report, and then click the **OK** button. The picture is inserted in the left side of the Report Header section, covering some of the report title text. See Figure 4-32.

Figure 4-32 — Picture inserted in the report

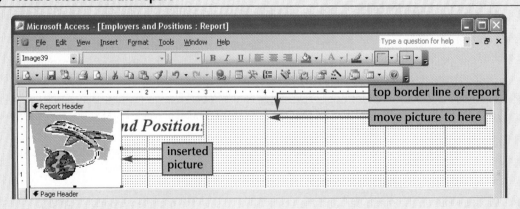

Notice that handles appear around the picture's border, indicating that the picture is selected and can be manipulated.

Zack wants the picture to appear to the right of the report title, so you need to move the picture using the mouse.

5. Position the pointer on the picture until the pointer changes to a 🖐 shape, and then click and drag the mouse to move the picture to the right so that its left edge aligns with the 4-inch mark on the horizontal ruler and its top edge is just below the top border line above the report title (see Figure 4-32).

6. Release the mouse button. The picture appears in the new position. Notice that the height of the Report Header section increased slightly to accommodate the picture. See Figure 4-33.

Repositioned picture in the report | **Figure 4-33**

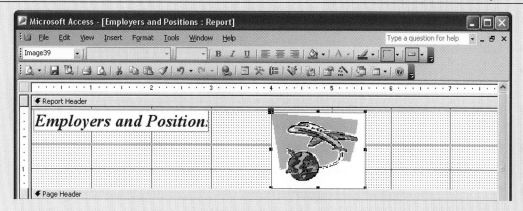

Trouble? If your picture appears in a different location from the one shown in Figure 4-33, use the pointer 🖐 to reposition the picture until it is in approximately the same position shown in the figure. Be sure that the top edge of the picture is below the top border line of the report.

7. Switch to Print Preview. The report now includes the inserted picture. If necessary, click the **Zoom** button 🔍 on the Print Preview toolbar to display the entire report page. See Figure 4-34.

Print Preview of report with picture | **Figure 4-34**

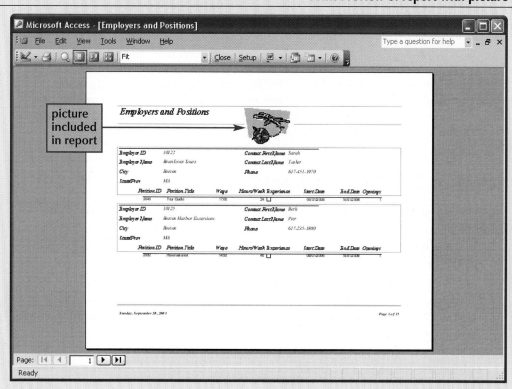

Trouble? If the picture covers the gray line at the top of the report, switch to Design view and use the pointer to position the picture in the correct location. Then repeat Step 7.

▶ **8.** Save the modified report.

The report is now completed. You'll print just the first page of the report so that Zack can review the report layout and the inserted picture.

To print page 1 of the report:

▶ **1.** Click **File** on the menu bar, and then click **Print**. The Print dialog box opens.

▶ **2.** In the Print Range section, click the **Pages** option button. The insertion point now appears in the From text box so that you can specify the range of pages to print.

▶ **3.** Type **1** in the From text box, press the **Tab** key to move to the To text box, and then type **1**. These settings specify that only page 1 of the report will be printed.

▶ **4.** Click the **OK** button. The Print dialog box closes, and the first page of the report is printed.

Zack approves of the report layout and contents, so you can close the report.

▶ **5.** Click the **Close Window** button ☒ on the menu bar. You return to the Database window.

Trouble? If you click the Close button on the Print Preview toolbar by mistake, you switch to Design view. Click the Close Window button ☒ on the menu bar.

Recall that when you created the report, you specified the name "Employers and Positions" so that this title would appear on the report. Now you need to rename the report object so that its name is consistent with the names of other database objects (that is, with no spaces in the object name). Renaming the report object will not affect the specified title of the report.

▶ **6.** Right-click **Employers and Positions** in the Database window, and then click **Rename**.

▶ **7.** Change the name of the report to **EmployersAndPositions**, and then press the **Enter** key.

▶ **8.** Close the Northeast database.

Elsa is satisfied that the forms you created—the PositionData form and the EmployerPositions form—will make it easier to enter, view, and update data in the Northeast database. The EmployersAndPositions report presents important information about NSJI's employer clients in an attractive and professional format, which will help Zack and his staff in their marketing efforts.

Review

To reinforce the tasks you learned in this session, go to the SAM 2003 Training Companion CD included with this text.

Session 4.2 Quick Check

1. In a form that contains a main form and a subform, what data is displayed in the main form and what data is displayed in the subform?

2. Describe how you use the navigation buttons to move through a form containing a main form and a subform.

3. Each item on a report in Design view is called a(n) _____.

4. The _____ button appears any time Access identifies a possible error in a report (or form) while you are working on the design of the report (or form).

5. To insert a picture in a report, the report must be displayed in _____.

6. Any text or pictures placed in the _____ section of a report will appear only on the first page of the report.

Review

Tutorial Summary

In this tutorial, you learned how to create a form using the Form Wizard and how to change the form's AutoFormat after you created it. Using the navigation buttons provided at the bottom of the form window and various keyboard techniques, you moved through the records in a form. You also used the Find command to locate specific form records, and included wildcard characters to search for records by specifying only a partial field value. In addition, you previewed and printed selected form records, and maintained table data using a form. With the one-to-many relationship already established between the necessary tables, you were able to create a form with a main form and a subform to display data from both tables at the same time. You also used the Report Wizard to create a report displaying data from two related tables. Working in Design view, you modified the report by resizing label and text box controls. You also learned about the new Error Checking Options button, which identifies potential design errors in a form or report and helps you to correct them, if necessary. Finally, you learned how to insert and reposition a picture in a report to add visual interest.

Key Terms

AutoForm Wizard	Form Wizard	Report Header section
AutoFormat	grouped report	Report Wizard
control	handles	subform
detail record	label control	text box control
Error Checking Options	main form	wildcard character
Find command		

Practice

Gain practice with the skills you learned in the tutorial using the same case scenario.

Review Assignments

Data Files needed for the Review Assignments: Recruits.mdb (*cont. from Tutorial 3*) and Travel.bmp

Elsa wants to enhance the Recruits database with forms and reports, and she asks you to complete the following:

1. Open the **Recruits** database located in the Brief\Review folder provided with your Data Files.
2. Use the Form Wizard to create a form based on the **Student** table. Select all fields for the form, the Columnar layout, the SandStone style, and the title **Student Data** for the form.
3. Use the form you created in the previous step to print the fifth form record. Change the AutoFormat to Sumi Painting, save the changed form, and then print the fifth form record again.
4. Use the **Student Data** form to update the Student table as follows:
   a. Use the Find command to move to the record with StudentID STO1323. Change the field values for FirstName to Nathaniel, City to Perth, and BirthDate to 4/2/85 for this record.
   b. Use the Find command to move to the record with StudentID KIE2760, and then delete the record.
   c. Add a new record with the following field values:
      StudentID: SAN2540
      FirstName: Pedro
      LastName: Sandes
      City: Barcelona

Nation: Spain
BirthDate: 5/1/85
Gender: M
SSN: 977-07-1798

   d. Print only this form record, and then close the form.

5. Rename the form object to **StudentData**.

6. Use the Form Wizard to create a form containing a main form and a subform. Select the FirstName, LastName, and SSN fields from the **Recruiter** table for the main form, and select all fields except SSN from the **Student** table for the subform. Use the Datasheet layout and the Sumi Painting style. Specify the title **Recruiter Students** for the main form and the title **Student Subform** for the subform. Resize all columns in the subform to their best fit. Use Design view to resize the main form and the subform so that all fields are visible in the subform at the same time. Resize the Form window in Form view, as necessary, so that all fields are visible at the same time. Print the fourth main form record and its subform records. Save and close the form. Rename the main form object to **RecruiterStudents** and the subform object to **StudentSubform**.

7. Use the Report Wizard to create a report based on the primary Recruiter table and the related Student table. Select all fields from the **Recruiter** table, and then select all fields from the **Student** table except SSN, in the following order: FirstName, LastName, City, Nation, BirthDate, Gender, StudentID. Sort the detail records in ascending order by Nation. Choose the Align Left 2 layout and the Formal style for the report. Specify the title **Recruiters and Students** for the report.

8. Display the **Recruiters and Students** report in Design view and maximize the Report window. Then do the following:

   a. Choose the error checking option to ignore the error identified for the Nation label control.

   b. Reduce the size of the Nation label control by one mark on the horizontal ruler (from the right); then widen the FirstName label control to the left so that it is fully displayed in the report.

   c. Reduce the size of both the City label control and its associated text box in the Detail section so that their left edges begin at the mark immediately before the 3-inch mark on the horizontal ruler. Then widen the LastName label control to the right so that it is fully displayed in the report.

   d. Widen the Gender label control to the right to the mark immediately after the 5-inch mark on the horizontal ruler; the Gender label control should touch the adjacent StudentID label control.

9. Switch to Print Preview and make sure that all the labels are completely displayed.

10. Insert the **Travel** picture, which is located in the Brief\Review folder provided with your Data Files, in the Report Header section of the **Recruiters and Students** report. Position the picture so that its left edge aligns with the 4-inch mark on the horizontal ruler and its top edge is just below the top border line of the report.

11. Print only the first page of the report, and then close and save the modified report.

12. Rename the report object to **RecruitersAndStudents**.

13. If your database is stored on a floppy disk, you will need to turn off the Compact on Close feature before closing the **Recruits** database because there isn't enough room on the disk to compact the database. If your database is stored on a hard drive or a network drive, no action is necessary.

14. Close the Recruits database.

Apply

Using what you learned in the tutorial, create forms and a report to work with and display data about video photography events.

Case Problem 1

Data Files needed for this Case Problem: Videos.mdb (*cont. from Tutorial 3*) **and Camcord.bmp**

Lim's Video Photography   Youngho Lim wants the Videos database to include forms and reports that will help him track and view information about his clients and their video shoot events. You'll create the necessary forms and reports by completing the following:

1. Open the **Videos** database located in the Brief\Case1 folder provided with your Data Files.
2. Use the Form Wizard to create a form based on the **Client** table. Select all fields for the form, the Columnar layout, and the Ricepaper style. Specify the title **Client Data** for the form.
3. Change the AutoFormat for the Client Data form to Standard.
4. Use the Find command to move to the record with ClientID 338, and then change the Address field value for this record to 2150 Brucewood Avenue.
5. Use the **Client Data** form to add a new record with the following field values:
   ClientID: 351
   ClientName: Peters, Amanda
   Address: 175 Washington Street
   City: Berkeley
   State: CA
   Zip: 94704
   Phone: 510-256-1007
   Print only this form record, and then save and close the form.
6. Rename the form object to **ClientData**.
7. Use the Form Wizard to create a form containing a main form and a subform. Select all the fields from the **Client** table for the main form, and select all fields except ClientID from the **Contract** table for the subform. Use the Tabular layout and the Standard style. Specify the title **Contracts by Client** for the main form and the title **Contract Subform** for the subform.
8. Print the seventh main form record and its subform records, and then close the **Contracts by Client** form.
9. Rename the main form object to **ContractsByClient** and the subform object to **ContractSubform**.
10. Use the Report Wizard to create a report based on the primary Client table and the related Contract table. Select all the fields from the **Client** table, and select all the fields from the **Contract** table except ClientID. Sort the detail records in ascending order by ContractID. Choose the Align Left 2 layout and the Casual style. Specify the title **Client Contracts** for the report.
11. Switch to Design view, and then widen the Phone text box control so that the Phone field values are completely displayed in the report, if necessary.
12. Insert the **Camcord** picture, which is located in the Brief\Case1 folder provided with your Data Files, in the Report Header section of the **Client Contracts** report. Position the picture so that its left edge aligns with the 4-inch mark on the horizontal ruler and its top edge is just below the top border line of the report.
13. Print only the first page of the report, and then close and save the modified report.
14. Rename the report object to **ClientContracts**.
15. Close the Videos database.

Challenge

Challenge yourself by creating and working with a form and a report for this fitness center.

Case Problem 2

Data Files needed for this Case Problem: Fitness.mdb *(cont. from Tutorial 3)* **and Weights.bmp**

Parkhurst Health & Fitness Center   Martha Parkhurst continues her work with the Fitness database to track and analyze the business activity of the fitness center members and their programs. To help her, you'll enhance the Fitness database by completing the following:

1. Open the **Fitness** database located in the Brief\Case2 folder provided with your Data Files.

2. Use the Form Wizard to create a form containing a main form and a subform. Select the ProgramID, MonthlyFee, and PhysicalRequired fields from the **Program** table for the main form, and select the MemberID, FirstName, LastName, City, Phone, and MembershipStatus fields from the **Member** table for the subform. Use the Datasheet layout and the Industrial style. Specify the title **Program Members** for the main form and the title **Member Subform** for the subform. Working in both Design view and Form view, as necessary, resize the subform so that all fields in it are visible. Then resize all columns in the subform to their best fit. Print the first main form record and its displayed subform records.

3. For the form you just created, change the AutoFormat to SandStone, save the changed form, and then print the first main form record and its subform records.

4. Navigate to the third record in the subform for the first main record, and then change the MembershipStatus field value to Active.

5. Navigate to the tenth record in the main form, and then the fourth subform record. Change the Phone field value for this record to 804-553-1275.

6. Rename the main form object to ProgramMembers and the subform object to MemberSubform.

Explore

7. Use the Report Wizard to create a report based on the primary Program table and the related Member table. Select all fields from the **Program** table, and then select the following fields from the **Member** table: MemberID, FirstName, LastName, City, Phone, DateJoined, and MembershipStatus. In the third Report Wizard dialog box, specify the City field as an additional grouping level. Sort the detail records by DateJoined in *descending* order. Choose the Align Left 1 layout, Landscape orientation, and the Bold style for the report. Specify the title **Programs and Members** for the report.

8. Insert the **Weights** picture, which is located in the Brief\Case2 folder provided with your Data Files, in the Report Header section of the **Programs and Members** report. Leave the picture in its original position at the left edge of the Report Header section.

Explore

9. Use the "Type a question for help" box to ask the following question: "How do I move a control in front of or behind other controls?" Click the topic "Move one or more controls," and then click the subtopic "Move a control in front of or behind other controls." Read the information and then close the Help window and the Search Results task pane. Verify that the **Weights** picture is still selected, and then move it behind the Programs and Members title.

Explore

10. Use the "Type a question for help" box to ask the following question: "How do I change the background color of a control?" Click the topic "Change the background color of a control or section." Read the information and then close the Help window and the Search Results task pane. Select the Programs and Members title object, and then change its background color to Transparent.

11. Display the report in Print Preview. Print just the first page of the report, and then close and save the report.

12. Rename the report object to **ProgramsAndMembers**.

13. Close the Fitness database.

Challenge

Use what you learned, plus some new skills, to create forms and a report to work with and display data about a zoo's patrons.

Case Problem 3

Data Files needed for this Case Problem: Redwood.mdb (*cont. from Tutorial 3*) and Animals.bmp

Redwood Zoo Michael Rosenfeld wants to create forms and reports for the Redwood database. You'll help him create these database objects by completing the following:

1. Open the **Redwood** database located in the Brief\Case3 folder provided with your Data Files.
2. If your Redwood database is stored on a floppy disk, you will need to delete the files **Redwood97.mdb** and **Redwood2002.mdb** from your disk so you will have enough room to complete the steps. If your database is stored on a hard drive or a network drive, no action is necessary.
3. Use the Form Wizard to create a form based on the **Pledge** table. Select all fields for the form, the Columnar layout, and the Blueprint style. Specify the title **Pledge Info** for the form.
4. Use the **Pledge Info** form to update the **Pledge** table as follows:
   a. Use the Find command to move to the record with PledgeID 2490, and then change the FundCode to B11 and the TotalPledged amount to 75.
   b. Add a new record with the following values:

PledgeID:	2977
DonorID:	59021
FundCode:	M23
PledgeDate:	12/15/2006
TotalPledged:	150
PaymentMethod:	C
PaymentSchedule:	S

   c. Print just this form record.
   d. Delete the record with PledgeID 2900.
5. Change the AutoFormat of the **Pledge Info** form to Expedition, save the changed form, and then use the form to print the last record in the **Pledge** table. Close the form.
6. Rename the form object to **PledgeInfo**.
7. Use the Form Wizard to create a form containing a main form and a subform. Select all the fields from the **Donor** table for the main form, and select the PledgeID, FundCode, PledgeDate, and TotalPledged fields from the **Pledge** table for the sub-form. Use the Datasheet layout and the Expedition style. Specify the title **Donors and Pledges** for the main form and the title **Pledge Subform** for the subform.
8. Display record 11 in the main form. Print the current main form record and its sub-form records, and then close the **Donors and Pledges** form.
9. Rename the main form object to **DonorsAndPledges** and the subform object to **PledgeSubform**.

Explore

10. Use the Report Wizard to create a report based on the primary Donor table and the related Pledge table. Select the DonorID, FirstName, LastName, and Class fields from the **Donor** table, and select all fields from the **Pledge** table except DonorID. In the third Report Wizard dialog box, specify the FundCode field as an additional grouping level. Sort the detail records in *descending* order by TotalPledged. Choose the Align Left 2 layout, Landscape orientation, and the Soft Gray style. Specify the title **Donors and Pledges** for the report.

11. Insert the **Animals** picture, which is located in the Brief\Case3 folder provided with your Data Files, in the Report Header section of the **Donors and Pledges** report. Position the picture so that its left edge aligns with the 4-inch mark on the horizontal ruler and its top edge is just below the top border line of the report.

Explore

12. Use the "Type a question for help" box to ask the following question: "How do I add a special effect to an object?" Click the topic "Make a control appear raised, sunken, shadowed, chiseled, or etched." Read the information, and then close the Help window and the Search Results task pane. Add the Shadowed special effect to the **Animals** picture, and then save the report.

Explore

13. Print only pages 1 and 7 of the report, and then close it.
14. Rename the report object to **DonorsAndPledges**.
15. If your database is stored on a floppy disk, you will need to turn off the Compact on Close feature before closing the **Redwood** database because there isn't enough room on the disk to compact the database. If your database is stored on a hard drive or a network drive, no action is necessary.
16. Close the **Redwood** database.

Create

With the figures provided as guides, create a form and a report to display and manage data for this luxury rental agency.

Case Problem 4

Data Files needed for this Case Problem: GEM.mdb *(cont. from Tutorial 3)* and Villa.bmp

GEM Ultimate Vacations Griffin and Emma MacElroy want to create forms and reports that will help them track and analyze data about their clients and the luxury properties they rent. Help them enhance the GEM database by completing the following:

1. Open the **GEM** database located in the Brief\Case4 folder provided with your Data Files.
2. Create the form shown in Figure 4-35. Be certain to resize all columns in the subform to their best fit.

Figure 4-35

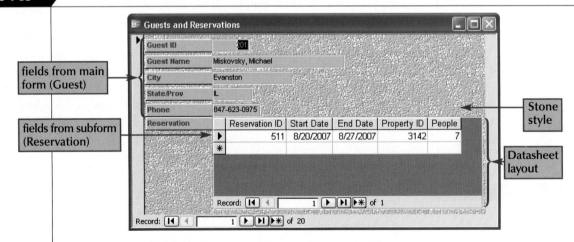

3. Using the form you just created, print the third main form record and its subform records.
4. Navigate to the second record in the subform for the third main record, and then change the People field value to 5.
5. Use the Find command to move to the record with GuestID 224, and then change the EndDate field value to 5/5/2007.
6. Use the appropriate wildcard character to find all records with a Phone value that begins with the area code 630. How many records did you find? Close the form.

7. Rename the form object to **GuestsAndReservations** and the subform object to **ReservationSubform**.
8. Use the Report Wizard to create the report shown in Figure 4-36.

Figure 4-36

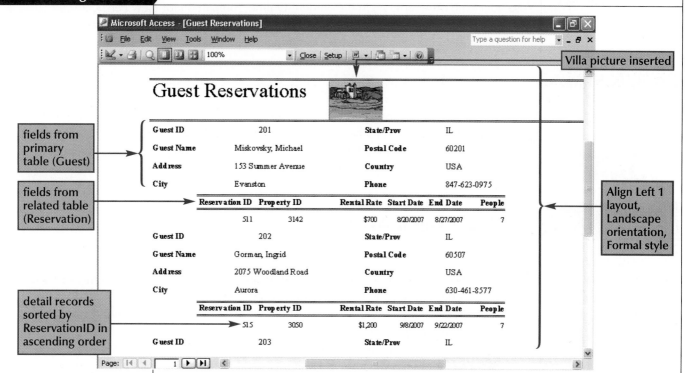

Hints: Resize the Phone text box control in order to display the Phone field values in the report fully. When inserting the Villa picture (located in the Brief\Case4 folder provided with your Data Files), position the picture so that its left edge aligns with the 3-inch mark on the horizontal ruler and its top edge is just below the top border line of the report. Also, use the bottom center or right handle (as necessary) to resize the Villa picture so that it fits within the lines of the report header.

Explore

9. Insert the same **Villa** picture in the Report Footer section of the **Guest Reservations** report. (Items placed in the Report Footer section appear only once, at the end of the report.) Position the picture so that its right edge aligns with the right edge of the report, at approximately the 6.5-inch mark on the horizontal ruler. Save the report.

Explore

10. View the first two pages of the report in Print Preview at the same time. (*Hint*: Use a toolbar button.) Use the Page navigation buttons to move through the report, displaying two pages at a time. Print only the first and last pages of the report, and then close the report.
11. Rename the report object to **GuestReservations**.
12. Close the GEM database.

Research

Use the Internet to find and work with data related to the topics presented in this tutorial.

Internet Assignments

The purpose of the Internet Assignments is to challenge you to find information on the Internet that you can use to work effectively with this software. The actual assignments are updated and maintained on the Course Technology Web site. Log on to the Internet and use your Web browser to go to the Student Online Companion for New Perspectives Office 2003 at **www.course.com/np/office2003**. Click the Internet Assignments link, and then navigate to the assignments for this tutorial.

Assess

SAM Assessment and Training

If your instructor has chosen to use the full online version of SAM 2003 Assessment and Training, you can go beyond the "just-in-time" training provided on the CD that accompanies this text. Simply log in to your SAM account (http://sam2003.course.com) to launch any assigned training activities or exams that relate to the skills covered in this tutorial.

Review

Quick Check Answers

Session 4.1

1. The AutoForm Wizard creates a form automatically using all the fields in the selected table or query; the Form Wizard allows you to choose some or all of the fields in the selected table or query, choose fields from other tables and queries, and display fields in any order on the form.
2. An AutoFormat is a predefined style for a form (or report). To change a form's AutoFormat, display the form in Design view, click the AutoFormat button on the Form Design toolbar, click the new AutoFormat in the Form AutoFormats list box, and then click the OK button.
3. the last record in the table
4. datasheet
5. the question mark (?)
6. as many form records as can fit on a printed page

Session 4.2

1. The main form displays the data from the primary table, and the subform displays the data from the related table.
2. You use the top set of navigation buttons to select and move through records from the related table in the subform, and the bottom set to select and move through records from the primary table in the main form.
3. control
4. Error Checking Options
5. Design view
6. Report Header

New Perspectives on

Integrating Microsoft® Office 2003

Tutorial 2   INT 2-3

Integrating Word, Excel, and Access

Creating a Brochure

Read This Before You Begin

Data Files

To complete the "Integrating Word, Excel, and Access" tutorial, you need the starting Data Files. See the inside back or front cover for information on downloading these files from course.com, or ask your instructor for assistance. The following table identifies each starting Data File and the folder it is stored in, as well as the ending files, which you create and save in each tutorial.

Folders		Starting Files	Ending Files
Tutorial .02	Tutorial	Hospital Letter1.doc, LHCBrochure.doc, LHCRequests.xls, LHCServices.xls	Lifestyles Services.mdb, New Services Brochure.doc, Request List.xls, Services Requested Query.rtf
	Review	LHCALDInfo.doc, LHCProducts.xls, LHCQuestions.doc, LHCServicesAndSolutions.xls	ALD Info Sheet.doc, ALD Products Workbook.xls, ALDProducts.mdb, Frequently Asked Questions.doc, Install Products.rtf, Product Prices.rtf
	Cases	LFCTextbooks.xls, MusicGrowth.xls, MusicLetter.doc, MusicMemo.doc	All Textbooks.xls, Outdated Texts.rtf, Renovations Memo.doc, Textbook Memo.doc, Textbooks.mdb

Storing Your Files

It is recommended that you store all your Data Files on a USB drive. Refer to the tutorial "Managing Your Files" for information on using USB drives. If you need to store your Data Files on floppy disks, you will need one high-density disk to store all the files for the "Integrating Word, Excel, and Access" tutorial.

SAM 2003 Training Companion CD

The SAM 2003 Training Companion CD that comes with this text gives you "just-in-time" training and reinforcement of important Microsoft Office skills. Look for the SAM CD logo throughout each tutorial for opportunities to complete the hands-on tasks included on this CD.

Integrating Word, Excel, and Access

Creating a Brochure

Case | Lifestyles Home Care, Inc.

Caitlin Sheehan, the founder and owner of Lifestyles Home Care, Inc., in Woburn, Massachusetts, decided to create a brochure to publicize the expanded services offered by her company. Caitlin realizes that many people are not even aware that services like the ones Lifestyles provides—to help elderly and disabled people stay in their homes rather than move into a nursing home—even exist. The brochure needs to communicate the services to potential new clients, give an overview of pricing, and explain the services clearly enough for people to see the benefits of helping loved ones remain in their own homes.

In addition to sending the new brochure to the social work departments at local hospitals, Caitlin decides to mail a copy to all of her current clients. She wants them to be aware of the new services, in case they would like additional services that the state won't pay for, or in case their circumstances change and they become ineligible for state-supported services.

Caitlin has drafted the text and established the general layout for the brochure in a Word document. She needs to insert the company logo into the brochure. Caitlin also wants to include a table summarizing the services she plans to offer and the fees for those services. Finally, she wants to include a sample package of services. The company logo and the list of services are contained in a Word letter and an Excel workbook. To create the sample package of services, Caitlin will import data she has stored in an Excel workbook into an Access database, where she can use Access tools to analyze the data. Then she can export the analysis into the brochure.

Objectives		SAM Training Tasks	
• Collect text from Office documents and place it on the Clipboard task pane • Paste selections from Office documents into Word • Find Office documents with the File Search task panes	• Learn about importing and exporting data • Import an Excel list into an Access database • Query an Access database • Export an Access query to a Word document	• Collect and paste using the Clipboard task pane • Copy and paste text • Copy cells	• Export data to Word • Import structured data into Access tables • Search for workbooks

For hands-on practice of key tasks in this tutorial, go to the SAM 2003 Training Companion CD included with this text.

You'll complete sections of the brochure for Caitlin using the tools and features of Microsoft Office 2003 that let you integrate information created in Word, Excel, and Access.

Planning the Brochure

Caitlin has already created a draft of the Lifestyles Home Care brochure in a Word document, but she needs to pull in graphics and data from other sources. She asks you to do this for her.

Figure 2-1 shows Caitlin's plan for the new brochure. Caitlin would like the company logo to appear on the first page of the brochure; a list of the company's services and fees to be included on the second page of the brochure; and a table showing frequently requested services to appear on the third page of the brochure. The fourth page does not require any changes.

| Figure 2-1 | Caitlin's plan for the new services brochure |

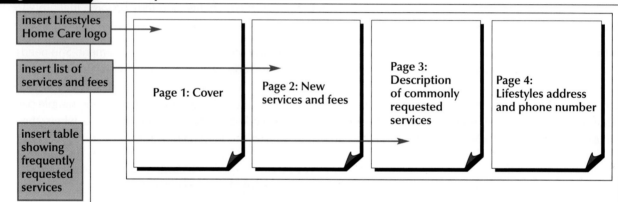

First, Caitlin wants you to insert the company logo on the cover of the brochure. You can do this by copying and pasting the logo from the letter Caitlin mailed to the hospital social work departments. Second, Caitlin wants you to insert a table listing the new services and fees. Caitlin cannot recall the name of this file, but she knows it's an Excel file. Once you find the table, you can copy and paste it into the brochure.

Finally, Caitlin wants you to include a table showing an example of a package of services a typical client might request. To create this table, you will need to analyze data Caitlin has stored in an Excel workbook. You realize the analysis of this data will be easier if the data is in the form of a table in an Access database, thereby allowing you to use the more sophisticated analytical tools available in Access. To use Access to analyze the data, you need to import the Excel data into an Access database. Importing data is different than the OLE methods you learned about in the first Integration tutorial. Recall that OLE is used to *share* data between Office programs. When you **import** data from one Office program to another, you are actually converting the data from its original source program format to a format that is supported by the destination program, which allows you to use the destination program's tools and features to view and manipulate the data in a new way. Once you have imported data from the Excel workbook into Access, you can create a query to determine the most requested services, and then export that information as a table into the brochure. When you **export** data, it is converted from one program's format to another, as in importing. However, when you import, you start in the destination program and import from the source program; when you export, you reverse this process— you start in the source program and export to the destination program.

Your first task is to collect the logo and the list of new services and fees to insert into the brochure. You'll use the Office task panes to streamline the process of finding and collecting information from different Office documents.

Using the Task Panes

Caitlin knows that she has stored some of the information she needs for the brochure in other Office documents. The company logo has been used in several letters she has written. She also knows that she has created a table of the new services and fees in an Excel worksheet.

Caitlin asks you to find these two pieces of information—the company logo and the table of services and fees—and insert them into the brochure where they belong. To integrate this material, you can use the Office task panes. Every Office program contains a number of task panes, including the Help, Clipboard, and Basic File Search task panes. The task panes include related options that you need to perform common tasks, such as simple and advanced options for finding a file.

You will start by using the Clipboard task pane to copy and paste the company logo into the brochure. Then you can use the File Search command to find the new services and fees table and insert that into the brochure.

Collecting Information on the Clipboard Task Pane

The **Clipboard task pane** allows you to access the Office Clipboard. You use the **Office Clipboard** to collect text and other items from Office documents, and then paste those items into any Office document. The collected items stay on the Office Clipboard until you clear it or exit Office. You can collect up to 24 items on the Office Clipboard. Once you cut or paste a 25th item to the Office Clipboard, the first item you collected is removed. The Office Clipboard is different from the system Clipboard. The **system Clipboard** is part of Windows, and it can contain only the last item cut or copied. Items that you cut or copy are put onto the system Clipboard, and each subsequent cut or copied item replaces the item that was on the system Clipboard previously.

To paste an item from the Office Clipboard, you must open the Clipboard task pane and click the item in the task pane that you want to paste. When you use the Paste command (either the menu command, the toolbar button, or the shortcut keys Ctrl + V), you paste only the last item cut or copied; in other words, you paste the item on the system Clipboard.

For the brochure, you'll copy the Lifestyles Home Care logo from one document, and then use the Office Clipboard to paste it into the brochure. First, you'll start Word and open the brochure document.

To open the brochure document:

1. Open the Word document **LHCBrochure**, located in the Tutorial.02\Tutorial folder included with your Data Files.

2. Save the document to the same folder with the name **New Services Brochure**. The brochure appears in Print Layout view.

3. If necessary, display nonprinting characters.

You'll start by copying the Lifestyles Home Care logo from a letter.

To copy the logo from a Word document:

1. Open the **Hospital Letter1** document, located in the Tutorial.02\Tutorial folder included with your Data Files. This is the document that contains the Lifestyles Home Care logo.

2. Click the **logo** in the document to select it. See Figure 2-2.

Figure 2-2   Lifestyles Home Care logo selected

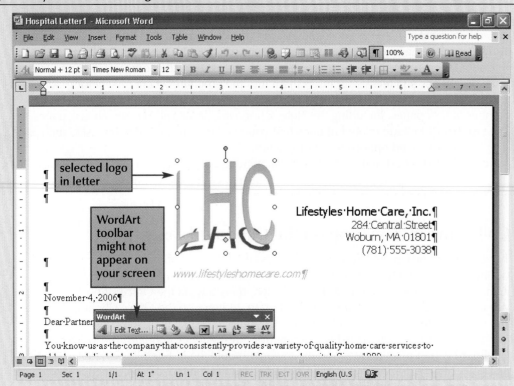

3. Click the **Copy** button 🖹 on the Standard toolbar. Word copies the logo to both the Office Clipboard and the system Clipboard, and a ScreenTip appears in the lower-right corner telling you that 1 of 24 items has been collected. See Figure 2-3.

Trouble? If the ScreenTip does not appear, click Edit on the menu bar, and then click Office Clipboard to open the Clipboard task pane. Click the Options button at the bottom of the task pane, and then click Show Status Near Taskbar When Copying. Click the Options button again, and then click Collect Without Showing Office Clipboard if it does not have a check next to it. If the LHC logo is not in the Clipboard task pane, close the task pane and then repeat Step 3; otherwise continue with Step 4.

Trouble? If the Clipboard task pane opens, skip Step 4.

Figure 2-3   Logo copied to Office Clipboard

Trouble? If the ScreenTip noted this was another item number other than 1, there are additional items on your Office Clipboard. This is not a problem.

4. Click **Edit** on the menu bar, and then click **Office Clipboard**. The Clipboard task pane opens with the logo pasted in it.

5. Close the Hospital Letter document.

The Clipboard task pane now contains one item—the company logo. Before you paste the logo into the brochure, you need to collect one more item—the services and fees table.

Finding Files Using the File Search Task Panes

Caitlin created the new services and fees table in an Excel workbook, but she does not remember what she named the file. Before you can copy this table to the Office Clipboard, you must find the file that contains it. You can use one of the search task panes to find the file. You use the **Basic File Search task pane** to find files that contain text you specify. You use the **Advanced File Search task pane** to find files based on their properties, such as who created the file or when. In either type of search, you enter your **search criteria**—the text or properties of the files you want to find. Caitlin wants to find the document that contains the text "new fee schedule."

To find the file containing the services and fees table:

1. In the New Services Brochure document, click **File** on the menu bar, and then click **File Search**. The Basic File Search task pane opens, as shown in Figure 2-4.

Basic File Search task pane   Figure 2-4

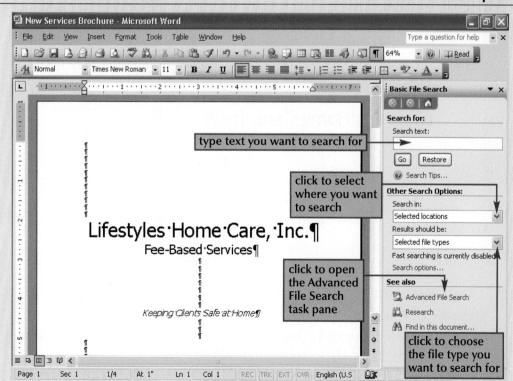

Trouble? If the Advanced File Search task pane opens instead of the Basic File Search task pane, click the Basic File Search link at the bottom of the Advanced File Search task pane.

2. Select any text in the **Search text** text box, if necessary, and then type **new fee schedule**. Caitlin knows that the file contains this phrase, so you can use it to find the file.

3. Click the **Search in** list arrow under Other Search Options, click the **My Network Places** and **Outlook** check boxes to clear them, if necessary, click the **My Computer** check box to check it, if necessary, and then click the **plus sign (+)** next to **My Computer** to open a list of locations on your computer. Notice that all of the check boxes are selected. If necessary, you could select only certain locations to narrow your search and speed up the search process. You should always check the search locations because Word remembers the settings from one session to the next.

4. Click the **My Documents** check box to clear it, and then click it again to select it. Now the My Documents check box is a single check box, which indicates that the search function will search for files matching the search criteria in the My Documents folder, but not within any subfolders stored in the My Documents folder. Note the other selected check boxes that look like there are two additional check boxes stacked underneath them. This indicates that the contents of any subfolder within those folders will be searched in addition to files within the folder itself. See Figure 2-5.

| Figure 2-5 | Search criteria set in Basic File Search task pane |

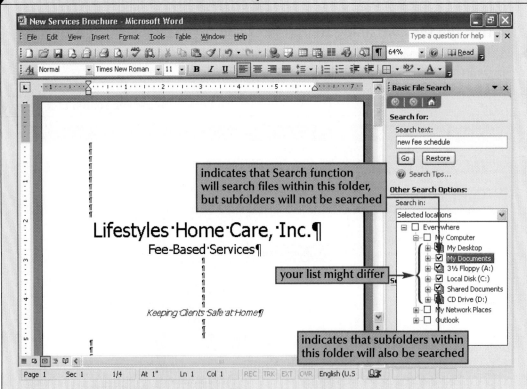

5. Click the **My Computer** check box to select it and all of the subfolders within it.

6. Click outside the Search in list box to close the list.

You can also narrow the search by selecting the type of document you want to find. Caitlin knows that the services and fees table is in an Excel workbook.

7. Click the **Results should be** list arrow, click the **plus sign (+)** next to Anything to expand the list, to show the list of file types, if necessary, and then click the **plus sign (+)** next to Office Files to expand that list, if necessary.

   Trouble? If you see only minus signs instead of plus signs, the lists are already expanded.

8. Click the **Office Files** check box to check it, if necessary, and then click the **Office Files** check box again to clear it. All of the file types under Office Files are cleared.

9. Click the **Excel Files** check box to select it.

10. Click the **Web Pages** check box to clear it, if necessary. (You might need to scroll down to see this check box.)

11. Click outside the Results should be list box to close the list, and then click the **Go** button in the task pane. The Search Results task pane opens in place of the Basic File Search task pane. After several moments, a list of the files it found based on the criteria you entered appears. See Figure 2-6. Note that this search may take a few minutes.

Search Results task pane ◀ Figure 2-6

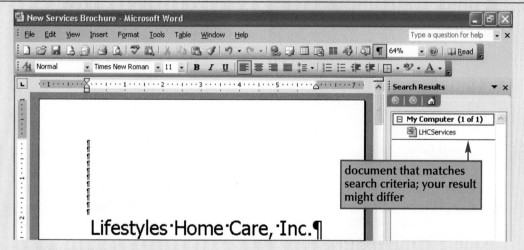

Trouble? If you see more than one file listed in the task pane on your screen, this just means that there are additional Excel files on your computer that contain the three words "new fee schedule" (although not necessarily as a phrase). The LHCServices file should appear at the top of the list.

Now you can open the workbook and copy the table to the Clipboard task pane.

To open the workbook and copy the fee schedule table:

1. In the Search Results task pane, click **LHCServices**. Excel starts and the LHCServices workbook opens.

2. Select cells **A6** to **C24**. These are the cells containing the services and fees table.

3. Click the **Copy** button 📋 on the Excel Standard toolbar to copy the services and fees table to the Clipboard task pane. The ScreenTip that appears in the lower-right tells you that you copied item 2 of 24 to the Clipboard.

4. Click the **Other Task Panes** list arrow, and then click **Clipboard** to switch to the Clipboard task pane. See Figure 2-7.

| Figure 2-7 | Cells to copy from LHCServices worksheet |

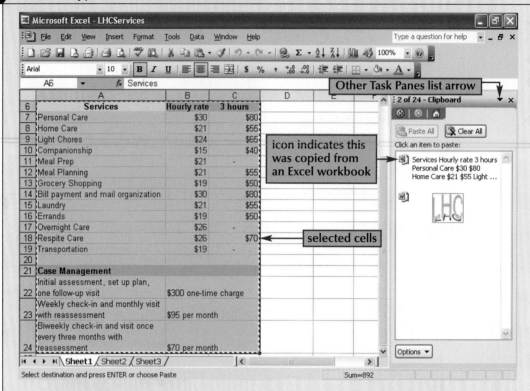

Trouble? If the Excel data in the Clipboard task pane does not have an Excel icon next to it, click the Copy button again to copy the data a second time, and then delete the item in the Clipboard task pane that does not have the Excel icon next to it by pointing to it, clicking the list arrow that appears, and then clicking Delete.

5. Close the **LHCServices** workbook, and then exit Excel.

The information you copied remains on the Office Clipboard even after you exit Excel.

You have collected two items for the brochure—the company logo and the table listing the new services and fees. Now you can paste these items into the brochure.

Pasting Items from the Clipboard Task Pane

To paste an item from the Clipboard task pane into a document, you open the document, click the location where you want to paste the item, and then click the item in the Clipboard task pane. The text or object then appears in the document. After you paste an item, the Paste Options button appears in the program window near the lower-right corner of the pasted item. Recall you use the Paste Options button to determine how the information you pasted should be formatted in the Word document.

You are ready to paste the selections you collected on the Clipboard.

To paste items from the Clipboard task pane:

1. Click the **New Services Brochure - Microsoft Word** button on the taskbar, if necessary, to make the New Services Brochure document active, click the **Other Task Panes** list arrow on the Search Results task pane title bar, and then click **Clipboard** to open the Clipboard task pane.

   First, you need to paste the logo you copied from the hospital letter into the brochure.

2. Click in the first blank paragraph in the brochure.

3. Click the **Lifestyles Home Care logo** in the Clipboard task pane. The logo is pasted into the Word document.

4. Click the pasted logo to select it, and then drag it to the top of the page and position it approximately centered over the word *Home*. See Figure 2-8.

Brochure with logo pasted | **Figure 2-8**

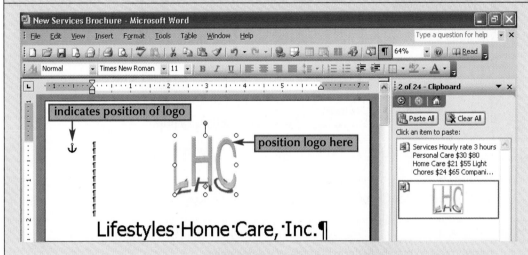

Next, you will paste the services and fees table into page 2 of the brochure.

5. Scroll down the document so that you can see the two paragraphs on page 2, and then click in the blank paragraph just above the page break on page 2.

6. Click the Excel item that begins **Services Hourly rate 3 hours** in the Clipboard task pane. The data is pasted into the brochure and retains the formatting of the original Excel worksheet. See Figure 2-9.

Figure 2-9 | **Services table copied into brochure**

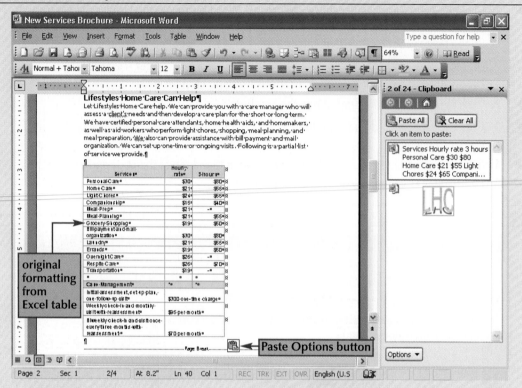

Trouble? If you have two copies of the data in the Clipboard task pane, make sure you click the item in the Clipboard task pane with the Excel icon.

The format of the table does not match the format of the rest of the text in the brochure; for example, the table text is smaller. You will use the Paste Options button to reformat the pasted table to match the format of the Word document.

7. Click the **Paste Options** button in the document. The options are similar to the ones you saw when you linked the Excel table to the Hospital Letter in the first Integration tutorial.

8. Click the **Match Destination Table Style** option button. The format of the table text now matches the format of the other paragraphs in the brochure.

9. Position the pointer over the table so that the **Select Table** button appears near the upper-left corner of the table, click the **Select Table** button in the document, click the **Center** button on the Formatting toolbar, and then click a blank area of the document to deselect the table. The table is centered horizontally on the page.

10. Click the **Close** button on the Clipboard task pane title bar to close the task pane, and then save the New Services Brochure document.

You have added all the information Caitlin needs in the first part of the brochure. Now Caitlin needs you to create the table listing the most frequently requested services, which you will then use to create a sample service package.

Using Excel Data in Access

About a year ago, Caitlin realized that her employees were reporting more and more instances of clients requesting additional services. Her employees also indicated that the clients, or the clients' families, often were willing to pay for the additional services. Caitlin tracked this information in an Excel workbook. She noted the services requested, the number of clients who requested the service, and the average amount the clients were willing to pay. She based her new business plan, in part, on the information in this worksheet.

Caitlin wants to add a table to page 3 of the brochure showing an example of a typical service package based on the services requested most often by clients. To determine which services are the most frequently requested, you will analyze the data in Caitlin's workbook. Although Excel is perfect for calculating totals and creating charts to track trends, Access is a better choice to use to extract information, such as which services are the most frequently requested. To find that information, you will import the Excel data into Access.

To create a table showing the most frequently requested services, you'll first import the list of requested services from the Excel worksheet into an Access database. Then you will perform a query in Access to determine which services were requested the most often. You will then export the results of the query to Word and insert them into the brochure.

Preparing an Excel List for Import

You can use lists of Excel data to build tables in Access. Then you can create forms, reports, queries, and other Access objects based on the tables. You can only import Excel data that is in the form of a list—a series of worksheet rows that contain related data, such as product names and prices or client names and phone numbers. Caitlin's worksheet showing the service requests is in the form of a list.

Before you import the Excel list, you should check the format of the data. The import will be seamless and error free if each column in the Excel worksheet has a label in the first row and the list of data contains no blank rows or columns. Caitlin asks you to prepare the worksheet before you import its data to Access.

To prepare the Excel data:

1. Open the Excel workbook **LHCRequests**, located in the Tutorial.02\Tutorial folder included with your Data Files. This is the Excel workbook that contains the information about the service requests.

2. Save the file as **Request List** in the Tutorial.02\Tutorial folder included with your Data Files.

   The first eight rows contain helpful information for someone reading the worksheet, but the first row of data needs to contain the column headings.

3. Select rows **1** through **8**, right-click the selection, click **Delete** on the shortcut menu to delete the selected rows, and then click the worksheet to deselect the cells. Excel deletes the rows and shifts the remaining data up eight rows.

   The first column does not have a column head. The column headings will become the field names in the table, so it is important that every column have a heading. You will add a heading to the first column.

4. Click **cell A1**, type **Service**, and then press the **Enter** key.

   It's a good idea for field names in Access not to contain any spaces, so you'll change the column headings now.

> **5.** Click **cell B1**, type **HowOftenRequested**, press the → key, type **AvgHourlyFee**, and then press the **Enter** key. See Figure 2-10.

| Figure 2-10 | **Excel worksheet prepared to be imported into Access** |

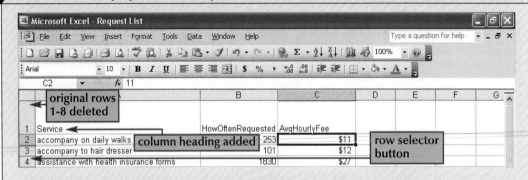

> **6.** Scroll down the worksheet to make sure there are no blank rows or other heading rows.

> **7.** Save and close the workbook.

Importing an Excel List into an Access Table

Now you're ready to import the Excel list into an Access table. To do this, you copy the data from Excel to Access, maintaining two separate versions of the data.

| Reference Window | **Importing Excel Data into Access** |

- Open the Access database where you want to import the Excel list.
- Click File on the menu bar, point to Get External Data, and then click Import.
- In the Import dialog box, click the Files of type list arrow, and then click Microsoft Excel.
- If necessary, click the Look in list arrow to locate the Excel workbook you want to use, and then double-click the workbook.
- Follow the directions in the Access Import Spreadsheet Wizard.

You will import the Excel list to a new table in a new database.

To import the Excel list to a table in a new database:

> **1.** Create a new, blank database in Access, name it **Lifestyles Services**, and save it in the Tutorial.02\Tutorial folder included with your Data Files.

> **2.** Click **File** on the menu bar, point to **Get External Data**, and then click **Import**. The Import dialog box opens.

> **3.** Click the **Files of type** list arrow, and then click **Microsoft Excel**.

> **4.** Click **Request List** located in the Tutorial.02\Tutorial folder, and then click the **Import** button. The first dialog box of the Import Spreadsheet Wizard opens, as shown in Figure 2-11.

First dialog box in Import Spreadsheet Wizard ◄ Figure 2-11

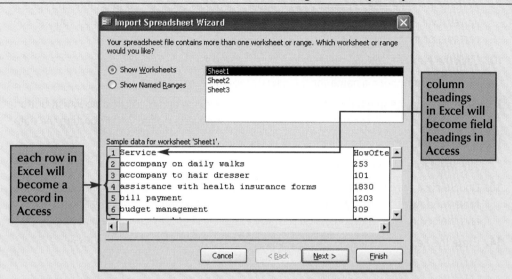

each row in Excel will become a record in Access

column headings in Excel will become field headings in Access

5. Make sure the **Show Worksheets** option button and **Sheet1** are selected, and then click the **Next** button.

6. In the second dialog box of the Import Spreadsheet Wizard, click the **First Row Contains Column Headings** check box to select it, if necessary. In the bottom half of the dialog box, notice that the gray column headings from the worksheet will become the field headings for the new Access table. Below those headings, you see how the Excel data will be organized into records (horizontal rows) and fields (vertical columns).

7. Click the **Next** button to continue to the third dialog box in the wizard. Use this dialog box to set where you want to store your data—in a new table or an existing table. You want to create a new table from the Excel worksheet.

8. Click the **Next** button to accept the default of storing the data in a new table. Now you can specify information about the fields you are importing. See Figure 2-12.

Specifying imported field information ◄ Figure 2-12

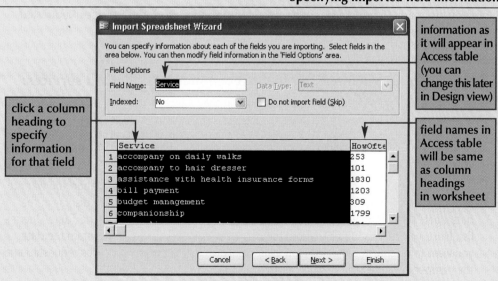

click a column heading to specify information for that field

information as it will appear in Access table (you can change this later in Design view)

field names in Access table will be same as column headings in worksheet

9. Click the **Next** button to accept the default field names and other field information.

The next dialog box in the wizard lets you assign a primary key to the data. When you are working in a database, a primary key uniquely identifies each record in a table and speeds up retrieval. Because the Request List worksheet does not contain information you can convert to a primary key, you can let Access add one to the table.

▶ **10.** Click the **Next** button to let Access add a primary key.

Now you can provide a name for the new Access table.

▶ **11.** Type **Services Requested** in the Import to Table text box, and then click the **Finish** button. After a moment, a dialog box opens telling you that Access has finished importing the data.

▶ **12.** Click the **OK** button in the dialog box.

The new table appears in the Database window.

▶ **13.** Double-click the **Services Requested** table icon to open the table, and then maximize the table window, if necessary. The Excel data has been imported into the new Access table, and the column headings are converted to field names and the row data to records.

▶ **14.** Close the Services Requested table. Leave the Lifestyles Services database open.

Now you are ready to query the table to determine the most requested services.

Using Access Data in a Word Document

As you recall from your work with Access, you use a query to extract information from a database. You create a query to search for records that meet your criteria, and then store them in a datasheet—a collection of data from a table, query, or other Access object, displayed in a row-and-column format. You can then export the datasheet into a Word document.

Caitlin wants to find the most requested services over the past year. She wants you to include all services that were requested more than 1500 times. You'll create a query to find this information. Access will store the results of the query in a datasheet, which you can then export to the new brochure.

Querying Data in an Access Database

Now you are ready to build a query to extract information from the Services Requested table you created in the new Lifestyles Services database.

To create a query to identify the most commonly requested services:

▶ **1.** In the Access Database window, click **Queries** in the Objects list.

You want to create a new query to find records in the Services Requested table.

▶ **2.** Double-click **Create query by using wizard**. The first dialog box of the Simple Query Wizard opens.

In this dialog box, you choose the table or query that contains the information you want to extract. Then you choose the fields in that table or query that you want to display in the datasheet. There is only one table in the new database, and it is listed in the Table/Queries list. Next, you choose the fields from the Services Requested table that contain the data you want to display in the datasheet. Caitlin only wants to show the services requested and the number of requests for each service.

3. Click **Service** in the Available Fields list box, click the **>** button, click **HowOftenRequested** in the Available Fields list box, and then click the **>** button to add those columns to the Selected Fields list box.

4. Click the **Next** button.

In the second dialog box of the wizard, you choose whether you want to view detail or summary information. Detail view shows every field of every record. To show a summary, you first choose how to summarize the information. For example, you could show the sum total of all the services requested instead of individual records. In this case, you need to show every field.

5. Click the **Next** button to accept the default of showing detail information. In the final dialog box of the wizard, you provide a title for the query. Access shows "Services Requested Query" for this query.

6. Click the **Finish** button to accept Services Requested Query as the query name. The query results appear in a datasheet.

7. Double-click the right column border on the Service column to expand the column to fit all of the entries, and then do the same to the second column. See Figure 2-13.

Results of the Services Requested Query ◄ **Figure 2-13**

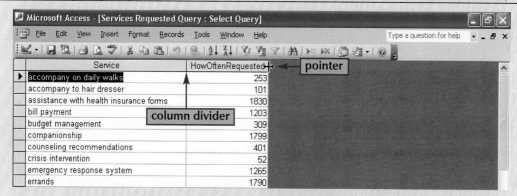

These results show all of the services requested. To set criteria to show only services requested more than 1500 times, you have to switch to Design view.

8. On the Query toolbar, click the **View** button. The query switches to Design view.

You need to set criteria to select only those records where the number of requests is greater than 1500. Although you need the HowOftenRequested field to select records based on that information, you don't want to show this field in the datasheet, only the Service Requested field. You can hide the HowOftenRequested field so it doesn't appear in the query results.

9. Click in the **Criteria** row of the HowOftenRequested column, and then type **>1500**.

10. Click the **Show** check box in the HowOftenRequested column to clear it. This hides the quantity information in the results. See Figure 2-14.

Figure 2-14 ▶ **Criteria set for query**

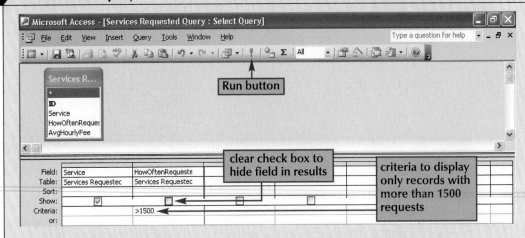

11. Click the **Run** button ⚡ on the Query Design toolbar. The query results appear in a new datasheet.

12. Double-click the right-column border of the Service column to expand the column width to accommodate all of the entries, if necessary. See Figure 2-15.

Figure 2-15 ▶ **Results of Services Requested Query after setting criteria**

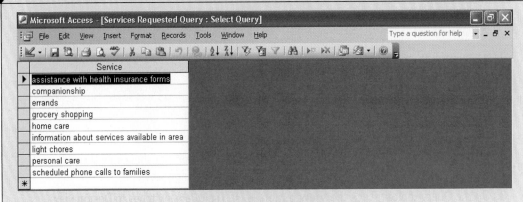

13. Save the query, and then close the Query Datasheet window.

Caitlin reviews the information and says it's just what she needs for the brochure. Now you can export the results of the query to the brochure document.

Exporting a Query from Access to Word

To export an Access query, you convert the query into **rich text format**, a special text format that preserves the layout of the data. The query becomes a text file with an .rtf extension, often called an RTF file. You can then insert the RTF file into a Word document.

Now that you have created and saved the Services Requested Query, you can export it and convert it into an RTF file. Then you'll switch to the brochure document and insert the query as a table.

To export a query and insert it into a Word document:

1. Click the **Services Requested Query** in the Database window to select it, if necessary, click **File** on the menu bar, and then click **Export**. The Export Query 'Services Requested Query' To dialog box opens.

2. Type **Services Requested Query** in the File name text box.

3. Click the **Save as type** list arrow, and then scroll to locate and click **Rich Text Format**.

4. If necessary, click the **Save in** list arrow to navigate to the Tutorial.02\Tutorial folder included with your Data Files.

5. Click the **Export** button. Access converts the Services Requested Query into an RTF file and stores it in the location you specified.

6. Close the Lifestyles Services database.

   Now you will insert the RTF file into the brochure.

7. Click the **New Services Brochure - Microsoft Word** button on the taskbar. The brochure appears in the Word window.

8. In the New Services Brochure document, scroll to page 3, and then click in the empty paragraph above the second paragraph.

9. Click **Insert** on the menu bar, and then click **File**. The Insert File dialog box opens.

10. Click the **Files of type** list arrow, and then scroll to locate and click **Rich Text Format**.

11. Click the **Look in** list arrow, and then navigate to the Tutorial.02\Tutorial folder included with your Data Files, if necessary.

12. Click **Services Requested Query**, and then click the **Insert** button. The query results are inserted into the document as a table.

    You need to center the table.

13. Position the pointer over the table, click the **Select Table** button ⊞, click the **Center** button ☰ on the Formatting toolbar, and then click in a blank area of the document. See Figure 2-16.

Figure 2-16   Query results inserted as table in brochure

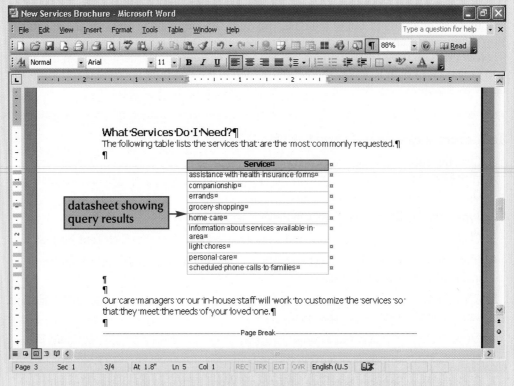

14. Save the **New Services Brochure** document, click the **Print Preview** button on the Standard toolbar, click the **Multiple Pages** button on the Print Preview toolbar, and then select **2 x 2 Pages** to view all four pages of the brochure. See Figure 2-17.

Figure 2-17   Completed brochure in Print Preview

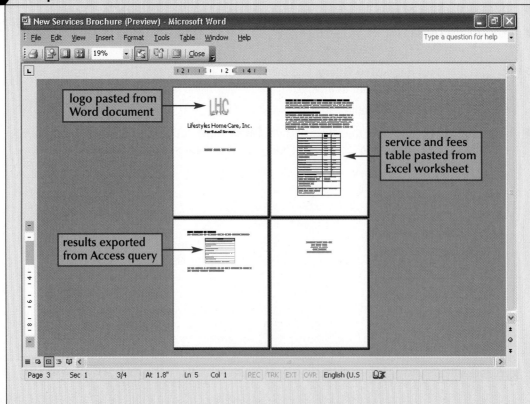

15. Print the **New Services Brochure** document, and then save and close the document.
16. Exit all open programs.

Review

To reinforce the tasks you learned in this tutorial, go to the SAM 2003 Training Companion CD included with this text.

Quick Check

1. Explain how to use the Office Clipboard to copy and paste multiple selections.
2. When searching for files, what is the difference between using the Basic File Search task pane and the Advanced File Search task pane?
3. Why would you import Excel data into an Access table?
4. Name two conditions Excel data must meet before you can import it into Access.
5. What do you use in Access to import data from Excel?
6. True or False: When you export, you convert data from a source program to a destination program.

Review

Tutorial Summary

In this tutorial, you learned how to use the Office Clipboard to copy and paste multiple items. You also learned how to search for a file containing specific text, in specific locations, or of a specific type. You prepared Excel data to be imported into an Access table, and then you imported the data. You then exported the results of a query from Access to a Word document.

Key Terms

Advanced File Search task pane	export	rich text format
Basic File Search task pane	import	search criteria
Clipboard task pane	Office Clipboard	system Clipboard

Practice

Practice the skills you learned in the tutorial using the same case scenario.

Review Assignments

Data Files needed for the Review Assignments: LHCQuestions.doc, LHCServicesAndSolutions.xls, LHCProducts.xls, LHCALDInfo.doc

Buena Oquendo, the community liaison for Lifestyles Home Care, has created several documents that she mails to people to try to answer commonly asked questions. One of these documents answers five frequently asked questions that people have about home care. Another document contains some information about assistive living devices—products that people can use in their homes to help them continue living independently. Some of the information she needs to include in these two documents already exists in other Office documents. Buena asks you to find and insert this information from the other Office documents.

To complete the documents:

1. Open the Word document **LHCQuestions** located in the Tutorial.02\Review folder included with your Data Files, and then save it as **Frequently Asked Questions** in the same folder.
2. Press the Ctrl + End keys to go to the end of the document, and then replace Buena Oquendo's name with your own.

3. Start Excel, and then open the **LHCServicesAndSolutions** workbook located in the Tutorial.02\Review folder included with your Data Files.
4. Copy the Lifestyles Home Care logo at the top of the Services worksheet to the Office Clipboard.
5. Click the Solutions worksheet tab, and then copy cells A7 through C26 to the Office Clipboard.
6. Close the workbook.
7. Switch back to the Frequently Asked Questions document, use the Office Clipboard to paste the logo at the top of the document, and then paste the Excel table in the paragraph below the answer to question 5. Keep the format of the table so it matches the source file.
8. Preview and print the document, save your changes, and then close the document.
9. In either open program, use the Basic File Search task pane to find a Data File that contains the text "assistive living devices." Restrict the search to the location where your Data Files are stored, but search for all Office file types. You should find the LHCProducts workbook and the LHCALDInfo document.
10. Open the **LHCProducts** workbook from the Search Results task pane, and then save it as **ALD Products Workbook** in the Tutorial.02\Review folder included with your Data Files.
11. Prepare the worksheet for importing into Access by deleting all the rows in the document above the column headings in Row 5 and deleting all blank rows.
12. Delete all the rows with a boldface identifier in column A (these rows do not have any data in columns B or C), add "Products" as a column heading to cell A1, delete space between the words in cells B1 and C1, and then save your changes and close the workbook.
13. Create a new, blank database in Access named **ALDProducts** and save it in the Tutorial.02\Review folder included with your Data Files.
14. Import Sheet 1 of the ALD Products Workbook to a new table in the ALDProducts database. Accept the defaults in the Import Spreadsheet Wizard, and name the new table **ALD List**.
15. Use the Simple Query Wizard to create a query that lists all of the products and whether they require installation. Save the query as **ALD List Query**, and then open it in Datasheet view.
16. Switch to Design view, and then modify the ALD List Query so that it displays only those products that require installation. (*Hint*: Type =Y in the Criteria row of the RequiresInstallation column.) Do not show the installation field in the results. Run the modified query, save it, and then close the query datasheet window.
17. Create another query that lists all of the products and their approximate cost. Save the query as **Product Prices Query**.
18. Modify the Product Prices Query in Design view so that it displays only those products whose cost is greater than $25. (*Hint*: Do not include the $ when you type the criteria.) Run the modified query, save it, and then close the query window.
19. Export the results of the ALD List Query to an RTF file called **Install Products** in the Tutorial.02\Review folder included with your Data Files.
20. Export the results of the Product Prices Query to an RTF file called **Product Prices** in the Tutorial.02\Review folder included with your Data Files.
21. Close the ALDProducts database, switch back to Word, open the **LHCALDInfo** document from the Search Results task pane, and then save it as **ALD Info Sheet** in the Tutorial.02\Review folder included with your Data Files.
22. Insert the **Install Products.rtf** file in the blank paragraph above the second paragraph in the document, and then center the table.
23. Insert the **Product Prices.rtf** file in the blank paragraph above the last paragraph in the document, and then center the table. Insert a space between "Approximate" and "Cost".
24. Save, preview, and print the ALD Info Sheet document, close the document and the Search Results task pane, and then exit all open programs.

Case Problem 1

Data Files needed for this Case Problem: MusicMemo.doc, MusicLetter.doc. MusicGrowth.xls

Making Music Caleb Jacobson, the owner of Making Music, recently applied for a loan to renovate his retail store and add additional practice rooms. He decides to send out a memo to his employees to explain the upcoming renovations. He has drafted the body of the memo, but he asks you to find and copy the company logo and a chart illustrating the store's growth. To complete the memo:

1. Open the Word document **MusicMemo** in the Tutorial.02\Cases folder included with your Data Files.
2. Replace Caleb Jacobson's name with your own, and then save the document as **Renovations Memo** in the same folder.
3. Use the Basic File Search task pane to locate a document containing the text "750 Main Street." (Make sure you type "Street" and not "St.") Restrict your search to the location where your Data Files are stored, but do not restrict the type of file for which to search. A document with the store's address in it is probably a letter and therefore will contain the logo. You should find the file MusicLetter.
4. Open the file **MusicLetter** from the Search Results task pane.
5. Copy the logo from the document to the Office Clipboard, and then close the MusicLetter document.
6. Use the Basic File Search task pane to search for a Word or Excel file containing the text "number of students." You should find the files MusicGrowth and MusicLetter as well as the current open document, Renovations Memo.
7. Open the file **MusicGrowth** from the Search Results task pane, copy the chart on the Number of Music Lessons worksheet to the Office Clipboard, copy the chart on the Lessons by Instrument worksheet to the Office Clipboard, and then close the workbook.
8. Switch back to the Renovations Memo document.
9. Paste the logo from the Clipboard task pane at the top of the memo and center it.
10. Paste the Number of Music Lessons chart (the column chart) to the first blank paragraph below the last paragraph in the memo, and then paste the Lessons by Instrument chart (the pie chart) in the blank paragraph above the chart you just pasted.
11. Save, preview, and print the Renovations Memo document.
12. Close the document, and then exit all open programs.

Case Problem 2

Data File needed for this Case Problem: LFCTextbooks.xls

Learning Fulfillment Centers The tutors at Learning Fulfillment Centers often recommend textbooks to their students. Nia Walker, the administrative assistant at the main office, started keeping a list of recommended textbooks in an Excel workbook. Enrique Garcia, the owner, has decided to review this list to make sure only texts with a copyright year after 2000 are recommended. You will search for the file that Nia created, import the list into Access, query the database to find the texts published in 2000 or earlier, and then export this information to a memo you will create in Word. To complete the memo:

1. Start Excel, if necessary.

2. Open the Advanced File Search task pane, and search for the file Nia Walker created. (*Hint*: Click the Property list arrow, click Author, type Nia Walker in the Value text box, and then click the Add button to add the search criteria to the list.) Restrict the search to Excel files. Also restrict the search to the location where your Data Files are stored. Make sure that if you select a folder that contains subfolders, you click the check box twice to make multiple check boxes appear so that the subfolders also will be searched. You should find the Excel file LFCTextbooks.

3. Open the Excel file **LFCTextbooks** from the Search Results task pane, and then save it as **All Textbooks** in the Tutorial.02\Cases folder included with your Data Files.
4. Set up the worksheet for Access to import so that row 1 includes column headings, and then save and close the workbook.
5. Create a new database in Access called **Textbooks** and save it in the Tutorial.02\Cases folder included with your Data Files.
6. Import Sheet1 of the All Textbooks workbook to a new table named **Recommended Texts**, and then save and close the table. Make sure you click the First Row Contains Column Headings check box to select it in the first dialog box of the Import Spreadsheet Wizard. (If a dialog box appears telling you that some of the data in row 1 cannot be used for valid field names, click the OK button to continue.)
7. Use the Simple Query Wizard to create a query to list all the texts. Add the Title, Edition, Author, Copyright, Publisher, and ISBN fields to the query, and accept all the other defaults in the wizard. Name the query **Recommended Texts Query**.
8. Modify the query to display only those textbooks that were published in 2000 or earlier, run the query, save the results, and then close the query window.
9. Export the query results to an RTF file named **Outdated Texts** and save this file in the Tutorial.02\Cases folder included with your Data Files, and then close the database.
10. Create a new Word document, and then type a memo to Enrique explaining that you found the information he requested.
11. Insert the RTF file **Outdated Texts** into the Textbook Memo.

Explore

12. Format the table so it fits nicely in the document. Select the entire table, click Format on the menu bar, click Paragraph, type 0 (zero) in the Left, Right, Before, and After text boxes, and then click the OK button. Make any other formatting changes to the table you like to make the table look nice in the document.
13. Save the memo as **Textbook Memo** in the Tutorial.02\Cases folder.
14. Preview and print the memo, close the document, and then exit all open programs.

Assess

SAM Assessment and Training

If your instructor has chosen to use the full online version of SAM 2003 Assessment and Training, you can go beyond the "just-in-time" training provided on the CD that accompanies this text. Simply log in to your SAM account (http://sam2003.course.com) to launch any assigned training activities or exams that relate to the skills covered in this tutorial.

Review

Quick Check Answers

1. Open the first document, and then select and copy text or other information to the Office Clipboard. Open other documents, and copy selections to the Clipboard task pane. Open the document where you want to paste the selections, click where you want to insert the selection, and then click the corresponding item on the Clipboard task pane. Paste other selections following this same procedure.
2. In the Basic File Search task pane, you search for files that contain text you specify. In the Advanced File Search task pane, you find files based on their properties, such as who created the file or when.
3. to extract information from the data
4. The Excel data should be in the form of a list with column headings in row 1 and no blank lines.
5. Import Spreadsheet Wizard
6. true

New Perspectives on
Microsoft® Office PowerPoint® 2003

Read This Before You Begin: Tutorials 1-2

Data Files

To complete PowerPoint Tutorials 1-2, you need the starting Data Files. See the inside back or front cover for information on downloading these files from course.com, or ask your instructor for assistance. The following table identifies each starting Data File and the folder it is stored in, as well as the ending files, which you create and save in each tutorial.

Folders		Starting Files	Ending Files
Tutorial .01	**Tutorial**	Lorena.ppt	Global Humanitarian Overview.ppt
	Review	VillageOP.ppt	Village Outreach Program.ppt
	Cases	LASIK.ppt, Library.ppt	Camellia LASIK.ppt, Digital Audio Player Review.ppt, e-Commerce Consultants.ppt, Public Library Outreach.ppt
Tutorial .02	**Tutorial**	GHLogo.jpg, MntTop.jpg, PeruExp2.ppt	Peru Expedition.ppt, PeruExp.ppt
	Review	Boots.jpg, Camera.jpg, Food.jpg, GHLogo.jpg, PackList.ppt, Personal.jpg, PrMeds.jpg, SlpBag.jpg, Vitamins.jpg	Peru Packing List.ppt
	Cases	Balmoral.jpg, Campsite.jpg, Castles.ppt, Craigievar.jpg, Edinburgh.jpg, Fraser.jpg, MenWithPacks.jpg, MountainLake.jpg, MountainMeadow.jpg, MountainRiver.jpg, Outfitter.ppt, PESLogo.jpg, PKPBadge.jpg, PKPKey.jpg, SBcam.jpg, SBfile.jpg, SBpages.jpg, SBpaper.jpg, SBpens.jpg, SBphoto.jpg, SBsciss.jpg, Urquhart.jpg	Backpacker's Outfitter.ppt, Honor Society.ppt, Sally's Scrapbooking.ppt, Scottish Castles.ppt

Storing Your Files

It is recommended that you store all your Data Files on a USB drive. Refer to the tutorial "Managing Your Files" for information on using USB drives. If you need to store your Data Files on floppy disks, you will need two high-density disks to store all the files for PowerPoint Tutorials 1-2.

SAM 2003 Training Companion CD

The SAM 2003 Training Companion CD that comes with this text gives you "just-in-time" training and reinforcement of important Microsoft Office skills. Look for the SAM CD logo throughout each tutorial for opportunities to complete the hands-on tasks included on this CD.

Creating a Presentation

Presenting Information About Humanitarian Projects

Case | Global Humanitarian, Austin Office

In 1985, a group of Austin, Texas business leaders established a nonprofit organization called Global Humanitarian. Its goal was to alleviate abject poverty in the third world through public awareness and personal involvement in sustainable self-help initiatives in third-world villages. Today, Global Humanitarian is a large umbrella organization and clearinghouse for national and international humanitarian organizations. Its five major functions are to help provide the following: entrepreneurial support, service expeditions, inventory surplus exchange, funding and grant proposals, and student internships.

The president of Global Humanitarian is Norma Flores, who sits on the board of directors and carries out its policies and procedures. The managing director of the Austin office is Miriam Schwartz, and the managing director in Latin America is Pablo Fuentes, who lives and works in Lima, Peru. Miriam wants you to use PowerPoint to develop a presentation to provide information about Global Humanitarian's current projects to potential donors, expedition participants, and student interns.

In this tutorial, you'll examine a presentation that Miriam created to become familiar with **Microsoft Office PowerPoint 2003** (or simply **PowerPoint**). You'll then create a presentation based on content that PowerPoint suggests by using the AutoContent Wizard. You'll modify the text in the presentation, and you'll add and delete slides. You'll check the spelling and style of the presentation, and then you'll view the completed slide show. Finally, you'll save the slide show and print handouts.

Session	Objectives		SAM Training Tasks	
Session 1.1	• Open and view an existing PowerPoint presentation • Switch views and navigate a presentation	• View a presentation in Slide Show view • Create a presentation using the AutoContent Wizard	• Create a specified type of slide • Create presentations from a blank presentation	• Create presentations using the AutoContent Wizard
Session 1.2	• Add, move, and delete slides • Promote and demote text in the Outline tab • Create speaker notes for slides	• Check the spelling and style in a presentation • Preview and print slides • Print outlines, handouts, and speaker notes	• Add and modify placeholders • Add notes • Change a bullet character and color on the Slide Master • Change the layout of individual slides • Change the order of slides in a presentation • Change the view to Slide Sorter view	• Check spelling • Delete slides from a presentation • Edit text on slides • Print an outline • Print handouts • Print slides • Print speaker notes • Use the Research Pane (Thesaurus)

Student Data Files   For a complete list of the Data Files needed for this tutorial, see page PPT 2.

Session 1.1

For hands-on practice of key tasks in this session, go to the SAM 2003 Training Companion CD included with this text.

What Is PowerPoint?

PowerPoint is a powerful presentation graphics program that provides everything you need to produce an effective presentation in the form of on-screen slides, a slide presentation on a Web site, black-and-white or color overheads, or 35-mm photographic slides. You may have already seen your instructors use PowerPoint presentations to enhance their classroom lectures.

Using PowerPoint, you can prepare each component of a presentation: individual slides, speaker notes, an outline, and audience handouts. The presentation you'll create for Miriam will include slides, notes, and handouts.

To start PowerPoint:

1. Click the **Start** button on the taskbar, point to **All Programs**, point to **Microsoft Office**, and then click **Microsoft Office PowerPoint 2003**. PowerPoint starts and the PowerPoint window opens. See Figure 1-1.

   Trouble? If you don't see the Microsoft Office PowerPoint 2003 option on the Microsoft Office submenu, look for it on a different submenu or as an option on the All Programs menu. If you still cannot find the Microsoft Office PowerPoint 2003 option, ask your instructor or technical support person for help.

Figure 1-1 | **Blank PowerPoint window**

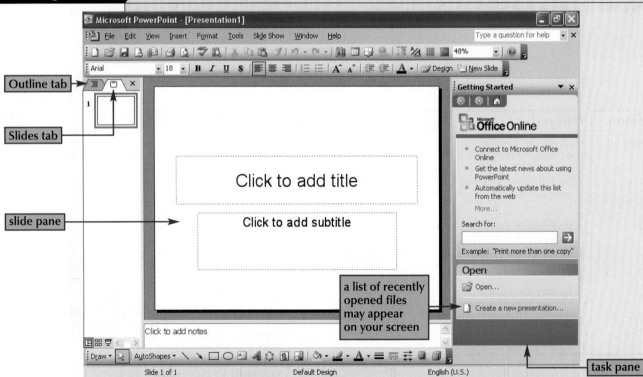

Trouble? If the PowerPoint program window is not maximized, click the Maximize button on the program window title bar.

Trouble? If the Office Assistant (an animated icon, usually a paper clip with eyes) opens when you start PowerPoint, right-click the Office Assistant, and then click Hide to close it.

Opening an Existing PowerPoint Presentation

Before you prepare the presentation on Global Humanitarian, Miriam suggests that you view an existing presentation recently prepared under Norma's and Miriam's direction as an example of PowerPoint features. When you examine the presentation, you'll learn about some PowerPoint capabilities that can help make your presentations more interesting and effective. You'll open the presentation now.

To open the existing presentation:

1. Make sure you have access to the Data Files in the Tutorial.01 folder.

   Trouble? If you don't have the PowerPoint Data Files, you need to get them before you can proceed. Your instructor will either give you the Data Files or ask you to obtain them from a specified location (such as a network drive). In either case, be sure that you make a backup copy of your Data Files before you start using them, so that the original files will be available on your copied disk in case you need to start over because of an error or problem. If you have any questions about the Data Files, see your instructor or technical support person for assistance.

2. Click the **Open** link under Open in the Getting Started task pane. The Open dialog box appears on the screen.

   Trouble? If you don't see the Open link, either click More or point to the small triangle at the bottom of the task pane to view additional links.

3. Click the **Look in** list arrow to display the list of disk drives on your computer, and then navigate to the **Tutorial.01\Tutorial** folder included with your Data Files.

4. Click **Lorena** (if necessary), and then click the **Open** button to display Miriam's presentation. The presentation opens in Normal view. See Figure 1-2.

PowerPoint window with presentation open   Figure 1-2

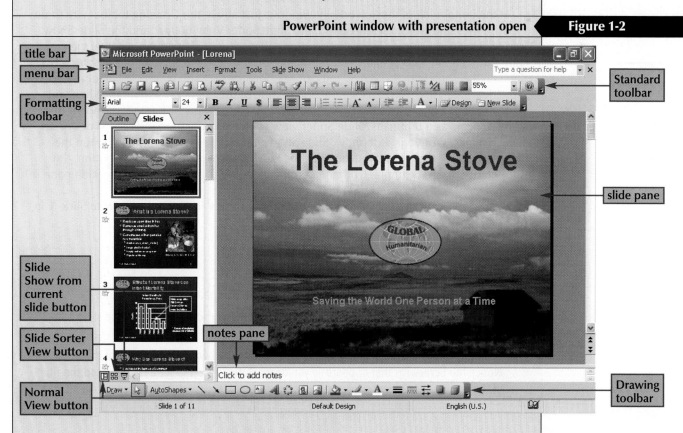

Trouble? If you see filename extensions on your screen (such as ".ppt" appended to "Lorena" in the filename), don't be concerned; they won't affect your work.

Trouble? If your screen doesn't show the Drawing toolbar, click View on the menu bar, point to Toolbars, and then click Drawing.

Trouble? If your screen shows the Standard toolbar and the Formatting toolbar on the same line, click Tools on the menu bar, click Customize, click the Options tab, click the Show Standard and Formatting toolbars on two rows check box to select it, and then click the Close button.

Switching Views and Navigating a Presentation

The PowerPoint window contains features common to all Windows programs, as well as features specific to PowerPoint. One obvious difference between the PowerPoint window and other Office programs is that the PowerPoint window is divided into sections. The section in the center of the screen, to the left of the task pane, is the slide pane. The **slide pane** shows the current slide as it will look during your slide show. Just below the slide pane is the notes pane. The **notes pane** contains notes (also called speaker notes) for the presenter; for example, the notes pane might contain specific points to cover or phrases to say during the presentation. During a slide show, the audience does not see the contents of the notes pane.

Along the left edge of the PowerPoint window, you can see two tabs, the Outline tab and the Slides tab. The **Slides tab** is on top when you first start PowerPoint. It shows a column of numbered slide **thumbnails** (miniature images) so you can see a visual representation of several slides at once. You can use the Slides tab to jump quickly to another slide in the slide pane by clicking the desired slide. The **Outline tab** shows an outline of the titles and text of each slide of your presentation.

At the bottom left of the PowerPoint window, just above the Drawing toolbar, are three view buttons: the Normal View button, the Slide Sorter View button, and the Slide Show from current slide button. These three buttons allow you to change the way you view a slide presentation. PowerPoint is currently in Normal view. Normal view is best for working with the content of the slides. You can see how the text and graphics look on each individual slide, and you can examine the outline of the entire presentation. When you switch to Slide Sorter view, the Slides and Outline tabs disappear from view and all of the slides appears as thumbnails. Slide Sorter view is an easy way to reorder the slides or set special features for your slide show. Slide Show view is the view in which you run the slide show presentation. When you click the Slide Show from current slide button, the presentation starts, beginning with the current slide (the slide currently in the slide pane in Normal view or the selected slide in Slide Sorter view).

Next you'll try switching views. PowerPoint is currently in Normal view with Slide 1 in the slide pane.

To switch views in PowerPoint:

1. Click the **Slide 2** thumbnail in the Slides tab. Slide 2 appears in the slide pane.

2. Click the **Next Slide** button ▼ at the bottom of the vertical scroll bar in the slide pane. Slide 3 appears in the slide pane.

3. Drag the scroll box in the slide pane vertical scroll bar down to the bottom of the scroll bar. Notice the ScreenTip that appears as you drag. It identifies the slide number and the title of the slide at the current position.

4. Click the **Outline** tab. The text outline of the current slide appears in the Outline tab.

5. Drag the scroll box in the vertical scroll bar of the Outline tab up to the top of the scroll bar, and then click the **slide icon** ▣ next to Slide 3. Slide 3 again appears in the slide pane.

6. Click the **Slides** tab. The Outline tab disappears behind the Slides tab.

7. Click the **Slide Sorter View** button ▦. Slide Sorter view appears, and Slide 3 has a colored frame around it to indicate that it is the current slide.

8. Position the pointer over the **Slide 2** thumbnail. A thin, colored frame appears around Slide 2.

9. Click the **Slide 2** thumbnail to make it the current slide.

10. Double-click the **Slide 1** thumbnail. The window switches back to Normal view and Slide 1 appears in the slide pane. You could also have clicked the Normal View button to switch back to Normal view.

Now that you're familiar with the PowerPoint window, you're ready to view Miriam's presentation.

Viewing a Presentation in Slide Show View

Slide Show view is the view you use when you present an on-screen presentation to an audience. When you click the Slide Show from current slide button or click the Slide Show command on the View menu, the slide show starts. If you click the Slide Show from current slide button, the current slide fills the screen, and if you click the Slide Show command on the View menu, the first slide fills the screen. No toolbars or other Windows elements are visible on the screen.

In Slide Show view, you move from one slide to the next by pressing the spacebar, clicking the left mouse button, or pressing the → key. Additionally, PowerPoint provides a method for jumping from one slide to any other slide in the presentation during the slide show: you can right-click anywhere on the screen, point to Go to Slide on the shortcut menu, and then click one of the slide titles in the list that appears to jump to that slide.

When you prepare a slide show, you can add special effects to the show. For example, you can add **slide transitions**, the manner in which a new slide appears on the screen during a slide show. You can also add **animations** to the elements on the slide; that is, each text or graphic object on the slide can appear on the slide in a special way or have a sound effect associated with it. A special type of animation is **progressive disclosure**, a technique in which each element on a slide appears one at a time after the slide background appears. Animations draw the audience's attention to the particular item on the screen.

You can also add a footer on the slides. A **footer** is a word or phrase that appears at the bottom of each slide in the presentation.

You want to see how Miriam's presentation will appear when she shows it in Slide Show view at Global Humanitarian's executive meeting. You'll then have a better understanding of how Miriam used PowerPoint features to make her presentation informative and interesting.

To view the presentation in Slide Show view:

▶ **1.** With Slide 1 in the slide pane, click the **Slide Show from current slide** button 🖳. The slide show begins by filling the entire viewing area of the screen with Slide 1 of Miriam's presentation. Watch as the slide title moves down the slide from the top and the Global Humanitarian logo and motto gradually appear on the screen.

As you view this first slide, you can already see some of the types of elements that PowerPoint allows you to place on a slide: text in different styles, sizes, and colors; graphics; and a background picture. You also saw an example of an animation when you watched the slide title slide down the screen and the logo and motto gradually appear.

▶ **2.** Press the **spacebar**. The slide show goes from Slide 1 to Slide 2. See Figure 1-3. Notice that during the transition from Slide 1 to Slide 2, the presentation displayed Slide 2 by scrolling down from the top of the screen and covering up Slide 1.

Figure 1-3 ▶ **Slide 2 in Slide Show view**

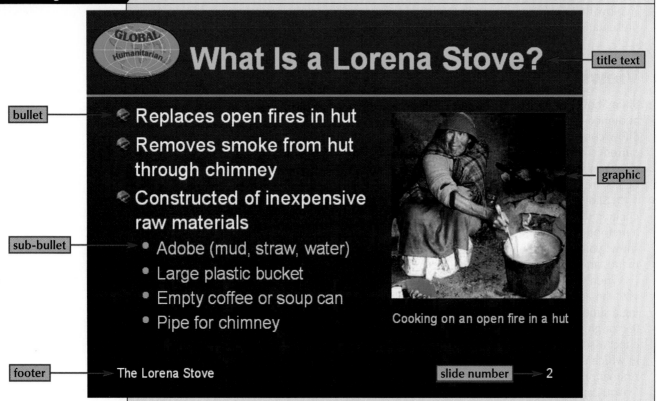

Trouble? If you missed the transition from Slide 1 to Slide 2, or if you want to see it again, press the ← key to redisplay Slide 1, and then press the spacebar to go to Slide 2 again.

Notice in Figure 1-3 that Slide 2 displays: (1) a colored background that varies in color across the slide, (2) Global Humanitarian's logo, (3) a title in large yellow text, (4) a bulleted list (with green textured bullets and white text, or solid cyan bullets with light yellow text), (5) a footer, (6) the slide number (in the lower-right corner of the slide), and (7) a photograph of a villager using an open fire.

▶ **3.** Click the left mouse button to proceed to Slide 3. During the transition from Slide 2 to Slide 3, you again see the slide scroll down onto the screen from the top. Once the slide appears on the screen, you see a chart slowly appear. PowerPoint supports features for creating and customizing this type of chart, as well as graphs, diagrams, tables, and organization charts.

4. Press the **spacebar**. The title of Slide 4 appears on screen. What you don't see on the screen is a bulleted list. That's because this slide is designed for progressive disclosure. Additional slide elements will appear on screen after you press the spacebar or click on the screen.

5. Press the **spacebar** to reveal the first bulleted item on Slide 4. The item is animated to fly onto the screen from the bottom.

6. Press the **spacebar** again to reveal the next bulleted item. As this item appears, the previous item dims. Dimming the previous bulleted items helps focus the audience's attention on the current bulleted item.

7. Press the **spacebar** again to cause the last bulleted item to dim.

So far, you've seen important PowerPoint features: slide transitions, progressive disclosure, animations, and graphics (photos and drawings). Now you'll finish the presentation and see custom animations and simple drawings.

To continue viewing the slide show:

1. Press the **spacebar** to go to Slide 5, and then press the **spacebar** again. The label "Fuel chamber" and its accompanying arrow appear gradually on the screen. This is another example of an animation.

2. Press the **spacebar** three more times, pausing between each to allow the label and arrow to appear gradually on the screen.

3. Press the **spacebar** once more. A graphic labeled "smoke" comes into view, and you hear the sound of wind (or a breeze). The smoke object is an example of a user-drawn graphic.

4. Press the **spacebar** again to animate the smoke graphic and repeat the sound effect. The smoke graphic travels from the fuel chamber up the stovepipe.

5. Go to **Slide 6**. The graphic on this slide is a simple diagram drawn using drawing tools on the Drawing toolbar, which include not only shapes like circles, ovals, squares, and rectangles, but also arrows, boxes, stars, and banners.

6. Continue moving through the slide show, looking at all the slides and pausing at each one to read the bulleted items and view the graphics, until you reach Slide 11, the last slide in the slide show.

7. Press the **spacebar** to move from Slide 11. A black, nearly blank, screen appears. This signals that the slide show is over, as indicated by the line of text on the screen.

8. Press the **spacebar** one more time to return to the view from which you started the slide show, in this case, Normal view.

9. Close the current presentation by clicking the **Close Window** button ☒ on the menu bar, and then click the **No** button when asked if you want to save changes.

As you can see from this slide show, PowerPoint has many powerful features. You'll learn how to use many of these features in your own presentations as you work through these tutorials.

You're now ready to create Miriam's presentation on general information about Global Humanitarian's current projects. Before you begin, however, you need to plan the presentation.

Planning a Presentation

Planning a presentation before you create it improves the quality of your presentation, makes your presentation more effective and enjoyable, and, in the long run, saves you time and effort. As you plan your presentation, you should answer several questions: What is my purpose or objective for this presentation? What type of presentation is needed? Who is the audience? What information does that audience need? What is the physical location of my presentation? What is the best format for presenting the information contained in this presentation, given its location?

In planning your presentation, you should determine the following aspects:

- **Purpose of the presentation**: to provide general information about Global Humanitarian
- **Type of presentation**: training (how to become involved with Global Humanitarian)
- **Audience for the presentation**: potential donors, potential participants in humanitarian expeditions, and potential student interns
- **Audience needs**: to understand Global Humanitarian's mission and how to join the effort
- **Location of the presentation**: small conference rooms to large classrooms
- **Format**: oral presentation accompanied by an electronic slide show of 10 to 12 slides

You have carefully planned your presentation. Now you'll use the PowerPoint AutoContent Wizard to create it.

Using the AutoContent Wizard

PowerPoint helps you quickly create effective presentations by using a wizard, a special window that asks you a series of questions about your tasks, and then helps you perform them. The AutoContent Wizard lets you choose a presentation category, such as "Training," "Recommending a Strategy," "Brainstorming Session," or "Selling a Product or Service." After you select the type of presentation you want, the AutoContent Wizard creates a general outline for you to follow and formats the slides using a built-in design template and predesigned layouts. A **design template** is a file that contains the colors and format of the background and the font style of the titles, accents, and other text. Once you start creating a presentation with a given design template, you can change to any other PowerPoint design template or create a custom design template. A **layout** is a predetermined way of organizing the objects on a slide. You can change the layout applied to a slide or you can customize the layout of objects on a screen by moving the objects.

In this tutorial, you'll use the AutoContent Wizard to create a presentation with the goal of training employees, volunteers, and prospective donors on Global Humanitarian's mission. Because "Training" is predefined, you'll use the AutoContent Wizard, which will automatically create a title slide and standard outline that you can then edit to fit Miriam's needs.

To create the presentation with the AutoContent Wizard:

1. Click **File** on the menu bar, and then click **New**. The New Presentation task pane opens on the right side of the PowerPoint window.

2. Click the **From AutoContent wizard** link in the New Presentation task pane. The first dialog box of the AutoContent Wizard opens on top of the PowerPoint program window. The green square on the left side of the window indicates where you are in the wizard.

3. Read the information in the Start dialog box of the AutoContent Wizard, and then click the **Next** button. The next dialog box in the AutoContent Wizard appears. Note that the green square on the left side of the dialog box moved from Start to Presentation type. The Presentation type dialog box allows you to select the type of presentation you want.

4. Click the **General** button, if necessary, and then click **Training**. See Figure 1-4.

Selecting the type of presentation in the AutoContent Wizard ◄ **Figure 1-4**

5. Click the **Next** button. The Presentation style dialog box opens with the question, "What type of output will you use?" You could also change this option after you create the presentation. As noted in your plan, you want to create an on-screen presentation.

Trouble? If a dialog box opens telling you that PowerPoint can't display the template used in this document because the feature is not currently installed, you must install the Training template before continuing. If you are working on your own computer, click the Yes button. If you are working in a lab, ask your instructor or technical support person for help.

6. Click the **On-screen presentation** option button to select it, if necessary, and then click the **Next** button. The Presentation options dialog box opens. In this dialog box, you specify the title and footer (if any) of the presentation.

7. Click in the **Presentation title** text box, type **Global Humanitarian**, press the **Tab** key to move the insertion point to the **Footer** text box, and then type **Overview of Global Humanitarian**.

The title will appear on the title slide (the first slide) of the presentation. The footer will appear on every slide (except the title slide) in the presentation. If the other two options are checked, they will appear on either side of the footer on the presentation slides.

8. Click the **Date last updated** check box to clear it, and leave the **Slide number** check box checked. You don't want to clutter the screen with information that is not pertinent for the audience. See Figure 1-5.

Selecting information in the AutoContent Wizard ◄ **Figure 1-5**

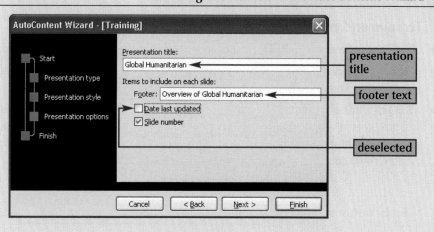

9. Click the **Next** button. The Finish dialog box opens, letting you know that you completed the questions for the AutoContent Wizard.

10. Click the **Finish** button. PowerPoint displays the AutoContent outline in the Outline tab and the title slide (Slide 1) in the slide pane. The filename in the title bar "Presentation" followed by a number is a temporary filename. See Figure 1-6.

| Figure 1-6 | Outline and slide after completing the AutoContent Wizard |

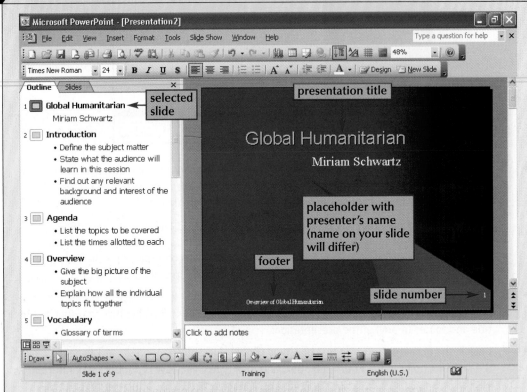

The AutoContent Wizard automatically displays the presenter's name (actually the name of the registered PowerPoint user) below the title in Slide 1. The name that appears on your screen will be different from the one shown in Figure 1-6.

Next, you'll save and name the presentation you created.

To save and name the presentation:

1. Click the **Save** button [icon] on the Standard toolbar. The Save As dialog box opens.

2. Click the **Save in** list arrow, and then navigate to the **Tutorial.01\Tutorial** folder included with your Data Files, if necessary.

3. Click immediately after Global Humanitarian, the default filename, in the **File name** text box, press the **spacebar**, type **Overview**, and then click the **Save** button. PowerPoint saves the presentation as Global Humanitarian Overview and displays that name in the title bar of the PowerPoint window.

In the next session, you'll edit the text of Miriam's presentation, as well as create notes.

Session 1.1 Quick Check

1. Describe the components of a PowerPoint presentation.
2. Name and describe the two panes and two tabs in the PowerPoint window in Normal view.
3. Define or describe the following:
   a. progressive disclosure
   b. slide transition
   c. design template
   d. layout
4. What are some of the questions that you should answer when planning a presentation?
5. Describe the purpose of the AutoContent Wizard.
6. Describe Slide Show view.

To reinforce the tasks you learned in this session, go to the SAM 2003 Training Companion CD included with this text.

Session 1.2

Modifying a Presentation

Now that you've used the AutoContent Wizard, you're ready to edit some of the words in the presentation to fit Miriam's specific needs. You'll keep the design template, which includes the blue background and the size and color of the text, used by the AutoContent Wizard.

The AutoContent Wizard automatically creates the title slide, as well as other slides, with suggested text located in placeholders. A **placeholder** is a region of a slide, or a location in an outline, reserved for inserting text or graphics. To edit the AutoContent outline to fit Miriam's needs, you must select the placeholders one at a time, and then replace them with other text. Text placeholders are a special kind of **text box**, which is a container for text. You can edit and format text in a text box, or you can manipulate the text box as a whole. When you manipulate the text box as a whole, the text box is treated as an **object**, something that can be manipulated or resized as a unit.

When text is selected, the text box is active and appears as hatched lines around the selected text with sizing handles (small circles) at each corner and on each side of the box. You drag **sizing handles** to make a text box or other object larger or smaller on the slide. When the entire text box is selected as a single object, the text box appears as a dotted outline with sizing handles.

Many of the slides that the AutoContent Wizard created in your presentation for Global Humanitarian contain bulleted lists. A **bulleted list** is a list of paragraphs with a special character (dot, circle, box, star, or other character) to the left of each paragraph. A **bulleted item** is one paragraph in a bulleted list. Bullets can appear at different outline levels. A **first-level bullet** is a main paragraph in a bulleted list; a **second-level bullet**—sometimes called a **sub-bullet**—is a bullet beneath (and indented from) a first-level bullet. Using bulleted lists reminds both the speaker and the audience of the main points of the presentation. In addition to bulleted lists, PowerPoint also supports numbered lists. A **numbered list** is a list of paragraphs that are numbered consecutively within the body text.

When you edit the text on the slides, keep in mind that the bulleted lists aren't meant to be the complete presentation; instead, they should emphasize the key points to the audience and remind the speaker of the points to emphasize. In all your presentations, you should follow the 6 × 6 rule as much as possible: Keep each bulleted item to no more than six words, and don't include more than six bulleted items on a slide.

For hands-on practice of key tasks in this session, go to the SAM 2003 Training Companion CD included with this text.

Reference Window

Creating Effective Text Presentations

- Think of your text presentation as a visual map of your oral presentation. Show your organization by using overviews, making headings larger than subheadings, including bulleted lists to highlight key points, and numbering steps to show sequences.
- Follow the 6 × 6 rule: Use six or fewer items per screen, and use phrases of six or fewer words. Omit unnecessary articles, pronouns, and adjectives.
- Keep phrases parallel.
- Make sure your text is appropriate for your purpose and audience.

Miriam reviewed your plans for your presentation and she has several suggestions for improvement. First, she wants you to replace the text that the AutoContent Wizard inserted with information about Global Humanitarian. She also wants you to delete unnecessary slides, and change the order of the slides in the presentation. You'll start by editing the text on the slides.

Editing Slides

Most of the slides in the presentation contain two placeholder text boxes. The slide **title text** is a text box at the top of the slide that gives the title of the information on that slide; the slide **body text** (also called the **main text**) is a large text box in which you type a bulleted or numbered list. In this presentation, you'll modify or create title text and body text in all but the title slide (Slide 1).

To edit the AutoContent outline to fit Miriam's needs, you must select text in each of the placeholders, and then replace that text with other text. You'll now begin to edit and replace the text to fit Miriam's presentation. The first text you'll change is the presenter's name placeholder.

To edit and replace text in the first slide:

1. If you took a break after the previous session, make sure PowerPoint is running, and then open the presentation **Global Humanitarian Overview** located in the Tutorial.01\Tutorial folder included with your Data Files. Slide 1 appears in the slide pane and the Outline tab is on top.

2. Position the pointer over the presenter's name (currently the registered PowerPoint user's name) in the slide pane so that the pointer changes to I, and then drag it across the text of the presenter's name to select the text. The text box becomes active, as indicated by the hatched lines around the box and the sizing handles at each corner and on each side of the text box, and the text becomes highlighted.

3. Type your first and last name (so your instructor can identify you as the author of this presentation), and then click anywhere else on the slide. As soon as you start to type, the selected text disappears, and the typed text appears in its place. (The figures in this book will show the name Miriam Schwartz.)

   Trouble? If PowerPoint marks your name with a red wavy underline, this indicates that the word is not found in the PowerPoint dictionary. Ignore the wavy line for now, because spelling will be covered later.

You'll now edit Slides 2 through 9 by replacing the placeholder text and adding new text, and by deleting slides that don't apply to your presentation.

To edit the text in the slides:

1. Click the **Next Slide** button ⬇ at the bottom of the vertical scroll bar in the slide pane. Slide 2 appears in the slide pane.

2. Drag across the word **Introduction** (the title text) to select it. See Figure 1-7.

Selecting title text ◀ Figure 1-7

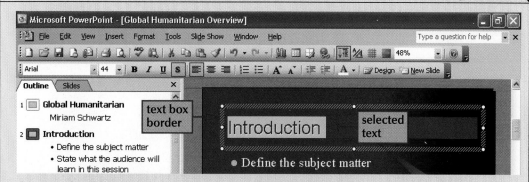

Now you're ready to type the desired title. As you perform the next step, notice not only that the words you type replace the selected text in the slide pane, but also that the slide title on the Outline tab changes.

3. Type **Are You Rich?** and then click in a blank space in the slide pane, just outside the edge of the slide, to deselect the text box. The hatched lines and sizing handles disappear. Notice that the slide title changed on the Outline tab as well.

   Trouble? If you clicked somewhere on the slide and selected another item, such as the bulleted list, click another place, preferably just outside the edge of the text box, to deselect all items.

   Now you're going to edit the text from the Outline tab.

4. In the Outline tab, select the text **Define the subject matter**. The text is highlighted by changing to white on black.

5. Type **Home has non-dirt floor: top 50%**. Don't include a period at the end of the phrase. This bulleted item is an incomplete sentence, short for "If you live in a home with a non-dirt floor, you're in the top 50% of the wealthiest people on earth."

6. Select the text of the second bulleted item in either the Outline tab or the slide pane, and then type **Home has more than one room: top 20%**. Again, don't include a period.

7. Select the text of the third bulleted item in the slide pane, and then type **Own more than one pair of shoes: top 5%**.

With the insertion point at the end of the third bulleted item, you're ready to create additional bulleted items.

To create additional bulleted items:

1. With the insertion point blinking at the end of the last bulleted item, press the **Enter** key. PowerPoint creates a new bullet and leaves the insertion point to the right of the indent after the bullet, waiting for you to type the text.

2. Type **Own a refrigerator: top 3%** and then press the **Enter** key.

3. Type **Own a car, computer, microwave, or VCR: top 1%**.

> 4. Click in a blank area of the slide pane to deselect the bulleted list text box. The completed Slide 2 should look like Figure 1-8.

Figure 1-8 | **Slide 2 after adding text**

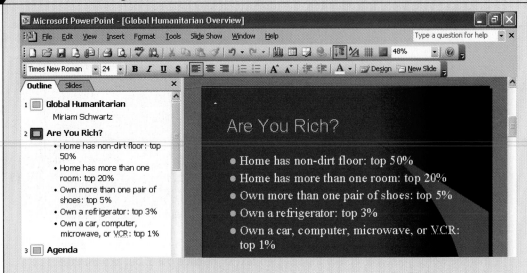

You're now ready to edit the text on another slide and create sub-bullets.

To create sub-bullets:

> 1. Click the **Next Slide** button ⬇ at the bottom of the vertical scroll bar four times to move to Slide 6. Slide 6 appears in the slide pane and on the Outline tab.
>
> 2. Select the title text **Topic One**, and then type **How You Can Help**.
>
> 3. Select all the text in the body text placeholder, not just the text of the first bulleted item.
>
> 4. Type **Become a member of Global Humanitarian**, press the **Enter** key, and then type **Contribute to humanitarian projects**. You've added two bulleted items to the body text.
>
>   Now you'll add some sub-bullets beneath the first-level bulleted item.
>
> 5. Press the **Enter** key to insert a new bullet, and then press the **Tab** key. The new bullet changes to a sub-bullet. In this design template, sub-bullets have a dash in front of them, which you won't be able to see until you start typing the text.
>
> 6. Type **Health and Education**, and then press the **Enter** key. The new bullet is a second-level bullet, the same level as the previous bullet.
>
> 7. Type **Water and Environment**, press the **Enter** key, type **Income Generation and Agriculture**, press the **Enter** key, and then type **Leadership and Cultural Enhancement**.
>
>   Now you want the next bullet to return to the first level.
>
> 8. Press the **Enter** key to create a new, second-level bullet, and then click the **Decrease Indent** button 🔣 on the Formatting toolbar. The bullet is converted to a first-level bullet. You can also press the Shift+Tab key combination to move a bullet up a level.
>
> 9. Type the remaining two first-level bulleted items: **Join a humanitarian expedition** and **Become a student intern**, and then click in a blank area of the slide to deselect the text box. See Figure 1-9.

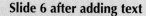

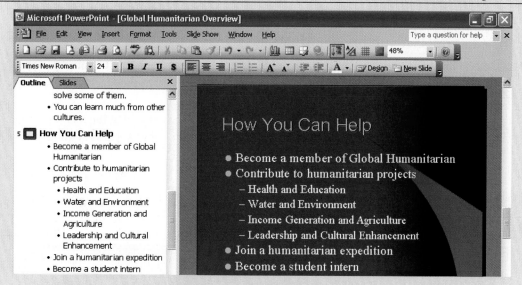

You have completed editing Slide 6. Miriam suggests that you delete the previous three slides, which are unnecessary for your presentation, before you edit the other slides.

Deleting Slides

When creating a presentation, you'll often delete slides. The AutoContent Wizard may create slides that you don't think are necessary, or you may create slides that you no longer want. You can delete slides in several ways: in Normal view, by clicking the slide thumbnail in the Slides tab or by clicking the slide icon in the Outline tab to select the slide, and then pressing the Delete key or using the Delete command on the shortcut or Edit menu; or in Slide Sorter view, by selecting the slide and then pressing the Delete key. Keep in mind that once you delete a slide, you can recover it by immediately clicking the Undo button on the Standard toolbar.

You need to delete Slide 3 ("Agenda"), Slide 4 ("Overview"), and Slide 5 ("Vocabulary").

To delete Slides 3 through 5:

1. With Slide 6 in the slide pane, click the **slide icon** 🔲 next to Slide 3 ("Agenda") on the Outline tab. You might need to drag the Outline pane scroll box up to view Slide 3. This causes Slide 3 to appear in the slide pane. Now you're ready to delete the slide.

2. Right-click the Slide 3 ("Agenda") **slide icon** 🔳 on the Outline tab, and then click **Delete Slide** on the shortcut menu. The entire slide is deleted from the presentation, and the rest of the slides are renumbered so that the slide that was Slide 4 becomes Slide 3, and so on. The renumbered Slide 3 ("Overview") appears in the slide pane.

3. Click the **Slides** tab. The Outline tab disappears and the Slides tab appears with thumbnails of all of the slides. With the Slides tab on top, notice that the labels identifying the Slides and Outline tabs change to icons.

4. With **Slide 3** ("Overview") selected in the Slides tab, press and hold the **Shift** key, and then click **Slide 4** on the Slides tab. Slides 3 and 4 are both selected on the Slides tab.

5. Click **Edit** on the menu bar, and then click **Delete Slide**. Both slides are deleted from the presentation. The new Slide 3, entitled "How You Can Help," now appears in the slide pane.

   Trouble? If the Delete Slide command is not on the Edit menu, click the double arrow at the bottom of the menu to display all of the commands on the menu.

Now you'll finish editing the presentation and save your work.

To edit and save the presentation:

▶ 1. Go to **Slide 4** ("Topic Two"), and then edit the title text to read **Benefits of Joining Global Humanitarian**. Notice that as you type the last word, PowerPoint automatically adjusts the size of the text to fit in the title text box.

   Trouble? If the font size of the text doesn't automatically adjust so that the text fits within the body text placeholder, click the AutoFit Options button ⊞ that appears in the slide pane, and then click the AutoFit Text to Placeholder option.

▶ 2. Select all the body text, not just the text of the first bulleted item, in the body text placeholder, and then type the bulleted items shown in Figure 1-10.

Figure 1-10	Completed Slide 4

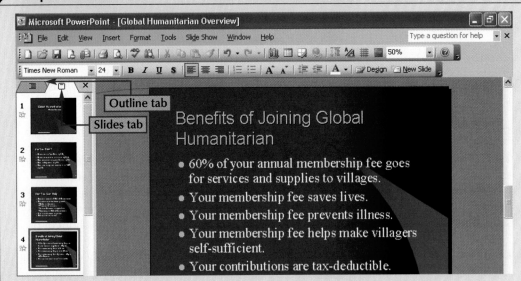

▶ 3. Go to **Slide 5**, and then modify the title and body text so that the slide looks like Figure 1-11.

Figure 1-11	Completed Slide 5

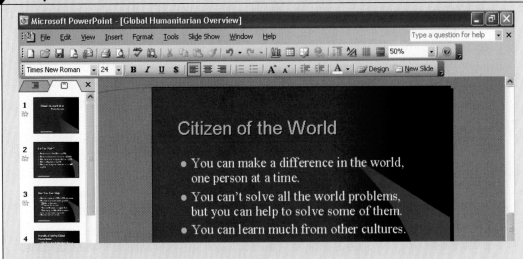

4. Delete **Slide 6** ("Where to Get More Information").

5. Click the **Save** button 🖫 on the Standard toolbar to save the presentation.

Miriam reviews your presentation and wants you to add a slide at the end of the presentation stating what action you want your readers to take as a result of your presentation.

Adding a New Slide and Choosing a Layout

Miriam suggests that you add a new slide at the end of the presentation explaining how individuals and families can join Global Humanitarian. When you add a new slide, PowerPoint formats the slide using a slide layout. PowerPoint supports four **text layouts**: Title Slide (placeholders for a title and a subtitle, usually used as the first slide in a presentation); Title Only (a title placeholder but not a body text placeholder); Title and Text (the default slide layout, with a title and a body text placeholder); and Title and 2-Column Text (same as Title and Text, but with two columns for text). PowerPoint also supports several **content layouts**—slide layouts that contain from zero to four charts, diagrams, images, tables, or movie clips. In addition, PowerPoint supports combination layouts, called **text and content layouts**, and several other types of layouts.

When you insert a new slide, it appears after the current one, and the Slide Layout task pane appears with a default layout already selected. This default layout is applied to the new slide. To use a different layout, you click it in the Slide Layout task pane.

To insert the new slide at the end of the presentation:

1. Because you want to add a slide after Slide 5, make sure Slide 5 is still in the slide pane.

2. Click the **New Slide** button on the Formatting toolbar. The Slide Layout task pane opens with the first layout in the second row under Text Layouts selected as the default, and a new Slide 6 appears in the slide pane with the default layout applied. See Figure 1-12.

New slide added ◀ **Figure 1-12**

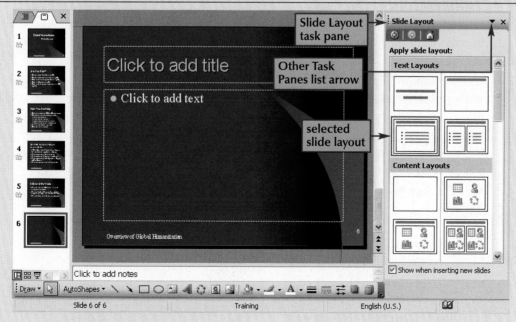

You'll accept the default layout for this slide. If you wanted a different layout, you would click the desired layout in the Slide Layout task pane.

Trouble? If the Slide Layout task pane does not appear, click View on the menu bar, click Task Pane, click the Other Task Panes list arrow at the top of the task pane, and then click Slide Layout. To make the Slide Layout task pane open automatically when you insert a new slide, click the Show when inserting new slides check box at the bottom of the task pane.

3. Position the pointer over the selected layout in the task pane. A ScreenTip appears, identifying this layout as the Title and Text layout.

   Next you'll close the Slide Layout task pane to provide a larger view of the slide pane.

4. Click the **Close** button ☒ in the Slide Layout task pane title bar to close the task pane.

   Trouble? If you accidentally click the Close button of the PowerPoint window or Presentation window, PowerPoint will ask you if you want to save the changes to your presentation. Click the Cancel button so that the presentation doesn't close, and then click the correct Close button on the task pane title bar.

The new slide contains text placeholders. On a new slide, you don't need to select the text on the slide to replace it with your text. You only need to click in the placeholder text box; the placeholder text will disappear and the insertion point will be placed in the text box, ready for you to type your text. Once you type your text, the dotted line outlining the edge of the text box will disappear. You'll add text to the new slide.

To add text to the new slide:

1. Click anywhere in the title text placeholder in the slide pane, where it says "Click to add title." The title placeholder text disappears and the insertion point blinks at the left of the title text box.

2. Type **Global Humanitarian Memmbership**. Make sure you type "Memmbership" with two *m*s in the middle. You'll correct this misspelling later. Again, the font size decreases to fit the text within the title placeholder.

3. Click anywhere in the body text placeholder. The placeholder text disappears and the insertion point appears just to the right of the first bullet.

4. Type **Individual membership: $75 per year**, press the **Enter** key, type **Family membership: $150 per year**, press the **Enter** key, type **Visit our Web site at www.globalhumanitarian.org**, and then press the **Enter** key.

   When you press the Enter key after typing the Web site address, PowerPoint automatically changes the Web site address (the URL) to a link. It formats the link by changing its color and underlining it. When you run the slide show, you can click this link to jump to that Web site if you are connected to the Internet.

5. Type **Call Sam Matagi, Volunteer Coordinator, at 523–555–SERV**.

You have inserted a new slide at the end of the presentation and added text to the slide. Next you'll create a new slide by promoting text in the Outline tab.

Promoting, Demoting, and Moving Outline Text

You can modify the text of a slide in the Outline tab as well as in the slide pane. Working in the Outline tab gives you more flexibility because you can see the outline of the entire presentation, not only the single slide currently in the slide pane. Working in the Outline tab allows you to easily move text from one slide to another or to create a new slide by promoting bulleted items from a slide so that they become the title and body text on a new slide.

To **promote** an item means to increase the outline level of that item—for example, to change a bulleted item into a slide title or to change a second-level bullet into a first-level bullet. To **demote** an item means to decrease the outline level—for example, to change a slide title into a bulleted item on the previous slide or to change a first-level bullet into a second-level bullet. You'll begin by promoting a bulleted item to a slide title, thus creating a new slide.

To create a new slide by promoting outline text:

1. Click the **Outline** tab. The outline of the presentation appears.

2. Drag the scroll box in the slide pane up until the ScreenTip displays "Slide: 3 of 6" and the title "How You Can Help." Slide 3 appears in the slide pane and the text of that slide appears at the top of the Outline tab.

3. In the Outline tab, move the pointer over the bullet to the left of "Contribute to humanitarian projects" so that the pointer becomes ✛, and then click the bullet. The text for that bullet and all its sub-bullets are selected.

   Now you'll promote the selected text so that it becomes the title text and first-level bullets on a new slide.

4. Click the **Decrease Indent** button 🔢 on the Formatting toolbar. PowerPoint promotes the selected text one level. Because the bullet you selected was a first-level bullet, the first-level bullet is promoted to a slide title on a new Slide 4, and the second-level bullets become first-level bullets on the new slide. See Figure 1-13.

Promoting a bulleted item to become a new slide ◀ **Figure 1-13**

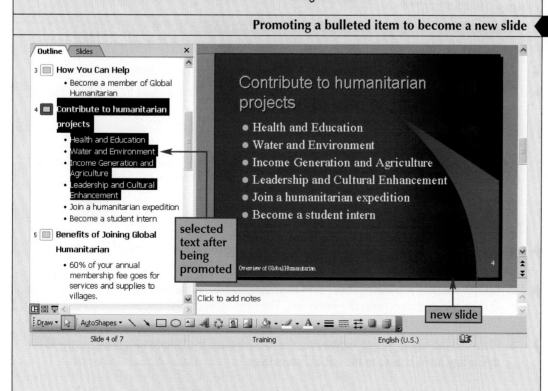

Now you'll edit this text, and then move some of the bulleted items to another slide.

5. Click anywhere to deselect the text, select the Slide 4 title text in the Outline tab, and then type **Types of Humanitarian Projects in Third-World Villages**. Notice that the title changes in the slide pane as well.

   Trouble? If all of the text on the slide becomes selected when you try to select the title text, make sure you position the pointer just to the left of the title text, and not over the slide icon, before you drag to select the text.

6. Click the bullet to the left of "Join a humanitarian expedition" (the fifth bullet in Slide 4) in the Outline tab, and then, while holding down the left mouse button, drag the bullet and its text up until the horizontal line position marker is just under the bulleted item "Become a member of Global Humanitarian" in Slide 3, as shown in Figure 1-14.

Figure 1-14	Moving text in the Outline tab

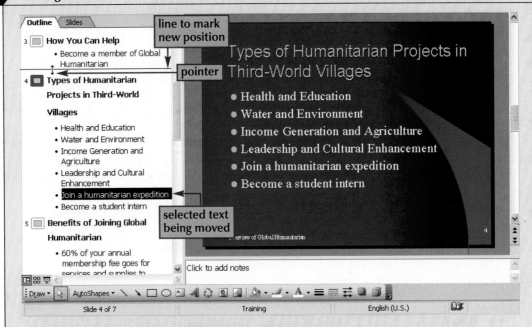

7. Release the mouse button. The bulleted item moves to the new position.

8. Using the same procedure, move the bulleted item "Become a student intern" from the end of Slide 4 to the end of Slide 3 in the Outline tab.

As you review your slides, you notice that in Slide 5, the phrase "Your membership fee" is repeated three times. You'll fix the problem by demoting some of the text.

To demote text on Slide 5:

1. Click the **slide icon** ▢ next to Slide 5 ("Benefits of Joining Global Humanitarian") in the Outline tab.

2. Click immediately to the right of "Your membership fee" in the second bulleted item in the Outline tab, and then press the **Enter** key. The item "saves lives" becomes a new bulleted item, but you want that item to appear indented at a lower outline level.

3. Press the **Tab** key to indent "saves lives," and then press the **Delete** key, if necessary, to delete any blank spaces to the left of "saves lives."

4. Click the bullet to the left of "Your membership fee prevents illness" in the Outline tab, press and hold down the **Shift** key, and then click the bullet to the left of "Your membership fee helps make villagers self-sufficient." This selects both bulleted items at the same time.

5. Click the **Increase Indent** button 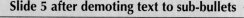 on the Formatting toolbar to demote the two bulleted items. Note this has the same effect as pressing the Tab key.

6. Delete the phrase "Your membership fee" and the space after it from the two items that you just demoted. Your slide should now look like Figure 1-15.

Slide 5 after demoting text to sub-bullets ◄ **Figure 1-15**

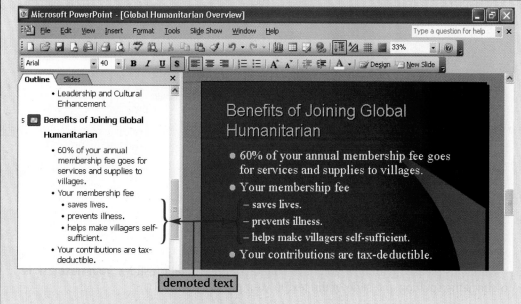

demoted text

   Miriam looks at your presentation and suggests that you move the current Slide 4 ahead of Slide 3. You could make this change by clicking the slide icon and dragging it above the slide icon for Slide 3 in the Outline tab. Instead, you'll move the slide in Slide Sorter view.

Moving Slides in Slide Sorter View

In Slide Sorter view, PowerPoint displays all the slides as thumbnails, so that several slides can appear on the screen at once. This view not only provides you with a good overview of your presentation, but also allows you to easily change the order of the slides and modify the slides in other ways.

To move Slide 4:

1. Click the **Slide Sorter View** button 🖿 at the bottom of the Outline tab. You now see your presentation in Slide Sorter view.

2. Click **Slide 4**. A thick colored frame appears around the slide, indicating that the slide is selected.

3. Press and hold down the left mouse button, drag the slide to the left so that the vertical line position marker appears on the left side of Slide 3, as shown in Figure 1-16.

| Figure 1-16 | Moving a slide in Slide Sorter view |

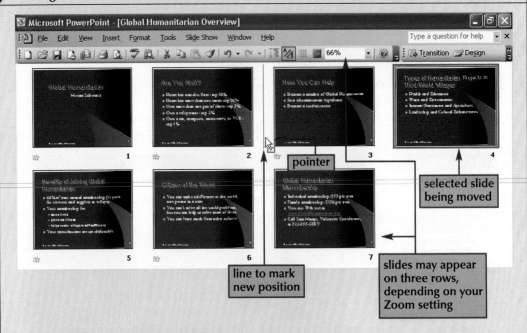

4. Release the mouse button. Slides 3 and 4 have switched places.

5. Click the **Normal View** button 🔲 to return to Normal view.

Miriam is pleased with how you have edited your presentation slides. Your next task is to check the spelling and style of the text in your presentation.

Checking the Spelling and Style in a Presentation

Before you print or present a slide show, you should always perform a final check of the spelling and style of all the slides in your presentation. This will help to ensure that your presentation is accurate and professional looking.

Checking the Spelling

If PowerPoint finds a word that's not in its dictionary, the word is underlined with a red wavy line in the slide pane. When you right-click the word, suggestions for alternate spellings appear on the shortcut menu, as well as commands for ignoring the misspelled word or opening the Spelling dialog box. You can also click the Spelling button on the Standard toolbar to check the spelling in the entire presentation.

You need to check the spelling in the Global Humanitarian presentation.

To check the spelling in the presentation:

1. Go to **Slide 7**. The spelling check always starts from the current slide.

2. Click the **Spelling** button 📝 on the Standard toolbar. The Spelling dialog box opens. The word you purposely mistyped earlier, "Memmbership," is highlighted in the Outline tab and listed in the Not in Dictionary text box in the Spelling dialog box. Two suggested spellings appear in the Suggestions list box, and the selected word in the Suggestions list box appears in the Change to text box.

3. With "Membership" selected in the Suggestions list box and in the Change to text box, click the **Change** button. If you knew that you misspelled that word throughout your presentation, you could click the Change All button to change all of the instances of the misspelling in the presentation to the corrected spelling.

The word is corrected, and the next word in the presentation that is not in the PowerPoint dictionary, Matagi, is flagged. This word is not misspelled; it is a surname.

4. Click the **Ignore** button. The word is not changed on the slide. If you wanted to ignore all the instances of that word in the presentation, you could click the Ignore All button. A dialog box opens telling you that the spelling check is complete.

Trouble? If another word in the presentation is flagged as misspelled, select the correct spelling in the Suggestions list, and then click the Change button. If your name on Slide 1 is flagged, click the Ignore button.

5. Click the **OK** button. The dialog box closes.

Next, you need to check the style in the presentation.

Using the Style Checker

The **Style Checker** checks your presentation for consistency in punctuation, capitalization, and visual elements and marks problems on a slide with a light bulb. For this feature to be active, you need to turn on the Style Checker.

To turn on the Style Checker:

1. Click **Tools** on the menu bar, click **Options** to open the Options dialog box, and then click the **Spelling and Style** tab.

2. Click the **Check style** check box to select it, if necessary. Now you'll check to make sure the necessary Style Checker options are selected.

Trouble? If a message appears telling you that the Style Checker needs to use the Office Assistant, click the Enable Assistant button. If another message appears telling you that PowerPoint can't display the Office Assistant because the feature is not installed, click the Yes button only if you are working on your own computer. If you are in a lab, ask your instructor or technical support person for assistance.

3. Click the **Style Options** button in the Options dialog box, click the **Slide title style** check box to select it, if necessary, click the list arrow to the right of this option, and then click **UPPERCASE**. When you run the Style Checker, it will suggest changing all of the titles to all uppercase.

4. Click the **Body text style** check box to select it, if necessary, click the list arrow to the right of this option, and then click **Sentence case**, if necessary. When you run the Style Checker, it will check to make sure that the text in each bullet in the body text has an uppercase letter as the first letter, and that the rest of the words in the body text start with a lowercase letter.

5. Click the bottom two check boxes under End punctuation to clear them, if necessary. Some of the bulleted lists in this presentation are complete sentences and some are not, so you want PowerPoint to allow variation in the end punctuation. See Figure 1-17.

Figure 1-17 Style Options dialog box

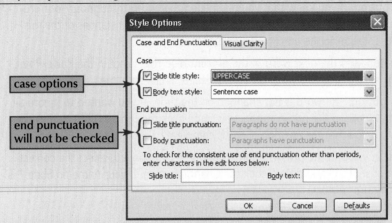

▶ **6.** Click the **OK** button to close the Style Options dialog box, and then click the **OK** button to close the Options dialog box.

From now on, PowerPoint will check the style in your presentation as you display each slide in the slide pane. Now you'll go through your presentation and check for style problems.

To fix problems marked by the Style Checker:

▶ **1.** Go to **Slide 1**. A light bulb appears next to the title. This indicates that the Style Checker found a problem with the slide title. Since you did not type any of the titles in all uppercase letters, a light bulb will appear on every slide marking the titles as not matching the style.

▶ **2.** Click the **light bulb**. The Office Assistant appears and displays a dialog box with a description of the problem and three options from which you can choose. See Figure 1-18.

Figure 1-18 Using the Style Checker

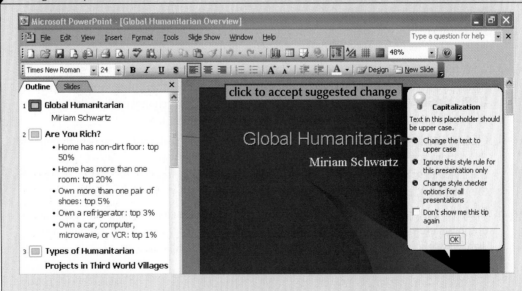

Trouble? If a message appears telling you that PowerPoint can't display the Office Assistant because the feature is not installed, click the Yes button only if you are working on your own computer. If you are in a lab, ask your instructor or technical support person for assistance.

▶ 3. Click the **Change the text to upper case** option button in the Office Assistant dialog box. All of the title text is now changed to uppercase.

▶ 4. Go to **Slide 2**.

▶ 5. Use the Style Checker to change the title text to uppercase.

▶ 6. Go to **Slide 3**, and then change the title text to uppercase. Another light bulb appears on Slide 3 next to the body text.

Trouble? If, in this or subsequent steps, the light bulb doesn't appear by the body text, go to the next or the previous slide, and then return to the current slide as a way of telling the Style Checker to recheck the slide.

▶ 7. Click the **light bulb** to see that the error in the body text is another capitalization error, and then click the **Change the text to sentence case** option button in the Office Assistant dialog box. All the words in the bulleted items are converted to lowercase (except the first word in each bulleted item); that is, all the bulleted items are converted to sentence case.

▶ 8. Go to **Slide 4**, change the title text to uppercase, and then click the **light bulb** next to the body text. The Style Checker detects that the first bulleted item is in mixed case (the words "Global Humanitarian" are capitalized), but the organization's name should remain capitalized, so you don't need to make any changes here.

▶ 9. Click the **OK** button in the Office Assistant dialog box. PowerPoint ignores the style for that slide, and the light bulb no longer appears.

▶ 10. Correct the title and body text on Slide 5, and the title text on Slide 6, and then go to Slide 7.

▶ 11. Correct the title text on Slide 7, but do not correct the capitalization in the body text on Slide 7. The words that start with an uppercase letter in the body text on this slide are proper nouns or are part of the phone number. Now you need to turn off the Style Checker.

▶ 12. Click **Tools** on the menu bar, click **Options**, click the **Check style** check box on the Spelling and Style tab to clear it, and then click the **OK** button. The Style Checker is turned off.

As you create your own presentations, watch for the problems marked by the Style Checker. Of course, in some cases, you might want a certain capitalization that the Style Checker detects as an error. In these cases, just ignore the light bulb, or click it, and then click the OK button. The light bulb never appears on the screen during a slide show or when you print a presentation.

Using the Research Task Pane

PowerPoint enables you to use the Research task pane to search online services or Internet sites for additional help in creating a presentation. Using these resources helps you make your presentations more professional. For example, you could look up specific words in a thesaurus. A **thesaurus** contains a list of words and their synonyms, antonyms, and other related words. Using a thesaurus is a good way to add variety to the words you use or to choose more precise words. You could also look up information in online encyclopedias, news services, libraries, and business sites.

Miriam thinks the word "rich" in Slide 2 may be too informal. She asks you to find an appropriate replacement word. You'll now look for synonyms in the Office thesaurus.

To do research using the thesaurus:

1. Go to **Slide 2**, and then highlight the word **RICH** in either the Outline tab or the slide pane. Be careful not to highlight the question mark at the end of the phrase.

2. Click the **Research** button on the Standard toolbar. The Research task pane opens with the word "RICH" in the Search for text box.

3. Click the list arrow next to All Reference Books in the task pane, and then click **Thesaurus: English (U.S.)**.

4. Click the **green arrow** button next to the Search for text box to begin a search for synonyms for the word "rich," if necessary. The thesaurus provides several suggestions in a list organized so that the most relevant words are in bold, and additional synonyms are indented under the bold terms.

5. Scroll down, if necessary, to see the word "full" in boldface, and then click the **minus sign** button next to "full (adj.)." The minus sign changes to a plus sign, and the list of words under "full" collapses.

   After looking over the list, Miriam decides that "full" and "opulent" do not convey the correct meaning. She decides that "wealthy" is the most appropriate synonym.

6. Position the pointer over the word **wealthy**, indented under the bold term **wealthy (adj.)**. A box appears around the term and a list arrow appears at the right side of the box.

7. Click the list arrow on the side of the box, as shown in Figure 1-19.

Figure 1-19 | **Using the Thesaurus in the Research task pane**

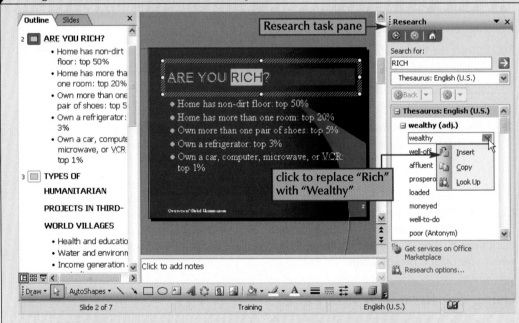

8. Click **Insert**. "WEALTHY" replaces "RICH" in the slide.

9. Close the task pane.

Creating Speaker Notes

When you show the presentation to Miriam, she is satisfied. Now you're ready to prepare the other parts of Miriam's presentation: the notes (also called speaker notes) and audience handouts (a printout of the slides). **Notes** are printed pages that contain a picture of and notes about each slide. They help the speaker remember what to say when a particular slide appears during the presentation. **Handouts** are printouts of the slides; these can be arranged with several slides printed on a page.

You'll create notes for only a few of the slides in the presentation. For example, Miriam wants to remember to acknowledge special guests or Global Humanitarian executives at any meeting where she might use this presentation. You'll create a note reminding her to do that.

To create notes:

▶ **1.** Click the **Slides** tab, and then click **Slide 1** in the Slides tab. Slide 1 appears in the slide pane. The notes pane currently contains placeholder text.

▶ **2.** Click in the notes pane, and then type **Acknowledge special guests and Global Humanitarian executives.** See Figure 1-20.

Notes on Slide 1 ◀ **Figure 1-20**

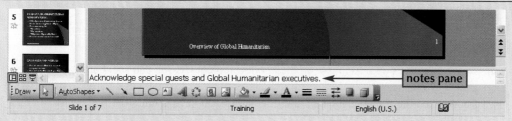

▶ **3.** Click **Slide 2** in the Slides tab, click in the notes pane, and then type **Everyone in this room is in the top one percent of wealthy people who have ever lived on earth.**

▶ **4.** Go to **Slide 3**, click in the notes pane, and then type **Give an example of each of these project types.** These are all the notes that Miriam wants.

▶ **5.** Click the **Save** button 🖫 on the Standard toolbar to save the changes to the presentation.

Before Miriam gives her presentation, she'll print the notes of the presentation so she'll have them available during her presentations. You can now view the completed presentation to make sure that it is accurate, informative, and visually pleasing.

To view the slide show:

▶ **1.** Go to **Slide 1**, and then click the **Slide Show from current slide** button 🖳 at the bottom of the Slides tab.

▶ **2.** Proceed through the slide show as you did earlier, clicking the left mouse button or pressing the spacebar to advance from one slide to the next.

▶ **3.** If you see a problem on one of your slides, press the **Esc** key to leave the slide show and display the current slide on the screen in Normal view, fix the problem on the slide, save your changes, and then click the **Slide Show from current slide** button 🖳 to resume the slide show from the current slide.

▶ **4.** When you reach the end of your slide show, press the **spacebar** to move to the blank screen, and then press the **spacebar** again to return to Normal view.

Now you're ready to preview and print your presentation.

Previewing and Printing a Presentation

Before you give your presentation, you may want to print it. PowerPoint provides several printing options. For example, you can print the slides in color using a color printer; print in grayscale or pure black and white using a black-and-white printer; print handouts with 2, 3, 4, 6, or 9 slides per page; or print the notes pages (the speaker notes printed below a picture of the corresponding slide). You can also format and then print the presentation onto overhead transparency film (available in most office supply stores).

Usually you'll want to open the Print dialog box by clicking File on the menu bar, and then clicking Print, rather than clicking the Print button on the Standard toolbar. If you click the Print button, the presentation prints with the options chosen last in the Print dialog box. If you're going to print your presentation on a black-and-white printer, you should first preview the presentation to make sure the text will be legible. You'll use Print Preview to see the slides as they will appear when they are printed.

To preview the presentation:

▶ 1. Go to **Slide 1**, if necessary, and then click the **Print Preview** button 🔍 on the Standard toolbar. The Preview window appears, displaying Slide 1.

▶ 2. Click the **Options** button on the Preview toolbar, point to **Color/Grayscale**, and then click **Grayscale**. The slide is displayed in grayscale.

▶ 3. Click the **Next Page** button 🔽 on the Preview toolbar. As you can see, part of the background graphic covers the text on Slide 2. See Figure 1-21. You'll need to remove the background from the slides so you can read them after you have printed them.

Figure 1-21 ▶ **Slide 2 in Preview window**

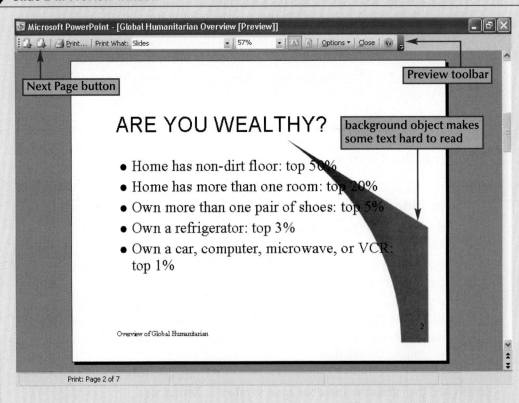

4. Click the **Close** button on the Preview toolbar to return to Normal view.

5. Click **Format** on the menu bar, click **Background** to display the Background dialog box, click the **Omit background graphics from master** check box, and then click the **Apply to All** button. The slide appears as before, but without the background graphic.

6. Click the **Print Preview** button 🔍 on the Standard toolbar, and then click the **Next Page** button 🔍 on the Preview toolbar. You can now easily read the text on Slide 2.

7. Click the **Print What** list arrow on the Preview toolbar, and then click **Handouts (4 slides per page)**. The preview changes to display four slides on a page.

8. Click the **Print** button on the Preview toolbar. The Print dialog box opens. See Figure 1-22.

Print dialog box ◀ **Figure 1-22**

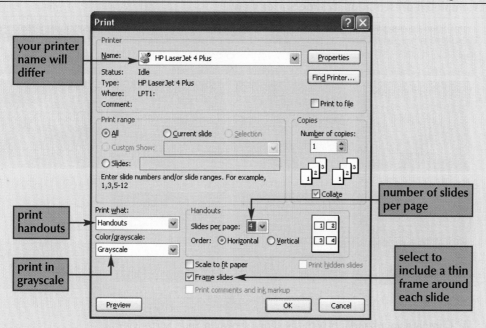

9. Compare your dialog box to the one shown in Figure 1-22, make any necessary changes, and then click the **OK** button to print the handouts on two pages. Now you're ready to print the notes.

10. Click the **Print What** list arrow on the Preview toolbar, and then click **Notes Pages**. The current slide is displayed as a notes page, with the slide on the top and the notes on the bottom.

11. Click the **Print** button on the Print Preview toolbar, click the **Slides** option button in the Print range section of the Print dialog box, and then type **1-3**. These are the only slides with notes on them, so you do not need to print all seven slides as notes pages.

12. Click the **OK** button to print the notes. Slides 1-3 print on three pieces of paper as notes pages.

13. Click the **Close** button on the Preview toolbar. The view returns to Normal view.

Your last task is to view the completed presentation in Slide Sorter view to see how all the slides look together. First, however, you'll restore the background graphics.

To restore the background graphics and view the completed presentation in Slide Sorter view:

1. Click **Format** on the menu bar, click **Background**, click the **Omit background graphics from master** check box to clear it, and then click the **Apply to All** button. The background graphics are restored to the slides.

2. Click the **Slide Sorter View** button 🔠 at the bottom of the Slides tab. The slides appear on the screen in several rows, depending on the current zoom percentage shown in the Zoom box on the Standard toolbar and on the size of your monitor. You need to see the content on the slides better.

3. Click the **Zoom** list arrow on the Standard toolbar, and then click **75%**. See Figure 1-23.

| Figure 1-23 | Completed presentation in Slide Sorter view |

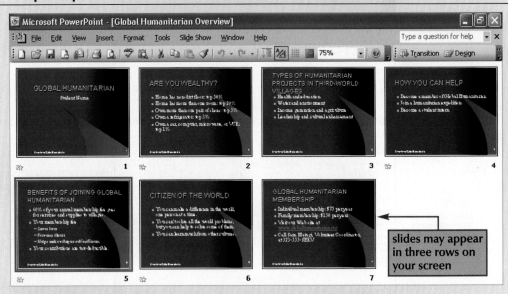

slides may appear in three rows on your screen

4. Compare your handouts with the slides shown in Slide Sorter view.

5. Click the **Close window** button ✕. A dialog box appears asking if you want to save your changes.

6. Click the **Yes** button to save the changes and close the presentation.

Review

To reinforce the tasks you learned in this session, go to the SAM 2003 Training Companion CD included with this text.

Session 1.2 Quick Check

1. Explain how to do the following in the Outline tab:
   a. move text up
   b. delete a slide
   c. change a first-level bullet to a second-level bullet
2. What does it mean to promote a bulleted item in the Outline tab? To demote a bulleted item?
3. Explain a benefit of using the Outline tab rather than the slide pane.

4. What is the Style Checker? What is an example of a consistency or style problem that it might mark?
5. What are notes? How do you create them?
6. Why is it beneficial to preview a presentation before printing it?

Review

Tutorial Summary

In this tutorial, you learned how to plan and create a PowerPoint presentation by modifying AutoContent slides. You learned how to edit the text in both the Outline tab and the slide pane; add a new slide and choose a slide layout; delete slides; and promote, demote and move text in your outline. You also learned how to check your presentation for consistency, create speaker notes, and preview and print your presentation.

Key Terms

animation	note	slide pane
body text	notes pane	slide transitions
bulleted item	numbered list	Slides tab
bulleted list	object	Style Checker
content layout	Outline tab	sub-bullet
demote	placeholder	text and content layout
design template	PowerPoint	text box
first-level bullet	progressive disclosure	text layout
footer	promote	thesaurus
handout	second-level bullet	thumbnail
layout	sizing handle	title text
main text		

Practice

Practice the skills you learned in the tutorial using the same case scenario.

Review Assignments

Data File needed for the Review Assignments: VillageOP.ppt

Miriam Schwartz, the managing director of the Austin, Texas headquarters of Global Humanitarian, asks you to prepare a PowerPoint presentation explaining the Village Outreach Program to potential donors and volunteers. She gives you a rough draft of a PowerPoint presentation. Your job is to edit the presentation. Complete the following:

1. Open the presentation **VillageOP** in the Tutorial.01\Review folder included with your Data Files.
2. Save the file as **Village Outreach Program** in the same folder.
3. In Slide 1, change the subtitle placeholder ("Global Humanitarian") to your name.
4. In Slide 2, use the Outline tab to demote the bulleted items "Health," "Education," "Clean water," and "Environment," so that they become second-level bulleted items.
5. Below the sub-bulleted item "Clean water," insert another second-level bulleted item: "Agriculture and Income-producing Projects."
6. In Slide 3, delete all occurrences of the word "the" to reduce the number of words in each bulleted item and thus approach the 6 × 6 rule.
7. Move the last bulleted item in Slide 3 ("Assist villagers in organizing health committees") in the Outline tab so it becomes the second bulleted item in the body text of Slide 3.

8. Go to Slide 5, and then promote the bulleted item "Agriculture and Income-produc-ing Opportunities" in the Outline tab so it becomes the title of a new slide (Slide 6).
9. Return to Slide 5 and promote the last three second-level bulleted items so they become bullets on the same level as "Help villagers build."
10. In Slide 7, move the second bulleted item ("Mobilize resources") so it becomes the fourth bulleted item.
11. Add a new Slide 8 with the default Title and Text layout.
12. In Slide 8, type the slide title "Village Projects."
13. Type the following as first-level bulleted items in Slide 8: "Wells," "Water Pumps," "Greenhouses," "Lorena Stoves," "First aid supplies," and "School supplies."
14. In Slide 2, add the following speaker note: "Relate personal experiences for each topic."
15. In Slide 3, add the following speaker note: "Explain that we need volunteers, espe-cially physicians, dentists, optometrists, and nurses."
16. Switch to Slide Sorter view, and then drag Slide 5 to the left of Slide 4.
17. Use the Research task pane to replace "Agriculture" on Slide 6 with another word, and then make this same change on Slide 2.
18. Check the spelling in the presentation and change or ignore each flagged word.
19. Turn on the Style Checker, set the Case options so that the slide title style is upper-case and the body text style is sentence case, and then examine the slides for ele-ments that the Style Checker flags, correcting slides as appropriate. Turn off the Style Checker when you are finished.
20. View the presentation in Slide Show view. Look carefully at each slide and check the content. If you see any errors, press the Esc key to end the slide show, fix the error, and then start the slide show again.
21. Go to Slide 6. When you viewed the presentation, did you notice the typographical error "load" in the final bulleted item? (It should be "loan.") If you did not fix this error already, fix it now.
22. Save the changes to the presentation, preview the presentation in grayscale, and then print the presentation in grayscale as handouts, four slides per page.
23. Print Slides 2 and 3 as notes pages in grayscale, and then close the file.

Case Problem 1

Apply

Apply the skills you learned to create a new presentation for an e-commerce company using the AutoContent Wizard, and then modify the content.

There are no Data Files needed for this Case Problem.

e-Commerce Consultants Kendall Koester founded e-Commerce Consultants, a consult-ing company that helps local businesses with their e-commerce needs, including Web page design, order fulfillment, and security. Kendall hired you to prepare a presentation to businesses to sell the services of e-Commerce Consultants. Complete the following:

1. Start PowerPoint, and then start the AutoContent Wizard.
2. In the Presentation type window, select the Sales/Marketing category, and then select Selling a Product or Service.
3. In the Presentation style window, select On-screen presentation.
4. In the Presentation options window, type "Developing Strategies for Your Future" as the presentation title, and type "e-Commerce Consultants" as the footer.
5. Omit the date last updated from the presentation, but include the slide number.
6. In Slide 1, change the subtitle placeholder to your name, if necessary.
7. In Slide 2 ("Objective"), replace the slide title with "What We Offer," and replace the body text with the following first-level bulleted items: "Overcoming barriers to e-commerce," "Surviving today's shaky market," "Setting up your Web site," and "Managing your orders."

8. In Slide 3 ("Customer Requirements"), leave the title text as is, and then replace the body text with the following bulleted items: "Web site design and development," "Order taking and fulfillment," "Security," and "Other." Don't modify or delete the radial diagram on the slide.

9. In Slide 4, change the slide title to "Meeting Your Needs," and then replace the body text with the following first-level bulleted items: "Promoting your product," "Securing startup funds," "Arranging for credit card accounts," and "Answering all your questions." Don't modify or delete the three pyramid diagrams.

10. Delete Slides 5 ("Cost Analysis") and 6 ("Our Strengths").

11. In the new Slide 5 ("Key Benefits"), leave the title text as is, and then replace the body text with the following first-level bulleted items: "You can focus on your products, your services, and your bottom line."; and "We'll help you sell your product on the Internet."

12. In Slide 6 ("Next Steps"), leave the title text as is, and then replace the body text with the following first-level bulleted items: "List what you want us to do," "Draw up an agreement," "Determine a timeline," "Establish the order-fulfillment process," and "Launch the Web-based e-commerce system."

13. Save the presentation as **e-Commerce Consultants** in the Tutorial.01\Cases folder included with your Data Files.

14. In Slide 2, indent (demote) "Managing your orders" so it is a sub-bullet under "Setting up your Web site," and then add another sub-bullet, "Handling online credit."

15. In Slide 3, add the following sub-bulleted items under "Web site design and development": "know-how," "graphic design," "software," and "programming."

16. In Slide 4, insert a new first bullet "We can help by," and then make all the other phrases the sub-bullets.

17. Move the last bulleted item "Answering all your questions" up to become the first sub-bullet.

18. In Slide 6 ("Next Steps"), delete excess words like "a," "an," and "the" to achieve the 6 × 6 rule as closely as possible.

19. Add a new slide after Slide 6 with the Title and Text layout, type "Your Account Representative" as the title text, and then type the following information in five bullets: Kendall Koester, e-Commerce Consultants, 1666 Winnebago St., Pecatonica, IL 61063, 555-WEB-PAGE. The city, state, and Zip code should all be part of the same bulleted item. (Note that the first letter of "e-Commerce" changes to an uppercase letter as soon as you press the spacebar. This is PowerPoint's AutoFormat.)

20. Replace the "E" in "E-Commerce" with "e."

21. Turn on the Style Checker, set the Case options so that the slide title style is title case and the body text style is sentence case, and then go through each slide of the presentation to see if the Style Checker marks any potential problems. (Don't forget to double-check each slide by moving to the next or previous slide and then back to the current slide to recheck it.) When you see the light bulb, click it, and then assess whether you want to accept or reject the suggested change. You'll want to accept most of the suggested changes, but make sure you leave words like "Web" and "Internet" capitalized, and don't change the capitalization of the address and phone number you typed on Slide 7. Turn off the Style Checker when you are finished.

22. Check the spelling in the presentation. Correct any misspellings, and ignore any words that are spelled correctly.

23. View the presentation in Slide Show view.

24. Save the presentation, preview it in grayscale, print the presentation in grayscale as handouts with four slides per page, and then close the file.

Apply

Apply the skills you learned to modify an existing presentation for a public library outreach program.

Case Problem 2

Data File needed for this Case Problem: Library.ppt

Carriage Path Public Library Davion McGechie is head of the Office of Community Outreach Services for the Carriage Path Public Library in Milford, Connecticut. Davion and his staff coordinate outreach services and develop programs in communities throughout the Long Island Sound. These services and programs depend on a large volunteer staff. Davion wants you to help him create a PowerPoint presentation to train his staff. Complete the following:

1. Open the file **Library** located in the Tutorial.01\Cases folder included with your Data Files, and save it as **Public Library Outreach** in the same folder.
2. In Slide 1, replace the subtitle placeholder ("Davion McGechie, Director") with your name.
3. In Slide 2, add the speaker's note "Mention that community groups include ethnic neighborhood councils, religious organizations, and civic groups."
4. Add a fourth bulleted item to Slide 2: "To implement outreach programs in the surrounding communities."
5. Move the second bulleted item ("To provide staff training") so that it becomes the last bulleted item.
6. In Slide 3, edit the second and third bulleted items so that "Four central libraries with in-depth collections" and "Six neighborhood Branch libraries" are second-level bulleted items below the main bullet.
7. Promote the bulleted item "Special Events & Programs" and its sub-bullets so that they become a new separate slide.
8. Use the Slides tab to move Slide 6 ("Branch Libraries") to become Slide 5.
9. Add a new slide after Slide 7 with the title "Volunteer Opportunities."
10. On Slide 8 (the new slide), create three bulleted items with the first line ("Literacy Tutors"), the second line ("Computer Instructors"), and the third line ("Children's Hour Story Tellers").
11. Under the third bullet, add the sub-bullets ("After-school story hour") and ("Bookmobile story hour").
12. Turn on the Style Checker, if necessary, and then go through all the slides, accepting all the suggested corrections of case (capitalization), except the following: "Deaf History Month: May," "National Literacy Month: September," "English as a Second Language (ESL)," and the names of the libraries.
13. Check the spelling in the presentation. Correct any spelling errors and ignore any words that are spelled correctly.
14. View the presentation in Slide Show view.
15. Go to Slide 2. When you viewed the presentation, did you notice the two typographical errors on this page? If you did not fix these errors, fix them now.
16. Save the presentation, preview it in grayscale, print the presentation in grayscale as handouts with four slides per page, and then close the file.

Challenge

Explore more advanced features of PowerPoint by formatting text, paragraphs, and lists, and by changing slide layouts and adding a design template.

Case Problem 3

Data File needed for this Case Problem: LASIK.ppt

Camellia Gardens Eye Center Dr. Carol Wang, head ophthalmologist at the Camellia Gardens Eye Center in Charleston, South Carolina, performs over 20 surgeries per week using laser-assisted in situ keratomileusis (LASIK) to correct vision problems of myopia (nearsightedness), hyperopia (farsightedness), and astigmatism. She asks you to help prepare a PowerPoint presentation to those interested in learning more about LASIK. Complete the following:

1. Open the file **LASIK** located in the Tutorial.01\Cases folder included with your Data Files, and then save it as **Camellia LASIK** in the same folder.
2. In Slide 1, replace the subtitle placeholder ("Camellia Gardens Eye Center") with your name.
3. In Slide 2, move the first bulleted item down to become the third bulleted item.
4. Edit the sub-bullets "Myopia," "Hyperopia," and "Astigmatism" in the first item so they're part of the first-level bullet and there are no sub-bullets. Be sure to add commas after the first two words, and add the word "and" before the last word.
5. Add a fourth bulleted item with the text "Patients no longer need corrective lenses."

Explore
6. Still in Slide 2, center the text in the title text box. (*Hint*: Click anywhere in the title text, and then position the pointer over the buttons on the Formatting toolbar to see the ScreenTips to find a button that will center the text.)

Explore
7. In Slide 3, change the bulleted list to a numbered list. (*Hint*: Select all of the body text, and then look for a button on the Formatting toolbar that will number the list.)

Explore
8. Have PowerPoint automatically split Slide 3 into two slides. (*Hint*: First, click the AutoFit Options button in the slide pane and click the Stop Fitting Text to This Placeholder option button. Then, with the insertion point in the body text box, click the AutoFit Options button again, and then click the appropriate option.)

Explore
9. On the new Slide 4, change the numbering so it continues the numbering from Slide 3 rather than starting over at number 1. (*Hint*: Right-click anywhere in the first item in the numbered list, click Bullets and Numbering on the shortcut menu, click the Numbered tab, and then change the Start at value.)
10. At the end of the title in Slide 4, add a space and "(cont.)," the abbreviation for continued.
11. In Slide 5, demote the two bullets under "With low to moderate myopia," so they become sub-bullets.

Explore
12. Still in Slide 5, tell the PowerPoint Spell Checker to ignore all occurrences of the word "hyperopia," which is not found in PowerPoint's dictionary. (*Hint*: Right-click the word to see a shortcut menu with spelling commands.)

Explore
13. If any of the bulleted text doesn't fit on the slide, but drops below the body text box, set the text box to AutoFit. (*Hint*: Click anywhere in the text box, click the AutoFit Options button that appears, and then click the desired option.)
14. In Slide 6, join the final two bullets to become one bullet. Be sure to add a semicolon between the two bullets and change the word "Other" to lowercase.
15. In Slide 8, move the second bullet "Schedule eye exam to determine" (along with its sub-bullets) up to become the first bullet.
16. In Slide 8, edit the bulleted item ("Analysis of . . .") so that "eye pressure," "shape of cornea," and "thickness of cornea" are sub-bullets below "Analysis of."

Explore
17. Change the layout of Slide 8 so that the body text appears in two columns. (*Hint*: Click the AutoFit Options button in the slide pane, and then click Change to Two-Column Layout.) Drag the last two bullets over to the second column in the body text. (*Hint*: After you select the bulleted item, position the pointer over the selected text instead of over the bullet, and then drag the pointer to immediately after the new bullet in the second column, using the vertical line indicator that appears to help guide you.)
18. Add a new Slide 9, and then apply the Title Only layout in the Text Layout section of the Slide Layout task pane.

Explore

19. In Slide 9, add the title "Camellia Gardens Eye Center," create a new text box near the center of the slide, and then add the address "8184 Camellia Drive" on the first line, "Charleston, SC 29406" on the second line, and the phone number "(843) 555-EYES" on the third line. (*Hint*: Click the Text Box button on the Drawing toolbar, and then click on the slide at the desired location.)

Explore

20. Change the size of the text in the new text box on Slide 9 so that it's 32 points. (*Hint*: Click the edge of the text box to select the entire text box and all of its contents, and then click the Font Size list arrow on the Formatting toolbar.)

Explore

21. Turn on the Style Checker, and then set the style options for end punctuation so that the Style Checker checks to make sure that slide titles do not have end punctuation, and that paragraphs in the body text have punctuation. Set the slide title style to title case and the body text style to sentence case. Also, set the Visual Clarity options so that the maximum number of bullets should not exceed six, the number of lines per title should not exceed two, and the number of lines per bulleted item should not exceed two. (*Hint*: Use the End punctuation section of the Case and End Punctuation tab and the Legibility section of the Visual Clarity tab in the Style Options dialog box.)

Explore

22. Go through all the slides, correcting problems of case (capitalization) and punctuation. Be sure not to let the Style Checker change the case for proper nouns. Let the Style Checker correct end punctuation for complete sentences, but you shouldn't allow (or you should remove) punctuation for words or phrases that don't form complete sentences. Do not accept the Style Checker's suggestions to remove question marks in the slide titles.

Explore

23. Change the Style Options back so that the next time the Style Checker is run, only the Slide title style and Body text style options on the Case and End Punctuation tab and the Fonts options on the Visual Clarity tab are selected, and then turn off the Style Checker.

24. Check the spelling in the presentation.

Explore

25. Apply the design template called "Watermark," which has a white background with violet circles. (*Hint*: Click the Design button on the Formatting toolbar, and then use the ScreenTips in the Slide Design task pane to find the Watermark design template.) If you can't find the Watermark design template, choose a different design template.

26. View the presentation in Slide Show view.

27. Save the presentation, preview it in grayscale, print the presentation in grayscale as handouts with four slides per page, and then close the file.

Research

Use the Internet to research MP3 players and prepare a review.

Case Problem 4

There are no Data Files needed for this Case Problem.

Portable Digital Audio Players   Your public speaking teacher instructs you to prepare a review of a portable digital audio player (for example, an MP3 player) for presentation to the class. If you are not familiar with portable digital audio players, your teacher suggests that you search the Internet or talk to other students for an explanation of what they are, how they work, and why so many people like them. You should then search the Internet for information or reviews about various brands and models of digital audio players. Alternatively, if you own a portable digital audio player, your instructor suggests you search the Internet for information about your player. You should organize your information into a PowerPoint presentation, with at least six slides. Complete the following:

1. Go to **www.google.com**, **yahoo.com**, or any other Web site that allows you to search the Web, and search using such terms as "digital audio player review" or "MP3 player review." You should read about various brands of players to get an idea of the most popular sellers.

2. Select one brand and model of digital audio player; search the Internet for more information and reviews about that player.

3. Use the AutoContent Wizard to begin developing slides for a presentation based on "Generic" in the General category of presentation types.

   a. Title the presentation "Review of" followed by the brand and model of your selected digital audio player. For example, the title might be "Review of Apple iPod," "Review of Rio Cali Sport MP3 Player," or "Review of Samsung Yepp YP-60V 256 MB MP3 Player."

   b. Include a footer with the text "Review of a digital audio player."

   c. Include both the date and the slide number in the footer.

4. In Slide 1, change the subtitle to your name, if necessary.

5. In Slide 2 ("Introduction"), include basic information about the digital audio player in the bulleted list. The information might include brand name, model name or number, capacity (for example, 128 MB or 256 MB), retail price, and street price.

6. In Slide 3 ("Topics of Discussion"), include categories of information used in reviewing the player, such as "General Description," "Features," "Audio File Formats," "Desktop Computer Software," "Ease of Use," "Technical Specifications," and "Reviewers' Comments."

7. Delete Slides 4 through 9. (*Hint*: Use Slide Sorter view.)

8. Create at least one slide for each topic you listed on Slide 3, and then include bulleted lists explaining that topic.

Explore ▶ 9. Use the Research Pane (by clicking the Research button on the Standard toolbar) to find additional information about the digital audio player you've chosen. (*Hint*: In the Research Pane, type the phrase "digital audio player" into the Search for text box, make sure your computer is connected to the Internet, select a research site such as eLibrary, if necessary, and click the green Start searching button.) You might want to create one or more new slides, cut and paste information into the new slides, and then edit the information into one or more appropriate bulleted lists.

10. Create a slide titled "Summary and Recommendation" as the last slide in your presentation, giving your overall impression of the player and your recommendation for whether the player is worth buying.

11. View the presentation on the Outline tab. If necessary, change the order of the bulleted items on slides, or change the order of slides.

Explore ▶ 12. If you see any slides with more than six or seven bulleted items, split the slide in two. (*Hint*: With the insertion point in the body text box, click the AutoFit Options button that appears near the lower-left corner of the text box, and click the appropriate command.)

13. Go through all the slides, correcting problems of case (capitalization), punctuation, number of bulleted items per slide, and number of lines per bulleted item. Be sure not to let the Style Checker change the case for proper nouns. Let the Style Checker correct end punctuation for complete sentences, but do not allow (or remove) punctuation for words or phrases that don't form complete sentences.

14. Check the spelling of your presentation.

15. View the presentation in Slide Show view. If you see any typographical errors or other problems, stop the slide show, correct the problems, and then continue the slide show. If you find slides that aren't necessary, delete them.

16. Save the presentation as **Digital Audio Player Review** in the Tutorial.01\Cases folder included with your Data Files.

17. Preview the presentation in grayscale, and print the presentation in grayscale as handouts with four slides per page. Print speaker notes if you created any, and then close the file.

Research

Go to the Web to find information you can use to create presentations.

Internet Assignments

The purpose of the Internet Assignments is to challenge you to find information on the Internet that you can use to work effectively with this software. The actual assignments are updated and maintained on the Course Technology Web site. Log on to the Internet and use your Web browser to go to the Student Online Companion for New Perspectives Office 2003 at **www.course.com/np/office2003**. Click the Internet Assignments link, and then navigate to the assignments for this tutorial.

Assess

SAM Assessment and Training

If your instructor has chosen to use the full online version of SAM 2003 Assessment and Training, you can go beyond the "just-in-time" training provided on the CD that accompanies this text. Simply log in to your SAM account (http://sam2003.course.com) to launch any assigned training activities or exams that relate to the skills covered in this tutorial.

Review

Quick Check Answers

Session 1.1

1. Individual slides, speaker notes, an outline, and audience handouts.
2. The slide pane shows the slide as it will look during your slide show. The notes pane contains speaker notes. The Outline tab shows an outline of your presentation. The Slides tab displays thumbnails of each slide.
3. a. a feature that causes each element on a slide to appear one at a time
   b. the manner in which a new slide appears on the screen during a slide show
   c. a file that contains the colors and format of the background and the font style of the titles, accents, and other text
   d. a predetermined way of organizing the objects on a slide
4. What is my purpose or objective? What type of presentation is needed? What is the physical location of my presentation? What is the best format my presentation?
5. The AutoContent Wizard lets you choose a presentation category and then creates a general outline of the presentation.
6. The view you use to present an on-screen presentation to an audience.

Session 1.2

1. a. Click a slide or bullet icon, and then drag the selected item up.
   b. Right-click the slide icon of the slide to be deleted in the Outline tab, and then click Delete Slide on the shortcut menu; or, move to the slide you want to delete in the slide pane, click Edit on the menu bar, and then click Delete Slide.
   c. Click the slide or bullet icon in the Outline tab, and then click the Decrease Indent button on the Formatting toolbar.
2. Promote means to decrease the level (for example, from level two to level one) of an outline item; demote means to increase the level of an outline item.
3. In the Outline tab, you can see the text of several slides at once, which makes it easier to work with text. In the slide pane, you can see the design and layout of the slide.
4. The Style Checker automatically checks your presentation for consistency and style. For example, it will check for consistency in punctuation.
5. Notes are notes for the presenter. They appear in the notes pane in Normal view or you can print notes pages, which contain a picture of and notes about each slide.
6. By previewing your presentation, you make sure that the slides are satisfactory, and that the presentation is legible in grayscale if you use a monochrome printer.

Applying and Modifying Text and Graphic Objects

Presenting and Preparing for an Expedition to Peru

Case | Global Humanitarian, Lima Office

The objectives of Global Humanitarian's expeditions are to help villagers build homes, schools, greenhouses, wells, culinary water systems, and Lorena adobe stoves; to provide medical and dental services; and to teach basic hygiene, literacy, and gardening skills. The village council of Paqarimuy, a small village in the puna (also called the altiplano, or high-altitude plains of the Andes Mountains), requested help in accomplishing some of these objectives. Therefore, Pablo Fuentes, the managing director of Global Humanitarian in Lima, Peru, is organizing a service expedition to that village. He plans the expedition as a two-week trip. To complete everything he hopes to accomplish, he needs approximately 25 volunteers. He thinks that the best way to recruit volunteers is to present a PowerPoint slide show to interested students at local colleges and universities. During the presentation, he can give an overview to the audience members so that they will have enough information to consider the trip. He can answer questions that the audience might have during and after the presentation. He asks you to help prepare a PowerPoint presentation to prospective expedition participants.

In this tutorial, you'll create a new presentation based on a design template, modify the design template, apply a design template to an existing presentation, and then enhance the presentation by adding graphics to the slides. You will also add a slide summarizing the content of the presentation.

Session	Objectives		SAM Training Tasks	
Session 2.1	• Create a presentation from a template • Apply a new template • Insert, resize, and recolor a clip-art image • Modify the design using the slide master • Insert a bitmap image on a slide	• Reformat text and resize text boxes • Apply a second design template • Insert tab stops to align text • Change the layouts of existing slides • Reposition text boxes	• Add a graphic image from a file • Add and format slide numbers on the slide master • Add clip art images to slides • Add information to the Date/Time area of the slide master • Add information to the Footer area of the slide master • Add information to the Number area of the slide master • Apply more than one design template to presentations • Change a bullet character and color on the slide master • Change the color of a PowerPoint object • Change the size of clip art	• Connect to the Microsoft Office Clip Art and Media Web site • Create a specified type of slide • Create presentations using Design templates • Delete title and subtitle text placeholders • Format slides differently in a single presentation • Format text in slides • Format text on the slide master • Modify presentation templates • Modify the format of slides independent of other slides • Remove a footer from the title slide • Use the Notes and Handouts sheet to add headers and footers
Session 2.2	• Create and modify a table • Create a diagram using the Diagram Gallery • Draw a simple graphic using AutoShapes	• Modify and rotate an AutoShape graphic • Insert and rotate text boxes • Create a summary slide	• Add and modify placeholders • Create a text box • Create tables on slides	• Format a table cell • Insert an AutoShape • Modify a text box

Student Data Files   For a complete list of the Data Files needed for this tutorial, see page PPT 2.

Session 2.1

For hands-on practice of key tasks in this session, go to the SAM 2003 Training Companion CD included with this text.

Planning a Presentation

Before creating his text presentation, Pablo and his staff planned the presentation as follows:

- **Purpose of the presentation**: to convince potential volunteers to apply for a position in the Peru expedition
- **Type of presentation**: an onscreen (electronic) information presentation
- **Audience**: students, health professionals, and other people interested in serving villages in a third-world country
- **Location of the presentation**: a conference room at the offices of Global Humanitarian, as well as classrooms and business offices
- **Audience needs**: to recognize the services they can provide and the adventure they can enjoy as expedition volunteers
- **Format**: one speaker presenting an onscreen slide show consisting of seven to 10 slides

After planning the presentation, Pablo and his staff discuss how they want the slides to look.

Creating a New Presentation from a Design Template

Plain white slides with normal text (such as black Times New Roman or Arial) often fail to hold an audience's attention. In today's information age, audiences expect more interesting color schemes, fonts, graphics, and other effects.

To make it easy to add color and style to your presentations, PowerPoint comes with design templates. A **design template** is a file that contains the color scheme, text formats, background colors and objects, and graphics in the presentation. The **color scheme** is the eight colors used in a design template. A **graphic** is a picture, clip art, photograph, shape, design, graph, chart, or diagram that you can add to a slide. A graphic, like a text box, is an object. Pablo asks you to create a new presentation with the Teamwork design template so that he can see what it looks like.

Reference Window	Creating a New Presentation from a Design Template

- Click File on the menu bar, and then click New.
- Click the From design template link in the New Presentation task pane.
- Click the design template you want to use.

You'll begin enhancing Pablo's presentation by changing the design template.

To create a new presentation from a design template:

1. Start PowerPoint, and then click the **Create a new presentation** link at the bottom of the Getting Started task pane. The New Presentation task pane opens.

   Trouble? If you don't see the Create a new presentation link in the Getting Started task pane, point to the small, downward-pointing triangle at the bottom of the task pane to scroll the task pane automatically so that you can see the commands at the bottom of the task pane.

Trouble? If PowerPoint is already running and the task pane is not open, click File on the menu bar, and then click New to open the New Presentation task pane.

2. Click the **From design template** link in the New Presentation task pane. Slide 1 (the title slide) of a new blank presentation opens in Normal view and the Slide Design task pane opens. Notice that Default Design appears in the status bar below the slide pane to indicate that this is the current design template. A thumbnail showing the Default Design template also appears in the Slide Design task pane under Used in This Presentation. In the Default Design template, the slides have black text on a plain white background.

3. Move the pointer over the **Default Design template** thumbnail under Used in This Presentation in the task pane. A ScreenTip appears, identifying the template. See Figure 2-1.

Blank presentation with Default Design template applied | **Figure 2-1**

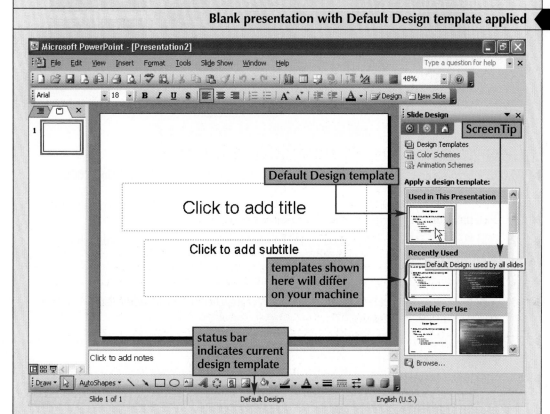

4. Scroll down through the thumbnail views of the design templates, and move the pointer over the thumbnails under **Available For Use** until you find **Teamwork**, a dark green thumbnail.

Trouble? If the Teamwork template is not in the task pane, you must install it. If you are working in a lab, ask your instructor or technical support person for help. If you are working on your own computer, click the Additional Design Templates thumbnail to install additional templates.

5. Click the **Teamwork** design template. The design template of the new presentation changes from Default Design to Teamwork. See Figure 2-2.

Figure 2-2 | **Teamwork design template applied**

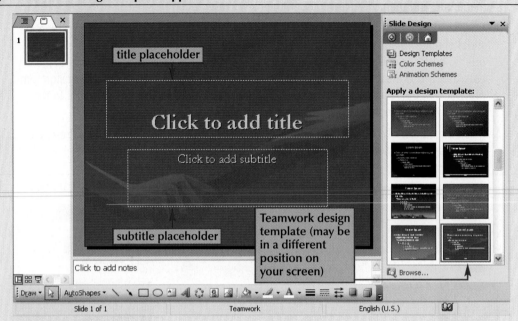

6. Click in the **title** placeholder in the slide pane, and then type **Peru Expedition 2006**.

7. Click in the **subtitle** placeholder and then type your own name.

8. Click the **Close** button ☒ in the Slide Design task pane.

9. Save the presentation as **PeruExp** in the Tutorial.02\Tutorial folder included with your Data Files.

10. Click **File** on the menu bar, and then click **Print** to open the Print dialog box.

11. Click the **Color/grayscale** list arrow, click **Grayscale**, click the **Print what** list arrow, and then click **Slides**, if necessary.

12. Click the **OK** button. The one-page presentation prints in full slide format (one slide fits the entire page).

13. Close the presentation (but leave PowerPoint running).

Pablo takes the new presentation you created, adds more slides to the presentation, and saves the file as PeruExp2. After considering the Teamwork design template, he decides that he doesn't like it because the hands in the background are hard to see. You'll change the design template now.

Applying a Design Template

The design template you choose for your presentation should reflect the content and the intended audience. For example, if you are presenting a new curriculum to a group of elementary school teachers, you might choose a template that uses bright, primary colors. Likewise, if you are presenting a new marketing plan to a mutual fund company, you might choose a plain-looking template that uses dark colors formatted in a way that appears sophisticated.

Although Pablo's presentation is serious, he wants to make the trip seem attractive to prospective participants. He decides that he wants to use a color scheme that includes a dark blue background with a color gradient and some graphics representing the Peruvian Andes Mountains. He thinks such a design would give his presentation more interest.

Applying a Different Design Template

- Display the Slide Design templates in the task pane by clicking the Design button on the Formatting toolbar.
- Scroll through the design template thumbnails until you see one you'd like to apply, and then click the design template thumbnail.

To change the design template:

1. Open the presentation file **PeruExp2** located in the Tutorial.02\Tutorial folder included with your Data Files.

2. Save the file in the same folder using the filename **Peru Expedition**. The presentation title slide appears in the slide pane.

3. Click the **Design** button on the Formatting toolbar to open the Slide Design task pane.

4. Scroll down through the thumbnail views of the design templates in the task pane under Available For Use, and then click the **Mountain Top** template. Don't forget to move the pointer over the templates to see their names. The design template of Peru Expedition changes from Teamwork to Mountain Top. See Figure 2-3.

Presentation with Mountain Top design template applied ◀ Figure 2-3

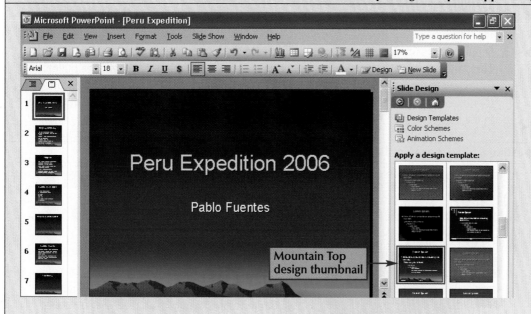

As you can see, the title slide has a dark blue background with varying color, and a background graphic of a mountain top along the bottom of the slide. Next, you'll modify this template to make it more appropriate for this presentation.

Understanding Graphics

Graphics add information, clarification, emphasis, variety, and even pizzazz to a PowerPoint presentation. PowerPoint enables you to include many types of graphics in your presentation: graphics created using another Windows program; scanned photographs, drawings, or cartoons; and other picture files or clip art located on a CD or other disk. You can also create graphics using the drawing tools in PowerPoint. In addition, you can add graphical bullets to a bulleted list.

Inserting Clip Art

Slide 6, "Expedition Information," has six bulleted items of text. Pablo wants to include some clip art to add interest to this slide. In PowerPoint, **clip art** refers specifically to images in the Media Gallery that accompanies Office 2003, or images that are available from the Clip Art and Media section of Microsoft Office Online. Pablo decides that an image of a globe would help emphasize the global aspects of the expedition.

To add clip art to a slide, you can use a slide layout that has a place for clip art, or you can insert the clip art as you would a picture. If you insert clip art using the Insert Clip Art button on the Drawing toolbar, the Clip Art task pane opens and you can search for clips that match keywords you type, and then browse the results. If you insert clip art by clicking a button on a layout that includes a placeholder for clip art, you can browse through all of the clips stored on your machine as well as search for clips that match keywords you type. You'll change the existing slide layout before adding clip art.

To change the layout of a slide and add clip art:

▶ 1. Go to **Slide 6** ("Expedition Information").

▶ 2. Click **Format** on the menu bar, and then click **Slide Layout** to display the Slide Layout task pane.

▶ 3. Scroll down the task pane until you see Text and Content Layouts, and then click the **Title, Text, and Content** layout (the first layout under Text and Content Layouts). The bulleted list moves to the left side of the slide and the content placeholder appears on the right of the slide. See Figure 2-4. Notice that PowerPoint automatically reduces the size of the text in the bulleted list so that it will fit properly within the reduced text box.

Figure 2-4   **Slide 6 after changing slide layout to Title, Text, and Content**

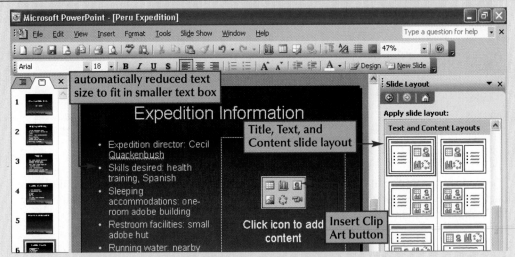

Trouble? If the text size doesn't automatically change or if it doesn't change to a small enough size, click anywhere in the body text, click the AutoFit Options button that appears near the lower-left corner of the body text, and then click the AutoFit Text to Placeholder option button.

4. Click the **Close** button ✕ in the task pane title bar to close the task pane.

5. Click the **Insert Clip Art** button 🖼 in the content placeholder. The Select Picture dialog box opens. If necessary, drag the box by its title bar so you can see all of it. Now you'll search for a piece of clip art that relates to a globe.

6. Type **globe** in the Search text box at the top of the dialog box, and then click the **Go** button. Depending upon how Office was installed on your computer, PowerPoint displays from just a few to over 250 pieces of clip art that contain a representation of a globe.

7. If necessary, drag the scroll button up to the top of the scroll bar in the Select Picture dialog box, and then double-click the image of a globe in the center of a red circular background. The Select Picture dialog box closes, the content placeholder disappears from the slide, and the clip art you selected appears in its place. See Figure 2-5.

Slide 6 with clip art inserted ◄ **Figure 2-5**

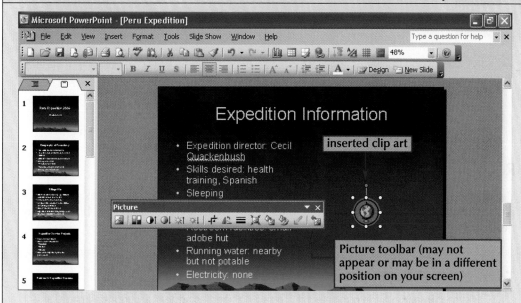

Now you'll modify this clip art image by changing its size and some of its colors.

Resizing Clip Art

The clip art is too small, and so is the body text box, making the autofit text in the bulleted list too small. You will increase the size of the clip art and the text box.

To resize the clip art image:

1. Drag the upper-right corner sizing handle of the globe clip art toward the upper-right corner of the slide until the image is approximately tripled in size.

2. Position the pointer over the selected clip art image so that it changes to ⬆, and then drag the entire clip art image so that it's centered between the top and bottom of the slide, and near the right edge of the slide. Compare your screen to Figure 2-6 and adjust the size or position of the graphic as necessary.

Figure 2-6 ▷ **Slide 6 with repositioned clip art**

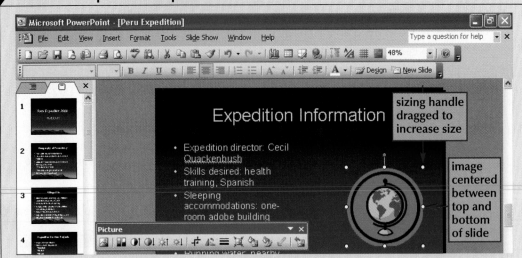

3. Click anywhere in the body text to display the text box and its sizing handles, and then drag the right-center sizing handle to the right until it just touches the left edge of the clip art.

With the clip art inserted and resized, you're ready to change some of the colors.

Recoloring Clip Art

Pablo thinks the red colors on the clip art don't match the blue hues of the design template, so he asks you to change the red to dark blue. You can recolor clip art, but you may not always be able to change the color on other types of pictures.

To recolor a clip art image:

1. Click the **clip art** in Slide 6 to select it. The sizing handles appear around the image, and the Picture toolbar appears.

Trouble? If the Picture toolbar doesn't appear automatically, click View on the menu bar, point to Toolbars, and then click Picture.

2. Click the **Recolor Picture** button 🖼 on the Picture toolbar to display the Recolor Picture dialog box. The colored rectangular tiles under Original are all of the colors used in this piece of clip art.

3. Drag the scroll box down to the bottom of the scroll bar in the dialog box so you can see the red and off-red tiles. See Figure 2-7.

Recolor Picture dialog box ◄ **Figure 2-7**

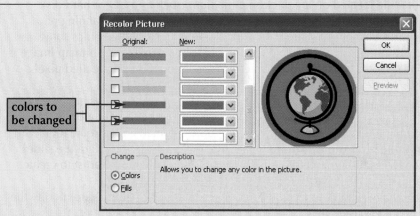

4. Click the **off-red color tile** list arrow in the New column, and then click the **light violet tile** on the palette of default colors. The **default colors** are those colors associated with the overall color scheme of the design template. The globe's shadow in the Preview box changes from off-red to light violet.

5. Change the **red tile** in the New column to the **royal blue tile** (not the dark blue tile) on the palette of default colors.

6. Click the **Preview** button in the Recolor Picture dialog box, and then drag the dialog box by its title bar so that you can see the colors applied to the clip art on the slide. The recolored clip art looks much better than the red colors did.

7. Click the **OK** button, and then click outside the selected object to deselect it. See Figure 2-8.

Recolored clip art and resized body text box ◄ **Figure 2-8**

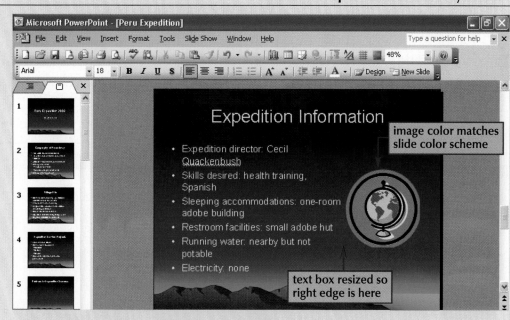

8. Click the **Save** button 🔲 on the Standard toolbar to save your changes.

You'll now add a picture to one of the slides. To add a picture to a slide, the picture must be a computer file located on an electronic medium, such as a CD or hard disk. Picture files are generated by taking photographs with a digital camera, scanning photographs taken with a conventional camera, or drawing pictures using graphics software (such as Microsoft Paint). These types of picture files are bitmap images. A **bitmap image** is a grid (or "map") of colored dots that form a picture. The colored dots are called **pixels**, which stands for picture elements.

Instead of using the current background graphic of the Mountain Top design template, Pablo prefers an actual photograph of the Andes Mountains, in the form of a bitmap image. To get a bitmap file of the Andes Mountains, Pablo scanned a picture he took with a 35mm camera. Pablo also wants to add Global Humanitarian's logo to all of the slides in the presentation. To get a bitmap file of the logo, Pablo hired a graphic artist to create the file using graphics software.

To make these changes to all of the slides in the presentation, you'll need to modify the design template in Slide Master view.

Modifying the Design Template in the Slide Master

A **master** is a slide that contains the elements and styles of the design template, including the text and other objects that appear on all the slides of the same type. Masters never appear when you show or print a presentation. PowerPoint presentations have four types of masters: the **title master**, which contains the objects that appear on the title slide (most presentations have only one title slide, but some have more than one); the **slide master**, which contains the objects that appear on all the slides except the title slide; the **handout master**, which contains the objects that appear on all the printed handouts; and the **notes master**, which contains the objects that appear on the notes pages.

You use slide and title masters so that all the slides in the presentation have a similar design and appearance. This ensures that your presentation is consistent. To make changes to the masters, you need to switch to Slide Master view. You'll do this now.

To switch to Slide Master view:

1. Click **View** on the menu bar, point to **Master**, and then click **Slide Master**. The view changes to Slide Master view, and the Slide Master View toolbar appears. See Figure 2-9.

Figure 2-9	Slide Master view

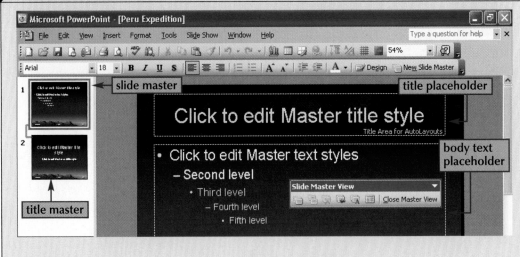

As you can see from the thumbnail slides in the Slides tab, Slide Master view includes two slides: the slide master (as Slide 1) and the title master (as Slide 2). The slide master is currently selected and appears in the slide pane. In Slide Master view, you always see both the slide master and the title master. They appear in Slide Master view as a set, and this is referred to as a **slide-title master pair**.

▶ 2. Click the **title master** (Slide 2) in the Slides tab. The slide pane now displays the master for the title slide.

▶ 3. Click **View** on the menu bar, point to **Master**, and then click **Handout Master**. The layout of handouts appears in the slide pane, and the Handout Master View toolbar appears. You can click the buttons on this toolbar to change the layout of the handout master.

▶ 4. Click **View** on the menu bar, point to **Master**, and then click **Notes Master**. The layout of the notes pages appears in the slide pane, and the Notes Master View toolbar opens.

▶ 5. Click the **Close Master View** button on the Notes Master View floating toolbar. PowerPoint returns to Normal view.

You can modify the slide and title master in Slide Master view by changing the size and design of the title and body text, adding or deleting graphics, and changing the background. You cannot delete or add objects to the background unless you are in Slide Master view.

Modifying Slide and Title Masters

Reference Window

- Click View on the menu bar, point to Master, and then click Slide Master; *or* press and hold the Shift key and then click the Normal View button at the bottom of the Slides or Outline tab to switch to Slide Master view.
- Click the thumbnail of the master slide type that you'd like to modify, either the slide master (Slide 1) or the title master (Slide 2).
- Make any changes to the slide or title master such as changing the background color; modifying the text size, color, font, or alignment; inserting clip art, bitmap images, or other graphics; and changing the size or location of text placeholders.
- Click the Normal View button or click the Close Master View button on the Slide Master View toolbar to return to Normal view.

Before you can insert Pablo's photograph of the Andes Mountains, you must delete the graphic of the mountains currently in the design template.

To modify the slide master:

▶ 1. Switch again to Slide Master view. The slide master appears.

You're going to delete the background image containing the mountain tops. The image is made up of three bitmaps that need to be deleted individually: the sky, the brown mountains, and the dark shading on the mountains.

▶ 2. Position the pointer over the bitmap image so that it changes to ⬚, and then click the teal-green area at the lower-right side of the slide as shown in Figure 2-10. Be careful not to click inside the placeholder titled Object Area for AutoLayouts or inside the placeholder for the Number Area. Sizing handles appear around the selected bitmap.

Figure 2-10 First bitmap in background image selected

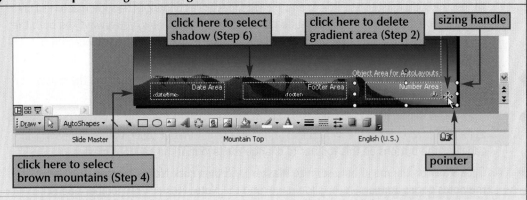

3. Press the **Delete** key. The selected bitmap is deleted.

   Trouble? If you accidentally deleted the Number Area placeholder, click the Undo button ↻ on the Standard toolbar, and then repeat Steps 2 and 3.

4. Click the brown mountain at the lower-left side of the slide as indicated in Figure 2-10. Be careful not to click inside the Date Area placeholder.

5. Press the **Delete** key. The bitmap of the mountains is deleted.

   Trouble? If you accidentally deleted the Date Area placeholder, click the Undo button ↻ on the Standard toolbar, and then repeat Steps 4 and 5.

6. Click the dark brown shadow in the area just above and to the left of the Footer Area placeholder, as indicated in Figure 2-10. Be careful not to click inside the Footer Area placeholder.

7. Press the **Delete** key. The last bitmap is deleted. The bottom of the slide no longer contains any graphics.

   Trouble? If you have difficulty selecting the shadow, click the Footer Area placeholder, press the ↓ key three times, and then repeat Steps 6 and 7. After you delete the shadow, click the Footer Area placeholder again, and then press the ↑ key three times to return the Footer Area placeholder to its original position.

8. Click the **Save** button ⊟ on the Standard toolbar to save your changes.

Because you deleted the mountain graphic in Slide Master view, it will be deleted from every slide in the presentation, except the title slide. Now you'll insert the new photo of the Andes Mountains on all of the slides.

Inserting and Modifying a Bitmap Image on a Slide

To add the new bitmap image to all of the slides, you will insert it on the slide master in Slide Master view. To insert a bitmap image on just one slide, you use the same procedure in Normal view.

Inserting a Graphic on a Slide

- If necessary, switch to Normal view, and then open the Slide Layout task pane by clicking Format on the menu bar and clicking Slide Layout.
- Click one of the Content layouts or one of the Text and Content layouts to change the layout of the current slide.
- Click the Insert Clip Art or Insert Picture button in the content placeholder, and then find the desired clip art or navigate to the folder containing the desired picture file.
- Double-click the graphic that you want to insert into the slide.
  or
- Click the Insert Picture button on the Drawing toolbar, navigate to and click the picture file you want to insert, and then click the Insert button.

To insert a graphic into a slide:

1. Click the **Insert Picture** button 🖻 on the Drawing toolbar. The Insert Picture dialog box opens.

2. Navigate to the Tutorial.02\Tutorial folder included with your Data Files.

3. Click **MntTop**, the bitmap image file of the photograph, and click the **Insert** button. The picture is inserted into your slide master in the middle of the slide, and the Picture toolbar appears.

   Trouble? If the Picture toolbar doesn't appear, click View on the menu bar, point to Toolbars, and then click Picture.

You need to move and resize the image to fit along the bottom of the slide master.

To reposition and resize a picture on a slide:

1. Position the pointer over the bitmap image so that it changes to ⌖, and then drag the photo to the lower-left corner of the slide. See Figure 2-11.

Slide master with bitmap image ◀ Figure 2-11

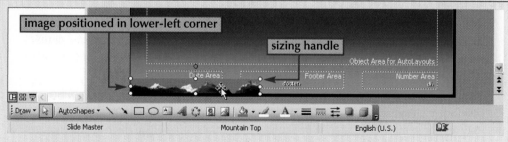

Trouble? If the Picture or Slide Master View toolbar covers the lower-left corner, drag the toolbar by its title bar to another location on the screen.

As you can see, the selected bitmap image has sizing handles in each corner and on each side of the picture. You'll drag a sizing handle to resize the image to the width of the slide.

2. Drag the upper-right sizing handle up and to the right until the width of the bitmap image is the same as the width of the slide, and approximately double its original height. See Figure 2-12. Because you are dragging a corner sizing handle, the height and width of the image resizes proportionally.

| Figure 2-12 | Resized picture of Andes Mountains |

You have two tasks left to perform on the bitmap image. First, the blue sky in the background of the photo interrupts the gradient colors in the background. You'll set a transparent color, which is a color on the bitmap image that becomes transparent (invisible). Second, you'll change the order of objects so that the bitmap image is behind the placeholders at the foot of the slide.

To set a color to transparent in a bitmap image:

1. Make sure the image is still selected, and then click the **Set Transparent Color** button on the Picture toolbar. The pointer changes to .

2. Click anywhere in the blue sky above the mountain tops in the bitmap image. The sky color becomes transparent so that the slide background color appears.

Now you want to make sure the mountain top picture is behind the three text placeholders at the bottom of the slide. To do this, you will change the order of the objects on the slide. Imagine each object is on a piece of paper and you lay each piece of paper down on the slide as you add objects. Objects you add last will be on top of the other objects on the slide.

To change the order of objects on a slide:

1. Make sure the image is still selected, click the **Draw** button on the Drawing toolbar, point to **Order**, and then click **Send to Back**. The bitmap image is sent to the back of all the objects on the slide master, including the slide background, so you can no longer see the mountains. Therefore, you need to move the mountains one object forward.

2. Make sure you can still see the sizing handles of the selected image, click the **Draw** button on the Drawing toolbar, point to **Order**, and then click **Bring Forward**. The mountains now properly appear in the slide master, in front of the background but behind the text placeholders.

   Trouble? If you accidentally deselected the mountain image before you brought it forward again, click the Undo button on the Standard toolbar to bring the image to the front again, and then repeat Steps 1 and 2.

As you can see, changing the drawing of mountaintops to a digital photograph of Andean mountaintops makes the background graphic more realistic. Now you'll make the same changes on the title master that you just made on the slide master.

To change the background graphic on the title master:

1. Make sure the resized bitmap image that you just added to the slide master is still selected, and then click the **Copy** button 🖻 on the Standard toolbar. The image is copied to the Clipboard.

2. Click the **title master** thumbnail (Slide 2) in the Slides tab. The title master appears in the slide pane. The original drawing of the mountain top appears at the bottom of the slide.

3. Delete all three components of the original mountain top drawing, as you did before.

4. Click the **Paste** button 🖺 on the Formatting toolbar to paste the bitmap image on the slide.

5. Send the image to the back, so that it's behind all the other objects on the title master, and then bring it forward one object to place it in front of the background. Now both the title master and the slide master have the bitmap image of Andean mountaintops as a background picture in the design template.

6. Click the **Save** button 🖫 on the Standard toolbar to save your changes.

Next, Pablo wants you to change the font of the body text on the slide master, and to modify the color of the title text on the slide master.

Modifying Text on a Slide

In PowerPoint, text is described in terms of the font, font size, and font style. A **font** is the design of a set of characters. Some names of fonts include Arial, Times New Roman, Helvetica, and Garamond. Font size is measured in **points**. Text in a book is typically printed in 10- or 12-point type. **Font style** refers to special attributes applied to the characters; for example, bold and italics are font styles.

Pablo wants you to replace the current subtitle and body text font (Arial) with a different font (Times New Roman), and to change the color of the title text from light violet to light blue. He also wants you to add the Global Humanitarian logo on the slides by placing it next to the title text on each slide.

Modifying the Format of Text on a Slide

To change the format of all the text in a text box, you first need to select the text box. To do this, you click the edge of it. This changes the text box border to a thick line composed of little dots. On the other hand, when you click *inside* a text box, you make the box active—that is, ready to accept text that you type or paste—but this doesn't select the text box, as indicated by the borders composed of slanted lines. When you select a text box (with a border of a thick line composed of little dots), any formatting changes you make are global formatting changes and are applied to all of the text in the text box. (This is different than if you select specific text within the text box and make a local formatting change to the selected text.)

You'll now select text boxes in the slide and title to change the font on all the slides.

To modify the fonts in text boxes on a slide:

1. Click the **slide master** thumbnail (Slide 1) in the Slides tab.

2. Click the dotted-line edge of the body text placeholder on the slide master in the slide pane. The entire placeholder text box is selected, as indicated by the border, which is now a thick line composed of little dots and sizing handles.

   Trouble? If the box surrounding the placeholder is composed of slanted lines, the text box is active, not selected. Click the edge of the text box to change it to a thick line composed of dots.

3. Click the **Font** list arrow Arial ▾ on the Formatting toolbar, scroll down, if necessary, and then click **Times New Roman** to change the body text font from Arial to Times New Roman.

4. Click the dotted-line edge of the title placeholder to select the entire text box, click the **Font Color** list arrow A ▾ on the Drawing or Formatting toolbar, click **More Colors** to open the Colors dialog box, and then click the **Standard** tab. You can now see a honeycomb of color cells from which to select a new font color. See Figure 2-13.

| Figure 2-13 | Standard tab in the Colors dialog box |

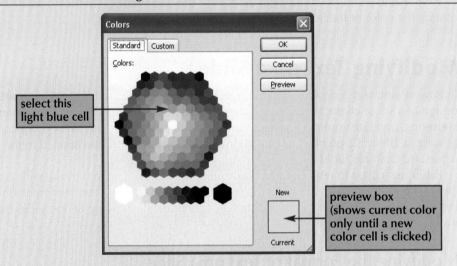

select this light blue cell

preview box (shows current color only until a new color cell is clicked)

5. Click the light blue cell, as indicated in Figure 2-13. The light blue color appears under New in the preview box in the lower-right corner of the dialog box.

6. Click the **OK** button. The font color of the title on the slide master changes from light violet to light blue. Now you'll change the text alignment so that the title text on the slide master is left-aligned rather than centered.

7. With the title text box still selected, click the **Align Left** button ▤ on the Formatting toolbar. The title text is now left-aligned.

8. Click the **title master** thumbnail (Slide 2) in the Slides tab. Note that the changes you made to the text boxes on the slide master have also been applied to the text boxes on the title master. Any changes you make to the format of the text on the slide master are also applied to the text on the title master. This does not, however, work in reverse; in other words, text-formatting changes that you make to the title master do not affect the text on the slide master.

   You don't want the title text on the title master left-aligned.

9. Select the **title** text box on the title master, and then click the **Center** button 🔲 on the Formatting toolbar. The text is center-aligned, while the title text on the slide master stays left-aligned.

Next, you need to resize the title text box on the slide so you can insert the Global Humanitarian logo next to the title.

Resizing a Text Box on a Slide

To resize a text box, you need to select it, and then drag a sizing handle. You'll resize the title text box on the slide master by dragging the left-center sizing handle. As with the formatting changes you made to the text, you would follow this same procedure to resize text boxes in Normal view.

To resize a text box:

1. Click the **slide master** thumbnail in the Slides tab, and then select the title text box. The sizing handles appear.

2. Drag the left-center sizing handle to the right approximately one inch, as shown in Figure 2-14, and then release the mouse button. This leaves room for the logo, which will go in the upper-left corner of the slide master, to the left of the title text box.

Resizing the title text placeholder ◀ **Figure 2-14**

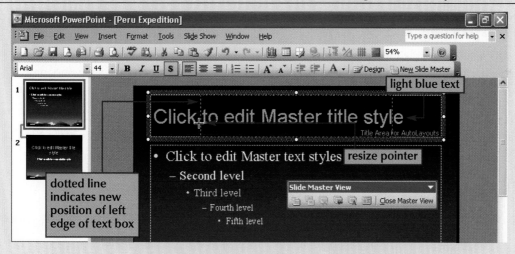

3. Insert the picture file **GHLogo**, located in the Tutorial.02\Tutorial folder included with your Data Files, into the slide master.

4. Drag the logo up near the upper-left corner of the slide, so that the top of the logo is aligned with the top of the title text box.

5. Drag the lower-right sizing handle up and to the left until the logo just fits in the space to the left of the title placeholder.

6. Set the black area surrounding the globe to transparent, and then click a blank area of the slide to deselect the logo. See Figure 2-15.

Figure 2-15 ▶ **Slide master after adding and reformatting logo**

Trouble? If your slide master does not look like the one shown in Figure 2-15, make any necessary adjustments now.

▶ 7. Click the **Close Master View** button on the Slide Master View toolbar. The presentation returns to Normal view.

▶ 8. Save the presentation.

Applying a Second Design Template

Normally all your slides in one presentation will have the same design template. On occasion, however, you might want to apply a second design template to only one, or a few, of the slides in your presentation. Pablo wants you to change the design template for Slide 8, "Expedition Costs (Per Person)" from the modified Mountain Top design template to the Globe design template. All of the other slides present points about the expedition itself. He wants this slide to stand out from the others because it lists the costs of the trip for each participant.

To apply a second design template to a presentation:

▶ 1. Go to **Slide 8** ("Expedition Costs (Per Person)"). When you want to apply a design template to only one slide, you'll usually want that slide to appear in the slide pane.

▶ 2. Click the **Design** button on the Formatting toolbar to open the Slide Design task pane.

▶ 3. Scroll the task pane until you locate the Globe design template, but do not click it. If you just click the Globe design template, it will appear on all the slides rather than just the selected slide.

▶ 4. Position the pointer over the **Globe** design template, and then click the **Design Template** list arrow. See Figure 2-16.

Applying a new design template to this slide only | **Figure 2-16**

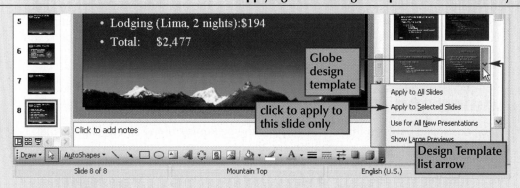

Trouble? If you clicked the design thumbnail instead of the Design Template list arrow, click the Undo button ⟲ on the Standard toolbar, and then repeat Step 4.

5. Click **Apply to Selected Slides**. Because Slide 8 is the only selected slide in the Slides tab, it's the only one to which the design template is applied.

6. Click the **Close** button ✕ in the Slide Design task pane, select the title text box in the slide pane, and then adjust the size and alignment of the title text box so that it's similar to the title text box on the other slides and so that the text doesn't overlap the Global Humanitarian logo. You need to change the body text font to match the other slide.

7. Select the body text box, change the font to Times New Roman, change the font size to 36, and then click a blank area of the slide. See Figure 2-17.

Slide 8 with Globe design template | **Figure 2-17**

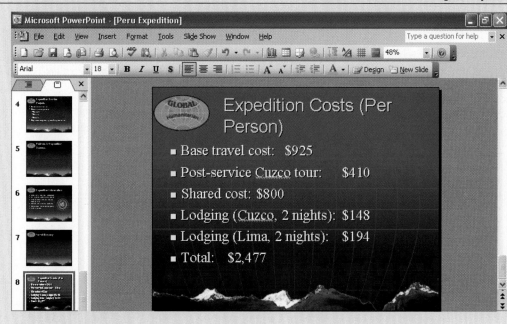

8. Save your changes.

You applied the Globe design template to only one slide in the presentation. The modified Mountain Top design remains on the other slides. The next time you switch to Slide Master view, you will see a second slide-title master pair for the Globe design template below the customized Mountain Top slide-title master pair. Now you need to modify the tab stops on Slide 8 to align the dollar amounts.

Adding and Modifying Tab Stops

A **tab** adds space between the left margin and the beginning of the text on a particular line, or between the text in one column and the text in another column. (When you create several long columns of data, however, you probably want to use a table instead of tabs.) For example, in Slide 8 ("Expedition Costs"), Pablo typed the cost description and a colon, pressed the Tab key to add space, and then typed the dollar amounts for each expense. A **tab stop** is the location where the insertion point moves (including any text to the right of it) when you press the Tab key. The default tab stops on a slide are set at one-inch intervals. You can add your own tab stops to override the default tab stops to align text on a slide. You can set tab stops so that the text left-aligns, right-aligns, center-aligns, or aligns on a decimal point.

The default tab stops on the ruler are left tabs, which position the left edge of text at the tab stop and extend the text to the right. However, you want to align the right sides of the dollar amounts in Slide 8, so you want to use a right tab stop, which positions the right edge of text at the tab stop and extends the text to the left. You'll change the tab stops on Slide 8 now.

To change the tab stops:

▶ **1.** Click **View** on the menu bar, and then click **Ruler**. Horizontal and vertical rulers appear on the screen.

Trouble? If rulers were already visible on your screen, then clicking Ruler on the View menu hid them. Click View on the menu bar, and then click Ruler again to redisplay the rulers.

▶ **2.** Click anywhere in the body text box. The default tab stops for the body text appear as light gray rectangles, or hash marks, under the ruler, and the Left Tab button appears to the left of the horizontal ruler. When Pablo typed the text on this slide, he pressed the Tab key after typing the colon in each line, so the dollar amounts on each line are aligned at the next available tab stop. See Figure 2-18.

Tabs for body text box on ruler 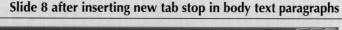 **Figure 2-18**

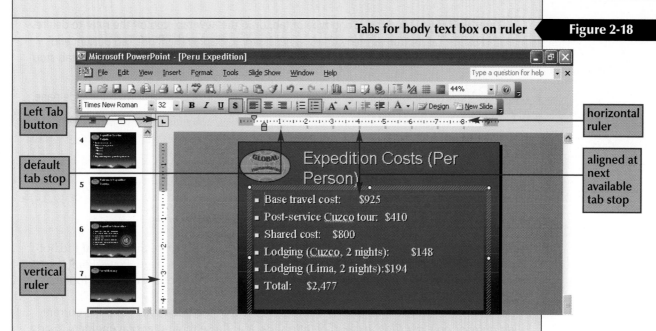

Trouble? If a button other than the Left Tab button appears to the left of the ruler, click the Tab button as many times as necessary until the Left Tab button appears.

3. Click the **Left Tab** button ⌞ to the left of the horizontal ruler so that the button changes to the Center Tab button ⊥, and then click the **Center Tab** button ⊥ to change it to the Right Tab button ⌟. If you were to click the Tab button again, the Decimal Tab button ⊥ would appear, and if you were to click once more, the Left Tab button would appear again.

4. Position the pointer immediately before the word "Base" in the first bulleted item, and then click and drag to the bottom of the body text to select all of the bulleted items. The selected text is highlighted.

5. Click just below the 8-inch mark in the white area of the horizontal ruler, and then click anywhere within the selected text. A new, right tab stop appears at the location you clicked, the default tab stops to the left of the new tab stop disappear, and the dollar amounts in the body text box become right-aligned at the new tab stop. See Figure 2-19.

Slide 8 after inserting new tab stop in body text paragraphs **Figure 2-19**

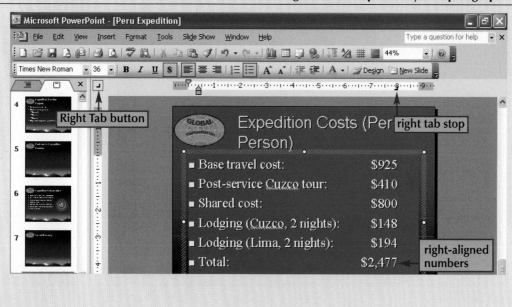

Trouble? If you used the wrong type of tab, drag the new tab stop off the ruler to delete it, click the Tab button as many times as necessary to display the Right Tab button, and then repeat Steps 4 and 5. If you clicked in the wrong place on the ruler, drag the tab stop character to the right or left until it's positioned where you want it.

▶ **6.** Click **View** on the menu bar, and then click **Ruler**. The rulers disappear from the slide pane.

▶ **7.** Click a blank area of the slide pane to deselect the text box, and then save your changes.

Next, you'll insert footers and slide numbers.

Inserting Footers and Slide Numbers

When you used the AutoContent wizard, you typed footer text to be displayed at the bottom of each slide. A **header** is text that appears at the top of each page. PowerPoint already provides a footer placeholder on the slide master, and both header and footer placeholders on the notes and handout masters.

As part of the overall slide design, Pablo wants you to include footers and the current slide number on each slide, except the title slide. You'll use the footer placeholders to add the footer and the slide number to each of the slides (except the title slide).

To insert a footer into your presentation:

▶ **1.** Click **View** on the menu bar, click **Header and Footer** to open the Header and Footer dialog box, and then click the **Slide** tab, if necessary, to display the slide footer information. In the Preview box in the lower-right corner of the dialog box, two of the rectangles at the bottom of the preview slide are black. These black rectangles correspond to the selected check boxes on the Slides tab, in this case, the Date and time and the Footer check boxes.

▶ **2.** Click the **Date and time** check box to clear it. The left rectangle in the Preview box turns white.

▶ **3.** Click the **Slide number** check box to select it. The right rectangle in the Preview box turns black. Now the slide number will appear on each slide.

▶ **4.** Make sure the Footer check box is selected, and then click in the **Footer** text box.

▶ **5.** Type **Peru Expedition 2006**, and then click the **Don't show on title slide** check box to select it. See Figure 2-20. The slide number and the text you typed in the Footer text box will appear on every slide except the title slide.

Header and Footer dialog box | **Figure 2-20**

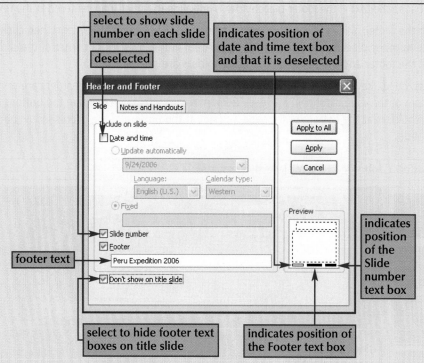

select to show slide number on each slide

indicates position of date and time text box and that it is deselected

deselected

footer text

select to hide footer text boxes on title slide

indicates position of the Footer text box

indicates position of the Slide number text box

▶ **6.** Click the **Apply to All** button in the Header and Footer dialog box. All the slides (except the title slide) now contain a footer.

The footer has several problems. First, after you applied the new design template to Slide 8, the mountains at the bottom of the slide appear in front of the footer. Second, the footer text isn't legible because the font is too small and its white color makes it unreadable against the white peak of an Andean mountaintop. You can solve these problems by modifying the slide master of the Globe design template, moving the footer on the slide master so that it appears on the left side of the slide, and increasing the font size of the text in the footer. Before you can reposition the footer placeholder text box, you need to delete the date and time placeholder text box.

To delete and reposition text boxes:

▶ **1.** Display the slide master, make sure the slide master of the Globe design (Slide 3 in the Slides tab) is selected, and send the mountain bitmap image to the back and bring it forward in front of the background, as before.

▶ **2.** On the same slide master, click the edge of the **date and time** placeholder (labeled Date Area) in the lower-left corner of the slide, and press the **Delete** key. The placeholder text box is deleted.

▶ **3.** Select the **footer** placeholder (labeled Footer Area), currently located in the bottom middle of the slide, and then press the ← key until the placeholder is aligned on the left with the body text placeholder. By using the ← key rather than dragging and dropping, you ensure that you move the placeholder horizontally but not vertically.

4. With the footer placeholder still selected, click the **Align Left** button ▤ on the Formatting toolbar so the text in the footer placeholder is left-aligned rather than centered in the text box.

5. With the footer placeholder still selected, press and hold the **Shift** key, and then click the **slide number** placeholder (labeled Number Area) in the lower-right corner of the slide. Both the footer and the slide number placeholders are selected.

6. Press the ↓ key two or three times until the bottoms of the two placeholders are on the bottom of the slide, as shown in Figure 2-21. Make sure that you position the bottom of the placeholders at the bottom of the slide and not at the bottom of the drop shadow behind the slide.

Figure 2-21	Reformatted Globe design template slide master

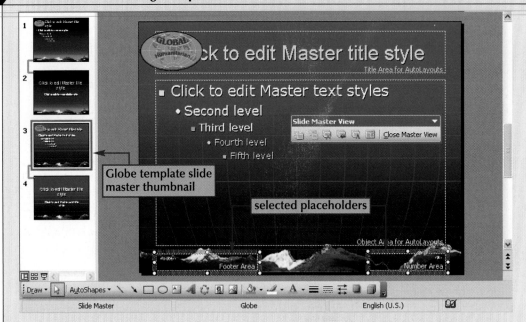

Trouble? If you can't position the text boxes where you want to, press and hold the Ctrl key while you press the ↓ key to nudge the placeholders in smaller increments than pressing the ↓ key alone.

7. With the footer and slide number placeholders still selected, click the **Font Size** list arrow 10 ▾ on the Formatting toolbar, and then click **24** to change the font size to 24 points.

8. Click the **Mountain Top slide master** (Slide 1) in the Slides tab and then repeat Steps 2 through 7 to make the same changes on the slide master of the Mountain Top design template.

9. Click the **Close Master View** button on the Slide Master View toolbar. Now you can read the footer text and the slide number, but the footer text wraps to a second line because the footer placeholder is too small to contain all the footer text on one line.

10. Switch back to Slide Master view, select the footer placeholder, and then drag the right-center sizing handle of the footer placeholder to the right until the right edge of the text box is near the center of the slide.

11. Repeat Step 10 on the Mountain Top slide master, and then click the **Normal View** button ▤ at the bottom of the Slides tab.

12. Go to **Slide 4** to make sure that you can read the footer and the slide number on a slide with the Mountain Top design template. See Figure 2-22.

Slide 4 with adjusted footer and slide number ◄ **Figure 2-22**

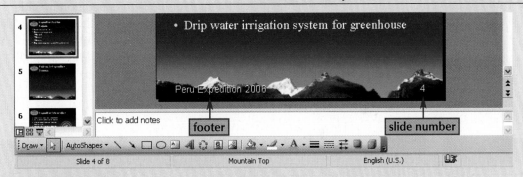

Trouble? If your footer and slide number aren't the same font size and color and in the same position as shown in Figure 2-22, return to Slide Master view and make any necessary adjustments.

13. Save the presentation.

Pablo is pleased with how the footer and page number appear at the bottom of each slide. You've completed most of Pablo's presentation. In Session 2.2, you'll finalize the slides by creating a table, diagram, and simple drawing.

Session 2.1 Quick Check

1. List at least three reasons to add graphics to your presentation.
2. Explain the meaning of the following terms:
   a. design template
   b. bitmap image
   c. graphic
   d. Default Design template
3. Describe how to do the following:
   a. make a text box active
   b. select a text box
   c. scale a graphic to change its size
   d. move an object on a slide
   e. apply a second design template to selected slides
   f. recolor clip art
4. What is the difference between the title master and the slide master?
5. What are tabs? What are tab stops? Describe how to insert a right tab stop on the ruler.
6. What are the three objects included in a footer on a slide as part of the master?

Review

To reinforce the tasks you learned in this session, go to the SAM 2003 Training Companion CD included with this text.

Session 2.2

For hands-on practice of key tasks in this session, go to the SAM 2003 Training Companion CD included with this text.

Creating a Table in a Slide

Pablo wants you to create a table listing the travel itinerary for the Peru expedition in Slide 7. A **table** is information arranged in horizontal rows and vertical columns. The area where a row and column intersect is called a **cell**. Each cell contains one piece of information and is identified by a column and row label; for example, the cell in the upper-left corner of a table is cell A1 (column A, row 1), the cell to the right of that is B1, the cell below A1 is A2, and so forth. A table's structure is indicated by borders, which are lines that outline the rows and columns.

Reference Window | **Inserting a Table on a Slide**

- Click Format on the menu bar, and then click Slide Layout to open the Slide Layout task pane.
- Change the slide layout of the desired slide to one of the Content layouts.
- Click the Insert Table button.
- Specify the desired table size—the numbers of columns and rows—and then click the OK button.
- Add information to the cells. Use the Tab key to move from one cell to the next, and the Shift+Tab keys to move to previous cells.
- Modify the borders as desired.
- Click in a blank area of the slide to deselect the table.

The itinerary table you'll create needs to have four columns: one for the date of travel, one for the departure or arrival city, one for the time of departure or arrival, and one for the flight number. The table needs to have nine rows: one row for column labels, and eight rows for the data. Now you'll create the travel itinerary table.

To create a table:

1. If you took a break after the previous session, make sure PowerPoint is running, and then open the presentation **Peru Expedition** located in the Tutorial.02\Tutorial folder included with your Data Files.

2. Go to **Slide 7** ("Travel Itinerary"), click **Format** on the menu bar, and then click **Slide Layout** to open the Slide Layout task pane.

3. Click the **Title and Content** layout. The layout of the current slide changes.

4. Click the **Insert Table** button 🖽 in the content placeholder in the slide pane. The Insert Table dialog box opens.

5. Type **4** in the Number of columns text box, press the **Tab** key to move the insertion point to the Number of rows text box, type **9**, and then click the **OK** button. A table made up of four columns and nine rows is inserted in the slide with the insertion point blinking in the first cell (cell A1), and the Tables and Borders toolbar opens.

   Trouble? If the table doesn't have four columns and nine rows, click the Undo button 🔄 on the Standard toolbar to undo your creation of the table, and then repeat Steps 4 and 5.

Trouble? If the Tables and Borders toolbar doesn't appear, click View on the main menu bar, point to Toolbars, and then click Tables and Borders.

6. Close the task pane.

Now you're ready to fill the blank cells with information. To enter data in a table, you click in the cell in which you want to enter data. Once you start typing in a cell, you can use the Tab and arrow keys to move from one cell to another. If you want to add a new row at the bottom of the table, move the insertion point to the last cell in the table, and then press the Tab key. A new row will be inserted automatically.

To add information to the table:

1. With the insertion point blinking in the first cell, type **Date**, press the **Tab** key to move to cell B1, type **City**, press the **Tab** key to move to cell C1, type **Time**, press the **Tab** key to move to cell D1 (the last cell in the first row), and then type **Flight**. This completes the column labels.

   Trouble? You might have to drag the Tables and Borders toolbar by its title bar to see the table cells.

2. Press the **Tab** key. The insertion point moves to cell A2.

3. Type **Dec. 25**, and then press the **Tab** key to move to cell B2.

4. Type **Lv Dallas** (short for "Leave Dallas") in cell B2, type **4:22 PM** in cell C2, and then type **AA 982** (short for American Airlines flight 982) in cell D2. This completes the first row of data.

5. Complete the information in the rest of the cells, as shown in Figure 2-23, and then click a blank area of the slide to deselect the table.

Slide 7 with completed table | **Figure 2-23**

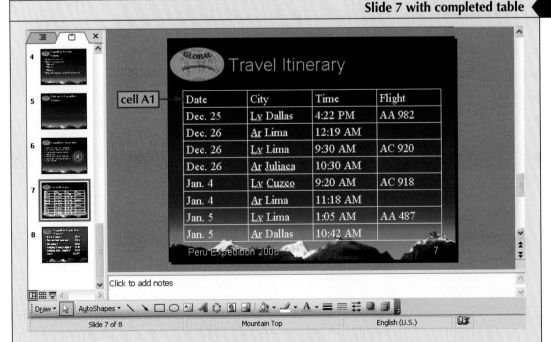

Trouble? If you pressed the Tab key after typing the last enty, you added a new row to the table. Click the Undo button [↺] on the Standard toolbar to remove the extra row.

To make the column labels appear visually separated from the data, you'll change the border below the top row so that it is more visible.

To draw a border:

▶ 1. Click anywhere in the table to make it active and display the Tables and Borders toolbar.

▶ 2. Click the **Draw Table** button 🖼 on the Tables and Borders toolbar, and then move the pointer off of the toolbar. The pointer changes to ⧸.

▶ 3. Click the **Border Width** list arrow 1 pt ▾ on the Tables and Borders toolbar, and then click **3 pt** to change the border line width to three points.

▶ 4. Click the **Border Color** button 🖉 on the Tables and Borders toolbar, and then click the light blue tile (the custom color *below* the main row of tiles). Now when you draw a border, it will be a 3-point, light blue line.

▶ 5. Drag ⧸ along the border between the first and second rows in the table. As you draw the border, a dotted line appears to indicate the border as it is drawn. When you release the mouse button, the light blue line appears.

▶ 6. Click the **Draw Table** button 🖼 on the Table and Borders toolbar to deselect it.

In addition to changing the border lines in a table, you can add and change diagonal lines within cells of a table. First, click the Table button on the Tables and Borders toolbar, click Borders and Fill, click the Borders tab, and then click one or both of the Diagonal Line buttons.

Although the colored border visually separates the column labels from the data in the table, the labels would stand out more if they were formatted differently from the data. You will format the text in the top row to be a light blue, bold, Arial font.

To modify the font in a table:

▶ 1. Drag I across all the text in the top row to select it.

▶ 2. Change the font to **Arial**, as you would any other type of text.

▶ 3. Click the **Bold** button **B** on the Formatting toolbar to make the selected text bold.

▶ 4. Click the **Font Color** list arrow **A ▾** on the Drawing or Formatting toolbar, and then click the light blue tile (the custom color *below* the main row of tiles).

▶ 5. Click a blank area of the slide pane to deselect the table. See Figure 2-24.

Table after modifying border and column headings   **Figure 2-24**

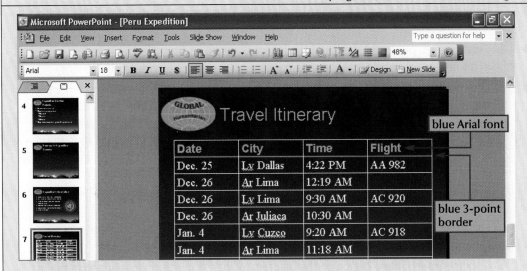

6. Save your changes.

You have completed the table that shows the flight itinerary for the Peru expedition. The Tables and Borders toolbar also lets you remove rows, add and remove columns, combine cells, split cells, and perform other modifications to the table. If you want to do any of these tasks, use PowerPoint's Help system. In addition, try right-clicking anywhere on the table to see a shortcut menu containing commands specific to working with tables.

Your next task is to create a diagram on Slide 5 to show the relationship between the four major parties involved in a humanitarian service project.

Creating a Diagram on a Slide

PowerPoint allows you to create the following types of diagrams on slides:

- **Cycle diagrams**—show a process that has a continuous cycle
- **Organizational charts**—show the relationship between individuals or units within an organization
- **Radial diagrams**—show the relationships of a core element
- **Pyramid diagrams**—show foundation-based relationships
- **Venn diagrams**—show areas of overlap between elements
- **Target diagrams**—show steps toward a goal

In the Peru Expedition presentation, Pablo wants you to add a Venn diagram on Slide 5 ("Partners in Expedition Success") to show the relationship between the four major parties involved in a humanitarian service project: the village for which the service is being performed, the volunteers who perform the service, the humanitarian organization that sponsors the service, and the donors who contribute money to support the service. You'll create the Venn diagram now.

To create a Venn diagram:

1. Go to **Slide 5**, and then change the layout to the **Title and Content** layout in the Content Layouts section.

2. Close the task pane, and then click the **Insert Diagram or Organization Chart** button in the content placeholder in the slide pane. The Diagram Gallery dialog box opens.

3. Click the **Venn Diagram** icon (the middle icon in the second row), and then click the **OK** button. A diagram with three intersecting circles and text box placeholders is added to the slide, and the Diagram toolbar opens. The text box placeholders are hard to see on the dark blue part of the background. Selection handles—gray circles with small *X*s in them—appear around the top circle in the diagram. When you see selection handles instead of sizing handles on a slide, it means that the selected object is part of a larger object, and although you can modify the selected object by changing its color or other attributes, you can't resize the individual object.

   Next, you'll edit the diagram by adding another circle, adding text, and modifying the circle colors.

4. Click the **Insert Shape** button on the Diagram toolbar. A fourth circle is added to the diagram. The new circle is the same color as the bottom circle. You'll change the color of the bottom circle.

5. Right-click the bottom circle, click **Format AutoShape** on the shortcut menu to open the Format AutoShape dialog box, and then click the **Colors and Lines** tab, if necessary.

6. Click the **Color** list arrow in the Fill section at the top of the dialog box, and then click the light blue tile (the custom color) located on its own row just above the More Colors command.

7. Click the **OK** button. The bottom circle is recolored light blue. See Figure 2-25.

Figure 2-25 ▶ **Venn diagram with new shape added**

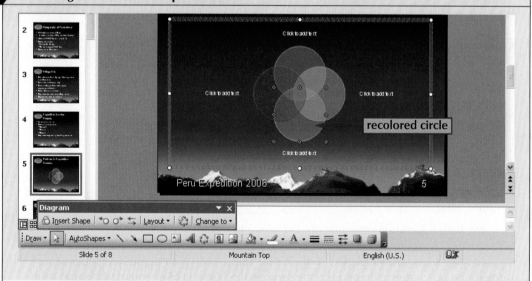

Now you'll label each circle in the Venn diagram.

To add and modify text in the Venn diagram:

1. Click in the text box placeholder (labeled "Click to add text") above the top circle, and then type **Village**.

2. Type **Volunteers** in the text box placeholder to the right of the right circle.

3. Click in the text box placeholder to the left of the left circle, type **Global**, press the **Enter** key, and then type **Humanitarian**.

4. Type **Donors** in the text box placeholder below the bottom circle.

   Because the font of the text around the Venn diagram is small, the text is hard to read. You'll increase the font size now.

5. Shift-click the four text boxes (press and hold the Shift key, and then click each of the text boxes) to select them all, and then change the font size to **24** points.

6. Click a blank area of the slide pane to deselect everything in the slide. See Figure 2-26.

Slide 5 with completed Venn diagram ◄ **Figure 2-26**

7. Save your changes.

This completes the diagram on Slide 5. When Pablo uses this slide show to give a presentation, he'll discuss how the roles of the village, volunteers, donors, and Global Humanitarian overlap to make a successful project.

Pablo now asks you to insert a new Slide 6, and create a shape in the slide.

Creating and Manipulating a Shape

For the last graphic to be included in his presentation, Pablo asks you to add an inverted triangle with labels along each side to a new Slide 6. The labels on each side of the triangle will list the three components of the Global Humanitarian strategy—village outreach projects, expeditions, and internships. Pablo wants you to use an equilateral triangle to point out that each of the three strategies is equally important. This graphic will be a strong visual reminder to potential Global Humanitarian contributors and volunteers of this threefold strategy.

To create the triangle, you'll use the triangle AutoShape. When you click the AutoShapes button on the Drawing toolbar, you are presented with the following categories of shapes from which to choose: lines, connectors, basic shapes (for example, rectangles and triangles), block arrows, flowchart shapes, stars and banners, callouts, and action buttons.

To insert a shape in a slide using AutoShapes:

1. Insert a new Slide 6, change the slide layout to **Title Only** (under Text Layouts), and then close the Slide Layout task pane.

2. Type **Global Humanitarian Strategy** in the title placeholder.

3. Click the **AutoShapes** button on the Drawing toolbar, and then point to **Basic Shapes**. The Basic Shapes palette opens.

4. Click the **Isosceles Triangle** button on the Basic Shapes palette, as indicated in Figure 2-27, and then position the pointer over the slide in the slide pane. The pointer changes to $+$.

Figure 2-27	Selecting an AutoShape

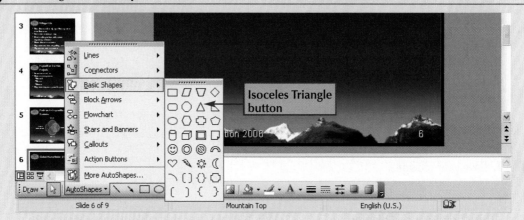

5. Position $+$ approximately one inch below the "o" in "Global" (in the title of the slide), press and hold down the **Shift** key, and then click and and drag the pointer down and to the right. The outline of a triangle appears as you drag. Pressing the Shift key while you drag makes the triangle equilateral—the three sides are of equal length. (Similarly, if you click the Oval button, you can press and hold the Shift key while you drag to draw a circle, and if you click the Rectangle button, you can press and hold the Shift key while you drag to draw a square.)

6. Release the mouse button and the Shift key when your triangle is approximately the same size and shape as the one shown in Figure 2-28.

Slide 6 with isosceles triangle shape | **Figure 2-28**

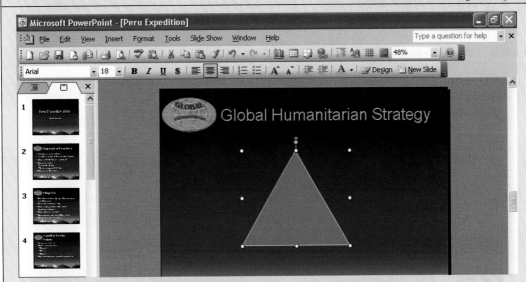

Trouble? If your triangle doesn't look like the one in Figure 2-28, you can move it by dragging it to a new location, resize or change its shape by dragging one or more of the sizing handles, or delete it by pressing the Delete key, and then repeating Steps 3 through 6 to redraw it.

In addition to the sizing handles, the selected triangle has a yellow diamond and a green circle at its top. The yellow diamond is an **adjustment handle**; if you drag it, the shape of the tip of the triangle changes without changing the overall size of the object. The green circle is the **rotate handle**, which you can drag to rotate the shape.

The default color of the drawn object is the blue color from the set of default colors, but Pablo prefers the same color of blue as the title text.

To change the fill color of an AutoShape:

1. With the triangle still selected, click the **Fill Color** list arrow on the Drawing toolbar. The color palette appears on the screen.

2. Click the light blue tile (the custom color located below the row of default tiles). The color of the triangle changes to light blue.

The triangle is the desired size and color, but Pablo wants you to flip (invert) the triangle so that it points down instead of up. You can use commands on the Draw menu on the Drawing toolbar to rotate and flip objects.

To flip an object:

▶ **1.** With the triangle still selected, click the **Draw** button on the Drawing toolbar, point to **Rotate or Flip**, and then click **Flip Vertical**.

▶ **2.** Click a blank region in the slide pane to deselect the triangle. Your triangle should be sized, positioned, colored, and oriented like the one shown in Figure 2-29.

| **Figure 2-29** | **Slide 6 after recoloring and flipping triangle** |

▶ **3.** Save the presentation.

Now you'll add the text labels along the sides of the triangle.

Inserting Text Boxes

Sometimes you need to add a text box in a different location than any of the text box placeholders on the layouts. You need to add text boxes on each of the three sides of the triangle in Slide 6.

Adding Text to the Diagram

You're ready to add the text naming the three strategies of Global Humanitarian on each side of the triangle. You'll now add three text boxes around the AutoShape triangle you just created.

To add a text box to the slide:

▶ **1.** Click the **Text Box** button 🔲 on the Drawing toolbar, and then position the pointer over the slide. The pointer changes to ↓.

▶ **2.** Position ↓ so it is just above and centered on the top side of the triangle, and then click. A small text box appears above the triangle with the insertion point blinking in it. The position doesn't have to be exact.

Trouble? If the insertion point is blinking in the middle of the triangle instead of in a new text box above the triangle, you clicked the edge of the triangle. Click the Undo button ↺ on the Standard toolbar, and then repeat Steps 1 and 2.

3. Click the **Center** button ≣ on the Formatting toolbar, and then type **Village Outreach Projects**.

4. Click the **Text Box** button ⃞ on the Drawing toolbar, click ↓ to the right of the triangle, and then type **Expeditions**.

5. Create a third text box to the left of the triangle, click the **Align Right** button ≣ on the Formatting toolbar, and then type **Internships**.

6. Click the **Text Box** button ⃞ again, and then drag to draw a text box *inside* the triangle.

7. Type **Global Humanitarian**.

   Trouble? If the text you type appears upside down, you did not drag to create the text box inside the triangle, you simply clicked. Click the Undo button on the Standard toolbar twice, and then repeat Steps 6 and 7.

8. If the text inside the triangle does not fit on one line, drag a sizing handle on the text box to increase the size of the text box.

9. Select the three text boxes that you created outside the triangle by Shift-clicking them, and then change the font size to **24** points.

10. Click in a blank area of the slide to deselect the text boxes. Your slide should now look similar to Figure 2-30.

Text boxes added in and around triangle ◄ **Figure 2-30**

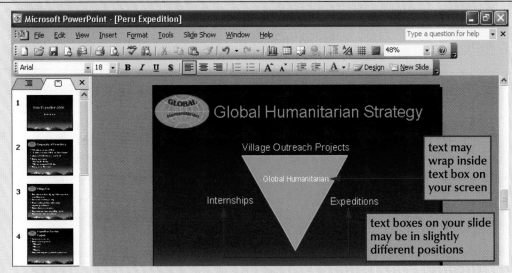

Next you'll rotate the text boxes to make them parallel to the sides of the triangle.

Rotating and Moving Text Boxes

The method for rotating text is similar to the one for rotating graphics (or rotating any other object). You use the Rotate or Flip commands on the Draw menu on the Drawing toolbar, or you drag the rotate handle on the object. You will rotate the text boxes on the left and right sides of the triangle.

To rotate and move the text boxes:

▶ **1.** Click anywhere within the "Expeditions" text box. The sizing handles and the rotate handle appear around the text box.

▶ **2.** Position the pointer over the rotate handle. The pointer becomes ⟳.

▶ **3.** Press and hold the **Shift** key, and then drag the rotate handle counterclockwise until the top edge of the box is parallel to the lower-right edge of the triangle. Holding down the Shift key causes the rotation to occur in 15-degree increments.

▶ **4.** Drag the "Expeditions" text box to position it against and centered on the lower-right edge of the triangle. See Figure 2-31.

Figure 2-31	Slide 6 with rotated and repositioned text box

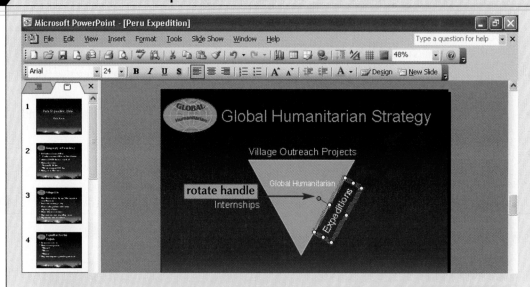

Trouble? If the edge of the text box isn't parallel to the edge of the triangle, you can repeat Steps 2 and 3 to fix the rotation. If necessary, try it without pressing the Shift key.

Trouble? If the text box jumps from one location to another as you drag it, and you can't position it exactly where you want it, hold down the Alt key as you drag the box. (The Alt key temporarily disables a feature that forces objects to snap to invisible gridlines on the slide.)

▶ **5.** Rotate the "Internships" text box clockwise so that the top edge of the text is parallel to the lower-left edge of the triangle, and then position the text box so it's against and centered on the left edge of the triangle.

▶ **6.** Adjust the position of (but don't rotate) the "Village Outreach Projects" text box so it's centered over the triangle.

▶ **7.** Reposition the text box inside the triangle so that it is centered in the triangle.

▶ **8.** Click a blank area of the slide pane to deselect the text box. Your slide should look like Figure 2-32.

Slide 6 with completed diagram ◄ **Figure 2-32**

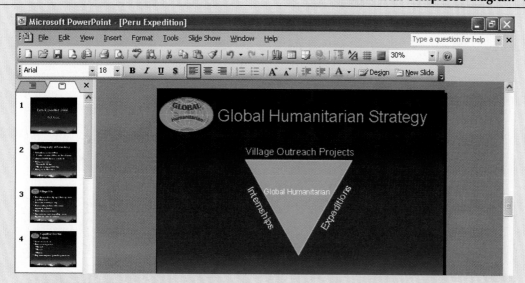

9. Save the presentation.

Pablo asks you to perform one final task before the presentation is finished. He wants you to add a summary at the end of the presentation.

Adding a Summary Slide

A **summary slide** is a slide containing the slide titles of selected slides in the presentation. PowerPoint helps you create a summary slide automatically. You'll do this now.

To create a summary slide:

▶ **1.** Click the **Slide Sorter View** button ⊞ at the bottom of the Slides tab. The presentation appears in Slide Sorter view.

▶ **2.** Click **Slide 2**, press and hold down the **Shift** key, and then click **Slide 9**. All of the slides except Slide 1 are selected. (If you wanted to select nonsequential slides, you would press and hold the Ctrl key while you clicked the desired slides.)

▶ **3.** Click the **Summary Slide** button 🖺 on the Slide Sorter toolbar. PowerPoint creates a new slide in front of the first selected slide with the title "Summary Slide" and body text consisting of a list of the titles of the selected slides.

   Trouble? If you don't see the Summary Slide button on the Slide Sorter toolbar, click the Toolbar Options button ⋮ on the Slide Sorter toolbar.

▶ **4.** Drag **Slide 2** (the new summary slide) to the right of Slide 10. Slide 2 becomes Slide 10, and the other slides are renumbered automatically.

▶ **5.** Double-click **Slide 10** to return to Normal view with Slide 10 in the slide pane.

▶ **6.** Double-click **Slide** in the title text to select the entire word, press the **Delete** key, and then deselect the text box. The selected text is deleted and the title becomes "Summary." See Figure 2-33.

Figure 2-33 New summary slide

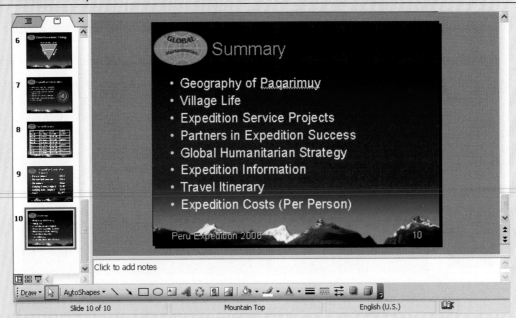

You have completed the entire presentation, so you should save the final version to the disk.

▶ **7.** Save the file.

As usual, you should finish up your presentation by checking the spelling, viewing it in Slide Show view, and printing it.

To check, view, and print the presentation:

▶ **1.** Click the **Spelling** button on the Standard toolbar to start checking the spelling of your presentation. Decide how to handle each word that is flagged because it was not found in the PowerPoint dictionary. (In most cases, you should click the Ignore All button because the words are proper nouns, such as "Paqarimuy" and "Cuzco.")

▶ **2.** Go to **Slide 1**, and then click the **Slide Show from current slide** button at the bottom of the Slides tab. The slide show starts.

▶ **3.** Press the **spacebar** or click the mouse button to advance through the slide show.

▶ **4.** If you see any problems while you are watching the slide show, press the **Esc** key to exit the slide show and return to Normal view, make the necessary corrections, and then return to Slide Show view.

▶ **5.** Go to **Slide 1**, and then replace Pablo's name with your own name.

▶ **6.** Print the presentation in grayscale as handouts, with six slides per page. Don't worry that the footers and one of the graphics are illegible in grayscale.

▶ **7.** Save the presentation, and then close the presentation.

Pablo is pleased with the additions and modifications you made to the presentation. He is anxious to use it to recruit volunteers for the next Peru expedition.

Session 2.2 Quick Check

1. How do you add a table to a slide?
2. Where is cell A1 in a table?
3. What is a Venn diagram?
4. How do you add a text box to a slide?
5. How do you draw a shape, such as a rectangle or a circle, on a slide?
6. How do you rotate or flip an object using menu commands?
7. How do you rotate an object without using menu commands?
8. Describe the Summary Slide command in PowerPoint.

Review

Tutorial Summary

In this tutorial, you learned how to create a new presentation using a design template, and how to apply a new design template to selected (or all) the slides in the presentation. You learned how to insert, format, and resize graphics, including clip art and photographs. You also learned how to modify the design template in the slide master and the title master. You learned how to add tab stops to align text on a slide. You learned how to insert footer information on slides. You also learned how to insert a table, a diagram, a shape, and a text box on slides. And finally, you learned how to add a summary slide to a presentation.

Key Terms

adjustment handle	font style	rotate handle
bitmap image	graphic	slide master
cell	handout master	slide-title master pair
clip art	header	summary slide
color scheme	master	tab
default colors	notes master	tab stop
design template	pixel	table
font	point	title master

Practice

Practice the skills you learned in the tutorial using the same case scenario.

Review Assignments

Data Files needed for the Review Assignments: PackList.jpg, GHLogo.jpg, SlpBag.jpg, Boots.ppt, Camera.jpg, Food.jpg, Personal.jpg, PrMeds.jpg, Vitamins.jpg

One of the common questions from volunteers who sign up for a service expedition is, "What items will I need for the trip?" In other words, they want to see a packing list to give them an idea of what they'll have to purchase and pack if they decide to go on the trip. Pablo decides to give a presentation to all volunteers to explain what they must take on the service expedition. He asks you to create a PowerPoint presentation on the Peru expedition packing list. Complete the following:

1. Open the file **PackList** located in the Tutorial.02\Review folder included with your Data Files, and then save it as **Peru Packing List** in the same folder.
2. Apply the design template titled "Teamwork," and then replace the subtitle in Slide 1 with your name.
3. Add the footer "Packing List" and slide numbers to all the slides except Slide 1.

4. In the title master, insert the logo file **GHLogo**, also located in the Tutorial.02\Review folder, position the graphic near the lower-right corner of the slide, just above the Number Area (the slide number placeholder text box), and then make the background of the logo transparent.

5. On both the title master and the slide master, change the title font color from light blue to the light yellow-green color found among the scheme colors. Switch back to Normal view when you are finished.

6. On Slide 2, change the slide layout so you can place clip art to the right of the bulleted list, search for clip art that deals with money, and then insert the piece of clip art that shows a dollar sign in an orange circle.

7. Recolor the clip art so that it is green (the third color from the right in the color palette).

8. Resize the clip art so it fits properly on the slide, and then resize the bulleted-list text box as needed so the text is as large as possible without overlapping the clip art. If the font size does not increase automatically when you increase the size of the text box, then use the Font Size button on the Formatting toolbar.

9. In Slide 3, insert the bitmap image file **SlpBag** ("sleeping bag") located in the Tutorial.02\Review folder.

10. Resize the sleeping bag image to increase its size so it fills more of the space on the right side of the slide, and then make the background of the image transparent.

11. In Slides 4 through 9, insert appropriate bitmap images located in the Tutorial.02\Review folder, resize the images as large as possible, and make the backgrounds transparent. Modify the layouts or resize the body text boxes as needed.

12. Add a new Slide 10 using the Title Only layout (under Text Layouts), type "Areas of Personal Preparation" as the title, draw a square in the middle of the blank area of the slide below the title, and change the fill color to the light blue color in the default color palette.

13. Add text just outside of the square on each of its four sides, using the words "Physical," "Mental," "Social," and "Spiritual." It doesn't matter which word you place on which side.

14. Rotate the text on the sides of the box so the bottom edges of the text boxes face toward the square. Adjust the text boxes so that each word is centered along the edge of the square and almost resting on the box. Resize the font to a readable size.

15. Add a new Slide 11 with the Title and Content layout, type "Discount Items" as the title, insert a table with three columns and five rows, and then add the text as follows:

Item	Regular Price	Discount Price
Boots	$198	$118
Sleeping bag	$162	$98
Water filter	$51	$32
Flashlight	$26	$16

16. Select the text and numbers in columns 2 and 3, and then right-align it.

17. Draw a light yellow-green, 4½ point border below the top row, and then modify the format of the text in the top row so it is 32 points and light yellow-green.

18. Drag the bottom-center sizing handle of the table up so that the table stays the same width but decreases in height so the text fits better in the cells of the table.

19. To Slide 11 only, apply the design template titled "Glass Layers," and then change the font and alignment of the title text on the slide master for this slide so that it matches the rest of the slides.

20. Add a new Slide 12 with the Title and Content layout, type "Thank You" as the title, and then insert a Pyramid diagram. Apply the teamwork design template to this slide.

21. Click the bottom placeholder in the diagram, type "You," click the middle place-holder, type "Global Humanitarian," click the top placeholder, type "The World," and then reformat all three labels to 28-point bold Arial.
22. Create a summary slide that includes titles from all the slides except Slides 1 and 12, and change the title to "Summary." Notice that PowerPoint creates two summary slides, because all of the slide titles will not fit on a single slide.
23. Check the spelling in the presentation, view the slide show, fix any problems you see, save the presentation, print it in grayscale as handouts with six slides per page, and then close the file.

Case Problem 1

Apply

Apply the skills you learned in this tutorial to modify a presenta-tion for a backpacking outfitter company.

Data Files needed for this Case Problem: Outfitter.ppt, MountainRiver.jpg, MountainLake.jpg, MenWithPacks.jpg, Campsite.jpg, MountainMeadow.jpg

The Backpacker's Outfitter Several years ago, Blake Stott received an M.S. degree in recre-ation management and started a new company, The Backpacker's Outfitter, which provides products and services for hiking, mountain climbing, rock climbing, and camping. The ser-vices include guided backpacking and climbing expeditions and courses on climbing and backpacking. The products include backpacking and climbing equipment and supplies. Blake uses PowerPoint to give presentations to businesses, youth groups (including Girl Scouts and Boy Scouts), clubs, and other organizations. He asks you to help him prepare a PowerPoint presentation explaining his products and services. Complete the following:

1. Open the file **Outfitter** located in the Tutorial.02\Cases folder included with your Data Files, and save it as **Backpacker's Outfitter** in the same folder.
2. Apply the design template titled "Cliff," and replace the subtitle in Slide 1 with your name. If "Cliff" is not installed on your computer, use the "Mountain Top" design template.
3. In the slide master, change the title text box so it is center-aligned rather than left-aligned. Make sure the title text box in the title master is also center-aligned.
4. In the slide master, between the title text box and the main text box, draw a horizontal line across the entire width of the slide.
5. Change line weight to 3-point and the line color to light yellow, the same as the title text color.
6. In Slide 2, change the slide layout to Title, Text, and Content. To the content place-holder, add the image **MountainRiver** located in the Tutorial.02\Cases folder included with your Data Files. Adjust the location of the picture so it's centered between the horizontal line and the bottom of the slide.
7. Repeat Step 6 for Slide 3, except insert the image **MountainLake** located in the Tutorial.02\Cases folder included with your Data Files. If necessary, click the main text box of Slide 3, click the AutoFit icon, and fit the text into the placeholder.
8. Repeat Step 7 for Slide 5, except insert the image **MenWithPacks** located in the Tutorial.02\Cases folder included with your Data Files.
9. In Slide 4, change the slide layout to Title and Text over Content. To the content place-holder, add the image **Campsite** located in the Tutorial.02\Cases folder included with your Data Files. Adjust the image size proportionally to 5.5 inches wide and center the image. If necessary, click the main text box, click the AutoFit icon, and fit the text into the placeholder. Increase the size of the text placeholder so that the bulleted text is 20 points and the sub-bulleted text is 18 points. (*Hint*: Drag the lower-center resize handle down about a half inch; the text should automatically resize.)

10. Repeat Step 9 for Slide 8, except insert the image **MountainMeadow** located in the Tutorial.02\Cases folder included with your Data Files, and adjust the text box size so the font is 24 point. Reposition the image, if necessary.
11. Insert a new Slide 7, change its layout to Title Only, and type the title "Phases of a Successful Backpacking Trip."
12. In Slide 7, draw a large equilateral regular pentagon in the middle of the blank area of the slide below the title.
13. Invert the pentagon so it's pointed down and change its fill color to light yellow.
14. Add white, 18-point Verdana (or Arial if your computer doesn't have Verdana) text just outside the pentagon on each of its five sides, using the phrases (starting at the top of the pentagon and going clockwise): "Planning," "Conditioning," "Training," "Equipment," and "Trip Site."
15. Rotate the text boxes so they are parallel to their respective sides of the pentagon. Adjust the size of the pentagon and the position of the text so that each phrase is centered along an edge, and almost resting on the shape.
16. Insert a new Slide 8, change the layout to Title and Content, type the title "Prices of Major Items," insert a table with two columns and five rows, and then add the text as follows:

Item	Typical Price
Backpack	$180
Tent	$150
Sleeping bag	$100
Boots	$160

Explore

17. Add a new row with "Total" in the left column and "$590" in the right column. (*Hint*: To add a row to an existing table, click in the last cell, in this case cell B5, and then press the Tab key.)
18. Drag the lower-center sizing handle of the table up so that the table stays the same width but decreases in height so the text fits better in the cells of the table.
19. Right-align the text and numbers in column 2.
20. Change the fill color of the top row of the table to brown. (*Hint*: Use the Fill Color button on the Tables and Borders toolbar.)
21. Check the spelling, view the slide show, fix any problems you see, and then save the presentation.
22. Print the presentation as grayscale handouts with six slides per page, and then close the file.

Challenge

Use the Internet to research information and apply the skills you learned to modify a presentation about the castles of Scotland.

Case Problem 2

Data Files needed for this Case Problem: Castles.ppt, Balmoral.jpg, Craigievar.jpg, Edinburgh.jpg, Fraser.jpg, Urquhart.jpg

Johnson Hodges Incorporated Moyra Torphins is a sales representative for Johnson Hodges Incorporated (JHI), a sales promotions company in Scarsdale, New York. JHI provides incentive packages and giveaways for large companies who hold internal sales competitions. Moyra, originally from Scotland, has been assigned to do research on castles in Scotland and to present her findings to the other sales representatives. You offer to help her prepare a PowerPoint presentation on castles of Scotland. Complete the following:

1. Open the file **Castles** located in the Tutorial.02\Cases folder included with your Data Files, and save it as **Scottish Castles** in the same folder.
2. Apply the design template titled "Globe," and then replace the subtitle in Slide 1 with your name.

3. In the title master and slide master, change the title text so it's the same color (light yellow) as the square bullets in the main text of the slide master.

Explore

4. In the slide master, add a gold 3-point border around the title text box. (*Hint*: Use the Fill Color button to change the shape to no fill, the Line Color button to change the color to gold—one of the default colors for this design template—and the Line Style button to change the thickness of the line.)

5. Add the footer "Scottish Castles" and slide numbering to all the slides.

6. Change the layout of Slide 2 to Title and Content, and then insert a Venn diagram consisting of three circles.

7. Add text labels next to each of the circles (in the designated placeholders), "Interesting Cultural Attractions," "Quality Accommodations," and "Accessible Location." Change the font size of these text boxes to 18 points.

8. Near the bottom of the slide and centered below the Venn diagram, insert a text box with the phrase "The Intersection of Success." Change the text to 24-point, light-yellow text.

Explore

9. Add a gold line border around the new text box. (*Hint*: Select the box and then click the Line Color button on the Drawing toolbar.)

Explore

10. Draw a 2¼ -point gold arrow from the text box to the center of the Venn diagram where the three circles overlap. (*Hint*: Use the Arrow and Line Style buttons on the Drawing toolbar.)

11. In Slide 3, change the layout to Title, Text, and Content, and then insert clip art that deals with travel (such as luggage or an airplane). If necessary, use the AutoFit option to fit the text in the placeholder.

12. Create Slide 4 with the title "Scottish Castles" and insert a table containing the following information. Change the text of the table to 20 points so it fits properly within each cell. Use the following table dimensions and text:

Castle	Nearest Major City	Approx. Year(s) of Construction	Open to Public
Balmoral	Aberdeen	1854	Mar to Aug 1
Craigievar			
Edinburgh			
Fraser			
Urquhart			

13. Use the Internet to find the information necessary to fill in the rest of the table. (*Note*: One of the following steps has you find other interesting information about each of these castles, so as you fill in the table, you might want to create individual slides about each of the castles.)

14. Center the text within the cells of the table.

15. If necessary, drag the lower-center sizing handle of the table up so that the table stays the same width but decreases in height so the text fits better in the cells of the table.

Explore

16. Select the top row of text, and change the vertical alignment so the text appears at the bottom of each cell in the row. (*Hint*: Use the Align Bottom button on the Tables and Borders toolbar.)

Explore

17. Change the fill color of the top row of the table to gold. (*Hint*: Use the Fill Color button on the Tables and Borders toolbar.) Change the font color of the text of the top row to blue (the same shade of blue as the top of the slide background).

18. Create a new Slide 5 with the title "Balmoral Castle." Change the layout to Title and Text over Content. In the content placeholder, insert the image of Balmoral Castle in the file **Balmoral** located in the Tutorial.02\Cases folder included with your Data Files.

19. Use the Internet to find information about Balmoral Castle to include as a bulleted list. Don't repeat the information given in the table in Slide 4. The bulleted list might include information such as "Located at Deeside (bank of the Dee River)," "Built of granite from the nearby quarries of Glen Gelder," "Summer home of British royalty," "Located on huge estate with much wildlife," and "Facilities include: Exhibitions, Gardens, Shops, Restaurant, Pony stable."

20. Create a new slide for each of the other four castles listed in the table on Slide 4 (thus you'll create Slides 6-9), change the slide layout to Title and Text over Content for Edinburgh and Urquhart castles, change the slide layout to Title, Content, and Text for the other two castles, and insert the appropriate image from the files located in the Tutorial.02\Cases folder included with your Data Files.

21. Find interesting information from the Internet about each castle and insert the information in a bulleted list.

22. Create a summary slide that includes titles from Slides 2 through 9, move the slide to the end of the presentation so it becomes Slide 10, and then change the title to "Summary."

23. Check the spelling, view the slide show, fix any problems you see, save the presentation, print the presentation as grayscale handouts with six slides per page, and then close the file.

Case Problem 3

Create

Create a new presentation about scrapbooking by using and expanding on the skills you learned in this tutorial.

Data Files needed for this Case Problem: SBcam.jpg, SBfile.jpg, SBpages.jpg, SBpaper.jpg, SBpens.jpg, SBphoto.jpg, SBsciss.jpg

Sally's Scrapbooking Four years ago, Brian and Sally DiQuattro started a business called Sally's Scrapbooking Supplies, which distributes wholesale scrapbooking supplies to retail stores in the Atlanta area. More recently, Brian and Sally opened their own specialty retail store (called Sally's Scrapbooking) and stocked it with scrapbooking supplies, which include binders, paper and plastic sheets and protectors, colored pens and markers, stickers and die cuts, stencils, scissors and cutting boards, glues and adhesives, and other miscellaneous items. As part of their marketing, Brian and Sally give presentations to scrapbooking clubs, women's clubs, crafts clubs, church groups, genealogical societies, and others interested in preserving their family histories through picture scrapbooks. The DiQuattros asked you to prepare a presentation for members of these organizations. The seven slides in your completed presentation should look like the slides shown in Figure 2-34.

Figure 2-34

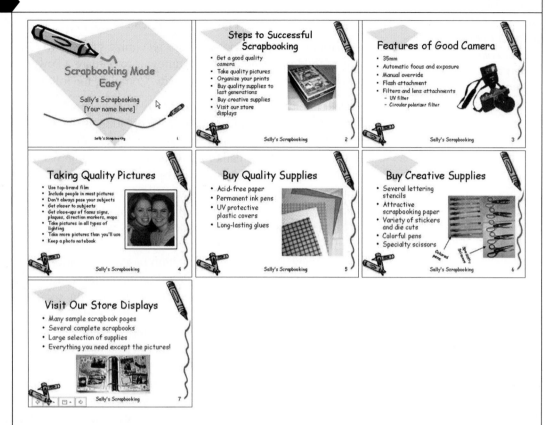

The following information will help you in creating the slide show. Read all the steps before you start creating your presentation.

1. The design template is called "Crayons."
2. The font is Comic Sans MS, the default font for the Crayons design template, but if your system doesn't support Comic Sans MS, you could use Eras Medium BT, Futura Bk BT, Kids, Microsoft Sans Serif, Technical, or some other font of your choosing.
3. In Slide 1, add your name in the subtitle placeholder.
4. Slides 2 through 7 contain one or more bitmap images. You'll find all these images in the Tutorial.02\Cases folder. You should use each image once.
5. The text at the bottom of the slides is a footer and an automatic slide number.
6. Modify the slide master so that the footer on your slides is in the same place as shown in the figure.
7. The content on Slides 2 through 7 reviews the following points:
   a. Quality supplies are critical in scrapbooking.
   b. Scrapbookers need acid-free and lignin-free paper to protect their photos from damage. (Ligni^n is a substance in paper that yellows over time.)
   c. Scrapbookers need archival-quality pens with ink that won't bleed through the paper.
   d. Page layout is easy with the right die cuts and stickers.
   e. Buy quality cutting tools and keep them sharpened.
   f. File photos in groups to prepare to lay out pages.
8. Remember to check the spelling in the final presentation, and to view the slide show.
9. Print the final presentation in grayscale as handouts with four slides per page.
10. Save the file as **Sally's Scrapbooking** to the Tutorial.02\Cases folder.

Research

Use the Internet to collect information about a collegiate honor society and create a new presentation based on this information.

Case Problem 4

Data Files you might use in this Case Problem: PESLogo.jpg, PKPBadge.jpg, PKPKey.jpg,

College Honor Society Honor societies recognize students who distinguish themselves in academics and leadership. Your assignment is to prepare a PowerPoint presentation on an honor society at your college or university. Complete the following:

1. Gather information on an honor society from honor society advisors, college advisement centers, or the office of the Dean of Students. For the names, locations, and phone numbers, call information at your college, or consult your student directory or catalog. You can also gather information from the Internet. For general information about members of the Association of College Honor Societies, including a list of most honor societies in the United States and Canada, consult **www.achsnatl.org**. For information on a specific national, nondiscipline-specific honor society, Phi Kappa Phi, consult **www.phikappaphi.org**. For a national freshman honor society, Phi Eta Sigma, consult **www.phietasigma.org**.

2. Create a new PowerPoint presentation based on an appropriate design template. Type the name of the society on the title slide, and type your name as the subtitle.

3. Create at least eight slides with information about the society. Information on your slides might include local and national names and addresses of advisors and officers, purposes, eligibility, activities, scholarships, recognition programs, famous members, history, meetings, local and national conventions, merchandise, and publications.

4. Modify the slide master by adding a text box or graphics object, changing the font attributes, or making some other desired change that will appear on all the slides.

5. Include the slide number and an appropriate footer on each slide, except the title slide. In the slide master, change the font style, size, and color, and change the position of the footer and slide number text.

6. Include in your presentation at least one piece of clip art.

Explore

7. Click Insert on the menu bar, point to Picture, and then click Clip Art to open the Clip Art task pane. Click the Clip Art on Office Online link in the task pane to go to Microsoft's Design Gallery Live, where you can search through hundreds of pieces of clip art. Find and insert at least one image connected specifically to the honor society you are describing. If you can't find the image on the Design Gallery Live site, look elsewhere on the Web, or request an image from the local chapter of the honor society. If you choose to describe Phi Kappa Phi or Phi Eta Sigma, bitmap images of their logos are located in the Tutorial.02\Cases folder.

8. Recolor the clip art you inserted to match the presentation color scheme or the colors of the other graphics in your presentation.

9. Include a table or an organizational chart in your presentation. (For information on organizational charts, use the PowerPoint Help system.) You might include a table with the name, description, location, and dates of chapter activities; a table listing the chapter merchandise and prices; or a table with names, addresses, phone numbers, and e-mail addresses of chapter officers. You might include an organizational chart showing the structure of officers in the honor society.

10. Include a drawing that you create from lines, arrows, AutoShapes, or text boxes. For example, you might create a diagram showing the procedure for becoming a member of the honor society, using text boxes and arrows.

11. Apply a second design template to one of the slides.

12. Create a summary slide, and change its title to "Summary of Phi Kappa Phi" (but use the name of your selected honor society).

13. Check the spelling in your presentation, view the slide show, and then save the presentation to the Tutorial.02\Cases folder using the filename **Honor Society**.

14. Print the presentation in grayscale as handouts with four slides per page, and then close the file.

Research

Go to the Web to find information you can use to create presentations.

Internet Assignments

The purpose of the Internet Assignments is to challenge you to find information on the Internet that you can use to work effectively with this software. The actual assignments are updated and maintained on the Course Technology Web site. Log on to the Internet and use your Web browser to go to the Student Online Companion for New Perspectives Office 2003 at **www.course.com/np/office2003**. Click the Internet Assignments link, and then navigate to the assignments for this tutorial.

Assess

SAM Assessment and Training

If your instructor has chosen to use the full online version of SAM 2003 Assessment and Training, you can go beyond the "just-in-time" training provided on the CD that accompanies this text. Simply log in to your SAM account (http://sam2003.course.com) to launch any assigned training activities or exams that relate to the skills covered in this tutorial.

Review

Quick Check Answers

Session 2.1

1. Graphics add information, clarification, emphasis, variety, and pizzazz.
2. a. a file that contains the color scheme, graphics, text formats, and background colors and objects in the presentation
   b. a grid (or "map") of colored dots that form a picture
   c. a picture, clip art, photograph, shape, design, graph, chart, or diagram
   d. the design template applied to a presentation if no other template is chosen (black text on a white background)
3. a. Click anywhere in the text box.
   b. Click the edge of the text box.
   c. Drag a sizing handle.
   d. Drag the object (or in the case of a text box, the edge of the box).
   e. Display the slide in the slide pane, click the list arrow of the desired design template in the Design Template task pane, and then click Apply to Selected Slides.
   f. Select the clip-art image, click the Recolor Picture button on the Picture toolbar, and modify the original colors to new colors.
4. The title master is a slide that contains the objects that appear on the title slide of the presentation. The slide master is a slide that contains the objects that appear on all the slides except the title slide.
5. Tabs add space between the left margin and the beginning of the text on a particular line, or between the text in one column and the text in another column. Tab stops are the locations where text moves when you press the Tab key. Click the Tab button until the Right Tab button appears, and then click the desired location on the ruler.
6. date and time, footer, and slide number

Session 2.2

1. Change the slide layout to a Content layout, click the Insert Table button, set the desired number of columns and rows, insert information into the cells, and modify the table format as desired.
2. upper-left corner
3. a diagram used to show overlap between different elements
4. Click the Text Box button on the Drawing toolbar, and click or drag at the desired location in the slide.
5. Click the AutoShapes list arrow on the Drawing toolbar, point to the appropriate category (such as Basic Shapes), click the desired shape button, move the pointer into the slide pane, and then drag the pointer to draw the figure.
6. Select the triangle, click the Draw button on the Drawing toolbar, point to Rotate or Flip, and then click the appropriate command.
7. Drag the rotate handle of the object in the slide pane.
8. a method for automatically creating a slide with the titles of the slides selected in Slide Sorter view

New Perspectives on
Integrating Microsoft®
Office 2003

Tutorial 3   INT 3-3
Integrating Word, Excel, Access, and PowerPoint
Creating a Form Letter and an Integrated Presentation

Read This Before You Begin

Data Files

To complete the "Integrating Word, Excel, Access, and PowerPoint" tutorial, you need the starting Data Files. See the inside back or front cover for information on downloading these files from course.com, or ask your instructor for assistance. The following table identifies each starting Data File and the folder it is stored in, as well as the ending files, which you create and save in each tutorial.

Folders		Starting Files	Ending Files
Tutorial .03	**Tutorial**	LHCLetter2.doc, LHCMostRequested.xls, LHCOutline.doc, LHCPresentation.ppt, LHCServices.mdb, SocialWorkContacts.mdb	Home Care Conference.ppt, Main Letter.doc, Merged Letters.doc, Outline for Slides.doc
	Review	LHCEmployees.ppt, LHCEmployeesOutline.doc, LHCGrowth2.xls, LHCServices.mdb, SocialWorkContacts.mdb	Employee Presentation.ppt, Main Labels.doc, Merged Labels.doc, Topics Outline.doc
	Cases	LFCFees.xls, LFCOutline.doc, MusicCustomers.mdb	LFC Presentation Outline.doc, Merge Envelope.doc, MusicCustomers.mdb, New Customer Presentation.ppt, Ridgefield Envelopes.doc

Storing Your Files

It is recommended that you store all your Data Files on a USB drive. Refer to the tutorial "Managing Your Files" for information on using USB drives. If you need to store your Data Files on floppy disks, you will need two high-density disks to store all the files for the "Integrating Word, Excel, Access, and PowerPoint" tutorial.

SAM 2003 Training Companion CD

The SAM 2003 Training Companion CD that comes with this text gives you "just-in-time" training and reinforcement of important Microsoft Office skills. Look for the SAM CD logo throughout each tutorial for opportunities to complete the hands-on tasks included on this CD.

Integrating Word, Excel, Access, and PowerPoint

Creating a Form Letter and an Integrated Presentation

Case | Lifestyles Home Care, Inc.

Caitlin Sheehan, owner of Lifestyles Home Care, has created a letter and brochure describing the new services her agency is planning to offer. She is ready to send her letter and brochure to the social work departments at all of the local hospitals. Her contacts in the social work departments are stored in an Access database.

Caitlin also needs to prepare a presentation for next month's National Home Care Conference. The demand for home care agencies that offer services for fees (rather than supplying services only to people who qualify under state income guidelines), is growing and conference organizers have asked her to discuss her business plan.

In this tutorial, you'll complete two separate tasks. First, you'll merge the letter to the hospitals with the names and addresses of the social work contacts stored in an Access database. Second, you'll create a presentation for Caitlin to use at the conference. You'll use Word to create an outline of the topics she wants to cover, and then you'll create a PowerPoint presentation from the outline. The presentation will also include an Access query and an Excel pie chart showing the most requested services. You'll use different integration methods to include these items in the presentation.

Objectives		SAM Training Tasks	
• Merge an Access query with a Word document • View merged documents • Preview and print a merged document • Create a Word outline	• Create PowerPoint slides from a Word outline • Copy and paste an Access query into a PowerPoint presentation • Link an Excel chart to a PowerPoint presentation	• Complete an entire mail merge process for form letters • Create an outline • Insert Excel charts in slides as linked objects	• Open a Word outline as a presentation • Send an outline to PowerPoint

Planning the Form Letter

A **form letter** is a Word document that contains standard paragraphs of text and a minimum of variable text, such as the names and addresses of the letter's recipients. The **main document** of a form letter contains the text and other information (including punctuation, spaces, and graphics) that you want to keep the same in each letter. It also includes merge fields. As you remember from Access, a field contains information that varies from one record to another. A **merge field** contains instructions for replacing the field placeholder with the information that changes from one letter to another, for example, the name and address of a contact. The variable information is contained in a **data source**, which can be a Word table, an Access database, or some other source. When you merge the main document with the data source, Word replaces the merge fields with the appropriate information from the data source. The process of combining the main document with the data source is called a **merge**. The term **mail merge** is used when you are merging a main document with a list of addresses from any data source.

In this case, Caitlin's letter is the main document, and the Access database containing the contact names in the social work departments and the addresses of the local hospitals is the data source. Figure 3-1 shows Caitlin's plan for the form letter.

Figure 3-1	Caitlin's plan for the form letter

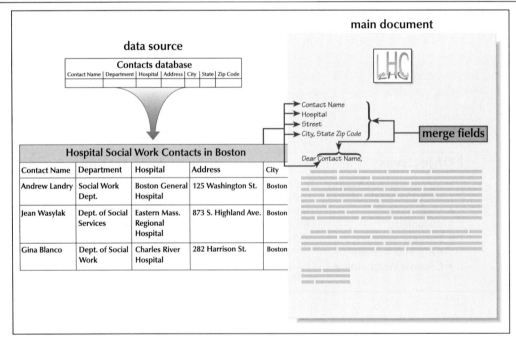

Merging Access Data with a Word Document

The first step in completing the mail merge is to specify the type of document you want to create, such as a form letter or mailing labels. Next, you select the main document, which Word also calls the **starting document**. Then you select recipients from the data source. When you specify an Access database as containing the data source for a mail merge, you select a table or query defined in the database as the actual data source.

Once you have identified the main document and the data source, you insert the merge fields into the main document. Finally, you preview the letters, make any needed changes, and merge the main document and the data source to produce customized form letters.

Selecting a Starting Document and Recipients

The main document of a mail merge can be a new or existing Word document. In this case, the starting document is Caitlin's existing letter to area hospitals. Caitlin modified the document you worked with in Integration Tutorial 1 to create a final version of the letter she wants to send. You'll begin by starting Word and opening the main document.

To open the main document:

▶ 1. Open the Word document **LHCLetter2**, which is located in the Tutorial.03\Tutorial folder included with your Data Files. The letter opens in Print Layout view.

▶ 2. Display nonprinting characters, if necessary.

▶ 3. Press the **Ctrl + End** keys to move to the end of the letter, and then replace Caitlin Sheehan's name with your own.

▶ 4. Press the **Ctrl + Home** keys to return to the beginning of the letter, and then save the file as **Main Letter** in the Tutorial.03\Tutorial folder included with your Data Files.

You need to start by selecting the type of document you want to create.

To select the main document and data source for the mail merge:

▶ 1. Click **Tools** on the menu bar, point to **Letters and Mailings**, and then click **Mail Merge**. The Mail Merge task pane opens, showing Step 1 of 6. See Figure 3-2. The Mail Merge task pane guides you through a series of six steps to create the final merged document. You navigate to the next or previous step by clicking the links at the bottom of the task pane.

Mail Merge task pane ◀ **Figure 3-2**

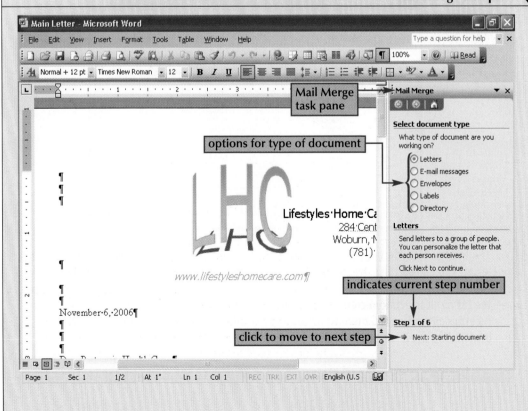

In Step 1 of the mail merge process, you select the type of document you want to create. The Letters option button is selected by default, but you can also create e-mail messages, envelopes, labels, or a directory containing the entire list.

2. Click the **Letters** option button, if necessary, and then click the **Next: Starting document** link. The Mail Merge task pane now shows the options for Step 2 of 6: Select starting document. You want to use the current document, Caitlin's letter to the hospitals, as the starting document.

3. Click the **Use the current document** option button, if necessary, and then click the **Next: Select recipients** link. The Mail Merge task pane changes to show the options for Step 3 of 6: Select recipients.

   You want to select recipients from an existing list in an Access database.

4. Click the **Use an existing list** option button, if necessary, and then click the **Browse** link. The Select Data Source dialog box opens, displaying a list of possible data sources. You need to locate the list of social worker contacts at the local hospitals, which is located in the Hospital Social Work Contacts table in the SocialWorkContacts database.

5. Click the **Look in** list arrow, navigate to the Tutorial.03\Tutorial folder included with your Data Files, click **SocialWorkContacts**, and then click the **Open** button. The Select Table dialog box opens with a list of all the tables and queries in the selected database (this database contains two tables and no queries). You need to choose a table or query in the selected database as the data source. If the database contained only one table, the Select Table dialog box would not open; instead, the Mail Merge Recipients dialog box would open immediately after you selected the database.

6. Click the **Hospital Social Work Contacts** table to select it, if necessary, and then click the **OK** button. The Mail Merge Recipients dialog box opens, as shown in Figure 3-3.

Figure 3-3 ▶ Mail Merge Recipients dialog box

You use the Mail Merge Recipients dialog box to select the people who will receive Caitlin's letter. You can sort this list by any field by clicking a column heading. For example, if you were doing a large mass mailing, you could sort the list by ZIP code. You can also narrow the list by deselecting records individually or filtering the list to include only records that meet specific criteria. Caitlin wants to send her initial mailing only to the hospitals in Boston. You decide to filter the list to include only those hospitals.

7. Click the **City** list arrow, and then click **(Advanced...)**. The Filter and Sort dialog box opens with the Filter Records tab selected.

8. Click the **Field** list arrow, scroll down, and then click **City**. You want to merge the main document only with those hospitals in Boston.

9. Click the **Comparison** list arrow, click **Equal to**, if necessary, click the **Compare to** text box, type **Boston**, and then click the **OK** button. The Filter and Sort dialog box closes and only the addresses for the Boston hospitals are displayed in the Mail Merge Recipients dialog box.

10. Click the **OK** button to close the Mail Merge Recipients dialog box. The Use an existing list section of the Mail Merge task pane now indicates that Word will select your recipients from the Hospital Social Work Contacts table in SocialWorkContacts.mdb. Your screen should look similar to Figure 3-4.

Recipients selected in the Mail Merge task pane | Figure 3-4

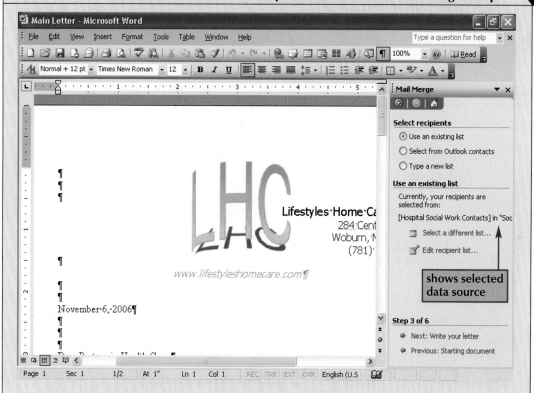

Trouble? If your screen does not show that your recipients are selected from the Hospital Social Work Contacts table in SocialWorkContacts.mdb, click the Select a different list link in the task pane, and then repeat Steps 4 through 10.

Next, you will insert the merge fields into the main document.

Inserting the Merge Fields

As noted earlier, a merge field is a special instruction that tells Word where to insert the variable information from the data source into the main document. For example, right now the letter does not have an inside address (the address for the recipient) at the top, as business letters usually do. Because this information will be different for each letter, you'll use merge fields to tell Word what information to pull from the data source.

The next step in the mail merge process is to insert the merge fields. For Caitlin's letter, you will insert the Address block and Greeting line merge fields. You then will check the merge fields to make sure they correspond with the fields in the Hospital Social Work Contacts table.

To insert the merge fields into the main document:

1. With the Mail Merge task pane showing Step 3 of 6, click the **Next: Write your letter** link. The Mail Merge task pane displays Step 4 of 6: Write your letter. Caitlin has already written the letter, but you need to add the recipient's name and address and a greeting line to personalize each copy of the letter.

2. Click in the second blank paragraph below the date in the letter. This is where the recipient's name and address will appear.

3. Click the **Address block** link in the Mail Merge task pane. The Insert Address Block dialog box opens, as shown in Figure 3-5.

Figure 3-5	Insert Address Block dialog box

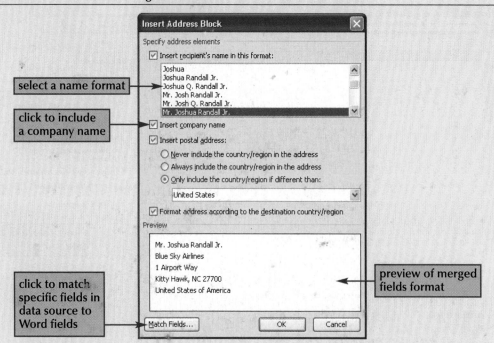

You use this dialog box to choose the format of the recipient's name and to specify whether to include the company name and country in the address. The content, tone, and style of the writing in Caitlin's customer letter is friendly and professional, so you decide to use a simple format of first and last name.

4. Click **Joshua Randall Jr.** in the Insert recipient's name in this format list box.

   After selecting address elements, you need to check to see how the fields in the Address block correspond to the fields in the Hospital Social Work Contacts table.

5. Click the **Match Fields** button. The Match Fields dialog box opens, as shown in Figure 3-6.

Match Fields dialog box ◄ **Figure 3-6**

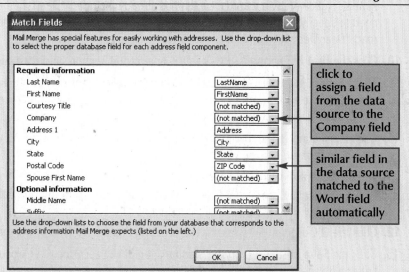

> click to assign a field from the data source to the Company field

> similar field in the data source matched to the Word field automatically

On the left are the fields Word expects in the Address block. On the right are the fields in the data source. Word automatically matches those fields that have the same or similar name; for example, it matches Postal Code with ZIP Code. Word did not find a match for the Company field. You want Word to match the Company field with the Hospital field in the Access table.

6. Click the **Company** list arrow, and then click **Hospital**.

7. Click the **OK** button to close the Match Fields dialog box, and then click the **OK** button to close the Insert Address Block dialog box. The Address block merge field appears in the main document between double chevrons («« »»).

   Trouble? If the Address block merge field appears between curly braces and includes additional text, such as {ADDRESSBLOCK \f}, Word is displaying field codes. Click Tools on the menu bar, click Options, click the View tab in the Options dialog box, and then click the Field codes check box to deselect it.

   Now you need to insert a greeting line to personalize the salutation.

8. In the letter, click and drag to select **Partner in Health Care:** (make sure you include the colon) in the salutation line, and then press the **Delete** key. Make sure you leave a space after "Dear." You will replace the generic text with each contact's first name.

9. In the Mail Merge task pane, click the **Greeting line** link. The Greeting Line dialog box opens, as shown in Figure 3-7.

Greeting Line dialog box ◄ **Figure 3-7**

> options for greeting line format

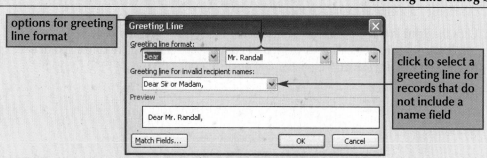

> click to select a greeting line for records that do not include a name field

The Greeting Line dialog box shows what Word will insert as the salutation "Dear Mr. Randall" followed by a comma. Caitlin has already included "Dear" in the letter, so you need to specify that Word does not include "Dear" as well; otherwise, the salutation will read "Dear Dear Mr. Randall."

▶ **10.** Click the **first list arrow** in the Greeting line format section, and then click **(none)**.

The greeting line would now read "Dear Mr. Randall"; however, Caitlin knows all of the contacts in the social work departments personally, and she would rather start with the first name, as in "Dear Joshua" followed by a comma.

▶ **11.** Click the **second list arrow** in the Greeting line format section, scroll down the list, and then click **Joshua**.

You can accept the other options in the Greeting Line dialog box—to end the salutation with a comma and to use "Dear Sir or Madam" for records in the Hospital Social Work Contacts table that do not include a contact name.

▶ **12.** Click the **OK** button. Word inserts the Greeting line merge field in the main document.

▶ **13.** Click the **Save** button 🔲 on the Standard toolbar to save the main document as Main Letter with the merge fields inserted.

Performing the Mail Merge

With the starting document and merge fields in place, you're ready to perform the mail merge. You can choose to merge the data to a new Word document or directly to a printer. Caitlin wants to proofread her final document before printing all of the merged documents, so you will print one copy of the merged letter, and then save the merge results in a new document. The new document you create with the merge results will contain one letter for each contact in the data source. Each letter will be identical, except for the merge fields, which will have the individual names and addresses.

To complete the mail merge:

▶ **1.** With the Mail Merge task pane showing Step 4 of 6, click the **Next: Preview your letters** link, and then scroll down the document so you can see both merged fields. The first merged form letter appears with Andrew Landry at Boston General Hospital as the first recipient.

▶ **2.** Click the **Next** button >> (next to Recipient: 1) in the Mail Merge task pane to preview the next recipient. The letter to Jean Wasylak at Eastern Mass. Regional Hospital appears.

You are ready to print a copy of the letter.

▶ **3.** Click the **Next: Complete the merge** link in the Mail Merge task pane. "Step 6: Complete the merge" appears in the task pane.

▶ **4.** Click the **Print** link in the Mail Merge task pane. The Merge to Printer dialog box opens in which you can specify the records you want to print. Make sure you are connected to a printer and that it is loaded with paper and ready to print.

5. Click the **Current record** option button, and then click the **OK** button. The print dialog box opens.

6. Click the **OK** button. Word prints one copy of the form letter—the letter to Jean Wasylak.

   Now you can create a new document containing all of the form letters.

7. In the Mail Merge task pane, click the **Edit individual letters** link. The Merge to New Document dialog box opens.

8. Click the **All** option button, if necessary, and then click the **OK** button. Word opens a new document with the temporary name "Letters" followed by a number. This document contains one letter for each of the recipients at the Boston hospitals; each letter is separated from the next by a section break.

9. Scroll through the merged document to see the merged addresses and salutations. Word replaced each merge field with the appropriate Access data. Notice that the merged document contains six pages: Each letter is two pages long, and there are three letters in all.

10. Click the **Save** button 🔲 on the Standard toolbar to open the Save As dialog box.

11. Save the document as **Merged Letters** in the Tutorial.03\Tutorial folder included with your Data Files, and then close the document. You return to the starting document.

12. Close the **Main Letter** document without saving changes.

   Because you saved the Main Letter document after you inserted the merged fields but before completing the merge, you can open it at any time, click the No button in the dialog box that opens asking if you want to run the SQL command (basically, complete the merge), open the Mail Merge task pane, and create new merged letters.

Caitlin plans to review the printed letter before she prints and mails the form letters. While she does that, Caitlin asks you to prepare her presentation for the National Home Care Conference to be held next month. In her presentation, Caitlin will explain her company's decision to add services for fees. She has already created the PowerPoint presentation file, selected a suitable template for the presentation, and created the title slide. She also quickly created a Word document in which she entered the topics for the remaining slides. She did not have time to properly organize the topics in an outline. To complete the presentation, you first need to create a Word outline from Caitlin's document.

Creating a Word Outline

You can create an outline in Word by typing text directly in Outline view in a new document. When you do, Word assigns heading styles to the text to format it as an outline. You can also format the text in an existing document by displaying it in Outline view and assigning each paragraph an appropriate heading style. You'll format Caitlin's document as an outline and then use this document to create the rest of the slides in Caitlin's PowerPoint presentation.

To open the document and display it in Outline view:

1. Open the Word document **LHCOutline**, located in the Tutorial.03\Tutorial folder included with your Data Files.

2. Save the document as **Outline for Slides** in the same folder. To format the document's text as an outline, you first need to switch to Outline view.

3. Click the **Outline View** button ⊞, located to the left of the horizontal scroll bar. The document switches to Outline view, and the Outlining toolbar is displayed. See Figure 3-8.

Figure 3-8 ▶ **Document displayed in Outline view**

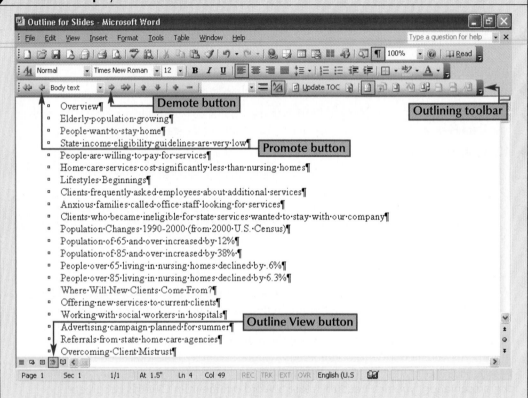

To format text as an outline, you use the Promote and Demote buttons on the Outlining toolbar. The Promote button **promotes**, or moves up, the selected paragraph to the next higher outline level. The Demote button **demotes**, or moves down, the selected paragraph to the next lower outline level. (Remember, Word refers to any text marked by a nonprinting, end-of-paragraph mark as a paragraph, even if the text consists of only one or two words, or if there is no text at all.)

The easiest way to format the text for Caitlin's outline is to select all of it and promote it to the first outline level. Then you can demote text as necessary. When you create PowerPoint slides from an outline, paragraphs at the first outline level become slide titles, paragraphs at the second outline level become first-level slide text, paragraphs at the third outline level become second-level slide text, and so on.

To format the text as a Word outline:

1. Click **Edit** on the menu bar, and then click **Select All**.

2. Click the **Promote** button [icon] on the Outlining toolbar. Word changes each paragraph to a first-level heading. Now you need to demote the necessary paragraphs to the next level.

3. Position the insertion point anywhere in the second paragraph (beginning with the word "Elderly").

4. Click the **Demote** button [icon] on the Outlining toolbar. The paragraph moves to the next lower outline level.

   Notice that the first paragraph now includes a plus sign to its left. This indicates that the first paragraph has subitems (paragraphs at a lower level) associated with it.

5. Drag to select the third through sixth paragraphs (beginning with "People" and ending with "nursing homes").

6. Press the **Tab** key. The selected paragraphs indent to the next lower outline level.

7. Refer to Figure 3-9 to format the next 14 paragraphs as indicated.

First part of formatted outline | **Figure 3-9**

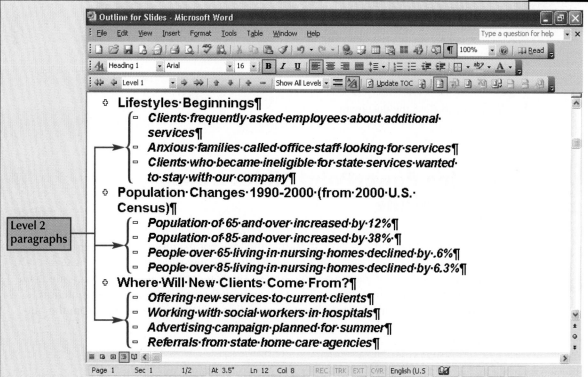

8. Scroll through the document, and then refer to Figure 3-10 to format the remaining paragraphs. Note that you must demote some paragraphs twice to move them to the appropriate level.

Figure 3-10	Remainder of formatted outline

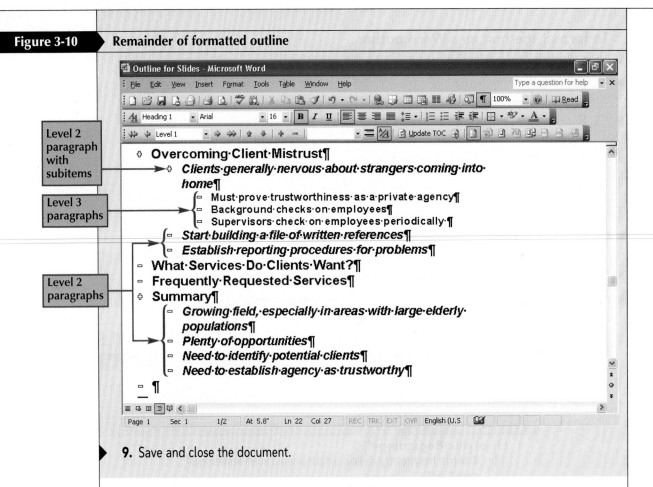

9. Save and close the document.

Creating PowerPoint Slides from a Word Outline

When you create slides from a Word outline, PowerPoint uses the heading styles in the Word document to determine how to format the text. For example, each paragraph formatted with the Heading 1 style becomes the title of a new slide, each Heading 2 becomes the first level of text on a slide, and so on. You can use an outline to create new slides in an existing presentation or to create an entirely new PowerPoint presentation. Now you can open Caitlin's PowerPoint presentation and create new slides from the outline you created.

To create new PowerPoint slides from a Word outline:

1. Open the PowerPoint file **LHCPresentation**, located in the Tutorial.03\Tutorial folder included with your Data Files. The presentation opens and displays its first and only slide, which contains the presentation title and the Lifestyles logo.

2. Save the presentation as **Home Care Conference** in the same folder.

   When you create slides from an outline (or other file), PowerPoint inserts them after the current slide. In this case, you want to insert them after the first (and only) slide in the presentation.

3. Click **Insert** on the menu bar, and then click **Slides from Outline**. The Insert Outline dialog box opens.

4. Click the **Look in** list arrow, navigate to the Tutorial.03\Tutorial folder included with your Data Files, click **Outline for Slides**, and then click the **Insert** button. PowerPoint inserts and formats the text of the Word outline to create Slides 2 through 10 and displays the first new slide (Slide 2). See Figure 3-11.

Slides inserted from outline | Figure 3-11

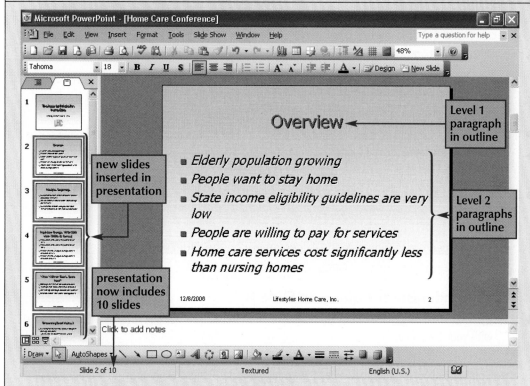

5. Click the **Next Slide** button in the slide pane scroll bar until you reach Slide 10. Notice that each Level 1 paragraph in the Word outline became a slide title, each Level 2 paragraph became a bulleted item, and each Level 3 paragraph became a subitem in a bulleted list. Also, note that PowerPoint automatically assigned the Title and Text layout to each slide.

   Slide 10 does not contain any text. There was a blank paragraph at the end of the Word outline.

6. With Slide 10 displayed in the slide pane, click **Edit** on the menu bar, and then click **Delete Slide**. Slide 10 is deleted.

7. Click the **Slide 6** thumbnail in the Slides tab. Slide 6 appears in the slide pane. The text on this slide looks a little crowded because it runs into the footer.

8. Double-click **Must** in the second bullet, press the **Delete** key twice, and then type **P**. The second bullet now is all on one line, and the rest of the text does not run into the footer.

9. Save the presentation.

   With the text for all the slides in place, you can now complete the presentation by adding the Updated Services Requested Query in the LHCServices database and a chart from the LHCMostRequested workbook.

Copying and Pasting an Access Query into a PowerPoint Presentation

Caitlin wants to include the list of most requested services on Slide 7 ("What Services Do Clients Want?"). This information is stored as an Access query in the LHCServices database. To include this information, copy and paste the Access query into the PowerPoint presentation.

Caitlin knows that the data in the query will not change before the conference, so she asks you to copy and paste the query onto Slide 7.

To prepare to copy and paste the query:

1. Move to **Slide 7** in the presentation.

   This slide will include only the slide title and the pasted Access query data; therefore, the current layout of the slide, Title and Text, is inappropriate. You need to change the layout of the slide before you copy and paste the query.

2. Click **Format** on the menu bar, and then click **Slide Layout**. The Slide Layout task pane opens.

3. Click the **Title Only** layout (column 2, row 1 in the Text Layouts section in the task pane). PowerPoint applies the layout to the slide.

4. Close the Slide Layout task pane.

   Now you can copy and paste the Access query on the slide.

To copy and paste the query on Slide 4:

1. Open the Access **LHCServices** database, located in the Tutorial.03\Tutorial folder included with your Data Files.

   Trouble? If a dialog box opens warning you that the database may not be safe, click the Open button. If a dialog box opens, warning you that Access can't open the database, see your instructor or technical support person.

2. Click **Queries** in the Database window, if necessary, to display the list of queries in the database, and then double-click **Updated Services Requested Query**. Access displays the results of the query in Datasheet view. See Figure 3-12.

Figure 3-12 ▶ **Updated Services Requested Query results**

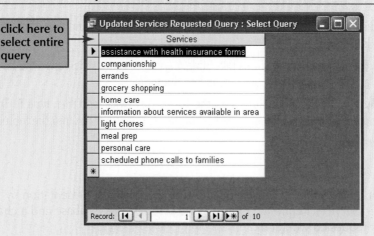

Caitlin wants all the data from the query to appear on the slide.

3. Click the **selector** to the left of the column heading (refer to Figure 3-12). Access selects all of the records in the query results window.

4. Click the **Copy** button 📋 on the Query Datasheet toolbar to copy the query results to the Clipboard.

5. Close the query and the database, and then click the **Microsoft PowerPoint - [Home Care Conference]** button on the taskbar. You return to the presentation.

Now you can paste the query on Slide 7.

6. Click in the slide pane in the blank area below the title text box, and then click the **Paste** button 📋 on the PowerPoint Standard toolbar. PowerPoint inserts the query results as a table on the slide. You need to reposition it on the slide and reformat it to match the style of the presentation.

7. Position the pointer over the edge of the table so that it changes to ⬚, and then click to select the entire table. See Figure 3-13. Make sure the selected table has a dotted outline. The dotted outline indicates that you can make changes to the entire table. A slanted line outline indicates that you can select parts of the table to change.

Access table selected on PowerPoint slide   **Figure 3-13**

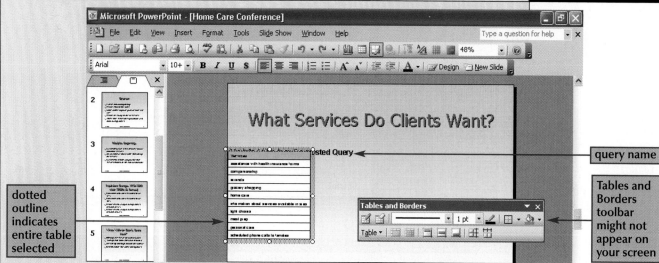

Trouble? If your table does not have a dotted outline as in Figure 3-13, click the slanted line outline.

8. Drag the table so that it is centered on the slide. Note that the query name was also pasted when you pasted the query results. You do not need this information on the slide.

Trouble? If the Tables and Borders toolbar is in the way, drag it out of the way by its title bar.

9. Click anywhere on the text **Updated Services Requested Query** to display the border of the text box, click on the slanted line border of the text box to change it to the dotted line border, and then press the **Delete** key.

You need to enlarge the table and the text in the table so that the table is easier to read.

10. Select the **table**, making sure the dotted line border appears, click the **Font Size** list arrow `10+ ▾` on the Formatting toolbar, and then click **20**.

11. Drag the **left** and **right sizing handles** on the table to stretch the table wide enough to accommodate the widest entry.

12. Click the word **Services** in the top row of the table, click the **Fill Color** list arrow `🖉 ▾` on the Tables and Borders toolbar, click **Automatic**, and then click the **Center** button `≣` on the Formatting toolbar. The color of the first row in the table changes to a dark tan to better match the slide design, and the column header is centered.

13. Click an empty area of the slide to deselect the table. See Figure 3-14.

Figure 3-14	Formatted Access table on PowerPoint slide

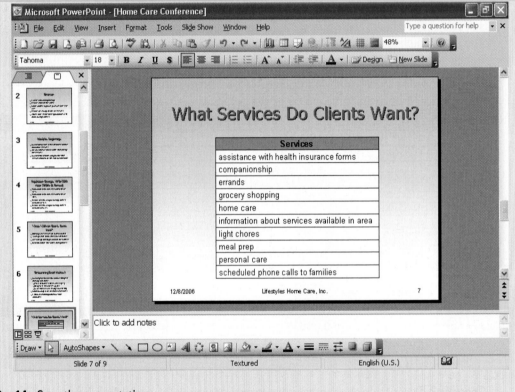

14. Save the presentation.

Now that you have inserted the Access query into Slide 7, you can complete the slide presentation by adding a chart to Slide 8.

Linking an Excel Chart to a PowerPoint Presentation

Caitlin wants to include an Excel column chart showing frequently requested services on Slide 8. She is still considering the format of the chart, so she asks you to link the chart to the presentation. This way, if she changes the chart, the revised chart will be automatically reflected in her presentation.

Linking Excel Data to a PowerPoint Presentation | Reference Window

- In Excel, select the information you want to insert into a PowerPoint presentation, and then click the Copy button on the Standard toolbar.
- In PowerPoint, click where you want to insert the Excel data, click Edit on the menu bar, and then click Paste Special.
- In the Paste Special dialog box, click Microsoft Excel Chart Object, if necessary, click the Paste link option button, and then click the OK button.

You will link the chart to the presentation now.

To link an Excel object to the presentation:

1. Move to **Slide 8** in the presentation. First, you need to change the slide layout to one appropriate for displaying the slide title and the linked chart.

2. Click **Format** on the menu bar, click **Slide Layout**, click the **Title Only** layout in the Slide Layout task pane, and then close the Slide Layout task pane.

3. Start Excel and then open the **LHCMostRequested** workbook located in the Tutorial.03\Tutorial folder included with your Data Files.

4. Scroll to the right and down so that you can see the chart, click the border of the chart area to select the entire chart (make sure the Chart toolbar displays "Chart Area" in the Chart Objects list box), and then click the **Copy** button 🖺 on the Standard toolbar. Do not close the workbook.

   Trouble? If the Chart toolbar displays "Plot Area" in the Chart Objects list box, click directly on the black border around the entire chart.

   Next, you need to switch back to the presentation and link the copied chart. Do not close the Excel workbook, or you will only be allowed to paste the chart instead of linking it.

5. Click the **Microsoft PowerPoint - [Home Care Conference]** button on the taskbar to switch back to the presentation.

6. Click **Edit** on the menu bar, and then click **Paste Special**. The Paste Special dialog box opens.

7. Make sure Microsoft Office Excel Chart Object is selected, click the **Paste link** option button, and then click the **OK** button. The chart is linked to the slide.

   Trouble? If the Paste link option button is not available (grayed out), then you closed the LHCMostRequested workbook. Switch back to Excel, open the workbook, copy the chart again, and then try pasting the link again.

   You need to resize the chart so it will be readable on the slide.

8. Drag the **corner sizing handles** to resize the chart so that it looks like the one shown in Figure 3-15. When you're finished, click an empty area on the slide to deselect the chart.

Figure 3-15	Linked Excel chart on PowerPoint slide after resizing

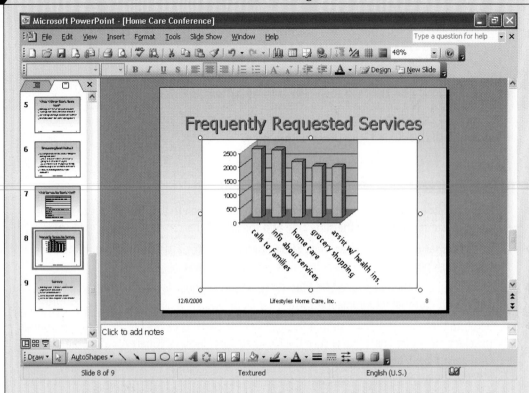

9. Save and close the presentation.

10. Click the **Microsoft Excel - LHCMostRequested** button on the taskbar, and then close the LHCMostRequested workbook.

11. Exit any open programs.

Caitlin is pleased with the finished letter and presentation. The integration features of Office make it easy for Caitlin to work with information created in different programs to produce exactly the results she wants.

Review

To reinforce the tasks you learned in this tutorial, go to the SAM 2003 Training Companion CD included with this text.

Quick Check

1. Describe how a mail merge works.
2. What is a merge field?
3. Why is a query a good data source for a mail merge?
4. Explain why you store the form letter with the merge fields in one document and the personalized form letter with individual names and addresses in another document.
5. How do you change heading levels in Outline view in Word?
6. What does the plus sign to the left of a paragraph in Outline view in Word indicate?
7. Describe the slide or slides that PowerPoint would create from a Word outline that has one Level 1 paragraph and three Level 2 paragraphs.

Review

Tutorial Summary

In this tutorial, you learned how to create a form letter that contains merge fields, and you learned how to merge data from a data source to the form letter. You learned how to filter only selected records from the data source into a final merged document. You also learned how to create a Word outline and then insert the outline as new slides in a PowerPoint presentation. Finally, you learned how to paste an Access query and link an Excel chart to a PowerPoint presentation.

Key Terms

data source	mail merge	merge field
demote	main document	promote
form letter	merge	starting document

Practice

Get hands-on practice of the skills you learned in the tutorial using the same case scenario.

Review Assignments

Data Files needed for the Review Assignments: SocialWorkContacts.mdb, LHCEmployeesOutline.doc, LHCEmployees.ppt, LHCGrowth2.xls, LHCServices.mdb

Now that the form letter is complete, Caitlin is ready to mail it. She needs to print the names and addresses on mailing labels that can be placed on the envelopes. Also, Caitlin wants to prepare a brief presentation to give to her employees at the next staff meeting. She wants to give the employees a thorough overview of the new services that they will be providing.

1. Open a new, blank document in Word, and then open the Mail Merge task pane so that it displays Step 1.
2. Select Labels as the document type, and then move to Step 2.
3. In Step 2, change the document layout and click the Label options link to open the Label Options dialog box. Select Avery standard in the Label products lists, and then scroll down the Product number list and choose product number 5160 - Address. Accept all other defaults in this dialog box, and then move to Step 3.
4. In Step 3, select recipients from an existing list in the Rehab Social Work Contacts table in the **SocialWorkContacts** database, which is stored in the Tutorial.03\Review folder included with your Data Files. You will print labels for all of the contacts in the list.
5. Move to Step 4. Lay out the first label by inserting the Address block item. Accept the defaults in the Insert Address Block dialog box. Match Word's Company field to the Hospital field in the table.
6. After you insert the Address block merge field in the first label, point to the small down arrow at the bottom of the task pane to scroll the task pane, if necessary, and then click the Update all labels button to copy the layout of the first label to the other labels on the page.
7. Save the main document (the one with the merge fields) as **Main Labels** in the Tutorial.03\Review folder included with your Data Files.
8. Move to Step 5 to preview the labels, and then move to Step 6 to complete the merge.
9. In Step 6, merge all of the labels to a new document. Scroll to the bottom of the page, click the first empty box on the left, and type your name. Save the document containing the merged labels as **Merged Labels** in the Tutorial.03\Review folder, print the document, and then close it. Close the Main Labels document without saving changes.

10. Open the Word document **LHCEmployeesOutline** located in the Tutorial.03\Review folder included with your Data Files, and save it as **Topics Outline** in the same folder.
11. Switch to Outline view, select all of the text, and demote all the text to Level 2.
12. Reformat the following paragraphs as Level 1 headings: Mission Statement, Overview, Why New Services?, New Services, Trust Issues, Current Employees, and Lifestyles Home Care, Inc.
13. Reformat the paragraphs in the following lists as Level 3 headings:
    Under the Level 1 heading "Why New Services?"
    - Many fewer people are eligible
    - People are willing to pay…
    Under the Level 1 heading "New Services"
    - Planning
    - Grocery Shopping
    - Meal Prep
    Under the Level 1 heading "Trust Issues"
    - Check quality…
    - Check for problems
    - Call supervisor…
    - Submit written report
    - Meet with supervisor…
    Under the Level 1 heading "Current Employees"
    - Will be offered…
    - Must attend training sessions
14. Save and close the Topics Outline document.
15. Open the PowerPoint presentation **LHCEmployees** located in the Tutorial.03\Review folder included with your Data Files, replace Caitlin's name with your own name, and then save it to the same folder as **Employee Presentation**.
16. Create new slides by inserting the Topics Outline document after Slide 1.
17. Go to Slide 3, insert a new slide as a new Slide 4 with the Title Only layout, click in the title text placeholder, and then type Current Services.
18. Open the Excel workbook **LHCGrowth2** located in the Tutorial.03\Review folder included with your Data Files, copy the range A6:F11 to the Clipboard, and then switch back to the Employee Presentation.
19. Link the contents of the Clipboard to Slide 4, and then resize the table as large as possible on the slide.
20. Insert a new slide after Slide 5 using the Title Only layout. Type **Services Requested Most Often** as the title.
21. Open the Access database **LHCServices** located in the Tutorial.03\Review folder included with your Data Files, copy the results of the Updated Services Requested Query to the Clipboard, close the query and the database, and then paste the contents of the Clipboard to the new Slide 6.
22. Center and reformat the query so that it matches the presentation design, and delete the query title.
23. Save the presentation, and then print it as handouts, six slides per page.
24. Close the presentation and the Excel workbook, and exit any open programs.

Challenge

Advance the skills you learned to merge addresses onto envelopes, and then update the merge fields for a letter to a music store's customers.

Case Problem 1

Data File needed for this Case Problem: MusicCustomers.mdb

Making Music Caleb Jacobson, the owner of Making Music, wrote a letter to his current customers providing information about the new lesson times he will be offering in the fall. He decides to send the letters in batches, using the cities as a sorting factor. Now he needs to send the letter to his customers in Ridgefield. You'll use the mail merge feature to create the envelopes for this mailing.

1. Open a new, blank document in Word, and then open the Mail Merge task pane so that it displays Step 1.
2. Select Envelopes as the document type, and then move to Step 2.

Explore

3. In Step 2, change the document layout and click the Envelope options link to open the Envelope Options dialog box. Change the Envelope Size to 6 3/4. (The address and return address should fit on your envelope with this setting, although its position will be off if you have a different size envelope. Alternately, you may select the size from the list that matches your envelope.)
4. Click the Printing Options tab, and then make sure that the Feed method will work on your printer. For example, does your printer print face up or face down, and in which position should you place the envelope to feed it into the printer? Click the OK button, and then move to Step 3.
5. Select recipients for the envelopes by using the Ridgefield Query in the **MusicCustomers** database, which is located in the Tutorial.03\Cases folder included with your Data Files. There is only one customer who lives in Ridgefield.

Explore

6. Move to Step 4, and arrange your envelopes by typing your name and address as the return address and then inserting the Address block in the middle of the envelope. Do not show the company name. Save the envelopes with the merge fields as **Merge Envelope** in the Tutorial.03\Cases folder included with your Data Files.
7. Preview the envelope.
8. Complete the merge by printing the envelope, and then merging the record to a new document. (If you do not have an envelope on which to print, print it on regular paper.) Save the document as **Ridgefield Envelopes** in the Tutorial.03\Cases folder included with your Data Files, and then close this document.
9. In the Merge Envelope document, go to Step 5 of 6 in the Mail Merge task pane.

Explore

10. Double-click the word "Rd," and then type "Ave." Open the **MusicCustomers** database, and then open the Ridgefield Query. Is the change you made in Word reflected in the Access query? Close the query and open the Mailing List table. Is the change you made reflected in Jose's record (record 3) here? Why or why not?

Explore

11. Change "Lincoln Rd." in Jose's address to "South Ave." Save and close the table and the database. Switch to the Merge Envelope document in Word, right-click anywhere on Jose's address, and then click Update Field. What happened? Why?
12. Go to Step 6, and then print the envelope. If you do not have an envelope, print it on a piece of paper.
13. Save and close the Merge Envelope document, and then exit any open program.

Case Problem 2

Data Files needed for this Case Problem: LFCOutline.doc, LFCFees.xls

Learning Fulfillment Centers Enrique Garcia has asked his assistant, Nia Walker, to prepare a presentation to give to potential customers. You'll prepare the presentation for Nia by completing the following:

1. Open the Word document **LFCOutline** located in the Tutorial.03\Cases folder included with your Data Files. Save it as **LFC Presentation Outline** in the same folder.
2. Use Outline view to adjust the topics so that they are grouped in a way that makes sense. Save your changes and close the document.
3. Create a new PowerPoint presentation using a design template of your choice. Create a title slide for the presentation. Include your name as the subtitle. Save the presentation as **New Customer Presentation** in the Tutorial.03\Cases folder.

4. Create new slides from the LFC Presentation Outline document. Scroll through the new slides.
5. Change the layout of the last two slides to one that can accommodate linked data from Excel.
6. Open the Excel file **LFCFees**, located in the Tutorial.03\Cases folder included with your Data Files. Link the appropriate data from this workbook to the appropriate slides in the presentation, and then resize and reposition the tables as needed. Does the color in the pasted table match the design you chose for the slides? If not, change the Fill Color of the table head in the workbook, and then update the link in the presentation.
7. Create a new final slide that includes the company's motto. (You can find the motto in the LFCFees workbook.)
8. Save the presentation, and then run the slide show.
9. Print the presentation slides as handouts, four slides per page.
10. Close the presentation and the open workbook, and then exit any open programs.

SAM Assessment and Training

Quick Check Answers

1. A mail merge combines a main or starting document that contains standard text and merge fields that indicate where to print variable information with a data source that contains the variable information.
2. special instructions that tell Word where to print the variable information
3. so that the merge will use your latest query instructions to retrieve the data
4. You use the form letter with the merge fields document to print other letters with a different data source or when the list of names and addresses in the data source changes. You use the personalized form letter to print and send to each recipient.
5. Click the Promote or Demote button on the Outlining toolbar.
6. that the paragraph has subitems (paragraphs at a lower level) associated with it
7. It becomes a slide with a title and three bullets of text.

New Perspectives on

Creating Web Pages with Microsoft® Office 2003

Using Word, Excel, Access, and PowerPoint to Create Web Pages

WEB 3

Read This Before You Begin

Data Files

To complete the "Creating Web Pages with Microsoft Office 2003" tutorial, you need the starting Data Files. See the inside back or front cover for information on downloading these files from course.com, or ask your instructor for assistance. The following table identifies each starting Data File and the folder it is stored in, as well as the ending files, which you create and save in each tutorial.

Folders		Starting Files	Ending Files
Web	Tutorial	Calculator.xls, Exercise.doc, Northeast.mdb, PeruExp.ppt	CalculatorWebPage.htm, Employer.htm, Employer Positions.html, ExerciseWebPage.htm, HealthHomePage.htm, Loan Calculator.xls, Mortgage Values.xls, MortgageWebPage.mht, Northeast.mdb, PeruExpedition.htm
	Review	Fund.xls, MPTour.ppt, Recruits.mdb, Stir-fry.doc	CalculatorPage.htm, ClassesHomePage.mht, College Calculator.xls, College Fund.xls, CollegeFundPage.htm, MachuPicchuTour.mht, Recruiter.html, Recruits.mdb, Stir-fryClass.mht, Student.htm

Storing Your Files

It is recommended that you store all your Data Files on a USB drive. Refer to the tutorial "Managing Your Files" for information on using USB drives. If you need to store your Data Files on floppy disks, you will need two high-density disks to store all the files for the "Creating Web Pages with Microsoft Office 2003" tutorial.

SAM 2003 Training Companion CD

The SAM 2003 Training Companion CD that comes with this text gives you "just-in-time" training and reinforcement of important Microsoft Office skills. Look for the SAM CD logo throughout each tutorial for opportunities to complete the hands-on tasks included on this CD.

Course Labs

The "Creating Web Pages with Microsoft Office 2003" tutorial features an interactive Course Lab to help you understand concepts related to Web pages and HTML. There are Lab Assignments at the end of the tutorial that relate to this lab. Contact your instructor or technical support person for assistance in accessing this lab.

Creating Web Pages with Microsoft Office 2003

Using Word, Excel, Access, and PowerPoint to Create Web Pages

Case | Temps Abound, Inc.

Temps Abound, Inc. is an agency that provides temporary office workers to businesses. Recently, Temps Abound has been getting requests for workers who can convert Office files into Web pages to be posted on the client's Web site or intranet. The latest requests have come from the following four clients: Bayside Health, Premier Finance, Northeast Seasonal Jobs International, and Global Humanitarian.

Bayside Health provides a variety of health-related services to corporations and other social service organizations. Susan Dague, publications director, develops newsletters on a variety of topics related to health and fitness. To broaden the audience for these newsletters, she wants to transform them into Web pages and add them to Bayside Health's Web site.

David Kowlske is a financial officer at Premier Finance, a lending company that is increasing its presence on the World Wide Web. David wants customers to be able to use the company's Web site to look up the current cost of a 20-year mortgage with a fixed interest rate. He also wants customers to be able to use the company's Web site to calculate mortgage payments based on the interest rate, the size of the mortgage, and the length of the loan. David has already created the Excel workbook that contains the values and formulas he wants to include on the Web pages.

Elsa Jensen is the founder of Northeast Seasonal Jobs International (NSJI), a company that contracts with hotels and resorts to supply their seasonal help. Elsa wants to create a Web page that lists the employers and their

Objectives		SAM Training Tasks	
• Learn how to share Office files online	• Create Web pages in Access	• Display your Web pages in a browser	• Hyperlink navigation with the mouse
• Create Web pages in Word	• Create Web pages in PowerPoint	• Format a Web page with themes	• Save a presentation as HTML
• Insert a hyperlink	• Publish Web pages to the Internet		
• Preview a Web page in a browser			
• Create Web pages in Excel			

Student Data Files For a complete list of the Data Files needed for this tutorial, see page WEB 2.

For hands-on practice of key tasks in this tutorial, go to the SAM 2003 Training Companion CD included with this text.

available positions. She will include this Web page on NSJI's company Web site so that this information will be available to NSJI employees when they work out of the office.

Global Humanitarian is a nonprofit organization that provides a variety of services to help people in less-developed countries, including organizing service expeditions. Miriam Schwartz, the managing director, wants to share a modified version of a PowerPoint presentation describing a recent expedition to Peru with potential volunteers and contributors. She wants people to be able to view the presentation on the organization's Web site.

In this tutorial, you'll create Web pages for all four of these clients.

Sharing Office Files Online

Most people are familiar with sharing Office files by printing and distributing paper copies of the file to others one at a time. However, as computers with network connections become more prevalent, it's becoming common to share Office files electronically as illustrated in Figure 1. One method is to send the Office file as an e-mail message or e-mail attachment to one person or a group of people simultaneously. Another method is to post the file as a Web page on an intranet or the Internet so that people can access the file as they need it.

Figure 1	Distribution methods for files

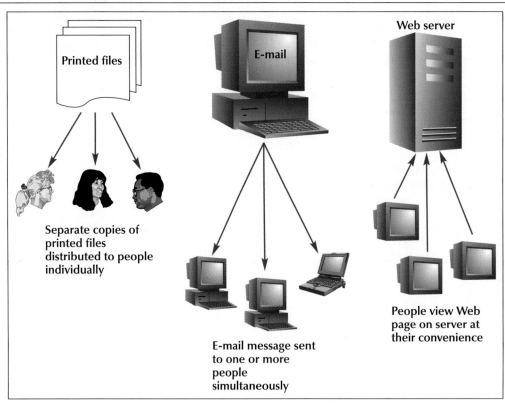

Most Web pages are created using the HTML programming language to describe the format of a Web page so that Web browsers know how to display the page. You can create a Web page by typing all of the necessary HTML code into a text document and saving the document with the .htm or .html file extension. Because a Web page contains HTML code, it is also called an **HTML document**. Professional designers create Web sites using a **Web page editor**, a software program designed specifically for that purpose, such as Macromedia Dreamweaver or Microsoft FrontPage. However, sometimes you'll want to quickly create a Web page from an existing Office file. Fortunately, you don't have to learn HTML to create Web pages; Word, Excel, Access, and PowerPoint can do the work for you.

Each Office program includes commands for saving a file as a Web page. To save a file as a Web page, you click File on the menu bar, choose the Save As or Save as Web Page command, and then change the Save as type option to Web page, Single File Web Page, or, in Word only, Web Page, Filtered.

If you save a file as a Web page, the file is saved as an HTML document and a new folder is created to contain all the supporting files (such as bullets, backgrounds, and graphics) for the Web page. For example, when you save a Web page with the filename "CompanyHomePage," a folder named "CompanyHomePage_files" is created. You use the Web page file format when you plan on creating multiple pages for a Web site.

A **single file Web page** is one file that contains the HTML document along with all the supporting files. The advantage of saving a file as a single file Web page is that you can send the single file Web page as an e-mail message or attachment and know that the recipient will have all the elements and supporting items referenced in the Web page. However, the file size of a single file Web page is larger than a Web page. Also, single file Web pages require Internet Explorer 4.0 or later.

A **filtered Web page** is an HTML document with the Office-related tags removed. Generally, you should not use filtered Web pages, which are available only in Word, unless you are experienced in creating Web pages and understand how HTML programming works.

Word creates a Web page from the entire file, and you can easily edit the content of the Web page in Word. With Excel, Access, and PowerPoint, you can choose to create a Web page from all or part of the file, but the editing ability may be more limited.

Creating Web Pages in Word

There are a few ways to create Web pages in Word. You can create a new, blank Web page document and then enter and format text and graphics as usual. You can create a Web page from a **template**, a special file that contains the design layout and tools for formatting page elements. You can also open an existing Word document and then save it as a Web page. You'll try the first and last method in this tutorial.

Creating Web Pages in Word	Reference Window

- Click Web page in the New area in the New Document task pane (*or* click the New button or the New Web Page button on the Standard toolbar *or* click the Open button and open an existing document).
- Click File on the menu bar, and then click Save as Web Page.
- Navigate to the location where you want to save the Web page.
- Type a new filename in the File name text box.
- Click the Save as type list arrow, and then click Web Page if you want to save the file as a Web page instead of a single file Web page.
- Click the Change Title button, type a page title, and then click the OK button.
- Click the Save button.

Susan (the publications director at Bayside Health) asks you to convert her current newsletter into a Web page for Bayside Health's new Web site. You'll open a blank Web page in Word, so that you can begin creating the Health News home page.

To create a new, blank Web page:

1. Start Word.
2. Click the **Show/Hide ¶** button ¶ on the Standard toolbar to display the nonprinting characters, if necessary.
3. Click **File** on the menu bar, and then click **New**. The New Document task pane opens.
4. Click the **Web page** link in the New area of the New Document task pane. A new, blank Web document opens, similar to a regular Word document. Note that the Web Layout View button is selected in the lower-left corner of the Document window, and the New button on the Standard toolbar is the New Web Page button.

As with other Word documents, you need to save the file to a storage disk. When you save the file as a Web page, you also need to specify the page title. The **page title** is the text that appears in the browser title bar each time the Web page is displayed in a browser. You should avoid using spaces in Web page filenames because some Web servers and browsers do not accept filenames with spaces.

You'll save the new document as a Web page.

To save a Web page:

1. Click **File** on the menu bar, and then click **Save as Web Page**. The Save As dialog box opens with Single File Web Page selected as the file type.
2. Click the **Save in** list arrow, and then navigate to the **Web\Tutorial** folder included with your Data Files.
3. Click the **Change Title** button. The Set Page Title dialog box opens.
4. Type **Health News Home Page** in the Page title text box, and then click the **OK** button.
5. Type **HealthHomePage** in the File name text box.
6. Click the **Save as type** list arrow, and then click **Web Page**. See Figure 2.

| Figure 2 | Completed Word Save As dialog box |

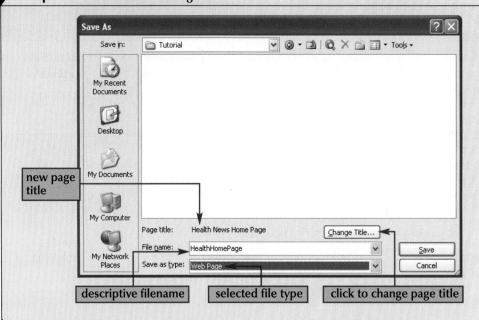

7. Click the **Save** button. The Web page is saved in the location you specified.

Word's basic editing and formatting features work the same in a Web page as they do in a regular Word document. You'll start typing the text of the home page.

To type the text of the home page:

1. Type **Bayside Health, Inc.**, and then press the **Enter** key twice.
2. Type **Welcome to our Health News Home Page**, and then press the **Enter** key twice.
3. Type **Our Health News Reports give you quick updates on these important topics:**, and then press the **Enter** key twice.
4. Click the **Bullets** button ☰ on the Formatting toolbar, and then type the following list:

   - **Exercise**
   - **Pain management**
   - **Low-fat cooking**

5. Press the **Enter** key three times, and then type your name.

You can manually transform the look of any aspect of the Web page as you would in an ordinary Word document, or you can apply a theme. A **theme** is a designed collection of formatting options that include colors, graphics, and background images.

The guidelines for formatting Web pages differ from those for documents. Although you can apply different fonts, font sizes, and colors to text, when people open your Web page in their browser, they may see something different, depending on their browser's settings. In addition, adding too many images, backgrounds, or other graphics can make the file size of the Web page large, leading to longer download times. If it takes too long, people might not wait for the page to load completely and instead jump to another page.

You'll format some of the text you typed, and then apply a theme.

To format the text of the home page:

1. Select the heading **Bayside Health, Inc.** and the subheading **Welcome to our Health News Home Page**.
2. Change the font to **Arial**, and then change the font size to **26**.
3. Click the **Font Color** button list arrow ▲▾ on the Formatting toolbar, and then click the red square in the third row, first column.
4. Center the heading and subheading, and then click outside the headings to deselect them. See Figure 3.

Figure 3	Formatted text of Web page

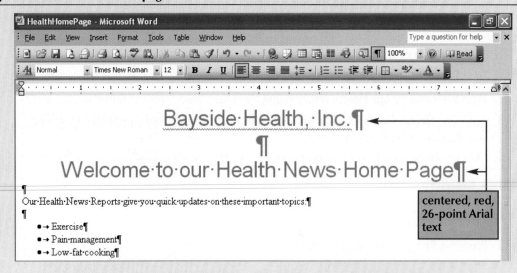

Trouble? If your document is not zoomed to 100%, click the Zoom list arrow on the Standard toolbar, and then click 100%.

Now that you have formatted the text, you'll select a theme. There are many themes available; however, some of the themes may need to be installed on first use.

To apply a theme to a Web page:

1. Click **Format** on the menu bar, and then click **Theme** to open the Theme dialog box.
2. Click **Capsules** in the Choose a Theme list box. See Figure 4.

Figure 4	Theme dialog box

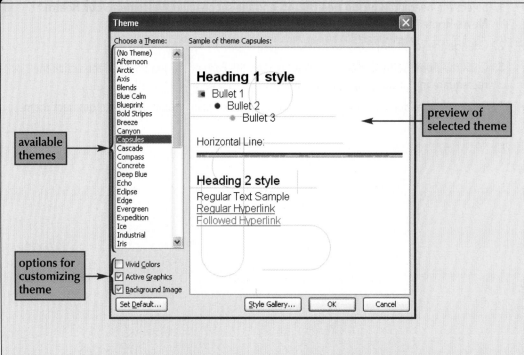

Trouble? If a dialog box opens, indicating that the Capsules theme is not installed on your computer, install the theme or select another theme.

3. Click the **OK** button. The Web page is now formatted as shown in Figure 5. The unformatted text is reformatted with the theme; however, the manual formatting you applied earlier remains intact, overriding the theme formatting.

Web page with theme ◄ **Figure 5**

4. Click the **Save** button 🔲 on the Standard toolbar to save your work.

When you have an existing document that you want share over the Web, you can save that document as a Web page rather than re-creating it in a blank Web page. Be aware, however, that not all elements you can create in a Word document convert to Web pages. One way to determine quickly which elements and features of a document will convert to a Web page and which will not is to view the page in Web Layout view.

One of the pages that Susan wants to include in the Web site will contain information about exercise. The information on exercise is currently stored as a desktop-published newsletter. You'll convert that Word document to a Web page.

To open the Exercise newsletter and view it in Web Layout view:

1. Open the **Exercise** document located in the **Web\Tutorial** folder included with your Data Files.

2. Click the **Print Layout View** button 🔲 in the lower-left corner of the Document window, if necessary, to display the document in Print Layout view.

3. Click the **Zoom** button list arrow `100%` on the Standard toolbar, and then click **Whole Page**. The newsletter is resized so that you can see the entire document on your screen.

4. Press the **Ctrl+End** keys to move the insertion point to the end of the document, press the **Enter** key three times, and then type your name. As you can see in Figure 6, this newsletter is set in two columns, and it contains a WordArt headline, a border, formatted headings, and a graphic (taken from Word's clip-art collection).

Figure 6 **Exercise newsletter**

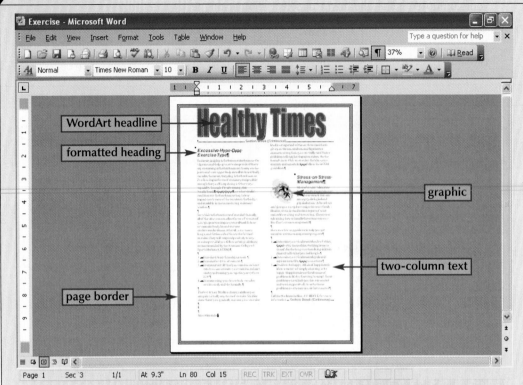

5. Click the **Web Layout View** button ⊡ in the lower-left corner of the Document window.

6. Scroll through the document to see how the Web page based on this document would look. The two-column portion of the document changes to a single column, and the border is hidden. The graphic moves to the top of the second section, under the heading "Excessive Hype Over Exercise Type."

You'll update the formatting and adjust the position of graphics after you save the newsletter as a Web page.

To save an existing document as a Web page:

1. Click **File** on the menu bar, and then click **Save as Web Page**. The Save As dialog box opens.

2. If necessary, click the **Save in** list arrow, and then navigate to the **Web\Tutorial** folder included with your Data Files.

3. Type **ExerciseWebPage** in the File name text box.

4. Click the **Save as type** list arrow, and then click **Web Page**. Remember, when you save the document as a Web page instead of a single file Web page, you create not only the single HTML document but also a folder with all of the associated files in it.

5. Click the **Change Title** button, type **Exercise News Report** in the Set Page title text box, and then click the **OK** button.

6. Click the **Save** button. A message informs you that some features of the original document (the desktop-published newsletter) cannot be displayed in Internet Explorer 4.0 or Netscape Navigator 4.0.

7. Click the **Continue** button. The document is saved as a Web page.

8. Drag the graphic down to position it after the first paragraph below the heading "Stress on Stress Management." See Figure 7.

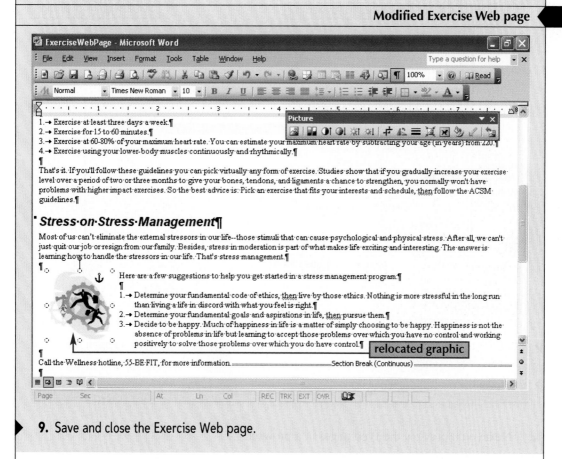

9. Save and close the Exercise Web page.

Next you'll insert hyperlinks.

Inserting Hyperlinks

Hyperlinks, or links, provide an easy way to navigate within and between Web pages. You can create a text link for each page using the appropriate text in the bulleted list. Once you change text to a link, it becomes colored and underlined, such as Exercise, and the pointer changes to 🖑 when positioned over the link. You can also use a graphic for a link; the only indicator that the graphic is a link is that the pointer changes shape when positioned over the graphic.

You'll change the Exercise bullet to a hyperlink so that the Exercise Web page opens when the Exercise bullet text is clicked.

To insert a text link:

1. Select **Exercise** in the bulleted list in the HealthHomePage document.

2. Click the **Insert Hyperlink** button 🔗 on the Standard toolbar. The Insert Hyperlink dialog box opens.

3. Click the **Look in** list arrow, and navigate to and click the **ExerciseWebPage** file you saved in the **Web\Tutorial** folder included with your Data Files. See Figure 8.

Figure 8 **Insert Hyperlink dialog box**

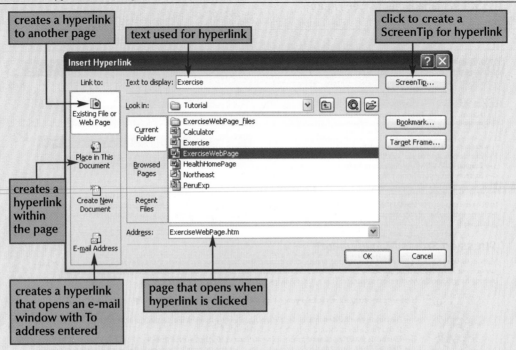

creates a hyperlink to another page

text used for hyperlink

click to create a ScreenTip for hyperlink

creates a hyperlink within the page

creates a hyperlink that opens an e-mail window with To address entered

page that opens when hyperlink is clicked

▶ **4.** Click the **OK** button. The Exercise text on the home page becomes a link to open the Exercise Web page.

▶ **5.** Save the HealthHomePage document.

Next you'll preview the Web pages in a browser.

Previewing Web Pages in a Browser

Before you publish Web pages for others to view, you should preview them in a Web browser to ensure that the pages look like you expect them to. Not all browsers display Web pages in the same way, so if you have access to more than one browser, you should preview your Web pages in the other browsers and, if possible, on other computers.

There are several ways to preview Web pages in a browser. You can use the Web Page Preview command on the File menu, you can display the Web toolbar and use the buttons on it to open the page in your default browser, or you can start your browser and use the Open command on the File menu. You'll preview the Web page you just created by using the Web Page Preview command. Because you will be viewing files stored on your computer, you don't have to be connected to the Internet to preview Web pages in a browser.

To preview Web pages in a browser:

▶ **1.** Click **File** on the menu bar, and then click **Web Page Preview**. The home page opens in the browser window.

▶ **2.** Maximize the browser window, if necessary. See Figure 9.

Web page previewed in Internet Explorer ◄ **Figure 9**

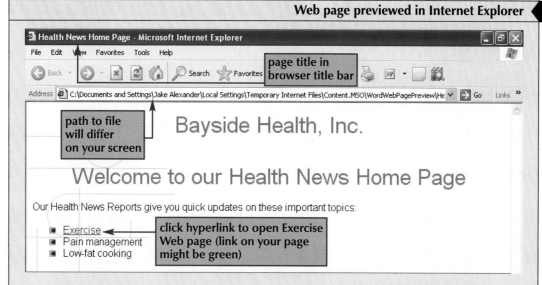

3. Click the **Exercise** link on the home page. The Exercise Web page opens in the browser window.

> **Trouble?** If the Exercise Web Page does not open, start your browser, open the HealthHomePage Web page, and then click the Exercise link. Close the browser when you are finished.

4. Click the **Close** button ⊠ on the browser window title bar to close the Web page and exit the browser.

5. Close the HealthHomePage document, and then exit Word.

Susan will later add more text and links to the two Web pages you created. She will ultimately publish all the Web pages on a Web server so that Bayside's clients can access them through the Internet.

Creating Web Pages in Excel

You can convert Excel workbooks into two types of Web pages: noninteractive and interactive. A **noninteractive Web page** allows users to scroll through and view the contents of an Excel workbook, but does not allow users to make any changes to the values displayed in the Web page. An **interactive Web page** provides tools for users to modify and format the values displayed in the Web page from their browsers. Any changes they make in the Web page do not affect the original workbook, so only the current user sees the changes being made. Also, changes do not last from one browser session to another.

You can also choose how much of the workbook to publish. In Excel, to **publish** means to save a workbook or portions of a workbook as a Web page.

If you need to modify the content of a Web page created in Excel, where you make those changes depends on whether the page is noninteractive or interactive. You can make changes to a noninteractive Web page in either the HTML document or in the workbook, which you then resave as a Web page. You should modify an interactive Web page only in the original workbook and then resave the workbook as a Web page. When you resave a Web page, you can select previously published items in the Publish as Web Page dialog box. If you publish to an existing Web page, you can click Replace file to copy over the page or you can click Add to file to append the new data at the end of the Web page.

Reference Window

Creating Web Pages in Excel

- Click the Open button and open an existing workbook that you want to save as a Web page.
- Click File on the menu bar, and then click Save as Web Page.
- Navigate to the location where you want to save the Web page.
- Type a new filename in the File name text box.
- Click the Save as type list arrow, and then click Single File Web Page if you want to save the file as a single file Web page.
- Click the Change Title button, type a page title, and then click the OK button.
- Check the Add interactivity check box to create an interactive Web page; leave it unchecked to create a noninteractive Web page.
- Click the Publish button, click the Choose list arrow, and then click what you want to include in the Web page.
- Check the AutoRepublish every time this workbook is saved check box.
- Check the Open published web page in browser check box to preview the Web page in a browser.
- Click the Publish button.

David (a financial officer at Premier Finance) has created a workbook that calculates the cost of a 20-year mortgage with a fixed interest rate of 5.5 percent. He wants you to convert this workbook to a Web page for Premier's Web site. You'll convert David's mortgage data into a noninteractive Web page that will display the values for a $100,000 mortgage for 20 years at a fixed 5.5 percent annual interest rate.

To open the Mortgage workbook:

1. Start Excel, and then open the **Calculator** workbook located in the **Web\Tutorial** folder included with your Data Files.

2. Review the contents of the workbook, and then return to the Documentation worksheet.

3. On the Documentation worksheet, enter the current date in cell B3 and enter your name in cell B4.

4. Save the Calculator workbook as **Mortgage Values** in the **Web\Tutorial** folder.

The Loan Values worksheet displays the current mortgage cost of a $100,000 loan, along with two embedded charts that show the declining balance on the principal over 240 payments and the breakdown between total interest payments and total principal payments. The Schedule worksheet displays a sample payment schedule for a 20-year mortgage. You'll save all of the data and charts on the Loan Values worksheet as a noninteractive Web page.

To create a noninteractive Web page:

1. Click **File** on the menu bar, and then click **Save as Web Page**. The Save As dialog box opens. See Figure 10.

Excel Save As dialog box | **Figure 10**

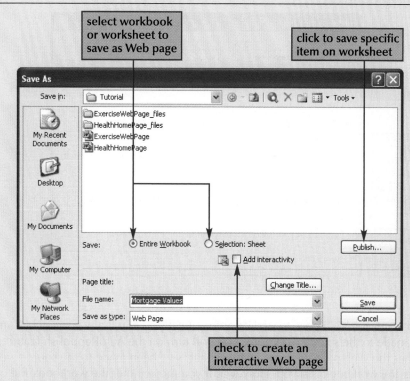

select workbook or worksheet to save as Web page

click to save specific item on worksheet

check to create an interactive Web page

2. Verify that the **Add interactivity** check box is unchecked.

3. Click the **Change Title** button to open the Set Page Title dialog box, type **Sample Mortgage Values** in the Page title text box, and then click the **OK** button. The page title appears in the Save As dialog box above the File name text box.

4. Type **MortgageWebPage** in the File name text box.

5. Click the **Save as type** list arrow, and then click **Single File Web Page**.

The next step is to choose which components of the workbook to publish. You can choose to publish either the entire workbook or the current selection in the active worksheet (which in this case is the entire Loan Values worksheet). Or, you can click the Publish button, which opens the Publish as Web Page dialog box, to make additional choices. In the Publish as Web Page dialog box, you can choose to publish the entire workbook; a specific worksheet in the workbook; an item on the selected worksheet, such as an embedded chart or a pivot table; a contiguous range of cells in a worksheet; or a previously published selection from the workbook.

David wants only the Loan Values worksheet published as a noninteractive Web page, and he wants to include both of the embedded charts on that worksheet.

To publish all of the items on a worksheet:

1. Click the **Publish** button. The Publish as Web Page dialog box opens.

2. Click the **Choose** list arrow, and then click **Items on Loan Values**. Excel displays three more options, each of which is based on the Loan Values worksheet. You can publish all the contents of the Loan Values worksheet or either of the two embedded charts.

3. Click **Sheet All contents of Loan Values** in the list. This has the same effect as clicking the Selection: Sheet option button in the Save As dialog box. See Figure 11.

Figure 11 ▶ Publish as Web Page dialog box

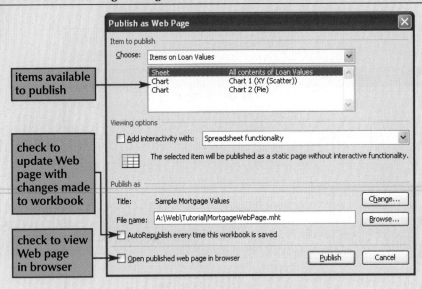

David wants the Web page to update automatically so that it always matches any changes made to the source workbook. You will turn on the AutoRepublish feature, which republishes the Web page with any changes that have been made to the source workbook whenever the workbook is saved. However, if you move either the workbook file or the Web page file, the AutoRepublish feature will not work.

To immediately view the Web page in your browser, you can check the Open published web page in browser check box. If you prefer not to immediately view the Web page, you can use the Web Page Preview command on the Web toolbar in Excel, or you can use the Open command in Internet Explorer to open the Web page file directly from the browser.

You'll turn on the AutoRepublish feature and open the Web page in the browser.

To turn on the AutoRepublish feature and open the Web page in the browser:

1. Click the **AutoRepublish every time this workbook is saved** check box to insert a check mark.

2. Click the **Open published web page in browser** check box to insert a check mark, if necessary.

3. Click the **Publish** button. The worksheet is saved as a single file Web page, and the Web page opens in a browser.

4. Click the **Maximize** button ▣ on the browser title bar to maximize the browser window, if necessary. See Figure 12.

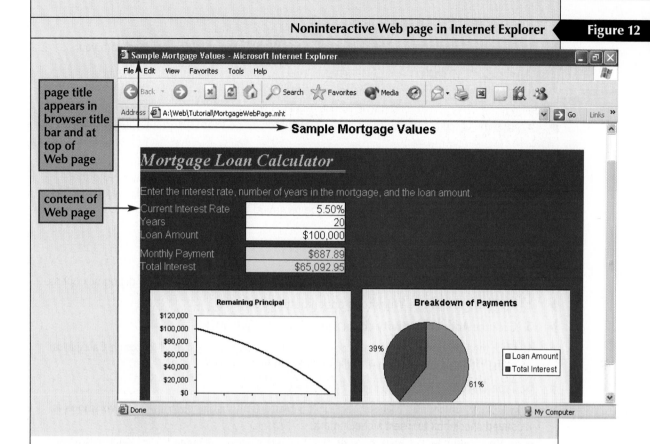

Noninteractive Web page in Internet Explorer | Figure 12

You'll close the Web browser and the workbook.

To close the browser and workbook:

1. Click the **Close** button ☒ on the browser title bar to close the Web browser and return to the Mortgage workbook.

2. Close the workbook without saving changes, but leave Excel running.

David wants to include an interactive Web page on Premier's Web site in which customers can enter different mortgage amounts to see how these values affect the overall cost of the mortgage. Users can enter data and perform calculations on an interactive Web page as long as they are using Internet Explorer 5.01 or later and have Excel on their computer. The interactivity available depends on what is in the workbook you are publishing, such as charts and pivot tables. You cannot open and modify interactive Web pages in Excel, so it's important to save a copy of the original workbook that you can modify and then republish as needed. Also, you can publish only the entire workbook with interactivity.

David already created the workbook from which he wants you to create the interactive Web page. This is the same workbook you opened when you created the noninteractive Web page.

To open the Calculator workbook:

▶ 1. Open the **Calculator** workbook located in the **Web\Tutorial** folder included with your Data Files.

▶ 2. On the Documentation worksheet, enter the current date in cell B3 and enter your name in cell B4.

▶ 3. Save the Calculator workbook as **Loan Calculator** in the **Web\Tutorial** folder.

This time, you'll publish the entire workbook as an interactive Web page. Note that Excel does not publish embedded charts or chart sheets in interactive Web pages, so the charts in the Loan Values worksheet will be removed during the conversion.

To create an interactive Web page:

▶ 1. Click **File** on the menu bar, and then click **Save as Web Page**. The Save As dialog box opens.

▶ 2. Verify that the **Entire Workbook** option button is selected.

▶ 3. Click the **Add interactivity** check box to insert a check mark.

▶ 4. Click the **Change Title** button to open the Set Title dialog box, type **Mortgage Calculator** in the Title text box, and then click the **OK** button.

▶ 5. Type **CalculatorWebPage** in the File name text box.

▶ 6. Click the **Publish** button, and then click the **AutoRepublish every time this workbook is saved** check box to insert a check mark.

▶ 7. Verify that the **Open published web page in browser** check box is checked.

▶ 8. Click the **Publish** button. The Mortgage Calculator Web page opens in your browser. It might take a minute or so to create the interactive Web page based on this workbook.

Trouble? If Netscape is your default browser, you will not be able to view the interactive Web page. Exit Excel, and then read the next set of steps, but do not complete them.

The contents of the workbook are placed on an interactive Web page as an object called the **spreadsheet component**. The initial size of the spreadsheet component fits the current dimensions of the Web browser window. If you resize the Web browser window, you might also need to refresh the window to resize the spreadsheet component. The spreadsheet component is a fully functioning workbook. You can enter new values or formulas, resize the rows or columns, and format the appearance of the worksheet cells. You move between worksheets in the spreadsheet component by clicking the tab at the bottom of the spreadsheet component and then clicking the desired sheet name from the list.

You'll view and test the interactive workbook by placing new values on the Mortgage Calculator Web page.

To view and test an interactive Web page:

▶ 1. Click the **Maximize** button 🔲 on the browser title bar. The Web browser enlarges to fit the entire screen, but the spreadsheet component does not change size.

▶ 2. Click the **Refresh** button 🗎 on the Standard Buttons toolbar. If necessary, the spreadsheet component enlarges to match the new dimensions of the browser window. See Figure 13.

Mortgage Calculator Web page in Internet Explorer   Figure 13

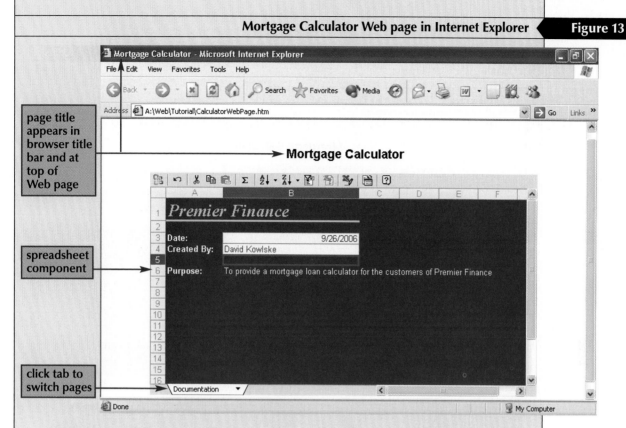

The spreadsheet component is a fully functioning object. You can enter new values or formulas, resize the rows or columns, and format the appearance of the worksheet cells. You move between worksheets in the spreadsheet component by clicking the tab at the bottom of the spreadsheet component and then clicking the desired sheet name from the list. You'll test the interactive workbook by placing new values on the Mortgage Calculator Web page.

3. Click the **Documentation** tab, and then click **Loan Values** in the list of worksheet names.

4. Click cell **B6**, type **15**, and then press the **Enter** key. The value of the monthly payment increases to $817.08, and the overall cost of the mortgage decreases to $47,075.02. See Figure 14.

Figure 14 ▶ **Interactive Web page updated**

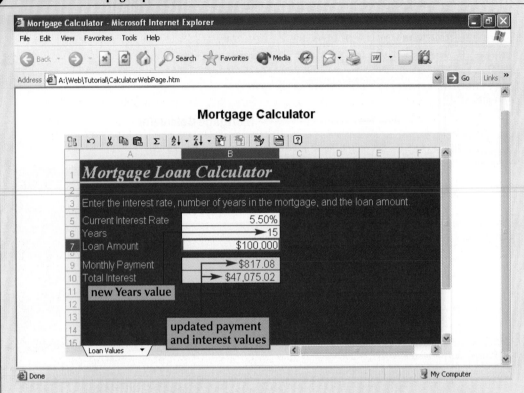

5. Click the **Close** button ⊠ on the browser title bar to close the Web browser and return to the Loan Calculator workbook in Excel.

6. Close the workbook without saving changes, and then exit Excel.

Although you can make changes to both the content and the appearance of an interactive Web page, these changes are not saved in the workbook. The original content and appearance will be displayed the next time you open the Web page.

Creating Web Pages in Access

You can create three types of Web pages based on Access database objects—a static HTML page, a dynamic HTML page, or a data access page. The type of Web page you create depends on how you want the information to be shared and manipulated by other users. Note that the Web Page and Single File Web Page options do not exist in Access.

A **static HTML page** (also called a static Web page) is a Web page based on a table, query, form, or report that shows the state of the database object at the time the page was created. Static HTML pages can be displayed in any Web browser that supports HTML version 3.2 or later.

A **dynamic HTML page** (also called a dynamic Web page) is a Web page based on a table, query, or form that is created each time the page is viewed or refreshed. Dynamic HTML pages can be displayed in any browser.

Similar to a dynamic HTML page, a **data access page** is a Web page that is linked to the data in the database. You can use a data access page to view, update, manipulate, or delete data in the Access database object on which the data access page is based. You create a data access page as a database object (table, query, form, report, page, macro, or module) that contains a shortcut to the location of the page's corresponding HTML file, which is stored outside the database. Users must have access to the database from which the data access page is created to view and make changes to the database. Data access pages require Microsoft Internet Explorer 5.01 with Service Pack 2 or later.

Elsa (the founder of Northeast Seasonal Jobs International) wants you to create a Web page that lists employers and their available positions. You'll create this Web page based on the Employer Positions query, which shows selected fields from both the Employer and Position tables. Because Elsa does not want the employees to be able to make changes to this information, you'll create a static Web page.

In Access, you create a static Web page by exporting a database object to an HTML document. In the Export dialog box, you specify the filename, file type, and location for the exported object. The exported HTML document does not exist in the database as a database object; it is a separate file stored in the location you specify.

The Save formatted option in the Export dialog box enables you to display the object in a format similar to its appearance in Datasheet view, with all the column headings, shading, and so on. If you do not choose this option, the object will appear without the field names as column headings and the appropriate spacing between columns.

Creating Static Web Pages in Access

Reference Window

- Click the Open button, open an existing database, and then display the object that you want to save as a static Web page.
- Right-click the object in the Database window, and then click Export.
- Navigate to the location where you want to save the Web page.
- Click the Save as type list arrow, and then click HTML Documents.
- Click the Save formatted check box.
- Click the Export button.
- Click the Default encoding option button, and then click the OK button.

To create the Web page Elsa requested, you'll save the Employer Positions query as an HTML document.

To export the Employer Positions query as an HTML document:

1. Start Access, and then open the **Northeast** database, located in the **Web\Tutorial** folder included with your Data Files.

   Trouble? If a dialog box opens with a message about installing the Microsoft Jet Service Pack, see your instructor or technical support person for assistance. You must have the appropriate Service Pack installed in order to open and work with Access databases safely.

   Trouble? If a dialog box opens warning you that the database may not be safe, click the Open button. If a dialog box opens, warning you that Access can't open the database due to security restrictions, click the OK button, click Tools on the menu bar, point to Macro, click Security, click the Medium option button, click the OK button, restart your computer if you're requested to do so, repeat Step 1, and then click the Open button if another dialog box opens telling you that the database may not be safe. When you're finished with this tutorial, change the macro security setting back to its original level.

2. Click **Queries** in the Objects bar of the Database window, right-click **Employer Positions**, and then click **Export** on the shortcut menu. The Export dialog box opens, displaying the type and name of the object you are exporting in its title bar (in this case, the Employer Positions query).

3. Verify that the Save in list box displays the **Web\Tutorial** folder.

4. Click the **Save as type** list arrow, and then click **HTML Documents**. The query name is added to the File name text box automatically.

5. Click the **Save formatted** check box. This is because Elsa wants the Employer Positions query to appear in datasheet format. See Figure 15. There is no option to change the page title; the page title will match the object name.

Figure 15 ▶ **Export dialog box**

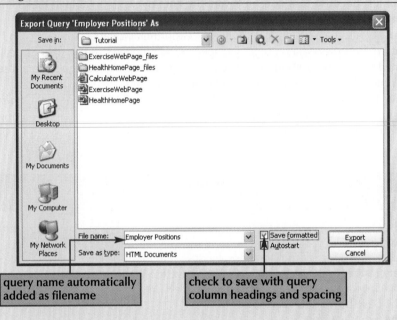

query name automatically added as filename

check to save with query column headings and spacing

6. Click the **Export** button. The HTML Output Options dialog box opens.

The HTML Output Options dialog box provides options for choosing an HTML template in which to display the Web page, or for using the default format. Elsa does not want to use a template for the Employer Positions query, so you can use the default settings.

7. Verify that the **Default encoding** option button is selected, and then click the **OK** button. Access exports the Employer Positions query to a new HTML document named Employer Positions in the Web\Tutorial folder, not in the Northeast database as a database object.

You will use the Web toolbar to open your browser and view the Web page you just created.

To view the Employer Positions query Web page:

1. Click **View** on the menu bar, point to **Toolbars**, and then click **Web**. The Web toolbar opens.

2. Click the **Go** button on the Web toolbar, and then click **Open Hyperlink**. The Open Internet Address dialog box opens, in which you enter the URL of the Web site or the name of the HTML document you want to view.

3. Click the **Browse** button to open the Browse dialog box, verify that the Look in list box displays the **Web\Tutorial** folder included with your Data Files, click **Employer Positions** in the list, and then click the **Open** button. The Address list box in the Open Internet Address dialog box displays the address for the Employer Positions HTML document.

4. Click the **OK** button. Internet Explorer starts and the Employer Positions Web page opens. See Figure 16.

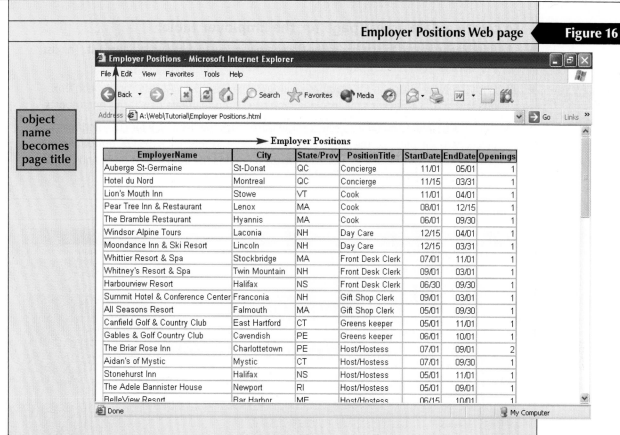

Employer Positions Web page — **Figure 16**

> **5.** Scroll through the Employer Positions Web page to view its contents.

> **6.** Click the **Close** button ☒ on the browser title bar to close the browser. You return to the database window in Access.

Because you created a static Web page, any future changes made to the underlying data in the Employer and Position tables will not appear in the Employer Positions Web page.

Next, Elsa wants you to create a Web page that shows the current information in the Employer table, and she wants changes made to the data in the Employer table to be reflected in the Web page. In addition, Elsa wants NSJI employees to be able to make changes to the Employer table from the Web page. To meet Elsa's needs, you'll create a data access page.

Creating Data Access Pages in Access

Reference Window

- Click the Open button, open an existing database, and then click Pages in the Objects bar of the Database window.
- Click the New button in the Database window.
- Click AutoPage: Columnar to select this wizard, select the table or query to use as the basis of the data access page, and then click the OK button.

You can create a data access page either in Design view or by using a wizard. To create the data access page for the Employer table, you'll use the AutoPage: Columnar Wizard.

To create a data access page for the Employer table:

1. Click **Pages** in the Objects bar of the Database window to display the Pages list. The list box does not contain any pages.

2. Click the **New** button in the Database window. The New Data Access Page dialog box opens. This dialog box is similar to ones you have used to create new forms and reports.

3. Click **AutoPage: Columnar** to select this wizard, click the list arrow for choosing the table or query as the basis for the page, click **Employer**, and then click the **OK** button. After a few moments, the AutoPage: Columnar Wizard creates the data access page and displays it in Page view. See Figure 17.

| Figure 17 | Employer data access page |

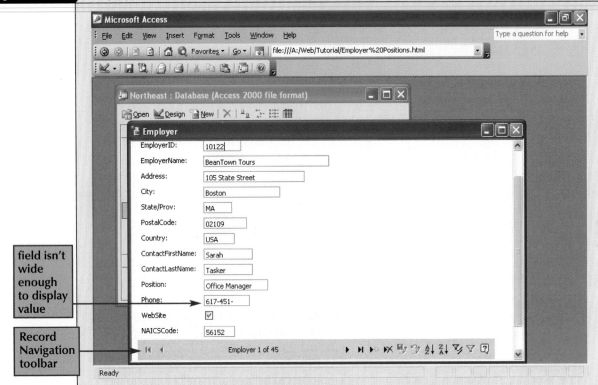

field isn't wide enough to display value

Record Navigation toolbar

Trouble? If your data access page appears with an AutoFormat applied to it, your screen will differ slightly from the one shown in the figure. This will not affect your work with the page; continue with the tutorial.

The Phone field value is not completely visible on the data access page. You can fix this quickly in Design view.

To modify the data access page in Design view:

1. Click the **View** button for Design view on the Page View toolbar. The data access page opens in Design view.

2. Click the **Phone** field's text box to select it, and then drag the center-right sizing handle to the right until the Phone text box is approximately the same size as the Position text box above it.

3. Click the **View** button for Page view on the Page Design toolbar to switch back to Page view. The Phone field value is now completely visible.

The Record Navigation toolbar, which appears below the record, provides buttons for moving between table records, similar to the buttons you use to move between records in a form, and buttons for adding and deleting records, sorting and filtering data, and so on. Before you continue, you'll save the data access page.

To save the data access page:

1. Click the **Save** button 🖫 on the Page View toolbar. The Save As Data Access Page dialog box opens.

2. Verify that the Save in list box displays the **Web\Tutorial** folder.

3. Click the **Save** button to save the data access page with the default name "Employer."

   Trouble? If a dialog box opens with a warning about the connection string, click the OK button.

Elsa has a change to make to one of the records in the Employer table. You can make the necessary changes directly in the data access page, which will simultaneously update the Employer table in the Northeast database. You can save changes you make to a record in a data access page either by moving to another record or by clicking the Save button on the Record Navigation toolbar.

To update the contact information in Page view:

1. Use the Record Navigation toolbar to move to record 3 (for the Bayside Inn & Country Club).

2. Double-click the entry **Mary** in the ContactFirstName field, type **Jeffrey**, double-click the entry **Russell** in the ContactLastName field, and then type **Hersha**.

3. Click the **Save** button 🖫 on the Record Navigation toolbar.

4. Click the **Close** button ☒ on the Employer window title bar. The data access page closes, and you return to the Database window. The Employer data access page is listed in the Pages list box.

Now, you'll see how the data access page looks in Internet Explorer.

To view the Employer data access page in Internet Explorer:

1. Right-click **Employer** in the Pages list box, and then click **Web Page Preview** on the shortcut menu. Internet Explorer starts and the Employer data access page opens. See Figure 18.

Figure 18 | **Employer data access page in Internet Explorer**

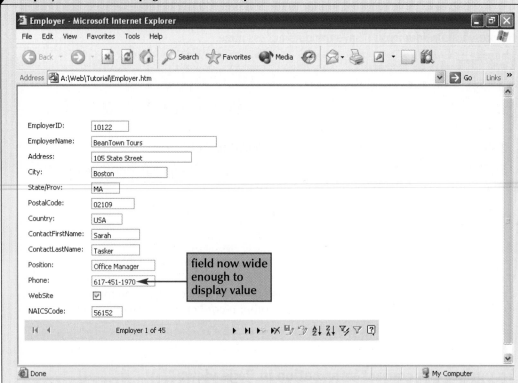

2. Click the **Close** button ⊠ on the browser title bar. The browser exits and you return to the Database window.

   To confirm that the changes you made earlier to the contact information are reflected in the Employer table, you'll open the table now and view the record.

3. Click **Tables** in the Objects bar of the Database window, and then open the **Employer** table in Datasheet view.

4. Scroll to the right and notice that the contact information for the Bayside Inn & Country Club is now Jeffrey Hersha.

5. Right-click the Web toolbar, click **Web** to close the Web toolbar, and then exit Access.

Now NSJI employees can use the company's intranet to view and update employer data in Internet Explorer.

Creating Web Pages in PowerPoint

Miriam (the managing director of Global Humanitarian) asks you to convert her Peru Expedition Report presentation to a Web page. When you save a presentation as a Web page or single file Web page, each slide is saved as an HTML document and a navigation frame is added to the left of the slide frame in the presentation. The **navigation frame**, also called the outline pane, contains links to each of the HTML documents (slides). There is also a toolbar, which contains buttons for hiding the outline of the presentation, hiding the notes pane, moving to the next or previous slide, and running the presentation as a slide show. If your presentation includes graphics, PowerPoint usually converts them to separate files in GIF or JPEG format.

If you want to edit the resulting HTML documents, you need to use either a word processing program that supports HTML editing (such as Word) or a dedicated HTML editor (such as Microsoft FrontPage). You cannot edit HTML documents directly in PowerPoint.

Creating Web Pages in PowerPoint

Reference Window

- Click the Open button and open an existing presentation that you want to save as a Web page.
- Click File on the menu bar, and then click Save as Web Page.
- Navigate to the location where you want to save the Web page.
- Type a new filename in the File name text box.
- Click the Save as type list arrow, and then click Single File Web Page or Web Page.
- Click the Publish button.
- Click the Complete presentation option button or click the Slide number option button and enter the slide numbers.
- Select an option in the Browser support area.
- Click the Change button, type a page title, and then click the OK button.
- Check the Open published Web page in browser check box to preview the Web page in a browser.
- Click the Publish button.

You'll open the Peru Expedition Report presentation and save it as a Web page.

To open the presentation:

1. Start PowerPoint, and then open the **PeruExp** presentation located in the **Web\Tutorial** folder included with your Data Files.

2. Replace Miriam's name in the subtitle box with your name.

3. Review the content of the presentation, which is similar to the Peru Expedition Report presentation you created in an earlier tutorial.

Next, you'll save the presentation as a Web page. You can choose to save either the entire presentation or a consecutive group of slides. Miriam asks you to include all the slides in the Web page.

To save a presentation as a Web page and preview it in a browser:

1. Click **File** on the menu bar, and then click **Save as Web Page**. The Save As dialog box opens.

2. Verify that the Save in location is the **Web\Tutorial** folder included with your Data Files, type **PeruExpedition** in the File name text box, click the **Save as type** list arrow, and then click **Web Page**.

3. Click the **Publish** button. The Publish as Web Page dialog box opens.

4. Verify that the **Complete presentation** option button is selected.

5. Click the **Microsoft Internet Explorer 4.0 or later (high fidelity)** option button in the Browser support area, if necessary.

6. Click the **Change** button, type **Peru Expedition Report** in the Set Page Title text box, and then click the **OK** button.

7. Verify that the **Open published Web page in browser** check box is checked. See Figure 19.

Figure 19 Publish as Web Page dialog box

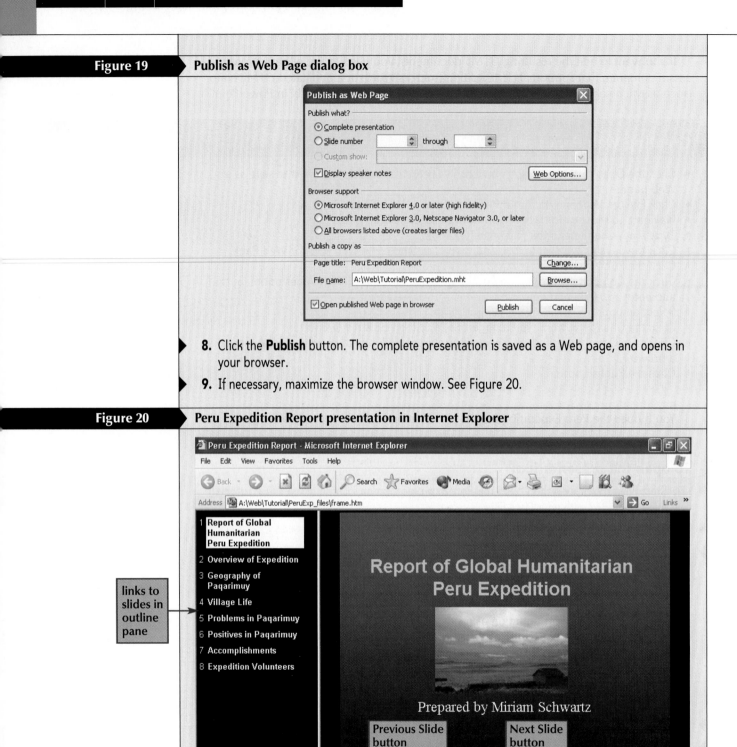

8. Click the **Publish** button. The complete presentation is saved as a Web page, and opens in your browser.

9. If necessary, maximize the browser window. See Figure 20.

Figure 20 Peru Expedition Report presentation in Internet Explorer

links to slides in outline pane

Trouble? If you don't see the outline, click the Outline button at the bottom of the screen.

The title slide of the Peru Expedition Report presentation appears in the slide pane, and an outline of the slides appears in the outline pane. Each outline item is a hyperlink to its corresponding slide. Also, a navigation bar appears at the bottom of the window. These hyperlinks and the navigation bar help you move through the presentation. The outline hyperlinks allow you to jump from one slide to any other in any order, whereas the navigation buttons help you to move one slide forward or backward.

To navigate a presentation Web page:

1. Click the **Next Slide** button ⇲ on the navigation bar at the bottom of the Web page. The slide pane displays Slide 2 of the presentation. Next, you'll test the hyperlinks that enable viewers to move between slides.

2. Click the **Accomplishments** hyperlink in the outline pane. The slide pane displays the Accomplishments slide (Slide 7).

3. Click the **Previous Slide** button ⇱ on the navigation bar at the bottom of the Web page. The Positives in Paqarimuy slide (Slide 6) appears in the slide pane.

4. Click the **Slide Show** button on the navigation bar to display the presentation full screen.

5. Click to display the next slide, press the **Esc** key to end the slide show, and then close the Web browser.

6. Exit PowerPoint without saving changes.

Once you create a Web page, you'll want others to be able to view it.

Publishing Web Pages

After you create a Web page, you need to copy the HTML file to a Web server or a network server so that others can view your Web pages over the World Wide Web or an intranet. If you used the Web Page option instead of the Single File Web Page option, you also need to copy the associated folder and its files. This process is called **publishing** the Web page to a server. Note that this use of the term *publish* is different from how Microsoft uses the term *publish* in Excel and PowerPoint. Publishing files to a server is also sometimes referred to as **uploading** files to a server.

You can copy the files for your Web pages to the appropriate server using a variety of methods, including FTP or Web folders. **FTP (file transfer protocol)** is a communication protocol that enables you to manipulate files and folders between remote computers. A **Web folder** is a folder from which you can transfer and manipulate files on a network server or a Web server. The actual location for the HTML files on the server, the file structure, and the filenames you use will differ depending on the server. Be sure to verify that you have permission to copy files to a server and contact your ISP or network administrator for the exact steps to follow before attempting to publish your Web pages to a server.

Also, you might need to rename the home page file to a specific filename, such as "index.htm" or "index.html," depending on the server. Ask the network administrator or ISP before publishing your Web page to a server. If you need to rename the file, be sure to test and update all links as necessary. You might need to resave the Web pages you created from Excel workbooks and any data access pages in Access, because these files contain references between the source file and the Web page.

Publishing Web Pages | Reference Window

- Contact your ISP or network administrator for the exact file structure, process, and location for publishing Web pages.
- Copy all the files and folders associated with the Web pages to the location specified by the administrator.
- View the published pages in different Web browsers and on several computer setups to test them.

After you publish Web pages to a server, you should test the pages by opening and viewing them using different Web browsers, different versions of the browsers, and several computer setups to ensure that the page content appears as you intended. Try to use the same browsers, versions, and computer setups that the people you intend to view the pages have. This final step will help to ensure that users can accurately see and use the information you published.

Review

To reinforce the tasks you learned in this tutorial, go to the SAM 2003 Training Companion CD included with this text.

Quick Check

1. What are three ways to share Office files?
2. What is a page title?
3. True or False: The font you apply to text on a Web page is always the same font that people see when they open that Web page in their browser.
4. What is the difference between a noninteractive Web page and an interactive Web page created from an Excel workbook?
5. If you want to link the data in a Web page to a database, what kind of Web page would you create?
6. True or False: You can create a Web page from only a complete PowerPoint presentation.
7. What should you do to test Web pages that you have published to a server?

Review

Tutorial Summary

You created Web pages from four Microsoft Office 2003 programs: Word, Excel, Access, and PowerPoint. You learned how to create a new Web page in Word, you learned how to apply a theme to that Web page, and you learned how to create a hyperlink from that page to another. You then learned how to create Web pages from existing Word documents, Excel workbooks, Access databases, and PowerPoint presentations. In addition, you learned how to create interactive Web pages from an Excel workbook, and how to create a data access page from an Access database. You also learned how to run a PowerPoint slide show from a Web page. You also learned how to preview Web pages in a browser. Finally, you learned how to publish Web pages to a server.

Key Terms

data access page	navigation frame	static HTML page
dynamic HTML page	noninteractive Web page	template
filtered Web page	page title	theme
FTP (file transfer protocol)	publish	upload
HTML document	single file Web page	Web folder
interactive Web page	spreadsheet component	Web page editor

Practice

Get hands-on practice of the skills you learned in the tutorial using the same case scenario.

Review Assignments

Data Files needed for the Review Assignments: Stir-fry.doc, Fund.xls, Recruits.mdb, and MPTour.ppt

The Temps Abound clients are pleased with the Web pages you created for them, and they've each asked you to create an additional Web page.

Bayside Health has recently been contracted to host a series of lectures on vegetarian cooking for college students. Susan asks you to begin creating a Web site that provides information on the classes. You'll need to use a desktop-published flier as the basis for one of the Web pages.

1. Start Word, and then open a new, blank Web page.
2. Add headings explaining the purpose of the Web page, and then type a paragraph of text introducing a series of vegetarian cooking classes. Add a bulleted list of class topics; include "The Fast Art of Stir-frying" as one of the topics.
3. Format the Web page using any theme. Adjust fonts and font sizes as necessary.
4. Add your name at the bottom of the document, and save the document as a Single File Web page with the filename **ClassesHomePage** in the **Web\Review** folder included with your Data Files and the page title "Cooking Classes." Leave the Web page file open.
5. Open the **Stir-fry** document located in the **Web\Review** folder.
6. Preview the document zoomed to Whole Page.
7. Preview the document in Web Layout view, and then save it as a Single File Web page named **Stir-fryClass** in the **Web\Review** folder with the page title "Fast Art of Stir-frying."
8. Format the new Web page to match the Cooking Classes page, and then save and close the Fast Art of Stir-frying page.
9. Create a hyperlink from the Stir-fry class bullet on the Cooking Classes page to the Stir-fry Class page and then save the page.
10. Preview the Cooking Classes page in your browser, click the Stir-fry class link to preview the Fast Art of Stir-frying page, exit your browser, and then exit Word.

David at Premier Finance has a workbook that displays sample values for a proposed college fund that he wants you to convert to Web pages. David wants customers to be able to view the return from monthly investments in a college savings plan. You will create both a noninteractive and an interactive version of David's workbook.

11. Start Excel, and then open the **Fund** workbook located in the **Web\Review** folder included with your Data Files.
12. Enter your name and the current date in the Documentation sheet, and then save the workbook as **College Fund** in the **Web\Review** folder.
13. Create a noninteractive Web page based on the workbook with "Sample College Fund" as the page title and **CollegeFundPage** as the filename. Publish only the contents of the Calculator worksheet, and select the options to republish the Web page every time the College Fund workbook is saved and to open the published Web page in the browser automatically.
14. Maximize the browser window, review the Web page, and then close the browser and close the College Fund workbook without saving changes.
15. Open the **Fund** workbook located in the **Web\Review** folder.
16. Enter your name and the current date in the Documentation sheet, and then save the workbook as **College Calculator** in the **Web\Review** folder.
17. Create an interactive Web page of the entire workbook with the page title "Fund Calculator" and the filename **CalculatorPage**. Make sure the Web page is republished each time the College Calculator workbook is saved, and make sure the Web page opens in the browser window automatically.
18. Maximize the browser window, refresh the screen, display the Calculator worksheet, and then enter $85,000 as the savings goal and 16 as the number of years.
19. Close the browser, and then exit Excel without saving changes.

Elsa is pleased with the Web pages you created for the Northeast database. Now she wants you to create Web pages based on objects in the Recruits database.

20. Start Access, and then open the **Recruits** database located in the **Web\Review** folder included with your Data Files.
21. Create a static Web page named **Recruiter** based on the Recruiter table, specifying the option for displaying the data in a datasheet format.
22. View the Web page in a browser, and then close the browser.

23. Use the AutoPage: Columnar Wizard to create a data access page based on the Student table.
24. Use the Record Navigation toolbar to move to the last record in the Student table (record 34), and then change the BirthDate field value for the last record to 11/16/84. Save your change using the appropriate Record Navigation toolbar button.
25. Save the data access page as **Student** in the **Web\Review** folder.
26. View the page in a browser, and then close the browser and exit Access.

Miriam has gotten positive feedback about the Peru Expedition Web page you created. Volunteers often choose to tour Cuzco and Machu Picchu following their service in a needy village, so she asks you to create a Web page giving a brief tour of Cuzco and Machu Picchu based on a modified version of an existing presentation.

27. Start PowerPoint, and then open the **MPTour** presentation located in the **Web\Review** folder included with your Data Files.
28. Replace the name in the subtitle with your name, save the presentation as a Single File Web page in the **Web\Review** folder, type **MachuPicchuTour** as the filename, enter "Tour of Machu Picchu" as the page title, include the complete presentation, optimize the browser for Microsoft Internet 4.0 or later (high fidelity), and open the published Web page in a browser automatically.
29. Review the presentation in the browser using the navigation button and links, and then view the presentation as a slide show.
30. Close the Web browser and exit PowerPoint without saving changes.

SAM Assessment and Training

Assess

If your instructor has chosen to use the full online version of SAM 2003 Assessment and Training, you can go beyond the "just-in-time" training provided on the CD that accompanies this text. Simply log in to your SAM account (http://sam2003.course.com) to launch any assigned training activities or exams that relate to the skills covered in this tutorial.

Lab Assignments

Reinforce

Web Pages & HTML

The New Perspectives Labs are designed to help you master some of the key concepts and skills presented in this text. The steps for completing this Lab are located on the Course Technology Web site. Log on to the Internet and use your Web browser to go to the Student Online Companion for New Perspectives Office 2003 at **www.course.com/np/office2003**. Click the Lab Assignments link, and then navigate to the assignments for this tutorial.

Quick Check Answers

Review

1. printing and distributing paper copies, sending as an e-mail message or attachment, and posting the file as a Web page on an intranet or the Internet
2. the text that appears in the browser title bar each time the Web page is displayed in a browser
3. False
4. A noninteractive Web page enables people to view the content without making any changes to the content. An interactive Web page enables people to modify and format the values in the Web page from their browser.
5. data access page
6. False
7. View them from different computer setups and with different Web browsers and different versions of those browsers.

Glossary/Index

L

label control A control that appears on a report (or other object) in Design view to identify the associated field value. AC 154

label text One of the three categories of chart text that includes the category names, the tick mark labels, and the legend text. EX 170

LAN. *See* local area network

landscape orientation A type of page orientation in which the page is wider than it is tall, so that text spans the widest part of the page. WD 60, WD 61, EX 40-41

laptop computer *See* notebook computer

laser printers A printer that transfers a temporary laser image onto paper with a powdery substance called toner. EC 12

layout A predetermined way of organizing the text and objects on a slide. PPT 10
    reports, AC 151

LCD. *See* liquid crystal display

left alignment A type of alignment in which text aligns on the left margin and is ragged on the right. WD 64

Left tab A tab alignment style that positions the left edge of text at the tab stop and extends the text to the right. WD 92

legend Used to identifying the format of the data marker used for each series in a chart. Used if the chart contains more than one data series. EX 154

less than operator (<), AC 102, EX 82

less than or equal to operator (<=), AC 102, EX 82

light bulb symbol, PPT 15, PPT 26line
    blank, inserting in documents, WD 12–13, WD 24
    multiple, selecting, WD 49
    selecting, WD 49

line charts, EX 149

line spacing The amount of vertical space between lines of text. changing, WD 62–63

line style The structure of a border. WD 119

line weight The thickness of a border. WD 119

link (n.). *See* hyperlink

link. *See* hyperlink

link 1.) (n.) A direct connection between a source and a destination program. INT 1–5
    between documents, breaking, INT 1–18—20

link 2.) (v.) To create a connection between source data and the copy in a new file; the copy in the new file is updated every time a change is made to the source data. EC 33, INT 1–5, INT 1–13—20
    updating linked objects, INT 1–16—18

linking objects from Excel to Word, INT 1–13—20
    updating linked objects, INT 1–16—18

Links dialog box, INT 1–19

liquid crystal display (LCD) A display that creates images by manipulating light within a layer of liquid crystal. EC 11

list
    bulleted, PPT 13, WD 68–69
    numbered, PPT 13, WD 69–70

list arrow An arrow that appears in a list box; you click the list arrow to view and select options. WIN 21–22

list box A box that displays a list of available choices from which you can select one item. WIN 21–22

loan analysis, financial functions, EX 74–82

local area network (LAN) Computers and peripheral devices that are located relatively close to each other and connected, usually with cables. EC 25

logging off To end your session with Windows XP but leave the computer turned on. WIN 11

Logical function Category of Excel functions that test, or evaluate, whether a condition, usually entered as an expression, is true or false. EX 82–84

logical operator In a query, an operator that allows you to combine two or more conditions. AC 107–109, AC 108, AC 110–112

login ID, BEB 23

Lookup Wizard data type, AC 39

M

magnetic storage devices Data storage devices that use oxide-coated plastic storage media called mylar. EC 18–20

magnification, worksheets, EX 62–63

mail merge The process of combining information from two separate documents to create many final documents, each containing customized information. INT 3-4—11, WD 167–174
    data source, WD 167, WD 169
    inserting merge fields, INT 3–7—10
    Mail Merge task pane, WD 168–169
    main document, WD 167
    merge fields, WD 167, WD 169–172
    merging Access data with Word documents, INT 3–4—11
    merging main document and data source, WD 173–174
    performing mail merge, INT 3–10—11
    previewing merged documents, WD 172–173
    selecting starting document, INT 3–5—7

Mail Merge Recipients dialog box, INT 3–6—7

Mail Merge task pane, INT 3–5, INT 3–7, WD 168–169

main document In a mail merge, a document that contains the standard text that will remain the same and the merge fields to contain the variable information; sometimes called the starting document. INT 3-4, WD 167
    merging with data source, WD 173–174

main form In a form based on two tables, the form that contains data from the primary table. AC 142–147

main text. *See* body text

mainframe A computer used to provide centralized storage, processing, and management for large amounts of data. EC 7, EC 8

maintaining (a database) The process of adding, changing, and deleting records in database tables to keep them current and accurate. AC 68–71

major gridline Lines that extend the tick marks across the plot area. EX 154

major tick mark The indication on the major units of increment on the x- or y-axis.

margin The space between the page content and the edges of the page. EX 126–127
    changing, WD 61–62

master Slide containing the elements and styles of the design template, including text and other objects that appear on all the slides of the same type. PPT 50. *See also* specific masters

Match Destination Table Style and Link to Excel command, INT 1–15

Match Destination Table Style command, INT 1–15

Match Fields dialog box, INT 3–8—9

Max function, AC 118

MAX function Excel function that calculates the maximum amounts for a given category and has a similar syntax to the AVERAGE and SUM functions. EX 54, EX 68–69

Maximize button, WIN 16, WIN 17

MEDIAN function, EX 54

megabyte (MB) 1,048,576 (approximately one million) bytes. EC 14

megahertz (MHz) Millions of cycles per second. EC 15

Memo data type, AC 39

memory A set of storage locations on the main circuit board which stores instructions and data; computers have four types of memory: random access memory (RAM), virtual memory, read-only memory (ROM), and complementary metal oxide semiconductor (CMOS) memory. EC 15–17

memory capacity. *See* storage

Task Reference

TASK	PAGE #	RECOMMENDED METHOD
Absolute reference, change press to relative	EX 58-59	Edit the formula, deleting the $ before the column and row references; or F4 to switch between absolute, relative, and mixed references
Access, start	AC 7	Click Start, point to All Programs, point to Microsoft Office, click Microsoft Office Access 2003
Action, redo	EX 34, WD 27	Click 🔁
Action, undo	EX 34, WD 27	Click 🔄
Actions, redo several	EX 34	Click 🔁 ▾, select the action(s) to redo
Actions, undo several	EX 34	Click 🔄 ▾, select the action(s) to undo
Address bar, display in My Computer window	WIN 27	Click View, point to Toolbars, click Address Bar to insert a check mark
Address book, open	BEB 31	Click the Addresses button on the Outlook Express toolbar
Aggregate functions, use in a query	AC 118	Display the query in Design view, click Σ
Auto Fill, copy formulas	EX 68	See Reference Window: Copying Formulas Using the Fill Handle
Auto Fill, create series	EX 71	Select the range, drag the fill handle down, release mouse button, click 🔳, click the option button to complete series
AutoContent Wizard, run	PPT 10	Click File, click New, click From AutoContent Wizard on New Presentation task pane, follow instructions
AutoCorrect, use	WD 20	Click 🔷 ▾, click correct spelling
AutoFormat, apply	EX 125	Select the range, click Format, click AutoFormat, select an AutoFormat design, click OK
AutoFormat, change	AC 133	*See* Reference Window: Changing a Form's AutoFormat
AutoShape, add text to	EX 183	See Reference Window: Inserting Text into an AutoShape
AutoShape, insert, reshape, resize, and rotate	EX 181	See Reference Window: Inserting an AutoShape
AutoSum, apply	EX 28	Click the cell in which you want the final value to appear, click Σ, select the AutoSum function to apply
Background color, apply	EX 112	Select the range, click the list arrow for 🎨 ▾, select a color square in the color palette
Background pattern, apply	EX 112	Open the Format Cells dialog box, click the Patterns tab, click the Pattern list arrow, click a pattern in the pattern gallery, click OK
Boldface, add to text	WD 72	Select text, click **B**
Border, change in table	WD 119	See Reference Window: Altering Table Borders
Border, create	EX 109	Click 🔲 ▾, select a border in the border gallery
Border, draw	EX 109	Click 🔲 ▾, click 🖉, draw the border using the Pencil tool
Border, draw around page	WD 163	Click Format, click Borders and Shading, click Page Border tab, click Options, click Measure from list arrow, click Text, adjust settings in Top, Bottom, Left and Right boxes, click OK, click OK.
Border of table, draw	PPT 68	Click 🖉, set desired border style and border width on Tables and Borders toolbar, drag 🖉 along border

TASK	PAGE #	RECOMMENDED METHOD
Bullets, add to paragraphs	WD 68	Select paragraphs, click ⊞
Calculated field, add to a query	AC 113	*See* Reference Window: Using Expression Builder
Cell, clear contents of	EX 32	Click Edit, point to Clear, click Contents; or press Delete
Cell, edit	EX 34	See Reference Window: Editing a Cell
Cell reference, change	EX 59	Press the F4 key to cycle through the difference cell reference modes
Cells, delete	EX 32	Select the cell or range, click Edit, click Delete, select a delete option, click OK; or select the cell or range, click-right the selection, click Delete, select a delete option, click OK
Cells, insert	EX 31	See Reference Window: Inserting Cells into a Worksheet
Cells, merge	EX 115	Select the adjacent cells, open the Format Cells dialog box, click the Alignment tab, select the Merge cells check box, click OK
Cells, merge and center	EX 115	Select the adjacent cells, click ⊞
Chart, add data label	EX 167	Select a data marker(s) or data series, click Chart, click Chart Options, click the Data Labels tab, select the data label type, click OK
Chart, add gridline	EX 167	Select the chart, click Chart, click Chart Options, click the Gridlines tab, click the check box for gridline option you want to select, click OK
Chart, add, remove, and revise data series	EX 164	See Reference Window: Editing the Data Source of a Chart
Chart, change 3-D elevation	EX 180	Select a 3-D chart, click Chart, click 3-D View, enter the elevation value or click the Elevation Up or Elevation Down button, click OK
Chart, change location	EX 166	Select the chart, click Chart, click Location, specify the new location
Chart, change scale	EX 176–177	Double-click a value on the y-axis, enter the minimum and maximum values for the scale, click OK
Chart, change to 3-D	EX 179	Select the chart, click Chart, click Chart Type, select a 3-D subtype, click OK
Chart, create with Chart Wizard	EX 148	See Reference Window: Creating a Chart Using the Chart Wizard
Chart, format data marker	EX 172	Double-click the data marker, select the formatting options using the tabs in the Format Data Series dialog box
Chart, move	EX 158	Select the chart, move the pointer over the chart area, drag the chart to its new location, release the mouse button
Chart, resize	EX 158	Select the chart, move the pointer over a selection handle, drag the handle to resize the chart, release the mouse button
Chart, select	EX 157	Move pointer over a blank area of the chart, and then click
Chart, update	EX 159	Enter new values for the chart's data source and the chart is automatically updated
Chart, use background image in	EX 175	Double-click the plot area, click the Patterns tab, click Fill Effects, click the Picture tab, click Select Picture, locate and select the background image file, click Insert, click OK twice
Chart axis title, add or edit	EX 155	Select the chart, click Chart, click Chart Options, click the Titles tab, click on the Category (X) axis text box and type the text for the title, click in the Values (Y) axis text box and type the text for the title, click OK
Chart data markers, change fill color	EX 172	Double-click the data marker, click the Patterns tab, click Fill Effects, click the Gradient tab, select the color and related color options, click OK

TASK	PAGE #	RECOMMENDED METHOD
Chart text, format	EX 168	Select the chart label, click a button on the Formatting toolbar; or double-click the chart label, select the formatting options using the tabs in the Format Data Label dialog box
Chart text, insert new unattached	EX 171	See Reference Window: Inserting Unattached Text into a Chart
Chart title, add or edit	EX 155	Select the chart, click Chart, click Chart Options, click the Titles tab, click in the Chart title text box type the text for title, click OK
Chart Wizard, start	EX 148	Click 📖
Clip art, crop	WD 154	Click clip art, click ⊣⊢, drag picture border to crop
Clip art, find	WD 150	Click 🖼 on Drawing toolbar, type search criteria, click Go
Clip art, insert	PPT 16	Change slide layout to a Content layout, click 🖼 in content placeholder, click clipart image, click OK
Clip art, insert in document	WD 150	Click 🖼 on Drawing toolbar, click Organize Clips, click picture, click Copy, click in document, click 📋
Clip art, recolor	PPT 47	Click clipart image, click 🖼, click color list arrow of color to change, click desired color, click OK
Clip art, resize	WD 153	Click clip art, drag resize handle
Clip art, rotate	WD 155	Click clip art, click 🔄 on the Picture toolbar
Clip art, wrap text around	WD 156	Click clip art, click 🖼 button on the Picture toolbar, click text wrapping option
Clipboard task pane, open	WD 54	Click Edit, click Office Clipboard
Clipboard task pane, use to cut, copy, and paste	WD 54	See Reference Window: Cutting or Copying and Pasting Text
Column, change width	EX 19	See Reference Window: Changing the Column Width or Row Height
Column, delete	EX 32	Select the column, click Edit, click Delete; or select the column, click-right the selection, click Delete
Column, hide	EX 116	Select the headings for the columns you want to hide, right-click the selection, click Hide
Column, insert	EX 31	See Reference Window: Inserting a Row and Column into a Worksheet
Column, insert in table	WD 112	Click Table, point to Insert, click Columns to Right or Columns to Left
Column, resize width in a datasheet	AC 64	Double-click ↔ on the right border of the column heading
Column, select	EX 25	Click the column heading of the column you want to select. To select a range of columns, click the first column heading in the range, hold down the Shift key and click the last column in the range.
Column, unhide	EX 116	Select the column headings left and right of the hidden columns, right-click the selection, click Unhide
Column width, change in table	WD 116	Double-click or drag border between columns; to see measurements, press and hold Alt while dragging
Columns, balance	WD 162	Click the end of the right-most column, click Insert, click Break, click Continuous, click OK
Columns, format text in	WD 147	Click where you want to insert columns, or select text to divide into columns, click Format, click Columns, select options, click OK
Columns, repeat in printout	EX 133	Open the Page Setup dialog box, click the Sheet tab, click the Column to repeat at left box, click the column that contains the information you want repeated, click OK

TASK	PAGE #	RECOMMENDED METHOD
Comment, display in Normal view	WD 76	Point to comment
Comment, insert	WD 75	Click insert, click Comment
Compressed files, extract	FM 19	Right-click compressed folder, click Extract All, click Next, select location, click Next, click Finish
Compressed folder, create	FM 19	Right-click a blank area of a folder window, point to New, click Compressed (zipped) Folder
Contact, add	BEB 31	See Reference Window: Adding a Contact to the Address Book
Data, find	AC 135	*See* Reference Window: Finding Data in a Form or Datasheet
Data access page, create in Access	WEB 23	See Reference Window: Creating Data Access Pages in Access
Database, compact and repair	AC 26	Click Tools, point to Database Utilities, click Compact and Repair Database
Database, compact on close	AC 26	*See* Reference Window: Compacting a Database Automatically
Database, convert to another Access version	AC 28	Click Tools, point to Database Utilities, point to Convert Database, click the format to convert to
Database, create a blank	AC 41	Click Create a new file in the task pane, click Blank database, type the database name, select the drive and folder, click Create
Database, create using a wizard	AC 41	Click 🗋 on the Database toolbar, click On my computer in the task pane, click the Databases tab, select a template, click OK, type the database name, select the drive and folder, click Create, follow the instructions in the wizard
Database, open	AC 8	Click Open (or More) in the task pane, select the database to open
Datasheet, print	AC 12	Click 🖨
Datasheet view, switch to	AC 53	Click 🖩
Date, insert current	EX 72	Insert the TODAY() or NOW() function
Date, insert with AutoComplete	WD 24	Start typing date, press Enter
Dates, fill in using Auto Fill	EX 71	Select the cell containing the initial date, drag and drop the fill handle to fill in the rest of the dates. Click 🖳, select option to fill in days, week-days, months, or years
Design template, apply	PPT 43	Click the Design button, click design thumbnail in task pane
Design template, apply to one slide or selected slides	PPT 58	Click the Design button, select slide(s), click design thumbnail list arrow, click Apply to Selected Slides
Design view, switch to	AC 57	Click 🖉
Diagram, create	PPT 70	Change slide layout to a Content layout, click 🔄, click desired diagram type, click OK, modify diagram as desired
Dictionary, create and select as default	WD 46	Click Tools, click Options, click Spelling & Grammar tab, click Custom Dictionaries, click New, type a name in the File name text box, click Save, click the name of the new dictionary, click Change Default, click OK.
Document, open	WD 43	Click 📂, select drive and folder, click filename, click open
Document, open new	WD 11	Click 🗋
Document, preview	WD 29	Click 🔍
Document, save with same name	WD 19	Click 💾
Drawing toolbar, display	EX 181	Click View, point to Toolbars, click Drawing; or click 🖎

TASK	PAGE #	RECOMMENDED METHOD
Drawing toolbar, open	WD 140	Click 📷
Drop cap, insert	WD 158	Click in paragraph, click Format, click Drop Cap, select options, click OK
E-mail message, attach a file to	BEB 33	Open the message, click the Attach button, navigate to the folder that contains the file, click the file name, click Attach
E-mail message, create and send	BEB 26	See Reference Window: Creating and Sending an E-mail Message
E-mail message, delete	BEB 30	Click the message header in the message list, and then click the Delete button
E-mail message, print	BEB 29	Click the Inbox folder, double-click the message header of the message to open it in its own window, click 🖨, specify the print settings, click Print
E-mail message, open in its own window	BEB 29	Double-click the message header in the message list
E-mail message, read	BEB 28	Click the Inbox folder, click (or double-click) the message header in the message list
E-mail message, receive	BEB 28	Click the Send/Recv button on the Outlook Express toolbar
E-mail message, reply to	BEB 29	Display the message in the message list or in its own window, click the Reply button, enter a reply message, click the Send button
E-mail message, view a sent	BEB 27	Click the Sent Items folder in the Folders list
E-mail message attachment, open	BEB 34	Open the e-mail message, click the paperclip icon, click the attachment file, click the Open it option button
Embedded object, create	INT 1-9	See Reference Window: Embedding an Object
Embedded object, edit	INT 1-12	Double-click the object, and then edit it using the source program's commands
Envelope, create	WD 30	Click Tools, point to Letters and Mailings, click Envelopes and Labels, click Envelopes tab, type delivery and return addresses, click Print
Excel, start	EX 5	Click Start, point to All Programs, point to Microsoft Office, click Microsoft Office Excel 2003
Excel chart, link to a PowerPoint slide	INT 3-19	See Reference Window: Linking Excel Data to a PowerPoint Presentation.
Excel data, import into Access	INT 2-14	See Reference Window: Importing Excel Data into Access
Favorite, create	BEB 15	Click the Add button in the Favorites Explorer Bar, accept the default name (or enter a new name), click OK
Favorite, delete	BEB 17	Right-click the Favorite you want to delete, click Delete on the shortcut menu, click Yes
Favorite, move to a folder	BEB 16	Click the Organize button in the Favorites Explorer bar, click the Move to Folder button, select the folder to move, click OK
Favorites, organize	BEB 16	See Reference Window: Organizing the Favorites list
Favorites Explorer Bar, close	BEB 17	Click ❎ on the Favorites Explorer bar
Favorites Explorer Bar, open	BEB 15	Click the Favorites button
Favorites folder, create	BEB 15	Click the Organize button in the Favorites Explorer bar, click the Create Folder button, enter a name for the folder, press Enter
Field, add to a table	AC 59	*See* Reference Window: Adding a Field Between Two Existing Fields
Field, define in a table	AC 43	*See* Reference Window: Defining a Field in a Table

TASK	PAGE #	RECOMMENDED METHOD
Field, delete from a table	AC 57	*See* Reference Window: Deleting a Field from a Table Structure
Field, move to a new location in a table	AC 58	Display the table in Design view, click the field's row selector, drag the field with the pointer
Field property change, update	AC 61	Click the list arrow for ⚡, select option for updating field property
File, close	OFF 21	Click the Close Window button ⊠ on the menu bar
File, copy	FM 16	*See* Reference Window: Copying a File or Folder in Windows Explorer or My Computer
File, delete	FM 18	Right-click the file, click Delete
File, move	FM 14	*See* Reference Window: Moving a File or Folder in Windows Explorer or My Computer
File, open	OFF 22	See Reference Window: Opening an Existing or a New File
File, print	OFF 29	See Reference Window: Printing a File
File, rename	FM 17	Right-click the file, click Rename, type the new name, press Enter
File, save	OFF 20	See Reference Window: Saving a File
File, switch between open	OFF 8	Click the taskbar button for the file you want to make active
Files, compress	FM 19	Drag files into a compressed folder
Files, find	INT 2-7	Click File, click File Search, type search text in the Basic File Search task pane or click the Advanced File Search link and set additional search criteria, set other search options, and then click Go
Files, sort by date	WIN 28	In Details view, click Date Modified button
Files, view details	WIN 28	Click Views button, click Details
Files, view tiles	WIN 29	Click Views button, click Tiles
Fill color, change	PPT 73	Click object to select it, click 🎨▾, select desired color
Filter By Selection, activate	AC 100	*See* Reference Window: Using Filter By Selection
Find and replace text	WD 58	See Reference Window: Finding and Replacing Text
Folder or drive contents, view in Windows Explorer	FM 10	Click ⊞
Folder, copy	FM 16	*See* Reference Window: Copying a File or Folder in Windows Explorer or My Computer
Folder, create	FM 13	*See* Reference Window: Creating a Folder Using Windows Explorer
Folder, move	FM 14	*See* Reference Window: Moving a File or Folder in Windows Explorer or My Computer
Folder, open	WIN 31	Double-click the folder
Folder, rename	FM 17	Right-click the folder, click Rename, type the new name, press Enter
Folders pane, open	WIN 30	Click View, point to Explorer Bar, click Folders
Font, change color	EX 104	Select the text, click **A**▾, select a color from the color palette
Font, change size	EX 103	Click 10 ▾, click a size
Font, change style	EX 103	Click **B**, click *I*, or click U
Font, change typeface	EX 103	Click Arial ▾, click a font
Font, modify	PPT 56	Click edge of text box, click Font list arrow, click font
Font, select default	WD 8	Click Format, click Font, click Font tab, click font name

TASK	PAGE #	RECOMMENDED METHOD
Font and font size, change	WD 70	See Reference Window: Changing the Font and Font Size
Font color, modify	PPT 56	Click edge of text box, click 🔺▾, click color (or click More Colors and click color, click OK)
Font size, select default	WD 8	Click Format, click Font, click Font tab, click font size
Footer, add	WD 101	Click View, click Header and Footer, click 🗐, type footer text, click Close
Footers, create	PPT 62	Click View, click Header and Footer, make sure there is a check mark in the Footer Check box, click Ⅰ in Footer text box, type text, click Apply to All
Form Wizard, activate	AC 130	Click Forms in the Objects bar, click New, click Form Wizard, choose the table or query for the form, click OK
Format, apply Currency Style, Percent Style, or Comma Style	EX 97-99	Click 💲, click % or click ❟, or open the Format Cells dialog box, click the Number tab, select a style, specify style-related options, click OK
Format, clear	EX 119	Click Edit, point to Clear, click Formats
Format, copy	WD 66	Select text with desired format, double-click 🖌, select paragraphs to format, click 🖌
Format, copy using Format Painter	EX 99	See Reference Window: Copying Formatting Using the Format Painter
Format, decrease decimal places	EX 97	Click 🔢
Format, find and replace	EX 120	See Reference Window: Finding and Replacing a Format
Format, increase decimal places	EX 99	Click 🔢
Format Cells dialog box, open	EX 101	Click Format, click Cells
Formula, copy	EX 56	See Reference Window: Copying and Pasting a Cell or Range
Formula, copy using the fill handle	EX 68	See Reference Window: Copying Formulas Using the Fill Handle
Formula, enter using keyboard	EX 15	See Reference Window: Entering a Formula
Formula, enter using mouse	EX 15	See Reference Window: Entering a Formula
Formula, insert	EX 15	See Reference Window: Entering a Formula
Formulas, show/hide	EX 42	Press the Ctrl + ` (grave accent) keys to display or hide the formulas in the worksheet cells
Function, insert using Insert Function dialog box	EX 65	Click *fx* on the Formula bar, select the function from the Insert Function dialog box, complete the Function Arguments dialog box
Getting Started task pane, open	OFF 16	Click the Home button 🏠 in the task pane
Graphic, crop	WD 154	Click graphic, click ⊹, drag to crop
Graphic, find	WD 150	Click 🖼 on Drawing toolbar, type search criteria, click Go
Graphic, resize	WD 153	Click graphic, drag resize handle
Graphic, rotate	WD 155	Click graphic, click 🔄 on the Picture toolbar
Graphic, wrap text around	WD 156	Click graphic, click 🖾 button on the Picture toolbar, click text wrapping option
Grayscale, preview presentation in	PPT 30	Click 🔲, click Grayscale
Handouts, print	PPT 31	Click File, click Print, click Print what list arrow, click Handouts, click Slides per page list arrow, click number, click OK
Header, add	WD 101	Click View, click Header and Footer, type header text, click Close
Header/footer, create	EX 128	Open the Page Setup dialog box, click the Header/Footer tab, click the Header list arrow or the Footer list arrow, select an available header or footer, click OK

TASK	PAGE #	RECOMMENDED METHOD
Header/footer, create custom	EX 129	Open Page Setup dialog box, click the Header/Footer tab, click the Custom Header or Customer Footer button, complete the header/footer related boxes, click OK
Help, display topic from the Home page	WIN 32	In Help and Support, click Home in the navigation bar
Help, display topic from the Index page	WIN 33	In Help and Support, click Index in the navigation bar, scroll to locate a topic or type a keyword, double-click the topic
Help, find topic	WIN 34	In Help and Support, click in the Search box, type word or phrase, click ➡
Help, start	WIN 31	Click Start, click Help and Support
Help task pane, use	OFF 26	See Reference Window: Getting Help from the Help Task Pane
History Explorer Bar, open	BEB 14	Click the History button
History list, view	BEB 14	Click the History button
Home page, return to	BEB 13	Click the Home button
Hotmail account, sign up	BEB 23	See Reference Window: Signing Up for a Hotmail Account
Hyperlink, add in document	WD 138	Type e-mail address or URL, press spacebar
Hyperlink, insert	WEB 11	Select text or graphic for link, click 🖼, navigate to linked page or file, click OK
Hyperlink, remove	WD 139	Right-click hyperlink, click Remove Hyperlink
Hyperlink, use	WD 138	Press Ctrl and click the hyperlink
Internet Explorer, start	BEB 7	Click the Start button, point to All Programs, click Internet Explorer
Italics, add to text	WD 73	Select text, click *I*
Layout, slide, change	PPT 46	Click Format, click Slide Layout, click desired layout
Line spacing, change	WD 63	Select text to change, press Ctrl+1 for single spacing, Ctrl+5 for 1.5 line spacing, or Ctrl+2 for double spacing
Linked object, break	INT 1-18	See Reference Window: Breaking the Link Between Linked Objects
Linked object, create	INT 1-14	See Reference Window: Linking an Object
Linked object, update	INT 1-16	Open the source file from within the source program, or double-click the linked object to open the source file, make changes in the source file and save the changes, right-click the linked object in the destination file, and then click Update Link
List box, scroll	WIN 21	Click the list arrow for the list box to display the list of options; click the scroll down or up arrow; or drag the scroll box
Logical function, insert	EX 83	Use the IF function
Magnification, changing	EX 62	See Reference Window: Changing the Zoom Magnification of the Workbook Window
Mail Merge, perform	WD 165	Click Tools, point to Letters and Mailings, click Mail Merge, follow steps in Mail Merge task pane
Mail Merge Wizard, start	INT 3-5	Click Tools, point to Letters and Mailings, click Mail Merge
Margins, change	WD 61	Click File, click Page Setup, click Margins tab, enter margin values, click OK
Master, slide or title, modify	PPT 51	Shift-click 🖼, make modifications, click 🖼
Menu command, select	WIN 8	Click the command on the menu; for submenus, point to a command on the menu

TASK	PAGE #	RECOMMENDED METHOD
Microsoft Office Online, use	OFF 28	Click the Connect to Microsoft Office Online link in the Help task pane
Mortgage, calculate monthly payment	EX 78	Use the PMT function
Mortgage, calculate the interest rate of	EX 80	Use the RATE function
Mortgage, calculate the number of payments	EX 80	Use the NPER function
Mortgage, calculate total value of	EX 80	Use the PV function
My Computer, open	WIN 25	Click Start, click My Computer
Nonprinting characters, show	WD 10	Click Show/ Hide ¶
Normal view, change to	WD 7	Click ≡
Notes, create	PPT 29	Click I in Notes pane, type text
Notes, print	PPT 31	Click File, click Print, click Print what list arrow, click Notes Pages, click OK
Numbering, add to paragraphs	WD 69	Select paragraphs, click ≣
Numbering, slide	PPT 62	Click View, click Header and Footer, click Slide Number check box
Object, change order	PPT 54	Click object, click the Draw button, point to Order, click desired layering order
Object, open	AC 10	Click the object's type in the Objects bar, click the object's name, click Open
Object, resize	PPT 47	Click object, drag sizing handle
Object, rotate	PPT 76	Click object to select it, drag rotate handle with ↻
Object, save	AC 12	Click 🖫, type the object name, click OK
Office Clipboard, using	INT 2-6	Click Edit, click Office Clipboard, copy or cut items, click items in Clipboard task pane to paste them
Outline text, demote	PPT 23	Click Outline tab (if necessary), click paragraph, click ⇥
Outline text, promote	PPT 21	Click Outline tab (if necessary), click paragraph, click ⇤
Outlook Express, start	BEB 24	Click the Start button, point to All Programs, click Outlook Express
Page, change orientation	EX 40	Open the Page Setup dialog box, click the Page tab, click the Landscape or Portrait option button
Page, preview more than one	WD 99	Click 🔍, click ▦
Page, set margins	EX 127	Open the Page Setup dialog box, click the Margins tab, specify the width of the margins, click OK
Page, vertically align	WD 100	Click File, click Page Setup, click Layout tab, click Vertical alignment list arrow, click Center
Page, view whole	WD 148	Click Zoom list arrow, click Whole Page
Page break, insert	WD 105	Click where you want to break the page, press Ctrl+Enter
Page break preview, switch to	EX 131	Click View on the menu bar, click Page Break Preview
Page number, insert	WD 102	Open header or footer, click 🔢 on Header/Footer toolbar
Page orientation, change	WD 60	Click File, click Page Setup, click Margins tab, click Landscape or Portrait icon, click OK.
Page Setup dialog box, open	EX 40	Click File, click Page Setup; or click the Setup button on the Print Preview toolbar
Paragraph, decrease indent	WD 65	Click ⇤

TASK	PAGE #	RECOMMENDED METHOD
Paragraph, indent	WD 65	Click ▤
Paragraph, move to the next-higher outline level	INT 3-13	Click ◆ on the Outlining toolbar in Word
Paragraph, move to the next-lower outline level	INT 3-13	Click ◆ on the Outlining toolbar in Word
Paste options, select	WD 53	Click ▤
Paste options, set	INT 2-12	Paste object into Word, click ▤, click desired option button
Picture, insert in a report	AC 158	In Design view, select the report section in which to insert the picture, click Insert, click Picture, select the picture file, click OK
Pie chart, create	EX 159	Select the row or column of data values to be charted, click , select Pie in the list of chart types, select a sub-type, complete the remaining Chart Wizard dialog boxes
Pie chart, explode piece(s)	EX 162	See Reference Window: Creating an Exploded Pie Chart
Pie chart, rotate	EX 161	Double-click the pie in the pie chart, click the Options tab, enter a new value in the Angle of First Slice box, click OK
PowerPoint, exit	PPT 12	Click ☒ on PowerPoint window
PowerPoint, start	PPT 4	Click Start button, point to All Programs, point to Microsoft Office, click Microsoft Office PowerPoint 2003
Presentation, close	PPT 9	Click ☒ on presentation window
Presentation, open	PPT 5	Click ▤, select disk and folder, click filename, click Open
Presentation, print	PPT 30	Click File, click Print, select options, click OK
Primary key, specify	AC 51	*See* Reference Window: Specifying a Primary Key for a Table
Print area, define	EX 131	Select the range, click File, point to Print Area, click Set Print Area
Print layout view, change to	WD 106	Click ▤
Program, close	WIN 12	Click ☒
Program, close inactive	WIN 14	Right-click the program button on the taskbar, click Close
Program, exit	OFF 30	Click the Close button ☒ on the title bar
Program, start	WIN 11	See Reference Window: Starting a Program
Program, switch to another	WIN 14	Click the program button on the taskbar
Programs, open	OFF 5	See Reference Window: Starting Office Programs
Programs, switch between open	OFF 8	Click the taskbar button for the program you want to make active
Property sheet, open	AC 116	Right-click the object or control, click Properties
Query, copy and paste into PowerPoint	INT 3-16	Open the query, click the selector to the left of the column headings to select the entire query, click ▤, switch to the PowerPoint slide, click ▤
Query, create with wizard	INT 2-17	Click Queries in the Objects list, and then double-click Create query by using wizard
Query, define	AC 82	Click Queries in the Objects bar, click New, click Design View, click OK
Query, export as RTF file	INT 2-19	Click File, click Export, type filename, click Save as type list arrow, click Rich Text Format, click Export
Query, import in RTF format to Word	INT 2-19	Click Insert in Word, click Insert File, click the Files of type list arrow, click Rich Text Format, click filename, click Insert, click file

TASK	PAGE #	RECOMMENDED METHOD
Query, run	AC 86	Click ⚠
Query results, sort	AC 97	*See* Reference Window: Sorting a Query Datasheet
Range, copy	EX 27	Select the cell or range, hold down the Ctrl key and drag the selection to the new location, release the Ctrl key and mouse button
Range, move	EX 26	Select the cell or range, drag the selection to the new location, release the mouse button
Range, select adjacent	EX 24	See Reference Window: Selecting Adjacent or Nonadjacent Ranges of Cells
Range, select nonadjacent	EX 24	See Reference Window: Selecting Adjacent or Nonadjacent Ranges of Cells
Record, add a new one	AC 63	Click ▶
Record, delete	AC 69	*See* Reference Window: Deleting a Record
Record, move to a specific one	AC 11	Type the record number in the record number box, press Enter
Record, move to first	AC 12	Click 【◄】
Record, move to last	AC 12	Click 【►】
Record, move to next	AC 12	Click 【►】
Record, move to previous	AC 12	Click 【◄】
Records, print selected in a form	AC 141	Click File, click Print, click Selected Record(s), click OK
Records, redisplay all after filter	AC 101	Click ▽
Recycle Bin, view contents of	WIN 8	Double-click the Recycle Bin icon
Redo command, use to redo multiple operations in a database object	AC 110	Click the list arrow for ↻, click the action(s) to redo
Relationship, define between database tables	AC 90	Click ᵯ
Relative reference, change to absolute	EX 58–59	Type $ before the column and row references; or press the F4 key
Report, check errors in Design view	AC 155	Click the list arrow for ◈, choose to correct or ignore errors
Report, print specific pages of	AC 23	Click File, click Print, click Pages, enter number of pages to print in the From and To boxes, click OK
Report Wizard, activate	AC 148	Click Reports in the Objects bar, click New, click Report Wizard, choose the table or query for the report, click OK
Research task pane, open	WD 76	Click 🔍.
Research task pane, use	OFF 17	See Reference Window: Using the Research Task Pane
Research task pane, use	WD 77	Connect to Internet, click 🔍, enter text in Search for text box, verify All Reference Books is selected in box below Search for text box, click ➡.
Row, change height	EX 19	See Reference Window: Changing the Column Width or Row Height
Row, delete	EX 33	Select the row, click Edit, click Delete; or select the row, right-click the selection, click Delete
Row, delete from table	WD 112	See Reference Window: Ways to Insert or Delete Table Rows and Columns
Row, hide	EX 116	Select the headings for the rows you want to hide, right-click the selection, click Hide
Row, insert	EX 31	See Reference Window: Inserting a Row or Column into a Worksheet

TASK	PAGE #	RECOMMENDED METHOD
Row, insert in table	WD 112	See Reference Window: Ways to Insert or Delete Table Rows and Columns
Row, select	EX 25	Click the heading of the row you want to select. To select a range of rows, click the first row heading in the range, hold down the Shift key and click the last row in the range
Row, unhide	EX 116	Select the rows headings above and below the hidden rows, right-click the selection, click Unhide
Row height, change in table	WD 115	Drag divider between rows; to see measurements, press and hold Alt while dragging
Rows, repeat in printout	EX 133	Open the Page Setup dialog box, click the Sheet tab, click the Row to repeat at top box, click the row that contains the information
Ruler, display	WD 8	Click View, click Ruler
Ruler, view (or hide)	PPT 60	Click View, click Ruler
ScreenTip, view	WIN 6	Position pointer over an object
Section, insert in document	WD 96	Click where you want to insert a section break, click Insert, click Break, click one of the Section break types option buttons, click OK
Section, vertically align	WD 99	Click File, click Page Setup, click Layout tab, click apply to list arrow, click This Section, click Vertical alignment list arrow, click Center, click OK
Shading, apply to table	WD 120	Select table area to shade, click Shading Color list arrow on Tables and Borders toolbar, click a color
Shape, create	PPT 72	Click the AutoShapes button, point to shape type, click desired shape, drag ┼ in slide
Sheet tabs, format	EX 119	Right-click the sheet tab, click Tab Color, select a color from the color palette
Shortcut menu, open	WIN 9	Right-click an object
Slide, add new	PPT 19	Click the New Slide button
Slide, delete	PPT 17	In Slide Pane, click Edit, click Delete Slide. In Outline tab, click [▦], press Delete. In Slide tab, click slide, press Delete
Slide, go to next	PPT 6	Click [▼]
Slide, go to previous	PPT 6	Click [▲]
Slide Show, view	PPT 8	Click [▢]
Slide Sorter View, switch to	PPT 7	Click [▦]
Slides, create from a Word outline	INT 3-15	Click Insert in PowerPoint, click Slides from Outline, click filename click Insert
Smart Tag, remove	WD 28	Click [ⓘ ▾], click Remove this Smart Tag
Sort, specify ascending in datasheet	AC 96	Click [A↓]
Sort, specify descending in datasheet	AC 96	Click [Z↓]
Speaker Notes, create	PPT 29	Click I in Notes Pane, type text
Special character, insert	WD 160	Click Insert, click Symbol, click Special Characters tab, click special character, click Insert, click Close
Spelling, check	EX 38	Click [ABC✓]
Spelling, correct individual word	WD 22	Right-click misspelled word (as indicated by a wavy red line), click correctly spelled word

TASK	PAGE #	RECOMMENDED METHOD
Spelling and grammar, check	WD 46	See Reference Window: Checking a Document for Spelling and Grammatical Errors
Standard Buttons toolbar, display in My Computer window	WIN 27	Click View, point to Toolbars, click Standard Buttons to insert a check mark
Start menu, open	WIN 7	Click Start
Static Web page, create in Access	WEB 21	See Reference Window: Creating Static Web Pages in Access
Style, apply	EX 123	Select the range, click Format, click Style, select a style, click OK
Style, create	EX 122	Select the cell that contains the formatting you want to use as the basis of the new style, click Format, click Style, type a name for the style, click Modify, specify format options using the Format Cells dialog box, click OK, click OK
Style, modify	EX 124	Select the range, click Format, click Style, click Modify, change style attributes, click OK
Style Checker, fix style problem	PPT 26	Click light bulb, click option to fix style problem
Style Checker, set options	PPT 25	Click Tools, click Options, click Spelling and Style tab, click Style Options, set options, click OK, click OK
Style Checker, turn on	PPT 25	Click Tools, click Options, click Spelling and Style tab, select Check style check box, click OK
Summary Slide, add	PPT 77	Switch to Slide Sorter view, select desired slides, click 🗐
Symbol, insert	WD 161	Click Insert, click Symbol, click desired symbol, click Insert, click Close
Tab stop, add	PPT 61	Select text box, click View, click Ruler, click tab stop alignment selector button to select desired tab stop style, click location on ruler
Tab stop, delete	PPT 62	Drag the tab stop off the ruler
Tab stop, move	PPT 62	Select text box, click View, click Ruler, drag tab stop to new location on ruler
Tab stop, set	WD 92	Click tab alignment selector, click ruler
Table, center on page	WD 121	Click in table, click Table, click Table Properties, click Table tab, click Center alignment option, click OK
Table, create in PowerPoint	PPT 66	Change slide layout to a Content layout, click 🖩, set number of columns and rows, fill in and format cells as desired
Table, create in Word	WD 105	Click 🖩, drag to select columns and rows; or click 🗹 on Tables and Borders toolbar, draw columns and rows
Table, create in a database	AC 42	Click Tables in the Objects bar, click New, click Design View, click OK
Table, import from another Access database	AC 67	Click File, point to Get External Data, click Import, select the folder, click Import, select the table, click OK
Table, open in a database	AC 10	Click Tables in the Objects bar, click the table name, click Open
Table, sort	WD 110	Click in the column you want to sort, click 🔼 or 🔽 on Tables and Borders toolbar
Table structure, save in a database	AC 52	*See* Reference Window: Saving a Table Structure
Tables and Borders toolbar, display	WD 109	Click 🗹
Task pane, close	OFF 15	Click the Close button ✕ on the task pane title bar
Task pane, display	OFF 15	Click View on the menu bar, click Task Pane
Task pane, navigate between	OFF 16	Click the Back button ⬅ or the Forward button ➡ in the task pane previously opened

TASK	PAGE #	RECOMMENDED METHOD
Task pane, open	OFF 16	Click the Other Task Panes button on the task pane title bar, click name of task pane you want to open
Task pane, open	WD 7	Click View, click Task Pane
Text, align	WD 64	Select text, click, ▤, ▤, ▤, or ▤
Text, align in table	WD 117	Click Align list arrow on Tables and Borders toolbar, click alignment option
Text, align within a cell	EX 105	Click ▤, click ▤, or click ▤; or open Format Cells dialog box, click the Alignment tab, select a text alignment, click OK
Text, copy and paste	WD 54	Select text, click 🔲 click at target location, click 🔲
Text, delete	WD 50	Press Backspace to delete character to left of Insertion point; press Delete to delete character to the right, press Ctrl+Backspace to delete to beginning of word; press Ctrl+Delete to delete to end of word
Text, enter into cell	EX 11	Click the cell, type text entry, press Enter
Text, enter multiple lines in a cell	EX 12	See Reference Window: Entering Multiple Lines of Text Within a Cell
Text, enter using AutoComplete	EX 17	Type the first letter of text entry you've entered in the worksheet, press Enter or Tab to complete the text entry displayed by AutoComplete
Text, increase or decrease indent of	EX 106	Click ▤ or ▤
Text, move by cut and paste	WD 54	Select text, click ✂ click at target location, click 🔲
Text, move by drag and drop	WD 52	Select text, drag selected text to target location, release mouse button
Text, select a block of	WD 49	Click at beginning of block, press and hold Shift and click at end of block
Text, select entire document	WD 49	Press Ctrl and click in selection bar
Text, select multiple adjacent lines	WD 49	Click and drag in selection bar
Text, select multiple nonadjacent lines	WD 49	Select text, press and hold Ctrl, and select next text
Text, select multiple paragraphs	WD 49	Click and drag in selection bar
Text, select paragraph	WD 49	Double-click in selection bar next to paragraph
Text, select sentence	WD 49	Press Ctrl and click in sentence
Text, wrap around WordArt	WD 144	Click WordArt, click 🔣 on the WordArt toolbar, click text wrap option
Text, wrap in cell	EX 107	Open the Format Cells dialog box, click the Alignment tab, select the Wrap text check box, click OK
Text box, add	PPT 74	Click 🔲, click ↓ in slide, type text
Text box, move	PPT 76	Click text box, drag edge (not sizing handle) of text box
Text box, resize	PPT 75	Click text box, drag sizing handle
Theme, apply to Web page	WEB 8	Click Format, click Theme, select theme, click OK
Toolbar, display	WD 7	Right-click any visible toolbar, click toolbar name
Toolbar, turn off personalized	OFF 14	Click the Toolbar Options button 🔻 on the right side of the toolbar, click the Show Buttons on Two Rows command
Transparent color, picture, set	PPT 54	Click picture, click 🔲, click color in picture
Type a question for help box, use	OFF 24	See Reference Window: Getting Help from the Type a Question for Help Box

TASK	PAGE #	RECOMMENDED METHOD
Underline, add to text	WD 73	Select text, click $\underline{U}$
Undo command, use to undo multiple operations in a database object	AC 110	Click the list arrow for ⟲, click the action(s) to undo
URL, enter	BEB 10	See Reference Window: Entering a URL in the Address Bar
Web Layout view, switch to	WEB 10	Click 🔲
Web page, create in Excel	WEB 14	See Reference Window: Creating Web Pages in Excel
Web page, create in PowerPoint	WEB 27	See Reference Window: Creating Web Pages in PowerPoint
Web page, create in Word	WEB 5	See Reference Window: Creating Web Pages in Word
Web page, go back to	BEB 12	Click the Back button
Web page, go forward to	BEB 12	Click the Forward button
Web page, preview in browser	WEB 12	Click File, and then click Web Page Preview
Web page, print	BEB 18	Click File, click Print, specify the print settings, click Print
Web page, publish	WEB 29	See Reference Window: Publishing Web Pages
Web page, reload	BEB 13	Click the Refresh button
Web page, save	BEB 18	Display the Web page, click File, click Save As, navigate to the folder in which you want to save the Web page, change the default filename if necessary, select the file format in which you want to save the Web page, click Save
Web page, stop transfer of	BEB 13	Click the Stop button
Web page graphic, save	BEB 19	See Reference Window: Saving an Image from a Web Page to a Disk
Web site, go to	BEB 10-11	Enter the URL in the Address Bar, and then press Enter; or click the link for the Web site
Web sites, display list of visited	BEB 13	Click the Back button list arrow or Forward button list arrow
Window, close	OFF 9	Click the Close button ✕
Window, maximize	OFF 10, WIN 17	Click ☐
Window, minimize	OFF 10, WIN 17	Click ▬
Window, move	WIN 18	Drag the title bar
Window, resize	WIN 18	Drag ⬛
Window, restore	OFF 10, WIN 17	Click ⧉
Windows Explorer, start	FM 9, WIN 29	Click Start, point to All Programs, point to Accessories, click Windows Explorer
Windows XP, shut down	WIN 34	Click Start, click Turn Off Computer, click Turn Off
Windows XP, start	WIN 4	Turn on the computer
Word, start	WD 5	Click 🔲 *start*, point to All Programs, point to Microsoft Office, click Microsoft Office Word 2003
WordArt, change shape	WD 143	Click WordArt, click 🅰 on the WordArt toolbar, click shape
WordArt, edit text	WD 142	Click WordArt, click Edit Text button on WordArt toolbar, edit text, click OK
WordArt, insert	WD 139	Click 🅰, click WordArt style, click OK, type WordArt text, select font, size, and style, click OK
WordArt, wrap text	WD 144	Click WordArt, click 🔲 on the WordArt toolbar, click text wrap option

TASK	PAGE #	RECOMMENDED METHOD
Workbook, preview	EX 39	Click 🔍; or click the Preview button in the Print dialog box
Workbook, print	EX 39	Click 🖨; or click File, click Print, select printer and print-related options, click OK
Workbook, save	EX 22	Click File, click Save, locate the folder and drive where you want to save the file, type a filename, click Save
Workbook, save in a different format	EX 22	Open the Save or Save As dialog box, display the location where you want to save the file, enter a filename, click the Save as type list arrow, select the file format you want to apply, click Save
Worksheet, add background image	EX 117	See Reference Window: Adding a Background Image to the Worksheet
Worksheet, copy	EX 37	See Reference Window: Moving or Copying a Worksheet
Worksheet, delete	EX 35	Click the sheet tab, click Edit, click Delete Sheet; or right-click the sheet tab, click Delete
Worksheet, insert	EX 35	Click Insert, click Worksheet; or right-click a sheet tab, click Insert, click Worksheet icon, click OK
Worksheet, rename	EX 36	Double-click the sheet tab that you want to rename, type a new name, press Enter
Worksheets, move	EX 37	See Reference Window: Moving or Copying a Worksheet
Worksheets, move between	EX 9	Click the sheet tab for the worksheet you want to view; or click one of the tab scrolling buttons and then click the sheet tab
Zoom setting, change	WD 8	Click Zoom list arrow, click zoom selection

SAM 2003 Training Companion Task Reference

This Task Reference provides a complete listing of all the training tasks available on the SAM 2003 Training Companion CD that accompanies this text. The Task Reference also shows which tutorial and session each training task maps to, as well as the pages in this book where the tasks are covered in more detail.

TUTORIAL	SAM TRAINING TASKS	PAGE #
Word Tutorial 2: Editing and Formatting a Document		
Session 2.1	Check grammar	WD 47–48
	Check spelling	WD 46–48
	Check spelling and grammar as you type	WD 46–48
	Collect and paste using the clipboard task pane	WD 54–57
	Copy and paste text	WD 55–56
	Cut and paste text	WD 54–55
	Cut text	WD 54
	Delete selected text from a document	WD 50–51
	Find and replace text	WD 58–60
	Move text	WD 51–55
	Open a document	WD 43–44
	Select a line	WD 49
	Select nonadjacent text	WD 49
	Select text	WD 49
	Set default dictionary	WD 46
	Use Save As	WD 45
	Use the Paste Options button	WD 53–55
Session 2.2	Add bullets	WD 68–69
	Add numbering	WD 68–70
	Add picture bullets to a list	WD 69
	Adjust line spacing	WD 62–63
	Bold text	WD 72
	Center a paragraph	WD 64
	Change font	WD 70–71
	Change font size	WD 70–71
	Change the page orientation	WD 60–62
	Create a hanging indent	WD 65
	Delete comments	WD 76
	Edit a comment	WD 76
	First-line indent paragraph	WD 64–66
	Indent paragraphs	WD 65–66
	Insert comments	WD 75–76
	Italicize text	WD 72–73
	Justify a paragraph	WD 64–65
	Modify page margins	WD 60–62
	Print documents	WD 74
	Right-align a paragraph	WD 64
	Underline a word	WD 73
	Use Format Painter	WD 66–68
	Use print preview	WD 74
	Use the Research task pane	WD 76–78
Word Tutorial 3: Creating a Multiple-Page Report		
Session 3.1	Change the vertical alignment of a section	WD 100
	Create a document header	WD 101–102
	Create a hanging indent	WD 93
	Create a header different from previous section header	WD 101–102
	Create tables	WD 105–108
	Delete a page break	WD 98
	Enter data into a Word table	WD 106–107
	First-line indent paragraph	WD 92–96
	Format sections	WD 96–100
	Insert a next page section break	WD 96–98
	Insert page breaks	WD 105–106
	Insert page numbers	WD 102
	Modify tabs	WD 95–96
	Set Decimal tabs	WD 92–93
	Use Page Setup options to format sections	WD 100
	Use print preview	WD 99
Session 3.2	Apply AutoFormats to tables	WD 115
	Delete table columns	WD 113–114

TUTORIAL	SAM TRAINING TASKS	PAGE #
	Insert rows in a table	WD 113
	Modify cell formats	WD 118–120
	Modify table borders	WD 118–120
	Modify table formats by merging table cells	WD 110
	Modify table formats by splitting table cells	WD 110
	Print documents	WD 124
	Rotate text in a table cell	WD 117
	Sort table data	WD 110–111
	Use formulas in tables	WD 110
	Use Reading layout and other views	WD 122–124
Word Tutorial 4: Desktop Publishing and Mail Merge		
Session 4.1	Apply columns	WD 147–148
	Convert a hyperlink to regular text	WD 139
	Create WordArt	WD 139–145
	Display the Web page associated with a hyperlink	WD 138
	Hide white space	WD 145
	Insert hyperlinks	WD 138
	Modify hyperlinks	WD 139
	Use advanced text wrapping	WD 144
Session 4.2	Add a page border	WD 163–164
	Apply the superscript font effect	WD 161
	Autoformat text as you type	WD 160–161
	Complete an entire mail merge process for form letters	WD 165–172
	Crop and rotate graphics	WD 154–155
	Flip a graphic	WD 155–156
	Format a letter as a drop cap	WD 158–159
	Insert a column break	WD 162
	Insert a symbol	WD 160–161
	Insert a symbol automatically	WD 160–161
	Insert Clip Art	WD 150–152
	Insert graphics in documents	WD 149–153
	Insert symbols	WD 160–161
	Modify a document footer	WD 164
	Modify graphics	WD 153–155
	Position a graphic	WD 157–158
	Resize a graphic	WD 153–154
	Revise column layout	WD 163
	Use AutoCorrect	WD 160–161
Excel Tutorial 1: Using Excel to Manage Data		
Session 1.1	Create formulas using the formula bar	EX 14–17
	Enter data in a selected range of cells	EX 11–14
	Enter formulas using Point mode	EX 17
	Enter numbers with format symbols	EX 14
	Go to a specific cell	EX 7–8
	Modify column widths	EX 19–21
	Modify row height	EX 19–20
	Range finder	EX 16
	Select a cell	EX 6–8
	Use Save	EX 22
	Use the Select All button to assign formats to the entire worksheet	EX 7
Session 1.2	Check spelling in a worksheet	EX 37–38
	Clear cell content	EX 32–33
	Copy cells	EX 27
	Create formulas using the SUM function	EX 28–30
	Delete a worksheet from a workbook	EX 35
	Delete rows and columns	EX 32–33
	Delete selected cells	EX 31–32
	Display formula contents	EX 41–43
	Edit a formula	EX 33–34
	Edit numbers in cells	EX 33–34
	Edit text in cells	EX 33–34

TUTORIAL	SAM TRAINING TASKS	PAGE #
	Delete records from a table using a datasheet	AC 68–69
	Edit records from a table using a datasheet	AC 69–71
	Enter records into a datasheet table	AC 53–56
	Format a table or query datasheet for display	AC 64
	Import a table from another Access database	AC 67–68
	Modify field properties for one or more tables in Table Design view	AC 60–63
	Move a field in a table structure	AC 58
	Resize to best fit	AC 64
	Use the New Record button to add a record	AC 63–64
Access Tutorial 3: Querying a Database		
Session 3.1	Add a table to the Design View query grid	AC 83, 94
	Create a multi-table query	AC 93–95
	Create a one-to-many relationship using the Relationships window	AC 90–93
	Create a query in design view	AC 83–85
	Enforce referential integrity in a one-to-many relationship	AC 91–93
	Filter datasheet by form	AC 100
	Filter datasheet by selection	AC 100–101
	Include all fields in a query	AC 82–84
	Include criteria in query for field not in results	AC 85
	Order records in datasheet view	AC 95–100
	Resize panes and field list in Query Design view	AC 90–91
	Restrict records in a join	AC 87, 92
	Sort a query on multiple fields in Design View	AC 95–100
	Sort records in a database	AC 95–96
	Specify referential integrity options	AC 89–93
	Use filter by form	AC 100
Session 3.2	Add a calculated field to a Select query	AC 112–116
	Build summary queries	AC 118–119
	Create calculated fields	AC 113–117
	Create queries using Wizards	AC 103
	Create queries with AND conditions	AC 107–109
	Create Select queries using the Simple Query Wizard	AC 103
	Format a table or query datasheet for display	AC 105–106
	Format results displayed in a calculated field	AC 116–117
	Use aggregate functions in queries to perform calculations	AC 117–119
	Use date and memo fields in a query	AC 103–104
	Use text data in criteria for a query	AC 108–109
	Use the AVG function in a query	AC 118–119
	Use Undo and Redo	AC 109–110
Access Tutorial 4: Creating Forms and Reports		
Session 4.1	Create forms using the Form Wizard	AC 130–132
	Delete records from a table using a form	AC 140
	Edit records from a table using a form	AC 139–140
	Enter records using a form	AC 140–141
	Use AutoFormats	AC 133–134
	Use navigation controls to move among records in a form	AC 135
Session 4.2	Align controls	AC 156–159
	Check errors in a report	AC 155–156
	Create a report using Report Wizard	AC 147–157
	Create a summary report using Report Wizard	AC 147–151
	Enter data in OLE fields	AC 158–159
	Insert a picture in a report	AC 158–159
	Modify a subform	AC 145–146
	Modify the properties of a form	AC 145–146
	Move controls	AC 159
	Preview a report	AC 151–153
	Print a report	AC 160
	Print specific pages of a report	AC 160
	Resize controls	AC 156–157
	Switch to landscape orientation	AC 151

Some of the exercises in this book require that you begin by opening a Data File. Follow one of the procedures below to obtain a copy of the Data Files you need.

Instructors

■ The Data Files are on the Instructor Resources CD under the category Data Files for Students, which you can copy to your school's network for student use.

■ Download the Data Files via the World Wide Web by following the instructions below.

■ Contact us via e-mail at reply@course.com.

■ Call Course Technology's Customer Service Department for fast and efficient delivery of the Data Files if you do not have access to a CD-ROM drive.

Students

■ Check with your instructor to determine the best way to obtain copies of the Data Files.

■ Download the Data Files via the World Wide Web by following the instructions below.

■ It is recommended that you store all your Data Files on a USB drive for maximum efficiency in organizing and working with the files.

Instructions for Downloading the Data Files from the World Wide Web

1. Start your browser and enter the URL www.course.com.

2. When the course.com Web site opens, click Student Downloads, and then search for your text by title or ISBN by entering the title or ISBN in the text box and then clicking the Go button.

3. If necessary, from the Search results page, select the title of the text you are using.

4. When the textbook page opens, click the Download Student Files link, and then click the link of the compressed files you want to download.

5. If the File Download – Security Warning dialog box opens, click Save. (NOTE: If the Save As dialog box opens, select a folder on your USB drive or hard disk to download the file to. Write down the folder name listed in the Save in box and the filename listed in the File name box.)

6. The filename of the compressed file appears in the Save As dialog box (e.g., 3500-8.exe, 0361-1d.exe).

7. Click either the OK button or the Save button, whichever choice your browser gives you.

8. When a dialog box opens indicating the download is complete, click the OK button (or the Close button, depending on which operating system you are using). Close your browser.

9. Open Windows Explorer and display the contents of the folder to which you downloaded the file. Double-click the downloaded filename on the right side of the Windows Explorer window. If the Open File – Security Warning dialog box opens, click Run.

10. In the WinZip Self-Extractor window, specify the appropriate drive and a folder name to unzip the files to. Click Unzip.

11. When the WinZip Self-Extractor displays the number of files unzipped, click the OK button. Click the Close button in the WinZip Self-Extractor dialog box. Close Windows Explorer.

12. Refer to the Read This Before You Begin page(s) in this book for more details on the Data Files for your text. You are now ready to open the required files.

Macintosh users should use a program to expand WinZip or PKZip archives. Students, ask your instructors or lab coordinators for assistance.

MICROSOFT®
Office 2003
First Course
PREMIUM EDITION

About the Premium Edition

The *New Perspectives on Microsoft Office 2003, First Course—Premium Edition* transforms the way students learn Microsoft Office skills with the following features, **new to this edition:**

- **SAM 2003 Training Companion CD!** This fully customized training companion is integrated with each tutorial in this book, providing students with hands-on practice and reinforcement of important skills. The SAM CD icon appears at key points throughout each tutorial, prompting students to go to the CD for "just-in-time" training on the tasks they are learning in that tutorial.
- **New listing of tutorial objectives and SAM training tasks!** The first page of each tutorial now includes a listing of the learning objectives for each tutorial session and the corresponding tasks on the SAM 2003 Training Companion CD. This map shows, at a glance, exactly which training tasks are available to students in each session to enhance their learning experience.
- **Enhanced Data File listings!** The "Read This Before You Begin" page, which appears at the beginning of each application section, now includes a complete listing of all the starting Data Files needed for that section, as well as the ending files, which students create and save. This new format makes it easy for students and instructors to ensure they have all the necessary files, both before working on a tutorial and upon completion of a tutorial. These redesigned pages also provide important information about storing Data Files, using the new SAM 2003 Training Companion CD, and completing any Course Labs available for the application.
- **SAM 2003 Training Companion Task Reference!** This task reference appears at the back of the book and provides a complete list of all the tasks available on the SAM 2003 Training Companion CD, which tutorial and session they map to, and which pages in the book students can go to for coverage of each task.
- **Increased emphasis on file management!** The "Managing Your Files" tutorial has been updated with coverage of USB drives and explains how students can use these popular storage devices. Also, the new tear-off File Management FastCARD on the back of the book offers students a handy way to have file management tips and techniques at their fingertips.

For additional information on what the New Perspectives Series has to offer, please visit: www.course.com/NewPerspectives

About the front cover image:
Commissioned to create a sculpture for the stairwell rotunda of the Safeco Corporate Headquarters building, artist Ed Carpenter (www.edcarpenter.net) utilized linear elements to guide visitors through the space. Integrated lighting on the aluminum rings projects subtle colors and broad patterns onto the ceiling of the rotunda through strips of copper, aluminum, and tempered glass. This installation offers visitors the opportunity to interact with atmospheric light effects as they move through the building. We invite you to look at light from a New Perspective.

SAM (Skills Assessment Manager) is a robust assessment and training system that enhances and expands upon the lessons in this text. A set of SAM skills ties directly to each tutorial in this book.

Other New Perspectives Titles

Microsoft Office 2003—
Brief, Second Edition
ISBN: 1-4188-6092-1

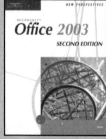

In 10 concise tutorials, this book covers essential skills of Microsoft Office 2003.

Microsoft Office 2003—
Second Course
ISBN: 0-619-20659-4

Builds from the First Course book to provide in-depth coverage of all of the Office applications and their integration.

About the New Perspectives Series
Our approach is all about critical thinking and problem solving. Without them, computer skills are learned but soon forgotten. With our case-based tutorials, step-by-step guidance, and extensive Instructor Resources, the New Perspectives Series has challenged students to apply what they have learned to real-life situations for over 10 years.